XC!

High School Cross Country in Michigan

1921-2019

By Jeff Hollobaugh

Table of Contents

Preface	1
Changes Through The Years	3
1. Boys Class A / Division 1	5
2. Boys Class B / Division 2	46
3. Boys Class C / Division 3	74
4. Boys Class D / Division 4	96
5. Boys Upper Peninsula	109
6. Girls Class A / Division 1	124
7. Girls Class B / Division 2	146
8. Girls Class C / Division 3	163
9. Girls Class D / Division 4	178
10. Girls Upper Peninsula	190
Legacy Ratings	199
All-Time Legacy Ratings By School – Boys	204
All-Time Legacy Ratings By School – Girls	221
Michigan at the Mideast Meet of Champions	234
Michigan at Foot Locker Nationals	240
Michigan at NXN	245
Michigan High Schoolers in International Competition	247

Front cover: Dathan Ritzenhein running the fastest 5K cross country race in U.S. history (John Brabbs/RunMichigan photo).

Back cover: Erin Finn winning the 2012 title, her second (Peter Draugalis photo).

@2020 by Jeff Hollobaugh

All rights reserved. This book or any portion thereof may not be reproduced or used in any manner whatsoever without the express written permission of the publisher except for the use of brief quotations in a book review.

ISBN: 9798645376178

At right, Duane Raffin—"Raff"—announcing the state finals through a troublesome flip phone connection, while the author spots for him.

Dedicated to Raff, my mentor in stat-keeping and cross country announcing and one of the best humans I've ever met. I wish I could have had this book done in time for you.

Preface

I was 14-years-old when I ran my first cross country race. I had no idea at the time that it would, in many ways, change the course of my life (even though stardom never came my way; I never won anything bigger than a dual meet). If you look, very carefully, you will find my name in the results in this book. Not that I earned it—I slipped it in there just to show future generations that I really did go to a state meet for reasons other than announcing it.

Still, since that day in 10th grade when I joined the team, fall to me has been that certain crisp breeze that always makes me say, "cross country weather."

Labor of love, you might call this book. It's taken more than 20 years to put together, though I confess there were some years I was too busy to even look at the project. As a history buff, it always frustrated me that so little of the history of my favorite sport was available. The athletes, the coaches, the races—all fascinating to me, and it's been a wonderful voyage of discovery to pull it all together. But honestly, the book's not done. Perhaps it will never be. I wanted to wait until the research was complete before I published. Now I realize that day may never come. There is no central repository of championship results in our state. Too often over the years have athletic departments dumped old files in the dumpster and old coaches have passed away without handing off that box full of old results to the next generation.

Indeed, in many of the years prior to 1995, I could not find information I needed. It might be just a name I am missing. In other cases, I have only the name of the individual winner, and in countless hours of scouring old microfilm, newspapers, yearbooks and scrapbooks, I have been unable to figure out who came in second place, let alone 40th. Luckily, I was able to come up with the complete team results of every Lower Peninsula championship since 1922.

One important reason to publish now is to get what I have out there, so that collectively we can finish this. Our sport, and the young people and their coaches who have labored at it—and reveled in it—deserve our recognition.

Special Thanks

I should give an extra nod to Jim Moyes, who somehow conned me into helping out with *The Fleet Feet of Spring: Michigan's High School State Championships in Track & Field*. Getting that book published made me realize that I needed to get off my rear-end and make this companion book a reality.

Many other people have contributed to this over the years. Special thanks to Kermit Ambrose, Kevin Behmer, Jacki Bilsborrow, Jim Cleverley, Walt Drenth, Jaime Dudash, Jim Gibbons, Emerson Green, Scott Hubbard, Charlie Janke, Jan Janke, Mike Jurasek, Tom Micallef, Tony Mifsud, Duane Raffin, Brian Salyers, Don Sleeman, Mike Timms, Miles Tomasaitis, Bryan Westfield—and yes, I'm sure I've forgotten more names.

My deep appreciation goes to our editorial crew: Mike Smith and George Tilt, who gave me support, encouragement, and fantastic proofreading.

What's In This Book?

Balance: All teams are created equal, so for the Lower Peninsula, I have listed every team that finished with a score, from 1922-on. For the Upper Peninsula, where there is no regional qualifying requirement, I listed the top 5 teams in each class/division. However, school sizes and participation numbers are not equal, and in listing individuals, I tried to list more names in the larger divisions. For instance, 40 deep for Class A/D1, 30 for

B/D2, 20 for C/D3 and 15 for D/D4 (and 5 deep for the UP races). The rationale? D1 schools have over 55% of the state's students, and probably a similar proportion of its cross country runners (D2=25.5%, D3 = 12.8%, D4 = 5.9%). The UP represents 3.2% of the state's overall population. So to be fair to individual runners, I naturally listed more in the bigger divisions.

Team members: For every winning team in the Lower Peninsula, I tried to include the names/results of all of the members who ran. Many names are still missing and I'd love to hear from those teams.

Athletes' Grades: For many athletes I have listed what grade they were in school. Many more are missing; that's not been a high priority for me to track them all down yet, but if you can fill in some blanks, please email! Same goes for missing first names.

Times: Many athletes and coaches naturally round their times down. Who wouldn't rather claim a 16:59 than a 17:00 when the official time was 16:59.9? But in keeping with ATFS guidelines for XC and road events, most of the times in this book are rounded up. A XC course simply cannot be measured to the level of precision that timing to the tenth implies. Unlike track, where you can be assured that most of the competitors ran pretty darn close to the advertised distance, cross country runners, even in the same race, run variable paths. And cross country courses change over time. Even in a single day at Michigan International Speedway, we have seen the course tweaked throughout the event. It's rarely the "same" course in the afternoon that it was in the morning, even before we account for the effect of the mud. However, in some of the write-ups, you will find me mentioning the tenths, because that can be helpful in understanding how close athletes are to each other in the same race.

Your help is needed: This is clearly a work in progress. For any meet result where you see an empty box (☐) next to the meet date, that means that there is more information I would like to include. If you have access to the original results, please get them to me! Emailing a scan or photo is fine. There will be annual updates of this book each winter and my hope is the book keeps getting better and more complete. Thanks in advance for your input!

Email: jeffhollobaugh@gmail.com

Many of the photos throughout the text have been provided by Peter Draugalis. Thank you for helping this look great!

From high school portraits to sports photography:

https://www.draugalisphotography.com

Thanks also to:

RunMichigan.com!
The Place To Run To First

Changes Through The Years

In the 1920s, when scholastic cross country got its start in the state of Michigan, the sport was a different beast than what we see today. For starters, half of a school's students—the girls—weren't even allowed to run. The distance started out at 2.5 miles for the first state meet, eventually dropping to an even 2 miles for the next 40+ years. In the 1920s and most of the 30s, boys had to be 16 before the first day of school in order to be eligible to race at regional or state meets. That ruled out 9th graders as well as most 10th graders. And while the top 5 runners scored, as they do today, teams were allowed to enter 6 runners, not 7. This was the case through at least 1949.

Also, there was one key difference with team scoring back in the early years. Runners from partial teams affected the team score; they were not removed from the scoring. Sometimes this had a dramatic effect. In the 1930 Class A race where Grand Rapids South tied Kalamazoo Central with 91 points, three schools sent single runners: Ferndale, Jackson, and Lansing Eastern. If those runners had been removed from the scoring, Grand Rapids South would have won by 3 points.

Here are some of the other major developments over the years:

1930—Detroit schools withdrew from the state tournaments in all sports. The conflict stemmed from differences over a variety of rules and procedures (for instance, the Detroit schools wanted to keep the state track meet a 2-day affair). Another factor was that at the time, and for years after, most of the state's best talent was in Detroit—why travel to compete with anyone else? At the time, Detroit's population was nearly a million, more than 6 times bigger than that of the next largest city, Grand Rapids.

1931—Since regionals were badly balanced, the number of teams advancing depended on the number competing at a particular regional. Eight or more teams meant that 4 would qualify. Six or 7 teams meant that three advanced. And 4 or 5 teams meant that 2 advanced. Three or less, only the winner would go. For individual qualification in Class A & B, as long as there were 3 or more schools, anyone in the top 5 could go to state as an individual. In Class C/D, all regional competitors were allowed to go to the state finals.

1932—The state finals were cancelled because of the Great Depression, but most of the usual Class A schools showed up in Ypsilanti and raced anyway.

1935 – In the waning years of the Depression, participation was down. Regionals were canceled for Class A and the state finals were open to any A teams.

1936—Again, no regionals for Class A. In the smaller classes, regionals were held, but all were allowed to advance to the finals. That remained the case through 1953.

1939—This was the last year that Upper Peninsula schools participated in the state finals. The anticipation that they would return to the fold following World War II never panned out, thus leaving Michigan as the only state in the country without a unified state final.

1949—After 26 years of being held on the campus of what would become Eastern Michigan University, the Lower Peninsula Finals moved to the Washtenaw Country Club in Ypsilanti. It would remain there through 1971.

1953—Regionals were once again deemed necessary for Class A and B. In C/D they were cancelled and any interested teams were allowed to go to the state finals.

1959—The number of qualifying teams from A and B regionals was adjusted; again, it was based on how many teams competed at a regionals. 5 or fewer teams=1 qualifier; 6-10=2 qualifiers; 11 or more=3 qualifiers.

1960—Because many felt that the Class A state meet was getting too big to run smoothly, the cross country committee began discussing adding a district competition to further thin the field. The discussion went nowhere.

1961—In A and B, the top 2 teams from each regional would qualify (there were still no regionals in C/D). In addition, the first 10 individuals who were not on those 2 teams would also qualify. For the first time at the state finals, there would be a separate individual race for the athletes without a complete team. Two separate state final races would remain a sad reality through 1995, denying fans many great matchups. Another factor in splitting the races up? The return of Detroit to MHSAA competition.

1965—Regionals were finally instituted in Class C/D, after a massive 36-team field destroyed the concept of an all-comers state finals the year before.

1970—The distance for regional and state championships was extended to 2.5 miles.

1972—The state finals left Washtenaw Country Club and were broken up into three separate events, with the different classes usually ending up at different sites. No longer could fans and reporters watch all the races at the same place. Also, the distance was extended again, this time to 3 miles.

1978—The MHSAA finally created a state championships for girls, though the first year it was an "all-class" event that pleased few of the smaller school programs.

1980—The distance was increased to 5K (3.11 miles), in keeping with the National Federation's move to metric distances. While regionals and state finals generally adhered to the change, for years a number of schools produced "fast" times on their home courses that remained at 3M.

1996—All of the Lower Peninsula championships were brought together at Michigan International Speedway, a move that helped to greatly increase media coverage of the sport. It was hailed as the largest sporting event in MHSAA history, with over 1,800 athletes participating. However, the move also created controversy, especially when spectators were confined to trackside seating. The next year, spectators were allowed onto the course, but coaches and fans remain fiercely divided on the subject of MIS. This year also marked the end of the separate team and individual races at the state finals, as computer scoring finally made it possible to keep accurate results and have all the best runners in the same race.

2000—The sport transitioned from the "class" system of categorizing schools to "divisions." Finally, an approximately equal number of schools competed in each of the four categories. At the top end, Class A/Division 1 athletes noticed few differences. However, the changes were more pronounced at the other end. The category for the smallest schools became much more competitive, for instance.

The Pioneers of Ann Arbor High School, the first state championship squad.

BOYS CLASS A / DIVISION 1

THE EARLY YEARS

The Detroit Athletic Club sponsored a cross country race on October 28, 1890, possibly the first cross country race ever in the state. The nine athletes—adults, presumably—covered between 5 and 6 miles with a winning time of about 55 minutes. Part of the course was along Detroit's Woodward Avenue, and athletes had to run through a number of fields.

In 1893, the DAC inaugurated an annual XC race of about 7 miles on Thanksgiving morning.

Collegiately, Princeton University started hosting its intercollegiate champnionships in 1899 and that led to the IC4A championships in 1909. The East Coast events got good play in the newspapers of the time—so track athletes and coaches were aware of the existance of the sport for years before efforts to make it a reality for Michigan high schoolers got going.

The University of Michigan started cross country as a varsity sport in 1919, but for years before that had a cross country club and races were held on campus as early as 1901. Michigan State, likewise, dates its varsity program to 1920, but had races as early as 1907—and intercollegiate competition in 1910.

Dr. Stewart Alfred McComber of Detroit University School (now Grosse Pointe Woods University Liggett) started the state's first high school program in 1904. He died at age 41, a victim of the 1918 influenza pandemic.

The first high school in the state to have a cross country club appears to have been the Detroit University School. In 1904 the cross country team was started by track coach Dr. S.A. McComber, who had held the high jump school record at Brown University. The club, captained by Gilbert Livingstone, traveled to Belle Isle several times a week for training runs of 4-6 miles. "In this way, the men will be kept in good condition until extreme weather sets in and necessitates a change to indoor work." Competiton, however, was not part of the program.

Eddie Hanavan of DUS might have been our first XC competitor. In June 1905 he placed second against the University of Michigan team in a cross country race. In the fall of 1905 there were plans to hold a race between DUS and Detroit Central, with Detroit Eastern also possibly participating.

The early prep runners were not afraid of distance. In November 1908, Detroit Central held its final XC run of the year on a course "about six miles in length." Mark Kennedy led the 13 finishers in 32:00 2/5.

Early distance runners faced challenges different than those of today. In 1914, runners at Hope College were ordered to stay off the roads after being implicated in several incidents where horses pulling carriages were spooked and ran away, in one case causing injury.

One cross country trend that thankfully didn't catch on came from Minnesota, where in 1915 young runners raced a half-mile over the broken ice of a waterway, leaping from ice floe to ice floe. No word on fatalities.

Muskegon was another early school with a team. In May, 1915, the coach there, Lewis Gudelsky, opined that his boys would beat all comers in a race at Hope College. He claimed that his top runners were regularly running a 4-mile loop faster than 20 minutes. At the time, the state record for 2 miles on the track was 10:18.4. The math did not lend credibility to his claim.

For some time, cross country also was a spring sport, and the Michigan spring championships were well-attended. In 1915, the Muskegon squad raced there, as well as 8 Detroit Cass Tech students wearing the YMCA colors. YMCA took runner-up honors ahead of Muskegon on the 5-mile course at Belle Isle. By 1917, the annual event (now hosted by the YMCA) drew "numerous distance runners from Detroit high schools."

In 1915 at the Thanksgiving Day race in Detroit, the top prep was Egbert Isbell of Detroit Northwestern, who placed 5th in 20:11 on the 3.5 mile course. Isbell later ran for Michigan where he won the 1922 Big 10 XC title and placed 7th in the Olympic Trials 5000 in 1924. (He later was a history professor at Eastern Michigan.)

Battle Creek Central and Kalamazoo Central both had early teams. The two schools waged an annual dual meet from 1913-on, with the winner of three-straight getting to keep a silver trophy. In 1919 the Bearcats grabbed the prize.

In the YMCA's Thanksgiving race of 1919, Ann Arbor High won with 29 points—a feat that the school lauded in its yearbook as a state championship win. We won't accord it that honor, as it was in a field of club and college teams that was limited to athletes age 17½ and older. It was the first of several straight wins by Ann Arbor.

In 1920, St. Clair, Marine City and Port Huron met for a 5M cross country race. Orville Chase of St. Clair won in 28:00.

Michigan Agricultural College (now MSU) hosted an annual college invitational. In 1920 Detroit Northern was allowed to compete, the high schoolers finishing last in the 6-team field over "five miles of the roughest territory in the vicinity of campus."

M. A. C. TO HOLD HIGH CROSS COUNTRY MEET

EAST LANSING, Nov. 3.—Every high school in the state has been invited by Athletic Director Brewer, of M. A. C. to enter the first interscholastic cross country run to be held at M. A. C. Nov. 11. This meet, the first of its kind in the history of state athletics, is expected to bring together the best long distance runners in Michigan schools.

The race will be over a three mile course, instead of the distance of five miles to be run by college athletes this week end. Floyd Rowe, state director of physical education, will be in charge.

The inaugural state meet that didn't happen.

1921

Michigan Agricultural College (now Michigan State University), set out to host the first-ever state meet in cross country, organized by Athletic Director Chester L. Brewer. According to one report, "While several schools, such as Battle Creek, Kalamazoo, Highland Park, Ypsilanti and others, are already strong in distance running, those in many other sections never go beyond the mile or possibly the two-mile in their track activities.

"Besides the trophy offered for the five-man team taking first place next Friday, ten individual medals will be given out—one gold, one silver and eight bronze. The visiting lads will have an opportunity to witness Armistice Day ceremonies now being planned."

Floyd Rowe, the state director of physical education, was to be in charge of the 3-mile event set for November 11. If nothing else, that would assure that the 1921 event would be the first official high school state championship. However, that week a heavy snowstorm hit Michigan. Lansing got 19 inches. Four days later—on the day that the meet was to be held—the *Lansing State Journal* complained that most of the city's streets were still impassable. The meet was cancelled, and the first-ever would have to wait a year, with another college taking charge.

1922 BOYS

Eight schools and 42 runners showed up for the first State Interscholastic Cross Country

Championship, a 2.5 mile race. It was organized by Lloyd Olds, the coach at Michigan Normal School (what is now Eastern Michigan University). Originally, Ann Arbor and Ypsilanti were scheduled to meet in a dual meet that day, but when a state championships was announced, both schools decided to run their dual concurrently with the championship.

Coach Homer Hanham's Ann Arbor team captured places 2-3-5-6-11 to win the silver cup handily. Hanham was in his first season of coaching, being a recent grad of Michigan Normal (now Eastern Michigan) and a jumper on the track team. The course started from the water tower near the front of the Ypsilanti campus and ran south on Summit Street to Recreation Park, where the athletes ran a lap around an old track before heading back to the water tower.

Some reports on the early meets have claimed that Olds merely invited local teams. However, the facts make it clear that he had every intent of making this a statewide meet from the onset. It wasn't the only MHSAA tournament that had its genesis at Michigan Normal. The first eight state gymnastics meets were held there (1925-32) only to be discontinued for 30 years. The first state basketball and tennis championships were also initiated by the athletics staff at the college.

Medals went to the first 7 runners.

While some might be disinclined to call this a "real" state championship because it predates the founding of the current MHSAA, note that the MHSAA recognized it as official in a number of its bulletins, carrying the winners of the early meets on its listing of all-time champions.

Ypsilanti, Nov. 11 ☐
1922 BOYS TEAMS
1. Ann Arbor 27
2. Detroit Northwestern 96
3. Battle Creek Central 101
4. Detroit Eastern 103
5. Kalamazoo Central 141
6. Detroit Northeastern 171
NS—Grand Rapids (4 finishers).

1922 BOYS INDIVIDUALS
1. Oscar Kutchinski (Grand Rapids Central)11 .... 13:28
2. Ted Hornberger (Ann Arbor)12 .... nt
3. Harold Scarlet (Ann Arbor)12 .... nt
4. Francis Stillwell (Detroit Eastern)12 .... nt
5. Joe Konupek (Ann Arbor)12 .... nt
6. Leslie Butler (Ann Arbor)12 .... nt
7. Garland Buck (Kalamazoo Central) .... nt
8. Lowell Blanchard (Detroit Northwestern)12 .... nt
9. Lawrence Tenhopen (Grand Rapids Central)12 ... nt
10. Willard Cooley (Kalamazoo Central)10 .... nt
11. Ted Wuerfel (Ann Arbor)10 .... nt
12. Seymour Blomfield (Detroit Northwestern) .... nt
13. Harold Vander Weyden (Grand Rapids Central)12. nt
14. Fred Beal (Battle Creek Central)12 .... nt
15. John Whitworth (Grand Rapids Central)12 .... nt
16. Rogers (Battle Creek Central) .... nt
17. ? (Battle Creek Central) .... nt
18. Powell (Detroit Eastern) .... nt
19. Smith (Detroit Northwestern) .... nt
20. Smith (Detroit Northwestern) .... nt
21. Joe Weslowski (Detroit Northeastern)11 .... nt
22. Panschoot (Detroit Northern) .... nt
23. Alfred Ruckstahl (Detroit Northwestern)11 .... nt
24. Roy Spaulding (Detroit Northwestern) .... nt
25. Melvin Voelker (Detroit Northwestern)12 .... nt
26. Tommy Belt (Detroit Eastern) .... nt
27. Clarke Lowber (Ann Arbor)12 .... nt
28. (Detroit Northwestern) .... nt
29. Bradford (Kalamazoo Central) .... nt
30. Jones (Battle Creek Central) .... nt
31. Thurston (Battle Creek Central) .... nt
32. Diller (Battle Creek Central) .... nt
33. (Detroit Northwestern) .... nt
34. Waits (Kalamazoo Central) .... nt
36. Ruxiaski (Detroit Northern) .... nt
37. Kasaynski (Detroit Northeastern) .... nt
38. Holmes () .... nt
39. (Detroit Northeastern) .... nt
40. Wright (Detroit Northeastern) .... nt

1923 BOYS

Ann Arbor made it 2-for-2 in the second annual meet, in Homer Hanham's last season of coaching before moving north to St. Johns. A total of 13 schools comprising 65 individuals entered; 57 finished in the muddy conditions. Every athlete at the meet got free entry into the Albion vs Michigan Normal football game that afternoon. The winner, Leroy Potter, was the dominant Michigan runner of the era. In 1925 he would set a state record in the mile by running 4:33.0 at the state championships.

Ypsilanti, Nov. 17 ☐
1923 BOYS TEAMS
1. Ann Arbor 59
2. Detroit Eastern 70
3. Detroit Northwestern 96
4. Detroit Southwestern 146
5. Detroit Central 162
6. Coldwater 172
7. Detroit Northeastern 219
NS (6 incomplete teams)—Highland Park, Kalamazoo Central, Linden, Oxford, Saginaw Eastern.

1923 BOYS INDIVIDUALS
1. Leroy Potter (Coldwater)11 .... 12:02
2. Francis Stillwell (Detroit Eastern) 12:07
3. Ralph Munson (Kalamazoo Central) .... nt
4. Ted Wuerfel (Ann Arbor)11 .... nt
5. Alfred Ruckstahl (Detroit Northwestern)12 . nt
6. Lloyd Cody (Ann Arbor)10 .... nt
7. Tommy Belt (Detroit Eastern) 12:21
8. Wayne Perrine (Ann Arbor) .... nt
9. Baker (Saginaw Eastern) .... nt
10. Scott (Oxford) .... nt
11. Peter DeVoogdt (Kalamazoo Central)12 .. nt
12. Joe Weslowski (Detroit Northwestern)12 .. nt
13. Leslie Brown (Detroit Central) .... nt
14. Walsh (Saginaw Eastern) .... nt
15. Seymour Blomfield (Detroit Northwestern) . nt
16. Banquier Aubrey (Ann Arbor) .... nt
17. Oxley (Detroit Northwestern) .... nt
18. Carnihay (Detroit Eastern) .... nt
19. Cecil Thurston (Kalamazoo Central)11 .... nt
20. Bennett (Coldwater) .... nt
21. Lange (Detroit Eastern) .... nt
22. Beyer (Detroit Eastern) .... nt
23. Brosson (Kalamazoo Central) .... nt
24. Angerilli (Detroit Northwestern) .... nt
25. Edwin Fenton (Ann Arbor) .... nt
26. Shurmur (Detroit Southwestern) .... nt
27. Flint (Detroit Central) .... nt
28. Gongon (Oxford) .... nt
29. Garney (Detroit Southwestern) .... nt
30. Crakowick (Detroit Southwestern) .... nt
31. Kaisinger (Detroit Northwestern) .... nt
32. Orth (Detroit Eastern) .... nt
33. Booth (Highland Park) .... nt
34. Joseph Lazarowski (Detroit Northwestern)12 . nt
35. MacGregor (Linden) .... nt
36. Demeter (Detroit Southwestern) .... nt
37. Welch (Linden) .... nt
38. Cox (Detroit Central) .... nt
39. Scheurman (Detroit Central) .... nt
40. Douglas Hammial (Ann Arbor) .... nt

1924 BOYS

The course was a 2.3 mile (other accounts say 2 miles, 395 yards, or 2.23M) out-and-back over dirt roads: "starting on Summit, just south of Ellis street, proceeding out Summit to the Saline road and into the county to the south, returning again via the Saline road and Summit street and finishing at the starting point." Reports said it was the same course as the previous year.

Coldwater's Leroy Potter, the first repeat champion.

A crowd of nearly 2,000 gathered at the finish of the Tuesday event and the college band played as the runners came home. "A crowded track made running conditions very unfavorable," according to one account. The winner, Roy Potter, was up before 5am to make it to the race on time. He won by more than 200 yards in 11:44 4/5 and had showered before the last of the 70+ runners had finished. Nine complete teams (they were limited to 6 runners each) competed in the Tuesday race, along with two partial squads. Potter's Coldwater team finished fourth.

The winning Ann Arbor squad, under Coach Meakin, had no returning runners from its victory the previous year, as star Ted Wuerfel was sick.

This was the first year that the MHSAA gave its official sanction to the meet, and hence it's the first meet listed in the MHSAA meet programs of today. However, it's interesting to note that the meet actually had a bigger field the previous year.

Ypsilanti, Nov. 11 ☐
1924 BOYS TEAMS
1. Ann Arbor 37
2. Kalamazoo Central 76
3. Detroit Southwestern 80
4. Coldwater 102
5. Battle Creek Central 129
6. Detroit Northwestern 159
7. Port Huron 205
8. Flint Central 217
9. Detroit Central 246
NS (incomplete teams)—Caro, Detroit Eastern.

1924 BOYS INDIVIDUALS
1. Leroy Potter (Coldwater)12 .... 11:45
2. Arthur Van Mere (Kalamazoo Central) .. c12:45
3. Carl Donner (Ann Arbor) .... nt
4. Banquier Aubrey (Ann Arbor) .... nt
5. Kaiser (Detroit Eastern) .... nt

6. Nelson Cody (Ann Arbor)11 .... nt
7. Wilfred Wells (Battle Creek Central) .... nt
8. McCarthy (Kalamazoo Central) .... nt
9. Kaizinger (Detroit Southwestern) .... nt
10. Kenneth Oxley (Detroit Northwestern) .... nt
11. Lloyd Cody (Ann Arbor) .... nt
12. Garney (Detroit Southwestern) .... nt
13. Wayne Perrine (Ann Arbor) .... nt
14. Small (Kalamazoo Central) .... nt
15. Schwendler (Detroit Southwestern) .... nt
24. Reginald Hankins (Ann Arbor) .... nt
29. Steele (Detroit Eastern) .... nt

1925 BOYS

A new course design greeted the athletes, who now ran a lap on Eastern Michigan's track before heading out for 2 miles on campus before returning for a final lap on the track.

Kalamazoo Central unseated three-time champ Ann Arbor and won the new trophy, a three-legged silver cup. The results were no surprise, as the Kalamazoo runners had earlier in the season defeated Ann Arbor in a dual. Lloyd Cody's time of 11:52.5, only eight seconds slower than the course record, was considered quite good "in view of the recent rains which slowed up the turf." Thirteen schools (60 athletes) had entered the 2.3 mile race on a Wednesday afternoon.

Earlier in the season, Cody had been defeated by Battle Creek Central's Howard Gatehouse in a dual meet over 3 miles, but Battle Creek Central did not travel to the state finals.

Saginaw Eastern finished five boys but wasn't counted in the team score, as the rules stated that a team needed six runners.

The runners faced a new course this year. They started with a lap around the college track and then covered nearly two miles on what would become Briggs Field before they returned for a finish on the track.

Ypsilanti, November 11 ☐
1925 BOYS TEAMS
1. Kalamazoo Central 36
2. Ann Arbor 52
3. Detroit Northwestern 61
4. Detroit Southwestern 104
5. Detroit Eastern 150
6. Mt Clemens 173
7. Monroe 182
8. Highland Park 210
9. Detroit Northern 224
NS (incomplete teams)—Baldwin, Saginaw Eastern, Ypsilanti Central, Ypsilanti Roosevelt.

1925 BOYS INDIVIDUALS
1. Lloyd Cody (Ann Arbor)12 .... 11:53*
(The Ypsilanti newspaper says Cody ran 11:53, while the MHSAA Bulletin says 12:00)
2. Arthur Van Mere (Kalamazoo Central) .... nt
3. Couse (Detroit Northwestern) .... nt
4. Francis Irey (Kalamazoo Central)11 .... nt
5. Leo Cavanaugh (Detroit Northwestern) .... nt
6. Garney (Detroit Southwestern) .... nt
7. DeYoung (Kalamazoo Central) .... nt
8. M. Etzel (Ann Arbor) .... nt
9. McDonald (Detroit Eastern) .... nt
10. Ralph Munson (Kalamazoo Central) .... nt
11. Waters (Ann Arbor) .... nt
12. Kaisinger (Detroit Southwestern) .... nt
13. Weaver (Kalamazoo Central)10 .... nt
14. Nelson Cody (Ann Arbor)12 .... nt
15. Gaunow (Detroit Northwestern) .... nt
16. Howard (Detroit Northwestern) .... nt
17. Reister (Kalamazoo Central) .... nt
18. Etzel (Ann Arbor) .... nt
19. Griffiths (Detroit Southwestern) .... nt
20. Kaiser (Detroit Eastern) .... nt

1926 BOYS

Teams from 18 schools entered the race (105 runners), and they ran a new course, this one measured at 2.5 miles. Pontiac's Val Criger went out fast, leading for the first 1.75M. That's where Ray Swartz passed him and went on to a 90-yard win. Criger held second until the last 300 yards, when McDonald unleashed a furious sprint to nab him. Swartz would go on to become a two-time state champ in the mile, breaking Leroy Potter's record with a 4:32.2 in 1928.

Ypsilanti, Nov. 11 ☐
1926 BOYS TEAMS
1. Kalamazoo Central 54
2. Detroit Northwestern 69
3. Detroit Cass Tech 128
4. Ann Arbor 132
5. Detroit Western 144
6. Detroit Eastern 181
7. Detroit Southwestern 206
8. Pontiac 206
9. Dearborn 241
10. Detroit Redford 247
11. Highland Park 254
12. Mt Morris 267
13. Three Rivers 324
14. Royal Oak 343
NS (incomplete teams)—Birmingham, Detroit U-D Jesuit, Mt Clemens, Ypsilanti Roosevelt.

Ray Swartz led Kalamazoo Central with wins in 1926 & 1927.

1926 BOYS INDIVIDUALS
1. Ray Swartz (Kalamazoo Central)10 .... 14:26
2. McDonald (Detroit Eastern) 14:41
3. Val Criger (Pontiac)11 .... 14:52
4. Nelson Cody (Ann Arbor) 14:56
5. Andrew DeYoung (Kalamazoo Central)11 .... 14:57
6. Leo Cavanaugh (Detroit Northwestern) 15:02
7. Clifford Whitney (Detroit Northwestern) 15:04
8. Jack Dant (Detroit Northwestern) 15:07
9. Marion Travis (Kalamazoo Central) 15:19
10. Gay (Mt Morris) 15:19
11. Arnold Goulder (Ann Arbor) .... nt
14. Walter Rogers (Kalamazoo Central)12 .... nt
25. Weaver (Kalamazoo Central)11 .... nt
29. Don Smith (Ypsilanti Roosevelt) .... nt

1927 CLASS A BOYS

This marked the first year that the races had to be separated by classes. To get into Class A, schools had to have 700 or more students enrolled. Twenty-seven teams competed, with Alonzo Stoddard's Kalamazoo Central team taking the win for the third straight year with a record low score of 25. It must be noted that under today's rules, the score would be 24, as Detroit Central did not finish 5 runners, and their 8th-placer would today be removed from the team totals.

Ypsilanti, Nov. 11 ☐
1927 BOYS CLASS A TEAMS
1. Kalamazoo Central 25
2. Detroit Eastern 99
3. Pontiac 117
4. Flint Central 121
5. Detroit Western 136
6. Ann Arbor 146
7. Detroit Cass Tech 165
8. Detroit Southeastern 166
9. Highland Park 207
10. Detroit Northern 242
NS (incomplete teams)—Detroit Central, Detroit Northwestern, Detroit Redford, Jackson.

1927 BOYS CLASS A INDIVIDUALS
1. Ray Swartz (Kalamazoo Central)11 .... 11:10
2. Charles Gould (Detroit Eastern) 11:33
3. McDonald (Detroit Eastern) 11:37
4. Otto Pongrace (Detroit Eastern)10 .... 11:38
5. Val Criger (Pontiac)12 .... 11:39
6. Marion Travis (Kalamazoo Central) 11:50
7. Harold Garrison (Kalamazoo Central)12 .... 11:54
8. Stone (Detroit Central) 11:55
9. Harold Ferris (Kalamazoo Central) 11:58
10. Braden (Flint) 11:59
11. Magoon (Ann Arbor) 12:27
12. Arnold (Detroit Western) 12:28
13. Skeen (Highland Park) 12:29
14. William DeBeauien (Pontiac)12 .... 12:30
15. Kienemienzy (Detroit Western) 13:11
16. Dickson (Detroit Eastern) 13:13
17. Parshall (Flint) 13:16
18. Gould (Detroit Western) 13:17
19. Brenner (Detroit Cass Tech) 13:18
20. Carr (Detroit Redford) 13:19
21. Goulder (Ann Arbor) .... nt
22. Matchett (Flint) .... nt
23. Poller (Detroit Cass Tech) .... nt
24. Ackerman (Detroit Southeastern) .... nt
25. Brusseau (Detroit Cass Tech) .... nt
26. Chase (Ann Arbor) .... nt
27. Francis VanHorn (Pontiac)10 .... nt
28. Fernyel (Detroit Redford) .... nt
29. Glowski (Flint) .... nt
30. Caston (Detroit Southeastern) .... nt
31. Keshishian (Highland Park) .... nt
32. Clickard (Detroit Redford) .... nt
33. Amluxen (Detroit Cass Tech) .... nt
34. Clark (Pontiac) .... nt
35. Muir (Detroit Northern) .... nt
36. Seth (Detroit Eastern) .... nt
37. McArthur (Pontiac) .... nt
38. D'Amour (Detroit Southeastern) .... nt
39. Bach (Ann Arbor) .... nt
40. Fredericks (Detroit Eastern) .... nt

1928 CLASS A BOYS

In Class A, 16 teams showed, 14 of them complete squads. The course was covered in snow. Two-time champion Ray Swartz of Kalamazoo Central was not eligible to run. In his absence, Flint Central's Jack Rutherford went to the front at the start and stayed there to win in 10:23. Runner-up Otto Pongrace of Detroit Eastern won the national mile title that spring and went on to a great career at Michigan State, placing 5th in the 1934 NCAA mile.

Ypsilanti, Nov. 10 ☐
1928 BOYS CLASS A TEAMS
1. Kalamazoo Central 51
2. Detroit Northwestern 59
3. Detroit Eastern 93

4. Detroit Southeastern 144
5. Flint Central 151
6. Detroit Redford 190
7. Ann Arbor 193
8. Highland Park 193
9. Detroit Northern 221
10. Pontiac 237
11. Grand Rapids South 250
12. Mt Clemens 291
13. Benton Harbor 307
14. Detroit Cass Tech 331
NS (partial teams)—Detroit Northeastern, Jackson.

1928 BOYS CLASS A INDIVIDUALS
1. Jack Rutherford (Flint Central)11 ....10:23
2. Otto Pongrace (Detroit Eastern)11.....................nt
3. Wesley Hurd (Detroit Northwestern)...................nt
4. Charles Gould (Kalamazoo Central) ....nt
5. Marion Travis (Kalamazoo Central) 10:37
6. Charles Giberson (Kalamazoo Central)12 ....nt
14. Lance Warner (Kalamazoo Central)11 ....nt
22. L. Loomis (Kalamazoo Central) ....nt
25. Laurence Kipp (Kalamazoo Central)11 ....nt

Wyanodtte's Earl Sonnenberg, 1929 winner.

1929 CLASS A BOYS
Earl Sonnenberg, a two-time state champion in the Class B 880, won his first Class A title here. Detroit Northwestern took Class A team honors with the highest winning score to that point. Class A runner-up Wesley Hurd went on to Michigan State and anchored the winning 4x1M and distance medley relays at the 1935 Penn Relays.

This was the first year that regionals were run (Class A & B only).

Ypsilanti, Nov. 9 □
1929 BOYS CLASS A TEAMS
1. Detroit Northwestern 66
2. Kalamazoo Central 97
3. Detroit Eastern 103
4. Flint Northern 104
5. Highland Park 106
6. Royal Oak 117
7. Detroit Southeastern 127
8. Wyandotte 129

1929 BOYS CLASS A INDIVIDUALS
1. Earl Sonnenberg (Wyandotte)12 ....10:26
2. Wesley Hurd (Detroit Northwestern)12 ....10:29
3. Otto Pongrace (Detroit Eastern)12 ....10:31
4. Lance Warner (Kalamazoo Central) 10:37
5. Bill Guy (Detroit Northwestern) 10:43
6. Blair (Highland Park) 10:43
7. Gabis (Detroit Eastern) 10:45
8. Johns (Wyandotte) 10:47
9. Auslander (Highland Park) 10:50
10. Dum (Royal Oak) 10:54
11. Sperry (Detroit Southeastern) ....nt
12. Coolman (Flint Northern) ....nt
13. Booshower (Flint Northern) ....nt
14. Wolcott (Royal Oak) ....nt
15. Wheame (Detroit Southeastern) ....nt
16. (Kalamazoo Central) ....nt
17. (Detroit Southeastern) ....nt
18. Speak (Royal Oak) ....nt
19. Hockenberry (Detroit Northwestern) ....nt
20. Care (Flint Northern) ....nt
21. (Detroit Eastern) ....nt
22. (Kalamazoo Central) ....nt
23. (Detroit Southeastern) ....nt
24. (Kalamazoo Central) ....nt
25. (Detroit Northwestern) ....nt
26. (Flint Northern) ....nt
27. (Highland Park) ....nt
28. (Highland Park) ....nt
29. (Detroit Eastern) ....nt
30. (Detroit Southeastern) ....nt
31. (Kalamazoo Central) ....nt
33. (Flint Northern) ....nt
35. (Wyandotte) ....nt
36. (Highland Park) ....nt
37. (Royal Oak) ....nt
38. (Royal Oak) ....nt

1930 CLASS A BOYS
At the state meet, Grand Rapids South and Kalamazoo Central battled to a tie. GRS had places 3-11-15-27-35, while KC had 12-16-18-21-24; no word on what their sixth runners did—or if they even had a sixth—so we can't tell how the tie would be broken under current rules.

The result surprised many, as Kalamazoo had beaten South at the regional, and had earlier crushed South in a dual, 15-43.

Note that at this point in history, Class A meant enrollments of 700 and over.

This was the first year that Detroit stayed out of the state championships, over a difference on policy matters. The absence would last 31 years, and deprive the meet of some of the finest competitors in the state's history.

The Detroit event was marked by cold winds that held the number of spectators to a minimum. The race covered a "nearly" 2-mile course. 17-year-old Stewart Fortner of Cooley won in 9:21 2/5 and had a 125-yard margin on second. Seventeen teams placed.

Ypsilanti, Nov. 8 □
1930 BOYS CLASS A TEAMS
=1. Grand Rapids South 91
=1. Kalamazoo Central 91
3. Flint Northern 106
4. Monroe 122
5. Ann Arbor 127
6. Flint Central 137
7. Mt Clemens 146
8. Dearborn Fordson 151
NS (partial teams)—Ferndale, Jackson, Lansing Eastern

1930 BOYS CLASS A INDIVIDUALS
1. Hoyt Servis (Ann Arbor)12 ....10:25
2. Jack Booth (Mt Clemens)12 ....10:35
3. Winfield Miller (Grand Rapids South) 10:36
4. Kenny Waite (Jackson) 10:43
5. Max Kaiser (Lansing Eastern)10 ....10:45
6. Erwin Steeb (Ann Arbor) 10:46
7. Edward Deinzer (Monroe) 10:47
8. Kane (Dearborn Fordson) 10:48
9. Pete Miller (Ferndale) 10:49
10. Henry Kuzewski (Monroe) 10:52
11. (Grand Rapids South) ....nt
12. (Kalamazoo Central) ....nt
13. Jacob Bohl (Flint Northern) ....nt
14. (Flint Central) ....nt
15. (Grand Rapids South) ....nt
16. (Kalamazoo Central) ....nt
17. (Mount Clemens) ....nt
18. (Kalamazoo Central) ....nt
19. Collick (Flint Northern) ....nt
20. (Dearborn Fordson) ....nt
21. (Kalamazoo Central) ....nt
22. Jordan (Flint Northern) ....nt
23. Proctor (Flint Northern) ....nt
24. (Kalamazoo Central) ....nt
25. (Flint Central) ....nt
26. ?
27. (Grand Rapids South) ....nt
28. Arnold Shavalia (Monroe) ....nt
29. Taylor (Flint Northern) ....nt
30. (Mount Clemens) ....nt
31. (Flint Central) ....nt
32. Ash (Flint Northern) ....nt
33. (Flint Central) ....nt
34. (Flint Central) ....nt
35. (Grand Rapids South) ....nt
36. (Dearborn Fordson) ....nt
37. (Ann Arbor) ....nt
38. Lyle Eshenroder (Monroe) ....nt
39. Charles Hill (Monroe) ....nt
40. (Ann Arbor) ....nt

Rouge Park, Oct. 31 □
1930 BOYS DETROIT TEAMS
1. Detroit Eastern 72
2. Highland Park 91
3. Detroit Southeastern 98
4. Detroit Cooley 130
5. Detroit Northwestern 147
6. Detroit Cass Tech 162
7. Detroit Central 168
8. Detroit Western 218
9. Detroit Northern 272
10. Hamtramck 277

1930 BOYS DETROIT TEAMS
1. Stewart Fortner (Detroit Cooley)12 ....9:22
2. William Zapalski (Detroit Western) c9:47
3. Longin Gabis (Detroit Eastern) c9:50
4. Montgomery Ostrander (Highland Park) ....nt
5. Talarowski (Detroit Eastern) ....nt
6. William Daley (Detroit Cass Tech)11 ....nt
7. George Webster (Detroit Northern) ....nt
8. Garmon (Detroit Southeastern) ....nt
9. Robert Withey (Highland Park) ....nt
10. Norman Lawton (Detroit Northwestern) ....nt

1931 CLASS A BOYS
Kalamazoo Central won its fifth Class A title, its men running 6-12-13-14-25, as Flint Northern was runner-up for the second-straight year on a day with excellent weather and course conditions.

Runner-up Max Kaiser was the regional runner-up behind Flint Northern's Jake Bohl. That race in Flint created headaches for the MHSAA when a rush of runners at the finish chute caught officials off-guard; they were unable to record any places beyond the top 12.

In Detroit, William Daly controlled the race, coming home the winner with a strong finish. He later starred at the University of Detroit. In 1935, he ran 4:16.6 for the mile, which made him the 12th fastest man in the world that year.

Ypsilanti, Nov. 7 □
1931 BOYS CLASS A TEAMS
1. Kalamazoo Central 70
2. Flint Northern 94

3. Monroe..97
4. Flint Central...104
5. Grand Rapids South 106
6. Ferndale...153
NS (partial teams)—Ann Arbor, Benton Harbor, Grand Rapids Creston, Jackson, Lansing Eastern, Mount Clemens

1931 BOYS CLASS A INDIVIDUALS
1. Ludlow Chase (Mt Clemens)12........................10:26
2. Max Kaiser (Lansing Eastern)11......................10:32
3. Erwin Steeb (Ann Arbor)12....................................nt
4. Robert Hills (Jackson).....................................10:34
5. Baulk (Monroe)..nt
6. Gerald Roberts (Kalamazoo Central)12...............nt
7. DeWitt (Flint Northern)...nt
8. Lautherhahn (Grand Rapids South)......................nt
9. Jake Bohl (Flint Northern)....................................nt
10. Dalby (Flint Central)..nt
11. (Monroe)
12. Arnold Baker (Kalamazoo Central)12..................nt
13. Randall Swartz (Kalamazoo Central)11..............nt
14. Bob Massey (Kalamazoo Central)12...................nt
15. (Grand Rapids South)...nt
16. (Grand Rapids Creston)......................................nt
17. (Flint Central)...nt
18. (Ferndale)..nt
19. (Monroe)...nt
20. (Flint Central)...nt
21. (Flint Northern)...nt
22. (Grand Rapids South)...nt
23. (Flint Central)...nt
24. (Grand Rapids South)...nt
25. George VanDerLester (Kalamazoo Central)........nt
26. (Monroe)...nt
27. (Benton Harbor)..nt
28. (Flint Northern)...nt
29. (Flint Northern)...nt
30. (Ferndale)..nt
31. ?..nt
32. (Ferndale)..nt
33. ?..nt
34. (Flint Central)...nt
35. (Ferndale)..nt
36. (Monroe)...nt
37. (Grand Rapids South)...nt
38. (Ferndale)..nt

Rouge Park, Oct. 29 □
1931 DETROIT TEAMS
1. Detroit Eastern..52
2. Detroit Southeastern.......................................56
3. Hamtramck..147
4. Detroit Northwestern.....................................153
5. Detroit Cass Tech..156
6. Highland Park..192
7. Detroit Redford..235
8. Detroit Southwestern....................................258
9. Detroit Cooley...274
10. Detroit Northeastern....................................278
A total of 18 complete teams competed

1931 BOYS DETROIT INDIVIDUALS
1. William Daly (Detroit Cass Tech)12.................9:48
2. Dragitz (Detroit Eastern)......................................nt
3. Mitchell (Detroit Eastern).....................................nt
4. Frieman (Detroit Eastern)....................................nt

1932 CLASS A BOYS

In 1932, the MHSAA Council voted to cancel the state meet. The Bulletin said, "Council voted to eliminate the state cross country run this year due to the apparent fact that the sport was being dropped by a considerable number of schools this fall." No numbers are available, but if so, that means that schools in the state were being hit hard by the Great Depression and had to make significant budget cuts.

According to the Ypsilanti paper of the time, the regional meet "is only being conducted this year because of the great demand of high school coaches and runners of this section. The local college each year has conducted the state meet, but the Michigan High School Athletic Association eliminated a state cross country meet from its program this year." Entries included 10 teams in Class A, six in Class B and four in Class C-D.

Of the three scheduled regionals, only the Ypsilanti race offered a Class A section, so it was a de facto Class A state championship. Every team that competed in the state finals the year before came. Some of the schools even referred to the meet as the "state championships" in their yearbooks.

Kalamazoo Central won the team title by 16 points, putting five in the top 15.

Kalamazoo's Alonzo Stoddard was the most successful coach of the era, with 8 state wins over a 9-year period.

A chilly, muddy day awaited harriers at the Detroit championships. The reporter for the *Detroit Times* wrote about one contestant that he "had so little athletic underwear that officials could find no place upon which to hang his number. He insisted on running, however, and as he was eligible the youngster started out. He was one of the 30 boys who failed to finish. Personally, I think he froze to death."

A sensation was created by young Art Gassaway, running in the first meet of his life. He looked a certain winner near the finish when "shivering spectators saw a large splash of mud. Gassaway had fallen into what appeared to be quicksand." Bill Hutchinson got ahead of him then, but Gassaway fought back, and the two crossed the line separated by inches.

Eastern Regional, Ypsilanti, Nov. 5 □
1932 BOYS CLASS A TEAMS
1. Kalamazoo Central..47
2. Lansing Eastern..63
3. Monroe..78
4. Flint Central...111
5. Ferndale..130
6. Flint Northern..161
7. Jackson...177
8. Royal Oak..196
NS (incomplete teams)—Ann Arbor, Saginaw Hill.

1932 BOYS CLASS A INDIVIDUALS
1. Max Kaiser (Lansing Eastern)12....................10:14
2. Forrest Spencer (Lansing Eastern)11..................nt
3. Forrest Spencer (Lansing Eastern)11..................nt
4. Randall Swartz (Kalamazoo Central)12................nt
8. Vern Baugher (Kalamazoo Central).....................nt
9. George VanDeLester (Kalamazoo Central)12......nt
12. Arthur Dungy (Kalamazoo Central)....................nt
13. Sanford Ladd (Ann Arbor)..................................nt
20. William Wikle (Ann Arbor)..................................nt
37. Bryant Limpert (Ann Arbor)................................nt

Rouge Park, Oct. 27 □
1932 BOYS DETROIT LEAGUE TEAMS
1. Detroit Northwestern..56
2. Detroit Cooley...92
3. Detroit Redford..144
4. Detroit Southwestern....................................147
5. Hamtramck..161
6. Detroit Eastern..174
7. Detroit Northeastern.....................................216
8. Detroit Mackenzie...216
9. Detroit Pershing..223
10. Highland Park..249
A total of 17 complete teams competed

1932 BOYS DETROIT LEAGUE INDIVIDUALS
1. Bill Hutchinson (Detroit Eastern)12.....................nt
2. Art Gassaway (Detroit Northeastern)11..............nt
3. Ben Kornowsky (Detroit Cooley).........................nt
4. Noble (Detroit Central)..nt
5. Hawn (Detroit Northwestern)..............................nt
6. Al Broschay (Detroit Southwestern)....................nt
7. Szalwinski (Hamtramck)......................................nt
8. R. Lafevrere (Detroit Redford).............................nt
9. Barkham (Detroit Cooley)....................................nt
10. Awkerman (Detroit Northwestern).....................nt

1933 CLASS A BOYS

For the second year, harriers in the state had to content themselves with regional meets but no state final. The Ypsilanti regional brought together all of the state's contending Class A teams. Many considered this the de-facto state meet, with the Lansing paper even calling Forrest Spencer the new state champion. He beat Lorimer Miles, 10:26.0-10:29.2, the winning time a new course record.

Again Kalamazoo Central won, placing its runners 2-9-16-17-36. Miles would win the state mile title the next spring in 4:31.3.

Eastern Regional, Ypsilanti, Nov. 4 □
1933 BOYS CLASS A TEAMS
1. Kalamazoo Central..80
2. Lansing Central...87
=3. Ann Arbor..88
=3. Ferndale..88
5. Jackson...100
6. Monroe..101
7. Lansing Eastern..125
8. Flint Central..160
NS—Royal Oak (2 finishers).

1933 BOYS CLASS A INDIVIDUALS
1. Forrest Spencer (Lansing Eastern)12............10:26
2. Lorimer Miles (Kalamazoo Central)11............10:30
3. Barron Hills (Jackson)....................................10:33
4. Lazenby (Ferndale)..10:43
5. Palmer (Ann Arbor)..10:45
6. Joseph Brzezinski (Jackson).........................10:45
9. (Kalamazoo Central)..nt
14. Bill Curtiss (Lansing Central).............................nt
16. (Kalamazoo Central)..nt
17. (Kalamazoo Central)..nt
18. Langley (Lansing Central)..................................nt
19. Chamberlain (Lansing Central)..........................nt
21. Barnes (Lansing Central)...................................nt
23. Chapman (Lansing Central)...............................nt
31. Gaudard (Lansing Eastern)................................nt
33. Melendy (Lansing Eastern)................................nt
36. (Kalamazoo Central)..nt
37. Baldwin (Lansing Eastern).................................nt

Rouge Park, Oct. 23 ☐
1933 BOYS DETROIT TEAMS
1. Detroit Southeastern ... 37
2. Detroit Northwestern ... 92
3. Detroit Redford ... 105
4. Detroit Pershing ... 116
5. Detroit Central ... 120
6. Hamtramck ... 171
7. Detroit Denby ... 198
8. Detroit Southwestern ... 210
9. Detroit Cooley ... 280
10. Detroit Mackenzie ... 340

A total of 17 complete teams competed

1933 BOYS DETROIT INDIVIDUALS
1. Art Gassaway (Detroit Northeastern)12 ... 11:27
2. Jack Thomas (Detroit Southeastern) ... 11:29
3. Wilfred Spencer (Detroit Southeastern) ... nt
6. Russ Bath (Detroit Southeastern) ... nt
8. William Husted (Detroit Southeastern) ... nt

1934 CLASS A BOYS

The MHSAA returned to having an official state finals. Jackson edged Lansing Eastern by just one point in Class A despite the fact that Kalamazoo Central had been picked to win and the Jackson squad was not even listed among the four possible challengers. Lorimer Miles stepped up for the win in a course record 10:20.4.

In Detroit, Joe Pacey stayed on the heels of Wilfred "Willie" Spencer from start to finish, but was never able to pass him. The two finished 50 yards ahead of the next runner. Spencer's Southeastern squad won with the lowest total ever in the meet. Prior to the race, a protest was filed that athletes under the age of 16 were entered. Four runners were pulled from the field after a quick investigation.

Ypsilanti, Nov. 3 ☐
1934 BOYS CLASS A TEAMS
1. Jackson ... 64
2. Lansing Eastern ... 65
3. Kalamazoo Central ... 70
4. Ferndale ... 81
5. Wyandotte ... 129
6. Flint Central ... 142
7. Ann Arbor ... 159
8. Flint Northern ... 206
9. Monroe ... 216
10. River Rouge ... 258

NS (partial team)—Lansing Central

1934 BOYS CLASS A INDIVIDUALS
1. Lorimer Miles (Kalamazoo Central)12 ... 10:21
2. James Brill (Ferndale) ... nt
3. Bob Lazenby (Ferndale) ... nt
4. Neil Gaudard (Lansing Eastern)12 ... nt
5. D. Palmer (Ann Arbor) ... nt
6. Vern Wolfe (Lansing Eastern)12 ... nt
7. Donald Bassler (Lansing Eastern)12 ... nt
8. Bernard Doonan (Kalamazoo Central) ... nt
9. Joe Brzezinski (Jackson)12 ... nt
10. Chuck Chamberlain (Lansing Central) ... nt
12. (Jackson) ... nt
13. (Jackson) ... nt
14. (Jackson) ... nt
16. (Jackson) ... nt
21. Elliott (Lansing Eastern) ... nt
27. Baldwin (Lansing Eastern) ... nt

Rouge Park, Oct. 23 ☐
1934 DETROIT TEAMS
1. Detroit Southeastern ... 22
2. Detroit Redford ... 88
3. Detroit Eastern ... 95
4. Detroit Cooley ... 99
5. Detroit Northwestern ... 103
6. Detroit Mackenzie ... 132

The 1934 Detroit champions from Southeastern. Individual winner Wilfred Spencer is in the middle of the back row.

1934 DETROIT INDIVIDUALS
1. Wilfred Spencer (Detroit Southeastern)12 ... 11:06
2. Joe Pacey (Detroit Eastern) ... nt
3. Bill Husted (Detroit Southeastern) ... nt
4. Irvine Dufour (Detroit Northwestern) ... nt
5. Art Baird (Detroit Southeastern) ... nt
6. Bill Ellis (Detroit Southeastern) ... nt
7. Dick Bell (Detroit Southeastern) ... nt
8. Alfonso Deposio (Detroit Redford) ... nt
9. Merrill Perkins (Detroit Redford) ... nt
10. Clif Brinkham (Detroit Southeastern) ... nt

1935 CLASS A BOYS

"There will be no regionals for Class A schools inasmuch as the number desiring to compete can be taken care of at the State Run without the necessity of Regional elimination," read the MHSAA Bulletin. Only 48 runners participated.

Regionals proceeded as scheduled for the other classes, though oddly enough, those races were far smaller at the state finals (24 runners in class B, 14 in C/D).

Kalamazoo Central lost its season opener to Jackson by a 34-21 score but came through for the state crown with a 4-point margin, despite having only one runner in the top 10. That was George Peck in fifth. The rest of the team placed 16-17-18-20. Jackson's Paul Herman missed the course record by a second. The next spring, he would win the Class A mile crown in 4:45.6.

In Detroit, Southeastern's Richard Bell won by 150 yards, but Redford put athletes in 2-3-6-8-10 to grab the team win. Bell's brother Bob placed 13th.

Ypsilanti, Nov. 2 ☐
1935 BOYS CLASS A TEAMS
1. Kalamazoo Central ... 76
2. Jackson ... 80
3. Flint Central ... 81
4. Monroe ... 102
5. Ferndale ... 108
6. Wyandotte ... 116
7. Ann Arbor ... 125
8. Lansing Eastern ... 151

1935 BOYS CLASS A INDIVIDUALS
1. Paul Herman (Jackson) ... 10:22
2. Barron Hills (Jackson) ... nt
3. Tom Weidenhammer (Monroe) ... nt
4. Burdell Elliott (Lansing Eastern) ... nt
5. George Peck (Kalamazoo Central) ... nt
6. William Welke (Wyandotte) ... nt
7. Don Carterline (Ann Arbor) ... nt
8. John Dargo (Wyandotte) ... nt
9. Sylvester Austeau (Monroe) ... nt
10. Bruce Champion (Ferndale) ... nt
12. (Jackson) ... nt
16. Ted Bennick (Kalamazoo Central) ... nt
17. Jake Bender (Kalamazoo Central) ... nt
18. Leonard Lesman (Kalamazoo Central) ... nt
20. Carl Rubert (Kalamazoo Central) ... nt
25. (Jackson) ... nt
40. (Jackson) ... nt

Rouge Park, Oct. 22 ☐
1935 DETROIT TEAMS
1. Detroit Redford ... 29
2. Detroit Southeastern ... 40
3. Hamtramck ... 71
4. Detroit Pershing ... 136
5. Detroit Cooley ... 140
6. Detroit Southwestern ... 153

1935 DETROIT INDIVIDUALS
1. Richard Bell (Detroit Southeastern)12 ... 11:00
2. Doug Pearse (Detroit Redford) ... nt
3. Orville Palmer (Detroit Redford) ... nt
4. Cyril Baird (Detroit Southeastern) ... nt
5. Stan Zasline (Hamtramck) ... nt
6. Chester Seller (Detroit Redford) ... nt
7. Charles Augularra (Detroit Southeastern) ... nt
8. Bill Breen (Detroit Redford) ... nt
10. Bob Mohr (Detroit Redford) ... nt

1936 CLASS A BOYS

Don Coffey and three of his teammates finished in the top 10 to pace coach Howard Gleason's Lansing Central squad to the Class A crown in the field of about 150 runners. They edged defending champion Kalamazoo Central by one point.

Again, no regionals were held in Class A.

In Detroit, the White brothers from Hamtramck ran together from the back, not emerging into the lead until the final half mile. According to the Free Press, Tait told his younger brother Johnny, "You keep up with me and we'll show these boys a few things."

Ypsilanti, Nov. 7 ☐
1936 BOYS CLASS A TEAMS
1. Lansing Central ... 52
2. Kalamazoo Central ... 53
3. Flint Central ... 71
4. Monroe ... 110
5. Jackson ... 129
6. Dearborn ... 139
7. River Rouge ... 164

1936 BOYS CLASS A INDIVIDUALS
1. Don Coffey (Lansing Central)12 ... 10:45
2. Sam Pool (Kalamazoo Central)11 ... nt
3. Norman Fossum (Lansing Central) ... nt
4. Duane Zemper (Flint Central)11 ... nt
5. Carl Rupert (Kalamazoo Central) ... nt
6. Chester Wilhelm (Monroe) ... nt
7. David Donaldson (Dearborn) ... nt
8. Ray Pinkham (Lansing Central) ... nt
9. Roosevelt Stieger (Jackson) ... nt
10. Howard Easterbrook (Lansing Central) ... nt
11. Herbert Boothe (Flint Central) ... nt
20. Keating (Jackson) ... nt
21. Jimmy Crane (Flint Central) ... nt
23. Lyle Glann (Flint Central) ... nt
27. Cooley (Jackson) ... nt
28. Paul Kelly (Flint Central) ... nt
30. Russell Ferbitz (Lansing Central) ... nt
36. Lacinski (Jackson) ... nt
37. Brzezinski (Jackson) ... nt
38. McMilling (Jackson) ... nt

Rouge Park, Oct. 15 ☐
1936 DETROIT TEAMS
1. Hamtramck ... 42
2. Detroit Redford ... 73
3. Detroit Cass Tech ... 91
4. Detroit Southeastern ... 95
5. Detroit Cooley ... 106
6. Detroit Northwestern ... 163

1936 DETROIT INDIVIDUALS

1. Tait White (Hamtramck)12 ....11:18
2. Johnny White (Hamtramck)10 ....c11:21
3. Orville Palmer (Detroit Redford)11 ....c11:22
4. Harry Blazkiewicz (Hamtramck) ....nt
5. Francis Turner (Detroit Pershing) ....nt
6. Gilbert Wittenberg (Detroit Cass Tech) ....nt
7. Stan Zasions (Hamtramck) ....nt
8. Charles Schuck (Detroit Cooley) ....nt
9. Warren Anderson (Detroit Northern) ....nt
10. Scotson Easson (Detroit Redford) ....nt

1937 CLASS A BOYS

Regionals were again scheduled for Class A, but because some schools had already lined up dual or league meets for that day, the regionals were declared optional.

Altogether, 12 schools entered 71 athletes in Class A. Champion Leroy Schwarzkopf won by 200 yards. He later starred at Yale and won the 1942 Penn Relays two-mile in 9:22.4. Flint Central's Indians won by 10 points; their Scotland-born coach, John Seaton, had come to America at age 6. A graduate of Central High and the University of Michigan, he never did sports but participated in the math club and the orchestra. Yet in a few short years he became one of the most successful distance coaches in the state.

Earlier in the season, Ann Arbor coach Tim Ryan experimented with a cross country distance medley. It was run at their dual with Jackson, with athletes covering varying distances. It was intended to be a starter event for beginning runners who could not handle the full two-mile distance. The next year Ryan used it in all but one of his duals.

In Detroit, coach Claude Snarey finally shook off a five-year jinx ("something always happens to my boys") and guided Cooley to the title. Warren Johnson was picked to duel it out with co-favorite John White of Hamtramck. They battled until the last 220, when White suddenly slowed to a walk. He finished 5th and collapsed at the line.

Ypsilanti, Nov. 6 □
1937 CLASS A TEAMS
1. Flint Central 69
2. Lansing Central 79
=3. Kalamazoo Central 93
=3. Saginaw Eastern 93
5. Lansing Eastern 99
6. Monroe 125
7. Flint Northern 158
8. Ann Arbor 191
9. Dearborn 196
10. Royal Oak 216

1937 CLASS A INDIVIDUALS
1. Leroy Schwarzkopf (Saginaw Eastern)12 ....10:28
2. Bill Nankervis (Flint Central) ....nt
2?. Stewart Graham (Royal Oak)10 ....nt
10. Jim Crane (Flint Central) ....nt
12. George Fechik (Flint Northern) ....nt
18. James Gardner (Flint Northern) ....nt
37. Richard Deane (Flint Northern) ....nt

Rouge Park, Oct. 27 □
1937 DETROIT TEAMS
1. Detroit Cooley 57
=2. Detroit Redford 71
=2. Detroit Southeastern 71
4. Highland Park 100
=5. Hamtramck 112
=5. Northwestern 112

1937 DETROIT INDIVIDUALS
1. Warren Johnson (Detroit Northwestern)12 ....11:05
2. Richard Baker (Detroit Redford) ....nt
3. Dale Brown (Detroit Southeastern) ....nt
4. Scotson Eason (Detroit Redford) ....nt
5. John White (Hamtramck) ....nt
6. Ed Crossley (Detroit Redford) ....nt
7. Roger Souilliere (Detroit Southeastern) ....nt
8. Dick Hart (Detroit Cooley) ....nt
9. Phil Crown (Highland Park) ....nt
10. Earl McIntosh (Detroit Cooley) ....nt

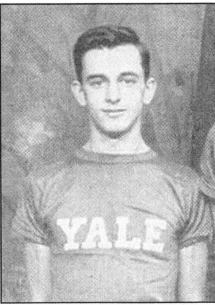

Saginaw Eastern's Leroy Schwarzkopf later starred for Yale.

1938 CLASS A BOYS

After 16 years of being guided by founder Lloyd Olds, the meet directorship passed to Eastern Michigan coach George Marshall. Stewart Graham moved up a step on the victory stand to lead Royal Oak to victory. The team was coached by Robert Dunn, who had competed while at Michigan Normal College. Thirteen schools and 92 runners participated (regional competition was again optional).

In Detroit, Mac Umstattd stunned. In his first (and last) season of prep cross country competition, the 16-year-old shattered the course record (his own 10:04 from the previous week) with apparent ease. A 1:58.8 half miler the previous season, Umstattd had not run cross country the previous year, since Detroit rules limited competition to those age 16 and over.

Ypsilanti, Nov. 5 □
1938 BOYS CLASS A TEAMS
1. Royal Oak 72
2. Flint Central 95
3. Lansing Eastern 97
4. Flint Northern 98
5. Kalamazoo Central 146
6. Jackson 149
7. Monroe 178
8. River Rouge 214
9. Lansing Central 223
10. Ferndale 251
11. Saginaw 261
12. Dearborn 315
13. Wyandotte 353

1938 BOYS CLASS A INDIVIDUALS
1. Stewart Graham (Royal Oak)11 ....10:39
2. Roy Lewis (River Rouge) 10:49
3. Joe Keating (Jackson) 10:51
4. Welles (Royal Oak) ....nt
5. Knapps (Royal Oak) ....nt
6. Walt Moore (Flint Central) 10:53
7. Bill Walter (Flint Northern) 10:54
8. Dick Foster (Lansing Eastern) ....nt
9. Don Merritt (Lansing Eastern) ....nt
11. George Fechik (Flint Northern) ....nt
13. Carl Herman (Jackson) ....nt
17. Lloyd Maidment (Flint Central) ....nt
18. Virgil Shreve (Flint Northern) ....nt
19. Vern Krebsbach (Flint Central) ....nt
22. Gerald Calhoun (Lansing Eastern) ....nt
23. George Byelick (Lansing Eastern) ....nt
23?. Lyle Gardner (Flint Northern) ....nt
24. Orrin Orde (Flint Central) ....nt
26. Jud Wickham (Lansing Central) ....nt
29. Warren Heddy (Flint Central) ....nt
30. Bob Smith (Flint Central) ....nt
35. Paul Cole (Lansing Eastern) ....nt
35?. Jim Mallett (Lansing Central) ....nt
36. Bob Elias (Flint Central) ....nt
36. Charles Snyder (Flint Northern) ....nt

Rouge Park, Oct. 20 □
1938 DETROIT TEAMS
1. Detroit Redford 29
2. Detroit Southeastern 68
3. Detroit Northwestern 96
4. Detroit Cooley 100
5. Detroit Cass Tech 101
6. Detroit Denby 155

1938 DETROIT INDIVIDUALS
1. Mac Umstattd (Detroit Northwestern)12 ....9:54
2. John White (Hamtramck)12 ....10:02
3. Ed Crossley (Detroit Redford) ....nt
4. Jack Addington (Detroit Redford) ....nt
5. Harold Garrick (Detroit Southeastern) ....nt
6. Dale Brown (Detroit Southeastern) ....nt
7. Scott Sasson (Detroit Redford) ....nt
8. Dick Baker (Detroit Redford) ....qnt
9. Bob Sullivan (Detroit Redford) ....nt
10. John Schlager (Detroit Cooley) ....nt

1939 CLASS A BOYS

In Class A, Dick Knapp needed every last bit of his torrid finishing kick to nab Bill Van Zandt at the line. Knapp had come onto the track for the final sprint in 4th place. He took the win in 10:40.4, with Van Zandt at 10:41.8.

The race was run in "ideal" weather conditions. Flint Central won with a 37-point total that was hailed as a record, with runners finishing 2-5-8-10-12.

In Detroit, 6-0/140lb Lux won his first race ever. Favored teammate Henry Lord led until the final 300 yards, then faded to 7th. Lux took over, chased by Crossley. He "faltered momentarily" in the last 50 yards, then recovered to win easily in the second-fastest time ever on the course.

Ypsilanti, Nov. 4 □
1939 BOYS CLASS A TEAMS
1. Flint Central 37
2. Flint Northern 129
3. Monroe 137
4. Kalamazoo Central 150
5. Jackson 174
6. Ann Arbor 182
7. Lansing Eastern 185
8. Ferndale 226
9. Royal Oak 252
10. Dearborn 265
11. River Rouge 329
12. Wyandotte 347

1939 BOYS CLASS A INDIVIDUALS
1. Dick Knapp (Royal Oak)12 ....10:40
2. Bill Van Zandt (Flint Central) 10:42
3. Bud Boers (Kalamazoo Central) ....nt

4. Jay Woolsey (Jackson)11 .... nt
5. Jack Chaplin (Flint Central) .... nt
6. Marshall (Plymouth) .... nt
7. Paul Cole (Lansing Eastern) .... nt
8. Millard Wells (Flint Central) .... nt
9. Jim Mallett (Lansing Central) .... nt
10. Joe Scukanec (Flint Central) .... nt
12. Warren Heddy (Flint Central) .... nt
14. Orrin Orde (Flint Central) .... nt
16. Lyle Gardner (Flint Northern) .... nt
18. Ted Jesionek (Flint Northern) .... nt
19. Frank Pritchard (Flint Central) .... nt
27. Bill Bowden (Lansing Eastern) .... nt
28. Joe MacKenzie (Lansing Central) .... nt
30. Sheridan Tucker (Flint Northern) .... nt
31. Harold Jacobs (Flint Northern) .... nt
34. Charles Snyder (Flint Northern) .... nt
38. Bob Carpenter (Lansing Eastern) .... nt
39. Roland Roberg (Flint Northern) .... nt

Rouge Park, Oct. 25 □
1939 DETROIT TEAMS
1. Detroit Cooley 46
2. Detroit Southeastern 52
3. Detroit Western 66
4. Detroit Redford 87
5. Detroit Cass Tech 132
6. Detroit Denby 145

1939 DETROIT INDIVIDUALS
1. Britton Lux (Detroit Cooley)12 .... 10:00
2. Ed Crossley (Detroit Redford) .... nt
3. Bob Shortle (Detroit Western) .... nt
4. Warren Ellsworth (Detroit Western) .... nt
5. Bill Fritz (Detroit Southeastern) .... nt
6. Bill Brown (Detroit Southeastern) .... nt
7. Henry Lord (Detroit Cooley)10 .... nt
8. Bill Bell (Detroit Southeastern) .... nt
9. Jack Webb (Detroit Cooley) .... nt
10. Bob Phippe (Detroit Southeastern) .... nt

1940 CLASS A BOYS

Weather and the course were both called ideal, though one newspaper referred to the "slippery" course. Class C-D champ the year before, 5-6/104lb Dominic Lecato moved up to Class A when he transferred to public schools, and he won another state title after taking the lead with a half-mile to go. Many felt that he would have broken the course record had it not been muddy.

Undefeated in high school competition both in cross country and track, Lecato left school in April of the following year to join the Navy, thus missing his senior state meet in track. He served on the aircraft carrier USS Yorktown and survived the sinking of the ship by enemy torpedoes at the Battle of Midway in 1942. He was a career Navy man and also served in Korea and Vietnam.

Royal Oak, meanwhile, avenged dual and regional meet losses to Flint Central with a narrow 3-point win here.

With 178 runners in all three classes combined, this was hailed as the biggest state meet ever.

Ypsilanti, Nov. 2 □
1940 BOYS CLASS A TEAMS
1. Royal Oak 58
2. Flint Central 61
3. Kalamazoo Central 114
4. Lansing Eastern 132
5. Ann Arbor 158
6. Monroe 237
7. River Rouge 239
8. Ferndale 240
=9. Dearborn 246
=9. Jackson 246
11. Plymouth 268
12. Lincoln Park 273
13. Wyandotte 316

Royal Oak's 1940 championship squad.

1940 BOYS CLASS A INDIVIDUALS
1. Dominic Lecato (Lansing Eastern)12 .... 10:54
2. Harold Hallman (Kalamazoo Central) c11:19
3. Bill Thomas (Royal Oak)11 .... nt
4. Clyde Johnson (Royal Oak) .... nt
5. Paul Cole (Lansing Eastern) .... nt
6. Bob Robinson (Royal Oak) .... nt
7. Joe Scukanec (Flint Central) .... nt
8. Art Adams (Jackson) 11:37
9. Jim Gibbard (Royal Oak)10 .... nt
10. Rutillo Enzastiga (Flint Central) .... nt
36. (Royal Oak) .... nt

Rouge Park, Oct. 17 □
1940 DETROIT TEAMS
1. Detroit Southeastern 26
2. Detroit Cooley 41
3. Detroit Western 120
4. Detroit Redford 122
5. Hamtramck 135
6. Detroit Pershing 135

1940 DETROIT INDIVIDUALS
1, Henry Lord (Detroit Cooley)11 .... 10:12
2. Bob Phipps (Detroit Southeastern) .... nt
3. Bill Brown (Detroit Southeastern) .... nt
4. Tom Collinson (Detroit Cooley) .... nt
5. Jack Longpre (Detroit Cooley) .... nt
6. Bill Fritz (Detroit Southeastern) .... nt
7. Box Blundell (Detroit Southeastern) .... nt
8. Jim Earl (Detroit Southeastern) .... nt
9. Don Curtis (Detroit Western) .... nt
10. James Rhoades (Detroit Northeastern) .... nt

1941 CLASS A BOYS

Cold rain and wind greeted the runners in Ypsilanti. Bill Thomas won by mere inches over Al Wehner and Jim Gibbard. "unfavorable course conditions kept times a full minute away from the records," said *the Detroit Free Press*. Thomas had slipped by Wehner, the leader, with only 50 yards to go. Flint Central dethroned defender Royal Oak by placing its men 6-8-15-19-20. This despite the fact that Central coach Seaton had resigned earlier in the year because of the war—his true calling was being a physicist and he went to work for the Naval Ordnance Laboratory in Washington, D.C.

In Detroit, favored Cooley took a backseat to Denby after Cooley's No. 2, junior Art Marx was spiked at the crowded start. With a three-inch gash in his foot, he stayed in the race, knowing that he was crucial to the team score. He limped home in 22nd place, 45 seconds off his best time. It wasn't enough to hold off Denby, but Cooley finished 2nd because of his heroics.

Ypsilanti, Nov. 1 □
1941 BOYS CLASS A TEAMS
1. Flint Central 68
2. Ann Arbor 107
3. Jackson 128
4. Kalamazoo Central 130
5. Lincoln Park 145
6. Monroe 147
7. Benton Harbor 160
8. Royal Oak 161
9. Dearborn 197
10. Wyandotte 210
11. River Rouge 271
12. Van Dyke 288

1941 BOYS CLASS A INDIVIDUALS
1. Bill Thomas (Royal Oak)12 .... 11:14
2. Al Wehner (Monroe) c11:15
3. Jim Gibbard (Royal Oak)11 .... c11:15
4. Wayne Larmee (Ann Arbor)10 .... nt
5. Hicks (Lincoln Park) .... nt
6. Rutilio Enzastiga (Flint Central) .... nt
7. Glen Shankland (Ann Arbor)11 .... nt
8. Jim Massar (Flint Central) .... nt
9. Melrose Hills (Jackson) .... nt
10. Bob Carter (Benton Harbor) .... nt
11. Gilbert McMickens (Kalamazoo Central) .... nt
12. Maghieise (Wyandotte) .... nt
13. Jesue (Lincoln Park) .... nt
14. Dick Lucking (Kalamazoo Central) .... nt
15. Bill Wells (Flint Central) .... nt
16. Cole (Jackson) .... nt
19. Steve Laporte (Flint Central) .... nt
20. Bill Stephenson (Flint Central) .... nt
21. Stanford McGlone (Flitnt Central) .... nt
23. Ed Peppel (Benton Harbor) .... nt
31. Charles Zletz (Flint Central) .... nt
36. Ray Clements (Benton Harbor) .... nt
38. Ed Burk (Benton Harbor) .... nt
(150 boys in field)

Rouge Park, Oct. 16 □
1941 DETROIT TEAMS
1. Detroit Denby 50
2. Detroit Cooley 66
3. Detroit Eastern 68
4. Detroit Southeastern 131
5. Detroit Northwestern 142
6. Detroit Western 145

1941 DETROIT INDIVIDUALS
1, Jack Longpree (Detroit Cooley)12 .... 10:09
2. Al Pingel (Detroit Denby) c10:12
3. George Kovatch (Detroit Eastern)12 .... nt
4. Jack Wessel (Detroit Eastern) .... nt
5. Bob Mettler (Detroit Denby) .... nt
6. Al Rigby (Detroit Eastern) .... nt
7. Jim Rhoades (Detroit Northeastern) .... nt
8. Jim Wesley (Hamtramck) .... nt
9. Bob Goletz (Detroit Cooley) .... nt
10. Ed Brugman (Detroit Redford) .... nt

1942 CLASS A BOYS

Because of wartime fuel restrictions, the MHSAA decided to cancel the regional meets and instead hold separate "final" meets that looked a lot like regionals. Schools were urged to attend the closest one.

The East Michigan Championship was held at the usual state meet site on the normal date, with 16 teams participating. Undefeated Jim Gibbard, a 125-lb senior, ran 3rd most of the way as Dick Lucking led, then sprinted past the others near the finish of the muddy course.

The West Michigan Championships was held in Kalamazoo, and apparently only two teams showed, making it a dual meet between Benton Harbor and Battle Creek Central. The Benton Harbor squad won in its only race of the season. Their previous coach, Don

Farnum, had departed to serve in the Navy. That left basketball coach Bill Perigo in charge.

The Detroit Metropolitan League moved its championships from Rouge Park to Palmer Park. The winner, in an automatic course record, was 6-6 Bob Edmondson. Only 17, it would be his last high school race, as the city indoor mile champ would graduate in January and miss his final season of track.

Briggs Field, Ypsilanti, Oct. 31 ☐
1942 BOYS EAST - CLASS A TEAMS
1. Kalamazoo Central.................................50
2. Jackson...58
3. Flint Central..87
4. Royal Oak...90
5. Ann Arbor...123
6. Wyandotte..167
7. Saginaw..174
8. Lincoln Park..176
9. Dearborn...214

1942 BOYS EAST - CLASS A INDIVIDUALS
1. Jim Gibbard (Royal Oak)12..................11:20
2. Gilbert McMickens (Kalamazoo Central)........c11:23
3. Dick Lucking (Kalamazoo Central)........c11:23
4. Walt Pittman (Jackson)........................11:27
7. Melrose Hills (Jackson)........................11:35
8. Tom Cole (Jackson).............................11:37
11. Louie Psumo (Kalamazoo Central)........... nt
14. Jack Dulworth (Jackson)....................11:55
16. Dick Dombos (Kalamazoo Central)11....... nt
18. Junior Wedell (Kalamazoo Central)........... nt
25. Don Wooley (Jackson)........................... nt
? Leon Koopsen (Kalamazoo Central)........... nt
? John Milroy (Kalamazoo Central)................ nt

Kalamazoo, (Oct 31?) ☐
60º, cloudy, slight wind, slick conditions.
1942 BOYS WEST – CLASS A TEAMS
1. Benton Harbor......................................21
2. Battle Creek Central............................37
(only teams entered)

1942 BOYS WEST – CLASS A INDIVIDUALS
1. Ivan Towns (Battle Creek Central)12........12:19
2. Leonard Newman (Benton Harbor)...........12:39
3. Stewart Jennings (Benton Harbor)...........12:40
4. Eddie Burks (Benton Harbor)..................13:07
5. Lyman Jewell (Benton Harbor)................13:24
6. Ernest Nichols (Battle Creek Central).......13:26
7. Tom Laity (Benton Harbor)....................13:33
8. Dick Chappell (Benton Harbor)...............13:40
9. Russell Brown (Battle Creek Central).......13:43
10. Delbert Vastbeinder (Battle Creek Central)......14:27
11. Keith McKeen (Battle Creek Central).......14:35
12. Gerald McCarthy (Battle Creek Central)......14:49

Palmer Park, Oct. 28 ☐
1942 DETROIT TEAMS
1. Detroit Southeastern............................32
2. Detroit Northwestern...........................71
3. Detroit Cooley......................................76
4. Detroit Denby....................................112
5. Detroit Mackenzie..............................130
6. Detroit Cass Tech...............................181

1942 DETROIT INDIVIDUALS
1. Bob Edmondson (Detroit Northwestern)12............9:42
2. Russ Foukes (Detroit Southeastern).......c9:44
3. Jack McGhie (Detroit Southeastern).......... nt
4. Jim Brummen (Detroit Southeastern)........ nt
5. Bob Mettler (Detroit Denby)..................... nt
6. Lester Smith (Detroit Mackenzie)............. nt
7. Earl Scott (Detroit Central)...................... nt
8. Gilmour Dalrymple (Detroit Southeastern)... nt
9. James Timms (Detroit Northwestern)........ nt
10. Bill Lintner (Detroit Cooley).................... nt

1943 CLASS A BOYS

Kalamazoo Central won its eighth title by tallying 33 points, a score bettered only twice in the meet's history. Dick Dombos led the squad with his win. The next spring, he won the Class A mile in 4:37.5.

This year, teams from the Upper Peninsula held their first officially separate "UP" Championship, canceling their travel to the Lower Peninsula because of severe wartime restrictions on gasoline usage.

In Detroit, Fred Stolliker won a poignant race. Weeks earlier, Redford AD and coach Frank "Hermie" Hermanson said, "No one can beat him." Sadly, Hermanson died just a few hours before the race. Stolliker said, "I was thinking about what Hermie had said about me. I thought about it when [Bill] Webb was pressing me near the finish and I knew I just couldn't let him down."

Briggs Field, Ypsilanti, Oct. 30 ☐
1943 BOYS CLASS A TEAMS
1. Kalamazoo Central 33
2. Dearborn 61
3. Lincoln Park 78
4. Royal Oak 94
5. Jackson 114
6. Flint Central 171
7. Lansing Eastern 209
8. Hazel Park 243

1943 BOYS CLASS A INDIVIDUALS
1. Dick Dombos (Kalamazoo Central)12.........11:02
2. Louie Psumo (Kalamazoo Central).........c11:05
6. Jack Green (Kalamazoo Central).................. nt
7. Bob Figley (Lansing Sexton)......................... nt
10. Floyd Sanford (Kalamazoo Central)............. nt
11. Dick Davis (Lansing Sexton)....................... nt
14. Bob Johnson (Kalamazoo Central)............... nt

Redford's Fred Stoliker dedicated his effort to his coach, "Hermie" Hermanson, who died before the race.

Palmer Park, Nov. 3 ☐
1943 DETROIT TEAMS
1. Detroit Cooley 36
2. Detroit Redford 54
3. Detroit Southeastern 105
4. Detroit Pershing 138
5. Detroit Eastern 138
6. Detroit Northwestern 138

1943 DETROIT INDIVIDUALS
1. Fred Stolliker (Detroit Redford)12 .... 9:52
2. Bill Webb (Detroit Eastern)......................c9:55
3. Alex Tait (Detroit Redford)........................... nt
4. Clark Jacot (Detroit Cooley)......................... nt
5. Howard Smith (Detroit Cooley).................... nt
6. Bob Davis (Detroit Cooley).......................... nt
7. Joe Metz (Detroit Redford).......................... nt
8. Norman Hanson (Detroit Chadsey)............... nt
9. Lloyd Graham (Detroit Northwestern).......... nt
10. Hank Cannon (Detroit Cooley).................... nt

1944 CLASS A BOYS

Lincoln Park left the state meet with the first-place trophy, and Royal Oak went home thinking it had lost. Some time later, a math error was discovered and Royal Oak was awarded the co-championship.

The Ann Arbor team had been slated to compete but had the last few meets of its schedule canceled due to a polio outbreak at the school.

Kalamazoo Central saw its hopes for a third straight win evaporate when one of its better runners, Robert Conrad, joined the Army the day before the meet.

80+ runners competed on a cold and windy day, with 10 teams represented (some reports say a total of 70 runners were there). Crowding on the course slowed the times.

In Detroit, coach Claude Snarey led his team to victory despite not having a single returning letter winner on the squad. Jim Carey, a half-miler in his first season of cross country, won by 50 yards. He would graduate the following January.

Ypsilanti, Nov. 4 ☐
1944 BOYS CLASS A TEAMS
=1. Lincoln Park..73
=1. Royal Oak...73
3. Kalamazoo Central 104
4. Jackson 129
5. Battle Creek Central 142
6. Dearborn 144
7. Lansing Eastern 147
8. Wyandotte 158
9. Saginaw Hill 198
10. Hazel Park 223

1944 BOYS CLASS A INDIVIDUALS
1. Clark Atcheson (Royal Oak)11 .... 11:16
4. Glen Alday (Battle Creek Central) .... nt
5. Robert Hyames (Kalamazoo Central)........... nt
8. Jerry Church (Wyandotte).......................... nt
12. Lloyd Jones (Jackson)............................... nt
14. Dale Babcock (Jackson)............................. nt
23. Dick Vandenberg (Jackson)........................ nt

Palmer Park, Oct. 25 ☐
1944 DETROIT TEAMS
1. Detroit Cooley.......................................47
2. Detroit Redford.....................................93
3. Detroit Pershing....................................98
4. Detroit Northwestern 102
5. Detroit Eastern 122
6. Detroit Southeastern.......................... 141

1944 DETROIT INDIVIDUALS
1. Jim Carey (Detroit Cooley)12 .... 9:57
2. Bill Mallory (Detroit Redford)................c10:06
3. Don Foukes (Detroit Southeastern).......c10:09
4. Gene Beeman (Detroit Cooley)................... nt
5. William Cook (Detroit Cooley).................... nt
6. Duane Jasper (Detroit Denby).................... nt
7. Dick Hoffman (Detroit Western)................. nt
8. Ken Murish (Detroit Pershing).................... nt
9. Frank Keuhn (Detroit Mackenzie)............... nt
10. Melvin Dawson (Detroit Northwestern)...... nt

1945 CLASS A BOYS

With the end of World War II, participation rebounded in Class A, with the biggest meet in years (96 runners). The 14 complete teams tied a record set in 1926 and again in 1928. Coach Glenn Mason's Saginaw Hill crew won with a record high score, led by Fred Meschke in 10:26.2. Teammate Bill Agre was close behind. The two had not been beaten all season.

Meschke was 16½ when he won the state title and shortly afterward he joined the armed forces to serve in the Pacific during the post-war period.

Though wartime rationing of gasoline had ended, the Upper Peninsula schools opted to not return to the state finals, though they did in other sports. Clearly, it reflected the low value the UP athletic directors placed on cross country.

In Detroit, Cooley won its third straight. It was the seventh win for coach Claude Snarey, who had coached Eastern to two championships and Cooley to five. Ross Smith capped an undefeated season and teammate Dave Rice surprised by finishing 2nd here after only a 17th at the West Side race the week before. A steady rain slowed the runners.

Ypsilanti, Oct. 27 ☐
1945 BOYS CLASS A TEAMS
1. Saginaw Hill 85
2. Battle Creek Central 104
3. Flint Northern 115
4. Lincoln Park 142
5. Ann Arbor 171
6. Midland 172
7. Royal Oak 196
=8. Jackson 197
=8. Monroe 197
10. Kalamazoo Central 206
11. Hazel Park 221
12. Dearborn 283
13. Wyandotte 301
14. Lansing Eastern 341

Fred Meschke joined the military shortly after winning the state title for Saginaw Hill.

1945 BOYS CLASS A INDIVIDUALS
1. Fred Meschke (Saginaw Hill) 10:27
2. Bill Agre (Saginaw Hill)11 .... c10:37
4. Roger Kessler (Ann Arbor) c10:59
7. Tom Goretzka (Battle Creek Central) 11:00
8. Don Cooper (Wyandotte) .... nt
15. Ronnie Flynn (Saginaw Hill) .... nt
16. Russell Smith (Battle Creek Central) 11:14
24. Pat O'Connell (Battle Creek Central) .... nt
26. John Edgerton (Battle Creek Central) .... nt
31. Linus Heydon (Saginaw Hill) .... nt
33. Ray Madison (Saginaw Hill)12 .... nt
34. Dean Raycraft (Saginaw Hill) .... nt
36. Bill Jeffrey (Battle Creek Central) .... nt
38. Bob Schmidt (Saginaw Hill) .... nt
58. Herb Izzo (Saginaw Hill) .... nt

Palmer Park, Oct. 25 ☐
1945 DETROIT TEAMS
1. Detroit Cooley 26
2. Detroit Mackenzie 94
3. Detroit Northwestern 100
4. Detroit Denby 123
5. Detroit Pershing 133
6. Detroit Cass Tech 181

1945 DETROIT INDIVIDUALS
1. Ross Smith (Detroit Cooley)12 .... 9:46
2. Dave Rice (Detroit Cooley) 9:58
3. Jim Payne (Detroit Denby) .... nt
4. Don Foukes (Detroit Southeastern) .... nt
5. Norman Jakust (Detroit Mackenzie) .... nt
6. Don Dickinson (Detroit Cooley) .... nt
7. Don Keeler (Detroit Cooley) .... nt
8. Sheldon Capp (Detroit Central) .... nt
9. Roy Link (Detroit Redford) .... nt
10. Eldon Dooley (Detroit Cooley) .... nt

1946 CLASS A BOYS

The Lower Peninsula races went off in perfect conditions, with 14 teams competing on the muddy course for Class A honors. Kalamazoo Central won title number nine with a record high 90-points.

Bill Agre of Arthur Hill edged Battle Creek Central's Tom Goretzka, 11:10.5-11:11.0. The 6-0 Agre was also a star basketball player, making first team All-State.

In these days the regular cross country season often stretched beyond the state finals. The winning team still had two more meets on its schedule, duels with Elkhart, Indiana, and Culver Military School.

In Detroit, Aaron Gordon capped an undefeated season, outkicking five other contenders in the last half mile. The previous year he injured his ankle in his first race and sat out the entire campaign.

This was the year that Quentin Brelsford won the NCAA Championship. A graduate of Birmingham High School, he was a noted half-miler as a prep. In 1938 he set a state record 1:55.4 that lasted for 23 years. But he never won a state cross country final. After fighting in World War II, he returned to attend Ohio Wesleyan University, and he stunned the NCAA field with his kick over the 4-mile course.

Ypsilanti, Oct. 26 ☐
1946 BOYS CLASS A TEAMS
1. Kalamazoo Central 90
2. Wyandotte 109
3. Monroe 119
4. Jackson 127
5. Battle Creek Central 146
6. Saginaw Hill 153
7. Flint Northern 176
8. Lincoln Park 179
9. Ann Arbor 215
10. Flint Central 229
11. Dearborn 230
12. Hazel Park 254
13. Royal Oak 323
14. Midland 330

1946 BOYS CLASS A INDIVIDUALS
1. Bill Agre (Saginaw Hill)12 .... 11:11
2. Tom Goretzka (Battle Creek Central) 11:11
3. Jerry Hein (Kalamazoo Central) .... nt
7. Don Cooper (Wyandotte) .... nt
9. John Koerts (Kalamazoo Central) .... nt
14. Fred Pitman (Wyandotte) .... nt
15. Bud Heydon (Wyandotte) .... nt
19. Dick Gerstner (Kalamazoo Central) .... nt
20. Dick Baber (Kalamazoo Central) .... nt
38. Burton Toornman (Kalamazoo Central) .... nt

Palmer Park, October 23 ☐
1946 DETROIT TEAMS
1. Detroit Cooley 44
2. Detroit Mackenzie 74
3. Detroit Redford 83
4. Detroit Cass Tech 110
5. Detroit Miller 123
6. Detroit Southeastern 131
NS (incomplete teams)—Detroit Central, Detroit Denby.

1946 DETROIT INDIVIDUALS
1. Aaron Gordon (Detroit Miller)11 .... 9:52
2. Bob Hahn (Detroit Cooley) c9:54
3. Jim White (Detroit Mackenzie) .... nt
4. Ken Wright (Detroit Denby) .... nt
5. Don Dickinson (Detroit Cooley) .... nt
6. Cal Richter (Detroit Redford) .... nt
7. Dick Osborne (Detroit Redford) .... nt
8. Bruce Vreeland (Detroit Redford) .... nt
9. Lynn DeSnyder (Detroit Cass Tech) .... nt
10. Willie Wilson (Detroit Southeastern) .... nt

1947 CLASS A BOYS

A wet, slippery course in Ypsilanti slowed runners at the LP meet. The field of 126 runners represented 18 teams, the largest field in meet history. Flint Central had been expected to contend for the title with Jackson, but the team fell victim to a series of "bad breaks."

Jackson's Dave Stevens caught Flint Central's Jack Crane 200 yards from the finish to win the big meet. A week later he fell to Battle Creek Central's Tom Goretzka in a dual meet, Goretzka breaking the Jackson course record with his 10:05.5, Stevens a foot behind.

In the PSL, Fields outkicked the heavily favored Gordon in the final 200 yards. Changes to the Palmer Park course allowed Fields to claim an automatic course record. Jimmy Russell's Northwestern squad took the win.

Briggs Field, Ypsilanti, Nov. 1 ☐
1947 BOYS CLASS A TEAMS
1. Jackson 45
2. Kalamazoo Central 103
3. Wyandotte 119
4. Dearborn 123
5. Battle Creek Central 189
6. Lansing Eastern 196
7. Flint Central 217
8. Lincoln Park 278
9. Ann Arbor 298
10. Monroe 301
11. Benton Harbor 302
12. Saginaw Hill 304
13. Pontiac 308
14. Royal Oak 311
15. Midland 317
16. Flint Northern 346
17. Saginaw 357
18. Hazel Park 409

1947 BOYS CLASS A INDIVIDUALS
1. Dave Stevens (Jackson)12 .... 10:52
2. Jack Crane (Flint Central)12 .... nt
3. Tom Goretzka (Battle Creek Central) .... nt
4. Paul Shaler (Jackson) .... nt
5. John Clark (Kalamazoo Central) .... nt
6?. Elroy Grahl (Wyandotte)11 .... nt
8. Sam Rodgers (Benton Harbor) 11:17
9. Ed Rutter (Benton Harbor) 11:18
12. Dick Vaughn (Jackson) .... nt
13. Dave Fultz (Jackson) .... nt

15. Dayle Stevens (Jackson) .... nt
20. Dick Hilderly (Jackson) .... nt
32. Ted Paychas (Jackson) .... nt
35. Bob Bennett (Battle Creek Central) .... nt
36. Wally Antuck (Battle Creek Central) .... nt

Palmer Park, Nov. 5 □
1947 DETROIT TEAMS
1. Detroit Northwestern 78
2. Detroit Pershing 80
3. Detroit Miller 87
4. Detroit Mackenzie 89
5. Detroit Cooley 98
6. Detroit Cass Tech 100

1947 DETROIT INDIVIDUALS
1. Stan Fields (Detroit Northwestern)12 .... 9:46
2. Aaron Gordon (Detroit Miller) c9:47
3. Chalmer Alexander (Detroit Cass Tech) .... nt
4. Jack Jones (Detroit Mackenzie) .... nt
5. Joe Pathe (Detroit Cooley) .... nt
6. Guido Sabella (Detroit Southeastern) .... nt
7. Jim White (Detroit Mackenzie) .... nt
8. Earl Ehrhart (Detroit Pershing) .... nt
9. Harold McEwen (Detroit Miller) .... nt
10. Don Langlois (Detroit Southeastern) .... nt

1948 CLASS A BOYS

With 25 teams (18 full) entered, this was the largest state meet yet. Muddy conditions and rain forced organizers to alter the course to avoid several clay patches that were deemed too slippery. Coach Chris Jensen's Jackson squad defended handily. Ann Arbor had earlier beaten runner-up Wyandotte in a dual meet, but ended up fourth here because lead runner Bob Burwell had to sit out with a broken arm.

Elroy Grahl capped his undefeated season with a win in 10:54 over the sloppy course.

In Detroit, coach Jimmy Russell's Northwestern squad won its second straight, this time in a heavy rain. Marvin Banks reversed the order with rival Joe Rosales, who had beaten him at the previous week's West Side meet. Banks, the city mile champion as a sophomore, prevailed by mere inches.

Marvin Banks won the 1948 Detroit title.

Briggs Field, Ypsilanti, Nov. 6 □
1948 BOYS CLASS A TEAMS
1. Jackson 53
2. Wyandotte 117
3. Flint Central 160
4. Ann Arbor 165
5. Flint Northern 165
6. Pontiac 176
7. Battle Creek Central 179
8. Monroe 194
9. Dearborn 201
10. Royal Oak 239
11. Saginaw Hill 287
12. Kalamazoo Central 290
13. Grand Rapids Catholic Central 305
14. Lansing Eastern 323
15. Midland 355
16. Lincoln Park 356
17. Hazel Park 424
18. Hamtramck 479

1948 BOYS CLASS A INDIVIDUALS
1. Elroy Grahl (Wyandotte)12 .... 10:54
3. Bruce Jacobs (Flint Northern)12 .... nt
4. Herb Copeland (Jackson) .... nt
5. Ray Palmer (Jackson) .... nt
11. Wally Server (Jackson) .... nt
14. Don Douglas (Ann Arbor) .... nt
16. Dick Hilderly (Jackson) .... nt
17. Alonzo Perrin (Jackson) .... nt
18. Jack Firestone (Ann Arbor) .... nt
21. Wally Antuck (Battle Creek Central) .... nt
24. Willie Jackson (Battle Creek Central) .... nt
34. Bill Romick (Battle Creek Central) .... nt
36. Bill Hicks (Ann Arbor) .... nt

Palmer Park, Nov. 3 □
1948 DETROIT TEAMS
1. Detroit Northwestern 38
2. Detroit Cass Tech 65
3. Detroit Redford 113
4. Detroit Miller 118
5. Detroit Denby 142
6. Detroit Cooley 143

1948 DETROIT INDIVIDUALS
1. Marvin Banks (Detroit Northwestern)11 .... 10:09
2. Joe Rosales (Detroit Western) 10:09
3. Roosevelt Evans (Detroit Northwestern)10 .. c10:11
4. Lang Moran (Detroit Cass Tech) .... nt
5. George Gaines (Detroit Northwestern) .... nt
7. George Harris (Detroit Miller) .... nt
8. Dan Simpson (Detroit Cooley) .... nt
9. George Bacalis (Detroit Cass Tech) .... nt
10. Scott Tetner (Detroit Redford) .... nt

1949 CLASS A BOYS

This was the year the race was moved from Briggs Field to the Washtenaw Country Club, because the event—with 55 total teams—had outgrown the tighter confines of campus.

Jackson won its third straight after a nearly undefeated season—the Vikings lost a dual meet to Battle Creek Central by one point.

In Detroit, Al Williams, an 18-year-old sophomore in his first season of cross country, took the lead from a half mile out and upset the favorites in a course record. He had finished only 5th in the West Side meet the week before. "They were just too fast for me," said the defender, Marvin Banks. The next spring Williams would break the state record in the mile with a 4:24.9.

Washtenaw Country Club, Ypsilanti, Nov. 5 □
1949 BOYS CLASS A TEAMS
1. Jackson 72
2. Battle Creek Central 110
3. Grand Rapids Catholic Central 127
4. Pontiac 139
5. Ann Arbor 156
=6. Dearborn 202
=6. Kalamazoo Central 202
8. Hazel Park 218
9. Flint Northern 239
10. Saginaw Hill 242
11. Flint Central 268
12. Royal Oak 290
13. Wyandotte 316
14. Lincoln Park 338
15. Bay City Central 408
16. Midland 463
17. Bay City Handy 504

1949 BOYS CLASS A INDIVIDUALS
1. Joe Host (Grand Rapids Catholic Central)11 .... 10:48
3. Roger Fulton (Jackson) .... nt
4. Jim Arnold (Battle Creek Central)11 .... nt
8. Howard Linders (Kalamazoo Central) .... nt
9. (Battle Creek Central) .... nt
10. Ray Palmer (Jackson) .... nt
13. Jim Bishop (Kalamazoo Central) .... nt
15. Jack Hoerath (Jackson) .... nt
17. (Battle Creek Central) .... nt
20. Harry Miller (Jackson) .... nt
24. Alonzo Perrin (Jackson) .... nt
29. Dick Hilderly (Jackson) .... nt
30. Jim Bishop (Kalamazoo Central) .... nt
31. Steve McCain (Jackson) .... nt

Palmer Park, Nov. 2 □
1949 DETROIT TEAMS
1. Detroit Northwestern 45
2. Detroit Cass Tech 90
3. Detroit Mackenzie 98
4. Detroit Cooley 110
5. Detroit Denby 145
6. Detroit Miller 148

1949 DETROIT INDIVIDUALS
1. Al Williams (Detroit Northwestern)10 .... 9:45
2. Roosevelt Evans (Detroit Northwestern)11 .. c9:51
3. Charles Irby (Detroit Northern) .... nt
4. Cliff Hatcher (Detroit Central) .... nt
5. Terry Iverson (Detroit Redford) .... nt
6. Ken Danison (Detroit Cooley) .... nt
7. Bob Skinner (Detroit Denby) .... nt
8. Dick Walton (Detroit Pershing) .... nt
9. Jim Clark (Detroit Mackenzie) .... nt
10. Marvin Banks (Detroit Northwestern)12 .... nt

1950 CLASS A BOYS

The Class A race this year earned the dubious distinction of being the only state title race run twice. Kalamazoo Central won the first race in heavy wind, sleet, and snow, in a large part because GR Catholic Central and Battle Creek missed the start, when starter Claude Snarey sent the runners off early (10 minutes early, according to the MHSAA Bulletin; 13 minutes early according to the *Battle Creek Enquirer*). Reported the *Ann Arbor News*: "Protests followed and the Michigan High School Athletic Association's unique decision was to run the race again and award duplicate team and individual trophies but to regard the first race… as official."

Battle Creek Central's Jim Arnold, once he saw the race was underway without him, charged onto the course, bypassing the starting line. Starting out in 80th place, he caught up to the pack and crossed the finish first. Officials gave him the first place award even though he hadn't covered the entire course.

For the second race, MHSAA paid school mileage expenses, but only 10 of the original 23 teams showed. The race was held just before the National Junior Championship, a 10,000m race over the same terrain (Michigan State won).

Perhaps understandably, Kalamazoo Central, the winner of the initial race, refused to run again. Arnold won again after running most of the way with defending champion Joe Host, producing a course record with the help of somewhat better weather. The course still had snow on it.

In Detroit, Roosevelt Evans, who had won the city half-mile title as a sophomore before switching sports and becoming a standout pitcher, won in a blistering 9:37.7 over a course described as "just short of two miles". He was the fourth straight winner for the Colts. Evans ran with his foot heavily taped to protect a bone bruise. In the sectional meet just a week before, he had covered the course in a record 9:36.4. Runner-up was Cliff Hatcher, one of the greatest quartermilers the state ever produced.

After graduating, Evans signed with the St. Louis Browns. He played in the minors for 8 years.

Washtenaw Country Club, Ypsilanti, Nov. 4 ☐
1950 BOYS CLASS A TEAMS – RACE 1
1. Kalamazoo Central 40
2. Ann Arbor 90
3. Royal Oak 100
4. Pontiac 174
5. Ypsilanti 212
6. Bay City Central 229
7. Jackson 237
8. Battle Creek Central 256
9. Flint Central 275
10. Saginaw Hill 296
11. Midland 325
12. Bay City Handy 332
13. Hazel Park 345
14. Flint Northern 348
15. Lincoln Park 379
16. Benton Harbor 395
17. Monroe 410
18. Dearborn 414
19. Grand Rapids Union 484
20. Hamtramck 505
21. Wyandotte 512
22. Wayne 555

Battle Creek Central's Jim Arnold won the state title twice in 1950.

1950 BOYS CLASS A INDIVIDUALS –RACE 1
1. Jim Arnold (Battle Creek Central)12 .... 10:45
2. Jim Bishop (Kalamazoo Central) .... nt
3. George Jayne (Ann Arbor) .... nt
4. Dave Ingle (Kalamazoo Central) .... nt
5. Dale Griffin (Jackson)10 .... nt
6. Willie McGee (Benton Harbor) .... nt
9. Charles Temple (Midland) .... nt
10. Ron Boegler (Kalamazoo Central) .... nt
11. Bud Decoster (Kalamazoo Central) .... nt
12. Jim Seidl (Ypsilanti)11 .... nt
13. Maclay Gearheart (Kalamazoo Central) .... nt
15. Dave Balcom (Kalamazoo Central) .... nt
22. Don Hamilton (Ypsilanti)12 .... nt
31. Steve McGain (Jackson) .... nt
40. Julius Sims (Kalamazoo Central) .... nt

Washtenaw Country Club, Ypsilanti, Nov. 11 ☐
1950 BOYS CLASS A TEAMS – RACE 2
1. Battle Creek Central 45
2. Ann Arbor 69
3. Grand Rapids Catholic Central 118
4. Pontiac 142
=5. Jackson 147
=5. Ypsilanti 147
7. Bay City Central 181
8. Hazel Park 210
9. Midland 214
10. Grand Rapids Union 263

1950 BOYS CLASS A INDIVIDUALS – RACE 2
1. Jim Arnold (Battle Creek Central)12 .... 10:40
2. George Jayne (Ann Arbor) .... nt
3. Joe Host (Grand Rapids Catholic Central)12 .... 10:59
5. Val Eichendaub (Battle Creek Central)12 .... 11:05
5?. Dale Griffin (Jackson)10 .... nt
6. Jim Seidl (Ypsilanti)11 .... nt
12. Ed Houldsworth (Battle Creek Central) 11:20
13. Preston Brown (Battle Creek Central) 11:20
14. Dave Dow (Ann Arbor) .... nt
15. Jim Young (Battle Creek Central) 11:22
16. Bob Winder (Ann Arbor) .... nt
18. Bob Gould (Ann Arbor) .... nt
19. Henry Haas (Ann Arbor) .... nt
20. Dale Farrall (Battle Creek Central) 11:30
21. Steve McCain (Jackson) .... nt
25. Duane Osborne (Battle Creek Central) 11:37
29. Leon Meyer (Ann Arbor) .... nt
30. Don Hamilton (Ypsilanti)12 .... nt
33. Pete Stamos (Ypsilanti)11 .... nt
34. Fred Henningsen (Jackson) .... nt
38. Roger Walker (Ypsilanti)12 .... nt
40. Joe Seidl (Ypsilanti)10 .... nt

Palmer Park, Nov. 1 ☐
1950 DETROIT TEAMS
1. Detroit Northwestern 49
2. Detroit Cass Tech 78
3. Detroit Cooley 91
4. Detroit Denby 102
5. Detroit Mackenzie 109
6. Detroit Miller 168

1950 DETROIT INDIVIDUALS
1. Roosevelt Evans (Detroit Northwestern)12 .... 9:38
2. Cliff Hatcher (Detroit Central) c9:47
3. Lou Kwiker (Detroit Central) .... nt
4. Jim Clark (Detroit Mackenzie) .... nt
5. Ken Danison (Detroit Cooley) .... nt
6. Jess Smith (Detroit Northwestern) .... nt
7. Bob Skinner (Detroit Denby) .... nt
8. Bob Babbs (Detroit Cass Tech) .... nt
9. Willie Atterberry (Detroit Eastern) .... nt
10. Jim Haggerty (Detroit Cooley) .... nt

1951 CLASS A BOYS

No one chased records as cold weather and a slippery course had the runners facing bigger challenges than the stopwatch. Dale Griffin, a hurdler during the track season (the 5-A league champion in both hurdle events as a soph), was only in 12th place at 1.25M. He started his drive then and won by nearly 100 yards. A total of 27 schools and 189 runners participated.

Pontiac, in what was described as a major upset, snatched the win by 9 points. Both Battle Creek Central and Kalamazoo Central had expected to finish higher up.

In Detroit, Northwestern's 32 points was hailed as the lowest winning score in the meet's history. The individual champion was Louis Kwiker, a six-foot tall 16-year-old who was the only athlete from Central to qualify for the finals. He took the lead early and won with a 25-yard margin. His time, 10:03, was called a course record, because the route had been changed from the previous year.

Washtenaw Country Club, Ypsilanti, Nov. 3 ☐
1951 BOYS CLASS A TEAMS
1. Pontiac 96
2. Ann Arbor 105
3. Bay City Central 107
4. Grand Rapids Union 163
5. Battle Creek Central 167
6. Jackson 206
7. Kalamazoo Central 244
8. Grand Rapids Catholic Central 247
9. Bay City Handy 295
10. Lincoln Park 305
11. Saginaw Hill 333
12. Hazel Park 360
13. Midland 369
14. Flint Northern 372
15. Royal Oak 388
16. Flint Central 432
17. Grand Rapids South 465
18. Dearborn 481
19. Ypsilanti 513
20. Benton Harbor 516
21. Wayne 551
22. Detroit St Joseph 581
23. Wyandotte 594
24. Van Dyke Lincoln 657
25. Detroit Catholic Central 686

1951 BOYS CLASS A INDIVIDUALS
1. Dale Griffin (Jackson)11 .... 10:53
2. Bill Boegler (Kalamazoo Central) c11:08
6. Terry Block (Grand Rapids Union) .... nt
11. Doug Hagen (Grand Rapids South) .... nt
13. Preston Brown (Battle Creek Central) .... nt
16. Dale Ferrall (Battle Creek Central) .... nt
21. Pete Stamos (Ypsilanti)12 .... nt
25. Jerry Host (Grand Rapids Catholic Central) .... nt
36. Tom Taube (Benton Harbor) .... nt

Palmer Park, Oct. 30 ☐
1951 DETROIT TEAMS
1. Detroit Northwestern 32
2. Detroit Cooley 75
3. Detroit Cass Tech 96
4. Detroit Redford 120
5. Detroit Southeastern 146
6. Detroit Denby 160

1951 DETROIT INDIVIDUALS
1. Louis Kwiker (Detroit Central)12 .... 10:03
2. Joe Babb (Detroit Cass Tech) c10:08
3. Adell Dukes (Detroit Northwestern) .... nt
4. Burle Huggins (Detroit Northwestern)11 .... nt
5. Willie Atterberry (Detroit Eastern) .... nt
6. Ken Santer (Detroit Redford) .... nt
7. Ed Gibson (Detroit Northwestern) .... nt
8. Bob Backus (Detroit Northwestern) .... nt
9. Ron Acton (Detroit Cooley) .... nt
10. Seabron Hall (Detroit Northwestern) .... nt

1952 CLASS A BOYS

Favored Kalamazoo Central fell far short as coach Lowell Palmer's Grand Rapids Union squad dominated in Class A. Twenty-six teams (190 runners) competed. Ron Den Uyl came from 6th place at halfway to challenge undefeated Terry Block near the finish, but the

Grand Rapids Union senior won by two seconds.

Jackson finished a surprise 3rd despite the fact that one of the Vikings' top runners, Bill Eagen, was spiked at the start and lost a shoe; he struggled to finish 132nd.

In Detroit, Cooley coach Claude Snarey acted as the scorer, and figured his own team for 67 points, which he thought would be unlikely to win. When all the teams but one had reported, Northwestern coach Jimmy Russell said, "Congratulations, Claude. If I have to lose I'd rather it be to you than anyone else." Snarey replied, "What are you talking about? We haven't beaten you." That's when Russell revealed that his favored team's total was one point shy of Cooley's.

Berle Huggins, Northwestern's individual winner, had captured the city mile the spring before in 4:30. He lost his senior season of track, however, when conflicting information arose as to whether he was 19 or 20 that spring. He had to leave the team and start attending night school.

Washtenaw Country Club, Ypsilanti, Nov. 1 ☐
1952 BOYS CLASS A TEAMS
1. Grand Rapids Union 67
2. Pontiac 154
3. Ann Arbor 173
4. Jackson 179
5. Bay City Central 196
6. Kalamazoo Central 204
7. Lansing Sexton 237
8. Grand Rapids Catholic Central 238
9. Plymouth 254
10. Battle Creek Central 266
11. Flint Central 274
12. Saginaw Hill 311
13. Midland 339
14. Lincoln Park 358
15. Ypsilanti 386
16. Dearborn 395
17. Detroit St Joseph 407
18. Hazel Park 422
19. Royal Oak 448
20. Lansing Eastern 450
21. Birmingham 568
22. Flint Northern 583
23. Holland 611
24. Bay City Handy 660
25. Wyandotte 666
26. Hamtramck 677

1952 BOYS CLASS A INDIVIDUALS
1. Terry Block (Grand Rapids Union)12 ....10:31
2. Ron Den Uyl (Holland) 10:33
3. Larry Favorite (Battle Creek Central) .... nt
4. Dale Vandenberg (Grand Rapids Catholic Central)... nt
7. Mel Harris (Jackson) .... nt
8. Bob Block (Grand Rapids Union) .... nt
11. Jerry Heller (Jackson) .... nt
16. Bert Korhonen (Grand Rapids Union) .... nt
18. Doug Horton (Grand Rapids Union) .... nt
23. Dick Block (Grand Rapids Union) .... nt
36. Ron Maher (Jackson) .... nt

Palmer Park, Oct. 29 ☐
1952 DETROIT TEAMS
1. Detroit Cooley 67
2. Detroit Northwestern 68
3. Detroit Redford 69
4. Detroit Pershing 123
5. Detroit Denby 126
6. Detroit Northeastern 129

1952 DETROIT INDIVIDUALS
1. Burle Huggins (Detroit Northwestern)12 ....10:08
2. Al Manser (Detroit Redford) c10:10
3. Ron Acton (Detroit Cooley) .... nt
4. Maurice Faller (Detroit Denby) .... nt
5. Stan Stankowvich (Detroit Northeastern) ..... nt
6. Bob Brantley (Detroit Cooley) .... nt
7. Harold Patton (Detroit Western) .... nt
8. Ken Santer (Detroit Redford) .... nt
9. Dick Blom (Detroit Cooley) .... nt
10. Charles Martin (Detroit Eastern) .... nt

1953 CLASS A BOYS

After a nearly 20-year stretch when regionals were either cancelled or optional, they once again were required. There were three sites: Birmingham, Grand Rapids and Lansing.

Soggy conditions—an inch of snow was on the course—ruled as Grand Rapids Union won its second straight title. Battle Creek Central's Larry Favorite produced the fastest time. The next spring he won the Class A mile in 4:28.9. Ernie Bennetts of Hazel Park, considered one of the pre-meet favorites, finished 10th.

In Detroit, favored Pershing won its first Metro title in 33 years. This in spite of the fact that Ron Hodge, one of the team's top men, was running with the leaders with 300 yards to go, took a bad spill, and had to be helped off the course. A light snow had been falling during the race.

Larry Favorite conquered the snow in 1953.

Washtenaw Country Club, Ypsilanti, Nov. 7 ☐
1953 BOYS CLASS A TEAMS
1. Grand Rapids Union 56
2. Jackson 140
3. Ann Arbor 146
4. Kalamazoo Central 148
5. Battle Creek Central 186
6. Midland 205
7. Lansing Sexton 206
8. Royal Oak 209
9. Pontiac 210
10. Mt Clemens 244
11. Hazel Park 279
12. Dearborn 313
13. Grand Rapids Catholic Central 315
14. Birmingham 343

1953 BOYS CLASS A INDIVIDUALS
1. Larry Favorite (Battle Creek Central)12 ....10:36
2. Dick Block (Grand Rapids Union) .... nt
3. Dale Vandenberg (Gran Rapids Catholic Central)..... nt
5. Burt Korhonen (Grand Rapids Union) .... nt
8. Arnold DeHaven (Grand Rapids Union) .... nt
9. Karl Parrish (Jackson) .... nt
10. Ernie Bennetts (Hazel Park) .... nt
12. Gary Warriner (Lansing Sexton) .... nt
15. Bob Block (Grand Rapids Union) .... nt
23. Bill Blake (Jackson) .... nt
26. Doug Horton (Grand Rapids Union) .... nt
29. Jerry Heller (Jackson) .... nt
39. Gene Shahan (Jackson) .... nt
40. Dale Gansmiller (Jackson) .... nt

Palmer Park, Nov. 4 ☐
1953 DETROIT TEAMS
1. Detroit Pershing 74
2. Detroit Northwestern 76
3. Detroit Cooley 87
4. Detroit Denby 136
5. Detroit Mackenzie 170
DQ—Detroit Miller (127).

1953 DETROIT INDIVIDUALS
1. Ron Wheeler (Detroit Pershing)11 ....10:16
2. Dick Ehrle (Detroit Redford) .... nt
3. Don Norwood (Detroit Western) .... nt
4. Fred Karn (Detroit Southeastern) .... nt
5. Gurney Beach (Detroit Pershing) .... nt
6. Al Bowser (Detroit Northwestern) .... nt
7. Pete Marudas (Detroit Miller) .... nt
8. Ernest Richardson (Detroit Miller) .... nt
9. Ernest Simms (Detroit Northwestern) .... nt
10. Bill Emerson (Detroit Cass Tech) .... nt

1954 CLASS A BOYS

Both Kalamazoo Cenral and Midland entered the state finals undefeated, but it was Kalamazoo that dominated despite its top runner, Bob Lake, being run down by Jackson's Karl Parrish in the final 150 yards. Parrish had led most of the early way before Lake made his own move with a quarter mile to go.

A fourth regional—in Trenton—was added to the line-up.

In Detroit, Ron Wheeler of Pershing broke his own course record of 9:58 after taking over the race at three quarters of a mile. Said coach Carl Holmes of Wheeler's beginnings two years earlier, "He was just a flat-footed slow plodder and I didn't think he would ever make a runner. Ron had more determination than anybody else on the squad and worked harder." Holmes added that Wheeler went so far as to train on weekends.

Washtenaw Country Club, Ypsilanti, Nov. 6 ☐
1954 BOYS CLASS A TEAMS
1. Kalamazoo Central 88
2. Midland 103
3. Pontiac 128
4. Jackson 135
5. Lincoln Park 199
6. Birmingham 201
7. Grand Rapids Ottawa Hills 241
8. Lansing Eastern 260
9. Lansing Sexton 269
10. Grand Rapids Union 279
11. Hazel Park 335
12. Monroe 338
13. Ann Arbor 349
14. Wyandotte 386

1954 BOYS CLASS A INDIVIDUALS
1. Karl Parrish (Jackson) 10:41
2. Bob Lake (Kalamazoo Central)11 ....c10:44
3. Dick Rogers (Midland) .... nt
10. Bill Blake (Jackson) .... nt
31. Mac Sargent (Jackson) .... nt
33. Rudy Kalafus (Jackson) .... nt

Palmer Park, Nov. 3 ☐
1954 DETROIT TEAMS
1. Detroit Northwestern 63
2. Detroit Denby 69
3. Detroit Redford 95
4. Detroit Pershing 96

5. Detroit Cooley 130
6. Detroit Miller 147

1954 DETROIT INDIVIDUALS
1. Ron Wheeler (Detroit Pershing)12 .... 9:57
2. Jerry Bocci (Detroit Denby) .... nt
3. Ernie Sims (Detroit Pershing) .... nt
4. Ernie Richardson (Detroit Miller) .... nt
5. Gurney Beach (Detroit Pershing) .... nt
6. Bill Minelli (Detroit Cooley) .... nt
7. Tom Scheffler (Detroit Denby) .... nt
8. Phil Eckman (Detroit Denby) .... nt
9. Sol Gaines (Detroit Northeastern) .... nt
10. Bob Patrick (Detroit Cody) .... nt

1955 CLASS A BOYS

First Lansing Eastern won its first 6-A conference title in 11 years. Then it topped the 14 other teams at the state finals. Winner Bob Lake, undefeated all fall, went on the following spring to win the Class A 880 in a meet record 1:58.9, after earlier running a 1:57.4 to win his conference. At Michigan State, he would win the Big 10 mile indoors and out in 1959.

In Detroit, Denby's Ralph Greene figured his team would win its first-ever title with 30 points. "I didn't guess all of the individual places, but the net result was the same," he said.

Denby's Jerry Bocci, who had won the city mile title in 4:32.0 the previous spring, took the individual victory.

Washtenaw Country Club, Ypsilanti, Nov. 5 □
1955 BOYS CLASS A TEAMS
1. Lansing Eastern 121
2. Pontiac 145
3. Kalamazoo Central 149
=4. Battle Creek Central 157
=4. Jackson 157
6. Birmingham 195
7. Lincoln Park 212
8. Grand Rapids Union 229
9. Saginaw Hill 272
10. Holland 281
11. Hazel Park 303
12. Dearborn 350
13. Southfield 358
14. Ypsilanti 389

1955 BOYS CLASS A INDIVIDUALS
1. Bob Lake (Kalamazoo)12 .... 10:29
2. Steve Rhodes (Grand Rapids Ottawa Hills) ...... nt
3. Earl Seamans (Battle Creek Central) .... nt
16. Paul Parrish (Jackson) .... nt
21. Sherri Shaffer (Holland) .... nt
25. Danny White (Battle Creek Central) .... nt
27. Mac Sargent (Jackson) .... nt
28. Max Rust (Battle Creek Central) .... nt
29. Gary Evan (Jackson) .... nt
34. Jan Robberst (Holland) .... nt
38. Ron Johnson (Jackson) .... nt
39. Daryl Gibbs (Battle Creek Central) .... nt
40. Ralph Harper (Ypsilanti)12 .... nt

Palmer Park, Nov. 2 □
1955 DETROIT TEAMS
1. Detroit Denby 30
2. Detroit Cass Tech 103
3. Detroit Central 104
4. Detroit Mackenzie 120
5. Detroit Northwestern 120
6. Detroit Miller 121

1955 DETROIT INDIVIDUALS
1. Jerry Bocci (Detroit Denby)12 .... 10:08
2. Tom Scheffler (Detroit Denby) c10:10
3. Stan Wheeler (Detroit Cass Tech) .... nt
4. Tom Bleakley (Detroit Denby) .... nt
5. Dave Tate (Detroit Denby) .... nt
6. Norman Young (Detroit Central)10 .... nt
7. Doug Beard (Detroit Northwestern) .... nt

8. Bob Swaney (Detroit Denby) .... nt
9. Felton Shaffer (Detroit Miller) .... nt
10. Leroy Arnold (Detroit Central) .... nt

1956 CLASS A BOYS

Berkley produced the top two runners in Class A despite not qualifying its entire team for the meet. Lansing Eastern successfully defended its Class A crown.

In Detroit, Tom Bleakley ran a longer course than his predecessors, as the Palmer Park course had been lengthened 200 yards to make it an actual two miles. Even so, he predicted a 10:25 race, eight seconds faster than he had run all season. His official time was 10:25.4. "I didn't realize I was running that fast," Bleakley (5-7, 141lb) said. "I was relaxed and might have done better if I had been pushed." At the quarter mile mark, he had been in last place in the 45-man field, but he took the lead at halfway.

Washtenaw Country Club, Ypsilanti, Nov. 3 □
1956 BOYS CLASS A TEAMS
1. Lansing Eastern 69
2. Saginaw Hill 128
3. Jackson 155
4. Flint Northern 179
5. Birmingham 234
6. Plymouth 244
7. Grand Rapids Creston 247
8. Pontiac Central 266
9. Wyandotte 278
10. Grand Rapids Catholic Central 279
11. Dearborn Edsel Ford 298
=12. Grand Rapids Central 346
=12. Mt Clemens 346
14. Allen Park 358
15. Royal Oak 376
16. Hazel Park 413
17. Grand Rapids Union 434
18. Dearborn 495

1956 BOYS CLASS A INDIVIDUALS
1. Jerry Young (Berkley)10 .... 10:31
2. Fred Chappel (Berkley)12 .... 10:32
3. Tom Davis (Port Huron)12 .... 10:42
4. Art Vaillencourt (Lansing Eastern)11 .... nt
5. Gary Bullock (Lansing Eastern)12 .... nt
6. Dave DeCoster (Plymouth) .... nt
9. Tom Blake (Jackson) .... nt
11. Paul Parrish (Jackson) .... nt
13. Don Goudard (Lansing Eastern)12 .... nt
17. Dave Brown (Lansing Eastern)12 .... nt
18. Jim Moore (Fliont Northern) .... nt
23. Joe Medina (Jackson) .... nt
29. Curt Stevens (Flint Northern) .... nt
30. Ron Selfridge (Lansing Eastern)11 .... nt
33. Bob Pearl (Lansing Eastern)11 .... nt
36. King Thomason (Port Huron)12 .... nt
57. Dick Stauffer (Lansing Eastern)11 .... nt

Palmer Park, Oct. 30 □
1956 DETROIT TEAMS
1. Detroit Denby 37
2. Detroit Central 64
3. Detroit Cass Tech 77
4. Detroit Redford 104
5. Detroit Mackenzie 131
6. Detroit Pershing 137

1956 DETROIT INDIVIDUALS
1. Tom Bleakley (Detroit Denby)11 .... 10:26
2. Norman Young (Detroit Central)11 .... 10:41
3. Bob Ouillette (Detroit Central) .... nt
4. Stan Wheeler (Detroit Cass Tech) .... nt
5. Bob Frey (Detroit Redford) .... nt
6. Luke Deman (Detroit Cass Tech) .... nt
7. Berry Tindle (Detroit Mackenzie) .... nt
8. Dick Mounts (Detroit Denby) .... nt
9. Jim Sciturro (Detroit Denby) .... nt

10. Roger Barkham (?) .... nt

Jerry Young being congratulated by his coach after winning his second title.

1957 CLASS A BOYS

Berkley's Jerry Young became only the third runner to successfully defend a Class A title, after running the first 1.5M with Benton Harbor's Paul Dodson before kicking to victory. In 1961, he would run two miles in 9:08.1 to capture the Big 10 Indoor title for MSU. Chuck Sweeney's Lansing Eastern squad got a scare earlier in the week when lead runner Art Vaillencourt got "23 stitches in his right hand as a result of tangling with a buzz saw." He recovered well enough to finish 10th, helping his teammates to their third-straight title.

In Detroit, Norman Young of Central said he wanted to win "more than anything else in my life." He reversed places with defender Tom Bleakley, who had beaten him the previous year. Added Young, "This is Central's centennial, and I hoped I could give the school a champion." Young had led most of the distance. Three times Bleakley passed him, and three times Young fought back. With 50 yards to go, he finally pulled a few steps ahead for a narrow win.

Washtenaw Country Club, Ypsilanti, Nov. 2 □
1957 BOYS CLASS A TEAMS
1. Lansing Eastern 118
2. Birmingham 141
3. Flint Central 160
4. Saginaw Hill 163
5. Jackson 177
6. Wayne Memorial 217
7. Lincoln Park 235
8. Allen Park 243
9. Royal Oak 271
10. Pontiac 275
11. Dearborn Edsel Ford 278
12. Grand Rapids Catholic Central 286
13. Dearborn 299
14. Redford Union 300
15. Wyandotte 364

16. Inkster	416
17. Hazel Park	419
18. Muskegon	438
19. Walled Lake	472
20. Kalamazoo Central	485

1957 BOYS CLASS A INDIVIDUAL
1. Jerry Young (Berkley)11	10:37
2. Larry Beamer (Pontiac)	10:40
3. Jerry Bashaw (Lincoln Park)11	10:43
7. Paul Dodson (Benton Harbor)	nt
10. Artt Vaillencourt (Lansing Eastern)	nt
11. Paul Parrish (Jackson)	nt
16. Joe Medina (Jackson)	nt
20. Dick Stauffer (Lansing Eastern)11	nt
22. Ron Selfridge (Lansing Eastern)	nt
30. Bob Pearl (Lansing Eastern)	nt
36. Ray Auvenshine (Lansing Eastern)	nt
40. Ron Eagan (Jackson)	nt

Palmer Park, Oct. 30 □
1957 DETROIT TEAMS
1. Detroit Denby	42
2. Detroit Redford	63
3. Detroit Central	97
4. Detroit Cody	100
5. Detroit Pershing	119
6. Detroit Northwestern	189

1957 DETROIT INDIVIDUALS
1. Norman Young (Detroit Central)12	10:39
2. Tom Bleakley (Detroit Denby)12	10:39
3. Frank Carissimi (Detroit Redford)10	10:43
4. Louis Molnar (Detroit Redford)	nt
5. Dick Mounts (Detroit Denby)	nt
6. Barrie Armstrong (Detroit Redford)	nt
7. George Rourke (Detroit Cody)	nt
8. Bob Kropf (Detroit Cody)	nt
9. Stephen Jarmon (Detroit Pershing)	nt
10. Joe Iskra (Detroit Cody)	nt

1958 CLASS A BOYS

A stomach ailment hit Flint Central's Bill Milum, who had been favored by many to win Class A; he finished 8th, while Jerry Bashaw pulled away from the field in the last three-quarters of a mile. Coach Varnard Gay's Flint Central squad still capped off an undefeated season with a 15-point win. The Class A race had 128 of the meet's 358 entrants.

Bashaw had been captain of the tennis team as a junior before switching to track and running a 4:33.4 mile.

A year earlier, there had been speculation that Berkley's Jerry Young would return for his senior year and attempt to win a record third straight. However, he graduated early and opted to join Michigan State's harrier team. In 1960 he placed 4th in the NCAA Championships.

In Detroit, Frank Carissimi opened eyes with a 50-yard win, missing the course record by three seconds despite a strong headwind. Said his coach, Ralph Greene, "Frank should wind up as one of the fastest runners we've had at Denby. He has more natural speed than anybody I've coached."

Said Carissimi, "I guess I'd rather run than do almost anything else, even eat. It's my only sport and I train two hours a day at school. On weekends I run around Belle Isle or through the woods with other members of my team."

The name of the meet itself changed this year, as the old Metropolitan League had become the Public School League.

Washtenaw Country Club, Ypsilanti, Nov. 1 □
1958 BOYS CLASS A TEAMS
1. Flint Central	114
2. Birmingham	129
3. Lincoln Park	175
4. Jackson	220
5. Wayne Memorial	228
6. Ann Arbor	269
7. Pontiac	270
8. Muskegon	281
9. Midland	305
10. Hazel Park	314
11. Redford Thurston	347
12. Dearborn	351
13. Grand Rapids Catholic Central	363
14. Wyandotte	425
15. Grand Rapids Christian	483

The day before the finals, Birmingham's runners decided to prank coach Kermit Ambrose, and Dave Pew showed up for school on crutches. No word on Ambrose's reaction. The next day Pew finished second, as did the team.

1958 BOYS CLASS A INDIVIDUALS
1. Jerry Bashaw (Lincoln Park)12	10:27
2. Dave Pew (Birmingham)	nt
3. George Friedreichsen (Flint Central)	nt
6. Jim Reilly (Birmingham)	nt
7. Bill Milum (Flint Central)	nt
8. Fraser Cocks (Birmingham)	nt
9. Gary Crenshaw (Flint Central)	nt
15. Jack Webb (Midland)	nt
18. Tim Butler (Port Huron)	nt
34. Ron Eagan (Jackson)	nt
36. Harlan Blomquist (Port Huron)	nt
38. Jerry Jernon (Jackson)	nt
47. Bill Foster (Flint Central)	nt
48. Buck Miley (Flint Central)	nt
53. Bob Lufcy (Flint Central)	nt
57. Bob Anthony (Flint Central)	nt

Palmer Park, Oct. 28 □
1958 DETROIT TEAMS
1. Detroit Redford	30
2. Detroit Pershing	76
3. Detroit Cody	110
4. Detroit Denby	112
5. Detroit Mumford	128
6. Detroit Cooley	130

1958 DETROIT INDIVIDUALS
1. Frank Carissimi (Detroit Dernby)11	10:29
2. Terry Moore (Detroit Redford)9	c10:39
3. Chuck Nowell (Detroit Central)	c10:40
4. Joe Iskra (Detroit Cody)	nt
5. Gary Chaplin (Detroit Redford)	nt
6. Hank Lennox (Detroit Redford)	nt
7. Butch Howie (Detroit Redford)	nt
8. Steve Jarmon (Detroit Pershing)	nt
9. Manley Ross (Detroit Mumford)	nt
10. Dick Rix (Detroit Redford)	nt

1959 CLASS A BOYS

According to Kermit Ambrose, in 1959 the course at Washtenaw Country Club was "drastically changed." Joe Anderson won going away in 10:24.5, a time that could be considered a new course record. Runner-up Carl Allen of Ann Arbor was in his first season of running. Two decades later, his son and namesake would deliver two runner-up performances for Ann Arbor Huron.

Ambrose's Maples delivered their first state win, putting up 73 points, the second-lowest winning total in 7 years.

In Detroit, Frank Carissimi challenged his coach, Ralph Green, as the team departed for the meet at Palmer Park: "How about some new spikes, coach? I'll break the record if I get them." Green gave him the spikes, though he felt his charge didn't have a chance to break the 10:18 record he had set at sectionals the previous week. Carissimi produced, however, cruising the "soggy" course a second faster than the record. In fourth place ran Redford's Terry Moore, who had run a 4:23.6 mile as a frosh but had to be lured from the football team.

Washtenaw Country Club, Ypsilanti, Nov. 7 □
1959 BOYS CLASS A TEAMS
1. Birmingham	73
2. Ann Arbor	145
3. Ypsilanti	159
4. Dearborn	171
5. Pontiac Central	180
6. Muskegon	200
7. Lincoln Park	210
8. Walled Lake	215
9. Flint Southwestern	242
10. Lansing Sexton	243
11. Grand Rapids Christian	283
12. Monroe	313
13. Grand Rapids Central	333
14. East Lansing	355
15. Detroit U-D Jesuit	360

1959 BOYS CLASS A INDIVIDUALS
1. Joe Anderson (Pontiac)11	10:25
2. Carl Allen (Ann Arbor)11	nt
3. Pat Stevens (Lansing Everett)12	nt
4. Dan Reid (Birmingham)	nt
5. Henning Anderson (Battle Creek Central)12	nt
6. Mac Poll (Lansing Sexton)	nt
10. Dick Kelley (Birmingham)	nt
12. Ted Kelly (Dearborn)	nt
15. Jock McPhee (Birmingham)	nt
17. Pat McDonald (Ypsilanti)12	nt
19. Ted Egner (Birmingham)	nt
25. Al Bauman (Birmingham)	nt
32. Ronnie Gillum (Ypsilanti)10	nt
36. Ernie Gillum (Ypsilanti)10	nt
41. Levi Hardwick (Ypsilanti)12	nt
43. Bob Barnes (Ypsilanti)11	nt

Palmer Park, Nov. 4 □
1959 DETROIT TEAMS
1. Detroit Denby	28
2. Detroit Northwestern	80
3. Detroit Mumford	89
4. Detroit Denby	92
5. Detroit Cody	124
6. Detroit Pershing	145

1959 DETROIT INDIVIDUALS
1. Frank Carissimi (Detroit Denby)12 ....10:17
2. Gary Chapin (Detroit Redford) 10:31
3. Chuck Nowell (Detroit Central) .... nt
4. Terry Moore (Detroit Redford) .... nt
5. Mike McMillan (Detroit Redford) .... nt
6. James Perry (Detroit Denby) .... nt
7. Peller Phillips (Detroit Northwestern) .... nt
8. Bill Stewart (Detroit Redford) .... nt
9. Dick Sharkey (Detroit Redford) .... nt
10. Jack Keating (Detroit Cody) .... nt

1960 CLASS A BOYS

Richard Lee's Ypsilanti squad won its first Class A title with a record high 141 points. The previous year they had gone undefeated until the state finals before finishing third. This year they had run up an 8-2 dual meet record and finished third in their league. Newspapers reported that temperatures were in the mid-thirties with snow flurries. Steve Meyer won at 10:04.5, beating Dennis "Spider" Johnson of Ann Arbor. Defending state champion Joe Anderson was not on Pontiac Central's team.

The original results had Wayne Memorial taking the runner-up trophy, but after a recount the Zebras were asked to return it.

Jeff Sonnenberg of Wyandotte was the nephew of '29 champ Earl Sonnenberg.

In Detroit, Dick Sharkey (5-6, 110lb) impressed with a 10:08 run that just missed the course record of 10:07 he set at the previous week's sectional meet. Said the winner, "Coach [Bruce] Waha told us last year that Herb Elliott, Australia's great miler, ran barefooted in sand to strengthen his legs and I decided to try it out. I ran two to five miles a day on the beach near our summer home in Oscoda. It helped my wind and toughened my feet."

Said Waha, "All of our boys trained during the summer, but not as hard or diligently."

Washtenaw Country Club, Ypsilanti, Nov. 5 □
1960 BOYS CLASS A TEAMS
1. Ypsilanti 141
2. Flint Southwestern 160
3. Dearborn Edsel Ford 161
4. Wayne Memorial 169
5. Birmingham Seaholm 195
6. Flint Central 197
7. Dearborn 198
8. Redford Thurston 228
9. Ann Arbor 247
=10. East Lansing 256
=10. Grand Rapids Central 256
12. Muskegon 285
13. Plymouth 289
14. Wyandotte 352
15. Grand Rapids Christian 357

1960 BOYS CLASS A INDIVIDUALS
1. Steve Meyer (Berkley)12 ....10:05
2. Dennis Johnson (Ann Arbor) 10:09
3. Roger Stevens (Kalamazoo Central) 10:10
4. Tony Klieman (Dearborn) 10:15
5. John Shaw (Flint Central) 10:16
6. Jack McPhee (Birmingham Seaholm) 10:18
7. Mike Felts (Garden City) 10:20
8. Paul Lamse (GR Central Christian) 10:23
9. Ted Egner (Birmingham Seaholm) 10:23
11. Pat Innes (Wayne Memorial)12 ....10:24
12. Jeff Sonnenberg (Wyandotte) 10:25
13. Ronnie Gillum (Ypsilanti)11 ....10:25
14. Dempsey Yearout (Wayne Memorial)11 ....10:26
15. Montie Hardy (Jackson) 10:27

Palmer Park, Nov. 2 □

1960 DETROIT TEAMS
1. Detroit Redford 29
2. Detroit Northwestern 89
=3. Detroit Denby 90
=3. Detroit Mumford 90
5. Detroit Cooley 134
6. Detroit Central 153

1960 DETROIT INDIVIDUALS
1. Dick Sharkey (Detroit Redford)11 .... 10:08
2. Shelton Douthard (Detroit Northwestern) 10:28
3. Dave Cox (Detroit Redford) ....nt
4. Tony Mifsud (Detroit Cody) ....nt
5. Brian Haynes (Detroit Redford) ....nt
6. Dick Mather (Detroit Redford) ....nt
7. Walter Foreman (Detroit Mumford) ....nt
8. Jim Carlson (Detroit Denby) ....nt
9. Ivan Sumner (Detroit Mackenzie) ....nt
10. Jim Perry (Detroit Denby) ....nt

When Detroit returned to the state finals in 1961, Redford's Dick Sharkey dominated, as did his team, coached by Bruce Waha.

1961 CLASS A BOYS

This year the Class A race was split into two different events, a section for teams only, and one for individuals who qualified for State without their teams. The MHSAA Bulletin commented, "It was felt that this race was successful in that it reduced the congestion at the finish line of the Class A Final Team Run while increasing, rather than decreasing, the number of qualifiers from Regionals to the Finals." Fifty-six athletes competed in the individual run.

This was also a landmark meet because of the return of the Detroit public schools to state athletic competition, 32 years after they had departed over a disagreement on policy. With the increase in statewide participation numbers as a result, two regionals were added for a total of 6, with three in the greater Detroit area.

Detroit schools took three of the top 10 slots at the finals, with its individuals running 1-2. It was abundantly clear to the 2,000 spectators that the state meet had missed some great performances over the previous three decades.

Dick Sharkey, all 118 pounds of him, put forth the best performance, a 9:57.2 that keyed a big team win by Bruce Waha's Redford squad. It was Sharkey's 20th straight victory in the past 2 years. Earlier in the week he had run 9:21 on a flatter course to win the PSL title. He had signaled early that he was the man to beat, running an eye-opening 9:07.4 on a new course at Rouge Park in his first race of the year; it was found out later the compeitors "unknowingly ran a shortened course."

A year later he would help Michigan State win the Big 10 Cross Country Championship and place fifth at NCAAs.

A record crowd of 2,000 gathered for the meet—possibly in part because of the addition of the Detroit schools, but also because of the pleasant weather—much better than the few years previously. An addition of a big hill on the WCC course made for new course records, though officials at the time insisted on keeping the old records as "official."

Washtenaw Country Club, Ypsilanti, Nov. 4 □
1961 BOYS CLASS A TEAMS
1. Detroit Redford 48
2. Ypsilanti 87
3. Flint Central 149
4. Midland 155
5. Monroe 159
6. Detroit Northwestern 164
7. Birmingham 174
8. Mt Clemens 187
9. Detroit Cody 190
10. Plymouth 209
11. Grand Rapids Christian 214
12. Grand Rapids Central 217

1961 BOYS CLASS A TEAM RACE
1. Dick Sharkey (Detroit Redford)12 .... 9:58
2. Tony Mifsud (Detroit Cody)12 .... 10:12
3. Bill Rieck (Mt Clemens) 10:29
4. Ernie Gillum (Ypsilanti)12 ....nt
5. Randolph Brewer (Ypsilanti)11 ....nt
6. Ed Bagley (Flint Central) ....nt
7. Ronnie Gillum (Ypsilanti)12 ....nt
8. Dick Mather (Detroit Redford) ....nt
9. William Diffon (Flint Central) ....nt
10. Brian Haynes (Detroit Redford) ....nt
14. Jamie McCallum (Detroit Redford) ....nt
15. Steve Martineau (Detroit Redford) ....nt

1961 BOYS CLASS A INDIVIDUAL RACE
1. Tom Florida (Flint Southwestern)11 .... 10:27
2. Norm Shaughnessey (Battle Creek Central)12 ... 10:27
3. Don Keller (Redford Thurston) 10:32
4. Tony Kliemann (Dearborn) ....nt
5. Dick Reamer (Detroit U-D Jesuit) ....nt
6. Jeff Sonnenberg (Wyandotte) ....nt
7. Dave Peck (Portage) ....nt
8. Lugauer Wolfgang (Ann Arbor) ....nt
9. Sam McMurray (Muskegon Heights) ....nt
10. Charles Lincoln (Mt Pleasant) 10:41
16. Ron Bowman (Benton Harbor) ....nt
23. Mike Gaunt (Muskegon Heights)11 ....nt
30. Ron Masters (Benton Harbor) ....nt

1962 CLASS A BOYS

The undefeated Redford squad again dominated after winning a fifth-straight city title. Flint Southwestern's Tom Florida capped his undefeated season with a 100-yard win in 10:01.

The individual race was even faster as Lou Scott, winner of the Class A mile title the previous spring in 4:17.4, turned his speed to cross country. He broke the course record at Washtenaw by two seconds with his 9:48.4. He took the state mile record down to 4:11.3 the following summer at the Freedom Festival track meet in Windsor. In 1968 he ran the 5000m in the Mexico City Olympics.

XC! High School Cross Country in Michigan

Redford won its second title in 1962. Only a failed millage vote the next year kept the team from winning a third-straight.

Washtenaw Country Club, Ypsilanti, Nov. 3 □
1962 BOYS CLASS A TEAMS
1. Detroit Redford 86
2. Flint Southwestern 122
3. Ypsilanti 131
4. Lincoln Park 152
5. Livonia Bentley 159
6. Birmingham Seaholm 162
7. Lansing Sexton 165
8. Dearborn 180
9. Detroit Central 182
10. Kalamazoo Norrix 186
11. Detroit Northwestern 186
12. Kalamazoo Central 187

1962 BOYS CLASS A TEAM RACE
1. Tom Florida (Flint Southwestern)12 .... 10:01
2. Art Link (Detroit Redford)11 .... 10:18
3. Randolph Brewer (Ypsilanti)12 .... 10:19
4. Ernie Slater (Ypsilanti)12 .... 10:26
5. Gordon Dewey (Lansing Sexton)12 .... nt
6. George Carlisle (Flint Southwestern)11 .... nt
7. Tom White (Detroit Redford)11 .... nt
8. Ken Halliburton (Detroit Northwestern) .... nt
9. Ron Stowall (Detroit Northwestern) .... nt
10. Bruce Anderson (Flint Southwestern)12 .... nt
11. Paul Reiker (Livonia Bentley)12 .... nt
12. John Eihner (Detroit Redford)11 .... nt
13. Bill Schoen (Birmingham Seaholm) .... nt
14. Jim Cleverley (Detroit Redford)12 .... nt
15. John Godre (Dearborn)12 .... nt
16. Bill Bacheler (Birmingham Seaholm) .... nt
20. Clarence Hollifield (Ypsilanti)12 .... 10:49
51. Pat Loagan (Detroit Redford)11 .... nt
53. Tim Cox (Detroit Redford)11 .... nt
54. John Kinsel (Detroit Redford)12 .... nt

1962 BOYS CLASS A INDIVIDUAL RACE
1. Lou Scott (Detroit Eastern)12 .... 9:49
2. Bob Richards (Bloomfield Hills)11 .... 9:54
3. Dick Beamer (Detroit U-D Jesuit) 10:00
4. Ron Marsiglio (Detroit Southeastern) .... nt
5. Joel Vore (Monroe)12 .... 10:22
6. Larry Adams (Detroit Northern) 10:25
7. Jack Addington (Detroit Cody) 10:26
8. Frank Grzyb (Detroit Ford) 10:27
9. Joe Garza (Detroit Western) .... nt
10. Ron Pulford (Berkley)11 .... nt
11. John Ziga (Detroit Cooley) .... nt
12. Barry Potter (Flint Central) .... nt
13. Lloyd Forsythe (GR Catholic Central)11 .... nt
14. Tom Hoopengardner (Bloomfield Hills) .... nt
15. Mike Gaunt (Muskegon Heights)12 .... nt

1963 CLASS A BOYS

Kermit Ambrose's Seaholm squad put together the lowest score in meet history, 41 points, to destroy the field. His top runners, Jamie Dennis and Bill Schoen went 1-2 (Schoen had run for Detroit Redford two years earlier as a sophomore).

Seaholm's fourth runner was Jim Olson, in 10:32. He ran a 4:22 mile the next spring despite injury troubles. The following year, he transferred to Kirkwood High School in Missouri, where he ran 4:06.5 in the mile. That made him the second-fastest prep in the nation that year after Jim Ryun.

In the individual race, Bob Richards ran a 9:46.1 to take two seconds off the course record of 9:48.4 set by Lou Scott a year earlier; he would later be an All-American for BYU. Running in second place was future Olympian Ron Kutchinski.

One disappointment of 1963 was the absence of Detroit Redford. The defending champions were arguably the best team in the state. However, the millage vote failed in Detroit and all non-revenue sports were canceled that school year. The team still trained and placed 6th in the *Track & Field News* National Postal Team Race, with Art Link running 9:39.4 (after a previous 9:32.4 on the track). Their fifth runner clocked 10:23.4.

Washtenaw Country Club, Ypsilanti, Nov. 2 □
1963 BOYS CLASS A TEAMS
1. Birmingham Seaholm 41
2. Grand Rapids Christian 89
3. Milford 115
4. Clio 118
5. Kalamazoo Central 133
6. Wyandotte 136
7. Ann Arbor 141
8. Flint Central 161
9. Detroit U-D Jesuit 197
10. Royal Oak Kimball 254

1963 BOYS CLASS A TEAM RACE
1. Jamie Dennis (Birmingham Seaholm)12 .... 10:10
2. Bill Schoen (Birmingham Seaholm)12 .... 10:13
3. Scott Lachniet (Grand Rapids Christian) 10:16
4. Ron Nehring (Kalamazoo Central)11 .... nt
5. Ben Madera (Wyandotte) .... nt
6. John Ziga (Ann Arbor) 10:23
7. Bill Brownlee (Kalamazoo Central)11 .... 10:24
8. Paul Schmitt (Detroit U-D Jesuit) .... nt
9. Paul Baker (Wyandotte) .... nt
10. Bill Nelson (Milford) .... nt
11. Pat Richardson (Birmingham Seaholm)12 ..... nt
13. Jim Olson (Birmingham Seaholm)11 .... nt
14. Bill Bacheler (Birmingham Seaholm) .... nt

1963 BOYS CLASS A INDIVIDUAL RACE
1. Bob Richards (Bloomfield Hills) 9:47
2. Ron Kutchinski (East Grand Rapids)11 ...... 10:11
3. Dion Stewart (East Lansing) 10:13
4. Dave Roberts (Southgate) .... nt
5. Jim Sugg (Temperance Bedford) 10:18
6. Jack Bantle (Detroit Austin) 10:18
7. Clarence Martin (Mt Clemens) .... nt
8. Dennis Hunt (Farmington) 10:19
9. Keith Reid (Redford Thurston) 10:20
10. Lloyd Forsythe (Grand Rapids Catholic) 10:21
11. Ed Bertrand (Detroit DeLaSalle)11 .... 10:22
13. John Cybulskis (Grand Rapids Catholic) .... nt
22. Tom Kearney (Bloomfield Hills)11 .... nt

1964 CLASS A BOYS

Royal Oak Kimball moved up from 10th the year before to win by a 12-point margin over Detroit Redford, now back from its one-year millage hiatus. Conditions were optimal, with Ron Nehring of Kalamazoo Central running a course record 9:47.7. That didn't last long, as in the next race, Cass Tech's Brian Moore captured individual honors in a record 9:40.2.

For reasons lost to history, Dearborn won its regional but top runner John Spain ended up in the individual race. Moore beat Spain by four seconds. Spain had plenty of speed, and would win the 1966 Big 10 half mile title in 1:48.0, anchoring the winning mile relay in the same meet.

Washtenaw Country Club, Ypsilanti, Nov. 7 □
1964 BOYS CLASS A TEAMS
1. Royal Oak Kimball 80
2. Detroit Redford 92
3. Wyandotte 113
4. Birmingham Seaholm 126
5. Ann Arbor 140
6. Milford 148
7. Muskegon Heights 180
8. Jackson Parkside 213
9. Kalamazoo Central 219
10. Midland 242
11. Mt Clemens 248
12. Detroit Catholic Central 256
13. Grand Rapids Christian 264

1964 BOYS CLASS A TEAM RACE
1. Ron Nehring (Kalamazoo Central)12 .... 9:48
2. Ben Madera (Wyandotte)12 .... 9:49
3. Paul Baker (Wyandotte)11 .... 9:56
4. Scott Bradley (Birmingham Seaholm) 9:57
5. John Groomes (Milford) 10:02
6. Donzell Neal (Muskegon Heights) 10:04
7. Mike Branic (Birmingham Seaholm)11 .... 10:05
8. Bill Nelson (Milford) 10:06
9. Richard Holloway (Detroit Redford) 10:07
10. Mark Gale (Jackson Parkside) 10:07
11. Rick Driefuss (Royal Oak Kimball) 10:07
12. Mick Beauchamp (Royal Oak Kimball) 10:07
13. Steve Burns (Ann Arbor) 10:07
14. Bruce Gaffney (Ann Arbor) 10:08
15. Jim Flatley (Detroit Redford) 10:09
16. Howard Allen (Royal Oak Kimball) 10:09
17. Jim Autman (Muskegon Heights) 10:09
18. Roger Stevens (Kalamazoo Central) 10:10
19. Pat Logan (Detroit Redford) 10:10
20. Neal Touran (Birmingham Seaholm) 10:11
21. Dick Falconer (Royal Oak Kimball) 10:12
22. Doug Mitchell (Detroit Redford) 10:12
23. Jerry Fountain (Kalamazoo Central) 10:16
24. Clarence Martin (Mt Clemens) 10:17
25. Lino Cassar (Royal Oak Kimball) 10:18

1964 BOYS CLASS A INDIVIDUAL RACE
1. Brian Moore (Detroit Cass Tech)12 .... 9:41
2. John Spain (Dearborn) 9:45
3. Bruce Shoup (Portage)12 .... 9:50
4. Tom Kearney (Bloomfield Hills)12 .... 9:52
5. Jack Magelsson (Flint Ainsworth) 9:54
6. Dave Roberts (Southgate) 9:59
7. John Daniel (Trenton) 10:03
8. Ken Leonowicz (Hazel Park) 10:07
9. Roger Cronin (Kalamazoo Norrix) 10:08
10. Daryl Burt (Lansing Eastern)12 .... 10:09
11. Ron Hirth (Grand Rapids Union) 10:10
12. Randy Dorris (Davison) 10:11
13. Jack Sulpher (Lansing Everett) 10:12
14. Paul Schmitt (Detroit U-D Jesuit) 10:12
15. Joe Watson (Farmington) 10:13

1965 CLASS A BOYS

A total of 356 runners competed in the Lower Peninsula meet, at a time when about 2,200 athletes in the L.P. competed in cross country overall.

Royal Oak Kimball pulled off a successful defense, topping Wyandotte by 13 points. Class A individual runner-up Hartman ran a 4:18.2 mile the next spring.

Roseville's Ivan Scholl leads Kim Hartman in the 1965 individual run. (photo courtesy of Bill Wehwein)

Washtenaw Country Club, Ypsilanti, Nov. 6 □

1965 BOYS CLASS A TEAMS

1. Royal Oak Kimball ... 63
2. Wyandotte ... 76
3. Jackson Parkside ... 124
4. Pontiac Northern ... 155
5. Birmingham Brother Rice ... 158
6. Hazel Park ... 180
7. Ann Arbor ... 213
8. Flint Central ... 221
9. Muskegon Heights ... 223
10. Pontiac Central ... 231
11. East Lansing ... 279
12. Detroit Redford ... 288
13. Ferndale ... 313
14. Grand Rapids Catholic Central ... 334
15. Kalamazoo Norrix ... 345
16. Berkley ... 347
17. Trenton ... 365
18. Mt Clemens ... 384

1965 BOYS CLASS A TEAM RACE

1. Al Ruffner (Wyandotte)11 ... 10:07
2. Ken Leonowicz (Hazel Park) ... 10:08
3. Jim Love (Flint Central) ... 10:13
4. Paul Baker (Wyandotte) ... 10:17
5. Jim Autman (Muskegon Heights) ... 10:18
6. Alan Garnsey (Royal Oak Kimball) ... 10:20
7. Bob Carpenter (Jackson Parkside) ... 10:22
8. Robert Hendricks (Wyandotte) ... 10:23
9. Lino Cassar (Royal Oak Kimball) ... 10:24
10. Jim Thorson (Birmingham Brother Rice) ... 10:25
11. Doug Hovey (Royal Oak Kimball) ... 10:26
12. Dave Kay (Pontiac Northern) ... 10:27
13. Dan Link (Detroit Redford) ... 10:28
14. Carl Little (Jackson Parkside) ... 10:29
15. Dan Simeck (Hazel Park) ... 10:29
16. Marc Dutton (Royal Oak Kimball) ... 10:29
17. Al Campbell (Ann Arbor) ... 10:30
18. Dave Johnson (Pontiac Northern) ... 10:31
19. Nick Ochoa (Pontiac Northern) ... 10:32
20. Douglas Bair (Birmingham Brother Rice) ... 10:32
21. Gary Buckheit (Livonia Clarenceville) ... 10:32
22. Bill Turkowski (Royal Oak Kimball) ... 10:33

1965 BOYS CLASS A INDIVIDUAL RACE

1. Ivan Scholl (Roseville)12 ... 10:00
2. Kim Hartman (Southfield)11 ... 10:05
3. Jack Magelsson (Flint Ainsworth) ... 10:06
4. John Bennett (St Clair Shores) ... 10:13
5. Calvin Williams (Detroit Northeastern) ... 10:18
6. Jim Lautenbach (GR Christian) ... 10:19
7. George Jenkins (Detroit Central) ... 10:20
8. Dan Ryan (Livonia Franklin) ... 10:21
9. Charles Gorman (Birmingham Seaholm) ... 10:22
10. Don Kleinow (Detroit Denby) ... 10;22
11. John Monigold (Detroit DeLaSalle) ... 10:23
12. Jim Lindler (Walled Lake) ... 10:24
13. Rens Verbeek (GR Cent Christ) ... 10;24
14. Ron Ludwig (Lansing Eastern) ... 10:25
15. Don Yehle (Midland) ... 10;25
16. John Wismer (St Joseph) ... 10:26
17. Sterling Speirn (Bloomfield Hills) ... 10:29
18. Richard Thornburn (Lincoln Park) ... 10:30
19. Vincent Smith (Detroit Western) ... 10:31

1966 CLASS A BOYS

The Lower Peninsula finals, originally scheduled for November 5, were delayed a week after a surprise 8-inch snowstorm hit the Wednesday and Thursday before the original date.

The races couldn't be closer. Forrest Jennings of Hazel Park won the team race in 9:54.7, with Al Ruffner of Wyandotte inches behind. Ken Howse of Detroit Finney took the individual race in 9:54.8, 11 days after winning the Detroit title in 9:22.9—two seconds away from Lou Scott's Rouge Park record. Howse would be among the first state champions in the two mile the next spring. The event had not been run officially in the state since 1910.

Washtenaw Country Club, Ypsilanti, Nov. 12 □

1966 BOYS CLASS A TEAMS

1. Hazel Park ... 82
2. Royal Oak Kimball ... 115
3. Wyandotte ... 137
4. Detroit Redford ... 168
5. Grand Rapids Christian ... 186
6. Ann Arbor ... 197

=7. Birmingham Seaholm ... 202
=7. Pontiac Central ... 202

9. Jackson Parkside ... 221
10. Kalamazoo Norrix ... 236
11. Flint Central ... 250
12. East Lansing ... 263
13. Redford Union ... 294
14. Adrian ... 301
15. Mt Clemens ... 305
16. Harper Woods Gallagher ... 318
17. Traverse City ... 353
18. Detroit Mumford ... 532

1966 BOYS CLASS A TEAM RACE

1. Forrest Jennings (Hazel Park)12 ... 9:55
2. Al Ruffner (Wyandotte)12 ... 9:55
3. Dan Simeck (Hazel Park)12 ... 10:00
4. Dan Link (Detroit Redford) ... 10:02
5. Jack Shepherd (Redford Union) ... 10:04
6. Bob Carpenter (Jackson Parkside) ... 10:05
7. Bill Lautenbach (Grand Rapids Christian) ... 10:06
8. William Turowski (Royal Oak Kimball) ... 10:07
9. John Mock (Mt Clemens) ... 10:08
10. Ralph Reed (Kalamazoo Norrix) ... 10:09
11. Brent Stone (Ann Arbor) ... 10:10
12. Bob Blachford (Detroit Redford) ... 10:10
13. Eric Bates (East Lansing) ... 10:11
14. Doug Hovey (Royal Oak Kimball) ... 10:12
15. Richard Breese (Detroit Redford) ... 10:12
16. Chip Gorman (Birmingham Seaholm) ... 10:14
17. Wayne Sailor (Wyandotte) ... 10:16
18. Dave Devere (Hazel Park)12 ... 10:18
19. Don Szatmary (Wyandotte) ... 10:19
20. Phil Hyre (Hazel Park)12 ... 10:21
21. Jack Schader (Royal Oak Kimball) ... 10:22
22. Marc Dutton (Royal Oak Kimball) ... 10:23
23. Steve Bell (Birmingham Seaholm) ... 10:25

? Allan Dowty (Hazel Park)12 ... nt
? Dan Cracchiolo (Hazel Park)11 ... nt
? Bob Woronko (Hazel Park)11 ... nt

1966 BOYS CLASS A INDIVIDUAL RACE

1. Ken Howse (Detroit Finney)12 ... 9:55
2. Kim Hartman (Southfield)12 ... 10:02
3. Don Estes (Southgate Schafer) ... 10:07
4. Jerome Myszkowski (Detroit U-D Jesuit) ... 10:09
5. Jim Lindler (Walled Lake) ... 10:11
6. Marion Pittman (Detroit Southwestern) ... 10:13
7. Roger Cleaver (Detroit Kettering) ... 10:15
8. Tom Boukout (Kalamazoo Central) ... 10:17
9. Jake Hill (Ypsilanti)11 ... 10:18
10. Steve Gorsalitz (Clio) ... 10:19
11. Don Yehle (Midland) ... 10:19
12. Charles Clark (Lansing Sexton) ... 10:20
13. Jim Morse (Flint Central) ... 10:20
14. Randy Cooley (Jackson) ... 10:21
15. Jim Love (Flint Central) ... 10:21
16. Bruce Evans (Bloomfield Hills) ... 10:22
17. Rich Freeland (Jackson) ... 10:24

1967 CLASS A BOYS

A light dusting of snow on top of damp ground greeted the runners at the Washtenaw Country Club.

Coach Ron Hornung's Trojans of East Lansing, only 12th the year before, topped the field by putting 5 in the top 20. Led by Jim Wrigley and Eric Bates, the team had prepped for its title running by winning its 14th-straight title at the Vicksburg regional.

Bates, the eventual 5th-placer, would later run for Princeton. His son Evan would take up ice dancing and become a two-time Olympian and World medalist.

Washtenaw Country Club, Ypsilanti, Nov. 4 □

30 degrees, wet.

1967 BOYS CLASS A TEAMS

1. East Lansing ... 50
2. Royal Oak Kimball ... 179
3. Pontiac Central ... 189
4. Birmingham Brother Rice ... 191
5. Hazel Park ... 193
6. Grand Rapids Christian ... 204
7. Wyandotte ... 210
8. Ypsilanti ... 231
9. Kalamazoo Norrix ... 243
10. Redford Union ... 247
11. Ferndale ... 266
12. Grand Blanc ... 280
13. Ecorse ... 294
14. Grand Rapids Union ... 297
15. Dearborn ... 322
16. Harper Woods Gallagher ... 335
17. Royal Oak Dondero ... 337
18. Clio ... 383

1967 BOYS CLASS A TEAM RACE

1. Warren Krueger (Hazel Park)11 ... 10:07
2. Dan Hague (Ecorse)12 ... 10:20
3. Steve Gorsalitz (Clio) ... 10:24
4. Jim Wrigley (East Lansing) ... 10:27
5. Eric Bates (East Lansing) ... 10:29
6. John Costello (Pontiac Central)11 ... 10:29
7. Jake Snell (East Lansing) ... nt
8. Greg Brawner (Royal Oak Kimball) ... nt
9. (Kalamazoo Norrix) ... nt
10. Tom Coombe (Ferndale)12 ... nt
12. Dwight Walls (Ypsilanti)12 ... nt
13. Jack Stevenson (Hazel Park)10 ... nt
14. Dale Arbour (East Lansing) ... nt
20. Dee Newton (East Lansing) ... nt
23. Matt Heumann (Ypsilanti)11 ... nt
28. Tom Johnson (Ypsilanti) ... nt
31. Rich Shankland (East Lansing) ... nt
34. Steve Brede (East Lansing) ... nt

1967 BOYS CLASS A INDIVIDUAL RACE

1. Bob Carpenter (Jackson Parkside)12 ... 10:06
2. Richard Gross (Grosse Pointe) ... 10:10
3. Greg Parrett (St Joseph) ... 10:14
4. Larry Williams (Farmington)11 ... 10:14

5. Duane Spitz (Lansing Eastern) 10:16
6. Rich Freeland (Jackson) 10:20
7. Mike Goodwin (Jackson Parkside)10 10:21
8. John Bambacht (Portage Central) 10:24
9. Ray Eddy (Adrian) 10:28

1968 CLASS A BOYS

Hazel Park was favored to run away with Class A honors, but Flint Kearsley shocked the field, running its best race when it counted. Kearsley's top runners placed 9-12-15-36-50. While Hazel Park fielded the individual champion in Warren Krueger, its next best competitor managed only 32nd place, and the team ended up fifth with 163 points. Still, that made three-straight individual wins for the Vikings.

Washtenaw Country Club, Ypsilanti, Nov. 2 ☐
Mid-50s, dry.

1968 BOYS CLASS A TEAMS

1. Flint Kearsley 122
2. St Joseph 130
=3. Battle Creek Lakeview 134
=3. Redford Union 134
5. Hazel Park 163
6. Adrian 165
7. Royal Oak Kimball 166
8. Pontiac Northern 179
9. Birmingham Brother Rice 184
10. Grand Blanc 236
11. Ann Arbor Pioneer 239
12. Grand Rapids Creston 291
13. Harper Woods Notre Dame 293
14. Lincoln Park 303
15. St Clair Shores South Lake 339
16. Grand Rapids Ottawa Hills 427
17. Detroit Catholic Central 450
18. Detroit U-D Jesuit 495

Hazel Park's Warren Krueger won in 1952.

1968 BOYS CLASS A TEAM RACE

1. Warren Krueger (Hazel Park)12 9:52
2. Mike McMahan (Lincoln Park) 9:59
3. Robert Junk (Redford Union) 10:07
4. Mike Shawver (Battle Creek Lakeview)12 10:14
5. Neil Dutton (Royal Oak Kimball) 10:18
6. Ken Barts (St Joseph) 10:18
7. Bob Bokka (Royal Oak Kimball) 10:20
8. Dave Eddy (Adrian) 10:20
9. Dave Baker (Flint Kearsley)10 10:20
10. Mike Parrett (St Joseph) 10:21
11. William Kuhn (Redford Union) 10:21
12. Kent Raysin (Flint Kearsley) 10:25
13. Charles Hotaling (Birmingham Brother Rice) 10:27
14. Dennis Keeney (Redford Union) 10:28
15. George Geisenhaver (Flint Kearsley) 10:29
16. Dave Mulder (Battle Creek Lakeview) 10:30
17. Frederick Pierce (Grand Blanc) 10:31
18. Gary Bean (St Joseph) 10:32
19. Scott Van Allsburg (Grand Rapids Creston) 10:34
20. Tom DeVos (Royal Oak Kimball) 10:35
21. Andrew Liddy (Pontiac Northern) 10:35
22. Tom Herrmann (St Clair Shores South Lake) 10:36
23. Thomas Knibbs (Pontiac Northern) 10:37
24. Skip Burck (Ann Arbor Pioneer) 10:38
25. Al Cornwell (Battle Creek Lakeview) 10:40
36. Ron Yuille (Flint Kearsley) 10:49
50. Mike Brunet (Flint Kearsley) 10:53
64. Terry Stewart (Flint Kearsley) 11:01
113. Kurt Zafiroff (Flint Kearsley) 11:27

1968 BOYS CLASS A INDIVIDUAL RACE

1. Larry Williams (Farmington)12 10:02
2. Jake Snell (East Lansing) 10:04
3. Ron Phillips (Detroit Denby)12 10:05
4. Rick Randall (North Farmington) 10:06
5. Richard Schott (Grosse Pointe South) 10:08
6. Randall Kilpatrick (Center Line) 10:09
7. Rich Freeland (Jackson) 10:13
8. Dallas Lincoln (Flushing) 10:15
9. Allen Smith (Detroit Cass Tech) 10:18
11. Matt Heumann (Ypsilanti)12 10:18
16. Mike Goodwin (Jackson Parkside)11 nt
23. Richard Meyer (Wayne Memorial) 10:40
27. Ray Torres (Wayne Memorial) 10:43

1969 CLASS A BOYS

Ann Arbor Huron, in only its third year of existence, upset defender Flint Kearsley with a great show of pack running. The top three River Rats came in 13-15-18 as heavy rains dogged the competition. In the A team race, defending two-mile champion Rick Schott of Grosse Pointe North dueled with Doug Brown until the last quarter mile, when Schott collapsed. He was briefly hospitalized for a severe bronchial ailment.

Washtenaw Country Club, Ypsilanti, Nov. 1 ⊠
Heavy rain.

1969 BOYS CLASS A TEAMS

1. Ann Arbor Huron 120
2. Flint Kearsley 142
3. Pontiac Northern 156
4. Harper Woods Notre Dame 160
5. Adrian 174
6. Grand Rapids Union 181
7. Birmingham Brother Rice 200
8. Royal Oak Dondero 219
9. Farmington 255
10. Kalamazoo Norrix 272
11. Grand Blanc 278
12. Grosse Pointe North 283
13. Royal Oak Kimball 290
14. St Joseph 295
15. Grand Rapids Creston 298
16. Lincoln Park 319
17. Redford Union 365
18. Detroit Cooley 436
19. Dearborn 452

1969 BOYS CLASS A TEAM RACE

1. Doug Brown (Harper Woods Notre Dame)12 9:59
2. Dave Eddy (Adrian) 10:03
3. Michael Parrett (St Joseph) 10:07
4. Mike McMahon (Lincoln Park) 10:08
5. Dave Baker (Flint Kearsley)11 10:12
6. Joe Evans (Royal Oak Dondero) 10:13
7. Bill Kuhn (Redford Union) 10:17
8. John Mathews (Birmingham Brother Rice) 10:18
9. Phil Ceeley (Royal Oak Kimball) 10:19
10. Scott Van Allsburg (Grand Rapids Creston) 10:19
11. George Coppens (Harper Woods Notre Dame) 10:19
12. Tom May (Dearborn) 10:26
13. Carl Tsigdinos (Ann Arbor Huron) 10:29
14. Mike Taylor (Pontiac Northern) 10:30
15. Ed Fisher (Ann Arbor Huron) 10:30
16. Kurt Gumerson (Flint Kearsley) 10:31
17. John Kussmaul (Adrian) 10:31
18. Andy Campbell (Ann Arbor Huron) 10:31
19. Jesse Little (Detroit Cooley) 10:32
20. Kurt Koepnik (Grand Rapids Union) 10:32
21. Fred Pierce (Grand Blanc) 10:33
22. Tom Jonsson (Royal Oak Dondero) 10:33
29. Adrian Newby (Ann Arbor Huron) 10:38
45. Martin Heuter (Ann Arbor Huron) 10:46
80. Scott Hubbard (Ann Arbor Huron) 11:06
81. Carl Heuter (Ann Arbor Huron) 11:08

1969 BOYS CLASS A INDIVIDUAL RACE

1. Mike Goodwin (Jackson Parkside)12 10:02
2. Steve Moffet (Pontiac Waterford) 10:05
3. Michael Brown (GR Ottawa Hills) 10:10
4. Doug Kurtis (Livonia Stevenson) 10:11
5. Mike Gilleran (Birmingham Seaholm) 10:15
6. Don Anderson (Garden City West) 10:17
7. Rick DeLeon (Battle Creek Central) 10:17
8. Rod Allen (Ypsilanti)12 10:18
9. Mike McNea (Flint Southwestern) 10:19
10. Dan Wilson (Fraser) 10:20
11. Sam Torres (Flint Southwestern) 10:21
12. Dave Gembel (Clio) 10:21
13. Pete Murtagh (Dearborn Edsel Ford) 10:22
14. Dave Mulder (Battle Creek Lakeview) 10:24
15. Keith Kline (Flint Central) 10:24
16. Fred Seyler (Clarkston) 10:25
17. Dave Burkhart (Southgate) 10:27
18. Paul Robinson (Jackson) 10:31
19. Brad Holst (Southfield) 10:32
20. Gary Schultz (Wayne Memorial) 10:33
32. Tom Levengood (Bay City Handy)10 10:43

1970 CLASS A BOYS

With the race distance increased to 2.5 miles, all eyes were on favored Ann Arbor Huron to take the Class A title. The River Rats ran only 5th, however, as Flint Kearsley strode to a two-point win with the help of music from its school band.

St Joseph had the team lead with a half mile to go, but John Sullivan—in 3rd for most of his 4:45 second mile—faded to 43rd place. "The pace was just too much for him," said coach Ron Waldvogel.

Said Kearsley coach Larry Wiltse, "This had to be a bigger thrill than winning in 1968. Then, we weren't that experienced and didn't know what to expect. But this year, we knew we had a chance and were more confident."

Washtenaw Country Club, Ypsilanti, Nov. 7 ☐

1970 BOYS CLASS A TEAMS

1. Flint Kearsley 111
2. St Joseph 113
3. Clarkston 136
4. Farmington 164
5. Ann Arbor Huron 171
6. Bay City Central 214
7. Pontiac Northern 217
8. Birmingham Brother Rice 229
9. Birmingham Seaholm 264
10. Grand Rapids Creston 273
11. Royal Oak Kimball 279
12. Grand Rapids Union 283
13. Howell 289
14. Taylor Center 322
15. Ann Arbor Pioneer 343
16. Grosse Pointe North 346
17. Battle Creek Lakeview 362
18. Harper Woods Notre Dame 419
19. Dearborn 437
20. Redford Borgess 485

1970 BOYS CLASS A TEAM RACE

1. Mike Gilleran (Birmingham Seaholm)11 ... 12:35
2. Dave Baker (Flint Kearsley)12 ... 12:40
3. Karl Tsigdinos (Ann Arbor Huron) ... 12:45
4. Bob Hunt (Bay City Central) ... 12:47
5. Tim Tobin (St Joseph) ... 12:52
6. Phil Ceeley (Royal Oak Kimball) ... 12:55
7. Scott Van Allsburg (GR Creston) ... 12:56
8. Fred Seyler (Clarkston) ... 12:59
9. Mike Taylor (Pontiac Northern) ... 13:02
11. Steve Norris (St Joseph) ... nt
14. Kurt Gummerson (Flint Kearsley)11 ... nt
19. Larry Gengler (Flint Kearsley)11 ... nt
25. Jim Lorah (St Joseph) ... nt
34. Dave Powell (Flint Kearsley)11 ... nt
42. Bill Freeman (Flint Kearsley) ... nt
46. Wayne Lechman (Flint Kearsley) ... nt
109. Bill Westenbarger (Flint Kearsley) ... nt

1970 BOYS CLASS A INDIVIDUAL RACE
1. Tom Levengood (Bay City Handy)11 ... 12:56
2. Dave Burkhart (Southgate) ... 12:57
3. Jeff Corneil (Lansing Eastern) ... 13:01
4. Jeff Dixon (East Grand Rapids) ... 13:03
5. Don Anderson (Garden City West) ... 13:03
6. Bob Reason (Birmingham Groves) ... 13:03
10. Greg Purrenhage (St Clair Shores Lakeview) ... nt
24. Phil Combs (Belleville) ... nt

1971 CLASS A BOYS

After near-misses in '68 and '70, St. Joseph, the smallest school in the Class A field, won the state title, led by Tim Tobin. "We didn't run a good race last year and were disappointed by our second-place finish. We were confident we would win if all the boys ran up to their capabilities," said coach Ron Waldvogel.

Tobin's twin, Pat, came in 7th place. Defending champ and course record holder Mike Gilleran finished a disappointed 9th after running with the leaders for the first half.

High winds and snow flurries were the order of the day. Nick Ellis had been leading the team race until a wrong turn cost him dearly.

Washtenaw Country Club, Ypsilanti, Nov. 6 □
Snowy, windy.

1971 BOYS CLASS A TEAMS
1. St Joseph ... 97
2. Flint Kearsley ... 120
3. Belleville ... 125
4. Ann Arbor Pioneer ... 139
5. West Bloomfield ... 186
6. Birmingham Seaholm ... 222
7. Grosse Pointe North ... 233
8. Pontiac Northern ... 237
9. Dearborn ... 241
10. Lincoln Park ... 242
11. Kalamazoo Norrix ... 248
12. Birmingham Brother Rice ... 302
13. Grand Rapids Union ... 314
14. Bay City Central ... 316
15. Livonia Stevenson ... 318
16. Harper Woods Notre Dame ... 335
17. Bloomfield Hills Lahser ... 338
18. Redford Borgess ... 427
19. Detroit Cooley ... 441

1971 BOYS CLASS A TEAM RACE
1. Tim Tobin (St Joseph)11 ... 12:49
2. Nick Ellis (Detroit Cooley)11 ... 12:59
3. Bob Hunt (Bay City Central) ... 13:09
4. Jon Cross (Belleville) ... nt
5. Kurt Gummerson (Flint Kearsley)12 ... 13:15
7. Pat Tobin (St Joseph) ... nt
8. Brian Hudson (St Joseph) ... nt
9. Mike Gilleran (Birmingham Seaholm) ... nt
12. Larry Gengler (Flint Kearsley)12 ... nt
18. Dave Morton (Ann Arbor Pioneer) ... nt
22. Tom Hughes (Ann Arbor Pioneer) ... nt
37. Jim Sullivan (St Joseph) ... nt
44. Steve Bond (St Joseph) ... nt

1971 BOYS CLASS A INDIVIDUAL RACE
1. Greg Meyer (GR West Catholic)11 ... 12:51
2. Dave Burkhart (Southgate) ... 12:55
3. Tom Levengood (Bay City Handy)12 ... 12:57
4. Bruce Petoskey (Jackson) ... 12:57
5. Joe Caruso (Temperance Bedford) ... 13:02
6. Carl Tsigdinos (Ann Arbor Huron) ... 13:03
7. Don Hubbard (Ann Arbor Huron)10 ... 13:05
8. Amos Brown (Detroit Northern) ... 13:09
9. Jim Berkeley (Grand Rapids Catholic) ... 13:09
10. Jeff Cornell (Lansing Eastern) ... 13:11
11. Rick Goodman (Lansing Sexton) ... 13:15
12. Rick Krinzman (Redford Union) ... 13:16
14. Jerry Salzwerdal (Forest Hills) ... nt

1972 CLASS A BOYS

The race distance increased to three miles the year that Flint Kearsley won its fourth team title. "We tried to get out hard and hang on, said coach Larry Wiltse. At the 1M mark, Kearsley was running 1-2-3.

At the meet, Dearborn and Portage Northern were called tied for third, but Dearborn's #6 was 68th, and Northern's was 91st.

Cass Benton Park, Redford, Nov. 4 □

1972 BOYS CLASS A TEAMS
1. Flint Kearsley ... 116
2. Livonia Stevenson ... 127
3. Dearborn ... 140
4. Portage Northern ... 140
5. West Bloomfield ... 153
6. Grosse Pointe North ... 154
7. Ann Arbor Pioneer ... 160
8. St Joseph ... 169
9. Mt Clemens ... 183
10. Royal Oak Kimball ... 201
11. Grand Blanc ... 257
12. Grand Ledge ... 309
13. Redford Borgess ... 333
14. East Lansing ... 341
15. Birmingham Brother Rice ... 353
16. Bay City Handy ... 370
17. Warren Cousino ... 373
18. Wyandotte ... 430

1972 BOYS CLASS A TEAM RACE
1. Tom Hammer (Grosse Pointe North)11 ... 15:53
2. Dave Mathia (Livonia Stevenson)12 ... 16:03
3. Tom Ellsperman (St Joseph)11 ... 16:04
4. Bill Leenhouts (Royal Oak Kimball) ... 16:05
5. Pat Davey (Birmingham Brother Rice) ... 16:05
6. Steve Bond (St Joseph) ... 16:06
7. Tony Costanzo (Dearborn) ... 16:11
8. Steve White (Livonia Stevenson) ... 16:14
9. Rich Hadler (Ann Arbor Pioneer) ... 16:14
10. Ed Grabowski (West Bloomfield) ... 16:15
12. Joe Dixson (Flint Kearsley)11 ... nt
14. Dana Garchow (Flint Kearsley)12 ... nt
17. Harold Cody (Grand Ledge) ... nt
22. Wayne Leckman (Flint Kearsley)12 ... nt
25. Gordon Drennan (Flint Kearsley)12 ... nt
30. Busch (Ann Arbor Pioneer) ... nt
43. Greg Wilson (Flint Kearsley)12 ... nt

1972 BOYS CLASS A INDIVIDUAL RACE
1. Walter Nowak (Wayne Memorial)12 ... 15:56
2. Mike McGuire (Farmington)11 ... 16:03
3. Dan Henry (Southfield)12 ... 16:10
4. Marc Nover (Owosso) ... 16:14
5. John Yurchis (Garden City East) ... 16:16
19. Julius Hobson (Flint Central) ... nt
20. Mike Raysin (Davison) ... nt

1973 CLASS A BOYS

Pat Davey's individual win came as no surprise, even with Mike McGuire in the field. A week earlier he had won the Catholic title in 14:45 at Rouge Park. Then at regionals at Royal Oak Kimball, he chopped 25 seconds off his own course record with a 14:53.

In the team race, the first-placer wasn't a shock, but his strategy was. At the regional, Flint Northern's Keith Young led from the start to beat West Bloomfield's Ed Grabowski in 14:43.5. Here, Young was coached by Norb Badar to stay behind until the final 50 yards, and he won it on the kick.

A week later, Pioneer coach Don Sleeman put together an all-star high school team that won the AAU Junior 10,000m race. Winning the race was Pat Davey in 30:48.6, a course record. McGuire took 2nd as the team put 5 in the top 12.

Flint Northern's Keith Young won it on the kick (Norb Badar photo)

Grand Blanc GC, Grand Blanc, Nov. 3 ☒

1973 BOYS CLASS A TEAMS
1. Grosse Pointe North ... 109
2. Ann Arbor Pioneer ... 111
3. Kalamazoo Norrix ... 140
4. Flint Northern ... 159
5. Royal Oak Kimball ... 173
6. Dearborn ... 184
7. Dearborn Edsel Ford ... 198
8. Livonia Stevenson ... 204
9. West Bloomfield ... 207
10. Flint Kearsley ... 235
11. Portage Northern ... 239
12. Midland ... 276
13. Ann Arbor Huron ... 289
14. Livonia Bentley ... 297
15. Warren Cousino ... 300
16. Westland Glenn ... 307
17. Wayne Memorial ... 415
18. Birmingham Groves ... 523

1973 BOYS CLASS A TEAM RACE
1. Keith Young (Flint Northern)11 ... 15:04
2. Ed Grabowski (West Bloomfield)12 ... 15:05
3. Jeff Randolph (Midland)11 ... 15:08
4. Steve White (Livonia Stevenson) ... 15:10
5. Dan Visscher (Dearborn) ... 15:18
6. Tom Hammer (Grosse Pointe North)12 ... 15:18
7. Dan Sheets (Warren Cousino) ... 15:20
8. Mike Watson (Dearborn Edsel Ford) ... 15:21
9. Chris Speer (Ann Arbor Pioneer) ... 15:22
10. Chip Hadler (Ann Arbor Pioneer) ... 15:24
11. Greg Savicke (Kalamazoo Norrix) ... 15:26
12. Don Seibert (Flint Kearsley)11 ... 15:30
13. Ed Brennan (Grosse Pointe North)12 ... 15:33

14. Frank Celeskey (Dearborn) 15:34
15. Mark Olson (Royal Oak Kimball) 15:35
16. Jim Fisher (Grosse Pointe North) 15:36
17. Peter Chetnik (Ann Arbor Pioneer) 15:37
18. Bryon Lilly (Kalamazoo Norrix) 15:38
25. John DiMercurio (Grosse Pointe North)12 ....15:50
49. Dave Maisteller (Grosse Pointe North)12 ....16:09
56. Rob Pelleman (Grosse Pointe North) 16:15
111. Steve Pohl (Grosse Pointe North) 17:09

1973 BOYS CLASS A INDIVIDUAL RACE

1. Pat Davey (Birmingham Brother Rice)12 ....15:04
2. Mike McGuire (Farmington)12 ....15:07
3. Harold Cody (Grand Ledge)12 ....15:16
4. Peter Maxwell (Port Huron) 15:19
5. Dan Zemper (Howell) 15:21
6. Ted Farmer (Lansing Sexton) 15:22
7. Jeff Searles (Warren Lincoln) 15:25
8. Bob Scholz (Bloomfield Hills Andover) 15:26
9. Mick McSween (Detroit Catholic Central) 15:27
10. Harold Carter (Ypsilanti) 15:29
11. Tom Munn (Troy) 15:30
12. Jeff Leestma (Birmingham Seaholm) 15:32
13. Paul Levengood (Bay City Handy) 15:32
14. Mark Oller (Redford Borgess) 15:32
15. Scott Minor (Kalamazoo Central) 15:32
16. Jim Baumgartner (Detroit U-D Jesuit) 15:32
17. Paul Zucker (Saginaw Hill) 15:34
18. Steve Elliott (Pontiac Central)11 ....15:35
19. Steve Banovic (Jackson) 15:36
20. Tom Calvert (Jackson) 15:38
21. Jeff Zylstra (Grandville) 15:39
22. John Bradburn (Flint Southwestern) 15:40

1974 CLASS A BOYS

Jackson placed a remarkable 3 in the top 5—and finished 6th (the Vikings' next two were 66th and 104th). Flint Northern took the win for coach Norb Badar. "I thought we could win," said Badar. "Why not? We were up for the race and we had won that tough Tri-State meet in Indiana."

Individually, both races were incredible, as Keith Young outlegged Steve Elliott in the team contest, while Jeff Randolph topped Sam James in the individual race. All built great resumes on the track. Young set an 880 record of 1:50.3 the next spring, and later starred at Tennessee with James. Elliott ran a still-standing mile record of 4:07.4, and was pushed by Randolph (4:09.2) at the A state track meet. Randolph later starred for Wisconsin, while Elliott competed for Michigan.

A week after the state finals, an all-star group of Michigan preps that reads like a Hall of Fame list got together and won the AAU Junior championship over a 10K course with a 2-3-5-6-7 finish. Keith Young led at 30:47 for 2nd place. Also on the team were Jack Sinclair of Grosse Ile, Jeff Randolph of Midland, Steve Elliott of Pontiac Central, and Jeff Zylstra of Grandville.

Grand Blanc GC, Grand Blanc, Nov. 2 ⊠
1974 BOYS CLASS A TEAMS

1. Flint Northern 74
2. St Joseph 104
3. Warren Cousino 116
4. Portage Northern 156
5. Grosse Pointe North 166
6. Jackson 182
7. Dearborn Edsel Ford 189
8. Birmingham Brother Rice 221
9. Farmington 251
10. Pontiac Central 254
11. Alpena 276
12. Temperance Bedford 284
13. Warren Fitzgerald 291
14. Wayne Memorial 319
15. Grand Ledge 329
16. Grand Blanc 341
17. Redford Union 344
18. Detroit Catholic Central 399

1974 BOYS CLASS A TEAM RACE

1. Keith Young (Flint Northern)12 ....14:38
2. Steve Elliott (Pontiac Central)12 ....14:47
3. Tom Calvert (Jackson) 14:57
4. Rich Bennett (Jackson) 15:02
5. Steve Banovic (Jackson) 15:19
6. Tim Dine (St Joseph)11 ....15:25
7. Dan Sheets (Warren Cousino) 15:27
8. Jon Grodzicki (Dearborn Edsel Ford) 15:28
9. Matt Henny (Portage Northern) 15:29
10. Dave Lewis (Grosse Pointe North) 15:30
11. Jim Fouchia (Warren Cousino) 15:30
12. Marty Kirk (St Joseph) 15:31
13. Jim Fisher (Grosse Pointe North) 15:32
14. Mike Watson (Dearborn Edsel Ford) 15:33
15. Ron Whitner (Flint Northern) 15:35
16. Mike Bowen (Flint Northern) 15:36
17. Mark Mohtbach (Temperance Bedford) 15:37
18. John Halford (Flint Northern) 15:38
19. Joe Pallazzolo (St Joseph) 15:39
24. Steve Branch (Flint Northern) 15:47
78. Anthony Sullivan (Flint Northern) 16:35
84. Richard MacInnes (Flint Northern) 16:38

1974 BOYS CLASS A INDIVIDUAL RACE

1. Jeff Randolph (Midland)12 ....14:47
2. Sam James (Highland Park)11 ....14:58
3. Jeff Zylstra (Grandville) 15:06
4. Tony Radalmenti (St Clair Shores Lakeview) 15:09
5. Jim Grabowski (West Bloomfield) 15:12
6. Tim Cummins (HW Notre Dame) 15:13
7. Dan Zemper (Howell) 15:15
8. Marvin Rus (Grand Rapids Christian) 15:24
9. Brad Goike (Mt Clemens L'Anse Creuse) 15:26
10. Art Kitze (Garden City East) 15:27
11. Mark Olson (Royal Oak Kimball) 15:28
12. John Harding (Southfield Lathrup) 15:29
13. Mark Booze (Lansing Waverly) 15:30
14. Bill Spencer (Grosse Pointe South) 15:31
15. Dan Heikkinen (Adrian) 15:32
16. Scott Stone (Southfield) 15:33
17. Gary Williams (Walled Lake Central) 15:34
18. Jeff Henderson (Flint Kearsley) 15:36
19. Al Vance (GR Ottawa Hills) 15:37
20. Rick Nash (Flint Southwestern) 15:38
21. Ken Brown (Livonia Stevenson) 15:39

1975 CLASS A BOYS

Highland Park's Sam James produced the fastest time in Class A, a 14:46. The next spring he won the Class A two mile in 9:04.7.

Both James and team winner Dan Heikkinen became All-American steeplechasers in college, James for Tennessee, Heikkinen for Michigan.

Grand Blanc GC, Grand Blanc, Nov. 1 ☐
1975 BOYS CLASS A TEAMS

1. Grosse Pointe North 81
2. Livonia Churchill 159
3. Kalamazoo Norrix 185
4. Dearborn 229
5. Mt Clemens 242
6. East Kentwood 254
7. Midland 277
8. Saginaw Eisenhower 293
9. Pontiac Central 295
10. Flint Kearsley 297
11. Ann Arbor Pioneer 313
12. Orchard Lake 335
13. Adrian 339
14. Dearborn Fordson 358
15. Inkster Cherry Hill 363
16. Grand Blanc 370
17. Westland Glenn 387
18. Birmingham Groves 408
19. Birmingham Brother Rice 413
20. Ann Arbor Huron 413
21. Rochester Adams 436
22. Temperance Bedford 442
23. St Joseph 457
24. East Detroit 483

1975 BOYS CLASS A TEAM RACE

1. Dan Heikkinen (Adrian)12 ....14:59
2. Dave Lewis (Grosse Pointe North)12 ....15:10
3. Jeff Henderson (Flint Kearsley)12 ....15:16
4. Paul Manza (Birmingham Brother Rice) 15:17
5. Joel Mangan (Birmingham Groves) 15:23
6. Ted Unold (Westland Glenn) 15:25
7. Steve Postema (Ann Arbor Pioneer) 15:27
15. Dan Beck (Grosse Pointe North) ....nt
17. Bill Weidenbach (Grosse Pointe North) ....nt
18. Jeff Stafford (Grosse Pointe North) ....nt
28. Dale Savage (Grosse Pointe North) ....nt
29. Luke Preslawski (Grosse Pointe North) ....nt
31. Rob Peleman (Grosse Pointe North)12 ....nt

Sam James of Highland Park produced a sizzling 14:46 over the 3M course.

1975 BOYS CLASS A INDIVIDUAL RACE

1. Sam James (Highland Park)11 ....14:46
2. Al Vance (Grand Rapids Ottawa Hills) 15:11
3. Calvin McQueen (Flint Northern) 15:12
4. Lou Cappo (Flushing) 15:16
5. Toby Hayes (Dearborn Edsel Ford) 15:17
6. Dick Northhuis (Grand Haven) 15:20
7. Todd Wint (Livonia Churchill) 15:22
8. Ed Ranes (Lansing Hill) 15:26
17. Mike Goree (East Lansing) ....nt

1976 CLASS A BOYS

The Norsemen of Grosse Pointe North defended their Class A title on a clear day with 39-degree temperatures. "This is a fantastic group of kids," said coach Tom Gauerke. "We try to have five kids run under 16 minutes in the state meet and all seven did that today."

Indian Trails GC, Grand Rapids, Nov. 6 ☐
1976 BOYS CLASS A TEAMS

1. Grosse Pointe North 94
2. Grand Blanc 118
3. Jackson 141
4. Dearborn Edsel Ford 189
5. Livonia Stevenson 219
6. Kalamazoo Norrix 232
7. West Bloomfield 233
8. Flint Kearsley 235
9. Brighton 240
10. Royal Oak Kimball 247
11. Mt Clemens 256
12. Garden City East 319
13. East Kentwood 325

14. Wayne Memorial 333
15. Dearborn Fordson 344
16. Adrian 358
17. Alpena 363
18. Milford 380
19. Grand Rapids Ottawa Hills 402
20. Birmingham Brother Rice 446
21. St Clair Shores Lake Shore 460

1976 BOYS CLASS A TEAM RACE
1. Tim Proulx (Brighton)12 .... 15:07
2. Michael White (Jackson)11 .... 15:11
3. Rich Kramer (West Bloomfield) 15:12
4. Ed Sullivan (Jackson) 15:17
5. Ed Hammer (Grosse Pointe North) 15:20
6. John Riebel (Kalamazoo Norrix) 15:23
7. Kevin Miller (Wayne Memorial) 15:25
8. Mike Gromko (East Kentwood) 15:26
9. Mark Devereaux (Jackson) 15:29
10. Mike Naas (Royal Oak Kimball) 15:29
11. Bill Weidenbach (Grosse Pointe North) 15:29
12. Rick Collard (Grand Blanc) 15:30
13. Steve Cousins (Flint Kearsley) 15:30
14. Jim Miller (Adrian) 15:30
15. Dan Beck (Grosse Pointe North) 15:30
16. Jeff Westray (Dearborn Edsel Ford) .. 15:34
17. Phil Stephenson (SCS Lake Shore) ... 15:37
18. John Robins (Grand Blanc) 15:41
19. Bill Wilkin (Livonia Stevenson) 15:42
20. Jay Tomaszewski (GR Ottawa Hills) .. 15:43
21. Rick Blaha (Wayne Memorial) 15:44
22. Dave Podsadecki (Flint Kearsley) 15:45
23. Joe Ciaravino (Grosse Pointe North) . 15:46
27. Jack McIntosh (Dearborn Edsel Ford) . 15:47
39. Mark Kennedy (Grosse Pointe North) . 15:55
50. Dale Savage (Grosse Pointe North) .. 16:06
67. Luke Przeslawski (Grosse Pointe North) 16:15

1976 BOYS CLASS A INDIVIDUAL RACE
1. Gary Carter (St Clair Shores Lake Shore)12 .... 15:19
2. Kerry Barnett (Pontiac Central) 15:20
3. Vic Wietecha (Livonia Churchill) 15:21
4. Gary Parenteau (Swartz Creek) 15:22
5. Terry Doherty (Davison) 15:24
6. Tobin Jones (Livonia Churchill) 15:27
7. Tim Baar (Dearborn Heights Crestwood) 15:30
8. Scott Kleam (Salem) 15:31
9. Robert Gould (Northville) 15:33
10. Doug Lancaster (Temperance Bedford) 15:36
11. Erik Henriksen (Portage Northern) 15:38
12. Dave Stimpson (Saginaw Eisenhower) 15:39
13. Gordon Sanders (Clarkston) 15:39
14. Ken Morris (Trenton) 15:41
15. Bill Morgan (Birmingham Groves) 15:42
18. Greg Hollobaugh (Allen Park)12 .... 15:48

1977 CLASS A BOYS

Coach Bob Stallcup's Grand Blanc squad moved up from runner-up to grab the crown this year, capping an undefeated season. Terry Doherty, undefeated and leading in the final stages, fell just before the finish line, allowing Grand Blanc's Mark Mesler to take the win by a half-second. Mesler had been 65th as a junior.

A week later at the Champion of Champions race at Saginaw Valley State, Mesler repeated his victory over Doherty.

Indian Trails GC, Grand Rapids, Nov. 5 □
1977 BOYS CLASS A TEAMS
1. Grand Blanc 51
2. Grosse Pointe North 86
3. Jackson 165
4. Royal Oak Kimball 200
5. Wayne Memorial 203
6. Flint Kearsley 209
7. Grand Haven 225
8. Dearborn Edsel Ford 262
9. Northville 274
10. Royal Oak Dondero 278
11. Brighton 287
12. Portage Northern 309
13. Alpena 338
14. Warren Tower 348
15. Birmingham Brother Rice 351
16. Sterling Heights Stevenson 353
17. Garden City East 364
18. Waterford Mott 367
19. Kalamazoo Norrix 389
20. Farmington 420
21. Livonia Stevenson 456

Coach Bob Stallcup's Grand Blanc squad dominated in 1977.

1977 BOYS CLASS A TEAM RACE
1. Mark Mesler (Grand Blanc)12 .... 14:49
2. Terry Doherty (Flint Kearsley)12 .... 14:49
3. Rick Blaha (Wayne Memorial) 14:52
4. Ed Hammer (Grosse Pointe North) 14:53
5. Erik Henriksen (Portage Northern) 14:57
6. Al Stefanski (Grand Blanc) 15:00
7. Doug Tolson (Wayne Memorial)10 ...... 15:01
8. Mark Devereaux (Jackson) 15:06
9. Ron Lessard (Royal Oak Dondero) 15:08
10. Mike Moore (Grand Blanc) 15:11
11. Steve Brandt (Grosse Pointe North) . 15:12
12. Mike White (Jackson) 15:15
13. Dave Denis (Grosse Pointe North) ... 15:16
14. Mike Lasley (Royal Oak Dondero) 15:17
15. Tim Hinterman (Grand Blanc) 15:19
19. John Robins (Grand Blanc) .... nt

1977 BOYS CLASS A INDIVIDUAL RACE
1. Curt Reynolds (Redford Thurston)12 . 14:48
2. Jim Miller (Adrian)11 .... 14:52
3. Phil Stevenson (SCS Lake Shore) 14:52
4. Kerry Barnett (Pontiac Central) 14:58
5. Gordon Sanders (Clarkston) 15:00
6. Kevin Tribbett (Battle Creek Lakeview) 15:12
7. Dennis Gilbert (Owosso) 15:13
8. Bob Church (Southfield) 15:14
9. Joe Cotner (Bloomfield Hills Andover) 15:15
10. Dean Johnston (Waterford Kettering) 15:16
11. David Schrader (West Bloomfield) 15:18
12. Brian Hess (Redford Thurston)12 ..... 15:20
13. Frank Yarde (Holland) 15:22
14. Junior Sostenaws (Lansing Eastern) . 15:28
15. Larry Genninger (Muskegon Mona Shores) 15:29

1978 CLASS A BOYS

A great race was missed in the Class A finals, as Adrian's Jim Miller and Wayne's Doug Tolson both clocked 14:47.4 on the Faulkwood Shores course. Unfortunately, they were in different races, and one can only speculate about who might have been the better runner that day.

Bob Ritzema's Brighton squad put 4 in the top 15 to win their first title by a 10-point margin. "We knew that we were a contender for the title because we could beat the others on paper, but we hadn't done it for real," said Ritzema.

Faulkwood Shores GC, Howell, Nov. 4 ⊠
1978 BOYS CLASS A TEAMS
1. Brighton 85
2. Grand Blanc 95
3. Royal Oak Kimball 194
4. Grosse Pointe North 207
5. Flint Kearsley 218
6. Kalamazoo Norrix 223
7. Jackson 231
8. Portage Northern 241
9. Northville 285
10. Grand Haven 286
11. Warren Tower 307
12. Sterling Heights Stevenson 325
13. Dearborn Edsel Ford 334
14. Southfield Lathrup 340
15. Dearborn Fordson 360
16. Flint Northern 395
17. West Bloomfield 409
18. Port Huron Northern 416
19. Wayne Memorial 443
20. Swartz Creek 444
21. Royal Oak Dondero 444
22. Walled Lake Central 463
23. Howell 490
24. Grosse Pointe South 494

1978 BOYS CLASS A TEAM RACE
1. Doug Tolson (Wayne Memorial)11 ...... 14:48
2. Todd Snow (Jackson) 14:52
3. Steve Orlando (Royal Oak Kimball) 14:58
4. Mike Moore (Grand Blanc) 15:00
5. Bryan Olsen (Jackson) 15:01
6. Bill Fluharty (Dearborn Edsel Ford) ... 15:02
7. Steve Leach (Brighton) 15:07
8. Rich Scharchburg (Grand Blanc)11 .... 15:08
9. Jeff Proulx (Brighton) 15:09
10. Larry Fischer (Grand Haven)12 .... 15:10
11. Kevin Hurley (Brighton) 15:11
12. Mike Lasley (Royal Oak Dondero) ... 15:17
13. Jim Schmidt (Grosse Pointe North) .. 15:18
14. Doug Moore (Brighton) 15:21
15. John Robins (Grand Blanc)12 .... 15:24
16. Dennis Truby (Royal Oak Kimball) ... 15:24
21. Mark Moleski (Grand Blanc) 15:30
44. Chris Rice (Brighton) 15:51
59. Ross Good (Brighton) 16:03
126. Louis Schmidt (Brighton) 16:47

1978 BOYS CLASS A INDIVIDUAL RACE
1. Jim Miller (Adrian)12 .... 14:48
2. Mike Kilpela (Ann Arbor Huron) 14:54
3. Kevin Tribbett (Battle Crk Lakeview)12 . 15:01
4. Chuck Broski (Hazel Park) 15:04
5. Scott Brasington (East Lansing) 15:08
6. Matt Barnard (Waterford Mott) 15:09
7. Gordon Sanders (Clarkston) 15:10
8. Bill Brady (Mt Clemens) 15:16
9. Steve Underwood (East Lansing) 15:19
10. Brian Murley (Lansing Sexton) 15:22
11. Chuck Pladerstone (Clio) 15:26
12. Johan Engholm (Farmington Hills Harrison) 15:26
13. Bryan Nevins (Rockford) 15:27
14. Tim Rauh (Dearborn) 15:28
15. Mark Davis (Waterford Mott) 15:30
16. Gary Berryman (Birmingham Groves) 15:34
17. Bob Oakley (Belleville)12 .... 15:37
18. Bill Courtney (Dearborn) 15:38
19. Mike Schumaker (East Kentwood) ... 15:38
20. Mike McKinney (Flint Southwestern) . 15:41
21. Tom Seidenwand (Warren Mott) 15:42
22. Bob Brock (Holland West Ottawa) ... 15:42
23. Ed Gray (Bridgeport) 15:42
24. Jerry Behl (Lansing Waverly) 15:43
49. Jeff Hollobaugh (Allen Park)12 .... 16:11

1979 CLASS A BOYS

Conditions were perfect as Doug Tolson, later an All-American at Tennessee, cruised the Class A course in 14:29, one of the fastest performances ever seen in the state.

Nearly a half-minute slower (14:57.7) was team race winner Peter Blickle, a German exchange student.

Bob Stallcup's Grand Blanc squad moved up from the runner-up position the year before; its 143 points was the highest winning total ever.

Faulkwood Shores GC, Howell, Nov. 3 ⊠
1979 BOYS CLASS A TEAMS

1. Grand Blanc 143
2. Flint Kearsley 166
3. Bloomfield Hills Lahser 188
4. Grosse Pointe North 197
5. Sterling Heights 236
6. Ann Arbor Pioneer 246
7. Warren Cousino 265
8. Jackson 266
9. Rockford 279
10. Alpena 300
11. Brighton 304
12. Detroit Catholic Central 311
13. Port Huron Northern 336
14. West Bloomfield 337
15. East Kentwood 381
16. Midland 395
17. Battle Creek Lakeview 403
18. Milford 413
19. Portage Northern 420
20. Birmingham Brother Rice 430
21. Birmingham Groves 434
22. Dearborn Fordson 454
23. Dearborn 455
24. Jenison 457
25. Adrian 519

1979 BOYS CLASS A TEAM RACE

1. Peter Blickle (Portage Northern)12 14:58
2. Andy Dillon (Detroit Catholic Central)12 15:04
3. Rick Scharchburg (Grand Blanc) 15:08
4. Kevin Hurley (Brighton) 15:08
5. Dan Adas (Flint Kearsley) 15:10
6. Mark Randolph (Midland) 15:16
7. Tom Kaltz (Warren Cousino) 15:22
8. Mark Moleski (Grand Blanc) 15:22
9. Brad Gapezynski (Sterling Heights) 15:25
10. Geoff Smith (Birmingham Groves) 15:25
11. Jerry Brabbs (Grand Blanc) 15:25
12. Doug Lambert (Bloomfield Hills Lahser) 15:26
13. Ed Matash (Alpena) 15:26
14. Cavin Councilor (Flint Kearsley) 15:28
15. Craig Dickenson (Flint Kearsley) 15:29
16. Eric Teutsch (Portage Northern) 15:30
17. Scott Arthur (Rockford) 15:31
18. Brian Bagans (Warren Cousino) 15:34
57. Robert Moore (Grand Blanc) 16:00
64. Scott Waller (Grand Blanc) 16:03
101. Mike Tobin (Grand Blanc) 16:18
117. Tom Brochu (Grand Blanc) 16:26

1979 BOYS CLASS A INDIVIDUAL RACE

1. Doug Tolson (Wayne Memorial)12 14:29
2. Carl Allen (Ann Arbor Huron)11 14:56
3. Scott Harper (Birmingham Seaholm) 15:01
4. Steve Orlando (Royal Oak Kimball) 15:06
5. Bill Brady (Mt Clemens) 15:09
6. Tom Seidenwand (Warren Mott) 15:11
7. Jeff Posthumus (Muskegon) 15:13
8. Dave Dunn (Kalamazoo Norrix) 15:17
9. Steve Underwood (East Lansing) 15:21
10. Will Riegle (Battle Creek Central) 15:22
11. Troy Oullette (Taylor Kennedy)12 15:23
12. David Crescio (Ypsilanti) 15:23
13. Paul Riegle (Battle Creek Central) 15:23
14. John Murphy (Farmington) 15:24
15. Bob Landry (Royal Oak Kimball) 15:25
16. Stace Alcala (Grand Haven) 15:30
17. Mike McKinney (Flint Southwestern) 15:30
18. Richard Stone (Warren Mott) 15:31
19. Paul Baize (Taylor Truman) 15:32
20. Jon McCormick (Kalamazoo Central) 15:33
21. Gordy Vonzellen (Sterling Heights Ford) 15:34
22. Steve Sutherland (Walled Lake Western) 15:35

1980 CLASS A BOYS

This marked the first year that all regionals and finals in the Lower Peninsula took place on 5000m courses. The day started out sunny before the clouds moved in. Flint Kearsley won the team title as expected.

In the individual race, Bill Brady and Carl Allen dueled the entire distance, with Brady having the stronger kick after a 9:37 at 2M. This was also the first year that timing in the thousandths showed up, even though the timers used hand timing. Brady's official time was given as 15:07.41.

In the team race, Holly coach Duane Raffin cautioned Matt Stack not to go out too fast: "We just told him to cool it until you know you could do something." He passed Kearsley's Cavin Councilor and Craig Dickinson near the 2M mark.

The winning Kearsley squad.

IMA Brookwood GC, Flint, Nov.1 ⊠
1980 BOYS CLASS A TEAMS

1. Flint Kearsley 100
2. Grosse Pointe North 132
3. Dearborn 189
4. Ann Arbor Pioneer 193
5. Milford 198
6. Birmingham Brother Rice 199
7. Rockford 214
8. East Kentwood 249
9. Sterling Heights Ford 307
10. Kalamazoo Norrix 307
11. Royal Oak Dondero 312
12. Davison 322
13. Lakeland 335
14. Warren Cousino 354
15. Holly 357
16. Jackson 358
17. Clio 384
18. Temperance Bedford 392
19. Battle Creek Lakeview 425
20. Sterling Heights 440
21. Traverse City 448
22. Northville 463
23. Canton 496
24. North Farmington 509

1980 BOYS CLASS A TEAM RACE

1. Matt Stack (Holly)11 15:23
2. Cavin Councilor (Flint Kearsley)12 15:34
3. Craig Dickinson (Flint Kearsley)12 15:35
4. Bill Courtney (Dearborn) 15:38
5. Clark Couyoumjian (Northville) 15:40
6. Jim Martin (Jackson) 15:42
7. Steve Van Dyke (Rockford) 15:45
8. Chris Corcey (Birmingham Brother Rice) 15:48
9. Jamie Elliott (Royal Oak Dondero)11 15:48
10. Chris Napolillo (East Kentwood) 15:48
11. Joe Morris (Milford) 15:51
12. Paul Johnson (Ann Arbor Pioneer) 15:53
13. Dan Hammer (Grosse Pointe North) 15:53
14. Jeff Weyerman (Rockford) 15:55
15. Joe Schmidt (Grosse Pointe North) 15:55
16. Joe Davey (Birmingham Brother Rice) 15:55
17. Mike Ulrich (Clio) 15:56
18. Cordy Vonzellen (Sterling Heights Ford) 15:58
19. Tim Sullivan (Birmingham Brother Rice) 16:00
20. Bob Addison (Davison) 16:00
21. Mark Rolain (Grosse Pointe North) 16:00
22. Rich Scofield (Flint Kearsley)12 16:01
34. Gregg MacInnis (Flint Kearsley)12 16:14
39. Kevin Gumerson (Flint Kearsley)12 16:17
95. Mike Wiltse (Flint Kearsley)10 16:52
114. Craig Adas (Flint Kearsley)11 17:02

1980 BOYS CLASS A INDIVIDUAL RACE

1. Bill Brady (Mt Clemens)12 15:08
2. Carl Allen (Ann Arbor Huron)12 15:21
3. Craig Higby (Grand Ledge) 15:36
4. Mike Parcha (Taylor Center) 15:37
5. Mike Mara (Midland Dow) 15:41
6. Geoff Smith (Birmingham Groves) 15:41
7. Dave Farlow (Owosso) 15:42
8. Lawrence Swift (Detroit Cass Tech) 15:43
9. Mike Maher (Kalamazoo Central) 15:49
10. Jim Marshall (Pontiac Central) 15:51
11. David Krafsur (Southfield Lathrup) 15:52
12. Bob Michiellitti (St Clair Shores Lakeview) 15:53
13. Greg Palardy (Dearborn Edsel Ford) 15:53
14. Paul Coburn (Livonia Franklin) 15:58
15. Klas Wallstrom (Bridgeport) 16:01
16. Mike McKinney (Flint Southwestern) 16:02
17. Dennis Keand (Berkley) 16:03
18. Mike Jewell (Swartz Creek) 16:05

1981 CLASS A BOYS

In Class A, under cloudy skies with a balmy 60-degree temperature, Dearborn Edsel Ford, coached by Skip Domke, won its first title ever. The team was led by senior Greg Palardy, who finished second overall.

IMA Brookwood GC, Flint, Oct. 31 ☐
1981 BOYS CLASS A TEAMS

1. Dearborn Edsel Ford 121
2. Flint Kearsley 140
3. Birmingham Brother Rice 192
4. Milford 194
5. Davison 238
6. Grosse Pointe North 266
7. Grand Blanc 267
8. Grand Rapids Union 276
9. Sterling Heights 283
10. Lansing Eastern 289
11. Royal Oak Dondero 292
12. Brighton 298
13. Temperance Bedford 317
14. Wayne Memorial 324
15. Traverse City 326
16. Kalamazoo Norrix 345
=17. Jackson 349
=17. Sterling Heights Stevenson 349
19. Warren Tower 361
20. Rockford 400
21. Rochester 446
22. Redford Union 453
24. Troy ?

1981 BOYS CLASS A TEAM RACE

1. Jamie Elliott (Royal Oak Dondero)12 15:42
2. Greg Palardy (Dearborn Edsel Ford)12 15:43
3. Joe Schmidt (Grosse Pointe North)11 15:44
4. David Cross (Kalamazoo Norrix) 15:44
5. Joe Davey (Birmingham Brother Rice) 15:45
6. Chris Borcey (Birmingham Brother Rice) 15:49
7. Jeff Olvin (Milford) 15:55
8. Chris Morgan (Davison) 15:56
9. Ed Matash (Flint Kearsley) 15:58
10. Glenn Klassa (Dearborn Edsel Ford) 15:59
11. Bob Jazwinski (Grand Rapids Union) 16:01
12. Bob Addison (Davison) 16:02
13. Joe Mihalic (Warren Tower) 16:02
14. Pat Fleenor (Brighton) 16:03
16. Jerry Kramer (Milford) 16:03

1981 BOYS CLASS A INDIVIDUAL RACE

1. Jeff Mundt (New Baltimore Anchor Bay)10 15:43
2. Fred Bunn (Grand Rapids Creston) 15:48

3. Mike Parcha (Taylor Center).................................15:52
4. Ricky Munoz (Flint Central)..................................16:00
5. Paul Pioszak (St Johns)......................................16:00
6. Rich Stetter (Warren Cousino)...............................16:02
7. Brad Quick (Niles)...16:03
17. Brian Weirick (Grandville)..................................16:19

1982 CLASS A BOYS

The Lower Peninsula finals were run in cold weather, temps barely rising above 30 with occasional snow showers. Grosse Pointe North, under coach Dave McEvers, put together a 64-point performance on the strength of a 1-2 finish. It was the fourth team title in nine years for the Norsemen. They had gone through the season undefeated, save for one loss at the Royal Oak Shrine Invitational.

Individual winner Phil Schoensee would qualify for the Foot Locker Nationals a few weeks later, only the second Michigan boy to do so since the meet's inception in 1979. He would place 19th in San Diego. Later he would be an All-American at Wisconsin.

IMA Brookwood GC, Flint, Nov. 6
1982 BOYS CLASS A TEAMS
1. Grosse Pointe North 64
2. Detroit Catholic Central 108
3. Warren Tower 139
4. Swartz Creek 184
5. Sterling Heights Stevenson 185
6. Dearborn Edsel Ford 187
7. Grand Blanc 205
8. Milford 217
9. Flint Kearsley 287
10. Jenison 323
11. Kalamazoo Norrix 346
12. East Lansing 348
13. Livonia Churchill 353
14. Temperance Bedford 354
15. Howell 362
16. Redford Union 368
17. East Kentwood 374
18. Birmingham Brother Rice 384
19. West Bloomfield 422
20. Wayne Memorial 448
21. Troy 480
22. Southfield Lathrup 497
23. Rochester 503
24. Southfield 634

1982 BOYS CLASS A TEAM RACE
1. Joe Schmidt (Grosse Pointe North)12............15:38
2. Mark Denis (Grosse Pointe North)12.............15:42
3. Joe Mihalic (Warren Tower)..........................15:49
4. Dan Schultz (Grand Blanc)...........................15:51
5. Marty Hegarty (Detroit Catholic Central) 15:51
6. Tim Mohr (Jenison)......................................15:52
7. Paul Buchanan (Detroit Catholic Central) 15:52
8. Mark Mitroka (Grand Blanc).........................15:57
9. Jeff Olvin (Milford).......................................15:58
10. Eric Koskinen (Swartz Creek).....................15:59
11. Murray Breeze (Kalamazoo Norrix).............16:00
12. Steve Shaver (Detroit Catholic Central) 16:00
13. Dave Roman (Sterling Heights Stevenson)........16:01
14. Scott Cooper (Grosse Pointe North)12........16:01
15. Darren Ezzo (Warren Tower).......................16:02
16. Jerry Kramer (Milford).................................16:03
17. Bob Thompson (Rochester).........................16:04
18. Scott Morell (Sterling Heights Stevenson)...16:04
19. Mark Parenti (Warren Tower)......................16:05
20. Eric Walker (Kalamazoo Norrix)...................16:06
21. Brian Boutell (Grosse Pointe North)12........16:08
22. Dan Miller (Livonia Churchill).......................16:09
23. Tom Bishop (Swartz Creek).........................16:10
24. Scott Klassa (Dearborn Edsel Ford)............16:11
26. Joe Carroll (Grosse Pointe North)11............16:13
69. Pete Strok (Grosse Pointe North) 16:47
82. Doug Schepke (Grosse Pointe North)..........16:57

1982 BOYS CLASS A INDIVIDUAL RACE
1. Phil Schoensee (Center Line)11 .... 15:31
2. Jeff Mundt (New Baltimore Anchor Bay)11 ......15:36
3. Don Johns (Center Line) 15:44
4. James Biskner (Bay City Glenn) 15:51
5. Eric Wittenberg (Birmingham Seaholm)........ 15:53
6. Joel Hernandez (Lansing Sexton) 15:57
7. Paul Smith (Jackson) 16:01
8. Dennis Dobbs (Lansing Eastern) 16:02
9. Rick Wood (Rochester Adams) 16:03
10. Orssie Bumpas (Detroit Catholic) 16:04
11. Dave Wysack (Wyandotte) 16:05
12. Bill Miller (Harper Woods Notre Dame)....... 16:06
13. Tom Gibson (Westland Glenn) 16:07
14. Todd Wright (Grand Haven) 16:08
15. David Swarts (Jackson) 16:09
16. Tim Root (Muskegon Mona Shores) 16:10
17. Robert Henderson (Pontiac Northern) 16:11

1983 CLASS A BOYS

Andy Ketch nipped Joe Mihalic at the finish of the team race, both clocking 15:35.7. It was the closest race in the history of the meet. Detroit Catholic Central, under Tony Magni, won its first state title.

"I've been saying all year that if our guys ran the way they were supposed to, the state meet wouldn't be that close," said Magni. "The field was the biggest they ever had and I was a little worried about that, but we pulled out in front early."

Catholic Central's winning margin of 118 points was the second-biggest in meet history.

Andy Ketch wasn't alone at the state finals, where he nipped Joe Mihalioc in the closest finish ever.

Eagle Creek GC, Hartland, Nov. 5
Clear and cool, 40 degrees.
1983 BOYS CLASS A TEAMS
1. Detroit Catholic Central 92
2. Grand Blanc 210
3. Warren Tower 214
4. Milford 264
5. White Lake Lakeland 284
6. Monroe 308
7. East Kentwood 309
8. Dearborn Fordson...................................... 314
9. Swartz Creek 317
10. Ann Arbor Pioneer 317
11. Portage Northern 323
12. Holland 335
13. East Lansing 342
14. Wayne Memorial 388
15. Hazel Park 395
16. Birmingham Brother Rice 402
17. Ferndale 403
18. Kalamazoo Norrix 409
19. Sterling Heights Stevenson 423
20. Brighton 471
21. Dearborn Edsel Ford 473
22. Holly 500
23. Dearborn 516
24. Warren Cousino 519
25. Livonia Churchill 535
26. Detroit Murray-Wright 535
27. Westland Glenn 585
28. Grosse Pointe South 621
29. Harper Woods Notre Dame 675
30. Bridgeport 722

1983 BOYS CLASS A TEAM RACE
1. Andy Ketch (Kalamazoo Norrix) 15:36
2. Joe Mihalic (Warren Tower) 15:36
3. Jeff Neal (Detroit Murray-Wright) 15:47
4. Steve Shaver (Detroit Catholic Central)..... 15:49
5. Erik Koskinen (Swartz Creek) 15:51
6. Kevin Psik (Dearborn Edsel Ford) 15:53
7. Marty Hegarty (Detroit Catholic Central)11 ...15:55
8. Tim Fraleigh (Ann Arbor Pioneer)11 .... 15:58
9. Geoff Clendening (Ferndale) 16:03
10. Ron Sprinkel (East Lansing) 16:03
11. Murray Breeze (Kalamazoo Norrix) 16:04
12. Mark Parenti (Warren Woods Tower) 16:09
13. Rob Helberg (Milford) 16:13
14. Bob Ray (Monroe) 16:14
15. Geoff Goolsby (Ferndale) 16:15
16. Rob Shaver (Detroit Catholic Central) 16:21
17. Doug Plachta (Livonia Churchill) 16:22
18. Mohamed Hazamy (Dearborn Fordson) ... 16:22
19. Mike Kazmierski (East Kentwood) 16:23
20. Tim Weber (Holland) 16:25
21. Jim Cauzillo (Detroit Catholic Central)11 ....16:25
22. Carl Caballero (Hazel Park)11 .... 16:26
23. Mark Mitroka (Grand Blanc) 16:27
24. Richard Lockhart (Grand Blanc)11 .... 16:27
25. Tom Asmas (Ferndale) 16:28
26. Alan Jaffray (Milford Lakeland) 16:29
44. Mark Anderson (Detroit Catholic Central).......16:43
74. Chris Hitts (Detroit Catholic Central) 16:57
93. Pat Isom (Detroit Catholic Central) 17:10

1983 BOYS CLASS A INDIVIDUAL RACE
1. Bob Thompson (Rochester) 15:32
2. Jeff Mundt (New Baltimore Anchor Bay)12 ......15:35
3. Jeff Wilson (Flint Kearsley) 15:53
4. Dave Kuritar (Howell) 16:00
5. Orssie Bumpas (Detroit Catholic) 16:03
6. Ken Dubois (Livonia Stevenson) 16:06
7. David Ciavenecia (Belleville) 16:08
8. Kyle Chura (Walled Lake Western) 16:10
9. Mark Tait (Detroit King) 16:18
10. Chris Mendoze (Detroit Ford) 16:19
11. Pat Martin (Jackson) 16:21
12. Lee (Grand Rapids) 16:21
13. Johnson (Ypsilanti) 16:21
14. Jay Hunt (Westland Glenn)11 .... 16:25

1984 CLASS A BOYS

Swartz Creek coach Dave Carey called it right before the race: "Catholic Central has the best five runners in the state and we have the best seven." Indeed, if all seven had scored, Swartz Creek would have won, 376-403. Instead Tony Magni's Shamrocks won by 30 points.

Said Magni, "I was wishing it was over after the first mile because we were winning and after the second mile because we were winning. I saw our fifth man was fading and we just hung on."

These are corrected results in the team race. According to Kermit Ambrose, "Numbers 23, 132, and 155 were not handed out. Number 190 came up twice (same school). I have re-scored the meet and what you find above is the correct result of the run." Ambrose's corrected version ran in the MITCA newsletter.

Dama Farms Golf Course, Howell, Nov. 3

50 degrees, partly cloudy.

1984 BOYS CLASS A TEAMS
1. Detroit Catholic Central 138
2. Swartz Creek 168
3. Hazel Park 212
4. Grand Blanc 227
5. Ann Arbor Pioneer 251
6. Dearborn 276
7. Monroe 297
8. Lakeland 297
9. Rochester 299
10. Dearborn Edsel Ford 309
11. Farmington 318
12. East Kentwood 320
13. Portage Northern 320
14. Holly 330
15. Milford 339
16. Birmingham Brother Rice 457
17. Utica Eisenhower 365
18. Dearborn Fordson 384
19. Flint Kearsley 432
20. Howell 434
21. Rockford 438
22. Jenison 451
23. Brighton 542
24. Warren Cousino 580
25. Westland Glenn 582
26. Redford Union 601
27. Grosse Pointe South 649
28. Harper Woods Notre Dame 713
29. Warren Woods Tower 724
30. Detroit Cass Tech 797

1984 BOYS CLASS A TEAM RACE
1. Tim Fraleigh (Ann Arbor Pioneer)12 ..... 15:25
2. Bob Thompson (Rochester)12 ..... 15:36
3. Erik Koskinen (Swartz Creek)12 ..... 15:38
4. Marty Hegarty (Detroit Catholic Central)12 ..... 15:40
5. Dan Carney (White Lake Lakeland)12 ..... 15:43
6. Guy Pace (Ann Arbor Pioneer)12 ..... 15:45
7. Steve Shaver (Detroit Catholic Central)12 ..... 15:46
8. Robert Abraham (Dearborn Fordson)12 ..... 15:51
9. Andy Klassa (Dearborn Edsel Ford)12 ..... 15:52
10. Scott Colvin (Grand Blanc)11 ..... 15:53
11. Greg Turgeon (Flint Kearsley)12 ..... 15:54
12. Jeff Wilson (Flint Kearsley)12 ..... 15:55
13. Richard Lockhart (Grand Blanc)12 ..... 15:56
14. Mark Zauel (Holly)11 ..... 15:58
15. Sean Falk (Monroe)12 ..... 16:03
16. Todd Williams (Monroe)10 ..... 16:06
17. Tom Royce (Milford)11 ..... 16:06
18. Mark Somerville (Dearborn)10 ..... 16:07
19. Chad Findley (Rochester)10 ..... 16:09
20. Harold Mueller (Swartz Creek)10 ..... 16:09
21. Chris Inch (Farmington)10 ..... 16:15
22. Ihab Hamka (Dearborn Fordson)10 ..... 16:16
23. Paul Roberts (Dearborn)12 ..... 16:16
24. Glen Jaffray (White Lake Lakeland)12 ..... 16:17
25. Mark Reinardy (East Kentwood)11 ..... 16:18
26. Charlie Parrish (White Lake Lakeland)11 ..... 16:19
27. Steve Broekstra (Rockford)12 ..... 16:19
28. Jim Cauzillo (Detroit Catholic Central)12 ..... 16:20
29. Kyle Rickard (Portage Northern)12 ..... 16:21
30. Art Main (Swartz Creek)11 ..... 16:25
31. Carl Caballero (Hazel Park)12 ..... 16:25
32. John Norton (Hazel Park)12 ..... 16:26
33. Andy Steele (Hazel Park)12 ..... 16:29

1984 BOYS CLASS A INDIVIDUAL RACE
1. Dave Homann (Garden City) 15:34
2. Geoff Goolsby (Royal Oak Kimball)12 ..... 15:42
3. Tim Moore (West Bloomfield) 15:59
4. Ron Lindstrom (Clio) 15:59
5. Tim Weber (Holland) 16:00
6. Todd Zielinski (Alpena) 16:01
7. Anthony Hamm (Flint Northern)10 ..... 16:02
8. Cliff Dwelle (Lake Orion) 16:08
9. Don Hoezee (GR Ottawwa Hills) 16:12
10. Steve Tschirhart (Waterford Kettering) 16:14

1985 CLASS A BOYS

Utica Eisenhower beat a Todd Williams-led Monroe squad, scoring a record-high 173 points. Said Eisenhower coach Mark Olin, "There's nothing special in the water out here. These kids run all year round… The kids are committed. They are the ones who put in all the lonely hours on the road."

The next spring Williams would win the 3200 crown in 9:11.63. Another great race was missed because of the split in the team and individual races, as Williams didn't run against rival Anthony Hamm of Flint Northern; they clocked the same 15:43 in separate races.

IMA Brookwood Golf Course, Flint, Nov. 2 ☒
1985 BOYS CLASS A TEAMS
1. Utica Eisenhower 173
2. Monroe 180
3. Rochester 184
4. Dearborn Edsel Ford 192
5. Okemos 243
6. Swartz Creek 262
7. Lakeland 290
8. Holly 292
9. Ann Arbor Pioneer 293
10. Farmington 305
11. East Kentwood 312
12. Birmingham Brother Rice 327
13. Davison 351
14. Lansing Waverly 356
15. Rochester Adams 356
16. Walled Lake Central 365
17. Kalamazoo Norrix 368
18. Hazel Park 369
19. Portage Northern 381
20. Holland 392
21. Adrian 404
22. Flint Kearsley 489
23. Detroit Catholic Central 501
24. Royal Oak Kimball 504
25. Dearborn 575
26. Grosse Pointe North 626
27. Harper Woods Notre Dame 647
28. Grosse Pointe South 656

1985 BOYS CLASS A TEAM RACE
1. Todd Williams (Monroe)11 ..... 15:43
2. Harold Mueller (Swartz Creek) 15:48
3. Chris Inch (Farmington) 15:51
4. Chad Findley (Rochester) 15:57
5. Rob Rinck (Lansing Waverly) 16:00
6. Chris Tolonen (Ann Arbor Pioneer) 16:01
7. Mark Zauel (Holly) 16:04
8. Al Stebbens (Farmington) 16:10
9. Sam Blumke (Hazel Park) 16:14
10. David Shamas (Utica Eisenhower) 16:17
11. Paul Sisovsky (Swartz Creek) 16:19
12. Eric Hammerberg (Dearborn Edsel Ford) 16:23
13. Bryan Whitmore (Okemos) 16:25
14. Phil Vanhull (Lakeland) 16:25
15. Andy Kazmierski (East Kentwood) 16:27
16. Matt Niesswender (Monroe) 16:27
17. Dave Wardwell (Portage Northern) 16:28
18. David Madrigal (Davison) 16:29
19. Mark Sommerville (Dearborn) 16:30
20. Mark Reinardy (East Kentwood) 16:31
21. Joe Hodson (Rochester) 16:31
22. Steve Littleson (Utica Eisenhower) 16:32
23. Jeff Madsen (Walled Lake Central) 16:32
24. Ed Hickey (Birmingham Brother Rice) 16:33
31. Doug Garden (Utica Eisenhower) 16:45
47. Mark Buckreis (Utica Eisenhower) 16:55
63. Gregg Sobocinski (Utica Eisenhower) 17:05
88. Chris White (Utica Eisenhower) 17:14
107. Eric Sorensen (Utica Eisenhower)10 ..... 17:23

1985 BOYS CLASS A INDIVIDUAL RACE
1. Anthony Hamm (Flint Northern)11 ..... 15:43
2. Cliff Dwelle (Lake Orion)11 ..... 15:59
3. Scott Colvin (Grand Blanc) 16:12
4. Matt Fogo (Troy) 16:14
5. Kirk Armstrong (North Farmington) 16:17
6. Jon Gill (Ferndale)10 ..... 16:19
7. Ron Tolson (Wayne Memorial) 16:20
8. Bruce Irvine (Warren DeLaSalle) 16:25
9. John Williams (Detroit Chadsey) 16:26
10. Carl Martin (Taylor Truman) 16:27
11. Jim Huff (Bloomfield Hills Lahser)10 ..... 16:28
12. Phil Antekeier (Ann Arbor Huron) 16:31
13. Bill Battle (Ypsilanti)11 ..... 16:32
14. Tom Royce (Milford) 16:32
15. Troy Greeley (Temperance Bedford) 16:34
16. Frank Wilkerson (Southfield) 16:34

After winning his second cross country title, Monroe's Todd Williams placed 2nd at nationals.

1986 CLASS A BOYS

This time Todd Williams and rival Anthony Hamm ran in the same race. Williams, the future Tennessee star and 2-time Olympian, broke Hamm early and sailed to 17-second win.

The individual race was won by Lake Orion's Cliff Dwelle. Said coach Stan Ford, "He's run by himself all year. We had hoped the team would be able to qualify so we could get him in with Williams and Hamm to give him some competition, because he's just been untouched this year."

A few weeks later, Williams would finish 2nd in the nation at the Foot Locker Nationals. Also in the race would be Dwelle (16th) and Chris Tolonen of Pioneer (27th).

IMA Brookwood Golf Course, Flint, Nov. 1 ☐
1986 BOYS CLASS A TEAMS
1. Swartz Creek 150
2. Farmington 157
3. Birmingham Brother Rice 168
4. Ann Arbor Pioneer 170
5. Lakeland 174
6. Traverse City 252
7. Monroe 256
8. Gibraltar Carlson 263
9. Rochester 269
10. Utica Eisenhower 288
11. Troy 328
12. Walled Lake Central 331
13. Flint Northern 353
14. Holland 358
15. Holt 361
16. Royal Oak Kimball 421
17. Kalamazoo Norrix 455

18. Milford 457
19. Dearborn Edsel Ford 463
20. Grand Ledge 465
21. Grandville 479
22. Warren DeLaSalle 497
23. Adrian 519
24. Clio 532
25. Fraser 570
26. Grosse Pointe North 573
27. Port Huron Northern 618
28. Grosse Pointe South 663

1986 BOYS CLASS A TEAM RACE

1. Todd Williams (Monroe)12 15:09
2. Anthony Hamm (Flint Northern)12 15:26
3. Harold Mueller (Swartz Creek) 15:36
4. Chris Inch (Farmington) 15:41
5. Chad Findley (Rochester) 15:44
6. Doug Goudie (Rochester) 15:47
7. Phil Vanhull (White Lake Lakeland) 15:51
8. Eric Sorensen (Utica Eisenhower)11 15:51
9. Tim Pitcher (Monroe) 15:54
10. Chris Tolonen (Ann Arbor Pioneer) 15:55
11. Jason Colvin (Ann Arbor Pioneer) 15:56
12. Doug Garden (Utica Eisenhower) 15:58
13. Paul Sisovsky (Swartz Creek) 15:58
14. Joe Marino (Ann Arbor Pioneer) 16:04
15. Paul DeLave (Warren DeLaSalle) 16:06
16. Eric Hammerberg (Dearborn Edsel Ford) 16:07
17. Chris Jonas (Grand Ledge) 16:13
18. Chris Pugh (White Lake Lakeland) 16:13
19. Derek Barg (Traverse City) 16:17
20. Al Stebbins (Farmington) 16:18
21. David Freeman (Swartz Creek) 16:18
22. Jeff Beyst (Gibraltar Carlson) 16:19

1986 BOYS CLASS A INDIVIDUAL RACE

1. Cliff Dwelle (Lake Orion)12 15:38
2. Joel Kaines (Flint Powers) 15:48
3. Ihab Hanka (Dearborn Fordson) 15:52
4. Sam Blumke (Hazel Park) 15:53
5. Carl Martin (Taylor Truman) 15:54
6. Jim Carlisle (Hazel Park) 15:57
7. Bill Battle (Ypsilanti)12 16:04
8. Jim Huff (Bloomfield Hills Lahser)11 16:05
9. Joe Tobin (Flint Kearsley) 16:05
10. Thomas Weiss (East Lansing) 16:05
11. Lee Christensen (Rockford) 16:06
12. Chris Langton (Waterford Mott) 16:08
13. Dan Liedel (Westland Glenn) 16:10
14. Frank Wilkerson (Southfield) 16:10
15. Kevin Kilkelly (Portage Northern) 16:11
16. Rich Schaffer (Lincoln Park) 16:18
17. Matt Smith (Redford Borgess) 16:19
18. Lorento Berlanga (Flint Carman-Ainsworth) 16:20

1987 CLASS A BOYS

Ann Arbor Pioneer won, its first victory since it took the 1924 trophy as Ann Arbor High School. "I have absolutely zero complaints," said coach Don Sleeman. "It was the greatest team effort that anybody could ask for. We did not have a single bad performance. Every single man did everything he could do."

Team race winner Paul Butterfield of Bridgeport had worries during the race: "My legs didn't feel strong today. I was just hoping my legs had enough in them to sprint to the finish and outkick [Colvin]."

Groesbeck GC, Lansing, Nov. 7 ⊠
1987 BOYS CLASS A TEAMS

1. Ann Arbor Pioneer 98
2. Monroe 126
3. Birmingham Brother Rice 164
4. Detroit Catholic Central 212
5. Ferndale 224
6. Lakeland 264
7. Kalamazoo Norrix 273
8. Farmington 287
9. Portage Northern 314
10. Okemos 320
11. Sterling Heights Stevenson 324
12. Sterling Heights Ford 332
13. Hazel Park 365
14. Ann Arbor Huron 387
15. Salem 392
16. East Kentwood 394
17. Grand Ledge 405
18. Gibraltar Carlson 429
19. Bloomfield Hills Lahser 437
20. Clio 451
21. Lansing Waverly 451
22. Bridgeport 472
23. Clinton Twp Chippewa Valley 476
24. Temperance Bedford 553
25. Swartz Creek 589
26. Harper Woods Notre Dame 630
27. Grosse Pointe North 708

1987 BOYS CLASS A TEAM RACE

1. Paul Butterfield (Bridgeport)12 15:37
2. Jason Colvin (Ann Arbor Pioneer)11 15:39
3. Jon Gill (Ferndale)12 15:49
4. Tim Pitcher (Monroe)11 15:50
5. Brandon Brownell (Okemos)12 16:02
6. Richard Gledhill (Clinton T Chippewa Valley)12 16:08
7. Jim Carlisle (Hazel Park)12 16:13
8. Jeff Beyst (Gibraltar Carlson)10 16:16
9. Kevin Kilkelly (Portage Northern)12 16:19
10. John Koppin (Birmingham Brother Rice)12 16:23
11. Nate Ford (Ann Arbor Pioneer)11 16:24
12. Dan Clevenger (Grand Ledge)11 16:26
13. Doug Vergari (Salem)12 16:28
14. Mike Bock (Ann Arbor Pioneer)12 16:31
15. Phil Sanborn (Monroe)11 16:32
16. Joel Dood (Okemos)12 16:34
17. Mike Burry (Birmingham Brother Rice)12 16:35
18. Matt Schroeder (Monroe)11 16:36
19. Jim Hensen (Ferndale)12 16:40
20. JohnElder (Grand Ledge)11 16:41
21. Tom Pier (Lansing Waverly)12 16:44
22. Matt Leighninger (Kalamazoo Norrix)12 16:45
23. Mike O'Brien (Birmingham Brother Rice)11 16:46
29. Eric Larson (Ann Arbor Pioneer)12 16:50
42. Hans Berg (Ann Arbor Pioneer)11 17:01
62. Jeff Louwsima (Ann Arbor Pioneer)10 17:14
72. Matt Knudvsvig (Ann Arbor Pioneer)12 17:19

1987 BOYS CLASS A INDIVIDUAL RACE

1. Brian Grosso (Walled Lake Western)11 15:51
2. Tom Weiss (East Lansing)11 16:02
3. John Frisbie (Northville)12 16:11
4. Rick Schaffer (Lincoln Park)12 16:12
5. Evan McGrath (Flint Carman-Ainsw)12 16:13
6. Doug Goudie (Rochester)12 16:14
7. Chris Buursma (Grandville)12 16:20
8. Steven Dean (Detroit Southeastern)11 16:20
9. Matt Smith (Redford Borgess)12 16:31
10. Jody Chism (Detroit Osborn)11 16:34
11. Dan Oden (Troy Athens)12 16:35
12. Jeff Blumenthal (Alpena)12 16:35
13. Derrick Allen (Wayne Memorial)12 16:35
14. Dan Kramer (Dearborn Fordson)11 16:36
15. Mike Jensen (Walled Lake Central)12 16:42
16. Rob Rasmussen (Novi)11 16:42
17. Tom Carney (Milford)11 16:44

1988 CLASS A BOYS

Todd Williams was gone, but Monroe could still run. The 39 points the Trojans tallied was the lowest score since 1939. The team boasted the two fastest runners, Phil Sanborn and Tim Pitcher.

"Unrelenting rain" had made the course especially difficult. Said Monroe coach Dave Bork, "We have a philosophy we run by, and that's do your best under the circumstances. We love weather like this becase we know that some teams and some kids will just bag it in and quit. But we try to take what comes."

In the Individual race, defending champion Brian Grosso took a wrong turn and ran significantly farther, ending up fifth in 16:53. A month later, at the Foot Locker national championships in San Diego, Grosso was a changed man. He pulled away from the field at midway to record a seven-second win in 15:03, becoming the first Michigander to win the prestigious title.

Yes, the 1988 race was wet.

IMA Brookwood Golf Course, Flint, Nov. 5 ⊠
1988 BOYS CLASS A TEAMS

1. Monroe 39
2. Ann Arbor Pioneer 112
3. Milford 127
4. Lakeland 155
5. Detroit Catholic Central 224
6. Troy 231
7. Sterling Heights Stevenson 255
8. Grand Ledge 287
9. Birmingham Brother Rice 299
10. Holly 331
11. Kalamazoo Norrix 344
12. Pontiac Central 346
13. Swartz Creek 348
14. Sterling Heights Ford 398
15. Dearborn Fordson 405
16. East Kentwood 449
17. Detroit U-D Jesuit 466
18. Wyandotte 481
19. Warren DeLaSalle 484
20. Davison 500
21. Rockford 521
22. East Detroit 539
23. Detroit Murray-Wright 539
24. Grosse Pointe South 593
25. Livonia Franklin 597
26. Portage Central 653
27. Muskegon Mona Shores 691

1988 BOYS CLASS A TEAM RACE

1. Phil Sanborn (Monroe)12 16:08
2. Tim Pitcher (Monroe)12 16:15
3. Jason Colvin (Ann Arbor Pioneer)12 16:16
4. Dan Kramer (Dearborn Fordson)12 16:23
5. Brian Hyde (East Kentwood)10 16:25
6. Matt Schroeder (Monroe)12 16:29
7. Sean Sweat (Monroe)12 16:30
8. Dave Clevenger (Grand Ledge)12 16:36
9. Bill Stricklin (Sterling Heights Ford)11 16:37
10. Mike Sheridan (Detroit Catholic Central)11 16:37
11. Lance Peterson (Lakeland)12 16:37
12. Rob Lee (Detroit U-D Jesuit)11 16:38
13. Nate Ford (Ann Arbor Pioneer)12 16:39
14. John Cowan (Birmingham Brother Rice)10 16:40
15. Matt Lee (Lakeland)11 16:42
16. Brian Pickl (Milford)9 16:47
17. Gabriel Shockley (Kalamazoo Norrix)12 16:48
18. John Rottenberk (Birmingham Brother Rice)11 16:49
19. Jason Minock (Milford)12 16:52
20. Mike Kramer (Troy)12 16:56
21. Tom Carney (Milford)12 16:58
22. Dean Rugh (Lakeland)9 16:59
23. Derek Bork (Monroe)12 16:59
24. Eddie Slaughter (Monroe)11 17:02
25. Jeffrey Dennard (Pontiac Central)11 17:03
26. Dave Rogers (Milford)12 17:05

27. John Elder (Grand Ledge)12 ... 17:08
84. Heath Laprad (Monroe)11 ... 17:46

1988 BOYS CLASS A INDIVIDUAL RACE

1. Dave Couch (Niles)12 ... 16:31
2. Tom Weiss (East Lansing)12 ... 16:41
3. Aaron Bruininks (Holland)11 ... 16:47
4. Chris Wooley (Wayne Memorial)12 ... 16:47
5. Brian Grosso (Walled Lake Western)12 ... 16:53
6. Steven Dean (Detroit Southeastern)12 ... 16:53
7. James Hanner (Brighton)12 ... 16:54
8. Robert Rasmussen (Novi)12 ... 16;54
9. Dave Richards (Wayne Memorial)12 ... 17:00
10. Rob Huff (Bloomfield Hills Lahser)11 ... 17:03
11. Brad Moore (Farmington)12 ... 17:03
12. Ben Goba (Farmington)10 ... 17:04
13. Dave Burke (Woodhaven)12 ... 17:06

As a senior, Brian Grosso was unable to win a second state title, but he bounced back a month later to win nationals.

1989 CLASS A BOYS

Detroit Catholic Central won its third state title, leading Ann Arbor Pioneer by 21 points. Said coach Tony Magni, "I told the kids that we've been here before and it was anybody's ballgame going into the state finals. I told them to stay tough and just keep coming at the end."

The only thing that went wrong for the Shamrocks was that they locked their keys in the team van and and couldn't leave when they had hoped to.

The individual race saw Brian Hyde grab the win for East Kentwood. He would later star at William & Mary (coached by 1976 Class C 3rd-placer Walt Drenth) and run the 1500m in 3:35.84.

IMA Brookwood Golf Course, Nov. 4 ☐
1989 BOYS CLASS A TEAMS

1. Detroit Catholic Central ... 124
2. Ann Arbor Pioneer ... 145
3. Milford ... 147
4. Lakeland ... 176
5. East Detroit ... 224
6. Salem ... 230
7. Canton ... 243
8. Monroe ... 253
9. Holly ... 297
10. Holland ... 319
11. Birmingham Brother Rice ... 326
12. Portage Northern ... 348
13. Grand Ledge ... 351
14. Sterling Heights Ford ... 364
15. Sterling Heights Stevenson ... 364
16. Ann Arbor Huron ... 426
17. Birmingham Groves ... 427
18. Swartz Creek ... 439
19. Flint Kearsley ... 440
20. Grand Haven ... 476
21. Traverse City ... 484
22. Troy ... 493
23. Sterling Heights ... 545
24. Grand Rapids Christian ... 580
25. Grosse Pointe South ... 594
26. Grosse Pointe North ... 603
27. Saginaw Hill ... 605

1989 BOYS CLASS A TEAM RACE

1. John Cowan (Birmingham Brother Rice)11 ... 15:34
2. Bill Stricklen (Sterling Heights Ford)12 ... 15:43
3. Mike Sheridan (Detroit Catholic Central)12 ... 15:49
4. Aaron Bruininks (Holland)12 ... 15:51
5. Aaron Lawson (Ann Arbor Pioneer)12 ... 15:53
6. Matt Lee (Lakeland)12 ... 15:57
7. Andy McCoubrey (Grand Ledge)11 ... 15:57
8. Mickey Hoose (Milford)12 ... 16:03
9. David Barkley (Swartz Creek)11 ... 16:03
10. Brian Beach (Canton)12 ... 16:06
11. Scott Collins (Grosse Pointe North)11 ... 16:08
12. John Nemens (East Detroit)11 ... 16:10
13. John Rotterberk (Birmingham Brother Rice)12 ... 16:11
14. Brian McEnhill (Grand Ledge)10 ... 16:11
15. Paul Rice (East Detroit)12 ... 16:12
16. Jay Schemanske (Detroit Catholic Central)12 ... 16:12
17. Craig Yank (East Detroit)12 ... 16:16
18. Matt Morgan (Monroe)11 ... 16:18
19. Chris Antczak (Detroit Catholic Central)12 ... 16:20
20. Brian Pickl (Milford)10 ... 16:21
21. Brad Haverkamp (GR Christian)11 ... 16:23
22. Todd Hill (Holly)12 ... 16:23
23. Dave Galvin (Detroit Catholic Central)12 ... 16:25
24. Mike Milliman (Ann Arbor Pioneer)11 ... 16:25
25. Heath Laprad (Monroe)12 ... 16:26
26. John Fundukian (Milford)12 ... 16:27
27. Jeff Louwsma (Ann Arbor Pioneer)12 ... 16:29
63. John Borke (Detroit Catholic Central) ... nt

1989 BOYS CLASS A INDIVIDUAL RACE

1. Brian Hyde (East Kentwood)11 ... 15:42
2. Che Moya (Bay City Handy)12 ... 15:42
3. Rob Lee (Detroit U-D Jesuit)12 ... 15:43
4. Ben Goba (Farmington)11 ... 15:59
5. Rob Huff (Bloomfield Hills Lahser)12 ... 16:01
6. Chris Priestaff (Dearborn Edsel Ford)11 ... 16:02
7. Brian Mollay (Novi)10 ... 16:11
8. Richard Gray (Flint Central)12 ... 16:13
9. Jeff Grosso (Walled Lake Western)11 ... 16:18
10. Dionne Finney (Pontiac Northern)11 ... 16:20
11. Derk Walkotten (Birm Seaholm)12 ... 16:21
12. Tim Black (Muskegon Reeths-Puffer)12 ... 16:25
13. Todd Snyder (Brighton)11 ... 16:28
14. Tim McElgunn (Warren DeLaSalle)12 ... 16:29

1990 CLASS A BOYS

After two years in the runner-up slot, Don Sleeman's Pioneer squad fought its way back to the top of the podium, putting four runners in the top 30. They had been ranked No. 1 all season.

The individual race featured a sterling match, with John Cowan, Brian Hyde and Ben Goba together with 400 left. They still had to climb one of the course's toughest hills. "I pulled ahead coming around the turn to the finish," said Cowan, who would later run for Notre Dame.

Many runners struggled with the unseasonal 75-degree heat, with dozens reporting heat-related cramps.

Eastern Michigan GC, Ypsilanti, Nov. 3 ☐
1990 BOYS CLASS A TEAMS

1. Ann Arbor Pioneer ... 110
2. Walled Lake Western ... 151
3. Milford ... 161
4. Dearborn ... 172
5. Lakeland ... 176
6. Monroe ... 182
7. Swartz Creek ... 255
8. Holland ... 304
9. Novi ... 322
10. Grand Rapids Christian ... 322
11. Grand Ledge ... 330
12. Grand Haven ... 331
13. Portage Northern ... 343
14. Traverse City ... 352
15. Rochester Adams ... 373
16. Royal Oak Dondero ... 374
17. Warren DeLaSalle ... 388
18. Clio ... 393
19. Okemos ... 394
20. Detroit U-D Jesuit ... 414
21. Salem ... 445
22. Port Huron Northern ... 502
23. Canton ... 512
24. Sterling Heights Ford ... 571
25. Grosse Pointe North ... 639
26. Dearborn Fordson ... 686
27. East Detroit ... 706

1990 BOYS CLASS A TEAM RACE

1. Brian Pickl (Milford)11 ... 16:00
2. Bill Crosby (Walled Lake Western)11 ... 16:14
3. Mike Milliman (Ann Arbor Pioneer)12 ... 16:18
4. Ron McEnhill (Grand Ledge)11 ... 16:29
5. Russell Inman (Detroit U-D Jesuit)12 ... 16:27
6. Jeff Grosso (Walled Lake Western)12 ... 16:28
7. Neil Murphy (Holland)11 ... 16:29
8. Jeff Dillon (Okemos)12 ... 16:32
9. John Button (Dearborn)12 ... 16:33
10. Bill Dietrich (Milford)11 ... 16:34
11. Edward Reilly (Royal Oak Dondero)11 ... 16:34
12. Nick Saracino (Detroit U-D Jesuit)9 ... 16:36
13. Jim Schwertfeger (Portage Northern)10 ... 16:37
14. Brian Molloy (Novi)11 ... 16:39
15. Dean Rugh (Lakeland)11 ... 16:41
16. Rob Cain (Ann Arbor Pioneer)12 ... 16:42
17. Scott Collins (Gross Pointe North)12 ... 16:44
18. Mike Ream (Canton)12 ... 16:48
19. Warren Johnson (White Lake Lakeland)11 ... 16:53
20. David Barkley (Berkley)12 ... 16:55
21. Glen Holevac (Berkley)12 ... 16:55
24. Terrance Vaughn (Ann Arbor Pioneer) ... 17:02
29. Andy White (Ann Arbor Pioneer) ... 17:06
38. Kevin Busack (Ann Arbor Pioneer) ... 17:12

1990 BOYS CLASS A INDIVIDUAL RACE

1. John Cowan (Birmingham Brother Rice)12 ... 15:40
2. Brian Hyde (East Kentwood)12 ... 15:49
3. Ben Goba (Farmington)12 ... 15:59
4. Chris Hincks (Romeo)10 ... 16:27
5. Dionne Finney (Pontiac Northern)11 ... 16:28
6. Brian Sponseller (Mt Pleasant)12 ... 16:29
7. Scott Noecker (Lansing Waverly)12 ... 16:32
8. Todd Snyder (Brighton)12 ... 16:35
9. Scott Glasgow (Troy Athens)12 ... 16:38
10. Jim Haviland (Clarkston)12 ... 16:40
11. Tom Shank (Lake Orion) ... 16:41
12. Gary Kinnee (Flint Kearsley)10 ... 16:42
13. Bill Garant (Flint Kearsley)12 ... 16:43
14. Fred Mattius (Holland West Ottawa)12 ... 16:45
15. Chris Priestaf (Dearborn Edsel Ford)12 ... 16:47
16. Jeff Ort (Niles)10 ... 16;52
17. Jason Kidwell (Belleville)11 ... 16:53
18. Brodie Laduc (Waterford Kettering)11 ... 16:54
19. Chris Kreple (Holland West Ottawa)11 ... 16:55

1991 CLASS A BOYS

The *Detroit News* offered a well-worded explanation for the slow times in Class A: "Runners at the Terra Verde Golf Course were hampered by snow and sleet-driven by 45-mph winds [sic]. The windchill factor was below zero. The 5,000-meter course also was inundated with water and mud."

White Lake Lakeland coach Randy Wilkins demonstrated the power of positive thinking: "I heard not one negative comment from any of our kids. This kind of weather is great. The worse it is, the better for us."

Walled Lake Western's Bill Crosby won the team race in 16:19, the fastest time of the day. "I knew I had done all the hard work to get here," he said.""I knew what I had to do."

Terre Verde Golf Course, Nunica, Nov. 2 ☒
1991 BOYS CLASS A TEAMS

1. White Lake Lakeland 144
2. Walled Lake Western 166
3. Monroe 168
4. Grand Rapids Christian 219
5. Milford 225
6. Ann Arbor Pioneer 225
7. Detroit Catholic Central 226
8. Royal Oak Dondero 239
9. Portage Northern 254
10. Sterling Heights Ford 286
11. Holland 291
12. Berkley 301
13. Swartz Creek 315
14. Adrian 320
15. Brighton 371
16. Muskegon Mona Shores 380
17. Belleville 419
18. Flint Kearsley 445
19. Traverse City 456
20. Port Huron Northern 457
21. Warren DeLaSalle 522
22. Birmingham Brother Rice 528
23. Flushing 530
24. Sterling Heights Stevenson 563
25. Detroit Osborn 605
26. Kalamazoo Central 614
27. Grosse Pointe South 700

1991 BOYS CLASS A TEAM RACE

1. Bill Crosby (Walled Lake Western)12 .... 16:19
2. Brian Pickl (Milford)12 .... 16:39
3. Ed Reilly (Royal Oak Dondero)12 .... 16:46
4. Dean Rugh (White Lake Lakeland)12 .... 16:49
5. Gary Kinnee (Flint Kearsley)11 .... 16:49
6. Warren Johnson (White Lake Lakeland)12 .... 16:51
7. Neil Murphy (Holland)12 .... 17:01
8. Matt Krupinski (Monroe)11 .... 17:02
9. Steve Witek (Detroit Catholic Central)12 .... 17:06
10. Phil Laprad (Monroe)10 .... 17:07
11. Chris Rudolph (Sterling Heights Ford)12 .... 17;08
12. Rick McDowell (Swartz Creek)11 .... 17:11
13. Jim Schwertfeger (Portage Northern)11 .... 17:11
14. Andy Hayes (Traverse City)12 .... 17:12
15. Stefan Roth (Ann Arbor Pioneer)12 .... 17:13
16. James Sweetman (Walled Lake Western)12 .... 17:16
17. Jason Runnels (White Lake Lakeland)12 .... 17:17
18. Jim Wyatt (Berkley)11 .... 17:20
19. Gregory Stephens (Adrian)11 .... 17:20
20. Ken Mayo (Sterling Heights Ford)12 .... 17;21
21. Corey Clausing (GR Christian)12 .... 17:22
22. Scott Vanderstell (Muskegon Mona Shores)12 . 17:23
23. Michael Allen (Port Huron Northern)12 .... 17:25
24. Brett Noordhoff (Muskegon Mona Shores)10 .... 17:28
25. Kent Young (Flushing)12 .... 17:28
26. Dave Park (Ann Arbor Pioneer)11 .... 17:29
53. Jeff Clarke (White Lake Lakeland)12 .... 17:56
64. Dave Collie (White Lake Lakeland)10 .... 18:02
82. Mark Nara (White Lake Lakeland)12 .... 18:17
103. Chris Kettle (White Lake Lakeland)10 .... 18:29

1991 BOYS CLASS A INDIVIDUAL RACE

1. Brodie Laduc (Waterford Kettering)12 .... 16:41
2. Jeff Ort (Niles) 16:59
3. Chris Hinckes (Romeo) 17:00
4. Ryan Kennedy (Rochester) 17:09
5. Bob Dickie (Grand Blanc) 17:15
6. Jeremy Hulbert (Flint Carman-Ainsworth) 17:15
7. John Crawford (Novi) 17:15
8. Geoff Nitterhouser (Romeo) 17:17
9. Chad Tibbets (Ann Arbor Huron) 17:22
10. Scott Lecy (Okemos) 17:24
11. Terry Price (West Bloomfield) 17:27
12. Mark Smith (West Bloomfield) 17:27
13. Shawn Mattingly (Kalamazoo Norrix) 17:28
14. Derek Cudini (Salem) 17:30

1992 CLASS A BOYS

Monroe unleashed a powerful punch on its way to the Class A title, running 2-3-4. "It is a talented team," said coach Dave Bork. "But like I always say, you can't win the Kentucky Derby riding a burro. They really work hard. The kids run at least 500 miles during the summer. I think that gives them a head start."

Lake Orion's Clint Verran won with the fastest time of the day, 15:54.3. A year earlier he had been running cross country on top of playing football. "I knew I had a lot more potential in running," he told the *Detroit Free Press*. "I wasn't going to play football after high school. I decided I wanted to be good at something. It wasn't an easy decision."

Terraverde Golf Club, Nunica, Nov. 7 ☒
1992 BOYS CLASS A TEAMS

1. Monroe 57
2. Detroit Catholic Central 109
3. Rochester Adams 163
4. Lakeland 188
5. Dearborn Fordson 210
6. Grand Rapids Christian 215
7. Brighton 240
8. Ann Arbor Pioneer 247
9. Cadillac 261
10. West Bloomfield 269
11. Berkley 313
12. Dearborn 316
13. Warren DeLaSalle 323
14. Flint Kearsley 365
15. Portage Northern 430
16. Sterling Heights Stevenson 435
17. Birmingham Brother Rice 437
18. Traverse City 462
19. Flushing 488
20. Niles 488
21. Temperance Bedford 510
22. Battle Creek Lakeview 550
23. Swartz Creek 568
24. Hazel Park 575
25. Port Huron Northern 642
26. Grosse Pointe South 667
27. East Pointe 761

1992 BOYS CLASS A TEAM RACE

1. Mike Mittman (Detroit Catholic Central)12 .... 15:56
2. Matt Krupinski (Monroe)12 .... 15:58
3. Phil Laprad (Monroe)11 .... 16:00
4. Andy Brittain (Monroe)10 .... 16;01
5. Gary Kinnee (Flint Kearsley)12 .... 16:02
6. Tim Gass (Birmingham Brother Rice)11 .... 16:02
7. Jeff Ort (Niles)12 .... 16:07
8. Chris Jordan (Brighton)10 .... 16:07
9. Stetson Steele (Dearborn)10 .... 16:07
10. Jim Schwertleger (Portage Northern)12 .... 16:13
11. Mark Smith (West Bloomfield)12 .... 16:14
12. Frank Sean (Battle Creek Lakeview)12 .... 16:14
13. Jeff Doyle (Rochester Adams)12 .... 16:19
14. Phil Sobeck (Warren DeLaSalle)10 .... 16:20
15. Don McLaughlin (Ann Arbor Pioneer)11 .... 16:21
16. Mark Leo (Detroit Catholic Central)11 .... 16:23
17. Jeremy Towne (Brighton)11 .... 16:26
18. Scott Scoles (Monroe)11 .... 16:26
19. Shelby Baecker (White Lake Lakeland)11 .... 16:26
20. Jon Christian (Dearborn)10 .... 16:27
21. Dave Park (Ann Arbor Pioneer)12 .... 16:27
22. Mike Vagnetti (Rochester Adams)12 .... 16:28
23. Jeff Kowalak (Rochester Adams)12 .... 16:29
30. Justin Schroeder (Monroe)10 .... 16:37
40. James Mell (Monroe)12 .... 16:42
57. Dustyn Bork (Monroe)10 .... 16:57

1992 BOYS CLASS A INDIVIDUAL RACE

1. Clint Verran (Lake Orion)12 .... 15:55
2. Chris Hincks (Romeo)12 .... 16:01
3. Jeff Ferrell (Waterford Mott)10 .... 16:05
4. Bob Dickie (Grand Blanc)12 .... 16:07
5. Greg Lynn (Muskegon Reeths-Puffer)12 .... 16:12
6. Jeff Rutkowski (Milford)10 .... 16:15
7. John Crawford (Novi)12 .... 16:17
8. Scott Grace (Lake Orion)11 .... 16:17
9. Justin Dreyer (Farmington Hills Harrison)12 .... 16:18
10. Jamie Reif (Flint Central)11 .... 16:19
11. Casey Lince (Pinckney)10 .... 16:19
12. Brant Lutz (Midland)12 .... 16:21
13. David Clinard (Farmington)12 .... 16:22
14. Rob Inglis (Birmingham Seaholm)10 .... 16:24
15. Scott Lecy (Okemos)11 .... 16:25
16. Robert Bray (Taylor Center)12 .... 16:28
17. Darin Grant (Muskegon Reeths-Puffer)12 .... 16:29

1993 CLASS A BOYS

Ranked No. 2 to Monroe coming in, Ann Arbor Pioneer upset the favorites by 29 points. It helped to put three runners in the top 10. Their No. 5 runner, Keith Braxton, managed 22nd place despite running in pain from an abcessed tooth. "He must have been 100th after a mile," said coach Don Sleeman. "But he just kept passing people."

Pioneer's Todd Snyder beat Fordson's Abdul Alzindani for the win. "I was feeling bad at the end and I thought he was going to get me," said Snyder. "I just hung on for dear life."

Saskatoon Golf Club, Alaska, Nov. 6 ☐
1993 BOYS CLASS A TEAMS

1. Ann Arbor Pioneer 56
2. Monroe 85
3. Brighton 126
4. Ann Arbor Huron 179
5. White Lake Lakeland 182
6. Dearborn Fordson 219
7. Grand Rapids Christian 249
8. Traverse City 278
9. Temperance Bedford 285
10. Detroit Catholic Central 311
11. Cadillac 312
12. Warren DeLaSalle 377
13. Port Huron Northern 407
14. Belleville 413
15. Grandville 413
16. Holly 414
17. Ferndale 427
18. Swartz Creek 473
19. Rochester Adams 479
20. Holt 500
21. Flint Kearsley 510
22. Berkley 521
23. Grosse Pointe North 551
24. Warren Cousino 557
25. Troy Athens 565
26. East Lansing 612
27. Grosse Pointe South 689

1993 BOYS CLASS A TEAM RACE

1. Todd Snyder (Ann Arbor Pioneer)11 .... 15:36
2. Abdul Alzindani (Dearborn Fordson)10 .... 15:38
3. Steve Schell (Dearborn Fordson)11 .... 15:46
4. Don McLaughlin (Ann Arbor Pioneer)12 .... 15:49
5. Phil Sobeck (Cadillac) 15:54
6. Andy Brittain (Monroe)11 .... 15:55
7. Rob Robeson (Ann Arbor Huron) 15:55
8. Shelby Baecker (White Lake Lakeland) 15:58
9. Joe Leo (Detroit Catholic Central) 16:02

10. Ben Ingram (Ann Arbor Pioneer) 16:03
11. Chris Jordan (Brighton) 16:04
12. Joe Monaghan (Ann Arbor Huron) 16:05
13. Eric Osborn (Port Huron Northern) 16:05
14. Phil Laprad (Monroe)12 ....16:08
15. Geoff Vandragt (Grand Rapids Christian) 16:08
16. Mark Scales (Monroe) 16:09
17. Brian Mockeridge (Belleville) 16:11
18. Jermey Towne (Brighton) 16:13
19. Ethan Conn (Ann Arbor Pioneer) 16:14
20. Ben Hunalt (Swartz Creek) 16:16
21. Dustin Bork (Monroe) 16:17
22. Keith Braxton (Ann Arbor Pioneer) 16:18
23. Hassan Jaafer (Dearborn Fordson) 16:18
24. Brandon Dutton (Brighton) 16:18
25. Jeff Clark (White Lake Lakeland) 16:19
26. Nate Fales (Cadillac) 16:20
27. Jeremy Hoogsteen (Grand Rapids Christian) 16:23
28. Justin Schroeder (Monroe) 16:24
29. Cameron Chapman (Port Huron Northern) 16:25

1993 BOYS CLASS A INDIVIDUAL RACE
1. Jeff Ferrell (Waterford Mott)11 ....15:40
2. Kevin Foltz (Flushing)10 ....15:45
3. Chris Wehrman (Pinckney)12 ....16:03
4. Jim Reif (Flint Central) 16:07
5. Stetsen Steele (Dearborn) 16:09
6. Scott Grace (Lake Orion) 16:12
7. Robert Inglis (Birmingham Seaholm) 16:20
8. Jeff Rutkowski (Milford) 16:25
9. Brett Noordhoff (Muskegon Mona Shores) 16:25
10. Brian Rajdi (North Farmington) 16:25
11. Pat Tyler (Niles) 16:26

1994 CLASS A BOYS

Defending individual champion Jeff Ferrell won after a regionals loss to Milford's Jeff Rutkowski (16th in the team race in 16:03) that had been his only defeat in two years. Steve Schell, second-place in the team race, placed eighth at the Foot Locker Nationals that fall.

Pioneer successfully defended, led by Todd Snyder, who had the fastest time of the day. He would later become a 2-time All-American for Michigan.

Saskatoon Golf Club, Alaska, Nov. 5
1994 BOYS CLASS A TEAMS
1. Ann Arbor Pioneer 72
2. White Lake Lakeland 113
3. Traverse City 132
4. Monroe 172
5. Milford 213
6. Brighton 215
7. Swartz Creek 234
8. Dearborn 308
9. Rochester 311
10. Dearborn Fordson 323
11. Rochester Adams 330
12. Detroit Catholic Central 356
13. Troy Athens 383
14. Flint Kearsley 412
15. Grandville 443
16. Canton 448
17. Grand Haven 457
18. Warren DeLaSalle 459
19. Sterling Heights Ford 460
20. North Farmington 491
21. Grand Ledge 513
22. Holt 527
23. East Kentwood 530
24. Grosse Pointe South 546
25. L'Anse Creuse 579
26. Grosse Pointe North 580
27. Flint Carman-Ainsnworth 651

1994 BOYS CLASS A TEAM RACE
1. Todd Snyder (Ann Arbor Pioneer)12 ....15:15
2. Steve Schell (Dearborn Fordson)12 ....15:19
3. Abdul Alzindani (Dearborn Fordson)11 ....15:31
4. Joe Leo (Detroit Catholic Central)11 ....15:34
5. Stetson Steele (Dearborn)12 ....15:36
6. Phil Sobeck (Warren DeLaSalle)12 ....15:38
7. Keith Braxton (Ann Arbor Pioneer)11 ....15:39
8. Charlie Wolf (Traverse City)11 ....15:51
9. Ben Hunalt (Swartz Creek)12 ....15:54
10. Justin Schroeder (Monroe)12 ....15:55
11. Nate Clay (Rochester Adams)12 ....15:55
12. Andy Brittain (Monroe)12 ....15:56
13. William Stevenson (Grosse Pointe North)12 ....15:58
14. Nick Gow (White Lake Lakeland)9 ....16:02
15. Mike Humes (Ann Arbor Pioneer)10 ....16:02
16. Jeff Rutkowski (Milford)12 ....16:03
17. Tony Digenova (Flint Kearsley)10 ....16:03
18. Ben Ingram (Ann Arbor Pioneer)12 ....16:05
19. Paul Kekel (Swartz Creek)11 ....16:06
20. Bob Sharpe (White Lake Lakeland)12 ....16:07
21. Tom Stamboulian (North Farmington)12 ....16:09
22. Christian Dorch (Rochester)12 ....16:10
23. Lance Binoniemi (White Lake Lakeland)10 ....16:12
24. Seth Washburn (White Lake Lakeland)11 ....16:12
25. Kevin Brokaw (Traverse City)12 ....16:13
26. Matt McCartney (Grand Haven)10 ....16:13
27. Jake Fortuna (Holt)11 ....16:13
28. Jeff Trembath (Brighton)11 ....16:14
29. Andy Ritter (Brighton)11 ....16:16
30. Eric Noughton (Traverse City)10 ....16:16
31. Anton Takken (Ann Arbor Pioneer)12 ....16:17
32. R.C. Edwards (White Lake Lakeland)12 ....16:18
33. Mike Keys (L'Anse Creuse)12 ....16:19
34. Mike Decker (Traverse City)12 ....16:20
35. Adam Wheeler (Traverse City)12 ....16:20
36. Ethan Conn (Ann Arbor Pioneer)12 ....16:20
52. Joshua Sanchez (Ann Arbor Pioneer)11 ....16:37

1994 BOYS CLASS A INDIVIDUAL RACE
1. Jeff Ferrell (Waterford Mott)12 ....15:47
2. Scott Pengelly (Salem)11 ....15:58
3. Reuben Zylstra (GR Christian)12 ....16:03
4. Jesse Elzinga (Temperance Bedford)10 ....16:05
5. Rob Radtke (West Bloomfield) 16:07
6. Brad Breining (Owosso) 16:17
7. Tom May (Farmington) 16:21
8. Brian Mockeridge (Belleville) 16:21
9. Jared Maxwell (Holly) 16:24
10. Doug Rupp (Lake Orion) 16:26

1995 CLASS A BOYS

Two inches of snow fell on some of the Lower Peninsula courses, all in the Grand Rapids area. That didn't keep Abdul Alzindani from recording the biggest winning margin in Class A history.

After finishing 2nd and 3rd in the two previous years, Alzindani was relieved to win. "It's been frustrating having a chance to win it and losing it at the end. I wasn't going to let anyone beat me this year."

The senior used frontrunning to good effect against statewide competition. That December, however, he used a mighty kick to win the Foot Locker national high school title.

Brighton took the team crown, its first since 1978, despite having No. 4 runner Matt Twork slip and fall near halfway. "We started off well," said coach Bob Ritsema. "At the three-quarter-mile mark, I told them we were in good position. About halfway through I hollered out, 'We're winning the meet!'"

He added, "Our kids thought it was neat to run in the snow."

Saskatoon Golf Club, Alaska, Nov. 4
1995 BOYS CLASS A TEAMS
1. Brighton 133
2. White Lake Lakeland 157
3. Traverse City 161
4. Temperance Bedford 162
5. Holly 184
6. Ann Arbor Pioneer 189
7. Monroe 244
8. Salem 247
9. Troy Athens 283
10. Grand Ledge 310
11. Swartz Creek 353
12. Wyandotte 355
13. Grand Haven 356
14. Flint Kearsley 361
15. Saline 361
16. Rockford 368
17. Rochester 369
18. Kalamazoo Central 442
19. Warren Cousino 453
20. St Johns 457
21. Detroit Catholic Central 477
22. Holt 547
23. Birmingham Brother Rice 547
24. Grosse Pointe South 553
25. Troy 639
26. Port Huron 671
27. Sterling Heights Ford 736

Fordson's Abdul Alzindni followed up his state win with another at Foot Locker Nationals.

1995 BOYS CLASS A TEAM RACE
1. Joe Leo (Detroit Catholic Central)12 ....15:42
2. Keith Braxton (Ann Arbor Pioneer)12 ....15:45
3. Mike Humes (Ann Arbor Pioneer)11 ....16:04
4. Scott Pengelly (Salem)12 ....16:07
5. Mike Cell (Traverse City)12 ....16:08
6. Gerald Newcomb (Holly)12 ....16:09
7. Jesse Elzinga (Temperance Bedford)11 ....16:12
8. Jeff Trembath (Brighton)12 ....16:16
9. Tony Digenova (Flint Kearsley)11 ....16:19
10. Jared Bienecki (Salem)12 ....16:19
11. Bryan Meyer (Troy Athens)11 ....16:22
12. Paul Kekel (Swartz Creek)12 ....16:23
13. Jared Maxwell (Holly)12 ....16:25
14. Eric Houghton (Traverse City)12 ....16:25
15. Matt Koepfer (Temperance Bedford)11 ....16:26
16. Mark Hansen (Brighton)11 ....16:28
17. Robert Haveman (Traverse City)11 ....16:31
18. Andy Ritter (Brighton)12 ....16:32
19. Matt Jackson (Troy Athens)11 ....16:33
20. Jacob Fortuna (Holt)12 ....16:33
21. Matt Meyer (Kalamazoo Central)11 ....16:35
22. Ryan Mol (Rockford)10 ....16:36
23. Nick Gow (White Lake Lakeland)10 ....16:39

24. Ryan Knowton (Grand Ledge)11 .... 16:39
25. Chris May (Temperance Bedford)12 .... 16:39
26. Mark Hoffman (Monroe)12 .... 16:40
27. Jason Hartmann (Rockford)9 .... 16:43
45. Matt Kriebel (Brighton)10 .... 17:06
46. Keith Erickson (Brighton)11 .... 17:06
59. Joe Ward (Brighton)12 .... 17:15
62. Matt Twork (Brighton)12 .... 17:17

1995 BOYS CLASS A INDIVIDUAL RACE

1. Abdul Alzindani (Dearborn Fordson)12 .... 15:20
2. Kevin Foltz (Flushing)12 .... 16:16
3. Matt Vennie (Flint Carman-Ainsworth)11 .... 16:19
4. Lyle Mayers (Charlotte)11 .... 16:22
5. Matt Jones (Muskegon Reeths-Puffer)11 .... 16:22
6. Jason Aspinell (Walled Lake Western)11 .... 16:26
7. Brian Wardlow (Pinckney)12 .... 16:29
8. Reed Steele (Dearborn)10 .... 16:31
9. Kevin Grant (Grosse Pointe North)12 .... 16:36
10. Josh Miller (Northwood)10 .... 16:40
11. Jared Roth (Farmington Hills Harrison)11 .... 16:41
12. Rick Bauer (Howell)10 .... 16:42
13. Ben Alford (Ferndale)12 .... 16:43
14. Shawn Delaney (Hazel Park)12 .... 16:43
15. Brian Rafdl (North Farmington)12 .... 16:43

1996 CLASS A BOYS

With all of the Lower Peninsula races brought together at the same site for the first time since 1971, the meet was trumpeted as the largest prep sports event in Michigan history (1,182 athletes, not to mention 8,500 spectators). For the first time since 1960, the team and individual athletes raced together. The medals had already been ordered for separate races, so officials awarded them as if the athletes had run separately. It was only a paper distinction. Sixth-placer Matt Jones (Muskegon Reeths-Puffer—15:54) was awarded the "individual" state championship.

Freezing temperatures and snow flurries had the athletes bundle up. The overall winner was Belgian foreign exchange student Augustine Forget of Hazel Park.

The placement of the meet at Michigan International Speedway got off to a rocky start, and controversy flared as soon as spectators realized they would not be allowed on the course. For most, that meant watching only the last few hundred yards of the race from the cold grandstands.

Michigan Int. Speedway, Brooklyn, Nov. 2 ⊠
1996 BOYS CLASS A TEAMS

1. White Lake Lakeland 94
2. Traverse City 99
3. Wyandotte 193
4. Grand Haven 241
5. Brighton 251
6. Wyandotte 268
7. Rockford 278
8. Monroe 299
9. Lake Orion 335
10. Troy Athens 339
11. Temperance Bedford 345
12. Dearborn Fordson 373
13. Swartz Creek 376
14. Sterling Heights 388
15. Grand Ledge 389
16. Warren Cousino 397
17. Detroit Catholic Central 403
18. Birmingham Brother Rice 417
19. Zeeland 431
20. Rochester Adams 445
21. Ann Arbor Pioneer 449
22. Flint Kearsley 455
23. Holland 476
24. St Johns 495
25. Jackson 500
26. Troy 585
27. Port Huron 609
28. Grosse Pointe South 659

1996 BOYS CLASS A INDIVIDUALS

1. Augustine Forget (Hazel Park-BELGIUM)12 .. 15:41
2. Jason Petipren (Warren Cousino)12 .... 15:48
3. Ben Evans (Birmingham Brother Rice)10 .... 15:49
4. Mark Hansen (Brighton)12 .... 15:50
5. Eric Houghton (Traverse City)12 .... 15:51
6. Lance Binoniemi (White Lake Lakeland)12 .... 15:53
7. Matt Jones (Muskegon Reeths-Puffer)12 .... 15:54
8. Anthony Spires (Detroit Mumford) 15:56
9. Jason Hartman (Rockford)10 .... 15:57
10. Ryan Piippo (Trenton) 16:00
11. Ryan Mol (Rockford)11 .... 16:01
12. Tony Digenova (Flint Kearsley)12 .... 16:01
13. Matt Vennie (Flint Carman-Ainsworth) 16:02
14. Matt McCartney (Grand Haven) 16:02
15. Justin Pfuender (Midland) 16:02
16. Chris Vranich (Traverse City) 16:05
17. Matthew Mayer (Kalamazoo Central) 16:06
18. Kevin Blacquiere (Zeeland) 16:06
19. Rick Bauer (Howell)11 .... 16:07
20. Christoper Dullock (Jackson) 16:07
21. Jordan Desilets (Lake Orion) 16:08
22. Ed Garza (Wyandotte) 16:09
23. Jason Aspinell (Walled Lake Western) 16:10
24. Ken Tracy (Rochester Adams) 16:11
25. Robert Haveman (Traverse City) 16:12
26. Phillip Andreadis (Portage Central) 16:13
27. Gary Goosen (Grand Haven) 16:13
28. Adam Cross (Rochester Adams) 16:14
29. Brian Dowry (Troy Athens) 16:15
30. Darin Piippo (Trenton) 16:16
31. Rich Oltesvig (White Lake Lakeland) 16:16
32. Mike Camilleri (White Lake Lakeland) 16:17
33. Ryan Johns (White Lake Lakeland) 16:18
34. Les Crosby (Battle Creek Lakeview) 16:19
35. Rich Hicks (Holly) 16:20
36. Matt Muskan (Dearborn Edsel Ford) 16:21
37. Joe Agostinelli (Traverse City) 16:25
38. Matt Koepfer (Temperance-Bedford) 16:25
39. Matt Jackson (Troy Athens) 16:25
40. Scott Kinczkowski (White Lake Lakeland) 16:26
42. Anthony Sager (White Lake Lakeland) 16:39

1997 CLASS A BOYS

The committee of Jackson-area coaches that organized the meet at Michigan International Speedway did much to right the problems of the previous year. Everyone's optimism, however, came down with the pouring rain that dogged the runners and made much of the course a quagmire. Between races, in fact, dump trucks brought in more dirt to give the runners better footing, and organizers had to make minor alterations to the course throughout the day.

The course was torn up when Jordan Desilets tried to run Jason Hartmann down in the final steps of the Class A race. He almost succeeded, but the lanky Rockford junior had just enough lean to hold him off, 16:17.1 to 16:17.1. This was the first year since 1960 that the MHSAA recognized only one individual champion in each class.

Randy Wilkins' Lakeland crew won its second straight (and four straight years in the top two). "We seem to thrive in these type of conditions," said Wilkins. "We focus better and compete even harder. We use the weather to our advantage."

Michigan Int. Speedway, Brooklyn, Nov. 1 ⊠
1997 BOYS CLASS A TEAMS

1. White Lake Lakeland 62
2. Rockford 84
3. Milford 189
4. Traverse City Central 206
5. Grand Ledge 230
6. Dearborn Fordson 237
7. Walled Lake Central 256
8. Salem 260
9. Ann Arbor Pioneer 265
10. Wyandotte 277
11. Detroit Catholic Central 291
12. Troy Athens 328
13. Monroe 347
14. Grand Haven 366
15. Rochester Adams 367
16. Holt 369
17. Detroit U-D Jesuit 438
18. Bay City Western 463
19. Coldwater 463
20. Midland Dow 475
21. Grosse Pointe South 494
22. Flint Carman-Ainsworth 513
23. Warren Cousino 517
24. Utica Eisenhower 553
25. Sterling Heights Ford 558
26. Portage Central 560
27. Grosse Pointe North 748

Jason Hartmann won by inches as a junior. The next year, he dominated.

1997 BOYS CLASS A INDIVIDUALS

1. Jason Hartmann (Rockford)11 .... 16:18
2. Jordan Desilets (Lake Orion)11 .... 16:18
3. Justin Momany-Pfruender (Midland)12 .... 16:18
4. Kevin Avenius (Novi)11 .... 16:20
5. Dathan Ritzenhein (Rockford)9 .... 16:23
6. Ian Searcy (Salem)12 .... 16:26
7. Anthony Sager (White Lake Lakeland)11 .... 16:26
8. Nick Gow (White Lake Lakeland)12 .... 16:29
9. Steven Crane (Taylor Truman)11 .... 16:29
10. Nick Allen (Salem)11 .... 16:30
11. Rob Block (Livonia Stevenson)12 .... 16:33
12. Ryan Mol (Rockford)12 .... 16:34
13. Rich Oltesvig (White Lake Lakeland)12 .... 16:34
14. Adam Cross (Rochester Adams)11 .... 16:35
15. Tom Greenless (Milford)10 .... 16:37
16. Corey Kellicut (Grand Ledge)12 .... 16:40
17. Travis Crawford (Traverse City Central)10 ... 16:41
18. Ben Evans (Birmingham Brother Rice) 16:43
19. Scott Kinezkowski (White Lake Lakeland) ... 16:45
20. David Sage (Clarkston)10 .... 16:46
21. Jon Little (Salem) 16:47
22. Shaun Moore (Canton) 16:48
23. Rick Bauer (Howell)12 .... 16:49
24. Phil Novack (Warren Cousino) 16:49
25. Ben Wojick (Wyandotte) 16:50
26. Kevin Arbuckle (Northville) 16:51
27. Paul Niedzewiecki (Adrian)10 .... 16:52
28. Jeff Davis (Temperance Bedford)11 .... 16:53
29. Andy Marsh (Grand Ledge)10 .... 16:54
30. Andrew Armstrong (Ann Arbor Pioneer) 16:54
31. Ryan Kennedy (Pinckney) 16:56
32. Matt Shannon (Detroit Catholic Central) 16:57
33. Doug Harger (Holt) 16:58

34. Todd Mobley (Walled Lake Central) 16:58
35. Ben Davis (Battle Creek Central)11 .... 17:00
36. Eric Lohr (Lake Orion) 17:02
37. Andy Martin (Rockford)10 .... 17:03
38. Jim Kenny (Rochester Adams) 17:03
39. Murwan Kadry (Dearborn Fordson) 17:05
40. Eric Salla (Wyandotte) 17:05
56. Pat Klein (White Lake Lakeland) 17:18

1998 CLASS A BOYS

Partly cloudy skies and temperatures in the mid-40s greeted the athletes at Michigan International Speedway. The ideal weather and hard, dry footing led to a new appreciation of the course on the part of many. The route was fast from the get-go. Records fell all day, but the speed of the course became quite clear to everybody when Jason Hartmann ripped through the mile in 4:31.7 and kept going. Splits of 9:24.8 and 14:23.3 saw him leave the field far behind. He crossed the finish in 14:51.8, more than 38 seconds under the course record and 20 seconds ahead of sophomore teammate Dathan Ritzenhein.

In all the LP classes combined, an unprecedented 74 boys broke 16:00. Organizers confirmed that nothing had changed about the course but the weather.

In the team race, Novi upset favored Rockford to win its first title ever. Coach Bob Smith's Wildcats featured three varsity runners in their first year in the sport. Said Smith, "You couldn't have asked for more from those guys. Coaching them has been a joy."

At Foot Locker Nationals in San Diego, Hartmann (4th) and Ritzenhein (8th) both broke into the top 10.

Michigan Int. Speedway, Brooklyn, Nov. 7
1998 BOYS CLASS A TEAMS
1. Novi 82
2. Rockford 87
3. Detroit Catholic Central 179
4. Traverse City Central 186
5. Grand Ledge 200
6. White Lake Lakeland 219
7. Sterling Heights 251
8. Lake Orion 251
9. Saline 266
10. Milford 281
11. Salem 290
12. East Kentwood 369
13. Portage Central 380
14. Birmingham Brother Rice 380
15. Warren Cousino 417
16. Midland Dow 421
17. Temperance Bedford 432
18. Rochester 441
19. Davison 458
20. Gaylord 491
21. Wyandotte 493
22. Utica Eisenhower 509
23. Sterling Heights Ford 523
24. St Johns 591
25. Dearborn Fordson 604
26. Grosse Pointe South 716
27. Grosse Pointe North 786

1998 BOYS CLASS A INDIVIDUALS
1. Jason Hartmann (Rockford)12 .... 14:52
2. Dathan Ritzenhein (Rockford)10 .... 15:12
3. Jordan Desilets (Lake Orion)12 .... 15:17
4. Ben Evans (Birmingham Brother Rice)12 ... 15:17
5. Adam Cross (Rochester Adams)12 .... 15:23
6. Todd Mobley (Walled Lake Central)11 .... 15:23
7. Kevin Avenius (Novi)12 .... 15:29
8. Dan Christopherson (Novi)12 .... 15:32
9. Jason Bruscha (Sterling Heights)12 .... 15:34
10. Anthony Sager (Lakeland)12 .... 15:35
11. Travis Crawford (Traverse City Central)11 ... 15:36
12. Andy Marsh (Grand Ledge)11 .... 15:37
13. Tom Greenless (Milford)11 .... 15:37
14. Nick Allen (Salem)12 .... 15:38
15. Jordan Emmorey (Gaylord)11 .... 15:40
16. John Digiovanni (Detroit Catholic Central)10 15:39
17. Andy Martin (Rockford)11 .... 15:39
18. Pat Klein (Lakeland)10 .... 15:41
19. Jeff Davis (Temperance Bedford)12 .... 15:41
20. David Sage (Clarkston)11 .... 15:42
21. Ben Davis (Battle Creek Central)12 .... 15:45
22. Kevin Lynn (Midland Dow)12 .... 15:47
23. Paul Niedzewiecki (Adrian)11 .... 15:47
24. John Hughes (Traverse City Central)11 ... 15:48
25. Scott Nagelkerke (Zeeland)12 .... 15:48
26. Shawn Edwards (Flushing)11 .... 15:50
27. Tim Moore (Novi)9 .... 15:51
28. Kevin Arbuckle (Northville)12 .... 15:53
29. Chris Toloff (Novi)10 .... 15:54
30. Rob DeWitte (Bloomfield Hills Lahser)12 . 15:54
31. Dan Jess (Detroit Catholic Central)12 ..... 15:55
32. Rick Oltesvig (Lakeland)12 .... 15:55
33. Ryan Wilman (Warren Cousino)12 .... 15:56
34. Nick Stanko (Wyandotte)12 .... 15:56
35. Sean Moore (Saline)10 .... 15:57
36. Kevin Pline (St Johns)12 .... 15:58
37. Joshua Burt (Livonia Franklin)12 .... 15:58
38. Eric Lohr (Lake Orion)12 .... 15:59
39. Matthew Haver (Clarkston)11 .... 16:01
40. Terrence Rindler (Portage Central)12 .... 16:03
41. Mike Burns (Novi)12 .... 16:04
54. Mark Avenius (Novi)10 .... 16:13
117. Eric Walle (Novi)10 .... 16:40

Dathan Ritzenhein made it three straight years of Rockford wins.

1999 CLASS A BOYS

Ideal conditions at Michigan International Speedway made for some of the fastest times ever on the course. Rockford's Dathan Ritzenhein ran unchallenged to win the Class A crown, but his favored Rockford team was upended for the second year straight by Novi. The Wildcats were led by sophomore Tim Moore, who placed third overall.

Said Novi coach Bob Smith, "It's psychological. The mind is a tremendous tool. We talked about how powerful the mind is coming here this morning, and they must have taken it to heart."

Ritzenhein noted, "I went our harder than I wanted to, but I had a good last mile."

At Foot Locker Nationals, Ritzenhein crushed the field with his 14:29 in Orlando. Also making it to the big show was Todd Mobley (18th in 15:20) and Tom Greenless (21st in 15:30).

Michigan Int. Speedway, Brooklyn, Nov. 6
1999 BOYS CLASS A TEAMS
1. Novi 68
2. Rockford 90
3. Saline 132
4. Clarkston 133
5. Grand Ledge 160
6. Detroit Catholic Central 178
7. Milford 242
8. Holland West Ottawa 247
9. Lake Orion 286
10. Grand Rapids Christian 313
11. Traverse City Central 317
12. Troy 332
13. Portage Northern 378
14. Rochester Adams 429
15. Temperance Bedford 440
16. Utica Eisenhower 441
17. Dearborn 445
18. Livonia Churchill 447
19. Bloomfield Hills Lahser 473
20. Sterling Heights 504
21. Warren Mott 550
22. Alpena 555
23. Grosse Pointe South 567
24. Midland 587
25. Grosse Pointe North 592
26. Wyandotte 598
27. Midland Dow 628

1999 BOYS CLASS A INDIVIDUALS
1. Dathan Ritzenhein (Rockford)11 .... 15:06
2. Todd Mobley (Walled Lake Central)12 .... 15:26
3. Tim Moore (Novi)10 .... 15:27
4. Tom Greenless (Milford)12 .... 15:41
5. Pat Klein (White Lake Lakeland)11 .... 15:41
6. Andy Marsh (Grand Ledge)12 .... 15:42
7. Chris Toloff (Novi)11 .... 15:43
8. Matt Daly (Detroit Catholic Central)11 .... 15:43
9. Paul Niedzwiecki (Adrian)12 .... 15:54
10. Jacob Crowe (Grand Ledge)12 .... 15:55
11. Andy Martin (Rockford)12 .... 15:56
12. Joe Whitman (Davison)11 .... 16:04
13. David Sage (Clarkston)12 .... 16:05
14. Ryan Malott (Hudsonville)12 .... 16:06
15. Dave Ruthven (Hudsonville)12 .... 16:06
16. Luke Mortensen (Midland Dow)12 .... 16:08
17. Mark Avenius (Novi)11 .... 16:10
18. Seth Folkertsma (Rockford)12 .... 16:10
19. Brandon Fisk (Utica Eisenhower)12 .... 16:11
20. Matthew Haver (Clarkston)12 .... 16:12
21. Ryan Detlor (Dearborn Edsel Ford)11 ..... 16:13
22. Eric Walle (Novi)11 .... 16:16
23. Nick Gillett (Troy)10 .... 16:17
24. Doug Gibbons (Detroit Catholic Central)11 . 16:17
25. Eric Walters (Howell)12 .... 16:18
26. Jake Hammerle (Woodhaven)10 .... 16:18
27. Chris Gumz (Rochester)10 .... 16:19
28. Tony Pate (Taylor Kennedy)12 .... 16:19
29. Matt Huyser (Holland)11 .... 16:20
30. Sean Moore (Saline)11 .... 16:21
31. Andrew Bauer (Bloomfield Hills Lahser)10 .. 16:21
32. Charlie Stamboulian (North Farmington)12 . 16:24
33. Brian Theut (White Lake Lakeland)10 ..... 16:25
34. Ed Davis (Saline)11 .... 16:26
35. Micheal Colt (Lake Orion)10 .... 16:27
36. Blake Terhune (Traverse City Central)11 ... 16:28
37. Kyle Fujimoto (Rockford)11 .... 16:29
38. Colin Vohlken (Holland West Ottawa)12 . 16:30
39. Richard Swor (Dearborn)11 .... 16:33
40. Travis Crawford (Traverse City Central)12 . 16:33
55. Nick Bassitt (Novi)12 .... 16:39
162. Evan Foster (Novi)10 .... 17:11
235. Mitch Erickson (Novi)10 .... 17:47

2000 D1 BOYS

Rockford made good on its promise and finally captured the Division 1 title. At the head of the charge was Dathan Ritzenhein, who produced the finest cross country run in Michigan history—and what many say is the best in U.S. history.

The senior pounded the field into submission with a 4:28.2 first mile, and whipped past 2M in 9:02.4. He hit 3M in 13:40.7 and finished nearly a minute ahead of one of the best fields ever, shattering the course record by 41 seconds with his 14:10.4. Behind him, Chris Toloff outkicked his junior Novi teammate, Tim Moore, to grab second.

Rockford's 56 points impressed. Coach Mark Nessner called the win "such a relief" after three-straight runner-up finishes.

This was the year that the sport, formerly separated into classes, was put into four divisions, with an equal number of teams in each. For the higher classes, it seemed a change in name only, and little looked different on the competitive scene.

At the Foot Locker Nationals in Orlando, Ritzenhein handily defended his title, clocking 14:35 (after winning the Midwest Regional in Kenosha in 14:35). Also making the race were Tim Moore (8th in 15:13) and Sean Moore of Saline (24th in 15:43).

Ritzenhein would go on to star at the Unversity of Colorado and make three U.S. Olympic teams. In 2003 he won the NCAA title in cross country; he later won three USA cross country titles. He held the U.S. record for 5000m on the track at 12:56.27.

Michigan Int. Speedway, Brooklyn, Nov. 4
2000 BOYS DIVISION 1 TEAMS
1. Rockford 56
2. Novi 89
3. Detroit Catholic Central 100
4. Saline 221
5. Milford 229
6. Traverse City Central 242
7. White Lake Lakeland 243
8. Portage Northern 267
9. Grand Blanc 324
10. Lake Orion 336
11. Traverse City West 353
12. Grand Ledge 354
13. Temperance Bedford 414
14. Sterling Heights 416
15. Grosse Pointe South 420
16. Okemos 436
17. Ann Arbor Pioneer 440
18. Livonia Stevenson 441
19. Birmingham Brother Rice 483
20. Dearborn 496
21. Detroit U-D Jesuit 518
22. Warren DeLaSalle 533
23. Clarkston 539
24. Zeeland 550
25. Grand Rapids Union 558
26. Troy 568
27. Utica Eisenhower 607

2000 BOYS DIVISION 1 INDIVIDUALS
1. Dathan Ritzenhein (Rockford)12 .... 14:11
2. Chris Toloff (Novi)12 .... 15:06
3. Tim Moore (Novi)11 .... 15:07
4. Pat Klein (White Lake Lakeland)12 .... 15:16
5. Brian Smith (Rockford)12 .... 15:21
6. Matt Daly (Detroit Catholic Central)12 ..... 15:23
7. Joe Swendrowski (Rockford)12 .... 15:24
8. Kyle Fujimoto (Rockford)12 .... 15:28
9. Sean Moore (Saline)12 .... 15:31
10. Blake Terhune (Traverse City Central)12 .. 15:34
11. Jon Wojcik (Wyandotte)12 .... 15:36
12. Ed Davis (Saline)12 .... 15:39
13. Jason Prowant (Muskegon Reeths-Puff)12 .. 15:46
14. Nicholas Kopczyk (Milford)11 .... 15:46
15. John Krawiec (Detroit Catholic Central)11 ... 15:47
16. Joseph Whitman (Davison)12 .... 15:48
17. Donnie Warner (Salem)12 .... 15:48
18. Matt French (Howell)11 .... 15:48
19. Dana Irrer (Okemos)11 .... 15:50
20. Adam Frezza (Lake Orion)12 .... 15:52
21. Jeff Draggich (Sterling Heights)10 .... 15:52
22. Mark Avenius (Novi)12 .... 15:54
23. Jake Hammerle (Woodhaven)11 .... 15:55
24. Chris Gumz (Rochester)12 .... 15:57
25. Brian Kelly (Roseville)12 .... 15:58
26. Kevin Gienapp (Brighton)10 .... 15:58
27. Dan Krawiec (Detroit Catholic Central)12 ... 15:58
28. Brendan Robinson (Grand Ledge)12 ..... 15:59
29. Lance Vanderberg (Muskegon Mona Sh)11 .. 15:59
30. Ryan Lowry (Detroit Catholic Central)11 ... 16:00
31. Brian Theut (White Lake Lakeland)11 ... 16:01
32. Nate McManus (Traverse City Central)12 .. 16:03
33. Richard Swor (Dearborn)12 .... 16:04
34. Kevin Naughton (Walled Lake Western)11 .. 16:05
35. Matt Johnson (Temperance Bedford)11 .. 16:06
36. Adam Roach (Port Huron)11 .... 16:06
37. Nick Gillett (Troy)11 .... 16:07
38. Cory Nowitzke (Monroe)11 .... 16:07
39. Patrick Miller (Milford)10 .... 16:07
40. Patrick Dantzer (Grosse Pointe South)11 .. 16:08
50. Phil Astras (Rockford)12 .... 16:15
59. Adam Druckenmiller (Rockford)12 .... 16:20
143. BJ Meyers (Rockford)9 .... 16:47

Novi's Tim Moore made it three years in a row that the winner of the state meet would also win the Foot Locker National title.

2001 D1 BOYS

Cool, clear conditions greeted the runners. With Ritzenhein graduated, Tim Moore was the only top 10 type returnee in the D1 race. He cruised to a 24-second win that presaged his national victory at Foot Locker a month later.

"I couldn't hear any runners behind me and I tried not to look back," said Moore. "I'm happy to win. It's been my goal since I was a freshman."

Moore would win nationals in Orlando with a 14:50 clocking.

In a dogfight of a team race, Tony Magni's Catholic Central squad won with the highest score in meet history after No. 1 runner Ryan Lowry was lost to a broken foot.

"The tough part was keeping focused on the team concept, but we had nothing to lose and everything to gain. We had to go from there," said coach Tony Magni.

Michigan Int. Speedway, Brooklyn, Nov. 3
2001 BOYS DIVISION 1 TEAMS
1. Detroit Catholic Central 186
2. Milford 205
3. Traverse City West 221
4. Grand Ledge 249
5. White Lake Lakeland 250
6. Portage Northern 257
7. Grand Blanc 258
8. Temperance Bedford 271
9. Traverse City Central 284
10. Novi 310
11. Saline 329
12. Birmingham Brother Rice 335
13. Lake Orion 337
14. Livonia Churchill 341
15. Muskegon Mona Shores 348
16. Utica Eisenhower 354
17. Ann Arbor Pioneer 361
18. Rockford 364
19. Grand Rapids Union 388
20. Rochester Adams 394
21. Troy 428
22. Canton 439
23. Detroit U-D Jesuit 471
24. Sterling Heights 521
25. Grandville 576
26. Troy Athens 629
27. Grosse Pointe South 700

2001 BOYS DIVISION 1 INDIVIDUALS
1. Tim Moore (Novi)12 .... 15:12
2. Jake Hammerle (Woodhaven)12 .... 15:36
3. Justin Zanotti (Macomb L'Anse Creuse N)12. 15:42
4. Matt French (Howell)12 .... 15:43
5. John Krawiec (Detroit Catholic Central)12 .. 15:48
6. Justin Hajduk (Salem)11 .... 15:50
7. Nick Gillett (Troy)12 .... 15:51
8. Dan Murray (Birmingham Brother Rice)12 .. 15:53
9. Lance Vanderberg (Muskegon Mona Sh)12 .. 15:55
10. David Lucas (Detroit Catholic Central)10 .. 15:57
11. Chris Catton (Grand Blanc)11 .... 15:58
12. Corey Nowitzke (Monroe)12 .... 15:58
13. Jason Schoener (Grand Blanc)12 .... 15:59
14. Troy Terry (Utica Eisenhower)12 .... 15:59
15. Dana Irrer (Okemos)12 .... 16:00
16. Nick Kopczyk (Milford)12 .... 16:00
17. Andrew Thorson (Grand Ledge)12 .... 16:01
18. Kevin Gienapp (Brighton)11 .... 16:02
19. Kevin Naughton (Walled Lake Western)12 .. 16:03
20. Adam Craig (White Lake Lakeland)11 ... 16:04
21. Dustin Voss (Saline)10 .... 16:05
22. Michael Colt (Lake Orion)12 .... 16:07
23. James Naughton (Ann Arbor Pioneer)12 .. 16:10
24. James Anai (Grand Ledge)10 .... 16:10
25. Tad Hulst (Zeeland)10 .... 16:11
26. Tim Marshall (Jackson)11 .... 16:13
27. William Chapman (Livonia Churchill)12 .. 16:14
28. Brian Theut (White Lake Lakeland)12 .... 16:14
29. Ryan Sucharski (Macomb Dakota)12 .... 16:15
30. Chris Welch (White Lake Lakeland)11 .. 16:16
31. Pat Miller (Milford)11 .... 16:16
32. Greg Haapala (Detroit U-D Jesuit)12 ..... 16:17
33. Ryan Gall (Livonia Churchill)12 .... 16:18
34. Andrew Manning (Traverse City Central)11 .. 16:19
35. Matt Johnson (Temperance Bedford)12 .. 16:22
36. Mick Tiffany (Traverse City Central)12 .. 16:22
37. Tim Kenny (Traverse City West)10 .... 16:22
38. Kevin Coch (East Kentwood)11 .... 16:24
39. Matthew Reed (Fraser)12 .... 16:25
40. Patrick Dantzer (Grosse Pointe South)12 .. 16:25
46. Kyle Jekot (Detroit Catholic Central)12 .. 16:31
96. Jon Marshall (Detroit Catholic Central)12 .. 16:52
117. Brian Doot (Detroit Catholic Central)11 .. 17:02
124. Brian Seymour (Detroit Catholic Central)12 17:05
173. Matt Esper (Detroit Catholic Central)12 .. 17:28

2002 D1 BOYS

Milford came into the meet as No. 1, but a spirited team performance by Mark Nessner's Rockford crew stole the win by two points.

"Nobody expected us to win today, so it's big," said Nessner. "It beat all my expectations. I was surprised we won. But they just put it all together today. It clicked for all of them."

Grand Blanc's Chris Catton won the race individually, in an official time of 15:18.85. "This is so much bigger than anything else," he exclaimed. The senior hit splits of 4:51.1 and 9:59.6, moving into the lead after the 2M.

Michigan Int. Speedway, Brooklyn, Nov. 2
2002 BOYS DIVISION 1 TEAMS
1. Rockford 133
2. Milford 135
3. Novi 161
4. Detroit Catholic Central 188
5. Traverse City West 209
6. Ann Arbor Huron 254
7. Saline 254
8. Temperance-Bedford 269
9. Traverse City Central 270
10. Utica Eisenhower 297
11. Grand Blanc 307
12. Birmingham Brother Rice 312
13. Lakeland 320
14. Muskegon Mona Shores 370
15. Zeeland 373
16. Dearborn Fordson 393
17. Sterling Heights 412
18. Livonia Stevenson 450
19. Troy Athens 467
20. Lansing Eastern 472
21. Salem 481
22. Troy 521
23. Rochester 549
24. Forest Hills Central 596
25. Kalamazoo Central 612
26. Detroit U-D Jesuit 632
27. Grosse Pointe South 753
28. Grosse Pointe North 819

2002 BOYS DIVISION 1 INDIVIDUALS
1. Chris Catton (Grand Blanc)12 .... 15:19
2. Dustin Voss (Saline)11 .... 15:22
3. Frank Tinney (Ann Arbor Huron)11 .... 15:25
4. Andrew Manning (Traverse City Central)12 .. 15:37
5. Kevin Gienapp (Brighton)12 .... 15:37
6. Matt Wish (Rockford)12 .... 15:46
7. Michael Hanlon (Ann Arbor Huron)12 ..... 15:47
8. Mark Moore (Novi)10 .... 15:48
9. Neil Atzinger (Saline)11 .... 15:48
10. Chris Welch (White Lake Lakeland)12 .... 15:49
11. Donnie Richmond (Oxford)11 .... 15:49
12. Tim Copacia (Utica Eisenhower)12 .... 15:50
13. Tim Kenny (Traverse City West)11 .... 15:50
14. Chris Mehay (New Baltimore Anchor B)12 .. 15:52
15. Adam Craig (White Lake Lakeland)12 .... 15:53
16. Jon Black (Birmingham Brother Rice)10 .. 15:53
17. Chris Hammer (Troy Athens) 15:55
18. Alex Wood (Traverse City West) 15:55
19. Brian Gilchrist (Novi) 15:56
20. Mark Sitko (Clarkston) 15:56
21. Matt Plaska (Zeeland) 15:57
22. Eric Graf (Rockford) 15:58
23. B.J. Meyers (Rockford) 15:59
24. James Erickson (Belleville) 16:00
25. Seth Thibodean (Milford) 16:00
26. Tim Kaijala (Muskegon Mona Shores) 16:01
27. Matt Gillespie (Livonia Stevenson) 16:02
28. Justin Hajduk (Salem) 16:04
29. Kyle Harris (Milford) 16:06
30. Alex Fritz (Temperance-Bedford) 16:07
31. Sean O'Halloran (Livonia Stevenson) 16:07
32. Chad Murray (Milford) 16:08
33. Cam Ross (Traverse City Central) 16:08
34. Chris Scott (Traverse City West) 16:10
35. Brian Doot (Detroit Catholic Central) 16:10
36. Dana Pitcock (Milford) 16:13
37. Jared Elmore (Clarkston) 16:13
38. David Lucas (Detroit Catholic Central) ... 16:13
39. Derek Scott (Grand Rapids Northview) .. 16:14
40. Mike Andersen (Milford) 16:14
44. Geoff Guthrie (Rockford) 16:18
72. Clark Richter (Rockford) 16:32
103. Todd Smith (Rockford) 16:48
126. Kevin Dorn (Rockford) 16:56

2003 D1 BOYS

After two-straight runner-up finishes, Brian Salyers' Milford crew finally made it to the top step, winning with a 59-point margin over Ann Arbor Huron.

"Hard work does pay off and he took it to another level," said Milford's athletic director—and previous coach—Gene Balawajder.

Saline's Dustin Voss exploded past the leader, Frank Tinney of Huron, in the final mile, covering that section in 4:38. He won by 13 seconds with his 14:54.45.

Saline's Dustin Voss blitzed the final mile. (Saline XC photo)

Michigan Int. Speedway, Brooklyn, Nov. 1
Cloudy, 52°, wind 5-7 mph.
2003 BOYS DIVISION 1 TEAMS
1. Milford 90
2. Ann Arbor Huron 149
3. Saline 166
4. Grand Ledge 201
5. Ann Arbor Pioneer 236
6. Pinckney 240
7. Novi 252
8. Muskegon Mona Shores 275
9. Portage Northern 276
10. Detroit Catholic Central 322
11. Rochester 323
12. Traverse City Central 325
13. Rockford 330
14. Holland West Ottawa 335
15. Traverse City West 338
16. Kalamazoo Central 347
17. Birmingham Brother Rice 385
18. Sterling Heights 407
19. Troy Athens 432
20. Grand Blanc 435
21. Salem 442
22. Detroit U-D Jesuit 492
23. Macomb L'Anse Creuse North 511
24. Grosse Pointe North 582
25. Grosse Pointe South 592
26. West Bloomfield 608
27. Livonia Stevenson 682

2003 BOYS DIVISION 1 INDIVIDUALS
1. Dustin Voss (Saline)12 .... 14:55
2. Frank Tinney (Ann Arbor Huron)12 .... 15:08
3. Justin Switzer (Waterford Kettering)11 ... 15:10
4. Neal Naughton (Walled Lake Western)12 . 15:15
5. Seth Thibodeau (Milford)12 .... 15:24
6. Tim Kaijala (Muskegon Mona Shores)12 . 15:25
7. Neil Atzinger (Saline)12 .... 15:26
8. Dan DeRusha (Milford)12 .... 15:27
9. Ryan McCarl (Muskegon Mona Shores)12 . 15:29
10. Mark Moore (Novi)11 .... 15:32
11. Jeff Hubbard (Ann Arbor Pioneer)12 ...... 15:32
12. Don Letts (Portage Northern)12 .... 15:32
13. Amol Huprikar (Novi)11 .... 15:34
14. Kyle Mena (Portage Northern)12 .... 15:35
15. David Lucas (Detroit Catholic Central)12 . 15:36
16. Riak Mabil (Grand Ledge)11 .... 15:37
17. John Black (Birmingham Brother Rice)11 . 15:38
18. Tim Kenny (Traverse City West)12 .... 15:38
19. Ian Boyle (Pinckney)11 .... 15:38
20. Luke Chrusciel (Grandville)12 .... 15:39
21. Jimmy Partridge (Sterling Heights)11 ..... 15:39
22. Tad Hulst (Zeeland)12 .... 15:39
23. Tim Dalton (Northville)12 .... 15:40
24. Abdullah Saleh (Dearborn Fordson)12 ... 15:42
25. Matt Chumbley (Rochester)12 .... 15:42
26. Adam Koepfer (Temperance Bedford)12 . 15:42
27. M Stensones-Fornaes (Ann Arbor Pion)11 .. 15:43
28. Nick Katsefaras (Pinckney)11 .... 15:43
29. James Erickson (Belleville)12 .... 15:45
30. Curtis Vollmar (Grand Blanc)11 .... 15:46
31. Dana Pitcock (Milford)11 .... 15:48
32. Ryan Grau (Kalamazoo Central)10 .... 15:48
33. Adam Daoud (Ann Arbor Huron)11 .... 15:49
34. Evan Lisull (Ann Arbor Huron)10 .... 15:52
35. John Wilson (Howell)11 .... 15:56
36. Kyle Harris (Milford)12 .... 15:57
37. Clark Richter (Rockford)12 .... 15:57
38. Jonathon Giarmo (Monroe)12 .... 16:00
39. Steve Leonard (Lakeland)11 .... 16:01
40. Nick Zendler (Flint Carman-Ainsworth)12 . 16:01
44. Chad Murray (Milford)11 .... 16:04
94. John Kuzmich (Milford)12 .... 16:33
122. Tim Wilkins (Milford)11 .... 16:46

2004 D1 BOYS

Milford's 3-4 provided the critical edge to top Pinckney in the team race to defend their title. The key, said Milford leader Dana Pitcock, was "We talked about running our type of race—no heroics."

Individually, Justin Switzer blasted the second mile to break the race open. "I was really hoping to go below 15:00," he told reporters, "but the mud around the turns slowed me down so much."

Michigan Int. Speedway, Brooklyn, Nov. 6
Clear, 60°, wind 14-20mph.
2004 BOYS DIVISION 1 TEAMS
1. Milford 108
2. Pinckney 120
3. Ann Arbor Huron 129
4. Novi 154
5. Ann Arbor Pioneer 188
6. Walled Lake Central 269
7. Lake Orion 289
8. Rockford 316
9. White Lake Lakeland 319
10. Monroe 339
11. Macomb L'Anse Creuse North 341
12. Traverse City Central 342
13. Howell 363
14. Salem 378
15. Livonia Churchill 396
16. Rochester 402
17. Grosse Pointe North 423
18. Holland West Ottawa 423
19. Traverse City West 423
20. Detroit U-D Jesuit 460
21. Jenison 467
22. Grosse Pointe South 509

23. Troy Athens 533
24. Grand Blanc 533
25. Clarkston 539
26. Sterling Heights 542
27. Muskegon Mona Shores 572

2004 BOYS DIVISION 1 INDIVIDUALS

1. Justin Switzer (Waterford Kettering)12 15:23
2. John Black (Birmingham Brother Rice)12 15:36
3. Mark Moore (Novi)12 15:39
4. Adam Daoud (Ann Arbor Huron)12 15:41
5. Riak Mabil (Grand Ledge)12 15:41
6. Nick Katsefaras (Pinckney)12 15:46
7. Dana Pitock (Milford)12 15:48
8. Amol Huprikar (Novi)12 15:48
9. Jordan Raetz (Rochester)12 15:50
10. Ian Boyle (Pinckney)12 15:55
11. Luke Heiman (White Lake Lakeland)10 15:59
12. Mike Anderson (Milford)12 16:01
13. Curtis Vollmar (Grand Blanc)12 16:01
14. Hadi Harp (Dearborn Fordson)12 16:02
15. Mark Jones (Saginaw Heritage)12 16:02
16. Jeff Kosters (Grandville)11 16:06
17. M Stensones-Fornaes (Ann Arb Pioneer)12 16:06
18. Maxwell Working (Detroit Catholic Cent)12 16:06
19. Takashi Gould (Ann Arbor Pioneer)12 16:07
20. Blake Figgins (Detroit Mumford)12 16:07
21. Chase Boggs-Smitley (Okemos)12 16:07
22. Connor Schultz (Livonia Churchill)12 16:07
23. Sean Maxwell (Walled Lake Central)11 16:08
24. Joel VanDerwarp (Milford)12 16:08
25. Colin Orr (West Bloomfield)12 16:09
26. Kenny Wassus (Monroe)12 16:09
27. Mike Carson (Jenison)12 16:15
28. Greg Farnum (Battle Creek Central)12 16:17
29. Evan Lisull (Ann Arbor Huron)11 16:21
30. Pat Sarver (Macomb L'Anse Creuse N)12 16:21
31. Sam Watson (Rochester)12 16:23
32. Billy Peterson (Lake Orion)12 16:24
33. Derek Shortt (Brighton)11 16:27
34. Kirk Leonard (Detroit U-D Jesuit)11 16:28
35. Rob Shinouskis (Lake Orion)11 16:29
36. Nick Anderson (Milford)9 16:29
37. Tyler Spagnuolo (Traverse City Central)12 16:30
38. Steve Breisach (Kalamazoo Central)11 16:30
39. Levi Hohl (Pinckney)9 16:31
40. Loren Ahonen (Temperance-Bedford)11 16:33
41. Brendan Marcum (Pinckney)10 16:34
85. Matt Picou (Milford)11 16:50
114. Matt Tupla (Milford)11 17:07
119. Tim Wilkins (Milford)12 17:11

2005 D1 BOYS

With only two runners in the top 50, Pinckney won its first state title. Coach Tom Carney's top runner, Brian Hankins, placed 17th. Teammate Mike Katsefaras finished 44th despite losing a shoe in the first mile. Carney later had it bronzed and handed it out as an annual award.

Individual winner Ryan Grau entered the MIS infield (2.5M) in about 14th place, and blistered his trip to the finish line. "It was all mental. I just went for it."

Michigan Int. Speedway, Brooklyn, Nov. 5 ⊠
Cloudy, 64°, winds 2-15mph.

2005 BOYS DIVISION 1 TEAMS

1. Pinckney 146
2. Ann Arbor Pioneer 176
3. Rockford 223
4. Walled Lake Central 249
5. Lake Orion 268
6. South Lyon 270
7. Milford 287
8. Portage Northern 337
9. Novi 339
10. Rochester Adams 356
11. Flushing 358
12. Grosse Pointe North 373
13. Detroit U-D Jesuit 375
14. Ann Arbor Huron 377
15. Lakeland 385
16. Okemos 391
17. Howell 392
18. Monroe 397
19. Rochester Hills Stoney Creek 401
20. Clarkston 415
21. Grosse Pointe South 427
22. Salem 438
23. Troy Athens 459
24. Macomb L'Anse Creuse North 470
25. Holland West Ottawa 474
26. Detroit Catholic Central 499
27. Traverse City West 549
28. Grand Haven 630

2005 BOYS DIVISION 1 INDIVIDUALS

1. Ryan Grau (Kalamazoo Central)12 15:35
2. Luke Heiman (White Lake Lakeland)11 15:37
3. Robbie Fisher (Grosse Pointe North)11 15:43
4. Dan Kapadia (Salem)12 15:46
5. Jacob Wernet (Grosse Pointe South)12 15:47
6. Pete Loy (Warren DeLaSalle)12 15:48
7. Cole Sanseverino (Monroe)11 15:48
8. Anthony Wile (Birmingham Brother Rice)11 15:49
9. Steve Breisach (Kalamazoo Central)12 15:49
10. Peter Christmas (Ann Arbor Pioneer)12 15:49
11. Rob Shinouskis (Lake Orion)12 15:50
12. Drew Collette (Lake Orion)12 15:50
13. Sean Maxwell (Walled Lake Central)12 15:53
14. Dave Dermes (Rochester Adams)11 15:54
15. Jake Hill (Walled Lake Central)11 15:54
16. Andrew Keller (South Lyon)12 15:57
17. Brian Hankins (Pinckney)10 15:58
18. Craig Marlatt (Ann Arbor Pioneer)12 15:58
19. Ross Solanskey (Berkley)12 15:59
20. Kirk Leonard (Detroit U-D Jesuit)12 15:59
21. Sam Breen (Woodhaven)12 15:59
22. Matt Picou (Milford)12 15:59
23. Karl Resch (Macomb L'Anse Creuse N)11 16:02
24. Mike Craze (Sterling Heights)11 16:02
25. Justin Heck (Monroe)10 16:03
26. Chris Wurster (Birmingham Brother Rice)12 16:04
27. Jeff Bonzheim (Jenison)11 16:04
28. Jon Bigelow (Jenison)11 16:04
29. Mike Wheat (Novi)11 16:05
30. Tony Sanfilippo (Walled L Central)11 16:05
31. Sean Johnston (Rockford)11 16:05
32. Evan Lisull (Ann Arbor Huron)12 16:07
33. Patrick Cooper (Portage Northern)12 16:07
34. Andrew Hawks (Rockford)11 16:08
35. Joe Cilluffo (Warren Mott)12 16:08
36. Tim Zeerip (Holland West Ottawa)12 16:08
37. Brad Anderson (Rochester Adams)12 16:11
38. Matt Neely (Brighton)10 16:12
39. Chuck Tully (Lincoln Park)12 16:13
40. Josh Lisiecki (Detroit U-D Jesuit)12 16:14
44. Mike Katsefaras (Pinckney)10 16:18
52. Jake Hohl (Pinckney)10 16:28
54. David Emery (Pinckney)11 16:29
61. Brendan Marcum (Pinckney)11 16:31
95. Matt Brunner (Pinckney)10 16:44
123. Matt Wines (Pinckney)9 16:54

2006 D1 BOYS

Pinckney repeated as D1 champs with a stunning performance, perhaps the finest team tally in meet history. The only better team score came back in 1927, when Kalamazoo Central scored 25 in a 10-team field. Said coach Tom Carney, "I'm very happy with what we've been able to accomplish."

Teammates David Emery and Mike Katsefaras ran 1-2, with four other teammates in the top 14. "You work all season for the state meet," said Emery. "You don't want to peak before that."

Michigan Int. Speedway, Brooklyn, Nov. 4 ⊠
Cloudy, 46°, winds 1-12mph.

2006 BOYS DIVISION 1 TEAMS

1. Pinckney 27
2. Novi 140
3. Traverse City Central 231
4. Traverse City West 231
5. Milford 246
6. Saline 271
7. Warren DeLaSalle 275
8. Portage Northern 285
9. Ann Arbor Pioneer 301
10. Lake Orion 302
11. Monroe 325
12. Plymouth 327
13. Rochester Adams 375
14. Rockford 378
15. Troy Athens 408
16. Grosse Pointe South 414
17. Detroit U-D Jesuit 430
18. Grosse Pointe North 442
19. Howell 447
20. Lakeland 455
21. Sterling Heights Ford 478
22. Livonia Churchill 519
23. Brighton 538
24. Hudsonville 545
25. Rochester Hills Stoney Creek 549
26. Holland West Ottawa 600
27. Detroit Mumford 750

David Emery, who couldn't break 20 as a 9th-grader, led Pinckney to a stunning team finish. (Pat Davey photo)

2006 BOYS DIVISION 1 INDIVIDUALS

1. David Emery (Pinckney)12 15:35
2. Mike Katsefaras (Pinckney)11 15:40
3. Cole Sanseverino (Monroe)12 15:46
4. Zach Romer (Midland)11 15:47
5. Neal Duggan (Troy Athens)12 15:51
6. Ben Miller (Warren DeLaSalle)10 15:54
7. Robbie Fisher (Grosse Pointe North)12 15:55
8. Brian Hankins (Pinckney)11 15:56
9. Steve Tobochnik (Kalamazoo Norrix)12 15:56
10. Jake Hohl (Pinckney)11 15:57
11. Jon Manby (East Kentwood)11 15:58
12. Matt Wines (Pinckney)10 15:59
13. Edwin Gay (Grosse Pointe South)10 15:59
14. Brenden Marcum (Pinckney)12 16:00
15. Anthony Scaparo (Plymouth)12 16:01
16. Gary Brownell (Woodhaven)11 16:02
17. Matt VanderRoest (Ann Arbor Huron)10 16:02
18. Ryan Ziolko (Lake Orion)10 16:02
19. Jon Hurrell (Bay City Western)10 16:02

20. Michael Wheat (Novi)12 ....16:02
21. Luke Heiman (Lakeland)12 ....16:03
22. Pablo Ruiz (Bay City Western)10 ....16:04
23. Adam Haag (Warren DeLaSalle)12 ....16:04
24. Chris Tassen (Troy Athens)12 ....16:05
25. Pat Cassady (Flushing)11 ....16:05
26. Joe Osentoski (Temperance Bedf)12 ....16:06
27. Jeff Bonzheim (Jenison)12 ....16:06
28. Alex Folk (Temperance Bedford)12 ....16:07
29. Matt Neely (Brighton)11 ....16:08
30. Devin McKeown (Milford)12 ....16:09
31. Nick Olson (Portage Northern)12 ....16:09
32. Alex Prasad (Novi)12 ....16:11
33. Kevin Tarczon (Traverse City C)12 ....16:12
34. Jesse Robbins (Muskegon MS)12 ....16:13
35. Alex Toloff (Detroit Catholic Central)10 ....16:13
36. Kevin Hagan (Okemos)12 ....16:15
37. Justin Heck (Monroe)11 ....16:15
38. John Gulbronson (Temperance B)12 ....16:16
39. Kyle Hines (Jackson)12 ....16:16
40. Jon Rock (Utica Eisenhower)11 ....16:17
60. Matt Brunner (Pinckney)11 ....16:25

2007 D1 BOYS

Brian Hankins, who played football as a freshman before switching to cross country, told the *Livingston Community News* that watching teammate David Emery win the year before taught him much, "He was patient. He made his move at the right time. I was real patient. I made one move to catch up. When I caught them, I knew it was anyone's race. I put in one final surge that I did not know that I had. I ended up pulling away."

Brian Hankins pulled away on the final stretch (Pete Draugalis photo)

Hankins keyed the third straight win for Pinckney—the first time that had happened in the big school race since Lansing Eastern in 1955-56-57. Commenting on the 17-point margin, Coach Tom Carney said, "We didn't just show up and somebody gave it to us. We had to earn it."

Michigan Int. Speedway, Brooklyn, Nov. 3
Clear, 55°, winds 15-20mph.
2007 BOYS DIVISION 1 TEAMS
1. Pinckney 124
2. Saline 141
3. Rochester Adams 213
4. Ann Arbor Pioneer 217
5. Ann Arbor Huron 230
6. Milford 253
7. Saginaw Heritage 260
8. Lake Orion 266
9. Northville 317
10. Detroit Catholic Central 342
11. Rockford 355
12. Grand Ledge 371
13. Salem 404
14. Canton 410
15. Traverse City Central 432
16. Hudsonville 436
17. Holland West Ottawa 441
18. Flushing 448
19. Detroit Mumford 449
20. White Lake Lakeland 469
21. Warren DeLaSalle 476
22. Grosse Pointe South 484
23. Portage Northern 493
24. Troy 497
25. Utica Eisenhower 499
26. Dearborn Fordson 511
27. Bay City Western 511
28. Detroit U-D Jesuit 514

2007 BOYS DIVISION 1 INDIVIDUALS
1. Brian Hankins (Pinckney)12 ....15:27
2. Gary Brownell (Woodhaven)12 ....15:34
3. Jon Rock (Utica Eisenhower)12 ....15:38
4. Blake Johnson (Saline)12 ....15:39
5. Ben Miller (Warren DeLaSalle)11 ....15:42
6. James Pearson (Detroit U-D Jesuit)12 ....15:43
7. Michael Murphy (Bloomfield Hills Rice)11 ....15:44
8. Justin Heck (Monroe)12 ....15:46
9. Pat Cassady (Flushing)12 ....15:47
10. Joseph Banyai (Royal Oak)12 ....15:49
11. Mike Katsefaras (Pinckney)12 ....15:51
12. Tim Huwer (Rochester Adams)12 ....15:51
13. Isaiah Ward (Detroit Mumford)12 ....15:52
14. Stephen Fuelling (Milford)12 ....15:52
15. Steve Miller (Rochester Adams)12 ....15:54
16. Zach Romer (Midland)12 ....15:54
17. Jordan Bauss (Sterling Heights Ford)12 ....15:54
18. Chris Paas (Rockford)12 ....15:55
19. Kenny Wall (Flushing)12 ....15:56
20. Kevin Debear (Salem)12 ....15:56
21. Charlie Cavell (Ann Arbor Pioneer)12 ....15:56
22. Bob Feigley (Milford)12 ....15:57
23. Nick Kern (Ann Arbor Pioneer)10 ....15:57
24. Stephen Walker (Midland Dow)11 ....15:58
25. Kyle Roche (Walled Lake Central)10 ....15:59
26. Matt Neely (Brighton)12 ....15:59
27. Ryan Ziolko (Lake Orion)11 ....15:59
29. Brian Conn (Saline)11 ....16:00
30. Arthur Acevedo (Saginaw Heritage)11 ....16:00
31. Mike Atchoo (Troy)10 ....16:01
32. Edwin Gay (Grosse Pointe South)11 ....16:01
33. Jake Hohl (Pinckney)12 ....16:03
34. Saeed Saleh (Dearborn Fordson)12 ....16:03
35. Sefan Morell (White Lake Lakeland)10 ......16:04
36. Shaun Slater (Portage Northern)11 ....16:08
37. Brockton Feltman (Grand Ledge)11 ....16:09
38. Tommy Hunt (Saline)11 ....16:10
39. Caleb Kline (Ann Arbor Huron)11 ....16:11
40. Keith Heyboer (Hudsonville)12 ....16:11
59. Matt Brunner (Pinckney)12 ....16:25
81. Matt Wines (Pinckney)11 ....16:31
104. Chris Lotz (Pinckney)11 ....16:38
195. Tanner Pesonen (Pinckney)10 ....17:24

2008 D1 BOYS

"I'm all smiles," Stephen Walker told the *Saginaw News* after his victory. "I didn't talk about a time goal; my main goal was just to win it. At about the two-mile mark I made my push."

Coach Jed Hopfensperger added, "Last year he was very nervous, but this year he was ready."

Pioneer captured the team crown with a big 63-point margin, as three-time champ Pinckney struggled after heavy graduation losses.

Dow's Stephen Walker – 2008 champion. (Pete Draugalis photo)

Michigan Int. Speedway, Brooklyn, Nov. 1
Partly cloudy, 59°, winds 2-7mph.
2008 BOYS DIVISION 1 TEAMS
1. Ann Arbor Pioneer 82
2. Saginaw Heritage 145
3. Bay City Western 185
4. Lake Orion 186
5. Ann Arbor Huron 228
6. Detroit Catholic Central 243
7. Rockford 277
8. Pinckney 279
9. Saline 290
10. Monroe 295
11. Rochester Adams 297
12. Plymouth 333
13. Novi 349
14. Caledonia 363
15. Rochester 411
16. Milford 417
17. East Kentwood 430
18. Grand Blanc 457
19. Holland West Ottawa 458
20. Warren DeLaSalle 462
21. Clarkston 473
22. Temperance Bedford 484
23. Portage Northern 512
24. White Lake Lakeland 529
25. Grosse Pointe South 579
26. Okemos 593
27. Grosse Pointe North 717

2008 BOYS DIVISION 1 INDIVIDUALS
1. Stephen Walker (Midland Dow)12 ....15:19
2. Mike Atchoo (Troy)11 ....15:23
3. Michael Murphy (Birmingham Rice)12 ....15:24
4. Edwin Gay (Grosse Pointe South)12 ....15:29
5. Kenny Laskowski (Rochester) 15:30
6. Matt Vander Roest (Ann Arbor Huron)12 ....15:32
7. Matt Wines (Pinckney)12 ....15:32
8. Nathan Karr (Ann Arbor Pioneer)11 ....15:35
9. Dan Culbertson (Ann Arbor Pioneer)12 ....15:36
10. Sean Bone (Lake Orion)11 ....15:38
11. Ryan Ziolko (Lake Orion)12 ....15:39
12. Jeremiah Hargett (Lake Orion) 15:40
13. Travis Borchard (Saginaw Heritage)12 ......15:41
14. Nate Huff (Milford)11 ....15:44

15. Omar Kaddurah (Grand Blanc)10 .... 15:44
16. Brett Burdick (Grand Blanc)12 .... 15:44
17. Jon Hurrell (Bay City Western)12 .... 15:44
18. Kyle Roche (Walled Lake Central)11............ 15:45
19. Michael Blaszczyk (Novi)11 .... 15:46
20. Nick Kern (Ann Arbor Pioneer)11 .... 15:47
21. Arthur Acevedo (Saginaw Heritage)12 .... 15:47
22. Ben Miller (Warren DeLaSalle)12 .... 15:49
23. Elmar Engholm (Plymouth)12 .... 15:49
24. Fasika Aklilu (East Kentwood)12 .... 15:50
25. Mike Reimann (Rochester Adams)12........... 15:50
26. Ricardo Galindo (Detroit Catholic Central)11 15:53
27. Tommy Valade (Temperance Bedford)11 .... 15:55
28. Anthony Sterzick (Caledonia)12 .... 15:56
29. Adam Kern (Ann Arbor Pioneer)11 .... 15:56
30. Brian Conn (Saline)12.................................... 15:58
31. Isaac Cox (East Kentwood)11 .... 15:59
32. Brockton Feltman (Grand Ledge)12 .... 15:59
33. Stephen Rich (Holland West Ottawa)10 ...... 16:00
34. Joe Duff (Grand Haven)10 .... 16:02
35. Alex Katona (Waterford Kettering)11 .... 16:02
36. Austin Whitelaw (Monroe)10 .... 16:03
37. David Wallington (Ann Arbor Pioneer)12..... 16:05
38. Brandon Cushman (Sag. Heritage)12 .... 16:06
39. Nathaniel Ellsworth (Sag. Heritage)11.......... 16:08
40. Jeremy Dickie (Swartz Creek)10 .... 16:10
80. Andres Sanz-Guerrero (Ann Arb Pioneer)1116:27
92. Joe Frakes (Ann Arbor Pioneer)11 .... 16:31

2009 D1 BOYS

The team race had shaped up to be a dogfight among Catholic Central, defending champ Pioneer and Pinckney—in fact, Pinckney had won the regional over CC. However, Coach Tony Magni's squad pulled off a near-perfect performance for a solid win.

D1 1600 champ Mike Atchoo ran a controlled race to win handily. Coach Eric Prowse told the Daily Tribune, "He understood he was going to be surrounded by a lot of talented runners. He didn't need to go out and blow everyone away early, partly out of respect for the competition, and because that wouldn't be a smart thing to do. He knew he was going to have to buckle down early, and when the time was right, use that 4:07 miler strength and finish strong."

Strong headwinds in the last half-mile blunted the kicks of many all day long.

Michigan Int. Speedway, Brooklyn, Nov. 7
Clear, 66°, winds gusting 18-25mph
2009 BOYS DIVISION 1 TEAMS
1. Detroit Catholic Central 68
2. Ann Arbor Pioneer............................... 96
3. Pinckney 155
4. Milford 167
5. Rockford 228
6. Saginaw Heritage 234
7. Lake Orion 263
8. Troy 264
9. Saline 266
10. Novi 281
11. Plymouth... 337
12. Grand Blanc 370
13. Grand Rapids Kenowa Hills 390
14. Ann Arbor Huron 398
15. Monroe 402
16. Temperance Bedford 403
17. Royal Oak... 417
18. Bloomfield Hills Brother Rice........... 424
19. Rochester Adams............................. 428
20. East Kentwood 443
21. Warren DeLaSalle 447
22. Okemos 459
23. Midland Dow 488
24. Rochester Hills Stoney Creek 639
25. Portage Central 639
26. Caledonia 641
27. Macomb Dakota 671

Troy's Mike Atchoo won big in 2009. (Jeff Hollobaugh photo)

2009 BOYS DIVISION 1 INDIVIDUALS
1. Mike Atchoo (Troy)12.......................................15:29
2. Jeremy Dickie (Swartz Creek)11 ....15:51
3. Ricardo Galindo (Detroit Catholic Central)12..15:52
4. Nick Kern (Ann Arbor Pioneer)12 ....16:00
5. Nathan Huff (Milford)12....................................16:02
6. Nick Kaiser (Temperance Bedford)11 ....16:02
7. Nick Perry (Woodhaven)12.............................16:03
8. Reed Kamyszek (GR Kenowa Hills)12............16:03
9. Andrew Cusmano (Warren DeLaSalle)11 ......16:04
10. Joe Duff (Grand Haven)11.............................16:06
11. Andrew Garcia-Garrison (Detroit Cath C)11 .16:08
12. Chad Norton (Walled Lake Central)12 ....16:09
13. Adam Kern (Ann Arbor Pioneer)12 ....16:09
14. Tanner Pesonen (Pinckney)12 ....16:10
15. Isaac Cox (East Kentwood)12 ....16:11
16. Christopher Platt (Walled Lake Northern)12.16:12
17. Scott Albaugh (Waterford Mott)11 ....16:14
18. Stefan Morell (White Lake Lakeland)12 ....16:15
19. Austin Whitelaw (Monroe)11..........................16:15
20. Kyle Roche (Walled Lake Central)12............16:15
21. Nathan Karr (Ann Arbor Pioneer)12 ....16:16
22. Alexander Katona (Waterford Kettering)12 ..16:17
23. Viktor Puskorius (Detroit Catholic Cent)12...16:18
24. Joe Porcari (Plymouth)11 ....16:18
25. T.J. Carey (Lake Orion)9................................16:19
26. Andrew Harper (Saline)12..............................16:19
27. Drake Veitenheimer (Rockford)12 ....16:20
28. Frank Griffiths (Northville)12..........................16:20
29. Ryan Konen (Grand Ledge)12.......................16:21
30. Evan Chiplock (Saginaw Heritage)10 ....16:22
31. Austin Zebrowski (Detroit Catholic Cent)11..16:22
32. Stephen Glinski (Warren DeLaSalle)12........16:23
33. Matthew Popielarz (Saginaw Heritage)12 ....16:23
34. Miles Felton (Canton)10.................................16:24
35. Nathaniel Ellsworth (Saginaw Heritage)12 ...16:24
36. John-Paul Zebrowski (Detroit Catholic C)11 16:24
37. Michael Lahner (Pinckney)12 ....16:24
38. Matt Kabacinski (Bay City Western)12 ....16:25
39. William Yau (Troy)10......................................16:29
40. Michael Blaszczyk (Novi)12...........................16:32
140. Mackenzie Boyd (Detroit Catholic Cent)11.17:23
237. Sean Carney (Detroit Catholic Central)12...19:46

2010 D1 BOYS

Waterford Mott's Scott Albaugh was shocked by his win: "I didn't know what was going to happen, truly," he told Mick McCabe of the Detroit Free Press. "I didn't want to get my hopes up, to be honest. I didn't know if I had it in me. It's amazing!

"I thought it was going to be faster at the start, but then I took the lead and I thought it was too easy, so I picked it up a little bit and it was still too easy."

Instructed by his coach, Ryan Robinson, to follow the pack, Albaugh got a warning at halfway, but responded with "the nod and a wink."

Monroe's Austin Whitelaw passed Albaugh on the infield, but Albaugh kicked back to the win on the final stretch.

Tony Magni's Catholic Central squad won its second straight: "Twice is nice. Being a defending champion, everyone is out to get you, and we got beat last week. I just told them to be positive."

The crucial moment as Scott Albaugh passes Austin Whitelaw on the final stretch. (Pete Draugalis photo)

Michigan Int. Speedway, Brooklyn, Nov. 6
2010 BOYS DIVISION 1 TEAMS
1. Detroit Catholic Central......................103
2. Dexter 114
3. Pinckney 146
4. Milford 155
5. Saline 180
6. Rockford 258
7. Temperance Bedford 282
8. Saginaw Heritage 295
9. Brighton...298
10. Grand Haven.....................................303
11. Grand Blanc 326
12. Rochester Hills Stoney Creek..........327
13. Waterford Mott..................................329
14. Macomb Dakota................................377
15. White Lake Lakeland 388
16. Bay City Western..............................400
17. Lake Orion 408
18. Traverse City West 426
19. Walled Lake Northern 439
20. Plymouth...449
21. Okemos 456
22. Portage Central 523
23. Ann Arbor Pioneer 541
24. Caledonia..587
25. Ann Arbor Huron 601
26. Macomb L'Anse Creuse North 627
27. Grosse Pointe South........................733

2010 BOYS DIVISION 1 INDIVIDUALS
1. Scott Albaugh (Waterford Mott)12 ....15:14
2. Austin Whitelaw (Monroe)12 ....15:16
3. Omar Kaddurah (Grand Blanc)12...................15:31
4. Nick Kaiser (Temperance Bedford)12 ....15:32
5. Evan Chiplock (Saginaw Heritage)11 ....15:33
6. Joe Duff (Grand Haven)12..............................15:33
7. Nick Renberg (Saline)11................................15:35
8. Austin Zebrowski (Detroit Catholic C)12.........15:35
9. John-Paul Zebrowski (Detroit Catholic C)12 ..15:40
10. Andrew Garcia-Garrison (Detroit Cath C)12.15:41
11. Taylor Neely (Dexter)11................................15:43
12. Evan Smallman (Milford)12 ....15:43
13. Tom Girardot (Birmingham Brother Rice)11.15:43
14. Colin Creagh (Macomb L'Anse Creuse N)1215:44
15. Alex Vermeulen (Dexter)10 ....14:45
16. Jeremy Cickie (Swartz Creek)12 ....15:46
17. Nathan Burnand (Waterford Mott)10 ....15:46
18. Zac Meston (Pinckney)12.............................15:46
19. Jeff Bajema (GR Kenowa Hills)10 ....15:46
20. Nicholas Culbertson (Macomb Dakota)12....15:47
21. Blake Bitner (GR Kenowa Hills)12................15:48
22. Spencer Gerber (Rockford)12 ....15:48
23. Stephen Fabian (Detroit U-D Jesuit)11 ....15:48
24. Andrew Barnett (Saline)12 ....15:49
25. T.J. Carey (Lake Orion)10 ....15:49
26. Eric Fegan (Pinckney)11...............................15:50
27. Joseph Porcari (Plymouth)12 ....15:51
28. Ian McGinn (Hartland)11...............................15:52
29. Nick Costello (Brighton)11............................15:52
30. Dan Thompson (Temperance Bedford)12....15:52
31. Ryan Duff (Grand Haven)11 ....15:54
32. Cody Snavely (Milford)10.............................15:55
33. Parker Latshaw (Dexter)12 ....15:56
34. Ben Reed (Midland)12..................................15:56
35. Garret Zuk (White Lake Lakeland)11............15:56
36. Nate Benton (Milford)...................................15:58
37. Matt Greve (Dexter)10 ....15:58
38. Mackenzie Boyd (Detroit Catholic C)12........16:00
39. Miles Felton (Canton)11...............................16:00
40. Casey Routledge (Walled Lk Northern)12....16:00
70. Ryan Boyd (Detroit Catholic C)11.................16:14
151. Jack Malinowski (Detroit Catholic C)10 ......16:50
155. Thomas Fagan (Detroit Catholic C)11 ....16:52

2011 D1 BOYS

The KLAA West conference dominated, taking 1-2, in addition to 5 and 13. "Our area is the mecca of cross country," said Milford coach Brian Salyers, who guided his team to a 128-point winning performance.

Lakeland's Garrett Zuk took the individual win in 15:22 on a muddy course after Evan Chiplock of Saginaw Heritage set a tough pace for the first 2M (9:47). Said Zuk, "He went out really hard and I think that helped me. I owe part of my win to him for doing that."

Chiplock faded to 38th, while Milford's Brian Kettle blistered the final stretch to finish 2nd.

Michigan Int. Speedway, Brooklyn, Nov. 5
2011 BOYS DIVISION 1 TEAMS
1. Milford...128
2. Hartland...172
3. Waterford Mott 177
4. Saline...186
5. White Lake Lakeland 188
6. Dexter..217
7. Rockford..220
8. Saginaw Heritage 231
9. Grand Blanc 260
10. Ann Arbor Pioneer 275
11. Lake Orion..282
12. Grand Haven 291
13. Pinckney..318
14. Clarkston...370
15. Romeo..383
16. Royal Oak..415
17. Bloomfield Hills Rice............................451
18. Traverse City Central 456
19. Detroit U-D Jesuit................................473
20. Okemos..497
21. Hudsonville..514
22. Temperance Bedford 535
23. East Kentwood 560
24. Grandville...613
25. Warren Mott 616
26. Caledonia...692
27. Wyandotte..715
28. Grosse Pointe South............................728

Garrett Zuk overcame the mud to win in 2011. (Pete Draugalis photo)

2011 BOYS DIVISION 1 INDIVIDUALS
1. Garret Zuk (White Lake Lakeland)12 ....15:22
2. Brian Kettle (Milford)10..................................15:25
3. Nick Renberg (Saline)12................................15:29
4. T.J. Carey (Lake Orion)11 ....15:33
5. Cody Snavely (Milford)11..............................15:38
6. Nathan Burnand (Waterford Mott)11 ....15:39
7. Thomas Girardot (Bloomfield Hills Rice)12 ...15:41
8. Jeff Bajema (GR Kenowa Hills)11 ....15:41
9. Sean Pengelly (Hartland)11 ....15:43
10. Ian McGinn (Hartland)12..............................15:49
11. Dan Smis (Northville)10...............................15:49
12. Derek Gielarowski (Plymouth)12..................15:51
13. Paul Ausum (Milford)12................................15:52
14. Ryan Duff (Grand Haven)12 ....15:53
15. Jacob Higle-Ralbovsky (Ann Arb Huron)12..15:54
16. Ahron Gunn (Woodhaven)12.......................15:55
17. Sam Tanielian (Clarkston)11........................15:55
18. Zachary Kughn (Grand Blanc)12 ....15:56
19. Matt Gilbert (Fenton)12................................15:57
20. David Diaz (Lake Orion)10 ....15:57
21. Stephen Biebelhausen (Roch. Adams)11 ...15:58
22. Matt Moss (Traverse City Central)12 ....15:58
23. Nick Costello (Brighton)12...........................15:58
24. Michael Cox (Pinckney)12 ....15:58
25. Sam Albaugh (Waterford Mott)9..................15:59
26. Spencer Bishop (Saline)12..........................15:59
27. Scott Neff (White Lake Lakeland)12............16:00
28. Ben Hill (Royal Oak)9 ....16:01
29. Nick Noles (Northville)9...............................16:02
30. William Yau (Troy)12....................................16:02
31. Galen Burrell (Ann Arbor Pioneer)11 ....16:03
32. Nicholas Lanzetta (Detroit Catholic Cent)11 16:03
33. Logan Wetzel (Saline)9...............................16:04
34. Eddie Komph (New Baltimore Anchor B)12.16:07
35. Irvin Wyche (Harrison T L'Anse Creuse)12.16:07
36. Brandon Carson (Waterford Mott)12 ....16:08
37. Eddie Codrington (Ann Arbor Pioneer)10....16:10
38. Evan Chiplock (Saginaw Heritage)12..........16:10
39. Austin Benoit (Rockford)11 ....16:12
40. Ryan Gillespie (Oxford)11...........................16:13
75. Chris Housel (Milford)11..............................16:28
78. Matt Graves (Milford)11...............................16:29
121. Steven Sloboda (Milford)12.......................16:48
182. Shawn Welch (Milford)12 ....17:15

2012 D1 BOYS

Milford's Brian Kettle took a fall halfway through the race, yet got up and worked for a half mile just to catch up to the lead pack. On the final stretch, he unleashed his kick—both knees bleeding—and stormed home to the win in 15:07.3.

"Things always come up where you have to adjust and plan accordingly," he said. "But as long as you can stay calm and focused and know what goal you have, it's still easy to see what you have to do."

Kettle's win keyed a repeat team victory for Milford, which put five in the top 33. "Every minute of every day we prepare for this thing," said Kettle.

Brian Kettle beat TJ Carey to win in 2012. (Milford XC photo)

Michigan Int. Speedway, Brooklyn, Nov. 3
2012 BOYS DIVISION 1 TEAMS
1. Milford...83
2. Waterford Mott 167
3. Rockford..186
4. Romeo..189
5. Ann Arbor Pioneer 211
6. Saline...223
7. Pinckney..271
8. Dexter..286
9. Hartland...296
10. Traverse City Central 305
11. Northville..308
12. Port Huron Northern 344
13. Clarkston..361
14. Walled Lake Northern..........................372
15. Grand Blanc 374
16. Royal Oak..375
17. Saginaw Heritage 436
18. Salem...440
19. Grand Haven 468
20. Hudsonville..471
21. Grand Ledge..494
22. Grand Rapids Kenowa Hills 508
23. Livonia Stevenson...............................516
24. Portage Central 556
25. Wyandotte..563
26. Troy..577
27. Grosse Pointe South 591

28. Portage Northern 750

2012 BOYS DIVISION 1 INDIVIDUALS
1. Brian Kettle (Milford)11 .... 15:08
2. T.J. Carey (Lake Orion)12 .... 15:10
3. Nathan Burnand (Waterford Mott)12 .... 15:15
4. Cody Snavely (Milford)12 .... 15:17
5. Jeff Bajema (GR Kenowa Hills)12 .... 15:22
6. Costa Willets (Ann Arbor Pioneer)11 .... 15:23
7. Stephen Biebelhausen (Rochester Adams)1215:27
8. Dan Sims (Northville)11 .... 15:29
9. Ryan Robinson (Waterford Mott)10 .... 15:29
10. Ben Hill (Royal Oak)10 .... 15:34
11. Trevor Sharnas (Romeo)12 .... 15:35
12. Esrom Woldemichael (GR Northview)12 ..... 15:55
13. Max Benoit (Royal Oak)12 .... 15:36
14. Max Kryza (Fenton)12 .... 15:37
15. Galen Burrell (Ann Arbor Pioneer)12 .... 15:37
16. Nicholas Lanzetta (Detroit Catholic C)12 ..... 15:39
17. Grant Praschan (Saline)12 .... 15:41
18. Alec Torecki (Romeo)11 .... 15:41
19. Jason Saliga (Romeo)12 .... 15:42
20. Mickey Davey (Warren DeLaSalle)10 .... 15:42
21. Conrad Schultz (Woodhaven)12 .... 15:43
22. Austin Benoit (Rockford)12 .... 15:43
23. Nathan Megge (Grand Ledge)11 .... 15:44
24. Tyler Sanders (Pinckney)12 .... 15:44
25. Blake Pozolo (Rochester)11 .... 15:44
26. Jareb Duggan (Hartland)11 .... 15:44
27. Justin Pippel (Grand Haven)12 .... 15:44
28. Matt Thomas (Port Huron Northern)10 .... 15:45
29. Drew Woznick (Rockford)12 .... 15:45
30. Blake McComas (White Lake Lakeland)10.. 15:46
31. Chris Housel (Milford)12 .... 15:47
32. Wesley Sanders (Pinckney)12 .... 15:47
33. Matt Graves (Milford)12 .... 15:48
34. Anthony Berry (Traverse City Central)9 ..... 15:48
35. Matt Greve (Dexter)12 .... 15:50
36. Sean Pengelly (Hartford)12 .... 15:50
37. Tyler DeLange (Port Huron Northern)12 ..... 15:51
38. Anthony Lamus (Saline)12 .... 15:54
39. Kyle Dotterer (Traverse City Central)11 ..... 15:55
40. Connor Wuori (Portage Central)10 .... 15:54
42. Kevin Black (Milford)11 .... 15:55
46. Clinton Caddell (Milford)11 .... 16:00
51. Jeffery Field (Milford)11 .... 16:06

2013 D1 BOYS

Grant Fisher of Grand Blanc missed the state finals the previous year because he was also on the soccer team, which had its own state finals on the same day.

"It's good to be back," he said. He led through 2M in 9:49, then put the pressure on, leaving defending champ Brian Kettle behind with a fast final mile to take a 18-second win. Fisher, who lost the 1600 title in the spring by a mere 0.006, added, "That was definitely on my mind today, knowing that Brian can close at any time."

Fisher would win the Foot Locker Nationals in San Diego five weeks later, becoming the fifth Michigan boy to do so.

Milford scored its third straight win, joining the short list of teams that have done so: Jackson ('47-49), Lansing Eastern ('55-57) and Pinckney ('05-07).

Michigan Int. Speedway, Brooklyn, Nov. 2
2013 BOYS DIVISION 1 TEAMS
1. Milford 165
2. Waterford Mott 170
3. Traverse City Central 180
4. Saline 196
5. Northville 202
6. Saginaw Heritage 205
7. Ann Arbor Pioneer 248
8. Pinckney 260
9. Birmingham Seaholm 285
10. Oxford 295
11. Hartland 302
12. Rockford 336
13. Lake Orion 338
14. Romeo 360
15. Holly 376
16. Walled Lake Northern 380
17. Plymouth 387
18. Grandville 436
19. Grand Blanc 464
20. Traverse City West 470
21. East Kentwood 516
22. Wyandotte 542
23. Wayne Memorial 548
24. Hudsonville 552
25. St Clair Shores Lakeview 574
26. Warren DeLaSalle 590
27. Troy 647

2013 BOYS DIVISION 1 INDIVIDUALS
1. Grant Fisher (Grand Blanc)11 .... 15:14
2. Brian Kettle (Milford)12 .... 15:32
3. Ben Hill (Royal Oak)11 .... 15:42
4. Ryan Robinson (Waterford Mott)11 .... 15:43
5. Daniel Kroth (Okemos)12 .... 15:44
6. Kyle Dotterer (Traverse City Central)12 .... 15:44
7. Costa Willets (Ann Arbor Pioneer)12 .... 15:49
8. Mickey Davey (Warren DeLaSalle)11 .... 15:50
9. Calum Ahmed (Royal Oak)12 .... 15:53
10. Dan Sims (Northville)12 .... 15:53
11. Anthonhy Berry (Traverse City Central)10 ..... 15:54
12. Connor Wuori (Portahe Central)11 .... 15:55
13. Justine Kiprotich (East Kentwood)12 .... 15:56
14. Sam Albaugh (Waterford Mott)11 .... 15:56
15. Cam McAuliffe (Traverse City Central)11 .... 15:57
16. Logan Wetzel (Saline)11 .... 15:58
17. Kevin Hall (Saline)11 .... 15:58
18. Alec Toreki (Romeo)11 .... 15:58
19. Vincent Cantu (Holly)12 .... 15:59
20. Donavan Brazier (GR Kenowa Hills)11 .... 15:59
21. Nick Noles (Northville)11 .... 15:59
22. Brian Moore (Howell)11 .... 16:00
23. Zane Berlanga (Plymouth)12 .... 16:02
24. Matt Thomas (Port Huron Northern)11 .... 16:02
25. Dietrich Hittner (East Lansing)12 .... 16:02
26. Lucas Arrivo (Ann Arbor Pioneer)11 .... 16:02
27. Michael Buffin (Grand Ledge)12 .... 16:04
28. Mitchell Dennis (Walled Lake Western)12 .... 16:05
29. Enael Woldemichael (GR Northview)10 .... 16:07
30. John Penington (Bloomfield Hills Rice)11 ..... 16:07
31. Isaac Harding (Rockford)10 .... 16:10
32. Kunal Tangri (Troy)11 .... 16:12
33. Parker Eisengruber (Saginaw Heritage)11 .. 16:15
34. Kael Fineout (Okemos)11 .... 16:16
35. Kyle Repetto (Rochester)11 .... 16:16
36. Grant Colligan (Holt)12 .... 16:18
37. Jacob Lee (Fenton)10 .... 16:18
38. Jareb Duggan (Hartland)12 .... 16:19
39. Ethan Davenport (Saginaw Heritage)12 .... 16:21
40. Jordan Steiff (Ann Arbor Huron)12 .... 16:21
49. Jeffery Field (Milford)12 .... 16:24
54. Sean Noone (Milford)11 .... 16:26
61. Kevin Black (Milford)12 .... 16:27
113. Clinton Caddell (Milford)12 .... 16:49
155. Alex Krasuski (Milford)12 .... 17:04
169. Kevin Bradsher (Milford)11 .... 17:09

2014 D1 BOYS

Any hopes Grant Fisher might have had to challenge Dathan Ritzenhein's course record of 14:10.4 blew away with the strong wind that challenged everyone at MIS. "The wind was kind of eating me up on the second mile. There's a bit of a stretch where you go straight into it, so I attacked it. We didn't know what it was going to be like, so the attack of the wind was tougher than what we expected."

That middle mile broke the race open. Fisher hit 2M in 9:26—Ryan Robinson of Waterford Mott was 2nd in 9:48. Fisher cruised home the winner in an impressive 14:52.5. Saline's Logan Wetzel kicked best for the runner-up spot, nearly 200m behind.

The Stanford-bound Fisher would soon defend his Foot Locker title and the next spring become the first Michigan prep to break the 4-minute mile with his 3:59.38.

After 12 years away from the top Rockford roared back to a 6-point win in a tight team battle.

Grand Blanc's Grant Fisher went undefeated as a senior, winning his second national title. The next spring he became the first Michigan prep to break the 4-minute mile. (Pete Draugalis photo)

Michigan Int. Speedway, Brooklyn, Nov. 1
2014 BOYS DIVISION 1 TEAMS
1. Rockford 140
2. White Lake Lakeland 146
3. Waterford Mott 148
4. Northville 165
5. Saline 203
6. Traverse City Central 223
7. Walled Lake Central 239
8. Pinckney 243
9. Grand Blanc 265
10. Rochester 293
11. Holly 300
12. Traverse City West 312
13. Ann Arbor Skyline 349
14. Okemos 349
15. Novi 356
16. Port Huron Northern 381
17. Detroit Catholic Central 391
18. Clarkston 397
19. Lake Orion 415
20. Ann Arbor Pioneer 432
21. Portage Central 452
22. Grand Haven 534
23. Hudsonville 548
24. Temperance Bedford 586
25. Macomb L'Anse Creuse North 635
26. St Clair Shores Lakeview 730
27. Grosse Pointe North 828

2014 BOYS DIVISION 1 TEAMS
1. Grant Fisher (Grand Blanc)12 .... 14:53
2. Logan Wetzel (Saline)12 .... 15:20
3. Anthony Berry (Traverse City Central)11 .... 15:22
4. Isaac Harding (Rockford)11 .... 15:24
5. Ryan Robinson (Waterford Mott)12 .... 15:24
6. Donavan Brazier (GR Kenowa Hills)12 .... 15:26

7. Connor Wuori (Portage Central)12 .... 15:26
8. Jon Russell (Ann Arbor Skyline)12 .... 15:28
9. Chaz Jeffress (Salem)11 .... 15:30
10. Andrew Lorant (Lake Orion)11 .... 15:32
11. Kevin Hall (Saline)12 .... 15:36
12. Jacob Greer (Midland)12 .... 15:39
13. Joost Plaetinck (Novi)11 .... 15:40
14. Mitchell Day (Alpena)10 .... 15:41
15. Parker Eisengruber (Saginaw Heritage)12 ... 15:41
16. Cole Johnson (Rockford)9 .... 15:41
17. Matt Thomas (Port Huron Northern)12 ..... 15:42
18. Mickey Davey (Warren DeLaSalle)12 .... 15:43
19. Logan Kleam (Woodhaven)11 .... 15:44
20. Dominic Davis (Wyandott Roosevelt)12 .... 15:45
21. Adam Beck (Rochester Adams)12 .... 15:46
22. Joe Renner (Davison)12 .... 15:46
23. Jackson Grzymkowski (WL Lakeland)11 ... 15:46
24. Jacob Domagalski (Romeo)12 .... 15:46
25. Matthew Pahl (Plymouth)12 .... 15:46
26. Nick Noles (Northville)12 .... 15:47
27. Bradley Mallory (Port Huron Northern)12 ... 15:47
28. Kunal Tangri (Troy)12 .... 15:47
29. Brian Moore (Howell)12 .... 15:48
30. Isaac Harris (Pinckney)12 .... 15:49
31. Jacob Stanton (East Lansing)11 .... 15:50
32. Conor Naughton (Northville)11 .... 15:51
33. Nick Schmidt (Davison)12 .... 15:54
34. Nick Hirschenberger (Traverse City W)11 ... 15:55
35. Blake McComas (White Lake Lakeland)12 .. 15:55
36. Kyle Garbovits (White Lake Lakeland)11 ... 15:58
37. Lynus Zullo (Ann Arbor Huron)12 .... 16:00
38. Jason Ferrante (Northville)12 .... 16:00
39. Dilon Lemond (Holly)11 .... 16:02
40. Nate Frasier (Holly)12 .... 16:03
57. Paul Burke (Rockford)12 .... 16:14
58. Grayson Harding (Rockford)11 .... 16:14
102. Grant Gabriel (Rockford)11 .... 16:31
169. Colin Reichenbach (Rockford)12 .... 17:02
207. Kirk Dickson (Rockford)12 .... 17:23

2015 D1 BOYS

The team race was a nail-biter, with Rockford defending by a slim 2 points against Northville. Said senior Isaac Harding, who won the individual race, "The coach came in and told us the news; everyone went really crazy. When we won last year [by 6 points] I didn't think it could get any closer."

Added Harding, "I knew the best thing I could do for my team was to do the best that I could individually and place first."

Michigan Int. Speedway, Brooklyn, Nov. 7
2015 BOYS DIVISION 1 TEAMS
1. Rockford 99
2. Northville 101
3. Novi 177
4. White Lake Lakeland 190
5. Rochester Adams 215
6. Saline 238
7. Milford 249
8. Detroit Catholic Central 283
9. Fenton 294
10. Birmingham Seaholm 311
11. Ann Arbor Skyline 334
12. Lake Orion 343
13. Pinckney 344
14. Bay City Western 349
15. Dexter 359
16. Traverse City Central 360
17. Monroe 368
18. Traverse City West 378
19. Clarkston 425
20. Grand Haven 454
21. Saginaw Heritage 487
22. Caledonia 502
23. Portage Central 537
24. Utica 562
25. Temperance Bedford 658
26. Troy 760
27. Royal Oak 779

saac Harding sprints away from the field at the finish; it was the fifth time a Rockford boy won the title. (Pete Draugalis photo)

2015 BOYS DIVISION 1 INDIVIDUALS
1. Isaac Harding (Rockford)12 .... 15:11
2. Mitchell Day (Alpena)11 .... 15:14
3. Cole Johnson (Rockford)10 .... 15:15
4. Enael Woldemichael (GR Northview)12 ... 15:17
5. Anthony Berry (Traverse City Central)12 ... 15:21
6. Joost Plaetinck (Novi)12 .... 15:24
7. Logan Kleam (Woodhaven)12 .... 15:30
8. Riad Rababeh (Dearborn)11 .... 15:31
9. Tony Floyd (Livonia Franklin)12 .... 15:32
10. Jacob Stanton (East Lansing)12 .... 15:34
11. Nick Hirschenberger (Traverse City W)12 ... 15:38
12. Jackson Grzymkowski (WL Lakeland)12 ... 15:40
13. Drew Wenger (White Lake Lakeland)10 ... 15:42
14. Ben Cracraft (Northville)11 .... 15:43
15. Conor Naughton (Northville)12 .... 15:43
16. Chaz Jeffress (Salem)12 .... 15:44
17. John Petruno (Walled Lake Western)11 ... 15:46
18. Matt Schram (Rochester Adams)11 .... 15:47
19. Jacob Lee (Fenton)12 .... 15:47
20. Jack Bleibtrey (Walled Lake Western)12 ... 15:47
21. Andrew Bill (Berkley)12 .... 15:48
22. Tim Osborne (Brighton)12 .... 15:49
23. Dominic Dimambro (Fenton)11 .... 15:49
24. Jared Hill (Walled Lake Central)11 .... 15:50
25. Christian Hubaker (Grand Ledge)11 ...... 15:50
26. Andrew Bond (Fenton)11 .... 15:52
27. Gabriel Mudel (Novi)10 .... 15:54
28. Austin Wicker (Pinckney)12 .... 15:54
29. Anthony Giannobile (Ann Arbor Skyline)10 .. 15:55
30. Evan Meyer (East Lansing)10 .... 15:57
31. Gabe Hogan (Oxford)12 .... 15:58
32. Jack Nicholson (Grand Haven)10 .... 15:58
33. Jordan Bennett (Caledonia)11 .... 16:00
34. Grant Gabriel (Rockford)12 .... 16:01
35. Ryan Talbott (Pinckney)11 .... 16:01
36. Tristan Williams (Ann Arbor Skyline)9 ... 16:02
37. Jonathan Voth (Grand Blanc)12 .... 16:04
38. Jack Halpin (Birmingham Seaholm)12 ... 16:05
39. Grayson Harding (Rockford)12 .... 16:05
40. Dilon Lemond (Holly)12 .... 16:05
84. Matthew MacGregor (Rockford)12 .... 16:25
103. Julian Kipke (Rockford)11 .... 16:32
145. Taylor Mrozinski (Rockford)12 .... 16:50

2016 D1 BOYS

Dearborn's Riad Rababeh made his big move just past the 2M mark on the long, gradual downhill leading back to the MIS infield. Running even with Alpena's Mitchell Day and Rockford's Cole Johnson as they passed 2M in 9:41, Rababeh finished with a 16-second margin after blistering the long infield curve.

"I just didn't look back and I took a little bit of control of the race there."

White Lake Lakeland surprised many by pulling out a convincing 73-point win over Saline despite only being ranked No. 4 in the final coaches' poll of the season.

Michigan Int. Speedway, Brooklyn, Nov. 5
2016 BOYS DIVISION 1 TEAMS
1. White Lake Lakeland 125
2. Saline 198
3. Bloomfield Hills Brother Rice 220
4. Novi 225
5. Ann Arbor Pioneer 237
6. Milford 243
7. Northville 257
8. Caledonia 309
9. Saginaw Heritage 316
10. Birmingham Seaholm 319
11. Bay City Western 343
12. Alpena 348
13. Grand Haven 356
14. Rockford 358
15. Clarkston 360
16. Lake Orion 360
17. Livonia Stevenson 376
18. Portage Central 389
19. Okemos 422
20. Macomb Dakota 434
21. Traverse City West 448
22. Dexter 473
23. Walled Lake Central 481
24. Portage Northern 541
25. Grosse Pointe North 556
26. Brighton 585
27. Temperance Bedford 615
28. Grand Blanc 667

Riad Rababeh of Dearborn. (Pete Draugalis photo)

2016 BOYS DIVISION 1 INDIVIDUALS
1. Riad Rababeh (Dearborn)12 .... 15:25
2. Mitchell Day (Alpena)12 .... 15:41
3. Harrison Grzymkowski (WL Lakeland)10 ... 15:52
4. Michael Jarvis (Lake Orion)12 .... 15:53
5. Tyler McCartney (Grand Ledge)12 .... 15:53
6. Matt Schram (Rochester Adams)12 .... 15:55
7. Andrew Bond (Fenton)12 .... 15:55
8. Tristan Williams (Ann Arbor Skyline)10 ..... 15:56
9. Abdi Ahmed (Forest Hills Northern)11 ...... 15:56
10. Ethan Byrnes (Plymouth)11 .... 15:56
11. Ben Cracraft (Northville)12 .... 15:57
12. Aden Smith (Alpena)10 .... 15:57
13. Jack Nicholson (Grand Haven)11 .... 15:58
14. Steven Stine (Fraser)12 .... 15:58
15. Zac Clark (Canton)12 .... 15:59
16. Ty Buckley (Detroit Catholic Central)12 ... 16:00
17. Nick Foster (Ann Arbor Pioneer)10 .... 16:01
18. Carter Solomon (Plymouth)9 .... 16:01
19. David Mitter (Howell)12 .... 16:02
20. Harrison Steen (Roch H Stoney Creek)11 ... 16:03

21. Jordan Bennett (Caledonia)12 ..... 16:03
22. Josh Smith (Alpena)10 ..... 16:03
23. Evan Meyer (East Lansing)11 ..... 16:03
24. Ben Williams (Birmingham Seaholm)12 ..... 16:04
25. Gannon Foley (Portage Central)12 ..... 16:05
26. Aidan Carichner (Saline)12 ..... 16:08
27. Austin Remick (Rochester)11 ..... 16:08
28. Zachary Stewart (Brighton)9 ..... 16:09
29. Saano Murembya (Okemos)11 ..... 16:11
30. Cameron Cooper (Oak Park)12 ..... 16:11
31. Michael Fiore (Saginaw Heritage)11 ..... 16:12
32. Michael Tremonti (Bloomfield Hills Rice)11 . 16:13
33. Christian Hubaker (Grand Ledge)12 ..... 16:13
34. Matthew Parran (Monroe)11 ..... 16:14
35. Robbie Lohr (Traverse City West)11 ..... 16:15
36. Anthony DeKraker (Saline)11 ..... 16:16
37. Jack Wilson (Romeo)9 ..... 16:17
38. Jack Shelley (Dexter)12 ..... 16:18
39. Dayton Brown (Rockford)11 ..... 16:19
40. Zack Werth (White Lake Lakeland)12 ..... 16:19
44. Joel Woody (White Lake Lakeland)12 ..... 16:23
45. Drew Wenger (White Lake Lakeland)11 ..... 16:24
79. Angelo Savich (White Lake Lakeland)11 .... 16:43
142. Luke Moore (White Lake Lakeland)12 ..... 17:08
173. Karl Stroup (White Lake Lakeland)12 ..... 17:20

2017 D1 BOYS

Rockford's Cole Johnson had the worst of experiences the previous year, fading from the lead to last in the final mile of the muddy course. As a senior, he was set to reinvent his relationship with the MIS course, staying at the front of the race before falling to the blistering kick of Ann Arbor Pioneer's Nick Foster on the final stretch.

Foster was motivated by team. The No. 1-ranked Pioneers hoped to bring home another title for Don Sleeman in his fiftieth year of coaching. Recounted Foster, "Yeah, we said, 'Let's do it for him,' but he said, 'No, don't do it for me—do it for each other.' He's a great coach and we want to make him happy."

Even though Pioneer was the favorite, Plymouth made the race very tight, coming within 3 points at the end.

Michigan Int. Speedway, Brooklyn, Nov. 4
2017 BOYS DIVISION 1 TEAMS
1. Ann Arbor Pioneer 107
2. Plymouth 110
3. White Lake Lakeland 130
4. Romeo 142
5. Saline 246
6. Saginaw Heritage 263
7. Ann Arbor Skyline 267
8. Clarkston 304
9. Rockford 340
10. Grand Haven 341
11. Okemos 346
12. Bloomfield Hills Brother Rice 356
13. Milford 359
14. Traverse City West 374
15. Rochester Hills Stoney Creek 382
16. Novi 385
17. Brighton 405
18. East Grand Rapids 411
19. Fenton 420
20. Salem 437
21. Troy 460
22. Temperance Bedford 488
23. Traverse City Central 513
24. Grosse Pointe North 518
25. East Kentwood 547
26. Kalamazoo Central 553
27. Portage Central 651

Nick Foster (left), just before he unleashed a mighty kick for the win over Cole Johnson (right). (Pete Draugalis photo)

2017 BOYS DIVISION 1 INDIVIDUALS
1. Nick Foster (Ann Arbor Pioneer)11 ..... 15:17
2. Cole Johnson (Rockford)12 ..... 15:19
3. Harrison Grzymkowski (WL Lakeland)11 ..... 15:19
4. Paul McKinley (Okemos)12 ..... 15:24
5. Carter Solomon (Plymouth)10 ..... 15:25
6. Gabriel Mudel (Novi)12 ..... 15:27
7. Harrison Steen (Roch. H Stoney Creek)12 ..... 15:27
8. Drew Wenger (White Lake Lakeland)12 ..... 15:27
9. Jack Wilson (Romeo)10 ..... 15:30
10. George Nummer (Birmingham Seaholm)11 .15:36
11. Anthony Giannobile (Ann Arbor Skyline)12 ..15:40
12. Austin Remick (Rochester)12 ..... 15:41
13. Abdi Ahmed (Forest Hills Northern)12 ..... 15:42
14. Andrew Nolan (Lake Orion)11 ..... 15:42
15. Zachary Stewart (Brighton)10 ..... 15:42
16. Brendan Allen (Romeo)12 ..... 15:43
17. Nick Trevisan (Farmington)12 ..... 15:44
18. Ethan Byrnes (Plymouth)12 ..... 15:44
19. Jack Nicholson (Grand Heven)12 ..... 15:45
20. Sam Martens (Holland)11 ..... 15:46
21. Dayton Brown (Rockford)12 ..... 15:49
22. Aden Smith (Alpena)11 ..... 15:50
23. Joseph Tavalieri (Fraser)10 ..... 15:50
24. Morgan McGrew (Traverse City Central)12..15:51
25. Nicholas Couyoumjian (Northville)11 ..... 15:51
26. Michael Zedan (New Balt. Anchor Bay)12...15:53
27. Anthony DeKraker (Saline)12 ..... 15:55
28. Robbie Lohr (Traverse City West)12 ..... 15:56
29. Jakob Sayers (Birmingham Seaholm)11 ..... 15:58
30. Brendan Favazza (Clarkston)10 ..... 15:58
31. Aldo Pando-Girard (Ann Arbor Pioneer)12..16:00
32. Dominic Bruce (Oxford)12 ..... 16:06
33. Evan Meyer (East Lansing)12 ..... 16:08
34. Adugna Moritz (Holt)9 ..... 16:09
35. Alec Miracle (Bloomfield Hills Rice)11 ..... 16:09
36. William Westveer (East Kentwood)12 ..... 16:10
37. Tristan Williams (Ann Arbor Skyline)11 ..... 16:11
38. Brandon Boyd (Plymouth)11 ..... 16:11
39. Mohammed Munassar (Dearborn E Ford)12 16:11
40. John Florence (Ann Arbor Pioneer)11 ..... 16:12
41. Jack Wallace (Ann Arbor Pioneer)12 ..... 16:12
51. Philip Valtadoros (Ann Arbor Pioneer)12 ..... 16:16
89. Ethan Mielock (Ann Arbor Pioneer)11 ..... 16:30
94. Michael Shkolnik (Ann Arbor Pioneer)12 ..... 16:33

2018 D1 BOYS

Nick Foster defended his title with another searing finish, showing the acceleration that would make him a 4:03.11 miler in the spring. With Plymouth's Carter Solomon alongside on the long final curve, Foster sprinted at the 3M mark and finished six seconds ahead.

Solomon had plenty to celebrated, as he and his teammates won the first title ever for Plymouth and coach Jon Mikosz.

"I'm so proud of those guys after last year being runner-up," said Mikosz. "To have the pressure on them all year and to be able to come back and pull it off is amazing."

The Wildcats needed everything they had, as Walled Lake Central was only 5 points behind at the finish.

Michigan Int. Speedway, Brooklyn, Nov. 3
Mostly cloudy, muddy, 40°, breezy.
2018 BOYS DIVISION 1 TEAMS
1. Plymouth 122
2. Walled Lake Central 127
3. Dexter 154
4. Clarkston 164
5. Ann Arbor Skyline 197
6. Ann Arbor Pioneer 236
7. Alpena 246
8. Milford 267
9. Saline 282
10. Brighton 295
11. Fenton 302
12. Grosse Pointe North 311
13. Hudsonville 316
14. Romeo 364
15. Northville 372
16. Rochester Hills Stoney Creek 390
17. Caledonia 429
18. Saginaw Heritage 447
19. Salem 457
20. Bloomfield Hills Brother Rice 475
21. Grand Haven 477
22. Traverse City Central 491
23. Royal Oak 507
24. Rockford 521
25. Portage Northern 555
26. Forest Hills Central 569
27. Temperance Bedford 684

2018 BOYS DIVISION 1 INDIVIDUALS
1. Nick Foster (Ann Arbor Pioneer)12 ..... 15:13
2. Carter Solomon (Plymouth)11 ..... 15:19
3. Harrison Grzymkowski (WL Lakeland)12 ..... 15:33
4. Zachary Stewart (Brighton)11 ..... 15:37
5. Brendan Favazza (Clarkston)11 ..... 15:40
6. Evan White (Milford)12 ..... 15:47
7. Alex Penski (Holt)11 ..... 15:49
8. Joey Tavalieri (Fraser)11 ..... 15:51
9. Alec Miracle (Bloomfield H Brother Rice)12 ..... 15:52
10. Sam Martens (Holland)12 ..... 15:53
11. Jack Wilson (Romeo)11 ..... 15:54
12. Tyler Pritchett (Midland)11 ..... 15:55
13. Andrew Nolan (Lake Orion)11 ..... 15:55
14. Drew Seabase (Alpena)10 ..... 15:56
15. Patrick Byrnes (Plymouth)10 ..... 15:57
16. Owen Huard (Dexter)11 ..... 15:57
17. Peter Baracco (Farmington)9 ..... 15:57
18. Jack Spamer (Brighton)11 ..... 15:57
19. Adugna Moritz (Holt)10 ..... 15:59
20. Luke Perelli (Detroit Catholic Central)11 ..... 16:00
21. Aden Smith (Alpena)12 ..... 16:01
22. Nathan Larson (Dexter)11 ..... 16:06
23. Adam Jesse (Fenton)11 ..... 16:08
24. Preston Navarre (Grosse Pointe North)10 ..16:09
25. Justin Hill (Walled Lake Central)11 ..... 16:10
26. Shawn Slater (Clarkston)12 ..... 16:10
27. Riley Hough (Hartland)9 ..... 16:11
28. Josh Smith (Alpena)12 ..... 16:11
29. Simon Pfeiffer (Saline)12 ..... 16:11
30. Nicholas Couyoumjian (Northville)12 ..... 16:12
31. George Nummer (Birmingham Seaholm)12.16:12
32. William Minnette (Saline)11 ..... 16:13
33. Brandon Boyd (Plymouth)12 ..... 16:14
34. Chris Allen (Walled Lake Central)12 ..... 16:15
35. Luke Haran (Salem)12 ..... 16:20
36. Hobbs Kessler (Ann Arbor Skyline)10 ..... 16:20
37. Jakob Sayers (Birmingham Seaholm)12 ..... 16:12
38. Mark Sprague (Clarkston)12 ..... 16:23
39. Thomas Young (Ann Arbor Skyline)11 ..... 16:25

40. Akshay Reddy (Walled Lake Central)11 .... 16:25
60. Jarrett Warner (Plymouth)12 .... 16:32
63. Tyler Mussen (Plymouth)11 .... 16:35
181. Basil Nyed (Plymouth)12 .... 17:30
218. Conner Davis (Plymouth)10 .... 18:02

Carter Solomon of Plymouth.

2019 D1 BOYS

Not since 1995 had Brighton ascended to the top of the podium. This year it was a special feat as any of several teams seemed to be in position to pull off the win. With seniors Jack Spamer and Zach Stewart pulling off a 3-4 finish, the Bulldogs had the edge.

Said Stewart, "I'd say coming into this we knew we had a really good shot. We knew we did last year and it didn't work out so well, but this year I think coming into it we just had to do what we needed to like it was any other meet."

Carter Solomon moved up a place to first. The Plymouth senior said, "I know those guys were coming for me. In my head, I was the third guy coming into this race. Those guys were legit. I wanted to race them and it worked out."

The depth of the field was underlined four weeks later when a record seven boys from Michigan finished in the top nine at the Foot Locker regionals and qualified for nationals. The previous high had been four.

Michigan Int. Speedway, Brooklyn, Nov. 2
2019 BOYS DIVISION 1 TEAMS
1. Brighton 138
2. Dexter 155
3. Clarkston 189
4. Saline 192
5. Traverse City Central 208
6. Rochester Hills Stoney Creek 216
7. Romeo 218
8. Ann Arbor Pioneer 239
9. Detroit Catholic Central 261
10. Caledonia 288
11. Fenton 304
12. Plymouth 309
13. Ann Arbor Skyline 329
14. Hartland 339
15. Zeeland West 355
16. Walled Lake Central 381
17. Cedar Springs 397
18. Rockford 423
19. Northville 477
20. Davison 499
21. Port Huron Northern 528
22. Dearborn 534
23. Royal Oak 537
24. Saginaw Heritage 547
25. Grandville 581
26. Troy 703
27. Warren DeLaSalle 731

2019 BOYS DIVISION 1 INDIVIDUALS
1. Carter Solomon (Plymouth)12 .... 15:02
2. Brendan Favazza (Clarkston)12 .... 15:06
3. Jack Spamer (Brighton)12 .... 15:18
4. Zach Stewart (Brighton)12 .... 15:31
5. Patrick Byrnes (Plymouth)11 .... 15:34
6. Hobbs Kessler (Ann Arbor Skyline)11 .... 15:37
7. Riley Hough (Hartland)10 .... 15:37
8. Jack Wilson (Romeo)12 .... 15:46
9. Will Minnette (Saline)12 .... 15:46
10. Luke Perelli (Detroit Catholic Central)12 ...... 15:48
11. Andrew Nolan (Lake Orion)12 .... 15:49
12. Connor Vachon (Jenison)11 .... 15:56
13. Jason Millis (Davison)12 .... 15:56
14. Kazuma Bowring (Milford)11 .... 15:56
15. Andrew Lane (East Lansing)12 .... 15:57
16. Ellis Mason (Greenville)12 .... 15:57
17. Drew Seabase (Traverse City Central)11 .... 15:57
18. Justin Hill (Walled Lake Central)12 .... 15:57
19. Peter Baracco (Farmington)10 .... 15:57
20. Gavin White (Pinckney)11 .... 15:59
21. Jozef Meyers (Kalamazoo Norrix)12 .... 15:59
22. Matt Whyte (Novi)12 .... 15:59
23. Preston Navarre (Grosse Pointe North)11 ... 16:00
24. Adam Jesse (Fenton)12 .... 16:00
25. Ethan Senti (Zeeland West)12 .... 16:01
26. Nathan Sesti (Clarkston)12 .... 16:03
27. Henry Monet Sano (Ann Arbor Pioneer)10 .. 16:03
28. Owen Huard (Dexter)12 .... 16:04
29. Nathan Larson (Dexter)12 .... 16:05
30. Tyler Mussen (Plymouth)12 .... 16:05
31. Scott Spaanstra (Brighton)12 .... 16:06
32. Jude Parks (Rockford)11 .... 16:07
33. Jack Kelke (Romeo)10 .... 16:07
34. Adugna Moritz (Holt)11 .... 16:09
35. Luke Venhuizen (Traverse City Central)10 .. 16:11
36. Charlie Frank (Dearborn)11 .... 16:11
37. Corey Bowers (Cedar Springs)11 .... 16:12
38. Caleb Jarema (Pinckney)10 .... 16:13
39. William Buller (Dexter)12 .... 16:14
40. Zachary Gerber (Traverse City Central)12 .. 16:14
47. Evan Ross (Brighton)10 .... 16:18
115. Andrew Hanna (Brighton)12 .... 16:46
149. Dan Campbell (Brighton)12 .... 17:01
189. Brady Matuszewski (Brighton)9 .... 17:20

CLASS A/D1 STATISTICS

TOP 25 CLOCKINGS AT MIS
14:11 Dathan Ritzenhein (Rockford)12 2000
14:52 Jason Hartmann (Rockford)12 1998
14:53 Grant Fisher (Grand Blanc)12 2014
14:55 Dustin Voss (Saline)12 2003
15:02 Carter Solomon (Plymouth)12 2019
15:06   D. Ritzenhein (Rockford)11 1999
15:06 Chris Toloff (Novi)12 2000
15:06 Brendan Favazza (Clarkston)12 2019
15:07 Tim Moore (Novi)11 2000
15:08 Frank Tinney (Ann Arbor Huron)12 2000
15:08 Brian Kettle (Milford)12 2000
15:10 Justin Switzer (Waterford Kettering)11 .. 2003
15:10 T.J. Carey (Lake Orion)12 2012
15:11 Isaac Harding (Rockford)12 2015
15:12   D. Ritzenhein (Rockford)10 1998
15:12   T. Moore (Novi)12 2001
15:13 Nick Foster (Ann Arbor Pioneer)12 2018
15:14 Scott Albaugh (Waterford Mott)12 2010
15:14   G. Fisher (Grand Blanc)11 2013
15:14 Mitchell Day (Alpena)11 2015
15:15 Neal Naughton (Walled Lk Western)12 .. 2003
15:15 Nathan Burnand (Waterford Mott)12 2012
15:15 Cole Johnson (Rockford)10 2015
15:16 Pat Klein (White Lake Lakeland)12 2000
15:16 Austin Whitelaw (Monroe)12 2010

BIGGEST WINNING MARGINS
60c   Leroy Potter/Arthur Van Mere 1924
56   Abdul Alzindani/Kevin Foltz .... 1995 I
26.7 Grant Fisher/Logan Wetzel 2014
26.6 Doug Tolson/Carl Allen 1979
24.3 Tim Moore/Jake Hammerle 2001

SMALLEST WINNING MARGINS
0.0   Andy Ketch/Joe Mihalic .... 1983 T
0.0   Jason Hartmann/Jordan Desilets 1997
0   Tom Florida/Norm Shaughnessy .... 1961 I
0   Forrest Jennings/Al Ruffner 1966
0.2   Keith Young/Ed Grabowski .... 1973 T
0.35 Brian Hyde/Che Moya .... 1989 I
0.5   Mark Mesler/Terry Doherty .... 1977 T
0.5   Bill Agre/Tom Goretzka 1946

LOWEST WINNING SCORES
25   Kalamazoo Central 1927
27   Ann Arbor 1922
27   Pinckney 2006
33   Kalamazoo Central 1943
36   Kalamazoo Central 1925
37   Ann Arbor 1924
37   Flint Central 1939
39   Monroe 1988
40   Kalamazoo Central 1950a
41   Birmingham Seaholm 1963

HIGHEST WINNING SCORES
186   Detroit Catholic Central 2001
173   Utica Eisenhower 1985
165   Milford 2013
150   Swartz Creek 1986
146   Pinckney 2005
144   White Lake Lakeland 1991
143   Grand Blanc 1979
141   Ypsilanti 1960
140   Rockford 2014
138   Detroit Catholic Central 1984
138   Brighton 2019

CLOSEST TEAM FINISH
0   Grand Rapids South/Kalamazoo Cent .. 1930
0   Lincoln Park/Royal Oak 1944
1   Jackson/Lansing Eastern 1934
1   Lansing Central/Kalamazoo Central 1936
2   Grosse Pointe North/Ann Arbor Pioneer 1973
2   Rockford/Milford 2002
2   Rockford/Northville 2015

BIGGEST WINNING TEAM MARGIN
129   East Lansing/Royal Oak Kimball 1967
118   Detroit Catholic Central/Grand Blanc 1983
113   Pinckney/Novi 2006
87   Grand Rapids Union/Pontiac 1952
84   Grand Rapids Union/Jackson 1953
84   Milford/Waterford Mott 2012

BOYS CLASS B / DIVISION 2

Dearborn won the first Class B state title. In front, from left: James McLellan, Eric Haglethorn, coach Leith Wetzel, Fred Lamke, Jack Calder. In back:: Spencer Wilkie, Willard Walker, Kenneth Hoganson, Robert Zahnow. Not pictured: Howard Purdy.

1927 CLASS B BOYS

This marked the first year that the races had to be separated by classes. Coach Leith Wetzel guided Dearborn to a 35-point win. Jimmie Crummey led the entire race until the final straightaway on the track, when Wyandotte's Earl Sonnenberg kicked past him for an 8-yard win.

Ypsilanti, Nov. 11 □
1927 BOYS CLASS B TEAMS
1. Dearborn 64
2. Ypsilanti Central 99
3. Royal Oak 114
4. Wyandotte 119
5. Detroit Holy Redeemer 125
6. Ferndale 136
7. Birmingham 155
NS (incomplete teams)—Clarksville, Grand Blanc, Iron Mountain, Kingsford, River Rouge, Sand Creek, Sibley, South Lake.

1927 BOYS CLASS B INDIVIDUALS
1. Earl Sonnenberg (Wyandotte)10 .... 11:40
2. Jimmie Crummey (Iron Mountain)11 ...... 11:42
3. Brown (Ferndale) 11:48
4. Griffith (Sand Creek) 11:53
5. Marcellus Barlage (Detroit Holy Redeemer)10 ... 11:58
6. Oliver Cejka (Kingsford) 12:02
7. James McClellan (Dearborn)10 .... 12:09
8. Cavel (Royal Oak) 12:11
9. Willard Walker (Dearborn)11 .... 12:17
10. Howard Purdy (Dearborn) 12:24
11. Mason (Royal Oak) 12:30
12. Parish (Ypsilanti) 12:32
13. Myhrs (Birmingham) 12:34
14. Crowley (Detroit Holy Redeemer) 12:37
15. Mason (South Lake) 13:10
16. Hubbard (Ypsilanti) 13:12
17. Walcott (Royal Oak) 13:18
18. Eric Haglethorn (Dearborn) 13:19
19. Williams (Ferndale) 13:23
20. Kenneth Hoganson (Dearborn) 14:12
21. Peters (Ypsilanti) .... nt
22. Minoch (Grand Blanc) .... nt
23. H. Gunliff (Wyandotte) .... nt
24. Richards (Ypsilanti) .... nt
25. Fred Lamke (Dearborn) .... nt
26. Cazier (Ypsilanti) .... nt
27. A. Gunliff (Wyandotte) .... nt
28. Kline (Grand Blanc) .... nt
29. Kuhn (Detroit Holy Redeemer) .... nt
30. Wimborn (Birmingham) .... nt

1928 CLASS B BOYS

Running on a "snow-clad pathway," Dearborn successfully defended its B title, this time by a margin of 38 points over Royal Oak. Marcellus Barrage defeated Wyandotte's defender, Earl Sonnenberg, by a "comfortable margin."

Ypsilanti, Nov. 10 □
1928 BOYS CLASS B TEAMS
1. Dearborn 62
2. Royal Oak 100
3. Wyandotte 116
4. Three Rivers 121
5. Ferndale 122
6. Birmingham 132
7. Detroit Holy Redeemer 145
8. Monroe 162
9. Dearborn Fordson 196
10. Ypsilanti Central 214

1928 BOYS CLASS B INDIVIDUALS
1. Marcellus Barlage (Detroit Holy Redeemer)11 .... 10:46
2. Earl Sonnenberg (Wyandotte)11 .... nt
3. Carr (Wyandotte) .... nt
4. James McClellen (Dearborn)11 .... nt
5. Willard Walker (Dearborn)12 .... nt

1929 CLASS B BOYS

James McClellan clipped 9 seconds off the meet record to help make it three in a row for Dearborn. Earl Sonnenberg of Wyandotte moved up to Class A where he was victorious.

Ypsilanti, Nov. 9 □
1929 BOYS CLASS B TEAMS
1. Dearborn 29
=2. Monroe 52
=2. Mt Clemens 52
4. Dearborn Fordson 108
5. Three Rivers 114
(Iron Mountain was listed as an entry also)

1929 BOYS CLASS B INDIVIDUALS
1. James McClellan (Dearborn)12 .... 10:37
2. Cleveland Hayes (Dearborn)11 .... 10:50
3. Booth (Mt Clemens) 10:51
4. Teil (Monroe) 10:55
5. Eric Hagelthorne (Dearborn)11 .... 11:01
6. Kuzwski (Monroe) 11:02
7. Kenneth Emery (Dearborn)11 .... 11:06
8. Tricoff (Dearborn Fordson) 11:10
9. Zimmerman (Monroe) 11:19
10. Lemke (Mt Clemens) 11:20
11. Hallem (Mt Clemens) .... nt
12. Hallis (Mt Clemens) .... nt
13. Hicks (Three Rivers) .... nt
14. Bernard McGuire (Dearborn) .... nt
15. Ruick (Monroe) .... nt
16. Lange (Mt Clemens) .... nt
17. Rocher (Mt Clemens) .... nt
18. Dieger (Monroe) .... nt
19. Wishowski (Midland) .... nt
20. Philip Newell (Dearborn)12 .... nt
21. (Dearborn Fordson) .... nt
22. (Dearborn Fordson) .... nt
23. (Three Rivers) .... nt
24. (Three Rivers) .... nt
26. (Three Rivers) .... nt

27. (Three Rivers) ....nt
28. (Dearborn Fordson) ....nt
29. (Dearborn Fordson) ....nt

1930 CLASS B BOYS

The Great Depression had an impact, with only two schools sending full teams to the state finals. Dearborn ran its streak to four straight. Monroe, runner-up the year before, had moved to Class A, along with Mount Clemens and Dearborn Fordson.

The Class B size requirements was that a school had to have an enrollment of 300-699.

Ypsilanti, Nov. 8 ☐
1930 BOYS CLASS B TEAMS
1. Dearborn 30
2. Three Rivers 57
NS (partial teams)—Howell, Rochester, Sault Ste Marie

1930 BOYS CLASS B INDIVIDUALS
1. Eric Hagelthorne (Dearborn)12 ....10:41
2. Robert Loughead (Sault Ste Marie)11 .....10:44
3. Perkins (Howell) 10:55
4. Hayes (Dearborn) 11:05
5. Emery (Dearborn) 11:06
6. Crocker (Rochester) 11:13
7. LeLao (Rochester) 11:15
8. Bingamen (Three Rivers) 11:35
9. Dodd (Dearborn) 11:41
10. Kemmerling (Three Rivers) 11:43
11. (Dearborn) ....nt
12. (Three Rivers) ....nt
13. (Three Rivers) ....nt
14. (Three Rivers) ....nt

1931 CLASS B BOYS

Robert Loughead of Sault Ste Marie captured the Class B crown and equalled the fastest time ever on the course. That helped the Soo team (1-9-10-12-23) take the win and break Dearborn's four-year hold on the trophy. Dearborn would have to wait 57 years before getting it back.

Ypsilanti, Nov. 7 ☐
1931 BOYS CLASS B TEAMS
1. Sault Ste Marie 55
2. South Haven 59
3. Niles 73
4. River Rouge 100
5. Dearborn 116
NS (partial team)—Birmingham, Rochester, Wayne

1931 BOYS CLASS B INDIVIDUALS
1. Robert Loughead (Sault Ste Marie)12 ....10:23
2. Claire Whitmore (Niles)12 ....nt
3. Hinz (South Haven) ....nt
4. Delao (Rochester) ....nt
5. Darking (South Haven) ....nt
6. Owens (Birmingham) ....nt
7. Gordon Sanderson (Wayne) ....nt
8. George Cronin (Niles) ....nt
9. Nash (Sault Ste Marie) ....nt
10. Cappricicao (Sault Ste Marie) ....nt
11. (South Haven) ....nt
12. Nelson (Sault Ste Marie) ....nt
13. (Dearborn) ....nt
14. (River Rouge) ....nt
15. (Dearborn) ....nt
16. (River Rouge) ....nt
17. (River Rouge) ....nt
18. (Niles) ....nt
19. (South Haven) ....nt
20. (Niles) ....nt
21. (South Haven) ....nt
22. ? ....nt
23. Graham (Sault Ste Marie) ....nt
24. ? ....nt

25. (Niles) ....nt
26. (River Rouge) ....nt
27. (River Rouge) ....nt
28. (Dearborn) ....nt
29. (Dearborn) ....nt
30. ? ....nt

1932 CLASS B BOYS

No state final was held because of the impact of the Great Depression, but three regionals were held around the state. Lloyd Jaroch's time in Kalamazoo, 10:31.3, was a new course record, beating Claire Whitmore's 10:54.5 from the previous year. The local paper described the course as having "fences and steep, slippery hills." Jaroch led from the start.

Eastern Regional, Ypsilanti, Nov. 1 ☐
1932 BOYS CLASS B TEAMS
1. Wayne 51
2. Dearborn 53
3. Rochester 54
4. Howell 103
5. River Rouge 110
6. Birmingham 112

1932 BOYS CLASS B INDIVIDUALS
1. Gordon Sanderson (Wayne) ....nt
5. (Wayne) ....nt
6. Schrepfer (Howell) ....nt
9. (Wayne) ....nt
13. (Wayne) ....nt
20. Steinacker (Howell) ....nt
21. Keeney (Howell) ....nt
23. (Wayne) ....nt
27. Hausheer (Howell) ....nt
29. Gates (Howell) ....nt

Western Regional, Kalamazoo, Nov. 5 ☐
1932 BOYS CLASS B TEAMS
1. Niles 26
2. South Haven 36
3. Three Rivers 58

1932 BOYS CLASS B INDIVIDUALS
1. Lloyd Jaroch (Niles)10 ....10:32
2. George Rathburn (Niles) ....nt
3. Hess (South Haven) ....nt
4. Thorn (Three Rivers) ....nt
5. Grimes (Niles) ....nt
6. Crawford (South Haven) ....nt
7. Harger (Niles) ....nt
8. Nordhoff (South Haven) ....nt
9. Dundee (South Haven) ....nt
10. Ward (South Haven) ....nt

UP Regional, Sault Ste Marie, Oct. 29 ☐
1932 BOYS CLASS B TEAMS
1. Sault Ste Marie 15
(only team entered)

1932 BOYS CLASS B INDIVIDUALS
1. Robert Loughead (Sault Ste Marie) 10:54
2. John Capricioso (Sault Ste Marie) 10:54
3. Garfield Thornsen (Sault Ste Marie) ....nt
4. Paul Miller (Sault Ste Marie) ....nt
5. Lawrence DeLucas (Sault Ste Marie) ....nt

1933 CLASS B BOYS

The state finals remained in mothballs and for a second year the runners had to console themselves with regional championships. At Kalamazoo, on the course of Western State Normal School (now Western Michigan), Ford Hess, the only non-Niles runner, led the entire way until they hit the track at the end, where the two Niles runners outsprinted the combo runner/football player.

In the Eastern Regional, Wayne's Gordon Sanderson defended his crown.

There was also a regional October 21 at Escanaba for which results are missing.

Eastern Regional, Ypsilanti, Nov. 4 ☐
1933 BOYS CLASS B TEAMS
1. Ecorse 43
2. Dearborn 50
3. Wayne 80
4. River Rouge 107
5. Howell 109
6. Rochester 130
7. Plymouth 162

1933 BOYS CLASS B INDIVIDUALS
1. Gordon Sanderson (Wayne) 10:49
2. Schrepfer (Howell) ....nt
3. Taylor (Ecorse) ....nt

Western Regional, Kalamazoo, Nov. 4 ☐
1933 BOYS CLASS B TEAMS
1. Niles 15
(only complete team)

1933 BOYS CLASS B INDIVIDUALS
1. George Rathburn (Niles)11 ....10:45
2. Franklin Grimes (Niles) ....nt
3. Ford Hess (South Haven)10 ....nt

George Grimes led Niles to victory in 1934 and 1935.

1934 CLASS B BOYS

Two weeks earlier, in a dual against Elkhart, Indiana, George Grimes presaged his win here with a trouncing of his teammate George Rathburn, running 10:13.9 to beat him by a "half city block." Rathburn had set the previous course record of 10:17 in 1932.

Ypsilanti, Nov. 3 ☐
1934 BOYS CLASS B TEAMS
1. Niles 26
2. Dearborn 43
3. Wayne 78

4. Ecorse 92
5. Ypsilanti 93

1934 BOYS CLASS B INDIVIDUALS
1. George Grimes (Niles) 10:34
2. George Rathburn (Niles)12 .... nt
3. K. Metzger (Niles) .... nt
4. Taylor (Ecorse) .... nt
5. Haynes (Dearborn) .... nt
6. Lee Thornton (Niles) .... nt
7. Bingham (Dearborn) .... nt
8. Bird (Dearborn) .... nt
9. Smith (Wayne) .... nt
10. Donaldson (Dearborn) .... nt

1935 CLASS B BOYS

George Grimes busted his own course record from the previous year, as Niles won its fourth straight (counting the regional wins of 1932-33). Only 24 runners participated.

Ypsilanti, Nov. 2 ☐
1935 BOYS CLASS B TEAMS
1. Niles 39
2. Dearborn 52
3. Ypsilanti 57
4. Wayne 90
5. Mt Clemens 92

1935 BOYS CLASS B INDIVIDUALS
1. George Grimes (Niles) 10:31
2. Keith Metzger (Niles) 10:37
3. H. Evans (Dearborn) .... nt
4. O. Hughes (Dearborn) .... nt
5. E. Herbst (Ypsilanti)12 .... nt
6. Martin Clapp (Niles) 11:16
7. R. Liddell (Dearborn) .... nt
8. Robert Lee (Ypsilanti)11 .... nt
9. C. Smith (Wayne) .... nt
10. Dick Crippen (Niles)10 .... 11:29
20. Joe Orias (Niles) .... nt

1936 CLASS B BOYS

Coach Joe Whitwam's Niles squad won with a dazzling record of 21 points; no team in that class has scored fewer since. First-year runner Phyl Drake won in 11:05.
Regionals were held in Dearborn, Escanaba and Kalamazoo. The UP race was held at halftime of the Escanaba-Iron Mountain football game. However, because of the small participation numbers at the previous year's finals, all regional participants were allowed to run at the state finals.

Ypsilanti, Nov. 7 ☐
1936 BOYS CLASS B TEAMS
1. Niles 21
2. Ypsilanti 49
3. Wayne 56
4. Plymouth 80

1936 BOYS CLASS B INDIVIDUALS
1. Phyl Drake (Niles)12 .... 11:05
2. Ed Foernier (Wayne) .... nt
3. Howard Pugh (Niles) .... nt
4. Jack Schick (Niles) .... nt
5. Jack Crawford (Ypsilanti)11 .... nt
6. Pascal Carr (Niles)11 .... nt
7. Larry Mathews (Niles) .... nt
8. Bob Borusch (Ypsilanti)11 .... nt
9. Henry Sutzer (Wayne) .... nt
10. Bill Tait (Ypsilanti)12 .... nt
11. Dick Crippen (Niles)11 .... nt

1937 CLASS B BOYS

Regional participation was required to compete at the state finals (unlike in Class A), but all teams were advanced.

Iron Mountain coach Dick Chard thought his runners were good enough to challenge the state's best. They were, triumphing by 6 points. After the meet they watched Michigan football beat Chicago by a point, then they rode the train to Chicago, returning home to the far north at 1:30 a.m. on Monday.
Albert Olds and his teammate Gerald Nelson finished with a huge 200-yard lead over the 34-runner field. All of the Mountaineers were underclassmen.

Ypsilanti, Nov. 6 ☐
1937 BOYS CLASS B TEAMS
1. Iron Mountain 36
2. Wayne 43
3. Niles 55
4. Ypsilanti 76

1937 BOYS CLASS B INDIVIDUALS
1. Albert Olds (Iron Mountain)11 .... 10:46
2. Gerald Nelson (Iron Mountain)10 .... 10:47
3. Robert Petro (Niles) 11:15
4. Bob Campbell (Ypsilanti)12 .... 11:16
9. Orville Osterberg (Iron Mountain)11 .... nt
10. Pascal Carr (Niles)12 .... nt
11. Fred Collick (Iron Mountain)11 .... nt
12. Dick Crippen (Niles)12 .... nt
13. Stevo Faccin (Iron Mountain)10 .... nt
14. Frank Petruska (Niles) .... nt
16. Robert VanWagoner (Niles) .... nt
21. Howard Pugh (Niles) .... nt

Dick Chard was the last UP coach to bring his teams below the bridge for the finals. His Iron Mountain squads won Class B in 1937 & 1938.

1938 CLASS B BOYS

Coach Dick Chard's Iron Mountain squad won on a windy day by putting five boys across the line in the top 10. Albert Olds perhaps lost his title when Clarence Snyder of Niles accidentally stepped on his heel and popped his shoe off with 100 yards to go. Olds stopped, tried to put it back on, and finally sprinted in holding the shoe. Snyder crossed the line in 11:01.4.
Once again, all teams advanced from regionals.

Ypsilanti, Nov. 5 ☐
1938 BOYS CLASS B TEAMS
1. Iron Mountain 33
2. Niles 42
3. Ypsilanti 85
4. Charlotte 86
5. Wayne 90

1938 BOYS CLASS B INDIVIDUALS
1. Clarence Snyder (Niles) 11:02
2. Albert Olds (Iron Mountain)12 .... nt
3. Love (Charlotte) .... nt
4. Kenneth Alquist (Iron Mountain) .... nt
6. Frank Petruska (Niles) .... nt
7. Robert Petro (Niles) .... nt
8. Fred Collick (Iron Mountain) .... nt
9. Richard Vicklund (Iron Mountain) .... nt
10. Orville Osterberg (Iron Mountain) .... nt
11. Art Blanchard (Ypsilanti)11 .... nt
12. Earl Koontz (Niles) .... nt
14. Art Lee (Ypsilanti)11 .... nt
16. Herbert White (Niles) .... nt
18. Ed Ring (Ypsilanti)12 .... nt
19. Clayton Williams (Niles) .... nt
21. Fred Wadke (Ypsilanti)12 .... nt
24. Tom Brooks (Ypsilanti)12 .... nt
27. Don Rust (Ypsilanti)12 .... nt
28. Russell Lyke (Ypsilanti)11 .... nt

1939 CLASS B BOYS

Ypsilanti's Art Lee led most of the way but ended up 4th after the sprinting was done. The race was held in "ideal" conditions. Clarence Snyder of Niles defended his title in 10:43.8 and brought his team back to the top after two years away.

Ypsilanti, Nov. 4 ☐
1939 BOYS CLASS B TEAMS
1. Niles 22
2. Iron Mountain 59
3. Wayne 70
4. Ypsilanti 80

1939 BOYS CLASS B INDIVIDUALS
1. Clarence Snyder (Niles) 10:44
2. Wallace Newlin (Wayne) 10:59
3. McCarthy (Niles) 11:11
4. Art Lee (Ypsilanti)12 .... 11:12
5. Glen Van Wagoner (Niles) 11:20
6. Robert Petro (Niles) 11:21
7. Earl Koontz (Niles) 11:22
8. Kenneth Alquist (Iron Mountain) 11:24
9. Richard Vickland (Iron Mountain) 11:26
10. Dick Petro (Niles) 11:27
11. (Iron Mountain) .... nt
12. John Lipp (Niles) .... nt
18. (Iron Mountain) .... nt

1940 CLASS B BOYS

Charlotte, coached by Kenneth Brown, had lost to Niles at the regional meet by 6 points, but turned it around at the state finals, winning by 16.

Ypsilanti, Nov. 2 ☐
1940 BOYS CLASS B TEAMS
1. Charlotte 53
2. Niles 69
3. Van Dyke 77
4. Alma 89
5. Bad Axe 113
6. Ypsilanti 117
7. Wayne 129

1940 BOYS CLASS B INDIVIDUALS
1. Russell Bradley (Charlotte)12 .... 11:19
2. Wallace Newlin (Wayne) .... nt
3. Fred Schnellenberger (Alma)11 .... nt
4. Ebright (Alma) .... nt
5. Dick Petro (Niles) .... nt
6. Stan Dusbiber (Ypsilanti)12 .... nt
7. Gerald Smith (Charlotte)12 .... nt
8. Elwood Martin (Charlotte)11 .... nt

9. McCarthy (Bad Axe) .... nt
10. Campbell (Van Dyke) .... nt

1941 CLASS B BOYS

Cold rain and wind greeted the runners in Ypsilanti. Martin Opem's Ypsilanti squad won Class B by placing 2-4-8-12-18. That was good enough to edge Niles by a mere point.

Ypsilanti, Nov. 1 □
1941 BOYS CLASS B TEAMS
1. Ypsilanti 44
2. Niles 45
3. Alma 57
4. Charlotte 93
5. Wayne 104

1941 BOYS CLASS B INDIVIDUALS
1. Fred Schnellenberger (Alma)12 .... 11:39
2. Robert Goss (Ypsilanti)12 .... c11:50
3. Richard Petro (Niles) .... nt
4. Mahlon Ellis (Ypsilanti)12 .... nt
5. Beall (Niles) .... nt
6. Carl Thomason (Wayne) .... nt
7. Duhamel (Alma) .... nt
8. Marshall Mosher (Ypsilanti)12 .... nt
9. Lockwood (Alma) .... nt
10. Kennedy (Niles) .... nt
12. John Wills (Ypsilanti)11 .... nt
18. Donald Furtney (Ypsilanti)12 .... nt

1942 CLASS B BOYS

Because of wartime fuel restrictions, the MHSAA decided to cancel the regional meets and instead hold separate "final" meets that looked a lot like regionals. Schools were urged to attend the closest one. An Upper Peninsula "final" was held in Escanaba on October 17 (see the UP section).

Hastings won the West Regional in its only meet of the season.

Briggs Field, Ypsilanti, Oct. 31 □
1942 BOYS LP EAST - CLASS B TEAMS
1. Birmingham 31
2. Wayne 44
3. Ypsilanti 54

1942 BOYS LP EAST - CLASS B INDIVIDUALS
1. Carl Thomason (Wayne) 11:38
2. John Willis (Ypsilanti)12 .... 11:49
7. Donald Gill (Ypsilanti)12 .... nt
14. William Seaton (Ypsilanti)11 .... nt
15. Donald Wesenberg (Ypsilanti)11 .... nt
16. Claude Hitt (Ypsilanti)12 .... nt

Kalamazoo, October 31 □
1942 BOYS LP WEST – CLASS B TEAMS
1. Hastings 15
(only full team that showed)

1942 BOYS LP WEST - CLASS B INDIVIDUALS
3. Dean Keeler (Hastings) .... nt

1943 CLASS B BOYS

The state finals returned even though World War II was still raging. Roger Kelly took the win in his first season on the team under coach E. A. Winston.

Briggs Field, Ypsilanti, Oct. 30 □
1943 BOYS CLASS B TEAMS
1. Ypsilanti 28
2. Birmingham 62
3. Charlotte 70
4. River Rouge 89
5. Trenton 99

1943 BOYS CLASS B INDIVIDUALS
1. Roger Kelly (Ypsilanti)12 .... 11:45
2. Lynn McAllister (Ypsilanti)12 .... 11:46
3. Russell Deland (Charlotte) 12:14
4. Milldrebrandt (Birmingham) 12:17
5. Batchelor (River Rouge) 12:18
6. Douglas Nowling (Ypsilanti)12 .... 12:18
7. Coryell (Birmingham) 12:30
8. Messer (Trenton) 12:32
9. Donald Wesenberg (Ypsilanti)12 .... 12:33
10. Tom Dixon (Ypsilanti)12 .... 12:37
11. Dick Fullerton (Charlotte) 12:42
12. Glenn Whitinger (Charlotte) 12:43
13. Kearns (River Rouge) 12:45
14. Moody (Birmingham) 12:50
15. Harrington (Birmingham) 12:51
16. William Seaton (Ypsilanti)12 .... 12:52
17. Guy Hubbard (Ypsilanti)12 .... 12:55
21. Eugene Royston (Charlotte) .... nt
23. Maurice Tharpe (Charlotte) .... nt
27. George Riddle (Charlotte) .... nt

1944 CLASS B BOYS

Reports described the race as "running under unfavorable weather conditions over a muddy course." The strong Charlotte squad was hampered as three of its top runners had leg injuries from playing on the football squad.

Maurice Hewlett's Kearsley squad won with a 32-point margin.

Ypsilanti, Nov. 4 □
1944 BOYS CLASS B TEAMS
1. Flint Kearsley 51
2. Birmingham 83
3. Plymouth 100
4. Charlotte 101
5. Redford Union 116
6. Ypsilanti 159
7. Wayne 164
8. River Rouge 202

1944 BOYS CLASS B INDIVIDUALS
1. Earl Kelly (Redford)11 .... 11:36
4. J. Pray (Charlotte .... nt
7. H. Krusell (Charlotte) .... nt
20. J. Thornton (Charlotte) .... nt
25. Junior King (Charlotte) .... nt

1945 CLASS B BOYS

Participation rebounded after the war. The 9 complete teams in Class B was the most since 1928's 10. In Coach Marshall's only year at the helm, the Ypsilanti boys defeated Charlotte for the win. Redford's Earl Kelly skipped a chance to defend his title, deciding not to go out for the team as a senior.

Ypsilanti, Oct. 27 □
1945 BOYS CLASS B TEAMS
1. Ypsilanti 74
2. Charlotte 89
=3. Birmingham 98
=3. Grand Blanc 98
5. Redford Union 102
6. Flint Kearsley 121
7. Plymouth 180
8. River Rouge 221
9. Bloomfield Hills Cranbrook 232

1945 BOYS CLASS B INDIVIDUALS
1. Harry Alcorn (Flint Kearsley)12 .... 10:38
2. Ted Stroud (East Lansing) .... nt
4. Elwyn Hughes (Grand Blanc)12 .... nt
6. Holmes (Charlotte) .... nt
7. Eugene Seidl (Ypsilanti)10 .... nt
8. Paul Rood (East Lansing) .... nt
9. Franklin Ossenheimer (Ypsilanti)11 .... nt
10. Furu (Charlotte) .... nt
11. Johansen (Charlotte) .... nt
13. J.W. Sifferman (Grand Blanc) .... nt

Nathan Moon, Fremont's 1946 winner, also played on the football team.

1946 CLASS B BOYS

Ypsilanti captured Class B honors again, despite the fact that one of its top runners, Franklin Ossenheimer, had a sore leg and could only manage 10th. A new coach took credit for the win this year, Ralph Deetz.

Ypsilanti, Oct. 26 □
1946 BOYS CLASS B TEAMS
1. Ypsilanti 62
2. Birmingham 68
3. Fremont 76
4. Charlotte 85
5. Flint Kearsley 119
6. Redford Union 126
7. Plymouth 195
8. Bloomfield Hills Cranbrook 209
9. Howell 262
10. River Rouge 275
11. Grand Blanc 309
12. Trenton 312

1946 BOYS CLASS B INDIVIDUALS
1. Nathan Moon (Fremont) 11:24
2. Eugene Seidl (Ypsilanti)11 .... 11:29
4. Lee Ossenheimer (Ypsilanti)12 .... nt
10. Franklin Ossenheimer (Ypsilanti)12 .... nt
15. Dick Phillips (Howell) 11:59
22. Bill Buck (Ypsilanti)11 .... nt
24. Bill Tully (Ypsilanti)11 .... nt

1947 CLASS B BOYS

A wet, slippery course in Ypsilanti slowed runners at the LP meet. Ralph Deetz's Ypsilanti squad gained revenge on Redford Union in Class B; not long before Redford Union had beaten Ypsi for conference honors. Eugene Seidl had a 30-yard lead when he hit the Huron track for the last 400 yards. Seidl won the Class B mile in 4:32.8 the next spring.

Briggs Field, Ypsilanti, Nov. 1 □
1947 BOYS CLASS B TEAMS
1. Ypsilanti 66
2. Redford Union 84
3. Plymouth 126
4. Birmingham 128
5. Bloomfield Hills Cranbrook 133
6. Hastings 147
7. Niles 174
8. Charlotte 187

9. Alma 190
10. River Rouge 211
11. Trenton 252
12. Howell 339
13. Flint Kearsley 389
14. Lansing Everett 409

1947 BOYS CLASS B INDIVIDUALS
1. Eugene Seidl (Ypsilanti)12 .... 10:56
2. James Anderson (Birmingham) .... nt
3. Leslie Teddams (Alma) .... nt
4. George Buddy (Plymouth) .... nt
5. Lee Wynn (Ypsilanti)10 .... nt
13. Bill Buck (Ypsilanti)11 .... nt
26. Dale Dolph (Ypsilanti)11 .... nt

1948 CLASS B BOYS

With 22 complete teams, this was the biggest field yet. The race was run in a cold rain. Somehow coach Tony Malinowski's Trenton squad pulled out a convincing win, despite earlier in the season losing a dual to Ypsilanti, 39-16 (and also dropping matches to Class A's Monroe and Wyandotte).

Briggs Field, Ypsilanti, Nov. 6 □
1948 BOYS CLASS B TEAMS
1. Trenton 91
2. Ypsilanti 123
3. Niles 133
4. Alma 150
5. Davison 184
6. Charlotte 189
7. Milford 224
8. Birmingham 258
9. Petoskey 290
10. Lansing Everett 317
11. Plymouth 328
12. Bloomfield Hills Cranbrook 329
13. Croswell-Lexington 330
14. Walled Lake 336
15. River Rouge 338
16. Mt Morris 416
17. Howell 422
18. East Lansing 428
19. Mt Pleasant 448
20. Flint Technical 491
21. Redford Union 498
22. Flint Kearsley 600

1948 BOYS CLASS B INDIVIDUALS
1. Lee Wynn (Ypsilanti)11 .... 11:00
19. Gordy Hyde (Alma) 11:30
28. Al Vandermark (Alma) .... nt

1949 CLASS B BOYS

Coach Homer Hatcher's Niles squad captured its first title since 1939 with the highest score in meet history. The Vikings dropped their first meet, a close one to Indiana's Mishewaka, but went undefeated after that. The weekend before the state finals, they showed their fitness with a score of 22 points at the 9-team Aquinas Invitational.

Washtenaw Country Club,Ypsilanti, Nov. 5 □
1949 BOYS CLASS B TEAMS
1. Niles 100
2. Ypsilanti 154
3. Mt Pleasant 164
4. Alma 237
5. Farmington 239
6. Charlotte 247
7. Ithaca 249
8. Trenton 267
=9. Lansing Everett 284
=9. Plymouth 284
11. Davison 288
12. Birmingham 291
13. Eaton Rapids 312

14. Walled Lake 323
15. Fremont 378
16. Howell 382
17. Flint Technical 385
18. Milford 415
19. Belleville 432
20. Croswell-Lexington 433
21. Mt Morris 436
22. Allegan 505
23. Lansing Resurrection 618

1949 BOYS CLASS B INDIVIDUALS
1. Jack Davis (Mt Pleasant) 11:07
2. Bud Davis (Bellevue) .... nt
3. Bobby Smith (Niles) .... nt
6. Joe Gessinger (Niles) .... nt
7. Jim Seidl (Ypsilanti)11 .... nt
17. Don Hamilton (Ypsilanti)11 .... nt
21. Ken Morris (Niles) .... nt
29. Lee Wynn (Ypsilanti)12 .... nt
33. Leonard Waugh (Niles) .... nt
37. Laudner Phillips (Niles) .... nt
38. Mal Williams (Niles) .... nt
41. Jim Pollock (Niles) .... nt

1950 CLASS B BOYS

After unseating Niles for the win, the Alma boys told reporters, "We did it for George."

George Chase was their "lanky, redheaded freckle-faced senior" captain, who trained longer and harder than any of the others and had clocked a school record 10:33 earlier in the season. He had only been beaten once all year.

The day of the state finals, George woke up sick. The team rallied, and their No. 2, Rocky Wolfgang, rose to the challenge for the victory. George struggled throughout, falling once and finishing 46th.

Coach Del Brenner's Panthers defeated rival Niles by just 5 points.

Washtenaw Country Club,Ypsilanti, Nov. 4 □
1950 BOYS CLASS B TEAMS
1. Alma 73
2. Niles 78
3. Farmington 100
4. Walled Lake 154
5. Plymouth 202
6. Grand Rapids Ottawa Hills 214
7. Howell 228
8. Birmingham 237
9. Mt Pleasant 277
10. Otsego 287
11. Petoskey 308
12. Mt Morris 323
13. Allegan 337
14. Milford 345
15. Croswell-Lexington 376
16. Belleville 377
17. Fenton 414
18. Trenton 496

1950 BOYS CLASS B INDIVIDUALS
1. Rocky Wolfgang (Alma)11 ....11:09
2. Milt Bowen (Alma) 11:09
3. Bob Nelson (Howell)12 .... nt
8. Lynn Holley (Holly)10 .... nt
15. John Goetz (Alma)11 .... nt
27. Junior Mailand (Alma)10 .... nt
28. Jim Cagala (Alma) .... nt
46. George Chase (Alma)12 .... nt

1951 CLASS B BOYS

Despite cold weather and a slippery course, three runners broke the Class B course record. They came to the finish together, with just a foot separating Bill Pyle and John Ballough, while Pyle's teammate Ray "Rocky" Wolfgang finished

40 yards back. Earlier in the season, Wolfgang had set a school record of 10:26.5.

In his first season of running, Alma's Bill Pyle won the state meet by 12 inches. He went on to become an All-American.

Washtenaw Country Club, Ypsilanti, Nov. 3
1951 BOYS CLASS B TEAMS
1. Alma 45
2. Niles 77
=3. Mt Pleasant 171
=3. Otsego 171
5. Walled Lake 203
6. Petoskey 206
=7. Davison 222
=7. Trenton 222
9. Plymouth 230
10. Howell 240
11. Farmington 279
12. Belleville 293
13. Adrian 294
14. Birmingham 348
15. Croswell 435
16. Livonia Bentley 443
17. Fenton 508
18. Redford Union 517
19. Lowell 542

1951 BOYS CLASS B INDIVIDUALS
1. Bill Pyle (Alma)11 ....10:53
2. John Ballough (Plymouth) c10:53
3. Rocky Wolfgang (Alma)12 ....c10:59
12. Sam King (Alma)10 .... nt
13. John Goetz (Alma)12 .... nt
16. Junior Mailland (Alma)11 .... nt
37. Ron Wolfgang (Alma)10 .... nt

1952 CLASS B BOYS

Bill Pyle charged to the lead after the gun and never looked back, en route to a 10:18, the fastest time recorded in any class on the Washtenaw course. The Class B mile champ the previous spring, he had set a course record on every course he ran that fall. He would go on to Western Michigan, where he would win the Mid-American title and become an All-American in 1956.

Alma's Panthers won their third straight with the biggest margin in meet history up to that time.

Washtenaw Country Club,Ypsilanti, Nov. 1 □
1952 BOYS CLASS B TEAMS
1. Alma 77
2. Belleville 143
3. Niles 151
4. Mt Pleasant 171
5. Farmington 201
6. Grand Ledge 209
7. Otsego 256
8. Trenton 273
9. Livonia Bentley 288

XC! High School Cross Country in Michigan

10. Petoskey 315
11. Redford Union 329
=12. Howell 331
=12. Walled Lake 331
14. Sturgis 336
15. Flint Kearsley 419
16. Davison 424
17. Livonia Clarenceville 442
18. Allegan 478
19. Portage 501
20. Milford 521
21. Adrian 631
22. Auburn Heights 648

1952 BOYS CLASS B INDIVIDUALS
1. Bill Pyle (Alma)12 .... 10:18
2. Wendell Gabier (Cadillac) .... nt
3. Sam King (Alma)11 .... nt
21. Cal Aumaugher (Alma)10 .... nt
24. Junior Mailland (Alma)12 .... nt
28. Ray Bovee (Alma) .... nt
29. Jack Schnepp (Alma)11 .... nt
55. Stan Curtis (Alma) .... nt

1953 CLASS B BOYS

Coached by Anthony Malinowski, the Trenton squad from Slocum Truax High School won it all on a sloppy, snow-covered course, with the highest winning score in history. The defending Alma squad had been decimated by graduation and the age rule (no 19-year-olds).

After a nearly 20-year stretch when regionals were either cancelled or optional, they once again were required. There were three sites: Birmingham, Grand Rapids and Lansing.

Trenton's championship team, running in formation in an awkwardly-posed yearbook photo.

Washtenaw Country Club, Ypsilanti, Nov. 7 □
1953 BOYS CLASS B TEAMS
1. Trenton 104
2. Alma 119
3. Walled Lake 125
4. Otsego 127
5. Livonia Bentley 136
6. Belleville 191
7. Howell 203
8. Allegan 225
9. Milford 244
10. Flint Kearsley 250

1953 BOYS CLASS B INDIVIDUALS
1. Bill Burgor (Trenton)12 .... 10:58
2. Richard Jackman (Milford) .... nt
12. Loren Eldred (Mt Pleasant) .... nt

16. Tony Curtis (Alma)12 .... 11:20
17. Tom DeRushia (Alma)10 .... nt
21. Ron Wolfgang (Alma)12 .... nt
28. Jack Schnepp (Alma)12 .... nt
27. Phil Langin (Alma)11 .... nt
? Joe Ohr (Alma)11 .... nt
?Jim Carneron (Trenton) .... nt
? Bill Sullivan (Trenton) .... nt
? Wally Leeper (Trenton) .... nt

1954 CLASS B BOYS

River Rouge produced the biggest winning margin ever to beat Alma by 104 points—quite an achievement for a school that hadn't sponsored cross country for six years. Harry Niner's team went undefeated, surviving its closest meet, against Lincoln Park, with a one-point margin.

One of Niner's top runners was Herman Ector, who was a basketball star and high jumper as well. He later served as a U.S. Army paratrooper. In 1967, when the Detroit riots erupted, he went to check on his mother and was shot to death on the sidewalk by an unlicensed security guard who suspected him of being a looter. A police investigation cleared Ector and recommended charges against the guard.

Washtenaw Country Club, Ypsilanti, Nov. 6 □
1954 BOYS CLASS B TEAMS
1. River Rouge 76
2. Alma 180
3. Livonia Bentley 185
4. Walled Lake 186
5. Lowell 227
6. Adrian 242
7. Farmington 270
8. Otsego 277
9. Romulus 287
10. Allegan 306
11. Davison 324
12. Mt Pleasant 332
13. Portage 355
14. Grand Rapids Central 364
15. Howell 384
16. Redford Union 385
17. Milford 435

1954 BOYS CLASS B INDIVIDUALS
1. Joe Ohr (Trenton)12 .... 10:53
5. Bob Scheffler (St Clair) 11:06
7. Loren Eldred (Mt Pleasant) .... nt
11. Clarence Voelm (Howell) .... nt
21. Dave Secord (Alma)12 .... 11:20

1955 CLASS B BOYS

The win went to Dick Wells of Adrian, who was a solid basketball player in the winter. In the spring, the places were reversed in the Class B mile, as Wally Schafer beat Wells in 4:37.4.

Washtenaw Country Club, Ypsilanti, Nov. 5 □
1955 BOYS CLASS B TEAMS
1. River Rouge 96
2. Walled Lake 123
3. Romulus 183
4. Farmington 190
5. Lowell 191
6. Inkster 231
7. Milford 237
8. Portage 241
9. Otsego 247
10. Trenton 248
11. Mt Pleasant 252
12. Charlotte 300

1955 BOYS CLASS B INDIVIDUALS
1. Dick Wells (Adrian)12 .... 10:52
2. Wally Schafer (Ludington) 10:54
11. Martin Buffin (Ludington) 11:17

1956 CLASS B BOYS

Wally Schafer led from the start but Bob Carrigan of Lowell sprinted past him just before the finish to win by a half second, 10:32.0 to 10:32.5. The Ludington coach said that Schafer didn't see Carrigan coming.

In the spring, Carrigan again pipped Schafer, winning the Class B mile in 4:37.4. Schafer, however, lost his shoe on the first lap and ran with one bare foot to a 4:37.8. A week later at the Champions of Champions meet, Carrigan again won, 4:32.8-4:32.9.

Washtenaw Country Club, Ypsilanti, Nov. 3 □
1956 BOYS CLASS B TEAMS
1. Portage 97
2. River Rouge 102
3. Walled Lake 213
4. Farmington 215
5. Trenton 230
6. Otsego 231
7. South Haven 232
8. Grand Ledge 234
9. Coldwater 241
10. Romulus 255
11. Redford Union 265
12. Lowell 293
13. Livonia Clarenceville 299
14. Howell 353
15. Mt Pleasant 454

1956 BOYS CLASS B INDIVIDUALS
1. Bob Carrigan (Lowell)12 .... 10:32
2. Wally Schafer (Ludington) 10:33
3. Randy Louritzen (Portage) 10:42

Roger Humbarger of Godwin Heights won two state titles without shoes. At Michigan State—with shoes—he helped the Spartans win two Big 10 titles.

1957 CLASS B BOYS

Roger Humbarger, 5-10/145, won in 10:49.8 running barefoot. He would go on to win the B mile crown the next spring. Eleven schools competed, but Livonia Clarenceville, which placed 4th originally, was disqualified for using an ineligible runner.

Washtenaw Country Club, Ypsilanti, Nov. 2 □
1957 BOYS CLASS B TEAMS
1. River Rouge 89

2. Howell 113
3. Grand Ledge 186
4. Lansing Resurrection 219
5. South Haven 224
6. Otsego 226
7. Marysville 227
8. Lansing Everett 246
9. Vicksburg 253
10. Lowell 295
dq—LivoniaClarenceville.

1957 BOYS CLASS B INDIVIDUAL
1. Roger Humbarger (Godwin Heights)11 .... 10:50
2. Gene Laws (Otsego) .... nt
3. Radak (Howell) .... nt
22. J. Delaney (Howell) .... nt
25. B. Hoel (Howell) .... nt

1958 CLASS B BOYS

Roger Humbarger defended in Class B in 10:26.9, again running barefoot. He said, "I figure that my shoes weigh about a half a pound and warmups proved to me that I could pace myself much better without them. For the last two years I've been running barefoot on sod, sidewalks and pavements. It's really toughened up my feet. Of course, though, I resort to my shoes when my runs are on cinder or gravel courses."

Four years later, Humbarger would place 19th in the NCAA for Michigan State.

For Humbarger's Godwin Heights, the victory was sweet, even with the highest winning score in meet history.

Washtenaw Country Club, Ypsilanti, Nov. 1 ☐
1958 BOYS CLASS B TEAMS
1. Wyoming Godwin Heights 123
2. River Rouge 149
3. Marysville 151
4. St Johns 175
5. Lansing Everett 181
6. Howell 198
7. Alma 210
8. South Haven 217
9. Lowell 278

1958 BOYS CLASS B INDIVIDUALS
1. Roger Humbarger (Godwin Heights)12 .... 10:27
2. Jan Bowen (Alma) 10:40
3. Craig Curtis (Coldwater) .... nt
6. Dick Polovich (Marysville) .... nt

1959 CLASS B BOYS

Jan Bowen of Alma produced the fastest time in the Lower Peninsula meet, moving up from his runner-up position the previous year. He signed with Michigan State and in 1963 captured the Big 10 mile title (4:14.3).

With only one returner, Howell was the classic Cinderella story. The Highlanders won four major meets en route to an upset win at the state finals. Said coach Robert Bloomer, "I'm very pleased and satisfied with the boys. They have been great not only in running, but also in their attitude."

Lead runner Jack Hardy heard the coach say this to the reporter and quipped, "Gee, that's the first time I've ever heard the coach say he was satisfied. He's always been just plain pleased."

Washtenaw Country Club, Ypsilanti, Nov. 7 ☐
1959 BOYS CLASS B TEAMS
1. Howell 97
2. St Johns 101
3. Bloomfield Hills 108
4. Grand Ledge 122
5. Milford 146
6. South Haven 154
7. Ecorse 190
8. Plainwell 192
9. Grand Rapids South Christian 213

1959 BOYS CLASS B INDIVIDUALS
1. Jan Bowen (Alma)11 .... 10:17
2. Russ Jacobus (Godwin Heights) .... nt
3. Rush Ring (Sparta) .... nt
6. Jack Hardy (Howell) 10:58
13. Lynn McKee (Howell) .... nt
14. Paul Brotz (Howell) .... nt
30. Rick Zemper (Howell) .... nt
34. Al Buckner (Howell) .... nt
? Matt Brady (Howell) .... nt
? Ralph Munson (Howell) .... nt

1960 CLASS B BOYS

Alma's Jan Bowen ran to a course record 9:50.9 in the Class B race amid snow flurries and temperatures in the mid-thirties. It was the best time in any class. One regional was eliminated this year for B, with only three being held: Farmington, Grand Rapids and Lansing.

Washtenaw Country Club, Ypsilanti, Nov. 5 ☐
1960 BOYS CLASS B TEAMS
1. Howell 88
2. St Johns 107
3. Milford 119
4. Ecorse 124
5. Croswell-Lexington 130
6. Otsego 148
7. Clio 158
8. Wyoming Park 167
9. Holland Christian 182

1960 BOYS CLASS B INDIVIDUALS
1. Jan Bowen (Alma)12 .... 9:51
2. Steve Smith (Wyoming Park)12 .... 10:18
3. Ted Nelson (Milford) .... nt
4. Rick Zemper (Howell) 10:28
19. Ralph Musson (Howell) .... nt
20. Al Buckner (Howell) .... nt
21. Craig Woodstock (Howell) .... nt
24. John Hoover (Howell) .... nt

1961 CLASS B BOYS

An addition of a big hill on the WCC course made for new course records, though officials at the time insisted on keeping the old records as "official."

Jeff Taylor of Otsego won in 10:16.8. The team title went by a 30-point margin to Frank Grimm's Wyoming Park team, the first in the school's history. The Vikings had gone undefeated on the season thanks to their top 5: Ken Coates, Dave Curtis, Jim Kidder, Rich Pullen and Dave Tardy.

Washtenaw Country Club, Ypsilanti, Nov. 4 ☐
1961 BOYS CLASS B TEAMS
1. Wyoming Park 103
2. Ecorse 133
3. Otsego 145
4. Sparta 155
5. Clio 159
6. Milford 167
7. St Johns 168
8. Howell 169
9. Riverview 178

1961 BOYS CLASS B INDIVIDUALS
1. Jeff Taylor (Otsego)12 .... 10:17
2. Ted Nelson (Milford) 10:23
3. Fred Ramsey (Holt) 10:31
4. Ron Vanatten (Plainwell) .... nt
5. Jim Kidder (Wyoming Park) .... nt
6. Bob Bean (Croswell) .... nt
7. Murill Bender (St Louis) .... nt
8. Dave Dobson (Marysville) .... nt
9. Ron Wilson (Lowell) .... nt
10. Bill Tucker (Ecorse) .... nt
12. Rick Zemper (Howell) .... nt
28. Ralph Musson (Howell) .... nt

Jeff Taylor, Otsego's 1961 winner.

1962 CLASS B BOYS

In one of the closest mass finishes ever, the placement of the top 10 teams all depended on the 5th man. Sparta came through victorious with the highest winning score ever. Fourth-placer Ron Kutchinski would go on to represent the United States over 800m in the Olympics.

Washtenaw Country Club, Ypsilanti, Nov. 3 ☐
1962 BOYS CLASS B TEAMS
1. Sparta 156
2. Riverview 175
3. Otsego 177
4. Fenton 179
5. Vicksburg 195
6. Riverside 199
7. Haslett 200
8. Grand Rapids South Christian 201
9. Wyoming Park 213
10. Howell 227
11. Lowell 241
12. Flushing 295

1962 BOYS CLASS B INDIVIDUALS
1. Steve Bishop (Vicksburg)10 .... 10:08
2. Leon Jasionowski (Detroit Servite) 10:14
3. Willard Reinstein (Riverview) 10:17
4. Ron Kutchinski (East Grand Rapids)10 .... nt
5. Ken Coates (Wyoming Park) .... nt
6. Gerri Stiles (Detroit Servite) .... nt
7. Frank Gibson (Otsego) .... nt
8. Roger Odell (Lowell) .... nt
9. Judd Rung (Sparta) .... nt
10. Ken Merkins (Coopersville) .... nt
11. Rick Niles (Grand Rapids Godwin Heights) .... nt
12. Charles Vreeland (Riverview) .... nt
13. Dave Tardy (Wyomng Park) .... nt
14. Edwin McKinney (Flushing) .... nt
17. Craig Woodstock (Howell) .... nt

1963 CLASS B BOYS

Tom Horn's Vicksburg squad came away with the team win, as defending champion Steve Bishop convincingly won the individual race.

Washtenaw Country Club, Ypsilanti, Nov. 2 ☐
1963 BOYS CLASS B TEAMS
1. Vicksburg 110
2. Grand Rapids South Christian 119
3. Dearborn Heights Riverside 123
4. Detroit Servite 138
5. Wyoming Park 145
6. Detroit St Joseph 159

7. Haslett 162
8. Wyoming Rogers 233
9. Holt 267
10. Coopersville 292
11. Kentwood 301
12. Croswell-Lexington 328

1963 BOYS CLASS B INDIVIDUALS
1. Steve Bishop (Vicksburg)11 .... 10:02
2. Ken Coates (Wyoming Park) 10:15
3. Leon Jasionowski (Detroit Servite) 10:22
4. Jim Raphael (Haslett) .... nt
5. Dan LeMay (Detroit Servite) .... nt
6. John Fradette (Detroit St Joseph) .... nt
7. John Schrader (Riverview) .... nt
8. Eric Skidmore (Vicksburg) .... nt
9. Charles Chabot (Holt) .... nt
10. Forest Meadows (Riverside) .... nt

Four years after winning the 1964 individual race, Ron Kutchinski of East Grand Rapids would be running the 800 in the Mexico City Olympics.

1964 CLASS B BOYS

The separate races for team and individual runners spread to Class B this year.

Two-time B champ Steve Bishop spent 11 weeks in Europe and reported late to practice. He lost five races during the season as he did two workouts a day to catch up. Said coach Tom Horn, "The day of the state finals his words were, 'Nobody is going to beat me,' and they didn't." He clocked 9:51.7. Ron Kutchinski won individual honors at 9:55.1.

Washtenaw Country Club, Ypsilanti, Nov. 7 □
1964 BOYS CLASS B TEAMS
1. Grand Rapids South Christian 77
2. Dearborn Heights Riverside 82
3. Holland Christian 88
4. Wyoming Rogers 91
5. Haslett 144
6. Detroit Lutheran West 145
7. Vicksburg 151
8. Flushing 177
9. Clio 179
10. Marshall 232

1964 BOYS CLASS B TEAM RACE
1. Steve Bishop (Vicksburg)12 .... 9:52
2. Dean Rosenberg (North Muskegon)12 ...9:56
3. John Schrader (Riverview) 10:10
4. Rich Stevens (Dearborn Hts Riverside)11 ..10:15
5. Ray Hendrikema (GR South Christian) ... 10:20
7. Russ Zoerhof (Holland Christian)12 .... nt
8. Ed Schlosser (Haslett) 10:22
9. Marv Apol (Grand Rapids South Christian) 10:26
10. (Grand Rapids South Christian) .... nt
14. Jerry O'Bryant (Haslett) 10:29
16. Hilbert Sybesma (Holland Christian)12 ...... nt

18. (Grand Rapids South Christian) .... nt
20. Larry Klaasen (Holland Christian)12 .... nt

1964 BOYS CLASS B INDIVIDUAL RACE
1. Ron Kutchinski (East Grand Rapids)12 ...... 9:56
2. Craig Rosenberger (Wyoming Rogers)12 ... 10:16
3. Denny Miles (Wyoming Kelloggsville) 10:16
4. Terry Jacht (Sparta) 10:17
5. Sam Butler (River Rouge) 10:20
6. Dan Vacisek (Reed City) 10:21
7. Don Reed (Three Rivers) 10:22
8. Larry Gross (Wyoming Rogers) 10:22
9. Joe Kruger (GR Forest Hills) 10:24
10. Aaron Wares (Dowagiac) 10:26
11. Jeff Sprague (Plainwell) 10:27
12. Norm Cepela (Wyoming Rogers) 10:27

1965 CLASS B BOYS

After losing the regional meet, Dearborn Heights Riverside bounced back with a resounding state win by 74 points. Wally McClarren won the team race in 10:09.0. Bob Crocker won the individual race in 10:08.8.

Washtenaw Country Club, Ypsilanti, Nov. 6 □
1965 BOYS CLASS B TEAMS
1. Dearborn Heights Riverside 73
2. East Grand Rapids 147
3. Livonia Clarenceville 152
4. Okemos 164
5. Wyoming Rogers 179
6. Grand Rapids East Christian 186
7. Lansing Waverly 209
8. Sparta 232
9. Harper Woods Gallagher 233
10. Vicksburg 246
11. Cedar Springs 269
12. Alma 277
13. Fenton 286
14. Plainwell 296
15. Sturgis 297
16. Marshall 308
17. Flushing 432

1965 BOYS CLASS B TEAM RACE
1. Wally McLarren (Dearborn Hts Riverside)12 ..10:09
2. Tom Yunck (Okemos) 10:14
3. Larry Buchheit (Livonia Clarenceville) ... 10:20
4. Rich Stevens (Dearborn Hts Riverside)12 ... 10:23
5. Denny Burns (Vicksburg) 10:24
6. Tom Johnson (HW Gallagher)10 .... 10:26
7. Norman Cepela (Wyoming Rogers) 10:27
8. Terry Jacht (Sparta) 10:29
9. Jay Muller (GR East Christian) 10:30
10. Greg Smith (Alma) 10:30
11. Dale Russell (Cedar Springs) 10:31
12. Jeff Sprague (Plainwell) 10:34
13. Richard Hoebeke (Wyoming Rogers) 10:37
14. Jim Vermeulen (Plainwell) 10:38
15. Mark Feighner (East Grand Rapids) 10:39
16. Lennie Voss (Lansing Waverly) 10:39
17. Steve Mackay (East Grand Rapids) 10:39
21. Paul Cooke (Dearborn Heights Riverside) ... 10:43
23. Mike Lorent (Dearborn Heights Riverside) .....nt
24. Ray Germain (Dearborn Heights Riverside) ...nt
26. Greg Frey (Dearborn Heights Riverside) ......nt
52. Bill Platt (Dearborn Heights Riverside) ....nt

1965 BOYS CLASS B INDIVIDUAL RACE
1. Bob Crocker (Paw Paw)12 .... 10:09
2. Ron Strang (Detroit Lutheran West)11 ... 10:13
3. Gary Bisbee (Grand Rapids Kentwood) ... 10:20
4. Warren Berridge (Chesaning) 10:21
5. Gary Powers (Detroit St Anthony) 10:23
6. Bob Woodliff (Wyoming Godwin) 10:24
7. Don Reed (Three Rivers) 10:31
8. Jim Hoban (Coopersville) 10:33
9. Charles Gardner (River Rouge) 10:34
10. Aaron Wares (Dowagiac) 10:36
11. Mike Vogel (Lansing O'Rafferty) 10:37
12. Ken Key (Coopersville) 10:38
13. Bill Ely (Mason) 10:39

(Ambrose has Ed Schlosser of Haslett running 10:19.1)

1966 CLASS B BOYS

The Lower Peninsula finals, originally scheduled for November 5, were delayed a week after a surprise 8-inch snowstorm hit the Wednesday and Thursday before the original date. Near-perfect weather brought 2,000 fans out. Ron Strang of Lutheran West won at 10:06.1.

In the team race, Holland Christian's Phil DeVries edged Brian Burns at the finish, 10:10.0 to 10:10.1.

Grand Rapids East Christian, a school that only stayed open for 8 years, won the team title in the second year of its program.

Washtenaw Country Club, Ypsilanti, Nov. 5 □
1966 BOYS CLASS B TEAMS
1. Grand Rapids East Christian 78
2. Dearborn Heights Riverside 114
3. Wyoming Rogers 119
4. Holland Christian 149
5. Sturgis 163
6. Howell 228
7. Greenville 230
8. Swartz Creek 233
9. Lansing Waverly 239
10. Okemos 242
11. Vicksburg 246
12. Detroit St Anthony 270
13. Flushing 285
14. Alma 299
15. Sparta 323
16. Ecorse 336
17. Plainwell 373
18. West Bloomfield 384

1966 BOYS CLASS B TEAM RACE
1. Phil DeVries (Holland Christian) 10:10
2. Brian Burns (Swartz Creek) 10:11
3. Jay Muller (GR East Christian) 10:14
4. Pat Hogle (Okemos) 10:19
5. Denny Burns (Vicksburg) 10:20
6. Gordon Frey (Dearborn Heights Riverside) ... 10:23
7. Paul Cooke (Dearborn Heights Riverside) 10:28
8. John Lasky (Detroit St Anthony) 10:29
9. Norm Cepela (Wyoming Rogers) 10:29
10. Robert Faber (Greenville) 10:30
11. Mike Ridge (Vicksburg) 10:30
12. Richard Hoebeke (Wyoming Rogers) 10:31

1966 BOYS CLASS B INDIVIDUAL RACE
1. Ron Strang (Detroit Lutheran West)12 ...... 10:07
2. Terry Furst (Niles Brandywine) 10:27
3. Ron Gould (Muskegon Reeths-Puffer) ... 10:28
4. Todd Smith (Coloma) .... nt
5. Tom Oberlin (Grand Rapids Forest Hills) ...... nt
6. Ed Schmidt (Coopersville) .... nt
7. Dave Holben (Wyoming) .... nt
10. Cliff Burke (Wyoming Kelloggsville) .... nt
14. Rob Cool (Grand Rapids Northview) .... nt
(Ambrose has Tom Johnson of Harper Woods Gallagher running 10:17 in 1966)

1967 CLASS B BOYS

Rob and Ron Cool of Grand Rapids Northview stood out in more than one way in the Class B team race. For starters, the twin brothers took the top two places. Even more notable is the fact that they both ran barefoot as they led the Wildcats to the team title..

Washtenaw Country Club, Ypsilanti, Nov. 4 □
1967 BOYS CLASS B TEAMS
1. Grand Rapids Northview 96
2. Dearborn Heights Riverside 135
3. Detroit St Anthony 160
4. Charlotte 161
5. Niles Brandywine 177

6. West Bloomfield 179
7. Sparta 182
8. Grand Rapids East Christian 191
9. Remus Chippewa Hills 196
10. Sturgis 200
11. East Jackson 220
12. Midland Bullock Creek 261
13. Plainwell 261
14. Vicksburg 268
15. Muskegon Heights 301
16. Oxford 377
17. Grosse Ile 470
18. Swartz Creek 481

1967 BOYS CLASS B TEAM RACE
1. Rob Cool (Grand Rapids Northview) 10:25
2. Ron Cool (Grand Rapids Northview) 10:27
3. Terry Furst (Niles Brandywine) 10:29
4. Lyle Warner (Remus Chippewa Hills) ... 10:32
5. Bill Chenoweth (Charlotte) 10:33
6. Paul Cooke (Dearborn Heights Riverside) 10:33
7. Curt Griffith (Sturgis) 10:36
8. Mike Ridge (Vicksburg) 10:41
9. Tom Bytwork (Charlotte) 10:46
10. Tom Badgerow (Sparta) 10:47
11. Ron Ascenzo (Detroit St Anthony) 10:47

1967 BOYS CLASS B INDIVIDUAL RACE
1. Steve Freese (Three Rivers) 10:20
2. Paul Baldwin (Flint Bendle) 10:32
3. Bart Cook (Marshall) 10:45
4. Mike Bratton (Detroit Lutheran West) ... 10:47
6. Randy Saliers (GR Kenowa Hills) .... nt
7. Todd Smith (Coloma) .... nt
8. Dave Clemo (Wyoming Rogers) .... nt
9. Ed Schmidt (Coopersville) .... nt

1968 CLASS B BOYS

Malcolm Gobel, already a legendary football coach, led his Charlotte team to the title, one of many accomplishments that would put the future Green Bay Packers scout into several different Halls of Fame. When told his was the team to beat that summer, he said, "We'll give them a run for their money, but…"

Only one of Gobel's top five was a senior. Said the coach, "I knew that it was going to take a mighty good team to beat us, but our kids were too strong."

Washtenaw Country Club, Ypsilanti, Nov. 2 □
1968 BOYS CLASS B TEAMS
1. Charlotte 65
2. Grand Rapids Northview 111
3. Detroit St Anthony 114
4. Detroit Lutheran West 172
5. Fenton 202
6. Vicksburg 229
7. Wyoming Rogers 239
8. Bullock Creek 249
9. Plainwell 253
10. St Louis 253
11. Dearborn Heights Annapolis 261
12. Zeeland 262
13. Sparta 273
14. Grosse Ile 277
15. Jackson Lumen Christi 281
16. Oxford 317
17. Battle Creek Harper Creek 319
18. Allegan 473

1968 BOYS CLASS B TEAM RACE
1. Jerry Sinkel (Detroit St Anthony) 10:07
2. Ralph Zoppa (St Louis) 10:08
3. Rob Cool (Grand Rapids Northview) 10:12
4. Ron Cool (Grand Rapids Northview) 10:17
5. Jim Goodfellow (Oxford) 10:17
6. Bill Chenowith (Charlotte) 10:18
7. Mike Wood (Plainwell) 10:19
8. Tom Bytwork (Charlotte) 10:28
9. Don Keswick (Fenton) 10:29
10. Gordon Preston (Sparta) 10:31

11. Steve Thompson (Charlotte) .... nt
17. Terry Bytwork (Charlotte) .... nt
23. Jim Chenoweth (Charlotte)9 .... nt

1968 BOYS CLASS B INDIVIDUAL RACE
1. Jim Anglin (Richland Gull Lake) 10:25
2. Randy Saliers (GR Kenowa Hills) 10:28
3. James Coyle (Ludington) 10:28
4. Chuck Campbell (Okemos) 10:29
5. Ben Tol (Grand Rapids Christian) 10:30
14. Roger Robertson (Eaton Rapids) .... nt
15. Dave Stiffler (Edwardsburg) 10:35
18. Bob Nordan (Dowagiac) .... nt

1969 CLASS B BOYS

Holt placed three in the top eight, but ended up tied for ninth when its next two runners came in at 113th and 119th. Charlotte came away with the successful defense of its crown in a race that was held in a steady rain.

Oxford's Jim Goodfellow outlegged Bill Chenoweth of Charlotte at the finish of the team race, 10:00.5-10:02.1, and the next spring he would also win the Class B 2-mile title in 9:28.2.

Washtenaw Country Club, Ypsilanti, Nov. 1 ⊠
1969 BOYS CLASS B TEAMS
1. Charlotte 58
2. Detroit East Catholic 127
3. Rochester Adams 134
4. Oxford 136
5. Wyoming Rogers 167
6. Fenton 175
7. Riverview 198
8. Grosse Ile 202
=9. Vicksburg 247
=9. Holt 247
11. Zeeland 285
12. Sparta 302
13. Coldwater 329
14. Muskegon Catholic 332
15. Bullock Creek 345
16. Sturgis 359
17. St Louis 397
18. Stevensville Lakeshore 413

1969 BOYS CLASS B TEAM RACE
1. Jim Goodfellow (Oxford) 10:01
2. Bill Chenoweth (Charlotte) 10:03
3. Mike Pettit (Holt) 10:20
4. Jerry Crane (Holt) 10:22
5. Don Keswick (Fenton) 10:23
6. Paul Wylie (Grosse Ile) 10:23
7. Ed Griffis (Rochester Adams) 10:24
8. Dennis Davis (Holt) 10:25
9. Steve Thompson (Charlotte) 10:27
10. Steve Brill (Oxford) 10:27
11. Jim Chenoweth (Charlotte)10 .... 10:28
12. Dave Arnold (Rochester Adams) 10:28
13. Dave Duba (Grosse Ile) 10:28
14. Rick Cain (Wyoming Rogers) 10:30
15. Frank Krisak (Detroit East Catholic) ... 10:31
16. Terry Bytwork (Charlotte) 10:32
17. Ed McClintec (St Louis) 10:33
20. Bill Bytwork (Charlotte) 10:36
75. David Rieben (Charlotte) 11:17
95. Howard Kane (Charlotte) 11:32

1969 BOYS CLASS B INDIVIDUAL RACE
1. Mike Woods (Plainwell) 10:17
2. Gary Klacking (WB Ogemaw Heights) .. 10:19
3. Don Tamminga (GR Catholic Central) .. 10:20
4. Randy Saliers (GR Ottawa Hills) 10:22
5. Dave Smith (Jackson Lumen Christi) ... 10:23
6. Randy Lawrence (Holland West Ottawa) ... 10:25
7. Tom Curtis (Wyoming) 10:27
8. Dennis Kurtis (Livonia Churchill) 10:28
9. Julius Aiello (Dearborn Heights Riverside) ... 10:29
10. Risto Maenpaa (Vassar) 10:29
11. Dave Wilson (Montrose) 10:29
12. Ron Doorn (Jenison) 10:30

13. Pail Aikins (Marshall) 10:33

1970 CLASS B BOYS

As the race distance increased to 2.5M, Grand Rapids West Catholic won its first harrier crown. Coach Leonard Skrycki's team was led by Greg Meyer, who placed 5th as a sophomore.

Running up front was Don Tamminga of Grand Rapids Central Catholic, who would win the Class B mile crown the next spring in 4:19.4. He outsprinted Fenton's Don Keswick, who had enough speed to win a state title in the half-mile (1:55.6).

Washtenaw Country Club, Ypsilanti, Nov. 7 □
1970 BOYS CLASS B TEAMS
1. Grand Rapids West Catholic 127
2. Fenton 135
3. Detroit East Catholic 143
4. Battle Creek Harper Creek 144
5. Rogers City 189
6. Muskegon Catholic 213
7. Riverview 214
8. Charlotte 219
9. Sturgis 223
10. Grand Rapids Christian 232
11. Oxford 246
12. Chesaning 254
13. Zeeland 267
14. Midland Bullock Creek 283
15. Otsego 327
16. Northville 341
17. Blissfield 350
18. Stevensville Lakeshore 411

Central Christian's Don Tamminga was fastest on the new 2.5M course.

1970 BOYS CLASS B TEAM RACE
1. Don Tamminga (Grand Rapids C Christian) .. 12:51
2. Don Keswick (Fenton) 12:54
3. Jonathan Warwick (Rogers City) 13:16
4. Doug O'Berry (Oxford) 13:19
5. Greg Meyer (Grand Rapids West Catholic)10 13:26
6. Bill Teachout (Battle Creek Harper Creek) 13:28
7. Rick Bell (Northville) 13:28
8. Bill Bytwork (Charlotte) 13:30
10. Frank Blissett (Fenton) .... nt
11. Dave Wilson (Montrose) .... nt

1970 BOYS CLASS B INDIVIDUAL RACE
1. Randy Lawrence (Holland West Ottawa) 13:14
2. Dave Smith (Jackson Lumen Christi) ... 13:23
3. Leonard Hoppe (Detroit Lutheran West) 13:26
4. Jim Weaver (Okemos) 13:27
5. Jerry Bartow (Croswell-Lexington) 13:27
6. Chuck Stamper (Carleton Airport) 13:30
7. Carl Ladd (Flint Bentley) 13:32
8. Roger Bradshaw (Ludington) .... nt

1971 CLASS B BOYS

Defending two-mile champ Doug O'Berry won the team race in 13:10, but his chances of defending on the track dimmed when Herb Lindsay won the individual race in 13:04. In the spring, Lindsay prevailed with a 9:22.9.

In the team race, Muskegon Catholic prevailed, thanks to the coaching of Joe LeMieux. Oxford and Avondale were given a tie for the runner-up spot initially, but Oxford's sixth man was 55th, Avondale's 90th.

Washtenaw Country Club, Ypsilanti, Nov. 6 □
1971 BOYS CLASS B TEAMS
1. Muskegon Catholic 80
2. Oxford 98
3. Auburn Hills Avondale 98
4. Alma 156
5. Rogers City 201
6. Kalamazoo Christian 206
7. Charlotte 222
8. Sturgis 232
9. New Boston Huron 243
10. Monroe Catholic Central 247
11. Otsego 253
12. Greenville 263
13. Okemos 302
14. Vassar 338
15. Harper Woods Lutheran East 355
16. Grand Rapids Central Christian 360
17. Dearborn Divine Child 378
18. Corunna 424

1971 BOYS CLASS B TEAM RACE
1. Doug O'Berry (Oxford) 13:11
2. Bill Bytwork (Charlotte) 13:16
3. James Dennis (Otsego) 13:34
4. Jon Warwick (Rogers City) 13:38
5. Jon Call (Avondale) 13:40
6. Joe Schmitt (Muskegon Catholic)12 ..... 13:41
10. Dennis Steffanik (Muskegon Catholic) ..... nt
12. Steve Bullard (Greenville) .... nt

1971 BOYS CLASS B INDIVIDUAL RACE
1. Herb Lindsay (Reed City) 13:04
2. Dave LaClair (Pinconning) 13:24
3. Jeff Doyle (Riverview) 13:32
4. Dave Bartels (South Haven) 13:35
5. Kim Stafford (Parchment) 13:36
6. Chuck Stamper (Carleton Airport) 13:37
7. Bob Frost (Allegan) 13:37
8. Gary Hinzman (Gibraltar Carlson) 13:38
9. Dan Block (Standish-Sterling) 13:38
13. Mark Mokma (Wyoming Park) .... nt
17. Elwyn Powers (Wyoming Park) .... nt

1972 CLASS B BOYS

The race distance increased to 3M the year that Flint Kearsley won its fourth team title on what the newspapers described as a "brisk and dreary day." Talent abounded. Tom Duits won the individual race. As a senior he would be the first Michigan prep to break 4:10 for the mile. After his college days at Western Michigan, he created a stir by running the fastest 1500m relay leg in world history, a 3:35.

Greg Meyer ran 27 seconds faster in the B team race. In 1978 he would become the first Michigander to break four minutes in the mile. He went on to win the 1983 Boston Marathon in 2:09:00. After his 15:21 win, Meyer said, "It was so muddy that you couldn't get any traction."

Auburn Hills Avondale won the team title with a sparkling 41-point performance.

Vicksburg High School, Vicksburg, Nov. 4 □
1972 BOYS CLASS B TEAMS
1. Auburn Heights Avondale 41
2. Linden 78
3. Muskegon Catholic 147
4. Grand Rapids West Catholic 170
5. Charlotte 190
6. Monroe Catholic Central 196
7. Grosse Ile 237
8. Battle Creek Central 245
9. Vassar 250
10. Alma 256
11. East Grand Rapids 268
12. Pinconning 273
13. Grand Rapids Northview 312
14. Royal Oak Shrine 326
15. Sturgis 332
16. Vicksburg 336
17. Whitehall 342
18. Flint Powers 385

1972 BOYS CLASS B TEAM RACE
1. Greg Meyer (GR West Catholic)12 .... 15:21
2. Devon Hind (Auburn Hills Avondale) 15:38
3. Tony Luttrell (Auburn Hills Avondale) ... 15:58
4. Jack VanSlambrouck (Monroe Catholic) 16:00
5. Jack Sinclair (Grosse Ile)10 .... 16:01
6. Dennis Stefanich (Muskegon Catholic) 16:01
7. Ray Murphy (Linden) 16:09
8. Dick Murphy (Linden) 16:09
9. John Call (Auburn Hills Avondale) 16:10
10. Bill Bytwortk (Charlotte) 16:13
11. (Auburn Hills Avondale) .... nt
15. Steve Sanders (GR West Catholic)10 ..... nt
16. (Auburn Hills Avondale) .... nt
21. Ron Bradstreet (Battle Creek Harper Creek) ..... nt

1972 BOYS CLASS B INDIVIDUAL RACE
1. Tom Duits (Hastings)11 .... 15:48
2. Robert Frost (Allegan) 15:55
3. Lorenzo Alcantar (Detroit Holy Redeemer) ... 16:02
4. Bill Donakowski (Dearborn Hts Riverside) 16:06
5. Mike Woolsey (Jackson Lumen Christi) 16:15
6. John Nelson (South Haven) 16:17
7. Mark Stevens (Kelloggsville) 16:19
8. Pete Savole (Remus Chippewa Hills) 16:21
9. Mark Fischer (Carrollton) 16:24
10. Mark Mokma (Wyoming Park) 16:25
13. Dan Cool (Grand Rapids Northview) .... nt

Shrine coach Lou Miramonti talking with his team captain, Vince Antonopoulos. The Knights won the state title by a slim 2 points.

1973 CLASS B BOYS

Royal Oak Shrine, coached by Lou Miramonti, made it to the top of the podium on a slim 2-point margin over Linden. It was the highest-scoring victory in meet history.

In cool, sunny weather, the 6-3 Tom Duits of Hastings lorded over the field, handily defeating Riverside's Bill Donakowski, a future national class runner himself.

This was the second year that coaches Ron Schultheiss of Charlotte and Jim Murray of Niles Brandywine organized the Meet of Champions on November 10 to bring together the best from every class. The race took place at the Charlotte Country Club, and Duits won in 14:47, topping Donakowski's 14:58.

Spring Meadows CC, Linden, Nov. 3 □
1973 BOYS CLASS B TEAMS
1. Royal Oak Shrine 165
2. Linden 167
3. Jackson Lumen Christi 173
4. Mt Pleasant 183
5. Grand Rapids West Catholic 190
6. Wyoming Kelloggsville 201
7. Harper Woods Gallagher 205
8. Charlotte 214
9. Sturgis 227
10. Grosse Ile 236
11. Muskegon Catholic 244
12. Saginaw Eisenhower 249
13. Ludington 265
14. Greenville 267
15. Holly 269
16. Paw Paw 298
17. Jackson Northwest 305
18. Livonia Clarenceville 418

1973 BOYS CLASS B TEAM RACE
1. Jack Sinclair (Grosse Ile)11 .... 15:16
2. Pat Fitzgerald (Jackson Lumen Christi) 15:26
3. Rick Murphy (Linden) 15:28
4. Steve Fountain (Mt Pleasant) 15:33
5. Tony Provenzola (Royal Oak Shrine) 15:44
6. Hugh Kuchta (Harper Woods Gallagher) 15:46
7. Harold Steele (Greenville) 15:47
8. Paul Singer (Saginaw Eisenhower) 15:48
9. Paul McGuire (Royal Oak Shrine) 15:49
10. Geoff Wilson (Holly) 15:50
11. Jim Adams (Grosse Ile) 15:52
33. Vince Antonopoulos (Royal Oak Shrine) 16:24
55. Ray Turczyn (Royal Oak Shrine) 16:39
63. Tom Williams (Royal Oak Shrine) 16:44
89. Duane Stewart (Royal Oak Shrine)10 ..... 16:58
107. Tim Kapala (Royal Oak Shrine) 17:08

1973 BOYS CLASS B INDIVIDUAL RACE
1. Tom Duits (Hastings)12 .... 14:57
2. Bill Donakowski (DH Riverside)12 .... 15:03
3. Rusty Burns (Vicksburg) 15:23
4. Matt Clark (Rockford) 15:31
5. Don McCoy (Hemlock) 15:33
6. Richard Howard (Lake Fenton) 15:36
7. John Monahan (Detroit Austin) 15:38
8. Mike Beisel (Saginaw MacArthur) 15:39
9. Dave Furst (Niles Brandywine) 15:40
10. Evan Harper (Brooklyn Columbia C) 15:40
11. Steve Oswald (Three Rivers) 15:41
12. Phil Vannette (Holland Christian)10 ..... 15:41
13. Ralph Dunman (Flint Hamady) 15:42
14. Don Schweiman (Flint Hamady) 15:42
15. Ken Russell (Wyoming Rogers) 15:44
16. Frank Lanciaux (Fremont) 15:45
17. Randy Ryan (Dearborn Divine Child) 15:46
18. Kevin McColley (Flint Powers) 15:47
19. Fred Aquirre (Detroit Holy Redeemer) 15:50
20. Bryan Dramer (Big Rapids) 15:52

1974 CLASS B BOYS

Catholic League champ Royal Oak Shrine successfully defended its B crown. Said coach Lou Miramonti, "It's just as good as the first time."

Jack Sinclair of Grosse Ile won again, this time in the individual race. "I don't run to win," he said. "Only to improve my time. I thought I could do 14:30, but I got sick. Big crowds and noise do that to me. It's nerves, tension. I had the heaves for nearly a mile."

Sinclair also had problems with the temperatures in the low 60s: "The sweat started running down my face. It was too warm. I carried my glasses the last mile in my hand."

Charlotte CC, Charlotte, Nov. 2 ☐
1974 BOYS CLASS B TEAMS
1. Royal Oak Shrine 85
2. Harper Woods Gallagher 112
3. Jackson Lumen Christi 159
4. Saginaw Eisenhower 176
5. Grand Rapids Catholic Central 182
6. Rockford 204
7. Grand Rapids West Catholic 210
8. Detroit Austin 224
9. Sturgis 227
10. Battle Creek Harper Creek 241
11. Vicksburg 248
12. Zeeland 262
13. Linden 266
14. Hemlock 273
15. Detroit DeLaSalle 284
16. Fenton 297
17. Corunna 358
18. Carrollton 503

1974 BOYS CLASS B TEAM RACE
1. Pat Fitzgerald (Jackson Lumen Christi) 15:09
2. Tony Provenzola (Royal Oak Shrine) 15:23
3. Rusty Burns (Vicksburg) 15:28
4. Paul McGuire (Royal Oak Shrine) 15:28
5. Mike Stephens (Linden) .... nt
6. Mike Thompson (Harper Woods Gallagher) .... nt
7. John Borgerding (Jackson Lumen Christi) .... nt
8. John Horgan (Grand Rapids Catholic Central) .... nt
9. Tony Lamay (Linden) .... nt
10. Steve Sanders (Grand Rapids West Catholic) .. nt
11. Lee Palonen (Battle Creek Harper Creek) .... nt
12. Paul Singer (Saginaw Eisenhower) .... nt
13. Jerry Zaccarbelli (Detroit DeLaSalle) .... nt
14. Eric Fernette (Corunna) .... nt
15. Mike Karasiewicz (Rockford) .... nt
16. Duane Stewart (Royal Oak Shrine) 15:59
20. Tom Walsh (Royal Oak Shrine) 16:04

1974 BOYS CLASS B INDIVIDUAL RACE
1. Jack Sinclair (Grosse Ile)12 .... 14:56
2. Phil Vannette (Holland Christian) 15:30
3. Rick Howard (Lake Fenton) 15:37
4. Doug Lautzenheiser (Charlotte) .... nt
5. Joe Jacobs (Essexville Garber) .... nt
6. Charles Brynselson (Paw Paw) 15:46
7. Tom Stark (Charlotte) .... nt
8. Rick Parsons (Wyoming Godwin Heights) .... nt
9. Eric Raynor (Petoskey) .... nt
10. Dick Rieth (Three Oaks River Valley) 15:55
11. Mike Woodbeck (Flint Powers) 15:55
12. Pete Colley (Lakeland) .... nt
13. David Dalton (Flint Hamady) .... nt
14. Ralph Dunman (Flint Hamady) .... nt
15. Tom Seavey (Holly) .... nt
16. John Markel (Marine City) 16:05
18. Tony David (Sturgis) .... nt

1975 CLASS B BOYS

"There's no better feeling than to know you're the best there is at what you do," said Sturgis coach Ralph Baker. "Hard work, determination, and a lot of desire was the reason for our success."

Charlotte's Tom Stark, on a 17-meet winning streak, took the lead in the first half mile of the individual race. He said he owed it all to coach Ron Schultheiss. "At first I couldn't see running three miles, but I liked Mr. Schultheiss so much that I tried out for the team."

Charlotte CC, Charlotte, Nov. 1 ☐
1975 BOYS CLASS B TEAMS
1. Sturgis 114
2. Harper Woods Gallagher 168
3. Royal Oak Shrine 199
4. Detroit Austin 204
5. Wyoming Park 257
6. Alma 267
7. Big Rapids 270
8. Grand Rapids South Christian 283
9. Rockford 286
10. Marshall 287
11. Sparta 293
12. New Boston Huron 302
=13. Carleton Airport 313
=13. Jackson Northwest 313
15. Otsego 345
16. Brighton 350
17. Mason 354
18. Grand Rapids Catholic Central 362
19. Lake Fenton 401
20. Dearborn Divine Child 426
21. Midland Bullock Creek 440
22. Flint Powers 467
23. Parchment 561

Carleton Airport's Bob Malone produced the fastest time of the day in 1975.

1975 BOYS CLASS B TEAM RACE
1. Bob Malone (Carelton Airport)12 .... 15:15
2. Tony Provenzola (Royal Oak Shrine) 15:20
3. Mike Thompson (HW Gallagher) 15:31
4. Bob Shown (Carleton Airport) 15:37
5. Jeff Okkonen (Sparta) 15:38
6. Curt Walker (Wyoming Park) 15:39
7. Neil Miller (Harper Woods Gallagher) 15:40
8. Chuck Love (Mason) 15:41
9. Dave Hartman (Sturgis) 15:46
10. Larry Quakkelaar (GR South Christian) 15:48
11. Dick Smith (Marshall) 15:49
12. Larry Karasiesz (Rockford) 15:50
13. Tony David (Sturgis) 15:52
14. John Horgan (GR Catholic Central) 15:53
15. Dan Dasen (Corunna) 15:54
23. Dan Marshall (Sturgis) 16:04
28. Mike Davis (Sturgis) 16:11
41. Steve Taylor (Sturgis) 16:24
87. Mark Meek (Sturgis) 16:56
90. Lee Taylor (Sturgis) 16:59

1975 BOYS CLASS B INDIVIDUAL RACE
1. Tom Stark (Charlotte) 15:22
2. Joel Jacobs (Essexville Garber) 15:33
3. Rich Parsons (Godwin Heights) 15:38
4. Pete Colley (White Lake Lakeland) 15:39
5. Phil Vannette (Holland Christian) 15:44
6. Chris Gilbert (Fenton) 15:47
7. Mike Mead (Stevensville Lakeshore) 15:52
8. Mark Poelman (Wyoming Rogers) 15:53
9. Steve Grimm (Grandville Calvin Christian) .. 15:54
10. Dave Ball (Battle Creek Harper Creek) 15:55
11. Lee Palonen (Battle Creek Harper Creek) ... 15:56
12. Larry Kostering (Zeeland) 15:58
13. Jacque Varty (Croswell-Lexington) 15:59
14. Clay Price (Saginaw MacArthur) 16:00
15. Kari Cindholm (Petoskey) 16:01

1976 CLASS B BOYS

The Fremont squad coached by Rich Tompkins crushed its opposition with a 75-point margin in blustery, 38-degree weather. "We knew we'd win this," said Tompkkins. "I said at the beginning of the year that this was a different bunch of kids."

The fastest time in Class B would go to Gerard Donakowski. His older brother Bill was a distance star at U-M, and his younger sister Donna would win the Class C 800, 1600, and 3200 in 1983. Gerard would go on to become a member of the U.S. World Championships team, and a sub-28:00 runner at 10,000m.

Green Valley GC, Sturgis, Nov. 6 ☐
1976 BOYS CLASS B TEAMS
1. Fremont 54
2. Detroit Austin 129
3. Holly 196
4. Rockford 199
5. New Boston Huron 227
6. Mason 230
7. Holt 235
8. Wyoming Rogers 247
9. Battle Creek Harper Creek 253
10. Sturgis 258
11. New Baltimore Anchor Bay 282
12. Zeeland 284
13. Carleton Airport 308
14. Flint Powers 317
15. Harper Woods Gallagher 324
16. Plainwell 335
17. Wyoming Kelloggsville 343
18. Alma 357
19. Greenville 394
20. Flint Hamady 439
21. Flint Ainsworth 443

1976 BOYS CLASS B TEAM RACE
1. Tim Schuman (New Boston Huron) 15:35
2. Neal Toward (New Baltimore Anchor Bay) 15:36
3. Kraig Morrison (Mason)12 .... 15:38
4. Tom Slocum (Fremont) 15:39
5. Dave Ball (Battle Creek Harper Creek) 15:39
6. Dave Hartman (Sturgis) 15:43
7. Kris Healy (Harper Woods Gallagher) 15:46
8. Mark Poelman (Wyoming Rogers) 15:52
9. Jim Featherstone (Fremont) 15:55
10. Dan Price (Fremont) 15:55
11. Jeff Lewis (Holly) 15:57
12. Matt Sliva (New Baltimore Anchor Bay) 15:58
13. Randy Alderink (Fremont) 15:58
14. David Denis (Detroit Austin) 15:59
15. Larry Kortering (Zeeland) .... nt
18. Bob VanderZel (Fremont) .... nt

1976 BOYS CLASS B INDIVIDUAL RACE
1. Gerard Donakowski (DH Riverside)11 .... 15:26
2. Steve Swarts (Port Huron Central) 15:32
3. Kevin Marcy (Dearborn Divine Child) 15:39
4. Curt Walker (Wyoming Park) 15:41
5. Dan Skinner (Hartland) 15:43
6. Chris Albert (Fenton) 15:46
7. Clay Price (Saginaw MacArthur) 15:48
8. Kurt Cunningham (Cadillac) 15:53
9. Tim Fountain (Mt Pleasant) 15:54
10. Rick Thompson (Sparta) 15:57
11. Kirk Lambers (Holland Christian) 15:57
12. Scott Miller (Parchment) 15:57
13. Brian Diemer (GR South Christian)10 .... 15:57
14. Eric Essique (Southgate Schafer) 15:58
15. Tom Burke (Detroit DeLaSalle) 15:58

1977 CLASS B BOYS

Riverside's Gerard Donakowski won the individual race, moving away from Brian Diemer in the last half mile as both broke the course record.

Said Diemer's coach, Paul Oosting of South Christian, "That was just too fast of a first mile. Brian was not used to such a fast pace early in the race. Donakowski was really fired up to win and it showed."

Holly, coached by Duane Raffin, piled up a 99-point margin, the second-largest in meet history.

Green Valley GC, Sturgis, Nov. 5 □
1977 BOYS CLASS B TEAMS
1. Holly 83
2. Battle Creek Harper Creek 182
3. Flint Ainsworth 202
4. Grand Rapids Christian 207
5. Rockford 210
6. New Baltimore Anchor Bay 212
7. Big Rapids 258
8. Jackson Lumen Christi 259
9. Plainwell 274
10. Otsego 275
11. Cedar Springs 299
12. Cadillac 300
13. Holt 303
14. Carleton Airport 304
15. Saginaw Eisenhower 304
16. Ludington 312
17. Marshall 314
18. Troy 315
19. Dearborn Divine Child 353
20. Inkster Cherry Hill 390
21. Harper Woods Gallagher 486

1977 BOYS CLASS B TEAM RACE
1. Dave Ball (Battle Creek Harper Creek) 15:12
2. Neal Toward (New Baltimore Anchor Bay) 15:15
3. Mark Smith (Cadillac)9 ....15:29
4. Jeff Lewis (Holly) 15:35
5. Dan Kelsh (Big Rapids) 15:39
6. Mark Blodger (Marshall) 15:40
7. Bill Lowande (Holly) 15:41
8. Al Ross (Ludington) 15:46
9. Mike Johnson (Flint Ainsworth) 15:50
10. Mike Mann (Cedar Springs) 15:51
11. John Brink (Grand Rapids Christian)11 ....15:51
12. Paul Peterson (Ludington) 15:53
13. Dave Simpson (Saginaw Eisenhower) 15:56
14. Larry Davidson (Holly) 15:59
15. Matt Sliva (New Baltimore Anchor Bay) 15:59
20. Mark Seavey (Holly) ....nt

1977 BOYS CLASS B INDIVIDUAL RACE
1. Gerard Donakowski (DH Riverside)12 ....14:58
2. Brian Diemer (GR South Christian)11 ....15:09
3. Tom Fountain (Mt Pleasant) 15:25
4. Kyle Spann (Midland Bullock Creek) 15:34
5. Dave Anderson (Sparta) 15:37
6. John Victor (Zeeland) 15:43
7. Kurt Mast (Holland Christian) 15:45
8. Ray McEwen (Southgate Schafer) 15:45
9. Dan Bilbrey (New Boston Huron) 15:45
10. Mark Poelman (Wyoming Rogers) 15:50
11. Phil Walcott (Jenison) 15:50
12. Pete Markel (Marine City) 15:52
13. John Foss (Delton Kellogg) 15:52
14. Don McCall (Pinckney) 15:52
15. Jerry Barnaby (Caledonia) 15:53

1978 CLASS B BOYS

"This is what I've wanted since last year," said Brian Diemer of Grand Rapids South Christian, of moving up from runner-up to winner. "A state championship. I also wanted the fastest time, but I don't know if I got it yet."

He didn't. In the team race, Cadillac's Mark Smith ran 16:11 on a course that newspapers described as 300 yards long.

Diemer would have to console himself with a legendary career at Michigan and a bronze medal in the Olympic steeplechase.

Holly's winning score of 169 was the highest in meet history.

Haslett HS, Haslett, Nov. 4 □
1978 BOYS CLASS B TEAMS
1. Holly 169
2. Grand Rapids Christian 181
3. Jackson Lumen Christi 185
4. Fremont 214
5. Holt 214
6. Flint Ainsworth 225
7. Cadillac 237
8. Midland Bullock Creek 238
9. Plainwell 243
10. Marshall 258
11. Dearborn Divine Child 266
12. Big Rapids 332
13. Otsego 347
14. Wyoming Rogers 361
15. Richland Gull Lake 362
16. Charlotte 363
17. Battle Creek Harper Creek 368
18. Port Huron 389
19. Harper Woods Gallagher 392
20. Troy 423
21. Forest Hills Central 436
22. Fenton 465
23. Riverview Richard 478
24. Inkster Cherry Hill 579

1978 BOYS CLASS B TEAM RACE
1. Mark Smith (Cadillac)10 ....16:11
2. John Determan (Flint Carman Ainsworth) 16:29
3. John Brink (Grand Rapids Christian) 16:35
4. Bill Stone (Holt) 16:40
5. Dan Kelsh (Big Rapids) 16:42
6. Kyle Spann (Midland Bullock Creek) 16:43
7. Terry Keyser (Midland Bullock Creek) 16:43
8. Bill Cook (Midland Bullock Creek) 16:45
9. Kevin Jewett (Fremont) 16:54
10. Ken Gamble (Big Rapids) 16:54
11. Glen Bradley (Charlotte) 16:58
12. Charles Den (Troy) 16:59
13. Fred Bisell (Marshall) 17:00
14. Matt Hatty (Dearborn Divine Child) 17:00
15. Don Fiero (Jackson Lumen Christi) 17:02

1978 BOYS CLASS B INDIVIDUAL RACE
1. Brian Diemer (GR South Christian)12 ....16:13
2. Kurt Mast (Holland Christian) 16:42
3. Al Ross (Ludington) 16:43
4. John Adams (Spring Lake) 16:47
5. Pete Markel (Marine City) 16:57
6. Phil Walcott (Jenison) 16:58
7. Glenn Craze (St Clair) 16:58
8. John Foss (Delton Kellogg) 16:58
9. Paul Blackwell (Lakeville) 16:59
10. Rick Stewart (Auburn Hills Avondale) 17:00
11. Jim MacDonald (East Grand Rapids) 17:01
12. Jim Shuster (Brooklyn Columbia Central) ...17:01
13. John Hister (Carleton Airport) 17:04
14. Dave Michael (Mt Morris) 17:05
15. Tim James (Hastings) 17:06

1979 CLASS B BOYS

Jackson Lumen Christi put three into the top five to key an impressive 53-point performance for coach Pat Arpino; that put the Titans 42 points ahead of the Holt team that had beaten them at the regional.

Cadillac's Mark Smith had the best time of the day at 15:09. He would go on to star at Eastern Michigan, becoming a 3-time All-American in the steeplechase. In 1988 he placed 4th in the Olympic Trials steeple.

Crockery GC, Spring Lake, Nov. 3 □
1979 BOYS CLASS B TEAMS
1. Jackson Lumen Christi 53
2. Holt 95
3. Charlotte 150
4. Fremont 179
5. Richland Gull Lake 239
6. Grand Rapids Christian 249
7. Dearborn Divine Child 266
8. Wyoming Rogers 274
9. St Johns 296
10. Wyoming Park 303
11. Port Huron 312
12. Caro 318
13. Cadillac 337
14. Flint Ainsworth 343
15. Detroit U-D Jesuit 360
16. Ludington 371
17. Carleton Airport 374
18. Madison Heights Foley 411
19. Otsego 414
20. Hartland 415
21. Chesaning 470
22. Stevensville Lakeshore 481
23. Monroe Catholic Central 513
24. New Boston Huron 556

Mark Smith won three in a row for Cadillac.

1979 BOYS CLASS B TEAM RACE
1. Mark Smith (Cadillac)11 ....15:09
2. Mike Wood (Jackson Lumen Christi) 15:13
3. John Adams (Jackson Lumen Christi) 15:22
4. Bill Stone (Holt) 15:23
5. Donald Fiero (Jackson Lumen Christi) 15:26
6. Vince Pruit (Caro) 15:26
7. Tom Clark (Holt) 15:36
8. Mark Mehlburg (Charlotte) ....nt
9. Mike Kwantes (Grand Rapids Christian) 15:43
10. Jim Lanciaux (Fremont) 15:44
11. Glen Craze (Port Huron Central) ....nt
12. Kevin Jewett (Fremont) 15:46
13. Keith Detlevich (Detroit U-D Jesuit) ....nt
14. Todd Long (Holt) ....nt
15. Peter Spencer (Jackson Lumen Christi) ....nt

1979 BOYS CLASS B INDIVIDUAL RACE

1. Kurt Russell (Flint Powers)....15:17
2. Tim Cannon (BH Cranbrook)11....15:20
3. Matt Stack (Holly)....15:24
4. Tom Ostrowski (Kenowa Hills)....15:33
5. David Hinkle (Mason)....15:34
6. Bruce Brogue (Dearborn Hts Robichaud)....15:36
7. Tracy Althide (Lapeer East)....15:36
8. Dave Papin (Ypsilanti Lincoln)....nt
9. David Ward (Albion)....nt
10. Todd Good (Parma Western)....nt
11. Mark Creswell (East Grand Rapids)....15:44
12. Fred Bisel (Marshall)....nt
13. Steve Ostrovich (Jackson Northwest)....nt
14. Craig Brown (Novi)....nt
15. Rich Kidder (Auburn Hills Avondale)....nt

1980 CLASS B BOYS

This marked the first year that all regionals and finals in the Lower Peninsula took place on 5,000m courses. The temperature on race day was 30-degrees. Mark Smith became the fifth person ever to win three state crowns, taking advantage of a mostly flat course to clock 15:26. In the spring he would run two miles in 9:01.2.

Lumen Christi might have lost the state crown when their lead runner, Mike Wood, tried to stay with Smith's ferocious pace. He lasted a mile, then faded to 17th.

It was coach Jeff Worman's Caro squad that took the big trophy with 155 points, toppinig Lumen Christi by 13.

Oxford Hills CC, Oxford, Nov. 1 □
1980 BOYS CLASS B TEAMS

1. Caro....155
2. Jackson Lumen Christi....168
3. Dearborn Divine Child....195
4. Detroit U-D Jesuit....197
5. Saginaw Eisenhower....218
6. Wyoming Rogers....225
7. Mason....228
8. Center Line....228
9. Otsego....255
10. St Joseph....269
11. Marysville....277
12. Charlotte....290
13. Sturgis....317
14. Hartland....320
15. Cadillac....324
16. Grand Rapids Christian....348
17. Linden....355
18. Bloomfield Hills Cranbrook....398
19. Ludington....425
20. Chelsea....441
21. Ann Arbor Richard....493
22. Fremont....521
23. Mt Pleasant....525
24. Essexville Garber....573

1980 BOYS CLASS B TEAM RACE

1. Mark Smith (Cadillac)12....15:26
2. John Adams (Jackson Lumen Christi)....15:51
3. Mark Mehlberg (Charlotte)....16:00
4. Dave Hinkle (Mason)....16:03
5. Vince Pratt (Caro)12....16:07
6. Keith Bellovich (Detroit U-D Jesuit)....16:13
7. Todd Nuerminger (Saginaw Eisenhower)....16:14
8. Dave Papin (Ypsilanti Lincoln)....16:16
9. Keith Keyser (Sturgis)10....16:20
10. Marty Newingham (Marysville)10....16:22
11. Dave Stephens (Linden)....16:26
14. Paul Mehlberg (Charlotte)....nt
20. Roberto Maiorana (Caro)12....nt
31. Rob Summersett (Caro)11....nt
49. Eric King (Caro)12....nt
50. Ken Bauer (Caro)11....nt

1980 BOYS CLASS B INDIVIDUAL RACE

1. Kurt Russell (Flint Powers)12....15:47
2. Mike Smith (Muskegon Reeths-Puffer)....16:10
3. Bill Stone (Holt)12....16:15
4. Pat McGinnis (Detroit DeLaSalle)....16:21
5. Tom Bobrowski (GR W Catholic)....16:26
6. Todd Koepke (Cedar Springs)....16:28
7. Neal Rogers (Eaton Rapids)....16:29
9. Doug Ogden (North Branch)....16:35
16. Tom Ostrowski (Kenowa Hills)....16:48

1981 CLASS B BOYS

Coach Barney Roy's harriers won their first state title at the tail end of an undefeated season. The Marshall squad ended up 24 points ahead of Grand Rapids Catholic Central.

Jeff Costello of the runner-up team had the best overall time at 15:56. He would win the Class B 2-mile at the state finals the next spring in 9:26.0.

Oxford Hills CC, Oxford, Oct. 31 □
1981 BOYS CLASS B TEAMS

1. Marshall....96
2. Grand Rapids Catholic Central....120
3. Grand Rapids Christian....200
4. Sturgis....206
5. Dearborn Divine Child....212
6. Otsego....214
7. Wyoming Rogers....227
8. Essexville Garber....247
9. Holly....257
10. Delton Kellogg....295
11. Royal Oak Shrine....314
12. Marysville....320
13. Jackson Lumen Christi....348
14. Battle Creek Lakeview....349
15. Caro....362
16. Hemlock....372
17. Chelsea....375
18. Tecumseh....415
19. Cadillac....427
20. Linden....429
21. Flint Ainsworth....467
22. Riverview Richard....480
23. Holland Christian....508
24. Saginaw Eisenhower....620

Team race winner Jeff Costello celebrating Catholic Central's runner-up finish.

1981 BOYS CLASS B TEAM RACE

1. Jeff Costello (GR Catholic Central)11....15:56
2. Marty Newingham (Marysville)11....16:06
3. John Loviska (Otsego)....16:07
4. Matt Stack (Holly)....16:08
5. Keith Keyser (Sturgis)11....16:10
6. Mark Brosnan (Chelsea)....16:13
7. Jeff Ash (Sturgis)11....16:18
8. Bab Haan (Grand Rapids Christian)....16:22
9. Tom Kelly (Marshall)....16:24
10. Ron Johnson (Marysville)11....16:28
11. Mike Skruch (Dearborn Divine Child)....16:30
12. Chris Kelly (Jackson Lumen Christi)....16:36
13. Bob Buchanan (Delton Kellogg)....16:38
14. Sean McGrath (GR Catholic Central)....16:38
15. Andy Reiser (Cadillac)....16:40

1981 BOYS CLASS B INDIVIDUAL RACE

1. Mike Benedict (Ludington)....16:16
2. Dan McCoy (Hillsdale)....16:21
3. Neil Rogers (Eaton Rapids)....16:21
4. Rusty Korhonen (Forest Hills Central)....16:22
5. Greg Shatney (Grand Rapids Northview)....16:22
6. Chuck Trese (Ortonville Brandon)....16:25
7. Rob Bockwell (Warren Woods)....16:27

1982 CLASS B BOYS

The finals were run in cold weather. Said Holly coach Duane Raffin, "I can't remember when it was this cold. The wind was the thing."

Grand Rapids Catholic Central was guided to the win by coach Jim Gardiner. Marysville's Ron Johnson led the race at 2M but was passed at the end by Chris Ingalls of Spring Lake. "Coach said, 'Look out for the Spring Lake kid; he's for real.' I was at a hill near the end when I lost my momentum, and he went by me like he just started the race."

Tyrone Hills GC, Linden, Nov. 6 □
1982 BOYS CLASS B TEAMS

1. Grand Rapids Catholic Central....145
2. Dearborn Divine Child....193
3. Essexville Garber....196
4. Hemlock....209
5. Marysville....209
6. Okemos....218
7. Mason....223
8. Warren Fitzgerald....243
9. Royal Oak Shrine....267
10. Holly....278
11. Fremont....287
12. Spring Lake....308
13. Sturgis....327
14. Flint Ainsworth....336
15. Grand Rapids Christian....342
16. Gaylord....357
17. Cadillac....389
18. Vicksburg....390
19. St Joseph....396
20. Battle Creek Lakeview....408
21. Chelsea....501
22. Saline....557
23. Ypsilanti Lincoln....603
24. Ecorse....604

1982 BOYS CLASS B TEAM RACE

1. Chris Ingalls (Spring Lake)....16:07
2. Ron Johnson (Marysville)12....16:13
3. Mark Brosnan (Chelsea)....16:15
4. Mark Pogliano (Saline)....16:21
5. Jeff Costello (Grand Rapids Catholic)12....16:25
6. Mike DesRosiers (Warren Fitzgerald)....16:26
7. Byron Oden (Ecorse)....16:26
8. Rick Prince (St Joseph)11....16:28
9. Marty Newingham (Marysville)12....16:30
10. Phil Van Dyke (Soring Lake)....16:31
11. Keith Keyser (Sturgis)....16:38
12. Brent McCumber (Cadillac)....16:42
13. Kyle Rambo (Essexville Garber)....16:43
14. Jeff Ash (Sturgis)....16:45
15. Fred Henderson (Fremont)....16:47
16. Denis McGrath (Grand Rapids Catholic)....16:48
17. Dave Arce (Royal Oak Shrine)....16:50
18. Todd Stone (Holly)....16:53
19. Carl Willits (Mason)....16:53
20. Tedd Stone (Holly)....16:54
21. Mike Skruch (Dearborn Divine Child)....16:55

1982 BOYS CLASS B INDIVIDUAL RACE

1. Rusty Korhonen (GR Forest Hills Central)....16:20
2. John Loviska (Otsego)....16:39
3. Tom Seagren (Saginaw Eisenhower)....16:44

4. John Haigh (Three Rivers) ... 16:45
5. Rick VanZile (Otsego) ... 16:48
6. Pete Trujillo (Ovid-Elsie) ... 16:49
7. Ken Campbell (Caro) ... 16:53
8. Thomas Kelly (Marshall) ... 16:54
9. Oscar Flores (North Branch) ... 16:55

1983 CLASS B BOYS

Fremont won, coached by Rich Tompkins, himself a former Class B 440 champ. "When you have everyone back, you have to set your sights high," he said.

Center Line dropped to Class B this season, which made Phil Schoensee the favorite. He won his regional in 15:24—a 46-second margin. At the finals he went out in 4:34 and held on to beat Forest Hills Central's Rusty Korhonen by three seconds. "I pretty much knew I was going to win," he said.

Tyrone Hills Golf Course, Linden, Nov. 5 ☒
1983 BOYS CLASS B TEAMS
1. Fremont ... 84
2. Grand Rapids Catholic Central ... 114
3. Parma Western ... 172
4. Okemos ... 213
5. Forest Hills Central ... 236
6. Caro ... 249
7. Dearborn Divine Child ... 261
8. St Joseph ... 274
9. Mason ... 280
10. Reed City ... 281
11. Jackson Lumen Christi ... 300
12. Coldwater ... 328
13. Mt Pleasant ... 331
14. Petoskey ... 340
15. Essexville Garber ... 360
16. Vicksburg ... 382
17. Carleton Airport ... 407
18. Linden ... 408
19. St Clair ... 408
20. Center Line ... 417
21. Monroe Catholic Central ... 439
22. Royal Oak Shrine ... 468
23. Marysville ... 494
24. Sturgis ... 574

1983 BOYS CLASS B TEAM RACE
1. Phil Schoensee (Center Line)12 ... 15:31
2. Rusty Korhonen (Forest Hills Central) ... 15:34
3. John Goble (Petoskey) ... 15:44
4. Lee Kingsley (Parma Western) ... 15:52
5. Rick Prince (St Joseph)12 ... 15:55
6. Rod Skittenhelm (Parma Western) ... 16:11
7. Kyle Rambo (Essexville Garber) ... 16:13
8. Bryan Whitmore (Okemos) ... 16:13
9. Fred Henderson (Fremont) ... 16:14
10. Mark Hale (Mason) ... 16:17
11. Steve Cashman (GR Catholic) ... 16:22
12. Steve MacDonald (GR Catholic) ... 16:23
13. Charles Miller (Mason) ... 16:25
14. John Somers (Fremont) ... 16:26
15. Pat Vandenberg (GR Catholic) ... 16:27
16. Summit (Coldwater) ... 16:30
17. Andy Snyder (Fremont) ... 16:31
18. Tom Frens (Fremont) ... 16:32
19. Gleason (Coldwater) ... 16:33
26. Baer (Fremont) ... 16:41
65. Shomwell (Fremont) ... 17:15
96. Riley (Fremont) ... 17:35

1983 BOYS CLASS B INDIVIDUAL RACE
1. Shaun Butler (Dearborn St Alphonsus) ... 16:09
2. Kevin Hoffman (Detroit Benedictine) ... 16:14
3. Dan McCoy (Hillsdale) ... 16:19
4. Greg Dykstra (Grand Rapids Christian) ... 16:21
5. Todd Vandenberg (GR Christian) ... 16:27
6. Mark Hulliberger (Corunna) ... 16:28
7. Mike Masters (Charlotte) ... 16:29
8. Ritter (Warren Fitzgerald) ... 16:29
9. Darrel Zeck (Saline) ... 16:31
10. Kurschat (Oxford) ... 16:33
11. Thomas (Gladwin) ... 16:34
13. John Fuller (East Grand Rapids) ... 16:36

1984 CLASS B BOYS

Grand Rapids Catholic Central captured its second crown in two years. Said coach Jim Gardiner, "I've had most of this bunch around for so long, it's just hard to describe. They worked so hard, and then to see them come out today and do it exactly the way we planned it."

Catholic Central's Steve Cashman took the lead at halfway, but ran out of steam with a quarter mile to go. Saline's Darrel Zeck kicked away for the win.

Tyrone Hills Golf Course, Linden, Nov. 3 ☐
1984 BOYS CLASS B TEAMS
1. Grand Rapids Catholic Central ... 64
2. Okemos ... 109
3. Jackson Lumen Christi ... 168
4. Fremont ... 235
5. Hillsdale ... 239
6. Bloomfield Hills Cranbrook ... 276
7. Reed City ... 286
8. Wyoming Rogers ... 295
9. Center Line ... 295
10. Three Rivers ... 297
11. Spring Lake ... 300
12. Monroe Catholic Central ... 301
13. Flint Ainsworth ... 375
14. Petoskey ... 384
15. Caro ... 393
16. St Joseph ... 404
17. Essexville Garber ... 404
18. Vicksburg ... 417
19. St Clair ... 436
20. Mt Pleasant ... 437
21. Saline ... 447
22. Hartland ... 487
23. Plainwell ... 502
24. Gibraltar Carlson ... 502
25. Chesaning ... 522
26. Dearborn Divine Child ... 589

1984 BOYS CLASS B TEAM RACE
1. Darrel Zeck (Saline) ... 16:05
2. Joe Parzych (Hillsdale) ... 16:15
3. Mike Bond (St Joseph) ... 16:16
4. Steve McDonald (GR Catholic) ... 16:29
5. Todd Sellon (Spring Lake) ... 16:31
6. Frank Maisano (Center Line) ... 16:32
7. Steve Cashman (GR Catholic) ... 16:32
8. Pat VandenBerg (GR Catholic) ... 16:33
9. Rob Cambran (Okemos) ... 16:34
10. Joe Warner (Reed City) ... 16:35
11. Ian Smith (Plainwell) ... 16:36
12. Roger Russell (Wyoming Rogers) ... 16:36

1984 BOYS CLASS B INDIVIDUAL RACE
1. Ron Rinck (Lansing Waverly) ... 16:13
2. Scott Gleason (Coldwater) ... 16:15
3. Greg Morey (North Branch) ... 16:25
4. Stanley Powell (Richland Gull Lake) ... 16:25
5. Kevin Hoffman (Detroit Benedictine) ... 16:30
6. Bob Schroeder (Melvindale) ... 16;31
7. Mike Kimball (Lansing Waverly) ... 16:36
9. Dan Lewis (Durand) ... nt

1985 CLASS B BOYS

Rich Tompkins' Fremont crew came back with a vengeance to take back the trophy after a year away. The Packers put four in the top 10.

Otsego's Brad Kirk had the fastest time of the day at 15:57.1. He would win the B 1600 title in the spring, but would take 2nd in the 3200 to Scott Ritter of Warren Fitzgerald, who won the individual race here.

Hudson Mills Metro Park, Chelsea, Nov. 2 ☐
1985 BOYS CLASS B TEAMS
1. Fremont ... 52
2. Bloomfield Hills Cranbrook ... 137
3. Center Line ... 169
4. Wyoming Rogers ... 194
5. Vicksburg ... 223
6. Saline ... 240
7. Jackson Lumen Christi ... 303
8. Essexville Garber ... 306
9. Holland Christian ... 308
10. Hartland ... 338
11. Fruitport ... 338
12. Hillsdale ... 346
13. East Grand Rapids ... 362
14. Sturgis ... 388
15. Hemlock ... 415
16. Hastings ... 429
17. Otsego ... 436
18. Petoskey ... 446
19. Dearborn Divine Child ... 447
20. Chelsea ... 454
21. Inkster ... 479
22. Royal Oak Shrine ... 481
23. Stevensville Lakeshore ... 482
24. Flint Ainsworth ... 499
25. Grand Rapids Christian ... 516
26. Oxford ... 520
27. Detroit U-D Jesuit ... 600

1985 BOYS CLASS B TEAM RACE
1. Brad Kirk (Otsego) ... 15:58
2. Collin Wisner (Fremont) ... 16:14
3. Paul Quick (Bloomfield Hills Cranbrook) ... 16:17
4. Roger Russell (Wyoming Rogers) ... 16:20
5. Curt Valentik (Center Line)12 ... 16:21
6. Joe Baer (Fremont) ... 16:24
7. Wayne Oom (Hastings)11 ... 16:25
8. Axel Mertz (Fremont) ... 16:29
9. Tim Bowdish (Chelsea) ... 16:32
10. Steve Eckert (Fremont) ... 16:34
11. Steve Driker (BH Cranbrook) ... 16:34
12. Mike Tenbusch (Detroit U-D Jesuit) ... 16:34
13. Scott Wood (Essexville Garber) ... 16:37
14. Kevin Eldridge (Inkster) ... 16:39
15. Pat McCarthy (East Grand Rapids) ... 16:41

Otsego's Brad Kirk went on to star at Western Michigan, making All-America in 1989.

1985 BOYS CLASS B INDIVIDUAL RACE
1. Scott Ritter (Warren Fitzgerald) ... 16:05
2. Eric Dickerson (Gaylord)10 ... 16:10

3. Scott Gleason (Coldwater) 16:12
4. Stanley Powell (Richland Gull Lake) 16:16
5. Tom Kuntzelman (Parma Western) 16:18
6. Seth Brown (Madison Heights Lamphere) 16:22
7. Josh Montei (Caro)11 16:27
8. Jeff Hough (Corunna)11 16:29
9. Bubba Zirker (Inkster Cherry Hill) 16:30
10. Ron Froeschke (St Joseph)10 16:31
11. Fred Nazar (Yale) 16:32
12. Ian Smith (Plainwell) 16:33
13. Glenn Judd (Mason) 16:35
14. Harold Calhoun (Detroit Northern) 16:37
15. Rich Cross (Lake Odessa Lakewood) 16:37

1986 CLASS B BOYS

Okemos won its first state title at Hudson Mills. "It wasn't an easy thing to do," said coach John Quiring. "We have been trying for four or five years to put one together."

The win came after a fortuitous dip in enrollment. Okemos was Class A the previous season and would go back to Class A the next. Corunna's Jeff Hough had the fastest time of the day; he would later be an All-MAC runner for Central Michigan.

Hudson Mills Metro Park, Dexter, Nov. 1 ☒
1986 BOYS CLASS B TEAMS
1. Okemos 102
2. Dearborn 138
3. Fremont 139
4. Big Rapids 189
5. Sturgis 193
6. Center Line 196
7. Hartland 234
8. St Joseph 275
9. Jackson Lumen Christi 280
10. Caledonia 296
11. Plainwell 304
12. Hillsdale 307
=13. Dearborn Divine Child 335
=13. Essexville Garber 335
15. Warren Fitzgerald 359
16. St Clair 396
17. Corunna 419
18. Grand Rapids West Catholic 433
19. Southgate Aquinas 435
20. Fruitport 445
21. Detroit U-D Jesuit 446
22. Wyoming Rogers 479
23. Farmington Hills Harrison 529
24. Algonac 547

Okemos receiving its first-ever XC state trophy.

1986 BOYS CLASS B TEAM RACE
1. Jeff Hough (Corunna)12 15:56
2. Ian Smith (Plainwell)12 16:01
3. Bryan Cross (Big Rapids)12 16:04
4. Ron Froeschke (St Joseph)11 16:20
5. Collin Wisner (Fremont)12 16:22
6. Scott Walsh (Warren Fitzgerald)11 16:26
7. Brandon Brownell (Okemos)11 16:26
8. Keith Wilkinson (Okemos)12 16:28
9. Rob Kania (Center Line)11 16:31
10. Joel Dood (Okemos)11 16:33
11. Dan Bergdahl (Dearborn)11 16:35
12. Grant Reed (Wyoming Rogers)11 16:36
13. Art Maisano (Center Line)12 16:37
14. Milos Horvat (Dearborn Divine Child)11 16:39
15. Keith Hayes (Dearborn)12 16:39
16. Jim Monty (Big Rapids)12 16:40
17. Mark Osbourne (Hillsdale)12 16:42
31. Jerry Graham (Okemos) 16:55
46. Bob Beekman (Okemos)12 17:07
95. Matt Nelson (Okemos)12 17:38
147. Matt Lydens (Okemos)11 18:39

1986 BOYS CLASS B INDIVIDUAL RACE
1. Josh Montei (Caro)12 16:07
2. Wayne Oom (Hastings)12 16:14
3. Jeff Boks (Bay City Handy)12 16:24
4. Dave Wichens (Fowlerville)12 16:26
5. Jeff Avery (GR South Christian)11 16:29
6. Ken Wolters (Hudsonville)12 16:32
7. Todd Davis (Hemlock)12 16:33
8. Scott Langford (Sparta)11 16:33
9. Eric Dickerson (Gaylord)11 16:35
10. Mike Kessler (Saline)12 16:39
11. Rich Benham (Muskegon Reeths-Puffer)12 16:40
12. Chris Facundo (Bay City Handy)10 16:40
13. Eric Pear (Saline)12 16:41

1987 CLASS B BOYS

It was a day for long overdue returns, as Dearborn returned to the Class B peak for the first time in 57 years. The team, coached by the legendary Bob Bridges, was ranked only No. 7 in the final coaches' poll before the meet. Said St. Joseph coach Ron Waldvogel, whose team had been favored, "We didn't lose the meet. Dearborn went out and won it. We couldn't have beaten Dearborn today."

Willow Metro Park, New Boston, Nov. 7 ☐
1987 BOYS CLASS B TEAMS
1. Dearborn 116
2. St Joseph 130
3. Sturgis 139
4. Fremont 173
5. Hartland 187
6. Caledonia 193
7. Hillsdale 301
8. Warren Fitzgerald 313
9. Forest Hills Central 319
10. Frankenmuth 322
11. Big Rapids 330
12. Ionia 335
13. Greenville 347
14. Essexville Garber 354
15. Dearborn Divine Child 354
16. Grand Rapids South Christian 363
17. Jackson Lumen Christi 370
18. Stevensville Lakeshore 374
19. Hemlock 413
20. Saline 440
21. Oxford 441
22. Mt Clemens 446
23. Southgate Aquinas 489
24. Bloomfield Hills Cranbrook 581

1987 BOYS CLASS B TEAM RACE
1. Mike Goodfellow (Oxford)11 15:55
2. Scott Walsh (Warren Fitzgerald)12 16:06
3. Jeff Granger (Frankenmuth)12 16:08
4. Carl Wades (Hartland)12 16:08
5. Ron Froeschke (St Joseph)12 16:15
6. Milas Horvath (Dearborn Divine Child)12 16:16
7. David Golpe (Warren Fitzgerald)10 16:18
8. Michael Hadous (Dearborn)12 16:20
9. Pressy Nieto (Greenville)11 16:22
10. John Odell (Sturgis)11 16:25
11. Toby LaFere (Jackson Lumen Christi)11 16:26
12. Dan Bergdahl (Dearborn)12 16:28
13. Scott Rector (Big Rapids)11 16:30
14. Rob Stanton (Big Rapids)11 16:30
15. John Barstis (Caledonia)12 16:31
16. McDowell (St Joseph)10 16:34
23. Kurt Barttell (Dearborn) nt
26. Mark Eix (Dearborn) nt
47. Michael Fink (Dearborn) nt

1987 BOYS CLASS B INDIVIDUAL RACE
1. Eric Dickerson (Gaylord)12 15:58
2. Rob Kania (Center Line)12 16:05
3. Bob Bates (Coldwater)10 16:07
4. Mark Donahue (Detroit U-D Jesuit)11 16:13
5. David Abebe (Battle Creek Harper Creek)11 16:20
6. Mike Langford (Sparta)12 16:22
7. Tim Klaes (Monroe St Mary)11 16:23
8. Shawn Burks (Mattawan)12 16:26
9. Keith Mulder (Holland Christian)12 16:29
10. Karl Gieber (Saginaw MacArthur)10 16:30
11. Meinychenko (Carleton Airport)11 16:30
12. Westfall (Three Rivers) 16:32
13. Tuggle (Fowlerville)11 16:32
14. Distelrath (St Clair)12 16:33

1988 CLASS B BOYS

On a cold and drizzly day Ron Waldvogel's St Joseph team finally claimed its title, the Bears' first since winning the Class A crown in 1971. It didn't come easy—they had to edge No. 1 Sturgis by a mere point to pull off the win.

Said Waldvogel, "It was one of the worst driving rain storms I've ever been in. Some of the runners had mud up to the middle of their thighs and they had to leap some puddles a foot-and-a-half deep.

"But our kids braved the elements. Everything just fell into place. I feel great for the kids. They put in a lot of hard work this season and it all paid off Saturday."

Scott Rector of Big Rapids had the fastest time of the day, a modest 16:51 on the normally fast Willow Park course which gives some indication of the challenging conditions.

Willow Metro Park, New Boston, Nov. 5 ☒
1988 BOYS CLASS B TEAMS
1. St Joseph 92
2. Sturgis 93
3. Big Rapids 106
4. Fremont 146
5. Dearborn Divine Child 181
6. Ionia 200
7. Dearborn 206
8. Essexville Garber 245
9. Jackson Lumen Christi 285
10. Sparta 286
11. Stockbridge 287
12. Saline 312
13. Grand Rapids South Christian 342
14. Gaylord 345
15. Mt Clemens 397
16. Pinckney 398
17. Grand Rapids Kenowa Hills 426
18. Vassar 450
19. Battle Creek Harper Creek 471
20. Bay City Handy 496
21. Bloomfield Hills Cranbrook 527
22. Mt Clemens Lutheran North 554
23. Durand 557
24. Ypsilanti Lincoln 583
25. Warren Fitzgerald 630

1988 BOYS CLASS B TEAM RACE
1. Scott Rector (Big Rapids)12 16:51
2. Rick Pott (Grand Rapids South Christian)12 16:56
3. Tony Perron (St Joseph)11 16:57
4. Ben Adler (St Joseph)12 17:05
5. Toby Lafere (Jackson Lumen Christi)12 17:10
6. Rob Stanton (Big Rapids)12 17:12
7. Tim Hildebrand (Essexville Garber)10 17:15
8. Pete McDowell (St Joseph)11 17:16
9. Tom Cosner-Apple (Sturgis)12 17:17
10. Joe Cronley (Sturgis)11 17:20
11. Ted Smith (Fremont)11 17:23
12. Alan Tyler (Durand)12 17:25
13. Chris Facundo (Bay City Handy)12 17:26
14. Jeffrey Kelke (Mt Clemens)12 17:27
15. Aaron Prussian (Saline)11 17:28
16. Mike Koebel (St Joseph)12 17:29

17. Kevin Selfridge (Ionia)11 .... 17:31
18. Mike Pepito (Sturgis)12 .... 17:34
19. Chris Hatty (Dearborn Divine Child) 17:35
20. Brad Charles (Fremont)9 .... 17:35
21. Michael Boruta (Dearborn)10 .... 17:35
61. Dave Sisson (St Joseph)11 .... 18:14
124. Mike Mahler (St Joseph)9 .... 19:03
166. Ben Bramwell (St Joseph)11 .... 20:27

1988 BOYS CLASS B INDIVIDUAL RACE
1. Mike Goodfellow (Oxford)12 .... 17:05
2. Tim Klaes (Monroe St Mary)12 .... 17:06
3. Bob Bates (Coldwater)11 .... 17:21
4. Jason Burndt (Ovid-Elsie)11 .... 17:30
5. Matt Weisdorfer (Oxford)12 .... 17:31
6. Pete Jennings (Ogemaw Heights)12 .... 17:32
7. Matthew Smit (GR West Catholic)12 .... 17:33
8. Jim Parzych (Hillsdale)10 .... 17:34
9. Trevor Smith (Allegan)10 .... 17:35

1989 CLASS B BOYS

Bob Bates of Coldwater won the team race in 16:05.3. Said coach Jim Billsborough, "Bob ran a smart race, and was in better shape with about a half mile to go… I think he got himself in the frame of mind that he was going to go there and win."

Rich Tompkins' Fremont squad put three in the top 13 and won going away with a 81-point margin.

Tyrone Hills Golf Course, Linden, Nov. 4 ☐
1989 BOYS CLASS B TEAMS
1. Fremont 96
2. Saline 177
3. Sturgis 203
4. Dearborn 212
5. Coldwater 215
6. Dearborn Divine Child 220
7. Stockbridge 262
8. Hudsonville Unity Christian 275
9. Beaverton 278
10. Warren Fitzgerald 308
11. Monroe Jefferson 353
12. Algonac 353
13. Oxford 360
14. Grand Rapids Catholic Central 362
15. Cadillac 369
16. Mt Clemens Lutheran North 373
17. Caledonia 385
18. Ionia 399
19. Perry 402
20. Lansing Catholic 409
21. Cedar Springs 410
22. Caro 410
23. Richland Gull Lake 414
24. Bloomfield Hills Cranbrook-Kingswood 426

1989 BOYS CLASS B TEAM RACE
1. Bob Bates (Coldwater)12 .... 16:06
2. Arbria Shepherd (Stockbridge)12 .... 16:12
3. Eric Gelino (Lansing Catholic)12 .... 16:20
4. Brad Charles (Fremont)12 .... 16:22
5. Jeff Christian (Beaverton)10 .... 16:26
6. Aaron Prussian (Saline)12 .... 16:27
7. Brian Smith (Sturgis)12 .... 16:33
8. John Button (Dearborn)11 .... 16:35
9. Ryan Burt (Dearborn Divine Child)10 .... 16:36
10. Joe Cronley (Sturgis)12 .... 16:37
11. Brent Springvloed (Hudsonville UC)12 .... 16:38
12. Ted Smith (Fremont)12 .... 16:42
13. Cliff Somers (Fremont)12 .... 16:45
14. Rich Chriscinske (Saline)10 .... 16:48
15. Larry Adams (Stockbridge)12 .... 16:49
16. Russ Hickey (Coldwater)9 .... 16:50
30. Troy Dekryger (Fremont) .... nt
37. Jeff Storms (Fremont) .... nt

1989 BOYS CLASS B INDIVIDUAL RACE
1. Pete McDowell (St Joseph)12 .... 16:15
2. Jeremy Bruskotter (Big Rapids)11 .... 16:20
3. Gar Eddings (Pinckney)12 .... 16:28
4. James Neumann (Center Line)11 .... 16:34
5. Arjay Schopoeray (Big Rapids)10 .... 16:40
6. Clay Vanderwarf (Lowell)11 .... 16:41
7. David Dolezal (Battle Creek Lakeview)12 .... 16:42
8. Mike Smedley (Buchanan)10 .... 16:43
9. Tim Hildebrand (Essexville Garber)11 .... 16:45
10. Gary Loubert (Hemlock)12 .... 16:46
11. Trevor Smith (Allegan)11 .... 16:46
12. Jack Rininger (Allegan)10 .... 16:47
13. John Baibak (DeWitt)12 .... 16:48
14. Jeff Smith (WB Ogemaw Heights)12 .... 16:48
15. Barry Deese (Linden)10 .... 16:50

1990 CLASS B BOYS

Big Rapids won its first-ever state title with a 50-point margin over Cedar Springs. Jeremy Bruskotter of Big Rapids, the favorite, finished 10 seconds ahead of Center Line's James Neumann to capture the team race win.

Third-placer Kris Eggle eventually competed for the University of Michigan and later served in the U.S. Border Patrol, where he died in the line of service.

Tyrone Hills Golf Course, Linden, Nov. 3 ☐
1990 BOYS CLASS B TEAMS
1. Big Rapids 131
2. Cedar Springs 181
3. Cadillac 182
4. Linden 190
5. Wyoming Godwin Heights 227
6. Plainwell 243
7. Lowell 254
8. Battle Creek Lakeview 256
9. Ortonville Brandon 271
10. Center Line 278
11. Caledonia 279
12. Kalamazoo Christian 290
13. Monroe St Mary 300
14. Dearborn Divine Child 310
15. Saline 318
16. Oxford 319
17. Allegan 339
18. Beaverton 365
19. Warren 392
20. Dearborn Heights Crestwood 406
21. Tecumseh 439
22. Haslett 486
23. Essexville Garber 601

1990 BOYS CLASS B TEAM RACE
1. Jeremy Bruskotter (Big Rapids)12 .... 15:42
2. James Neumann (Center Line)12 .... 15:52
3. Kris Eggle (Cadillac)12 .... 15:55
4. Bob Paulsen (Cadillac)12 .... 16:13
5. Cliff Robinson (Big Rapids)11 .... 16:18
6. Jason Deese (Linden)12 .... 16:19
7. Barry Deese (Linden)11 .... 16:24
8. Jeff McCaul (Caledonia)12 .... 16:28
9. Rich Chriscinske (Saline)11 .... 16:31
10. Jim Marcero (Monroe St Mary)10 .... 16:32
11. Trevor Smith (Allegan)12 .... 16:33
12. Andy Brazee (Plainwell)12 .... 16:35
13. Jason Schrock (Wyoming Godwin Heights)12 .... 16:36
14. Marzuki Stevens (BH Cranbrook)11 .... 16:38
15. David Dolezal (Battle Creek Lakeview)12 .... 16:43
16. Jeff Christian (Beaverton)11 .... 16:48
17. Jesse Laginess (Center Line)11 .... 16:50
18. Larry Wells (Wyoming Godwin Heights)10 .... 16:51
19. Marc Norman (Warren)12 .... 16:51
20. Clay VanderWarf (Lowell)12 .... 16:51
21. Guy Whitaker (Ortonville Brandon) 16:54
22. Ken Fisk (Cedar Springs) 16:55
23. Todd Whitwam (Caledonia) 16:55
24. Arjay Schopieray (Big Rapids) 17:00
36. Eric Wozniak (Big Rapids) 17:16

1990 BOYS CLASS B INDIVIDUAL RACE
1. Randy Logan (Richland Gull Lake)12 .... 16:15
2. Jason Schaefer (Mt Clemens Clintondale)11 .... 16:38
3. Bill Cahill (GR Kenowa Hills)12 .... 16:39
4. Todd Richman (Comstock)11 .... 16:47
5. Matt Angle (Perry)10 .... 16:48
6. Trinity Townsend (Muskegon Heights)11 .... 16:48
7. Joe Martin (Petoskey)10 .... 16:49
8. Adam Kuzinski (Hartland)11 .... 16:49
9. Eric VanHevel (Macomb Lutheran North)12 .... 16:55

1991 CLASS B BOYS

Russ Hickey of Coldwater sprinted past Marzuki Stevens with 200 yards left. Said the winner, "I tried to draft off him to stay out of the wind. Coming out of the woods, it hit so hard. The last 200 yards, I lost all comprehension of where the finish line was."

Over 2,000 fans watched in windy, snowy, 29-degree weather as Fremont won its second title in three years.

Winters Creek GC, Big Rapids, Nov. 2 ☐
1991 BOYS CLASS B TEAMS
1. Fremont 122
2. Saline 160
3. St Joseph 201
4. Jackson Lumen Christi 204
5. Big Rapids 219
6. Cedar Springs 247
7. Coldwater 251
8. Ortonville Brandon 262
9. Dearborn Divine Child 263
10. Caledonia 294
11. Algonac 306
12. Linden 337
13. Farmington Hills Harrison 351
14. Edwardsburg 357
15. Plainwell 368
16. Monroe St Mary 373
17. South Haven 375
18. Bloomfield Hills Cranbrook 398
19. Oxford 422
20. Gladwin 438
21. Marysville 483
22. Sanford Meridian 503
23. West Branch Ogemaw Heights 515
24. Ionia 540
25. Warren Cousino 545

Rich Topkins won the quarter-mile state title for Hart in 1964. As a coach, he guided Fremont to six state titles in cross country.

1991 BOYS CLASS B TEAM RACE
1. Russ Hickey (Coldwater)11 .... 16:25
2. Marzuki Stevens (BH Cranbrook)12 .... 16:29
3. Jim Marcero (Monroe St Mary)11 .... 16:46

4. Cliff Robison (Big Rapids)....16:50
5. Brad Charles (Fremont)....16:51
6. Rich Chriscinske (Saline)....16;52
7. Ryan Burt (Dearborn Divine Child)12....16:53
8. Arjay Schoperay (Big Rapids)....17:11
9. Steve Marcero (Monroe St Mary)....17;13
10. Barry Deese (Linden)12....17:13
11. Phil St Clair (Plainwell)....17:14
12. Mark Goodfellow (Oxford)....17:15
13. Chris Lewis (South Haven)....17;21
14. Ed Kerns (Fremont)....17:21
15. Anthony Fazekas (Jackson Lumen Christi)....17:22
16. Kevin Van Tiem (Gladwin)....17:25
17. Vichs Mattson (Edwardsburg)....17:25
25. Brent Luchies (Fremont)....17:34
32. Rob Klomp (Fremont)....17:39
46. Mike Kelly (Fremont)....17:50

1991 BOYS CLASS B INDIVIDUAL RACE

1. Jeff Christian (Beaverton)12....16:39
2. Bob Busquaert (St Clair S Lake Shore)11....17:01
3. Matt Angle (Perry)....17:08
4. Keizo Takahashi (Tecumseh)....17:15
5. Fred Bedore (Durand)....17;17
6. Michael Hayes (DeWitt)....17:18
7. Daryl Rose (Muskegon Orchard View)....17:18
8. Larry Wells (Godwin Heights)....17:19
9. Ryan Donley (Ludington)....17:20
10. Merrek Sakwa (Bloomfield Hills Andover)....17:21
11. Kevin Niemic (Manistee)....17:22
12. Jeremy Hurley (Wyoming Park)....17:23
13. Erik Randall (Auburn Hills Avondale)....17:24
14. Robert Hyde (Godwin Heights)....17:25
15. Adam Goodrow (Tecumseh)....17:25

1992 BOYS CLASS B BOYS

South Haven captured the B crown. Coach Mark Robinson remarked, "We were 2-13 my first year at South Haven. We've come a long way. The kids never gave up… and we had enough to be there at the end."

Tyrone Hills GC, Linden, Nov. 7 □
1992 BOYS CLASS B TEAMS

1. South Haven....142
2. Coldwater....183
3. Oxford....203
4. Dearborn Divine Child....207
5. Chelsea....209
6. Fremont....214
7. Grant....230
8. St Joseph....252
9. Zeeland....265
10. Caledonia....266
11. Bloomfield Hills Cranbrook....286
12. Jackson Lumen Christi....292
13. West Branch Ogemaw Heights....312
14. Algonac....337
15. Gaylord....357
16. Cedar Springs....377
17. Grosse Ile....387
18. Ortonville....393
19. Buchanan....416
20. Belding....423
21. Big Rapids....425
22. Warren Cousino....432
23. Bloomfield Hills Andover....546
24. Vassar....554

1992 BOYS CLASS B TEAM RACE

1. Joe O'Connor (Ogemaw Heights)11....16:11
2. Russ Hickey (Coldwater)....16:11
3. Mark Goodfellow (Oxford)12....16:31
4. Jon Davis (Gaylord)....16:40
5. Pete Parbel (Caledonia)....16:41
6. Nathan Lewis (South Haven)....16:44
7. Merrek Sakwa (Bloomfield Hills Andover)....16:47
8. Paul Altesleben (Dearborn Divine Child)....16:48
9. Mike Colston (St Joseph)....16:48
10. Jon Marson (Algonac)....16:49
11. Guy Whittaker (Ortonville Brandon)....16:50
12. Will Sherwood (Coldwater)....16:53
13. Ryan Schultz (Chelsea)....16:54
14. Cory Neehan (Bloomfield Hills Cranbrook)....16:57
15. Christopher Lewis (South Haven)....16:57
16. Jason Zimmerman (Grant)....nt
28. David Antonnson (South Haven)....nt
41. Brian Nordin (South Haven)....nt
52. Eddie Foley (South Haven)....nt

1992 BOYS CLASS B INDIVIDUAL RACE

1. Bob Busquaert (St Clair Shores Lakeview)12....16:09
2. David Riemersma (Godwin Heights)12....16:32
3. Jim Marcero (Monroe St Mary)12....16:35
4. Michael Cranmer (Fruitport)....16:35
5. Bill Schutt (Richmond)12....16:39
6. Tom Chorny (Fruitport)....16:39
7. Troy Levely (Caro)....16:42
8. Robert Hyde (Godwin Heights)....16:46
9. Derrik Vruggink (Hudsonville)....16:49
10. Matt Angle (Perry)....16:49
11. Joel Anderson (Spring Lake)....16:53
12. Tommy Clark (Stockbridge)....16:54
13. Ion Hallahan (Albion)....16:55
14. Mike Walczuk (Auburn Hills Avondale)....16:57

1993 CLASS B BOYS

Fremont won its sixth title in Class B. Said coach Rich Tompkins, "This was one of our stronger teams."

Tom Chorny of Fruitport, winner of the individual race, went on to become a successful steeplechaser. He won the 2001 USA title and later became a coach in the collegiate ranks.

Grand Rapids GC, Grand Rapids, Nov. 6 □
1993 BOYS CLASS B TEAMS

1. Fremont....69
2. Dearborn Divine Child....141
3. Bloomfield Hills Cranbrook Kingwood....214
4. Coldwater....231
5. Gaylord....239
6. West Branch Ogemaw Heights....252
7. Oxford....253
8. Albion....300
9. Ypsilanti Lincoln....300
10. Spring Lake....326
11. Zeeland....352
12. Ionia....359
13. Grand Rapids Catholic Central....375
14. St Joseph....380
15. Cedar Springs....382
16. Grosse Ile....386
17. Yale....406
18. Jackson Lumen Christi....416
19. Fowlerville....418
20. Stockbridge....421
21. Ortonville-Brtandon....425
22. Harper Woods....447
23. Grand Rapids South Christian....542
24. Paw Paw....548
25. Frankenmuth....550
26. Allegan....581
27. Bloomfield Hills....584

1993 BOYS CLASS B TEAM RACE

1. Joe O'Connor (Ogemaw Heights)12....15:57
2. Nicholas Lee (Bloomfield Hills Cranbrook)....16:06
3. Paul Altesleben (Dearborn Divine Child)....16:10
4. Ryan Watson (Cedar Springs)....16:14
5. Mitch Arend (Fremont)....16:29
6. Mike Coltson (St Joseph)....16:31
7. Ian Hallahan (Albion)....16:36
8. Josh Mourer (Ionia)11....16:36
9. Eric Stoll (Ypsilanti Lincoln)....16:37
10. Jeremy Eastwood (Fowlerville)11....16:40
11. Brent Luchens (Fremont)....16:40
12. Kent Frens (Fremont)....16:41
13. Joe Anderson (Spring Lake)....16:42
14. Aaron Vandewege (Zeeland)....16:42
15. Jason Quist (Cedar Springs)....16:43
18. Rob Klomp (Fremont)....16:50
23. Scott Waterstrodt (Fremont)....16:59

1993 BOYS CLASS B INDIVIDUAL RACE

1. Tom Chorny (Fruitport)11....16:10
2. Peter Parbel (Caledonia)12....16:18
3. Timothy Tottingham (Linden)....16:25
4. Cory Brown (Chelsea)....16:25
5. Jeff Evans (Marshall)....16:26
6. Troy Levely (Caro)....16:27
7. Mike Barbee (Coloma)....16:30
8. Jeremy Hurley (Wyoming Park)....16:33
9. Jason Ballard (Otisville Lakeland)....16:34
10. Jeffery Cross (Linden)....16:34
11. Robert Curtis (Warren Woods)....16:35
12. Ken Baginski (Center Line)....16:36
13. Justin Pilzer (Algonac)....16:37
14. Derek Vruggink (Hudsonville)....16:42
15. Mike Walczuk (Auburn Hills Avondale)....16:48

1994 BOYS

"I don't think I could have run any faster," said St Joe's Mike Colston, winner of the team race. "The conditions were perfect for me—mud, water and a cool day to run. What a great way to finish out my cross country career. I couldn't have dreamed of a better ending."

Tom Chorny, who repeated as the individual race winner, qualified a few weeks later for Foot Locker Nationals, where he placed 23rd in 15:33.

Coach Jim Lister's Stockbridge squad won the title in only its fourth appearance at the state finals, a year after placing 20th.

Grand Rapids GC, Grand Rapids, Nov. 5 □
1994 BOYS CLASS B TEAMS

1. Stockbridge....143
2. Fremont....177
3. Grand Rapids Catholic Central....178
4. Caledonia....187
5. Brooklyn Columbia Central....253
6. St Joseph....257
7. Chelsea....268
8. West Branch Ogemaw Heights....285
9. Zeeland....311
10. Gaylord....313
11. Coldwater....328
12. Cadillac....341
13. Cedar Springs....345
14. Harper Woods Notre Dame....357
15. Otsego....391
16. Dearborn Divine Child....423
17. Oxford....428
18. Caro....429
19. Grosse Ile....435
20. Ionia....439
21. Trenton....452
22. Bloomfield Hills Andover....454
23. Lowell....459
24. Eaton Rapids....463
25. Vassar....514
26. Croswell....546
27. Clawson....561

1994 BOYS CLASS B TEAM RACE

1. Mike Colston (St Joseph)....16:22
2. Ryan Watson (Cedar Springs)....16:30
3. Troy Levely (Caro)....16:37
4. Ryan Schultz (Chelsea)....16:46
5. Jeff Billsborrow (Coldwater)....16:48
6. Frens Kent (Fremont)....16:49
7. Josh Mourer (Ionia)12....16:51
8. Justin Holzscv (Gaylord)....16:52
9. Ben Thompson (Caledonia)....16:54
10. Kevin Rottier (Fremont)....16:55
11. Kevin Schultz (Clawson)....16:56
12. Bradford Wright (Cadillac)....16:56
13. Jeremy Clark (Stockbridge)11....16:57
14. Phil Lemieux (Brooklyn Columbia Central)....16:58
15. Steve Long (Coldwater)....16:58
16. Phil Lemieux (Brooklyn Columbia Central)....16:58
17. Brent Miedema (Zeeland)....17:00
21. David Allison (Stockbridge)....17:17

23. Matt Ashby (Stockbridge) 17:20
35. Jamey Lister (Stockbridge)9 17:34
51. Nathan Schultz (Stockbridge) 17:45

1994 BOYS CLASS B INDIVIDUAL RACE

1. Tom Chorny (Fruitport)12 16:09
2. Tim Tottingham (Linden) 16:33
3. Ken Baginski (Center Line) 16:40
4. Josh Woodwyk (Houghton Lake) 16:50
5. Jeremy Eastwood (Fowlerville) 16:52
6. Charleten Morgan (Albion) 16:53
7. Jacob Brundage (Stanton-Central Montcalm) 16:58
8. Corey Meehan (Bloomfield Hills Cranbrook) 17:00
9. Jeff Evans (Marshall) 17:01
10. Robert Curtis (Warren Woods Tower) 17:02
11. Kevin Morris (Hillsdale) 17:08
12. Josh Breimayer (Wyoming Rogers) 17:09
13. Steve Short (Saginaw Swan Valley) 17:11
14. Jeffery Cross (Linden) 17:14
15. Keith Vroman (Ludington) 17:15

1995 CLASS B BOYS

Running on a snow-covered course in "bone-chilling" temperatures, Stockbridge pulled off the repeat win for coach Jim Lister, with three runners in the top 25, led by Lister's son, Jamey, in 7th.

"We were the only team I was worried about," said the elder Lister. "With everyone back from the state championship team, I figured that if we ran our best we'd win.

"There was about an inch of snow on the ground and people were falling all over the place. But our guys didn't worry about that. They just went out there and ran."

The winning margin for Stockbridge over second-placer Gaylord was 106 points, the largest in meet history.

Grand Rapids GC, Grand Rapids, Nov. 4 ☐
1995 BOYS CLASS B TEAMS

1. Stockbridge 115
2. Gaylord 221
3. Ida 227
3. Clawson 246
4. Fremont 257
6. Trenton 260
7. St Joseph 270
8. Caledonia 300
9. Eaton Rapids 307
10. West Branch Ogemaw Heights 308
11. Grosse Ile 308
12. Dearborn Heights Crestwood 316
13. Harper Woods Notre Dame 321
14. Coldwater 335
15. Cedar Springs 372
16. Oxford 396
17. Shepherd 400
18. Wayland 403
19. Petoskey 415
20. Marshall 422
21. Dexter 432
22. Wyoming Park 436
23. Grant 447
24. Lowell 521
25. Madison Heights Lamphere 551
26. Richland Gull Lake 589
27. Haslett 639

1995 BOYS CLASS B TEAM RACE

1. Matthew Hantung (HW Notre Dame)12 15:39
2. Kevin Schultz (Clawson)12 15:44
3. Jeff Evans (Marshall) 15:53
4. Gary Schultz (Clawson)12 15:55
5. Jason Thomas (Gaylord)12 15:59
6. Justin Holzschu (Gaylord)11 16:03
7. Jamey Lister (Stockbridge)10 16:04
8. Ryan Piippo (Trenton)11 16:06
9. Steve Long (Coldwater)12 16:08
10. Jason Joloszynski (Shepherd) 16:08
11. Joe Droste (St Joseph)12 16:08
12. Jake Swinehart (Grant)11 16:09
13. Mark Bradley (Eaton Rapids)11 16:11
14. Tim Boring (Stockbridge)11 16:12
17. Gene Barnes (Fremont)12 16:13
25. David Allison (Stockbridge)12 16:25
31. Jeremy Clark (Stockbridge)12 16:32
38. Matt Ashny (Stockbridge)12 16:41
52. Shawn Demint (Stockbridge)10 16:54
89. Brian Boos (Stockbridge)11 17:17

1995 BOYS CLASS B INDIVIDUAL RACE

1. Robert Curtis (Warren Woods)12 15:26
2. Gene Lebron (Albion)12 15:34
3. Ken Baginski (Center Line)12 15:35
4. Kevin Rossiter (Monroe St Mary)12 15:39
5. Ryan Greutman (Carleton Airport)11121 15:39
6. John Hazelbrook (Hudsonville) 15:56
7. Jon Purwin (Grand Rapids West Catholic)11 15:56
8. Kevin Morris (Hillsdale)12 15:57
9. Vinod Aravind (Detroit Country Day)11 15:59
10. Chuck Knuth (Marysville)12 16:02
11. Joe Bertschinger (GR Kenowa Hills)12 16:05
12. Jeremiah McNeilly (Big Rapids)10 16:06
13. Jack Phillips (Coopersville)11 16:12
14. Matt Grulke (Corunna)11 16:13
15. James Carlson (Ludington)11 16:14

1996 CLASS B BOYS

Once the meet moved to Michigan International Speedway, officials took their timing/scoring game up a notch and it was once more feasible to have a single race instead of dividing competitors into team and individual runs. The event featured 1,182 runners from all classes, making it the biggest gathering of high school athletes in MHSAA history.

Despite wind chills in the 20s and light snow, Charlotte's Lyle Mayers won in a thrilling sprint finish over Russ Gerbers of Wyoming Park, 15:37.40 to 15:38.29. "It was hard at the end, but I felt confident I had a good kick. That's what got me here."

Third-placer Tim Boring of Stockbridge was given an award as individual winner of the team race, as the the MHSAA still recognized—on paper at least—separate team and individual champions.

Caledonia, coached by John Soderman, scored its first state win.

Michigan Int. Speedway, Brooklyn, Nov. 2 ☒
1996 BOYS CLASS B TEAMS

1. Caledonia 94
2. Stockbridge 116
3. Corunna 133
4. Gaylord 187
5. Eaton Rapids 208
6. Ypsilanti 264
7. Grosse Ile 285
8. Richland Gull Lake 298
9. West Branch Ogemaw Heights 303
10. Muskegon Orchard View 331
11. Grand Rapids Catholic Central 335
12. Ida 337
13. Big Rapids 339
14. Petoskey 340
15. Clawson 371
16. St Joseph 401
17. Spring Lake 422
18. Bloomfield Hills Cranbrook 423
19. Sparta 449
20. Marysville 464
21. Jackson Lumen Christi 469
22. Jackson Northwest 495
23. Croswell-Lexington 503
24. Harper Woods Notre Dame 527
25. Dexter 528
26. North Branch 561
27. Edwardsburg 686

1996 BOYS CLASS B INDIVIDUALS

1. Lyle Mayers (Charlotte)12 15:38
2. Russ Gerbers (Wyoming Park)12 15:39
3. Tim Boring (Stockbridge)12 15:50
4. Jaime Burke (Dexter) 16:04
5. Justin Hulzschu (Gaylord)12 16:06
6. Matt Grulke (Corunna)12 16:08
7. Jason Moore (Wayland) 16:11
8. Jack Philips (Coopersville)12 16:12
9. Justin Andre (Ypsilanti) 16:13
10. Jared Aldrich (Corunna) 16:13
11. David Vandenberg (Caledonia) 16:14
12. Rick Hornbaker (Algonac) 16:14
13. Nick Brockway (Richlaand Gull Lake)11 16:15
14. Tim Morehouse (Clawson) 16:16
15. Lucus Humphrey (Central Montcalm) 16:17
16. Charlie MacLean (Muskegon Orchard View) 16:17
17. Jamey Lister (Stockbridge)11 16:19
18. John Bruder (Shepard) 16:20
19. Brian Wilson (North Branch) 16:21
20. Mike Wilusz (Royal Oak Dondero) 16:22
21. David Friedrich (Caledonia) 16:23
22. Jacob Russlow (Monroe St. Marys) 16:23
23. Rob Lillie (Caledonia) 16:23
24. Nathan Hoffman (Allegan) 16:24
25. Andrew Vynke (Marysville) 16:24
26. Chris Bien (Oxford) 16:25
27. Todd St Clair (Perry) 16:27
28. Chris Stine (Lamphere) 16:29
29. Michael Paisley (Grosse Ile) 16:30
30. Andy Paiz (GR Catholic Central) 16:31
36. Andy Schupp (Caledonia) 16:35
73. Joe Lyllie (Caledonia) 16:54
149. Ryan Ogle (Caledonia) 17:27
229. Phil VanLaan (Caledonia) 18:03

Gull Lake's Nick Brockway was the best mudder in 1997.

1997 CLASS B BOYS

Nick Brockway of Gull Lake churned over the muddy course in 16:04 for the win. "My body is pretty tired, but inside I feel real good. I shared the lead pretty much all the way. I knew who the top runners would be.

"I didn't want to be a jerk about it, but I kind of knew I could win. I was just thinking this could be my race."

Gordie Aldrich's Corunna squad put three in the top 10 to seal a 74-point win, leaving Lumen Christi 87 points behind.

Michigan Int. Speedway, Brooklyn, Nov. 1
1997 BOYS CLASS B TEAMS
1. Corunna 74
2. Jackson Lumen Christi 161
3. Grand Rapids Catholic Central 162
4. Stockbridge 227
5. St Joseph 238
6. Big Rapids 259
7. Haslett 280
8. Fremont 299
9. Clawson 301
10. Howard City Tri-County 324
11. Richland Gull Lake 328
12. Sparta 340
13. Flint Powers 341
14. Muskegon Orchard View 356
15. Dearborn Heights Crestwood 361
16. Petoskey 380
17. West Branch Ogemaw Heights 394
18. Albion 425
19. Wayland 432
20. Ida 434
21. Harper Woods Notre Dame 447
22. Oscoda 462
23. Hemlock 463
24. Dearborn Divine Child 529
25. Imlay City 579
26. Parma Western 609
27. Bloomfield Hills Andover 700

1997 BOYS CLASS B INDIVIDUALS
1. Nick Brockway (Richland Gull Lake)12 .... 16:04
2. Jamey Lister (Stockbridge)12 .... 16:10
3. Andy Vyncke (Marysville)12 .... 16:19
4. Jarred Aldrich (Corunna)11 .... 16:36
5. Aaron Lindell (Corunna)11 .... 16:38
6. Tim Morehouse (Clawson)12 .... 16:39
7. Jason Moore (Wayland)12 .... 16:42
8. Todd St. Clair (Perry)11 .... 16:42
9. Jed Hindes (Fremont)12 .... 16:43
10. Jeremy Canze (Corunna)11 .... 16:45
11. William Monnett (Clawson)12 .... 16:49
12. Matthew Zissler (Hemlock)12 .... 16:50
13. Shawn Gast (St Joseph)12 .... 16:50
14. Sasha Voight (Haslett)12 .... 16:51
15. Mario Marquez (Dearborn Heights Crestwood).16:52
16. Chris Stine (Madison Heights Lamphere) 16:53
17. Shane Overbey (Dexter)12 .... 16:54
18. John Hall (Clawson)12 .... 16:55
19. Adam Wilson (Stevensville Lakeshore) 16:55
20. Cyrus Fisher (Howard City Tri-County) 16:56
21. Justin Perez (Flint Powers)12 .... 16:57
22. Joe Dolson (Jackson Lumen Christi) 16:58
23. Rick Hornbaker (Algonac)12 .... 17:01
24. Paul Pobursky (Ida)12 .... 17:02
25. Mike Richardson (Godwin Heights)12 .... 17:03
26. Kevin Rathbun (Corunna)12 .... 17:03
27. Steven Sheffer (Muskegon Orchard View) .17:05
28. Max McGonegal (Jackson Lumen Christi) .17:05
29. Ryan Inks (Tecumseh)12 .... 17:06
30. John Dolson (Jackson Lumen Christi) 17:07
63. Andrew Mackay (Corunna)12 .... 17:32
209. Mike Grulke (Corunna)12 .... 18:33
253. Joe Grulke (Corunna)12 .... 19:09

1998 CLASS B BOYS

Corunna, with a key man out with injury, lost a tiebreaker to Gull Lake despite putting three in the top seven. Tom DeVault, the Gull Lake coach, said, "A team wins titles in cross country and we did it with an entire team."

It was the first time in Class B history that officials had to go to the tiebreaker for first place.

The Blue Devils' race was keyed by soph Kurtis Marlowe, a 4:23.39 performer at 1600, now in his first season of cross country.

Corunna's Jared Aldrich won the individual crown.

Michigan Int. Speedway, Brooklyn, Nov. 7
1998 BOYS CLASS B TEAMS
1. Richland Gull Lake 128
2. Corunna 128
3. Marysville 132
4. Muskegon Orchard View 198
5. Petoskey 221
6. West Branch Ogemaw Heights 249
7. Flint Powers 277
8. Big Rapids 287
9. Ida 289
10. Battle Creek Lakeview 292
11. Jackson Lumen Christi 298
12. Coldwater 334
13. Hudsonville Unity Christian 347
14. Perry 349
15. Williamston 351
16. Grand Rapids Catholic Central 355
17. Trenton 357
18. Holland Christian 392
19. St. Joseph 430
20. Essexville Garber 450
21. South Haven 476
22. Gladwin 488
23. Imlay City 502
24. Orchard Lake St. Mary's 515
25. Dearborn Heights Crestwood 658
26. Bloomfield Hills Andover 702
27. Clawson 764

Corunna's Jared Aldrich won big in 1998. (Corunna XC photo)

1998 BOYS CLASS B INDIVIDUALS
1. Jared Aldrich (Corunna)12 .... 15:13
2. Kurtis Marlowe (Richland Gull Lake)10 ...... 15:29
3. Andy Vyncke (Marysville)12 .... 15:31
4. Jeremy Canze (Corunna)12 .... 15:34
5. Mike Richardson (Godwin Heights)gel)12 .. 15:35
6. Brian Wilson (North Branch)12 .... 15:35
7. Aaron Lundell (Corunna)12 .... 15:39
8. Joel David (Wyoming Kelloggsville) 15:40
9. Ryan Hesselink (Middleville TK)12 .... 15:40
10. Patrick Roberts (Trenton)10 .... 15:40
11. Steve Sheffer (Muskegon Orchard View)12 . 15:41
12. Chris Stine (Madison Heights Lamphere)12 .. 15:43
13. Lucas Humphrey (Central Montcalm)12 ... 15:43
14. Jeff Mulder (Haslett)12 .... 15:43
15. Dave Haagsma (GR South Christian)11 ... 15:44
16. Tim Ross (Caledonia)9 .... 15:45
17. Dan Wilkerson (Marysville)12 .... 15:48
18. Todd St. Clair (Perry)12 .... 15:50
19. Adam Tumele (Muskegon Orchard View)12 ..... 15:51
20. Josh Neal (Marysville)9 .... 15:51
21. Justin Perez (Flint Powers)11 .... 15:54
22. Alan Bruder (WB Ogemaw Heights)12 .... 15:56
23. Paul Pobursky (Ida)12 .... 15:56
24. Graham Wellman (Frankenmuth)10 .... 15:58
25. Brendan Gary (GR Catholic Central)12 ... 16:02
26. Nicholas Carson (Fowlerville)11 .... 16:04
27. Dan Kasprowicz (Godwin Heights)11 ...... 16:04
28. Tony McHerron (South Haven)11 .... 16:04
29. Garnet Johnson (WB Ogemaw Heights)12 ... 16:05
30. Charles Penninger (Edwardsburg)11 ...... 16:06
41. Robert Urmy (Richland Gull Lake)12 ...... 16:12
42. Charles Massey (Richland Gull Lake)12 .. 16:12
51. Brian Mauzy (Richland Gull Lake)12 ...... 16:19
65. Kristopher Krzyminski (Corunna)9 .... 16:25
79. Luke Fiordalis (Richland Gull Lake)11 .... 16:31
85. Steve Saterlee (Richland Gull Lake)11 ... 16:33
116. David Haglund (Richland Gull Lake)11 . 16:44
140. Robert Currie (Corunna)12 .... 16:52
211. Judd Robertson (Corunna)11 .... 17:29
213. Ian Faber (Corunna)9 .... 17:32

1999 CLASS B BOYS

Flint Powers took the team title with a 18-point margin, helped along by Justin Perez. The senior finished first, topping Kurtis Marlowe, and keeping Gull Lake from having the individual winner for three straight years.

Said Perez, "It's great. I can't explain it. It's just amazing. I was ranked fourth going into the race and I knew I could be up there with everyone else."

Michigan Int. Speedway, Brooklyn, Nov. 6
1999 BOYS CLASS B TEAMS
1. Flint Powers 144
2. Holland Christian 162
3. Big Rapids 170
4. Trenton 199
5. Ida 211
6. Richland Gull Lake 234
7. Caledonia 248
8. Gaylord 294
9. Perry 298
10. South Haven 298
11. Stockbridge 316
12. Harper Woods Notre Dame 318
13. Chelsea 334
14. Tecumseh 341
15. Williamston 364
16. Coldwater 379
17. Sparta 385
18. Petoskey 386
19. St. Joseph 408
20. Dearborn Divine Child 410
21. Richmond 448
22. Howard City Tri-County 514
23. Gladwin 526
24. Bad Axe 552
25. Imlay City 595
26. Warren Woods-Tower 602
27. Tawas City 733

1999 BOYS CLASS B INDIVIDUALS
1. Justin Perez (Flint Powers)12 .... 15:20
2. Kurtis Marlowe (Richland Gull Lake)11 ..... 15:29
3. Jordan Emmorey (Gaylord)12 .... 15:34
4. Tim Ross (Caledonia)10 .... 15:37
5. Brian Maat (Holland Christian)10 .... 15:43
6. Pat Roberts (Trenton)11 .... 15:45
7. Justin Blakely (Big Rapids)12 .... 15:46
8. Steve Cuttita (Flint Powers)12 .... 15:48
9. Adam Ludwig (St Joseph)10 .... 15:49
10. Tim DuBuc (Onsted)10 .... 15:56
11. Michael Grammes (Tecumseh)11 .... 16:00

12. Dave Hagsma (GR South Christian)12 16:04
13. Tony McHerron (South Haven)12 16:07
14. Dan Kasprowicz (Godwin Heights)12 16:08
15. Mike Linch (Stevensville Lakeshore)11 16:08
16. John Cook (St Clair)11 16:09
17. Charles Penninger (Edwardsburg)12 16:11
18. Jason Stover (Williamston)11 16:11
19. Don Wilkins (Trenton)12 16:12
20. Andy Brickel (Richmond)10 16:12
21. Dave Ernsberger (Petoskey)12 16:13
22. Mitch Petz (Caledonia)12 16:15
23. Marc Michaels (HW Notre Dame)11 16:15
24. Graham Wellman (Frankenmuth)11 16:19
25. Craig Potter (Cedar Springs)11 16:21
26. Todd Peabody (Perry)12 16:23
27. Luke Fiordalis (Richland Gull Lake)12 16:25
28. Jon O'Connor (WB Ogemaw Heights)12 16:26
29. Mark Lubbers (Holland Christian)12 16:27
30. John Montri (Ida)12 16:28
34. Leo Foley (Flint Powers)12 16:31
63. Kyle Pennell (Flint Powers)10 16:46
133. Jesse Gould (Flint Powers)9 17:12
183. Mike Cushman (Flint Powers)12 17:38
251. Matt Cuttitta (Flint Powers)10 18:36

2000 D2 BOYS

Kurtis Marlowe finally got his win, making it three years out of four for Gull Lake. "My sophomore year, it was great to finish second. Then last year, I knew how bad it felt to finish second when I was favored. This year I haven't run awesome, but I'm still there and I feel like people aren't really giving me a chance."

Big Rapids, coached by Brad Kahrs, moved up from 3rd for the team win.This was the first year that the sport moved to divisional classifications, with approximately the same number of schools in each division.

Michigan Int. Speedway, Brooklyn, Nov. 4 ⊠
2000 BOYS DIVISION 2 TEAMS

1. Big Rapids 103
2. St Clair 110
3. Holland Christian 148
4. Flint Powers 157
5. Petoskey 241
6. Ionia 243
7. Fremont 303
8. Lake Odessa Lakewood 306
9. Farmington 330
10. Chelsea 334
11. Tecumseh 349
12. Caro 357
13. Richland Gull Lake 362
14. Bloomfield Hills Cranbrook 379
15. Dearborn Divine Child 410
16. Remus Chippewa Hills 411
17. Flint Kearsley 429
18. East Lansing 433
19. Harper Woods Notre Dame 438
20. Birmingham Seaholm 453
21. Allegan 461
22. Three Rivers 463
23. Grosse Ile 472
24. Oxford 478
25. Carleton Airport 491
26. St. Joseph 559
27. Madison Heights Lamphere 631

2000 BOYS DIVISION 2 INDIVIDUALS

1. Kurtis Marlowe (Richland Gull Lake)12 15:03
2. Tim Ross (Caledonia)11 15:17
3. Adam Ludwig (St Joseph)11 15:27
4. Brian Maat (Holland Christian)12 15:28
5. Andrew Bauer (Bloomfield Hills Lahser)11 15:38
6. John Cook (St Clair)12 15:47
7. Pat Roberts (Trenton)12 15:52
8. Tim O'Hara (Big Rapids)11 15:54
9. Ben Salvette (Cranbrook-Kingswood)11 15:55
10. Josh Huyser-Honig (GR Christian)11 15:56
11. Michael Pierce (Dearborn Divine Child)12 15:58
12. Scott Evans (Fremont)12 16:03
13. Ryan Hurley (Coldwater)12 16:05
14. Matt Casillas (East Grand Rapids)11 16:06
15. Michael Grammes (Tecumseh)12 16:07
16. Timothy Kelsh (Remus Chippewa Hills)...1016:07
17. Lawrence McElroy (St Clair)10 16:08
18. James Jones (Fremont)11 16:08
19. Jacob Baron (Monroe Jefferson)11 16:09
20. Mike Walls (Warren Woods-Tower)12 16:12
21. Kyle Pennell (Flint Powers) 16:14
22. Lance Betts (Big Rapids)11 16:15
23. Derek Meiring (Carleton Airport)11 16:15
24. Chris Kirwin (Big Rapids)11 16:16
25. Jesse Gould (Flint Powers)10 16:16
26. Tyler Zwagerman (Holland Christian)11 16:17
27. Jeff Riggleman (Tecumseh)11 16:19
28. Richard Vogelzang (Holland Christian)11 16:21
29. Craig Potter (Cedar Springs)12 16:21
30. Josh Miller (Belding)12 16:22
50. Geoff May (Big Rapids)11 16:36
59. Corey Reinke (Big Rapids)11 16:42
80. Nate VandeMark (Big Rapids)11 16:53
99. Sam Shewan (Big Rapids)10 17:02

2001 D2 BOYS

The day's fastest race at MIS went to Tim Ross, who hammered through the first two mile markers in 4:29 and 9:23 before finishing in 15:04. He later placed 5th at Foot Locker nationals in 14:58. Said Ross, "The race went exactly how I wanted it to go. I went out and got a big lead by the mile mark. I just wanted to go out fast and then try to hold on."

Ross's 37.5-second winning margin broke the record for the biggest in meet history.

Big Rapids held onto its team title, winning by 49 points over powerhouse Fremont as an expected challenge from St. Clair didn't materialize.

Michigan Int. Speedway, Brooklyn, Nov. 3 ⊠
2001 BOYS DIVISION 2 TEAMS

1. Big Rapids 81
2. Fremont 130
3. Flint Powers 168
4. Bloomfield Hills Lahser 223
5. St Clair 239
6. Dexter 262
7. Lake Odessa Lakewood 266
8. East Lansing 271
9. East Grand Rapids 299
10. Petoskey 318
11. Grand Rapids Christian 344
12. Stevensville Lakeshore 344
13. Monroe Jefferson 344
14. Corunna 349
15. Haslett 353
16. Bloomfield Hills Cranbrook 401
17. Sparta 408
18. Madison Heights Lamphere 416
19. Oxford 424
20. Richland Gull Lake 434
21. Ionia 447
22. Grosse Ile 448
23. Cadillac 469
24. Carleton Airport 487
25. Orchard Lake St. Mary's 592
26. Sturgis 617
27. Harper Woods Notre Dame 663

2001 BOYS DIVISION 2 INDIVIDUALS

1. Tim Ross (Caledonia)12 15:04
2. Andrew Bauer (BH Lahser)12 15:42
3. Adam Ludwig (St Joseph)12 15:55
4. Scott Kallgren (Trenton)12 15:59
5. Tyler Zwagerman (Holland Christian)12 16:01
6. Lance Betts (Big Rapids)12 16:07
7. Tim O'Hara (Big Rapids)12 16:07
8. Ben Salvette (Cranbrook Kingswood)12 16:11
9. Jacob Baron (Monroe Jefferson)12 16:11
10. Luke Walker (Flint Powers)10 16:12
11. Dennis Rathke (East Lansing)12 16:14
12. Jim Pancoast (Stevensville Lakeshore) 16:16
13. Matt Casillas (East Grand Rapids)12 16:16
14. Curtis Christensen (Flint Kearsley)10 16:16
15. James Jones (Fremont)12 16:19
16. Josh Huyser-Honig (GR Christian)12 16:21
17. Timothy Kelsh (Remus Chippewa Hills)11 16:22
18. Jesse Gould (Flint Powers)11 16:23
19. Sean Derby (Cadillac)12 16:23
20. Matt Sackrider (Battle Creek Harper Creek)1216:23
21. Nick Lewis (Gaylord)10 16:24
22. Robby Young (Wayland)11 16:24
23. Riley Klingel (Fremont)9 16:25
24. Sam Shewan (Big Rapids)11 16:26
25. Jeff Byrne (Bay City John Glenn)11 16:27
26. Justin Kessler (Ionia)12 16:28
27. Jeff Riggleman (Tecumseh)12 16:28
28. Derek Scott (Grand Rapids Northview)11 16:29
29. Nathen Straathof (Fremont)10 16:29
30. Travis Williams (Lake Odessa Lakewood)1216:30
36. Nate VandeMark (Big Rapids)12 16:36
57. Corey Reinke (Big Rapids)12 16:50
107. Cody Chupp (Big Rapids)11 17:16
214. Chris Kirwin (Big Rapids)12 18:33

2002 D2 BOYS

Sophomore Riley Klingel of Fremont scored the win over Bay City Glenn's Jeff Byrne, 15:25.10 to 15:25.55. Luke Walker of Flint Powers had led early, but Klingel started moving at the 2M mark and outraced Byrne to the line.

Dexter won its first boys title—the Dreadnaughts had won the girls meet in 1981. Coach Jaime Dudash's team finished 32 points ahead of Powers Catholic.

Michigan Int. Speedway, Brooklyn, Nov. 2 ⊠
2002 BOYS DIVISION 2 TEAMS

1. Dexter 70
2. Flint Powers 102
3. Bloomfield Hills Lahser 188
4. Fremont 198
5. Grosse Ile 200
6. Haslett 264
7. Chelsea 273
8. Sparta 275
9. Grand Rapids Christian 281
10. St Clair 292
11. Grand Rapids Catholic Central 297
12. Big Rapids 301
13. Allegan 331
14. East Grand Rapids 333
15. Richland Gull Lake 361
16. Croswell-Lexington 394
17. Petoskey 398
18. Fenton 436
19. Dearborn Heights Crestwood 443
20. Coldwater 476
21. Orchard Lake St. Mary's 495
22. Center Line 511
23. Cadillac 530
24. Dearborn Divine Child 560
25. Greenville 620
26. Farmington Hills Harrison 682
27. St Clair Shores Lakeview 753

2002 BOYS DIVISION 2 INDIVIDUALS

1. Riley Klingel (Fremont)10 15:26
2. Jeff Byrne (Bay City Glenn)12 15:26
3. Jared Kelsch (Remus Chippewa Hills)11 15:41
4. Luke Walker (Flint Powers)11 15:44
5. Christopher Burke (Dexter)12 15:47
6. Dan Meyer (Dexter)11 15:54
7. Larz McElroy (St Clair)12 15:55
8. Nick Lewis (Gaylord)11 15:56
9. Jon Hodge (Grosse Ile)12 15:56
10. Timothy Kelsh (Remus Chippea Hills)12 15:57
11. Riak Mabil (Charlotte) 15:58
12. Corey Thelen (Lake Odessa-Lakewood) 15:58
13. Jack DaSilva (Tecumseh) 15:59
14. Dan Roberts (Vicksburg) 16:03
15. AJ McConnell (Sparta) 16:04

16. Michael Barrows (Flint Powers) 16:07
17. Dan Cramer (Cedar Springs) 16:07
18. Sam Shewan (Big Rapids) 16:09
19. Tony Nalli (Dexter) 16:10
20. Curtis Christensen (Flint Kearsley) 16:11
21. Jesse Gould (Flint Powers) 16:11
22. Emory Nelkie (WB Ogemaw Heights) 16:12
23. Jon Hans (Dearborn Heights Crestwood) 16:12
24. Bruce Kaczmarek (BH Lahser) 16:12
25. Mark Vandermeer (Wyoming Park) 16:17
26. Jim Pancoast (Stevensville Lakeshore) 16:18
27. Nathen Straathof (Fremont) 16:18
28. Daniel Morris (Lake Odessa Lakewood) 16:18
29. Mike Quick (Bloomfield Hills Lahser) 16:19
30. Ben Piercy (Richland Gull Lake) 16:21
36. Ryan Boluyt (Dexter) 16:23
54. Lex Williams (Dexter) 16:40
74. Andrew Porinsky (Dexter) 16:52
121. TJ LaRosa (Dexter) 17:12

2003 D2 BOYS

A successful defense for Dexter was helped along by its top two, Tony Nalli and Dan Meyer, placing in the top six. Nalli led for the first half of the race before Luke Walker of Flint Powers went by him at the 2M mark.

Michigan Int. Speedway, Brooklyn, Nov. 1 ⊠
2003 BOYS DIVISION 2 TEAMS

1. Dexter 76
2. Bloomfield Hills Lahser 128
3. Flint Powers 130
4. Grand Rapids Christian 147
5. Gaylord 228
6. Fremont 229
7. Petoskey 273
8. East Grand Rapids 323
9. Cedar Springs 325
10. Fenton 341
11. Grand Rapids Catholic Central 342
12. Mattawan 347
13. Center Line 366
14. Richland Gull Lake 381
15. Dearborn Heights Crestwood 381
16. East Lansing 382
17. Coldwater 400
18. Chelsea 426
19. St. Clair 429
20. Croswell-Lexington 469
21. Mt Pleasant 509
22. Dearborn Divine Child 516
23. Orchard Lake St. Mary's 538
24. Carleton Airport 566
25. Hazel Park 590
26. Sparta 606
27. Redford Thurston 782

2003 BOYS DIVISION 2 INDIVIDUALS

1. Luke Walker (Flint Powers)12 .... 15:13
2. Tony Nalli (Dexter)11 .... 15:27
3. Daniel Roberts (Vicksburg)10 .... 15:33
4. Corey Thelen (Lake Odessa Lakewood)11 ... 15:35
5. Riley Klingel (Fremont)11 .... 15:36
6. Dan Meyer (Dexter)12 .... 15:37
7. Nick Lewis (Gaylord)12 .... 15:41
8. Dan Cramer (Cedar Springs)11 .... 15:45
9. Dave Vandenberge (GR Christian)12 .... 15:45
10. Chris Baker (Mattawan)12 .... 15:46
11. Jon Hans (Dearborn Heights Crestwood)12 15:46
12. Joel Schut (Grand Rapids Christian)11 .... 15:48
13. Nate Dehaan (GR South Christian)11 .... 15:50
14. Christopher Olds (Gaylord)10 .... 15:51
15. Dale Staudaker (Croswell-Lexington)11 .... 15:52
16. Mathew Willings (Flint Powers)11 .... 15:52
17. Bruce Kaczmarek (Bloomfield H Lahser)11. 15:52
18. Jeff Standfest (St. Clair)11 .... 15:53
19. Lex Williams (Dexter)11 .... 15:55
20. Nathan Straathof (Fremont)12 .... 15:55
21. Matthew Rose (Bloomfield Hills Lahser)12 .. 15:58
22. Michael Quick (Bloomfield Hills Lahser)10 .. 16:00
23. Ryan Boluyt (Dexter)12 .... 16:01
24. Joel Dehaan (GR South Christian)12 .... 16:01
25. Mike Walker (Fenton)12 .... 16:02
26. Abraham Mach (East Lansing)12 .... 16:03
27. Nathan Watts (Haslett)12 .... 16:05
28. Timothy Horst (Trenton)11 .... 16:07
29. Trevor Bach (Chelsea)12 .... 16:09
30. Andrew Lawrick (Stevensville)11 .... 16:09
45. TJ LaRosa (Dexter)11 .... 16:27
79. Ryan Neely (Dexter)9 .... 16:48
106. Dan Jackson (Dexter)9 .... 17:00

2004 D2 BOYS

Vicksburg junior Daniel Roberts pulled out the win over Riley Klingel on a windy day. "Riley and I stayed with each other until the last 200 or 300 and I pulled away from him. It was a really long battle until the end and it was definitely a struggle. I knew I had God on my side and that I could pull through."

Roberts noted that the ground was soft and "we weren't sure how to approach the race."

Later that fall Roberts qualified for the Foot Locker Nationals where he placed 18th. For his senior year he moved to Colorado and improved his national placing to 12th.

Klingel tragically died in the spring of 2005 in an auto accident on his way to school for a morning run. He had signed with Michigan State where had had been expected to make an impact. Said Fremont coach Cliff Somers, "Our school is just devastated."

Vicksburg's Daniel Roberts kicked best.

Michigan Int. Speedway, Brooklyn, Nov. 6 ⊠
2004 BOYS DIVISION 2 TEAMS

1. Dexter 93
2. Fremont 128
3. Bloomfield Hills Lahser 174
4. Flint Powers 230
5. Sparta 260
6. Coldwater 272
7. Grand Rapids Christian 275
8. Forest Hills Northern 275
9. Chelsea 277
10. Richland Gull Lake 283
11. Petoskey 299
12. Corunna 304
13. East Grand Rapids 311
14. Birmingham Seaholm 319
15. St Clair 350
16. Hazel Park 355
17. Lowell 373
18. Three Rivers 425
19. Fenton 429
20. Vicksburg 444
21. Big Rapids 495
22. Orchard Lake St Mary's 498
23. Ferndale 600
24. Carleton Airport 616
25. Royal Oak Kimball 651
26. Dearborn Heights Crestwood 703
27. Ypsilanti 703

2004 BOYS DIVISION 2 INDIVIDUALS

1. Daniel Roberts (Vicksburg)11 .... 15:20
2. Riley Klingel (Fremont)12 .... 15:23
3. Dan Cramer (Cedar Springs)12 .... 15:39
4. Lex Williams (Dexter)12 .... 15:43
5. Patrick Grosskopf (Corunna)11 .... 15:47
6. Van Tate (Petoskey)11 .... 15:47
7. Tony Nalli (Dexter)12 .... 15:54
8. Jeff Standfest (St Clair)12 .... 15:56
9. Corey Thelen (Lake Odessa-Lakew)12 .... 15:58
10. Robert Gunn (Detroit Central)12 .... 16:01
11. Nate Poirier (Center Line) 16:02
12. Jameson Bilsborrow (Coldwater) 16:04
13. Andrew Ropp (Flint Powers) 16:05
14. Ross Faasse (Forest Hills Northern) 16:06
15. Joel Schut (Grand Rapids Christian) 16:08
16. Tim Horst (Trenton) 16:11
17. Andrew Lawrick (Stevensville) 16:12
18. Mike Quick (Bloomfield Hills Lahser) 16:14
19. Ian Girard (Chelsea) 16:14
20. Nate DeHaan (GR South Christian) 16:15
21. Mathew Willings (Flint Powers) 16:16
22. Mitchell Hoffman (St. Johns) 16:17
23. Craig Vachon (GR Catholic Central) 16:18
24. Justin Kelly (Ferndale) 16:19
25. Ryan Reiterman (Warren Lincoln) 16:19
26. Patrick Liederbach (Petoskey) 16:20
27. Simon Nyang (Forest Hills Northern) 16:21
28. Peter Wilson (Richland Gull Lake) 16:22
29. Dan Jackson (Dexter)10 .... 16:24
30. Erik Westbrook (Fremont) 16:25
40. TJ LaRosa (Dexter) 16:37
58. Bobby Aprill (Dexter)9 .... 16:53
100. Ryan Neely (Dexter)10 .... 17:17
106. Charles Wolcott (Dexter) 17:20

2005 D2 BOYS

Landon Peacock, who sat out the 2004 season after transferring to Cedar Rapids, captured the individual title: "I wanted this state championship ever since I was a freshman. I guess it was my time to do it."

Peacock would go on to star at Wisconsin, where he was a 2-time All-American and the 2010 Big 10 champion in cross country.

Dexter won its fourth-straight title under the coaching of Jamie Dudash; that tied the record for most consecutive wins set by Dearborn in the meet's first four years, 1927-30.

Michigan Int. Speedway, Brooklyn, Nov. 5 ⊠
2005 BOYS DIVISION 2 TEAMS

1. Dexter 95
2. Bloomfield Hills Lahser 130
3. Flint Powers 180
4. Sparta 184
5. Coldwater 205
6. Petoskey 222
7. Corunna 281
8. Three Rivers 283
9. St Clair 299
10. Fremont 300
11. Forest Hills Northern 305
12. Grand Rapids Christian 329
13. Mattawan 337
14. Fenton 349
15. Birmingham Seaholm 359

16. Chelsea	360	
17. Holland Christian	419	
18. East Grand Rapids	425	
19. Ypsilanti	466	
20. Vicksburg	472	
21. Dearborn Divine Child	484	
22. Bangor Glenn	511	
23. Royal Oak Kimball	532	
24. Hazel Park	562	
25. Bloomfield Hills Cranbrook	569	
26. Carleton Airport	588	
27. Farmington Hills Harrison	628	

2005 BOYS DIVISION 2 INDIVIDUALS
1. Landon Peacock (Cedar Springs)12 ... 15:10
2. Patrick Grosskopf (Corunna)12 ... 15:19
3. Van Tate (Petoskey)12 ... 15:25
4. Dan Jackson (Dexter)11 ... 15:31
5. Ian Girard (Chelsea)12 ... 15:39
6. Mitchell Hoffman (St Johns)12 ... 15:39
7. Addis Habtewold (St Clair)10 ... 15:41
8. Bobby Aprill (Dexter)10 ... 15:42
9. Simon Nyang (Forest Hills Northern)12 ... 15:43
10. Patrick Liederbach (Petoskey)11 ... 15:52
11. Willy Dague (Monroe Jefferson) ... 15:55
12. Nathan Poirier (Center Line) ... 15:55
13. Jay Bilsborrow (Coldwater) ... 15:58
14. Michael Quick (Bloomfield Hills Lahser) ... 15:58
15. Andrew Ropp (Flint Powers) ... 16:03
16. Tyler Emmorey (Cedar Springs) ... 16:03
17. Eric Stouten (Sparta) ... 16:04
18. James Lanciaux (Fremont) ... 16:04
19. Jason Bishop (Dexter)9 ... 16:04
20. Alex Donaghy (Greenville) ... 16:06
21. Tom Posner (Center Line) ... 16:06
22. Henry Frey (East Lansing) ... 16:07
23. Trent Denhof (Grant) ... 16:08
24. Steve Bates (Corunna) ... 16:09
25. Ryan Reiterman (Warren Lincoln) ... 16:09
26. Joseph Grace (Bloomfield Hills Lahser) ... 16:10
27. Blaise Henning (Petoskey) ... 16:11
28. Gregory Bodfish (South Haven) ... 16:11
29. Ted Howard (Birmingham Seaholm) ... 16:12
30. Brett Busuttil (Algonac) ... 16:12
50. Ryan Neely (Dexter)11 ... 16:28
71. Charles Wolcott (Dexter) ... 16:40
110. Andrew Martin (Dexter)11 ... 16:59
165. Alex Hess (Dexter)10 ... 17:24

2006 D2 BOYS

Dexter won its record fifth in a row in the most impressive fashion, with Bobby Aprill and Dan Jackson going 1-2, sophomore Jason Bishop in 5th, Ryan Neely in 8th and Ben Steavenson in 13th.

"There's a lot of pressure because people expected a lot from us," said Steavenson. "Bad races are not an option."

Media was quick to call the score a "state record," ignoring three lower scores by Niles in the 1930s, plus another 28 by Ypsilanti in 1943. While that was long ago and the meet was much smaller then, a record is a record.

One achievementot was indisputed: the Dreadnaughts' margin over Sparta was the biggest ever, at 114.

Michigan Int. Speedway, Brooklyn, Nov. 4 ☒
2006 BOYS DIVISION 2 TEAMS
1. Dexter ... 28
2. Sparta ... 142
3. Fremont ... 157
4. Fenton ... 175
5. Linden ... 221
6. Bloomfield Hills Lahser ... 253
7. Three Rivers ... 267
8. Forest Hills Eastern ... 275
9. Caledonia ... 291
10. Petoskey ... 312
11. Richmond ... 318
12. Birmingham Seaholm ... 331

13. Muskegon Orchard View ... 347
14. St Clair ... 350
15. Sturgis ... 361
16. Bloomfield Hills Cranbrook ... 386
17. Chelsea ... 394
18. Eaton Rapids ... 399
19. Grand Rapids Christian ... 425
20. Corunna ... 444
21. South Haven ... 446
22. Coldwater ... 446
23. Alma ... 553
24. Remus Chippewa Hills ... 557
25. Ferndale ... 665
26. Carleton Airport ... 677
27. Dearborn Heights Annapolis ... 750
28. Farmington Hills Harrison ... 809

2006 BOYS DIVISION 2 INDIVIDUALS
1. Bobby Aprill (Dexter)11 ... 15:16
2. Dan Jackson (Dexter)12 ... 15:16
3. Addis Habtewold (St Clair)11 ... 15:22
4. Eric Stouten Jr. (Sparta)12 ... 15:28
5. Jason Bishop (Dexter)10 ... 15:34
6. James Lanciaux (Fremont)11 ... 15:34
7. Joe Dimambro (Fenton)12 ... 15:34
8. Ryan Neely (Dexter)12 ... 15:40
9. Pat Liederbach (Petoskey)12 ... 15:48
10. Neil Grundman (Croswell-Lexington)12 ... 15:48
11. Jesse Anderson (Fenton)11 ... 15:51
12. Ted Howard (Birmingham Seaholm)11 ... 15:56
13. Ben Steavenson (Dexter)11 ... 15:57
14. Mike Morgan (Fremont)11 ... 15:59
15. Nate Knisely (Coldwater)12 ... 16:00
16. Michael Skinner (Linden)11 ... 16:02
17. Nathan Martin (Three Rivers)11 ... 16:02
18. Brad Ferrara (Linden)11 ... 16:02
19. Nick Krol (Bloomfield Hills Lahser)12 ... 16:03
20. Brendan Smith (Chelsea)12 ... 16:04
21. Mike Fish (Mattawan)12 ... 16:05
22. Erik Westbrook (Fremont)11 ... 16:06
23. Tyler Emmorey (Cedar Springs)12 ... 16:08
24. Henry Frey (East Lansing)11 ... 16:11
25. Billy Stone (Fruitport)12 ... 16:12
26. Chris McCarty (Richmond)12 ... 16:13
27. Joey Grace (Bloomfield Hills Lahser)11 ... 16:13
28. Chris Pratt (North Branch)12 ... 16:14
29. Adam Yost (Sparta)12 ... 16:15
30. Brad Dauber (Sparta)12 ... 16:18
52. Andrew Martin (Dexter)12 ... 16:37
102. Alex Hess (Dexter)11 ... 16:57

2007 D2 BOYS

Addis Habtewold of St Clair kicked past defending champion Bobby April in the final stretch to claim the win. Said Habtewold, "It kind of scared me when he took the lead for a while. But I went after him, he kind of slowed down and I caught up to him. I didn't even look back, I just went all out."

After crossing the finish, Habtewold was overcome with emotion. "I fell to the ground and started crying. I was shaking. I didn't believe it."

Fremont ended Dexter's reign on top, outscoring the Dreadnaughts 105-138, despite Dexter putting three in the top five. Pointing out the Packer top four were all seniors, lead runner Erik Westbrook said, "It was a perfect way to end our careers."

Michigan Int. Speedway, Brooklyn, Nov. 3 ☒
2007 BOYS DIVISION 2 TEAMS
1. Fremont ... 105
2. Dexter ... 138
3. Linden ... 147
4. Forest Hills Eastern ... 157
5. Grand Rapids Christian ... 201
6. Petoskey ... 224
7. Caledonia ... 240
8. Chelsea ... 241
9. Bloomfield Hills Lahser ... 261

10. St Clair ... 277
11. Vicksburg ... 284
12. Fenton ... 292
13. Alma ... 324
14. St Joseph ... 343
15. Three Rivers ... 364
16. Eaton Rapids ... 367
17. Sparta ... 421
18. Flint Powers ... 462
19. Trenton ... 469
20. Spring Lake ... 503
21. Carleton Airport ... 517
22. Otsego ... 572
23. Tecumseh ... 590
24. Flint Kearsley ... 593
25. Ferndale ... 669
26. St Clair Shores Lake Shore ... 675
27. Madison Heights Lamphere ... 848

Addis Habtewold of St. Clair topped defending champion Bobby Aprill of Dexter. (Pete Draugalis photo)

2007 BOYS DIVISION 2 INDIVIDUALS
1. Addis Habtewold (St Clair)12 ... 15:11
2. Bobby Aprill (Dexter)12 ... 15:17
3. Jason Bishop (Dexter)11 ... 15:30
4. Nathan Martin (Three Rivers)12 ... 15:37
5. Ben Steavenson (Dexter)12 ... 15:44
6. Ted Howard (Birmingham Seaholm)12 ... 15:49
7. Joey Kryza (Fenton)12 ... 15:51
8. Isaiah Stone (Muskegon OV)12 ... 15:53
9. Brad Ferrara (Linden)11 ... 15:55
10. Jesse Anderson (Fenton)12 ... 15:56
11. Erik Westbrook (Fremont)12 ... 15:58
12. Joey Grace (Bloomfield Hills Lahser)12 ... 16:00
13. Mike Morgan (Fremont)12 ... 16:02
14. Henry Frey (East Lansing)12 ... 16:02
15. Jeff MacMillan (Mattawan)11 ... 16:07
16. Jacob Batch (Fruitport)12 ... 16:08
17. Reed Kamyszek (GR Kenowa Hills)10 ... 16:09
18. James Lanciaux (Fremont) 12 ... 16:11
19. Blaise Henning (Petoskey)12 ... 16:13
20. Anthony Sterzick (Caledonia)11 ... 16:13
21. Edward Seymour (Wayland)12 ... 16:14
22. Alex Bergquist (Forest Hills Eastern)12 ... 16:14
23. Xavier Manalo (SCS Lake Shore)11 ... 16:15
24. Brandon Hoffman (Parma Western)11 ... 16:16
25. Michael Dunn (Trenton)12 ... 16:16
26. Chad Scott (Forest Hills Eastern)10 ... 16:16
27. Chris Ryan (Vicksburg)11 ... 16:16
28. August Pappas (Chelsea)9 ... 16:17
29. James Kirschner (St. Joseph)11 ... 16:17

30. Isaac Webb (Ferndale)12 .... 16:18
43. Davis Lindsay (Fremont)12 .... 16:27
63. Nick Butcher (Fremont)9 .... 16:40
133. Charlie Fias (Fremont)9 .... 17:22
134 Matt Carlson (Fremont)11 .... 17:22

2008 D2 BOYS

With the cupboard nearly bare in Dexter and Fremont decimated by graduation, a new champion was preordained. Clint Lawhorne's Linden team didn't just win by default, however. A powerful 59-point performance gave the Eagles a winning margin of 115 points. It broke Dexter's 2006 record for the biggest margin ever by a single point.

"I felt we were mentally prepared to go," said Lawhorne. "We had a lot of experience returning and most had run this course before. But this is still a new experience for us, to be ranked No. 1 since the beginning of the season. We've always run as the underdog."

Reed Kamyszek of Kenowa Hills topped Mattawan's Jeff MacMillan, 15:32.2-15:34.7. "Even though I had teammates here for support… it can make things a little more nervous not having your team in the race, especially at the beginning."

Reed Kamyszek nearing the finish. (Pete Draugalis photo)

Michigan Int. Speedway, Brooklyn, Nov. 1 ⊠
2008 BOYS DIVISION 2 TEAMS
1. Linden 59
2. Vicksburg 174
3. Otsego 191
4. Chelsea 215
5. Forest Hills Eastern 222
6. Williamston 225
7. Fremont 266
8. Ionia 281
9. Fenton 288
10. Flint Powers 302
11. St Johns 313
12. Grand Rapids South Christian 339
13. Mattawan 340
14. Grand Rapids Christian 341
15. Sturgis 346
16. Byron Center 355
17. East Lansing 374
18. Alma 424
19. St Clair 447
20. Sparta 513
21. Cadillac 517
22. Pontiac Notre Dame 540
23. West Branch Ogemaw Heights 541

24. Tecumseh 568
25. Lapeer East 636
26. Carleton Airport 654
27. Trenton 664
28. Richmond 693

2008 BOYS DIVISION 2 INDIVIDUALS
1. Reed Kamyszek (GR Kenowa Hills)11 .... 15:33
2. Jeff MacMillan (Mattawan)12 .... 15:35
3. Jake Hord (Linden)11 .... 15:43
4. Mike Darnell (Gibraltar Carlson)11 .... 15:46
5. Brad Ferrara (Linden)12 .... 15:46
6. Garrett Cullen (Forest Hills Eastern)11 ...... 15:46
7. August Pappas (Chelsea)10 .... 15:50
8. Matt Hoshal (East Lansing)11 .... 15:50
9. Kyle Slaughter (Ionia)12 .... 15:50
10. Jake Batch (Fruitport)12 .... 15:52
11. Tommy Brinn (Otsego)12 .... 15:52
12. Brendan Sage (Linden)11 .... 15:53
13. Xavier Manalo (SCS Lake Shore)12 .... 15:54
14. Ben Carruthers (Dexter)11 .... 15:56
15. Daniel Suber (BH Cranbrook)12 .... 15:56
16. Chris Ryan (Vicksburg)12 .... 15:57
17. Joseph Maki (Flint Powers)12 .... 15:58
18. Nick Butcher (Fremont)10 .... 15:58
19. Mark Beams (Vicksburg)11 .... 15:58
20. Ian Hancke (Haslett)11 .... 15:59
21. Alex Salemi (St. Johns)11 .... 15:59
22. Robbie Pemberton (Petoskey)12 .... 16:02
23. John Rlsch (Williamston)12 .... 16:03
24. Brandon Hoffman (Parma Western)12 .... 16:04
25. Kyle LeMieux (Linden)12 .... 16:04
26. Morsi Rayyan (St. Johns)11 .... 16:04
27. Kyle Anderson (Milan)12 .... 16:05
28. Jimmy Mckeiver (GR Catholic Central)12 ... 16:05
29. Kevin Barry (Lansing Waverly)12 .... 16:06
30. Derrick Laparl (St. Clair)11 .... 16:09
41. Dylan Ryan (Linden)11 .... 16:22
73. Mark Wright (Linden)10 .... 16:41
136. Garret Chappell (Linden)11 .... 17:11

2009 D2 BOYS

Kenowa Hills and its '08 champion, Reed Kamyszek, moved up to Division I, opening the door for Chris Burns of Pontiac Note Dame. "I wanted to go out with the pack, but not be the first out because it was windy," said Burns. "[Mark] Beams made a move, so I just tried sticking with him. I noticed the pace was slowing down, so I picked it up going into the stadium. I wanted this more than anything."

A year after not qualifying a team, Dexter came back as a contender but was beaten into second by a superlative performance from Ionia. It was the first time the Bulldogs had ever broken into the top fve.

The key to the win for Chris Young's team may have been top runner Austin Alcala, who was only 33rd at regionals because of a case of the flu. He rebounded for 13th place at MIS.

Michigan Int. Speedway, Brooklyn, Nov. 7 ⊠
2009 BOYS DIVISION 2 TEAMS
1. Ionia 92
2. Dexter 184
3. Flint Powers 201
4. Grand Rapids West Catholic 204
5. Vicksburg 217
6. Gaylord 221
7. Linden 222
8. Forest Hills Eastern 225
9. Williamston 226
10. St. Joseph 248
11. Forest Hills Northern 253
12. Sturgis 281
13. Alma 287
14. Croswell-Lexington 377
15. St Clair 401
16. Chelsea 413
17. Grand Rapids Christian 414
18. Fremont 419

19. Grand Rapids Catholic Central 425
20. Big Rapids 441
21. West Branch Ogemaw Heights 485
22. Dearborn Divine Child 570
23. Bloomfield Hills Lahser 573
24. Trenton 643
25. Yale 646
26. Carleton Airport 678
27. Orchard Lake St Mary's 764

Chris Burns pulls away from Jacob Hord off the final turn. (Pete Draugalis photo)

2009 BOYS DIVISION 2 INDIVIDUALS
1. Chris Burns (Pontiac Notre Dame)12 .... 15:48
2. Jacob Hord (Linden)12 .... 15:51
3. Mark Beams (Vicksburg)12 .... 15:58
4. August Pappas (Chelsea)11 .... 16:04
5. Morsi Rayyan (St Johns)12 .... 16:10
6. Matt Hoshal (East Lansing)12 .... 16:11
7. Ben Carruthers (Dexter)12 .... 16:12
8. Alex Standiford (Mattawan)11 .... 16:15
9. Taylor Compton (Hamilton)11 .... 16:18
10. Martin Nelkie (WB Ogemaw Heights)12 .. 16:18
11. Garrett Cullen (Forest Hills Eastern)12 ... 16:22
12. Ian Hancke (Haslett)12 .... 16:22
13. Austin Alcala (Ionia)12 .... 16:23
14. Chris Schulist (Zeeland West)12 .... 16:23
15. Connor Mora (Cedar Springs)9 .... 16:24
16. Sam Felton (St Joseph)12 .... 16:25
17. Cameron Dobson (Croswell-Lexington)11 ... 16:26
18. Jeff Sattler (Byron Center)11 .... 16:27
19. Bryce Bradley (Chelsea)10 .... 16:28
20. Morgan Timiney (Plainwell)12 .... 16:28
21. Nick Butcher (Fremont)11 .... 16:29
22. Michael Stewart (Mason)12 .... 16:30
23. Zeke Timmer (GR West Catholic)11 .... 16:30
24. Don Blight (Ionia)11 .... 16:31
25. John Webb (Monroe Jefferson)11 .... 16:31
26. Spencer Ferris (Forest Hills Eastern)11 .. 16:32
27. Blake Bitner (GR West Catholic)11 .... 16:36
28. Josh Clark (Edwardsburg)10 .... 16:36
29. Clark Ruiz (Big Rapids)9 .... 16:38
30. Spencer Pioszak (Williamston)12 .... 16:43
36. Nick Wharry (Ionia)10 .... 16:48
41. Connor Montgomery (Ionia)10 .... 16:54
44. Brandon Winter (Ionia)9 .... 16:57
48. Cody Kasper (Ionia)11 .... 17:00
114. Tyler Ellis (Ionia)11 .... 17:30

2010 D2 BOYS

"I worked on my kick a lot in practice," said Mattawan's Alex Standiford. It showed, as the senior put away Chelsea's Bryce Bradley in the final 600m. "It pays off in a situation like this."

Forest Hills Northern put together a clutch effort to win the big trophy for the first time. Said coach Joe Curcuru, "We ran the second, third, fifth and sixth best times in school history today."

Alex Standiford prepared for a big finish. (Pete Draugalis photo)

Michigan Int. Speedway, Brooklyn, Nov. 6
2010 BOYS DIVISION 2 TEAMS
1. Forest Hills Northern 108
2. Mason 163
3. Grand Rapids Christian 202
4. Fremont 213
5. Ionia 216
6. Sparta 238
7. St Joseph 239
8. Otsego 264
9. East Lansing 264
10. Haslett 266
11. Mattawan 280
12. St Clair 288
13. Richland Gull Lake 290
14. Gaylord 331
15. Byron Center 349
16. Dearborn Divine Child 353
17. Chelsea 388
18. Croswell-Lexington 411
19. Linden 412
20. Alma 434
21. Adrian 450
22. Trenton 588
23. Corunna 632
24. Marine City 666
25. Mt Pleasant 682
26. Detroit Country Day 713
27. South Lyon East 731

2010 BOYS DIVISION 2 INDIVIDUALS
1. Alex Standiford (Mattawan)12 .... 15:20
2. Bryce Bradley (Chelsea)11 .... 15:27
3. Nicholas Soter (Dearborn Divine Child)11 ...... 15:28
4. Nick Butcher (Fremont)12 .... 15:38
5. Connor Mora (Cedar Springs)10 .... 15:39
6. Robbie Glew (East Lansing)12 .... 15:40
7. August Pappas (Chelsea)12 .... 15:42
8. Jeff Sattler (Byron Center)12 .... 15:44
9. George O'Connor (Croswell-Lexington)11 ..... 15:46
10. Cameron Dobson (Croswell-Lexington)12 ... 15:48
11. Jacob Towne (Forest Hills Northern)11 .... 15:51
12. Don Blight (Ionia)12 .... 15:54
13. Rick Perez (Adrian)12 .... 15:55
14. Alex Vancamp (Haslett)11 .... 15:56
15. Kenny Wherry (Easton Rapids)10 ... 15:58
16. Taylor Compton (Hamilton)12 .... 15:59
17. Alex Whitmer (Mason)10 .... 16:00
18. Zach Stepanovich (Forest Hills Northern)12 16:04
19. Clark Ruiz (Big Rapids)10 .... 16:04
20. Bryan Harvey (Otsego)11 .... 16:05
21. Brennan Shafer (St Clair)10 .... 16:06
22. Luke Johnson (Ludington)10 .... 16:06
23. William Trice (Forest Hills Northern)11 .... 16:07
24. Eric Veldcamp (Grand Rapids Christian)11 . 16:07
25. Jake Featherstone (Fremont)12 .... 16:08
26. Esrom Woldemichael (GR Northview)10 ..... 16:09
27. Greg Madendorp (Whitehall)12 .... 16:10
28. Tanner Hinkle (Mason)10 .... 16:10
29. Ryan Beyea (Haslett)11 .... 16:11
30. Josh Clark (Edwardsburg)11 .... 16:11
32. Ben LaFave (Forest Hills Northern)11 .... 16:13
65. Grant Cook (Forest Hills Northern)11 .... 16:36
172. Gabe Stepanovich (Forest H Northern)11.. 17:28
173. Nate Dwarshuis (Forest Hills Northern)12.. 17:28

2011 D2 BOYS

Mason, coached by Charles Miller, moved up from the previous year's runner-up position to capture its first state title. Miller called it before the meet: "I think we're ready. Everyone's ready, feeling good and looking forward to it."

Chelsea's Bryce Bradley also moved up from the second spot, winning a close one against Divine Child's Nicholas Soter, 15:20.6-15:21.9. Said Bradley, who was wearing a knee wrap: "I was dying. I could not go any faster. I just didn't want to lose. I just started kicking. I had never lost to Soter before and didn't want to lose to him here."

Michigan Int. Speedway, Brooklyn, Nov. 5
2011 BOYS DIVISION 2 TEAMS
1. Mason 92
2. St Joseph 129
3. Ionia 134
4. Cedar Springs 205
5. Grand Rapids Christian 209
6. Sparta 236
7. St Clair 253
8. Chelsea 262
9. Linden 272
10. Richland Gull Lake 301
11. Haslett 305
12. Forest Hills Northern 310
13. Dearborn Divine Child 320
14. Forest Hills Eastern 350
15. Sturgis 376
16. Vicksburg 383
17. Gaylord 402
18. Zeeland East 426
19. Clio 439
20. Grand Rapids South Christian 441
21. Milan 474
22. Croswell-Lexington 518
23. Monroe Jefferson 539
24. Marine City 575
25. Bloomfield Hills Lahser 667
26. Detroit Country Day 719
27. Ferndale 734

2011 BOYS DIVISION 2 INDIVIDUALS
1. Bryce Bradley (Chelsea)12 .... 15:21
2. Nicholas Soter (Dearborn Divine Child)12 ... 15:22
3. Connor Mora (Cedar Springs)11 .... 15:34
4. Tanner Hinkle (Mason)11 .... 15:42
5. Clark Ruiz (Big Rapids)11 .... 15:54
6. Alex Whitmer (Mason)11 .... 15:55
7. Joey Fici (Vicksburg)11 .... 15:56
8. David Berry (St Joseph)11 .... 16:03
9. Dallas Shields (Hazel Park)11 .... 16:03
10. Kenny Wherry (Easton Rapids)11 ... 16:05
11. Joe Cecil (Mason)12 .... 16:06
12. Brandon Winter (Ionia)12 .... 16:06
13. Griffin Miller (Dearborn Divine Child)11 ..... 16:07
14. Wuoi Mach (Grand Rapids Christian)11 ..... 16:07
15. Connor Montgomery (Ionia)12 .... 16:08
16. Cody Smith (St Clair)12 .... 16:08
17. Ryan Beyea (Haslett)12 .... 16:09
18. Dustin Brummel (Middleville TK)12 .. 16:11
19. Roger Phillips (Linden)11 .... 16:12
20. Brice Brown (Ionia)11 .... 16:13
21. Adam Birkeland (Sparta)12 .... 16:13
22. Austin Horn (Chelsea)11 .... 16:15
23. Alex McCormick (Haslett)10 .... 16:17
24. Ryan Hearth (Cadillac)11 .... 16:17
25. Mason VanDyke (Mason)10 .... 16:19
26. Nick Wharry (Ionia)10 .... 16:19
27. Charlie Felton (St Joseph)10 .... 16:20
28. Ben Deuling (Muskegon Orchard View)12... 16:21
29. Brandon George (Sparta)12 .... 16:22
30. Danny Hughes (Vicksburg)12 .... 16:22
77. Jacob Hanson (Mason)10 .... 16:51
162. Preston Tickner (Mason)9 .... 17:36
237. Paul Pioszak (Mason)10 .... 19:10

2012 D2 BOYS

Connor Mora of Cedar Springs decided to play this one by ear. "I went in ready to adjust my strategy with whatever the race threw at me. When [Tanner] Hinkle took it out hard, I decided to sit back and wait until the 2M to see where he would take it."

Mora went into the lead with 800 left. "I thought, 'Just go. It's the right time and I need to start hitting it now.' I had to go.

"I gave it all I had, and if he had a better ending, then that was it."

St. Clair took the team title; it was coach Jon Davidson's 100th career win. Top runner Brennan Schafer waited for the official results. "It felt like an hour and they finally posted it. I couldn't see it, but the St. Joe coach turned around and said, 'Congrats, you guys are state champs.'"

Connor Mora later captained Michigan's cross country team and won All-America honors in track. (Pete Draugalis photo)

Michigan Int. Speedway, Brooklyn, Nov. 3
2012 BOYS DIVISION 2 TEAMS
1. St Clair 114
2. Linden 128
3. St Joseph 153
4. Cedar Springs 201
5. Mason 242
6. Chelsea 244
7. Richland Gull Lake 261
8. Grand Rapids Christian 271
9. Otsego 283
10. Ionia 307
11. Sturgis 334
12. Forest Hills Northern 339
13. East Grand Rapids 356
14. Bloomfield Hills Lahser 393
15. St Johns 393
16. Croswell-Lexington 409
17. Clio 411
18. Riverview 472
19. Owosso 489
20. Dearborn Divine Child 497
21. Gaylord 508
22. Whitehall 511
23. South Haven 522
24. Milan 532
25. Zeeland West 628
26. Bloomfield Hills Andover 629
27. Marine City 638
28. Orchard Lake St Mary's 655

2012 BOYS DIVISION 2 INDIVIDUALS
1. Connor Mora (Cedar Springs)12 .... 15:05
2. Tanner Hinkle (Mason)12 .... 15:10
3. Clark Ruiz (Big Rapids)12 .... 15:33
4. Mason VanDyke (Mason)11 .... 15:34
5. Kenny Wherry (Eaton Rapids)12 .... 15:34
6. Roger Phillips (Linden)12 .... 15:36
7. Alex Whitmer (Mason)12 .... 15:36
8. Chris Koon (Clio)12 .... 15:36
9. Mowgli Crosby (Forest Hills Eastern)12 .... 15:38
10. Brennan Shafer (St Clair)12 .... 15:40
11. Brandon Winter (Ionia)12 .... 15:41
12. Austin Horn (Chelsea)12 .... 15:44
13. Aaron Baumgarten (Williamston)12 .... 15:45
14. Dallas Shields (Hazel Park)12 .... 15:50
15. Cody Smith (St Clair)11 .... 15:52
16. Graham Elliott (Linden)12 .... 15:52
17. Brice Brown (Ionia)12 .... 15:53
18. Luke Johnson (Ludington)12 .... 15:53
19. Brad Hoekstra (Allendale)11 .... 15:54
20. Justin Starr (Otsego)11 .... 15:54
21. Codey Cook (St Johns)10 .... 15:54
22. John Sattler (Byron Center)11 .... 15:54
23. Zach LeMieux (Linden)12 .... 15:55
24. Charlend Howard (Gaylord)12 .... 15:55
25. Jacob Stubbs (Chelsea)11 .... 15:58
26. Steven Griffith (Sturgis)12 .... 15:59
27. Austin Sargent (Cedar Springs)10 .... 15:59
28. Griffin Miller (Dearborn Divine Child)12 .... 16:00
29. Charlie Felton (St Joseph)11 .... 16:00
30. David Berry (St Joseph)12 .... 16:00
39. Trevor Holowaty (St Clair)11 .... 16:10
45. Dakota Hazel (St Clair)12 .... 16:18
47. Andrew Snider (St Clair)12 .... 16:19
68. Nathan Leonard (St Clair)12 .... 16:31
88. Buddy Broskey (St Clair)9 .... 16:40

2013 D2 BOYS

"The race went how I planned," said winner Austin Sargent of Cedar Springs. "I wanted to stay with the group until about 2M and then make my move. Third mile was strong, except for the finish. That was really hard."

After losing four seniors from its top 6 the year before, one might have thought that St. Clair would have a tough time defending. Said senior Cody Smith, "At the end of last year we weren't sure how things would turn out this year. But as summer training went on and the season started, we began to get our hopes back up. The mentality we had last year carried over into this year."

Michigan Int. Speedway, Brooklyn, Nov. 2
2013 BOYS DIVISION 2 TEAMS
1. St Clair 106
2. St Joseph 127
3. Grand Rapids Christian 180
4. Linden 198
5. Otsego 226
6. Chelsea 246
7. Forest Hills Northern 252
8. East Grand Rapids 276
9. Forest Hills Eastern 289
10. Sturgis 299
11. Croswell-Lexington 318
12. Mason 326
13. Clio 363
14. Orchard Lake St Mary's 369
15. Milan 371
16. Corunna 389
17. Ludington 403
18. Whitehall 405
19. Dearborn Divine Child 416
20. Petoskey 463
21. South Haven 463
22. Grand Rapids Catholic Central 492
23. Pontiac Notre Dame 496
24. Flat Rock 595
25. Essexville Garber 606
26. Bloomfield Hills Cranbrook-Kingswood 687
27. Ferndale 688

Austin Sargent made it two individual wins in a row for Cedar Springs. (Pete Draugalis photo)

2013 BOYS DIVISION 2 INDIVIDUALS
1. Austin Sargent (Cedar Springs)11 .... 15:43
2. Mason VanDyke (Mason)12 .... 15:49
3. Blake Watson (Corunna)10 .... 15:53
4. Alex McCormick (Haslett)12 .... 15:59
5. Justin Starr (Otsego)12 .... 16:00
6. Cody Smith (St Clair)12 .... 16:07
7. Codey Cook (St Johns)11 .... 16:09
8. Cal Morgan (Forest Hills Northern)12 .... 16:11
9. Benny Briseno (Grand Rapids Christian)11 .. 16:12
10. David Trimas (Chelsea)11 .... 16:13
11. Trevor Holowaty (St Clair)12 .... 16:13
12. Morgan Beadlescomb (Algonac)10 .... 16:14
13. Joey Humes (Milan)10 .... 16:14
14. Keaton Smith (Whitehall)11 .... 16:16
15. Erik Edwards (St Joseph)11 .... 16:16
16. Paul Pioszak (Mason)12 .... 16:17
17. Adam Gizowski (St Clair)12 .... 16:20
18. Nolan Redetzke (Forest Hills Eastern)12 .. 16:21
19. Tyler Starr (Otsego)12 .... 16:22
20. John Sattler (Byron Center)12 .... 16:23
21. Sam Butler (Richland Gull Lake)12 .... 16:24
22. Andrew Wittland (Forest Hills Northern)11 .. 16:24
23. Matthew Ritter (Ludington)12 .... 16:26
24. Joe Gallagher (Orchard Lake St Mary's)11 .. 16:26
25. Dave Doyle (Linden)12 .... 16:28
26. Mark DeJong (Grand Rapids Christian)12 .. 16:28
27. Nathan Mylenek (Pontiac Notre Dame)10 .. 16:29
28. Nick Jewell (St Joseph)11 .... 16:30
29. Stephen Pfahler (St Joseph)12 .... 16:31
30. Kapo Suarez (Coopersville)11 .... 16:32
38. Paul Schneider (St Clair)12 .... 16:39
73. Austin Kromroy (St Clair)12 .... 17:01
91. Ryan Parslow (St Clair)12 .... 17:08
150. Buddy Brosky (St Clair)10 .... 17:34

2014 D2 BOYS

Junior Morgan Beadlescomb didn't know how safe his lead was on the final stretch. "I heard the announcer; that's the one thing I remember hearing. I heard the announcer say that I would be the future state champion when I still had 100 meters to go."

Beadlescomb had run alongside defending champion Austin Sargent until the 3M mark, when he turned a convincing sprint into a 12-second win.

Grand Rapids Christian won its first state title, topping Fremont by 21 points.

Morgan Beadlscomb of Algonac won the first of two titles in 2014. (Pete Draugalis photo)

Michigan Int. Speedway, Brooklyn, Nov. 1
2014 BOYS DIVISION 2 TEAMS
1. Grand Rapids Christian 83
2. Fremont 104
3. East Grand Rapids 199
4. Clio 208
5. St Joseph 228
6. Chelsea 255
7. Linden 263
8. Corunna 269
9. Forest Hills Northern 305
10. Sparta 310
11. Otsego 314
12. Sturgis 314
13. Orchard Lake St Mary's 320
14. Pontiac Notre Dame 351
15. Zeeland West 373
16. Parma Western 397
17. St Clair 426
18. St Johns 456
19. Richland Gull Lake 463
20. Petoskey 476
21. Allen Park 500
22. Dearborn Divine Child 538
23. Grand Rapids South Christian 593
24. Ann Arbor Richard 595
25. Armada 615
26. Bloomfield Hills Cranbrook-Kingswood 701
27. Ferndale 735
28. Detroit Country Day 789

2014 BOYS DIVISION 2 INDIVIDUALS
1. Morgan Beadlescomb (Algonac)11 ....15:31
2. Austin Sargent (Cedar Springs)12 ....15:43
3. Daniel Steele (Sturgis)11 ....15:44
4. Matthew Zerfas (Fremont)10 ....15:53
5. Noah Jacobs (Corunna)10 ....15:57
6. Thomas VanSlembrouck (Pinckney)12 ....15:58
7. Nathan Mylenek (Pontiac Notre Dame)11 ....16:01
8. Benny Briseno (Grand Rapids Christian)12 ...16:02
9. Sam Kaastra (Fremont)10 ....16:04
10. Alex Stowell (Freeland)12 ....16:04
11. ColinKemner (Adrian)12 ....16:08
12. Codey Cook (St Johns)12 ....16:11
13. Justin Varineau (Grand Rapids Christian)10 16:12
14. Shawn Bell (Sturgis)11 ....16:12
15. Skyler Arthur (St Joseph)12 ....16:12
16. Ethan Taljonick (Clio)11 ....16:15
17. Miles Garn (Charlotte)12 ....16:17
18. Jim VanDyke (Grand Rapids Christian)12 ...16:17
19. Jacob Starr (Otsego)11 ....16:17
20. Alec Keaton (Allen Park)12 ....16:17
21. Mitch Kolito (DeWitt)12 ....16:18
22. Erik Edwards (St Joseph)12 ....16:18
23. Brendan Fraser (Pontiac Notre Dame)10 ....16:18
24. Brad Thomas (Battle Crk Harper Creek)12 ..16:20
25. Matthew Levitt (East Grand Rapids)11 ....16:21
26. Brandon Urban (Carleton Airport)12 ....16:21
27. Keaton Smith (Whitehall)12 ....16:21
28. Colin McNally (Ann Arbor Richard)12 ....16:21
29. Josiah Quinn (St Johns)11 ....16:21
30. Ryan Torok (Linden)12 ....16:22
36. Leland Robertson (GR Christian)12 ....16:27
45. Patrick Jonker (Grand Rapids Christian)12 ..16:32
55. Aaron Brink (Grand Rapids Christian)10 .....16:40
65. Zach Terpstra (Grand Rapids Christian)12 ..16:46

2015 D2 BOYS

Getting spiked in the early going did not hold Morgan Beadlescomb back from winning his second title. With windy conditions, no one had staged a breakaway early and the Algonac senior entered the stadium with Noah Jacobs, Brendan Fraser and Nathan Mylenek.

On the run in, no one was stronger than Beadlescomb.

"That was my goal all year and it feels really good to come here and take it like I did. It was a really big pack and I was still able to kick it in," said the Algonac senior.

Beadlescomb would star at Michigan State, earning cross country All-American honors as a junior in 2019.

With four runners in the top 19, Fremont easily won its eighth title over a surprising runner-up Otsego squad that had come in ranked No. 9.

Michigan Int. Speedway, Brooklyn, Nov. 7
2015 BOYS DIVISION 2 TEAMS
1. Fremont..69
2. Otsego..162
3. Clio..171
4. Coldwater...173
5. Corunna..174
6. Grand Rapids Christian.........................191
7. St Clair..216
8. East Grand Rapids................................249
9. Pontiac Notre Dame..............................259
10. Spring Lake..319
11. Richland Gull Lake...............................330
12. St Johns..331
13. Orchard Lake St Mary's.......................379
14. Williamston...429
15. Yale...446
16. Linden...456
17. Hamilton..461
18. Big Rapids..465
19. Chelsea...483
20. Forest Hills Eastern.............................494
21. Grosse Ile...496
22. Sturgis...499
23. Allen Park...506
24. Sparta...545
25. Parma Western....................................555
26. Croswell-Lexington..............................587
27. Hudsonville Unity Christian.................603
28. Essexville Garber.................................646

2015 BOYS DIVISION 2 INDIVIDUALS
1. Morgan Beadlescomb (Algonac)12 ....15:27
2. Noah Jacobs (Corunna)11 ....15:31
3. Brendan Fraser (Pontiac Notre Dame)11.....15:40
4. Nathan Mylenek (Pontiac Notre Dame)12....15:41
5. Matthew Zerfas (Fremnt)11 ....15:45
6. Joey Humes (Milan)12 ....15:47
7. Justin Varineau (Grand Rapids Christian)11 .15:54
8. Shuaib Aljabaly (Coldwater)10 ....15:58
9. Reid Parsons (Comstock Park)10 ....16:00
10. Mark Freyhof (Hamilton)12 ....16:02
11. Dillan Haviland (St Johns)10 ....16:02
12. Blake Watson (Corunna)12 ....16:03
13. Alex Comerford (Otsego)9 ....16:05
14. Sam Kaastra (Fremont)11 ....16:06
15. Dylan Sykes (GR Catholic Central)11 ....16:07
16. Cole Hamilton (Fremont)11 ....16:08
17. Ethan Taljonick (Clio)12 ....16:10
18. Will Finch (Otsego)10 ....16:10
19. Ben Schmidt (Fremont)11 ....16:12
20. Joey Dawson (Richland Gull Lake)12 ....16:13
21. Ben Geer (Mason)12 ....16:13
22. Jacob Inosencio (Parma Western)12 ....16:14
23. Jacob Starr (Otsego)12 ....16:16
24. Shawn Bell (Sturgis)12 ....16:17
25. Zack Murphy (Coldwater)11 ....16:17
26. Jack Keais (St Clair)12 ....16:17
27. Josiah Quinn (St Johns)12 ....16:18
28. Ben Fagen (Coldwater)10 ....16:21
29. Lewis Tate (Paw Paw)11 ....16:21
30. Ben Zaremba (Auburn Hills Avondale)11....16:22
35. Sam Stitt (Fremont)11 ....16:27
176. Benjamin Deuling (Fremont)12 ....17:42
177. Ben Devries (Fremont)10 ....17:44

2016 D2 BOYS

Noah Jacobs came to MIS with an undefeated season and he left the same way after leading his Corunna teammates to their second state crown in an upset of favored Fremont.

"It's really special," said Jacobs. "It's the culmination of everything that I've worked for throughout my high school career. I came in as a freshman and saw times and went up to my coach and said, 'I really want to win a state championship.' At first he kind of thought it was a joke and then he looked at me and said, 'OK, let's do this.'"

Jacobs had hoped to break 15 minutes but the soft course and the wind made that impossible. "It was one of the harder races I've ever run. Nobody really wanted to push the pace… Got in the stadium and the wind was in my face. It was a battle the last mile."

Michigan Int. Speedway, Brooklyn, Nov. 5
2016 BOYS DIVISION 2 TEAMS
1. Corunna..92
2. Fremont..99
3. Grand Rapids Christian.........................139
4. Coldwater...195
5. Otsego..236
6. Fruitport..249
7. Pontiac Notre Dame..............................260
8. St Clair..268
9. Chelsea...273
10. East Grand Rapids..............................287
11. St Johns..319
12. Spring Lake..337
13. Croswell-Lexington..............................359
14. Hamilton..372
15. Lake Fenton..373
16. Grosse Ile...394
17. Dearborn Divine Child..........................414
18. Battle Creek Harper Creek..................467
19. Howard City Tri-County.......................469
20. Linden...476
21. Parma Western....................................486
22. Flint Powers..499
23. Clio..526
24. Sparta...539
25. Forest Hills Eastern.............................546
26. St Joseph...581
27. Macomb Lutheran North.....................612

Noah Jacobs of Corunna.
(Pete Draugalis photo)

2016 BOYS DIVISION 2 INDIVIDUALS
1. Noah Jacobs (Corunna)12 .... 15:28
2. Brendan Fraser (Pontiac Notre Dame)12 ...... 15:40
3. Shuaib Aljabaly (Coldwater)11 .... 15:46
4. Justin Varineau (Grand Rapids Christian)12 . 15:50
5. James Gedris (Grosse Ile)10 .... 15:56
6. Jack Schafer (Adrian)12 .... 15:57
7. Dillan Haviland (St Johns)11 .... 16:00
8. Ben Jacobs (Corunna)10 .... 16:02
9. Alex Comerford (Otsego)10 .... 16:03
10. Ben Schmidt (Fremont)11 .... 16:05
11. Lewis Tate (Paw Paw)12 .... 16:05
12. Chandler Lorf (Flint Powers)11 .... 16:08
13. Sam Borisch (Comstock Park)12 .... 16:09
14. Reid Parsons (Comstock Park)11 .... 16:10
15. Garrett Novak (Flat Rock Summit Acad)12 .. 16:11
16. Brennan Mudd (Midland Bullock Creek)11 .. 16:12
17. Aaron Simot (Fruitport)12 .... 16:13
18. Brendan Parr (St Clair)11 .... 16:13
19. Nick Holbrook (New Boston Huron)12 .... 16:13
20. Adam Sawicki (Grosse Ile)12 .... 16:14
21. Andrew Hylen (Spring Lake)10 .... 16:15
22. Evan Bishop (East Grand Rapids)9 .... 16:16
23. Michael Hancock (Dearborn Divine Child)9 . 16:24
24. Cole Hamiton (Fremont)12 .... 16:25
25. Dakota Hundley (Corunna)11 .... 16:25
26. Ben Zaremba (Auburn Hills Avondale)12 .... 16:25
27. Mike Hyatt (Muskegon Orchard View)11 ..... 16:25
28. Sam Kaastra (Fremont)12 .... 16:26
29. Matthew Converse (Zeeland West)10.......... 16:26
30. Luke Noah (Middleville TK)12 .... 16:31
50. Charlie Bruckman (Corunna)10 .... 16:45
52. Kyle Mesh (Corunna)12 .... 16:47
72. Miles Petersen (Corunna)11 .... 16:56
80. Ryan Schwab (Corunna)11 .... 17:01

2017 D2 BOYS

Stormy weather and a delay because of lightning didn't keep Shuaib Aljabaly from his goal at MIS. "At the 2M mark, it was just me and another runner, and I told myself, 'This is where it ends.' One of us is taking it from here to the end and I decided to go."

Chelsea—wearing its Kenyan flag shorts—raced to its first team victory for coach Eric Swager. It was the 23rd time the Bulldogs had made it to the finals.

Shuaib Aljabaly put together a strong final mile. (Pete Draugalis photo)

Michigan Int. Speedway, Brooklyn, Nov. 4
2017 BOYS DIVISION 2 TEAMS
1. Chelsea 96
2. Corunna 110
3. Lansing Catholic 165
4. St Clair 166
5. Pontiac Notre Dame 206
6. Fremont 232
7. Linden 284
8. St Johns 289
9. Flint Powers 292
10. Cedar Springs 314
11. Zeeland East 328
12. Grand Rapids Christian 337
13. Spring Lake 340
14. Dearborn Divine Child 354
15. Lake Fenton 371
16. Zeeland West 379
17. Grand Rapids South Christian 437
18. West Branch Ogemaw Heights 445
19. Croswell-Lexington 490
20. Grosse Ile 498
21. Essexville Garber 500
22. Marshall 501
23. Yale 545
24. Parma Western 559
25. Vicksburg 559
26. Mason 585
27. Allegan 643

2017 BOYS DIVISION 2 INDIVIDUALS
1. Shuaib Aljabaly (Coldwater)12 .... 15:13
2. Alex Comerford (Otsego)11 .... 15:25
3. Ben Jacobs (Corunna)11 .... 15:36
4. Ben Schmidt (Fremont)12 .... 15:39
5. Tom Oates (Chelsea)12 .... 15:39
6. Tyler Buchanan (Linden)10 .... 15:43
7. Will Finch (Otsego)12 .... 15:48
8. Michael Hancock (Dearborn Divine Child)10 . 15:48
9. Anthony Hancock (Dearborn Divine Child)10 . 15:49
10. Brendan Parr (St Clair)12 .... 15:50
11. Jensen Holm (Chelsea)11 .... 15:52
12. Dillan Haviland (St Johns)12 .... 15:53
13. Cameron Oleen (Fruitport)12 .... 15:53
14. Chandler Lorf (Flint Powers)12 .... 15:54
15. James Gedris (Grosse Ile)11 .... 15:55
16. Reid Parsons (Comstock Park)12 .... 15:55
17. Josiah Morse (Essexville Garber)12 ... 15:56
18. Micah VanderKooi (GR South Christian)10 .. 15:57
19. Andrew Hylen (Spring Lake)11 .... 16:00
20. Robert Diebold (Riverview)12 .... 16:05
21. Hunter Zartman (Otsego)10 .... 16:05
22. James Ohlsson (Pontiac Notre Dame)10 .. 16:08
23. Caleb Velzen (Hudsonville Unity Christ)12 . 16:10
24. Dakota Hundley (Corunna)12 .... 16:11
25. Shawn Little (Dowagiac)10 .... 16:11
26. Casron Rabbitt (Chelsea)11 .... 16:13
27. John Pieper (Pontiac Notre Dame)12 .. 16:17
28. Nathan Walker (Fremont)9 .... 16:18
29. Brennan Mudd (Midland Bullock Creek)12 . 16:20
30. Chris Davis (Fowlerville)12 .... 16:21
42. Connor Gilbreath (Chelsea)12 .... 16:30
59. Foster Thorburn (Chelsea)11 .... 16:42
87. Will Scott (Chelsea)10 .... 17:00
228. Jeremy Northrop (Chelsea)12 .... 18:47

2018 D2 BOYS

Chelsea did it again, this time nipping Fremont by just 13 points, helped along by the lead pack of Carson Rabbit (11th), Foster Thorburn (12rth) and Will Scott (14th).

Alex Comerford dominated the individual racing with a powerful mid-race surge, running 4:49 for the middle mile. "I don't always have the last half mile that the other guys do," explained the Otsego senior. "I really had to make a hard move with two miles to go. I felt like I could sustain that pace for a long time."

Michigan Int. Speedway, Brooklyn, Nov. 3
Mostly cloudy, muddy, 40°, breezy.
2018 BOYS DIVISION 2 TEAMS
1. Chelsea 121
2. Fremont 134
3. Spring Lake 199
4. Zeeland West 201
5. Otsego 202
6. Corunna 226
7. Cedar Springs 243
8. Haslett 253
9. East Grand Rapids 267
10. Grand Rapids Christian 330
11. Dearborn Divine Child 331
12. Goodrich 336
13. Big Rapids 349
14. Lake Fenton 376
15. Lansing Catholic 382
16. Parma Western 404
17. Armada 404
18. St Johns 438
19. Grand Rapids South Christian 471
20. Yale 477
21. Zeeland East 490
22. Flint Powers 501
23. Linden 514
24. Holland Christian 519
25. Alma 520
26. Grosse Ile 527
27. St Clair 616

2018 BOYS DIVISION 2 INDIVIDUALS
1. Alex Comerford (Otsego)12 .... 15:24
2. Evan Bishop (East Grand Rapids)11 ... 15:36
3. Ben Jacobs (Corunna)12 .... 15:44
4. Anthony Hancock (Dearborn Divine Child)11 . 15:49
5. Nathan Walker (Fremont)10 .... 15:56
6. Michael Hancock (Dearborn Divine Child)11 . 16:03
7. Andrew Hylen (Spring Lake)12 .... 16:04
8. Ben Hylen (Spring Lake)12 .... 16:05
9. Tyler Buchanan (Linden)11 .... 16:05
10. Ethan Senti (Zeeland West)11 .... 16:10
11. Carson Rabbitt (Chelsea)12 .... 16:16
12. Foster Thorburn (Chelsea)12 .... 16:17
13. Matthew Graver (Grosse Ile)12 .... 16:18
14. Will Scott (Chelsea)11 .... 16:19
15. Colten Covington (Grant)12 .... 16:20
16. James Ohlsson (Pontiac Notre Dame)11 .. 16:22
17. Shawn Little (Dowagiac)11 .... 16:23
18. Andrew Periard (East Grand Rapids)12 .... 16:23
19. Bryson DenUyl (Marysville)11 .... 16:23
20. Ethan Rockburh (Belding)10 .... 16:24
21. Hunter Zartman (Otsego)11 .... 16:27
22. Sam Baustert (Whitehall)12 .... 16:27
23. Jack Leman (Edwardsburg)11 .... 16:27
24. Will Peters (Lansing Catholic)12 .... 16:27
25. Ben Paige (Fremont)10 .... 16:27
26. Gezahegn Starr (Parma Western)12 ... 16:28
27. Tommy Hufton (Lake Fenton)12 .... 16:28
28. Jaydon Moleski (Cedar Springs)11 ..... 16:29
29. Thomas Westrick (Forest Hills Eastern)12 . 16:29
30. Matthew Converse (Zeeland West)12 ... 16:32
56. Zander Hartsuff (Chelsea)11 .... 16:55
65. Joseph Norwood (Chelsea)11 .... 16:59
72. Owen Smith (Chelsea)10 .... 17:02
100. Erik Reiber (Chelsea)10 .... 17:11

Otsego's Alex Comerford, runner-up the year before, surged to the win in 2018. (Pete Draugalis photo)

2019 D2 BOYS

Evan Bishop used a fast close to seal the win on a soft course. "Once I took the lead, I really wanted to make a decisive move and power all the way to the finish," the East Grand Rapids senior said.

"I just tried to play to my strong suit and leave it all out there… This season, the biggest goal for me was winning this race."

Bishop had taken the lead just before the 2M after testing the field a half mile earlier. On the final stretch, the footing was his biggest challenge. "It was rough. I almost wiped out."

Fremont captured title No. 9 by putting four of its runners into the top 20. That gave Cliff Somers' crew a margin of 108 points over Otsego.

Michigan Int. Speedway, Brooklyn, Nov. 2
Mostly cloudy, muddy.
2019 BOYS DIVISION 2 TEAMS
1. Fremont 68
2. Otsego 176
3. Haslett 191
4. Chelsea 218
5. Dearborn Divine Child 226
6. Grand Rapids Christian 227

7. East Grand Rapids 265
8. St Johns 269
9. Yale 281
10. Sparta 325
11. Linden 327
12. Holland Christian 351
13. Adrian 356
14. Petoskey 360
15. St Clair 378
16. Armada 438
17. Hastings 447
18. Spring Lake 457
19. Berrien Springs 470
20. Battle Creek Harper Creek 492
21. Flint Powers 510
22. Lake Fenton 511
23. Marshall 518
24. Goodrich 524
25. Alma 529
26. Allendale 586
27. Corunna 674

Evan Bishop talks to reporters after his win.

2019 BOYS DIVISION 2 INDIVIDUALS
1. Evan Bishop (East Grand Rapids)12 .... 15:13
2. Anthony Hancock (Dearborn Divine Child)12.15:19
3. Michael Hancock (Dearborn Divine Child)12..15:24
4. Nathan Walker (Fremont)11 .... 15:24
5. Koby Fraaza (Richland Gull Lake)11 .... 15:51
6. Tyler Buchanan (Linden)12 .... 15:58
7. Shawn Little (Dowagiac)12 .... 15:59
8. Conor Somers (Fremont)10 .... 16:02
9. Colin Mulder (Otsego)11 .... 16:07
10. Joseph Farley (Petoskey)12 .... 16:12
11. Hunter Zartman (Otsego)12 .... 16:19
12. Ben Clason (Forest Hills Eastern)11 .... 16:20
13. Braydon Honsinger (Freeland)9 .... 16:20
14. Parker Lambers (Holland Christian)10 .... 16:21
15. Matthew McClelland (Yale)11 .... 16:21
16. Elijah Becker (East Grand Rapids)12 .... 16:21
17. Stephen Henry (Haslett)12 .... 16:23
18. Adam Ward (Holland Christian)11 .... 16:23
19. Michael Hegarty (Dearborn Divine Child)9 .. 16:24
20. Ben Paige (Fremont)11 .... 16:24
21. Kyle Korte (Forest Hills Eastern)12 .... 16:26
22. Aidan Makled (Hastings)12 .... 16:27
23. Jack Luymes (Grand Rapids Christian)12 ... 16:27
24. Callen Carrier (Spring Lake)11 .... 16:27
25. Havi Carroll (Hamilton)12 .... 16:27
26. Joseph Norwood (Chelsea)12 .... 16:28
27. Caleb Gaffner (Hudonsville Unity Chr)12 .... 16:28
28. Ethan Wilstermann (GR Christian)12 .... 16:29
29. Alex Mitchell (Holland Christian)12 .... 16:29
30. Ian Hill (Spring Lake)10 .... 16:32
36. Mikko Vesma (Fremont)12 .... 16:41
43. Joshua Zerfas (Fremont)11 .... 16:47
100. Colton Best (Fremont)11 .... 17:19

CLASS B/D2 STATISTICS

TOP 25 CLOCKINGS AT MIS
15:03 Kurtis Marlowe (Richland Gull Lake)12 .. 2000
15:04 Tim Ross (Caledonia)12 2001
15:05 Connor Mora (Cedar Springs)12 2012
15:10 Landon Peacock (Cedar Springs)12 2005
15:10 Tanner Hinkle (Mason)12 2012
15:11 Addis Habtewold (St Clair)12 2007
15:13 Jared Aldrich (Corunna)12 1998
15:13 Luke Walker (Flint Powers)12 2003
15:13 Shuaib Aljabaly (Coldwater)12 2017
15:13 Evan Bishop (East Grand Rapids)12 2019
15:16 Bobby Aprill (Dexter)11 2006
15:16 Dan Jackson (Dexter)12 2006
15:17 T. Ross (Caledonia)11 2000
15:17 B. Aprill (Dexter)12 2007
15:19 Patrick Grosskopf (Corunna)12 2005
15:19 Anthony Hancock (Dearborn DC)12 2019
15:20 Justin Perez (Flint Powers)12 1999
15:20 Daniel Roberts (Vicksburg)11 2004
15:20 Alex Standiford (Mattawan)12 2010
15:21 Bryce Bradley (Chelsea)12 2011
15:22 A. Habtewold (St Clair)11 2006
15:22 Nicholas Soter (Dearborn Divine C)12 . 2011
15:23 Riley Klingel (Fremont)12 2004
15:24 Alex Comerford (Otsego)12 2018
15:24 Michael Hancock (Dearborn DC)12 2019
15:24 Nathan Walker (Fremont)11 2019

BIGGEST WINNING MARGINS
37.5 Tim Ross/Andrew Bauer .... 2001 I
34 Jack Sinclair/Phil Vannette .... 1974 I
29 Brian Diemer/Kurt Mast .... 1978 T
25 Mark Smith/John Adams .... 1980 T
24 Tom Chorny/Tim Tottingham .... 1994 I

SMALLEST WINNING MARGINS
0 Rocky Wolfgang/Milt Bowen 1950
0c Bill Pyle/John Ballough (12 inches) 1951
0 Joe O'Connor/Russ Hickey .... 1992 T
0.1 Phil DeVries/Brian Burns .... 1966 T
0.2c Albert Olds/Gerald Nelson (1 stride) 1937
0.45 Riley Klingel/Jeff Byrne 2002
0.5 Bob Carrigan/Wally Schafer 1956
0.6 Bobby Aprill/Dan Jackson 2006
0.89 Lyle Mayers/Russ Gerbers 1996

LOWEST WINNING SCORES
21 Niles 1936
22 Niles 1939
26 Niles 1934
28 Ypsilanti 1943
28 Dexter 2006
29 Dearborn 1929
30 Dearborn/Three Rivers 1930
33 Iron Mountain 1938
36 Iron Mountain 1937
39 Niles 1935

HIGHEST WINNING SCORES
169 Holly 1978
165 Royal Oak Shrine 1973
156 Sparta 1962
155 Caro 1980
145 Grand Rapids Catholic Central 1982
144 Flint Powers 1999
143 Stockbridge 1994
142 South Haven 1992
131 Big Rapids 1990
128 Richland Gull Lake 1998

CLOSEST TEAM FINISH
0 Richland Gull Lake/Corunna 1998
1 Ypsilanti/Niles 1941
1 St Joseph/Sturgis 1988
2 Royal Oak Shrine/Linden 1973
4 Sault Ste Marie/South Haven 1931
4 Howell/St Johns 1959

BIGGEST WINNING TEAM MARGIN
115 Linden/Vicksburg 2008
114 Dexter/Sparta 2006
108 Fremont/Otsego 2019
106 Stockbridge/Gaylord 1995
104 River Rouge/Alma 1954

1940 Champ: Russell Bradley of Charlotte.

1945 B Champ: Harry Alcorn of Flint Kearsley.

BOYS CLASS C / DIVISION 3

1928 CLASS C/D BOYS

A C-D race was added this year, but the rationale isn't clear. Perhaps it had something to do with school size as opposed to demand because only five teams competed. Parma only entered one boy, and Waldron and Lexington each failed to finish five. Waldron somehow got the nod for third place and went home with a trophy.

Ypsilanti, Nov. 10 □
1928 BOYS CLASS C/D TEAMS
1. Ypsilanti Roosevelt 32
2. Alanson 48
NS—Lexington, Parma, Waldron.

1928 BOYS CLASS C/D INDIVIDUALS
1. Leland Tompkins (Parma)11 ..... 11:52
2. Doering, Jr (Ypsilanti Roosevelt) ..... nt
3. Hubbard (Ypsilanti Roosevelt) ..... nt
4. H. Moore (Alanson) ..... nt
5. H. Bunz (Alanson) ..... nt

1929 CLASS C/D BOYS

Roosevelt High defended its title. The school was founded in 1900 as a laboratory school by what is now Eastern Michigan University. In 1924 it got a new building and the Roosevelt name. It was closed in 1969 and the structure is now a classroom building for the university.

Ypsilanti, Nov. 9 □
1929 BOYS CLASS C/D TEAMS
1. Ypsilanti Roosevelt 41
2. Alanson 57
3. Clarksville 67
4. Parma 75
NS (incomplete teams)—Croswell, Lexington.

1929 BOYS CLASS C/D INDIVIDUALS
1. Leland Tompkins (Parma)12 ..... 11:33
2. Hubbard (Ypsilanti Roosevelt) 11:33
3. Kitchen (Alanson) 11:34
4. Lewis (Croswell) 11:47
5. Neil (Ypsilanti) 12:00
6. Ramsby (Alanson) 12:05
7. Stahl (Clarksville) 12:07
8. McCalla (Ypsilanti) 12:11
9. Kaufman (Clarksville) 12:19
10. Ordway (Alanson) 12:23
11. P. Sullivan (Clarksville) ..... nt
12. Oscar (Ypsilanti Roosevelt) ..... nt
13. Rotter (Alanson) ..... nt
14. Mayer (Ypsilanti Roosevelt) ..... nt
15. Gilbert (Parma) ..... nt
16. Pulling (Parma) ..... nt
17. Whitfield (Ypsilanti Roosevelt) ..... nt
18. Gregg (Clarksville) ..... nt
19. Lentz (Lexington) ..... nt
20. Bidwell (Parma) ..... nt

1930 CLASS C/D BOYS

The meet grew in size, as more teams from small schools entered; at the time, the requirement for C/D was a student population of fewer than 300.

Clarksville's Truman Kauffman won the battle down the stretch against Milford's Aaron Gooding. Croswell won the team title in its first year with a full squad.

Ypsilanti, Nov. 8 □
1930 BOYS CLASS C/D TEAMS
1. Croswell 77
2. Milford 93
3. Romulus 119
4. Napoleon 119
5. Ypsilanti Roosevelt 144
6. Olanson 162
7. Saranac 182
8. Lincoln 199
9. Fowlerville 200
NS (partial teams)—Clarksville, Okemos, Sand Creek

1930 BOYS CLASS C/D INDIVIDUALS
1. Truman Kauffman (Clarksville)11 ..... 11:01
2. Aaron Gooding (Milford) 11:04
3. Hubbard (Ypsilanti Roosevelt) 11:06
4. Betzoldt (Romulus) 11:10
5. Lewis (Croswell) 11:12
6. Currier (Okemos) 11:14
7. Elliot (Milford) 11:24
8. E. White (Romulus) 11:25
9. Colovin (Alanson) 11:30
10. Fisher (Napoleon) 11:31
11. (Napoleon) ..... nt
12. (Fowlerville) ..... nt
13. (Sand Creek) ..... nt
14. (Milford) ..... nt
15. (Croswell) ..... nt
16. (Lincoln) ..... nt
17. (Croswell) ..... nt
18. (Milford) ..... nt
19. (Croswell) ..... nt
20. (Alanson) ..... nt
21. (Croswell) ..... nt

1931 CLASS C/D BOYS

Clarksville's Truman Kauffman successfully defended his title. That spring he tried his hand(s) at boxing as a welterweight (140-147lb) only to discover that running was his best sport.

Napoleon captured its first title.

Ypsilanti, Nov. 7 □
1931 BOYS CLASS C/D TEAMS
1. Napoleon 55
2. Sand Creek 73
3. Clarksville 102
4. Saranac 131
5. Hanover 142
6. Centreville 142
7. Romulus 145
8. Croswell 161
9. Fowlerville 207
10. Mackinaw City 212
NS (partial team)—Ypsilanti Roosevelt

1931 BOYS CLASS C/D INDIVIDUALS
1. Truman Kauffman (Clarksville)12 ..... 10:45
2. Uehmeier (Sand Creek) ..... nt
3. Howard Densmore (Hanover) 11:01
4. R. Snow (Napoleon) ..... nt
5. Hall (Sand Creek) ..... nt
6. Fisher (Napoleon) ..... nt
7. Marsh (Napoleon) ..... nt
8. Huyck (Sand Creek) ..... nt
9. Ratcliff (Napoleon) ..... nt
10. Awe (Centreville) ..... nt
11. (Clarksville) ..... nt
12. (Ypsilanti Roosevelt) ..... nt
13. (Romulus) ..... nt
14. (Saranac) ..... nt
15. (Saranac) ..... nt
16. (Hanover) ..... nt
17. (Centerville) ..... nt
18. (Hanover) ..... nt
19. (Croswell) ..... nt
20. (Fowlerville) ..... nt
29. Snider (Napoleon) ..... nt
31. Harfurd (Napoleon) ..... nt

1932 CLASS C/D BOYS

Because of the Great Depression, the state meet was canceled in 1932 and '33. Class C/D regionals were held at three sites. Escanaba and Iron Mountain skipped their regional, having scheduled their annual dual for the same day. Escanaba won, 15-40.

Eastern Regional, Ypsilanti, Nov. 1 □
1932 BOYS CLASS C/D TEAMS
1. Napoleon 46
2. Sand Creek 60
3. Fowlerville 73
NS (incomplete teams)—Hanover, Romulus.

1932 BOYS CLASS C/D INDIVIDUALS
1. Raymond Snow (Napoleon)12 ..... 11:09

Western Regional, Kalamazoo, Nov. 1 □
1932 BOYS CLASS C/D TEAMS
Results needed

1932 BOYS CLASS C/D INDIVIDUALS
Results needed

UP Regional, Sault Ste Marie, October 29 □
1932 BOYS CLASS C/D TEAMS
1. DeTour 21
2. Rudyard 34
(only 2 teams)

1932 BOYS CLASS C/D INDIVIDUALS
1. N. Hawkins (DeTour)12 ..... 12:23
2. I. Pitko (DeTour) c13:00
3. J. Bergama (Rudyard) ..... nt
4. L. St Onge (DeTour) ..... nt
5. J. McLarney (DeTour) ..... nt
6. M. Koski (Rudyard) ..... nt
7. H. Ruona (Rudyard) ..... nt
8. C. Postma (Rudyard) ..... nt
9. J. Kominski (DeTour) ..... nt
10. T. Millen (DeTour) ..... nt
11. B. Nayback (Rudyard) ..... nt

1933 CLASS C/D BOYS

Again, there was no state final, but regionals were held at Ypsilanti and Kalamazoo on the same day.

Arnold Borders set a course record to lead Napoleon to its third-straight win at Ypsilanti. The previous spring he had won the Class D state title in the mile at 4:53.9.

Eastern Regional, Ypsilanti, Nov. 4 □
1933 BOYS CLASS C/D TEAMS
1. Napoleon 28
2. Sand Creek 59
3. Romulus 62
NS—Hanover (2 finishers).

1933 BOYS CLASS C/D INDIVIDUALS
1. Arnold Borders (Napoleon)11 ..... 11:03

Western Regional, Kalamazoo, Nov. 1 □
1933 BOYS CLASS C/D TEAMS
1. Kalamazoo State 34
2. Clarksville 41
(only complete teams entered)

1933 BOYS CLASS C/D INDIVIDUALS
1. Leverett VanHalst (Okemos)10 ..... 11:18

2. Towbridge (Clarksville) ....nt
4. Bennink (Kalamazoo State) ....nt
5. Councell (Kalamazoo State) ....nt
6. McGee (Kalamazoo State) ....nt
9. Hope (Kalamazoo State) ....nt
10. Heimstra (Kalamazoo State) ....nt

1934 CLASS C/D BOYS

The *Jackson Citizen-Patriot* put the damper on the Napoleon win, pointing out that their local school might not have won had Onekama or Okemos fielded full teams.

Onekama's Lawrence Kelly won in 1934.

Ypsilanti, Nov. 3 ☐
1934 BOYS CLASS C/D TEAMS
1. Napoleon 40
2. Kalamazoo Western State 43
NS (partial teams)—Okemos, Onekama.

1934 BOYS CLASS C/D INDIVIDUALS
1. Lawrence Kelly (Onekama)12 ....11:01
2. Arnold Borders (Napoleon)12 ....nt
3. Van Halst (Okemos) ....nt
4. King (Okemos) ....nt
5. Hudson (Kalamazoo Western State) ....nt
6. G. Earley (Napoleon) ....nt
7. McGee (Kalamazoo Western State) ....nt
8. Counsell (Kalamazoo Western State) ....nt
9. Leland (Napoleon) ....nt
10. Miller (Napoleon) ....nt
13. (Napoleon) ....nt

1935 CLASS C/D BOYS

Marvin Nichols, the only runner entered from Lambertville (present-day Bedford), broke the course record by 8 seconds. Only 14 runners participated. Nichols would later serve in World War II as a medic before returning to his Monroe County farm.

Napoleon, coached by Virgil Roberson, won what was essentially a dual meet.

Ypsilanti, Nov. 2 ☐
1935 BOYS CLASS C/D TEAMS
1. Napoleon 25
2. Brooklyn 60
NS (partial teams)—Lambertville, Lansing Everett, Romulus.

1935 BOYS CLASS C/D INDIVIDUALS
1. Marvin Nichols (Lambertville)12 ....10:53
2. Steve Kostek (Romulus)10 ....nt
3. Roy Snider (Napoleon) ....nt
4. W. Deland (Napoleon) ....nt

5. Ronald Earley (Napoleon) ....nt
6. Milo Palen (Napoleon) ....nt
7. Lyle Smoyer (Napoleon) ....nt

1936 CLASS C/D BOYS

Napoleon, under new coach Oliver Byam, won its sixth-straight title (The newspapers at the time counted the two years when only regionals were available). Because of the small participation numbers at the previous year's finals, all regional participants were allowed to run at the state finals.

Ypsilanti, Nov. 7 ☐
1936 BOYS C/D TEAMS
1. Napoleon 32
2. Romulus 63
3. Lambertville 81
4. Flint Bendle 86
5. Brooklyn 90

1936 BOYS CLASS C/D INDIVIDUALS
1. Steve Kostek (Romulus)11 ....10:56
2. Keith Cruikshank (Bendle) ....nt
3. Milo Palen (Napoleon) ....nt
4. Roy Snider (Napoleon) ....nt
5. Stanley Ksionzek (Napoleon) ....nt
6. Charlee Wright (Brooklyn) ....nt
7. Robert Smith (Romulus) ....nt
8. Charles Weigand (Lambertville) ....nt
9. Ronald Early (Napoleon) ....nt
10. Gilbert Yerder (Brooklyn) ....nt

1937 CLASS C/D BOYS

Regional participation was required to compete at the state finals (unlike in Class A), but all teams were advanced.

Steve Kostek of Romulus was the star of the Lower Peninsula production. Running in the Class C-D event, Kostek recorded a far better time than the bigger classes saw, chopping the C-D course record by more than a half-minute.

Coach Leo McFarlane's Lansing St. Mary's squad won the team race with a low 23-points.

Ypsilanti, Nov. 6 ☐
1937 BOYS CLASS C/D TEAMS
1. Lansing St Mary 23
2. Napoleon 54
3. Lambertville 65
4. Romulus 80

1937 BOYS CLASS C/D INDIVIDUALS
1. Steve Kostek (Romulus)12 ....10:22

1938 CLASS C/D BOYS

Once again, all teams advanced from regionals. Lansing St. Mary defended its title by 8-points from its same-name challengers out of the Flint area.

Individual winner Kenneth Bohr ran a modest 10:58 in the rain, with temperatures nearing freezing.

Ypsilanti, Nov. 5 ☐
1938 BOYS CLASS C/D TEAMS
1. Lansing St Mary 50
2. Mt Morris St Mary 58
3. Brooklyn 96
4. Chesaning 101
5. Lambertville 113
6. Napoleon 121

1938 BOYS CLASS C/D INDIVIDUALS
1. Kenneth Bohr (Brooklyn)12 ....10:58
2. Dominic Lecato (Lansing St Mary)10 ....10:?
6. Jim LaFontaine (Lansing St Mary) ....nt
8. George Jakovac (Lansing St Mary) ....nt
9. Dick Foster (Lansing Eastern) ....nt
10. Don Merritt (Lansing Eastern) ....nt

13. Vito Nelli (Lansing St Mary) ....nt
20. Sam Pizzo (Lansing St Mary) ....nt
26. Walt Ozanich (Lansing St Mary) ....nt

1939 CLASS C/D BOYS

Ideal weather conditions greeted runners in Ypsilanti. Dominic Lecato won alone. The previous year, he had been part of a team championship. When six of those seven graduated, however, Lecato had to do it by himself. He did, and shortly afterward transferred to larger Lansing Central.

Napoleon, under new coach Stuart Leigh, won again, this time against local rival East Jackson.

Ypsilanti, Nov. 5 ☐
1939 BOYS CLASS C/D TEAMS
1. Napoleon 42
2. East Jackson 50
3. Lambertville 83

1939 BOYS CLASS C/D INDIVIDUALS
1. Dominic Lecato (Lansing St Mary)11 ....10:57
2. Willard Farr (Michigan Center) ....nt
3. Lyle Sherwood (Napoleon) ....nt
4. Cummings (Michigan Central) ....nt
5. Sotak (East Jackson) ....nt
6. Pattison (Lambertville) ....nt
7. Dick Fransted (Napoleon) ....nt
7?. Walter McUmber (Napoleon) ....nt
8. Bob Smith (East Jackson) ....nt
9. Bob Adams (Napoleon) ....nt

1940 CLASS C/D BOYS

Napoleon captured its eighth title in 10 years. Flint Hoover (which eventually became part of the Carman-Ainsworth district) produced individual winner Harold Flynn. The next spring Flynn would win the Class C mile crown in 4:37.6.

Ypsilanti, Nov. 2 ☐
1940 BOYS CLASS C/D TEAMS
1. Napoleon 36
2. East Jackson 50
3. Flint Hoover 57
4. Blanchard 71

1940 BOYS CLASS C/D INDIVIDUALS
1. Harold Flynn (Flint Hoover)12 ....11:30
2. Bailey (East Jackson) 11:46
3. Lyle Sherwood (Napoleon) 11:53
4. Adams (Napoleon) ....nt
5. Burke (East Jackson) ....nt
6. Grim (Blanchard) ....nt
7. Mcumber (Napoleon) ....nt
8. Birdsall (East Jackson) ....nt
9. Wilhite (Flint Hoover) ....nt
10. Franstad (Napoleon) ....nt

1941 CLASS C/D BOYS

Imlay City, coached by rookie Thurlow King, won the crown in its first year of cross country competition. Napoleon, which had won 8 of the previous 11 years, had been heavily favored. Weather was windy and rainy, and harriers faced plenty of mud.

John Sisson won the title in his first year of cross country.

Ypsilanti, Nov. 1 ☐
1941 BOYS CLASS C/D TEAMS
1. Imlay City 55
2. Napoleon 63
3. Flint Kearsley 65
4. Blanchard 71
5. East Jackson 105
6. Ludington St. Simon 129

1941 BOYS CLASS C/D INDIVIDUALS
1. John Sisson (Imlay City)12 ....11:41
2. Hank Worthy (Imlay City) ....nt
3. Copenhauer (Flint Kearsley) ....nt
4. Barnes (Blanchard) ....nt
5. Lyle Sherwood (Napoleon) ....nt
6. Cartier (Ludington Catholic) ....nt
7. Bob Jones (Imlay City) ....nt
8. Bandur (Flint Kearsley) ....nt
9. Miles (Napoleon) ....nt
10. E. Grim (Blanchard) ....nt
11. Eddie Fransted (Napoleon) ....nt
12. Elmer Burke (East Jackson) ....nt
13. Andy Sotak (East Jackson) ....nt
17. Charles Birdsell (East Jackson) ....nt
20. Lyn Sherwood (Napoleon) ....nt

1942 CLASS C/D BOYS

No state meet was held in 1942 because of World War II, but the East Regional was held in the usual time and place, while only Sparta attended the West Regional in Kalamazoo. Napoleon scored the East win, with Bob Jones of Imlay City finishing first on a dry day with temperatures in the low 40s.

Briggs Field, Ypsilanti, Oct. 31 □
1942 BOYS LP EAST - CLASS C/D TEAMS
1. Napoleon ....ns
2. Imlay City ....ns
3. Flint Kearsley ....ns

1942 BOYS LP EAST - CLASS C/D INDIVIDUALS
1. Bob Jones (Imlay City)12 ....nt

Western Michigan College, Kalamazoo, Oct. 31 □
1942 BOYS LP WEST – CLASS C/D TEAMS
1. Sparta 15
(only entrant)

1942 BOYS LP WEST – CLASS C/D INDIVIDUALS
Winner unknown

1943 CLASS C/D BOYS

The MHSAA again slapped the "state" label on the annual meet. Napoleon beat Flint Kearsley for title No. 10, led by Keith Griffin.

Briggs Field, Ypsilanti, Oct. 30 □
1943 BOYS CLASS C/D TEAMS
1. Napoleon 32
2. Flint Kearsley 43
3. Imlay City 45

1943 BOYS CLASS C/D INDIVIDUALS
1. Keith Griffin (Napoleon)11 .... 11:48

1944 CLASS C/D BOYS

World War II had a huge effect on the financial status of small communities. In addition, so many young men joined the war effort that it was difficult for some schools to field full teams. Hence the 1944 CD State Final was a dual meet, with Napoleon winning title 11 and Keith Griffin repeating as well. Like many of his classmates, Griffin joined the Army after graduation to serve in World War II and later taught science at Montague High School for many years.

Ypsilanti, Oct. 28 □
1944 BOYS CLASS C/D TEAMS
1. Napoleon 25
2. Imlay City 31
(only two teams entered)

1944 BOYS CLASS C/D INDIVIDUALS
1. Keith Griffin (Napoleon)12 .... 11:40

1945 CLASS C/D BOYS

The war was over, but by the fall the high school sports scene had not bounced back. This time, Lester Luce's Imlay City team edged Napoleon by a mere point. Neil Dean finished first.

Ypsilanti, Oct. 27 □
1945 BOYS CLASS C/D TEAMS
1. Imlay City 27
2. Napoleon 28
(only two teams entered)

1945 BOYS CLASS C/D INDIVIDUALS
1. Neil Dean (Napoleon)12 .... 11:46
2. Elmer Brinker (Imlay City) ....nt
3. Stewart Bachus (Imlay City) ....nt
4. Arthur Layher (Napoleon) ....nt
5. Vincent Layher (Napoleon) ....nt
6. Bob Willey (Imlay City) ....nt
7. Norman VanPutten (Imlay City) ....nt
8. L. Brown (Napoleon) ....nt
9. Wayne Dahn (Imlay City) ....nt
10. Harry Hayden (Napoleon) ....nt
12. Perry Wearthby (Napoleon) ....nt
13. Fred Wagner (Imlay City) ....nt
14. Norman Reece (Napoleon) ....nt

1946 CLASS C/D BOYS

Hemlock joined the party as the sport resurged in 1946, winning the CD title with a sparkling 30 points, under coach Leonard Burns. Ivan Davis of Merrill finished first.

Ypsilanti, Oct. 26 □
1946 BOYS CLASS C/D TEAMS
1. Hemlock 30
2. Merrill 58
3. Romulus 73
4. Napoleon 77
5. Imlay City 124
6. Birch Run 150

1946 BOYS CLASS C/D INDIVIDUALS
1. Ivan Davis (Merrill) ....nt

1947 CLASS C/D BOYS

Ivan Davis once again won; this time he would lead his Merrill team to the championship. The next spring he won the Class D mile in 4:44.9. He would go on to run for Western Michigan before transferring to Central Michigan, where he was captain of the cross country and track teams.

Briggs Field, Ypsilanti, Nov. 1 □
1947 BOYS CLASS C/D TEAMS
1. Merrill 53
2. Napoleon 79
3. Flint Utley 108
4. Albion-Starr Commonwealth 112
5. Hemlock 113
6. Whitehall 127
7. Birch Run 184
8. East Jackson 216

1947 BOYS CLASS C/D INDIVIDUALS
1. Ivan Davis (Merrill)12 .... 11:04
2. Homer Huffman (Napoleon) ....nt
3. Ray Palmer (Star Commonwealth) ....nt
4. Denzel Dockley (Flint Utley) ....nt
5. Norval Boyd (Hemlock) ....nt

1948 CLASS C/D BOYS

Ithaca won its first state title, led by senior Tom Turnbull. Running through a downpour, Dick Page's team eked out a 4-point win over Napoleon.

Briggs Field, Ypsilanti, Nov. 6 □
1948 BOYS CLASS C/D TEAMS
1. Ithaca 68
2. Napoleon 72
3. Hemlock 115
4. Merrill 125
5. Albion Starr Commonwealth 127
6. Milan 135
7. Flint Utley 151
8. Ypsilanti Roosevelt 160
9. Merrill Sacred Heart 262
10. Detroit St Charles 287
11. Birch Run 296
12. Columbiaville 346

1948 BOYS CLASS CD INDIVIDUALS
1. Tom Turnbull (Ithaca)12 .... 11:13
2. Homer Huffman (Napoleon) ....nt
3. Dick Raby (Napoleon) ....nt
6. Duane Humm (Ithaca) ....nt
7. Dan Robbins (Ithaca) ....nt
16. Dick Parling (Ithaca) ....nt
38. Duane Vernon (Ithaca) ....nt
56. Ray Ringle (Ithaca) ....nt

Jerry Leland, the "unattached" 1949 winner, went on to compete for Western Michigan.

1949 CLASS C/D BOYS

Class C-D winner Jerry Leland of Ypsilanti Roosevelt may have been the only unattached runner ever to win a state title. This was his first and only race of the year, because his school did not sponsor cross country. Officials saw no problem with letting him jump in.

The race had been moved from Briggs Field to the Washtenaw Country Club, because the event—with 55 total teams—had outgrown the tighter confines of campus. Perhaps Leland, a local, had an advantage in knowing the course better than his rivals. The two lead runners for much of the race—Homer Huffman of Napoleon and Bill Lenahan of St Augustine—went off course, and controversy ensued when they were disqualified after finishing 34th & 35th respectively. Leland, who had been far behind, went home with the win.

Napoleon, coached by Gordon Smith, pulled off the team win despite the DQ of its top runner.

Washtenaw Country Club, Ypsilanti, Nov. 5
1949 BOYS CLASS C/D TEAMS
1. Napoleon 58
2. Hemlock 75
3. Merrill 83
4. Kalamazoo St Augustine 91
5. Birch Run 146
6. Pontiac Dublin 149
7. Central Lake 181

1949 BOYS CLASS C/D INDIVIDUALS
1. Jerry Leland (Ypsilanti Roosevelt)12 .... 11:34
3. Dick Raby (Napoleon) .... nt
6. Tom Kendall (Napoleon) .... nt
8. Don Harris (Napoleon) .... nt
18. Clarence Brown (Napoleon) .... nt
23. Jack Fransted (Napoleon) .... nt
DQ—Homer Huffman (Napoleon) & Bill Lenahan (Kalamazoo St Augustine).

1950 CLASS C/D BOYS

Chuck Sweeney's Lansing Everett crew dropped down from Class B the year before and was able to score a low 36 points and take the victory.

Coach Chuck Sweeney and his first championship team.

Jim Chapman of Spring Arbor held off Everett's two top runners to score the win. The future minister ran for Albion College and twice won MIAA titles in both the mile and two mile, as well as one in cross country.

Washtenaw Country Club, Ypsilanti, Nov. 4
1950 BOYS CLASS C/D TEAMS
1. Lansing Everett 36
2. New Lothrop Maple Grove 64
3. Merrill 118
4. Napoleon 121
5. Livonia Clarenceville 147
6. Spring Arbor 156
7. Birch Run 162
8. Grosse Ile 187
9. Pontiac Dublin 201
10. Kalamazoo St Augustine 231

1950 BOYS CLASS C/D INDIVIDUALS
1. Jim Chapman (Spring Arbor)12 .... 11:10
2. Ed Townsend (Lansing Everett)12 .... nt
3. Tom Hoffmeyer (Lansing Everett)12 .... nt
7. Ellis Nobel (Lansing Everett)11 .... nt
9. Clarence Brown (Napoleon) .... nt
10. Jim Diederichs (Lansing Everett)10 .... nt
13. Tom Kendall (Napoleon) .... nt
14. Ron Wilson (Lansing Everett)11 .... nt
23. Elton Brink (Lansing Everett)11 .... nt
32. Richard Green (Lansing Everett)12 .... nt

1951 CLASS C/D BOYS

Everett defended its title with a slim 3-point margin ahead of Morrie (Maurice) Ruddy of New Lothrop St. Michael. Ruddy won the D mile crown the next spring (4:59.4) and later taught and coached at his alma mater.

Washtenaw Country Club, Ypsilanti, Nov. 3
1951 BOYS CLASS C/D TEAMS
1. Lansing Everett 53
2. New Lothrop St Michael 56
3. Napoleon 94
4. Spring Arbor 135
5. Kalamazoo St Augustine 141
6. Gaylord 177
7. Merritt 229
8. Birch Run 232

1951 BOYS CLASS C/D INDIVIDUALS
1. Morrie Ruddy (New Lothrop St Michael)12 .... 11:24
2. Ellis Noble (Lansing Everett)12 .... 11:26
7. Elton Brink (Lansing Everett)11 .... nt
10. Jim Diederichs (Lansing Everett)11 .... nt
11. Ron Wilson (Lansing Everett)12 .... nt
23. Harold Rouse (Lansing Everett)11 .... nt

1952 CLASS C/D BOYS

Lansing Everett joined Napoleon as the only schools to win three in a row. Evart's Gaylord Denslow took the individual win. He would later place 4th in the NCAA cross country race, helping Michigan State to the national title.

Washtenaw Country Club, Ypsilanti, Nov. 1
1952 BOYS CLASS C/D TEAMS
1. Lansing Everett 57
2. Spring Arbor 75
3. Napoleon 99
4. New Lothrop St Michael 112
5. Merrill 157
6. Gaylord 197
7. Petoskey St Francis 207
8. Kalamazoo St Augustine 213
9. Keego Harbor 227
10. Linden 231

1952 BOYS CLASS C/D INDIVIDUALS
1. Gaylord Denslow (Evart)12 .... 11:03
4. Jerry Rider (Lansing Everett)10 .... nt
9. Jim Diederichs (Lansing Everett)12 .... nt
10. Bob Prince (Lansing Everett)11 .... nt
15. Syd Bokovy (Lansing Everett) .... nt
19. Jerry Rosecrans (Lansing Everett) .... nt
? Bill Woodland (Lansing Everett)12 .... nt
? Jim Harmon (Lansing Everett)12 .... nt

1953 CLASS C/D BOYS

Spring Arbor won its first title; the seminary school west of Jackson eventually morphed into what is now Spring Arbor University. It stopped offering high school classes in 1960.

Washtenaw Country Club, Ypsilanti, Nov. 7
1953 BOYS CLASS C/D TEAMS
1. Spring Arbor 40
2. Lansing Everett 61
3. Napoleon 93
4. New Lothrop St Michael 112
5. Keego Harbor 160
6. Fenton 166
7. Kalamazoo St Augustine 194

1953 BOYS CLASS C/D INDIVIDUALS
1. Frank Dawson (Spring Arbor)11 .... 11:14

1954 CLASS C/D BOYS

Coach Don McDonald's Blue Jays from Spring Arbor captured another big win with a low score of 31 points. Individual winner Jim Chernenko would win the Class C mile the next spring in 4:36.9.

Washtenaw Country Club, Ypsilanti, Nov. 6
1954 BOYS CLASS C/D TEAMS
1. Spring Arbor 31
2. New Lothrop St Michael 92
3. Edwardsburg 129
4. Wyoming Lee 134
5. Lake Odessa 152
6. Camden-Frontier 165
7. Keego Harbor 172
8. Tustin 245
9. Napoleon 249
10. Dexter 276

1954 BOYS CLASS C/D INDIVIDUALS
1. Jim Chernenko (Capac)11 .... 11:07
3. Charles Minnis (Spring Arbor)11 .... nt
4. Frank Dawson (Spring Arbor)12 .... nt
6. Gordon Fitzgerald (Spring Arbor)11 .... nt
8. Fred Whims (Spring Arbor)12 .... nt
10. Gordon Holton (Spring Arbor)10 .... nt
11. Vee Radebaugh (Edwardsburg) .... nt
12. Ray Radebaugh (Edwardsburg) .... nt
19. Neale Lundsford (Edwardsburg) .... nt

Capac's Jim Chernenko won in 1954; the next year, football beat him up too much.

1955 CLASS C/D BOYS

Spring Arbor won its third in a row as the top three runners all broke the course record.

The previous year's individual champion, Jim Chernenko of Capac, competed in both cross country and football. In a mid-October gridiron game he found himself with broken ribs and a cracked vertebrae, ending his seasons in both sports, though his coach reassured the newspapers he would be back for basketball. The next spring he defended his C mile title in 4:38.8.

Washtenaw Country Club, Ypsilanti, Nov. 5
1955 BOYS CLASS C/D TEAMS
1. Spring Arbor 38
2. Lansing Everett 50
3. Lake Odessa 76
4. Camden-Frontier 97
5. Edwardsburg 185
6. Plainwell 186
7. New Lothrop St Michael 192
8. Fowlerville 222
9. Wyoming Lee 244
10. Dexter 260
11. McBain 273
12. Keego Harbor 310

1955 BOYS CLASS C/D INDIVIDUALS
1. Ron Hopkins (Lansing Everett)11 .... 10:51
2. Gordon Fitzgerald (Spring Arbor)12 .... 10:55
3. Paul Andrews (Spring Arbor)12 .... 10:57
8. Darrell Dunckel (Spring Arbor)10 .... nt
12. Gordon Holton (Spring Arbor)11 .... nt
13. Howard Snyder (Spring Arbor)10 .... nt

20. Wade Bailor (Spring Arbor)11 .... nt
28. Wilbur Shorb (Spring Arbor)12 .... nt

1956 CLASS C/D BOYS

With five in the top 10, Lansing Everett crushed the scoring record, tallying a mere 22 points to leave the rest of the 7-team field in its dust. The win capped a season that had seen the Vikings only lose twice, both times to Class A champ Lansing Eastern.

Ron Hopkins repeated his win of the previous year. In the spring he would win the Class C half mile in 2:03.0. He would attend Western Michigan, and ran in the NCAA cross country championships three times for the Broncos.

Washtenaw Country Club, Ypsilanti, Nov. 3 ☐
1956 BOYS CLASS C/D TEAMS
1. Lansing Everett 22
2. Spring Arbor 70
3. Camden-Frontier 78
4. McBain 109
5. New Lothrop St Michael 114
6. Grand Rapids Rogers 190
7. Crystal 232

1956 BOYS CLASS C/D INDIVIDUALS
1. Ron Hopkins (Lansing Everett)12 .... 11:03
2. Gene Hoffmeyer (Lansing Everett)12 ..... 11:06
3. Don Block (Winegars) 11:24
4. Chuck Swinehart (Lansing Everett)11 .... nt
5. Conroy Underwood (Lansing Everett)12 ..... nt
6. Howard Snyder (Spring Arbor)11 .... nt
7. Gordon Holton (Spring Arbor)12 .... nt
8. Buzz Schact (Spring Arbor)11 .... nt
10. Doug Milliman (Lansing Everett)12 .... nt

1957 CLASS C/D BOYS

Coach Keith Griffin's Camden-Frontier team won its first title as Lansing Everett moved up to Class B. Lake Odessa finished only two points behind.

John Myjak of Burton Atherton.

Washtenaw Country Club, Ypsilanti, Nov. 2 ☐
1957 BOYS CLASS C/D TEAMS
1. Camden-Frontier 80
2. Lake Odessa 82
3. East Jackson 101
4. New Lothrop St Michael 130
5. Wyoming Rogers 145
6. Burton Atherton 162
7. Spring Arbor 165
8. Orchard Lake St Mary's 214
9. Covert 220
10. Okemos 250
11. McBain 270
12. Haslett 335
13. Crystal 337
14. Holt 353

1957 BOYS CLASS C/D INDIVIDUAL
1. John Myjak (Burton Atherton)12 .... 11:09
2. Gary Martin (East Jackson) .... nt

1958 CLASS C/D BOYS

East Jackson, in only its second year of cross country, won under the guidance of coach Dick Fults. Runner-up Pewamo-Westphalia, in its first season of cross country, went undefeated until placing second at the state finals.

C/D teams could go to the state meet without having a regionals, which as the sport grew, started to have an effect. The C/D race had more teams and competitors than A or B.

Washtenaw Country Club, Ypsilanti, Nov. 1 ☐
1958 BOYS CLASS C/D TEAMS
1. East Jackson 84
2. Pewamo-Westphalia 112
3. Camden-Frontier 118
4. Wyoming Rogers 149
5. New Lothrop St Michael 157
6. Burton Atherton 172
7. Swartz Creek 197
8. Covert 216
9. Spring Arbor 248
10. Orchard Lake St Mary's 279
11. Brown City 287
12. Napoleon 301
13. Haslett 322
14. Lake Odessa 378
15. Crystal 403
16. Muskegon Christian 404

1958 BOYS CLASS C/D INDIVIDUALS
1. Ron Mitchell (Covert)12 .... 10:41
2. Ernest Callard (Swartz Creek) .... nt
3. Dick Pickering (East Jackson)11 .... c10:45
4. Jim English (Swartz Creek) .... nt
5. Gary Gray (Ypsilanti Roosevelt) .... nt
10. Larry Hamilton (East Jackson) .... nt
13. Al Rich (Buton Atherton) .... nt
15. Gary Martin (East Jackson) .... nt
16. Bill McCullough (East Jackson) .... nt
40. Dave Duguid (East Jackson) .... nt
93. Harry Sprangel (East Jackson) .... nt

1959 CLASS C/D BOYS

Pewamo-Westphalia, in only its second trip to the finals, came away with the win, scoring just 49 points to the 89 of defending champion East Jackson. Coach Ken Click guided the team to an undefeated season, helped by his lead runners, Ken Schafer and Amby Fox. Six of the seven Pewamo runners had broken 11:00 during the season.

Washtenaw Country Club, Ypsilanti, Nov. 7 ☐
1959 BOYS CLASS C/D TEAMS
1. Pewamo-Westphalia 49
2. East Jackson 89
3. Camden-Frontier 104
4. New Lothrop St Michael 110
5. Hale 114
6. Brown City 184
7. Burton Atherton 199
8. Napoleon 224
9. Orchard Lake St Mary's 238
10. Boyne City 277
11. Haslett 296
12. Adrian Madison 323
13. Spring Arbor 340
14. Covert 343
15. Detroit Country Day 449

1959 BOYS CLASS C/D INDIVIDUALS
1. Dick Pickering (East Jackson)12 .... 10:51
6. Larry Hamilton (East Jackson) .... nt
9. Larry Hicks (East Jackson) .... nt
32. Larry Ruede (East Jackson)11 .... nt
41. Terry Tubbs (East Jackson)11 .... nt

1960 CLASS C/D BOYS

Jerry Smith of team winner East Jackson avenged his only loss of the year to Tom Sheets of Boyne City, winning by a 20-yard margin, after trailing by 20 yards with a half mile to go. Sheets had earlier beaten Smith at the Albion Invitational. For Smith it was an incredible rookie year in the sport. The next spring he was regional champ in the mile at 4:37.7.

Washtenaw Country Club, Ypsilanti, Nov. 5 ☐
1960 BOYS CLASS C/D TEAMS
1. East Jackson 54
2. Pewamo-Westphalia 130
3. Camden-Frontier 135
=4. Napoleon 170
=4. New Lothrop St Michael 170
6. Haslett 206
7. Brown City 214
8. McBain 217
9. Muskegon Christian 236
10. Fennville 251
11. Jackson Northwest 281
12. Orchard Lake St Mary's 300
13. Williamston 335
14. Burton Atherton 359
15. Covert 393
16. Grosse Pointe University 449

1960 BOYS CLASS C/D INDIVIDUALS
1. Jerry Smith (East Jackson)12 .... 10:29
2. Tom Sheets (Boyne City) c10:35
3. Norm Shaughnessey (Jackson Northwest)11 ..... nt
7. Larry Hamilton (East Jackson)12 .... nt
11. Pat Schram (Napoleon) .... nt
12. Larry Ruede (East Jackson)12 .... nt
15. Terry Tubbs (East Jackson)12 .... nt
19. Dave DeLaet (East Jackson)11 .... nt
30. Ron Worden (East Jackson)12 .... nt
61. Chuck Hoover (East Jackson)11 .... nt

1961 CLASS C/D BOYS

In its first appearance at the state finals, the Warriors of Remus Chippewa Hills took a slim 92-96 victory over Napoleon, with East Jackson (103) and Fennville (104) very close behind. Coached by Arnold Schellenbarger, Remus Chippewa Hills managed the win without putting any runners into the top 10.

Washtenaw Country Club, Ypsilanti, Nov. 4 ☐
1961 BOYS CLASS C/D TEAMS
1. Remus Chippewa Hills 92
2. Napoleon 96
3. East Jackson 103
4. Fennville 104
5. Ann Arbor St Thomas 180
6. Portland St Patrick 188
7. Haslett 217
8. Camden-Frontier 224
9. Muskegon Christian 240
10. Lake Odessa 256
11. Montague 258
12. DeWitt 276
13. Adrian Madison 360
14. New Lothrop St Michael 420
15. Battle Creek Springfield 493
16. Glen Arbor Leelanau 510
17. Springport 531
18. Brown City 550
19. Covert 563

21. Bellaire	569
22. Saranac	581
23. Kentwood	589
24. Grosse Pointe University	617
25. North Farmington	640

1961 BOYS CLASS C/D INDIVIDUALS

1. Maurice Carr (Ann Arbor St Thomas)	11:07
2. Pat Schram (Napoleon)11	11:13
3. Bill Gooding (Fennville)10	nt
4. Steve Hector (Springport)	nt
5. Ken Cummer (East Lansing)	nt
6. Paul Pung (Portland St Patrick)	nt
7. William Chamberlain (Montague)	nt
8. Bill Werner (Pewamo-Westphalia)	nt
9. Jim Barron (Fennville)11	nt
10. Jack Brake (Lake Odessa)	nt
11. Tom Lingard (Napoleon)11	nt
13. Dave DeLaet (East Jackson)	nt

1962 CLASS C/D BOYS

Led by individual winner Ivan Palmer, Remus Chippewa Hills defended its title, topping Fennville by 20 points. Palmer, a transfer from nearby Vestaburg High, nipped Fennville's Bill Gooding as both clocked 10:44.

Washtenaw Country Club, Ypsilanti, Nov. 3 □
1962 BOYS CLASS C/D TEAMS

1. Remus Chippewa Hills	55
2. Fennville	75
3. Napoleon	126
4. Ann Arbor St Thomas	149
5. Portland St Patrick	149
6. Adrian Madison	236
7. Lake Odessa	249
8. Montague	252
9. Muskegon Heights	279
10. DeWitt	289
11. Saranac	290
12. Brown City	294
13. Covert	306
14. Reese	326
15. Carson City	354
16. Alba	360
17. Camden-Frontier	396
18. White Pigeon	496
19. Detroit Country Day	543
20. Wayne St Mary	560

1962 BOYS CLASS C/D INDIVIDUALS

1. Ivan Palmer (Remus Chippewa Hills)12	10:44
2. Bill Gooding (Fennville)11	10:44
3. Tom Lingard (Napoleon)12	11:00
4. William Warfield (Camden-Frontier)	nt
5. James Shaw (Remus Chippewa Hills)	nt
6. Paul Pung (Portland St Patrick)	nt
7. Phil Beagle (Fennville)12	nt
8. Jim Barron (Fennville)12	nt
9. Ray Childers (Brown City)	nt
10. Jack Brake (Lake Odessa)	nt
11. Bob DeLaLuz (Fennville)11	nt
12. Pat Schram (Napoleon)12	nt
13. Dale Sage (Reese)	nt
14. Robert Reynolds (Carson City)	nt

1963 CLASS C/D BOYS

Ann Arbor's St. Thomas put five runners in the top 12 to score a low 40 points, with a 95-point winning margin, the biggest ever. Coach Bernie Ryan said it was a response to some bragging the previous year by the winning Remus Chippewa Hills team. "We had two goals after they started needling us about it. We wanted to be the best in the state and we wanted to win by less than 55 points."

Washtenaw Country Club, Ypsilanti, Nov. 2 □
1963 BOYS CLASS C/D TEAMS

1. Ann Arbor St Thomas	40
=2. Napoleon	135
=2. Remus Chippewa Hills	135
4. Reese	170
5. Adrian Madison	197
6. Covert	201
7. Brown City	235
8. Fennville	237
9. Springport	260
10. DeWitt	261
11. New Lothrop St Michael	295
12. Elsie	302
13. Lawton	317
14. Muskegon Christian	320
15. Saranac	355
16. Tustin	361
17. Lake City	388
18. Alba	394
19. Detroit Country Day	476
20. Camden	505
21. Kent City	543
22. Onaway	598
23. Grosse Pointe University	640

1963 BOYS CLASS C/D INDIVIDUALS

1. Jack Hall (Ann Arbor St Thomas)10	10:37
2. Bill Harden (Elsie)	10:47
3. Ray Childers (Brown City)	nt
4. Bill Fountain (Remus Chippewa Hills)	nt
5. Craig Van Vorhees (Fennville)	nt
6. Dale Sage (Reese)	nt
7. Dick Deighton (Ann Arbor St Thomas)	nt
8. Gary Bowen (Alma)	nt
9. Jim Carr (Ann Arbor St Thomas)	nt
10. Bob Schram (Napoleon)	nt
11. (Ann Arbor St Thomas)	nt
12. (Ann Arbor St Thomas)	nt

Kalamazoo University's Jim Giachino ran away with the 1964 crown.

1964 CLASS C/D BOYS

This is the year that killed the "no regionals" concept for Class C/D. For years it had essentially been an all-comers affair, with officials saying that participation wasn't big enough to justify regional elimination. They maintained this even as the C/D race grew bigger than A and B.

However, when 36 teams showed up at the starting line this year, officials realized the situation had exploded. It was the biggest state final race in history. Following the meet the MHSAA told schools to expect regionals in 1965.

Jim Giachino of Kalamazoo University, who had set marks of 1:58.5 and 4:28.7 the previous spring before winning the Class C mile crown at 4:30.2, won at 9:51.5. The next spring he would run a 4:20.1 mile. He later would become a successful tennis coach in the NCAA, retiring after nine seasons at Sam Houston State.

Reese, coached by John Osler, took the team title by 98 points.

Washtenaw Country Club, Ypsilanti, Nov. 7 □
1964 BOYS CLASS C/D TEAMS

1. Reese	71
2. Ann Arbor St Thomas	169
3. Remus Chippewa Hills	184
4. Wyoming Lee	203
5. Lawton	209
6. Napoleon	224
7. Capac	241
=8. Shepherd	283
=8. Springport	283
10. Muskegon Christian	295
11. Morenci	296
12. Fennville	374
13. Covert	384
14. Kalamazoo University	417
15. Homer	434
16. Pittsford	455
17. Montague	464
18. Saranac	467
19. White Pigeon	473
20. Fairview	489
21. Byron Center	501
22. Adrian Madison	529
23. Tustin	535
24. Lake City	602
25. DeWitt	652
26. Freesoil	676
27. Clinton	721
28. Essexville Garber	724
29. Flint Hamady	736
30. Camden-Frontier	775
31. Detroit Country Day	791
32. Whittemore-Prescott	796
33. Galien	816
34. Fowlerville	819
35. Schoolcraft	944
36. Grosse Pointe University	1015

1964 BOYS CLASS C/D INDIVIDUALS

1. Jim Giachino (Kalamazoo University)12	9:52
2. Jack Hall (Ann Arbor St Thomas)	10:07
3. Dale Sage (Reese)12	10:11
4. Craig Van Vorhees (Fennville)	10:24
8. Ed Schlosser (Haslett)11	10:22?
14. Jerry O'Bryant (Haslett)	10:29
20. Phil Heath (Napoleon)	10:55

1965 CLASS C/D BOYS

As promised, four regional races were held, which helped officials cut the state finals race by a massive two-thirds.

Springport, coached by Henry Tinkham, lost its regional race but bounced back to win here by 42 points. The team was led by junior Jim Gibbs, who would later coach at Michigan State.

Washtenaw Country Club, Ypsilanti, Nov. 6 □
1965 BOYS CLASS C/D TEAMS

1. Springport	84
2. Haslett	126
3. Napoleon	137
4. Shepherd	170
5. Orchard Lake St Mary's	173
6. Reese	191

7. Ann Arbor St Thomas 194
8. Lawton 206
9. Byron Center 231
10. Remus Chippewa Hills 248
11. Lake City 319
12. Covert 327

1965 BOYS CLASS C/D INDIVIDUALS
1. Ed Schlosser (Haslett)12 .... 10:20
2. Richard Towne (Morenci) 10:32
3. Jim Gibbs (Springport)11 .... 10:46
4. Roger Towne (Ypsilanti) 10:47
5. Tom Payne (Wyoming Lee) 10:50

1966 CLASS C/D BOYS

Coach Gene Bednarowski led the Blue Devils to the first state title in school history. C/D third-placer Nick Wellburn would be among the first state champions in the two mile the next spring. The event had not been run officially in the state since 1910.

Terry Doxey of Gobles just edged Jim Gibbs of Springport for the individual crown.

Washtenaw Country Club, Ypsilanti, Nov. 12 □
1966 BOYS CLASS C/D TEAMS
1. Lawton 64
2. Reese 110
3. Napoleon 111
4. Remus Chippewa Hills 142
5. Shepherd 156
6. Springport 190
7. Mayville 205
8. Bangor 234
9. Concord 257
10. Wyoming Lee 267
11. Orchard Lake St Mary's 279
12. North Muskegon 361

1966 BOYS CLASS C/D INDIVIDUALS
1. Terry Doxey (Gobles)11 .... 10:29
2. Jim Gibbs (Springport)12 .... 10:30
3. Nick Welburn (Lawton) 10:32
4. Keith Schultz (Napoleon) 10:38
5. Gerald Wesaw (Bangor) 10:40
6. Lyle Warner (Remus Chippewa Hills) 10:42
7. Phil Paige (Covert) 10:44
8. Dewayne Hall (Reese) 10:46
9. Stanley Bober (Napoleon) 10:48
10. Clare Kreger (Mayville) 10:50
11. Robert Sugden (Mayville) 10:52
12. Thomas Atwater (Lawton) 10:54
13. William McFadden (Lawton) 10:55
14. Ray Towne (Morenci) 10:56
15. Manuel Rangel (Reese) 10:57
17. Gary Wellburn (Lawton) .... nt
19. John Schur (Lawton) .... nt
23. Dave Dudeck (Lawton) .... nt
45. Bill Britt (Lawton) .... nt

1967 CLASS C/D BOYS

The cold and snowy conditions hampered some of the teams, but Lawton produced a clutch race. Coach Gene Bednarowski's Blue Devils beat New Haven by 14 points. It was the highest winning total in meet history.

Mayville's Clare Kreger was the toughest on the wet, slippery course. Reportedly on the final hill to the finish, a number of runners slipped and were passed.

Washtenaw Country Club, Ypsilanti, Nov. 4 □
30-degrees, cold, snowy.
1967 BOYS CLASS C/D TEAMS
1. Lawton 97
2. New Haven 111
3. Ann Arbor St Thomas 156
4. Mayville 156
5. Bellevue 171
6. Napoleon 178
7. Shepherd 223
8. Wyoming Lee 231
9. Adrian Madison 232
10. Perry 250
11. McBain 284
12. Kingsley 287

1967 BOYS CLASS C/D INDIVIDUALS
1. Clare Kreger (Mayville)11 .... 10:43
2. Nick Welburn (Lawton) 10:45
3. Terry Doxey (Gobles)12 .... 10:49
4. Tom Broughton (New Haven) 10:52
5. Tom Atwater (Lawton) 10:53
6. Frank Dusett (New Haven) .... nt
7. Douglas Stevens (New Haven) .... nt
8. Manuel Rangel (Reese) .... nt
9. Mark Sackrider (Bellevue) .... nt
10. Steve Haney (Centerville) .... nt
11. Al Adams (Napoleon) .... nt
12. Ed Fishtler (New Haven) .... nt
13. Jon Brower (Napoleon) .... nt
14. Bob Sugden (Mayville) .... nt
15. Gary Miller (New Haven) .... nt
20. Gary Welbum (Lawton) .... nt
29. John Schur (Lawton) .... nt
41. Nathan Bitley (Lawton) .... nt

Tracey Elliott, Cherryland's only champion ever.

1968 CLASS C/D BOYS

Tracey Elliott of Elk Rapids Cherryland moved into the lead at the halfway mark and was never threatened, winning by 15 meters.

He would be the first and last champion from Cherryland High. Two years later, construction began on a new high school, Cherryland became a middle school building, and Elk Rapids High became the new school name.

Elliott would repeat as the Class D two-mile champ in the spring at 9:44.1. He would go on to star for Bowling Green and was one of Dave Wottle's training partners in the lead-up to Wottle's Olympic 800 win in 1972.

East Jackson, coached by William Fitch, won the team title with 127 points, the highest winning total ever.

Washtenaw Country Club, Ypsilanti, Nov. 2 □
1968 BOYS CLASS C/D TEAMS
1. East Jackson 127
2. Napoleon 135
3. Montrose 161
4. North Branch 175
5. Battle Creek St Philip 176
6. Grosse Pointe St Paul 186
7. Wyoming Lee 189
8. Elk Rapids Cherryland 194
9. Ann Arbor St Thomas 202
10. White Pigeon 258
11. Shepherd 272
12. Fairview 294

1968 BOYS CLASS C/D INDIVIDUALS
1. Tracy Elliott (Elk Rapids Cherryland)12 .... 10:25
2. Al Adams (Napoleon) 10:28
3. Jim Casazza (Grosse Pointe St Paul) 10:32
4. Dennis Valentine (East Jackson)11 .... 10:34
5. Jon Brower (Napoleon) 10:35
6. Mike Hamilton (Manchester) 10:36
7. Terry Valentine (East Jackson) 10:36
8. Tony Hubbarth (Grosse Pointe St Paul) 10:37
9. Clare Kreger (Mayville)12 .... 10:39
10. Tom Atwater (Lawton) 10:39
11. Richard Fleece (Battle Creek St Philip) .. 10:41
12. David Bauman (Battle Creek St Philip) ... 10:42
13. Dan Garcia (Adrian Madison) 10:45
14. Tom Darga (Ann Arbor St Thomas) 10:49
15. Gary Johnson (Montrose)11 .... 10:53

1969 CLASS C/D BOYS

Coach William Fitch's boys from East Jackson successfully defended in a steady rain on the rolling two-mile course. Senior Dennis Valentine moved up from 4th a year earlier to take the top award, just edging Floyd Hassett of Elk Rapids.

Washtenaw Country Club, Ypsilanti, Nov. 1 ⊠
1969 BOYS CLASS C/D TEAMS
1. East Jackson 123
2. Battle Creek St Phillip 198
3. Litchfield 238
4. North Branch 241
5. Dansville 251
6. Grosse Pointe St Paul 256
7. Vandercook Lake 264
8. Elk Rapids 269
9. Fairview 283
10. Shepherd 291
11. Mayville 337
12. Flint Bendle 359
13. Concord 361
14. DeWitt 364
15. Montague 393
16. Reese 395
17. North Muskegon 425
18. Ravenna 436

1969 BOYS CLASS C/D INDIVIDUALS
1. Dennis Valentine (East Jackson)12 .... 10:12
2. Floyd Hassett (Elk Rapids)12 .... 10:13
3. Mike Hamilton (Manchester) 10:16
4. Steve Rockey (Litchfield) 10:22
5. Dick Vandenberg (Muskegon Christian) ... 10:36
6. Tom Darga (Ann Arbor St Thomas) 10:36
7. Dan Adams (Dansville) 10:36
8. Frank Dusett (New Haven) 10:36
9. Larry Brigham (Concord) 10:37
10. Jon Brower (Napoleon) 10:40
11. Steve Palma (Central Montcalm) 10:40
12. Daryl Tessin (Hemlock) 10:41
13. Jerry Grose (Elk Rapids Cherryland) 10:41
14. Bob Curell (North Branch) 10:43
15. Tim Emerson (Battle Creek St Philip) 10:45
16. Mike Dolby (DeWitt) 10:46
17. Doug Mohre (Vandercook Lake) 10:48
18. Ron Haag (Grosse Pointe St Paul) 10:48
19. Dave Young (East Jackson) 10:49
20. Charles Freeburn (Litchfield) 10:50
28. Dave Hinz (East Jackson) 10:59
34. Don Willard (East Jackson) 11:06
42. Gary Majchrowski (East Jackson) 11:12
59. Ron Lukasik (East Jackson) 11:24
77. Bob Serafin (East Jackson) 11:39

1970 CLASS C/D BOYS

Vandercook Lake, coached by Chuck Conrad, put in a combined 10,000+ miles of training to win the team title, jhust a year after making it to the state finals for the first time. With no runners making All-State (top 15), the undefeated team was led to victory by seniors Dave McIntee, Ken Dinges, George Spencer and Pat Quinlan.

Winner Mike Burns would go on to win two state titles in the mile for Carson City-Crystal. It would be his company that would handle the "chip" timing for the state meets for many years. Runner-up Dave Hinz ran a 2:12:06 marathon in 1983 and the next year was 12th in the Olympic Trials marathon. Third-placer Herb Lindsay was the best road racer in the world in the early 1980s.

Washtenaw Country Club, Ypsilanti, Nov. 7 ☐
1970 BOYS CLASS C/D TEAMS
1. Vandercook Lake 183
2. Shepherd 209
3. Mason County Central 230
=4. Bangor 238
=4. Wayne St Mary 238
6. Dearborn St Alphonsus 243
7. Wyoming Lee 248
8. Muskegon Christian 248
9. Mayville 275
10. Reed City 305
11. Addison 325
12. Buckley 341
13. Hudson 342
14. Watervliet 347
15. Williamston 358
16. Battle Creek St Philip 403
17. Middleton-Fulton 421
18. Ann Arbor St Thomas 446

Mike Burns won in 1970 for Carson City-Crystal. He went on to star at Central Michigan and in 1996 led the crew that introduced chip timing to the state finals.

1970 BOYS CLASS C/D INDIVIDUALS
1. Mike Burns (Carson City-Crystal)11 ...... 13:02
2. Dave Hinz (East Jackson) 13:07
3. Herb Lindsay (Reed City) 13:18
4. Richard Theisen (Dearborn St Alphonsus) 13:34
5. Dale Johnson (Muskegon Christian) 13:35
6. Lee Davies (Williamston) 13:36
7. Dick Vandenburg (Muskegon Christian) 13:37
8. Chris Villadsen (Mason County Central) 13:42
9. Ryan Sexton (Wayne St Mary) 13:43
10. Jeff Kastner (Hopkins) 13:44
11. Bob Norman (Addison) 13:44
12. Joe Hennigan (DeWitt) 13:45
13. Daryl DeLabbi (Wayne St Mary) 13:46
14. Dave Patterson (Maryville) 13:48
15. David Pais (Dearborn St Alphonsus) 13:49

1971 CLASS C/D BOYS

Officials finally decided it was time to split up the Class C/D field into team and individual races. They had been doing it in Class A and B for a decade. On the one hand, it made life easier for officials tasked with scoring the meet; on the other, it deprived fans and competitors of many great races, as the top talent was often split up.

Wyoming Lee took the team title, and of the two races, Mike Burns of runner-up Carson City-Crystal had the fastest time overall, winning by an astounding 45-second margin

Washtenaw Country Club, Ypsilanti, Nov. 6 ☐
1971 BOYS CLASS C/D TEAMS
1. Wyoming Lee 81
2. Carson City-Crystal 100
3. Fennville 137
4. Mayville 162
5. Fairview 172
6. Shepherd 172
7. Vandercook Lake 174
8. Watervliet 175
9. Hartford 180
10. Ann Arbor St Thomas 182
11. Orchard Lake St Mary's 193
12. Dansville 210

1971 BOYS CLASS C/D TEAM RACE
1. Mike Burns (Carson City-Crystal)12 ...... 12:57
2. Doug Mohre (Vandercook Lake) 13:42
3. Timothy Karas (Orchard Lake St Mary's) 13:45
4. Chris Glowacki (Shepherd) 13:48
5. Paul Carroll (Ann Arbor St Thomas) 14:00
6. Jim Sexton (Fennville) 14:01
9. Greg Lowing (Wyoming Lee) ...... nt
12. Lyle Bordeaux (Wyoming Lee) ...... nt
15. Dave Boyd (Fennville) ...... nt
16. Bruce Kale (Wyoming Lee) ...... nt
20. Tom Cook (Wyoming Lee) ...... nt
24. Brian Robinson (Wyoming Lee) ...... nt

1971 BOYS CLASS C/D INDIVIDUAL RACE
1. Lee Davies (Williamston)11 ...... 13:28
2. Greg Sanderson (Lawton) 13:35
3. Ken Lynn (Onsted) 13:38
4. Ron Denny (Bangor) 13:45
5. Gordon Freestone (Bangor) 13:51
6. Dan Farver (Reese) 13:52
7. Roy Heminger (Litchfield) 13:53
8. Edmund Flores (Shelby) 13:59
9. Gary Ray (North Muskegon) 14:02
12. Dave Bartels (South Haven) ...... nt

1972 CLASS C/D BOYS

Wyoming Lee got beat at regionals by Mason County Central but turned the tables at the state finals.

The winning margins in both races were the biggest ever seen in Class C/D.

In the individual race, Herb Lindsay rocketed out from the start to win by 47 seconds. He went on to be a 2-time All-American at Michigan State. He was the U.S. champion at 10,000 in 1979 and in 1981 set a World Record of 61:47 for the half marathon.

Vandercook Lake HS, Jackson, Nov. 4 ☐
1972 BOYS CLASS C/D TEAMS
1. Wyoming Lee 91
2. Carson City-Crystal 95
3. Rogers City 110
4. Watervliet 111
5. Kalamazoo Christian 132
6. Dansville 138
7. Akron-Fairgrove 157
8. Mason County Central 165
9. Addison 178
10. Harper Woods Lutheran East 213
11. Concord 222
12. Mayville 287

1972 BOYS CLASS C/D TEAM RACE
1. Dale Darling (Dansville)12 ...... 16:26
2. Bill Wilson (Addison) 16:38
3. Roger LaPratt (Akron-Fairgrove) 16:46
4. Mark Kelly (Carson City-Crystal) 16:52
5. Eidean Hummel (Dansville) 17:00
6. Don Triemstra (Kalamazoo Christian) 17:03
7. Michael Lynch (Watervliet) 17:04
8. Lyle Bordeaux (Wyoming Lee) 17:05
9. David Null (Watervliet) 17:05
10. John Dennis (Casron City Crystal) 17:07
16. Bryan Robinson (Wyoming Lee) 17:13
18. Paul Noel (Wyoming Lee) 17:15
21. Greg Popma (Wyoming Lee) 17:18
28. Tom Cook (Wyoming Lee) 17:28

1972 BOYS CLASS C/D INDIVIDUAL RACE
1. Herb Lindsay (Reed City)12 ...... 15:36
2. Jeff Pullen (Leroy Pine River)11 ...... 16:23
3. Justin Wilson (Muskegon WM Christian) 16:31
4. Lee Davies (Williamston) 16:32
5. Chris Glowacki (Shepherd) 16:33
6. Sam Myer (Shepherd) 16:34
7. Brian Thiede (Vandercook Lake) 16:40
8. Ron Ensing (McBain) 16:46
9. Steve Bunn (Hartford) 16:49
10. Dan Nelson (Lakeview) 16:52
11. Edmund Flores (Shelby) 16:53

1973 CLASS C/D BOYS

After runner-up finishes the two previous years, Carson City-Crystal finally made it to the top, beating Watervliet by 29 points. Two solid races were a treat for fans but did nothing to resolve who the better runner was: Justin Wilson of Western Michigan Christian (15:12 in the team race) or Jeff Pullen of Leroy Pine River (15:04 in the individual run). In the state track meet that spring, Pullen decisively beat Wilson in the two mile, after earlier running a 9:12.3.

Way back in 62nd in the team race was one Darroll Gatson. Better known as a quarter-miler, he ran a 45.12 for Alabama in 1978 and later was head track coach at Michigan State.

Haslett HS, Haslett, Nov. 3 ☐
1973 BOYS CLASS C/D TEAMS
1. Carson City-Crystal 78
2. Watervliet 107
3. Montrose 138
4. Shepherd 149
5. Wyoming Lee 182
6. Vassar 188
7. Addison 196
8. Rogers City 209
9. Muskegon Western Michigan Christian 223
10. Benzie Central 266
11. Buckley 279
12. Blissfield 279
13. Detroit East Catholic 284
14. Concord 292
15. White Cloud 320
16. Manchester 366
17. Kalamazoo Christian 383
18. Dansville 397

1973 BOYS CLASS C/D TEAM RACE
1. Justin Wilson (Muskegon WM Christian)11 ...... 15:12
2. Sam Meyer (Shepherd) 15:29
3. Bill Wilson (Addison) 15:30

4. David Null (Watervliet) 15:45
5. Loe Hoekstra (Kalamazoo Christian) 15:48
6. Mike Faber (Shepherd) 15:52
7. Mike Lynch (Watervliet) 15:54
8. Kevin Cusack (Carson City-Crystal) 15:59
9. Randy Weber (Buckley) 16:01
10. Lyle Bordeaux (Wyoming Lee) 16:06
11. (duplicate) ...
12. Mark Tyan (Carson City-Crystal) 16:08
13. John Dennis (Carson City-Crystal) 16:09
14. Doug Spiece (Carson City-Crystal) 16:12
31. Clark Duerr (Carson City-Crystal) 16:34
48. Al Spiece (Carson City-Crystal) 16:52
62. Darroll Gatson (Detroit East Catholic) 17:06
66. Fred Hargett (Carson City-Crystal) 17:09

1973 BOYS CLASS C/D INDIVIDUAL RACE
1. Jeff Pullen (Leroy Pine River)12 .... 15:04
2. Ken St John (Morrice) 15:31
3. Steve Bunn (Hartford) 15:33
4. Robert Darcy (Ravenna) 15:40
5. Ken Hollenbeck (Elk Rapids) 15:57
6. Tobin Wine (Kingsley) 15:57
7. Andy Kovac (St Louis) 15:59
8. Charles Fairless (Dearborn Sacred Heart) .. 16:00
9. Don Wilson (North Branch) 16:01
10. Paul Strasel (Merrill) 16:02
11. Richard Martinez (Fennville) 16:03
15. Dan Isenhoff (Hopkins) .... nt

1974 CLASS C BOYS

With the Class D contingent finally getting their own race—paired with Class A at another site—Class C runners got a little more elbow room. Justin Wilson led Muskegon Western Michigan Christian to the win with an 18-point margin over rival Carson City-Crystal.

Wilson, who ran 15:44, was just a notch ahead of the 15:45 winning time Charles Fairless of Dearborn Sacred Heart in the individual race.

Western Michigan Christian's Justin Wilson had the fastest time of the day.

Charlotte CC, Charlotte, Nov. 2 ☐
1974 BOYS CLASS C TEAMS
1. Muskegon Western Michigan Christian 86
2. Carson City-Crystal 104
3. Mayville 123
4. White Cloud 136
5. Clare 146
6. Battle Creek Lakeview 149
7. Mason County Central 176
8. Unionville-Sebewaing 178
9. Bath 206
10. Ida 215
11. Watervliet 242
12. Concord 248
13. St Joseph Lake Michigan Catholic 253
14. Manchester 326

1974 BOYS CLASS C TEAM RACE
1. Justin Wilson (Muskegon WM Christian)12 .... 15:44
2. Mike Solis (Battle Creek Lakeview)11 .... 15:49
3. Steve Ford Battle Creek (Lakeview) 15:57
4. Ed LaBair (Mayville) .... nt
5. Ken Jezierski (Unionville-Sebewaing) .... nt
6. Mark Hanson (Bath) .... nt
7. Clyde Harris (Muskegon W. Michigan Christ.) .. nt
8. Gary Vowman (Ida) .... nt
9. Marv Ryan (Carson City-Crystal) .... nt
10. Tim Androl (Unionville-Sebewaing) .... nt
11. Doug Krudop (Carson City-Crystal) .... nt
12. Al DeYoung (Muskegon W. Michigan Christ.) .. nt
13. Mike Lynch (Watervliet) 16:22
14. William McClintock (White Cloud) .... nt

1974 BOYS CLASS C INDIVIDUAL RACE
1. Charles Fairless (Dearborn Sacred Heart)12 .. 15:45
2. Charles Hueber (Saginaw Michigan Lutheran) .. 15:53
3. Mark Herbers (St Charles) 15:56
4. Don Isenhoff (Hopkins) .... nt
5. Paul Drake (Reese) .... nt
6. Mike Saber (Shepherd) .... nt
7. William Elliott (Rogers City) .... nt
8. Vem Halford (Wyoming Lee) .... nt
9. Tim Fall (Vassar) .... nt
10. Brad Shaw (Addison) .... nt

1975 CLASS C BOYS

Mayville, guided by coach Robert Weaver, won its first state trophy with 148 points.

The tie for 2nd between Wyoming Lee and Central Montcalm was broken by the fastest time for their 4th-place runners.

Charlotte CC, Charlotte, Nov. 1 ☐
1975 BOYS CLASS C TEAMS
1. Mayville 148
2. Wyoming Lee 173
3. Stanton-Central Montcalm 173
4. Bath 195
5. Addison 198
6. DeWitt 201
7. Mason County Central 210
8. Michigan Center .... ns
9. Clare .... ns
10. Allen Park Cabrini .... ns
11. Edwardsburg 246
12. Dearborn St Alphonsus .... ns
13. Kent City .... ns
14. Montrose .... nt
15. Benzie Central 360
16. White Cloud .... ns
17. St Louis .... ns
18. St Joseph Lake Michigan Catholic 369
=19. Reese 385
=19. Three Oaks River Valley 385
21. Manchester .... ns

1975 BOYS CLASS C TEAM RACE
1. Neal Davis (Clare)11 .... 15:49
2. Brad Shaw (Addison) 15:53
3. Ed LaBair (Mayville)11 .... 15:54
4. Ken Theisen (Dearborn St Alphonsus) 15:58
5. Rick Alward (Bath) 16:03
6. Todd Moss (Benzie Central) 16:05

1975 BOYS CLASS C INDIVIDUAL RACE
1. Mike Solis (Battle Creek Lakeview)12 .... 15:34
2. Ken Owens (Gladwin) 15:46
3. Paul Drake (Muskegon Reeths-Puffer) 15:54
4. Clyde Harris (Muskegon Christian) 15:57
5. Kim Sharp (Flat Rock) 15:58
6. Richard Holmes (Pine River) 15:59
7. Bob Mena (Leslie) 16:00
8. Steve Ford (Battle Creek Lakeview) 16:04
9. Mark Ryan (Carson City-Crystal) 16:05

1976 CLASS C BOYS

Mason County Central had apparently won the meet, but its fourth runner, Kevin Gancarz, was disqualified after finishing 34th. The Spartans dropped to 4th place and the title went to Breckenridge.

According to coach Steve Bishop, Gancarz was with a group of six runners that failed to go around a small tree on the golf course. "Just a couple of yards that gave him absolutely no advantage," said Bishop.

"What really makes me mad is that after the team run, the first run on the course, the same official that disqualified Kevin and a couple of other boys yelled warnings and upon occasion physically grabbed runners to force them to run back around the tree. Martin Schulist from Whitehall, who won the individual race, was one that was warned and retraced his steps around the little tree."

Said Ludington coach Ruben Gomez, "I have never seen so many disqualifications in a state meet… The Spartans were the champions. Everyone there knew it."

Benzie Central had been favored to do much better, but four of its members sat out the race for disciplinary reasons. A parent drove all night to get two additional runners to the meet, where the team finished last.

Green Valley Golf Course, Sturgis, Nov. 6 ☐
1976 BOYS CLASS C TEAMS
1. Breckenridge 120
2. DeWitt 160
3. Grandville Calvin Christian 164
4. Mason County Central 169
5. Edwardsburg 187
6. Mayville 188
7. Allen Park Cabrini 190
8. Kent City 217
9. Clare 220
10. Bath 223
11. Union City 229
12. Manchester 231
13. Akron-Fairgrove 246
14. Capac 255
15. Shepherd 305
16. Dearborn St Alphonsus 359
17. Kalamazoo Christian 411
18. Benzie Central 425

1976 BOYS CLASS C TEAM RACE
1. Ed LaBair (Mayville)12 .... 15:43
2. Dan Heslip (Manchester) 15:49
3. Steve Grim (Grandville Calvin Christian) ... 15:52
4. Dave MacLean (Mason County Central) ... 15:52
5. Jerry Curtis (Akron-Fairgrove) 15:55
6. Dale Hool (Mayville) 15:55
7. Kurt Smith (Breckenridge) 15:55
8. Ron Buchanan (Allen Park Cabrini)12 .... 16:00
9. Dave Cronkrite (Breckenridge) 16:01
10. Leo Kennedy (Breckenridge) 16:02
11. Dale Tarrant (Bath) 16:02
12. Dave Wilson (DeWitt) 16:02
13. Duane Ingraham (Mason County Central) .. 16:03
14. Darrell Tarrant (Bath) 16:02
15. Michael LeFleur (Capac) 16:06

1976 BOYS CLASS C INDIVIDUAL RACE
1. Martin Schulist (Whitehall)11 .... 15:34
2. Richard Friday (Montague) 15:48
3. Walt Drenth (Charlevoix) 15:58
4. Richard Poppe (Muskegon W Mi Christian) .. 16:00
5. Brad Shaw (Addison) 16:02

1977 CLASS C BOYS

Tom Mauro's DeWitt squad used a 1-2-5 finish to nail down a 40-point winning margin. Teammates Dave Wilson and Ron Hensley crossed together in 15:29.7.

John Henning of Allen Park Cabrini took the individual race in the faster time, 15:22.

Green Valley GC, Sturgis, Nov. 5 □
1977 BOYS CLASS C TEAMS
1. DeWitt 62
2. Clare 102
3. Breckenridge 111
4. St Louis 116
5. Edwardsburg 163
6. Wyoming Lee 167
7. Capac 218
8. Mattawan 263
9. Pewamo-Westphalia 274
10. Clinton 282
11. Mason County Central 290
12. Royal Oak Shrine 302
13. East Jackson 309
14. Marlette 315
15. Charlevoix 326
16. Manchester 331
17. Bangor 364
18. Muskegon Oakridge 390

1977 BOYS CLASS C TEAM RACE
1. Dave Wilson (DeWitt)12 .... 15:30
2. Ron Hensley (DeWitt) 15:30
3. Phil Robar (St Louis) 15:37
4. Dave Foster (Clare) 15:42
5. Roland Hensley (DeWitt) 15:43
6. Perry Henscke (Mattawan) 15:49
7. Leo Kennedy (Breckenridge) 15:57
8. Mark Hoffman (Breckenridge) 15:57

John Henning won Cabrini's only title.

1977 BOYS CLASS C INDIVIDUAL RACE
1. John Henning (Allen Park Cabrini)11 .... 15:22
2. Dan Shamiyeh (Freeland)11 .... 15:29
3. Martin Schulist (Whitehall)12 .... 15:37
4. Dale Tarrant (Bath) 15:38
5. John Galarno (Carrollton) 15:42
6. Mike Maike (White Cloud) 15:43
7. John Darga (Burton Atherton) 15:44
8. Dale Hool (Mayville) 15:44
9. Francis Burch (Whitehall) 15:49
10. Steve Habegger (Middleville TK) 15:54
11. Dan Morton (Union City) 15:57
12. Max Curtis (Shepherd) 15:57

1978 CLASS C BOYS

"I didn't think we'd win it," said Wyoming Lee coach Art Kraai. "Breckenridge was favored. They were No. 1 all season."

Freeland's Dan Shamiyeh unseated defending champion John Henning. He would later star for Eastern Michigan and ran on the distance medley team that won the NCAA Indoor title in 1984.

Haslett HS, Haslett, Nov. 4 □
1978 BOYS CLASS C TEAMS
1. Wyoming Lee 123
2. Breckenridge 135
3. Freeland 161
4. DeWitt 164
5. Charlevoix 167
6. St Louis 177
7. East Jackson 199
8. Clare 202
9. Onsted 274
10. Rogers City 288
11. Hart 290
12. Watervliet 296
13. Allen Park Cabrini 296
14. Mattawan 306
15. Clinton 327
16. Grandville Calvin Christian 360
17. Marlette 395
18. Springport 442
19. Capac 453
20. Bangor 457
21. Hudson 469

1978 BOYS CLASS C TEAM RACE
1. Dan Shamiyeh (Freeland)12 .... 16:17
2. John Henning (Allen Park Cabrini)12 ...... 16:25
3. Leo Kennedy (Breckenridge) 16:31
4. Max Curtis (Breckenridge) 16:34
5. Ron Hensley (DeWitt) 16:49
6. Bill Bainbridge (Wyoming Lee) 16:50
7. Jeff Drenth (Charlevoix) 16:53
8. Jim Gillis (Breckenridge) 16:53
9. Bob Love (Rogers City) 16:54
10. Craig Higby (St Louis) 16:57
11. Todd Griffith (Onsted) 16:58
12. Mark Russell (Charlevoix) 17:01
13. Roland Hensley (DeWitt) 17:02
14. Mike LaFleur (Capac) 17:05
15. Matt Lamourie (Allen Park Cabrini) 17:06
21. Jody Lowing (Wyoming Lee) .... nt
26. Wendell Ratliff (Wyoming Lee) .... nt
30. Jim Melinn (Wyoming Lee) .... nt
40. Scott Holford (Wyoming Lee) .... nt

1978 BOYS CLASS C INDIVIDUAL RACE
1. Ken Jabe (Flat Rock)12 .... 16:42
2. Mike Maike (White Cloud) 16:52
3. Francis Burch (Whitehall) 17:01
4. Bryan Burns (Carson City-Crystal) 17:03
5. Rod Howard (Galesburg-Augusta) 17:07

1979 CLASS C BOYS

Jerry Mayer's St. Louis team brought home its first state title—barely. In the final tally Freeland was only two points behind the Sharks' 86-point score.

"We weren't sure who our toughest competition would be," said Mayer. "We're just glad to get the win. The kids really deserved it."

Perhaps it's an understatement to say that conditions were fast. Craig Higby of St. Louis won the team race in 14:49; Guy Jacobsen of Whitehall the individual race in 14:54. They were the first sub-15 times in Class C Finals history.

County Clare GC, Clare, Nov. 3 □
1979 BOYS CLASS C TEAMS
1. St Louis 86
2. Freeland 88
3. Clare 151
4. Springport 162
5. Mattawan 200
6. Fulton-Middleton 274
7. Reese 282
8. Mason County Central 295
9. East Jackson 297
10. Three Oaks River Valley 306
11. Mancelona 319
12. Charlevoix 324
13. Haslett 341
14. Olivet 347
15. Stockbridge 371
16. Leslie 374
17. Bangor 375
18. Marlette 380
19. Wyoming Lee 389
20. Muskegon Oakridge 422
21. Buchanan 424
22. Allen Park Cabrini 437
23. Kent City 498
24. Detroit Holy Redeemer 574

1979 BOYS CLASS C TEAM RACE
1. Craig Higby (St Louis) 14:49
2. Phil Bedford (Clare)12 .... 15:09
3. Rich Hunter (Freeland) 15:15
4. Armanda Garta (St Louis) 15:25
5. Greg Barnett (Mason County Central) 15:30
6. Paul Diaz (St Louis) 15:32
7. Troy Hillman (Mattawan) 15:32
8. Bill Romusier (Marlette) 15:34
9. James Slavik (Fulton-Middleton) 15:35
10. Doug Borden (St Louis) 15:36
65. Steve Crumbaugh (St Louis) .... nt

1979 BOYS CLASS C INDIVIDUAL RACE
1. Guy Jacobson (Whitehall)12 .... 14:54
2. Bob Stanfield (Williamston)11 .... 15:32
3. Randy Lyons (Hudson) 15:33
4. Dave Dumonte (Hart) 15:34
5. Rich Bean (Quincy) 15:35
6. Eric Stuber (Williamston) 15:36
7. Tom Broekema (Kalamazoo Christian) 15:37
8. Ed Ford (Forest Hills Northern) .... nt
9. Bob Vandenburg (Middleville TK) .... nt
10. Kevin German (Concord) .... nt

1980 CLASS C BOYS

This marked the first year that all regionals and finals in the Lower Peninsula took place on 5,000m courses. Williamston's Eric Stuber took his time getting to the lead. He was worse than 20th at the half-mile mark, and 5th at the mile. He finally took the lead at the halfway point.

Coach Chuck King put his top 5 runners all from places 17-39 to grab the win for Concord. The plight of Concord was one shared by many schools of the time. In the yearbook, six pages were devoted to their football team that had a 3-6 record. Zero mention of their state championship cross country team. Sigh.

County Clare GC, Clare, Nov. 1 □
1980 BOYS CLASS C TEAMS
1. Concord 136
2. Reese 182
3. Napoleon 187
4. Kalamazoo Christian 193
5. Charlevoix 231
6. Muskegon Oakridge 232
7. DeWitt 242
8. Stockbridge 249
9. Rogers City 257

10. Grandville Calvin Christian 265
11. Unionville-Sebewaing 294
12. Williamston 295
13. St Louis 302
14. Olivet 310
15. Mattawan 315
16. Lakeview 319
17. Hartford 356
18. Benzie Central 366
19. Mancelona 371
20. Edwardsburg 388
21. Allen Park Cabrini 397

1980 BOYS CLASS C TEAM RACE
1. Eric Stuber (Williamston)12 .... 15:34
2. Richard Bradshaw (Stockbridge) 15:40
3. Bob Stanfield (Williamston)12 .... 16:04
4. Dana Howard (Napoleon) 16:06
5. Jim Schuster (Napoleon) 16:07
6. Jay Swartwout (Charlevoix) 16:10
7. Mark McFoley (Reese) 16:10
8. Dan Dixon (Napoleon) 16:11
9. Ted Wissner (DeWitt) .... nt
10. Tom Broekema (Kalamazoo Christian) .... nt
17. Steve Hubbard (Concord) 16:36
20. Kevin Gorman (Concord) 16:39
27. Tim Buehler (Concord) 16:44
33. Chuck Grimes (Concord) 16:52
39. Mike Kraus (Concord) 16:57
66. Dan Bush (Concord) 17:23
76. Bill Baird (Concord) 17:27

1980 BOYS CLASS C INDIVIDUAL RACE
1. Bob Vandenburg (Middleville TK)11 .... 15:59
2. Brian Olling (Breckenridge) 16:04
3. Klinger (Leslie) 16:08
4. Jenks (Leslie) 16:17
5. Matt Thesarrow (Burton Atherton) 16:19
6. Brian Rayburn (Clare) 16:20
7. John Card (Freeland) 16:20

1981 CLASS C BOYS

Kalamazoo Christian convincingly won its first title with a record margin of 101 points. The margin might have been smaller but for a frightening incident near the finish line. Stockbridge's top runner, senior Jon Fillmore, was running near the leaders when he collapsed 100 meters from the finish. He was taken to ths hospital and later released. Stockbridge finished second in the team tallies; its fifth man finished 88th, so Fillmore's DNF did not affect the team placing.

Ron Simpson of Redford St Mary produced the fastest time, 15:53. He would win the 800 (1:53.7) and 1600 (4:13.5) the next spring at the Class C finals. At Michigan he would win All Big 10 honors several times.

Watervliet HS, Watervliet, Oct. 31 ☐
1981 BOYS CLASS C TEAMS
1. Kalamazoo Christian 55
2. Stockbridge 156
3. St Louis 182
4. Benzie Central 187
5. Muskegon Oakridge 202
6. DeWitt 203
7. Napoleon 205
8. Allen Park Cabrini 214
9. Charlevoix 226
10. Shepherd 263
11. Caledonia 282
12. Orchard Lake St Mary's 289
13. Rogers City 291
14. Onsted 301
15. Grandville Calvin Christian 321
16. Marlette 344
17. Niles Brandywine 360
18. Edwardsburg 386
19. Mt Clemens Lutheran North 466
20. Cass City 488
21. Quincy 576

1981 BOYS CLASS C TEAM RACE
1. Rich Bradshaw (Stockbridge)10 .... 16:21
2. Paul Ward (Orchard Lake St Mary's) 16:27
3. Greg Bliss (Cass City) 16:28
4. Dan Nixon (Napoleon) 16:28
5. Tom Broekema (Kalamazoo Christian) 16:38
6. Ted Wisner (DeWitt) 16:44
7. Dan Veen (Kalamazoo Christian) 16:48
8. Haley (Allen Park Cabrini) .... nt
9. Fouts (Kalamazoo Central) .... nt
10. Bumpus (Stockbridge) .... nt
11. Jeff Sanborn (Edwardsburg) 17:03
13. Tod Richard (Edwardsburg) 17:05

1981 BOYS CLASS C INDIVIDUAL RACE
1. Ron Simpson (Redford St Mary)12 .... 15:53
2. Bob Vandenberg (Middleville TK) 16:08
3. Brian Olling (Breckenridge) 16:30
4. John Card (Freeland) 16:32
5. Jon Johnson (Berrien Springs) 16:34
6. Jim Gilbert (Comstock Park) 16:34
7. Mitch Hartnagle (Bullock Creek) 16:37
8. Dan Clark (Montrose) 16:40
9. Kevin Olling (Breckenridge) 16:46

1982 CLASS C BOYS

Coach Pete Spieles and assistant Walt Drenth guided Charlevoix to its first state title, the Rayders finishing 57 points ahead of defending champion Kalamazoo Christian.

Perry teammates Marty Alward and Mike Kloss battled to the finish of the individual run, with Alward winning, 17:08.1-17:08.9.

Coach Pete Spieles (right) and assistant Walt Drenth (left) bookend the first-ever state championship team from Charlevoix.

Watervliet HS, Watervliet, Nov. 6 ☐
1982 BOYS CLASS C TEAMS
1. Charlevoix 73
2. Kalamazoo Christian 130
3. Napoleon 150
4. Reed City 182
5. Bath 186
6. Midland Bullock Creek 198
7. Vandercook Lake 229
8. Benzie Central 267
9. Orchard Lake 271
10. Edwardsburg 277
11. Rogers City 277
12. Unionville-Sebewaing 303
13. Cass City 320
14. Onsted 321
15. Niles Brandywine 328
16. Detroit Lutheran West 392
17. Elkton-Pigeon-Bayport 392
18. Grandville 398
19. Capac 399
20. St Joseph Lake Michigan Catholic 431
21. Mattawan 448

1982 BOYS CLASS C TEAM RACE
1. Greg Bliss (Cass City)11 .... 16:43
2. Kirk Scharich (Unionville-Sebewaing) 16:54
3. Bill Taylor (Charlevoix)11 .... 17:00
5. Dave Mittan (Edwardsburg) 17:08
10. Brad Abendroth (Bath) .... nt
12. Vaughn Svendsen (Bath) .... nt

1982 BOYS CLASS C INDIVIDUAL RACE
1. Marty Alward (Perry)12 .... 17:09
2. Mike Kloss (Perry)12 .... 17:09
3. Pat Green (Shepherd) 17:17
4. Allen Bryson (Leslie) .... nt
5. Jon Johnson (Berrien Springs) 17:20
13. Pat Daugherty (Buchanan) 17:40

1983 CLASS C BOYS

No. 1-ranked Charlevoix repeated as team champions, this time by an even larger margin of 85 points. Bill Taylor dominated with a 15:46 win. A month later he would placed 23rd at Foot Locker Nationals in 15:46.9.

Katke GC, Big Rapids, Nov. 5 ☒
1983 BOYS CLASS C TEAMS
1. Charlevoix 76
2. Rogers City 161
3. Bullock Creek 194
4. Orchard Lake St Mary's 196
5. Bath 196
6. Clinton 201
7. Napoleon 202
8. DeWitt 226
9. Grandville Calvin Christian 233
10. Benzie Central 266
11. Detroit Lutheran West 277
12. Cass City 284
13. Union City 308
14. Grand Rapids South Christian 309
15. Sandusky 319
16. Marlette 335
17. Forest Hills Northern 347
18. Muskegon Oakridge 366
19. St Joseph Lake Michigan Catholic 374
20. Edwardsburg 390

1983 BOYS CLASS C TEAM RACE
1. Bill Taylor (Charlevoix)12 .... 15:46
2. Maxwell Hogan (Rogers City) 16:10
3. John Tunison (Charlevoix) 16:16
4. Randy Johnson (GR South Christian) 16:23
5. Greg Bliss (Cass City)12 .... 16:26
6. Scott Long (Sandusky) 16:26
7. Dennis Topolinski (Orchard Lake St Mary) 16:27
8. Brad Abendroth (Bath) 16:38
9. Mike Price (DeWitt) 16:39
10. Lee Allard (Charlevoix)12 .... 16:42
11. David McKay (Clinton) 16:44
14. Matt Landon (Charlevoix)12 .... 16:50
48. Rick Gallant (Charlervoix)12 .... 17:35
61. Mike Dohm (Charlevoix)9 .... 17:46
85. Dave Hendrickson (Charlevoix)12 .... 18:07

1983 BOYS CLASS C INDIVIDUAL RACE
1. John Sehl (Saginaw Valley Lutheran) 16:22
2. Jesse McGuire (Bronson)10 .... 16:26
3. Chuck Bumpus (Stockbridge) 16:31
4. Bob Jones (Saginaw St Peter & Paul) 16:33
5. Jeff Barnett (Mason County Central) 16:33
6. Greg Marvin (Mattawan) 16:36
7. Rich Pewe (Olivet) 16:38
8. Jeff Szentoriklosi (Addison) 16:40
9. Tony Nickel (Michigan Center) 16:42

1984 CLASS C BOYS

Bronson's Jesse McGuire, undefeated all year, handily topped challenger Jeff Barnett of Mason County Central. He would blossom in college, twice winning All-America honors at Western Michigan.

Benzie Central, after not having placed in the top 3 before, won its first team title under Eldon "Pete" Moss.

Katke GC, Big Rapids, Nov. 3
1984 BOYS CLASS C TEAMS
1. Benzie Central 67
2. Mason County Central 120

3. Charlevoix 128
4. Bath 139
5. Muskegon Oakridge 201
6. Unionville-Sebewaing 203
7. Detroit Lutheran West 237
8. Shepherd 249
9. Orchard Lake St Mary's 260
10. Goodrich 266
11. Hartford 281
12. Cass City 283
13. Bronson 296
14. Edwardsburg 301
15. Williamston 304
16. Clinton 313
17. Fennville 326
18. Michigan Center 338

1984 BOYS CLASS C TEAM RACE

1. Jesse McGuire (Bronson)11 .... 15:47
2. Jeff Barnett (Mason County Central)11 .... 15:55
3. Dennis Topolinski (Orchard Lake St Mary) 16:28
4. Tom Johnson (Mason County Central) 16:29
5. Eric Kemner (Clinton) 16:43
6. Todd Kuluwiak (Benzie Central) 16:45
7. Andy MacDonald (Williamston) 16:48
8. Pat Green (Shepherd) 16:55
9. Dave Keefer (Mason County Central) 16:57
10. Jeff Frostic (Benzie Central) 17:00
11. Brad Pullman (Bath) 17:03
12. Jon Lawniczak (Goodrich) 17:09
13. Dave Ambsprang (Michigan Center) 17:10

1984 BOYS CLASS C INDIVIDUAL RACE

1. Greg Parker (Capac)10 .... 16:33
2. Scott Long (Sandusky) 16:52
3. Eric Grimm (Grandville Calvin Christian) 16:57
4. Alan Banaszak (Bay City All Saints) 17:02
5. Dana Dewitt (DeWitt) 17:05
6. Mike Seppi (Napoleon) 17:08
7. Dan Brunk (Carson City-Crystal) 17:11

Bronson's Jesse McGuire won the team race in 1984, the individual race the next year. He would go on to win two Mid-American XC titles for Western Michigan.

1985 CLASS C BOYS

Benzie Central faced a tough battle with Charlevoix but prevailed by a slim four points.

Capac's Greg Parker and Bronson's Jesse McGuire each won again, but they switched races, with Parker in the team race and McGuire in the individual.

Parker trailed the leaders early, including Mason County Central's Jeff Barnett, the Class C 3200 champ, explaining "I let them break the wind for me. I figured I could pass them in the final kick, but I did get a little nervous because they really started to pick it up in the final quarter mile."

Cass City HS & Rolling Hills, Cass City, Nov. 2 ☐

1985 BOYS CLASS C TEAMS

1. Benzie Central 87
2. Charlevoix 91
3. Mason County Central 117
4. Carson City-Crystal 175
5. Ann Arbor Richard 211
6. Unionville-Sebewaing 214
7. Grandville Calvin Christian 234
8. Bath 251
9. Concord 252
10. Niles Brandywine 253
11. Williamston 255
12. Detroit Lutheran West 269
13. Sandusky 284
14. Muskegon Oakridge 324
15. Orchard Lake St Mary's 343
16. Hudson 348
17. Edwardsburg 373
18. Capac 421
19. Vandercook Lake 447
20. Bangor 484

1985 BOYS CLASS C TEAM RACE

1. Greg Parker (Capac)11 .... 15:52
2. Jeff Barnett (Mason County Central)12 .... 16:00
3. Tom Johnson (Mason County Central) 16:07
4. Matt Johnson (Benzie Central) 16:26
5. Scott Long (Sandusky) 16:31
6. Tony Hill (Concord) 16:33
7. Doug Bergmann (Charlevoix) 16:36
8. Mark Quist (Grandville Calvin Christian) 16:39
9. Bill Huddleston (Benzie Central) 16:41
10. Todd Kulawjak (Benzie Central) 16:43
11. Andy McDonald (Williamston) 16:45
12. Pat Rajewski (Charlevoix) 16:46
13. (Benzie Central) .... nt
51. (Benzie Central) .... nt
52. (Benzie Central) .... nt
71. (Benzie Central) .... nt

1985 BOYS CLASS C INDIVIDUAL RACE

1. Jesse McGuire (Bronson)12 .... 15:56
2. Jeff Thomas (Mancelona) 15:57
3. Adam Norman (Kalkaska)11 .... 16:28
4. Bill Arnold (Beaverton) 16:29
5. Trent Hostetler (Marlette) 16:42
6. Todd Taylor (Morenci) 16:47
7. Gordy Smith (Parchment) 16:48
8. David Havarter (Leslie) 16:50

1986 CLASS C BOYS

Running in the cold rain, Capac's Greg Parker captured his third-straight title.He pulled away after a fast first mile. "I like to get pushed early, but after I pulled away I was just trying to finish," he explained. "My legs felt good. With the cold and the rain, my arms stiffened and my hands were cold."

Kalkaska's Adam Norman won the individual race in a faster time, 15:55. The next spring he would defeat Parker to take the Class C 3200,

Also grabbing a third-straight was Benzie Central, achieving something that hadn't been done in Class C since Lansing Everett and Spring Arbor in the 1950s.

Cass City HS & Rolling Hills, Cass City, Nov. 5 ☐

1986 BOYS CLASS C TEAMS

1. Benzie Central 86
2. Charlevoix 98
3. Williamston 170
4. Olivet 201
5. Capac 208
6. Onsted 209
7. Unionville-Sebewaing 225
8. Rogers City 232
9. Sandusky 235
10. Carson City-Crystal 247
11. Shepherd 255
12. Three Oaks River Valley 264
13. Leslie 276
14. St Joseph Lake Michigan Catholic 297
15. Edwardsburg 329
16. Detroit Lutheran West 331
17. Michigan Center 352
18. Mason County Central 373

1986 BOYS CLASS C TEAM RACE

1. Greg Parker (Capac)12 .... 15:58
2. Todd Kulawjak (Benzie Central) 16:08
3. Matt Johnson (Benzie Central)11 .... 16:11
4. Bill Huddleston (Benzie Central)11 .... 16:11
5. Hank Walker (Sandusky)11 .... 16:25
6. Pat Rajewski (Charlevoix)11 .... 16:29
7. Eric Ramsey (Onsted)11 .... 16:34
8. Marcus Tarver (Detroit Lutheran West)12 .... 16:35
9. Jeff Hohlbein (Shepherd)12 .... 16:40
10. David Abke (Unionville-Sebewaing)11 .... 16:41
11. Jim Behnke (Capac)11 .... 16:41
12. Mike Reed (Olivet)10 .... 16:42
13. David Hahn (Three Oaks River Valley)11 .... 16:43
26. Brian (Benzie Central) 17:05
51. Roth (Benzie Central) 17:36
63. Martin (Benzie Central) 17:48
84. Reed (Benzie Central) 18:14

1986 BOYS CLASS C INDIVIDUAL RACE

1. Adam Norman (Kalkaska)12 .... 15:55
2. Gordie Smith (Parchment)12 .... 16:17
3. Greg Spiegel (Blissfield)12 .... 16:25
4. Bill Arnold (Beaverton)12 .... 16:34
5. Joseph Wardie (Fenton)12 .... 16:38
6. Steve Laninga (White Cloud)10 .... 16:41
7. Scott Norman (Kalkaska)11 .... 16:42

1987 CLASS C BOYS

Charlevoix stormed back to the top, putting four runners in the top 25 to come out 35 ahead of three-time champ Benzie Central. Onsted's Eric Ramsey captured the team race in the fastest time of the day, 15:45.1.

Bath HS, Bath, Nov. 7 ☐

1987 BOYS CLASS C TEAMS

1. Charlevoix 85
2. Benzie Central 120
3. Williamston 137
4. Kalkaska 156
5. Sandusky 165
6. Unionville-Sebewaing 180
7. Onsted 236
8. Ann Arbor Richard 236
9. Clare 249
10. Stockbridge 258
11. Edwardsburg 258
12. Marlette 270
13. Beaverton 281
14. Shepherd 335
15. Southfield Christian 342
16. Centreville 344
17. Leslie 356
18. St Joseph Lake Michigan Catholic 409

1987 BOYS CLASS C TEAM RACE

1. Eric Ramsey (Onsted)12 .... 15:46
2. Pat Rajewski (Charlevoix)12 .... 15:52
3. Bill Huddleston (Benzie Central)12 .... 15:59
4. David Abke (Unionville-Sebewaing)12 .... 16:00
5. Scott Miller (Charlevoix)10 .... 16:03
6. Chris Long (Sandusky)11 .... 16:05
7. Scott Norman (Kalkaska)12 .... 16:05
8. Jason Hunt (Onsted)12 .... 16:06
9. James Newman (Unionville-Sebewaing)12 .... 16:08
10. Hank Walker (Sandusky)12 .... 16:12
11. Tony Achenbach (Unionville-Sebewaing)11 .... 16:15
12. Matt Johnson (Benzie Central)12 .... 16:16
13. Aric Prudden (Williamston)12 .... 16:16
14. Jeff Slumway (Ann Arbor Richard)11 .... 16:24
15. Gurvinder Singh (Ann Arbor Richard)11 .... 16:25
16. Arbria Sheppard (Stockbridge)10 .... 16:25
22. Gehry Wiesner (Charlevoix) .... nt
23. Tom Merta (Charlevoix) .... nt
33. Sean Henne (Charlevoix) .... nt

1987 BOYS CLASS C INDIVIDUAL RACE
1. David Hahn (Three Oaks River Valley)12............16:03
2. Gordie Maitland (GP University Liggett)12............16:09
3. Tim Brennan (East Jordan)11............16:16
4. Mike Smith (Grant)12............16:27

1988 CLASS C BOYS

Charlevoix captured its second-straight title, this time on a muddy course. Lead runner Scott Miller won in 16:43 after sprinting away from Sandusky's Chris Long in the final 800. It was the first loss of the year Long.

Said Sandusky runner Derrick Lee, "We ran our best. Charlevoix was just too strong for us. The course was so muddy you couldn't get any traction."

Bath HS, Bath, Nov. 5 ☒
1988 BOYS CLASS C TEAMS
1. Charlevoix 69
2. Sandusky 97
3. Beaverton 107
4. Olivet 119
5. Clare 145
6. Mason County Central 152
7. Williamston 220
8. Edwardsburg 221
9. Orchard Lake St Mary's 222
10. Hudson 237
11. Marlette 284
12. Concord 297
13. Grandville Calvin Christian 331
14. Carson City-Crystal 351
15. Napoleon 358
16. Union City 400
17. Wyoming Godwin Heights 407
18. Hartford 502

1988 BOYS CLASS C TEAM RACE
1. Scott Miller (Charlevoix)11..................16:43
2. Chris Long (Sandusky)12....................16:55
3. Jeff Christian (Beaverton)9.................17:18
4. Jay Bruse (Beaverton)11....................17:19
5. Dennis Miller (Clare)12......................17:24
6. Rob Oldt (Clare)12.............................17:30
7. Gehry Wiesner (Charlevoix)11............17:31
8. Ryan Ortega (Godwin Heights)11........17:36
9. Jeff Patterson (Mason County Central)11..17:38
10. Kurt Long (Sandusky)10...................17:39
11. Joe Janecke (Williamston)12............17:42
12. Mike Heisler (Olivet)12....................17:45
13. Michael Ball (Hudson)9...................17:46
14. Mike Reed (Olivet)12......................17:48
15. Robert Fisher (Orchard Lake St Mary's)12..17:50
16. Pat Etherington (Edwardsburg)11....17:51
17. Marc Zweedyk (Grandville Calvin Christian)12..17:52
18. Dylan Stewart (Charlevoix)12..........17:57
21. Paul Walculat (Charlevoix)10..........18:03
22. Bill Crook (Charlevoix)12...............18:07
27. Bill Burns (Charlevoix)12...............18:15
61. Tim Henne (Charflevoix)11.............19:09

1988 BOYS CLASS C INDIVIDUAL RACE
1. Tim Brennan (East Jordan)12............17:12
2. Andre Lumbreras (Saginaw Nouvelle)10..17:29
3. Jaime Dudash (Kingsley)11................17:32
4. Jared Glover (Kingsley)11..................17:54

1989 CLASS C BOYS

Charlevoix made history by tying the mark for the longest streak at three straight. Scott Miller defended his title in 16:03.

In the individual race, Steve Johnson of Breckenridge would produce the fastest time of the day at 16:00. He would win the C 1600 on the track the next spring in 4:23.02.

Kingsley's Jaime Dudash, 5th in the team race, would go on to coach the Dexter boys to a record 5 straight wins in Division 2.

Torrey Pines Golf Course, Lake Fenton, Nov. 4 ☐
1989 BOYS CLASS C TEAMS
1. Charlevoix 70
2. Edwardsburg 97
3. Wyoming Godwin Heights 132
4. Sandusky 171
5. Onsted 177
6. Orchard Lake St Mary's 178
7. Kingsley 183
8. Williamston 186
9. Newaygo 241
10. Mason County Central 261
11. Benzie Central 266
12. Mayville 316
13. Bridgman 320
14. Addison 339
15. Centreville 345
16. Leslie 353
17. Napoleon 382
18. Marlette 429

1989 BOYS CLASS C TEAM RACE
1. Scott Miller (Charlevoix)12................16:03
2. Jared Glover (Kingsley)12..................16:05
3. Ryan Ortega (Godwin Heights)12......16:23
4. Jason Schrock (Godwin Heights)11...16:24
5. Jaime Dudash (Kingsley)11................16:28
6. Kurt Long (Sandusky)11....................16:41
7. Pat Etherington (Edwardsburg)12.....16:43
8. Chuck Cosnowski (Orchard Lake St Mary's)11..16:56
9. Derick Lee (Sandusky)12..................16:57
10. Ryan Cameron (Mason County C)12..17:01
11. Bill Crook (Charlevoix)12................17:02
12. Vic Mattson (Edwardsburg)10.........17:04
13. Shawn Neff (Edwardsburg)12..........17:07
15. Mike Sevenski (Charlevoix)............17:11
21. Chris Meier (Charlevoix).................nt
22. Paul Wakulat (Charlevoix)...............nt

1989 BOYS CLASS C INDIVIDUAL RACE
1. Steve Johnson (Breckenridge)12.......16:00
2. Michael Ball (Hudson)10..................16:23
3. Jay Caruso (Whitmore Lake)12........16:36
4. Andre Kumbreras (Saginaw Nouvel)11..16:53
5. Marty Arends (Grant)10...................17:03
6. Brig Cobb (Southfield Christian)11..17:04
7. Chris Lloyd (Union City)11...............17:04

1990 CLASS C BOYS

Two years earlier, after losing the title to Charlevoix by 28 points, Sandusky coach Wayne Roberts said, "It looks like Sandusky and Charlevoix will have a grudge match next year."

He was off by 12 months as the big battle between the two powerhouses happened in 1990, Charlevoix taking a record fourth-straight victory by one point.

Torrey Pines Golf Course, Lake Fenton, Nov. 3 ☐
1990 BOYS CLASS C TEAMS
1. Charlevoix 101
2. Sandusky 102
3. Flat Rock 130
4. Carson City-Crystal 141
5. Grant 154
6. Marlette 170
7. Leslie 196
8. Orchard Lake St Mary's 200
9. Onsted 211
10. Jonesville 257
11. Centreville 274
12. Farwell 279
13. Clare 300
14. Mason County Central 318
15. Bridgman 346
16. Napoleon 382
17. Mayville 392
18. Schoolcraft 409

1990 BOYS CLASS C TEAM RACE
1. Michael Vischer (Onsted)12..............16:06
2. Kurt Long (Sandusky)12....................16:23
3. Mike Sevensky (Charlevoix)..............16:30
4. Blaine Dinsmore (Carson City-Crystal)12..16:36
5. Marty Arends (Grant)11.....................16:43
6. Jason Chappel (Marlette)10..............16:49
7. Chad Rich (Sandusky)9.....................16:52
8. Chris Meier (Charlevoix)....................16:53
9. Edwardo Miller (Centreville)10..........16:54
15. Paul Wakulat (Charlevoix)...............17:15
36. Matt Stargardt (Charlevoix).............17:39
39. Zack Pajhtas (Charlevoix)................17:41

1990 BOYS CLASS C INDIVIDUAL RACE
1. Michael Ball (Hudson)11...................15:58
2. Chris Johnson (Saginaw Michigan Lutheran)10..16:13
3. Michael Lake (Berrien Springs)12.....16:21
4. Michael Smedley (Buchanan)11........16:34
5. Bouce Littlefield (Hartford)10............16:37
6. Chris Lloyd (Union City)12.................16:38
7. Kevin Elliot (Kent City)11..................16:41
8. Eric Ellis (Addison)10........................16:50
9. Brig Cobb (Southfield Christian)12...16:52
10. Jeremy O'Shea (Benzie Central)......16:53
11. Tim Himburg (Ida)12........................16:54
12. Victor Mattson (Edwardsburg)11.....16:54

1991 CLASS C BOYS

Pete Spieles' Charlevoix team did the unprecedented in Class C, winning a fifth-straight title by 14 points over challenger Carson City-Crystal.

The team run was won by Buchanan's Michael Smedley (16:49), who celebrated a double win with his sister Megan capturing the girls' race by 54 seconds. Michael Smedley would go on to run at Notre Dame before switching to the triathlon. In 2004 he placed 4th in the Olympic Trials in that event, just missing the team.

In the individual race, Michael Ball of Hudson defended in a much-faster 16:22.

Memorial Park, Frankenmuth, Nov. 2 ☐
1991 BOYS CLASS C TEAMS
1. Charlevoix 76
2. Carson City-Crystal 90
3. Grant 144
4. Leslie 153
5. Buchanan 172
6. Clare 193
7. Mayville 212
8. Riverview Richard 220
9. Sandusky 222
10. Flat Rock 224
11. Kalamazoo Christian 269
12. Bath 281
13. Onsted 287
14. Marlette 300
15. Michigan Center 338
16. Kingsley 371
17. Quincy 404
18. Lakeview 447

1991 BOYS CLASS C TEAM RACE
1. Michael Smedley (Buchanan)12.......16:49
2. Mike Sevenski (Charlevoix)..............16:55
3. Robert Ross (Onsted)........................16:59
4. Lance Aldrich (Carson City-Crystal)10..17:03
5. Chad Rich (Sandusky).......................17:03
6. Matt Smith (Charlevoix).....................17:04
7. Justin Curry (Carson City-Crystal)9..17:09
8. Martin Arends (Grant)........................17:10
9. Bret Clements (Bath).........................17:13
10. Denny Creisher (Leslie)...................17:14
11. Brian McClaine (Michigan Center)..17:14
12. Mitchell Arends (Grant)...................17:15
13. Jeremy Bogard (Kalamazoo Christian)..17:16
28. Canh Tran (Buchanan).....................17:39
30. Eric Ostrander (Buchanan)...............17:40
48. Danus Hubbard (Buchanan).............18:02

1991 BOYS CLASS C INDIVIDUAL RACE
1. Michael Ball (Hudson)12...................16:22

2. Chris Johnson (Saginaw Mich. Luth)11 .... 16:27
3. Chris Heggelun (Laingsburg) 16:58
4. Boyce Littlefield (Hartford) 17:07
5. Eric Ellis (Addison) 17:09
6. Jeremy O'Shea (Benzie Central) 17:16
7. Jonathan Hess (Tri-County) 17:20

1992 CLASS C BOYS

Finally Sandusky was able to topple the Charlevoix juggernaut, bringing a long-awaited win to coach Wayne Roberts. Team race winner Chad Rich broke away from the pack after the two-mile mark.

"I looked back thinking maybe I went out too hard," he said, "but I felt fine, so I kept up the pace. I was glad I won, but then I thought about the team. I watched for our other guys to come in."

Running in buzzcuts with the double CC/arrow design shaved on the backs of their heads, the Redskins rose to the occasion. Said Roberts, "We couldn't afford to have somebody fall back a long ways and coming in 50th. You do that and there's not much chance to win... We've had some good teams here at Sandusky, but this was the best team ever."

Memorial Park, Frankenmuth, Nov. 7 ☐
1992 BOYS CLASS C TEAMS
1. Sandusky 86
2. Suttons Bay 102
3. Carson City-Crystal 121
4. Leslie 134
5. Charlevoix 163
6. Kalamazoo Christian 175
7. Clare 180
8. Onsted 231
9. Napoleon 238
10. Lakeview 258
11. Sanford Meridian 263
12. Mayville 277
13. Erie-Mason 312
14. Centreville 348
15. Edwardsburg 360
16. Burton Atherton 384
17. Flat Rock 385
18. Ann Arbor Richard 414

1992 BOYS CLASS C TEAM RACE
1. Chad Rich (Sandusky)11 .... 16:37
2. Matt Smith (Charlevoix)12 .... 16:43
3. Jeremy Bogard (Kalamazoo Christian) 16:51
4. Lance Aldrich (Carson City-Crystal)11 .... 16:52
5. Ben Pickel (Lakeview) 16:53
6. Matt Livingston (Sandusky)12 .... 16:53
7. Justin Curry (Carson City-Crystal)10 .... 16:55
8. Joe Crawford (Clare) 17:01
9. Kyle Stallman (Suttons Bay) 17:04
10. Denny Creisher (Leslie) 17:04
11. Paul Whitchurch (Carson City-Crystal) 17:08
13. Rich Brinker (Sandusky)11 .... 17:12
29. TJ Camburn (Sandusky)12 .... nt
37. Jon Livingtson (Sandusky)9 .... nt
47. Matt Bissett (Sandusky) .... nt
88. Dan Beatty (Sandusky) .... nt

1992 BOYS CLASS C INDIVIDUAL RACE
1. Boyce Littlefield (Hartford)12 .... 16:25
2. Chris Johnson (Saginaw Mich Luth)12 .... 16:34
3. Anthony Lambert (Kingsley) 16:56
4. Eric Ellis (Addison) 16:58
5. M. McFellin (Summerfield) 16:59
6. Casey Rokoczy (Coleman) 17:00
7. Chris Stoik (Marlette)11 .... 17:03
8. Jason Maurer (Breckenridge) 17:04
9. Terry McKown (Concord) 17:06
10. Jeff Michalski (Orchard Lake St Mary's) 17:08

1993 CLASS C BOYS

Leslie won its first title, notching the third-highest score ever. "We finally got over that hump," said coach Jim Hanson. "We won this on the basis of a good performance of five runners. A lot of teams in the state were equal, with a lot of talent. We didn't have some of the superstars, but no other team had five runners as close together as ours."

Candlestone Golf Club, Lowell, Nov. 6 ☐
1993 BOYS CLASS C TEAMS
1. Leslie 147
2. Carson City-Crystal 157
3. Charlevoix 161
4. Suttons Bay 187
5. Clare 207
6. Sandusky 219
7. Jonesville 243
8. Newaygo 254
9. Mayville 257
10. Kalamazoo Christian 258
11. Bangor 281
12. Saginaw Valley Lutheran 290
13. Onsted 298
14. Hudson 313
15. Goodrich 322
16. Lakeview 328
17. Flat Rock 349
18. Grandville Calvin Christian 358
19. Bath 382
20. Muskegon Oakridge 404
21. Lutheran Westland 412

1993 BOYS CLASS C TEAM RACE
1. Justin Curry (Carson City-Crystal)11 .... 16:37
2. Mike Bush (Charlevoix)11 .... 16:44
3. Art Smith (Bangor) 16:46
4. Rich Brinker (Sandusky)12 .... 16:50
5. Mike Cell (Suttons Bay) 16:59
6. Lance Aldrich (Carson City)12 .... 17:02
7. Ben Pickel (Lakeview) 17:05
8. Matt Dickinson (Charlevoix) 17:09
9. B. Pokinghome (Lutheran Westland) 17:10
10. Joe Crawford (Clare) 17:11
11. Jeremy Bogard (Kalamazoo Christian) 17:14
12. Chad Rich (Sandusky)12 .... 17:16
13. Ben Darling (Leslie)10 .... 17:17
14. Corey Green (Jonesville) 17:18
19. Allen Bradley (Leslie) 17:35
27. Keith Shoemaker (Leslie) 17:47
28. Bill Darling (Leslie) 17:48
? Damon Place (Leslie) .... nt

1993 BOYS CLASS C INDIVIDUAL RACE
1. Michael McFellin (Petersburg-Summerfield)12 .... 17:00
2. Jeff Brown (Napoleon) 17:12
3. Cam Montgomery (Kent City) 17:14
4. Charles Slates (St Louis) 17:14
5. Luis Vasquez (Hartford) 17:15
6. Derek Michael (Hart) 17:16
7. Terry McKown (Concord) 17:18
8. David Van Acker (Ida) 17:18

1994 CLASS C BOYS

One newspaper described the Lowell course as a "mud bog." Senior Justin Curry defended his title to lead his Carson City-Crystal team to a 22-point win over the defending champs from Leslie. Earlier in the year Curry had won the C title at 3200 with his 9:33.81. Leslie's Ben Darling was 4th in that race and runner-up in the cross country finals.

Lowell HS, Lowell, Nov. 5 ☐
1994 BOYS CLASS C TEAMS
1. Carson City-Crystal 92
2. Leslie 114
3. Charlevoix 136
4. East Jordan 170
5. Benzie Central 216
6. Sandusky 251
7. Shepherd 262
8. Kalamazoo Hackett 274
9. Concord 292
10. Orchard Lake St Mary's 293
11. Jonesville 303
12. Bangor 310
13. Ida 312
14. Saginaw Valley Lutheran 313
15. Lutheran Westland 343
16. Breckenridge 345
17. Comstock Park 351
18. Goodrich 367
19. Onsted 361
20. Hartford 381
21. Elkton-Pigeon-Bayport 425

1994 BOYS CLASS C TEAM RACE
1. Justin Curry (Carson City-Crystal)12 .... 17:06
2. Ben Darling (Leslie)11 .... 17:25
3. Mike Bush (Charlevoix) 17:31
4. Jason Maurer (Breckenridge) 17:42
5. Jason Jaluszinski (Shepherd) 17:51
6. Aaron Shefler (Carson City-Crystal) 17:56
7. Mikie Newrirk (East Jordan) 17:59
8. Keith Shoemaker (Leslie) 18:01
9. Luis Vasquez (Hartford) 18:09
10. Kevin Rossiter (Orchard Lake St Mary's) 18:12
11. Leonard Young (Elkton-Pigeon-Bayport) 18:14
12. John Broder (Shepherd) 18:17
27. Shiloh Cunningham (Carson City-Crystal) 18:37
28. Marcos Marla (Carson City-Crystal) 18:38
30. Dan Clark (Carson City-Crystal) 18:40

1994 BOYS CLASS C INDIVIDUAL RACE
1. Matthew Waldfogel (Erie-Mason)11 .... 17:25
2. Craig Beerens (McBain) 17:52
3. Ben Pickel (Lakeview) 17:56
4. Kurt Laansma (Allendale) 17:58
5. Matt Lafave (Sanford Meridian) 17:59
6. Mike Cell (Suttons Bay) 18:10
7. Charles Slates (St Louis) 18:14
8. Jon Dodson (Buchanan) 18:17

1995 CLASS C BOYS

Ben Darling finally got his title, rolling to a convincing 15:42 win over Erie-Mason's Matthew Waldfogel.

Coach Eldon "Pete" Moss's Benzie Central squad captured the team win despite only having one senior in its top 5.

Lowell HS, Lowell, Nov. 4 ☒
1995 BOYS CLASS C TEAMS
1. Benzie Central 104
2. Lutheran Westland 141
3. McBain 152
4. Carson City-Crystal 180
5. Clare 205
6. Kalamazoo Hackett 226
7. Bath 231
8. Saginaw Valley Lutheran 240
9. Jonesville 258
10. Kalamazoo Christian 259
11. Breckenridge 271
12. Sanford Meridian 272
13. Concord 257
14. Leslie 296
15. Goodrich 318
16. Erie-Mason 324
17. Hartford 406
18. Harrison 420
19. Bangor 471
20. Sandusky 480
21. Marcellus 525
22. Burton Atherton 542

1995 BOYS CLASS C TEAM RACE
1. Ben Darling (Leslie)12 .... 15:42
2. Matthew Waldfogel (Erie-Mason)12 .... 16:03
3. Craig Beerens (McBain)12 .... 16:06
4. Jason Maurer (Breckenridge)12 .... 16:12
5. Matt LaFave (Sanford Meridian)12 .... 16:13
6. Dan Hoekstra (Kalamazoo Christian)11 .... 16:17
7. Aaron Shepler (Carson City-Crystal)12 .... 16:20
8. Zack Cooley (Bath)12 .... 16:21
9. Jason Fazekas (Jonesville)11 .... 16:30
10. Jason Saarm (Benzie Central)11 .... 16:34

11. Nick James (Kalamazoo Hackett)11 ... 16:37
12. Dylan Wade (Benzie Central)10 ... 16:38
13. Brad Polkinghorne (Lutheran Westland)12 ... 16:40
14. Nates Hanes (Concord)10 ... 16:41
18. Jeremiah Saier (Benzie Central)9 ... 16:47
29. Peter Bissell (Benzie Central)12 ... 17:03
35. Andy Rosa (Benzie Central)11 ... 17:07
43. David Struble (Benzie Central)10 ... 17:16
45. Sean Herron (Benzie Central)12 ... 17:16

1995 BOYS CLASS C INDIVIDUAL RACE

1. Joe Veldman (Three Oaks River Valley)11 ... 16:08
2. Tiran Bailey (Bear Lake)11 ... 16:16
3. Josiah Middaugh (East Jordan)12 ... 16:21
4. Chris Vranich (Elk Rapids)11 ... 16:22
5. Wes Witte (Comstok Park)12 ... 16:32
6. Kurt Laansma (Allendale)12 ... 16:42

1996 CLASS C BOYS

Light snow flurries and 30-degree, windy conditions greeted Class C runners in their first meet at Michigan International Speedway. The individual and team races were combined for the first time since 1970. However, because the awards had already been ordered and paid for, race officials gave 4th-placer Nate Hanes the title of "individual" state champion.

McBain, coached by John Ensing, won its first state title.

Joe Veldman of Three Oaks River Valley won again, just a second faster than the previous year.

Michigan Int. Speedway, Brooklyn, Nov. 2 ⊠
1996 BOYS CLASS C TEAMS

1. McBain ... 113
2. Benzie Central ... 121
3. Saginaw Valley Lutheran ... 133
4. St Louis ... 148
5. Three Oaks River Valley ... 203
6. Carson-City Crystal ... 203
7. Kalamazoo Hackett ... 225
8. Jonesville ... 240
9. Howard City Tri County ... 267
10. Hemlock ... 279
11. Leslie ... 282
12. Mason County Central ... 285
13. Quincy ... 295
14. Wyoming Kelloggsville ... 312
15. Addison ... 344
16. Sanford Meridian ... 347
17. Sandusky ... 379
18. Goodrich ... 400
19. Constantine ... 408
20. Manchester ... 441
21. Flat Rock ... 465
22. Bangor ... 548

1996 BOYS CLASS C INDIVIDUALS

1. Joe Veldman (Three Oaks River Valley)12 ... 16:07
2. Tom Hoeflinger (Quincy)12 ... 16:17
3. Curtis King (Mason County Central)11 ... 16:19
4. Nate Hanes (Concord)11 ... 16:40
5. Jacob Fazekas (Jonesville)12 ... 16:41
6. Matt Zissler (Hemlock)11 ... 16:44
7. Nick Boak (Jonesville)12 ... 16:45
8. Ron David (Constantine)12 ... 16:48
9. Nathan Hildner (Frankenmuth) ... 16:48
10. Marcus Marek (Carson-City Crystal)11 ... 16:53
11. Paul Vansweden (Howard City Tri County) ... 16:55
12. Joshua Ravary (Erie-Mason) ... 16:55
13. John Ferguson (Saginaw M Lutheran) ... 16:57
14. Jeff Bode (Shelby) ... 17:02
15. Terry Dykhouse (McBain)12 ... 17:02
16. Ryan Lantzer (St. Louis) ... 17:02
17. Josh Helsel (Lake City) ... 17:05
18. Brhett Butler (Concord)12 ... 17:07
19. Dan Hoekstra (Kalamazoo Christian)12 ... 17:07
20. Ben Jenks (Carson-City Crystal)11 ... 17:08
23. Kevin Dykhouse (McBain)12 ... 17:10
34. Rick Naerehout (McBain)12 ... 17:24
36. Derek Byrne (McBain) ... 17:26
68. Jason Eisenga (McBain)12 ... 17:46
135. Greg Bonham (McBain) ... 18:21
206. Jered Benthem (McBain) ... 19:54

1997 CLASS C BOYS

"When you're ranked No. 1 at the start of the season, there's a lot to prove," said Benzie coach Pete Moss. "There's pressure associated with that and this team had to deal with that. But they handled it well."

On a muddy day, Benzie packed a powerful punch in sophomore winner Jake Flynn and 4th-placer Dylan Wade.

Michigan Int. Speedway, Brooklyn, Nov. 1 ⊠
1997 BOYS CLASS C TEAMS

1. Benzie Central ... 92
2. Sandusky ... 169
3. St Louis ... 175
4. Saginaw Valley Lutheran ... 187
5. Wyoming Kelloggsville ... 215
6. Carson City-Crystal ... 217
7. East Jordan ... 219
8. Sanford Meridian ... 223
9. Mason County Central ... 230
10. Concord ... 232
11. Bangor ... 268
12. Leslie ... 278
13. Bath ... 292
14. Lutheran Westland ... 312
15. Jonesville ... 349
16. Ann Arbor Richard ... 364
17. Kalamazoo Hackett ... 366
18. Pittsford ... 370
19. Erie-Mason ... 386
20. Three Oaks River Valley ... 407
21. Unionville-Sebewaing ... 556

1997 BOYS CLASS C INDIVIDUALS

1. Jake Flynn (Benzie Central)10 ... 16:09
2. John Schiemann (Saginaw Valley Lutheran)12 ... 16:21
3. Nate Hanes (Concord)12 ... 16:33
4. Dylan Wade (Benzie Central)12 ... 16:37
5. Mike Gray (Sanford Meridian)11 ... 16:39
6. Ryan Cole (Sanford Meridian)11 ... 16:41
7. Joel David (Wyoming Kelloggsville) ... 16:44
8. Adam Booth (Homer)11 ... 16:44
9. Shane Higgins (Sandusky)11 ... 16:51
10. Jacob Grice (Sandusky)10 ... 16:51
11. Joshua Ravary (Erie-Mason) ... 16:52
12. Pat McCarty (Carson City-Crystal) ... 16:52
13. Jeff Bode (Shelby) ... 16:53
14. Kenneth Zimmerman (Lake Fenton) ... 16:54
15. Brent Wrisley (St Louis)11 ... 16:55
16. Steven Kettler (Lake Fenton) ... 16:55
17. Tristen Perlberg (Saginaw Valley Lutheran)11 ... 16:57
18. Ben Jenks (Carson City-Crystal) ... 16:58
19. Jason Werner (Pewamo-Westphalia) ... 16:58
20. Tom Heine (St Louis) ... 16:59
33. David Struble (Benzie Central) ... 17:17
37. Jeremiah Saier (Benzie Central) ... 17:20
57. Matt Lyon (Benzie Central) ... 17:34
58. Mike Cline (Benzie Central) ... 17:34
175. Jeremiah Avery (Benzie Central) ... 18:53

1998 CLASS C BOYS

Perfectly fast conditions were welcomed by the runners as PRs galore fell. East Jordan won with a high 145, just 20 points ahead of Jonesville, which had the same score as third-place Hemlock.

Jake Flynn repeated his victory, this time destroying the Class C course record by 55 seconds. The next spring he would win the Class C 3200 title in 9:33.15.

"I just sat back, relaxed and ran my heart out and ended up in the lead in the first corner and that's what I was aiming to do," said Flynn, who hit 4:42 at the mile.

Michigan Int. Speedway, Brooklyn, Nov. 7 ⊠
1998 BOYS CLASS C TEAMS

1. East Jordan ... 145
2. Jonesville ... 165
3. Hemlock ... 165
4. Sandusky ... 169
5. Bath ... 178
6. Benzie Central ... 199
7. Saginaw Valley Lutheran ... 216
8. Albion ... 230
9. Bangor ... 240
10. Sanford Meridian ... 248
11. Allendale ... 254
12. Rogers City ... 254
13. Breckenridge ... 308
14. Berrien Springs ... 327
15. Vandercook Lake ... 356
16. Hesperia ... 385
17. Lutheran Westland ... 403
18. Kalamazoo Christian ... 405
19. Erie-Mason ... 427
20. Laingsburg ... 434
21. Allen Park Cabrini ... 459

Benzie's Jake Flynn won a record three straight.

1998 BOYS CLASS C INDIVIDUALS

1. Jake Flynn (Benzie Central)11 ... 15:12
2. Ryan Cole (Sanford Meridian)11 ... 15:24
3. Justin Kibbey (Maple City Glen Lake)10 ... 15:35
4. Kevin Sule (Hemlock)11 ... 15:42
5. Brent Wrisley (St Louis)11 ... 15:48
6. Jeremiah Saier (Benzie Central)12 ... 15:51
7. Shane Higgins (Sandusky)11 ... 15:54
8. Derek Byrne (McBain)11 ... 15:56
9. Aaron Rogers (Berrien Springs)11 ... 15:57
10. Mike Gray (Sanford Meridian)11 ... 15:58
11. Tristen Perlberg (Saginaw Valley Lutheran)11 ... 15:58
12. Matt Kaczor (Freeland)11 ... 15:59
13. Jeremy Smith (Concord)12 ... 16:01
14. Steve Kettler (Lake Fenton)11 ... 16:03
15. Joe VanHorn (Allendale)11 ... 16:03
16. Kevin Hughes (Clare)12 ... 16:04
17. Steve Grajewski (Ann Arbor Greenhills)12 ... 16:04
18. Matt Anderla (Albion)11 ... 16:05
19. Ryan Blake (Three Oaks River Valley)12 ... 16:06
20. Walter Aslakson (Hesperia)11 ... 16:08
24. Tarn Leach (East Jordan)10 ... 16:14
36. Chris Bearden (East Jordan)12 ... 16:33
37. Kevin Penzian (East Jordan)11 ... 16:34
70. Micah Middaugh (East Jordan)10 ... 16:56
102. Dustin Tinney (East Jordan)12 ... 17:12
120. Matt Shaw (East Jordan)12 ... 17:19
157. Jeremy Booze (East Jordan)9 ... 17:39

1999 CLASS C BOYS

Jake Flynn won his third-straight, a record for class C. His 15:16 indicated he might have provided some strong competition for Ritzenhein had the two raced each other. The Rockford star had clocked 15:06 in Class A.

Dale Buist's Allendale squad managed a 20-point win over defending champion East Jordan.

Michigan Int. Speedway, Brooklyn, Nov. 6 ☒

1999 BOYS CLASS C TEAMS

1. Allendale ... 104
2. East Jordan ... 124
3. Hemlock ... 135
4. St Louis ... 144
5. Benzie Central ... 174
6. Sanford Meridian ... 185
7. Sandusky ... 188
8. Albion ... 213
9. Hesperia ... 234
10. McBain ... 249
11. Leslie ... 250
12. Marlette ... 299
13. Laingsburg ... 316
14. Kalamazoo Hackett ... 341
15. Berrien Springs ... 351
16. Jonesville ... 372
17. Addison ... 411
18. Kalamazoo Christian ... 436
19. Allen Park Cabrini ... 444
20. Lutheran Westland ... 479
21. Dundee ... 534

1999 BOYS CLASS C INDIVIDUALS

1. Jake Flynn (Benzie Central)12 ... 15:16
2. Ryan Cole (Sanford Meridian)12 ... 15:20
3. Aaron Rogers (Berrien Springs)12 ... 15:41
4. Kevin Sule (Hemlock)12 ... 15:45
5. Derek Byrne (McBain)12 ... 15:49
6. Mike Gray (Sanford Meridian)12 ... 15:57
7. Joe VanHorn (Allendale)12 ... 15:58
8. Jacob Grice (Sandusky)11 ... 15:58
9. Justin Kibbey (Maple City Glen Lake)11 ... 16:00
10. Tristen Perlberg (Saginaw Valley Lutheran)12 ... 16:00
11. Adam Booth (Homer)12 ... 16:01
12. Tarn Leach (East Jordan)11 ... 16:04
13. Jason Barbachyn (Kent City)12 ... 16:04
14. Matthew Kaczor (Freeland)12 ... 16:06
15. Brent Wrisley (St Louis)12 ... 16:10
16. Exekiel DeBacker (Pittsford)12 ... 16:17
17. Luke Williams (Hopkins)12 ... 16:20
18. Walter Aslakson (Hesperia)12 ... 16:20
19. Will Boylan-Pett (Bath)11 ... 16:21
20. Shane Higgins (Sandusky)12 ... 16:24
30. Ryan Klingeman (Allendale)12 ... 16:40
34. Aaron Smeckert (Allendale)12 ... 16:47
44. Jesse VanderSchuur (Allendale)12 ... 16:58
56. Ben Watson (Allendale)10 ... 17:07
63. Colbert Baron (Allendale)12 ... 17:11

2000 D3 BOYS

Williamston, 15th in Class B the year before, found itself in Division 3 and had an immediate impact, with Paul Nilsson's team winning by 33 points and Jason Stover taking the individual crown in 15:25.

At the Greater Lansing meet, Stover had been knocked down "numerous times" and he was hoping to stay out of trouble at MIS. The previous year, in Class B, he lost a shoe.

"Jason should serve as an inspiration to a lot of runners," said Nilsson. "He was a guy struggling to break 19 minutes as a freshman, and now he's state champion as a senior."

Michigan Int. Speedway, Brooklyn, Nov. 4 ☒

2000 BOYS DIVISION 3 TEAMS

1. Williamston ... 62
2. Hemlock ... 95
3. Stockbridge ... 103
4. Benzie Central ... 177
5. Charlevoix ... 188
6. Sandusky ... 214
7. Kalamazoo Hackett ... 267
8. Bangor ... 305
9. Goodrich ... 317
10. Ida ... 325
11. Bad Axe ... 335
12. Whitehall ... 353
13. Gladwin ... 354
14. Ovid-Elsie ... 365
15. Vassar ... 366
16. Addison ... 373
17. Spring Lake ... 439
18. Perry ... 443
19. Wyoming Kelloggsville ... 444
20. Schoolcraft ... 465
21. Howard City Tri County ... 482
22. Sanford Meridian ... 482
23. Clare ... 488
24. Erie-Mason ... 564
25. Lake Fenton ... 577
26. Dundee ... 678
27. Lake City ... 752

2000 BOYS DIVISION 3 INDIVIDUALS

1. Jason Stover (Williamston)12 ... 15:25
2. Phil McClellan (Stockbridge)12 ... 15:48
3. Jacob Grice (Sandusky)12 ... 15:48
4. Tom Clifford (GR West Catholic)12 ... 15:54
5. Warren Krueger (Stockbridge)12 ... 15:57
6. Troy Sanchez (Hemlock)12 ... 16:02
7. Brandon Grybas (Stockbridge)11 ... 16:09
8. Curt Campbell (Stockbridge)12 ... 16:14
9. Chris Schiemann (Saginaw Valley Lutheran)12 .. 16:15
10. Daniel Sultz (Benzie Central) ... 16:18
11. Andrew Goodenough (Hemlock)12 ... 16:18
12. Pat Maynard (Williamston)12 ... 16:19
13. Lawrence Cornell (Albion)12 ... 16:19
14. Albert Engle (Brooklyn Columbia Central)12 ... 16:19
15. John Jurgensen (Gladwin)12 ... 16:20
16. Mike Salisbury (Williamston)12 ... 16:20
17. Nick Oertel (Goodrich)11 ... 16:20
18. Antonio Munoz (Bangor)11 ... 16:20
19. Andrew Brickel (Richmond)12 ... 16:21
20. David Youngman (Lakeview)12 ... 16:22
26. David Bills (Williamston)9 ... 16:26
33. Mike Delaney (Williamston)9 ... 16:35
120. Nick Marlatt (Williamston)12 ... 17:29
158. Benjamin Pankow (Williamston)10 ... 17:52

2001 D3 BOYS

Hemlock won its first title since 1946 under the direction of William Agresta, topping Benzie Central by 24 points.

Brandon Grybas of Stockbridge and Pennfield's Aaron Nasers battled for nearly the entire way before Grybas sprinted for the win in the final 200. Nasers fell across the finish line, barely holding off Hemlock's Steve Czymbor. "I used everything I had to get over that line in second," said Nasers. "I remember falling and that's it."

Michigan Int. Speedway, Brooklyn, Nov. 3 ☒

2001 BOYS DIVISION 3 TEAMS

1. Hemlock ... 137
2. Benzie Central ... 161
3. Charlevoix ... 162
4. Williamston ... 178
5. Jackson Lumen Christi ... 188
6. Constantine ... 226
7. Caro ... 228
8. Elk Rapids ... 240
9. Stockbridge ... 243
10. Ovid-Elsie ... 317
11. Kalamazoo Hackett ... 345
12. Tawas City ... 345
13. Goodrich ... 352
14. Grand Rapids Baptist ... 355
15. Grand Rapids West Catholic ... 371
16. Hillsdale ... 377
17. Bangor ... 414
18. Morley-Stanwood ... 441
19. Ida ... 445
20. Perry ... 461
21. Spring Lake ... 463
22. Lake Fenton ... 473
23. Bad Axe ... 559
24. Essexville Garber ... 569
25. Yale ... 603
26. Onsted ... 622
27. Riverview Richard ... 726

2001 BOYS DIVISION 3 INDIVIDUALS

1. Brandon Grybas (Stockbridge)12 ... 15:58
2. Aaron Nasers (Battle Creek Pennfield)12 ... 16:03
3. Steve Czymbor (Hemlock)11 ... 16:04
4. David Bills (Williamston)10 ... 16:13
5. Dan Campbell (Grand Rapids Baptist)12 ... 16:14
6. Shawn Jordan (Constantine)10 ... 16:16
7. Nicholas Puchacz (Hemlock)11 ... 16:24
8. Greg Schmit (Leslie)11 ... 16:28
9. Josh Wheelock (Benzie Central)11 ... 16:31
10. Gordie Selph (Charlevoix)12 ... 16:31
11. Jacob Dolson (Jackson Lumen Christi)12 ... 16:31
12. Zachary Schnitta (Berrien Springs)11 ... 16:34
13. Paul Lange (Laingsburg)9 ... 16:36
14. Luke Ten hoppen (Kalkaska)11 ... 16:37
15. Fil Marlatt (Williamston)11 ... 16:38
16. Jason Mantey (Caro)10 ... 16:39
17. Enoch Sayers (Caro)12 ... 16:39
18. Ben Hammer (Elk Rapids)11 ... 16:40
19. Nick Oertel (Goodrich)12 ... 16:43
20. Peter Gorkiewicz (Charlevoix)11 ... 16:44
62. Craig Madaleno (Hemlock)11 ... 17:12
72. Joseph Frost (Hemlock)11 ... 17:15
90. Rob Slate (Hemlock)12 ... 17:30
141. Andrew Henne (Hemlock)11 ... 17:57
220. George Drown (Hemlock)12 ... 18:52

2002 D3 BOYS

Hemlock defended the D3 crown, topping rival Williamston by 23 points, even though Williamston's David Bills was able to outleg two pursuers from Hemlock at the finish.

"It went according to plan," said Bills. "But the last half mile along the inside of the track was pretty tough."

Michigan Int. Speedway, Brooklyn, Nov. 2 ☒

2002 BOYS DIVISION 3 TEAMS

1. Hemlock ... 90
2. Williamston ... 113
3. Grand Rapids West Catholic ... 115
4. Benzie Central ... 195
5. Stockbridge ... 222
6. Hart ... 247
7. Jackson Lumen Christi ... 271
8. Kalamazoo Hackett ... 296
9. Shepherd ... 298
10. Hesperia ... 308
11. Essexville Garber ... 336
12. Constantine ... 341
13. Hudson ... 365
14. Wyoming Kelloggsville ... 385
15. Allendale ... 399
16. Corunna ... 413
17. Kalkaska ... 443
18. Beaverton ... 445
19. Bronson ... 467
20. Lake Fenton ... 475
21. Onsted ... 478
22. Dearborn Heights Annapolis ... 499
23. Ida ... 552
24. Frankenmuth ... 577
25. Reese ... 584
26. Yale ... 634
27. Goodrich ... 644

2002 BOYS DIVISION 3 INDIVIDUALS

1. David Bills (Williamston)11 ... 15:36
2. Steve Czymbor (Hemlock)12 ... 15:39
3. Nicholas Puchasz (Hemlock)12 ... 15:50
4. Peter Gorkiewicz (Charlevoix)12 ... 15:51
5. Josh Perrin (Hillsdale)11 ... 15:53

6. Zachary Schnitta (Berrien Springs)12 .... 15:59
7. Luke TenHopen (Kalkaska)12 .... 16:05
8. Joe Zick (Durand)12 .... 16:06
9. Kyle Shropshire (Stockbridge)10 .... 16:08
10. Brian Murphy (Corunna)11 .... 16:08
11. Shawn Jordan (Constantine)12 .... 16:15
12. Garrett Romero (East Jordan)12 .... 16:15
13. Sean Beckwith (Corunna)11 .... 16:19
14. Steve Harpold (GR West Catholic)12 .... 16:20
15. Josh Wheelock (Benzie Central)12 .... 16:21
16. Adam Smith (Ovid-Elsie)10 .... 16:22
17. Joe Heine (St. Louis)12 .... 16:23
18. Greg Schmit (Leslie)12 .... 16:26
19. Paul Lange (Laingsburg)10 .... 16:26
20. Joseph Frost (Hemlock)12 .... 16:29
37. Craig Madaleno (Hemlock)12 .... 16:47
83. Adam Beyersdorf (Hemlock)12 .... 17:14
115. Andrew Henne (Hemlock)12 .... 17:32
132. Brent Drown (Hemlock)10 .... 17:42

2003 D3 BOYS

Grand Rapids West Catholic moved to the top. Said Williamston's Paul Nilsson, "To beat us, [they] had to run their greatest race of the season."

It was the Falcons' first win since the 1970 Class B title. Said coach Denny Scully, "We felt we were the team to beat, but we had to be perfect because everyone else was. This course brings out the best in everybody and every one of our athletes did what we asked of them coming into this race."

Josh Perrin of Hillsdale took the lead before the mile and lengthened his margin through, 2M in 9:42. Defending champion David Bills whittled that gap down near the end, but Perrin summoned a strong kick for a 10-second win in 15:18.

Hillsdale's Josh Perrin won by a big margin.

Michigan Int. Speedway, Brooklyn, Nov. 1
2003 BOYS DIVISION 3 TEAMS
1. Grand Rapids West Catholic 113
2. Williamston 133
3. Shepherd 150
4. Hillsdale 204
5. Allendale 219
6. Benzie Central 224
7. Corunna 257
8. Mason County Central 265
9. Essexville Garber 289
10. Morley-Stanwood 296
11. Hart 298

12. Carson City-Crystal 315
13. Onsted 317
14. Beaverton 324
15. Jackson Lumen Christi 344
16. Three Oaks River Valley 403
17. Erie-Mason 409
18. Kent City 443
19. Albion 445
20. Capac 507
21. Constantine 515
22. Lake Fenton 524
23. Kalkaska 559
24. Dundee 586
25. Armada 653
26. Delton Kellogg 705
27. Reese 735

2003 BOYS DIVISION 3 INDIVIDUALS
1. Josh Perrin (Hillsdale)12 .... 15:18
2. David Bills (Williamston)12 .... 15:28
3. Landon Peacock (Morley-Stanwood)10 ...... 15:46
4. Daniel Clark (Jackson Lumen Christi)11 ..... 15:53
5. Travis Nash (Onsted)12 .... 16:03
6. Nathan Mester (Beaverton)10 .... 16:05
7. Zac Gallagher (Essexville Garber)10 .... 16:06
8. Michael O'Shaughnessey (Elk Rapids)11 ..... 16:06
9. Patrick Grosskopf (Corunna)12 .... 16:07
10. Kevin Christensen (Battle Creek Pennfield)12 ... 16:10
11. Dave Smith (Byron)12 .... 16:10
12. Brian Murphy (Corunna)12 .... 16:11
13. Mitch Zost (Allendale)11 .... 16:11
14. Erich Tanis (GR West Catholic)12 .... 16:19
15. Jacob. Dubois (East Jackson)12 .... 16:20
16. Tom Ray (Constantine)11 .... 16:25
17. Sam Passenger (GR West Catholic)10 ...... 16:25
18. Ben Miller (Benzie Central)11 .... 16:25
19. Kyle Shropshire (Stockbridge)11 .... 16:26
20. Steve Terry (Three Oaks River Valley)12 ... 16:27
32. Ed DeVries (GR West Catholic)11 .... 16:35
44. Andrew Vereecke (GR West Catholic)10 ... 16:45
51. Nick Preston (GR West Catholic)10 .... 16:47
52. Andrew Bissonette (GR West Catholic)10 .. 16:47
73. Chris Leikert (GR West Catholic)11 .... 17:03

2004 D3 BOYS

Harbor Springs—the champs the previous year in D4—edged defending champion West Catholic by 14 points to win the title in its first year in D3.

Josh Hofbauer led his team to the win, battling with Zac Gallagher for the first two miles (10:05) before pulling away. "I knew I had to get away," he told RunMichigan. "I surged and kept it. I had to do it, I've been working since I was a sophomore."

Michigan Int. Speedway, Brooklyn, Nov. 6
2004 BOYS DIVISION 3 TEAMS
1. Harbor Springs 91
2. Grand Rapids West Catholic 105
3. Williamston 125
4. Jackson Lumen Christi 157
5. Allendale 162
6. Shepherd 164
7. Carson City-Crystal 282
8. Erie-Mason 293
9. Beaverton 298
10. Benzie Central 320
11. St Louis 325
12. Hillsdale 328
13. Essexville Garber 346
14. Kent City 363
15. Mason County Central 379
16. Lansing Catholic 389
17. Freeland 390
18. Richmond 425
19. Hemlock 469
20. Onsted 481
21. Armada 535
22. Constantine 564
23. Monroe St Mary 577
24. Schoolcraft 613
25. Capac 617

26. Bronson 695
27. Detroit Country Day 731
28. Durand 734

2004 BOYS DIVISION 3 INDIVIDUALS
1. Josh Hofbauer (Harbor Springs)12 .... 15:49
2. Zac Gallagher (Essexville Garber)11 .... 15:54
3. Mike O'Shaughnessy (Elk Rapids)12 .... 15:58
4. Mitchell Zost (Allendale)12 .... 16:03
5. Kyle Shropshire (Stockbridge)12 .... 16:04
6. Dave Brent (Monroe St Mary)12 .... 16:11
7. Dan Clark (Jackson Lumen Christi)12 .... 16:13
8. Maverick Darling (Ovid-Elsie)9 .... 16:14
9. Sam Passenger (GR West Catholic)11 .... 16:15
10. Zack Jones (Leroy-Pine River)11 .... 16:15
11. Joe Ruffing (Jackson Lumen Christi)12 ..... 16:16
12. Spencer Beatty (Harbor Springs)11 .... 16:18
13. Mike Mayday (Hanover-Horton)11 .... 16:19
14. Ben Miller (Benzie Central)12 .... 16:20
15. Alex Russeau (Erie-Mason)10 .... 16:20
16. Ben Ruthruff (Olivet)12 .... 16:20
17. Andrew Bissonette (GR West Catholic)11 .. 16:20
18. Jeff Maxfield (Hillsdale)11 .... 16:20
19. Strohkirch Jordan (Gladwin)10 .... 16:21
20. Trent Denhof (Grant)10 .... 16:21
24. Eric Hart (Harbor Springs)12 .... 16:24
49. Chad Wenz (Harbor Springs)11 .... 16:56
54. Trey Graham (Harbor Springs)9 .... 17:00
89. Nick Allerding (Harbor Springs)10 .... 17:23
149. Brian McGuiness (Harbor Springs)9 .... 17:56

2005 D3 BOYS

A pair of sophomores battled at the front, Ovid-Elsie's Maverick Darling edging Williamston's Matt Lutzke at the finish, 15:49.9 to 15:50.5. With the top six all within 3.3 seconds at the finish, the kicks on the final stretch determined the order.

Said Darling of his plan, "Just pace myself the first bit and then take care of it from there and keep moving up."

Teamwise, Williamston returned to the winner's circle after five years away, scoring a narrow 5-point win over West Catholic, runners-up for the second-straight year.

Michigan Int. Speedway, Brooklyn, Nov. 5
2005 BOYS DIVISION 3 TEAMS
1. Williamston 78
2. Grand Rapids West Catholic 83
3. Jackson Lumen Christi 187
4. Lansing Catholic 223
5. Erie-Mason 224
6. Kalkaska 259
7. Carson City-Crystal 267
8. Benzie Central 269
9. Hillsdale 301
10. Shepherd 311
11. Allendale 318
12. Freeland 330
13. Cass City 365
14. Kent City 381
15. Leroy Pine River 411
16. Albion 424
17. Capac 427
18. Bangor 436
19. Napoleon 460
20. Hemlock 462
21. Kalamazoo Hackett 478
22. Lake Fenton 513
23. Macomb Lutheran North 572
24. Saginaw Swan Valley 574
25. Marlette 595
26. Riverview Richard 602
27. Stanton-Central Montcalm 636
28. Kalamazoo Christian 646

2005 BOYS DIVISION 3 INDIVIDUALS
1. Maverick Darling (Ovid-Elsie)10 .... 15:50
2. Matt Lutzke (Williamston)10 .... 15:51
3. Mike Mayday (Hanover-Horton)12 .... 15:52
4. Nick Tecca (Parchment)11 .... 15:53
5. Paul Grieve (Kalkaska)11 .... 15:53

6. Kyle Smith (Lake Fenton)12 .... 15:54
7. Ryan Scott (Grand Rapids West Catholic)10 . 15:58
8. Brandon Griffin (Erie-Mason)11 .... 15:58
9. Aaron Simoneau (Manistee)11 .... 16:01
10. Devon Duflo (Carson City-Crystal)11 .... 16:05
11. Zac Gallagher (Essexville Garber)12 .... 16:05
12. Zack Jones (Leroy Pine River)12 .... 16:08
13. Daniel Nix (Williamston)10 .... 16:12
14. Spencer Beatty (Harbor Springs)12 .... 16:12
15. Ben Miller (Benzie Central)12 .... 16:16
16. Chris Baier (Kingsley)12 .... 16:17
17. Christopher Pankow (Williamston)12 .... 16:17
18. Nicholas Tomsic (Bangor)12 .... 16:18
19. Evan Lowry (Hanover-Horton)11 .... 16:18
20. Andrew Bissonette (GR West Catholic)12 .... 16:19
36. Tyler Sharp (Williamston)12 .... 16:34
55. David Ash (Williamston)11 .... 16:51
109. Luke Theis (Williamston)11 .... 17:19
174. Steffen Carlisle (Williamston)11 .... 17:58

2006 D3 BOYS

Coached by Justin Keyes, Erie-Mason scored its first win ever, topping the defending champs by 13 points.

Maverick Darling won his second title, blasting the middle mile in 4:57 to rip through 2M (9:57) with a 40-meter lead.

"I got boxed in the first 800," said Darling, "so it was a little slow the first mile. But I wanted to get under 15:30 and I did."

Michigan Int. Speedway, Brooklyn, Nov. 4 ☒
2006 BOYS DIVISION 3 TEAMS

1. Erie-Mason 77
2. Williamston 90
3. Jackson Lumen Christi 175
4. Kalkaska 181
5. Benzie Central 188
6. Grand Rapids West Catholic 220
7. Kalamazoo Hackett 250
8. Bangor 256
9. Allendale 278
10. Elk Rapids 304
11. Flint Powers 317
12. Lansing Catholic 322
13. Capac 370
14. Freeland 393
15. Kent City 441
16. Durand 445
17. Cass City 481
18. Gladwin 498
19. Saginaw Swan Valley 514
20. Dundee 526
21. Albion 527
22. Shepherd 527
23. Riverview Richard 541
24. Detroit Crockett 580
25. Berrien Springs 582
26. Macomb Lutheran North 624
27. Mayville 722

2006 BOYS DIVISION 3 INDIVIDUALS

1. Maverick Darling (Ovid-Elsie)11 .... 15:24
2. Paul Grieve (Kalkaska)12 .... 15:31
3. Aaron Simoneau (Manistee)12 .... 15:34
4. Matt Lutzke (Williamston)11 .... 15:39
5. Josh McAlary (Jackson Lumen Christi)11 ...... 15:41
6. Brandon Griffin (Erie-Mason)12 .... 15:50
7. Dan Nix (Williamston)11 .... 15:54
8. Nick Tecca (Parchment)12 .... 15:57
9. Wes Stoody (Flint Powers)12 .... 15:57
10. Trenton Denhof (Grant)12 .... 16:00
11. Mike Gravelyn (GR West Catholic)11 .... 16:06
12. Jordan Strohkirch (Gladwin)12 .... 16:08
13. Joshua Brent (Monroe St Mary)11 .... 16:08
14. Alex Roth (Benzie Central)12 .... 16:10
15. Ian Mcdowell (Lansing Catholic)12 .... 16:11
16. Garrett Lacy (Carson City-Crystal)11 .... 16:13
17. Jeff Nordquist (Parchment)12 .... 16:13
18. Mike Hall (Vermontville Maple Valley)12 ...... 16:13
19. Billy Neri (Blissfield)12 .... 16:14
20. Jesiah Rodriguez (Erie-Mason)12 .... 16:15
29. Alex Russeau (Erie-Mason)12 .... 16:26
35. Justin Trychel (Erie-Mason)10 .... 16:31
52. Nick Petro (Erie-Mason)10 .... 16:41
80. Dan Mizell (Erie-Mason)12 .... 16:57
136. Kris Williamson (Erie-Mason)12 .... 17:29

2007 D3 BOYS

For his grand finale, Maverick Darling of Ovid-Elsie put on a display of pure domination, winning his third-straight title by a massive 40 seconds. He became the fifth boy in Lower Peninsula history to score three wins. It was the fastest time in any divison, by far,and the third-fastest time in MIS history.

"It hurts," said the victor, who ran splits of 4:35 and 9:29 en route. "It's not easy. But it's a great feeling seeing that clock at the finish line."

Darling would go on to finish 10th at Foot Locker nationals, before taking his talents to Wisconsin. As a Badger, he was a four-time All-Big 10 pick and made All-American in 2012.

Said coach Paul Nilsson of his winning Williamston squad, "These guys ran as a team and not as individuals, and believe me, that's two different things. The kids held back until the last tenth of a mile, playing [the strategy] to ge the best team score."

Michigan Int. Speedway, Brooklyn, Nov. 3 ☒
2007 BOYS DIVISION 3 TEAMS

1. Williamston 63
2. Grand Rapids West Catholic 89
3. Bangor 198
4. Kent City 234
5. Hillsdale 237
6. Jackson Lumen Christi 249
7. Shepherd 268
8. Benzie Central 281
9. Elk Rapids 288
10. Saginaw Swan Valley 294
11. Kalamazoo Hackett 300
12. Harrison 344
13. Hanover-Horton 349
14. Whitmore Lake 362
15. Caro 377
16. Monroe St Mary 377
17. Whitehall 408
18. Lansing Catholic 423
19. Cass City 432
20. Carson City-Crystal 457
21. Ann Arbor Richard 492
22. Schoolcraft 511
23. Macomb Lutheran North 549
24. Riverview Richard 560
25. Ithaca 566
26. Grosse Ile 735

2007 BOYS DIVISION 3 INDIVIDUALS

1. Maverick Darling (Ovid-Elsie)12 .... 14:53
2. Mike Gravelyn (GR West Catholic)12 .... 15:33
3. Matt Lutzke (Williamston)12 .... 15:38
4. Isaiah Vandoorne (Grant)12 .... 15:48
5. Josh McAlary (Jackson Lumen Christi)12 ...... 15:50
6. James Hughes (Manchester)12 .... 15:55
7. Alex Wilson (Kent City)10 .... 15:55
8. Nick Ekel (Ovid-Elsie)12 .... 15:55
9. John Person (Williamston)12 .... 15:55
10. Alex Vanias (Leroy Pine River)12 .... 15:58
11. Travis Gere (Caro)12 .... 16:01
12. Joe McAvoy (Hillsdale)11 .... 16:03
13. Antonio Schafer (GR West Catholic)11 .... 16:03
14. Dan Nix (Williamston)12 .... 16:07
15. David Madrigal (Durand)10 .... 16:09
16. Edwin Wainaina (Grandville Calvin Chr)11 .. 16:10
17. Blake Allison (Harrison)10 .... 16:12
18. Tyler Noble (Shepherd)11 .... 16:15
19. Michael O'Brien (Kalamazoo Hackett)12 ..... 16:15
20. Donny Freed (Addison)12 .... 16:16
31. Travis Barczak (Williamston)12 .... 16:27
45. John Risch (Williamston)11 .... 16:39
63. Robin McGrathlle (Williamston)12 .... 16:49
118. Spencer Pioszak (Williamston)10 .... 17:20

2008 D3 BOYS

Tony Schafer of West Catholic broke away after the 2M mark to grab the win by 5 seconds and a PR by some 25 seconds. Said coach Denny Scully, "The fact that he had competition had everything to do with his great time. This kid lives and breathes for running."

Rick Cahoon's Shepherd squad grabbed the win by a slim 4 points over Hillsdale. "They ended up that way because everyone was pushing for everyone," he said.

Michigan Int. Speedway, Brooklyn, Nov. 3 ☒
2008 BOYS DIVISION 3 TEAMS

1. Shepherd 117
2. Hillsdale 121
3. Benzie Central 157
4. Freeland 195
5. Grand Rapids West Catholic 241
6. Grandville Calvin Christian 250
7. Mason County Central 284
8. Jackson Lumen Christi 291
9. Whitmore Lake 294
10. Bangor 294
11. Elk Rapids 322
12. Lansing Catholic 332
13. Monroe St Mary 349
14. Charlevoix 382
15. Cass City 426
16. Albion 439
17. Macomb Lutheran North 444
18. Kent City 454
19. Ann Arbor Richard 465
20. Kalamazoo Hackett 482
21. Sanford Meridian 500
22. Armada 504
23. Laingsburg 527
24. Detroit Communication Media Arts 529
25. Schoolcraft 589
26. Frankenmuth 604
27. Caro 652
28. Saginaw Nouvel 742

2008 BOYS DIVISION 3 INDIVIDUALS

1. Tony Schafer (GR West Catholic)12 .... 15:24
2. Blake Allison (Harrison)11 .... 15:29
3. Alex Wilson (Kent City)11 .... 15:31
4. Paul Lewis (Albion)11 .... 15:42
5. David Madrigal (Durand)11 .... 15:49
6. Joe McAvoy (Hillsdale)12 .... 15:52
7. Justin Bateson (Blissfield)11 .... 15:56
8. Anthony Miller (Freeland)12 .... 16:00
9. Zach Carpenter (Whitmore Lake)11 .... 16:06
10. Edwin Wainaina (Grandville Calvin Chr)12 .. 16:08
11. Jim Janisse (Elk Rapids)12 .... 16:09
12. Stephen Tennis (Hudson)11 .... 16:10
13. Caleb Rhynard (Shepherd)10 .... 16:10
14. Gareth Gose (Leslie)12 .... 16:10
15. Jared Lauber (Mason County Central)11 ..... 16:11
16. Andreas Koerner (Macomb Lutheran N)12 .. 16:14
17. Josh Moskalewski (Allendale)12 .... 16:15
18. Trevor Denton (Chesaning)10 .... 16:15
19. Mike Falvey (Ann Arbor Richard)11 .... 16:15
20. Lyle Kafer (Hillsdale)11 .... 16:17
36. David Silversmith (Shepherd)12 .... 16:29
37. Josh Kyser (Shepherd)12 .... 16:30
39. Tyler Noble (Shepherd)12 .... 16:32
49. Jared Gilbert (Shepherd)12 .... 16:38
95. Kurtis Hall (Shepherd)9 .... 17:01
111. Lynn Jones (Shepherd)12 .... 17:15

2009 BOYS D3 BOYS

"There was no way I was going to get outkicked," said David Madrigal of Durand after he outsprinted Blake Allison and Paul Lewis down the final stretch. "After every practice I did eight to 10 100-meter sprints. The wind was tough out there today, but I kind of drafted off the other two guys."

Benzie Central captured its first team win since 1997.

Michigan Int. Speedway, Brooklyn, Nov. 7
2009 BOYS DIVISION 3 TEAMS
1. Benzie Central 164
2. Grandville Calvin Christian 180
3. Hillsdale 212
4. Kent City 232
5. Mason County Central 259
6. Jackson Lumen Christi 267
7. Whitmore Lake 280
8. Freeland 281
9. Chesaning 286
10. Lansing Catholic 334
11. Durand 350
12. Stockbridge 360
13. Charlevoix 360
14. Albion 368
15. Monroe St Mary 374
16. Ida 379
17. Byron 407
18. Allendale 408
19. Armada 445
20. Erie-Mason 467
21. Bangor 471
22. Frankenmuth 483
23. Kalamazoo Hackett 515
24. Roscommon 526
25. Almont 550
26. Caro 552
27. Bloomingdale 597
28. Clare 616
29. Delton Kellogg 630

*Durand's David Madrigal won in 2009.
(Pete Draugalis photo)*

2009 BOYS DIVISION 3 INDIVIDUALS
1. David Madrigal (Durand)12 .... 15:43
2. Blake Allison (Harrison)12 .... 15:46
3. Paul Lewis (Albion)12 .... 15:50
4. Alex Wilson (Kent City)12 .... 16:00
5. Zach Carpenter (Whitmore Lake)12 .. 16:14
6. Caleb Rhynard (Shepherd)11 .... 16:18
7. Sebastian Reisch (Hillsdale)12 .... 16:18
8. Lyle Kafer (Hillsdale)12 .... 16:25
9. Taylor Heath (Hanover-Horton)12 ..... 16:28
10. Spencer Pageau (Jackson Lumen Chr)11 .. 16:28
11. Andrew Reidsma (Grandville Calvin Chr)12 16:31
12. Gary Ezzo (Armada)12 .... 16:33
13. Nick Smith (Ida)12 .... 16:35
14. Charlton Craig (Schoolcraft)11 .... 16:36
15. Tommy Matuszak (Caro) 16:36
16. Kenny Harris (Albion)11 .... 16:37
17. Lucas Baylis (Belding)12 .... 16:37
18. Trevor Denton (Chesaning)11 .... 16:38
19. Eric Buday (Charlevoix)11 .... 16:39
20. Mark List (Laingsburg)12 .... 16:40
40. Robert Kirby (Benzie Central)12 .... 17:05
41. Tom Smeltzer (Benzie Central)12 ...... 17:08
44. Travis Clous (Benzie Central)10 .... 17:10
59. David Rhodes (Benzie Central)12 ...... 17:20
68. Rick Jones (Benzie Central)12 .... 17:25
91. William Huddleston (Benzie Central)10 .. 17:37
102. Talon Morris (Benzie Central)12 .... 17:41

2010 D3 BOYS

Caleb Rhynard of Shepherd, undefeated all season, set the pace from the start, passing the mile in 4:46. "I just wanted to go out and run my race and do what I could."

The team win went to Grandville Calvin Christian. Said coach Laurens TenKate, "This is our first state title and we've only got one senior in our top 15. It was a solid race by all our guys."

*Caleb Rhyard of Shepherd.
(Pete Draugalis photo)*

Michigan Int. Speedway, Brooklyn, Nov. 6
2010 BOYS DIVISION 3 TEAMS
1. Grandville Calvin Christian 107
2. Lansing Catholic 192
3. Shepherd 212
4. Frankenmuth 212
5. Jackson Lumen Christi 242
6. Hillsdale 250
7. Perry 263
8. Mason County Central 288
9. Flint Powers 289
10. Benzie Central 299
11. Schoolcraft 304
12. Napoleon 320
13. Freeland 336
14. Hemlock 340
15. Evart 350
16. Allendale 353
17. Whitmore Lake 374
18. Delton Kellogg 379
19. Almont 429
20. Grand Rapids NorthPointe Christian . 434
21. Kalamazoo Hackett 454
22. Monroe St Mary 455
23. Roscommon 469
24. Reese 569
25. Ida 599
26. Allen Park Cabrini 606
27. Kingsley 660

2010 BOYS DIVISION 3 INDIVIDUALS
1. Caleb Rhynard (Shepherd)12 .... 15:27
2. Dylan Creger (Almont)12 .... 15:49
3. Ben Sievert (Frankenmuth)12 .... 15:57
4. Brayden Border (St Louis)12 .... 15:59
5. Blake Garver (Napoleon)12 .... 16:03
6. Spencer Pageau (Jackson Lumen Christi)12 16:05
7. David Zinger (Evart)10 .... 16:05
8. Zac Nowicki (Grandville Calvin Christian)10 .. 16:06
9. Thomas Bambach (Allendale)12 .... 16:07
10. Trevor Denton (Chesaning)12 .... 16:09
11. Eric Edmond (Frankenmuth)11 .... 16:09
12. William Huddleston (Benzie Central)11 .. 16:10
13. Stuart Crowell (Parchment)12 .... 16:10
14. Charlton Craig (Schoolcraft)12 .... 16:10
15. Justus Pinckney (Grandville Calvin Chr)11 . 16:14
16. Justin Krauss (Perry)12 .... 16:15
17. Bryce Stroede (Hanover-Horton)10 ... 16:15
18. John Bell (Perry)11 .... 16:16
19. Josh Kersjes (Grandville Calvin Chr)11 .. 16:17
20. Chase Barnett (Mason County Central)9 .. 16:17
31. Simon Reidsma (Grandville Calvin Chr)11 .. 16:33
87. Andrew Rylaarsdam (Grandville Calv C)10 . 17:07
99. Steven Haagsma (Grandville Calvin Chr)12 17:15
132. Michael Brecker (Grandville Calvin Chr)11 17:34

2011 D3 BOYS

Zachary Zingsheim of Lansing Catholic surprised many by taking the win with an impressive kick. "It was muddy with really bad footing... I knew it was going to be close and tough... I said 'I'm going to go now, with everything I have left, and if he beats me I know I gave myself a chance.'"

Zingsheim, a sub-50 second 400 runner, prevailed by more than six seconds.

Grandville Calvin Christian used a 9-point margin to defend its title.

Michigan Int. Speedway, Brooklyn, Nov. 5
2011 BOYS DIVISION 3 TEAMS
1. Grandville Calvin Christian 56
2. Lansing Catholic 65
3. Hemlock 195
4. Benzie Central 244
5. Chesaning 248
6. Clare 249
7. Stockbridge 271
8. Pewamo-Westphalia 293
9. Grand Rapids NorthPointe Christian . 305
10. Frankenmuth 333
11. Marlette 339
12. Freeland 353
13. Hillsdale 353
14. Jackson Lumen Christi 374
15. Kingsley 388
16. Charlevoix 420
17. Watervliet 438
18. Erie-Mason 441
19. Bridgman 442
20. Ida 444
21. Clinton 456
22. Perry 463
23. Almont 519
24. Newaygo 545
25. Schoolcraft 557
26. Macomb Lutheran North 590
27. Byron 649

2011 BOYS DIVISION 3 INDIVIDUALS
1. Zachary Zingsheim (Lansing Catholic)12 ..... 15:49
2. Chase Barnett (Mason County Central)10 ... 15:55
3. Josh Kersjes (Grandville Calvin Christian)12 15:57
4. Nick Raymond (Erie-Mason)11 .... 15:59
5. Zac Nowicki (Grandville Calvin Christian)11 .. 16:00
6. Bryce Stroede (Hanover-Horton)11 .... 16:01
7. Jacob Bowman (Marlette)11 .... 16:03
8. Simon Reidsma (Grandville Calvin Chr)12 .. 16:04
9. Keenan Rebera (Lansing Catholic)9 .. 16:06
10. Justus Pinckney (Grandville Calvin Chr)12 . 16:09
11. Andy Bowman (Marlette)11 .... 16:11
12. Jimmy Hicks (Lansing Catholic)12 ..... 16:14
13. Zach Hardway (Hillsdale)10 .... 16:15
14. Ben Hemstreet (Pinconning)11 .... 16:18
15. Tyler Sobleskey (Olivet)12 .... 16:19
16. Joe Oehrli (Reed City)12 .... 16:22
17. Kyle Losey (Stockbridge)12 .... 16:24
18. Will Wilson (Kent City)10 .... 16:24
19. Kurtis Hall (Shepherd)12 .... 16:24

20. Eric Edmond (Frankenmuth)12......16:26
59. Andrew Rylaarsdam (Grandville Calv C)11..17:04
65. Logan Jurgens (Grandville Calvin Chr)9 ......17:09
122. Alex Clark (Grandville Calvin Chr)11..........17:39

2012 D3 BOYS

Nick Raymond of Erie-Mason did everything right this year. "Last year I went out and I was leading the race and I was a little confused because I wasn't expecting to. I kind of died and fell back. This time I was prepared to go out for the lead and just take it."

It worked. He won in 15:06, the second-fastest Class C/D3 time since the finals moved to MIS.

Jackson Lumen Christi, coached by Dave Miller, won its first title in 33 years.

Michigan Int. Speedway, Brooklyn, Nov. 3
2012 BOYS DIVISION 3 TEAMS
1. Jackson Lumen Christi.................129
2. Marlette..................137
3. Grandville Calvin Christian.................147
4. Benzie Central.................187
5. Freeland.................196
6. Ithaca.................216
7. Mason County Central.................223
8. Watervliet.................250
9. Stockbridge.................261
10. Lansing Catholic.................312
11. Hemlock.................324
12. Saranac.................338
13. Clare.................344
14. Dundee.................374
15. Manistee.................375
16. Erie-Mason.................378
17. Napoleon.................393
18. Hanover-Horton.................445
19. Schoolcraft.................464
20. Ida.................502
21. Bangor.................506
22. Farwell.................512
23. Newaygo.................546
24. Reese.................567
25. Caro.................643
26. Ann Arbor Richard.................679
27. Macomb Lutheran North.................701

2012 BOYS DIVISION 3 INDIVIDUALS
1. Nick Raymond (Erie-Mason)12..........15:06
2. Bryce Stroede (Hanover-Horton)12..........15:23
3. Chase Barnett (Mason County Central)11..........15:29
4. Jacob Bowman (Marlette)12..........15:38
5. Keenan Rebera (Lansing Catholic)10..........15:43
6. Andy Bowman (Marlette)12..........15:49
7. Zac Nowicki (Grandville Calvin Christian)12..15:55
8. Andrew Rylaarsdam (Grandville Calv Chr)12.16:00
9. Jake Keena (Kingsley)10..........16:04
10. Zach Scheich (Dundee)12..........16:04
11. Mitchell Hoffman (Hemlock)12..........16:11
12. Tim Young (Saranac)12..........16:11
13. Dominic Muessig (Clinton)12..........16:13
14. Cameron Bredice (Bridgman)11..........16:14
15. Tyler Jensen (Ovid-Elsie)12..........16:14
16. Will Wilson (Kent City)11..........16:16
17. Zach Hardway (Hillsdale)11..........16:17
18. Ben Hemstreet (Pinconning)12..........16:17
19. Karl Berkemeier (Jackson Lumen Christi)11.16:17
20. Charlie Ludlow (Jackson Lumen Christi)12..16:18
28. Ryan Gibson (Jackson Lumen Christi)10....16:25
48. Patrick Soltis (Jackson Lumen Christi)11....16:51
83. Canyon Raburn (Jackson Lumen Christi)11.17:11
170. Alex Hoop (Jackson Lumen Christi)10 ....17:56
230. Kristopher Cavender (Jackson Lum C)10 ..19:06

2013 D3 BOYS

On a muddy day, Lansing Catholic's Keenan Rebera was fastest on his feet, winning by nearly 30 seconds. "I came back here with a grudge against this course," he said. "After the first hill, I realized it was going to be a little bit slow, so I wanted to keep up the pace."

Benzie Central, guided by Asa Kelly, captured its seventh title

Michigan Int. Speedway, Brooklyn, Nov. 2
2013 BOYS DIVISION 3 TEAMS
1. Benzie Central.................111
2. Stockbridge.................129
3. Lansing Catholic.................189
4. Clare.................192
5. Grandville Calvin Christian.................219
6. Hanover-Horton.................276
7. Watervliet.................282
8. Jackson Lumen Christi.................282
9. St Louis.................292
10. Mason County Central.................295
11. Midland Bullock Creek.................332
12. Charlevoix.................349
13. Napoleon.................352
14. Holland Black River.................355
15. Bridgman.................355
16. Dundee.................360
17. Hemlock.................363
18. Schoolcraft.................387
19. Newaygo.................413
20. Freeland.................459
21. Caro.................476
22. Ida.................533
23. Marlette.................541
24. Almont.................607
25. Carrollton.................624
26. Macomb Lutheran North.................693
27. Capac.................732

2013 BOYS DIVISION 3 INDIVIDUALS
1. Keenan Rebera (Lansing Catholic)11..........15:31
2. Chase Barnett (Mason County Central)12....16:01
3. Ben Utz (Michigan Center)11..........16:05
4. Will Wilson (Kent City)12..........16:07
5. Zac Benham (Mason County Central)10........16:08
6. Jake Keena (Kingsley)11..........16:11
7. Zach Wehner (Schoolcraft)12..........16:12
8. Nathaniel Baird (Stockbridge)10..........16:13
9. Zack Richards (Comstock)11..........16:13
10. Cameron Bredice (Bridgman)12..........16:14
11. James Sira (Midland Bullock Creek)12........16:16
12. Bobby Haskin (GR West Catholic)10..........16:20
13. Logan Jurgens (Grandville Calvin Chr)11..16:24
14. Hunter Nivison (Clare)12..........16:28
15. Abe Visser (Grandville Calvin Chr)10..........16:28
16. Jarren Guy (Durand)12..........16:33
17. Alex Stowell (Freeland)11..........16:33
18. Damien Halverson (Hesperia)11..........16:34
19. Mike Westra (GR Covenant Christian)12....16:34
20. Zach Hardway (Hillsdale)12..........16:35
23. Kyle Bailey (Benzie Central)11..........16:40
27. Brayden Huddleston (Benzie Central)9........16:42
31. Max Gaft (Benzie Central)12..........16:49
51. Ismael Halaweh (Benzie Central)12..........17:08
52. Jake Williams (Benzie Central)10..........17:09
53. Noah Robotham (Benzie Central)10..........17:09
84. Andrew Hayden (Benzie Central)12..........17:28

2014 D3 BOYS

Both Benzie Central and Lansing Catholic's Keenan Rebera successfully defended titles. For Benzie, three runners in the top 25 helped seal a 54-point win over Lansing Catholic.

Said Rebera, "It was my last time here. I really wanted to make the most of it. I had three goals: win, beat my time from last year and not have my shoes come untied.

"The conditions today were worse than last year. That's what makes it fun. The last mile was pretty lonely, but that's the nature of this sport."

Michigan Int. Speedway, Brooklyn, Nov. 2
2014 BOYS DIVISION 3 TEAMS
1. Benzie Central.................87
2. Lansing Catholic.................141
3. Hanover-Horton.................188
4. Stockbridge.................191
5. Shepherd.................205
6. Bridgman.................215
7. Grandville Calvin Christian.................233
8. Clare.................241
9. Dundee.................271
10. Holland Black River.................273
11. Jackson Lumen Christi.................275
12. Adrian Madison.................315
13. Bangor.................357
14. Ovid-Elsie.................371
15. Grand Rapids Covenant Christian.................392
16. Watervliet.................409
17. Jonesville.................418
18. Pewamo-Westphalia.................430
19. Mason County Central.................441
20. Boyne City.................444
21. Caro.................452
22. Carrollton.................538
23. Macomb Lutheran North.................602
24. Reese.................627
25. Sandusky.................647
26. Almont.................650
27. Byron.................714

Keenan Rebera won two straight for Lansing Catholic. (Pete Draugalis photo)

2014 BOYS DIVISION 3 INDIVIDUALS
1. Keenan Rebera (Lansing Catholic)12..........15:31
2. Zac Benham (Mason County Central)11........15:45
3. Abe Visser (Grandville Calvin Christian)11....15:49
4. Bransen Stimpfel (Cass City)11..........15:57
5. Ben Utz (Michigan Center)12..........15:58
6. Bobby Haskin (GR West Catholic)11..........16:01
7. Logan Jurgens (Grandville Calvin Chr)12......16:05
8. Austin Fillmore (Stockbridge)12..........16:07
9. Brayden Huddleston (Benzie Central)10........16:09
10. Kyler Phillips (Clare)12..........16:10
11. Arik LaFave (Hesperia)11..........16:10
12. Ryan Hilbrandt (Hemlock)11..........16:16
13. Dylan Richards (Burton-Bendle)12..........16:18
14. Brock Eves (Hillsdale)11..........16:20
15. Evan Goodell (St Louis)10..........16:21
16. Walker Priest (Shepherd)11..........16:24
17. Fraser Wilson (Kent City)9..........16:25
18. Damien Halverson (Hesperia)12..........16:30
19. Kyle Bailey (Benzie Central)12..........16:31
20. Brian Njuguna (Bridgman)10..........16:31
25. Jake Williams (Benzie Central)11..........16:33
34. Noah Robotham (Benzie Central)11..........16:43
57. Jeffery Crouch (Benzie Central)10..........17:10
200. Kyle Smith (Benzie Central)11..........18:45
202. Zane Brooks (Benzie Central)12..........18:46

2015 D3 BOYS

Tim Simpson's Lansing Catholic crew had been runners-up three times, but finally eked out a 3-point win over defending champion Benzie Central.

"They went all out and ran like they've been running all year, " said Simpson of his Cougars. "We're not the team with a bunch of frontrunners like Benzie. We've got a pack, and I knew if our guys raced aggressively for them we'd be okay."

Calvin Christian's Abe Visser took the individual win after running with James McCann for much of the race. "With a half mile left I decided to just go, get it done."

Michigan Int. Speedway, Brooklyn, Nov. 7
2015 BOYS DIVISION 3 TEAMS
1. Lansing Catholic 124
2. Benzie Central 127
3. Holland Black River 149
4. Shepherd 171
5. Hanover-Horton 171
6. Bridgman 191
7. Grand Rapids Covenant Christian 222
8. Clare 266
9. Stockbridge 295
10. Charlevoix 298
11. Hemlock 309
12. Cass City 333
13. Grandville Calvin Christian 348
14. Caro 364
15. Mason County Central 386
16. Bangor 404
17. Erie-Mason 429
18. Pewamo-Westphalia 432
19. Dundee 438
20. Blissfield 484
21. Watervliet 507
22. Napoleon 562
23. Standish-Sterling 576
24. Bronson 589
25. Almont 590
26. Marlette 660
27. Montrose 740

Calvin Christian's Abe Visser.
(Pete Draugalis photo)

2015 BOYS DIVISION 3 INDIVIDUALS
1. Abe Visser (Grandville Calvin Christian)12 .... 15:35
2. James McCann (Holland Black River)12 .... 15:49
3. Brayden Huddleston (Benzie Central)11 .... 15:56
4. Bransen Stimpfel (Cass City)12 .... 15:57
5. Arik LaFave (Hesperia)12 .... 15:59
6. Evan Goodell (St Louis)11 .... 16:00
7. Ryan Hilbrandt (Hemlock)12 .... 16:03
8. Yami Albrecht (Caro)9 .... 16:04
9. Fraser Wilson (Kent City)10 .... 16:05
10. Braxton Snuffer (Muskegon WM Chr)12 ..... 16:10
11. Jesse Saxton (Grant)12 .... 16:11
12. Zac Wright-Fisher (Mason Co Central)12 ... 16:12
13. Brian Njuguna (Bridgman)11 .... 16:14
14. Walker Priest (Shepherd)12 .... 16:15
15. Jake Williams (Benzie Central)12 .... 16:17
16. Zakaria Drews (Caro)11 .... 16:18
17. Dominic Paoletti (Monroe St. Mary)11 .... 16:19
18. Jake Chapman (Stockbridge)12 .... 16:20
19. D'Anthony Goodwin (Carrollton)11 .... 16:24
20. Ethan Markey (Lansing Catholic)11 .... 16:26
26. Will Peters (Lansing Catholic)9 .... 16:33
28. Ryan Schroeder (Lansing Catholic)10 .... 16:34
46. Eric Warriner (Lansing Catholic)9 .... 17:00
72. Sammy Migaldi (Lansing Catholic)10 .... 17:10
90. Gavin Jager (Lansing Catholic)12 .... 17:21
122. Bobby Reid (Lansing Catholic)12 .... 17:42

2016 D3 BOYS

Sophomore Yami Albrecht kicked his way to the win. "It's the longest straightaway of the year on a cross country course, but I knew how it was going to be and I was prepared for it. Coming down the straightaway I felt pretty strong. And anyone after me I felt was dead because there was mud back there."

Rick Bauer, himself a three-time All-Stater for Howell in Class A, guided his Saugatuck team to its first D3 win. The Indians had won in D4 twice before.

Michigan Int. Speedway, Brooklyn, Nov. 5
2016 BOYS DIVISION 3 TEAMS
1. Saugatuck 61
2. Lansing Catholic 137
3. Hanover-Horton 182
4. Stockbridge 192
5. Caro 198
6. Holland Black River 204
7. Shepherd 249
8. Erie-Mason 255
9. Benzie Central 274
10. McBain 279
11. Grand Rapids West Michigan Aviation 304
12. North Muskegon 335
13. Almont 376
14. Charlevoix 390
15. Clare 400
16. Monroe St Mary 403
17. Bangor 415
18. Traverse City St Francis 480
19. Onsted 490
20. Beaverton 500
21. Dundee 513
22. Bath 519
23. Sanford Meridian 537
24. Olivet 566
25. Sandusky 618
26. Madison Heights Foley 636
27. Berrien Springs 650

2016 BOYS DIVISION 3 INDIVIDUALS
1. Yami Albrecht (Caro)10 .... 15:48
2. Brian Njuguna (Bridgman)12 .... 15:51
3. Evan Goodell (St Louis)12 .... 15:53
4. Corey Gorgas (Saugatuck)10 .... 16:03
5. Zachary Pettinga (Saugatuck)12 .... 16:07
6. Landon Melling (Hanover-Horton)11 .... 16:09
7. Brayden Huddleston (Benzie Central)12 ..... 16:14
8. Dominic Paoletti (Monroe St. Mary)12 .... 16:21
9. Grant Gayan (GR W Michigan Aviation)12 .. 16:28
10. Joshua Fink (Holland Black River)11 .... 16:36
11. Paul Dusabe (GR W Michigan Aviation)12 . 16:37
12. Nick Butch (Saugatuck)12 .... 16:37
13. D'Anthony Goodwin (Carrollton)12 .... 16:38
14. Colin Kane (Dundee)10 .... 16:38
15. Kole Hanke (Bridgman)12 .... 16:39
16. Trey Cucuro (Whitmore Lake)12 .... 16:39
17. Aiden McLaughlin (Morley-Stanwood)9 .... 16:39
18. Corbin Healey (Erie-Mason)11 .... 16:40
19. Jake Chapman (Stockbridge)12 .... 16:41
20. Ryan Schroeder (Lansing Catholic)11 ...... 16:41
27. Orlando Carrion (Saugatuck)12 .... 16:45
37. Keegan Seifert (Saugatuck)11 .... 17:01
76. Jacob VanderRoest (Saugatuck)12 .... 17:30
131. Evan Hotary (Saugatuck)12 .... 17:53

2017 D3 BOYS

Yami Albrecht captured his second-straight win for Caro, but that wasn't enough to lift his teammates to the win. It was Hanover-Horton that took the big trophy, topping the Tigers, 122-128.

Dean Blackledge, the winning coach, told RunMichigan, "This is the first boys cross country championship we've had and they focused on it for the whole year and it paid dividends today."

Yami Albrecht won twice for Caro.
(Pete Draugalis photo)

Michigan Int. Speedway, Brooklyn, Nov. 4
2017 BOYS DIVISION 3 TEAMS
1. Hanover-Horton 122
2. Caro 128
3. Holland Black River 149
4. Erie-Mason 241
5. Harbor Springs 257
6. Kent City 258
7. Shepherd 261
8. Hart 280
9. Grant 285
10. Pewamo-Westphalia 286
11. Montrose 296
12. Saugatuck 323
13. Clare 338
14. Ithaca 402
15. Berrien Springs 411
16. Ann Arbor Greenhills 422
17. Manton 452
18. Onsted 462
19. Dundee 486
20. Jonesville 487
21. Whitmore Lake 493
22. Stockbridge 496
23. Leslie 542
24. Charlevoix 544
25. Bangor 567
26. Bad Axe 587
27. Traverse City St Francis 613
28. Almont 620
29. Memphis 728

2017 BOYS DIVISION 3 INDIVIDUALS
1. Yami Albrecht (Caro)11 .... 15:45
2. Jeremy Kloss (Harbor Springs)11 .... 15:48
3. Landon Melling (Hanover-Horton)12 .... 15:55
4. Corey Gorgas (Saugatuck)11 .... 16:00
5. Fraser Wilson (Kent City)12 .... 16:02
6. Colin Kane (Dundee)11 .... 16:03
7. Aiden McLaughlin (Morley-Stanwood)10 .... 16:14
8. Ransom Allen (Ithaca)11 .... 16:19
9. Bo Shepherd (Hanover-Horton)12 .... 16:21
10. Nik Pettinga (Saugatuck)9 .... 16:22
11. Sam Sharnas (Holland Black River)11 ..... 16:23
12. Colten Covington (Grant)11 .... 16:28
13. Corbin Healey (Erie-Mason)12 .... 16:29
14. Micah Beauregard (Stockbridge)10 .... 16:30
15. Zach Hoekstra (Grandville Calvin Christ)12 . 16:31
16. Kevin McNeil (Morley-Stanwood)12 .... 16:32

17. David Knarian (Bad Axe)11 ....16:34
18. Peyton Tipton (Montrose)12 ....16:34
19. Tyler Kintigh (Benzie Central)10 ....16:35
20. Aaron Hulburt (Caro)11 ....16:35
42. Andy Swihart (Hanover-Horton)10 ....16:58
47. Bradley Guenther (Hanover-Horton)12 ....17:04
70. Donovan Kennedy (Hanover-Horton)11 ....17:16
80. Garrett Melling (Hanover-Horton)10 ....17:20
108. Dean Reynolds (Hanover-Horton)9 ....17:32

2018 D3 BOYS

It had been a long time coming for Caro. The Tigers won the 1980 Class B crown. In 2017, they were runners-up, but narrowly missed the win. This time, behind Yami Albrecht's third-straight individual win, they cruised to the victory with 61 points. Albrecht became the seventh boy in Lower Peninsula history to win three straight.

The muddy course worked to Albrecht's advantage as he battled Jeremy Kloss on the final stretch. "We were next to each other the whole way around. At the 3M mark, Jeremy stepped in the mud and he got stuck. I saw his leg got stuck inthere. I went for it at that point," said the winner.

Michigan Int. Speedway, Brooklyn, Nov. 3 ⊠
2018 BOYS DIVISION 3 TEAMS
1. Caro 61
2. Pewamo-Westphalia 100
3. Shepherd 195
4. Hanover-Horton 206
5. Grandville Calvin Christian 215
6. Hart 220
7. McBain 244
8. Berrien Springs 267
9. Dundee 303
10. Charlevoix 326
11. Ann Arbor Greenhills 352
12. Ithaca 375
13. Harbor Springs 393
14. Kent City 395
15. Benzie Central 403
16. Bloomingdale 410
17. Montrose 414
18. Clare 436
19. Jonesville 447
20. Holland Black River 458
21. Sandusky 481
22. Traverse City St Francis 492
23. Ida 503
24. Bangor 503
25. Onsted 541
26. Byron 639
27. Madison Heights Foley 733

2018 BOYS DIVISION 3 INDIVIDUALS
1. Yami Albrecht (Caro)12 ....15:41
2. Jeremy Kloss (Harbor Springs)12 ....15:46
3. Colin Kane (Dundee)12 ....15:59
4. David Knarian (Bad Axe)12 ....16:14
5. Ransom Allen (Ithaca)12 ....16:15
6. Cole Jensen (Montague)12 ....16:20
7. Hayden Germain (Pewamo-Westphalia)11 ....16:22
8. Carson Laney (Jonesville)11 ....16:25
9. Aiden McLaughlin (Morley-Stanwood)11 ....16:27
10. Brandon Wirth (Reed City)12 ....16:30
11. Alex Enns (Hart)10 ....16:33
12. Caleb Cotton (Caro)12 ....16:39
13. Sam Sharnas (Holland Black River)12 ....16:41
14. Ashton Walker (Pewamo-Westphalia)11 .....16:41
15. Logan Brown (Caro)10 ....16:43
16. Keegan O'Malley (McBain)12 ....16:44
17. Ashton Sheline (Berrien Springs)10 ....16:44
18. Mitchell Bjorne (Bath)12 ....16:45
19. Micah Beauregard (Stockbridge)11 ....16:45
20. Mitch Nurenberg (Pewamo-Westphalia)12 ..16:46
28. Bryden Miller (Caro)12 ....16:55
33. Aaron Hulburt (Caro)12 ....17:01
43. Kevin Wilson (Caro)10 ....17:11
116. Cole Moen (Caro)10 ....17:57

2019 D3 BOYS

With 8th grade state records in the 1600 (4:32.00) and 3200 (9:34.52), Hunter Jones didn't surprise many with his first high school cross country season. Still, the Benze frosh made history by being the first boys 9th grade winner in any division since Ryan Shay in the 1993 Class D race. A 9th-grader had never before won the Class C/D3 race.

Earlier in the season, Jones had told a reporter for the *Record-Eagle*, "I didn't think I would get this fast this quick, but all the work we are doing in practice has led me to excel. It made it a lot easier."

Said coach Asa Kelly, "I don't know what's inside of him, but it's unreal. That kid has the highest pain threshold I have ever seen."

Eighth-placer Garrett Melling led Hanover-Horton to its second win in three years: "We know what we can do and we just wanted to go out and get it again this year, and we did," he told Jared Purcell of MLive.

Michigan Int. Speedway, Brooklyn, Nov. 2 ⊠
2019 BOYS DIVISION 3 TEAMS
1. Hanover-Horton 146
2. Grandville Calvin Christian 183
3. Charlevoix 184
4. Traverse City St Francis 200
5. Hart 202
6. St Louis 231
7. Benzie Central 239
8. Harbor Springs 257
9. Caro 281
10. Saugatuck 290
11. Shepherd 293
12. Montrose 297
13. Bloomingdale 309
14. Grand Rapids Covenant Christian 335
15. Parchment 350
16. Pewamo-Westphalia 354
17. Napoleon 434
18. Montague 457
19. Jonesville 475
20. Manistee 483
21. Madison Heights Foley 533
22. Memphis 535
23. Erie-Mason 542
24. Clinton 572
25. Sanford Meridian 600
26. Dundee 613
27. Byron 675

2019 BOYS DIVISION 3 INDIVIDUALS
1. Hunter Jones (Benzie Central)9 ....15:45
2. Andrew Frohm (Vandercook Lake)12 ....16:14
3. Carson Hersch (New Lothrop)11 ....16:16
4. Ashton Walker (Pewamo-Westphalia)12 ....16:17
5. Hayden Germain (Pewamo-Westphalia)12 ...16:19
6. Alex Enns (Hart)11 ....16:21
7. Braxton Lamey (Ithaca)11 ....16:21
8. Garrett Melling (Hanover-Horton)12 ....16:22
9. Aiden McLaughlin (Morley-Stanwood)12 ......16:27
10. Dean Reynolds (Hanover-Horton)11 ....16:28
11. Carson Laney (Jonesville)12 ....16:30
12. Tyler Guggemos (Kalkaska)10 ....16:34
13. Thomas Richards (TC St Francis)10 ....16:34
14. Luke Witvliet (Grandville Calvin Christian)11 16:38
15. Ryan O'Neill (Perry)12 ....16:39
16. Alec Shaw (Homer)12 ....16:39
17. Garrett Winter (Parchment)10 ....16:40
18. Tyler Carlson (Memphis)11 ....16:40
19. Zach Wright (Potterville)11 ....16:42
20. Joe Furlan (Bloomingdale)11 ....16:43
62. Rogan Melling (Hanover-Horton)9 ....17:17
72. Andy Swihart (Hanover-Horton)12 ....17:29
89. Logan Shepherd (Hanover-Horton)11 ....17:42
108. Shane Sauber (Hanover-Horton)12 ....17:52
140. Richard Haislip (Hanover-Horton)12 ....18:15

CLASS C/D3 STATISTICS

TOP 25 CLOCKINGS AT MIS
14:53	Maverick Darling (Ovid-Elsie)12	2007
15:06	Nick Raymond (Erie-Mason)12	2012
15:12	Jake Flynn (Benzie Central)11	1998
15:16	J. Flynn (Benzie Central)12	1999
15:18	Josh Perrin (Hillsdale)12	2003
15:20	Ryan Cole (Sanford Meridian)12	1999
15:23	Bryce Stroede (Hanover-Horton)12	2012
15:24	R. Cole (Sanford Meridian)11	1998
15:24	M. Darling (Ovid-Elsie)11	2006
15:24	Tony Schafer (GR West Catholic)12	2008
15:25	Jason Stover (Williamston)12	2000
15:27	Caleb Rhynard (Shepherd)12	2010
15:28	David Bills (Williamston)12	2003
15:29	Blake Allison (Harrison)11	2008
15:29	Chase Barnett (Mason Co Central)11	2012
15:31	Paul Grieve (Kalkaska)12	2006
15:31	Alex Wilson (Kent City)11	2008
15:31	Keenan Rebera (Lansing Catholic)11	2013
15:31	K. Rebera (Lansing Catholic)12	2014
15:33	Mike Gravelyn (GR West Catholic)12	2007
15:34	Aaron Simoneau (Manistee)12	2006
15:35	Justin Kibbey (Maple City Glen Lk)10	1998
15:35	Abe Visser (Grandville Calvin Chr)12	2015
15:36	David Bills (Williamston)11	2002
15:38	Matt Lutzke (Williamston)12	2007
15:38	Jacob Bowman (Marlette)12	2012

BIGGEST WINNING MARGINS
47	Herb Lindsay/Jeff Pullen	1972 I
45	Mike Burns/Doug Mohre	1971 T
39.3	Maverick Darling/Mike Gravelyn	2007
38	Guy Jacobson/Bob Stanfield	1979 I
29.9	Keenan Rebera/Chase Barnett	2013

SMALLEST WINNING MARGINS
0.0	Dave Wilson/Ron Hensley	1977 T
0	Leland Tompkins/Hubbard	1929
0	Ivan Palmer/Bill Gooding	1962
0.6	Maverick Darling/Matt Lutzke	2005
0.8	Marty Alward/Mike Kloss	1982 I
0.8	Jesse McGuire/Jeff Thomas	1985 I

LOWEST WINNING SCORES
22	Lansing Everett	1956
23	Lansing St Mary	1937
25	Napoleon	1935
25	Napoleon	1944
27	Imlay City	1945
30	Hemlock	1946
31	Spring Arbor	1954
32	Ypsilanti Roosevelt	1928
32	Napoleon	1936
32	Napoleon	1943

HIGHEST WINNING SCORES
183	Vandercook Lake	1970
164	Benzie Central	2009
148	Mayville	1975
147	Leslie	1993
146	Hanover-Horton	2019
145	East Jordan	1998
137	Hemlock	2001

CLOSEST TEAM FINISH
1	Imlay City/Napoleon	1945
1	Charlevoix/Sandusky	1990
2	Camden-Frontier/Lake Odessa	1957
2	St Louis/Freeland	1979

BIGGEST WINNING TEAM MARGIN
101	Kalamazoo Christian/Stockbridge	1981
99	Reese/AA St Thomas	1964
95	AA St Thomas/Napoleon & Remus CH	1963
85	Charlevoix/Rogers City	1983
85	Grandville Calvin Ch/Lansing Catholic	2010

BOYS CLASS D / DIVISION 4

Coach Rob Glover (back, dark shirt) guided Kingsley to the first Class D state title.

1974 CLASS D BOYS

The first Class D state championships was run at the same site as the Class A race. Kingsley coach Rob Glover told his local paper, "The win Saturday will pull a lot more guys for cross country. I'm kind of disappointed not all the schools in our conference offer cross country, because that holds the competition down. These kids rank right up there with football and basketball players."

It was the first state title for Kingsley in any sport; on their return to town the team was escorted by the community's firetrucks.

Grand Blanc Golf Club, Grand Blanc, Nov. 2
"Ideal" weather.
1974 BOYS CLASS D TEAMS
1. Kingsley 121
2. Buckley 126
3. Grass Lake 131
4. Centreville 145
5. Dansville 158
6. Hesperia 182

1974 BOYS CLASS D INDIVIDUALS
1. Ken St John (Morrice)12 .... 15:44
2. Matt Pringle (Buckley) 15:46
3. Stan Sidor (Kingsley)12 .... 16:01
4. Bill Lannen (Mt Pleasant Sacred Heart)11 .. 16:04
5. Dale Buist (Allendale) 16:14
6. Ken Christmas (Covert) 16:18
7. Tom Stuart (Mason County Eastern) 16:20
8. Randy Webber (Buckley) 16:21
9. Tony Candy (Flint Holy Rosary) 16:27
10. Gerald Glinsky (Grass Lake) 16:31
11. Don Dewald (Akron-Fairgrove) 16:34
12. Larry Crouch (Grass Lake) 16:36
13. John Seppala (Lawton) 16:37
14. Toebin Wine (Kingsley)12 .... 16:38
15. Woody Tyler (North Muskegon) 16:39
23. Dave Heim (Kingsley)10 .... 16:59
29. Mike Zenner (Kingsley)10 .... 17:12
52. Dan Hawley (Kingsley)12 .... 18:08
54. Robin Wine (Kingsley) 18:14
56. Bob Milne (Kingsley)12 .... 18:21
(74 runners)

1975 CLASS D BOYS

Sacred Heart's Bill Lannen, who had won his regional in 15:35, stayed true to form to capture the state final race in 15:34. The next spring he would win the Class D mile in 4:24.5.

Chuck King's Concord crew, 12th in Class C the previous year, moved down to score a 13-point win over Elk Rapids. Mike Jurasek, in third overall, was named the team race champion as Lannen and Bob Duerkson were both running as individuals. Later on Jurasek would become a successful coach at Albion and Concord, and would also direct the Michigan Indoor Track Series.

Grand Blanc Golf Club, Grand Blanc, Nov. 1
1975 BOYS CLASS D TEAMS
1. Concord 56
2. Elk Rapids 69
3. Centreville 83
4. Grass Lake .... ns
5. Bear Lake .... ns
6. Dansville .... ns
7. Kingsley .... ns
8. Flint Holy Rosary .... ns
9. Fulton-Middleton .... ns

1975 BOYS CLASS D INDIVIDUALS
1. Bill Lannen (Mt Pleasant Sacred Heart)12 ..... 15:34
2. Bob Duerkson (Mancelona) 15:49
3. Mike Jurasek (Concord)12 .... 15:50
4. Alfonso Vasquez (Elk Rapids) .... nt
6. Don Marker (Elk Rapids) .... nt
8. Dean Christiansen (Potterville) .... nt
8?. Tony Candy (Flint Holy Rosary) .... nt
10. Mike Zenner (Kingsley) .... nt

1976 CLASS D BOYS

In Class D, the race was finally split so that the team race could be scored without worrying about individual qualifiers. Potterville's Kim Dahlgren, second in the team race, had played nearly the entire football game the night before, but still led his team to the win.

Dahlgren had taken a hard hit on an out-of-bounds play the night before. Said coach Tom Swanson, "It took a minute for Kim to get up and I said, 'Oh no, there goes the state championship,' but he shook it off and came back real tough today."

Bear Lake's chances were diminished the week before when its Nos. 1 and 3 runners were in a car accident.

Indian Trails GC, Grand Rapids, Nov. 6 □
1976 BOYS CLASS D TEAMS
1. Potterville 68
2. Concord 101
3. Kingsley 119
4. Bear Lake 128
5. Dansville 135
6. Centreville 144
7. Mt Pleasant Sacred Heart 147
8. Detroit Temple Christian 154
9. Ann Arbor Greenhills 163
10. Southfield Christian 187

1976 BOYS CLASS D TEAM RACE
1. Cameron Owens (Concord)12 .... 16:11
2. Kim Dahlgren (Potterville) 16:22
3. Dean Christiansen (Potterville) 16:31
4. Mike Zenner (Kingsley) 16:33
5. Robert Kuntzman (Southfield Christian) ... 16:34
6. Rob Utterbach (Mt Pleasant Sacred Heart) ... 16:36
7. Kevin Larson (Southfield Christian) 16:37
8. Tom Seyler (Kingsley) 16:43
9. Steve VanLotan (Potterville) 16:45
10. Dave Watters (Mt Pleasant Sacred Heart) ... 16:47
11. Randy Mister (Bear Lake) 16:49

1976 BOYS CLASS D INDIVIDUAL RACE
1. Randy Perkins (Webberville)11 .... 16:05
2. Bob Duerkson (Mancelona)11 .... 16:19
3. John Whitney (Alanson) 16:30
4. David VanHouten (McBain Christian) 16:48

1977 CLASS D BOYS

The top two teams in Class D tied, with the tie-breaker going to four-man scoring. Sacred Heart came out on top, 26-28.

Randy Perkins of Webberville ran to a dominating individual win, despite being only second in his regional.

Indian Trails GC, Grand Rapids, Nov. 5 □
1977 BOYS CLASS D TEAMS
1. Mt Pleasant Sacred Heart 46
2. Akron-Fairgrove 46
3. Concord 104
4. Southfield Christian 144
5. Potterville 157
6. Fulton-Middleton 163
7. Bear Lake 169
8. Mancelona 197
9. Ann Arbor Greenhills 202
10. Lansing Christian 213
11. Ann Arbor Richard 230
12. Kingsley 308

1977 BOYS CLASS D TEAM RACE
1. Jerry Curtis (Akron-Fairgrove)12 .... 15:42
2. Jim Hubbard (Concord) 16:03
3. Bob Duerkson (Mancelona) 15:46
4. Phil Bedford (Akron-Fairgrove)10 .... 16:07
5. Bob Utterbach (Mt Pleasant Sacred H) .. 16:10
6. Dave Watters (Mt Pleasant Sacred H) ... 16:12
7. Dennis Cruz (Mt Pleasant Sacred H) 16:13
8. Rusty Schaefer (Mt Pleasant Sacred H) .. 16:15
9. James Slavik (Fulton-Middleton) 16:20
10. Bill Hubbard (Concord) 16:24
11. Kyle Detmers (Akron-Fairgrove) 16:27

1977 BOYS CLASS D INDIVIDUAL RACE
1. Randy Perkins (Webberville)12 .... 15:23
2. Rod Brevard (Detroit East Catholic)11 .. 15:56
3. Matt Valding (Detroit Country Day) 16:11
4. Roger Smith (Litchfield) 16:22

1978 CLASS D BOYS

East Catholic's Rod Brevard had the fastest time of the day in the team race at 15:19, but the most exciting racing came in the individual run, where Sacred Heart's Rusty Schafer and Morrice's Brad McPherson went to the wire, each clocking 15:43.9.

Akron-Fairgrove, coached by Jerry Lasceski, made it to the top of the team standings, but just barely, edging Mancelona by three, with Ann Arbor Greenhills another point back.

Faulkwood Shores GC, Howell, Nov. 4 □
1978 BOYS CLASS D TEAMS
1. Akron-Fairgove 96
2. Mancelona 99
3. Ann Arbor Greenhills 100
4. Flint Holy Rosary 107
5. Bear Lake 137
6. Concord 173
7. Detroit Country Day 179
8. Kingsley 199
9. Ann Arbor Richard 224
10. Lansing Christian 228
11. Lawton 235
12. Detroit DePorres 249
13. Detroit East Catholic 280
14. Southfield Christian 342

1978 BOYS CLASS D TEAM RACE
1. Rod Brevard (Detroit East Catholic)12 ... 15:19
2. Phil Bedford (Akron-Fairgove)11 .... 15:31
3. Eric Miller (Ann Arbor Greenhills) 15:59
4. Paul Ziehm (Bear Lake) 16:03
5. Kevin Gorman (Concord) 16:11
6. Kirk Becker (Akron-Fairgove) 16:14
7. Tom Seyler (Kingsley) 16:16
8. Jim Hubbard (Concord) 16:19
9. Dan Biehl (Mancelona) 16:20
10. Kyle Detmers (Akron-Fairgove) 16:21
11. Mark Salgat (Flint Holy Rosary) 16:24

1978 BOYS CLASS D INDIVIDUAL RACE
1. Rusty Schafer (Mt Pleasant Sacred Heart)11 15:44
2. Brad McPherson (Morrice) 15:44
3. Duane Baas (McBain Christian) 16:09
4. Jon deGroot (Dansville) 16:20

1979 CLASS D BOYS

With lead runner Eric Miller finishing first, Ann Arbor Greenhills, coached by future Eastern Michigan University head John Goodridge, won convincingly with 67 points.

In the individual run, Rusty Schafer defended his title with the fastest time of the day.

Potterville HS, Potterville, Nov. 3 □
1979 BOYS CLASS D TEAMS
1. Ann Arbor Greenhills 67
2. Lansing Christian 101
3. Kingsley 113
4. Detroit Country Day 116
5. Fairview 123
6. Saranac 130
7. Ann Arbor Richard 138
8. Potterville 148
9. Bear Lake 167

1979 BOYS CLASS D TEAM RACE
1. Eric Miller (Ann Arbor Greenhills)12 ..... 15:47
2. Greg Miller (Potterville)11 .... 15:52
3. Andy Moyad (Ann Arbor Greenhills) 16:00
4. Bob Bills (Fairview) 16:01
5. John Seyler (Kingsley) 16:04
6. Mike Carr (Ann Arbor Richard) 16:05
7. Trent Chipman (Saranac) 16:07
8. Matt Balding (Detroit Country Day) 16:08
9. Mark King (Kingsley) 16:13

1979 BOYS CLASS D INDIVIDUAL RACE
1. Rusty Schafer (Mt Pleasant Sacred Heart)12 ... 15:43

2. Carl Mayhand (Mason County Eastern)9 ... 15:57
3. Rob Moore (Allendale) 16:06
4. Stan Iseler (Kinde North Huron) 16:09
5. Hayne Luck (Centreville) 16:10
6. Tom Kirkman (Saginaw Mich Lutheran) ... 16:13

1980 CLASS D BOYS

Coach Rob Glover guided Kingsley to another Class D win, topping Centreville by 13 points. "Our goals were high and our expectations even higher," said the coach.

For the second year in a row, it was two Millers in front. This time St. Philip's Tim Miller dueled for most of the distance with Potterville's Greg Miller. With 100 yards to go, Greg shot into the lead, but Tim recovered to catch him at the line.

Said St. Philip coach Dave Barrett, "I would have to say this was Tim's best race. He ran as hard as he could."

Mason Count Eastern's Carl Mayhand dominated the individual run.

Potterville HS, Potterville, Nov. 1 □
1980 BOYS CLASS D TEAMS
1. Kingsley 97
2. Centreville 110
3. Ann Arbor Greenhills 116
4. Detroit Country Day 117
5. Battle Creek St Philip 138
6. Lansing Christian 141
7. Saginaw Valley Lutheran 143
8. Potterville 156
9. Fairview 176
10. Alanson 211
11. Walkerville 237

1980 BOYS CLASS D TEAM RACE
1. Tim Miller (Battle Creek St Phillip)11 .... 16:20
2. Greg Miller (Potterville)12 .... 16:21
3. Bill Duren (Ann Arbor Greenhills) 16:34
4. Bob Mills (Fairview) 16:39
5. Mark King (Kingsley)12 .... 16:40
6. George Sehl (Saginaw Valley Lutheran) ... 16:43
7. Matt Balding (Detroit Country Day) 16:44
8. Alan Bradford (Alanson) 16:46
9. Don Cook (Detroit Country Day) 16:48
10. Perry Horton (Centreville) 16:48
11. Randy Payne (Walkerville) .... nt
12. Tm Roekle (Saginaw Valley Lutheran) ..... nt
16. John Van Hoose (Kingsley)10 .... 17:10
18. John Seyler (Kingsley)10 .... 17:15

28. Scott Hoeflin (Kingsley)12 .... 17:33
38. Gary Rawlings (Kingsley)11 .... 17:36
48. Bill Belmore (Kingsley)11 .... 18:04
60. Tom Strong (Kingsley)10 .... 18:24

1980 BOYS CLASS D INDIVIDUAL RACE

1. Carl Mayhand (Mason County Eastern)10 .... 16:07
2. Kevin Morey (Morrice) 16:35
3. John Mullally (Flint Holy Rosary) 16:41
4. Dave Himlin (Ann Arbor Richard) 16:45
5. Mark Salgat (Flint Holy Rosary) 16:46
7. Ron Landry (Oakland Christian) 16:52
10. Mike Miller (Pontiac Catholic) 17:03
11. Joe VanBonn (Ann Arbor Richard) 17:09
15. Matt Anhut (Ann Arbor Richard) 17:17

1981 CLASS D BOYS

After winning the Class C title the year before, Chuck King's Concord squad captured Class D honors with a 22-point margin.

Tim Miller of Battle Creek St. Philip defended his individual race title with the fastest time of the day.

Johnson Park, Wyoming, Oct. 31 ☐
1981 BOYS CLASS D TEAMS

1. Concord 76
2. Centreville 98
3. Ann Arbor Greenhills 102
4. Lansing Christian 111
5. Dansville 126
6. Potterville 144
7. Flint Holy Rosary 155
8. Ann Arbor Richard 168
9. Southfield Christian 206
10. Kingsley 213
11. Suttons Bay 241
12. Mason County Eastern 326

1981 BOYS CLASS D TEAM RACE

1. Ben Szporluk (Ann Arbor Greenhills)12 .... 16:38
2. Charles Grimes (Concord) 16:55
3. Dave Waterstradt (Dansville) 16:51
4. Steve Hubbard (Concord) 16:51
5. John Mullally (Flint Holy Rosary) 16:53
6. Doug Kirby (Centreville) 17:07
7. J. Greers (Lansing Christian) 17:08
8. P. Ross (Ann Arbor Greenhills) 17:10
9. C. Ruthruft (Potterville) 17:12

1981 BOYS CLASS D INDIVIDUAL RACE

1. Tim Miller (Battle Creek St Phillip)12 .... 16:18
2. Rob Moore (Allendale) 16:56
3. Ron Landry (Oakland Christian) 17:01
4. M. Miller (Pontiac Catholic) 17:03
5. K. Morfy (Morrice) 17:08
6. S. Messenger (Reading) 17:09
7. J. Barden (Kingston) 17:12
8. D. Simmons (Ann Arbor Richard) 17:12

1982 CLASS D BOYS

In Class D, Steve Hubbard of Concord upset heavily favored Rob Moore. "I was just as surprised as anyone else," said Hubbard. Coach Chuck King's Concord boys won their second straight, this time with only one senior in his top 5; Concord also made history by winning the girls' title as well. Times were slowed significantly by snow and ice.

In the individual run, Paul Beasley finished 2nd despite suffering a fractured skull earlier in the season.

Johnson Park, Wyoming, Nov. 6 ☐
1982 BOYS CLASS D TEAMS

1. Concord 55
2. Southfield Christian 91
3. Potterville 108
4. Wyoming Lee 127
5. Lansing Christian 136
6. Centreville 138
7. Ann Arbor Greenhills 166
8. Fairview 187
9. Allendale 193
10. Pontiac Christian 227
11. Manton 228
12. Ann Arbor Richard 253

1982 BOYS CLASS D TEAM RACE

1. Steve Hubbard (Concord)11 .... 16:57
2. Rob Moore (Allendale) 17:12
3. Doug Kirby (Centreville) 17:14
4. P. Ross (Ann Arbor Greenhills) 17:17
5. J. Walsh (Southfield Christian) 17:24
6. K. Christianson (Potterville) 17:31
7. Mike Kraus (Concord)11 .... 17:33
8. D. Harkema (Lansing Christian) 17:34
9. P. Horton (Centreville) 17:35
10. R. Evans (Fairview) 17:39
12. Tom Baird (Concord)12 .... 17:41
16. Kevin Schupbach (Concord)11 .... 17:45
18. Tony Hill (Concord)9 .... 17:53
56. Jeff Bauman (Concord)11 .... nt
57. Rusty Pelham (Concord)10 .... nt

1982 BOYS CLASS D INDIVIDUAL RACE

1. Dan Ebright (Suttons Bay)11 .... 17:00
2. Paul Beasley (Battle Creek St Phillip)10 .... 17:12
3. Scott Voelker (Flint Holy Rosary) 17:28
4. J. Mullally (Flint Holy Rosary) 17:33
5. D. Huckins (Dansville) 17:35

1983 CLASS D BOYS

Ann Arbor Greenhills won by just 7 points in a record for the lowest score ever. Said coach Bruce Dyer, "It's a nice ending to a long season. We reached our peak earlier in the season and I was a little worried after the regional meet. I felt we may not have been strong enough to win the state, but our kids came through."

Great Lakes Bible College, Lansing, Nov. 5 ☒
1983 BOYS CLASS D TEAMS

1. Ann Arbor Greenhills 44
2. Concord 51
3. Southfield Christian 84
4. Battle Creek St Phillip 136
5. Kingsley 141
6. Lansing Christian 143
7. Reading 154
8. Morrice 183
9. Akron-Fairgrove 187
10. Manton 218

1983 BOYS CLASS D TEAM RACE

1. Steve Hubbard (Concord)12 .... 15:59
2. Peter Ross (Ann Arbor Greenhills) 16:16
3. Shawn Messenger (Reading) 16:22
4. Voorhees (Ann Arbor Greenhills) 16:22
5. Paul Beasley (Battle Creek St Phillip)11 .... 16:25
6. Rosenthal (Ann Arbor Greenhills) 16:44
7. Attard (Southfield Christian) 16:46
8. O'Daniel (Battle Creek St Phillip) 16:50
9. Dace (Southfield Christian) 16:53
10. Pelham (Concord) 16:54
14. David Dubin (Ann Arbor Greenhills)10 .... 17:01
18. David Dimcheff (Ann Arbor Greenhills) 17:11
23. Fadiman (Ann Arbor Greenhills) 17:23
59. Bjorn Fadiman (Ann Arbor Greenhills)10 .... 18:50

1983 BOYS CLASS D INDIVIDUAL RACE

1. Dan Ebright (Suttons Bay)12 .... 16:11
2. Ron Lichti (Potterville) 16:45
3. David Huckins (Dansville) 16:48
4. Ringmar (Centreville) 16:52
5. Kiessel (Suttons Bay) 16:57

1984 CLASS D BOYS

After placing second the year before, Concord bounced back to the top spot with an impressive 65-point performance. The Yellowjackets also captured the girls' title.

"When it happened in '82," said coach Chuck King, "I thought it was a once-in-a-lifetime thing. This is just super. Both the boys and girls ran as a team. Nobody ran for themselves. That was the key."

Jeff Thomas, a Mancelona sophomore, had the best time of the day. Said coach Mark Nixon, "He hasn't realized his full potential. In all his races, there was no one to push him."

Grace Bible College, Lansing, Nov. 3 ☐
1984 BOYS CLASS D TEAMS

1. Concord 65
2. Mancelona 72
3. Ann Arbor Greenhills 83
4. Morrice 105
5. Suttons Bay 120
6. Kingsley 128
7. Battle Creek St Phillip 136
8. Southfield Christian 158

1984 BOYS CLASS D TEAM RACE

1. Jeff Thomas (Mancelona)10 .... 16:05
2. Tony Hill (Concord)11 .... 16:19
3. Dave Dubin (Ann Arbor Greenhills)11 .... 16:31
4. Rick Hughes (Suttons Bay) 16:35
5. Rusty Pelham (Concord)12 .... 16:47
6. Ed Kiessel (Suttons Bay) 16:51
7. Matt Holappa (Ann Arbor Greenhills) 16:59
8. Dan Cobb (Southfield Christian) 17.05
9. David Dimcheff (Ann Arbor Greenhills) 17:06
10. Ryan Watson (Mancelona) 17:09
14. Richard Felkey (Concord)10 .... 17:17
18. Ron Roth (Concord)11 .... 17:28
26. Mike Szamrej (Concord)10 .... 17:55
33. Todd Nichols (Concord)9 .... nt
51. Paul Nichols (Concord)12 .... nt

1984 BOYS CLASS D INDIVIDUAL RACE

1. Dan Dukes (Detroit East Catholic)12 .... 16:45
2. Steve Bierstetel (Fowler)10 .... 16:49
3. Ed Chalut (Flint Holy Rosary) 17:07
4. Corey Champion (Reading) 17:08
5. Ernie Mack (Detroit Bethesda) 17:10

1985 B CLASS D BOYS

Greenhills prevailed, holding off Fowler by 10 points. It was the first trip to the state finals for the Fowler team.

Fowler's Steve Bierstetel, runner-up in the individual race the year before, came through for the win.

West Shore CC, Muskegon, Nov. 2 ☐
1985 BOYS CLASS D TEAMS

1. Ann Arbor Greenhills 52
2. Fowler 62
3. Kingsley 78
4. Colon 87
5. Potterville 144
6. Webberville 164
7. Akron-Fairgrove 166
8. Mason County Eastern 167
9. Alba 216

1985 BOYS CLASS D TEAM RACE

1. Steve Bierstetel (Fowler)11 .... 17:30
2. Scott Kaukonen (Colon) 17:41
3. Ben Travis (Kingsley) 17:50
4. Matt Holappa (Ann Arbor Greenhills) 17:57
5. David Dimcheff (Ann Arbor Greenhills) 18:06
6. Steve Kaukonen (Colon) 18:16
7. David Dubin (Ann Arbor Greenhills)12 .... 18:21
8. Troy Irrer (Fowler)10 .... 18:22
9. Jon Hayes (Potterville) 18:22
15. John Ramsburgh (Ann Arbor Greenhills) 18:34
21. (Ann Arbor Greenhills) .... nt
29. (Ann Arbor Greenhills) .... nt
53. (Ann Arbor Greenills) .... nt

1985 BOYS CLASS D INDIVIDUAL RACE

1. Bob Brent (Hale)11 .... 17:29

2. Darrell Springer (Manton)........17:37
3. Greg O'Daniel (Battle Creek St Phillip)........17:44
4. Dan Cobb (Southfield Christian)........17:48
5. Darrell Hart (Morrice)........17:52
6. Hal Page (Reading)........18:12
7. Kevin Drummond (Morrice)........18:15

1986 CLASS D BOYS

The Class D race was the closest ever, with the tie between the top two teams being broken by the sixth man, 24th to 39th, Third place was only two points back.

Individually, Mancelona's Jeff Thomas recaptured the title he had first won as a 10th grader. He had to beat defending champion Steve Bierstetel of Fowler to do it.

West Shore Comm. College, Muskegon, Nov. 1 ☐
1986 BOYS CLASS D TEAMS
1. Concord........84
2. Kingsley........84
3. Fowler........86
4. Colon........94
5. Mancelona........104
6. Mason County Eastern........148
7. Whitmore Lake........159
8. Saginaw Michigan Lutheran........165
9. Ann Arbor Greenhills........170

1986 BOYS CLASS D TEAM RACE
1. Jeff Thomas (Mancelona)12........16:47
2. Steve Bierstetel (Fowler)12........17:00
3. Jared Glover (Kingsley)........17:04
4. John Rumsburgh (Ann Arbor Greenhills)........17:05
5. Ken Matzea (Mason County Eastern)........17:11
6. Scott Kaukonen (Colon)........17:24
7. Mike Szamrej (Concord)12........17:25
8. Brisa Ely (Whitmore Lake)........17:27
9. Troy Irrer (Fowler)........17:28
10. Steve Kaukonen (Colon)........17:34
15. Richard Felkey (Concord)12........17:47
16. Mike Bauman (Concord)........17:50
21. Todd Nichols (Concord)11........18:07
25. David Jordon (Concord)........18:22
27. Nichols (Concord)........18:24
29. English (Concord)........18:33

1986 BOYS CLASS D INDIVIDUAL RACE
1. Bob Brent (Hale)12........17:12
2. Gordon Maitland (GP University Liggett)........17:22
3. Jon Hayes (Potterville)........17:25
4. Rob Kauffman (Schoolcraft)........17:29
5. Rob Thomas (Kingston)........17:31

1987 CLASS D BOYS

After losing on a tiebreaker the year before, Rob Glover's Kingsley team managed a 19-point win over Suttons Bay. It would be their last year in Class D, as their enrollment would boost them to Class C the following year.

Morrice junior Keith McGuire produced the day's fastest time for the win. His favorite sport, he told the papers, was basketball.

Wyoming, Nov. 7 ☐
1987 BOYS CLASS D TEAMS
1. Kingsley........84
2. Suttons Bay........103
3. Colon........135
4. Potterville........137
5. Fowler........163
6. Concord........171
7. Lutheran Westland........174
8. Mason County Eastern........192
9. Reading........210
10. Whitmore Lake........230
11. Mesick........264
12. Akron-Fairgrove........281
13. Morrice........292
14. White Cloud........298
15. Fairview........357

1987 BOYS CLASS D TEAM RACE
1. Keith McGuire (Morrice)11........16:41
2. Pat Hoban (Suttons Bay)12........16:53
3. Ken Matzen (Mason County Eastern)12........16:54
4. Steve Laninga (White Cloud)11........17:04
5. Troy Irrer (Fowler)12........17:09
6. Jon Hayes (Potterville)12........17:15
7. Steve Kaukonen (Colon)12........17:21
8. Jared Glover (Kingsley)10........17:23
9. Shawn Hoban (Suttons Bay)12........17:31
10. Brian Muth (Kingsley)12........17:34
11. Gerber (Fairview)12........17:35
12. Becker (Fowler)11........17:38
13. Adam Schoech (Kingsley)10........17:39
25. Jaime Dudash (Kingsley)10........18:03
28. Dennis Muth (Kingsley)11........18:12
50. Steve McGregor (Kingsley)12........nt
51. Dale Muth (Kingsley)10........nt

1987 BOYS CLASS D INDIVIDUAL RACE
1. Matt Joseph (Ann Arbor Greenhills)12........17:05
2. Mike Shepardson (Wyoming Lee)12........17:29
3. Kurt Hanke (Bridgman)12........17:55

1988 CLASS D BOYS

Fowler won big with its 52-point tally; it was the school's first. Guided by Kim Spalsbury, the Eagles put together a 42-point margin ahead of Gabriel Richard.

In the individual race, Keith McGuire of Morrice was able to defend his title, but knee problems had curtailed his running. The next spring he would skip track to play baseball for the first time.

Memorial Park Frankenmuth, Nov. 5 ⊠
1988 BOYS CLASS D TEAMS
1. Fowler........52
2. Ann Arbor Richard........94
3. Whitmore Lake........106
4. Mason County Eastern........133
5. Potterville........147
6. Reading........174
7. Lutheran Westland........205
8. Manton........210
9. Pentwater........216
10. Akron-Fairgrove........231
11. Schoolcraft........240
12. Mesick........265
13. Webberville........294
14. Alanson........333

1988 BOYS CLASS D TEAM RACE
1. Gurvinder Singh (Ann Arbor Richard)12........17:00
2. Tim Becker (Fowler)........17:29
3. Jay Caruso (Whitmore Lake)........17:37
4. Tom Becker (Fowler)........17:42
5. Jeff Shumway (Ann Arbor Richard)........17:47
6. Rick Weslock (Schoolcraft)........17:50
7. Wayne Moffit (Manton)........17:51
8. Preston Pike (Mesick)........17:57
9. Bruce Ely (Whitmore Lake)........17:58
10. Stephen Hankins (Mason County Eastern)........18:02
11. Doug Corcoran (Reading)10........18:03
12. Robert Tucker (Potterville)........18:04
13. Garrick Pahl (Fowler)........18:09
14. Terry Schneider (Fowler)........18:11
19. Brian Thelen (Fowler)........18:25
23. Kevin Hainer (Fowler)........18:35
29. Tony Feldpausch (Fowler)........18:47

1988 BOYS CLASS D INDIVIDUAL RACE
1. Keith McGuire (Morrice)12........17:47
2. Jason Eisenlohr (Bear Lake)9........18:04
3. Kevin Way (Pittsford)12........18:20

1989 CLASS D BOYS

Fowler repeated, this time with an even better score.

Bear Lake's Jason Eisenlohr won the team race, and Mesick's Preston Pike the individual run. Their times, nearly identical, led fans to wonder who would have prevailed in a combined race.

Memorial Park, Frankenmuth, Nov. 4 ☐
1989 BOYS CLASS D TEAMS
1. Fowler........47
2. Pentwater........80
3. Potterville........109
4. Suttons Bay........130
5. Manton........167
6. Lutheran Westland........194
7. Fairview........211
8. Webberville........215
9. Burr Oak........243
10. Ann Arbor Richard........246
11. Detroit Holy Redeemer........251
12. Alanson........264
13. Bear Lake........277
14. Colon........328
15. Grass Lake........396

1989 BOYS CLASS D TEAM RACE
1. Jason Eisenlohr (Bear Lake)10........16:56
2. Mike Kremsreiter (Potterville)11........17:06
3. Ted Feldpausch (Fowler)10........17:20
4. Tom Becker (Fowler)11........17:20
5. Steve Lloyd-Jones (Pentwater)10........17:32
6. Terry Schneider (Fowler)11........17:36
7. Steve Watkins (Lutheran Westland)11........17:42
8. Jim McHugh (Pentwater)12........17:44
9. Pat Kohler (Suttons Bay)10........17:44
10. Erin Irwin (Detroit Holy Redeemer)12........17:47
11. Don Johnson (Manton)11........17:48
16. Tony Feldpausch (Fowler)........nt
18. Bryan Thelen (Fowler)........nt

1989 BOYS CLASS D INDIVIDUAL RACE
1. Preston Pike (Mesick)12........16:55
2. Doug Corcoran (Reading)11........16:58
3. Mike Richardson (Central Lake)11........16:58
4. Ryan Stevens (Allendale)12........17:48

1990 CLASS D BOYS

Kim Spalsbury's Fowler squad did it again, this time in the lowest score in meet history to capture a record third-straight. "The kids were outstanding, and really ran like this all season," he said. "The seven seniors on the team gave us tremendous leadership."

Central Lake's Mike Richardson, running in the individual race, had the fastest time. He said, "I wanted to do better than last year. I felt satisfied. It's what I've worked for, for two years."

Memorial Park, Frankenmuth, Nov. 3 ☐
1990 BOYS CLASS D TEAMS
1. Fowler........42
2. Pentwater........153
3. Burr Oak........156
4. Reading........170
5. Whitmore Lake........172
6. Potterville........185
7. Grass Lake........192
8. Camden-Frontier........195
9. Bear Lake........197
10. Suttons Bay........246
11. Fairview........250
12. Manton........253
13. Ann Arbor Richard........290
14. Akron-Fairgrove........308
15. Boyne Falls........318
16. Ann Arbor Greenhills........360

1990 BOYS CLASS D TEAM RACE
1. Doug Corcoran (Reading)12........16:49
2. Ted Feldpausch (Fowler)11........16:56
3. Jason Eisenlohr (Bear Lake)11........17:00
4. Lloyd Jones (Pentwater)........17:04
5. Tom Becker (Fowler)........17:06
6. Nordijk (Whitmore Lake)........17:10
7. Eric Bierstetel (Fowler)9........17:11
8. McGinn (Grass Lake)........17:11

9. Miller (Camden-Frontier) ...17:18
10. Androl (Akron-Fairgrove) ...17:23
11. McHall (Burr Oak) ...17:26
12. Terry Schnieder (Fowler) ...17:33
13. Mike Kremstreiter (Potterville) ...17:34

1990 BOYS CLASS D INDIVIDUAL RACE
1. Mike Richardson (Central Lake)12 ...16:42
2. Casey Shay (Central Lake)10 ...17:25
3. Dave Babcock (Webberville) ...17:52

1991 CLASS D BOYS

The Fowler streak ended, and Bear Lake did it convincingly, breaking the record for lowest score in meet history. The Lakers put five into the top 14.

Soph Eric Bierstetel led a Fowler 1-2 in the bitter cold despite finishing 2nd at his regional and 3rd at his conference.

"I was happy with my run," said Bierstetel. "For a day like today, Ted and I ran well. We thought that maybe the cold could work as an advantage for our team. Everyone has to run in this weather too. You just needed the right attitude."

Bath HS, Bath, Nov. 2 ☐
1991 BOYS CLASS D TEAMS
1. Bear Lake ...40
2. Suttons Bay ...78
3. Fowler ...93
4. Fairview ...154
5. Manton ...187
6. Whitmore Lake ...193
7. Akron-Fairgrove ...212
8. Grass Lake ...228
9. Boyne Falls ...242
10. Reading ...245
11. Ann Arbor Richard ...249
12. Schoolcraft ...270
13. Camden-Frontier ...270
14. Ann Arbor Greenhills ...274
15. Pittsford ...285

1991 BOYS CLASS D TEAM RACE
1. Eric Bierstetel (Fowler)10 ...16:32
2. Ted Feldpausch (Fowler)12 ...16:41
3. Jason Eisenlohr (Bear Lake)12 ...16:56
4. Kyle Stallman (Suttons Bay) ...16:56
5. Jason Major (Fairview) ...16:56
6. Ryan Sink (Bear Lake) ...16:57
7. Tom Parks (Suttons Bay) ...17:02
8. Dan Geeting (Bear Lake) ...17:03
9. Steve Milliron (Bear Lake) ...17:06
10. Joe Westerbrook (Boyne Falls) ...17:09
11. Jason Bissonette (Whitmore Lake) ...17:14
12. Jay Sieland (Fairview) ...17:15
13. John Parks (Suttons Bay) ...17:16
14. Jason Vaughn (Bear Lake) ...17:16
15. Marty Ginn (Grass Lake) ...17:17

1991 BOYS CLASS D INDIVIDUAL RACE
1. Casey Shay (Central Lake)11 ...17:10
2. Tom Read (Traverse City St Francis) ...17:17
3. Adam Dusseau (Ottawa Lake Whiteford) ...17:19

1992 CLASS D BOYS

Under cloudy skies with temperatures in the mid-30s, Bear Lake defended its title handily, beating Fowler by 51 points.

Fowler's Eric Bierstetel took the lead at the mile mark and rolled to a 9-second win. "I wanted to get out kind of slow at the mile, but I kind of got dragged out pretty quick and that took me away from my strategy," he said. "But it worked pretty well. I felt really good."

Bath HS, Bath, Nov. 7 ☐
1992 BOYS CLASS D TEAMS
1. Bear Lake ...55
2. Fowler ...106
3. Pittsford ...127
4. Bath ...183
5. Akron-Fairgrove ...190
6. Whitmore Lake ...195
7. Ann Arbor Richard ...201
8. McBain ...210
9. Grass Lake ...215
10. Camden-Frontier ...232
11. Manton ...239
12. Reading ...257
13. Burr Oak ...266
14. Mason County Eastern ...285
15. Boyne Falls ...331

1992 BOYS CLASS D TEAM RACE
1. Eric Bierstetel (Fowler)11 ...16:15
2. Marty McGinn (Grass Lake)11 ...16:24
3. Jason Vaughn (Bear Lake) ...16:32
4. Jake Snyder (Camden-Frontier) ...16:36
5. Matt Carr (Pittsford) ...16:37
6. Ryan Fink (Bear Lake) ...16:37
7. Jason Bisonette (Whitmore Lake) ...16:38
8. Jason Smith (Fowler) ...16:39
9. Jeff Beuche (Ann Arbor Richard) ...16:45
10. Steven Milliron (Bear Lake) ...16:47
11. Daniel Eeting (Bear Lake) ...16:51
12. Joe Ensing (McBain) ...16:52
13. Mark Becker (Akron-Fairgrove) ...16:55
25. Brian McCarthy (Bear Lake) ...17:36

1992 BOYS CLASS D INDIVIDUAL RACE
1. Casey Shay (Central Lake)12 ...16:27
2. Tom Read (Traverse City St Francis) ...16:41
3. Matt Shasta (Miles) ...16:55

1993 CLASS D BOYS

Coach Pat Richardson's Grass Lake team put together a dazzling 49-point performance to win its first state title.

Grass Lake's Marty McGinn took the win after two-time champ Eric Bierstetel was spiked midway through the race; he dropped from the lead and limped home in 2nd, ankle bleeding.

Winning the individual run was Central Lake Ryan Shay, who became the first 9th-grader to win a Class D title.

Marty McGinn led Grass Lake to its first title.

Pando Recreation Area, Wyoming, Nov. 6 ☐
1993 BOYS CLASS D TEAMS
1. Grass Lake ...49
2. Bear Lake ...68
3. McBain ...89
4. Fowler ...143
5. Akron-Fairgrove ...168
6. Reading ...202
7. Pittsford ...205
8. Camden-Frontier ...218
9. Burr Oak ...219
10. Fairview ...234
11. St Joseph Lake Michigan Catholic ...244
12. Detroit Holy Redeemer ...289
13. Boyne Falls ...305
14. Buckley ...318

1993 BOYS CLASS D TEAM RACE
1. Marty McGinn (Grass Lake)12 ...16:49
2. Eric Bierstetel (Fowler)12 ...17:31
3. Craig Beerens (McBain) ...17:49
4. Tigran Bailey (Bear Lake) ...17:49
5. Joe Ensing (McBain) ...18:01
6. Matt Carr (Pittsford) ...18:02
7. Adam Delaney (Grass Lake)10 ...18:15
8. Chad Wehrran (Akron-Fairgrove) ...18:27
9. Trevor McGinn (Grass Lake)9 ...18:42
10. Jason Vaughn (Bear Lake) ...18:48
14. Justin Klavon (Grass Lake)10 ...18:57
18. Kevin Rogan (Grass Lake)9 ...19:11
24. Phil Shaltis (Grass Lake) ...19:27
48. ? (Grass Lake) ...20:14

1993 BOYS CLASS D INDIVIDUAL RACE
1. Ryan Shay (Central Lake)9 ...17:48
2. Grant Hill (New Buffalo) ...18:11
3. Aaron Woudenberg (Atlanta) ...18:23
4. Chad Stepaniuk (Freesoil) ...18:32
5. Tim Mahon (Harper Woods) ...18:42

1994 CLASS D BOYS

Trevor McGinn won the team race for Grass Lake, following up his older brother as the champion. The team scoring favored Bath, though, as coach Mel Comeau's Fighting Bees finished 34 points ahead of the defending Grass Lake squad.

Said Comeau before the race, "We've been in this situation before. I feel confident about this team and think we have a solid shot at winning the title."

Christian Reformed RC, Wyoming, Nov. 5 ☐
1994 BOYS CLASS D TEAMS
1. Bath ...54
2. Grass Lake ...88
3. Fowler ...103
4. Bear Lake ...109
5. Akron-Fairgrove ...155
6. Burr Oak ...170
7. New Buffalo ...183
8. Ann Arbor Greenhills ...188
9. Boyne Falls ...208
10. Ann Arbor Richard ...249
11. Manton ...269
12. Detroit Holy Redeemer ...280
13. Mason County Central ...311
14. Buckley ...319
15. Wyoming Lee ...344

1994 BOYS CLASS D TEAM RACE
1. Trevor McGinn (Grass Lake)10 ...16:44
2. Grant Hill (New Buffalo) ...16:58
3. Tigron Baler (Bear Lake) ...17:08
4. Jason Vaughan (Bear Lake) ...17:15
5. Zack Cooley (Bath)11 ...17:22
6. Chad Wehrman (Akron-Fairgrove) ...17:25
7. Joe DeVoogt (Ann Arbor Richard) ...17:28
8. Jim McKenna (Bath)12 ...17:34
9. Jarrod Miller (Fowler)11 ...17:34
10. Tim Clements (Bath)11 ...17:41
11. Scott Clark (Bath)12 ...17:44
20. Wayne Sager (Bath) ...18:14

1994 BOYS CLASS D INDIVIDUAL RACE
1. Ryan Shay (Central Lake)10 ...16:34
2. Elijah Eversole (Bridgman) ...17:31
3. Joshua Johnson (Bridgman) ...17:33
4. Marty Klein (Mendon) ...17:38

5. Steven Hendershot (Lansing Christian)12 ....17:43

1995 CLASS D BOYS

Ryan Shay of Central Lake won number three convincingly in 16:01 on the snowy course. On the team side, coach Pat Richardson guided Grass Lake to the top again in a one-point sqeaker against Fowler.

Said runner-up coach Kim Spalsbury, "There is nothing more disappointing than a one-point loss. The kids might be a little disappointed right now. They might not realize it tomorrow, or the next day, or next week, but somewhere down the line, they will realize that a second-place finish… is a magnificent accomplishment."

Christian Reformed RC, Wyoming, Nov. 4
1995 BOYS CLASS D TEAMS
1. Grass Lake...61
2. Fowler...62
3. Ann Arbor Greenhills................................116
4. Fairview..159
5. Pittsford..165
6. New Buffalo..208
7. Camden-Frontier....................................212
8. Detroit Holy Redeemer..........................229
9. Boyne Falls...234
10. Litchfield...242
11. Wyoming Lee..245
12. Mason County Eastern..........................245
13. Ann Arbor Richard.................................265
14. Central Lake..277
15. Buckley..346

1995 BOYS CLASS D TEAM RACE
1. Ryan Shay (Central Lake)11 ....16:01
2. Trevor McGinn (Grass Lake)11 ....16:16
3. Adam George (Fowler)12 ....17:02
4. Kris Brown (Ann Arbor Greenhills)10......17:09
5. Colin Dunham (Grass Lake)10 ....17:10
6. Ryan Bills (Litchifield)11 ....17:15
7. Jarred Miller (Fowler)12 ....17:15
8. John Shoup (Mason County Eastern)12........17:17
9. Sean Enneking (Fowler)11 ....17:16
10. Josh McDowell (Pittsford)10 ....17:33
11. Luke Robinson (Fairview)12 ....17:38
12. Kevin Rogan (Grass Lake)11 ....17:40
14. Aaron Usher (Grass Lake)12 ....17:42
28. Russell Rogan (Grass Lake)9 ....18:06
44. Ben Latocki (Grass Lake)10 ....18:36
75. Jon O'Neill (Grass Lake)9 ....19:37

1995 BOYS CLASS D INDIVIDUAL RACE
1. Alvin Marshall (Genessee)11..................17:11
2. Eric Potter (Adrian Lenawee Christian)11..........17:15
3. Nathan Woudenburg (Atlanta)12 ....17:20
4. Tony Herrera (Walkerville)11..................17:39

1996 CLASS D BOYS

With all of the Lower Peninsula races brought together at the same site for the first time since 1971, the meet was trumpeted as the largest prep sports event in Michigan history (1,800+ athletes). For the first time since 1960, the team and individual athletes raced together.

The medals had already been ordered for separate races, so officials awarded them as if the athletes had run separately. It was only a paper distinction. In Class D, 10th-placer Alvin Marshall (Genesee—17:01) was awarded the "individual" state championship.

Freezing temperatures and snow flurries had the athletes bundle up. The hottest erformance came from Ryan Shay of Central Lake, who became the first boy to win four individual cross country titles. Running solo, he covered the course faster than anyone in the bigger divisions.

Shay went on to become a 9-time All-American at Notre Dame. As a pro he won five USATF road titles and won the USA Running Circuit overall two years in a row. While running in Olympic Marathon Trials at the New York City Marathon in 2007, he tragically collapsed and died from a pre-existing enlarged heart condition.

Michigan Int. Speedway, Brooklyn, Nov. 2
1996 BOYS CLASS D TEAMS
1. Grass Lake...68
2. Pittsford..114
3. Ann Arbor Greenhills................................115
4. New Buffalo..151
5. Ann Arbor Richard..................................152
6. Whitmore Lake.......................................162
7. Walkerville...168
8. Detroit Holy Redeemer..........................188
9. Bear Lake...226
10. Fowler..232
11. Litchfield...242
12. Central Lake..263
13. Wolverine..284
14. Traverse City St Francis.........................395
15. Fairview...428

Central Lake's Ryan Shay became the first boy to win four individual state titles. He went on to star for Notre Dame and later became of the top marathoners in the U.S.

1996 BOYS CLASS D INDIVIDUALS
1. Ryan Shay (Central Lake)12 ....15:30
2. Trevor McGinn (Grass Lake)12 ....16:37
3. Ryan Bills (Litchfield)12 ....16:47
4. Kris Brown (Ann Arbor Greenhills)11 .....16:55
5. Colin Dunhan (Grass Lake)11................16:56
6. Tony Herrera (Walkerville)....................16:56
7. Nathan Shay (Central Lake)10...............16:57
8. Patrick Butler (New Buffalo)..................16:58
9. Sean Enneking (Fowler)12 ....17:00
=10. Alvin Marshall (Genessee)12 ....17:01
=10. David Gonzalas (Detroit Holy Redeemer)12....17:01
12. Kyle Lindley (New Buffalo)11 ....17:02
13. Adam Booth (Homer) 17:03
14. Robert Mitchell (Ubly)..........................17:06
15. Chris Ray (Ann Arbor Richard)11 ....17:08
17. Ryan Mayer (Grass Lake)10 ....17:17
30. Kevin Rogan (Grass Lake)12 ....17:36
37. Russell Rogan (Grass Lake)10 ....17:45
87. Tim Nylen (Grass Lake) 18:36
104. Jon O'Neill (Grass Lake)10 ....19:08

1997 CLASS D BOYS

With a steady rain falling and a mud-covered course, Grass Lake tied the record for consecutive wins at three straight. The battle went down to the wire, as New Buffalo, with the individual winner and 4th place, finished just six points behind.

"Looking at the regional results, we would have lost a dual meet to New Buffalo by three points," said coach Pat Richardson. "We knew it would be close. But we're blessed with some real tough kids who stayed aggressive and wouldn't lose."

Michigan Int. Speedway, Brooklyn, Nov. 1
1997 BOYS CLASS D TEAMS
1. Grass Lake...63
2. New Buffalo..69
3. Litchfield...129
4. Bear Lake...124
5. Whitmore Lake.......................................129
6. Walkerville...166
7. Central Lake..187
8. Wolverine...231
9. Buckley..238
10. Fowler..241
11. Colon...251
12. Detroit Holy Redeemer.........................316
13. Atlanta..316
14. Genesee..356
15. Carsonville-Port Sanilac.......................391

1997 BOYS CLASS D INDIVIDUALS
1. Kyle Lindley (New Buffalo)12 ....16:47
2. Colin Dunham (Grass Lake)12...............16:51
3. Nathan Shay (Central Lake)11 ....17:06
4. Patrick Butler (New Buffalo) 17:16
5. Michael Fultz (Burr Oak) 17:18
6. Aaron Compton (Whitmore Lake)..........17:21
7. Ryan Mayer (Grass Lake)11 ....17:23
8. Ron Hein (Galien)11...............................17:24
9. Ricardo Miller (Centreville)....................17:25
10. Josh Fuentes (Walkerville)10 ....17:26
11. Gabe Wordell (Warren Bethesda)11 ....17:27
12. Ryan O'Connor (Wolverine)11 ....17:32
13. Jason Whitney (Mendon) 17:32
14. Rick Mitsunaga (Harper Wds Gallagher)11 .17:38
15. Timothy Schroeder (Whitmore Lake) ...17:38
23. Nathan Usher (Grass Lake)10 ....17:45
25. Eric Ball (Grass Lake) 17:49
28. Russell Rogan (Grass Lake)11 ....17:52
34. Tim Nylen (Grass Lake) 18:03
41. Kris Kane (Grass Lake)9 ....18:13

1998 CLASS D BOYS

Bear Lake made it back to the winner's circle after six years away, ending the Grass Lake streak at three.

Galien's Ron Hein won, even if he had his doubts going up against Central Lake's Nathan Shay, who won the 3200 title the previous spring. "He was concerned aboput Shay because, being in another region, we never get to see him," said coach Matt Remmo. "We just saw he had a good time."

But Hein pulled away after the mile mark to win handily. "He ran very, very well."

Michigan Int. Speedway, Brooklyn, Nov. 7
1998 BOYS CLASS D TEAMS
1. Bear Lake..64
2. Grass Lake...81
3. New Buffalo..108
4. Wolverine...129
5. Litchfield..152
6. Galien..154
7. Detroit Holy Redeemer..........................186
8. Vanderbilt...212

9. Lawrence...249
10. Buckley...251
11. Fowler...254
12. Genesee..293
13. Plymouth Christian................................293
14. Pentwater..327
15. New Lothrop..429

1998 BOYS CLASS D INDIVIDUALS
1. Ron Hein (Galien)12...............................16:07
2. Nathan Shay (Central Lake)12................16:21
3. Nathan Usher (Grass Lake)11................16:34
4. Jimmy Hein (Galien)11...........................16:43
5. Aaron Romero (Detroit Holy Redeemer)11........16:44
6. Gabe Wordell (Warren Bethesda)12................16:50
7. Mike VanPatten (Litchfield)12..................16:57
8. John Calo (New Buffalo)11.....................17:00
9. Brett Vanderveen (Bear Lake)12..............17:01
10. Juan Serrata (Detroit Holy Redeemer)12......17:02
11. Aaron Morden (Bear Lake)12.................17:04
12. Ryan Mayer (Grass Lake)12...................17:06
13. Mike Richmond (Bear Lake)10................17:06
14. Jordan Roose (Plymouth Christian)11........17:08
15. Kris Kane (Grass Lake)10......................17:13
18. Ted Brown (Bear Lake)11.......................17:22
28. Jeremy Hejl (Bear Lake)12.....................17:35
67. Adam Werts (Bear Lake)9......................18:23
85. Tony Shrum (Bear Lake)12.....................18:55

1999 CLASS D BOYS

New Buffalo edged Bear Lake with soph Mike Putzke taking the win. It was quite the experience for rookie coach Vance Price, who credited previous coach Terry Keyser for building the program.

"The guys ran great today. Our guys came in really strong, passing lots of guys. They knew they had to go out today and run like champions and they did."

Michigan Int. Speedway, Brooklyn, Nov. 6 ⊠
1999 BOYS CLASS D TEAMS
1. New Buffalo..79
2. Bear Lake..87
3. Litchfield...122
4. Lawrence..133
5. Buckley...181
6. Detroit Holy Redeemer............................188
7. Fowler..199
8. Galien...209
9. Mason County Eastern............................213
10. Atlanta..221
11. Pentwater...236
12. Rochester Hills Lutheran Northwest.......237
13. New Lothrop...299
14. Auburn Hills Oakland Christian..............327
15. Wyandotte Mt Carmel............................353

1999 BOYS CLASS D INDIVIDUALS
1. Mike Putzke (New Buffalo)10..................16:49
2. David Harrand (Buckley)12....................16:50
3. Mike Richmond (Bear Lake)11...............17:03
4. Aaron Ritsema (Wyoming Tri-Unity)12....17:07
5. Nathan Egger (Lansing Christian)11.......17:14
6. Mike Vanderstraeten (Colon)12...............17:16
7. Raymond Perez (Detroit Holy Redeemer)9....17:21
8. Tim Sukta (Jackson Christian)10............17:23
9. Joe Feldpausch (Fowler)12....................17:24
10. Matt Hillman (Lawrence)10..................17:24
11. John Calo (New Buffalo)12...................17:26
12. Lance Vidak (Mason County Eastern)11....17:26
13. Jeff Havens (Litchfield)12.....................17:28
14. Keith Fisher (Colon)11.........................17:29
15. Aaron Romero (Detroit Holy Redeemer)12....17:30
22. Rich Mrozek (New Buffalo)12................17:49
25. Chad Curtis (New Buffalo)12................17:52
59. Mike Irwin (New Buffalo)9....................18:28
70. Bob Sprental (New Buffalo)10...............18:46
72. Brent Hoag (New Buffalo)10..................18:49

2000 D4 BOYS

In a controversial move, the sport moved from classes and into equal-sized divisions. For the higher classes, it seemed a change in name only, and little changed on the competitive scene. For the smallest class, however, the changes were dramatic. Not only were far more teams included in the state finals (27 in Division 4, compared to Class D's 15 the previous year), but the make-up of those teams was different. None of the top 10 teams from 1999 made it into 2000's top 10.

East Jordan—2nd in Class C the year before—took a 12-point win over Ubly. Individually, Bath's Will Boylan-Pett—19th the previous year in C—moved down for the win.

Michigan Int. Speedway, Brooklyn, Nov. 4 ⊠
2000 BOYS DIVISION 4 TEAMS
1. East Jordan..96
2. Ubly..108
3. St Louis..116
4. Lawton...184
5. Rogers City..188
6. Jonesville...219
7. Vandercook Lake...................................244
8. Grass Lake...245
9. Concord...246
10. Maple City Glen Lake..........................323
11. Hanover-Horton....................................324
12. Grand Rapids Baptist...........................366
13. Ann Arbor Greenhills............................372
14. Bear Lake...388
15. Harbor Springs.....................................408
16. Lawrence...436
17. Brown City...447
18. Allen Park Cabrini................................465
19. Mt Pleasant Sacred Heart....................477
20. Buckley..482
21. Saranac...524
22. Carsonville-Port Sanilac......................525
23. Mendon...533
24. Detroit Benedictine..............................591
25. Grosse Pointe Woods University Liggett....591
26. Wyandotte Mt Carmel..........................616
27. Detroit Holy Redeemer........................743

2000 BOYS DIVISION 4 INDIVIDUALS
1. Will Boylan-Pett (Bath)12......................15:43
2. Andy Duemling (Ubly)12.......................15:44
3. Jeff Luehm (St Louis)12........................15:51
4. Jason Jaques (Jonesville)12.................15:59
5. Matt Kibbey (Maple City Glen Lake)10....16:01
6. Justin Kibbey (Maple City Glen Lake)12....16:03
7. Tarn Leach (East Jordan)......................16:03
8. Mike Putzke (New Buffalo)11................16:16
9. Micah Middaugh (East Jordan)..............16:17
10. Scott Rumzek (Ubly)12........................16:18
11. Kris Kane (Grass Lake)12....................16:23
12. Gaben Moore (Concord)12..................16:34
13. Keith Longuski (Ubly)11......................16:35
14. Dan Campbell (Grand Rapids Baptist)11....16:36
15. Christian Weder (Ann Arbor Greenhills)....16:36
20. Jeremy Booze (East Jordan)...............16:39
44. Jeremy Penzien (East Jordan).............17:07
59. Garrett Romero (East Jordan).............17:22
144. Brian Kirby (East Jordan)...................18:22
148. Matt Smith (East Jordan)...................18:25

2001 D4 BOYS

Two years after his sophomore victory, New Buffalo's Mike Putzke returned to the top with a PR 15:49.

Lawton won its first title since its victories in the C/D division in 1966-67. Said coach Kris Bullock, "The championship is a bit of a surprise because I didn't think we ran terribly well at regional. I was a little concerned after that. But the state championship was our goal at the beginning of the season. We're very happy we attained our goal, because you don't do that many times in life."

Michigan Int. Speedway, Brooklyn, Nov. 3 ⊠
2001 BOYS DIVISION 4 TEAMS
1. Lawton...143
2. Bear Lake...213
3. Harbor Springs.......................................219
4. Central Lake..228
5. Vandercook Lake...................................234
6. Brown City...239
7. Jonesville...242
8. Ann Arbor Greenhills..............................254
9. Bath...262
10. Unionville-Sebewaing..........................267
11. East Jordan...268
12. Allen Park Cabrini................................300
13. Saranac...325
14. Buckley..329
15. Breckenridge.......................................387
16. New Buffalo...387
17. McBain...393
18. Ubly...405
19. Mt Pleasant Sacred Heart....................435
20. Southfield Christian..............................458
21. Reading...462
22. Marcellus...482
23. Morenci..564
24. Grosse Pointe Woods University Liggett........564
25. Saugatuck..579
26. Detroit Holy Redeemer........................618
27. Detroit Benedictine..............................632

Two-time winner Mike Putzke of New Buffalo.

2001 BOYS DIVISION 4 INDIVIDUALS
1. Mike Putzke (New Buffalo)12................15:49
2. Frank Therrian (Holton)12.....................16:12
3. Stephan Shay (Central Lake)10.............16:25
4. Kyle Eisenga (McBain)12......................16:30
5. Keith Longuski (Ubly)12........................16:33
6. Jacob Kloss (Harbor Springs)10............16:37
7. Matt Kibby (Maple City Glen Lake)11....16:39
8. Gregory Martus (Brown City)12.............16:42
9. Daniel Orozco (Lawton)11....................16:46
10. Joshua Simmons (Hale)10..................16:47
11. Chad Zitzelsberger (Mt Pleasant SH)12....16:50
12. Todd Ptacek (St Joseph L Mich Catholic)11....16:52
13. Christian Weder (Ann Arbor Greenhills)....16:54
14. Bryant Haist (Unionville-Sebewaing)12....16:54
15. Bryce Slavik (Fulton-Middleton)12........16:56
16. Jens Berdahl (Lawton)12.....................16:57
29. Tim Ferguson (Lawton)11....................17:13
76. Jose Carrizales (Lawton)10.................18:06
83. John Kuiper (Lawton)10.......................18:10
111. William Thorsberg (Lawton)11............18:27
133. Ryan Armstrong (Lawton)10..............18:44

2002 D4 BOYS

For the second time in meet history, a brother won the title. Liam Boylan-Pett's victory came two years after his brother Will's win. He later starred at Columbia, and in 2009 became the 315th American to break the 4-minute mile. Boylan-Pett said he got some good advice from his brother.

"We talk about twice a week on the phone, and we talked about winning this race. He gave me a lot of good tips."

It was the first win ever for Harbor Springs, coached by Mike Kloss.

Michigan Int. Speedway, Brooklyn, Nov. 2
2002 BOYS DIVISION 4 TEAMS
1. Harbor Springs 113
2. Lawton 142
3. Bath 176
4. Jonesville 230
5. Bear Lake-Onekama 240
6. Central Lake 268
7. Vandercook Lake 272
8. Saranac 283
9. Hale 308
10. Allen Park Cabrini 318
11. Southfield Christian 329
12. Brown City 344
13. Beal City 358
14. Ubly 369
15. Maple City Glen Lake 376
16. Athens 389
17. Coleman 434
18. Gaylord St Mary 434
19. Ann Arbor Greenhills 436
20. Marion 453
21. Colon 460
22. Jackson Christian 493
23. St Joseph Lake Michigan Catholic 506
24. Auburn Hills Oakland Christian 512
25. Gobles 543
26. Grosse Pointe Woods University Liggett ... 612
27. Detroit Holy Redeemer 631

2002 BOYS DIVISION 4 INDIVIDUALS
1. Liam Boylan-Pett (Bath)11 .... 16:08
2. Matt Kibbey (Maple City Glen Lake)12 ..... 16:11
3. Daniel Orozco (Lawton)12 .... 16:19
4. Todd Ptacek (Lake Mich Catholic)12 .... 16:22
5. Stephan Shay (Central Lake)11 .... 16:26
6. Jacob Kloss (Harbor Springs)11 .... 16:27
7. Adam Sprangel (Vandercook Lake)11 ..... 16:34
8. Joshuwa Hofbauer (Harbor Springs)10 ... 16:34
9. Shelby Nousain (Concord)12 .... 16:43
10. Korey Kuhl (Vandercook Lake)12 .... 16:45
11. Elliott Shay (Central Lake)12 .... 16:45
12. Dan Richmond (Bear Lake)12 .... 16:46
13. Bradley Bohlinger (GP Univ Liggett)12 .. 16:46
14. Lance Jones (Saranac)12 .... 16:47
15. Kyle Walsh (Ubly)12 .... 16:51
21. Sanders Frye (Harbor Springs)12 .... 16:59
23. Erik Hart (Harbor Springs)10 .... 17:00
91. Kevin Ronk (Harbor Springs)12 .... 17:55
107. Chad Wenz (Harbor Springs)9 .... 18:04
144. Kyle Newbury (Harbor Springs)11 .... 18:37

2003 D4 BOYS

"I should have won, but I didn't," said defending champ Liam Boylan-Pett. "No excuses."

The winner was Central Lake's Stephan Shay, the younger brother of 4-time winner Ryan Shay. He would go on to run for Michigan State and BYU and become a professional road racer himself.

Harbor Springs repeated, thanks to three runners in the top 10.

Michigan Int. Speedway, Brooklyn, Nov. 1
2003 BOYS DIVISION 4 TEAMS
1. Harbor Springs 73
2. Hudson 127
3. Vandercook Lake 164
4. Bath 165
5. Hale 173
6. Bear Lake 192
7. Traverse City St Francis 277
8. Southfield Christian 302
9. Lawton 347
10. Ann Arbor Greenhills 354
11. Bridgman 362
12. Boyne Falls 372
13. Fairview 402
14. Brown City 402
15. Ann Arbor Richard 413
16. Colon 415
17. Grand Rapids Covenant Christian 415
18. Bellevue 438
19. Wyoming Tri-Unity Christian 440
20. Sand Creek 441
21. Coleman 449
22. Jonesville 470
23. Saginaw Michigan Lutheran 515
24. Lutheran Westland 519
25. Carsonville-Port Sanilac 566
26. Auburn Hills Oakland Christian 607
No score--Grosse Pointe Woods University Liggett

Stephan Shay took the win for Central Lake.

2003 BOYS DIVISION 4 INDIVIDUALS
1. Stephen Shay (Central Lake)12 .... 15:35
2. Liam Boylan-Pett (Bath)12 .... 15:51
3. Josh Hofbauer (Harbor Springs)11 .... 15:52
4. Adam Sprangel (Vandercook Lake)12 ... 15:59
5. Ben Tarbutton (Gaylord St. Mary)12 ...... 16:12
6. Jacob Kloss (Harbor Springs)12 .... 16:14
7. Luke Hutchins (Southfield Christian)12 . 16:30
8. Spencer Beatty (Harbor Springs)10 ...... 16:31
9. Dustin Dodge (Bellevue)10 .... 16:32
10. Chris Stoddard (Bath)11 .... 16:33
11. Curtis Barclay (Hale)11 .... 16:35
12. Robert Deo (Hudson)12 .... 16:36
13. Benjiman Smith (Athens)12 .... 16:38
14. Caleb Erway (Morenci)11 .... 16:44
15. Nicholas Evans (Bridgman)12 .... 16:45
34. Chad Wenz (Harbor Springs)10 .... 17:00
57. Mark Morse (Harbor Springs)12 .... 17:31
77. Erik Hart (Harbor Springs)11 .... 17:46
133. Nicholas Allerding (Harbor Springs)12 . 18:28

2004 D4 BOYS

"I was more focusing on placing in the top 30. I just wanted to make all-state," confessed Justin Todd. The senior, in his first year of running cross country—and the first year of Climax-Scotts having a team—had the fastest time at regionals but still didn't expect to be a big factor.

"A little past the mile I took off and tried to break the other guy mentally. That didn't work, so I thought I'd better try something else.

Before the 2M I started to lose the guy in front of me. I got worried."

After the 2M, Todd took off on the downhill stretch. "I'm not very strong going up hills, but going down I'm pretty good. I took off and I kept going."

Doug Baird's Hesperia squad inched ahead of Bear Lake-Onekama to win by a single point.

Michigan Int. Speedway, Brooklyn, Nov. 6
2004 BOYS DIVISION 4 TEAMS
1. Hesperia 124
2. Bear Lake-Onekama 125
3. Potterville 191
4. Colon 234
5. Ann Arbor Greenhills 251
6. Vandercook Lake 272
7. Grand Rapids Covenant Christian 272
8. Saginaw Valley Lutheran 308
9. Bellevue 308
10. Mason County Eastern 335
11. Southfield Christian 338
12. Mendon 356
13. Grand Rapids NorthPointe Christian 373
14. Hale 381
15. Gobles 388
16. Auburn Hills Oakland Christian 400
17. Hudson 404
18. Wyoming Tri-Unity Christian 420
19. Mackinaw City 430
20. Saginaw Michigan Lutheran 455
21. Ellsworth 474
22. Marcellus 489
23. Lutheran Westland 522
24. Whitmore Lake 528
25. Detroit Holy Redeemer 549
26. Brown City 556
27. Lawrence 631
28. Royal Oak Shrine 693

2004 BOYS DIVISION 4 INDIVIDUALS
1. Justin Todd (Climax-Scotts)12 .... 16:29
2. Curtis Barclay (Hale)12 .... 16:34
3. Loren Milbrath (Saginaw Mich Lutheran)11 . 16:35
4. Aaron Hunt (Potterville)11 .... 16:35
5. Josh Groenwald (Bear Lake)11 .... 16:36
6. Chris Stoddard (Bath)12 .... 16:43
7. Jason Busch (Mancelona)11 .... 16:45
8. Wes Muller (GR NorthPointe Christian) . 16:46
9. Seth Campbell (GR NorthPointe Christian)12 16:46
10. Caleb Erway (Morenci)12 .... 16:47
11. Mike Glinski (Sand Creek)11 .... 16:47
12. Peter Hamp (Ann Arbor Greenhills)11 .. 16:50
13. Andy Rumsey (Hesperia)12 .... 16:51
14. Paul Oliver (Jonesville)12 .... 16:54
15. Matthew Hanko (GR Covenant Christian)11 16:55
18. Brett Billings (Hesperia) 17:01
53. Brandon Billings (Hesperia)9 .... 17:45
56. B.J. Whelan (Hesperia)9 .... 17:48
66. Chuck Breuker (Hesperia)11 .... 17:55
78. Jordan Slate (Hesperia)9 .... 17:59
102. Jake Kraley (Hesperia)11 .... 18:13

2005 D4 BOYS

St. Louis hadn't made it to the top since it captured the Class C crown 26 years earlier. Coach Steve Kelly guided the Sharks to a 38-point margin over Bellevue.

"I really thought we were down a ways," said a surprised Kelly. But little things like having our sixth guy from last week come in as our third today made a huge difference."

Matt Hanko of Covenant Christian, only 15th the year before, pulled off the win.

Michigan Int. Speedway, Brooklyn, Nov. 5
2005 BOYS DIVISION 4 TEAMS
1. St Louis 127
2. Bellevue 165
3. Bear Lake-Onekama 167
4. Grand Rapids Covenant Christian 191

5. Vandercook Lake 194
6. Hesperia 217
7. Potterville 226
8. Pittsford 275
9. Mendon 286
10. Hudson 300
11. Ann Arbor Greenhills 306
12. Saranac 358
13. Saginaw Michigan Lutheran 371
14. Colon 378
15. Brethren 395
16. Gobles 398
17. Mackinaw City 419
18. Unionville-Sebewaing 428
19. Mason County Eastern 484
20. Fairview 486
21. St Joseph Lake Michigan Catholic 498
22. Royal Oak Shrine 543
23. Ellsworth 545
24. Mayville 571
25. Lawrence 614
26. Southfield Christian 623
27. Detroit Chavez Academy 758

2005 BOYS DIVISION 4 INDIVIDUALS

1. Matt Hanko (GR Covenant Christian)12 16:15
2. Loren Milbrath (Saginaw Mich Lutheran)12 16:18
3. Mike Glinski (Sand Creek)12 16:23
4. Alex Harris (Royal Oak Shrine)11 16:28
5. Nick Swisher (Bear Lake)11 16:31
6. Brett Domeyer (Bath)12 16:36
7. Josh Groenwald (Bear Lake)12 16:39
8. Peter Hamp (Ann Arbor Greenhills)12 16:41
9. John Koser (Hudson)11 16:42
10. Cody Hoffman (Bellevue)12 16:42
11. Jake Green (Bellevue)12 16:46
12. Aaron Hunt (Potterville)12 16:48
13. Kenny Hugenell (Decatur)11 16:49
14. Alex Best (St Louis)11 16:50
15. Jon Hatfield (Pittsford)10 16:50
20. Trevor Sova (St Louis)12 16:55
40. Max Ramirez (St Louis)12 17:19
52. Nick Davaloz (St Louis)10 17:26
60. Zach Drater (St Louis)12 17:32
77. Tim Snyder (St Louis)10 17:41
116. Matt Creswell (St Louis)9 18:01

2006 D4 BOYS

Waldron's Tim Jagielski kept looking over his shoulder in the final mile. "I was just making sure I could hold onto the lead. I've led every race I've been in this year but was a little worried today," he told the *Detroit Free Press*.

Only 31st the year before, Jagielski made his break before the first mile.

Hesperia won its second title in three years, this time with the highest score in meet history. Said coach Doug Baird, "Our guys just pulled it together and ran their tails off. What a great moment for our team."

Michigan Int. Speedway, Brooklyn, Nov. 4 ⊠
2006 BOYS DIVISION 4 TEAMS

1. Hesperia 148
2. Hudson 160
3. Whitmore Lake 162
4. Saugatuck 194
5. Bear Lake-Onekama 201
6. Saranac 214
7. St Louis 232
8. Mendon 263
9. Colon 289
10. Potterville 299
11. Harbor Springs 304
12. Hart 331
13. Vandercook Lake 335
14. Ellsworth 351
15. Grand Rapids Covenant Christian 374
16. McBain 377
17. Mt Pleasant Sacred Heart 419
18. Mason County Eastern 450
19. Royal Oak Shrine 458
20. Mackinaw City 464
21. Eau Claire 522
22. Saginaw Valley Lutheran 528
23. Lawrence 552
24. Concord 571
25. Unionville-Sebewaing 614
26. Auburn Hills Oakland Christian 633
27. Ubly 710
28. Southfield Christian 832

2006 BOYS DIVISION 4 INDIVIDUALS

1. Tim Jagielski (Waldron)11 16:07
2. Alex Harris (Royal Oak Shrine)12 16:15
3. Kevin Oblinger (Mt Pleasant Sacred Heart)10 16:20
4. Alex Best (St. Louis)12 16:22
5. Zach Carpenter (Whitmore Lake)9 16:25
6. Derek Childs (Breckenridge)12 16:26
7. John Koser (Hudson)12 16:29
8. Ashton Fisher (Ellsworth)10 16:36
9. Trey Graham (Harbor Springs)11 16:36
10. Kyle Daugherty (Jackson Christian)11 16:39
11. Nick Swisher (Bear Lake-Onekama)12 16:40
12. Nate Panicacci (Whitmore Lake)11 16:40
13. Stephen Ryder (Hart)11 16:41
14. Ryan Pohl (Pewamo-Westphalia)10 16:42
15. Louis Borton (Morenci)12 16:42
33. Jordan Slate (Hesperia)11 16:59
34. Brandon Billings (Hesperia)11 17:00
47. B.J. Whelan (Hesperia)11 17:14
51. Phil Khozein (Hesperia)12 17:16
53. Dakota Cooper (Hesperia)11 17:18
152. Jeb Moritz (Hesperia)11 18:32
162. Justin Zeerip (Hesperia)12 18:45

2007 D4 BOYS

Sacred Heart's Kevin Oblinger played it careful in his matchup with defending champion Tim Jagielski of Waldron. "You want to go crazy and stay with him. But I know if I go out with him, I won't have much at the end, so I stayed conservative."

Oblinger didn't move to the lead until the final half-mile, winning by seven seconds.

Potterville won its first title in 31 years. The team rallied around coach Dan Brunk, whose 3-year-old son Carson was fighting cancer. They shaved their heads in September when the toddler started on chemotherapy. (In 2019, Carson Brunk ran on the varsity squad.)

Michigan Int. Speedway, Brooklyn, Nov. 3 ⊠
2007 BOYS DIVISION 4 TEAMS

1. Potterville 144
2. Hesperia 150
3. St Louis 184
4. Saugatuck 188
5. Saranac 219
6. Ellsworth 241
7. Harbor Springs 265
8. Hudson 270
9. Ann Arbor Greenhills 274
10. Grand Rapids Covenant Christian 278
11. Mendon 284
12. Saginaw Valley Lutheran 319
13. Bridgman 327
14. Adrian Lenawee Christian 334
15. Bear Lake 345
16. Reese 402
17. Colon 416
18. Hillsdale Academy 439
19. Mackinaw City 468
20. Lawrence 504
21. North Muskegon 508
22. Suttons Bay 521
23. Traverse City St Francis 532
24. Southfield Christian 542
25. Brown City 557
26. Lutheran Westland 652
27. Newport Lutheran South 757

2007 BOYS DIVISION 4 INDIVIDUALS

1. Kevin Oblinger (Mt Pleasant Sacred Heart)11 15:50
2. Kyle Stacks (Concord)10 15:57
3. Tim Jagielski (Waldron)12 16:03
4. Christian Birky (Saugatuck)11 16:05
5. Tec Adams (Harbor Springs)11 16:09
6. Ashton Fisher (Ellsworth)11 16:21
7. Ben Wynsma (Suttons Bay)10 16:23
8. Brayden Border (St Louis)9 16:25
9. Josiah Snellink (Hudsonville Freedom Baptist)12 16:30
10. Kent Jones (Saranac)12 16:31
11. Ben Rueger (Saginaw Valley Lutheran)12 16:31
12. Stephen Tennis (Hudson)10 16:33
13. Marcus Feldpausch (Fowler)11 16:34
14. Victor Allen (Southfield Christian)9 16:34
15. Nick Flietstra (Potterville)10 16:35
26. Larry Julson (Potterville)11 16:40
33. Collin Ward (Potterville)11 16:52
76. Mikel Strieff (Potterville)10 17:31
91. Jerry Zimmerman (Potterville)10 17:41
94. Tyler Carter (Potterville)10 17:43
147. Nick Dilernia (Potterville)12 18:13

2008 D4 BOYS

For the second year in a row, the defending individual champion lost. This time, Harbor Springs' Tec Adams blistered a winning pace from the start. "I wanted to go out fast and set the pace. And I knew I wanted a good second mile, so I had to go out by myself. I couldn't hold myself back."

The top two both dipped under Ryan Shay's 1996 course record.

Potterville coach Dan Brunk said the second win was tougher than the first. "I think just because of that No. 1 ranking all season. It was something that we never had to deal with before, but the boys handled it very maturely. We did what we had to do on the most important day of the year."

Michigan Int. Speedway, Brooklyn, Nov. 1 ⊠
2008 BOYS DIVISION 4 TEAMS

1. Potterville 129
2. Adrian Lenawee Christian 131
3. Harbor Springs 145
4. Hesperia 182
5. Saugatuck 190
6. Concord 195
7. Bridgman 250
8. Ann Arbor Greenhills 255
9. Bear Lake-Onekama 268
10. Saranac 280
11. Mendon 330
12. Wolverine 341
13. Hillsdale Academy 370
14. Fowler 372
15. North Muskegon 376
16. Suttons Bay 387
17. Onaway 460
18. Lawrence 463
19. Traverse City St Francis 474
20. Royal Oak Shrine 481
21. Southfield Christian 503
22. Bellevue 518
23. Sand Creek 539
24. Ubly 564
25. Saginaw Michigan Lutheran 653
26. Unionville-Sebewaing 665
27. Detroit Weston Prep 685

2008 BOYS DIVISION 4 INDIVIDUALS

1. Tec Adams (Harbor Springs)12 15:23
2. Kevin Oblinger (MP Sacred Heart)12 15:26
3. Christian Birky (Saugatuck)12 15:30
4. Kyle Stacks (Concord)11 15:31
5. Ben Wynsma (Suttons Bay)11 15:49
6. Larry Julson (Potterville)12 15:56
7. Ashton Fisher (Ellsworth)12 16:01
8. Tyler Slentz (Saugatuck)12 16:01
9. Victor Allen (Southfield Christian)10 16:07
10. Luke Operhall (Wolverine)12 16:11
11. Ryan Pohl (Pewamo-Westphalia)12 16:13
12. Nick Flietstra (Potterville)11 16:15
13. Michael Schulte (MP Sacred Heart)12 16:17

14. Spencer Nousain (Concord)9 ....16:23
15. Mitchell Dale (Oakland Christian)11 ....16:26
18. Collin Ward (Potterville)12 ....16:28
66. Tyler Carter (Potterville)11 ....17:19
84. Andrew Dilernia (Potterville)10 ....17:31
89. Nathan Laduke (Potterville)10 ....17:34
179. Kyle Lamb (Potterville)10 ....18:50

2009 D4 BOYS

Concord went 1-2 to seal the team win for head coach David Jordon, topping Bridgman by 35 points. "It was really nice to go 1-2," said Kyle Stacks. "We always had this dream a couple of years ago that we would go 1-2, and it was really nice to see that happen. As a team, all of our hard work really paid off."

Michigan Int. Speedway, Brooklyn, Nov. 7
2009 BOYS DIVISION 4 TEAMS
1. Concord 109
2. Bridgman 144
3. North Muskegon 165
4. Potterville 168
5. Saranac 202
6. Bear Lake-Onekama 228
7. Hesperia 230
8. Harbor Springs 231
9. Bellevue 272
10. Mt Pleasant Sacred Heart 293
11. Hudson 314
12. Southfield Christian 376
13. Suttons Bay 379
14. Evart 384
15. Mendon 397
16. Holton 404
17. St Joseph Lake Michigan Catholic 407
18. Ann Arbor Greenhills 407
19. Onaway 487
20. Blanchard-Montabella 526
21. Carsonville-Port-Sanilac 530
22. Sand Creek 541
23. Central Lake 544
24. Royal Oak Shrine 579
25. Morenci 610
26. Ottawa Lake Whiteford 635
27. Rochester Hills Lutheran Northwest 728

2009 BOYS DIVISION 4 INDIVIDUALS
1. Kyle Stacks (Concord)12 ....15:55
2. Spencer Nousain (Concord)10 ....16:10
3. Ben Wynsma (Suttons Bay)12 ....16:18
4. Matt Proctor (Brown City)11 ....16:27
5. Jeffrey Bord (Ann Arbor Greenhills)11 ....16:34
6. Mitchell Dale (Auburn Hills Oakland Chr)12 ...16:35
7. Mark Haukereid (Bridgman)12 ....16:44
8. Ethan Lievense (Saugatuck)12 ....16:44
9. Victor Allen (Southfield Christian)11 ....16:47
10. Steve Tennis (Hudson)12 ....16:48
11. Sean Kelly (Saugatuck)9 ....16:49
12. Noah Haverdink (Hudsonville Free. Bapt)11 16:49
13. James Vance (Saranac)12 ....16:53
14. Nicholas Flietstra (Potterville)12 ....16:56
15. Ethan VanDePerre (Blanchard Montab.)12 ..16:57
30. Joseph Brubaker (Concord)12 ....17:10
55. Ian Miller (Concord)11 ....17:47
64. Kyle Grimes (Concord)12 ....17:55
136. Parker Saenz (Concord)9 ....18:55
170. Kylan Boehlke (Concord)12 ....19:25

2010 D4 BOYS

Kyle Tait took the individual win for Big Rapids Crossroads but claimed his injured twin Aaron was the better runner. "Aaron's faster than me. He probably would have beaten me."

Tait's performance fell just short of the course record. "I left a lot out there," he said. "I missed the record by three seconds, so my coach is going to be mad. I should have pushed myself more. It's so hard to push yourself when you're running from the front."

It was the first-ever team win for North Muskegon. Said coach Gary Neal, "We had four runners turn in their personal bests. We were ranked No. 1 throughout the season, so there was the bullseye factor."

Michigan Int. Speedway, Brooklyn, Nov. 6
2010 BOYS DIVISION 4 TEAMS
1. North Muskegon 89
2. Bridgman 121
3. Harbor Springs 138
4. Potterville 171
5. Concord 191
6. Hesperia 208
7. Pewamo-Westphalia 262
8. Mt Pleasant Sacred Heart 268
9. Unionville-Sebewaing 313
10. Hillsdale Academy 325
11. Saugatuck 326
12. Albion 330
13. Mendon 339
14. Royal Oak Shrine 356
15. Southfield Christian 384
16. Grand Traverse Academy 400
17. Bear Lake 405
18. Brown City 412
19. Carsonville-Port Sanilac 422
20. Eau Claire 465
21. Mason County Eastern 552
22. Sand Creek 588
23. Ellsworth 596
24. Lutheran Westland 605
25. Auburn Hills Oakland Christian 633
26. Rogers City 635
27. Newport Lutheran South 741

2010 BOYS DIVISION 4 INDIVIDUALS
1. Kyle Tait (Big Rapids Crossroads)12 ....15:26
2. Spencer Nousain (Concord)11 ....15:52
3. Victor Allen (Southfield Christian)12 ....15:57
4. Noah Haverdink (Hudsonville Free. Chr)12 ..16:14
5. Matt Proctor (Brown City)12 ....16:15
6. Nick Vanderkooi (Fremont Providence)10 ...16:17
7. Sean Kelly (Saugatuck)10 ....16:20
8. Cammeron Magro (Bridgman)12 ....16:22
9. Andrew Dilernia (Potterville)12 ....16:24
10. Dominick Reed (Athens)12 ....16:29
11. Mathias Waterstradt (North Muskegon)11 ..16:29
12. Jeff Cherry (Hesperia)11 ....16:30
13. Nick Moon (Dansville)12 ....16:31
14. Ben Kloss (Harbor Springs)11 ....16:32
15. Casey Voisin (Mt Pleasant Sacred Heart)11 16:33
20. Alex Benham (North Muskegon)11 ....16:39
23. Jacob Chovaz (North Muskegon)10 ....16:43
33. Ryan O'Keefe (North Muskegon)12 ....16:58
39. Joe Potter (North Muskegon)12 ....17:12
55. Thayer Lowe (North Muskegon)11 ....17:27

2011 D4 BOYS

Concord scored another win—its fifth boys' state title ever. After being runner-up for two straight years, Spencer Nousain finally got the win for the Yellowjackets.

"I wanted to run the first mile strong and try to pull away before I got to the 3M mark," said Noussain. "The team state title my senior year is something I've been looking forward to for a long time. Those guys have been working hard."

Michigan Int. Speedway, Brooklyn, Nov. 5
2011 BOYS DIVISION 4 TEAMS
1. Concord 64
2. Mt Pleasant Sacred Heart 99
3. North Muskegon 131
4. Potterville 165
5. Evart 192
6. Hesperia 206
7. Unionville-Sebewaing 226
8. Kalamazoo Hackett 229
9. Breckenridge 252
10. Grand Traverse Academy 302
11. Saugatuck 324
12. Holland Black River 341
13. Eau Claire 416
14. Royal Oak Shrine 417
15. Bear Lake 430
16. Hudson 461
17. Albion 466
18. Rogers City 480
19. Mendon 500
20. Mackinaw City 509
21. Plymouth Christian 510
22. Lutheran Westland 528
23. Auburn Hills Oakland Christian 555
24. Boyne Falls 564
25. Sand Creek 569
26. Waterford Our Lady of the Lakes 585
27. Carsonville-Port Sanilac 692

Spencer Nousain of Concord topped Saugatuck's Sean Kelly. (Pete Draugalis photo)

2011 BOYS DIVISION 4 INDIVIDUALS
1. Spencer Nousain (Concord)12 ....15:56
2. Sean Kelly (Saugatuck)11 ....16:01
3. David Zinger Evart)11 ....16:07
4. Jeff Cherry (Hesperia)12 ....16:18
5. Stephan Biggs (Addison)12 ....16:20
6. Casey Voisin (Mt Pleasant Sacred Heart)12 .16:21
7. David Dantuma (Big Rapids Crossroads)12 .. 16:25
8. Jacob Chovaz (North Muskegon)11 ....16:33
9. Austin Wigent (Reading)12 ....16:33
10. Ben Schilling (Mt Pleasant Sacred Heart)12 16:34
11. Nick Vanderkooi (Fremont Prov. Chr)11 ....16:34
12. Joel Calvert (Hillsdale Academy)12 ....16:36
13. Joey Southgate (Unionville-Sebewaing)12 ..16:38
14. Michael Myers (Kalamazoo Hackett)11 .....16:40
15. Bohdan Hartman (Fulton Middleton)9 ......16:40
17. Jacob Hall (Concord)9 ....16:40
19. Jesse Hersha (Concord)9 ....16:41
20. Parker Saenz (Concord)10 ....16:42
37. Mason Nousain (Concord)10 ....17:11
40. Sam Comden (Concord)11 ....17:14
73. Tyler Neu (Concord)11 ....17:37

2012 D4 BOYS

Concord won another team title and produced a new individual winner in sophomore Jesse Hersha, making it three different individual champions in four years for the Yellowjackets.

Said Hersha, who placed 19th the year before, "If you would have told me after state last year when I was a freshman, I never would have thought of this. I may have expected top eight, but I never thought I'd win it. It's amazing."

Michigan Int. Speedway, Brooklyn, Nov. 3
2012 BOYS DIVISION 4 TEAMS
1. Concord 61
2. Evart 100
3. Pewamo-Westphalia 117
4. Saugatuck 140
5. Breckenridge 147
6. Kalamazoo Hackett 225
7. Mt Pleasant Sacred Heart 240
8. Mendon 263
9. Bear Lake 267
10. Hesperia 307
11. Harbor Springs 316
12. Saginaw Michigan Lutheran 346
13. Royal Oak Shrine 380
14. Mancelona 414
15. Waterford Our Lady of the Lakes 416
16. Kalamazoo Christian 418
17. Traverse City St Francis 424
18. Unionville-Sebewaing 459
19. Eau Claire 485
20. Grand Traverse Academy 498
21. Plymouth Christian 506
22. Lutheran Westland 528
23. Albion 538
24. Grosse Pointe Woods University Liggett ... 596
25. Sand Creek 598
26. New Lothrop 672
27. Rogers City 685

2012 BOYS DIVISION 4 INDIVIDUALS
1. Jesse Hersha (Concord)10 .... 15:33
2. David Zinger (Evart)12 .... 15:53
3. Sean Kelly (Saugatuck)12 .... 15:59
4. Nick Vanderkooi (Fremont Prov. Chr)12 .... 16:07
5. Michael Myers (Kalamazoo Hackett)12 .... 16:09
6. Jacob Chovaz (North Muskegon)12 .... 16:10
7. Zach Kerr (Saugatuck)12 .... 16:12
8. Ben Kendell (Royal Oak Shrine)11 .... 16:13
9. Max Hodges (Evart)11 .... 16:22
10. Tanner Droste (Pewamo-Westphalia)11 ..... 16:22
11. Josiah Ottolini (Concord)9 .... 16:23
12. Joseph Newcomb (Tekonsha)12 .... 16:25
13. Evan Carter (Southfield Christian)12 .... 16:27
14. Parker Saenz (Concord)12 .... 16:27
15. Daniel Ridley (Deckerville)11 .... 16:28
18. Tyler Neu (Concord)12 .... 16:30
47. Sam Comden (Concord)12 .... 17:06
108. Joey Hutchins (Concord)10 .... 17:51
146. Tucker Ward (Concord)9 .... 18:24

2013 D4 BOYS

Jesse Hersha won the individual crown again, this time by 44 seconds on a sloppy, wet day. "I was focusing on the team result, hoping we'd do better. I just wanted to come out here and do what I can do. I wasn't looking for a huge day individually."

Saugatuck won its first state title. Said lead runner Jacob Pettinga, "The team did really well. A lot of people stepped up and we came out with the win."

Michigan Int. Speedway, Brooklyn, Nov. 2
2013 BOYS DIVISION 4 TEAMS
1. Saugatuck 113
2. Mt Pleasant Sacred Heart 121
3. Concord 134
4. Bear Lake 159
5. Evart 159
6. Pewamo-Westphalia 162
7. Beal City 242
8. Deckerville 324
9. Kalamazoo Christian 332
10. Sandusky 340
11. Mendon 343
12. Hillsdale Academy 361
13. Potterville 384
14. Saginaw Michigan Lutheran 411
15. New Buffalo 435
16. Sand Creek 443
17. Manton 449
18. Indian River Inland Lakes 467
19. Pellston 469
20. Grand Traverse Academy 471
21. Hudson 483
22. Jackson Christian 500
23. Britton Deerfield 534
24. Boyne Falls 542
25. Rochester Hills Lutheran Northwest ... 565
26. Grosse Pointe Woods University Liggett ... 577
27. Royal Oak Shrine 597

2013 BOYS DIVISION 4 INDIVIDUALS
1. Jesse Hersha (Concord)11 .... 15:50
2. Josh Wojan (East Jordan)12 .... 16:34
3. Jacob Pettinga (Saugatuck)11 .... 16:37
4. Cooper Terry (Mt Pleasant Sacred Heart)12 .. 16:40
5. Tanner Droste (Pewamo-Westphalia)12 ...... 16:44
6. Jacob Hall (Concord)11 .... 16:52
7. Daniel Ridley (Deckerville)12 .... 16:53
8. Clayton Springer (Saugatuck)12 .... 16:54
9. Winter Romeyn (Ellsworth)11 .... 16:56
10. Nick Pung (Beal City)11 .... 16:57
11. Zach Feldpausch (Fowler)12 .... 16:58
12. Jim English (Mt Pleasant Sacred Heart)12 .. 16:59
13. Luke Anderson (Harbor Beach)11 .... 16:59
14. Braxton Snuffer (Muskegon WM Christ)10 .. 16:59
15. John Girven (Bear Lake)12 .... 16:59
38. Nick Butch (Saugatuck)9 .... 17:27
56. Zachary Pettinga (Saugatuck)9 .... 17:49
60. Joe Brown (Saugatuck)11 .... 17:53
104. Orlando Carrion (Saugatuck)9 .... 18:28
133. Michael Granzotto (Saugatuck)12 .... 18:46

Jesse Hersha won a record three-straight for Concord. He would later star at Michigan State. (Pete Draugalis photo)

2014 D4 BOYS

Concord's Jesse Hersha became the sixth runner in Lower Peninsula history to win three straight—with Concord winning five of the last 6 D4 individual titles. Along the way the MSU-bound senior tied the D4 course record—though the reporters that day called it a near miss, not having rounded Tec Adams' 2008 clocking up properly (Adams 15:22.4 should be listed as a 15:23, just as Hersha's 15:23.0 would be).

"When I won it my sophomore year, the first thing I thought was, 'All right, I've got to go through and do it,' It really didn't feel real until now that I'm a 3-time state champion."

Beal City upended defending champion Saugatuck by a mere 4 points for the win.

Michigan Int. Speedway, Brooklyn, Nov. 1
2014 BOYS DIVISION 4 TEAMS
1. Beal City 105
2. Saugatuck 109
3. Bear Lake-Onekama 121
4. Concord 123
5. Hudson 226
6. Mendon 240
7. Kalamazoo Christian 260
8. Harbor Springs 277
9. Ubly 281
10. North Muskegon 327
11. Manton 341
12. Plymouth Christian 353
13. Breckenridge 366
14. Evart 377
15. Eau Claire 397
16. Ottawa Lake Whiteford 398
17. Potterville 407
18. Fairview 429
19. Lansing Christian 429
20. Hillsdale Academy 479
21. Ellsworth 515
22. Frankfort 528
23. Centreville 540
24. Southfield Christian 548
25. Grosse Pointe Woods University Liggett ... 556
26. Rochester Hills Lutheran Northwest ... 629
27. Riverview Richard 719

2014 BOYS DIVISION 4 INDIVIDUALS
1. Jesse Hersha (Concord)12 .... 15:23
2. Santana Scott (Evart)11 .... 15:55
3. Nick Pung (Beal City)12 .... 16:20
4. Adam Grifka Ubly)12 .... 16:30
5. Doug Hollett (Kalamazoo Christian)12 .... 16:32
6. Bohdan Hartman (Fulton)12 .... 16:32
7. Ethan Schafer (Beal City)11 .... 16:34
8. Luke Anderson (Harbor Beach)12 .... 16:35
9. Aaron Peters (Sand Creek)11 .... 16:38
10. Braxton Snuffer (Muskegon WM Christ11 .. 16:38
11. Jacob Hall (Concord)12 .... 16:39
12. Denver Cade (Buckley)9 .... 16:41
13. Winter Romeyn (Ellsworth)12 .... 16:45
14. Jordan Anderson (Bear Lake-Onekama)11 .. 16:48
15. Zachary Pettinga (Saugatuck)10 .... 16:48
39. David Reihl (Beal City)10 .... 17:29
51. James Kolb (Beal City)12 .... 17:38
59. Brendan Carrick (Beal City)12 .... 17:45
106. Zach Bellinger (Beal City)12 .... 18:20
134. Apollo Schafer (Beal City)11 .... 18:37

2015 D4 BOYS

Saugatuck fought its way back to the top, this time with an impressive 51-point showing, putting five in the top 15. It was the lowest score since the move to a divisional format and a larger meet in 2000.

Evart's Santana Scott, head shaven down the middle, streaked to a big win after being runner-up the year before. He explained the haircut: "We've done something unique together for the last five years and it's my senior year so I got to help decide, and this is what we determined. It made me feel more awesome."

As for the race, he said, "I thought it was closer, so I was trying to keep the lead I had."

Quipped runner-up Zachary Pettinga, "The top of his head blinded me. I lost my footing and everything."

Michigan Int. Speedway, Brooklyn, Nov. 7
2015 BOYS DIVISION 4 TEAMS
1. Saugatuck 51
2. Bear Lake-Onekama 92
3. Harbor Springs 179
4. Concord 198
5. Lansing Christian 203

6. Mendon 211
7. Hudson 214
8. Evart 236
9. Mt Pleasant Sacred Heart 246
10. Beal City 248
11. Plymouth Christian 297
12. Sand Creek 319
13. Manton 376
14. Ubly 388
15. Kalamazoo Christian 394
16. Kalamazoo Hackett 416
17. Potterville 442
18. Riverview Richard 442
19. Ellsworth 501
20. Ottawa Lake Whiteford 503
21. Holton 513
22. Lutheran Westland 543
23. Frankfort 595
24. Eau Claire 605
25. Grosse Pointe Woods University Liggett 608
26. Auburn Hills Oakland Christian 628
27. Indian River Inland Lakes 658

Santana Scott sported a new haircut for his 2015 victory. (Pete Draugalis photo)

2015 BOYS DIVISION 4 INDIVIDUALS
1. Santana Scott (Evart)12 .... 16:06
2. Zachary Pettinga (Saugatuck)11 .... 16:23
3. Ethan Schafer (Beal City)12 .... 16:30
4. Aaron Peters (Sand Creek)12 .... 16:31
5. Daniel Holder (Hudson)10 .... 16:34
6. Jacob Tanner Holton)11 .... 16:35
7. Jeremy Kloss (Harbor Springs)9 .... 16:38
8. Jordan Anderson (Bear Lake-Onekama)12 .. 16:41
9. Kaiden Hejl (Bear Lake-Onekama)10 ... 16:41
10. Quentin Genaw (Mancelona)10 .... 16:42
11. Corey Gorgas (Saugatuck)9 .... 16:42
12. Gary McBride (Bear Lake-Onekama)10 .. 16:44
13. Nick Butch (Saugatuck)11 .... 16:47
14. Orlando Carrion (Saugatuck)11 .... 16:50
15. Keegan Seifert (Saugatuck)10 .... 16:52
39. Eldon Garvelink (Saugatuck)11 .... 17:22
87. Jacob VanderRoest (Saugatuck)11 ..... 17:56

2016 D4 BOYS

The theme of the race seemed to be last year's D3 teams coming down to D4 to wreak havoc. Pewamo-Westphalia, coached by Scott Werner, had been 6th in D3 the previous year. The team eked out a 13-point win over Harbor Springs to win its first state title since the 1959 C/D crown. The Pirates' 2-6 runners all finished within an impressive 11 seconds.

Individually, CarLee Stimpfel of Cass City ran to the win. He had also previously been in D3, and had never made all-state. He said, "Once I had a big enough gap, I knew I was going to be able to push it on in. All season I didn't have much competition. I won every race except for two, so it's just one of those things."

Michigan Int. Speedway, Brooklyn, Nov. 5
2016 BOYS DIVISION 4 TEAMS
1. Pewamo-Westphalia 131
2. Harbor Springs 144
3. Bear Lake-Onekama 181
4. Concord 234
5. Beal City 251
6. Manton 254
7. Holton 268
8. Evart 294
9. Hudson 344
10. Mt Pleasant Sacred Heart 355
11. Cass City 355
12. Potterville 359
13. Lansing Christian 361
14. Mendon 377
15. Hale 379
16. Hesperia 382
17. Walkerville 412
18. Battle Creek St Philip 421
19. Plymouth Christian 421
20. Sand Creek 433
21. Ellsworth 437
22. Ubly 439
23. Fairview 482
24. Grosse Pointe Woods University Liggett 504
25. Southfield Christian 527
26. Kingston 567
27. Kalamazoo Hackett 568
28. Frankfort 668

Cass City's CarLee Stimpfel. (Pete Draugalis photo)

2016 BOYS DIVISION 4 INDIVIDUALS
1. CarLee Stimpfel (Cass City)11 .... 16:03
2. Jeremy Kloss (Harbor Springs)10 .... 16:13
3. Jacob Tanner (Holton)12 .... 16:20
4. Noah Heckenlively (Hillsdale Academy)12 .. 16:38
5. Alex Grifka (Ubly)11 .... 16:39
6. Ashton Walker (Portland St. Patrick)9 .. 16:42
7. Bryce Thelen (Pewamo-Westphalia)12 .. 16:44
8. Gary McBride (Bear Lake-Onekama)11 .. 16:47
9. Justin Detgen (Concord)12 .... 16:48
10. Davis Tebben (Lansing Christian)11 ... 16:49
11. Alex Taylor (Beal City)10 .... 16:49
12. Kaiden Hejl (Bear Lake-Onekama)11 .. 16:51
13. Kyler Korstanje (Holton)11 .... 16:52
14. Matt Bartels (Saginaw Nouvel)12 .... 16:52
15. Daniel Holder (Hudson)11 .... 16:53
35. Mitch Nurenberg (Pewamo-Westphalia)10 .. 17:19
36. Brock Simon (Pewamo-Westphalia)12 .. 17:20
38. Kyle Hengesbach (Pewamo-Westphalia)10 .. 17:22
43. Trent Barker (Pewamo-Westphalia)11 .. 17:29
46. Zach Schmitz (Pewamo-Westphalia)12 .. 17:30
47. Daniel Mikovits (Concord)12 .... 17:30
226. Troy Hagen (Pewamo-Westphalia)9 .. 20:54

2017 D4 BOYS

CarLee Stimpfel of Cass City returned to successfully defend his title, becoming the eleventh runner to win more than once in Class D/D4. Said the champ, "It was definitely a lot tougher race than last year. I don't know what it was. I think it was more mental."

Mt. Pleasant Sacred Heart, coached by Mark Zitzelsberger, won its first title since 1977, putting its first five across with a 40-second spread.

Michigan Int. Speedway, Brooklyn, Nov. 4
2017 BOYS DIVISION 4 TEAMS
1. Mt Pleasant Sacred Heart 126
2. Potterville 185
3. Beal City 204
4. Ellsworth 255
5. Ubly 280
6. East Jordan 281
7. Sand Creek 282
8. Cass City 284
9. Plymouth Christian 285
10. Battle Creek St Philip 294
11. Bear Lake-Onekama 315
12. Dansville 350
13. Carson City-Crystal 366
14. Walkerville 369
15. Johannesburg-Lewiston 376
16. Deckerville 412
17. Hudson 427
18. Muskegon Western Michigan Christian .. 430
19. Lutheran Westland 432
20. Hillsdale Academy 443
21. Mendon 468
22. Maple City Glen Lake 474
23. White Cloud 483
24. Gobles 488
25. Bridgman 528
26. Hesperia 562
27. Rochester Hills Lutheran Northwest ... 585
28. Auburn Hills Oakland Christian 738

2017 BOYS DIVISION 4 INDIVIDUALS
1. CarLee Stimpfel (Cass City)12 .... 16:08
2. Luke Pohl (Plymouth Christian)11 .... 16:14
3. Alex Grifka (Ubly)12 .... 16:24
4. Tylor Ross (Fairview)12 .... 16:34
5. Shane Achterhof (Walkerville)10 .... 16:36
6. Zane Aldrich (Whittemore-Prescott)12 .. 16:39
7. Carlos Gascho (Johannesburg-Lewiston)9 .. 16:44
8. Gary McBride (Bear Lake-Onekama)12 .. 16:45
9. Davis Tebben Lansing Christian)12 ..... 16:46
10. Seth Windle (Plymouth Christian)12 ... 16:48
11. Nicholas Swanson (Ubly)12 .... 16:48
12. Alex Taylor (Beal City)11 .... 16:48
13. Kaiden Hejl (Bear Lake-Onekama)12 .. 16:50
14. David Frederick (Tekonsha)11 .... 16:51
15. Ben Perry (Marine City Mooney)12 ..... 16:52
25. TJ Moore (Mt Pleasant Sacred H)11 ... 17:04
31. Chase Nelson (Mt Pleasant Sacred H)11 .. 17:10
40. Josh Lynch (Mt Pleasant Sacred H)10 .. 17:30
46. Matthew Nowak (Mt Pleasant Sacred H)9 .. 17:34
54. Noah Schafer (Mt Pleasant Sacred H)12 .. 17:44
65. Zach Ervin (Mt Pleasant Sacred Heart)11 .. 17:51
96. Xavier Addison (Mt Pleasant Sacred H)11 .. 18:14

2018 D4 BOYS

Saugatuck won its third state title, with team leader Corey Gorgas winning the individual title as well. "I'm just so happy right now we pulled this off," he said.

"We were going against the defending champ. They have a great team, great coach, great program. We knew they were going to be tough to beat. We put in a lot of work this summer."

Two-time runner-up Luke Pohl had gone out hard, leading the field past the 800 mark before Pettinga took over.

Michigan Int. Speedway, Brooklyn, Nov. 3

2018 BOYS DIVISION 4 TEAMS
1. Saugatuck 62
2. Mt Pleasant Sacred Heart 102
3. East Jordan 153
4. Breckenridge 157
5. Unionville-Sebewaing 227
6. Muskegon Western Michigan Christian 266
7. Dryden 293
8. Plymouth Christian 295
9. Potterville 295
10. Hillsdale Academy 301
11. Beal City 333
12. Bridgman 388
13. Concord 391
14. Lutheran Westland 408
15. Mayville 411
16. Saranac 422
17. Lake Leelanau St Mary 426
18. Ellsworth 429
19. Kalamazoo Christian 430
20. Hudson 471
21. Rochester Hills Lutheran Northwest 475
22. Gobles 495
23. Mason County Eastern 523
24. Bear Lake-Onekama 532
25. Addison 545
26. Johannesburg-Lewiston 575
27. Mendon 626

2018 BOYS DIVISION 4 INDIVIDUALS
1. Corey Gorgas (Saugatuck)12 .... 15:34
2. Luke Pohl (Plymouth Christian)12 .... 16:14
3. Nik Pettinga (Saugatuck)10 .... 16:18
4. Alex Taylor (Beal City)12 .... 16:19
5. Coleman Clark (Carson City-Crystal)10 ...... 16:23
6. Mason Sumner (Breckenridge)9 .... 16:23
7. Shane Acherthof (Walkerville)11 .... 16:30
8. Carlos Gascho (Johannesburg-Lewiston)10 . 16:34
9. Hunter Adams (Adrian Lenawee Christian)12 16:45
10. Reginald Richmond (White Cloud)11 .... 16:46
11. Brenden Knuth (Dryden)12 .... 17:01
12. Bentley Alderson (Unionville-Sebewaing)10 17:04
13. Ethan Rozanski (Dryden)12 .... 17:04
14. Wyatt Emmons (Mayville)10 .... 17:04
15. Max Sharnas (Saugatuck)9 .... 17:05
28. Ray Bartlett (Saugatuck)12 .... 17:12
30. Winston Marcy (Saugatuck)11 .... 17:17
73. Tristan Ashley (Saugatuck)9 .... 18:08
84. Adam Martinson (Saugatuck)9 .... 18:15

Corey Gorgas led his Saugatuck teammates to the victory. (Pete Draugalis photo)

2019 D4 BOYS

Breckenridge came away with the big trophy, 43 years after the school last won at the 1976 Class C finals. "We set this goal two years ago and the kids completely bought it," said coach Kurt Gulick. "I knew we had it by the halfway point of the race. The boys ran really well."

Junior Mason Sumner took the individual win for the Huskies, moving away from the pack after a 10:28 at the 2M mark. "It went well; it went how I wanted it to go," he told RunMichigan.

Michigan Int. Speedway, Brooklyn, Nov. 2

2019 BOYS DIVISION 4 TEAMS
1. Breckenridge 72
2. Unionville-Sebewaing 131
3. East Jordan 166
4. Carson City-Crystal 192
5. Petoskey St Michael 211
6. Wyoming Potter's House 227
7. Mt Pleasant Sacred Heart 230
8. Concord 276
9. Mason County Eastern 320
10. Webberville 341
11. Bridgman 341
12. Beal City 366
13. Morrice 373
14. Dansville 378
15. Muskegon Western Michigan Christian 396
16. Mendon 409
17. Kalamazoo Christian 414
18. Whitmore Lake 436
19. Allen Park Cabrini 442
20. Johannesburg-Lewiston 449
21. Hillsdale Academy 453
22. Deckerville 484
23. Lawrence 499
24. Plymouth Christian 521
25. Frankfort 582
26. Rochester Hills Lutheran Northwest 600
27. Sand Creek 644
28. Maple City Glen Lake 721

2019 BOYS DIVISION 4 INDIVIDUALS
1. Mason Sumner (Breckenridge)10 .... 16:08
2. Coleman Clark (Carson City-Crystal)11 ..... 16:17
3. Nathan Lott (Webberville)10 .... 16:18
4. Jonathan Mikovits (Concord)10 .... 16:26
5. Carlos Gascho (Johannesburg-Lewiston)11 . 16:29
6. Matthew Nowak (MP Sacred Heart)11 .... 16:33
7. Shane Acherthof (Walkerville)12 .... 16:45
8. Wyatt Emmmons (Mayville)11 .... 16:47
9. Josh Lynch (Mt Pleasant Sacred Heart)12 . 16:54
10. Jalen Nelson (Dansville)11 .... 16:55
11. Caleb Stout (Wyoming Potter's House)12 . 16:55
12. Colttion Vine (Breckenridge)11 .... 16:57
13. Grayson Rasmus (Saranac)11 .... 16:59
14. Caleb Rivers (Morrice)11 .... 17:03
15. Reginald Richmond (White Cloud)12 .... 17:04
18. Trent Carter (Breckenridge)10 .... 17:08
26. Ashton Gillis (Breckenridge)12 .... 17:16
40. Colton Chovanec (Breckenridge)12 .... 17:34
108. Jonathan Markley (Breckenridge)12 ...... 18:27
180. Weston Wise (Breckenridge)12 .... 19:17

CLASS D/D4 STATISTICS

TOP 25 CLOCKINGS AT MIS
15:23 Tec Adams (Harbor Springs)12 2008
15:23 Jesse Hersha (Concord)12 2014
15:26 Kevin Oblinger (MP Sacred Heart)12 2008
15:26 Kyle Tait (Big Rapids Crossroads)12 2010
15:30 Ryan Shay (Central Lake)12 1996
15:30 Christian Birky (Saugatuck)12 2008
15:31 Kyle Stacks (Concord)11 2008
15:33 J. Hersha (Concord)10 2012
15:34 Corey Gorgas (Saugatuck)12 2018
15:35 Stephen Shay (Central Lake)12 2003
15:43 Will Boylan-Pett (Bath)12 2000
15:44 Andy Duemling (Ubly)12 2000
15:49 Mike Putzke (New Buffalo)12 2001
15:49 Ben Wynsma (Suttons Bay)11 2008
15:50 K. Oblinger (MP Sacred Heart)11 2007
15:50 J. Hersha (Concord)11 2013
15:51 Jeff Luehm (St Louis)12 2000
15:51 Liam Boylan-Pett (Bath)12 2003
15:52 Josh Hofbauer (Harbor Springs)11 2003
15:52 Spencer Nousain (Concord)11 2010
15:53 David Zinger (Evart)12 2012
15:55 K. Stacks (Concord)12 2009
15:55 Santana Scott (Evart)11 2014
15:56 Larry Julson (Potterville)12 2008
15:56 S. Nousain (Concord)12 2011

BIGGEST WINNING MARGINS
66.1 Ryan Shay/Trevor McGinn 1996
57 Ryan Shay/Elijah Eversole .... 1994 I
44.4 Jesse Hersha/Josh Wojan 2013
43 Mike Richardson/Casey Shay .... 1990 I
42 Marty McGinn/Eric Bierstetel .... 1993 T

SMALLEST WINNING MARGINS
0.3 Mike Putzke/David Harrand 1999
1 Tim Miller/Greg Miller .... 1980 T
1.0 Will Boylan-Pett/Andy Duemling 2000
2 Ken St John/Matt Pringle 1974
2.6 Matt Hanko/Loren Milbrath 2005
3 Preston Pike/Doug Corcoran .... 1989 I
3.05 Liam Boylan-Pett/Matt Kibbey 2002
3.3 Tec Adams/Kevin Oblinger 2008

LOWEST WINNING SCORES
40 Bear Lake 1991
42 Fowler 1990
44 Ann Arbor Greenhills 1983
46 Mt Pleasant Sacred Heart 1977
47 Fowler 1989
49 Grass Lake 1993
51 Saugatuck 2015
52 Ann Arbor Greenhills 1985
52 Fowler 1988
54 Bath 1994

HIGHEST WINNING SCORES
148 Hesperia 2006
144 Potterville 2007
143 Lawton 2001
131 Pewamo-Westphalia 2016
129 Potterville 2008
127 St Louis 2005
126 Mt Pleasant Sacred Heart 2017
124 Hesperia 2004
121 Kingsley 1974
113 Harbor Springs 2002
113 Saugatuck 2013

CLOSEST TEAM FINISH
0 MP Sacred Heart/Akron-Fairgrove 1977
0 Concord/Kingsley 1986
1 Grass Lake/Fowler 1995
1 Hesperia/Bear Lake-Onekama 2004
2 Potterville/Adrian Lenawee Christian 2008

BIGGEST WINNING TEAM MARGIN
111 Fowler/Pentwater 1990
70 Lawton 2001
59 MP Sacred Heart/Potterville 2017
59 Breckenridge/Unionville-Sebewaing 2019
54 Harbor Springs/Hudson 2003

UPPER PENINSULA BOYS

The Beginnings
In the UP, the term "cross country" was more often paired with cross country skiing, a sport imported by the many Finns who settled in the area.

An Upper Peninsula championships began in 1927 when it was won by Iron Mountain's Jimmie Crummey. Four weeks later Crummey and his teammates traveled to the state championships in Ypsilanti, where Crummey was runner-up in the Class B race.

Jimmie Crummey of Iron Mountain.

In 1931, the Sault Ste. Marie squad won the state championship in Class B, led by individual winner Robert Loughead. Then in the late '30s, Iron Mountain went on a tear under the coaching of Dick Chard, winning Class B titles in 1937 and 1938 and placing second in 1939.

In 1940 and 1941, no UP teams traveled south to the state finals. World War II marked the end of UP teams participating in the state finals. Originally the trips south were stopped on the basis of fuel rationing for the wartime effort. But with the end of the war, there was no interest among UP athletic directors to rejoin the fold. To this day, Michigan is the only state that does not offer an actual state championship in the sport.

This history tracks the UP championships from the beginning of World War II.

1942 UP BOYS
The forerunner of the separate UP Finals came in 1942. Because of wartime fuel restrictions, the MHSAA decided to cancel the regional meets and instead hold separate "final" meets that looked a lot like regionals. Schools were urged to attend the closest one. Only one was scheduled for the UP, and it was a de facto peninsula championship.

Escanaba, October 17 ☐
1942 UP FINAL – CLASS B TEAMS
1. Iron Mountain 18
2. Escanaba 37

1943 UP BOYS
In a similar set-up to the previous year, a final was held in the UP. However, it was still considered a temporary wartime situation. As per tradition, it was held at halftime of the Iron Mountain-Escanaba football game.

Iron Mountain, Oct. 16 ☒
1943 BOYS UPPER PENINSULA TEAMS
1. Escanaba 23
2. Kingsford 50
3. Iron Mountain 54

1943 BOYS UPPER PENINSULA INDIVIDUALS
1. Harris (Escanaba) .... nt
2. Williams (Escanaba) .... nt
3. McConaughy (Iron Mountain) .... nt
4. Pesavento (Iron Mountain) .... nt
5. Johnson (Escanaba) .... nt

1944 UP BOYS
In the annual halftime race, Iron Mountain made it a clean sweep of the top 5 places. Escanaba's Dan Anderson, placed 6th.

Escanaba, Oct. 21 ☒
1944 BOYS UP CLASS B TEAMS
1. Iron Mountain 15
2. Escanaba 44
(only two teams entered)

1944 BOYS UP CLASS B INDIVIDUALS
1. David McConaughy (Iron Mountain) .... nt
2. William Pesavent (Iron Mountain) .... nt
3. John McConaughy (Iron Mountain) .... nt
4. John Trembreull (Iron Mountain) .... nt
5. Raymond Hughes (Iron Mountain) .... nt

1944 BOYS UP CLASS C/D/E TEAMS
1. Baraga 24
(only complete team entered)

1944 BOYS UP CLASS C/D/E INDIVIDUALS
1. David Bryers (McMillan) .... nt
2. Waino Tervo (Baraga) .... nt
3. Walter Williams (McMillan) .... nt
4. Earl Jacobson (Baraga) .... nt
5. Richard Lytikainen (Baraga) .... nt

1945 UP BOYS
Iron Mountain's Dave Siegel, favored for the win in Class B, had his right shoe fall off an amazing eight times. He noted that he had to pass some of the runners seven times. Not surprisingly, he finished far back in the pack.

Iron Mountain, Oct. 20 ☐
1945 BOYS UP CLASS B TEAMS
1. Iron Mountain 27
2. Escanaba 37
(only two teams entered)

1945 BOYS UP CLASS B INDIVIDUALS
1. Duane Carlson (Iron Mountain) 10:55
2. Glen Porterfield (Menominee) .... nt
3. Robert Weiser (Iron Mountain) .... nt
4. John McConaughy (Iron Mountain) .... nt
5. Robert Ostrum (Escanaba) .... nt

1945 BOYS UP CLASS C/D/E TEAMS
1. Baraga .... ns
(only full team entered)

1946 UP BOYS
Menominee placed 1-2 in the B race to roll to a 31-point performance, led by Glenn Porterfield.

Escanaba, Oct. 19 ☐
1946 BOYS UP CLASS B TEAMS
1. Menominee 31
2. Escanaba 51
3. Iron Mountain 64
(no other complete teams)

1946 BOYS UP CLASS B INDIVIDUALS
1. Glenn Porterfield (Menominee) 9:48
2. Edward Tappan (Menominee) .... nt
3. Robert Ostrom (Escanaba) .... nt

1946 BOYS UP CLASS C/D/E TEAMS
1. Eben 21
2. Baraga 36
(only two teams entered)

1946 BOYS UP CLASS C/D/E INDIVIDUALS
1. Paul Nykanen (Eben) 10:31
2. Bernart Frigard (Eben) .... nt

1947 UP BOYS
Bill Tappan led Menominee to its second-straight win.

Iron Mountain, Oct. 18 ☐
1947 BOYS UP CLASS B TEAMS
1. Menominee 23
2. Iron Mountain 47
3. Escanaba 53

1947 BOYS UP CLASS B INDIVIDUALS
1. Bill Tappan (Menominee) 10:29
2. R. Ostrom (Escanaba) .... nt
3. J. Foley (Menominee) .... nt

1947 BOYS UP CLASS C/D/E TEAMS
1. Eben 18
2. Baraga 41
(only two teams entered)

1947 BOYS UP CLASS C/D/E INDIVIDUALS
1. C. Johnson (Eben) 10:29
2. P. Nykane (Eben) .... nt
3. Wesley Tervo (Baraga) .... nt

1948 UP BOYS
Bill Tappan won his second-straight title as Memoninee won No. 3 in a row.

Escanaba HS, Escanaba, Oct. 16 ☐
1948 BOYS UP CLASS B TEAMS

1. Menominee 18
2. Escanaba 49
3. Manistique 61
4. Iron Mountain 98

1948 BOYS UP CLASS B INDIVIDUALS
1. Bill Tappan (Menominee) 11:05
2. Dan Lysakowski (Menominee) .... nt
3. Dan Lasnoski (Escanaba) .... nt

1948 BOYS UP CLASS C/D/E TEAMS
1. Chatham-Eben 25
2. Baraga 35
(only two teams entered)

1948 BOYS UP CLASS C/D/E INDIVIDUALS
1. Wesley Tervo (Baraga) 11:38
2. Ralph Turunen (Baraga) .... nt
3. Leslie Aho (Eben) .... nt

Menominee's championship squad, 1948.

1949 BOYS
According to newspaper reports, the athletes ran 2.75 miles, which seems unlikely given the fast time. Tom Hazen finished the last quarter mile minus his left shoe.

Iron Mountain, Oct. 15 □
1949 BOYS UP CLASS B TEAMS
1. Menominee 21
2. Manistique 51
3. Escanaba 82
4. Iron Mountain 88
5. Marquette 125

1949 BOYS UP CLASS B INDIVIDUALS
1. Tom Hazen (Menominee) 10:29
2. Ronald Bauer (Menominee) .... nt
3. Don Lysakowski (Menominee) .... nt
4. W. LaBar (Manistique) .... nt
5. Supanich (Calumet) .... nt

1949 BOYS UP CLASS C/D/E TEAMS
1. Baraga 27
2. Eben 30
(only two teams entered)

1949 BOYS UP CLASS C/D/E INDIVIDUALS
1. Don Johnston (Eben) 11:04

1950 UP BOYS
Escanaba, coached by Harry Wylie, put five in the top 15 to replace 4-time champ Menominee—which did not send a team.

Escanaba HS, Escanaba, Oct. 14 □
1950 BOYS UP CLASS B TEAMS
1. Escanaba 45
2. Manistique 51
3. Ironwood 54
4. Marquette 69

1950 BOYS UP CLASS B INDIVIDUALS
1. Rodney Mattson (Ironwood) 10:43
2. Dale Kangas (Ironwood) .... nt
3. Jack Quinn (Marquette) .... nt

1950 BOYS UP CLASS C/D/E TEAMS
1. Baraga 22
2. Chatham 36

1950 BOYS UP CLASS C/D/E INDIVIDUALS
1. Donald Johnson (Eben) 11:28
2. James Archambeau (Eben) .... nt
3. John Dorsky (Eben) .... nt

1951 UP BOYS
Sault Ste. Marie prevailed with a 16-point margin over defending champ Escanaba.

Iron Mountain, Oct. 13 □
1951 BOYS UP CLASS B TEAMS
1. Sault Ste Marie 42
2. Escanaba 58
3. Ironwood 76
4. Menominee 85
5. Manistique 101

1951 BOYS UP CLASS B INDIVIDUALS
1. T. VanLuven (Sault Ste Marie) 10:43

1951 BOYS UP CLASS C/D/E TEAMS
1. Eben 19
2. Baraga 36

1951 BOYS UP CLASS C/D/E INDIVIDUALS
1. Vartti (Eben) 11:20

1952 UP BOYS
Still run during halftime of the Escanaba-Iron mountain football game, the meet saw the runners from the Soo defend their title successfully. Dick Casey sprinted away from runner-up Jack Quinn and broke the course record. Quinn had a lead of 150-feet when they entered the stadium, but Casey ran him down.

Escanaba, Oct. 11 □
1952 BOYS UP CLASS B TEAMS
1. Sault Ste Marie 58
2. Escanaba 66
3. Ironwood 82
4. Manistique 96
5. Menominee 117

1952 BOYS UP CLASS B INDIVIDUALS
1. Dick Casey (Escanaba) 10:37
2. Jack Quinn (Manistique) .... nt
3. Carl Seneglee (Sault Ste Marie) .... nt
4. Glenn Bumstead (Sault Ste Marie) .... nt
5. Arnold Kero (Ironwood) .... nt

1952 BOYS UP CLASS C/D/E TEAMS
1. Baraga 31
2. Houghton 42
3. Eben 55

1952 BOYS UP CLASS C/D/E INDIVIDUALS
1. Edwin Jalonen (Eben) 11:22
3. Norman Juntunen (Baraga) .... nt

1953 UP BOYS
Ron Groleau won the C-D-E crown in his first season of running, winning by 300 yards. Houghton won its first-ever state title.

Iron Mountain, Oct. 10 □
1953 BOYS UP CLASS B TEAMS
1. Menominee 44
2. Saulte Ste Marie 45
3. Ishpeming 49
4. Ironwood 93
5. Escanaba 141

1953 BOYS UP CLASS B INDIVIDUALS
1. Phil Poquette (Menominee) 10:56

1953 BOYS UP CLASS C/D/E TEAMS
1. Houghton 26
2. Nahma 48
3. Baraga 63
4. Vulcan .... ?
5. Chatham .... ?

1953 BOYS UP CLASS C/D/E INDIVIDUALS
1. Ron Grouleau (Nahma) 11:10

1954 UP BOYS
Rapid River was indeed rapid as it scored a perfect 15 points to capture the UP CDE championship, run at halftime in the Escanaba-Iron Mountain football game. Bill Lundin (4th) and Larry Paul (5th) joined the top three in the unprecedented sweep. In Class B, Sault Ste. Marie grabbed the three top places.

Escanaba HS, Escanaba, Oct. 16 ⊠
1954 BOYS UP CLASS B TEAMS
1. Sault Ste Marie 24
2. Menominee 40
3. Escanaba 85
4. Ishpeming 107
5. Ironwood 127

1954 BOYS UP CLASS B INDIVIDUALS
1. Ove Lundgren (Sault Ste Marie) 10.55
2. Jim Long (Sault Ste Marie) .... nt
3. Jim Stafford (Sault Ste Marie) .... nt
4. George Quaal (Ishpeming) .... nt
5. Pete Tessier (Menominee) .... nt

1954 BOYS UP CLASS C/D/E TEAMS
1. Rapid River 15
2. Nahma 72
3. Houghton 86
4. Vulcan 91
5. Baraga 113

1954 BOYS UP CLASS C/D/E INDIVIDUALS
1. Ken Harwood (Rapid River) 11:06
2. Steve Johnson (Rapid River) .... nt
3. Jim Greenlund (Rapid River) .... nt
4. Bill Lundin (Rapid River) .... nt
5. Larry Paul (Rapid River) .... nt

1955 UP BOYS
The Class C-D-E race went off first, so Steve Johnson got credit for the first course record (on a new course this year). Class B's Jim Stafford earned a tie minutes later.

Iron Mountain HS, Iron Mountain, Oct. 15 □
1955 BOYS UP CLASS B TEAMS
1. Sault Ste Marie 25
2. Escanaba 36
3. Ironwood 61
4. Marquette .... ?

1955 BOYS UP CLASS B INDIVIDUALS
1. Jim Stafford (Sault Ste Marie) 10:24
4. Eugene Gamache (Escanaba) .... nt
5. Bob Rohde (Escanaba) .... nt

1955 BOYS UP CLASS C/D/E TEAMS
1. Pickford 28
2. Rapid River 43
3. Baraga 76
4. Nahama .... ?
5. Cooks .... ?

1955 BOYS UP CLASS C/D/E INDIVIDUALS
1. Steve Johnson (Rapid River)11 .... 10:24
2. Ken Harwood (Rapid River)11 .... nt

1956 UP BOYS
In CDE, Kan Harwood nipped his teammate Steve Johnson after trailing him earlier in the race.

Escanaba, Oct. 13
1956 BOYS UP CLASS B TEAMS
1. Escanaba 36
2. Marquette Graveraet 53
3. Sault Ste Marie 59
4. Kingsford 76

1956 BOYS UP CLASS B INDIVIDUALS
1. Jim Brunelle (Escanaba) 11:23
2. Bob Anderson (Escanaba) .... nt
3. Fred White (Marquette) .... nt
4. Bernhard Johnson (Kingsford) .... nt
5. Larry Maki (Marquette) .... nt

1956 BOYS UP CLASS C/D/E TEAMS
1. Rapid River 52
2. Pickford 82
3. Baraga 90
4. Nahma .... ns
5. Dollar Bay .... ns

1956 BOYS UP CLASS C/D/E INDIVIDUALS
1. Ken Harwood (Rapid River) 11:14
2. Steve Johnson (Rapid River) .... nt
3. Roger Wahl (Pickford) .... nt
4. Sven Backman (Dollar Bay) .... nt
5. Ted O'Brien (Pickford) .... nt

1957 UP BOYS

Still apparently held at halftime of the big football game, the UP meet reached a low point when the Class B race was cancelled because only one team showed.

Escanaba, Oct. 12
1957 BOYS UP CLASS B – Cancelled; only one team showed.

1957 BOYS UP CLASS C/D/E TEAMS
1. Pickford 52
2. Rapid River 73
3. Baraga 76
4. Marquette Baraga 110
5. Dollar Bay 119

1957 BOYS UP CLASS C/D/E INDIVIDUAL
1. Douglas Treado (Marquette Baraga) 11:05

1958 UP BOYS

After the previous year's debacle, the football halftime years were over. The meet moved to a date two weeks later and to the Marquette Golf and Country Club, a course that won favorable reviews from the attending coaches. Escanaba won Class B with 18 points, the third lowest total ever.

Marquette Golf & GC, Marquette, Oct. 25
1958 BOYS UP CLASS B TEAMS
1. Escanaba 18
2. Kingsford 43
(only two teams entered)

1958 BOYS UP CLASS B INDIVIDUALS
1. Pete Ladoucher (Escanaba) 11:29
2. Clinton Schroeder (Escanaba) .... nt
3. David Klasell (Escanaba) .... nt
4. Dick Arntzen (Escanaba) .... nt

1958 BOYS UP CLASS C/D/E TEAMS
1. Pickford 25
2. Rapid River 67
3. Vulcan 90
4. Baraga 100
5. Marquette Baraga 112

1958 BOYS UP CLASS C/D/E INDIVIDUALS
1. Anthony Lee (DeTour) 11:27
2. Mike McCarthy (Pickford) .... nt
3. Ken Stevenson (Pickford) .... nt
4. Bruce Taylor (Pickford) .... nt

1959 UP BOYS

The course at the Marquette GCC was "slightly revised", so that the finish was on a slightly downhill stretch instead of the previous year's uphill location. The meet was run a week earlier as well. Only three teams contested the Class B title, still a significant improvement over the previous few years. The weather was described as "bitter cold."

Marquette Golf and CC, Marquette, Oct. 17
1959 BOYS UP CLASS A/B TEAMS
1. Escanaba 23
2. Marquette Graveraet 43
3. Newberry 56

1959 BOYS UP CLASS A/B INDIVIDUALS
1. Pete Ladoucher (Escanaba) 12:31
2. Doug Nelson (Escanaba) .... nt
3. Pete Schroeder (Escanaba) .... nt
4. Jim Anderson (Marquette Graveraet) ... nt
5. Joe Hebert (Escanaba) .... nt

1959 BOYS UP CLASS C/D TEAMS
1. Rapid River 46
2. Vulcan 55
3. Pickford 56
4. Brimley 87
5. DeTour 118

1959 BOYS UP CLASS C/D INDIVIDUALS
1. Ronald Rapson (Pickford)10 .... 11:28
2. Dwight Harwood (Rapid River) .... nt
3. Anthony Lee (DeTour) .... nt
4. Gerry Arnold (Vulcan) .... nt
5. Jack Barry (Vulcan) .... nt

1960 UP BOYS

The meet was co-sponsored by Northern Michigan College. Four schools entered the B Run. In C/D, Vulcan--which no longer exists--won its first and only state title. The former mining town is now part of the Norway school district.

Marquette Golf & CC, Marquette, Oct. 15
1960 BOYS UP CLASS A/B TEAMS
=1. Escanaba 40
=1. Kingsford 40
3. Marquette Graveraet 42
4. Sault Ste. Marie 105

1960 BOYS UP CLASS A/B INDIVIDUALS
1. Kenny Johnson (Marquette Graveraet) 11:54
2. Joe Hebert (Escanaba) 12:08
4. Mike Oates (Marquette Graveraet) .... nt

1960 BOYS UP CLASS C/D TEAMS
1. Vulcan 43
2. Rudyard 56
3. Rapid River 91
4. Pickford 102
5. Baraga 112

1960 BOYS UP CLASS C/D INDIVIDUALS
1. Dwight Harwood (Rapid River) 11:12
2. Joe Haferkorn (Vulcan) 11:30
3. Marshall Kuivinen (Baraga) .... nt

1961 UP BOYS

Newspapers reported excellent conditions for the UP runs. According to reports, at least 9 of the Class B runners broke the old course record of 11:31.

Marquette Golf & CC, Marquette, Oct. 21
1961 BOYS UP CLASS A/B TEAMS
1. Escanaba 31
2. Marquette Graveraet 48
3. Sault Ste Marie 65
4. Kingsford 81

1961 BOYS UP CLASS A/B INDIVIDUALS
1. Kenny Johnson (Marquette Graveraet) 11:07
2. Meyers (Marquette Graveraet) .... nt
3. Dick Ball (Sault Ste Marie) .... nt
4. Fred Ivens (Escanaba) .... nt
5. Doug Nelson (Escanaba) .... nt

1961 BOYS UP CLASS C/D TEAMS
1. Rudyard 63
2. Pickford 64
3. Rapid River 84
4. Vulcan 97
5. Baraga 109

1961 BOYS UP CLASS C/D INDIVIDUALS
1. Marshall Kuivinen (Baraga) 10:58
2. Ed Broclaw (Vulcan) .... nt
3. Paul Olson (Rapid River) .... nt
4. Dave Braden (Rudyard) .... nt
5. Don Gattra (Vulcan) .... nt

1962 UP BOYS

Rudyard won honors for the quickest transition ever to big school status. The Class C-D champions the previous year, the school had been promoted to Class B only two weeks before this race, and won it by six points. Class A-B winner Thomas Chestnut returned to Ishpeming after two years away.

Marquette Golf & CC, Marquette, Oct. 13
1962 BOYS UP CLASS A/B TEAMS
1. Rudyard 32
2. Sault Ste Marie 38
3. Escanaba 84
4. Marquette 109

1962 BOYS UP CLASS A/B INDIVIDUALS
1. Thomas Chestnut (Ishpeming) 11:08
2. Jim Postma (Rudyard) .... nt
3. Dick Ball (Sault Ste Marie) .... nt
4. Louis Thorne (Sault St Marie) .... nt
5. Ron Hintz (Rudyard) .... nt

1962 BOYS UP CLASS C/D TEAMS
1. Vulcan 60
2. DeTour 79
3. Rapid River 80
4. Pickford 92
5. Perkins 132

1962 BOYS UP CLASS C/D INDIVIDUALS
1. Paul Olson (Rapid River) 10:59
2. Ed Breclaw (Vulcan) .... nt
3. Marshall Kuivinen (Baraga) .... nt
4. Don Gattra (Vulcan) .... nt

The Rudyard 1963 team.

1963 UP BOYS

Rudyard, led by Jeff Kamper, easily topped the Class B field. In Class C/D, DeTour won its first team title ever.

Marquette Golf & CC, Marquette, Oct. 19
1963 BOYS UP CLASS A/B TEAMS
1. Rudyard 39
2. Ishpeming 80

3. Sault Ste Marie 84
=4. Escanaba 99
=4. Marquette Graveraet 99

1963 BOYS UP CLASS A/B INDIVIDUALS
1. Jeff Kamper (Rudyard) 10:47
2. Ron Hintz (Rudyard) .... nt
3. Rod LaFond (Newberry) .... nt
5. Dennis Burkman (Marquette Graveraet) ...... nt

1963 BOYS UP CLASS C/D TEAMS
1. DeTour 62
2. Cooks 78
3. Perkins 79
4. Pickford .... ?
5. Rapid River .... ?

1963 BOYS UP CLASS C/D INDIVIDUALS
1. Walter Roberts (Cooks) 10:56
2. Doug Ehle (Cedarville) .... nt
3. Tom Teeple (Perkins) .... nt
4. Steve Simonsen (Perkins) .... nt
5. Ron Zwolinski (DeTour) .... nt

1964 UP BOYS
Runners faced fierce winds and a snow-covered course that by the end of the day was labelled "treacherous." Ishpeming survived best, winning its first-ever state championship.

Ishpeming's first championship team.

Marquette CC, Marquette, Oct. 10
1964 BOYS UP CLASS A/B TEAMS
1. Ishpeming 55
2. Escanaba 66
3. Sault Ste Marie 68
4. Menominee 110
5. Gladstone 116

1964 BOYS UP CLASS A/B INDIVIDUALS
1. Bruce Ellison (Gladstone) 11:17
2. Tom McCutchen (Newberry) .... nt
3. Gary Vandeville (Escanaba) .... nt
4. Gordon Leppanen (Ishpeming)10 .... nt
5. Rodney Montcalm (Ishpeming)12 .... nt

1964 BOYS UP CLASS C/D TEAMS
1. Pickford 43
2. DeTour 58
3. Cooks 109
4. Brimley .... ns
5. Rapid River .... ns

1964 BOYS UP CLASS C/D INDIVIDUALS
1. John Krzycky (Pickford) 11:38
2. Greg Leedy (DeTour) 11:43
3. John Stano (Ironwood St Ambrose)12 ...... 11:44

1965 UP BOYS
Ishpeming won a second-straight title with a 31-point performance.

Northern Michigan Univ., Marquette, Oct. 16
1965 BOYS UP CLASS A/B TEAMS
1. Ishpeming 31
2. Rudyard 87
3. Sault Ste Marie 96

1965 BOYS UP CLASS A/B INDIVIDUALS
1. Gene Cyrus (Ishpeming) 10:57

1965 BOYS UP CLASS C/D TEAMS
1. DeTour 48
2. Cooks 119
3. Painesdale-Jeffers 130

1965 BOYS UP CLASS C/D INDIVIDUALS
1. Greg Ledy (DeTour) 11:18
5. Jim Richards (Ironwood St Ambrose) 11:34

1966 UP BOYS
Ishpeming got even better, winning No. 3 in a row with a dominant 26 points.

Marquette Golf & CC, Marquette, Oct. 22
1966 BOYS UP CLASS A/B TEAMS
1. Ishpeming 26
2. Menominee 37
3. Gladstone 71

1966 BOYS UP CLASS A/B INDIVIDUALS
1. Gordon Pekuri (Menominee)10 .... 10:33

1966 BOYS UP CLASS C/D TEAMS
1. Rudyard 63
2. DeTour 80
3. Cooks 86

1966 BOYS UP CLASS C/D INDIVIDUALS
1. Greg Ledy (DeTour) 10:50

1967 UP BOYS
Menominee unseated three-time champion Ishpeming, 50-72.

Northern Michigan Univ., Marquette, Oct. 14
1967 BOYS UP CLASS A/B TEAMS
1. Menominee 50
2. Ishpeming 72
3. Gladstone 80

1967 BOYS UP CLASS A/B INDIVIDUALS
1. Gordon Pekuri (Menominee)11 .... 10:35

1967 BOYS UP CLASS C/D TEAMS
1. Eben Junction 58
2. Pickford 63
3. DeTour 64

1967 BOYS UP CLASS C/D INDIVIDUALS
1. Michael Skytta (Champion) 11:02

1968 UP BOYS
Gordon Pekuri defended his Class A-B title, but for Ironwood this time, as his family had moved in the interim.

Northern Michigan Univ., Marquette, Oct. 19
1968 BOYS UP CLASS A/B TEAMS
1. Ishpeming 43
2. Ironwood 68
3. Menominee 70
4. Gladstone 82
5. Escanaba 130

1968 BOYS UP CLASS A/B INDIVIDUALS
1. Gordon Pekuri (Ironwood)12 .... 10:39
2. Jim Nelson (Ishpeming) .... nt
5. Mike Koldewey (Ishpeming) .... nt

1968 BOYS UP CLASS C/D TEAMS
1. Pickford 42
2. Brimley 101
3. DeTour 113
4. Rapid River 132
5. Big Bay de Noc 144

1968 BOYS UP CLASS C/D INDIVIDUALS
1. LeRoy Picciano (Baraga) 11:30
4. Bob Jacquart (Ironwood Catholic) .... nt

1969 UP BOYS
The Ishpeming Hematites put three in the top 10 to easily win the Class A/B crown.

Marquette Golf & CC, Marquette, Oct. 25
1969 BOYS UP CLASS A/B TEAMS
1. Ishpeming 47
2. Menominee 78
3. Calumet 107
4. Escanaba 121
5. Escanaba Holy Name 123

1969 BOYS UP CLASS A/B INDIVIDUALS
1. Paul Williams (Newberry) 10:39
2. Ivan Plude (Menominee) .... nt
3. Arlon Goforth (Sault Ste Marie) .... nt
4. James Nelson (Ishpeming) .... nt
5. Gary Patrick (Calumet) .... nt

1969 BOYS UP CLASS C/D TEAMS
1. Rudyard 77
2. Pickford 81
3. St Ignace 107
4. Big Bay de Noc 108
5. Rapid River 127

1969 BOYS UP CLASS C/D INDIVIDUALS
1. Fred Teddy (L'Anse)10 .... 10:43
2. Bob Jacquart (Ironwood Catholic) 10:57
5. Brian Dalko (Munising) .... nt

1970 UP BOYS
In the first year on a 2.5M course, Gary Patrick of Calumet won Class A/B in an automatic course record 12:57.

Marquette Golf & CC, Marquette, Oct. 24
1970 BOYS UP CLASS A/B TEAMS
1. Ishpeming 43
2. Menominee 48
3. Calumet 82
4. Escanaba 138
5. Rudyard 145

1970 BOYS UP CLASS A/B INDIVIDUALS
1. Gary Patrick (Calumet) 12:57
2. Garland Mattson (Ishpeming) .... nt
3. Gary Santti (Ishpeming) .... nt
4. Bryon Francom (Menominee) .... nt
5. Ivan Plude (Menominee) .... nt

1970 BOYS UP CLASS C/D TEAMS
1. Pickford 32
2. L'Anse 44
3. Ironwood Catholic 133
4. St Ignace .... ?
5. DeTour .... ?

1970 BOYS UP CLASS C/D INDIVIDUALS
1. Fred Teddy (L'Anse)11 .... 13:05
2. Dana Hill (Pickford) .... nt
3. Brian Aho (Painesdale-Jeffers) .... nt
4. Bill Skinner (Pickford) .... nt
5. Jim Hagen (St Ignace) .... nt

1971 UP BOYS
In a thrilling race, Paul Erspamer of Marquette beat defending champ Gary Patrick of Calumet as Ishpeming won its second-straight team title. Fred Teddy of L'Anse crushed the course record in the C/D race.

Marquette Country Club, Marquette, Oct. 9
1971 BOYS UP CLASS A/B TEAMS
1. Ishpeming 50
2. Calumet 54
3. Marquette 69
4. Escanaba 100
5. Menominee 132

1971 BOYS UP CLASS A/B INDIVIDUALS
1. Paul Erspamer (Marquette) 13:04

2. Gary Patrick (Calumet) 13:07
3. Maurice Simons (Escanaba)..........................nt

1971 BOYS UP CLASS C/D TEAMS
1. Pickford 64
2. L'Anse 90
3. Chassell 108
4. Ironwood Catholic 164

1971 BOYS UP CLASS C/D INDIVIDUALS
1. Fred Teddy (L'Anse)12 ....12:29
2. Pierre Soumis (Chassell) ....nt
3. Jim Skinner (Pickford) ....nt

1972 UP BOYS

Cold and wind caused the runners to produce slower times than expected over the lengthened course. Lloyd Hooper of Ishpeming upset favored teammate Glenn Santti to capture the A-B crown. It was the first year the distance was changed to 3M.

Northern Michigan Univ., Marquette, Oct. 21 □
1972 BOYS UP CLASS A/B TEAMS
1. Ishpeming 40
2. Menominee 58
3. Calumet 91
4. Sault Ste Marie..107
5. Escanaba 150

1972 BOYS UP CLASS A/B INDIVIDUALS
1. Lloyd Hooper (Ishpeming)12 ....16:50
2. Glenn Santti (Ishpeming) ....nt
3. Dan Leskela (Calumet) ....nt
4. Dave Baker (Ironwood) ....nt
5. Lee Aderman (Menominee) ....nt

Pickford's 1972 squad, with coach Web Morrison in upper right.

1972 BOYS UP CLASS C/D TEAMS
1. Pickford 66
2. Chassell 92
3. Perkins 136
4. Rudyard ....?
5. Crystal Falls ....?

1972 BOYS UP CLASS C/D INDIVIDUALS
1. Pierre Suomis (Chassell)12 ....16:42
2. Jim Skinner (Pickford).......................................nt
3. Terry Verbrigghe (Perkins) ....nt
4. Rick Brownell (Watersmeet) ....nt
5. Roger Thompson (Pickford) ....nt

1973 UP BOYS

Escanaba and Ironwood ran to a tie in Class A-B, and officials did not go to a tiebreaker. Escanaba took the trophy home on a coin flip, with Ironwood having to await a duplicate. Brad Benam of Munising ran a course record 15:37 to win C-D.

Northern Michigan Univ., Marquette, Oct. 20 □
1973 BOYS UP CLASS A/B TEAMS
=1. Escanaba 65
=1. Ironwood 65
3. Calumet 68
4. Ishpeming ....?
5. Sault Ste Marie..?

1973 BOYS UP CLASS A/B INDIVIDUALS
1. Dave Baker (Ironwood)................................15:41
2. Rob Cavalieri (Kingsford) 15:43
3. Dean Benoit (Escanaba)...................................nt
4. Tim Kennedy (Ironwood) ....nt
5. Wayne Kolesar (Ironwood) ....nt

1973 BOYS UP CLASS C/D TEAMS
1. Munising 72
2. Norway 94
3. Perkins 113
4. Chassell ....?
5. Pickford ....?

1973 BOYS UP CLASS C/D INDIVIDUALS
1. Brad Benam (Munising)...............................15:37
2. Tim Skinner (Pickford) ....nt
3. Brian Wing (Stephenson) ....nt

1974 BOYS UP BOYS

The meet was restructured with Class C and D being split into different races. The fastest runner of the day, Terry Verbrigghe, helped former Class E champion Perkins to its highest "D" finish ever.

Northern Michigan Univ., Marquette, Oct. 16 □
1974 BOYS UP CLASS A/B TEAMS
1. Escanaba 53
2. Menominee 60
3. Calumet 81
4. Ironwood 114
5. Ishpeming 118

1974 BOYS UP CLASS A/B INDIVIDUALS
1. Dean Benoit (Escanaba).............................16:06
2. Wayne Beckman (Ironwood) 16:08
3. Paul Peterson (Escanaba) ....nt
4. Tom Theoret (Gladstone) ....nt
5. Tony Stupping (Menominee) ....nt

1974 BOYS UP CLASS C TEAMS
1. Norway 34
2. Rudyard 74
3. Ishpeming Westwood 86
4. Munising 93
5. Hancock 97

1974 BOYS UP CLASS C INDIVIDUALS
1. Greg Harger (Munising) 16:18
2. Mike Degenear (Norway) ....nt
3. John Vanderworth (Rudyard) ....nt
4. Jeff Johnson (Ishpeming Westwood) ....nt
5. Mik Phillips (Norway) ....nt

1974 BOYS UP CLASS D TEAMS
1. Chassell 42
2. Perkins 65
3. Painesdale-Jeffers 135
4. Watersmeet ....?
5. Pickford ....?

1974 BOYS UP CLASS D INDIVIDUALS
1. Terry Verbrigghe (Perkins)11 ....16:02
2. Mark Palosaari (Chassell) ....nt
3. Craig Chartier (Eben)..nt

1975 UP BOYS

Escanaba won the Class A-B title after briefly losing its team because of millage problems the previous month. "It was just a tremendous team effort," said coach Dick Burroughs. In Class C, Greg Harger of Munising ran the fastest time ever in the UP state meet.

Marquette Golf & CC, Marquette, Oct. 15 □
1975 BOYS UP CLASS A/B TEAMS
1. Escanaba 41
2. Marquette 63
3. Calumet 99
4. Gladstone 125
5. Ironwood 129

1975 BOYS UP CLASS A/B INDIVIDUALS
1. Wayne Beckman (Ironwood) 15:42
2. Kurt Malmgren (Marquette)11 ....nt
3. Tom Theoret (Gladstone) ....nt
4. Ron McKenzie (Sault Ste Marie) ....nt

1975 BOYS UP CLASS C TEAMS
1. Norway 58
2. Ishpeming 81
3. Hancock 103
4. Rudyard 115
5. Ishpeming Westwood 123

1975 BOYS UP CLASS C INDIVIDUALS
1. Greg Harger (Munising) 15:37
2. Chuck Cloninger (Ishpeming Westwood)..........nt
3. Pat Clancy (Ishpeming) ....nt
4. Tom Wright (Hancock) ....nt
5. John Rothier (Stephenson) ....nt

1975 BOYS UP CLASS D TEAMS
1. Chassell 37
2. Painesdale-Jeffers 72
3. Detour 82
4. Perkins 139
5. Watersmeet 180

1975 BOYS UP CLASS D INDIVIDUALS
1. Terry Verbrigghe (Perkins)12 ....15:59
2. Ron Carlson (DeTour) ....nt
3. Mark Palosaari (Chassell) ....nt
4. Terry Kangas (Painesdale-Jeffers) ....nt

1976 UP BOYS

On a course that was "slowed by cold weather and 4-6 inches of snow, Kurt Malmgren and Tom Theoret staged a close battle in Class A-B, with Marquette's Malmgren emerging the winner. In the team race, Escanaba won top honors for the fourth straight year.

Marquette Golf & CC, Marquette, Oct. 20 □
1976 BOYS UP CLASS A/B TEAMS
1. Escanaba 50
2. Menominee 53
3. Ironwood 83
4. Gladstone 85
5. Calumet 97

1976 BOYS UP CLASS A/B INDIVIDUALS
1. Kurt Malmgren (Marquette)12 ....16:12
2. Tom Theoret (Gladstone) ....nt
3. Ken Sakely (Escanaba) ....nt
4. David Kanipes (Ironwood) 16:48

1976 BOYS UP CLASS C TEAMS
1. Ishpeming 50
2. Hancock 55
3. Rudyard 60
4. St Ignace 105
5. Norway 107

1976 BOYS UP CLASS C INDIVIDUALS
1. Tom Wright (Hancock)12 ....16:22
2. Ken Verheckey (Rudyard) ....nt
3. Mike Degener (Norway) ....nt
4. Pat Clancy (Ishpeming) ....nt
5. Bob Nettell (Hancock).......................................nt

1976 BOYS UP CLASS D TEAMS
1. Painesdale-Jeffers 65
2. Chassell 75
3. DeTour 79

1976 BOYS UP CLASS D INDIVIDUALS
1. Terry Kangas (Painesdale-Jeffers) 16:55
3. Andre Soumis (Chassell)9 ....17:05

1977 UP BOYS

Gwinn shocked in its first year of cross country. Coached by Janet Mihelich, the team ended Marquette's four-year streak in Class A-B while topping pre-race favorite Gladstone. Said Mihelich of her 15 runners, "We started slow and sure and made steady forward progress. I'm so excited. I've never been best at anything."

Menominee's Mike Photenhauer posted the fastest time, but the biggest individual surprise came when unheralded Kevin King of Ishpeming beat two of his favored teammates and won the C crown.

Gladstone GC, Gladstone, Oct. 19
1977 BOYS UP CLASS A/B TEAMS
1. Gwinn 68
2. Marquette 75
3. Gladstone 76
4. Escanaba 112
5. Menominee 117

1977 BOYS UP CLASS A/B INDIVIDUALS
1. Mike Photenhauer (Menominee)10 .... 16:09
2. Craig Braue (Gwinn) 16:26
3. Dwayne Livermore (Gladstone)12 .... 16:31
4. Dave Kanipes (Ironwood) 16:53
5. Marty Dugard (Gwinn) 17:00

1977 BOYS UP CLASS C TEAMS
1. Ishpeming 28
2. Hancock 57
3. St Ignace 103
4. West Iron County 112
5. Houghton 141

1977 BOYS UP CLASS C INDIVIDUALS
1. Kevin King (Ishpeming)12 .... 16:18
2. Jeff Mount (Hancock)12 .... 16:22
3. Pat Clancy (Ishpeming)12 .... 16:28
4. Dave Kahan (Houghton) 16:33
5. Paul Orchard (West Iron County) 16:34

1977 BOYS UP CLASS D TEAMS
1. Painesdale-Jeffers 45
2. Rudyard 76
3. Chassell 129
4. Ironwood Catholic 137
5. Watersmeet 153

1977 BOYS UP CLASS D INDIVIDUALS
1. Al Olsen (Painesdale-Jeffers) 16:41
2. Steve Semenak (Ironwood Catholic) 16:50
3. Steve Nelson (Rapid River) 17:09
4. Richard Postma (Rudyard) 17:37
5. Doug Kaver (Rudyard) 17:40

1978 UP BOYS

Gladstone topped upstart Gwinn for its first Class A-B state title ever. "They worked hard for it," said Braves coach Dave Lahtinen. Pierre Ogea of Ishpeming won the C crown in 15:56, just a tick slower than Mike Photenhauer's clocking in Class A-B. Class D went to Andre Soumis of Chassell, who explained his choice of sports by saying, "We don't have football at Chassell."

Gladstone GC, Gladstone, Oct. 18 □
UP CLASS A/B TEAMS
1. Gladstone 50
2. Gwinn 62
3. Marquette 88
4. Menominee 91
5. Calumet 109

1978 BOYS UP CLASS A/B INDIVIDUALS
1. Mike Photenhauer (Menominee)11 .... 15:55
2. Dean Borg (Gwinn)11 .... 16:05
3. Steve Tackman (Gladstone) 16:22
4. Ken Becker (Gladstone) .... nt

1978 BOYS UP CLASS C TEAMS
1. Hancock 59
2. Ishpeming 61
3. Houghton 76
4. Ishpeming Westwood 101
5. St Ignace 128

1978 BOYS UP CLASS C INDIVIDUALS
1. Pierre Ogea (Ishpeming)12 .... 15:56
2. Dan Kahan (Houghton)12 .... 16:00
3. Mark Horwitz (Norway)11 .... 16:03
4. Jeff Mount (Hancock) .... nt
5. Steve Pohlman (Ishpeming) .... nt

1978 BOYS UP CLASS D TEAMS
1. Painesdale-Jeffers 31
2. DeTour 114
3. Chassell 119
4. Rudyard 133
5. Rock-Mid Peninsula 133

1978 BOYS UP CLASS D INDIVIDUALS
1. Andre Soumis (Chassell)11 .... 16:32*
2. Richard Postma (Rudyard) 16:45
3. Doug Bernard (Big Bay de Noc) 16:56
(*=MHSAA Bulletin says Soumis's time was 16:23)

1979 UP BOYS

Mike Photenhauer won his third straight A-B crown with a meet record 15:48. On the team side, Marquette won its first title with a 10-point margin over Gwinn. Ishpeming won Class C honors over Munising and crosstown rival Westwood. Said coach Norm Andrew, "We felt Westwood and us would be neck-and-neck all the way, then we broke away at about the halfway point."

Marquette's 1979 champions.

Gladstone GC, Gladstone, Oct. 17
1979 BOYS UP CLASS A/B TEAMS
1. Marquette 36
2. Gwinn 46
3. Menominee 82
4. Gladstone 93
5. Calumet 117

1979 BOYS UP CLASS A/B INDIVIDUALS
1. Mike Photenhauer (Menominee)12 .... 15:48
2. Dean Borg (Gwinn)12 .... 16:17
3. Paul Couture (Gwinn) 16:18
4. Jon Kingston (Marquette) 16:27
5. Jeff Martin (Marquette) 16:32

1979 BOYS UP CLASS C TEAMS
1. Ishpeming 40
2. Munising 84
3. Ishpeming Westwood 93
4. Hancock 95
5. Houghton 125

1979 BOYS UP CLASS C INDIVIDUALS
1. Rick Miller (Ishpeming)11 .... 16:10
2. Tom Verme (Munising) 16:20
3. Steve Pohlman (Ishpeming) 16:28
4. Al LaCosse (Westwood) 16:36
5. Kirk Harger (Munising) 16:39

1979 BOYS UP CLASS D TEAMS
1. Painesdale-Jeffers 73
2. Chassell 97
3. Cedarville 100
4. Pickford 129
5. Rudyard 139

1979 BOYS UP CLASS D INDIVIDUALS
1. Joe Hebert (Norway)11 .... 15:51
2. Mark Horowitz (Norway)12 .... 16:04
3. Andre Soumis (Chassell)12 .... 16:29
4. Richard Postma (Rudyard) 16:34
5. Mike Cobe (Painesdale-Jeffers) 16:52

1980 BOYS UP BOYS

The races remained at three miles when the Lower Peninsula went to 5K. The big shocker was Norway in the Class D race. Joe Hebert had been picked to win, but no one expected his teammates to come through. In Class C, Westwood won a two-point victory over its crosstown rival by putting four runners in the top 11. The front of the C race was especially thrilling, as the lead changed three times in the last 100 yards. In Class A-B, Al LaFountain and John Kingston of Marquette broke away with three-quarters of a mile to go.

Gladstone GC, Gladstone, Oct. 15
1980 BOYS UP CLASS A/B TEAMS
1. Marquette 25
2. Menominee 68
3. Calumet 89
4. Gwinn 97
5. Gladstone 123

1980 BOYS UP CLASS A/B INDIVIDUALS
1. Al LaFountain (Marquette)12 .... 15:55
2. John Kingston (Marquette)11 .... 16:04
3. Jim Harris (Escanaba)12 .... 16:15
4. Paul Couture (Gwinn) 16:25
5. Ron Specker (Marquette) 16:30

1980 BOYS UP CLASS C TEAMS
1. Ishpeming Westwood 55
2. Ishpeming 57
3. Munising 96
4. Houghton 100
5. St Ignace 106

1980 BOYS UP CLASS C INDIVIDUALS
1. Rick Miller (Ishpeming) 16:05
2. Dan Kahan (Houghton) 16:06
3. Al LaCosse (Ishpeming Westwood)11 ...... 16:13
4. Steve Pohlmna (Ishpeming) 16:14
5. Mike Miller (Munising) 16:18

1980 BOYS UP CLASS D TEAMS
1. Norway 67
2. Painesdale-Jeffers 81
3. Cedarville 109
4. Watersmeet 112
5. Rudyard 114
6. Big Bay de Noc 126
7. Mid-Peninsula 135
8. Rapid River 152
9. Brimley 217

1980 BOYS UP CLASS D INDIVIDUALS
1. Joe Hebert (Norway) 16:29
2. Neil Gottsacker (Watersmeet) 16:33
3. Frank Gourneau (Painesdale-Jeffers) 16:57
4. Eugene Soumis (Chassell) 17:23
5. Jeff Cason (Cedarville) 17:29

1981 UP BOYS

Steve Ostrenga of Menominee narrowly escaped the final charge of Marquette's John

Kingston. The race was so close that officials had to meet over a "photo finish machine" to decide it. Marquette brought home the team trophy, however, on a misty day. In Class D, Chassell won by one point over Painesdale-Jeffers. The Chassell coach, Lou Braun, was a Jeffers grad, so he had some mixed feelings. "I was sweating it out until our final runner came in," he said. "Today happened to be our day."

Marquette Golf & CC, Marquette, Oct. 14
1981 BOYS UP CLASS A/B TEAMS
1. Marquette 23
2. Menominee 44
3. Gladstone 73
4. Gwinn 96
5. Escanaba 126

1981 BOYS UP CLASS A/B INDIVIDUALS
1. Steve Ostrenga (Menominee)11 .... 15:53
2. John Kingston (Marquette)12 .... 15:53
3. Jay Kastar (Marquette)11 .... 16:18
4. Tracy Lokken (Gwinn) 16:21
5. Jon Ottoson (Marquette) 16:29

1981 BOYS UP CLASS C TEAMS
1. Ishpeming 68
2. Negaunee 96
3. Iron Mountain 112
4. Hancock 121
5. St Ignace 121

1981 BOYS UP CLASS C INDIVIDUALS
1. Jim Albee (Hancock) 15:51
2. Tony Gregorich (Calumet) 15:57
3. Al LaCosse (Ishpeming Westwood)12 .. 16:14
4. Kirk Nichols (Ishpeming) 16:25
5. Harold Plattenberg (Negaunee) 16:26

1981 BOYS UP CLASS D TEAMS
1. Chassell 38
2. Painesdale-Jeffers 39
=3. Norway 104
=3. Rudyard 104
5. Big Bay de Noc 139

1981 BOYS UP CLASS D INDIVIDUALS
1. Eugene Suomis (Chassell) 16:21
2. Frank Gourneau (Painesdale-Jeffers) .. 16:38
3. Andy Moore (Big Bay de Noc) 17:08
4. Steve Butline (Painesdale-Jeffers) 17:10
5. Bruce Perander (Chassell) 17:15

1982 UP BOYS

Menominee was slightly favored over defender Marquette, after beating them twice the week before. Marquette won the big one, however. Said retiring Menominee coach Rick Lund, "I don't know what was with our boys, but they were nervous." Jon Otteson hadn't beaten favored Steve Ostrenga once all year, but he managed to do it when it counted. Said coach Dale Phillips, "He broke away in the last mile and just widened his lead."

Days River GC, Gladstone, Oct. 13
1982 BOYS UP CLASS A/B TEAMS
1. Marquette 35
2. Menominee 43
3. Gladstone 73
4. Gwinn 86
5. Escanaba 124

1982 BOYS UP CLASS A/B INDIVIDUALS
1. Jon Otteson (Marquette)12 .... 15:26
2. Steve Ostrenga (Menominee)12 .... 15:33
3. Ron Thompson (Gladstone) 15:56
4. Brian Anderson (Menominee) 15:58
5. Mike Gustafson (Gladstone) 16:03

1982 BOYS UP CLASS C TEAMS
1. Ishpeming 38
2. Negaunee 78
3. Calumet 94
4. Ishpeming Westwood 125
5. Hancock 130

1982 BOYS UP CLASS C INDIVIDUALS
1. Mike Wasson (Negaunee) 15:23
2. Jim Albee (Hancock)12 .... 15:32
3. Todd Pohlman (Ishpeming)10 .... 15:33
4. Tim Stadler (Ishpeming) 15:47
5. Tony Gregorich (Calumet) 15:56

1982 BOYS UP CLASS D TEAMS
1. Chassell 31
2. Jeffers 41
3. Norway 69
4. Rock-Mid Peninsula 90
5. Big Bay de Noc 135

1982 BOYS UP CLASS D INDIVIDUALS
1. Eugene Suomis (Chassell) 15:40
2. Dan Giessen (Norway) 15:41
3. Steve Butina (Painesdale-Jeffers) 16:33
4. Rick Simpson (Painesdale-Jeffers) 16:36
5. Steve Krug (Chassell) 16:50

1983 UP BOYS

Cold and rainy conditions didn't keep Menominee from putting four runners in the top 10 to score a win in Class A-B. In Class C, Negaunee put seven in the top 15. "That even surprised me," said coach Duane Palomaki. The athletes ran on a newly devised 5000m course that had been soaked by two inches of rainfall.

Marquette Golf & CC, Marquette, Oct. 12
1983 BOYS UP CLASS A/B TEAMS
1. Menominee 41
2. Escanaba 57
3. Gwinn 72
4. Marquette 78
5. Gladstone 90

1983 BOYS UP CLASS A/B INDIVIDUALS
1. Tracy Lokken (Gwinn)12 .... 17:06
2. Fran Champeau (Menominee)11 .... 17:16
3. Gustafson (Gladstone) 17:36
4. Ken Eubank (Gladstone) 17:45
5. Stan Hill (Marquette) 17:46

1983 BOYS UP CLASS C TEAMS
1. Negaunee 27
2. Ishpeming 59
3. Ishpeming Westwood 77
4. Calumet 115
5. Hancock 148

1983 BOYS UP CLASS C INDIVIDUALS
1. Todd Pohlman (Ishpeming)11 .... 16:47
2. Larry Gray (Ishpeming Westwood) 16:48
3. Todd Reynolds (Negaunee) 16:55
4. Harold Plattenberg (Negaunee) 17:15
5. David Tillly (Negaunee) 17:32

1983 BOYS UP CLASS D TEAMS
1. Painesdale-Jeffers 29
2. Chassell 42
3. Rock-Mid Peninsula 71

1983 BOYS UP CLASS D INDIVIDUALS
1. Bruce Perander (Chassell) 18:06
2. Tim Tahtinen (Painesdale-Jeffers) 18:17
3. Jeff Simpson (Painesdale-Jeffers) 18:23
4. Arts (Rock Mid-Peninsula) 18:41
5. Mills (Rudyard) 18:53

1984 UP BOYS

Hancock won its second title ever in Class D. Coach Arne Henderson said, "The key to winning was the way we bunched our runners." Certainly, placing 2-3-4-5-6 didn't hurt. Class C's Arnie Kinnunen and Todd Pohlman battled from start to finish, Kinnunen only getting the advantage on the final stretch.

Marquette Golf & CC, Marquette, Oct. 10
1984 BOYS UP CLASS A/B TEAMS
1. Gladstone 44
2. Marquette 54
3. Escanaba 59
4. Menominee 60
5. Gwinn 126

1984 BOYS UP CLASS A/B INDIVIDUALS
1. Ray Theoret (Gladstone)10 .... 16:02
2. Fran Champeau (Menominee) 16:04
3. Matt Roth (Marquette)12 .... 16:20
4. Pete Plouff (Gladstone) 16:21
5. Glenn Gregg (Escanaba) 16:22

1984 BOYS UP CLASS C TEAMS
1. Ishpeming Westwood 53
2. Stephenson 66
3. Ishpeming 77
4. Calumet 91
5. Negaunee 119

1984 BOYS UP CLASS C INDIVIDUALS
1. Arnie Kinnunen (Calumet)12 .... 16:21
2. Todd Pohlman (Ishpeming) 16:23
3. Adam Cook (West Iron County) 16:34
4. Larry Gray (Ishpeming Westwood) 16:38
5. Pete Marcotte (Ishpeming Westwood) . 16:39

1984 BOYS UP CLASS D TEAMS
1. Hancock 20
2. Crystal Falls Forest Park 65
3. Painesdale-Jeffers 67
4. Chassell 107
5. Rock-Mid Peninsula 113

1984 BOYS UP CLASS D INDIVIDUALS
1. Charles Cox (Painesdale-Jeffers) 16:57
2. Mike Regula (Hancock)10 .... 17:03
3. Paul Heinonen (Hancock) 17:20
4. Greg Nakkula (Hancock) 17:27
5. Shannon Taucher (Hancock) 17:30

1985 UP BOYS

Dan Beudry won Class A-B after pulling away with a surge at 2M. "I felt good about my chances when I still had the lead on top of the last hill." Defender Ray Theoret was ill and finished only 30th.

Gladstone GC, Gladstone, Oct. 19
1985 BOYS UP CLASS A/B TEAMS
1. Marquette 40
2. Gladstone 68
3. Escanaba 69
4. Gwinn 106
5. Menominee 111
6. Kingsford 114

1985 BOYS UP CLASS A/B INDIVIDUALS
1. Dan Beaudry (Escanaba)12 .... 15:40
2. Geoff Osowski (Marquette)10 .... 15:44
3. Jay Richer (Gladstone) 15:55
4. Dennis Murvich (Kingsford) 16:02
5. Eric Kittinen (Marquette) 16:05

1985 BOYS UP CLASS C TEAMS
1. Ishpeming Westwood 45
2. Stephenson 92
3. Iron Mountain 96
4. Ishpeming 102
5. Calumet 112

1985 BOYS UP CLASS C INDIVIDUALS
1. Tim Goliversic (Ishpeming) 15:37
2. Peter Marcotte (Ishpeming Westwood)10 .. 15:53
3. Mike Brodeur (Houghton) 16:00
4. Dave Berg (Ishpeming) 16:04
5. Shannon Taucher (Houghton) 16:08

1985 BOYS UP CLASS D TEAMS
1. Painesdale-Jeffers 30
2. Crystal Falls 43
3. Rock-Mid Peninsula 58
4. Chassell 106

1985 BOYS UP CLASS D INDIVIDUALS
1. Charles Cox (Crystal Falls) 16:19
2. Jeff Simpson (Painesdale-Jeffers) 16:46
3. Dean Koski (Rock-Mid Peninsula) 16:51
4. Dean Aberly (Crystal Falls-Forest Park) .. 16:56
5. Dean Blom (Painesdale-Jeffers) 17:04

1986 UP BOYS

Fine weather greeted the runners. Marquette won again in Class A-B. Said coach Dale Phillips, "Our kids just wanted it a little more." In Class C, Pete Marcotte led most of the distance, but was outkicked by Houghton's Mike Brodeur on the final stretch.

Gladstone Golf Course, Gladstone, Oct. 18
1986 BOYS UP CLASS A/B TEAMS
1. Marquette 38
2. Escanaba 47
3. Kingsford 75
4. Gladstone 85
5. Gwinn 104

1986 BOYS UP CLASS A/B INDIVIDUALS
1. Gary Gregg (Escanaba)12 .... 15:57
2. Dennis Murvich (Kingsford) 16:11
3. Geoff Osowski (Marquette)11 .... 16:12
4. Glenn Gregg (Escanaba) 16:22
5. Peter Easton (Marquette) 16:31

1986 BOYS UP CLASS C TEAMS
1. Stephenson 67
2. Iron Mountain 73
3. Calumet 85
4. Ishpeming 113
5. Ironwood 126

1986 BOYS UP CLASS C INDIVIDUALS
1. Mike Brodeur (Houghton) 16:04
2. Peter Marcotte (Ishpeming Westwood)11 .... 16:06
3. Jeff Legeret (Iron Mountain) 16:10
4. Bob Schnell (Stephenson) 16:16
5. Carl Hanson (Stephenson) 16:24

1986 BOYS UP CLASS D TEAMS
1. Hancock 29
2. Eben 65
3. Painesdale-Jeffers 74
4. Crystal Falls Forest Park 87
5. Chassell 124

1986 BOYS UP CLASS D INDIVIDUALS
1. Shannon Taucher (Hancock) 16:50
2. Mike Regula (Hancock) 16:53
3. Blake Penberthy (Eben) 17:10
4. Nowicki (Crystal Falls Forest Park) 17:18
5. Stevens (Painesdale-Jeffers) 17:25

1987 UP BOYS

Finally, the Upper Peninsula meet moved from Wednesday to a Saturday. Geoff Osowski upset favored Rhett Fisher in the homestretch to win the A-B crown. In Class C, Peter Marcotte took the course record down from 16:02, and Class D's Deren Pershinske also dipped under the old best.

Marquette Golf and GC, Marquette, Oct. 24
1987 BOYS UP CLASS A/B TEAMS
1. Marquette 26
2. Gladstone 67
3. Kingsford 88
4. Sault Ste Marie 98
5. Escanaba 99

1987 BOYS UP CLASS A/B INDIVIDUALS
1. Geoff Osowski (Marquette)12 .... 16:04
2. Rhett Fisher (Escanaba)12 .... 16:09
3. Eric Kiltinen (Marquette)11 .... 16:12
4. Dan Bovin (Gladstone) 16:24
5. Travis Hunt (Gwinn) 16:34

1987 BOYS UP CLASS C TEAMS
1. Iron Mountain 56
2. Ishpeming Westwood 92
3. Calumet 101
4. Stephenson 118
5. Ironwood 121

1987 BOYS UP CLASS C INDIVIDUALS
1. Pete Marcotte (Ishpeming Westwood)12 ... 15:42
2. Bob Schnell (Stephenson)11 .... 16:12
3. Jeff Legeret (Iron Mountain) 16:14
4. Steve Smithson (Iron Mountain) 16:27
5. Ron Williams (Ishpeming) 16:36

1987 BOYS UP CLASS D TEAMS
1. Eben - Superior Central 40
2. Crystal Falls Forest Park 70
3. White Pine 73
4. Carney-Nadeau 87
5. Painesdale-Jeffers 101

Engadine's Darrin Pershinske crushed the Class D field by more than a minute.

1987 BOYS UP CLASS D INDIVIDUALS
1. Deren Pershinske (Engadine) 15:53
2. Glenn Avena (Crystal Falls Forest Park)11 .... 17:03
3. Mark Nowicki (Crystal Falls Forest Park) ... 17:06
4. Blake Penberthy (Eben Junction-Superior C).17:11
5. Scott Strahl (Carney-Nadeau) 17:14

1988 UP BOYS

Dan Bovin won Class A-B honors. "It was a hard race," he said. "The pace was unbelievable. There was no time to relax."

Marquette Golf & CC, Marquette, Oct. 22
1988 BOYS UP CLASS A/B TEAMS
1. Marquette 31
2. Sault Ste Marie 78
3. Gladstone 88
4. Escanaba 93
5. Menominee 97

1988 BOYS UP CLASS A/B INDIVIDUALS
1. Dan Bovin (Gladstone)11 .... 16:11
2. Mike Argeropoulos (Marquette)12 .... 16:15
3. Bruce Wright (Kingsford)12 .... 16:20
4. Bryan Bjork (Marquette)11 .... 16:28
5. Eric Kiltinen (Marquette)12 .... 16:29

1988 BOYS UP CLASS C TEAMS
1. Stephenson 63
2. Ironwood 75
3. Calumet 95
4. Hancock 99
5. Ishpeming 114

1988 BOYS UP CLASS C INDIVIDUALS
1. Bob Schnell (Stephenson)12 .... 15:41
2. Chris Lett (Houghton)10 .... 15:58
3. Dan Schnell (Stephenson)10 .... 16:43
4. Ron Williams (Ishpeming Westwood)11 .. 16:44
5. Tom Fioruicci (Iron Mountain)12 .... 16:45

1988 BOYS UP CLASS D TEAMS
1. Eben Junction-Superior Central 39
2. Painesdale-Jeffers 65
3. White Pine 73
4. Carney Nadeau 85
5. Crystal Falls Forest Park 108

1988 BOYS UP CLASS D INDIVIDUALS
1. Glenn Avena (CF Forest Park)12 .... 16:40
2. Tim Piche (Carney-Nadeau)12 .... 16:41
3. Gary Spolarich (White Pine)10 .... 16:56
4. Jon Butina (Painesdale-Jeffers)9 .... 17:10
5. Tom Cox (Superior Central)12 .... 17:10

1989 UP BOYS

Dale Phillips' Marquette squad won its fifth title in a row in Class A-B. The fastest time of the day went to Brian Anderson of Escanaba in 17:26.

Gladstone Golf & CC, Gladstone, Oct. 21
1989 BOYS UP CLASS A/B TEAMS
1. Marquette 47
2. Escanaba 71
3. Sault Ste Marie 88
4. Ironwood 92
5. Menominee 99

1989 BOYS UP CLASS A/B INDIVIDUALS
1. Brian Anderson (Escanaba) 17:26
2. Chad Waucauch (Sault Ste Marie) 17:42
3. Dan Bovin (Gladstone) 18:09
4. Bryan Bjork (Marquette) 18:34
5. Jim Clow (Sault Ste Marie) 18:36

1989 BOYS UP CLASS C TEAMS
1. Houghton 55
2. Stephenson 60
3. Calumet 66
4. Hancock 74
5. Ishpeming 85

1989 BOYS UP CLASS C INDIVIDUALS
1. Chris Lett (Houghton)11 .... 17:39
2. Ron Williams (Ishpeming)11 .... 18:09
3. Dan Schnell (Stephenson)11 .... 18:18
4. Tim Nordin (Stephenson)11 .... 18:19
5. Abe Aho (Houghton)12 .... 18:30

1989 BOYS UP CLASS D TEAMS
1. Eben Junction-Superior Central 26
2. Carney-Nadeau 82
3. Painesdale-Jeffers 88
4. Crystal Falls Forest Park 103
5. White Pine 136

1989 BOYS UP CLASS D INDIVIDUALS
1. Jeff Jacobson (Carney-Nadeau) 18:34
2. Gary Spolarich (White Pine)11 .... 19:06
3. Aaron Anderson (Eben-Superior C)11 .... 19:37
4. Darrell Nummela (Eben-Superior Central) .. 20:05
5. Jason Maki (Eben-Superior Central) 20:16

1990 UP BOYS

Runners faced a difficult course. "The conditions were muddy. It rained a lot and there was a head wind at different points," described Marquette coach Dale Phillips. It was the sixth Marquette win in a row. The top performance went to Chris Lett of Houghton, who later starred at Michigan State.

Gladstone Golf & CC, Gladstone, Oct. 20
1990 BOYS UP CLASS A/B TEAMS
1. Marquette 45
2. Menominee 68
3. Ironwood 103
4. Sault Ste Marie 105
5. Kingsford 114

1990 BOYS UP CLASS A/B INDIVIDUALS
1. Chad Waucaush (Sault Ste Marie)12 .... 17:18
2. Jason Ladd (Menominee) 17:51
3. Bruce Anderson (Menominee) 18:01
4. Kelly Keefe (Marquette) 18:04
5. Dimitri Jajich (Marquette) 18:07

1990 BOYS UP CLASS C TEAMS
1. Stephenson 43
2. Hancock 63
3. Ishpeming Westwood 86
4. Houghton 92
5. Ishpeming 131

1990 BOYS UP CLASS C INDIVIDUALS
1. Chris Lett (Houghton)12 .... 17:01
2. Matt Rodeheffer (Hancock)10 .... 17:37
3. David Bouchard (Newberry) 17:39
4. Dan Schnell (Stephenson) 17:51
5. Ryan Potila (Isphemimg Westwood) 17:54

1990 BOYS UP CLASS D TEAMS
1. Painesdale Jeffers 42
2. Carney-Nadeau 56
3. Eben-Superior Central 65
4. Forest Park 89
5. White Pine 139

1990 BOYS UP CLASS D INDIVIDUALS
1. Dan Malanao (Eben-Superior Central) 17:48
2. Gary Spolarich (White Pine)12 .... 17:54
3. Don Wettanen (Carney-Nadeau) 18:22
4. Steve Laurila (Painesdale-Jeffers) 18:30
5. Filip Martin (Crystal Falls-Forest Park) 18:31

1991 UP BOYS

Escanaba won a close one, with Gwinn a point behind and Menominee only three back. Coach John Prokos, in his last state meet, called it, "one of those Cinderella finishes." One of his runners, expected to lead, ran only 15th in the sunny, just-above-freezing conditions. Another failed to finish after spraining an ankle on a tree root.

In Class D, Stephenson and Ishpeming both tallied 60 points, but Stephenson's number six runner finished two places ahead of Ishpeming's.

Marquette Golf & CC, Marquette, Oct. 19
1991 BOYS UP CLASS A/B TEAMS
1. Escanaba 77
2. Gwinn 78
3. Menominee 80
4. Marquette 86
5. Kingsford 126

1991 BOYS UP CLASS A/B INDIVIDUALS
1. Ryan Potila (Ishpeming Westwood)10 .... 16:52
2. Bob Knapp (Kingsford)11 .... 16:59
3. Brad Dubord (Escanaba) 17:00
4. Jason Ladd (Menominee) 17:16
5. Kurt Hiller (Menominee) 17:16

1991 BOYS UP CLASS C TEAMS
1. Stephenson 60
2. Ishpeming 60
3. Ironwood 73
4. Houghton 92
5. Negaunee 120

1991 BOYS UP CLASS C INDIVIDUALS
1. Matt Rodeheffer (Hancock)11 .... 16:23
2. Dan Kaukola (Ishpeming)12 .... 17:03
3. Erik Racine (Ishpeming)12 .... 17:04
4. Petr Belej (Hancock) 17:17
5. Chad Christensen (West Iron County) 17:23

1991 BOYS UP CLASS D TEAMS
1. Painesdale-Jeffers 30
2. Carney-Nadeau 55
3. Chassell 108
4. Crystal Falls 112
5. Superior Central 113

1991 BOYS UP CLASS D INDIVIDUALS
1. Don Wettanen (Carney-Nadeau) 17:31
2. Tom Wesa (Painesdale-Jeffers) 17:50
3. John Pietila (Painesdale-Jeffers) 18:00
4. Matt Rondeau (Eben-Superior Central) 18:05
5. Jeff Rautiola (Painesdale-Jeffers) 18:06

1992 UP BOYS

Ryan Potila won Class A-B in 15:38, breaking Matt Rodeheffer's 1992 course record of 15:40. No matter. In the next race, Rodeheffer ran 15:26 and grabbed the record back. Temperatures were in the high 40s.

Presque Ile Park, Marquette, Oct. 24
1992 BOYS UP CLASS A/B TEAMS
1. Gwinn 48
2. Escanaba 80
3. Marquette 84
4. Ishpeming Westwood 94
5. Gladstone 136

1992 BOYS UP CLASS A/B INDIVIDUALS
1. Ryan Potila (Ishpeming Westwood)11 ...... 15:38
2. Bob Knapp (Kingsford)11 .... 15:53
3. Mike Sandretto (Ishpeming Westwood) 16:00
4. Tony Fornetti (Escanaba) 16:11
5. Eric Turner (Gwinn) 16:20

1992 BOYS UP CLASS C TEAMS
1. Stephenson 67
2. Ironwood 79
3. Houghton 112
4. Hancock 114
5. Calumet 128

1992 BOYS UP CLASS C INDIVIDUALS
1. Matt Rodeheffer (Hancock)12 .... 15:26
2. Dave Delisle (Munising)11 .... 15:58
3. Bruce Carlson (Ishpeming) 16:05
4. Dave Everson (Houghton) 16:09
5. David Bouchard (Newberry) 16:17

1992 BOYS UP CLASS D TEAMS
1. Painesdale-Jeffers 26
2. Carney-Nadeau 49
3. Chassell 82
4. Crystal Falls Forest Park 99
5. Republic-Michigamme 122

1992 BOYS UP CLASS D INDIVIDUALS
1. Tom Wesa (Painesdale-Jeffers) 16:29
2. Jason Maki (Superior Central)11 .... 16:31
3. Don Wettalen (Carney-Nadeau) 16:35
4. Mark Randell (Painesdale-Jeffers) 16:43
5. Jeff Rautiola (Painesdale-Jeffers) 16:53

1993 BOYS

Ryan Potila won his third straight Class A-B race. Ironwood won Class C: "The boys definitely saved their best for last," said coach Bruce Beckman. In Class D, Jason Maki was 20 yards behind Tom Wesa with six-tenths of a mile left, but he ran him down for the win. The Marquette course was 140 yards longer than in previous years, to make it "more accurate".

Presque Ile Park, Marquette, Oct. 23
1993 BOYS UP CLASS A/B TEAMS
1. Marquette 35
2. Kingsford 74
3. Ishpeming Westwood 117
4. Sault Ste Marie 125
5. Escanaba 128

1993 BOYS UP CLASS A/B INDIVIDUALS
1. Ryan Potila (Ishpeming Westwood)12 ...... 16:12
2. Bob Knapp (Kingsford)12 .... 16:33
3. Andy Ramos (Gwinn)10 .... 16:42
4. Ty Sheksy (Marquette) 16:53
5. Robin Martin (Marquette) 17:05

1993 BOYS UP CLASS C TEAMS
1. Ironwood 62
2. Calumet 88
3. Ishpeming 122
4. Stephenson 134
5. Newberry 139

1993 BOYS UP CLASS C INDIVIDUALS
1. Dave DeLisle (Munising)12 .... 15:49
2. Chad Christiansen (West Iron County) 16:39
3. Dave Evenson (Houghton) 16:47
4. Tony Lupino (Ironwood)12 .... 16:50
6. Steve Aho (Ironwood) 16:52

1993 BOYS UP CLASS D TEAMS
1. Painesdale-Jeffers 33
2. Chassell 65
3. Carney-Nadeau 74
4. Eben-Superior Central 75
5. Republic-Michigamme 92

1993 BOYS UP CLASS D INDIVIDUALS
1. Jason Maki (Superior Central)12 .... 17:01
2. Tom Wesa (Painesdale-Jeffers) 17:13
3. Jeff Rautiola (Painesdale-Jeffers) 17:33
4. Charlie Dillion (Republic-Michigamme) 17:46
5. Jeremy Szapa (Carney-Nadeau) 17:47

1994 UP BOYS

Marquette's Robin Martin produced the fastest time of the day. He would go on to become a NCAA Division I All-American at 800m (1:47.10) for the University of Pennsylvania.

Gladstone Golf & CC, Gladstone, Oct. 22
1994 BOYS UP CLASS A/B TEAMS
1. Marquette 33
2. Kingsford 57
3. Menominee 62
4. Ishpeming-Westwood 117
5. Escanaba 121

1994 BOYS UP CLASS A/B INDIVIDUALS
1. Robin Martin (Marquette)12 .... 17:43
2. Warren Ross (Menominee)11 .... 17:44
3. Andrew Thierry (Marquette)12 .... 18:02
4. Kevin Landmark (Negaunee) 18:03
5. Jason Homa (Menominee) 18:06

1994 BOYS UP CLASS C TEAMS
1. Calumet 74
2. Ironwood 88
3. Munising 103
4. Houghton 135
5. Stephenson 159

1994 BOYS UP CLASS C INDIVIDUALS
1. Dave Elwing (Munising)11 .... 17:24
2. Tom Miller (Houghton) 17:39
3. Kevin Knierem (Newberry) 17:56
4. Dan Munoz (Munising) 18:02
5. Ryan Kangas (Calumet) 18:08

1994 BOYS UP CLASS D TEAMS

1. Republic-Michigamme 22
2. Carney-Nadeau 42
3. Chassell 69
4. Eben Junction – Superior Central 105
5. Rock-Mid Peninsula 116

1994 BOYS UP CLASS D INDIVIDUALS
1. Roy Andrews (Carney-Nadeau) 18:30
2. Charlie Dillon (Republic-Michigamme) 18:54
3. Kevin Delliss (Republic-Michigamme) 18:56
4. Jason Tapio (Republic-Michigamme) 19:02
5. Phil Gravedoni (Republic-Michigamme) 19:21

1995 UP BOYS

It was the third-straight win for Marquette—and No. 13 for head coach Dale Phillips. Dave Elwing of Munising had the fastest time of the day.

Red Fox Run GC, Sawyer, Oct. 21
1995 BOYS UP CLASS A/B TEAMS
1. Marquette 61
2. Ishpeming Westwood 68
3. Menominee 69
4. Kingsford 113
5. Gwinn 122

1995 BOYS UP CLASS A/B INDIVIDUALS
1. Steve Campbell (Menominee)10 .... 17:29
2. Andy Ramos (Gwinn)11 .... 17:33
3. Warren Ross (Menominee)12 .... 17:44
4. Pete Remien (Ishpeming Westwood)10 .... 17:55
5. Bob Britton (Menominee) 17:57

1995 BOYS UP CLASS C TEAMS
1. Munising 64
2. Newberry 95
3. Ironwood 104
4. Stephenson 115
5. Calumet 125

1995 BOYS UP CLASS C INDIVIDUALS
1. Dave Elwing (Munising)12 .... 16:51
2. Dan Munoz (Munising)12 .... 17:02
3. Mark Kujat (St Ignace) 17:11
4. Ryan Kangas (Calumet) 17:38
5. Aaron Litzner (St Ignace) 17:40

1995 BOYS UP CLASS D TEAMS
1. Republic-Michigamme 26
2. Carney-Nadeau 52
3. Rock-Mid Peninsula 56
4. Eben-Superior Central 111
5. Chassell 139

1995 BOYS UP CLASS D INDIVIDUALS
1. Roy Andrews (Carney-Nadeau) 18:09
2. Charlie Dillon (Rock-Mid Peninsula) 18:35
3. Philip Gravedoni (Rock-Mid Peninsula) 18:41
4. Matt Barron (Rock-Mid Peninsula) 18:43
5. Kevin Delliss (Republic-Michigamme) 19:14

1996 UP BOYS

Menominee, coached by Randy Verkeke, upended Marquette by 23 points. Pete Remien of Ishpeming Westwood had the fastest time at 16:51.

Red Fox Run GC, Sawyer, Oct. 19
Clear and cool.
1996 BOYS UP CLASS A/B TEAMS
1. Menominee 35
2. Marquette 58
3. Ishpeming Westwood 80
4. Escanaba 95
5. Kingsford 103

1996 BOYS UP CLASS A/B INDIVIDUALS
1. Pete Remien (Ishpeming Westwood)11 .... 16:51
2. Steve Campbell (Menominee) 17:22
3. Adam Weasler (Escanaba) 17:43
4. Dave Ross (Menominee) 17:47
5. Gabe Disbrow (Ishpeming Westwood) 17:49

1996 BOYS UP CLASS C TEAMS
1. Calumet 69
2. Newberry 85
3. Stephenson 100
4. Negaunee 114
5. Ironwood 128

1996 BOYS UP CLASS C INDIVIDUALS
1. Aaron Litzner (St Ignace)11 .... 16:59
2. Brett Nepper (Iron Mountain) 17:29
3. Mike Wilman (Ironwood)11 .... 17:30
4. Caden Ruohomaki (Negaunee) 17:39
5. Ryan Kangas (Calumet) 17:42

1996 BOYS UP CLASS D TEAMS
1. Republic-Michigamme 30
2. Carney-Nadeau 51
3. Eben-Superior Central 66
4. Crystal Falls Forest Park 95
5. Painesdale-Jeffers 133

1996 BOYS UP CLASS D INDIVIDUALS
1. Tom Dillon (Rock-Mid Peninsula) 17:54
2. Josh Palmer (Crystal Falls Forest Park) 17:56
3. Mike Spaton (Rock-Mid Peninsula) 18:32
4. Thomas Verbrigghe (Eben-Superior Central) .. 18:38
5. Matt Barron (Rock-Mid Peninsula) 18:44

1997 UP BOYS

Pete Remien wrapped up his prep cross country career with a 16:34 win in Class C. By the time he graduated from Ishpeming Westwood, he would have two UP titles in cross country and 9 in track. He was later a Mid-American Conference champion for Central Michigan.

Class D winner Aaron Litzner would go on to set a GLIAC record in the 5000 for Lake Superior State.

Red Fox Run GC, Sawyer, Oct. 18
1997 BOYS UP CLASS A/B TEAMS
1. Menominee 33
2. Escanaba 55
3. Marquette 76
4. Negaunee 122
5. Sault Ste Marie 132

1997 BOYS UP CLASS A/B INDIVIDUALS
1. Caden Ruohomaki (Negaunee)12 .... 17:11
2. Dave Ross (Menominee)12 .... 17:30
3. Steve Campbell (Menominee)12 .... 17:34
4. John Blake (Menominee) 17:36
5. John Gannon (Escanaba) 17:58

1997 BOYS UP CLASS C TEAMS
1. Calumet 48
2. Newberry 86
3. Munising 94
4. Ironwood 106
5. Ishpeming Westwood 106

1997 BOYS UP CLASS C INDIVIDUALS
1. Pete Remien (Ishpeming Westwood)12 .... 16:34
2. Dave Campbell (Calumet)11 .... 17:13
3. Mike Wilman (Ironwood)12 .... 17:27
4. Chris Labadie (Newberry) 17:32
5. Ken Burley (Munising) 17:35

1997 BOYS UP CLASS D TEAMS
1. Carney-Nadeau 56
2. Republic Michigamme 58
3. Chassell 109
4. Crystal Falls Forest Park 112
5. St Ignace 125

1997 BOYS UP CLASS D INDIVIDUALS
1. Aaron Litzner (St Ignace)12 .... 16:52
2. T.J. Verbrigghe (Eben-Superior Central)11 .... 17:51
3. Nick Schaedig (Cedarville)9 .... 17:53
4. Seann Duffin (Carney-Nadeau) 17:53
5. Tim Dillon (Republic-Michigamme) 18:11

1998 UP BOYS

Escanaba moved up from 2nd place in 1997 to capture the A/B crown. In Class C, Calumet won its third consecutive championship. Calumet's David Campbell ran the fastest time of the day (17:23). moving up from his runner-up finish the previous year.

Red Fox Run GC, Sawyer, Oct. 17
1998 BOYS UP CLASS A/B TEAMS
1. Escanaba 38
2. Marquette 54
3. Menominee 86
4. Sault Ste Marie 89
5. Iron Mountain-Kingsford 119

1998 BOYS UP CLASS A/B INDIVIDUALS
1. Mark Ammel (Escanaba)12 .... 17:50
2. Joey Graci (Marquette)10 .... 18:07
3. Paul Ammel (Escanaba)11 .... 18:12
4. Andy Verhamme (Escanaba) 18:17
5. David Paul (Gladstone) 18:18

1998 BOYS UP CLASS C TEAMS
1. Calumet 43
2. Munising 58
3. Houghton 88
4. Stephenson 150
5. Newberry 157

1998 BOYS UP CLASS C INDIVIDUALS
1. David Campbell (Calumet)12 .... 17:23
2. Matt Sturos (Calumet)12 .... 17:48
3. Ken Burley (Munising)12 .... 17:57
4. Scott Carhoun (Stephenson) 18:00
5. Dave Harvey (Munising) 18:44

1998 BOYS UP CLASS D TEAMS
1. Carney-Nadeau 37
2. Chassell 59
3. Superior Central 70
4. Republic-Michigamme 74
5. North Central 129

1998 BOYS UP CLASS D INDIVIDUALS
1. Seann Duffin (Carney-Nadeau)11 .... 18:07
2. Jake Denkins (Big Bay de Noc)11 .... 18:14
3. Jeff Papineau (Superior Central)10 .... 18:24
4. Adam Sworski (North Central) 18:34
5. Jake Polfus (Carney-Nadeau) 18:38

1999 UP BOYS

The weather for the Finals could not have been worse. Rain, snow, ice, and winds howling up to 60mph challenged the runners. Jim Martin's crew from the Sault won its first title in 44 years. In Class D, Seann Duffin won his second straight crown.

Pictured Rocks CC, Munising, Oct. 23
1999 BOYS UP CLASS A/B TEAMS
1. Sault Ste. Marie 27
2. Escanaba 77
3. Marquette 77
4. Kingsford 93
5. Menominee 93

1999 BOYS UP CLASS A/B INDIVIDUALS
1. Tom Shannon (Sault Ste Marie)12 .... 17:49
2. John Gannon (Escanaba)12 .... 17:58
3. Joe Graci (Marquette)11 .... 18:01
4. Anthony Abramson (Sault) 18:03
5. Clifton Lindsey (Sault) 18:11

1999 BOYS UP CLASS C TEAMS
1. Ishpeming 24
2. Houghton 71
3. Munising 72
4. Newberry 172
5. Calumet 173

1999 BOYS UP CLASS C INDIVIDUALS
1. Jim Miller (Houghton)12 ....18:04
2. Paul Olen (Ishpeming)12 ....18:13
3. Ryan Krueger (Ishpeming)10 ....18:19
4. Anthony Carello (Ishpeming) 18:20
5. Brian Hart (Ishpeming) 18:21

1999 BOYS UP CLASS D TEAMS
1. Carney-Nadeau 30
2. Chassell 49
3. Superior Central 63
4. Republic-Michigamme 103
5. Powers North Central 126

1999 BOYS UP CLASS D INDIVIDUALS
1. Seann Duffin (Carney-Nadeau)12 ....18:15
2. Nick Schaedig (Cedarville)11 ....18:23
3. Alan Granroth (Chassell)11 ....18:32
4. Gary Merkling (Carney-Nadeau) 18:46
5. Jake Denkins (Big Bay de Noc) 18:50

2000 UP BOYS

The Upper Peninsula schools joined the rest of the state in going with a divisional format, but it was just a change in name only, as the three levels were no different than the previous set-up. In Division 3, Carney-Nadeau won a record fourth-straight and the Sault repeated from 1999 with a very low 24-point score.

Red Fox Run GC, Sawyer, Oct. 17
2000 BOYS UP DIVISION 1 TEAMS
1. Sault Ste Marie 24
2. Marquette 44
3. Menominee 106
4. Gladstone 115
5. Kingsford 141

2000 BOYS UP DIVISION 1 INDIVIDUALS
1. Jamie Cihak (Marquette)11 ....16:40
2. Cliff Lindsay (Sault Ste Marie)12 ....16:54
3. Joe Graci (Marquette)12 ....17:08
4. Anthony Abramson (Sault) 17:16
5. Dan Brown (Sault) 17:17

2000 BOYS UP DIVISION 2 TEAMS
1. Munising 50
2. Ishpeming 52
3. Ishpeming Westwood 110
4. Newberry 115
5. Rudyard 125

2000 BOYS UP DIVISION 2 INDIVIDUALS
1. Matt Anderson (Munising)11 ....17:08
2. Ryan Krueger (Ishpeming)11 ....17:14
3. Dave Harvey (Munising)12 ....17:21
4. Erick Palo (Ishpeming) 17:26
5. Curt Van (Stephenson) 17:29

2000 BOYS UP DIVISION 3 TEAMS
1. Carney-Nadeau 33
2. Republic-Michigamme 78
3. Superior Central 85
4. Chassell 90
5. Crystal Falls Forest Park 93

2000 BOYS UP DIVISION 3 INDIVIDUALS
1. Nick Schaedig (Cedarville)12 ....17:33
2. Brent Jurmu (Carney-Nadeau)10 ....17:43
3. Gary Merkling (Carney-Nadeau)11 ....17:50
4. Joss Martin (Crystal Falls Forest Park) 17:58
5. Nathanel Holsworth (Republic Michigamme) .18:08

2001 UP BOYS

Jamie Cihak won his second straight title, this time with a margin of more than one minute over teammate Stuart Kramer.

It was a three-peat for Sault Ste Marie in D1 despite being ranked second to Marquette all season. Coach Jim Martin told *The Evening News*, "We had some kids step up. They beat us on the uphills, but we beat them on the downhills. This course was suited for our style of running. We told our kids to get out there right away because they aren't used to coming from behind… We had nothing to lose. Marquette is a real strong team. I don't think they lost it. We won it."

In D4, Carney-Nadeau made it five straight.

Gladstone Golf Course, Gladstone, Oct. 20
2001 BOYS UP DIVISION 1 TEAMS
1. Sault Ste Marie 29
2. Marquette 35
3. Menominee 115
4. Negaunee 119
5. Gladstone 152

2001 BOYS UP DIVISION 1 INDIVIDUALS
1. Jamie Cihak (Marquette)12 ....17:02
2. Stuart Kramer (Marquette)10 ....18:07
3. Daniel Brown (Sault Ste Marie)11 ....18:08
4. Nick Richer (Negaunee) 18:09
5. Adam Gurnoe (Sault) 18:16

2001 BOYS UP DIVISION 2 TEAMS
1. Ishpeming 48
2. Westwood 86
3. Rudyard 111
4. Ironwood 118
5. Stephenson 148

2001 BOYS UP DIVISION 2 INDIVIDUALS
1. Brent Malaski (Rudyard)11 ....17:35
2. Ryan Kruger (Ishpeming)10 ....17:36
3. Jesse Daniels (Ironwood)11 ....18:01
4. Tony Barnes (Ishpeming) 18:06
5. Matt Anderson (Munising) 18:13

2001 BOYS UP DIVISION 3 TEAMS
1. Carney-Nadeau 36
2. Pickford 59
3. Powers-North Central 74
4. Superior Central 104
5. Crystal Falls 106

2001 BOYS UP DIVISION 3 INDIVIDUALS
1. Joss Martin (Crystal Falls)10 ....18:09
2. Sam Kilpela (Jeffers)10 ....18:35
3. Brent Jurmu (Carney-Nadeau)11 ....18:38
4. Dan Miller (Rapid River) 18:39
5. Gary Merkling (Carney-Nadeau) 18:56

2002 UP BOYS

Coach Dale Phillips put himself back in the win column when his Marquette squad beat Sault Ste. Marie by 40 points. It was win No. 14 in Phillips' coaching career.

Carney-Nadeau's win streak in D3 continued as it beat second place Pickford by 25 points. Joss Martin of Crystal Falls had the fastest time, winning D3 in 16:51.

Gladstone, Oct. 19
2002 BOYS UP DIVISION 1 TEAMS
1. Marquette 36
2. Sault Ste. Marie 76
3. Negaunee 88
4. Kingsford 136
5. Calumet 152

2002 BOYS UP DIVISION 1 INDIVIDUALS
1. Beau Poquette (Kingsford)11 ....16:59
2. Nick Richer (Negaunee)12 ....17:00
3. Stuart Kramer (Marquette)11 ....17:18
4. Derik Sundberg (Marquette) 17:31
5. Andy Brzoznowski (West Iron County) 17:38

2002 BOYS UP DIVISION 2 TEAMS
1. Ishpeming Westwood 32
2. Stephenson 87
3. Ironwood 94
4. Ishpeming 102
5. Rudyard 131

2002 BOYS UP DIVISION 2 INDIVIDUALS
1. Jesse Daniels (Ironwood)12 ....16:56
2. Brent Malaski (Rudyard)12 ....17:31
3. Curt Van (Stephenson)12 ....17:34
4. Jake Rankinen (Ishpeming Westwood) 17:51
5. Andrew Danny Hill (Ishpeming Westwood) 18:20

2002 BOYS UP DIVISION 3 TEAMS
1. Carney-Nadeau 65
2. Pickford 80
3. Powers-North Central 84
4. Crystal Falls Forest Park 88
5. Painesdale-Jeffers 93

2002 BOYS UP DIVISION 3 INDIVIDUALS
1. Joss Martin (Crystal Falls)11 ....16:51
2. Brad Hunter (Pickford)12 ....17:24
3. Adam Christopherson (Powers NC)11 ....17:50
4. Samuel Kilpela (Painesdale-JHeffers) 18:02
5. Darren Grondin (Carney-Nadeau) 18:22

Counting both boys and girls teams, Marquette's Dale Phillips coached his way to a stunning 42 UP team titles.

2003 UP BOYS

Marquette easily defended its title with a 24-point margin. The team was led by Stuart Kramer, who had the fastest time of the day in 16:45.

D2 third-placer Matt Wyble distinguished himself two years later by running with a teammate across the United States to raise money to help children in Africa.

For the first time since 1997, D3 had a champion not named Carney-Nadeau as Cedarville beat Painesdale-Jeffers on a tie-breaker with the Cedarville 6th man more than a minute ahead of his counterpart.

Fountain XC Course, Banat, Oct. 18
2003 BOYS UP DIVISION 1 TEAMS
1. Marquette 36
2. Sault Ste Marie 60
3. Gladstone 93
4. Menominee 134
5. Ironwood 138

2003 BOYS UP DIVISION 1 INDIVIDUALS
1. Stuart Kramer (Marquette)12 ....16:45
2. Derek Sundberg (Negaunee)12 ....17:00
3. Chris Davis (Gladstone)11 ....17:19
4. Alex Tiseo (Marquette) 17:27
5. Craig Cooper (Sault) 17:31

2003 BOYS UP DIVISION 2 TEAMS
1. Stephenson 27
2. Ishpeming Westwood 57
3. Ishpeming 100
4. Rudyard 109
5. Hancock 122

2003 BOYS UP DIVISION 2 INDIVIDUALS
1. Lucas Hodges (Hancock)12 .... 17:23
2. Danny Hill (Ishpeming Westwood)12 ..... 17:36
3. Matt Wyble (Stephenson)12 .... 17:43
4. Brandon Newlin (Stephenson) 17:45
5. Ernesto Dela Rosa (Stephenson) 17:59

2003 BOYS UP DIVISION 3 TEAMS
1. Cedarville 55
2. Painesdale-Jeffers 55
3. Crystal Falls-Forest Park 99
4. Powers North Central 104
5. Carney-Nadeau 115

2003 BOYS UP DIVISION 3 INDIVIDUALS
1. Joss Martin (CF Forest Park)12 .... 16:50
2. Samuel Kilpela (Painesdale-Jeffers)12 .. 17:00
3. Jason Sweeney (Cedarville)12 .... 17:26
4. Chad Schlosser (Cedarville)10 .... 17:38
5. Mike Turton (Eben Superior Central)10 .. 17:39

2004 UP BOYS

Marquette won again, this time toppling Calumet by 50, and Cedarville won again in D3. Sophomore Brad Bruce of Munising won D2 in 16:48, the day's fastest time.

Fountain XC Course, Banat, Oct. 23
2004 BOYS UP DIVISION 1 TEAMS
1. Marquette 37
2. Calumet 87
3. Sault Ste Marie 92
4. Gladstone 111
5. Houghton 136

2004 BOYS UP DIVISION 1 INDIVIDUALS
1. Nik Klena (Marquette)9 .... 17:10
2. Chris Davis (Gladstone)12 .... 17:14
3. Greg Peterson (Houghton)10 .... 17:22
4. Ben Montgomery (Marquette)11 .... 17:30
5. Jared Helminen (Calumet)10 .... 17:40

2004 BOYS UP DIVISION 2 TEAMS
1. Ishpeming Westwood 52
2. Munising 88
3. Stephenson 93
4. Ironwood 99
5. Rudyard 114

2004 BOYS UP DIVISION 2 INDIVIDUALS
1. Brad Bruce (Munising)10 .... 16:48
2. Taggert Bradley (Ishpeming Westwood)9 ..... 17:23
3. Scott Bond (Munising)10 .... 17:24
4. Lucas Hodges (Hancock)12 .... 17:24
5. Mark Kinnunen (Munising)11 .... 17:26

2004 BOYS UP DIVISION 3 TEAMS
1. Cedarville 47
2. Painesdale-Jeffers 74
3. Pickford 94
4. Powers North Central 95
5. Rapid River 105

2004 BOYS UP DIVISION 3 INDIVIDUALS
1. Chad Schlosser (Cedarville)11 .... 16:57
2. Cody Juntikka (Painesdale-Jeffers)12 ... 17:05
3. Carl Morrison (Pickford)12 .... 17:19
4. Michael Turton (Eben-Superior Central)11 .. 17:51
5. Tyler Crossman (Rapid River)9 .... 17:54

2005 UP BOYS

Mark Kinnunen won D2 in 16:49, leading Munising to the team title with a 38-point performance, topping defending champ Ishpeming Westwood by 28.

In D1, Marquette made it four in a row.

Michigan Tech, Houghton, Oct. 22
2005 BOYS UP DIVISION 1 TEAMS
1. Marquette 70
2. Calumet 76
3. Sault Ste Marie 78
4. Houghton 84
5. Gladstone 127

2005 BOYS UP DIVISION 1 INDIVIDUALS
1. Greg Peterson (Houghton)11 .... 17:16
2. Keith Helminen (Calumet)11 .... 17:18
3. Eric Koppana (Calumet)12 .... 17:42
4. Chris Lynch (Negaunee)10 .... 17:51
5. Jacob Bennette (Sault)9 .... 17:56

2005 BOYS UP DIVISION 2 TEAMS
1. Munising 42
2. Ishpeming Westwood 50
3. Stephenson 67
4. Ironwood 93
5. St Ignace 169

2005 BOYS UP DIVISION 2 INDIVIDUALS
1. Mark Kinnunen (Munising)12 .... 16:49
2. Brad Bruce (Munising)11 .... 17:14
3. Scott Bond (Munising)11 .... 17:19
4. Craig Tessmer (Stephenson)10 .... 17:31
5. Matt Sundberg (Ishpeming Westwood)11 ... 17:49

2005 BOYS UP DIVISION 3 TEAMS
1. Rapid River 38
2. Painesdale-Jeffers 66
3. Cedarville 94
4. Eben Superior Central 101
5. Pickford 127

2005 BOYS UP DIVISION 3 INDIVIDUALS
1. Tyler Crossman (Rapid River)10 .... 17:15
2. David Kilpela (Painesdale-Jeffers)11 ..... 17:57
3. Jonathon Kilpela (Painesdale-Jeffers)9 ... 18:08
4. Mike Jenkins (Carney-Nadeau)12 .... 18:18
5. Mike Turton (Eben-Superior Central)12 ... 18:36

2006 UP BOYS

Escanaba picked up a solid win in D1. Coached by Joe Royer, it was the first win for the Eskymos since 1998. Munising repeated as champions in D2.

Michigan Tech, Houghton, Oct. 21
2006 BOYS UP DIVISION 1 TEAMS
1. Escanaba 56
2. Sault Ste Marie 83
3. Houghton 109
4. Marquette 118
5. Gladstone 133

2006 BOYS UP DIVISION 1 INDIVIDUALS
1. Jacob Bennette (Sault Ste Marie)10 ...... 17:05
2. Alan Peterson (Ironwood)9 .... 17:05
3. Stuart Chipman (Sault Ste Marie)12 ...... 17:17
4. John Jacisin (Ironwood)11 .... 17:35
5. Derek Saari (Escanaba)12 .... 17:38

2006 BOYS UP DIVISION 2 TEAMS
1. Munising 46
2. Westwood 50
3. Stephenson 58
4. Rudyard 89
5. Newberry 130

2006 BOYS UP DIVISION 2 INDIVIDUALS
1. Scott Bond (Munising)12 .... 17:06
2. Brad Bruce (Munising)12 .... 17:29
3. Cody Robinson (Westwood)12 .... 17:29
4. Isiah Otten (Rudyard)11 .... 17:41
5. Alex Zaleski (Munising)10 .... 17:42

2006 BOYS UP DIVISION 3 TEAMS
1. Painesdale-Jeffers 41
2. Rapid River 48
3. Chassell 96
4. Pickford 110
5. DeTour 111

2006 BOYS UP DIVISION 3 INDIVIDUALS
1. Tyler Crossman (Rapid River)11 .... 17:12
2. Jonathon Kilpela (Painesdale-Jeffers)10 ... 17:33
3. David Kilpela (Painesdale-Jeffers)12 ..... 18:04
4. Richard Gibson (Pickford)11 .... 18:22
5. Blair Suave (Rapid River)11 .... 18:33

2007 UP BOYS

Houghton, coached by Traci Filpus, won its first state meet since the 1989 Class C title. Alan Peterson of Ironwood had the fastest time of the day, 16:47, to win D2. He later starred at Grand Valley and would compete in the 2020 Olympic Trials Marathon.

Stephenson movewd up from 3rd the previous year to take D2, and in D3 Rapid River won after being runner-up in 2006.

Sault Ste Marie, Oct. 20
2007 BOYS UP DIVISION 1 TEAMS
1. Houghton 45
2. Marquette 73
3. Sault Ste Marie 76
4. Escanaba 84
5. Menominee 117

2007 BOYS UP DIVISION 1 INDIVIDUALS
1. Jacob Bennette (Sault Ste Marie)11 ...... 17:04
2. Evan Griffith (Houghton)10 .... 17:06
3. Nathan Manderfield (Houghton)11 .... 17:23
4. Ben Jaszczak (Houghton)10 .... 17:34
5. Tom McFadden (Marquette)12 .... 17:39

2007 BOYS UP DIVISION 2 TEAMS
1. Stephenson 45
2. Munising 61
3. Ironwood 65
4. Rudyard 97
5. Newberry 137

2007 BOYS UP DIVISION 2 INDIVIDUALS
1. Alan Peterson (Ironwood)10 .... 16:47
2. Craig Tessmer (Stephenson)12 .... 16:57
3. John Jacisin (Ironwood)12 .... 17:13
4. Alex Zaleski (Munising)11 .... 17:22
5. Andrew Nuttall (Stephenson)12 .... 17:46

2007 BOYS UP DIVISION 3 TEAMS
1. Rapid River 71
2. Painesdale-Jeffers 87
3. Eben Junction-Superior Central 91
4. Pickford 120
5. Powers-North Central 127

2007 BOYS UP DIVISION 3 INDIVIDUALS
1. Tyler Crossman (Rapid River)12 .... 17:18
2. Jonathon Kilpela (Painesdale-Jeffers)11 ... 17:38
3. Teryn Miller (Detour)11 .... 18:08
4. Richard Gibson (Pickford)12 .... 18:30
5. Troy Rynnanen (Chassell)11 .... 18:36

2008 UP BOYS

Marquette, coached by Mike Leanes, won big in D1 with a 23-point team performance. The Redmen were led by Mickey Sanders. The sophomore had the day's fastest time at 16:35. Munising won its third title in four years in D2.

Sault Ste Marie, Oct. 18
2008 BOYS UP DIVISION 1 TEAMS
1. Marquette 23
2. Gladstone 66
3. Houghton 103
4. Escanaba 123
5. Sault Ste Marie 134

2008 BOYS UP DIVISION 1 INDIVIDUALS
1. Mickey Sanders (Marquette)10 .... 16:35
2. Evan Griffith (Houghton)11 .... 16:49

3. Reed Payant (Marquette)10 ....17:01
4. Austin Wissler (Marquette)10 ....17:17
5. Clinton Bergman (Gwinn)11 ....17:28

2008 BOYS UP DIVISION 2 TEAMS
1. Munising 29
2. L'Anse 100
3. Rudyard 107
4. Ironwood 107
5. Stephenson 148

2008 BOYS UP DIVISION 2 INDIVIDUALS
1. Alan Peterson (Ishpeming)11 ....16:46
2. Alex Zaleski (Munising)12 ....16:49
3. Corey Gage (Newberry)11 ....17:02
4. Jacob Mahoski (Munising)10 ....17:06
5. Dominic Beckman (Ironwood)12 ....17:15

2008 BOYS UP DIVISION 3 TEAMS
1. Eben-Superior Central 51
2. Chassell 73
3. Painesdale-Jeffers 79
4. Cedarville 104
5. Detour 108

2008 BOYS UP DIVISION 3 INDIVIDUALS
1. Jonathan Kilpela (Painesdale-Jeffers)12 ....16:38
2. Tyler Veraghen (North Central)12 ....17:42
3. Teryn Miller (Detour)12 ....17:47
4. Tim Wolfe (Eben-Superior Central)11 ....18:14
5. Troy Rynnanen (Chassell)12 ....18:16

2009 UP BOYS

Teammate Reed Payant beat defending champion Mickey Sanders by 30 seconds as the Redmen of Marquette tallied a sterling 24 points, finishing 1-2-3.

Sault Ste Marie, Oct. 24
2009 BOYS UP DIVISION 1 TEAMS
1. Marquette 24
2. Houghton 98
3. Sault Ste Marie 99
4. Escanaba 113
5. Gladstone 114

2009 BOYS UP DIVISION 1 INDIVIDUALS
1. Reed Payant (Marquette)11 ....16:21
2. Mickey Sanders (Marquette)11 ....16:51
3. Austin Wissler (Marquette)11 ....17:01
4. Clinton Bergmann (Gwinn)12 ....17:09
5. Caleb Cox (Gladstone) 17:55

2009 BOYS UP DIVISION 2 TEAMS
1. Rudyard 37
2. Munising 50
3. L'Anse 81
4. Stephenson 90
5. Norway 148

2009 BOYS UP DIVISION 2 INDIVIDUALS
1. Alan Peterson (Ishpeming)12 ....16:20
2. Jacob Mahoski (Munising)11 ....16:35
3. Andrew Otten (Rudyard) 17:00
4. Ryan Goings (Munising) 17:18
5. David Jarvie (Rudyard) 17:32

2009 BOYS UP DIVISION 3 TEAMS
1. Painesdale-Jeffers 65
2. Eben-Superior Central 72
3. Cedarville 83
4. Rapid River 90
5. Hancock 91

2009 BOYS UP DIVISION 3 INDIVIDUALS
1. Matthew Schlosser (Cedarville) 18:38
2. Tyler Mercier (Powers-North Central) 18:48
3. Darrell Kohli (Rapid River) 18:53
4. Jeffery Laux (Hancock) 19:00
5. Lukas Maki (Eben-Superior Central) 19:00

2010 UP BOYS

In D1, Mickey Sanders of Marquette recaptured the title he had grabbed two years earlier, beating defending champion and teammate Reed Payant, 16:27-16:37. It was Marquette's thirde consecutive win and its seventh in the last nine years.

Escanaba, Oct. 23
2010 BOYS UP DIVISION 1 TEAMS
1. Marquette 47
2. Houghton 88
3. Escanaba 94
4. Sault Ste Marie 123
5. Negaunee 160

Marquette's Mickey Sanders.

2010 BOYS UP DIVISION 1 INDIVIDUALS
1. Mickey Sanders (Marquette)12 ....16:27
2. Reed Payant (Marquette)12 ....16:37
3. Austin Wissler (Marquette)12 ....16:49
4. Evan Griffith (Houghton) 16:54
5. Corey Mullins (Houghton) 16:56

2010 BOYS UP DIVISION 2 TEAMS
1. Stephenson 52
2. Rudyard 78
3. L'Anse 97
4. St Ignace 130
5. Hancock 146

2010 BOYS UP DIVISION 2 INDIVIDUALS
1. David Hebert (West Iron County) 16:55
2. Trevor Vetort (Stephenson)12 ....16:58
3. David Jarvie (Rudyard) 17:17
4. Kenny Peterson (Ishpeming) 17:39
5. Jono Newlin (Stephenson)11 ....17:48

2010 BOYS UP DIVISION 3 TEAMS
1. Eben-Superior Central 41
2. Cedarville 48
3. Munising 75
4. Rapid River 76
5. Carney-Nadeau 134

2010 BOYS UP DIVISION 3 INDIVIDUALS
1. Jake Mahoski (Munising) 16:48
2. Andrew Kelto (Munising)11 ....17:35
3. Maki Lukas (Eben-Superior Central) 17:53

4. Josh Hester (Cedarville)10 ....17:57
5. Nick Maki (Eben-Superior Central)9 ....18:00

2011 UP BOYS

Marquette, after three straight D1 wins, dropped to 10th place. It would be the year for Houghton, as Traci Filpus's squad would win by 39 points, led by senior Dylan Turpeinen.

Pictured Rocks GC, Munising, Oct. 22
2011 BOYS UP DIVISION 1 TEAMS
1. Houghton 41
2. Kingsford 80
3. Escanaba 105
4. Menominee 144
5. Sault Ste Marie 146

2011 BOYS UP DIVISION 1 INDIVIDUALS
1. Dylan Turpeinen (Houghton)12 ....17:02
2. Devin Berg (Calumet)10 ....17:04
3. Daniel Kulas (Kingsford)11 ....17:10
4. Davey Luplow (Menominee)10 ....17:12
5. Jacob Colling (Houghton)9 ....17:21

2011 BOYS UP DIVISION 2 TEAMS
1. Stephenson 36
2. St Ignace LaSalle 70
3. Norway 81
4. Rudyard 119
5. Ironwood 121

2011 BOYS UP DIVISION 2 INDIVIDUALS
1. Jono Newlin (Stephenson)12 ....17:32
2. Bennett Paul (St Ignace LaSalle)12 ....17:37
3. Jared Joki (Ironwood)9 ....18:11
4. Ken Truitt (Stephenson)10 ....18:19
5. Dusty Seavoy (L'Anse)11 ....18:19

2011 BOYS UP DIVISION 3 TEAMS
1. Munising 36
2. Cedarville 46
3. Pickford 84
4. Carney-Nadeau 96
5. Painesdale-Jeffers 111

2011 BOYS UP DIVISION 3 INDIVIDUALS
1. Andrew Kelto (Munising)12 ....17:48
2. Josh Hester (Cedarville)11 ....18:04
3. Skyler Lloyd (Eben-Superior Central)11 ....18:41
4. Brett Houle (Dollar Bay)11 ....18:44
5. Izaak Mahoski (Munising)9 ....18:55

2012 UP BOYS

"The weather was great, but the course was a little wet," freshman D1 winner Parker Scott told John Vrancic of the MHSAA. "The slippery footing slowed everything down."

Sault Ste. Marie, coached by Jim Martin, won its first title in 11 years, and Stephenson won its third-straight D2 title. In D3 freshman Brett Hannah took first and led Munising to a repeat win.

Pictured Rocks GC, Munising, Oct. 20
2012 BOYS UP DIVISION 1 TEAMS
1. Sault Ste Marie 65
2. Escanaba 72
3. Kingsford 101
4. Menominee 102
5. Houghton 105

2012 BOYS UP DIVISION 1 INDIVIDUALS
1. Parker Scott (Sault Ste Marie)9 ....16:51
2. Daniel Kulas (Kingsford)12 ....16:59
3. Jacob Colling (Houghton)10 ....17:00
4. Lance Rambo (Marquette)9 ....17:19
5. Davey Luplow (Menominee)11 ....17:20

2012 BOYS UP DIVISION 2 TEAMS
1. Stephenson 52
2. Norway 67
3. Hancock 76

4. Ironwood 84
5. Manistique 84

2012 BOYS UP DIVISION 2 INDIVIDUALS
1. Connor Cappaert (Stephenson)10 .... 17:26
2. Jared Joki (Ironwood)10 .... 17:44
3. Tyler Pomeroy (Manistique)12 .... 18:14
4. Bryson Lawrence (Manistique)12 .... 18:38
5. Ken Truitt (Stephenson)11 .... 18:43

2012 BOYS UP DIVISION 3 TEAMS
1. Munising 55
2. Cedarville 72
3. St Ignace LaSalle 90
4. Pickford 103
5. Dollar Bay 106

2012 BOYS UP DIVISION 3 INDIVIDUALS
1. Brett Hannah (Munising)9 .... 17:55
2. Josh Hester (Cedarville)12 .... 18:01
3. Izaak Mahoski (Munising)10 .... 18:01
4. Zachary Mazurek (Bessemer)10 .... 18:10
5. Brett Houle (Dollar Bay)12 .... 18:23

2013 UP BOYS

"The course was very slippery and the times were slow," Lance Rambo, the D1 winner from Marquette, said. "The water at Mile 2 made it challenging. But the most challenging part was in the end. You just had to push through it."

Marquette, once again coached by Dale Phillips (title No. 18), won by 33 points over Escanaba.

Gentz's Homestead GC, Harvey, Oct. 19
2013 BOYS UP DIVISION 1 TEAMS
1. Marquette 42
2. Escanaba 75
3. Houghton 86
4. Sault Ste Marie 108
5. Calumet 110

2013 BOYS UP DIVISION 1 INDIVIDUALS
1. Lance Rambo (Marquette)10 .... 16:57
2. Robert Reiboldt (Marquette) 17:08
3. David Jazsczak (Houghton)11 .... 17:23
4. Nate Carey (Kingsford)10 .... 17:27
5. Joey Wolfe (Escanaba)9 .... 17:30

2013 BOYS UP DIVISION 2 TEAMS
1. St Ignace 57
2. Hancock 67
3. Ishpeming 69
4. Ironwood 81
5. Norway 121

2013 BOYS UP DIVISION 2 INDIVIDUALS
1. Jared Joki (Ironwood)11 .... 17:10
2. Bradley Gustafson (St Ignace)12 .... 16:19
3. Andrew Sjogren (St Ignace)12 .... 18:24
4. Justin Anderson (Norway)11 .... 18:46
5. Jacob Sjogren (St Ignace)12 .... 18:47

2013 BOYS UP DIVISION 3 TEAMS
1. Powers-North Central 66
2. Pickford 68
3. Cedarville 109
4. Dollar Bay 111
5. Painesdale-Jeffers 112

2013 BOYS UP DIVISION 3 INDIVIDUALS
1. Connor Cappaert (Stephenson)11 .... 17:40
2. Zach Mazurek (Bessemer)11 .... 17:58
3. Seth Polfus (Powers-North Central)9 .... 18:19
4. Bryce Holle (Powers-North Central)10 .... 18:23
5. Nick Maki (Eben-Superior Central)12 .... 18:28

2014 UP BOYS

Chassell won D3, its first state win since the 1982 Class D title. "Chassell cross country went away for a few years, but now it looks like it's back stronger than ever," coach Marco Guidotti told the MHSAA's John Vrancic.

Marquette won D1 by 10 points. It would be the final boys career win—19 in all—for legendary coach Dale Phillips.

Gentz's Homestead GC, Harvey, Oct. 18
2014 BOYS UP DIVISION 1 TEAMS
1. Marquette 59
2. Escanaba 69
3. Houghton 95
4. Sault Ste Marie 102
5. Negaunee 125

2014 BOYS UP DIVISION 1 INDIVIDUALS
1. Nate Carey (Kingsford)11 .... 17:20
2. Lance Rambo (Marquette)11 .... 17:26
3. Joey Wolfe (Escanaba)10 .... 17:28
4. David Jazsczak (Houghton)12 .... 17:45
5. Eric Cousineau (Escanaba)12 .... 17:48

2014 BOYS UP DIVISION 2 TEAMS
1. Ishpeming 53
2. Powers-North Central 67
3. Ironwood 68
4. Ishpeming Westwood 105
5. Gwinn 119

2014 BOYS UP DIVISION 2 INDIVIDUALS
1. Jared Joki (Ironwood)12 .... 16:46
2. Bryce Holle (Powers-North Central)11 .... 18:31
3. Kazmine Langness (Ishpeming)11 .... 19:13
4. Phillip Hagenson (Manistique)9 .... 19:32
5. Justin Anderson (Norway)12 .... 19:33

2014 BOYS UP DIVISION 3 TEAMS
1. Chassell 78
2. Stephenson 84
3. Munising 85
4. Dollar Bay 104
5. Cedarville 147

2014 BOYS UP DIVISION 3 INDIVIDUALS
1. Grady Kerst (Munising)10 .... 17:22
2. Connor Cappaert (Stephenson)12 .... 18:05
3. Brett Hannah (Munising)11 .... 18:14
4. Zak Mazurek (Bessemer)12 .... 18:26
5. Sam Dean (Wakefield-Marenisco)11 .... 18:31

2015 UP BOYS

Negaunee won its first title since 1983's Class C crown. The race up front was fast, with Marquette's Lance Rambo winning his second title in 16:11 as the top five in D1 all bettered 17:00.

"Our guys really wanted it. They went out and attacked," Negaunee coach Lisa Bigalk told John Vrancic. "This was such an incredible season. The guys didn't have an off-day all year."

Beachamp's Grove, Flat Rock, Oct. 24
2015 BOYS UP DIVISION 1 TEAMS
1. Negaunee 43
2. Sault Ste Marie 85
3. Marquette 93
4. Houghton 110
5. Escanaba 115

2015 BOYS UP DIVISION 1 INDIVIDUALS
1. Lance Rambo (Marquette)12 .... 16:11
2. Colton Yesney (Negaunee)10 .... 16:33
3. Joey Wolfe (Escanaba)11 .... 16:50
4. Nate Carey (Kingsford)12 .... 16:52
5. Mitchell Delong (Calumet)11 .... 16:53

2015 BOYS UP DIVISION 2 TEAMS
1. Ishpeming 28
2. Wakefield-Marenisco/Bessemer 61
3. Powers-North Central 62
4. Ironwood 81
5. Hancock 133

2015 BOYS UP DIVISION 2 INDIVIDUALS
1. Sam Dean (Wakefield-Marenisco/Bess)12 ..... 17:15
2. Spencer Giroux (Ishpeming)9 .... 17:23
3. Nick Niemi (Ironwood)9 .... 17:31
4. Bryce Holle (Powers-North Central)12 .... 17:59
5. Derek Mahoski (Ishpeming)12 .... 18:12

2015 BOYS UP DIVISION 3 TEAMS
1. Chassell 51
2. Dollar Bay 69
3. Cedarville 96
4. Munising 134
5. Stephenson 141

2015 BOYS UP DIVISION 3 INDIVIDUALS
1. Brett Hannah (Munising)12 .... 16:53
2. Michael Brown (Marquette North Star)12 ...... 17:49
3. Abraham Gockenbach (Chassell)9 .... 17:55
4. Brendan Leclaire (Dollar Bay)9 .... 18:10
5. Jacob Iacono (Dollar Bay)10 .... 18:11

Lance Rambo won two titles for Marquette.

2016 UP BOYS

Negaunee made it two in a row, topping Houghton by 18 points in D1.

The Miners were led by junior Colton Yesney, whose 15:50 won by 36 seconds.

Grady Kerst, D3 champion from Munising in 2014, had moved to Ishpeming and won the title in D2, leading his team to its third consecutive win. In D3, Chassell also won its third-straight.

Beachamp's Grove, Flat Rock, Oct. 22
2016 BOYS UP DIVISION 1 TEAMS
1. Negaunee 38
2. Houghton 56
3. Marquette 92
4. Sault Ste Marie 96
5. Calumet 160

2016 BOYS UP DIVISION 1 INDIVIDUALS
1. Colton Yesney (Negaunee)11 .... 15:50
2. Garrett Rudden (Marquette)11 .... 16:26

3. Clayton Sayen (Houghton)11 .... 16:28
4. Thomas Ziegler (Negaunee)12 .... 16:31
5. Seth Helman (Houghton)11 .... 16:43

2016 BOYS UP DIVISION 2 TEAMS
1. Ishpeming 29
2. Wakefield-Marenisco/Bessemer 41
3. Newberry 106
4. Ironwood 110
5. Hancock 136

2016 BOYS UP DIVISION 2 INDIVIDUALS
1. Grady Kerst (Ishpeming)12 .... 16:25
2. Spencer Giroux (Ishpeming)10 .... 16:36
3. Kindred Griffis (Newberry)12 .... 16:38
4. Isaiah Aili (Wakefield-Marenisco/Bess)11 .... 16:53
5. Nick Niemi (Ironwood)10 .... 16:53

2016 BOYS UP DIVISION 3 TEAMS
1. Chassell 54
2. Brimley 77
3. Stephenson 81
4. Cedarville 126
5. Powers-North Central 149

2016 BOYS UP DIVISION 3 INDIVIDUALS
1. Austin Plotkin (Brimley)9 .... 17:02
2. Brendan Leclaire (Dollar Bay)10 .... 17:25
3. Ben Tuomi (Chassell)10 .... 17:37
4. Thomas Bohn (Cedarville)9 .... 17:39
5. Hunter Rautiola (Chassell)12 .... 17:44

2017 UP BOYS

Clayton Sayen of Houghton edged Marquette's Garrett Rudden after an uphill sprint to the finish line by a mere tenth, 16:25.7-16:25.8 as Houghton took the team win.

"I knew it was going to be a battle," said Sayen, "and I gave it every ounce I could."

The D3 tie between Brimley and Chassell went to the No. 6 man to break. Brimley's was 30th, 9 places and 29 seconds ahead of Chassell's.

Pictured Rocks GC, Munising, Oct. 21
2017 BOYS UP DIVISION 1 TEAMS
1. Houghton 39
2. Marquette 54
3. Sault Ste Marie 98
4. Gladstone 113
5. Negaunee 119

2017 BOYS UP DIVISION 1 INDIVIDUALS
1. Clayton Sayen (Houghton)12 .... 16:26
2. Garrett Rudden (Marquette)12 .... 16:26
3. Luke Rambo (Marquette)12 .... 16:29
4. Adam Bruce (Gladstone)11 .... 16:39
5. Seth Helman (Houghton)12 .... 16:57

2017 BOYS UP DIVISION 2 TEAMS
1. Wakefield-Marenisco/Bessemer 22
2. Ishpeming 36
3. Ironwood 99
4. Newberry 102
5. Hancock 143

2017 BOYS UP DIVISION 2 INDIVIDUALS
1. Spencer Giroux (Ishpeming)11 .... 17:04
2. Isaiah Aili (Wakefield-Marenisco/Bess)12 .... 17:45
3. Uriah Aili (Wakefield-Marenisco/Bess)11 .... 17:49
4. Devon Byers (Wakefield-Marenisco/Bess)11 . 17:50
5. Jonah Broberg (Ishpeming)10 .... 17:53

2017 BOYS UP DIVISION 3 TEAMS
1. Brimley 60
2. Chassell 60
3. Rudyard 118
4. Munising 134
5. Stephenson 165

2017 BOYS UP DIVISION 3 INDIVIDUALS
1. Austin Plotkin (Brimley)10 .... 17:08

2. Thomas Bohn (Cedarville)10 .... 17:17
3. Ben Tuomi (Chassell)11 .... 17:39
4. Michael Satchell (Pickford)12 .... 17:58
5. Ethan Brown (Stephenson)12 .... 18:08

2018 UP BOYS

On a windy, cold day with snow squalls coming off the lake, Sault Ste. Marie put five in the top 14. "We've been banged up all year," said coach Jim Martin, "but the kids never stopped believing."

Uriah Aili of Wakefield-Marenisco/Bessemer had the fastest time of the day in winning D2, after running much of the race with teammate Devon Byers. "Devon and I were going to run together and see what happened," he said. "We started pulling away at about 1.5M."

In D3, Chassell made it four wins in five years.

Pictured Rocks GC, Munising, Oct. 20
2018 BOYS UP DIVISION 1 TEAMS
1. Sault Ste Marie 42
2. Houghton 65
3. Gladstone 70
4. Marquette 71
5. Menominee 160

Gladstone's Adam Bruce.

2018 BOYS UP DIVISION 1 INDIVIDUALS
1. Adam Bruce (Gladstone)12 .... 17:06
2. Joe Wood (Houghton)11 .... 17:36
3. Jake Strasler (Gladstone)12 .... 17:41
4. Kaaleb Ranta (Sault Ste Marie)11 .... 17:48
5. Giovanni Mathews (Gladstone)9 .... 17:48

2018 BOYS UP DIVISION 2 TEAMS
1. Ishpeming 32
2. Wakefield-Marenisco/Bessemer 47
3. Newberry 70
4. Ironwood 82

2018 BOYS UP DIVISION 2 INDIVIDUALS
1. Uriah Aili (Wakefield-Marenisco/Bess)12 .... 17:03
2. Devon Byers (Wakefield-Marenisco/Bess)12. 17:16
3. Spencer Giroux (Ishpeming)12 .... 17:34
4. Jonah Broberg (Ishpeming)11 .... 18:01
5. Jordan Longtine (Ishpeming)10 .... 18:07

2018 BOYS UP DIVISION 3 TEAMS
1. Chassell 41
2. Brimley 54
3. Rudyard 72
4. Rapid River 156
5. Stephenson 164

2018 BOYS UP DIVISION 3 INDIVIDUALS
1. Austin Plotkin (Brimley)11 .... 17:24
2. Thomas Bohn (Cedarville)11 .... 17:30
3. Cameron Hoornstra (Brimley)10 .... 17:47
4. Ben Tuomi (Chassell)12 .... 17:56
5. Davin Hill (Dollar Bay)10 .... 18:05

2019 UP BOYS

The Ishpeming Hematites won a second-straight in D2 with an impressive 27 points under the coaching of P.J. Pruett. "We have a lot of runners coming back next year," said Pruett. "The future looks bright."

Houghton's Joe Wood won D1 with the fastest time of the day, 16:51. "I wanted to stay with the front pack at the beginning," said Wood. "I made my move a little after the mile mark."

Gentz's Homestead GC, Harvey, Oct. 19
2019 BOYS UP DIVISION 1 TEAMS
1. Marquette 51
2. Sault Ste Marie 57
3. Houghton 63
4. Gladstone 103
5. Menominee 131

2019 BOYS UP DIVISION 1 INDIVIDUALS
1. Joe Wood (Houghton)12 .... 16:58
2. Giovanni Mathews (Gladstone)10 .... 17:28
3. Jaron Wyma (Sault Ste Marie)11 .... 17:31
4. Kaaleb Ranta (Sault Ste Marie)12 .... 17:33
5. Drew Hughes (Gladstone)9 .... 17:34

2019 BOYS UP DIVISION 2 TEAMS
1. Ishpeming 27
2. Ironwood 51
3. Wakefield-Marenisco/Bessemer 67
4. Norway 92

Jonah Broberg led Ishpeming to the win. (Ishpeming XC photo)

2019 BOYS UP DIVISION 2 INDIVIDUALS
1. Jonah Broberg (Ishpeming)12 .... 17:30
2. Adam Cavagnetto (Norway)10 .... 17:34
3. Jordan Longtine (Ishpeming)11 .... 17:49
4. Adam Mazurek (Wakefield-Marenisco/B)12 .. 17:55
5. Joseph King (Ishpeming)11 .... 16:03

2019 BOYS UP DIVISION 3 TEAMS
1. Rudyard 72
2. Dollar Bay 93
3. Brimley 96
4. Painesdale-Jeffers 101
5. Chassell 115

2019 BOYS UP DIVISION 3 INDIVIDUALS
1. Austin Plotkin (Brimley)12 .... 17:21
2. Thomas Bohn (Cedarville)12 .... 17:32
3. Cameron Hoornstra (Brimley)11 .... 18:01
4. Nik Thomas (Ewen Trout Creek)10 .... 18:11
5. Hayden Mills (Rudyard)11 .... 18:21

GIRLS CLASS A / DIVISION 1

The Wolverine Parkettes, based in Lincoln Park, won the 1970 AAU Senior Women's National title. From left: Jacki Ford, Pam Bagian, Cheryl Bridges, Theresa Rulison and Kathy Moore. Rulison and Moore were still in high school at this point. Two years earlier, the Parkettes won the national senior title with a team composed entirely of Lincoln Park High School students: Moore, Jacki Ford, Bagian, Sherice Duchamp and Patti Ford.

THE EARLY YEARS

While in the Detroit schools, girls got their start in track in the 1920s, there was no move to let females try cross country. Indeed, statewide, the development of the girls side of the sport trailed the boys side by decades.

In the Upper Peninsula, cross country ski competitions for girls took off in the 1940s, but running? Nope.

It wasn't until the 1960s that girls in Michigan started participating in AAU club cross country, with 1965 being the first year with a state meet. Among the prime movers in this movement were the Michigammes, founded by Red Simmons in Ann Arbor, and the Wolverine Parkettes, founded by Richard Beyst in Lincoln Park in 1965. Other important clubs included Joe Smetanka's Lipke Track Club in Detroit; the Motor City Track Club of Detroit, founded by Richard Ford and Bettye Robinson; the Fleet Feet Club of Midland; and the Flint Track Club.

Note: team scoring for these early AAU races was based on the team's top 3 finishers.

The open winner in 1968, Sperry Jones, was a 1962 graduate of the University of Michigan and qualified for the 1968 Olympics as a kayaker.

1965 AAU STATE CHAMPIONSHIPS
Rouge Park, Detroit, November 12

Novice Division 1M course
1. Janie Schulte (SEM-Ann Arbor)9 .... 6:09
2. Debbie Babridge (DTC-Detroit Kettering) 6:13
3. Joyce Regan (Roadrunners-Detroit Denby)10 .... 6:15
4. Connie Bilicki (unat-Detroit Cody)10 .... 6:27
5. Mary Maganas (unat-Redford)9 .... 6:29

Open Division (14-up) 1.5M course
1. Sperry Jones (SEM-Michigan) 9:06
2. Francie Kraker (SEM-Ann Arbor 65 grad) 9:10
3. Vonnie Perrine (SEM-Whitmore Lake)12 .... 9:19
4. Anna Payne (LL-Lansing Gabriels 65 grad) 9:25
5. Carol Dickinson (Uticettes-Utica)11 .... 9:29

1966 AAU STATE CHAMPIONSHIPS
Rouge Park, Detroit, November 12

Novice Division 1M course
1. Mary Ann Kincke (DTC) 6:04
2. Glenda Micoi (MW) 6:14
3. Roxy Clair (DTC-Detroit Cody)10 .... 6:22
4. Mary Maganas (MM-Redford)10 .... 6:42
5. Chris Dudley (LL-East Lansing)9 .... 6:48
Teams: 1. Detroit TC 10.

Open Division (14-up) 1.5M course
1. Francie Kraker (SEM-Ann Arbor 65 grad) 8:42
2. Pam Bagian (WP-Lincoln Park)9 .... 9:08
3. Janie Schulte (SEM-Ann Arbor)10 .... 9:31

4. Jacki Ford (WP-Lincoln Park)9................9:47
5. Mary Dudley (LL-East Lansing)10............9:51
Teams: 1. Southeast Michigammes 10; 2. Wolverine Parkettes 15.

1967 AAU STATE CHAMPIONSHIPS
Rouge Park, Detroit, November 18

Girls Division (ages 14-17) 1.5M course
Teams: 1. Wolverine Parkettes.

Open Division (14-up) 2M course
3. Jacki Ford (WP-Lincoln Park)10..............12:00
Teams: 1. Wolverine Parkettes.

In November 1967, Kathy Moore, then a 14-year-old 9th-grader at Lincoln Park, finished 6th in the AAU Women's Nationals and qualified to run in an international cross country championship. However, appendicitis struck and she was unable to travel.

1968 AAU STATE CHAMPIONSHIPS
Lake Kearsley, Flint, October 26
42°, windy

Girls Division (ages 14-17) 1.5M course
1. Carol Frederick (SEM-Ann Arbor)9..............9:06
2. Sue Bylicki (MC-Detroit St Mary of Redford)10 ......9:22
3. Janie Schulte (SEM-Ann Arbor)11..............9:23
4. Mary Ann Fahlgren (SEM-Ann Arbor)10..........9:48
5. Alice Steinicke (SEM-Ann Arbor)11.............9:52
Teams: 1. Southeast Michigammes 8; 2. Motor City TC 19; 3. Flint TC 24

Open Division (14-up) 2M course
1. Pam Bagian (WP-Lincoln Park)11.............12:19
2. Kathy Moore (WP-Lincoln Park)10............12:26
3. Jacki Ford (WP-Lincoln Park)11..............12:30
4. Sherice DuChamp (WP-Lincoln Park)9.........12:43
5. Patti Ford (WP-Lincoln Park)10...............13:18
Teams: 1. Wolverine Parkettes A 6; 2. Wolverine Parkettes B 16; 3. Wolverine Parkettes C 27.

On November 30, 1968, the Parkettes took 2nd at the AAU Senior Championships in Frederick, Maryland, missing the win by just one point. The team was composed entirely of Lincoln Park High School students. Their places and times on the 2M course: 14. Kathy Moore 11:40; 18. Jacki Ford 11:49; 20. Pam Bagian 11:52; 36. Sherice Duchamp 12:15; 37. Patti Ford 12:16.

1969 AAU STATE CHAMPIONSHIPS
Cass Benton, Redford, October 25
62° and clear

Girls Division (ages 14-17) 1.5M course
1. Theresa Rulison (WP-East Lansing)9.............9:01
2. Karen Zimmerman (WP-Lincoln Park)9..........9:04
3. Patti Ford (WP-Lincoln Park)11..................9:10
4. Pat Darish (MC)..................................9:17
5. Marcia Rall (WP-East Lansing)10................9:26
Teams: 1. Wolverine Parkettes A 21; 2. Wolverine Parkettes B 24; 3. Motor City TC 43.

Open Division (14-up) 2M course
1. Cheryl Bridges (unattached).....................10:59
2. Pam Bagian (WP-Lincoln Park)12...............11:18
3. Jacki Ford (WP-Lincoln Park)12.................11:39
4. Kathy Moore (WP-Lincoln Park)11..............12:01
4. Carol Frederick (SEM-Ann Arbor)10............12:16
Teams: 1. Wolverine Parkettes 16; 2. Southeast Michigammes 29; 3. Fleet Feet 50.

In November 1969, Pam Bagian of Lincoln Park/Wolverine Parkettes finished 3rd in the AAU Nationals, running 11:15 on a two-mile course, qualifying for the World team. The Parkettes won the national AAU team title with 35 points, helped along by runner-up Cheryl Bridges from Indiana (an early World Record holder in the marathon and mother of Olympic medalist Shalane Flanagan). Also on the team were Lincoln Park's Jacki Ford (13th in 11:39), and Kathy Moore (11:59). Theresa Rulison, a Parkette from East Lansing, ran 12:10.

That same meet the Wolverine squad also won the national 14-17 race, led by 5th-placer Karen Zimmerman. Vicki Slater placed 10th and Patti Ford 12th.

Bagian ran 15:45 for 4K to finish 14th at the 1970 International in Frederick, Maryland (there were two international championships that year, the other in France) while still a senior at Lincoln Park. She was named the Outstanding Woman Athlete in the state that year by the AAU.

Said Bagian, "I haven't always had this kind of success. I started running when I was in 8th grade because some of my girlfriends were in Mr. Beyst's class and he got them interested in running. I just kind of tagged along."

1970 AAU STATE CHAMPIONSHIPS
Orchard Lake, October 24

Girls Division (ages 14-17) 1.5M course
1. Mickey Tupper (MC-Detroit Redford)9..............8:43
2. Denise Green (WP-Lansing?)...................9:01
3. Theresa Rulison (WP-East Lansing)10...........9:09
4. Karen Zimmerman (WP-Lincoln Park)10..........9:11
5. Ann Forshee (SEM-AA Huron)9..................9:24

Open Division (14-up) 2M course
1. Pam Bagian (WP-Lincoln Park 70 grad).........11:50
2. Jacki Ford (WP-Lincoln Park 70 grad)..........12:08
3. Vickie Slater (WP-Lincoln Park)10..............12:53
4. Sue Parks (WP-Ypsilanti)9......................12:56
5. Lynn Olson (WP-Lincoln Park)11................13:01

In late 1970 the Parkettes again won the national title with recent grads Pam Bagian and Jacki Ford on the team.

At this point, we've been unable to locate AAU State results from 1971-74.

In November 1974 at the AAU Nationals in Bellbrook, Ohio, sophomore Mary Ann Opalewski (Fleet Feet-Saginaw MacArthur) placed 3rd in the 14-17 Division.

XC IN THE SCHOOLS

By 1973, girls cross country was fairly widespread at the high school level in Michigan, though many of the girls were running as part of the boys teams. However, the MHSAA was in no hurry to sanction it, despite the fact there were major invitationals for girls at Ann Arbor Pioneer, Delta College, Fennville, Grand Ledge, Saginaw Eisenhower, West Bloomfield and Ypsilanti.

Said Ann Arbor Huron's Ken Hillis in 1975, "This is a serious problem. The MHSAA doesn't have any glamorous meets for talented high school girls. They won't allow us to run in the better organized AAU meets and they haven't provided an official state meet.

"Their argument is that there is not interest, but if you had been at the Pioneer Invitational [11 teams competed], you could never say that. The other side of the coin is that if you won't recognize a sport then you are keeping other schools from building up their programs, so it works both ways."

In the same 1975 *Ann Arbor News* article, Ann Arbor Pioneer coach Lincoln Schoch said, "It's hard to blame the state at this point. Right now we're only talking about 175-200 runners. But it would be a shame if they didn't recognize us next year and sponsor a state meet. The girls growth rate seems to be doubling every year.

"Right now, we're having recognition problems. A lot of people haven't accepted girls running two and three miles yet. We have the disadvantage of not only being a minor sport but being a girls minor sport. What Ken and I are doing is trying to get people to knock down that image and to see girls cross country is a viable sport."

Hillis and Schoch joined forces to organize the first de-facto state championships for girls in 1975, with Ted Wilson acting as meet director.

1975 CLASS A GIRLS

The pre-MHSAA state finals was held on a Wednesday at Pioneer High School over a 2.25M course. Coach Carl Chapman's heavily-favored team from Grand Ledge won the title. Ann Arbor Huron might have been able to win, but Leslie Laviolette was unable to run because of injury. Huron coach Ken Hillis said she would have been a top 10 finisher.

There were 84 runners in Class A, so it was fairly well attended. At least the top four ran faster than the course record of 14:11 held by Pioneer's Pat Schott.

Teams were allowed more than seven entries each; Huron, for instance, ran nine, while Pioneer ran 15.

The Grand Ledge team had an 8-0 record that first season, indicating that there were a decent number of competitive opportunities leading up to the state finals.

Results are incomplete; if you have more please let me know.

Grand Ledge Class A state champs

Pioneer HS, Ann Arbor, November 5 □
1975 GIRLS CLASS A TEAMS
1. Grand Ledge 46
2. Ann Arbor Huron 56
3. Ann Arbor Pioneer 95
=4. Pontiac Central 99
=4. Redford Union 99

Other schools with entries: Adrian, Bay City Western, Clio, Fowlerville, Kalamazoo Central, Livonia Stevenson, Midland, Clinton Twp Chippewa Valley, Muskegon Mona Shores, Owosso, Pontiac Central, Portage Northern, Royal Oak Kimball, Saginaw Eisenhower, Southfield, St Clair Shores South Lake, Walled Lake Western, West Bloomfield,

1975 GIRLS CLASS A INDIVIDUALS
1. Joanne Singer (Saginaw Eisenhower)12..............13:37
2. Theresa Lawless (Grand Ledge)12 ....13:48
3. Karla Amble (Ann Arbor Huron)12 ....13:49
4. Pat Schott (Ann Arbor Pioneer) 13:52
5. Peg Dyer (Grand Ledge)12 .... nt
7. Aini Maripuu (Ann Arbor Huron) 14:16
10. Cindy Damon (Ann Arbor Huron)12 ....14:32
11. Angelia Ilieff (Grand Ledge)12 .... nt
15. Linda Moreno (Grand Ledge)12 .... nt
22. Melissa Knopf (Ann Arbor Huron) 15:03
?. Debbie Mayotte (Ann Arbor Pioneer) 15:30
? Amy Conlin (Ann Arbor Pioneer) .... nt
? Carol Summerfield (Ann Arbor Pioneer).................... nt
? Barbara Willoughby (Ann Arbor Pioneer)..............15:34
41. Pat Dyer (Grand Ledge)12 .... nt

Saginaw Eisenhower's Joanne Singer was the first state champion in a state finals with school teams.

1976 CLASS A GIRLS
Another de-facto state championships for girls came in Ann Arbor. Twelve teams battled in 35-degree temps, plus 24 individuals who weren't on scoring teams.

Saginaw Eisenhower produced its second-straight state champion, despite having only two girls on the team. Kelly Spatz would go on to star at Michigan State, where she was named Sportswoman of the Year in 1981. She held the Spartan school record in the mile for many years at 4:49.56. She placed 21st in the AIAW Nationals (that was pre-NCAA for women) in 1980.

Ann Arbor, November 3 ☐
1976 GIRLS CLASS A TEAMS
1. Livonia Stevenson...41
2. Ann Arbor Pioneer..69
3. Royal Oak Kimball...104
4. Ann Arbor Huron..145
5. Redford Union..160
6. White Lake Lakeland.....................................168
7. Milford...169
8. Midland...170

9. Pontiac Central..203
10. Royal Oak Dondero.....................................212
11. Midland Dow..249
12. Kalamazoo Norrix..297

1976 GIRLS CLASS A INDIVIDUALS
1. Kelly Spatz (Saginaw Eisenhower)12 .... 18:00
2. Julie Voyles (Livonia Stevenson)11...................18:15
3. Beth Huff (Ann Arbor Pioneer)9 .... 18:24
4. Charla Gardner (Swartz Creek) 18:31
5. Carie Pierce (Portage Northern) 18:33
6. Carol Brotherton (Milford Lakeland) 18:43
7. Marcy Nesbitt (Birmingham Groves) 18:44
8. Kathy Dubois (Livonia Stevenson)................... 18:48
9. Jane Foote (Milford).. 18:54
10. Kerri Ericksen (West Bloomfield) 19:03
11. Pamela Allen (Kalamazoo Central) 19:03
12. Dana Loesche (Ann Arbor Pioneer)10............ 19:03
13. Debbie Morehouse (Royal Oak Kimball) 19:10
14. Carol Molesky (Saginaw Eisenhower)9 .... 19:10
15. Pam Draper (Flint Kearsley) 19:20
16. Aini Maripuu (Ann Arbor Huron) 19:21
17. Sue Ostrander (Livonia Stevenson)............... 19:23
18. Kathy Schmidt (Livonia Stevenson) 19:39
19. Ann Krumrey (Pontiac Central) 19:40
20. Martha Carlson (Ann Arbor Pioneer).............. 19:47
21. Cathy Bjork (Midland).................................... 19:54
22. Julie Clifford (Redford Union) 19:55
23. M. Weld (Royal Oak Kimball) 19:57
24. J. Bogue (Royal Oak Kimball) 20:01
25. Jan Niemiec (Livonia Stevenson) 20:12
26. Debbie Gillig (Owosso) 20:12
27. Deborah Froelich (Midland)........................... 20:16
28. Dorothy Matusik (Milford)............................... 20:24
29. Shannon Mara (Midland Dow) 20:25
30. Nancy Liponaga (Royal Oak Dondero).......... 20:25
31. Less Doll (Grand Ledge) 20:27
32. Carol Thrane (Ann Arbpr Pioneer)................. 20:31
33. Carol Sionkowski (Redford Union) 20:33
34. Carol Cunningham (Adrian).......................... 20:34
35. Melissa Knopf (Ann Arbor Huron).................. 20:36
36. Linda Dyer (Grand Ledge)............................ 20:41
37. Jilie Reitz (Royal Oak Kimball) 20:42
38. Joyce Kraft (Milford Lakeland)....................... 20:43
39. Jane Santinga (Ann Arbor Pioneer) 20:44
40. Karen Schmidt (Livonia Stevenson).............. 20:47

1977 CLASS A GIRLS
MITCA sponsored a well-attended invitational state championships. The meet was directed by Karyn Cribley. Some 49 teams competed. The most impressive run came from Port Huron junior Miriam Boyd, who ripped three miles in 16:43, a performance that still would be mind-boggling. The next spring Boyd would win the A title at two miles in 10:36.8, a state record that would last 18 years.

Ann Arbor Huron won the team title under coach Ken Hillis. However, Hillis found out at the meet that the MHSAA wasn't planning on making girls cross country official until the 1980 season. The MHSAA stance was that it wouldn't become an "official" sport until there were three straight years with 10% or more of the schools in the state competing.

"We've been supplying them with records for the past three years but they say they'll start keeping them beginning with this season."

Hills added, "Just because the state didn't make it an official state title doesn't mean we couldn't enjoy it. We enjoyed the win as much as we would have if the state would have given us the trophy."

Potterville, Oct. 22 ▨
1977 GIRLS CLASS A TEAMS
1. Ann Arbor Huron... 71
2. Redford Union 110
3. Ann Arbor Pioneer 116
4. Royal Oak Kimball 164
5. Farmington Hills 176

6. Royal Oak Dondero...177
7. East Lansing...189
8. Midland...199
9. Livonia Stevenson...202
10. Kalamazoo Norrix..256
11. White Lake Lakeland......................................208
12. Adrian..280
13. Pontiac Central..324
14. Kalamazoo Central..367
15. Westland Glenn...380
16. Lansing Everett...454

1977 GIRLS CLASS A INDIVIDUALS
1. Miriam Boyd (Port Huron)11 .... 16:43
2. Carol Schenk (Flint Kearsley)12 .... 17:07
3. Beth Huff (Ann Arbor Pioneer)10..................... 17:43
4. Michelle Collins (Farmington Hills Mercy)........ 18:04
5. Brenda Clark (Grand Haven) 18:07
6. Sue Heinlen (Farmington Hills Mercy) 18:15
7. Voyles (Livonia Stevenson)............................. 18:16
8. Liz Woodley (Redford Thurston) 18:20
9. Susan Brown (Brighton)9 .... 18:26
10. Ellen Birkhimer (Midland).............................. 18:27
11. Barb Richards (Traverse City) 18:28
12. Debbie Morehouse (Royal Oak) 18:31
13. Shelly Clark (Grand Haven) 18:36
14. Brenda Lucas (Grand Rapids Creston).......... 18:41
15. Ruth Hubbard (Walled Lake Western)............ 18:42
16. Sue Frederick (Ann Arbor Huron)11 .... 18:53
17. Dana Loesche (Ann Arbor Pioneer)............... 18:54
18. Betty Davis (Redford Union) 19:02
19. Josie VonVoightlander (Ann Arbor Huron)..... 19:05
20. Janine Crawley (East Lansing) 19:12
21. Kandi Laird (Redford Union) 19:15
22. Cindy Bjornderg (Royal Oak) 19:17
23. Sue Smith (Livonia Stevenson) 19:20
24. Nancy Liponaga (Royal Oak)......................... 19:21
25. Missy Knopf (Ann Arbor Huron) 19:24
26. Katie Brown (Clinton Twp Chippewa Valley) 19:27
27. Aini Maripuu (Ann Arbor Huron) 19:31
28. Deb Froelich (Midland).................................. 19:41
29. Ann Krumrey (Pontiac Central) 19:42
30. Melissa Ropek (Westland Glenn).................. 19:44
31. Laura Browne (Redford Borgess) 19:47
32. Kelly Mann (Ann Arbor Huron) 19:50
33. Karen Klein (Kalamazoo Norrix) 19:51
34. Sue Riley (Redford Union) 19:55
35. Sue Jacques (Redford Union) 19:56
36. Jolynette Disson (Pontiac Northern) 19:57
37. Lisa Jenkins (East Lansing) 19:58
38. Laurie Fookes (Midland)................................ 19:59
39. Julie Hammerstein (Adrian)........................... 20:00
40. Linda Larson (White Lake Lakeland) 20:01
57. Betty Peters (Ann Arbor Huron)..................... 20:21
66. Cindy Osmun (Ann Arbor Huron) 20:36

1978 ALL-CLASSES GIRLS
This first year of official MHSAA cross country saw 122 of the 247 invited schools in the Lower Peninsula send teams to regionals. All the classes were mixed at the finals, despite the previous year's exhibition which had apparently showed enough participation in all four classes for separate championships.

Coach Hal Commerson's Rochester squad went down as the first winning team in MHSAA annals, beating Pioneer by 16.

The only non-Class A teams to qualify were Carleton Airport (B), Decatur (C), St. Louis (C), DeWitt (C), Three Oaks River Valley (C) and Hillsdale (C).

Port Huron did not compete, so '77 champion Miriam Boyd, who had run a two-mile state record of 10:36.8 in the spring, did not run. However, a week later she won the state Junior Olympic title with an impressive 17:06 for 3M at Cass Benton.

Two weeks earlier, MITCA hosted a state meet for classes at Potterville High School. Elsewhere in this history, we carry those results as de-facto state championship races for Classes B, C and D. However for Class A, where representation wasn't as strong, the race was no more significant than a good invitational (just 10 of the A teams at Potterville qualified for the MHSAA meet).

Livonia Stevenson won the MITCA meet with 95 points, beating Brighton, Grosse Pointe North, Farmington Hills Mercy, Grand Haven and 14 other schools. Lori Bennett of Stevenson (she transferred from Ladywood) led all finishers with her 17:55. Brenda Clark of Grand Haven ran second, Susan Brown of Brighton third.

Pioneer's Beth Huff was the first champion of the MHSAA era.

Haslett HS, Haslett, Nov. 4 ☐
1978 GIRLS LP TEAMS
1. Rochester 133
2. Ann Arbor Pioneer 149
3. Brighton 169
4. Livonia Stevenson 187
5. Redford Union 194
6. Carleton Airport (B) 198
7. Farmington Hills Mercy 250
8. Midland 259
9. Decatur (C) 259
10. Grand Haven 266
11. Portage Northern 273
12. Flint Kearsley 292
13. St Louis (C) 296
14. Flushing 318
15. Ann Arbor Huron 335
16. Muskegon Mona Shores 392
17. DeWitt (C)) 392
18. East Lansing 401
19. Three Oaks River Valley (C) 419
20. Grand Ledge 466
21. Pontiac Central 490
22. Hillsdale (B) 496
23. Traverse City 533
24. Saginaw Hill 543

1978 GIRLS LP TEAM RACE
1. Beth Huff (Ann Arbor Pioneer)11 .... 18:48
2. Brenda Clark (Grand Haven) 19:02
3. Sheila Varga (Three Oaks River Valley) ... 19:19
4. Susan Brown (Brighton)10 .... 19:31
5. Pat Hamparian (Brighton) 19:35
6. Jill Washburn (Rochester) 19:41
7. Melinda Fisher (Grand Haven) 19:44
8. Sue Frederick (Ann Arbor Huron) 19:47

9. Kathy Seibel (Decatur) 19:47
10. Janet Fulkerson (Midland) 19:48
11. Sue Heinlen (Farmington Hills Mercy) .. 19:49
12. Laurie Bennett (Livonia Stevenson) 19:56
13. Lisa Franseen (Rochester) 19:58
14. Dawn Clark (Grand Haven) 20:00
15. Wendy Tipton (Livonia Stevenson) 20:03
16. Dana Loesche (Ann Arbor Pioneer) 20:07
17. Michelle Collins (Farmington Hills Mercy) .... nt
18. Karen Curtic (Rochester) .... nt
19. Ellen Burkhimer (Midland) .... nt
20. Betty Davis (Redford Union) .... nt
21. Aimee Landry (Rochester) .... nt
22. Dana Loesche (Ann Arbor Pioneer) ..... nt
23. Sherry Turco (Muskegon Mona Shores) ... nt
24. Cindy Litwin (Carleton Airport) .... nt
25. Kandi Laird (Redford Union) .... nt

1978 GIRLS LP INDIVIDUAL RACE
1. Gail Burch (Whitehall)9 .... 18:46
2. Melanie Weaver (Mason County Central)12 ... 19:13
3. Anne Pewe (Olivet) 19:22
4. Lisa Last (Alma) 19:31
5. Nora Green (Shepherd) 19:46
6. Julie Stansberry (Yale) 20:03
7. Nancy Liponoga (Royal Oak Dondero) .. 20:08
8. Cheryl Scheffer (South Lyon) 20:18
9. Janie Barner (Holt) 20:21
10. Cheri Warchock (Kalkaska) 20:21
11. Geri Gaines (Breckenridge) 20:22
12. Robin Magee (Ann Arbor Greenhills) ... 20:31
13. Karen Klein (Kalamazoo Norrix) 20:33
14. Teresa Brink (Okemos) 20:45
15. Liz Skomch (Dearborn Divine Child) ... 20:46

1979 CLASS A GIRLS

Gary Meehan coached No. 2 Brighton to an impressive 71 points in Class A, led by undefeated Pat Hamparian's 17:16 victory.

"They saved the best for last," said Meehan. Kayla Skelly, later a two-time Mid-American Conference champion for Western Michigan, won the individual run.

Defending team race champion Beth Huff had moved to Wisconsin for her senior year.

The two champions faced off at the Junior Olympics at Cass Benton a week later, Hamparian topping Skelly by 15 seconds over 2.5 miles

Faulkwood Shores GC, Howell, Nov. 3 ☒
1979 GIRLS CLASS A TEAMS
1. Brighton 49
2. Rochester 120
3. Grand Haven 120
4. Clio 139
5. Milford 173
6. Ann Arbor Pioneer 200
7. Redford Union 221
8. Royal Oak Kimball 234
9. East Lansing 240
10. Portage Northern 246
11. Grosse Pointe North 251
12. West Bloomfield 275
13. Farmington Hills Mercy 326
14. Warren Cousino 338
15. Kalamazoo Norrix 340
16. Royal Oak Dondero 355
17. Hazel Park 363

1979 GIRLS CLASS A TEAM RACE
1. Pat Hamparian (Brighton)10 .... 17:16
2. Kelly Shumate (Clio)9 .... 17:30
3. Sue Paquette (Hazel Park) 17:35
4. Brenda Clark (Grand Haven) 17:46
5. Karen Curtis (Rochester) 17:55
6. Lisa Franseen (Rochester) 17:59
7. Rosie Hamparian (Brighton) 18:01
8. Susan Brown (Brighton)11 .... 18:02
9. Lisa Burger (Clio) 18:02
10. Liz Watch (Royal Oak Kimball) 18:08
11. Dawn Clark (Grand Haven) 18:17
12. Karen Klein (Kalamazoo Norrix) 18:23

13. Angie Mogielski (Redford Union) 18:24
14. Kathy Barnum (Ann Arbor Pioneer) 18:28
15. Ginny Patrick (Brighton) 18:34
16. Cindy Poly (West Bloomfield) 18:37
17. Martha Whitaker (Grosse Pointe North) ... 18:37
18. Lisa Clark (Brighton) 18:44
19. Lisa Kugler (Grand Haven) 18:45
20. Ingrid Rader (Ann Arbor Pioneer) 18:46
21. Sue Nabozny (Milford) 18:46
22. Mary Reed (West Bloomfield) 18:50
23. Donna Tremper (Milford) 18:51
24. Sue Stortz (Warren Cousino) 18:54
25. Julie Misekow (Clio) 18:54
26. Aimee Landry (Rochester) 18:59
39. Jenny Lancour (Brighton) 19:21
41. Beth Pominville (Brighton) 19:22

1979 GIRLS CLASS A INDIVIDUAL RACE
1. Kayla Skelly (Midland)10 .... 17:46
2. Janet Fulkerson (Midland) 17:56
3. Judy Yuhn (Walled Lake Western) 17:58
4. Leslie Olin (Flushing) 17:59
5. Marti Bissinger (Lansing Waverly) 18:06
6. Tina Jordan (Detroit Mumford) 18:10
7. Ann Boyd (Port Huron) 18:12
8. Marti Vanacker (Lansing Eastern) 18:18
9. Tish Kriechel (Flint Kearsley) 18:23
10. Brenda Schenk (Flint Kearsley) 18:28
11. Lori Bennett (Livonia Stevenson) 19:30
12. Dawn VanBrocklin (Flushing) 18:32
13. Mary Gleason (Davison) 18:50
14. Tammy Huntman (Flushing) 18:57
15. Lisa Thocher (Lansing Eastern) 19:00

1980 CLASS A GIRLS

Brighton's Pat Hamparian produced the fastest time in the first year the finals went to 5000m. That came after a see-saw battle with Clio's Kelly Shumate, who was in the lead with a half mile to go.

Brighton coach Gary Meehan noted that a contingent of Bulldog fans had followed the team. "There were probably 50-100 fans there. Its's nice to have their support."

In the individual race, Kayla Skelly led from wire to wire on the cold and windy day.

IMA Brookwood GC, Flint, Nov.1 ☐
1980 GIRLS CLASS A TEAMS
1. Brighton 85
2. Clio 103
3. Rochester 157
4. Milford 157
5. Grosse Pointe North 182
6. East Lansing 204
7. Redford Union 206
8. Portage Northern 237
9. Troy Athens 259
10. Trenton 275
11. Davison 294
12. St Clair Shores Lakeview 298
13. Walled Lake Western 312
14. Jackson Parkside 319
15. Bloomfield Hills Lahser 331
16. Grand Haven 353
17. Ann Arbor Huron 364
18. Grosse Pointe South 383
19. Livonia Stevenson 412

1980 GIRLS CLASS A TEAM RACE
1. Pat Hamparian (Brighton)11 .... 17:55
2. Kelly Shumate (Clio)10 .... 18:03
3. Judy Yuhn (Walled Lake Western) 18:07
4. Lisa Franseen (Rochester) 18:10
5. Erna Messenger (East Lansing) 18:16
6. Aimee Landry (Rochester) 18:31
7. Cathy Schmidt (Grosse Pointe North) 18:43
8. Sue Brown (Brighton)12 .... 18:54
9. Lisa Reimund (Troy Athens) 18:57
13. Beth Gilmore (Milford) 19:05
15. Rosy Hamparian (Brighton) 19:13
23. Donna Tremper (Milford) 19:31
24. Betsy Schneider (East Lansing) .... nt

25. Wendy Taylor (Milford) 19:36
26. Lisa Clark (Brighton) 19:37
28. Nancy Ingram (East Lansing) ....nt
35. Tish Schmidt (Brighton) 19:56
49. Jenny Lancour (Brighton) 20:21
54. Beth Pominville (Brighton) 20:29

1980 GIRLS CLASS A INDIVIDUAL RACE
1. Kayla Skelly (Midland)11 ....18:00
2. Sue Paquette (Hazel Park) 18:08
3. Patti Whynott (East Kentwood) 18:36
4. Anna Bauer (Birmingham Seaholm) 18:44
5. Brenda Schenk (Flint Kearsley) 18:49
6. Janet Fulkerson (Midland) 18:58
7. Sherry Jelsone (East Detroit) 19:01

1981 CLASS A GIRLS

Kayla Skelly won her third title, matching Gail Burch as a three-time winner. Norb Badar's Flint Northern team held off Davison by two points, the smallest winning margin in meet history.

Defending team race champion Pat Hamparian was troubled much of the season by an ankle injury.

IMA-Brookwood GC, Flint, Oct. 31 □
1981 GIRLS CLASS A TEAMS
1. Flint Northern 114
2. Davison 116
3. Redford Union 129
4. Flushing 140
5. Brighton 193
6. Clio 196
7. Temperance Bedford 201
8. Ann Arbor Huron 239
9. Troy Athens 242
10. Warren Cousino 255
11. Livonia Churchill 258
12. Walled Lake Central 292
13. Milford 305
14. Kalamazoo Norrix 306
15. Portage Northern 390
16. Berkley 397
17. Royal Oak Kimball 431
18. Grosse Pointe South 438
19. Benton Harbor 449
20. Traverse City 473
21. Grosse Pointe North 498
22. St Clair Shores Lakeview 541

1981 GIRLS CLASS A TEAM RACE
1. Kelly Shumate (Clio)11 ....18:29
2. Kara Walcher (Temperance Bedford) 18:45
3. Carlene Isabelle (Flint Northern) 18:53
4. Bonnie McDonald (Kalamazoo Norrix) 19:01
5. Jayne Johnston (Davison) 19:02
6. Martha Whitaker (Grosse Pointe North) 19:04
7. Debbie Thomas (Warren Cousino) 19:06
8. Lisa Burger (Clio) 19:07
9. Robin Champagne (Warren Cousino) 19:09
10. Kim Warsaw (Temperance Bedford) 19:10
11. Julie Recla (Livonia Churchill) 19:12
12. Mary Gleason (Davison) 19:15
13. Leslie Olin (Flushing) ....nt
15. Marlene Isabell (Flint Northern) ....nt
16. Denise Seeley (Davison) ....nt
18. Beth Reynolds (Clio) ....nt
20. Dawn VanBrocklin (Flushing) ....nt
21. Tina Williams (Flint Northern)12 ....nt

1981 GIRLS CLASS A INDIVIDUAL RACE
1. Kayla Skelly (Midland)12 ....18:43
2. Larissa Szporluk (Ann Arbor Pioneer) 19:01
3. Kim Harris (Warren Mott) 19:12
4. Chris Bale (Holland West Ottawa) 19:15
5. Lisa Greb (Sterling Heights Ford) 19:17
6. Debbie Ledesma (Lansing Sexton) 19:18
7. Mini Baker (Bloomfield Hills Lahser) 19:19
8. Jill Shavers (East Kentwood) 19:19

1982 CLASS A GIRLS

Kelly Shumate crossed the line nearly 200m clear of the field in 18:01.2. Temperance Bedford, coached by Gary Duhaime, topped Brighton for the win.

Clio's Kelly Shumate ended her prep career with two state XC wins—along with two runner-up finishes.

In the individual race, Howell's Jeanette Kot took the win, despite placing second in her league meet two weeks earlier. Coach Bruce Powelson called it "Her finest race of the season."

IMA Brookwood GC, Flint, Nov. 6 ▣
1982 GIRLS CLASS A TEAMS
1. Temperance Bedford 108
2. Brighton 132
3. Flint Northern 173
4. Livonia Churchill 194
5. Grand Blanc 236
6. Redford Union 240
7. Clio 244
8. Berkley 273
9. Troy Athens 281
10. Kalamazoo Norrix 281
11. Dearborn Edsel Ford 282
12. Jackson 287
13. Grosse Pointe North 291
14. Ann Arbor Huron 319
15. East Kentwood 338
16. Portage Northern 345
17. Sterling Heights Stevenson 364
18. Grosse Pointe South 404
19. Birmingham Seaholm 433
20. Bloomfield Hills Lahser 470
21. Farmington Hills Mercy 477
22. Warren Mott 493
23. Clarkston 513

1982 GIRLS CLASS A TEAM RACE
1. Kelly Shumate (Clio)12 ....18:02
2. Kara Walcher (Temperance Bedford) 18:38
3. Lisa Clark (Brighton) 18:44
4. Carlene Isabelle (Flint Northern) 18:47
5. Heather Meyer (Berkley) 18:53
6. Angie Mogielski (Redford Union) 18:57
7. Mary Peruski (Dearborn Edsel Ford) 18:57
8. Julie Recla (Livonia Churchill) 19:01
9. Christie Penny (Temperance Bedford) 19:01
10. Meg Moisen (Grosse Pointe South) 19:07
11. Anne Knott (Ann Arbor Huron) 19:09
12. Darlene Calvin (Kalamazoo Norrix) 19:11
13. Kami Laird (Redford Union) 19:15
14. Kris Ollila (Warren Mott) 19:16
15. Chris Reed (Portage Northern) 19:19
16. Marlene Isabelle (Flint Northern) 19:20
17. Yvette Carriere (Grand Blanc) 19:24
18. Janet Wesselman (Grosse Pointe North) 19:26
19. Beth Reynolds (Clio) 19:28
20. Jill Shaver (East Kentwood) 19:29
21. Tisch Schmidt (Brighton) 19:31
22. Kim Warsaw (Temperance Bedford) 19:35
23. Martha Whitaker (Grosse Pointe North) 19:37
24. Jill Thauvette (Troy Athens) 19:38
25. Dawn Hedding (Grand Blanc) 19:39
26. Ellen McCarthy (Farmington Hills Mercy) 19:39
27. Colleen Cady (Flint Northern) 19:41
28. Kathy Curtiss (Livonia Churchill) 19:47
37. Sandy Snary (Temperance Bedford) 19:59
38. Kathy Gladieux (Temperance Bedford) 19:59
45. Marie Young (Temperance Bedford) 20:09
74. Chris Sugg (Temperance Bedford) 20:52

1982 GIRLS CLASS A INDIVIDUAL RACE
1. Jeanette Kot (Howell)11 .... 18:43
2. Debbie Thomas (Warren Cousino) 19:05
3. Leslie Kinczkowski (Taylor Center) 19:07
4. Jennifer Ostrom (Flint Kearsley) 19:14
5. Kathy Kubicki (Rochester Adams) 19:22
6. Tina Simon (St Johns) 19:23
7. Debbie Rode (Traverse City) 19:27
8. Kelly Wool (Northville) 19:29
9. Dawn Tosh (Taylor Center) 19:33
10. Ada Udvatia (Lansing Everett) 19:38
11. Beth Lawrence (Royal Oak Kimball) 19:45
12. LaRinda Heavner (Davison) 19:46
13. Colleen Mara (Midland Dow) 19:47

1983 CLASS A GIRLS

Australian exchange student Michelle Bews ran the fastest time of the day, 18:11, to win the Class A team race. She had missed much of the previous two years of running because of bone chips in her ankle.

Gary Meehan's Brighton crew took its third win in five years. "I'm very pleased. They came in very close together and ran a good race." In the early going, Edsel Ford looked strong, but Meehan said, "I stopped worrying when I saw that seven of my girls were ahead of their fifth."

Eagle Creek GC, Hartland, Nov. 5 ▣
1983 GIRLS CLASS A TEAMS
1. Brighton 97
2. Dearborn Edsel Ford 128
3. Portage Northern 176
4. Birmingham Seaholm 184
5. Sterling Heights Stevenson 211
6. Rochester Adams 218
7. Milford 232
8. Ann Arbor Pioneer 244
9. Troy Athens 257
10. Berkley 275
11. Grand Blanc 309
12. Livonia Churchill 345
13. Flushing 345
14. Clio 346
15. Westland Glenn 346
16. Temperance Bedford 386
17. Traverse City 392
18. Ann Arbor Huron 420
19. Kalamazoo Norrix 434
20. Grosse Pointe South 440
21. Romeo 446
22. Grosse Pointe North 456
23. Clinton Twp Chippewa Valley 523
24. Royal Oak Kimball 553

1983 GIRLS CLASS A TEAM RACE
1. Michelle Bews (Birmingham Seaholm)12 .... 18:11

2. Debbie Zonca (Sterling Heights Stevenson)..........18:35
3. Mary Peruski (Dearborn Edsel Ford)..........18:46
4. Elizabeth Lohenbauer (Dearborn Edsel Ford)..........18:55
5. Heather Meyer (Berkley)..........19:01
6. Kelly Petzold (Sterling Heights Stevenson)..........19:09
7. Marchall Zorlen (Romeo)..........19:09
8. Kathy Kubicki (Rochester Adams)..........19:15
9. Cindy Repella (Brighton)11..........19:21
10. Yvette Carriere (Grand Blanc)..........19:25
11. Kris Salt (Dearborn Edsel Ford)..........19:26
12. Adrienne Karpell (Ann Arbor Pioneer)..........19:30
13. Anna Knott (Ann Arbor Huron)..........19:32
14. Chris Reed (Portage Northern)..........19:33
15. Jenny Rae (Portage Northern)..........19:34
16. Janell Sheets (Brighton)12..........19:35
17. Marcia Whidden (Grand Blanc)..........19:36
18. Beth Reynolds (Clio)..........19:39
19. Amy Raasch (Brighton)10..........19:40
20. Terese Lemanski (Milford)..........19:40
21. Nancy Solterisch (Grosse Pointe South)..........19:47
22. Nancy Wernica (Rochester Adams)..........19:51
23. Carolyn Schroeder (Dearborn Edsel Ford)..........19:53
24. Debbie Palmer (Rochester Adams)..........19:54
25. Carrie Cain (Ann Arbor Pioneer)..........19:55
26. Debbie Nowak (Brighton)10..........19:55
27. Barb Saaristo (Brighton)10..........19:56
59. Colleen Hurley (Brighton)..........20:34
64. Tara Tiedman (Brighton)9..........20:38

1983 GIRLS CLASS A INDIVIDUAL RACE
1. Jenny Wilcox (Lansing Sexton)9..........18:39
2. Laura Matson (Bloomfield Hills Andover)11..........19:03
3. Lisa Greb (Sterling Heights Ford)..........19:15
4. Brenda Elibri (Warren Woods Tower)..........19:33
5. Bonnie Fitzpatrick (Warren)..........19:38
6. Cindy Panowicz (Northville)..........19:40
7. Julie Adair (Monroe)..........19:42
8. Simmon (St Johns)..........19:43
9. Lake (Holland)..........19:46
10. Sue Anderson (Niles)..........19:47
11. McVicar (Royal Oak Dondero)..........19:49
12. Chura (Saginaw Eisenhower)..........19:53
13. Ostrom (Flint Kearsley)..........19:54
14. Sivacek (Battle Creek Central)..........19:55

1984 CLASS A GIRLS

Mary Peruski, Elizabeth Lehenbauer and Kris Salt led an Edsel Ford charge as they finished 1-2-3, the first time any team had swept the top three places. The Thunderbirds finished with the lowest score in meet history up to that time.

Said coach Bob Champine, "We weren't really worried about teams. We were just worried about putting it all together on this day. In this wind and weather, anything can happen."

Dama Farms GC, Howell, Nov. 3 ⊠
1984 GIRLS CLASS A TEAMS
1. Dearborn Edsel Ford..........32
2. Milford..........151
3. Grosse Pointe North..........196
4. Brighton..........201
5. Portage Northern..........207
6. Ann Arbor Pioneer..........245
7. Sterling Heights Stevenson..........269
8. Grosse Pointe South..........274
9. Utica Eisenhower..........276
10. Monroe..........300
11. Ann Arbor Huron..........314
12. Bloomfield Hills Lahser..........327
13. Berkley..........373
14. Redford Union..........396
15. Flint Kearsley..........403
16. East Kentwood..........416
17. Traverse City..........447
18. Clio..........456
19. Livonia Churchill..........468
20. Rochester..........487
21. Sterling Heights Ford..........492
22. Salem..........492
23. Northville..........508
24. Livonia Stevenson..........541
25. Bay City Western..........545

1984 GIRLS CLASS A TEAM RACE
1. Mary Peruski (Dearborn Edsel Ford)12..........18:11
2. Elizabeth Lehenbauer (Dearborn Edsel Ford)..........18:26
3. Kris Salt (Dearborn Edsel Ford)10..........18:27
4. Heather Meyer (Berkley)..........18:30
5. Debbie Nowak (Brighton)..........19:01
6. Nancy Solterisch (Grosse Pointe South)..........19:04
7. Terese Lemanski (Milford)..........19:10
8. Leanne Rose (Dearborn Edsel Ford)10..........19:14
9. Adrienne Harpell (Ann Arbor Pioneer)..........19:16
10. Lisa Kopacka (Grosse Pointe North)..........19:18
11. Molly Stuart (Clio)..........19:26
12. Amy Bennett (Ann Arbor Huron)..........19:32
13. Stacie Ray (Milford)..........19:32
14. Kelly Chura (Utica Eisenhower)..........19:33
15. Amy Edwards (Portage Northern)..........19:34
16. Denise Durrer (Salem)..........19:35
17. Janis Bilinski (Redford Union)..........19:38
18. Jill Rothert (Dearborn Edsel Ford)..........19:44
19. Kate Pampreen (Bloomfield Hills Lahser)..........19:47
20. Holly Spohn (Bloomfield Hills Lahser)..........19:48
21. Kim Griffin (Utica Eisenhower)..........19:49
22. Julie Adair (Monroe)..........19:50
23. Allegra Alexander (Ann Arbor Pioneer)..........19:50
24. Yvette Pierce (East Kentwood)..........19:50
25. Laura Marr (Monroe)..........19:54
26. Amy Pettibone (Sterling Heights Ford)..........19:55
27. Cammy Potter (Traverse City)..........19:55
28. Amy Raasch (Brighton)..........19:57
29. Karla Wescott (Portage Northern)..........20:00
30. Kathy Wojewski (Ann Arbor Huron)..........20:00
46. Klassa (Dearborn Edsel Ford)..........20:16
99. Hanke (Dearborn Edsel Ford)..........21:04

Andover's Laura Matson won big her junior year. The next spring she would run a state record 4:39.4 in the 1600.

1984 GIRLS CLASS A INDIVIDUAL RACE
1. Laura Matson (Bloomfield Hills Andover)11..........18:10
2. Brenda Pippel (Holland)..........18:56
3. Sharon Armstrong (Detroit Kettering)..........19:07
4. Ada Udvadia (Lansing Everett)..........19:09
5. Kathleen McInnis (Clarkston)..........19:10
6. Jill Thauvette (Troy Athens)..........19:17
7. Jenny Wilcox (Lansing Sexton)10..........19:19
8. Janet Reinowski (Dearborn)..........19:21
9. DeAnna McVicar (Royal Oak Dondero)..........19:24
10. Ann Lampkin (Detroit Redford)..........19:25

1985 CLASS A GIRLS

Stevenson coach Kevin Hanson guided his team to its first title, topping Ann Arbor Pioneer by 27 points.

Kris Salt made it two Edsel Ford wins in a row at the front of the team race.

In the individual run, Denys Adams of Okemos topped defending champion Laura Matson, who had set a state record of 4:39.4 in the 1600 the previous spring. Adams had taken the lead in the first mile and never eased up.

"I never looked back," said Adams. "But I tried to imagine that Laura was breathing down my neck. I was hoping she wouldn't be there. If you put me in a half mile against her, there's no way I could keep up. But this race is closer to my speciality."

Matson collapsed at the finish line and later said, "I just wanted to finish without fainting. Denys really started to stretch it out near the end. It's not embarrassing to finish second to her."

IMA Brookwood Golf Course, Flint, Nov. 2 ⊠
1985 GIRLS CLASS A TEAMS
1. Sterling Heights Stevenson..........127
2. Ann Arbor Pioneer..........154
3. Grosse Pointe South..........189
4. Milford..........207
5. Utica Eisenhower..........223
6. Ann Arbor Huron..........238
7. Temperance Bedford..........240
8. Portage Northern..........241
9. Dearborn Edsel Ford..........251
10. Rochester..........256
11. East Lansing..........273
12. Howell..........288
13. Waterford Kettering..........378
14. Dearborn..........379
15. Brighton..........402
16. Grandville..........416
17. South Lyon..........418
18. Grosse Pointe North..........425
19. Farmington..........436
20. Clio..........483
21. Battle Creek Central..........486
22. Livonia Stevenson..........490
23. Bay City Western..........517
24. Walled Lake Central..........538
25. Novi..........539
26. Flint Kearsley..........715

1985 GIRLS CLASS A TEAM RACE
1. Kris Salt (Dearborn Edsel Ford)11..........18:33
2. Danielle Harpell (Ann Arbor Pioneer)10..........18:47
3. Nancy Solterisch (Grosse Pointe South)..........18:58
4. Jill Rothert (Dearborn Edsel Ford)..........19:00
5. Mara Matuszak (Ann Arbor Huron)..........19:02
6. Janet Beinowski (Dearborn)..........19:06
7. Seana Arnold (Ann Arbor Pioneer)10..........19:08
8. Rebecca Sivacek (Battle Creek Central)..........19:13
9. Theresa Pierfelice (Sterling Hts Stevenson)..........19:15
10. Kim Moffatt (Rochester)..........19:17
11. Meredith Saillant (Dearborn Edsel Ford)..........19:20
12. Jenny Schank (Howell)10..........19:21
13. Wendy Gordon (Howell)..........19:24
14. Amy White (Sterling Heights Stevenson)..........19:34
15. Jennifer Heilman (Utica Eisenhower)..........19:35
16. Kim Hirai (East Lansing)..........19:40
17. Therese Lemanski (Milford)11..........19:42
18. Amy Parsil (Temperance Bedford)..........19:43
19. Kelesta Whitfield (Battle Creek Central)..........19:44
20. Ellen Mayer (Grosse Pointe South)..........19:46
21. Allegra Alexander (Ann Arbor Pioneer)11..........19:49
22. Kris Schultz (South Lyon)..........19:51
23. Liz Earle (Ann Arbor Pioneer)12..........19:51
24. Peggy Martin (Temperance Bedford)..........19:51
30. Jill Johnson (Sterling Heights Stevenson)..........19:57
31. Kris Stork (Sterling Heights Stevenson)..........19:59
43. Stacey Tevlin (Sterling Heights Stevenson)..........20:14
87. Karen Kantzer (Sterling Heights Stevenson)..........21:12

113. Pam Bokmiller (Sterling Heights Stevenson) ... 21:41

1985 GIRLS CLASS A INDIVIDUAL RACE

1. Denys Adams (Okemos)12 ... 18:20
2. Laura Matson (Bloomfield Hills Andover)12 ... 18:53
3. Lisa Lis (Jackson) ... 19:07
4. Brenda Pippel (Holland) ... 19:19
5. Holly Spohn (Bloomfield Hills Lahser) ... 19:21
6. Liz Lange (Birmingham Groves) ... 19:27
7. Kathleen McInnes (Clarkston) ... 19:32
8. Yvette Pierce (East Kentwood) ... 19;35
9. Kristen Zanetti (Trenton) ... 19:36
10. Ruth Fellingham (Bloomfield Hills Andover) ... 19:37
11. Lori Wissmueller (Bay City Glenn) ... 19:38
12. Pamela Kroll (Anchor Bay) ... 19:38
13. Karen Opp (Westland Glenn) ... 19:39
14. Karen Vantor (Livonia Churchill) ... 19:41
15. Linda Filar (Fraser) ... 19:44
16. Adair (Monroe) ... 19:50

1986 CLASS A GIRLS

Ann Arbor Pioneer won the title initially. Said coach Bryan Westfield, "They have been running well all year. They're just good, dedicated kids who have a lot of faith, a lot of courage and a lot of strength in their faith. That's what makes them good."

However, it later came out that Pioneer's No. 5 runner, Rachel Mann, who had attended Canton High the previous year, had moved with her father to a friend's house in Ann Arbor that fall. The house was in the Huron district, rendering Mann ineligible.

MHSAA assistant director Fred Sible, noting that Pioneer would have to forfeit the title, said, "I can't see any way around it."

When the decision came down, instead of elevating Sterling Heights Stevenson to the top spot, the MHSAA decided to leave it vacant.

"We are going to try to plead our case to see if we can get another standing," said Stevenson coach Kevin Hanson.

Bill Bupp, another MHSAA assistant director, refused to budge. "It's a matter of practicality. There are so many unanswered questions it doesn't become practical to pursue it."

[Note: for the purposes of the statistics in this book, all teams have been moved up, and Stevenson is recognized as the rightful champion.]

Kris Salt won her second straight in 1986. She later became an All-ACC runner for Clemson.

IMA Brookwood Golf Course, Flint, Nov. 1 ⊠
1986 GIRLS CLASS A TEAMS

1. [Ann Arbor Pioneer -- title vacated] ... 91]
2. Sterling Heights Stevenson ... 125
3. Portage Northern ... 205
4. Dearborn Edsel Ford ... 220
5. Ann Arbor Huron ... 226
6. Farmington ... 232
7. Traverse City ... 254
8. Milford ... 268
9. Harper Woods Regina ... 311
10. Rochester ... 326
11. Walled Lake Central ... 344
12. Clarkston ... 368
13. Kalamazoo Norrix ... 392
14. Grosse Pointe North ... 395
15. Jackson ... 406
16. Trenton ... 413
17. West Bloomfield ... 413
18. Temperance Bedford ... 420
19. Bay City Western ... 438
20. Flushing ... 439
21. Grosse Pointe South ... 451
22. Swartz Creek ... 478
23. Troy ... 487
24. Bloomfield Hills Andover ... 530
25. Detroit Kettering ... 548
26. Lansing Everett ... 618
27. Belleville ... 661
28. Bloomfield Hills Lahser ... 669

1986 GIRLS CLASS A TEAM RACE

1. Kris Salt (Dearborn Edsel Ford)12 ... 17:58
2. Theresa Pierfelice (Sterling Heights Stevenson) . 18:20
3. Seana Arnold (Ann Arbor Pioneer)11 ... 18:29
4. Danielle Harpell (Ann Arbor Pioneer)11 ... 18:38
5. Sara Braunreiter (Jackson) ... 18:46
6. Ann Mudgett (Traverse City) ... 18:46
7. June Alosisio (Dearborn Edsel Ford)9 ... 18:59
8. Laura Franklin (Jackson) ... 19:00
9. Gabrielle Brown (Ann Arbor Pioneer) ... 19:06
10. Mara Matuszak (Ann Arbor Huron) ... 19:13
11. Amber Crawford (Rochester) ... 19:16
12. Ruth Fellingham (Bloomfield Hills Andover) ... 19:17
13. Jenny Payne (Traverse City) ... 19:18
14. Jill Rother (Dearborn Edsel Ford)11 ... 19:21
15. Amy Edwards (Portage Northern) ... 19:25
16. Allegra Alexander (Ann Arbor Pioneer) ... 19:28
17. Kay Ruessman (Sterling Heights Stevenson) ... 19:28
18. Therese Lemanski (Milford) ... 19:29
19. Theresa Bunker (Milford) ... 19:30
20. Amy Bennett (Ann Arbor Huron) ... 19:32
21. Colleen Yuhn (Walled Lake Central) ... 19:32
22. Lisa Chalmers (Walled Lake Central) ... 19:33
23. Laura Simmering (Ann Arbor Huron) ... 19:33
24. Amy Iannuzzi (Harper Woods Regina) ... 19:34
25. Holly Spohn (Bloomfield Hills Lahser) ... 19:35
26. Stacy Abbott (West Bloomfield) ... 19:35
27. Bonnie Stecker (Farmington) ... 19:36
28. Kristen Zanetti (Trenton) ... 19:37
29. Kim Richert (Sterling Heights Stevenson) ... 19:38
30. Kathleen McInnis (Clarkston) ... 19:39
32. Stork (Sterling Heights Stevenson) ... 19:41
45. Chappelle (Sterling Heights Stevenson) ... 20:02
59. Rachel Mann (Ann Arbor Pioneer)11 ... 20:21
70. Childs (Sterling Heights Stevenson) ... 20:30
123. Rogalski (Sterling Heights Stevenson) ... 21:17
126. Carrie Dibble (Ann Arbor Pioneer) ... 21:19
134. Delahunty (Ann Arbor Pioneer) ... 21:27

1986 GIRLS CLASS A INDIVIDUAL RACE

1. Jenny Schank (Howell)11 ... 19:00
2. Mary Whynott (East Kentwood) ... 19:13
3. Sandra Terrell (St Johns) ... 19:15
4. Becky Turbin (Howell) ... 19:22
5. Karen Kantor (Livonia Churchill) ... 19:25
6. Mary Demock (Grand Haven) ... 19:26
7. Michelle Wheeler (Owosso) ... 19:31
8. Jenny Wilcox (Lansing Sexton)12 ... 19:36
9. Jill Dutkiewicz (Jenison) ... 19:38
10. Carlene Mighty (Ypsilanti) ... 19:39

1987 CLASS A GIRLS

This time around, Bryan Westfield's Pioneer team used a 1-2 punch to win by 72 points, and there were no cries of foul.

A challenging course made the going tough for many, even though temperatures were nicely in the lower 50s. Said team race winner Danielle Harpell, "My legs were stumbling. I wasn't sure I was going to make it. We ran really hard the whole race though and by the end I didn't have anything left."

Groesbeck Golf Course, Lansing, Nov. 7 ⊠
1987 GIRLS CLASS A TEAMS

1. Ann Arbor Pioneer ... 67
2. West Bloomfield ... 149
3. Portage Northern ... 178
4. Dearborn Edsel Ford ... 195
5. Rochester Adams ... 208
6. Jackson ... 229
7. Sterling Heights Stevenson ... 238
8. Kalamazoo Norrix ... 248
9. Troy ... 294
10. Clarkston ... 294
11. Canton ... 339
12. Farmington ... 363
13. Port Huron ... 365
14. Grosse Pointe South ... 375
15. Temperance Bedford ... 381
16. Brighton ... 387
17. Swartz Creek ... 439
18. Owosso ... 452
19. Trenton ... 474
20. Mt Pleasant ... 488
21. East Kentwood ... 492
22. Holly ... 532
23. Grand Haven ... 535
24. Grand Ledge ... 536
25. Farmington Hills Mercy ... 540
26. Grosse Pointe North ... 557
27. Redford Borgess ... 617
28. Detroit Pershing ... 764

1987 GIRLS CLASS A TEAM RACE

1. Danielle Harpell (Ann Arbor Pioneer)12 ... 18:42
2. Gabrielle Brown (Ann Arbor Pioneer)11 ... 18:49
3. Mary Whynott (East Kentwood)10 ... 18:55
4. Sherri Chatters (Jackson)10 ... 18:57
5. Jill Rothert (Dearborn Edsel Ford)12 ... 19:14
6. Stacy Abbott (West Bloomfield)10 ... 19:14
7. Michelle Schaefer (Kalamazoo Norrix)9 ... 19:15
8. Karen Perry (Kalamazoo Norrix) ... 19:22
9. Michelle Hoskins (Portage Northern)11 ... 19:27
10. Elizabeth Bolden (Grosse Pointe North)11 ... 19:29
11. Theresa Pierfelice (Sterling H Stevenson)12 ... 19:30
12. Laura Franklin (Jackson)11 ... 19:30
13. Melissa Hanley (Rochester Adams)11 ... 19:31
14. Delachaise Roosevelt (Port Huron)10 ... 19:31
15. Tracy Abbott (West Bloomfield)10 ... 19;32
16. Lara Grimes (Brighton)9 ... 19:40
17. Sara Braunreiter (Jackson)12 ... 19:43
18. Seana Arnold (Ann Arbor Pioneer)12 ... 19:46
19. Sonya Schaffer (Clarkston)10 ... 19:49
20. Meredith Saillant (Dearborn Edsel Ford)11 ... 19:49
21. Kay Ruessman (Sterling Hts Stevenson)12 ... 19:50
22. Carrie Dibble (Ann Arbor Pioneer)11 ... 19:50
23. Megan Flaharty (West Bloomfield)9 ... 19:51
24. Tera Furst (Ann Arbor Pioneer)10 ... 19:53
25. Amy Edwards (Portage Northern)12 ... 19:56
26. June Alosio (Dearborn Edsel Ford)10 ... 19:57
27. Michelle Wheeler (Owosso)10 ... 19:57
28. Marie Mizeur (Portage Northern)9 ... 19:58
29. Rachal Mann (Ann Arbor Pioneer)12 ... 19:59
92. Megan Dellhanty (Ann Arbor Pioneer)12 ... 21:27

1987 GIRLS CLASS A INDIVIDUAL RACE

1. Jenny Schank (Howell)12 ... 19:19
2. Laura Simmering (Ann Arbor Huron)12 ... 19:26
3. Mayrie Richards (Rochester)9 ... 19:37
4. Mara Matuszak (Ann Arbor Huron)12 ... 19:49
5. Janet Novallo (Macomb L'Anse Creuse North)10 19:54
6. Deanna Schulte (Walled Lake Central)9 ... 19:57
7. Colleen Yuhn (Walled Lake Central)11 ... 20:01
8. Theresa Bunker (Lake Orion)12 ... 20:02
9. Valentine Stumpf (Belleville)9 ... 20;03
10. Tina Gallagher (Bay City Glenn)12 ... 20:03
11. Angela Williams (Pontiac Central)11 ... 20:04

1988 CLASS A GIRLS

Pioneer won its second-straight as Gabrielle Brown moved up a spot to take the win in the team race. Sylvia Marino, normally Pioneer's

No.2, competed in a cast because of a pulled muscle and a fracture in her fibula, didn't make it into the top five on her team, but coach Bryan Westfield's squad still finished 17 points ahead of Edsel Ford.

Westfield credited the win to No. 5 runner Megan Delahunty, a senior who had never made the top five before. "We never had to count on her before and all of a sudden in her senior year she has to run her most important race at the state meet. She was running with pressure and everyone else rose to the occasion."

IMA Brookwood Golf Course, Flint, Nov. 5 ⊠
1988 GIRLS CLASS A TEAMS

1. Ann Arbor Pioneer 100
2. Dearborn Edsel Ford 117
3. Troy 159
4. Kalamazoo Norrix 172
5. Grand Haven 223
6. Traverse City 233
7. West Bloomfield 260
8. Sterling Heights Stevenson 265
9. Canton 276
10. East Kentwood 294
11. Utica 307
12. Greenville 315
13. Jackson 364
14. Woodhaven 365
15. Swartz Creek 399
16. Monroe 435
17. Flint Kearsley 462
18. Grosse Pointe South 481
19. Redford Union 490
20. Rochester Adams 508
21. Port Huron Northern 515
22. Warren Mott 531
23. Grosse Pointe North 556
24. Trenton 581
25. Berkley 600
26. Detroit Cass Tech 633
27. Clio 661
28. Farmington Hills Mercy 728

1988 GIRLS CLASS A TEAM RACE

1. Gabrielle Brown (Ann Arbor Pioneer)12 19:05
2. Meredith Saillant (Dearborn Edsel Ford)12 19:14
3. Laura Franklin (Jackson)12 19:19
4. Kristi McKimson (Troy)12 19:24
5. Alison Dodge (Traverse City)12 19:30
6. Cindy Arrendondo (Grand Haven)11 19:32
7. Carrie Dibble (Ann Arbor Pioneer)12 19:37
8. Karen Perry (Kalamazoo Norrix)12 19:38
9. Christina McKinney (Kalamazoo Norrix)12 19:39
10. Molly Lori (East Kentwood)9 19:40
11. Catherine Edwards (Utica)11 19:45
12. June Aloisio (Dearborn Edsel Ford)11 19:49
13. Stacy Abbott (West Bloomfield)11 19:50
14. Beth Zimmer (Ann Arbor Pioneer)12 19:50
15. Tera Furst (Ann Arbor Pioneer)11 19:51
16. Tracy Abbott (West Bloomfield)11 19:52
17. Sheri Chatters (Jackson)11 19:59
18. Jennifer Cole (Utica)12 20:00
19. Julie Nichols (Grosse Pointe South)12 20:12
20. Michele Schaefer (Kalamazoo Norrix)10 20:18
21. Stephanie Walton (Traverse City)10 20:18
22. Kathleen Doherty (Greenville)12 20:21
63. Megan Delahanty (Ann Arbor Pioneer)12 21:03
84. Carrie Osterwisch (Ann Arbor Pioneer)10 21:33
92. Sylvia Marino (Ann Arbor Pioneer)10 21:40

1988 GIRLS CLASS A INDIVIDUAL RACE

1. Allison Mendyk (Midland)12 19:33
2. Colleen Yuhn (Walled Lake Central)12 19:37
3. Jessica Kluge (St Johns)11 19:38
4. Jodi Shay (Mt Pleasant)12 19:41
5. Jennifer Kiel (Farmington)11 19:46
6. Lisa Rives (North Farmington)11 19:48
7. Tiphanie Crane (Howell)10 19:53
8. Julie Moore (Lakeland)12 19:56
9. Kristi Wink (Brighton)11 19:57
10. Kathryn Scieszia (East Lansing)9 19:57
11. Angela Williams (Pontiac Central)12 20:01
12. Ginny Martin (Temperance Bedford)9 20:02
13. Melissa Modderman (Grandville)12 20:07
14. Mavrie Richards (Rochester)10 20;12
15. Rena Palmer (Grand Blanc)11 20:14
16. Janet Novallo (Macomb L'Anse Creuse N)12 20:14
17. Erin Racht (Niles)9 20:19
18. Jill Dutkiewicz (Jenison)12 20:21

1989 CLASS A GIRLS

Pioneer's Bridget Mann, just a frosh, stormed over the IMA Brookwood course in a stunning 18:13, leaving teammate (and runner-up) Tera Furst 43 seconds behind. Even with the 1-2, however, Pioneer finished second to West Bloomfield in the team standings.

Said West Bloomfield coach Lee Averill, "It's been a long time. I always pictured what it would be like to stand up here, but I'm just kind of numb right now."

Pioneer frosh Bridget Mann won by a huge margin.

IMA Brookwood GC, Flint, Nov. 4 ☐
1989 GIRLS CLASS A TEAMS

1. West Bloomfield 96
2. Ann Arbor Pioneer 104
3. Brighton 133
4. Grandville 199
5. Farmington 217
6. Kalamazoo Norrix 266
7. Milford 285
8. Traverse City 288
9. Grosse Pointe North 294
10. Dearborn Edsel Ford 308
11. Holland 322
12. Canton 370
13. Grosse Pointe South 373
14. Sterling Heights Stevenson 382
15. Ann Arbor Huron 387
16. East Lansing 420
17. Troy 456
18. Clinton Twp Chippewa Valley 463
19. Novi 492
20. Port Huron 501
21. Clio 518
22. Rochester Adams 534
23. Flint Kearsley 539
24. Mt Pleasant 568
25. Hazel Park 579
26. Port Huron Northern 579
27. Troy Athens 582
28. Grand Haven 592

1989 GIRLS CLASS A TEAM RACE

1. Bridget Mann (Ann Arbor Pioneer)9 18:13
2. Tera Furst (Ann Arbor Pioneer)12 18:56
3. Jennifer Kiel (Farmington)12 19:04
4. Robyn Brandow (Grandville)10 19:04
5. Kristi Wink (Brighton)12 19:11
6. Dela Roosevelt (Port Huron)12 19:18
7. Sylvia Marino (Ann Arbor Pioneer)11 19:20
8. Kathryn Scieszka (East Lansing)10 19:24
9. Monica O'Maila (Brighton)12 19:25
10. Carolyn Shosey (Brighton)10 19:25
11. Michelle Schaefer (Kalamazoo Norrix)11 19:26
12. Tracy Robinson (Rochester Adams)11 19:30
13. Nichole VanOppens (Grosse Pointe North)12 19:31
14. Amy Fidelman (West Bloomfield)10 19:35
15. Tracy Abbott (West Bloomfield)12 19:36
16. Amy Parker (Troy)10 19:44
17. Amy Smith (Canton)10 19:50
18. Shannon McCabe (Hazel Park)10 19:55
19. Laura Howell (Grandville)10 19:55
20. Stephanie Gorman (Kalamazoo Norrix)10 19:56
21. Karen Reed (West Bloomfield)9 19:56
22. Megan Flaherty (West Bloomfield)11 19:57
23. Laurin Schultz (Grosse Pointe North)12 19:58
24. Stacy Abbott (West Bloomfield)12 20:00
25. Lara Grimes (Brighton)11 20:01

1989 GIRLS CLASS A INDIVIDUAL RACE

1. Lisa Rives (North Farmington)12 18:46
2. Jennifer Ray (Walled Lake Western)9 19:01
3. Anne Gray (Belleville)9 19:02
4. Julie Banks (Utica)11 19:16
5. Sheri Chatters (Jackson)12 19:29
6. Tiphanie Crane (Howell)11 19:31
7. Jessica Kluge (St Johns)12 19:34
8. Mary Whynott (East Kentwood)12 19:35
9. Wendy Proos (Walled Lake Western)10 19:40
10. Michelle Wheeler (Owosso)12 19:41
11. Catherine Edwards (Utica)12 19:42
12. Carrie Vanisacker (Monroe)11 19:45
13. Missy Reinardy (East Kentwood)12 19:45
14. Ijnanya Alhamasi (Detroit Ford)11 19:49
15. Rena Palmer (Grand Blanc)12 19:59

1990 CLASS A GIRLS

Holly busted the record for the highest winning score ever, but coach Duane Raffin couldn't complain. The Broncos topped Pioneer by six points, the second-closest race in meet history.

"I realize after 30 years of coaching that anything can happen at the state meet," said Raffin. "We ran just as we expected, maybe just a little bit better."

Molly Lori of East Kentwood had the fastest time of the day in winning the individual race. "This course is kind of like our home course," she said. "I rehearsed it mentally and I think I was prepared fairly well."

University of Michigan GC, Ann Arbor, Nov. 3 ☐
1990 GIRLS CLASS A TEAMS

1. Holly 146
2. Ann Arbor Pioneer 152
3. Milford 153
4. Traverse City 169
5. Redford Union 230
6. Grosse Pointe South 234
7. Sterling Heights Stevenson 271
8. Dearborn Edsel Ford 300
9. Grosse Pointe North 316
10. Portage Northern 325
11. Grandville 335
12. Brighton 335
13. Greenville 337
14. Kalamazoo Norrix 358
15. Flint Kearsley 360

16. Mt Pleasant 393
17. East Lansing 397
18. Salem 403
19. Clinton Twp Chippewa Valley 415
20. Monroe 460
21. Rochester 462
22. West Bloomfield 471
23. Livonia Stevenson 472
24. Okemos 546
25. Mt Clemens 631
26. Sterling Heights Ford 636
27. Hazel Park 641
28. Troy Athens 652

1990 GIRLS CLASS A TEAM RACE

1. Kathryn Sciestka (East Lansing)11 .... 19:22
2. Bridget Mann (Ann Arbor Pioneer)10 .... 19:50
3. Robyn Brandow (Grandville)11 .... 19:50
4. Rachel O'Byrne (Grosse Pointe South)9 .... 19:50
5. Colleen Danes (Dearborn Edsel Ford)12 .... 19:51
6. Karlene Kurtz (Traverse City)10 .... 19:54
7. Tracey Priska (Sterling Heights Stevenson)11 .... 19:57
8. Nicole Pannecouck (Sterling Hts Stevenson)12 .... 19:57
9. Sylvia Marino (Ann Arbor Pioneer)12 .... 19:58
10. Carrie Vanisacker (Monroe)12 .... 19:59
11. Mary Mick (Holly)12 .... 19:59
12. Tina Shively (Milford)12 .... 20:14
13. Andrea Cantu (Flint Kearsley)12 .... 20:17
14. Jennifer Wiesdorfer (Holly)11 .... 20:19
15. Jessica McLalin (Grosse Pointe North)10 .... 20:31
16. Karen Reed (West Bloomfield)10 .... 20:34
17. Erika Schimik (Traverse City)10 .... 20:37
18. Jenna DeWaelsche (Holly)11 .... 20:37
19. Sherrie Schotter (Flint Kearsley)12 .... 20:38
20. Amy Fidelman (West Bloomfield)11 .... 20:39
21. Lori Kungelsmith (Traverse City)11 .... 20:39
22. Mindy Longjohn (Portage Northern)10 .... 20:41
28. Deborah Barton (Holly)10 .... 21:00
75. Michelle Parker (Holly) 22:02
154. Cherie Klinkenberger (Holly)12 .... 23:44
173. Krista Henn (Holly)12 .... 25:31

East Kentwood's Molly Lori: the fastest in 1990.

1990 GIRLS CLASS A INDIVIDUAL RACE

1. Molly Lori (East Kentwood)11 .... 18:55
2. Amy Doucette (Warren Cousino)12 .... 19:15
3. Jennifer Roy (Walled Lake Western)10 .... 19:29
4. Renae Bluekamp (Holland West Ottawa)12 .... 19:29
5. Trachsel (Holland West Ottawa)9 .... 19:40
6. Thompson (Royal Oak Dondero)10 .... 19:44
7. Anne Gray (Belleville)10 .... 19:46
8. Julie Banks (Utica)12 .... 19:51
9. Stacie Cecil (Swartz Creek)11 .... 19:59
10. Rebecca Caldwell (Wyandotte)9 .... 20:04
11. Tabithe Belcher (Walled Lake Central)10 .... 20:08
12. Sara Havenga (Forest Hills)11 .... 20:10
13. Julie Jorgenson (Muskegon Mona Shores)12 .... 20;15
14. Reaves (Southfield)9 .... 20:21
15. Dixon (Livonia Ladywood)10 .... 20:27
16. Dain (Birmingham Seaholm)12 .... 20:36
17. Myrand (Woodhaven)11 .... 20:40
18. McLellan (Davison)10 .... 20:41

1991 CLASS A GIRLS

Horrible conditions greeted athletes at Terre Verde Golf Course east of Grand Haven. It was 24-degrees, snowy, with winds gusting to 40mph. Wind chill -4. Favored Traverse City won. Said coach Mark Fries, "We covered all aspects of the race and we were prepared for anything.

"I knew it was going to be cold, but I thought it would be more difficult," said individual race winner Elke Thompson.

Terre Verde GC, Nunica, Nov. 2 ⊠
1991 GIRLS CLASS A TEAMS

1. Traverse City 110
2. Dearborn Edsel Ford 121
3. Brighton 141
4. Walled Lake Western 202
5. Clinton Twp Chippewa Valley 234
6. Mt Pleasant 249
7. Ann Arbor Pioneer 251
8. Grandville 260
9. Livonia Stevenson 281
10. Sterling Heights Stevenson 281
11. Grosse Pointe South 282
12. Milford 325
13. East Kentwood 336
14. Woodhaven 344
15. Troy 367
16. Holly 376
17. Monroe 414
18. Portage Northern 414
19. Holland West Ottawa 418
20. Okemos 446
21. Swartz Creek 529
22. Grosse Pointe North 537
23. Port Huron Northern 581
24. Troy Athens 607
25. Flint Carman-Ainsworth 610
26. Birmingham Seaholm 638
27. Detroit Redford 662

1991 GIRLS CLASS A TEAM RACE

1. Christy Goodison (Sterling Hts Stevenson)10 .... 19:18
2. Molly Lori (East Kentwood)12 .... 19:32
3. Tracey Priska (Sterling Heights Stevenson)12 .... 20:06
4. Koritnick (Livonia Stevenson)11 .... 20:19
5. Bridget Mann (Ann Arbor Pioneer)11 .... 20:24
6. Green (Brighton)9 .... 20:27
7. Allyson Mann (Ann Arbor Pioneer)11 .... 20:34
8. Karlene Kurtz (Traverse City)11 .... 20:38
9. Shosey (Brighton)12 .... 20:42
10. Ray (Walled Lake Western)11 .... 20:47
11. O'Byrne (Grosse Pointe South)10 .... 20:48
12. Trachel (Holland West Ottawa)10 .... 20:49
13. Byrne (Walled Lake Western)9 .... 20:50
14. Lori Klingelsmiht (Traverse City)12 .... 20:54
15. Erika Schimik (Traverse City)11 .... 20:56
16. Onorato (Dearborn Edsel Ford)10 .... 20:56
17. Myrand (Woodhaven)12 .... 20:57
18. Klotkowski (Dearborn Edsel Ford)11 .... 21:02
19. Mulligan (Clinton Twp Chippewa Valley)12 .... 21:02
20. Wise (Grosse Pointe South)9 .... 21:03
21. MacKinnon (Livonia Stevenson)10 .... 21:08
22. Gorden (Dearborn Edsel Ford)11 .... 21:11
23. Finger (Troy Athens)12 .... 21:12
24. Parker (Troy)12 .... 21:12
25. Schwestfeger (Portage Northern)10 .... 21:12
34. Jenny Peters (Traverse City)12 .... 21:24
39. Sara Jefferson (Traverse City)10 .... 21:32
56. Libby Hackett (Traverse City)10 .... 21:45
112. Kerry Mead (Traverse City)11 .... 22:46

1991 GIRLS CLASS A INDIVIDUAL RACE

1. Elke Thompson (Royal Oak Dondero)11 .... 20:05
2. Anne Gray (Belleville)11 .... 20:28
3. Becky Caldwell (Wyandotte)10 .... 20:36
4. Dixon (Livonia Ladywood)11 .... 20:36
5. Ouillette (Bay City Western) 20:38
6. Graff (Utica)11 .... 20:40
7. Keefover (North Farmington)10 .... 20:44
8. Shively (North Farmington)11 .... 20:51
9. Reis (West Bloomfield)9 .... 20:51
10. Hartwig (Trenton)12 .... 20:51
11. Boroditsch (Canton)10 .... 20:58
12. Cates (Adrian)9 .... 21:01
13. Schmitt (Taylor Truman)12 .... 21:01
14. Moore (Salem)9 .... 21:02
15. Belcher (Walled Lake)11 .... 21:05

1992 CLASS A GIRLS

Traverse City, coached by Mark Fries, successfully defended its title, topping Brighton by 43 points.

Christi Goodison of Sterling Heights Stevenson, won her second straight team race in the fastest time of the day.

Terre Verde GC, Nunica, Nov. 7 □
1992 GIRLS CLASS A TEAMS

1. Traverse City 117
2. Brighton 160
3. Ann Arbor Huron 221
4. Walled Lake Western 235
5. Monroe 240
6. West Bloomfield 252
7. East Kentwood 254
8. Troy 254
9. Milford 255
10. Cadillac 268
11. Dearborn Edsel Ford 280
12. Grosse Pointe South 296
13. Clinton Township Chippewa Valley 320
14. Berkley 348
15. Holland West Ottawa 367
16. Grandville 423
17. Rochester Adams 439
18. Sterling Heights Stevenson 461
19. Port Huron 461
20. Utica Eisenhower 467
21. Flint Kearsley 481
22. Bloomfield Hills Lahser 540
23. Portage Central 549
24. Okemos 569
25. Belleville 581
26. Flushing 602
27. Grosse Pointe North 711

1992 GIRLS CLASS A TEAM RACE

1. Christy Goodison (Sterling Hts Stevenson)11 .... 18:49
2. Hillary Green (Brighton)10 .... 19:01
3. Kristy Kolozsvary (Clinton Twp Chippewa Vl)10 .... 19:03
4. Wendy Robertson (Troy) 19:06
5. Kim Russell (East Kentwood) 19:07
6. Anne Gray (Belleville) 19:16
7. Jenny Ray (Walled Lake Western) 19:28
8. Andrea Boyer (Brighton) 19:31
9. Erika Schimek (Traverse City) 19:34
10. Heidi Wise (Grosse Pointe South) 19:36
11. Karlene Kurtz (Traverse City)12 .... 19:36
12. Monica Goodwill (Clinton TChippewa Valley) 19:37
13. Bridget Byrne (Walled Lake Western) 19:39
14. Jessica McClean (West Bloomfield) 19:40
15. Michelle Knapp (East Kentwood) 19:47
16. Sara Jefferson (Traverse City) 19:48
17. Lara Reis (West Bloomfield) 19:50
18. Alana McQueen (Ann Arbor Huron) 19:56
19. Chrissy Garst (Troy) 19:56
20. Karen Reed (West Bloomfield) 19:57
21. Collen Juhl (Milford) 19:58
22. Jenny Sisk (Monroe) 19:59
23. Janelle Shepherd (Flint Kearsley) 19:59
40. Libby Hackett (Traverse City)11 .... 20:26
41. Kerry Mead (Traverse City)12 .... 20:30
49. Sonya Mahaney (Traverse City) 20:38

1992 GIRLS CLASS A INDIVIDUAL RACE

1. Alexis Lund (Muskegon Reeths-Puffer)9 .... 18:53
2. Anjanette Korotnik (Livonia Stevenson)12 .... 18:55
3. Eileen Fleck (East Lansing)11 .... 18:59
4. Becky Caldwell (Wyandotte) 19:03
5. Erin Keenan (Rockford) 19:08
6. Sarah Prasad (Farmington Hills Mercy) 19:19
7. Deborah Barton (Holly) 19:20
8. Emily Shively (North Farmington) 19:23
9. Heather Moore (Hartland) 19:26
10. Amy Freund (Farmington Hills Mercy) 19:27

11. Inrgid Oullette (Bay City Western) 19:32
12. Danielle Kovac (Holly) 19:34
13. Leah Scharl (Clarkston) 19:34
14. Melissa Ide (Grand Haven) 19:39
15. Brooke Vandermeulen (GR Union) 19:40
16. Alison Klemmer (Troy Athens) 19:55
17. L. Retherford (Salem) 20:00

1993 CLASS A GIRLS

East Lansing's Eileen Fleck captured the individual race with a winning margin of 49 seconds, the largest in Class A history. The next spring she would run an impressive 10:35.13 for 3200 to win the Midwest Meet of Champions.

Fleck had been racing Christi Goodison's splits. Goodison had run in the team race a half hour earlier.

"I would have liked to have had the lowest time, but I'm happy with the win," said Fleck, who ended up with the largest winning margin in meet history, a year after losing in the closest race ever.

Goodison, who ran 11 seconds faster, said, "If someone else would have been there, I think I could have gone faster."

Troy, under coach Kevin Spencer, took the team title by 30 points. "Everybody had to go out and run their best time and they did," he said. "We knew we had a good 1-2 combination. Three, four and five would make up the difference."

Saskatoon Golf Club, Alaska, Nov. 6 ☐
1993 GIRLS CLASS A TEAMS
1. Troy 112
2. Brighton 142
3. Monroe 148
4. Rochester Adams 201
5. West Bloomfield 210
6. Troy Athens 229
7. Farmington Mercy 296
8. Flushing 331
9. Sterling Heights Stevenson 332
10. Port Huron Northern 340
11. Rockford 347
12. Jenison 357
13. Berkley 375
14. Grosse Pointe South 375
15. East Kentwood 404
16. Milford 410
17. Pinckney 410
18. Dearborn Edsel Ford 411
19. Utica Eisenhower 428
20. Mt Pleasant 428
21. Belleville 449
22. Holland 518
23. Grandville 544
24. Flint Kearsley 615
25. St Johns 721
26. Warren Mott 724

1993 GIRLS CLASS A TEAM RACE
1. Christy Goodison (SH Stevenson)12 ....17:52
2. Jan Rothenberg (West Bloomfield)9 ....18:27
3. Allison Klemmer (Troy Athens)10 ....18:37
4. Chrissy Garst (Troy) 18:43
5. Hilary Green (Brighton) 18:51
6. Andrea Pullen (Jenison) 18:56
7. Andrea Boyer (Brighton) 19:00
8. Wendy Robertson (Troy) 19:01
9. E. O'Connell (Farmington Hills Mercy) 19:08
10. Andrea Rosema (Jenison) 19:08
22. Sonja Heubner (Holland) 19:35
32. Laura Pomp (Holland) 19:48

1993 GIRLS CLASS A INDIVIDUAL RACE
1. Eileen Fleck (East Lansing)12 ....18:03
2. Alexis Lund (Muskegon Reeths-Puffer)10 ....18:52
3. B. Mackinnon (Livonia Stevenson)12 ....19:02
4. J. Hampton (Novi) 19:18
5. Becky Caldwell (Wyandotte) 19:19
6. Alana McQueen (Ann Arbor Huron) 19:21
7. Bridget Byrne (Walled Lake Western) 19:25
8. Maria Merikak (Ann Arbor Pioneer) 19:26
9. Elizabeth Fernandez (Birmingham Marian) 19:28
10. Carrie Brecht (Midland Dow) 19:28

1994 CLASS A GIRLS

In Class A, Troy Athens captured the crown that crosstown rival Troy had the year before. Coach Debbie Zonca remarked, "Some of the other coaches were asking what's in the water."

Sophomore Andrea Rosema of Jenison took the lead early en route to her win in the team race. Portage Northern frosh Sharon Van Tuyl ran nearly as fast, 18:18, to win the individual title.

Saskatoon Golf Club, Alaska, Nov. 5 ☐
1994 GIRLS CLASS A TEAMS
1. Troy Athens 97
2. Ann Arbor Pioneer 129
3. Novi 161
4. Livonia Stevenson 197
5. Sterling Heights Stevenson 215
6. Monroe 230
7. Brighton 278
8. Rockford 283
9. Holt 319
10. Troy 325
11. Jenison 327
12. Flushing 355
13. Rochester Adams 358
14. Farmington 396
15. Ann Arbor Huron 416
16. Grand Haven 419
17. Traverse City 422
18. Holland West Ottawa 426
19. Swartz Creek 443
20. Grosse Pointe South 452
21. Clinton Twp Chippewa Valley 483
22. Milford 485
23. Utica Eisenhower 488
24. Pinckney 515
25. Berkley 566
26. Port Huron Northern 627
27. Grosse Pointe North 684
28. Okemos 710

1994 GIRLS CLASS A TEAM RACE
1. Andrea Rosema (Jenison)10 ....18:17
2. Katie Horner (Troy Athens)10 ....18:37
3. Lisa Timmer (Ann Arbor Pioneer) 18:45
4. Kelly Travis (Livonia Stevenson)9 ....18:52
5. Traci Owczarek (Troy Athens)12 ....18:54
6. Lorana Camp (Novi) 19:00
7. Katie Ryan (Rochester Adams) 19:01
8. Jenny Hampton (Novi) 19:01
9. Brook Kosanic (Grand Haven) 19:05
10. Andrea Pullen (Jenison) 19:11
11. Emily Magner (Ann Arbor Pioneer) 19:14
12. Aimee Vasse (Grosse Pointe South) 19:15
13. Jenny Sisk (Monroe) 19:17
14. Katie Szopo (Brighton) 19:20
15. Alison Klemmer (Troy Athens) 19:20
16. Jamie Grant (Holt) 19:21
17. Erin Leonard (Ann Arbor Pioneer)9 ....19:29
18. Melissa Granger (Swartz Creek) 19:31
19. Amy Worges (Swartz Creek) 19:31
20. Kelly McNeilance (Livonia Stevenson) 19:34
21. Vanessa Spencer (Holt)12 ....19:35
22. Laura Harger (Holt)11 ....19:36
23. Janine Chura (Utica Eisenhower) 19:36
24. Tracy Raymond (Rockford) 19:37
25. Hilary Green (Brighton) 19:37
37. Jenny Wegner (Troy Athens) 19:48
38. Kristtin Lenderman (Troy Athens) 19:50

1994 GIRLS CLASS A INDIVIDUAL RACE
1. Sharon Van Tuyl (Portage Northern)9 ....18:18
2. Eileen O'Connel (Farmington Hills Mercy)12 ....18:48
3. Laura Edwardson (Kalamazoo Norrix) 18:59
4. Shauna Pennington (Greenville) 19:00
5. Leah Scharl (Clarkston) 19:15
6. Alexis Lund (Muskegon Reeths-Puffer)11 ....19:19
7. Sharon Dickie (Grand Blanc)9 ....19:20
8. Rita Arndt (Saline) 19:23
9. Aimmee Tow (Sterling Heights Ford) 19:24
10. Heather Moore (Hartland) 19:24
11. Lara Reis (West Bloomfield) 19:30
12. Kerrie Price (Grandville) 19:33
13. Natalia Celuch (Harper Woods Regina) 19:33
14. Sara Ellis (Mt Pleasant) 19:33
15. Kristen Kiley (White Lake Lakeland) 19:35

1995 CLASS A GIRLS

Snow and cold set the tone as Troy Athens defended its crown. "I told the girls that no one was going to hand them a trophy," said coach Debbie Zonca.

Prior to the race, the Athens team played in the snow. "They had fun with it and realized that it was the same for everyone. We weren't going to throw away our goals just because Mother Nature threw some white stuff at us."

Saskatoon Golf Club, Alaska, Nov. 4 ☒
1995 GIRLS CLASS A TEAMS
1. Troy Athens 102
2. Livonia Stevenson 113
3. Sterling Heights Stevenson 126
4. Clarkston 230
5. Farmington 257
6. Port Huron Northern 259
7. Greenville 264
8. Novi 298
9. Grosse Pointe South 302
10. Flushing 306
11. Rockford 307
12. Brighton 323
13. Holland West Ottawa 332
14. Pinckney 345
15. Jenison 375
16. Grand Haven 381
17. Rochester 382
18. Troy 427
19. Temperance Bedford 443
20. Portage Central 459
21. Birmingham Seaholm 494
22. Rochester Adams 500
23. Belleville 511
24. Swartz Creek 536
25. Midland 585
26. Lincoln Park 639
27. New Baltimore Anchor Bay 702

1995 GIRLS CLASS A TEAM RACE
1. Alison Klemmer (Troy Athens)12 ....18:31
2. Andrea Rosema (Jenison)11 ....18:54
3. Megan Fitzgerald (SH Stevenson)9 ....18:54
4. Stephanie Burklow (Clarkston)12 ....19:01
5. Kelly Travis (Livonia Stevenson)10 ....19:01
6. Patty Langworthy (Holland West Ottawa)11 ....19:13
7. Traci Owczarek (Troy Athens)12 ....19:16
8. Shauna Pennington (Greenville)10 ....19:17
9. Andrea Pullen (Jenison)12 ....19:22
10. Christina Garst (Troy)12 ....19:23
11. Katie Horner (Troy Athens)11 ....19:24
12. Rebecca Tavierne (Sterling Hts Stevenson)9 ....19:27
13. Aimee Vasse (Grosse Pointe South)12 ....19:28
14. Jennifer Lyijnen (Sterling Hts Stevenson)11 ....19:31
15. Amy Brown (Port Huron Northern)12 ....19:37
16. Kim McNeilance (Livonia Stevenson)9 ....19:39
17. Jennifer Denkins (Flushing)12 ....19:40
18. Lorna Camp (Novi)11 ....19:42
19. Krissy Love (Holland West Ottawa)10 ....19:44
20. Natsasha Mindera (Temperance Bedford)12 ....19:45
21. Chrystal Moyer (Greenville)11 ....19:48
22. Elizabeth Cook (Clarkston)10 ....19:49
23. Ashley Carter (Birmingham Seaholm)9 ....19:51
24. Katie Easton (Port Huron Northern)9 ....19:52
25. Kris Lawrence (Pinckney)12 ....19:53
30. Katie Markey (Troy Athens)12 ....20:03
53. Kristin Lederman (Troy Athens)10 ....20:22
73. Janine Waltereit (Troy Athens)10 ....20:38

96. Laura Elder (Troy Athens)9 ... 20:50

1995 GIRLS CLASS A INDIVIDUAL RACE

1. Sharon Van Tuyl (Portage Northern)10 ... 18:21
2. Alexis Lund (Muskegon Reeths-Puffer)12 ... 18:57
3. Shawn Kemp (Milford)9 ... 19:04
4. Rita Arndt (Saline) ... 19:17
5. Jackie Bucholz (Holly) ... 19:20
6. Emily Magner (Ann Arbor Pioneer) ... 19:21
7. Aimee Tow (Utica) ... 19:23
8. Jennifer Waiczuk (Waterford Mott) ... 19:26
9. Laura Harger (Holt)12 ... 19:32
10. Lisa Timmer (Ann Arbor Pioneer) ... 19:32

Portage Northern's Sharon Van Tuyl.

1996 CLASS A GIRLS

No one impressed more here than Sharon Van Tuyl, three weeks after coming back from a stress fracture. The junior won her third straight title with a 17:53 run, 41 seconds ahead of Andrea Rosema. The next track season, Van Tuyl would win the National Scholastic two mile in a state record 10:25.59.

For the first tme ever on the girls' side, there was only one race, as the individual and team categories were combined. Technology made it possible to finally be able to do the team scoring accurately with the inclusion of the individuals. For this year only, separate recognition was given to both the team and individual winners, even though they were in the same race. After two years as the individual winner, Sharon Van Tuyl ran in the team category. Andrea Rosema of Jenison, the team winner from '94, was credited as the individual winner though she finished second to Van Tuyl.

Sterling Heights Stevenson returned to the top for the first time since the 1986 race for which it was never credited.

Michigan Int. Speedway, Brooklyn, Nov. 2 ⊠
1996 GIRLS CLASS A TEAMS

1. Sterling Heights Stevenson ... 104
2. Livonia Stevenson ... 126
3. Novi ... 182
4. Traverse City ... 184
5. Rockford ... 190
6. Grosse Pointe South ... 199
7. Birmingham Seaholm ... 200
8. Brighton ... 211
9. Milford ... 275
10. Holland West Ottawa ... 323
11. Sterling Heights Ford ... 323
12. Salem ... 368
13. Rochester Adams ... 425
14. Belleville ... 428
15. Grand Rapids Christian ... 432
16. Port Huron Northern ... 433
17. Clarkston ... 454
18. Portage Northern ... 455
19. Flushing ... 458
20. Temperance Bedford ... 497
21. Hudsonville ... 507
22. Swartz Creek ... 522
23. Dearborn Edsel Ford ... 533
24. Midland ... 562
25. Troy ... 567
26. Warren Mott ... 666
27. Rochester ... 723

1996 GIRLS CLASS A INDIVIDUALS

1. Sharon Van Tuyl (Portage Northern)11 ... 17:53
2. Andrea Rosema (Jenison)12 ... 18:34
3. Aimee Tow (Sterling Heights Ford)12 ... 18:48
4. Cami Moll (Hudsonville) ... 18:48
5. Kelly Travis (Livonia Stevenson)11 ... 18:49
6. Dayna Herr (Milford) ... 18:49
7. Marne Smiley (Sterling Hts Stevenson) ... 18:50
8. Megan Fitzgerald (Sterling Hts Stevenson) ... 18:51
9. Marjori Brocks (Westland Glenn) ... 18:51
10. Patty Langworthy (West Ottawa) ... 18:53
11. Rachel Sturtz (Traverse City) ... 18:57
12. Jackie Bucholz (Holly) ... 18:57
13. Laura Hayden (Rochester Adams) ... 18:59
14. Kate Crowley (Grosse Pointe South) ... 18:59
15. Rachel Smith (Monroe)11 ... 19:00
16. Brooke Albright (Novi) ... 19:02
17. Erin Kenyon (Birmingham Seaholm) ... 19:08
18. Beth Auty (Grosse Pointe South) ... 19:09
19. Kate Atheris (Farmington) ... 19:09
20. Jonnie Vasse (Grosse Pointe South)11 ... 19:09
21. Julie Schmidt (Romeo) ... 19:09
22. Megan Plante (Clarkston) ... 19:11
23. Kelly McNeilance (Livonia Stevenson) ... 19:11
24. Rachel Brown (Port Huron Northern) ... 19:13
25. Ashley Fillion (Livonia Churchhill) ... 19:13
26. Ashley Carter (Birmingham Seaholm) ... 19:16
27. Kimberly McNeilance (Livonia Stevenson) ... 19:17
28. Shawn Kemp (Milford) ... 19:19
29. Laura Girz (Ann Arbor Huron) ... 19:20
30. Nora Colligan (Rockford) ... 19:20
31. April DeKorte (Grand Rapids Christian) ... 19:21
32. Jennifer Hampton (Novi) ... 19:22
33. Michelle Suszek (Alpena) ... 19:23
34. Shannon Stephens (SH Stevenson) ... 19:25
35. Kerrie Card (Rockford) ... 19:26
36. Lisa Chaps (Brighton) ... 19:27
37. Jennifer Bolton (Salem) ... 19:27
38. Hidi Jasch (Holland)11 ... 19:27
39. Jennifer Wakczuk (Waterford Mott) ... 19:28
40. Katie Chapman (Detroit Cass Tech) ... 19:29
41. Jennifer Lyijnen (Sterling Heights Stevenson) ... 19:30
56. Rebecca Tavierne (Sterling Hts Stevenson)10 .. 19:42
109. Katie Fitzgerald (Sterling Heights Stevenson) . 20:12

1997 CLASS A GIRLS

The cold, driving rain wasn't to everyone's liking in the second edition of the state finals at MIS. The biggest shocker was not who won, but who lost. Sharon Van Tuyl of Portage Northern, a heavy favorite for a fourth straight Class A title, led for half the distance before the pack caught her and she folded. She later described becoming disoriented and falling in the last half mile. She picked herself up to trudge home 54th in 20:36.

The upset winner in Class A, Katie Boyles of Rochester Adams, was just a frosh. "I didn't think winning was possible," she said. "I had heard about all the great runners here. I just waited and picked my spots. I'm on such an adrelaline rush right now, I feel wonderful."

Ann Arbor Pioneer won its third title a year after if failed to qualify a team, upsetting favored Rockford.

Michigan Int. Speedway, Brooklyn, Nov. 1 ⊠
1997 GIRLS CLASS A TEAMS

1. Ann Arbor Pioneer ... 68
2. Rockford ... 114
3. Livonia Stevenson ... 169
4. Milford ... 172
5. Grosse Pointe South ... 205
6. Brighton ... 211
7. Traverse City Central ... 213
8. Grand Haven ... 267
9. Novi ... 283
10. Midland ... 296
11. Rochester Adams ... 301
12. Sterling Heights Stevenson ... 304
13. Temperance Bedford ... 376
14. Mason ... 378
15. Monroe ... 382
16. Mt Pleasant ... 406
17. Birmingham Seaholm ... 426
18. Port Huron Northern ... 432
19. Troy Athens ... 447
20. Portage Central ... 478
21. Okemos ... 486
22. Sterling Heights Ford ... 527
23. Grosse Pointe North ... 584
24. St Johns ... 589
25. Rochester ... 636
26. Flushing ... 677
27. Dearborn Edsel Ford ... 699

1997 GIRLS CLASS A INDIVIDUALS

1. Katie Boyles (Rochester Adams)9 ... 19:08
2. Cami Moll (Hudsonville)11 ... 19:12
3. Laura Girz (Ann Arbor Huron)11 ... 19:22
4. Marne Smiley (Sterling H Stevenson) ... 19:26
5. Sharon Dickie (Grand Blanc)12 ... 19:27
6. Andrea Parker (Livonia Stevenson) ... 19:33
7. Sara DeBruyn (Traverse City Central) ... 19:33
8. Emily Magner (Ann Arbor Pioneer) ... 19:33
9. Stacic Selich (Midland Dow) ... 19:33
10. Emily Blakeslee (Rockford)11 ... 19:36
11. Rachel Smith (Monroe)12 ... 19:36
12. Hidi Jasch (Holland)12 ... 19:37
13. Rachel Brown (Port Huron Northern) ... 19:38
14. Amber Culp (Ann Arbor Pioneer) ... 19:38
15. Rachel Sturtz (Traverse City Central) ... 19:40
16. Julia Schmidt (Romeo) ... 19:41
17. Megan Fitzgerald (SH Stevenson) ... 19:42
18. Jonnie Vasse (Grosse Pointe South)12 ... 19:43
19. Erin Leonard (Ann Arbor Pioneer)12 ... 19:51
20. April Smith (Charlotte)12 ... 19:52
21. Elizabeth Auty (Grosse Pointe South) ... 19:54
22. Iris Slater (Brighton) ... 19:57
23. Mariann Hop (Grand Haven) ... 20:02
24. Shawn Kemp (Milford) ... 20:04
25. Leah Cressman (Ann Arbor Pioneer) ... 20:05
26. Kristyn Kern (White Lake Lakeland) ... 20:05
27. Karin Wandler (Milford) ... 20:07
28. Claire Romanski (Okemos) ... 20:09
29. Kalin Toedenbusch (Rockford)9 ... 20:09
30. Heidi Crowley (Grosse Pointe South) ... 20:10
31. Jennifer Hanley (Ann Arbor Pioneer) ... 20:11
32. Nora Colligan (Rockford) ... 20:13
33. Laura Hayden (Rochester Adams) ... 20:14
34. Molly Hobey (East Lansing) ... 20:16
35. Ashley Carter (Birmingham Seaholm) ... 20:18
36. Anna Wiking (Milford) ... 20:19
37. Martha Graham (Midland) ... 20:19
38. Jordan Hartmann (Rockford) ... 20:20
39. Michele Suszek (Alpena) ... 20:22
40. Kelly McNeilance (Livonia Stevenson) ... 20:23
47. Anne Richtmyer (Ann Arbor Pioneer) ... 20:32
152. Claudia Sell (Ann Arbor Pioneer) ... 21:27

1998 CLASS A GIRLS

MIS course conditions were lightning fast, and 38 girls broke 19 minutes. The Rockford Rams dominated the race. At times four of them, led by Emily Blakeslee, were at the front of the pack. In the end, defending champ Katie Boyles got around Blakeslee for a course record win, but the Rams still won with a record 25-point performance.

"I had to dig deep in the end," said Boyles, who had been 15th at the mile and only took the lead in the final qurter mile. "That's usually how I run. I don't like leading because I have a really strong kick at the end and some speed I like to use."

Michigan Int. Speedway, Brooklyn, Nov. 7 ⊠
1998 GIRLS CLASS A TEAMS

1. Rockford 25
2. Sterling Heights Stevenson 95
3. Ann Arbor Pioneer 133
4. Grand Haven 150
5. Traverse City Central 220
6. Grosse Pointe South 251
7. Mt Pleasant 281
8. Brighton 302
9. Livonia Stevenson 307
10. Troy Athens 327
11. Romeo 330
12. Portage Central 391
13. Rochester Adams 395
14. Saline 397
15. Temperance Bedford 406
16. Midland 437
17. Rochester 442
18. Port Huron Northern 448
19. Flushing 475
20. Dearborn Edsel Ford 478
21. Gaylord 484
22. South Lyon 496
23. Birmingham Seaholm 512
24. Troy 544
25. Alpena 558
26. Warren Cousino 644
27. Belleville 703

Katie Boyles won four straight for Rochester Adams.

1998 GIRLS CLASS A INDIVIDUALS

1. Katie Boyles (Rochester Adams)10 17:52
2. Emily Blakeslee (Rockford)11 18:01
3. Kalin Toedebusch (Rockford)10 18:10
4. Linsey Blaisdell (Rockford)10 18:12
5. Michelle Ruggero (Sterling Heights Ford)12 18:14
6. Nora Colligan (Rockford)11 18:14
7. Jenny Fitzgerald (Sterling Hts Stevenson)10 18:15
8. Rachel Campbell (Sterling Hts Stevenson)12 18:21
9. Teresa Bongiovanni (Romeo)9 18:28
10. Andrea Parker (Livonia Stevenson)11 18:29
11. Amber Culp (Ann Arbor Pioneer)11 18:32
12. Jordan Hartmann (Rockford)11 18:33
13. Anne Zuelke (Grand Haven)10 18:35
14. Megan Fitzgerald (Sterling Hts Stevenson)12 18:36
15. Marne Smiley (Sterling Hts Stevenson)11 18:38
16. Courtney Meeker (Rochester)9 18:40
17. Beth Auty (Grosse Pointe South)11 18:42
18. Kendra Snyder (Holland)10 18:42
19. Karen Leroy (Oxford)11 18:42
20. Julia Schmidt (Romeo)11 18:43
21. Kristin Echols (Novi)11 18:43
22. Jenny Gerteisen (Portage Central)11 18:45
23. Lori VanderMeulen (Grand Rapids Union)12 18:46
24. Leah Cressman (Ann Arbor Pioneer)11 18:46
25. Anne Richtmyer (Ann Arbor Pioneer)12 18:46
26. Kate Gaylord (Mason)10 18:47
27. Heidi Crowley (Grosse Pointe South)11 18:48
28. Rachel Sturtz (Traverse City Central)12 18:48
29. Michelle Suszek (Alpena)11 18:51
30. Amanda Lee (South Lyon)11 18:51
31. Claire Romanski (Okemos)11 18:54
32. Jenny Weber (Gaylord)9 18:56
33. Kellie Nicholson (Temperance Bedford)10 18:56
34. Kristen Post (Holland West Ottawa)12 18:57
35. Katie Erdman (Cadillac)9 18:57
36. Rachel Brown (Port Huron Northern)12 18:58
37. Sarah Sherman (Grand Haven)11 18:58
38. Jane Martineau (Mt Pleasant)12 18:58
39. Shawn Kemp (Milford)12 19:01
40. Alyson Flohr (Northville)10 19:03
46. Renae Sobie (Rockford)11 19:08
73. Amanda Dusendang (Rockford)12 19:29

1999 CLASS A GIRLS

A stunning 83 girls bettered 20:00 on a day when temperatures were in the low 50s and the wind was steady. The course surface was hard and fast, and conspiracy theories aside, the course remained substantially the same as previous years. Katie Boyles got the last laugh on her doubters by coming through for a third straight title, tying the record for Class A.

"I felt confident coming into the race; all I had to do was give it my best," said Boyles, who moved into the lead around the final long turn of the infield.

Teamwise, Rockford, coached by Brad Prins, again dominated, its 40 points giving the Rams a 112-point margin—the second-biggest in meet history—over runner-up Rochester Adams.

Michigan Int. Speedway, Brooklyn, Nov. 6 ⊠
1999 GIRLS CLASS A TEAMS

1. Rockford 40
2. Rochester Adams 152
3. Traverse City Central 216
4. Ann Arbor Pioneer 218
5. Grosse Pointe South 223
6. Traverse City West 237
7. Portage Central 237
8. Saline 246
9. Sterling Heights Stevenson 269
10. Romeo 285
11. Troy 285
12. Milford 346
13. Brighton 347
14. Livonia Stevenson 347
15. Flushing 363
16. Temperance Bedford 411
17. Alpena 432
18. Lowell 439
19. Battle Creek Lakeview 461
20. Rochester 477
21. Dearborn Edsel Ford 481
22. Swartz Creek 484
23. Sterling Heights 530
24. Grosse Pointe North 622
25. Berkley 635
26. Port Huron 686
27. Wyandotte 786

1999 GIRLS CLASS A INDIVIDUALS

1. Katie Boyles (Rochester Adams)11 17:56
2. Teresa Bongiovanni (Romeo)10 18:01
3. Kalin Toedebusch (Rockford)11 18:02
4. Linsey Blaisdell (Rockford)11 18:08
5. Emily Blakeslee (Rockford)12 18:34
6. Julia Schmidt (Romeo)12 18:42
7. Michelle Suszek (Alpena)12 18:45
8. Katie Kramer (Milford)9 18:46
9. Brittany Ballard (Midland)10 18:47
10. Karen Leroy (Oxford)12 18:50
11. Andrea Parker (Livonia Stevenson)12 18:51
12. Amber Culp (Ann Arbor Pioneer)12 18:51
13. Renae Sobie (Rockford)12 18:51
14. Rachel Cox (Battle Creek Lakeview)12 18:53
15. Stephanie Sayler (Romeo)10 18:57
16. Jenny Gertaisen (Portage Central)12 18:58
17. Marne Smiley (SH Stevenson)12 18:58
18. Kendra Snyder (Holland)12 19:00
19. Elise Elzinga (Temperance Bedford)11 19:05
20. Melanie Batey (Davison)12 19:07
21. Sarah Sherman (Grand Haven)12 19:07
22. Nina Schmitt (Novi)9 19:08
23. Jordan Hartmann (Rockford)12 19:11
24. Danielle Chase (Saline)10 19:14
25. Chelsea Loomis (Traverse City West)11 19:15
26. Kelsey Toedebusch (Rockford)9 19:17
27. Shannon Stanley (Rochester Adams)9 19:19
28. Mimi Speyer (Grand Rapids Christian)11 19:19
29. Jaclyn House (Berkley)11 19:22
30. Megan Newton (East Lansing)9 19:24
31. Megan Lewis (Traverse City Central)10 19:25
32. Nicolette Merritt (Greenville)9 19:27
33. Sarah Hastings (Traverse City Central)12 19:28
34. Heidi Crowley (Grosse Pointe South)12 19:29
35. Lori VanderMeulen (Grand Rapids Union)12 19:29
36. Ryan Hittle (Brighton)12 19:30
37. Megan Coughlin (Waterford Mott)10 19:31
38. Taylor Bones (Bloomfield Hills Lahser)10 19:32
39. Kellie Nicholson (Temperance Bedford)11 19:34
40. Kristyn Kern (White Lake Lakeland)11 19:35
95. Nora Colligan (Rockford)12 20:05

2000 D1 GIRLS

The fastest race ever opened many eyes. The Rockford girls went out more slowly than the previous year, waiting for Katie Boyles's inevitable late-race drive. Yet Boyles could not be stopped. She came from behind after the second mile and hammered home to a 17:18 that crushed the course record by 34 seconds. Behind her, four other girls also dipped under 17:40. The most surprising of them was Boyles's sophomore teammate, Shannon Stanley, who kicked past Rockford's top three just before the line to grab second.

"I feel really excited, pretty giddy," said Boyles. "When I got into cross country my freshman year, I never thought I would do anything like this. It's by far the biggest athletic accomplishment of my life."

The was the first year of divisions, a new classification system that had little effect on the largest schools. Rockford won a record third-straight title.

Michigan Int. Speedway, Brooklyn, Nov. 4 ⊠
2000 GIRLS DIVISION 1 TEAMS

1. Rockford 35
2. Milford 112
3. Troy 232
4. Romeo 235
5. Rochester Adams 242
6. Grand Haven 276
7. Brighton 283
8. Sterling Heights Stevenson 289
9. Portage Central 315
10. Saline 324
11. Kalamazoo Norrix 353
12. Okemos 364
13. Livonia Churchill 372
14. Traverse City Central 372
15. Swartz Creek 374
16. Ann Arbor Pioneer 379
17. Livonia Stevenson 392
18. Rochester 417
19. Walled Lake Central 436
20. Traverse City West 457
21. Grosse Pointe South 459
22. Sterling Heights 536
23. Temperance Bedford 545
24. Ann Arbor Huron 546
25. Holland 572
26. Warren Mott 623
27. Troy Athens 627

2000 GIRLS DIVISION 1 INDIVIDUALS
1. Katie Boyles (Rochester Adams)12 .... 17:18
2. Shannon Stanley (Rochester Adams)10 .... 17:32
3. Linsey Blaisdell (Rockford)12 .... 17:33
4. Kalin Toedebusch (Rockford)12 .... 17:34
5. Nikki Bohnsack (Rockford)9 .... 17:58
6. Teresa Bongiovanni (Romeo)11 .... 17:58
7. Katie Kramer (Milford)10 .... 18:12
8. Jentry Soule (Grand Haven)11 .... 18:13
9. Kelsey Toedebusch (Rockford)10 .... 18:19
10. Elisa Zemlick (Kalamazoo Norrix)9 .... 18:21
11. Brittany Ballard (Midland)11 .... 18:30
12. Lisa Canty (Milford)9 .... 18:30
13. Michelle Kinkela (Sterling Hts Stevenson)12 .. 18:33
14. Claire Otwell (Traverse City Central)9 ...... 18:41
15. Aimee Keenan (Rockford)12 .... 18:42
16. Kendra Snyder (Holland)12 .... 18:43
17. Catherine Schmidt (Romeo)12 .... 18:44
18. Kristyn Kern (White Lake Lakeland)12 ...... 18:45
19. Chelsea Loomis (Traverse City West)12 ... 18:45
20. Theresa Martin (Troy Athens)9 .... 18:46
21. Karyn Erkfritz (Clarkston)12 .... 18:52
22. Kristy Powers (Rockford)9 .... 18:54
23. Anne Zuelke (Grand Haven)12 .... 18:55
24. Katie Buckham (Kalamazoo Central)10 .... 18:55
25. Erin Geldhof (Troy)10 .... 18:59
26. Lauren Puretz (Okemos)12 .... 19:03
27. Tiffany Kaid (Milford)9 .... 19:05
28. Stephanie Sayler (Romeo)11 .... 19:10
29. Lisa Montgomery (Livonia Stevenson)9 .... 19:11
30. Kellie Nicholson (Temperance Bedford)12 . 19:11
31. Laura Larivee (Troy)12 .... 19:12
32. Susan Duncan (Livonia Churchill)11 .... 19:14
33. Julie Puschmann (Port Huron)12 .... 19:16
34. Dana Larivee (Troy)12 .... 19:16
35. Meredith Alexander (Portage Central)9 ..... 19:17
36. Leigha Christian (Rochester)11 .... 19:17
37. Jessie Stewart (Kalamazoo Norrix)11 .... 19:17
38. Sarah Pilon (Livonia Stevenson)10 .... 19:18
39. Colleen Johnson (Milford)11 .... 19:18
40. Kristy Brown (Lansing Eastern)10 .... 19:18
57. Brittany Ogden (Rockford)11 .... 19:31

Remember the famous "Stop Pre" shirts? Boyles couldn't help having a little fun after proving her many doubters wrong.

2001 D1 GIRLS

A record four straight for the Rockford girls, who topped powerhouse Sterling Heights Stevenson by 45 points.

Sophomore Nikki Bohnsack won in 17:41, with Shannon Stanley of Rochester Adams taking the runner-up spot for the second year. Bohnsack led through the mile and 2M (11:14)

Michigan Int. Speedway, Brooklyn, Nov. 3 ⌧

2001 GIRLS DIVISION 1 TEAMS
1. Rockford 76
2. Sterling Heights Stevenson 121
3. Ann Arbor Pioneer 136
4. Rochester Adams 218
5. Romeo 221
6. Clarkston 251
7. Milford 261
8. Brighton 272
9. Livonia Churchill 276
10. Kalamazoo Norrix 284
11. Grosse Pointe South 290
12. Grand Ledge 303
13. Saline 317
14. Livonia Stevenson 353
15. Northville 377
16. Traverse City West 409
17. Forest Hills Northern 426
18. Grand Haven 426
19. Portage Central 475
20. Traverse City Central 475
21. Ann Arbor Huron 527
22. Troy 565
23. Grosse Pointe North 591
24. North Farmington 607
25. Farmington 660
26. Midland Dow 704
27. Canton 798

2001 GIRLS DIVISION 1 INDIVIDUALS
1. Nikki Bohnsack (Rockford)10 .... 17:41
2. Shannon Stanley (Rochester Adams)11 ...... 18:08
3. Elisa Zemlick (Kalamazoo Norrix)10 .... 18:17
4. Katie Danyko (Sterling Heights Stevenson)12 .. 18:28
5. Teresa Bongiovanni (Romeo)12 .... 18:46
6. Kelsey Toedebusch (Rockford)11 .... 18:52
7. Kristi Boerman-Powers (Rockford)10 .... 18:57
8. Lisa Canty (Milford)10 .... 18:57
9. Nina Schmitt (Novi)11 .... 18:59
10. Kristin Granroth (Milford)10 .... 18:59
11. Liz Mengyan (Clarkston)9 .... 19:00
12. Ashley Patten (Lake Orion)12 .... 19:00
13. Devon Rupley (Northville)10 .... 19:03
14. Jessie Stewart (Kalamazoo Norrix)12 .... 19:05
15. Nicole Blake (Sterling Heights Stevenson)11 .. 19:08
16. Susan Duncan (Livonia Churchill)12 .... 19:09
17. Renee Vela (Sterling Heights Stevenson)12 . 19:11
18. Rachel Eyler (Ann Arbor Pioneer)12 .... 19:13
19. Andrea Moreland (Rochester Adams)12 ... 19:14
20. Erica Nichols (Grand Ledge)12 .... 19:18
21. Jentry Soule (Grand Haven)12 .... 19:19
22. Amy Marsh (Grand Ledge)11 .... 19:19
23. Carrie Hadler (Ann Arbor Pioneer)12 .... 19:21
24. Anne Oltman (Clarkston)9 .... 19:22
25. Melissa Moncion (Romeo)12 .... 19:22
26. Erin Kelly (East Kentwood)12 .... 19:23
27. Michelle Harrold (Rockford)10 .... 19:23
28. Briana Wade (Ann Arbor Pioneer)12 .... 19:24
29. Rachel Bumann (Brighton)11 .... 19:24
30. Rebecca Propst (Romeo)9 .... 19:25
31. Sarah Bolton (Rochester Adams)11 .... 19:25
32. Anne Hoekstra (Kalamazoo Norrix)10 ...... 19:33
33. Colleen Johnson (Milford)12 .... 19:35
34. Bontje Zangerling (Belleville)12 .... 19:37
35. Megan Lewis (Traverse City Central)12 ... 19:38
36. Heather Moehle (Northville)11 .... 19:39
37. Clarissa Codrington (Ann Arbor Pioneer)12 .. 19:40
38. Katie Nicholson (Temperance Bedford)9 .. 19:41
39. Danielle Lewis (Livonia Stevenson)12 ..... 19:45
40. Brittany Gregory (Traverse City West)12 . 19:45
45. Brittinie Ogden (Rockford)12 .... 19:49
48. Laura Nelson (Rockford)12 .... 19:51
62. Lindsay Stebbins (Rockford)10 .... 20:00

2002 D1 GIRLS

The Rams of Rockford, after a tumultuous winter, managed to win a record fifth-straight crown. Brad Prins, the coach that led them to four victories, resigned in February after the *Grand Rapids Press* brought forth parent complaints of Prins allegedly giving supplements to student-athletes. The controversy divided the Rockford running community, with some, most notably Dathan Ritzenhein, voicing full support for Prins.

Dave Hodkinson and Ken Raymond earned the coaching credit for the latest Rams win.

Nikki Bohnsack captured first place again, saying, "I ran an awesome time, better than last year, so I don't have anything to complain about."

On a cold windy day, Shannon Stanley of Rochester Adams finished 2nd for the third-straight year.

Michigan Int. Speedway, Brooklyn, Nov. 2 ⌧

2002 GIRLS DIVISION 1 TEAMS
1. Rockford 57
2. Clarkston 110
3. Brighton 116
4. Milford 135
5. Grosse Pointe South 194
6. Livonia Stevenson 271
7. Ann Arbor Pioneer 274
8. Saline 275
9. Portage Central 299
10. Traverse City Central 322
11. Sterling Heights Stevenson 347
12. Traverse City West 365
13. Rochester Adams 367
14. Forest Hills Central 405
15. Ann Arbor Huron 409
16. Grand Blanc 419
17. Grandville 430
18. Grand Haven 443
19. Romeo 447
20. Troy Athens 452
21. Livonia Churchill 483
22. Troy 559
23. Grosse Pointe North 574
24. Holt 585
25. Canton 598
26. Birmingham Groves 626
27. Harper Woods Regina 863

2002 GIRLS DIVISION 1 INDIVIDUALS
1. Nikki Bohnsack (Rockford)11 .... 17:44
2. Shannon Stanley (Rochester Adams)12 ...... 17:57
3. Elisa Zemlick (Kalamazoo Norrix)11 .... 18:04
4. Lisa Canty (Milford)11 .... 18:32
5. Liz Mengyan (Clarkston)10 .... 18:33
6. Shari Rogers (Utica Eisenhower)10 .... 18:39
7. Mo Kuhta (Clarkston)11 .... 18:41
8. Kristi Boerman-Powers (Rockford)11 .... 18:44
9. Erica D'Angelo (Clinton Twp Chippewa Valley)9. 18:46
10. Danielle Underwood (Forest Hills Northern)10 .. 18:47
11. Eileen Creutz (Saline)9 .... 18:47
12. Heather Sirko (Livonia Stevenson)10 .... 18:48
13. Rachel Bumann (Brighton)12 .... 18:48
14. Lindsey Stebbins (Rockford)11 .... 18:49
15. Amy Markham (Rockford)10 .... 18:49
16. Rebecca Propst (Romeo)10 .... 18:50
17. Laura Fisher (Grosse Pointe North)12 ...... 18:51
18. Jennifer Culbertson (Macomb Dakota)12 . 18:51
19. Kristin Granroth (Milford)11 .... 18:51
20. Lyndsay Smith (Clarkston)9 .... 18:51
21. Madison Bangert (Midland Dow)10 .... 18:52
22. Katelyn Johnston (Temperance Bedford)9 . 18:54
23. Valerie Stansbury (Romeo)12 .... 18:56
24. Susanna Rivard (Brighton)11 .... 18:57
25. Rachel Ward (Brighton)12 .... 18:59
26. Theresa Martin (Troy Athens)11 .... 19:02
27. Rebecca Thelen (Grand Ledge)11 .... 19:05
28. Liz Petit (Grosse Pointe South)11 .... 19:06
29. Mollie Harms (Sterling Heights Stevenson)12 . 19:08

30. Elizabeth Otto (Portage Central)11 ...... 19:08
31. Jessica Palffy (Grosse Pointe South)10 ...... 19:09
32. Liz Baxter (Grosse Pointe South)10 ...... 19:09
33. Kristina Olsen (Jackson)9 ...... 19:09
34. Anne Oltman (Clarkston)10 ...... 19:09
35. Nicole Blake (Sterling Heights Stevenson)12 ...... 19:10
36. Claire Otwell (Traverse City Central)11 ...... 19:11
37. Annie Otwell (Traverse City Central)12 ...... 19:13
38. Kelsey Toedebusch (Rockford)12 ...... 19:13
39. Rebecca Szopo (Brighton)9 ...... 19:14
40. Tiffany Kaid (Milford)11 ...... 19:14
50. Andi Ruth Owens (Rockford)9 ...... 19:23
71. Lisa Kreuger (Rockford)12 ...... 19:38

2003 D1 GIRLS

After an unprecedented run at the top, Rockford finally fell. The Clarkston girls, coached by Jamie LaBrosse, captured the title with a 29-point edge on the Rams.

Two-time champion Nikki Bohnsack from Rockford struggled with injury during the season and could only finish 8th. In her stead, frosh teammate Rachel Wittum won the race with a solid 12-second margin over Saline's Eileen Creutz.

Michigan Int. Speedway, Brooklyn, Nov. 1
2003 GIRLS DIVISION 1 TEAMS
1. Clarkston 102
2. Rockford 131
3. Milford 139
4. Traverse City Central 156
5. Saline 180
6. Grandville 185
7. Brighton 200
8. Grosse Pointe South 247
9. Livonia Stevenson 269
10. Temperance Bedford 291
11. Davison 324
12. Okemos 360
13. Dearborn 373
14. Traverse City West 387
15. Troy 398
16. Salem 399
17. Livonia Churchill 421
18. Rochester Adams 456
19. Troy Athens 480
20. Rochester 507
21. Farmington 512
22. Portage Central 523
23. Portage Northern 526
24. Grand Haven 528
25. Sterling Heights Stevenson 579
26. Grosse Pointe North 724
27. Fraser 903

2003 GIRLS DIVISION 1 INDIVIDUALS
1. Rachel Wittum (Rockford)9 ...... 17:56
2. Eileen Creutz (Saline)10 ...... 18:08
3. Lisa Canty (Milford)12 ...... 18:13
4. Kristina Olsen. (Jackson)10 ...... 18:19
5. Annie Otwell (Traverse City Central)10 ...... 18:24
6. Lindsey Gaudard (Lake Orion)11 ...... 18:25
7. Lisa Senakiewich (Davison)12 ...... 18:30
8. Nikki Bohnsack (Rockford)12 ...... 18:36
9. Lyndsay Smith (Clarkston)10 ...... 18:37
10. Elizabeth Hoefing (Rochester)12 ...... 18:38
11. Erica D'Angelo (Clinton T Chippewa Valley)10 ..18:38
12. Katelyn Johnston (Temperance Bedford)10 ...... 18:39
13. Rachael Button (Farmington)12 ...... 18:40
14. Kristen Frey (Livonia Stevenson)9 ...... 18:41
15. Kelsey Bristol (Grandville)11 ...... 18:42
16. Kelsey Campbell (Traverse City Central)10 ...... 18:43
17. Emily Langenberg (Grand Ledge)9 ...... 18:44
18. Stephanie Viener (Brighton)10 ...... 18:46
19. Claire Otwell (Traverse City Central)12 ...... 18:47
20. Emily Goddard (Davison)11 ...... 18:47
21. Emily McLaughlin (Grosse Pointe South)9 ...... 18:49
22. Danielle Dakroub (Okemos)9 ...... 18:49
23. Gillian Nordquist (Clarkston)11 ...... 18:50
24. Katie Nicholson (Temperance Bedford)11 ...... 18:51
25. Jessie Hemming (Traverse City West)10 ...... 18:51
26. Susie Rivard (Brighton)12 ...... 18:51

27. Liz Mengyan (Clarkston)11 ...... 18:52
28. Shari Rogers (Utica Eisenhower)11 ...... 18:52
29. Mo Kuhta (Clarkston)12 ...... 18:54
30. Kirstian Tyler (Livonia Franklin)12 ...... 18:56
31. Megan Jambeck (Milford)11 ...... 18:57
32. Kristin Granroth (Milford)12 ...... 18:57
33. Mallory Farnum (Milford)11 ...... 18:58
34. Ashley Lehmann (Grandville)11 ...... 19:07
35. Stephanie Huber (Sterling Heights)11 ...... 19:12
36. Jenna Leach (Clarkston)9 ...... 19:12
37. Anne Oltman (Clarkston)12 ...... 19:12
38. Juanita Espinoza (Macomb L'Anse Creuse N)11 19:13
39. Anne Hoekstra (Kalamazoo Norrix)12 ...... 19:14
40. Ashley Scullion (East Kentwood)11 ...... 19:14
98. Beth Hoekstra (Clarkston)10 ...... 19:57

2004 D1 GIRLS

Clarkston did it again, despite hitting disaster in the first 200 meters. A pile-up of around 25 runners put five of the Wolves on the ground.

"They got up, composed themselves, and ran as hard and fast as they could," said coach Jamie LaBrosse.

Saline's Eileen Creutz won the individual crown after battling with defending champ Rachel Wittum and Clarkston's Liz Mengyan most of the way. Mengyan, ahead at 3M, stopped at that clocl, thinking in her fatigue that it was the finish line. Both Creutz and Wittum streaked past her as she recovered for 3rd. Said Creutz, "I felt awesome. It was amazing. Best race ever."

Michigan Int. Speedway, Brooklyn, Nov. 6
2004 GIRLS DIVISION 1 TEAMS
1. Clarkston 132
2. Traverse City Central 172
3. Okemos 179
4. Rockford 184
5. Livonia Stevenson 196
6. Saline 199
7. Grosse Pointe South 208
8. Milford 213
9. Livonia Churchill 327
10. Salem 335
11. Grand Haven 353
12. Temperance Bedford 370
13. Grandville 379
14. Utica Eisenhower 383
15. Novi 396
16. Sterling Heights Stevenson 421
17. Troy 426
18. Traverse City West 465
19. White Lake Lakeland 474
20. Rochester Adams 476
21. Grand Blanc 476
22. Ann Arbor Pioneer 484
23. Troy Athens 518
24. Brighton 578
25. Grosse Pointe North 581
26. Portage Northern 585
27. Farmington Hills Mercy 630
28. Fraser 944

2004 GIRLS DIVISION 1 INDIVIDUALS
1. Eileen Creutz (Saline)11 ...... 18:03
2. Rachel Wittum (Rockford)10 ...... 18:12
3. Liz Mengyan (Clarkston)12 ...... 18:17
4. Carlie Green (Milford)10 ...... 18:19
5. Amber Brunmeier (Holland West Ottawa)10 ...... 18:31
6. Emily Langenberg (Grand Ledge)10 ...... 18:33
7. Kristen Frey (Livonia Stevenson)10 ...... 18:33
8. Kellee Lemke (Sterling Heights Stevenson)11 ...... 18:36
9. Erica D'Angelo (Clinton T Chippewa Valley)11 ...... 18:38
10. Nora Kiilunen (Brighton)9 ...... 18:40
11. Katie Haines (Rockford)9 ...... 18:41
12. Emily Goddard (Davison)12 ...... 18:46
13. Betsy Graney (Grosse Pointe North)10 ...... 18:47
14. Allie Pugh (Okemos)10 ...... 18:49
15. Megan Pines (Troy)9 ...... 18:50
16. Katelyn Johnston (Temperance-Bedford)11 ...... 18:51
17. Michelle Rogers (Utica Eisenhower)9 ...... 18:56

18. Danielle Dakroub (Okemos)10 ...... 18:58
19. Nicole Hammer (Troy Athens)9 ...... 18:58
20. Kim Secord (Rochester)9 ...... 18:59
21. Darcy Dubuc (Grand Haven)9 ...... 18:59
22. Jillian McLaughlin (Grosse Pointe South)11 ...... 19:00
23. Stephanie Huber (Sterling Heights)12 ...... 19:00
24. Jenny Morgan (Clarkston)11 ...... 19:00
25. Natalie Humphry (Grosse Pointe South)12 ...... 19:04
26. Natalie Webb (Woodhaven)9 ...... 19:04
27. Kristina Olsen (Jackson)11 ...... 19:10
28. Rachel Patterson (Rochester Adams)10 ...... 19:11
29. Katie Reilly (Lake Orion)12 ...... 19:11
30. Megan Brackins (Waterford Kettering)9 ...... 19:14
31. Jessica Lupinacci (Walled Lake Western)11 ...... 19:14
32. Shari Rogers (Utica Eisenhower)12 ...... 19:15
33. Kara Butler (Okemos)12 ...... 19:16
34. Lynsey Ardingo (Pinckney)12 ...... 19:16
35. Heather Sirko (Livonia Stevenson)12 ...... 19:18
36. Jamie Chapman (Traverse City Central)12 ...... 19:18
37. Michaela Crew (White Lake Lakeland)9 ...... 19:20
38. Stephanie Skowneski (Clint Chippewa Valley)9 19:20
39. Kelsey Campbell (Traverse City Central)11 ...... 19:20
40. Emily McLaughlin (Grosse Pointe South)10 ...... 19:22
48. Anne Oltman (Clarkston)12 ...... 19:30
53. Lyndsay Smith (Clarkston)11 ...... 19:37
61. Gillian Nordquist (Clarkston)12 ...... 19:42
69. Jenna Leach (Clarkston)10 ...... 19:45
121. Beth Hoekstra (Clarkston)11 ...... 20:20

Eileen Creutz of Saline won two in a row.

2005 D1 GIRLS

"We all came back to the tent and we didn't know what the resuls were going to be," said Clarkston senior Lyndsay Smith.

The news that the Wolves had won a third-straight was welcome. Said Jenny Morgan, who had placed 4th despite it being her first race in a month following a lung illness, "We didn't run a perfect race, but we ran a solid race and it won us a state championship."

Up front, Saline's Eileen Creutz successfully defended in 17:41. She had been cross training the two weeks prior to the meet because of a flare-up of tendinitis. "I didn't know what to expect today," she said.

Michigan Int. Speedway, Brooklyn, Nov. 5
2005 GIRLS DIVISION 1 TEAMS
1. Clarkston 123
2. Okemos 138
3. Rockford 140
4. Livonia Churchill 215
5. Traverse City Central 220
6. Rochester Adams 256
7. Saline 272
8. Grand Haven 275
9. Livonia Stevenson 284
10. Milford 335
11. Rochester 345
12. Grandville 350
13. Sterling Heights Stevenson 354
14. Troy Athens 355
15. Grand Ledge 361
16. Salem 371
17. Troy 376
18. Walled Lake Northern 388
19. Jackson 407
20. Temperance Bedford 432
21. Ann Arbor Pioneer 444
22. Holland West Ottawa 446
23. Rochester Hills Stoney Creek 500
24. Grosse Pointe North 525
25. Grosse Pointe South 563
26. Midland 618
27. Detroit King 891

2005 GIRLS DIVISION 1 INDIVIDUALS
1. Eileen Creutz (Saline)12 .... 17:41
2. Katie Haines (Rockford)10 .... 17:48
3. Becca Addison (Grand Haven)9 .... 17:55
4. Jenny Morgan (Clarkston)12 .... 17:55
5. Courtney Calka (Livonia Stevenson)9 .... 17:56
6. Stephanie Morgan (Clarkston)9 .... 17:57
7. Rachel Patterson (Rochester Adams)11 ... 18:01
8. Emily Langenberg (Grand Ledge)11 .... 18:06
9. Carlie Green (Milford)11 .... 18:08
10. Danielle Dakroub (Okemos)11 .... 18:12
11. Allison Rademacher (Grand Ledge)10 .... 18:13
12. Audrey Huth (Utica)9 .... 18:13
13. Amber Brunmeier (Holland West Ottawa)11 .. 18:18
14. Missy Darling (Holt)12 .... 18:22
15. Kristina Olsen (Jackson)12 .... 18:22
16. Erica D'Angelo (Clinton T Chippewa Valley)12 .. 18:26
17. Allie Pugh (Okemos)11 .... 18:27
18. Joanne Gabl (Saline)12 .... 18:29
19. Shelly Rogers (Utica Eisenhower)10 .... 18:32
20. Kellee Lemcke (Sterling Heights Stevenson)12 . 18:32
21. Nicole Hammer (Troy Athens)10 .... 18:32
22. Natalie Webb (Woodhaven)10 .... 18:33
23. Emily Van Wasshenova (Monroe)12 .... 18:34
24. Leah Borns (Grand Haven)12 .... 18:34
25. Betsy Graney (Grosse Pointe North)11 .. 18:34
26. Alina Gatowsky (Birmingham Groves)11 . 18:35
27. Sara Lieblein (Lake Orion)12 .... 18:36
28. Rachel McFarlane (Livonia Churchill)10 . 18:36
29. Nora Kiilunen (Brighton)10 .... 18:38
30. Annie Otwell (Traverse City Central)12 .. 18:38
31. Brittany Dixon (Rockford)11 .... 18:39
32. Lyndsay Smith (Clarkston)12 .... 18:41
33. Teresa Buiocchi (Okemos)11 .... 18:43
34. Allie Hock (Lake Orion)10 .... 18:43
35. Rachel Wittum (Rockford)11 .... 18:44
36. Elle Munoa (Holland West Ottawa)11 ..... 18:47
37. Taylor Mattarella (Traverse City Central)9 .. 18:50
38. Rachel Quaintance (Walled Lake Northern)9 . 18:50
39. Cally Macumber (Rochester Adams)9 .... 18:52
40. Shaniece Pinkston (Detroit Mumford)9 ... 18:52
57. Kristien Smith (Clarkston)9 .... 19:10
66. Jenna Leach (Clarkston)11 .... 19:17
134. Beth Hoekstra (Clarkston)12 .... 20:00
155. Rachel Blenc (Clarkston)10 .... 20:14

2006 D1 GIRLS

Carlie Green came in ahead of Rachel Patterson to grab individual honors for Milford, but Patterson could take consolation that she could celebrate the team win with her Rochester Adams teammates and coach Bud Cicciarelli.

It was the closest team finish ever in D1, with the tie being broken when Adams' No. 6 runner crossed more than 30 seconds ahead of the No. 6 for Churchill.

Michigan Int. Speedway, Brooklyn, Nov. 4
2006 GIRLS DIVISION 1 TEAMS
1. Rochester Adams 112
2. Livonia Churchill 112
3. Rockford 199
4. Saline 201
5. Rochester 215
6. Clarkston 260
7. Milford 271
8. Traverse City Central 292
9. Okemos 293
10. Troy 314
11. Ann Arbor Huron 380
12. Sterling Heights Stevenson 382
13. East Kentwood 386
14. Ann Arbor Pioneer 387
15. Holland West Ottawa 389
16. Troy Athens 407
17. Grandville 425
18. Grand Blanc 432
19. Utica 443
20. Grand Haven 455
21. Brighton 476
22. Grosse Pointe South 511
23. Grosse Pointe North 512
24. Grand Ledge 518
25. Livonia Stevenson 550
26. Detroit Mumford 550
27. Northville 554
28. Flushing 582

Milford's Carlie Green (Marvin Goodwin photo)

2006 GIRLS DIVISION 1 INDIVIDUALS
1. Carlie Green (Milford)12 .... 17:50
2. Rachel Patterson (Rochester Adams)12 ... 17:53
3. Katie Haines (Rockford)11 .... 17:54
4. Nicole Hammer (Troy Athens)11 .... 18:07
5. Tiffany Abrahamian (Rochester)11 .... 18:07
6. Emily Langenberg (Grand Ledge)12 .... 18:10
7. Megan Maceratini (Livonia Churchill)12 ... 18:13
8. Alex Leptich (Saline)9 .... 18:15
9. Christina Capriccioso (West Bloomfield)10 . 18:16
10. Cally Macumber (Rochester Adams)10 .. 18:21
11. Alyssa Mira (Livonia Churchill)10 .... 18:23
12. Audrey Huth (Utica)10 .... 18:23
13. Betsy Graney (Grosse Pointe North)12 .. 18:24
14. Rachel McFarlane (Livonia Churchill)11 . 18:25
15. Krista Parks (East Kentwood)9 .... 18:25
16. Jennifer Snelgrove (Grand Ledge)9 .... 18:27
17. Taylor Mattarella (Traverse City Central)10 .. 18:28
18. Sara Kroll (Livonia Churchill)9 .... 18:28
19. Kim Secord (Rochester)11 .... 18:29
20. Kristen Smith (Clarkston)10 .... 18:29
21. Emily Morgridge (Milford)11 .... 18:30
22. Kate Carter (Saline)9 .... 18:31
23. Alison White (Midland Dow)9 .... 18:33
24. Becca Addison (Grand Haven)10 .... 18:38
25. Allie Hock (Lake Orion)11 .... 18:39
26. Courtney Calka (Livonia Stevenson)10 .. 18:40
27. Michaela Crew (White Lake Lakeland)11 .. 18:40
28. Jennifer Yee (Troy)11 .... 18:41
29. Grace Green (Troy)10 .... 18:41
30. Elle Munoa (Holland West Ottawa)12 ..... 18:46
31. Brittany Dixon (Rockford)12 .... 18:50
32. Elizabeth Kelley (Rochester Adams)11 .. 18:51
33. Rachel Quaintance (Walled Lake N)10 .. 18:53
34. Danielle Tepper (Grandville)10 .... 18:55
35. Lindsey Hilton (Rochester Adams)10 ...... 18:56
36. Danielle Dakroub (Okemos)12 .... 18:57
37. Hannah Cavicchio (Salem)12 .... 18:59
38. Shannon Kohlitz (Jackson)12 .... 19:00
39. Kayla Boyes (Pinckney)9 .... 19:00
40. Megan Goethals (Rochester)9 .... 19:01
57. Kristin Byrne (Rochester Adams)12 .... 19:13
84. Amy Bush (Rochester Adams)10 .... 19:32
173. Nicole Rheinlander (Rochester Adams)11 .. 20:18

2007 D1 GIRLS

A year after crosstown rival Rochester Adams won, the Falcons of Rochester, coached by Larry Adams, grabbed their first title. "They've worked hard," he said. "They've fought through injuries, sickness… They just continued to persevere because they wanted to win a state championship."

Shannon Osika, a frosh from Waterford Mott, won what would be her only state title in cross country. She would win the 3200 the next spring for her only title in track. If anything, that's an indicator of how ferocious the competition was getting in Michigan girls distance running.

Osika would go on to star at Michigan, winning two individual Big 10 titles and making All-American six times. As a pro, she would run the fastest-ever 1500 by a Michigander, 4:01.80.

Shannon Osika only won as a frosh, but would go on to world-class efforts on the track. (Pete Draugalis photo)

Michigan Int. Speedway, Brooklyn, Nov. 3
2007 GIRLS DIVISION 1 TEAMS
1. Rochester 108
2. Grand Haven 154
3. Traverse City Central 166

4. Rochester Adams	188
5. Saline	193
6. Rockford	209
7. Livonia Churchill	225
8. Troy	240
9. Brighton	258
10. Ann Arbor Huron	277
11. Grand Blanc	298
12. Milford	306
13. Lake Orion	311
14. Grand Ledge	313
15. Pinckney	355
16. Woodhaven	379
17. Clarkston	401
18. Livonia Stevenson	422
19. Holland West Ottawa	479
20. Walled Lake Western	488
21. Canton	494
22. Grosse Pointe South	552
23. Okemos	560
24. Bay City Western	564
25. Flushing	709
26. Grosse Pointe North	717

2007 GIRLS DIVISION 1 INDIVIDUALS

1. Shannon Osika (Waterford Mott)9	17:36
2. Audrey Huth (Utica)11	17:40
3. Cally Macumber (Rochester Adams)11	17:46
4. Gabrielle Anzalone (Grand Blanc)9	17:47
5. Tiffany Abrahamian (Rochester)12	17:50
6. Allison Rademacher (Grand Ledge)12	18:02
7. Kristen Smith (Clarkston)11	18:05
8. Grace Green (Troy)(11	18:07
9. Taylor Mattarella (Traverse City Central)11	18:10
10. Katie Haines (Rockford)12	18:16
11. Kristen Emmorey (Brighton)9	18:16
12. Julia Otwell (Traverse City Central)10	18:20
13. Brittni Hutton (Milford)12	18:22
14. Mollie Pozolo (Rochester)11	18:23
15. Rachel McFarlane (Livonia Churchill)12	18:23
16. Becca Addison (Grand Haven)11	18:24
17. Courtney Calka (Livonia Stevenson)11	18:28
18. Lindsey Hilton (Rochester Adams)11	18:29
19. Rachel Quaintance (Walled Lake Northern)11	18:29
20. Michelle Moriset (Troy)10	18:31
21. Alex Leptich (Saline)10	18:32
22. Leah Shepherd (East Kentwood)9	18:33
23. Megan Goethals (Rochester)10	18:33
24. Kate Carter (Saline)10	18:34
25. Lindsey Gakenheimer (Monroe)12	18:37
26. Alison White (Midland Dow)10	18:38
27. Emily Morgridge (Milford)12	18:39
28. Allie Hock (Lake Orion)12	18:39
29. Katie Perkins (Traverse City Central)10	18:43
30. Cristina Perez (Grand Haven)12	18:45
31. Alexandria Dawson (Grand Blanc)10	18:46
32. Laura Addison (Grand Haven)9	18:48
33. Jen Rock (Utica Eisenhower)12	18:49
34. Darcy Dubuc (Grand Haven)12	18:51
35. Natalie Webb (Woodhaven)12	18:53
36. Kelly Taylor (Rochester Hills Stoney Creek)11	18:54
37. Kim Secord (Rochester)12	18:57
38. Sarah Thomas (Canton)11	18:57
39. Lindsay Clark (Walled Lake Western)9	18:58
40. Tiffany Kincaid (Clarkston)11	18:58
55. Brook Handler (Rochester)9	19:11
80. Kaitlin Baarck (Rochester)12	19:26
159. Amy Tranchida (Rochester)12	20:28

2008 D1 GIRLS

An epic contest in near-perfect conditions between Megan Goethals of Rochester and defending champ Shannon Osika of Waterford Mott led to the fastest time ever run on the MIS course.

"It was a battle all the way to the end," said Larry Adams, the Rochester coach.

Traverse City Central won its first team title for coach Lisa Taylor, who as an athlete was Class B runner-up for Alma in 1979.

Michigan Int. Speedway, Brooklyn, Nov. 1
2008 GIRLS DIVISION 1 TEAMS

1. Traverse City Central	129
2. Grand Haven	148
3. East Kentwood	189
4. Rockford	195
5. Brighton	220
6. Saline	221
7. Troy	225
8. Livonia Churchill	232
9. Rochester Adams	249
10. Novi	249
11. Ann Arbor Huron	251
12. Clarkston	285
13. Rochester	297
14. Pinckney	326
15. Waterford Mott	401
16. Grand Blanc	421
17. Okemos	435
18. Ann Arbor Pioneer	449
19. Battle Creek Lakeview	452
20. White Lake Lakeland	471
21. Traverse City West	474
22. Grand Ledge	517
23. Grosse Pointe South	578
24. Wyandotte	651
25. Woodhaven	678
26. Grosse Pointe North	708
27. Macomb L'Anse Creuse North	761

2008 GIRLS DIVISION 1 INDIVIDUALS

1. Megan Goethals (Rochester)11	17:11
2. Shannon Osika (Waterford Mott)10	17:18
3. Rebecca Addison (Grand Haven)12	17:29
4. Audrey Huth (Utica)12	17:36
5. Gabrielle Anzalone (Grand Blanc)10	17:37
6. Cally Macumber (Rochester Adams)12	17:51
7. Sara Kroll (Livonia Churchill)11	17:54
8. Courtney Calka (Livonia Stevenson)12	17:56
9. Kristen Smith (Clarkston)12	18:00
10. Lindsey Hilton (Rochester Adams)12	18:14
11. Alissa Williams (East Kentwood)10	18:17
12. Lindsay Clark (Walled Lake Western)10	18:18
13. Amanda Mergaert (Utica)12	18:19
14. Amanda Southwell (Livonia Churchill)11	18:25
15. Sharon Hecker (Grandville)12	18:26
16. Mollie Pozolo (Rochester)12	18:26
17. Allison White (Midland Dow)11	18:27
18. Annie-Norah Beveridge (Ann Arbor Huron)10	18:29
19. Elle Robinson (Novi)12	18:30
20. Katie Perkins (Traverse City Central)11	18:30
21. Catie Rietseam (Rockford)10	18:30
22. Jennifer Snelgrove (Grand Ledge)11	18:31
23. Natalie Smith (Clarkston)9	18:32
24. Julia Valencia (Walled Lake Western)9	18:35
25. Danielle Tepper (Grandville)12	18:35
26. Elizabeth Kingshott (Brighton)9	18:37
27. Alex Leptich (Saline)11	18:39
28. Grace Green (Troy)12	18:43
29. Rachael Steil (Grandville)11	18:45
30. Emily Thomas (Grand Haven)12	18:48
31. Kate Carter (Saline)11	18:49
32. Megan Mcpherson (Livonia Franklin)10	18:50
33. Krista Parks (East Kentwood)11	18:52
34. Julia Otwell (Traverse City Central)11	18:54
35. Marina Aguilera (Monroe)9	18:55
36. Bianca Kubicki (Canton)10	18:55
37. Becky Allor (White Lake Lakeland)12	18:57
38. Taylor Mattarella (Traverse City Central)12	18:58
39. Ellory Green (Brighton)12	18:59
40. Kelcie Severson (Rockford)12	19:01
44. Maren Bahra (Traverse City Central)11	19:06
49. Sam Ehle (Traverse City Central)10	19:08
94. Aimee Marsh (Rochester Adams)10	19:40
140. Alison Ostema (Traverse City Central)12	20:07

2009 D1 GIRLS

The footing was soft, the wind was howling. Yet Megan Goethals of Rochester delivered the finest—and fastest cross country performance in state history.

Ripping through splits of 5:27 and 10:53, the senior destroyed the field in racking up the biggest winning margin in meet history. Not only was she the only athlete under 17:00, she was the only one under 18:00 with her official time of 16:54.8.

And it was not as if she was running against an untalented field. In her wake were athletes who would become NCAA Div. All-Americans in cross country (Avery Evenson, Jamie Morrisey), All-Americans in track (Brook Handler, Morrisey, Shannon Osika), and Big 10 individual champions (Sara Kroll, Haley Meier, Hannah Meier, Morrisey, Osika).

Goethals did it despite the wind. "That was awful. Once you go onto the track it was like a wind tunnel. I kept telling myself, 'Almost there, almost there.'

"I looked back once and someone yelled, 'Don't look back again!' I never knew how close or far they were from me. There was so much noise out here, I kept thinking they were right behind me.

"This was probably the most determined I've been. I've been focused on this race the whole season. I knew my goal was to break 17 here,."

Mike Smith's Saline squad took the team win with a 51-point margin over Rockford. The win also created perhaps an unprecedented father-son coaching connection, as Mike Smith's father Gordon coached Napoleon to the boys Class CD title in 1949.

Megan Goethals became the first girl to break 17:00 on the MIS course. She won by more than a minute. (Pete Draugalis photo)

Michigan Int. Speedway, Brooklyn, Nov. 7
2009 GIRLS DIVISION 1 TEAMS

1. Saline	141
2. Rockford	192
3. Grosse Pointe South	212
4. Traverse City Central	218
5. Pinckney	253
6. Troy	257
7. Grandville	294
8. Salem	317
9. Birmingham Seaholm	325
10. Ann Arbor Pioneer	332
11. Livonia Churchill	334
12. Grand Haven	341
13. East Kentwood	347
14. Grand Ledge	375
15. Hartland	375

16. Waterford Mott....... 396
17. Rochester....... 400
18. Milford....... 409
19. Alpena....... 417
20. Romeo....... 422
21. Northville....... 435
22. Sterling Heights Stevenson....... 438
23. Brighton....... 501
24. Midland....... 517
25. Monroe....... 543
26. Midland Dow....... 549
27. Rochester Hills Stoney Creek....... 630
28. Temperance Bedford....... 680

2009 GIRLS DIVISION 1 INDIVIDUALS
1. Megan Goethals (Rochester)12....... 16:55
2. Avery Evenson (Hartland)9....... 18:11
3. Sara Kroll (Livonia Churchill)12....... 18:11
4. Hannah Meier (Grosse Pointe South)9....... 18:18
5. Alex Leptich (Saline)12....... 18:20
6. Michelle Moriset (Troy)12....... 18:24
7. Shannon Osika (Waterford Mott)11....... 18:31
8. Haley Meier (Grosse Pointe South)9....... 18:35
9. Alissa Williams (East Kentwood)11....... 18:36
10. Kate Carter (Saline)12....... 18:40
11. Krista Parks (East Kentwood)12....... 18:42
12. Jackie Mullins (Novi)9....... 18:43
13. Brook Handler (Rochester)11....... 18:46
14. Taylor Stepanski (Alpena)10....... 18:47
15. Elizaveta Boudreau (Ann Arbor Pioneer)12. 18:51
16. Allison White (Midland Dow)12....... 18:56
17. Jamie Morrissey (Rochester Adams)9....... 18:58
18. Jane Hawks (Rockford)10....... 18:59
19. Brooke Kovacic (Oxford)9....... 19:00
20. Julia Valencia (Walled Lake Western)10....... 19:01
21. Julia Otwell (Traverse City Central)12....... 19:07
22. Tess Wilberding (Birmingham Seaholm)9 ... 19:08
23. Karyn Rapundalo (Ann Arbor Huron)11....... 19:10
24. Lauren Kettle (Milford)11....... 19:11
25. Mallory Wilberding (Birmingham Seaholm)9 19:12
26. Rachael Steil (Grandville)12....... 19:15
27. Sammy Mondry (Grandville)9....... 19:16
28. Lindsay Clark (Walled Lake Western)11....... 19:17
29. Leah Shepherd (East Kentwood)11....... 19:18
30. Annie-Norah Beveridge (Ann Arb Huron)11 19:19
31. Victoria Tripp (Salem)11....... 19:25
32. Katie Carlson (Rockford)12....... 19:29
33. Sarah Johnson (Rochester Adams)10....... 19:30
34. Melanie Brender (Sterling H Stevenson)12. 19:31
35. Bianca Kubicki (Canton)11....... 19:31
36. Shelby Jackson (Romeo)10....... 19:31
37. Chirstina Firl (Grosse Pointe South)9....... 19:32
38. Laura Addison (Grand Haven)11....... 19:32
39. Marina Aguilera (Monroe)10....... 19:33
40. Alyssa Cummings (Saline)9....... 19:34
50. Emily Reyst (Saline)9....... 19:46
69. Katie Colosimo (Saline)10....... 20:03
137. Amy Creutz (Saline)10....... 20:49
174. Chelsea Noble (Saline)12....... 21:16

2010 D1 GIRLS

It came down to the final sprint between Rochester's Brook Handler and Grand Blanc senior Gabi Anzalone. After following Anzalone through splits of 5:23 and 10:55, Handler mounted the best drive to the line, winning 17:00.2 to 17:01.7.

"It's crazy. I never expected this," Handler told RunMichigan. "I never imagined I could drop a minute and a half in a year."

Handler described it as a battle. "Especially the last mile. She threw in some really good surges. There were a couple of times I didn't know if I was going to be able to answer. And then when we got to the 3M mark, I knew I had 160m to go. I just really wanted it. I knew I had the sprinting ability."

Grand Haven, coached by Greg Russick, won its first-ever team title. The squad was led by frosh Claire Borchers, who despite not running on the track team, went on to become an All-American steeplechaser for Michigan.

Michigan Int. Speedway, Brooklyn, Nov. 6 ⊠
2010 GIRLS DIVISION 1 TEAMS
1. Grand Haven....... 135
2. Traverse City Central....... 154
3. Rockford....... 167
4. Northville....... 169
5. Pinckney....... 174
6. Grosse Pointe South....... 200
7. Saline....... 224
8. Midland Dow....... 274
9. Grand Blanc....... 305
10. Salem....... 318
11. Rochester Hills Stoney Creek....... 340
12. Midland....... 344
13. Troy....... 355
14. Milford....... 381
15. Dexter....... 382
16. Brighton....... 448
17. Caledonia....... 448
18. Monroe....... 471
19. Livonia Franklin....... 474
20. Lake Orion....... 481
21. Hudsonville....... 481
22. Ann Arbor Pioneer....... 488
23. Waterford Mott....... 506
24. Walled Lake Northern....... 508
25. Grand Ledge....... 624
26. Grosse Pointe North....... 651
27. Sterling Heights Stevenson....... 675

Brook Handler won the homestretch battle with Grand Blanc's Gabrielle Anzalone. (Pete Draugalis photo)

2010 GIRLS DIVISION 1 INDIVIDUALS
1. Brook Handler (Rochester)12....... 17:01
2. Gabrielle Anzalone (Grand Blanc)12....... 17:02
3. Hannah Meier (Grosse Pointe South)10....... 17:22
4. Erin Finn (West Bloomfield)10....... 17:31
5. Shannon Osika (Waterford Mott)12....... 17:38
6. Lindsay Clark (Walled Lake Western)12....... 17:53
7. Haley Meier (Grosse Pointe South)10....... 17:55
8. Alissa Williams (East Kentwood)12....... 17:59
9. Callie Clark (Pinckney)12....... 18:00
10. Claire Borchers (Grand Haven)9....... 18:01
11. Avery Evenson (Hartland)10....... 18:02
12. Brooke Kovacic (Oxford)10....... 18:03
13. Megan McPherson (Livonia Franklin)12....... 18:03
14. Rachel Clark (Pinckney)12....... 18:09
15. Taylor Manett (Rockford)11....... 18:09
16. Rachel Barrett (Milford)9....... 18:10
17. Tess Wilberding (Birmingham Seaholm)10 .. 18:11
18. Morgan Bridgewater (White Lk Lakeland)11 18:13
19. Jamie Morrissey (Rochester Adams)10....... 18:16
20. Christina Firl (Grosse Pointe South)10....... 18:17
21. Miranda Belcher (Traverse City Central)11 .. 18:18
22. Anna Pasternak (Hartland)12....... 18:19
23. Bianca Kubicki (Canton)12....... 18:19
24. Laura Addison (Grand Haven)12....... 18:21
25. Julia Valencia (Walled Lake Western)11....... 18:24
26. Lauren Marsh (Traverse City Central)9....... 18:25
27. Kayla Kavulich (Salem)9....... 18:26
28. Kerri McMahan (Novi)9....... 18:32
29. Annie-Norah Beveridge (Ann Arb Huron)12. 18:33
30. Sammy Mondry (Grandville)10....... 18:34
31. Jordan Storer (Midland Dow)9....... 18:36
32. Shannon Boyce (Romeo)10....... 18:37
33. Catie Rietsema (Rockford)12....... 18:44
34. Aubrey Wilberding (Birm. Seaholm)10....... 18:45
35. Lauren Halpern (Ann Arbor Skyline)10....... 18:46
36. Julia Stock (Grand Haven)11....... 18:46
37. Kellie Mussell (Midland Dow)12....... 18:48
38. Amy Creutz (Saline)11....... 18:49
39. Nicole Mosteller Northville)9....... 18:51
40. Kailey Sickmiller (Grosse Pointe North)12 ... 18:52
77. Cristina Perez (Grand Haven)12....... 19:17
82. Kristi King (Grand Haven)11....... 19:19
109. Priscilla Vanheest (Grand Haven)11....... 19:34
162. Natalie Myers (Grand Haven)12....... 20:01

2011 D1 GIRLS

It took a while for it to hit Erin Finn. "I finished the race and I was talking and I was like, 'OK, cool, it was a good race.' Then it was a couple of minutes after I thought, 'Oh my gosh, I just won the state championship race.' I have been dreaming about it since I could walk. It's just incredible."

The finish was the closest ever in meet history, with Finn, who had led through splits of 5:31 and 11:04—and had a 6-second edge at the 3M mark—surviving the fast finishes of Rockford's Taylor Manett and Grosse Pointe South's Hannah Meier. Finn clocked 17:22.6, with Manett at 17:24.0 and Meier at 17:24.1.

Grosse Pointe South, coached by Steve Zaranek, won the title with a slim 5-point margin over Saline. Said Meier of some of the team's younger runners, "They dropped their times by about 15 seconds and they knew it was up to them to get there, to get their places down if we wanted to get near the top."

Michigan Int. Speedway, Brooklyn, Nov. 5 ⊠
2011 GIRLS DIVISION 1 TEAMS
1. Grosse Pointe South....... 106
2. Saline....... 111
3. Grand Haven....... 163
4. Birmingham Seaholm....... 185
5. Rockford....... 232
6. Rochester Adams....... 232
7. Traverse City Central....... 235
8. Northville....... 259
9. Hudsonville....... 286
10. Grand Ledge....... 293
11. Oxford....... 306
12. Troy....... 336
13. Midland Dow....... 361
14. Livonia Churchill....... 373
15. Brighton....... 375
16. Clarkston....... 381
17. East Kentwood....... 465
18. Caledonia....... 474
19. Temperance Bedford....... 474
20. Sterling Heights Stevenson....... 482
21. Traverse City West....... 492
22. Dexter....... 514
23. Hartland....... 521
24. Pinckney....... 531
25. Waterford Mott....... 568
26. Grosse Pointe North....... 671
27. Okemos....... 757
28. Woodhaven....... 760

2011 GIRLS DIVISION 1 INDIVIDUALS
1. Erin Finn (West Bloomfield)11....... 17:23
2. Taylor Manett (Rockford)12....... 17:24
3. Hannah Meier (Grosse Pointe South)11....... 17:25
4. Shelby Jackson (Romeo)12....... 17:45

5. Avery Evenson (Hartland)11 ... 17:58
6. Brooke Kovacic (Oxford)11 ... 18:04
7. Bailey Parmelee Greenville)12 ... 18:11
8. Gabby Thivierge (Rochester Adams)11 ... 18:12
9. Jamie Morrissey (Rochester Adams)11 ... 18:19
10. Kelsie Schwartz (Grosse Pointe South)10 ... 18:22
11. Aubrey Wilberding (Birming Seaholm)11 ... 18:24
12. Haley Meier (Grosse Pointe South)11 ... 18:25
13. Julia Valencia (Walled Lake Western)12 ... 18:25
14. Jordan Storer (Midland Dow)10 ... 18:26
15. Rachel Barrett (Milford)10 ... 18:31
16. Claire Borchers (Grand Haven)10 ... 18:33
17. Roxy Glasser (Grand Haven)10 ... 18:34
18. Natalie Smith Clarkston)12 ... 18:36
19. Sammy Mondry (Grandville)11 ... 18:40
20. Kerigan Riley (Livonia Churchill)11 ... 18:41
21. Ersula Farrow (Grosse Pointe South)9 ... 18:42
22. Jane Hawks (Rockford)12 ... 18:43
23. Abby Rentschler (Saline)9 ... 18:43
24. Nicole Kowalchick (Roch. Hills Stoney C)10 18:44
25. Lauren Green (Saline)9 ... 18:45
26. Morgan Bridgewater (White L Lakeland)12 .. 18:45
27. Jessica Goethals (Rochester)10 ... 18:46
28. Maria Lepore (Rochester)12 ... 18:48
29. Christy Snelgrove Grand Ledge)11 ... 18:51
30. Amy Creutz (Saline)12 ... 18:52
31. Molly Peregrine (Traverse City Central)10 ... 18:55
32. Lauren Miller (Troy)10 ... 18:56
33. Elianna Shwayder (Saline)10 ... 18:58
34. Julia Demko (Birmingham Seaholm)9 ... 18:59
35. Audrey Belf (Birmingham Seaholm)9 ... 19:00
36. Heather Smith Farmington Hills Mercy)12 ... 19:00
37. Jackie Mullins (Novi)11 ... 19:01
38. Brittany Johnson (Oxford)12 ... 19:02
39. Sarah Johnson (Rochester Adams)12 ... 19:02
40. Hayley Williamson Brighton)11 ... 19:03
102. Megan Sklarski (Grosse Pointe South)9 ... 19:42
175. Carolyn Sullivan (Grosse Pointe South)12 . 20:33
221. Nicole Keller (Grosse Pointe South)11 ... 21:28

West Bloomfield's Erin Finn won her second title in 2012. (Pete Draugalis photo)

2012 D1 GIRLS

Erin Finn successfully defended her title, dominating the race after battling anemia much of the season. "With my iron problem that I've had all season, I don't have the speed that these other girls have and I knew it would kill me if I went out with them. So I held back and went at my race pace until I caught up with Hannah [Meier]."

Finn caught Meier before the mile (5:18) and had a 14-second lead at the 2M (10:57). "Once I passed Hannah and she didn't go with me I knew it was mine," she said. I could tell she spent a lot in the first K and I was barely getting started. I knew I was not going to let her pass me no matter what."

Birmingham Seaholm, coached by Jeff Devantier, upset defended Grosse Pointe South for the team title.

Michigan Int. Speedway, Brooklyn, Nov. 3 ⊠
2012 GIRLS DIVISION 1 TEAMS
1. Birmingham Seaholm ... 69
2. Grosse Pointe South ... 88
3. Saline ... 101
4. Traverse City Central ... 244
5. Northville ... 265
6. Sterling Heights Stevenson ... 273
7. Brighton ... 277
8. Salem ... 297
9. Grand Haven ... 306
10. Rockford ... 313
11. Rochester Adams ... 338
12. Grandville ... 343
13. Oxford ... 365
14. Clarkston ... 373
15. Hudsonville ... 374
16. Caledonia ... 422
17. Midland Dow ... 425
18. Grand Ledge ... 426
19. Milford ... 434
20. Waterford Mott ... 449
21. Livonia Churchill ... 469
22. East Lansing ... 475
23. Dexter ... 503
24. Troy ... 520
25. Temperance Bedford ... 691
26. Davison ... 738
27. Woodhaven ... 761

2012 GIRLS DIVISION 1 INDIVIDUALS
1. Erin Finn (West Bloomfield)12 ... 17:08
2. Hannah Meier (Grosse Pointe South)12 ... 17:35
3. Jamie Morrissey (Rochester Adams)12 ... 17:49
4. Aubrey Wilberding (Birm. Seaholm)12 ... 17:56
5. Gabrielle Thiviergg (Rochester Adams)12 ... 17:57
6. Elianna Shwayder (Saline)11 ... 18:03
7. Brooke Kovacic (Oxford)12 ... 18:05
8. Ersula Farrow (Grosse Pointe South)10 ... 18:06
9. Jessica Goethals (Rochester)11 ... 18:10
10. Alex Berends (Hudsonville)11 ... 18:14
11. Kayla Kavulich (Salem)11 ... 18:16
12. Tess Wilberding (Birmingham Seaholm)12 .. 18:17
13. Addie May (Flushing)10 ... 18:19
14. Kelsie Schwartz (Grosse Pointe South)11 ... 18:23
15. Marissa Dobry (Birmingham Seaholm)9 ... 18:24
16. Valerie Wierenga (Grandville)9 ... 18:25
17. Hannah Schroder (Caledonia)12 ... 18:26
18. Roxy Glasser (Grand Haven)11 ... 18:27
19. Allison Shannon (Sterling Hts Stevenson)9 . 18:27
20. Rachel DaDamio (Birmingham Seaholm)10 18:28
21. Jackie Feist (Birmingham Groves)11 ... 18:29
22. Rachel Walny (Clinton T Chippewa Vall)11 . 18:29
23. Alexandria Cell (Ann Arbor Huron)11 ... 18:30
24. Molly Peregrine (Traverse City Central)11 ... 18:30
25. Lauren Green (Saline)10 ... 18:31
26. Gillian Walter (Saline)9 ... 18:31
27. Olivia Bordewyk (Caledonia)10 ... 18:32
28. Claire Borchers (Grand Haven)11 ... 18:32
29. Daya Wagh (Waterford Mott)12 ... 18:32
30. Samantha Hanson (Sterling H Stevenson)9 18:33
31. Gloria Park (Saline)11 ... 18:33
32. Haley Meier (Grosse Pointe South)12 ... 18:33
33. Audrey Belf (Birmingham Seaholm)10 ... 18:33
34. Sarah Goble (East Lansing)10 ... 18:34
35. Ellie Leonard (Jenison)11 ... 18:34
36. Bailey Johnson (Jenison)10 ... 18:37
37. Kallie Dent (Midland Dow)11 ... 18:39
38. Kerigan Riley (Livonia Churchill)12 ... 18:40
39. Serena Gale-Butto (Muskegon M Shores)12 18:40
40. Nicole Hanson (Clarkston)9 ... 18:41
104. Julia Demko (Birmingham Seaholm)10 ... 19:21
129. Hannah Kenny (Grand Haven)9 ... 19:39

2013 D1 GIRLS

Seaholm tried to make it two in a row, but this was the year of Nancy Smith's Northville squad The Mustang lead pack of four was separated by only 10.8 seconds on a muddy day at MIS.

"We have a great pack," said Smith. "We have seven girls that can really pack together. That is truly what won it today. We worked as a team."

Seaholm did get the individual winner in junior Audrey Belf. "I never had that much pressure in my life," she said. "I kind of stopped using the Internet for a week. I didn't want to see anything or have any reason ro psyche myself out. I wanted to go into the race with a clear head."

Michigan Int. Speedway, Brooklyn, Nov. 2 ⊠
2013 GIRLS DIVISION 1 TEAMS
1. Northville ... 107
2. Saline ... 139
3. Hudsonville ... 164
4. Birmingham Seaholm ... 165
5. Rockford ... 169
6. Traverse City Central ... 170
7. Grosse Pointe South ... 236
8. Brighton ... 255
9. Milford ... 322
10. Salem ... 339
11. Jenison ... 341
12. Midland Dow ... 357
13. Walled Lake Northern ... 374
14. Grandville ... 382
15. Sterling Heights Stevenson ... 399
16. Utica Eisenhower ... 427
17. East Lansing ... 439
18. Grand Haven ... 451
19. Dexter ... 470
20. Grosse Pointe North ... 492
21. Bay City Western ... 511
22. Bloomfield Hills ... 524
23. Forest Hills Central ... 535
24. Lake Orion ... 561
25. Clarkston ... 572
26. Troy ... 587
27. Temperance Bedford ... 609
28. Ann Arbor Pioneer ... 609

2013 GIRLS DIVISION 1 INDIVIDUALS
1. Audrey Belf (Birmingham Seaholm)11 ... 17:32
2. Lauren Brasure (Rockford)12 ... 17:41
3. Valerie Wierenga (Grandville)10 ... 17:58
4. Elianna Shwayder (Saline)12 ... 18:07
5. Jordan Storer (Midland Dow)12 ... 18:09
6. Ellie Leonard (Jenison)12 ... 18:10
7. Ersula Farrow (Grosse Pointe South)11 ... 18:13
8. Marissa Dobry (Birmingham Seaholm)10 ... 18:18
9. Kali Dent (Midland Dow)12 ... 18:21
10. Rachel Coleman (Northville)12 ... 18:24
11. Alex Berends (Hudsonville)12 ... 18:25
12. Ashley Ko (Traverse City Central)11 ... 18:27
13. Lexa Barrott (Northville)10 ... 18:27
14. Taleen Shahrigian (Northville)12 ... 18:31
15. Rachel Barrett (Milford)12 ... 18:31
16. Gillian Walter (Saline)10 ... 18:32
17. Kerianne Schoff (Rockford)11 ... 18:32
18. Claire Borchers (Grand Haven)12 ... 18:32
19. Hannah Cummings (Saline)10 ... 18:33
20. Jessica Goethals (Rochester)12 ... 18:34
21. Kelli Jackson (Hudsonville)11 ... 18:34
22. Cayla Eckenroth (Northville)9 ... 18:35
23. Jennifer Rogers (Farmington)12 ... 18:35
24. Samantha Allmacher (Utica Eisenhower)11 18:36
25. Molly Peregrine (Traverse City Central)12 ... 18:36
26. Nicole Kowalchick (Roch. H Stoney Crk)12. 18:37
27. Kelsie Schwartz (Grosse Pointe South)12 ... 18:38
28. Abby Green (Troy)12 ... 18:38
29. Danielle Bentzley (Birmingham Seaholm)12 18:40
30. Marah Pugh (Macomb Dakota)12 ... 18:40
31. Gloria Park (Saline)12 ... 18:44
32. Samantha Hanson (SH Stevenson)10 ... 18:46
33. Andrea Crowe (Brighton)9 ... 18:47
34. Morgan Harney (Rockford)12 ... 18:47
35. Alexandria Cell (Ann Arbor Huron)12 ... 18:49
36. Alexis Munley (Waterford Mott)9 ... 18:49
37. Mallory Barrett (Milford)9 ... 18:50

38. Nicole Hanson (Clarkston)10 .... 18:51
39. Hannah Lonergan (Novi)11 .... 18:52
40. Brianna Mulrooney (Walled Lk Northern)9 .. 18:52
61. Nicole Mosteller (Northville)12 .... 19:11
66. Erin Zimmer (Northville)12 .... 19:12
100. Emma Herrmann (Northville)10 .... 19:33

2014 D1 GIRLS

Seniors Audrey Belf and Rachel DaDamio led Seaholm to the win over Traverse City Central with a 1-2 punch.

"I wanted to stay behind a little bit at the start," Belf told Bill Khan, "but people were not going out as fast as I'd hoped, so I kind of just took it there. In the second mile, I got caught up in the wind. I felt I should have pushed through more and finished strong, but I can't complain."

Notably, DaDamio finished out her high school career with a strong runner-up performance, despite never having won a race in high school. "It doesn't make a difference to me," she said. "I just want to constantly improve for myself."

Belf would go on to win All-Big East honors at Georgetown before transferring to Michigan. DaDamio would win All-ACC honors for Notre Dame.

Audrey Belf repeated in 2014. (Pete Draugalis photo)

Michigan Int. Speedway, Brooklyn, Nov. 1
2014 GIRLS DIVISION 1 TEAMS
1. Birmingham Seaholm 88
2. Traverse City Central 115
3. Northville 135
4. Milford 169
5. Saline 230
6. Rockford 258
7. Sterling Heights Stevenson 264
8. Clarkston 272
9. Brighton 317
10. Woodhaven 356
11. Salem 358
12. Grand Rapids Kenowa Hills 368
13. Grosse Pointe South 371
14. Hudsonville 410
15. Waterford Mott 417
16. Ann Arbor Pioneer 426

17. Dexter 454
18. Rochester 467
19. Grandville 473
20. Grand Haven 483
21. Flushing 492
22. Lake Orion 501
23. Walled Lake Northern 512
24. Livonia Churchill 527
25. Davison 566
26. Grosse Pointe North 657
27. Macomb L'Anse Creuse North 674

2014 GIRLS DIVISION 1 INDIVIDUALS
1. Audrey Belf (Birmingham Seaholm)12 .... 17:19
2. Rachel DaDamio (Birmingham Seaholm)12 ... 17:30
3. Karenna Duffey (Macomb L'Anse Creuse N)9 17:34
4. Rachel Bonner (Port Huron)11 .... 17:55
5. Sielle Kearney (Traverse City Central)9 .... 17:58
6. Ersula Farrow (Oak Park)12 .... 17:58
7. Anne Forsyth (Ann Arbor Pioneer)9 .... 17:59
8. Ashley Ko (Traverse City Central)12 .... 17:59
9. Kelli Jackson (Hudsonville)12 .... 18:01
10. Emma Wilson (Romeo)11 .... 18:05
11. Cayla Eckenroth (Northville)10 .... 18:09
12. Maddy Trevisan (Farmington)11 .... 18:13
13. Madison Troy (Grandville)9 .... 18:16
14. Lynsie Gram (Clarkston)12 .... 18:17
15. Lexa Barrott (Northville)11 .... 18:19
16. Samantha Hanson (SH Stevenson)11 .... 18:20
17. Mallory Barrett (Milford)10 .... 18:20
18. Brianna Mulrooney (Walled Lake N)10 .... 18:22
19. Bailey Johnson (Jenison)12 .... 18:21
20. Julia Demko (Birmingham Seaholm)12 .... 18:22
21. Hannah Lonergan (Novi)12 .... 18:22
22. Grace Cutler (Royal Oak)10 .... 18:22
23. Nicole Hanson (Clarkston)11 .... 18:24
24. Hannah Cummings (Saline)11 .... 18:24
25. Madeline Wesley (Clinton Chippewa Val)12 18:26
26. Nicole Grindling (Milford)9 .... 18:32
27. Hailey Harris (Northville)11 .... 18:33
28. Madison Paquette (Milford)12 .... 18:34
29. Madison Goen (GR Kenowa Hills)11 .... 18:35
30. Clarissa Hoye (Woodhaven)9 .... 18:36
31. Allison Shannon (Sterling H Stevenson)11 .. 18:39
32. Emmalyne Tarsa (Traverse City Central)10 . 18:41
33. Emma Herrmann (Northville)11 .... 18:47
34. Alexis Munley (Waterford Mott)10 .... 18:49
35. Camryn Gabriel (Rockford)9 .... 18:50
36. Lauren Arquette (Salem)11 .... 18:50
37. Madison Marciniak (Bay City Western)12 .... 18:50
38. Gillian Walter (Saline)11 .... 18:51
39. Lauren Kaliszewski (Rochester)10 .... 18:52
40. Audrey Ladd (Birmingham Seaholm)10 .... 18:52
54. Mary Sanders (Birmingham Seaholm)11 ..... 19:01
63. Patty Girardot (Birmingham Seaholm)11 ..... 19:09
68. Rachel McCardell (Birmingham Seaholm)9 .19:17

2015 D1 GIRLS

The year after graduating the winner and runner-up from the previous year, Seaholm managed to win again, this time by 46 points over Brighton.

"Coming into this season, we were not expecting to win," said lead runner Audrey Ladd. "We lost our top three from last year and they were all so professional about how they ran. So our goal was maybe top three… Then slowly throughout the season we got confident we could actually do this, so it means a lot. Every girl in our top seven contributed so much to this race."

Sophomore Madison Troy of Grandville outkicked Saline's Jessi Larson and Farmington's Maddi Trevisan for the individual win. "Our group of three kinda kicked in and sprinted it out."

Michigan Int. Speedway, Brooklyn, Nov. 7
2015 GIRLS DIVISION 1 TEAMS
1. Birmingham Seaholm 90
2. Brighton 136
3. Milford 149

4. Northville 150
5. Saline 186
6. Waterford Mott 211
7. Rockford 291
8. Ann Arbor Pioneer 301
9. Traverse City Central 303
10. Pinckney 320
11. Clarkston 346
12. Rochester Adams 352
13. Grosse Pointe South 369
14. Portage Northern 378
15. Salem 404
16. Grand Haven 408
17. Farmington 425
18. Grandville 426
19. Midland Dow 441
20. Lake Orion 504
21. Forest Hills Central 508
22. Troy 516
23. Wyandotte 553
24. Saginaw Heritage 556
25. Bay City Western 562
26. Monroe 614
27. Grosse Pointe North 699

Madison Troy won a close one in 2015, outlegging Maddy Trevison and Jessi Larson (left) in the stretch. (Pete Draugalis photo)

2015 GIRLS DIVISION 1 INDIVIDUALS
1. Madison Troy (Grandville)10 .... 17:29
2. Jessi Larson (Saline)10 .... 17:31
3. Maddy Trevisan (Farmington)12 .... 17:32
4. Sielle Kearney (Traverse City Central)10 ...... 17:42
5. Emma Wilson (Romeo)12 .... 17:42
6. Grace Cutler (Royal Oak)11 .... 17:46
7. Mallory Barrett (Milford)11 .... 17:48
8. Lexa Barrott (Northville)12 .... 18:01
9. Rachel Bonner (Port Huron)12 .... 18:04
10. Victoria Heiligenthal (Milford)9 .... 18:05
11. Audrey Ladd (Birmingham Seaholm)11 ...... 18:07
12. Abby Inch (Farmington)9 .... 18:14
13. Anne Forsyth (Ann Arbor Pioneer)10 .... 18:20
14. Karenna Duffey (Mac L'Anse Creuse N)10 .. 18:21
15. Rylee Robinson (Waterford Mott)9 .... 18:22
16. Rachel McCardell (Birmingham Seaholm)10 18:22
17. Gabby Hentemann (Grand Haven)9 .... 18:22
18. Mary Sanders (Birmingham Seaholm)12 ..... 18:22
19. Patty Girardot (Birmingham Seaholm)12 ..... 18:23
20. Alexa Vanderhoff (Portage Northern)12 ...... 18:24
21. Emily Wall (Midland Dow)11 .... 18:25
22. Natalie Douglas (Livonia Franklin)12 .... 18:28
23. Anna Piccione (Grosse Pointe South)12 ..... 18:29
24. Olivia Clymer (White Lake Lakeland)10 ...... 18:29
25. Samantha Hanson (SH Stevenson)12 .... 18:31
26. Jacalyn Overdier (Ann Arbor Pioneer)11 ..... 18:32
27. Peyton Witt (Portage Northern)9 .... 18:32
28. Kirsten McGahan (Brighton)12 .... 18:33
29. Miranda Reynolds (Brighton)11 .... 18:33
30. Jenna Sica (Brighton)12 .... 18:35
31. Madeline Rehm (White Lake Lakeland)9 .... 18:37
32. Camryn Gabriel (Rockford)10 .... 18:37
33. Nicole Hanson (Clarkston)12 .... 18:40

34. Hannah Cummings (Saline)12 ...... 18:42
35. Courtney Jarema (Pinckney)9 ...... 18:42
36. Katie Osika (Waterford Mott)10 ...... 18:43
37. Brianna Mulrooney (Walled Lk Northern)11 .18:43
38. Stephanie Vanis (East Lansing)12 ...... 18:43
39. Jessica Gockley (Traverse City West)12...... 18:43
40. Emma Herrmann (Northville)12 ...... 18:44
53. Emily Rooney (Birmingham Seaholm)10...... 18:55
67. Kati Beckeman (Birmingham Seaholm)10...... 19:06
104. Lily Tripp (Birmingham Seaholm)9 ...... 19:35

2016 D1 GIRLS

Only 93rd a year before, Battle Creek Lakeview's Maggie Farrell improved phenomenally as a senior, crusing to a solid win over Pioneer's Anne Forsyth.

"I felt like I ran pretty smart. I started out with the pack up until the 2M mark and started to pull away at the end. It kind of got a little rough at the end because it was a really muddy day here, especially near the track."

Milford won its first girls title by 18 points over Pioneer. The Mavericks' 150 points was the highest winning tally in meet history. Said lead runner Mallory Barrett: "We weren't sure how good we could be, and coming in nobody was talking about us. We were definitely under the radar."

Lakeview's Maggie Farrell.
(Pete Draugalis photo)

Michigan Int. Speedway, Brooklyn, Nov. 5 ⌧
2016 GIRLS DIVISION 1 TEAMS
1. Milford 150
2. Ann Arbor Pioneer 172
3. Northville 178
4. Birmingham Seaholm 188
5. Pinckney 258
6. Battle Creek Lakeview 266
7. Traverse City Central 269
8. Troy 297
9. Saline 298
10. Clarkston 299
11. Brighton 302
12. Grand Haven 304
13. Midland Dow 319
14. Rockford 328
15. White Lake Lakeland 334
16. Waterford Mott 373
17. Livonia Churchill 396
18. Salem 459
19. Flushing 461
20. Oxford 468
21. Holland West Ottawa 475
22. Saginaw Heritage 505
23. Okemos 511
24. Wyandotte 538
25. Grosse Pointe South 561
26. Romeo 562
27. Hudsonville 582

2016 GIRLS DIVISION 1 INDIVIDUALS
1. Maggie Farrell (Battle Creek Lakeview)12 ..... 17:26
2. Anne Forsyth (Ann Arbor Pioneer)11 ...... 17:35
3. Karenna Duffey (Mac L'Anse Creuse N)11 ... 18:01
4. Kyla Christopher-Moody (W Bloomfield)10 ... 18:01
5. Madison Malon (Grandville)10 ...... 18:05
6. Anna Jensen (Midland Dow)9 ...... 18:07
7. Sielle Kearney (Traverse City Central)11 ...... 18:17
8. Rylee Robinson (Waterford Mott)10 ...... 18:17
9. Mallory Barrett (Milford)12 ...... 18:17
10. Audrey Ladd (Birmingham Seaholm)12 ...... 18:17
11. Katie Osika (Waterford Mott)11 ...... 18:21
12. Olivia Schroder (Caledonia)12 ...... 18:21
13. Rachel McCardell (Birmingham Seaholm)11 18:25
14. Victoria Heiligenthal (Milford)10 ...... 18:27
15. Jessi Lindstrom (Flushing)12 ...... 18:31
16. Cambria Tiemann (Fenton)10 ...... 18:32
17. Alexa Keiser (Fenton)9 ...... 18:36
18. Gabby Hentemann (Grand Haven)10 ...... 18:36
19. Logann Haluszka (Battle Crk Lakeview)11 .. 18:36
20. Jenna Magness (Grand Ledge)12 ...... 18:38
21. Jessi Larson (Saline)11 ...... 18:41
22. Peyton Witt (Portage Northern)10 ...... 18:43
23. Madeline Rehm (White Lake Lakeland)10 .. 18:44
24. Maija Rettelle (Midland Dow)11 ...... 18:45
25. Ana Barrott (Northville)11 ...... 18:45
26. Samantha Tran (Forest Hills Northern)10 .... 18:46
27. Abby Inch (Farmington)10 ...... 18:48
28. Makayla Perez (Allen Park)11 ...... 18:49
29. Olivia Clymer (White Lake Lakeland)11 ...... 18:49
30. Emily Rooney (Birmingham Seaholm)11 ..... 18:50
31. Cayla Eckenroth (Northville)12 ...... 18:55
32. Ashley Defrain (Port Huron Northern)11 ..... 18:58
33. Nicole Cybul (Northville)10 ...... 19:05
34. Camryn Gabriel (Rockford)11 ...... 19:05
35. Megan Worrel (Troy)11 ...... 19:06
36. Kathleen George (Livonia Churchill)12 .... 19:06
37. Maggie Pawelczyk (Wyandotte)12 ...... 19:08
38. Jacalyn Overdier (Ann Arbor Pioneer)12 ..... 19:09
39. Sydney Dawes (Ann Arbor Pioneer)12 ...... 19:11
40. Caroline George (Livonia Churchill)12 .... 19:17
45. Nicole Grindling (Milford)11 ...... 19:22
62. Natalie Black (Milford)10 ...... 19:33
84. Regan Lobodzinski (Milford)11 ...... 19:48
153. Rachel O'Rourke (Milford)12 ...... 20:26
209. Paige Saiz (Milford)10 ...... 21:11

2017 D1 GIRLS

Ericka VanderLende emerged as a major force. Only 99th the year before, the Rockford junior crushed a 17:17 to win decisively. "It's been a really good season," she said. "I stayed a lot more consistent with my races. Last year, I was kind of all over the place."

Troy, coached by Matt Richardson, surprised many to win the team title by 5 points over Northville. "We knew it was going to be a close race coming in, being ranked third" said Megan Worrel.

Michigan Int. Speedway, Brooklyn, Nov. 4 ⌧
2017 GIRLS DIVISION 1 TEAMS
1. Troy 127
2. Northville 132
3. Rockford 153
4. Ann Arbor Pioneer 180
5. Milford 234
6. Traverse City Central 235
7. Birmingham Seaholm 238
8. Clarkston 257
9. Traverse City West 259
10. Saline 277
11. Pinckney 289
12. Brighton 332
13. East Grand Rapids 336
14. Waterford Mott 377
15. Bay City Western 402
16. Holland West Ottawa 405
17. Lake Orion 418
18. Salem 423
19. Caledonia 453
20. Fenton 471
21. Temperance Bedford 480
22. Grand Haven 497
23. Ann Arbor Skyline 540
24. Rochester Hills Stoney Creek 562
25. Hudsonville 573
26. Berkley 641
27. Bloomfield Hills 690

2017 GIRLS DIVISION 1 INDIVIDUALS
1. Ericka VanderLende (Rockford)11 ...... 17:17
2. Sielle Kearney (Traverse City Central)12 ...... 17:31
3. Rylee Robinson (Waterford Mott)11 ...... 17:35
4. Jessi Larson (Saline)12 ...... 17:49
5. Karenna Duffey (Mac L'Anse Creuse N)12 .... 17:52
6. Rachel McCardell (Birmingham Seaholm)12 . 17:52
7. Kyla Christopher-Moody (West Bloomfield)11 17:54
8. Gabby Hentemann (Grand Haven)11 ...... 17:59
9. Yasmine Mansi (Northville)9 ...... 18:00
10. Madeline Rehm (White Lake Lakeland)11 ... 18:02
11. Abby Inch (Farmington)11 ...... 18:07
12. Victoria Heiligenthal (Milford)11 ...... 18:08
13. Alexa Keiser (Fenton)10 ...... 18:08
14. Megan Worrel (Troy)12 ...... 18:08
15. Anne Forsyth (Ann Arbor Pioneer)12 ...... 18:10
16. Peyton Witt (Portage Northern)11 ...... 18:10
17. Anastasia Tucker (Midland Dow)11 ...... 18:11
18. Nicole Cybul (Northville)11 ...... 18:11
19. Madelyn Malczewski (Romeo)10 ...... 18:13
20. Zofia Dudek (Ann Arbor Pioneer)10 ...... 18:13
21. Camryn Gabriel (Rockford)12 ...... 18:15
22. Leah Socks (Traverse City Central)10 .... 18:15
23. Katie Osika (Waterford Mott)12 ...... 18:16
24. Mia Patria (Clarkston)11 ...... 18:19
25. Ashley Defrain (Port Huron Northern)12 ...... 18:20
26. Hannah Smith (Traverse City West)9 .... 18:22
27. Ana Barrott (Northville)12 ...... 18:24
28. Sophie Novak Lake Orion)9 ...... 18:26
29. Anna Fischer (St Joseph)12 ...... 18:26
30. Emily Rooney (Birmingham Seaholm)12 ...... 18:27
31. Elizabeth Dalrymple (Clarkston)11 ...... 18:28
32. Olivia Clymer (White Lake Lakeland)12 ...... 18:31
33. Ashlyn Nagel (Bay City Western)10 ...... 18:35
34. Andrea Ruiz (Holly)9 ...... 18:40
35. Vivi Eddings (Pinckney)9 ...... 18:41
36. Cambria Tiemann (Fenton)11 ...... 18:41
37. Hannah Palomino (Troy)12 ...... 18:43
38. Kayla Fortino (Saline)11 ...... 18:43
39. Rachel Kempf (Saginaw Heritage)12 ...... 18:43
40. Abby Olson (Holland West Ottawa)10 ...... 18:44
41. Paige Anderson (Troy)9 ...... 18:45
42. Meghan Monaghan (Troy)12 ...... 18:45
44. Katie Scoles (Troy)11 ...... 18:47
85. Lauren Fulcher (Troy)11 ...... 19:13
205. Abby Kerr (Troy)11 ...... 20:30

2018 D1 GIRLS

For Rockford's Ericka VanderLende, the heavy favorite after an undefeated season and a 16:43.3 regional win (which would have qualified her for the boys D1 final—a possibly unprecedented achievement), there was only one strategy: to run away. That she did, having a clear lead as the runners left the stadium at the 800 mark. By the mile (5:23) it was an insurmountable 16-second gap over the large trailing pack.

By 2M (10:56), VanderLende led Pioneer's Zofia Dudek by 30 seconds, Dudek's race keyed a strong Pioneer team effort, with her even being on the team a bit of a surprise. The previous year, the Polish student ran for Pioneer while her father was a visiting professor at Michigan, a one-year appointment. But when that position was renewed, Dudek happily came back for another year.

Inside the MIS oval, the ground became mushier, thanks to the rains that fell all week. VanderLende appeared to have little difficulty with the footing, winning by 50 seconds with her 17:08.4. In a strong burst at the finish, West Bloomfield's Kayla Christopher-Moody tagged Dudek for the runnerup position.

Clarkston surprised many by taking the win over Pioneer, 134-152. Pre-meet favorite Northville struggled to 8th.

Michigan In. Speedway, Brooklyn, Nov. 3
Mostly cloudy, muddy, 40°, breezy.
2018 GIRLS DIVISION 1 TEAMS
1. Clarkston 134
2. Ann Arbor Pioneer 152
3. Pinckney 206
4. Traverse City Central 208
5. Bay City Western 234
6. Saline 239
7. Rockford 241
8. Northville 252
9. Fenton 269
10. Salem 310
11. Holland West Ottawa 352
12. Traverse City West 366
13. Temperance Bedford 383
14. Romeo 388
15. Milford 392
16. Bloomfield Hills 413
17. White Lake Lakeland 424
18. Forest Hills Northern 436
19. Plymouth 446
20. Lake Orion 451
21. Caledonia 454
22. Hudsonville 458
23. Grand Rapids Ottawa Hills 516
24. Troy 519
25. Birmingham Seaholm 539
26. Brighton 583
27. Howell 683

Ericka VanderLende successfully defended for Rockford, making it a total of five girls individual titles for the Rams. (Pete Draugalis)

2018 GIRLS DIVISION 1 INDIVIDUALS
1. Ericka VanderLende (Rockford)12 ....17:09
2. Kyla Christopher-Moody (West Bloomfield)12 .....17:59
3. Zofia Dudek (Ann Arbor Pioneer-POLAND)11 .....18:00
4. Madeline Rehm (White Lake Lakeland)12 ....18:00
5. Sophie Novak (Lake Orion)10 ....18:02
6. Ashlyn Nagel (Bay City Western)11 ....18:07
7. Victoria Heiligenthal (Milford)12 ....18:07
8. Gabby Hentemann (Grand Haven)12 ....18:08
9. Noelle Adriaens (Pinckney)12 ....18:09
10. Julia Flynn (Traverse City Central)9 ....18:10
11. Audrey DaDamio (Birmingham Seaholm)10 .....18:10
12. Abby Inch (Farmington)12 ....18:11
13. Samantha Tran (Forest Hills Northern)12 .....18:11
14. Rylee Robinson (Waterford Mott)12 ....18:13
15. Mia Patria (Clarkston)11 ....18:14

16. Grace Nolan (Clarkston)12 ....18:16
17. Adit Dau (GR Ottawa Hills)9 ....18:25
18. Alexa Keiser (Fenton)11 ....18:29
19. Maryam Sheena (Walled Lake Western)11 .....18:30
20. Lauren Kiley (Plymouth)9 ....18:33
21. Vivi Eddings (Pinckney)10 ....18:33
22. Emma Everhart-Deckard (Rockford)12 ....18:33
23. Hannah Smith (Traverse City West)10 ....18:36
24. Maddy Boyd (Alpena)12 ....18:39
25. Caitlin Rose (Grand Blanc)12 ....18:42
26. Sarah Forsyth (Ann Arbor Pioneer)9 ....18:43
27. Anastasia Tucker (Midland Dow)12 ....18:43
28. Kayla Fortino (Saline)12 ....18:44
29. Nicole Cybul (Northville)12 ....18:44
30. Emily Gordon (Northville)10 ....18:44
31. Allison Sherman (Lake Orion)12 ....18:45
32. Andrea Ruiz (Holly)10 ....18:46
33. Madison Ebright (GR Ottawa Hills)10 ....18:47
34. Madi Wood (Saline)9 ....18:50
35. Jocelyn Henridricks (GR Northview)10 .....18:51
36. Reagan Justice (Salem)10 ....18:52
37. Elizabeth Bulat (Rochester)12 ....18:54
38. Ellie Reynolds (Flushing)10 ....18:55
39. Anna Vogel (Ann Arbor Pioneer)11 ....18:56
40. Elizabeth Dalrymple (Clarkston)12 ....18:59
59. Mallory Ferguson (Clarkston)12 ....19:12
60. Mattie Drennan (Clarkston)10 ....19:13
72. Emily Ferguson (Clarkston)12 ....19:21
208. Elise Wilhelm (Clarkston)9 ....21:04

2019 D1 GIRLS

Zofia Dudek blasted out at the start and never looked back. At 1M (5:23) she led by 11 seconds. At 2M (10:50), the margin was 29 seconds. When she hit the finish in an official time of 17:00.4, she won by 52.6 seconds, the third-biggest margin in meet history. It was a notable performance for a cold, muddy day.

Of the finishing stretch, she said, "It was hard. The wind was really strong. Especially on the curve, where there was really nobody there, it was hard… The conditions weren't perfect."

Ann Arbor Pioneer also celebrated its first win in 22 years—and the first in the post-Bryan Westfield era—after two runner-up finishes in the three previous years.

Six weeks later, Dudek kicked her way to the Foot Locker national title, clocking 16:45 in the San Diego race.

Pioneer's Zofia Dudek won by a stunning 52 seconds. (Pete Draugalis photo)

Michigan In. Speedway, Brooklyn, Nov. 2
2019 GIRLS DIVISION 1 TEAMS
1. Ann Arbor Pioneer 80
2. Traverse City Central 113
3. Saline 182

4. Brighton 197
5. Bay City Western 213
6. Northville 231
7. Holland West Ottawa 237
8. Romeo 282
9. Troy 290
10. Temperance Bedford 374
11. Clarkston 375
12. Grand Blanc 383
13. Jenison 393
14. Caledonia 399
15. Salem 399
16. Rockford 402
17. Forest Hills Northern 404
18. Plymouth 407
19. Fenton 407
20. Milford 466
21. Birmingham Seaholm 187
22. Howell 497
23. Bloomfield Hills 499
24. Rochester Hills Stoney Creek 523
25. Rochester Adams 556
26. Okemos 565
27. Royal Oak 713
28. Sterling Heights Stevenson 787

2019 GIRLS DIVISION 1 INDIVIDUALS
1. Zofia Dudek (Ann Arbor Pioneer-POLAND)12 .... 17:01
2. Arianne Olson (Holland West Ottawa)9 ...... 17:53
3. Julia Flynn (Traverse City Central)10 .... 18:00
4. Madi Wood (Saline)10 .... 18:03
5. Audrey DaDamio (Birmingham Seaholm)11 ..... 18:09
6. Mia Patria (Clarkston)12 .... 18:11
7. Elizabeth Babcock (Novi)11 .... 18:11
8. Alexa Keiser (Fenton)12 .... 18:14
9. Sarah Forsyth (Ann Arbor Pioneer)10 ...... 18:15
10. Maryam Sheena (Walled Lake Western)12 ..... 18:15
11. Lauren Kiley (Plymouth)10 .... 18:15
12. Madison Ebright (Grand Rapids Ottawa Hills)11 18:16
13. Sophie Novak (Lake Orion)11 .... 18:17
14. Abbie Draheim (East Lansing)11 .... 18:21
15. Leah Socks (Traverse City Central)12 ...... 18:24
16. Abby Olson (Holland West Ottawa)12 ...... 18:24
17. Avery McLean (Traverse City Central)11 .... 18:25
18. Londyn Swenson (Plymouth)11 .... 18:25
19. Yasmine Mansi (Northville)11 .... 18:27
20. Adit Dau (Grand Rapids Ottawa Hills)10 ..... 18:28
21. Allison Cornell (Forest Hills Northern)9 ..... 18:28
22. Katie Carothers (Brighton)10 .... 18:28
23. Whitney Currie (Forest Hills Central)11 ..... 18:31
24. Madelyn Malczewski (Romeo)12 .... 18:33
25. Ellie Voetberg (Portage Central)11 .... 18:34
26. Elsa Rusthoven (DeWitt)11 .... 18:35
27. Kaitlyn Hynes (DeWitt)11 .... 18:35
28. Maya Guikema (Jenison)9 .... 18:37
29. Abbie Haupt (Livonia Churchill)11 .... 18:38
30. Paige Anderson (Troy)11 .... 18:46
31. Lindsey Peters (Caledonia)11 .... 18:49
32. Cookie Baugh (Ann Arbor Pioneer)10 ...... 18:51
33. Morgan Crompton (Brighton)11 .... 18:55
34. Chloe Wall (Waterford Kettering)10 .... 18:55
35. Emily Gordon (Northville)11 .... 19:00
36. Anna Vogel (Ann Arbor Pioneer)12 .... 19:02
37. Andrea Ruiz (Holly)11 .... 19:02
38. Ashlyn Nagel (Bay City Western)12 .... 19:04
39. Charlotte Batra (Ann Arbor Pioneer)10 ..... 19:08
40. Marin Stevens (Bay City Western)10 .... 19:10
58. Anna Dudek (Ann Arbpr Pioneer)11 .... 19:25
149. Danielle Armstrong (Ann Arbor Pioneer)12 ..... 20:14

CLASS A/D1 STATISTICS

TOP 25 CLOCKINGS AT MIS
16:55 Megan Goethals (Rochester)12 2009
17:01 Brook Handler (Rochester)12 2010
17:01 Zofia Dudek (Ann Arbor Pioneer)12 2019
17:02 Gabi Anzalone (Grand Blanc)12 2010

Time	Athlete	Year
17:08	Erin Finn (West Bloomfield)12	2012
17:09	Ericka VanderLende (Rockford)12	2018
17:11	Goethals (Rochester)11	2008
17:17	Ericka VanderLende (Rockford)11	2017
17:18	Katie Boyles (Rochester Adams)12	2000
17:18	Shannon Osika (Waterford Mott)10	2008
17:19	Audrey Belf (Birmingham Seaholm)12	2014
17:22	Hannah Meier (Grosse Pointe S)10	2010
17:23	Finn (West Bloomfield)11	2011
17:24	Taylor Manett (Rockford)12	2011
17:25	Meier (Grosse Pointe South)11	2011
17:26	Maggie Farrell (Battle Crk Lakeview)12	2016
17:29	Rebecca Addison (Grand Haven)12	2008
17:29	Madison Troy (Grandville)10	2015
17:30	Rachel DaDamio (Birm. Seaholm)12	2014
17:31	Finn (West Bloomfield)10	2010
17:31	Jessi Larson (Saline)10	2015
17:31	Sielle Kearney (Traverse City C)12	2017
17:32	Shannon Stanley (Roch. Adams)10	2000
17:32	Belf (Birmingham Seaholm)11	2013
17:32	Maddi Trevisan (Farmington)12	2015

BIGGEST WINNING MARGINS

65.5	Megan Goethals/Avery Evenson	2009
52.6	Zofia Dudek/Arianne Olson	2019
50.2	Ericka VanderLende/K Christopher-M	2018
49.06	Eileen Fleck/Alexis Lund	1993 I
46.1	Laura Matson/Brenda Pippel	1984 I

SMALLEST WINNING MARGINS

1.4	Erin Finn/Taylor Manett	2011
1.5	Brook Handler/Gabi Anzalone	2010
2.43	Alexis Lund/Anjanette Korotnik	1992 I
3.0	Carlie Green/Rachel Peterson	2006
3.73	Allison Mendyk/Colleen Yuhn	1988 I
3.8	Shannon Osika/Audrey Huth	2007
4.3	Katie Boyles/Cami Moll	1997

LOWEST WINNING SCORES

25	Rockford	1998
32	Dearborn Edsel Ford	1984
35	Rockford	2000
40	Rockford	1999
41	Livonia Stevenson	1976
46	Grand Ledge	1975
49	Brighton	1979
57	Rockford	2002
67	Ann Arbor Pioneer	1987
68	Ann Arbor Pioneer	1997
69	Birmingham Seaholm	2012

HIGHEST WINNING SCORES

150	Milford	2016
146	Holly	1990
141	Saline	2009
135	Grand Haven	2010
134	Clarkston	2018
133	Rochester	1978
132	Clarkston	2004
129	Traverse City Central	2008
127	Sterling Heights Stevenson	1985
127	Troy	2017

CLOSEST TEAM FINISH

0	Rochester Adams/Livonia Churchill	2006
2	Flint Northern/Davison	1981
5	Grosse Pointe South/Saline	2011
5	Troy/Northville	2017
6	Holly/Ann Arbor Pioneer	1990

BIGGEST WINNING TEAM MARGIN

119	Dearborn Edsel Ford/Milford	1984
112	Rockford/Rochester Adams	1999
82	Ann Arbor Pioneer/West Bloomfield	1987
77	Rockford	2000
71	Brighton/Rochester	1979

Saline's 2009 D1 Champions, coach Mike Smith at right.

GIRLS CLASS B / DIVISION 2

1975 CLASS B GIRLS
The girls ran on a 2.25M course at the first state meet, organized by coaches on a Wednesday at Pioneer High School. The first winner, Bonnie Arnold, trained with the Pennfield boys team, coached by Richard Everson.

The Hillsdale team was coached by Bill Tefft, who said, "We're really proud of the gals. I think a lot of credit goes to the 500 miles they ran last summer. They've worked so hard all year. This was just an excellent finish."

Pioneer HS, Ann Arbor, November 5 ☐
1975 GIRLS CLASS B TEAMS
1. Hillsdale 36
2. Milford 49
3. Saginaw Swan Valley 69

Other schools with entries: Battle Creek Pennfield, Detroit Holy Redeemer, Hastings, Milford, Monroe St Mary, Sparta, Tecumseh, Whitehall, White Lake Lakeland.

Pennfield's Bonnie Arnold, the first Class B state champ.

1976 GIRLS CLASS B INDIVIDUALS
1. Bonnie Arnold (Battle Creek Pennfield)10 ....14:16
3. Cindy Nelson (Hastings)...14:24
6. Linda Masserant (Hillsdale)....................................14:38
7. Ann Heinowski (Hillsdale).......................................15:21
11. Candi VanDusen (Hillsdale)..................................15:53
14. Jane Foote (Milford)...nt
16. Jane Post (Hillsdale)..16:37
19. Debbie Stemen (Hillsdale)....................................16:52

1976 CLASS B GIRLS
Hillsdale repeated at the top, holding off Hastings by 13 points. Saginaw MacArthur's Mary Ann Opalewski, who dominated by over a minute. Opalewski was well known to running fans, having run a 5:01.2 mile in 1975 and won the Class B two-mile crown in 11:00.0 the next year. (MacArthur High was merged with Eisenhower in 1988 to form Heritage High. The former MacArthur building now houses White Pine Middle School.)

Pioneer HS, Ann Arbor, November 3 ☐
1976 GIRLS CLASS B TEAMS
1. Hillsdale 52
2. Hastings 65
3. Carleton Airport 71
4. Oscoda 95
5. Milan 96
6. Midland Bullock Creek 97

1976 GIRLS CLASS B INDIVIDUALS
1. Mary Ann Opalewski (Saginaw MacArthur)12 ..... 17:44
2. Cindy Nelson (Hastings) 18:52
3. Bonnie Arnold (Battle Creek Pennfield)11 .... 19:13
4. Laura Okkonen (Sparta) 19:15
5. Kelly Yesmunt (Midland Bullock Creek) 19:16
6. Linda Masserant (Hillsdale) 19:24
7. Debbie Love (Carleton Airport) 19:33
8. Sheila Varga (Three Oaks River Valley) 19:38
9. Anne Heinowski (Hillsdale) 19:54
10. Janel Mumme (Tecumseh) 20:05
11. Julie Anne Conley (Birch Run) 20:18
12. Paula Pederson (Hastings) 20:23
13. Shelly Phillips (Milan) 20:24
14. Belinda Manar (Carleton Airport) 20:29
15. Julie Willson (Hillsdale) 20:37
16. Elizabeth Brown (Oscoda) 20:54
17. Donna Shackleton (Oscoda) 21:01
18. Susan Haas (Oscoda) 21:01
19. Tammy Campau (Hartland) 21:01
20. Denise Oleynik (Carleton Airport) 21:06
21. Diane Oleynik (Carleton Airport) 21:10
22. Chris Favorite (Hastings) 21:32
23. Holly Porter (Hillsdale) 21:43
24. Ellen Beckley (Alma) 21:49
25. Kathy Powers (Hastings) 22:01
26. Lori Bidwell (Milan) 22:06
27. Laurie Baily (Hartland) 22:06
28. Lana Beilfuss (Hillsdale).......................................22:15
29. Linda Trumbull (Midland Bullock Creek) 22:19
30. Joan Popp (Midland Bullock Creek) 22:24

1977 CLASS B GIRLS
MITCA took over the de-facto state championships for girls. Directed by Karyn Cribley, the Saturday event was well-attended. Cheryl Scheffer of South Lyon finished 12 seconds ahead of Ladywood frosh Lori Bennett. Two months later Bennett would run 4:58.7 in a college meet at Eastern Michigan; it lasted as the state indoor record for 6 years. The following spring Scheffer won the Class B two mile in 11:05.5; Bennett took the mile in 5:00.3.

Potterville, Oct. 22 ☐
1977 GIRLS CLASS B TEAMS
1. Livonia Ladywood 62
2. Oscoda 94
3. Hillsdale 125
4. Milan 132
5. Hastings 167
6. Bullock Creek 175
7. Madison Heights Foley 179
8. Monroe St Mary 205
9. Holt 217
10. Jackson Northwest 227
11. Carleton Airport 233
12. Dearborn Divine Child 237
13. Tecumseh 277
14. Alma 288

1977 GIRLS CLASS B INDIVIDUALS
1. Cheryl Scheffer (South Lyon)10 ....17:38
2. Lori Bennett (Livonia Ladywood)9 ....17:50
3. Bonnie Arnold (Battle Creek Pennfield)12 ....18:02
4. Sheila Varga (Three Oaks River Valley)...............18:12
5. Frances Reilly (Oscoda) 18:35
6. Sue Jarvis (Livonia Ladywood) 18:37
7. Lee Ann Yank (Madison Heights Foley)...............18:45
8. Shelly Phillips (Milan) 18:47
9. Linda Masserant (Hillsdale) 18:58
10. Melinda Roberts (Mt Morris)................. 18:59

1978 CLASS B GIRLS
The first year of MHSAA-sponsored girls cross country combined all the classes into one race. Officials said the numbers did not justify separate races, despite the solid turnout for the previous year's event, which brought together 370 girls from all classes and 45 complete teams. See Class A for the results of the MHSAA race.

Potterville decided to again host separate races by class, called the "Girls' State Open Cross Country Championships." On the Class B level, most of the state's top teams competed (9 of 14 from the previous year's meet).

Carleton Airport won handily, and two weeks later was the top Class B school at the MHSAA all-class championships. Joan DeMaat of Grand Rapids Christian beat defending champion Cheryl Scheffer with her 17:31 over the three-mile course.

Potterville HS, Potterville, October 21 ☐
1978 GIRLS CLASS B TEAMS
1. Carleton Airport 122
2. Milan 186
3. Holt 196
4. Dearborn Divine Child 197
5. Hillsdale 221
6. Saline 235
7. Fremont 240
8. Okemos 251
9. Madison Heights Foley 279
10. Monroe St Mary 284
11. Linden 297
12. Jackson Northwest 317
13. Midland Bullock Creek 393
14. Tecumseh 449

Incomplete squads: Battle Creek Pennfield, Big Rapids, Charlotte, Grand Rapids Christian, Gwinn, Mt Morris, St Johns, South Lyon.

1978 GIRLS CLASS B TEAM RACE
1. Joan DeMaat (Grand Rapids Christian)............... 17:31
2. Cheryl Scheffer (South Lyon)11 ....nt
3. Debbie Love (Carleton Airport) ....nt
4. Janie Barner (Hillsdale) ....nt
5. Teresa Brink (Okemos) ....nt
6. Tara DeVries (Grand Rapids Christian) ....nt
7. Tracy Arion (Linden) ....nt
8. Kris Zdanowski (South Lyon) ....nt
9. Ann Rouman (Big Rapids) ....nt
10. Cindy Litwin (Carleton Airport) ....nt

1979 CLASS B GIRLS
"We scouted every team and checked the times for every runner here," said John Warners, the Grand Rapids Christian coach. "We had a set position for each one of our girls to finish. We knew who we had to beat."

Joan DeMaat led the team in 5th place despite having her appendix out three weeks earlier.

Crockery GC, Spring Lake, Nov. 3
1979 GIRLS CLASS B TEAMS
1. Grand Rapids Christian 109
2. Hillsdale 175
3. Fenton 181
4. Dearborn Divine Child 184
5. Fremont 190
6. Milan 223
7. Jackson Northwest 231
8. Vicksburg 241
9. Linden 241
10. Holt 263
11. Jackson Lumen Christi 272
12. Madison Heights Foley 274
13. Mt Morris 274
14. Carleton Airport 281
15. Alma 292
16. Gladwin 295
17. Chesaning 314
18. Croswell-Lexington 316

South Lyon's Cheryl Scheffer broke 18-minutes on the 3M course—the last year that distance would be run.

1979 GIRLS CLASS B TEAM RACE
1. Kim Koviack (Chesaning)9 .... 18:14
2. Lisa Last (Alma) 18:23
3. JoAnn Van Ryewk (Vicksburg) 18:32
4. Kim Southworth (Jackson Northwest) 18:34
5. Joan DeMast (Grand Rapids Christian) 18:40
6. Lyn Walters (Fenton) 18:52
7. Mary Newhof (Grand Rapids Christian) 18:55
8. Tina Manning (Gladwin) 18:57
9. Kathy Kline (Vicksburg) 18:57
10. Renee Filistraut (Dearborn Divine Child) .. 18:58
11. Janine Banner (Holt) 19:01
12. Jennifer Pratt (Milan) 19:02
13. Melinda Roberts (Mt Morris) 19:08
14. Laura Wilson (Hillsdale) 19:08
15. Laurette Reeves (Chesaning) 19:08
16. Joan Lanclaux (Fremont) 19:09
17. Shelly Ramont (Holt) 19:10
18. Julie Willson (Hillsdale) 19:12
19. Diane Michael (Mt Morris) 19:13
20. Beth DeMaat (Grand Rapids Christian) .... nt
21. Elizabeth Skruch (Dearborn Divine Child) .. nt
30. Kim Kragt (Grand Rapids Christian) .... nt
47. Lara DeVries (Grand Rapids Christian) .... nt
55. Beth Sneller (Grand Rapids Christian) ...... nt
76. Kris Engelhard (Grand Rapid Christian) .... nt

1979 GIRLS CLASS B INDIVIDUAL RACE
1. Cheryl Scheffer (South Lyon)12 .... 17:59
2. Kelly McKillen (Dexter)9 .... 18:00
3. Julie Stansberry (Yale)11 .... 18:44
4. Teresa Brink (Okemos) 18:46
5. Tammi Begerowski (Yale)9 .... 19:03
6. Lynn Wedge (Marysville) 19:12
7. Leslie Burgess (Anchor Bay) 19:23
8. Mary Ann Russelll (Flint Powers) 19:24
9. Judy Reynolds (Charlotte) 19:30

1980 CLASS B GIRLS

Cold weather (30-degrees) and a mostly flat course saw Ladywood, coached by Ray Prosser, demolish the women's field. Kelly Champagne, later a star at the University of Texas, overtook leader Tami Begerowski in the last mile.

"I knew she was there, because she kept trying to pass me on the straightaways," said Begerowski.

This was the year of the switch to the 5K distance at all regionals and state final sites.

Oxford Hills CC, Oxford, Nov. 1
1980 GIRLS CLASS B TEAMS
1. Livonia Ladywood 62
2. Hartland 125
3. Jackson Lumen Christi 135
4. Carleton Airport 199
5. Holt 225
6. Dexter 230
7. Milan 241
8. Hillsdale 255
9. Mt Morris 269
10. Grand Rapids Christian 270
11. Marysville 271
12. Dearborn Divine Child 276
13. Gladwin 288
14. Hemlock 326
15. Yale 335
16. Madison Heights Foley 352
17. Croswell-Lexington 377
18. Lowell 391
19. Allegan 458
20. Grand Rapids Forest Hills 483
21. Holland Christian 486
22. Richland Gull Lake 617

1980 GIRLS CLASS B TEAM RACE
1. Kelly Champagne (Livonia Ladywood)10 .... 18:38
2. Tami Begerowski (Yale)10 .... 18:43
3. Julie Stansberry (Yale)12 .... 19:33
4. Kelly McKillen (Dexter)10 .... 19:34
5. Lynn Wedge (Marysville) 19:35
6. Diane Michael (Mt Morris) 19:48
7. Jennifer Rioux (Livonia Ladywood)10 ...... 19:50
8. Jennifer Pratt (Milan) 19:53
14. Tina Schwab (Marysville)9 .... 20:05
18. Shelly Ramont (Holt) .... nt
?. Colleen Lee (Livonia Ladywood) .... nt
?. Lisa Bagdady (Livonia Ladywood) .... nt
?. Katy Harley (Livonia Ladywood) .... nt

1980 GIRLS CLASS B INDIVIDUAL RACE
1. Joann Lanciaux (Fremont) 18:26
2. Chris Sharp (Grand Rapids Northview) 19:11
3. Christa Willson (Ludington)9 .... 19:12
4. Kim Koviack (Chesaning)10 .... 19:14
5. Anne Walker (Royal Oak Shrine) 19:15
6. Karen Gamble (Big Rapids) 19:40
7. Tere Stouffer (Avondale) 19:47
8. Kris Zdanowski (South Lyon) 19:50
10. Teresa Brink (Okemos) .... nt
15. Nola Rogers (Eaton Rapids) .... nt

1981 CLASS B GIRLS

Jennifer Rioux of Ladywood dominated the team run in 19:01 but frosh Valari Ambrose ran even faster in the individual run at 18:56. Rioux would go on to be a cross country All-American for Wake Forest. Dexter, coached by Jim Jawarski, won the team title by 18 points.

Oxford Hills CC, Oxford, Oct. 31
1981 GIRLS CLASS B TEAMS
1. Dexter 90
2. Jackson Lumen Christi 108
3. Hartland 130
4. Royal Oak Shrine 146
5. Livonia Ladywood 191
6. St Joseph 217
7. Milan 260
8. Grand Rapids Christian 268
9. Wyoming Park 291
10. Richland Gull Lake 298
11. Marysville 303
12. Muskegon Catholic 318
13. Flint Powers 319
14. Detroit Northern 327
15. Jackson Northwest 356
16. Jackson Parkside 400
17. Yale 440
18. Holland Christian 450
19. Parma Western 456
20. Petoskey 479
21. Gladwin 480
22. Remus Chippewa Hills 482
23. Three Rivers 525
24. Mt Morris 541

1981 GIRLS CLASS B TEAM RACE
1. Jennifer Rioux (Livonia Ladywood)11 ...... 19:01
2. Ann Walker (Royal Oak Shrine) 19:22
3. Lynn Wedge (Marysville) 19:25
4. Kelly Champagne (Livonia Ladywood) 19:25
5. Lori Dunnigan (Jackson Lumen Christi) 19:33
6. Kelly McKillen (Dexter)11 .... 19:41
7. Yale Langley (Muskegon Catholic) 19:41
8. Sara Peopples (Dexter) 19:42
9. Laura Leiblein (Jackson Parkside) 19:43
10. Jenna DeVries (Grand Rapids Christian) .. 19:44
11. Tina Schwab (Marysville) 19:44
12. Lorrie Konopacki (Jackson Lumen Christi) .. 19:46
13. Tammy Begerowski (Yale) 19:47
14. Lisa Goletman (Dexter) 19:49
15. Julie Langley (Muskegon Catholic) 19:58
16. Barb Wallace (Jackson Lumen Christi) 20:00
17. Rebecca ASmith (Wyoming Park) 20:02
18. Dianna Beauchamp (Hartland) 20:05
27. (Dexter) .... nt
35. (Dexter) .... nt

1981 GIRLS CLASS B INDIVIDUAL RACE
1. Valari Ambrose (Riverview Richard)9 ...... 18:56
2. Chris Sharp (Grand Rapids Northview) 19:08
3. Sheryl Koeltzow (Saginaw Swan Valley) 19:12
4. Nels Rogers (Eaton Rapids) 19:22
5. Kim Kovlack (Chesaning)11 .... 19:35
6. Arden Dexter (Mason) 19:43
7. Tere Stouffer (Auburn Hills Avondale) 19:45
8. Brenda Thorne (Bay City Handy) 19:54
9. Karen Gamble (Big Rapids) 19:56
10. Karen Pantse (Otsego) 19:59
11. Liesl Charron (Charlotte) 20:00
12. Karen Twichel (Ortonville Brandon) 20:00

1982 CLASS B GIRLS

Mike Woolsey's Lumen Christi earned its first win, topping Hartland by 31 points. Kelly McKillen of Dexter beat defending champion Jennifer Rioux by 11 seconds. In the individual run, Valari Ambrose made it two in a row. Said second placer Bobbi Sue Johnson of Algonac, "I didn't even see her."

In the spring it would be Kelly Champagne of Ladywood who would win the B 3200 title. McKillen would finish 2nd in both that race and the 1600 (to Kim Adent of St. Joseph).

Tyrone Hills GC, Linden, Nov. 6
1982 GIRLS CLASS B TEAMS

1. Jackson Lumen Christi 99
2. Hartland 130
3. Dexter 144
4. Muskegon Catholic 166
5. Gladwin 236
6. Livonia Ladywood 237
7. Marysville 240
8. Mason 255
9. Royal Oak Shrine 256
10. Grand Rapids Christian 266
11. Flint Powers 272
12. St Joseph 278
13. Ionia 310
14. Jackson Northwest 315
15. Hemlock 333
16. Wyoming Rogers 344
17. Richland Gull Lake 377
18. Cadillac 396
19. Three Rivers 423
20. Essexville Garber 445
21. Saline 488
22. Monroe St Mary 503

Mike Woolsey, Lumen Christi Class of '74, has coached his alma mater to 9 girls state titles.

1982 GIRLS CLASS B TEAM RACE
1. Kelly McKillen (Dexter)12 .... 18:55
2. Jennifer Rioux (Livonia Ladywood)12 .... 19:06
3. Kelly Champagne (Livonia Ladywood)12 .... 19:20
4. Anne Walker (Royal Oak Shrine) 19:26
5. Cathy Burkhart (Flint Powers) 19:41
6. Julie Watson (Hemlock) 19:46
7. Lorrie Konopacki (Jackson Lumen Christi)10 .... 19:46
8. Chris Tenaglia (Hartland) 19:50
9. Jamie Grant (Mason) 19:52
10. Kay Gemrich (Richland Gull Lake) 19:55
11. Diane Devereaux (Flint Powers) 19:57
12. LuAnn Henry (Cadillac) 19:58
13. Jean Wyckoff (Gladwin) 19:59
14. Val Langley (Muskegon Catholic) 20:07
15. Cindy Wilson (Mason) 20:16
16. Teri Stouffer (Royal Oak Shrine) 20:27
17. Barb Wallace (Jackson Lumen Christi)12 ...... 20:29
18. Lisa Forner (Jackson Lumen Christi)10 .... 20:31
23. Julie Ziegler (Jackson Lumen Christi)10 .... 20:40
32. Mary DeWitt (Jackson Lumen Christi)10 .... 21:03
44. Lori Dunigan (Jackson Lumen Christi)11 ...... 21:23
49. Sheila Dobbin (Jackson Lumen Christi)11 .... 21:28

1982 GIRLS CLASS B INDIVIDUAL RACE
1. Valari Ambrose (Riverview Richard)10 .... 19:37
2. Bobbi Sue Johnson (Algonac)11 .... 19:57
3. Michelle Chapman (Grosse Ile) 19:59
4. Karen Gamble (Big Rapids) 19:59
5. Sheryl Koeltzow (Saginaw Swan Valley) 20:00
6. Sandre Frame (Chelsea) 20:00

7. Tami Bergerowski (Yale) 20:01
8. Michelle VanHeulen (Wyoming Park) 20:01
9. Liesl Charron (Charlotte) 20:02
10. Karen Panse (Otsego) 20:03
11. Sue Cashman (Grand Rapids Catholic) 20:16
12. Laura Cighowski (SCS South Lake) 20:17
13. Lisa Somes (Mt Pleasant) 20;25
14. Melissa Fleming (Allegan) 20:26

1983 CLASS B GIRLS

St. Joseph senior Kim Adent, regional champ and one of the possible favorites, missed the meet because of a stomach problem. She had missed the year before with a leg injury.

Even before the Adent news hit, Shrine's Tere Stouffer was considered the strong favorite. The senior did not disappoint, roaring to a 36-second victory.

Lumen Christi captured its second team title, showing all the makings of a dynasty. It's 89-point margin was the biggest in meet history.

Tyrone Hills Golf Course, Linden, Nov. 5
1983 GIRLS CLASS B TEAMS
1. Jackson Lumen Christi 91
2. Hartland 180
3. Gladwin 181
4. Grand Rapids Christian 210
5. Richland Gull Lake 226
6. Flint Powers 267
7. Muskegon Catholic 270
8. Chelsea 295
9. Marysville 297
10. Mason 300
11. Essexville Garber 316
12. Big Rapids 316
13. Grand Rapids Catholic Central 331
14. Alma 342
15. Dexter 348
16. St Joseph 356
17. Okemos 370
18. Royal Oak Shrine 408
19. Allen Park Cabrini 412
20. Novi 439
21. Algonac 486
22. Riverview 499
23. Holland Christian 527
24. Dearborn Divine Child 561

1983 GIRLS CLASS B TEAM RACE
1. Tere Stouffer (Royal Oak Shrine)12 .... 18:31
2. Cathy Buckart (Flint Powers) 19:08
3. Lori Dunigan (Jackson Lumen Christi)12 .... 19:13
4. Sally Reinink (Holland Christian) 19:21
5. Kay Gremerich (Richland Gull Lake) 19:23
6. Kristen Gilbert (Big Rapids) 19:31
7. Tama Jones (Grand Rapids Christian) 19:32
8. Bonnie Sue Johnson (Algonac) 19:33
9. Vonnie Dood (Okemos) 19:34
10. Barbara Bacon (Big Rapids) 19:36
11. Chris Bringedahl (Muskegon Catholic) 19:37
12. Susan Neiswinter (Hartland) 19:38
13. Melissa Schutte (Grand Rapids Christian) .. 19:40
14. Linda Garder (Dexter) 19:45
15. Jamie Grant (Mason) 19:49
16. Helen Johnson (Marysville)9 .... 19:53
17. Roberta McKean (Richland Gull Lake) 19:56
18. Julie Langley (Muskegon Catholic) 19:57
19. Lorrie Konopacki (Jackson Lumen Christi)11 .. 19:58
21. Julie Ziegler (Jackson Lumen Christi)11 .... 20:00
23. Lisa Forner (Jackson Lumen Christi)11 ...... 20:02
25. Ruth Navarre (Jackson Lumen Christi)10 .... 20:12
26. Cecilie Gehring (Jackson Lumen Christi)11 .. 20:16
30. Mary DeWitt (Jackson Lumen Christi)11 ..... 20:31

1983 GIRLS CLASS B INDIVIDUAL RACE
1. Valari Ambrose (Riverview Richard)11 .... 18:59
2. Amy Blok (Wyoming Park) 19:13
3. Julie Watson (Hemlock) 19:27
4. Sharon Kinsler (Saginaw MacArthur) 19:35
5. Michelle VanHeulen (Wyoming Park) 19:41
6. Diane Weaver (Marshall) 19:44
7. Pam Boots (Oxford) 19:45

8. Nola Rogers (Eaton Rapids) 19:46
9. Liesl Charron (Charlotte) 19:51
10. Erin Gillespie (Jackson Northwest) 19:52
11. Lori Jewell (Kenowa Hills) 19:56
12. Melissa Fleming (Allegan) 19:57

1984 CLASS B GIRLS

Valari Ambrose won a record fourth-straight title in 18:41, her fastest time ever at the state fnals, and faster than Marysville's Helen Johnson, who won the team run. She went on to become an All-American for Hillsdale College.

Johnson had learned from her ninth grade season. Said Marysville coach Mary Mantai, "She knew she had to get out fast from her expericen last year. With a mile and a half to go, she had the lead of about 10 yards. No one got close to her."

The Lumen Christi girls won a record third-straight.

Tyrone Hills Golf Course, Linden, Nov. 3
1984 GIRLS CLASS B TEAMS
1. Jackson Lumen Christi 84
2. Gladwin 125
3. Grand Rapids Christian 134
4. Chelsea 169
5. Hillsdale 201
6. Alma 203
7. Hartland 224
8. Oxford 239
9. Grand Rapids Catholic Central 252
10. Mt Clemens Lutheran North 261
11. Petoskey 300
12. Richland Gull Lake 328
13. Jackson Northwest 338
14. Saline 371
15. Marysville 394
16. Hemlock 399
17. Otsego 423
18. Grosse Ile 425
19. Caro 449
20. Vicksburg 452
21. Dearborn Divine Child 454
22. Greenville 481

1984 GIRLS CLASS B TEAM RACE
1. Helen Johnson (Marysville)10 .... 19:08
2. Anne VanDam (Petoskey)11 .... 19:26
3. Susan Cashman (GR Catholic Central)11 ..... 19:35
4. Dawn Toth (Saline)11 .... 19:40
5. Julie Watson (Hemlock)12 .... 19:41
6. Erin Gillespie (Jackson Northwest)12 .... 19:46
7. Kerry Gremel (Mt Clemens Lutheran North)10 .. 19:51
8. Laura Tenaglia (Hartland)12 .... 19:52
9. Jean Wyckoff (Gladwin) 19:52
10. Kari Frederick (Jackson Lumen Christi)9 .... 19:55
11. Patty Ziolkowski (Jackson Lumen Christi)10 .. 20:00
12. Shari VanderHorn (Grand Rapids Christian)12. 20:00
13. Kim Horton (Gladwin) 20:00
14. Katy Fromer (Gladwin) 20:03
15. Patty Anzaldua (Otsego)11 .... 20:09
16. Renee Wendzel (Richland Gull Lake)9 .... 20:17
17. Shannon Sowell (Mt Clemens Lutheran N)10 .. 20:17
18. Ruth Navarre (Jackson Lumen Christi)11 .... 20:24
22. Julie Ziegler (Jackson Lumen Christi)12 ..... 20:29
23. Lisa Forner (Jackson Lumen Christi)12 ...... 20:33
61. Cecilie Gehring (Jackson Lumen Christi)12 .. 21:25
99. Susie Crowley (Jackson Lumen Christi) 22:07

1984 GIRLS CLASS B INDIVIDUAL RACE
1. Valari Ambrose (Riverview Richard)12 .... 18:41
2. Denys Adams (Okemos)11 .... 19:09
3. Sarah Sargent (Midland Bullock Creek) 19:28
4. Jenny Ledrick (Forest Hills Central) 19:38
5. Cindy Wilson (Mason) 19:44
6. Jamie Grant (Mason) 19:57
7. Vonnie Dood (Okemos) 19:57
8.
9. Melanie Medina (Saginaw Swan Valley)10 .... 20:09
10. Sharon Kinsler (Saginaw MacArthur)11 .... 20:10

11. Jill Lamountain (Saginaw Swan Valley) 20:12
12.
13. Tina Allard (Ludington) 20:18

1985 CLASS B GIRLS

Helen Johnson staged a dramatic come-from-behind finish. The Marysville junior was about 30 yards behind Bullock Creek's Sarah Sargent with less than a quarter mile to go when she launched an incredible kick to deliver a 9-second win.

"When she passed me at the 2M mark, I thought I had lost for sure. I thought maybe second wouldn't be too bad," she admitted. "Then I heard some people saying, 'Get the Marysville girl, Kerry!' [to eventual third-placer Kerry Grimes of Mt. Clemens] I said, 'No way!'… That got me going. Then the girl in front of me started getting closer. I knew I had her because she didn't even fight back."

It was a big day for the Johnson family, as Helen's older brother Ron won the Mid-American Conference title for Central Michigan that same morning. He had never placed higher than second at the high school state meet.

Hillsdale dethroned Lumen Christi for the team title, 82-100, on what was described as a "cold and misty day."

Hudson Mills Metro Park, Dexter, Nov. 2 □
1985 GIRLS CLASS B TEAMS
1. Hillsdale 82
2. Jackson Lumen Christi 100
3. Chelsea 192
4. Grand Rapids Christian 195
5. Alma 209
6. Mt Clemens 217
7. Saline 236
8. Oxford 245
9. Grand Rapids Catholic Central 267
10. Essexville Garber 275
11. Marysville 283
12. Coldwater 300
13. Petoskey 341
14. Midland Bullock Creek 372
15. Hartland 387
16. Greenville 401
17. Otsego 405
18. Yale 408
19. Cadillac 413
20. Richland Gull Lake 429
21. Mason 440
22. Caro 470
23. Dearborn Divine Child 552
24. Dearborn St Alphonsus 714

1985 GIRLS CLASS B TEAM RACE
1. Helen Johnson (Marysville)11 ....18:37
2. Sarah Sargent (Midland Bullock Creek) 18:46
3. Kerry Greme (Mt Clemens) 18:59
4. Nicole Butler (Hillsdale) 19:00
5. Kris Butler (Hillsdale) 19:02
6. Cathy Acus (Hillsdale)11 ....19:24
7. Kasey Anderson (Chelsea)10 ....19:34
8. Wendy Dutcher (Essexville Garber) 19:39
9. Shannon Sowell (Mt Clemens) 19:40
10. Jill Strawser (Coldwater)9 ....19:42
11. Dawn Toth (Saline) 19:44
12. Kari Frederick (Jackson Lumen Christi)10 ....19:45
13. Kate Conlen (Oxford) 19:46
14. Toni Enbody (Greenville)11 ....19:49
15. Heather Huhn (Mason)10 ....19:55
16. Rhonda Wendzel (Richland Gull Lake)10 ...19:57
20. Patty Anzaldua (Otsego) 20:11

1985 GIRLS CLASS B INDIVIDUAL RACE
1. Sharon Kinsler (Saginaw MacArthur)12 .....18:54
2. Jenny Ledrick (GR Forest Hills Central) 19:29
3. Pam Pollie (Caledonia) 19:42
4. Barb Kookier (Holland Christian)11 ....19:46
5. Sharon Veneklase (Grand Rapids W Cath) 19:54
6. Becky Duda (Goodrich)10 ....19:57
7. Jennifer Wytko (Battle Creek Lakeview)12 ....20:01
8. Amy Blok (Wyoming Park) 20:01
9. Wendy Hower (Milan) 20:12
10. Angie Case (Montrose) 20:13
11. Pat Hernandez (Montrose) 20:13
12. Christine Weaver (Sturgis)9 ....20:14
13. Sheila Carnisay (Royal Oak Shrine) 20:16

1986 CLASS B GIRLS

Jackson Lumen Christi scored its fourth win in five years, in the closest finish in meet history, beating Chelsea by just one point.

Jill Strawser of Coldwater won the team run. Said coach Jim Billsborrow, "She just took control of the race. I think she had to be one of the favorites. I don't think people expected her to do it, though."

Hudson Mills Metro Park, Dexter, Nov. 1 ⊠
1986 GIRLS CLASS B TEAMS
1. Jackson Lumen Christi 141
2. Chelsea 142
3. Milan 152
4. Dearborn 158
5. Grand Rapids Christian 169
6. Coldwater 232
7. Cadillac 245
8. Grand Rapids Catholic Central 273
9. Mt Clemens Lutheran North 278
10. Saline 282
11. Greenville 298
12. Stanton-Central Montcalm 304
13. Sturgis 311
14. Marysville 327
15. Yale 360
16. Richland Gull Lake 368
17. Holland Christian 375
18. Livonia Ladywood 379
19. Standish-Sterling 392
20. Vicksburg 426
21. Midland Bullock Creek 458
22. Essexville Garber 461
23. Farmington Hills Harrison 579
24. Madison Heights Foley 739

1986 GIRLS CLASS B TEAM RACE
1. Jill Strawser (Coldwater)10 ....19:16
2. Kasey Anderson (Chelsea)11 ....19:22
3. Janet Reinowski (Dearborn)11 ....19:22
4. Rhonda Wendzel (Richland Gull Lake)11 ...19:32
5. Megan Fisher (Grand Rapids Catholic)11 ..19:41
6. Sherri Prince (Grand Rapids Christian)12 ..19:49
7. Helen Johnson (Marysville)12 ....19:49
8. Toni Enbody (Greenville)12 ....19:49
9. Janine Kloc (Livonia Ladywood)12 ....19:51
10. Patty Ziolkowski (Jackson Lumen Christi)12 ....19:53
11. Emilie Sargent (Bullock Creek)10 ....19:58
12. Jaime Webster (Saline)11 ....19:58
13. Jennifer Rossi (Chelsea)11 ....20:02
14. Kari Frederick (Jackson Lumen Christi)11 ....20:04
15. Kerry Gremel (Mt Clemens Lutheran North)12 ....20:06
16. Rochelle Smetka (Milan)12 ....20:11
17. Nancy Olkowski (Dearborn)10 ....20:14
18. Dawn Valle (Coldwater)12 ....20:21
28. Jennifer Jenks (Jackson Lumen Christi)9 ....20:47
42. Ellen Gibson (Jackson Lumen Christi)11 ....21:08
47. Joanna Gleeson (Jackson Lumen Christi)12 .....21:14
54. Marcie Holda (Jackson Lumen Christi)10 ....21:23
89. Becky Frederick (Jackson Lumen Christi)11 ......22:10

1986 GIRLS CLASS B INDIVIDUAL RACE
1. Heather Huhn (Mason)11 ....19:15
2. Jenny Ledrick (Forest Hills Central)12 ....19:26
3. Kellie Wright (Parma Western)9 ....19:46
4. Antoinette Smith (Alma)12 ....19:48
5. Gloria Durisin (Melvindale)12 ....19:55
6. Angela Thomas (Sparta)9 ....19:55
7. Sandy Potter (Hartland)11 ....19:58
8. Carri Ham (Big Rapids)11 ....20:02
9. Cathy Acus (Hillsdale)12 ....20:03
10. Janet Holverstott (Riverview Richard)10 ..20:09
11. Lucinda Holloway (Warren Fitzgerald)10 ...20:15
12. Karen Jeppesen (Brooklyn Columbia Central) .. 20:17

1987 CLASS B GIRLS

Heather Slay of East Grand Rapids, who had won the 1600 title the previous spring, captured the team run in a fast 18:43. The next spring she would win both the 1600 (5:00.77) and 3200 (meet record 10:49.59). She would later star for Yale.

Big Rapids' Carrie Ham took the individual run in 19:06. In college at Hillsdale she would win an NAIA national title in the 4x8.

Grand Rapids Catholic Central came in ranked No. 1 and ran true to form, beating defender Lumen Christi by 22 points.

Heather Slay of East Grand Rapids.

Willow Metro Park, New Boston, Nov. 7 □
1987 GIRLS CLASS B TEAMS
1. Grand Rapids Catholic Central 112
2. Jackson Lumen Christi 134
3. Chelsea 204
4. Grand Rapids Christian 223
5. Milan 245
6. Sturgis 253
7. Petoskey 254
8. Dearborn 264
9. Mt Clemens Lutheran North 270
10. Caro 271
11. Greenville 273
12. Gladwin 283
13. Gaylord 288
14. Saline 305
15. Yale 322
16. East Grand Rapids 326
17. Vicksburg 361
18. Dearborn Divine Child 437
19. Midland Bullock Creek 442
20. Fowlerville 443
21. Alma 454
22. Lakeview 472
23. Dearborn Heights Crestwood 639
24. Mt Clemens 703

1987 GIRLS CLASS B TEAM RACE

1. Heather Slay (East Grand Rapids)11 ... 18:43
2. Kasey Anderson (Chelsea)12 ... 18:56
3. Meagen Fisher (GR Catholic Central)12 ... 19:04
4. Janet Reinowski (Dearborn)12 ... 19:05
5. Wendy Hower (Milan)11 ... 19:33
6. Kara Wires (Sturgis)12 ... 19:35
7. Kathleen Doherty (Greenville)11 ... 19:47
8. Emilie Sargent (Bullock Creek) ... 19:48
9. Marci Holba (Jackson Lumen Christi)11 ... 19:49
10. Linda Fitzpatrick (Mt Clemens Lutheran N)12 ... 19:52
11. Erica Adams (Gladwin)9 ... 19:53
12. Carol Flickinger (Milan)9 ... 19:55
13. Lisa Snyder (GR Catholic Central)9 ... 19:59
14. Lisa Reid (Yale)11 ... 20:08
15. Amy Blaising (Battle Creek Lakeview)12 ... 20:09
16. Lisa Daugin (GR Catholic Central)9 ... 20:14
25. Tina Barnes (GR Catholic Central)11 ... 20:40
55. Margaret Robach (GR Catholic Central) ... 21:13
65. Hope Calati (GR Catholic Central)10 ... 21:22
125. Pam Hillary (GR Catholic Central)12 ... 23:06

1987 GIRLS CLASS B INDIVIDUAL RACE

1. Carrie Ham (Big Rapids)12 ... 19:06
2. Heather Huhn (Mason)12 ... 19:14
3. Karen Jeppesen (Brooklyn Columbia Central)12 ... 19:25
4. Jill Strawser (Coldwater)11 ... 19:37
5. Amy Lathrop (Jackson Northwest)9 ... 19:41
6. Rhonda Wendzel (Richland Gull Lake)12 ... 19:52
7. Joy Strawser (Coldwater)9 ... 19:57
8. Kelly Litchfield (Portland) ... 19:59
9. Kerry Radcliff (Durand)12 ... 20:00
10. Jennifer Duthler (Imlay City)10 ... 20:01
11. Kellie Wright (Parma Western)10 ... 20:02
12. Angie Decan (Fruitport)12 ... 20:02
13. Andrea Cantu (Flint Kearsley)9 ... 20:04
14. Kim Blouw (Wyoming Park)10 ... 20:05
15. Sharon Veneklase (Grand Rapids W Catholic) ... 20:06

1988 CLASS B GIRLS

Buchanan junior Jeni Vite surprised many when she beat defending champion Heather Slay by 26 seconds in the team run. Said coach Mike Rouse, "The key was she ran a smart race. She stayed with the leader and didn't let her get away. Then she made her move at around the 2M mark."

Steve Porter's Milan squad won the team title in resounding fashion over East Grand Rapids. The margin was 91 points, the biggest in meet history.

Buchanan's Jeni Vite.

Willow Metro Park, New Boston, Nov. 5 ⊠
1988 GIRLS CLASS B TEAMS

1. Milan ... 114
2. East Grand Rapids ... 205
3. Grand Rapids Christian ... 208
4. Gladwin ... 212
5. Sturgis ... 251
6. Gaylord ... 259
7. Jackson Lumen Christi ... 274
8. Petoskey ... 277
9. Grand Rapids Catholic Central ... 286
10. Jackson Northwest ... 289
11. Buchanan ... 294
12. Alma ... 296
13. Coldwater ... 306
14. Fremont ... 309
15. Yale ... 324
16. Cadillac ... 338
17. Caro ... 348
18. Saline ... 384
19. Allen Park Cabrini ... 403
20. Richland Gull Lake ... 438
21. Dearborn Divine Child ... 439
22. Dearborn ... 461
23. Marysville ... 538
24. Redford Borgess ... 550
25. Imlay City ... 652
26. Mt Clemens ... 753

1988 GIRLS CLASS B TEAM RACE

1. Jeni Vite (Buchanan)11 ... 19:23
2. Heather Slay (East Grand Rapids)12 ... 19:49
3. Lisa Snyder (Grand Rapids Catholic C)10 ... 19:53
4. Cara Luchies (Fremont)11 ... 20:04
5. Erica Adams (Gladwin)10 ... 20;05
6. Jill Strawser (Coldwater)12 ... 20:06
7. Wendy Hower (Milan)12 ... 20:10
8. Becky Shively (Fremont)9 ... 20:14
9. Jean Zylka (Allen Park Cabrini)12 ... 20:18
10. Carol Flickinger (Milan)10 ... 20:20
11. Joy Strawser (Coldwater)11 ... 20:25
12. Jodie Cuson (Grand Rapids Christian)9 ... 20:31
13. Wendy Johnecheck (Petoskey)10 ... 20:34
14. Lisa Reid (Yale)12 ... 20:35
15. Jennifer Mast (Jackson Northwest)11 ... 20:36
16. Amy Lathrop (Jackson Northwest)10 ... 20:40
17. Theresa Foster (Richland Gull Lake)11 ... 20:41
18. Kati Holborn (Gaylord)10 ... 20:50
19. Kelly Beschoner (Yale)10 ... 20:56
20. Michelle Gayney (Redford Borgess)12 ... 20:57
29. Cindy Hasselbring (Milan)10 ... 21:06
33. Annie Thompson (Milan)10 ... 21:10
35. Pam Hoffman (Milan)12 ... 21:17
94. Kathie Michelin (Milan)12 ... 22:19
146. Lara Woods (Milan) ... 23:43

1988 GIRLS CLASS B INDIVIDUAL RACE

1. Jennifer Barber (Frankenmuth)9 ... 19:56
2. Laura Bell (Otisville Lake Ville)10 ... 20:21
3. Tobi McKern (Chesaning)9 ... 20:33
4. Kim Blouw (Wyoming Park)11 ... 20:38
5. Amber Steiner (Clawson)9 ... 20:40
6. Kelley DeLange (Algonac)11 ... 20:41
7. Rena Hassing (Allegan)11 ... 20;45
8. Amy Sytsma (Holland Christian)9 ... 20:47
9. Angie Thomas (Sparta)11 ... 20:49
10. Sharon Veneklase (GR West Catholic)12 ... 20:52

1989 CLASS B GIRLS

Ninth-grader Lisa Monti led Chelsea to victory, as Pat Clarke's Bulldogs tied the record for the highest winning score ever. Fremont finished just 5 points behind. It was the closest Class B meet ever.

Another frosh, Tecumseh's Nicole Randolph, took the individual run.

Tyrone Hills Golf Course, Linden, Nov. 4 ⊠
1989 GIRLS CLASS B TEAMS

1. Chelsea ... 141
2. Fremont ... 146
3. Jackson Northwest ... 172
4. East Grand Rapids ... 216
5. Jackson Lumen Christi ... 245
6. Petoskey ... 251
7. Algonac ... 259
8. Grand Rapids South Christian ... 261
9. Lowell ... 267
10. Grand Rapids Catholic Central ... 270
11. Gladwin ... 329
12. Gaylord ... 332
13. Corunna ... 339
14. Mattawan ... 350
15. Marysville ... 358
16. Dearborn Divine Child ... 371
17. Milan ... 371
18. Yale ... 381
19. Grosse Ile ... 386
20. Warren Mott ... 408
21. Otisville LakeVille ... 426
22. Caledonia ... 449
23. Fowlerville ... 456
24. Allegan ... 470
25. Clawson ... 700
26. Marine City ... 702

1989 GIRLS CLASS B TEAM RACE

1. Lisa Monti (Chelsea)9 ... 19:08
2. Michele Radcliffe (Corunna)11 ... 19:14
3. Amy Lothrop (Jackson Northwest)11 ... 19:15
4. Lisa Kuiper (Grand Rapids S Christian)12 ... 19:32
5. Becky Beland (Caledonia)9 ... 19:36
6. Hillari Kirsch (Lowell)11 ... 19:38
7. Vonda Meder (Corunna)12 ... 19:44
8. Lisa Snyder (Grand Rapids Catholic C)11 ... 19:44
9. Carol Flickinger (Milan)11 ... 19:44
10. Sheila Rottier (Fremont)11 ... 19:47
11. Roxanne Swanson (Algonac)11 ... 19:48
12. Jennifer Mast (Jackson Northwest)12 ... 19:52
13. Shanon Kilgore (Algonac)10 ... 19:53
14. Kelly DeLange (Algonac)12 ... 19:54
15. Wendy Johncheck (Petoskey)11 ... 20:00
23, Valerie Bullock (Chelsea)9 ... 20:23
35. Kim Roberts (Chelsea)12 ... 20:48
37. Sarah Grau (Chelsea)12 ... 20:54
45. Vicki Bullock (Chelsea)12 ... 21:03
106. Christine Mignano (Chelsea)11 ... 22:13
129. Teddi Hauck (Chelsea)9 ... 22:44

1989 GIRLS CLASS B INDIVIDUAL RACE

1. Nicole Randolph (Tecumseh)9 ... 18:57
2. Kim Blouw (Wyoming Park)12 ... 19:15
3. Jeni Vite (Buchanan)12 ... 19:21
4. Joy Strawser (Coldwater)11 ... 19:22
5. Julie Hay (Three Rivers)11 ... 19:40
6. Amy Sytsma (Holland Christian)10 ... 19:47
7. Jenny Konnacker (Richland Gull Lake)10 ... 19:49
8. Eileen Mikloiche (Mt Clemens Lutheran N)11 ... 19:53
9. Megan Young (Cadillac)10 ... 19:54
10. Tobi McKern (Chesaning)10 ... 19:56
11. Terry Osborn (DeWitt)12 ... 19:57
12. Julie Owen (Alma)10 ... 19:58
13. Agapita Arizola (Croswell-Lexington)9 ... 20:02
14. Erica Shepard (Redford Borgess)9 ... 20:03
15. Angela Thomas (Sparta)12 ... 20:04

1990 CLASS B GIRLS

The team run saw a close finish between Kelly Smith--later an All-American 1500m runner for Colorado--and Laura Bell. Smith prevailed on the sprint by one second.

Jackson Lumen Christi notched a record-high score for Class B. It was state win No. 6 for the team, coached by Mike Woolsey. The winning margin—a scant 1 point—was the smallest ever.

Tyrone Hills Golf Course, Linden, Nov. 3⊠
1990 GIRLS CLASS B TEAMS

1. Jackson Lumen Christi ... 144
2. Caledonia ... 145
3. Fremont ... 150
4. Petoskey ... 163
5. Chelsea ... 190
6. Mason ... 201
7. Mattawan ... 218
8. Gaylord ... 298
9. Plainwell ... 314
10. Richland Gull Lake ... 323
11. Lowell ... 341
12. Otisville LakeVille ... 346

13. Marysville 350
14. Grosse Ile 369
15. Alma 385
16. Jackson Northwest 390
17. Algonac 391
18. Grand Rapids Catholic Central 407
19. New Boston Huron 414
20. East Grand Rapids 421
21. Milan 435
22. Yale 440
23. Dearborn Divine Child 511
24. Marine City 600
25. Warren Mott 604

1990 GIRLS CLASS B TEAM RACE
1. Kelly Smith (Petoskey)9 ....18:54
2. Laura Bell (Otisville Lake Ville)12 ....18:55
3. Lisa Monti (Chelsea)10 ....19:12
4. Jenny Kornacker (Richland Gull Lake)11 ....19:13
5. Amy Leatherman (Caledonia)12 ....19:28
6. Amy Lathrop (Jackson Northwest)12 ....19:33
7. Wendy Johnecheck (Petoskey)12 ....19:40
8. Lisa Buytendorp (Mattawan)10 ....19:42
9. Sheila Rottier (Fremont)12 ....19:43
10. Michelle Oliver (Lowell)9 ....19:44
11. Marci Beeke (Plainwell)12 ....19:44
12. Korey Hofman (Caledonia)12 ....19:47
13. Valerie Bullock (Chelsea)10 ....19:49
14. Julie Kokoczka (Jackson Lumen Christi)11 ....19:50
15. Kathy McGill (Alma)12 ....19:55
16. Becky Shively (Fremont)11 ....19:56
17. Judeth Meriwether (Richland Gull Lake)12 ....19:57
18. Djohariah Stevens (Petoskey)12 ....20:00
19. Kelly Beschoner (Yale)12 ....20:03
20. Hillari Kirsch (Lowell)12 ....20:06
21. Roxanne Swanson (Algonac)12 ....20:10
25. Mary Gibson (Jackson Lumen Christi)11 ....20:18
29. Cathy Jackson (Jackson Lumen Christi)10 ....20:33
32. Laura Welch (Jackson Lumen Christi)12 ....20:38
44. Colleen McGrath (Jackson Lumen Christi)10 ....20:56
? Angie Aerts (Jackson Lumen Christi)12 .... nt
? Andrea Ramp (Jackson Lumen Christi)10 .... nt

1990 GIRLS CLASS B INDIVIDUAL RACE
1. Jennifer Barber (Frankenmuth)11 ....18:53
2. Erica Adams (Gladwin)12 ....19:17
3. Annie Erlewine (Big Rapids)10 ....19:24
4. Julie Hay (Three Rivers)12 ....19:29
5. Sara Stanton (Big Rapids)10 ....19:35
6. Becky Dykehouse (Grand Rapids S Christian)11 19:43
7. Jill Strawser (Coldwater)12 ....20:02
8. Melanie Kaczur (Southgate Aquinas)11 ....20:03
9. Nicole Randolph (Tecumseh)10 ....20:08
10. Peggy Lang (WB Ogemaw Heights)12 ....20:10

1991 CLASS B GIRLS

Annie Erlewine won the team run for Big Rapids, her 19:33 giving her a 75-yard margin at the finish over Chelsea's Lisa Monti.

Even though Chelsea was ranked No. 1 coming in, Lumen Christi successfully defended its title, making for a total of 7. The tie between Chelsea and Big Rapids for 2nd was broken by the sixth runner.

After finishing 9th the year before, Tecumseh's Nicole Randolph won the individual run by a much bigger margin than when she won two years earlier.

Winters Creek Golf Course, Big Rapids, Nov. 2 ⊠
1991 GIRLS CLASS B TEAMS
1. Jackson Lumen Christi 95
2. Chelsea 134
3. Big Rapids 134
4. Fremont 175
5. Mattawan 202
6. Hillsdale 208
7. Petoskey 226
8. Grand Rapids South Christian 299
9. Gaylord 302
10. Southgate Aquinas 304
11. Caledonia 307
12. Grosse Ile 316
13. Perry 339
14. Plainwell 343
15. Gladwin 344
16. Monroe St Mary 359
17. Edwardsburg 382
18. Bloomfield Hills Andover 435
19. Yale 468
20. Otisville Lakeville 480
21. Algonac 496
22. Stanton-Central Montcalm 510
23. Caro 544
24. Dearborn Divine Child 610
25. Marine City 680

1991 GIRLS CLASS B TEAM RACE
1. Annie Erlewine (Big Rapids)11 ....19:33
2. Lisa Monti (Chelsea)11 ....19:47
3. Kelly Smith (Petoskey)10 ....20:07
4. Shannon Dye (Hillsdale) 20:09
5. Ann Byland (Fremont) 20:10
6. Sara Stanton (Big Rapids)10 ....10:11
7. Valeria Bullock (Chelsea) 20:17
8. Julie Kokoczka (Jackson Lumen Christi)12 ....20:19
9. Summer Adolf (Big Rapids)9 ....20:19
10. Amanda Spiller (Yale) 20:20
11. Emily Kaiser (Otisville Lakeville) 20:22
12. Becky Shively (Fremont) 20:31
13. Betsy Haverkamp (GR South Christian) 20:33
14. Katy Hollbacher (Petoskey) 20:36
15. Jennifer Brewer (Southgate Aquinas) 20:39
16. Jennifer Welch (Monroe St Mary) 20:41
17. Cathy Jackson (Jackson Lumen Christi)11 ....20:42
18. Marlene Micinski (Edwardsburg) 20:45
19. Becky Hand (Jackson Lumen Christi)9 ....20:46
20. Megan Powers (Jackson Lumen Christi)9 ....20:49
31. Mary Gibson (Jackson Lumen Christi)12 ....21:13
43. Lisa Krejcick (Jackson Lumen Christi)9 ....21:36
89. Kris Kuenz (Jackson Lumen Christi)12 ....22:34

1991 GIRLS CLASS B INDIVIDUAL RACE
1. Nicole Randolph (Tecumseh)11 ....19:42
2. Rhonda Wolf (Sturgis) 20:19
3. Erin McCarthy (Flint Powers) 20:30
4. Jennifer Komacker (Richland Gull Lake)12 ....20:36
5. Julianne Raack (Dexter) 20:38
6. Michelle St Louis (Sturgis) 20:39
7. Jennifer Lalonde (Grand Rapdis Catholic) 20:40
8. Christine Brubaker (Monroe Jefferson)10 ....20:43
9. Agapita Arizola (Croswell-Lexington) 20:45
10. Heather Moore (Hartland)9 ....20:48
11. Paula Kangas (Saline) 20:49

1992 CLASS B GIRLS

Defending champion Annie Erlewine was beaten in the team race, but her Big Rapids squad won the overall crown, as did the Big Rapids boys. "Believe me, it feels much, much better being on a state championship team than it does being a state champion by yourself," she said.

Kelly Smith took the individual run in 18:46, after following the leaders for the first two miles before breaking away for a 29-second win. "She came through with a tremendous race," said coach Don Dickmann.

Lisa Monti finishe her career for Chelsea with a win. In four years she never finished lower than 3rd at the state finals.

Tyrone Hills Golf Course, Linden, Nov. 7 ⊠
1992 GIRLS CLASS B TEAMS
1. Big Rapids 101
2. Caledonia 114
3. Gaylord 115
4. Chelsea 120
5. Saline 159
6. Jackson Lumen Christi 184
7. West Branch Ogemaw Heights 267
8. Monroe St Mary 290
9. Flint Powers 295
10. Yale 299
11. Hudsonville 307
12. Perry 328
13. Plainwell 339
14. Holland Christian 367
15. Hastings 395
16. Fremont 403
17. Vicksburg 422
18. Cedar Springs 425
19. Vassar 449
20. Grosse Ile 476
21. Bloomfield Hills Andover 490
22. Milan 531
23. Algonac 573
24. Marine City 695

1992 GIRLS CLASS B TEAM RACE
1. Lisa Monti (Chelsea)12 ....19:14
2. Annie Erlewine (Big Rapids)12 ....19:28
3. Edith Kortekaas (Hastings)12 ....19:42
4. Summer Adolph (Big Rapids)10 ....19:46
5. Kate Fall (Vassar)9 ....19:53
6. Ann Welch (Monroe St Mary) 19:56
7. Katie Sobczak (Caledonia) 20:00
8. Sara Stanton (Big Rapids)11 ....20:08
9. Stacey Lenard (Hudsonville)10 ....20:09
10. Sarah Flegal (Caledonia) 20:11
11. Becky Beland (Caledonia) 20:11
12. Cathy Carr (Plainwell)12 ....20:13
13. Ann Byland (Fremont) 20:13
14. Amanda Spiller (Yale) 20:15
15. Jennifer Welch (Monroe St Mary) 20:20
16. Rta Arndt (Saline)9 ....20:22
17. Kate Halgren (Gaylord)10 ....20:23
18. Megan Powers (Jackson Lumen Christi)10 ....20:30
41. Becky Tuttle (Big Rapids) 21:11
46. Janna Muccio (Big Rapids) 21:21
47. Karen Jefts (Big Rapids) 21:21
50. Jenny Smith (Big Rapids) 21:23

1992 GIRLS CLASS B INDIVIDUAL RACE
1. Kelly Smith (Petoskey)11 ....18:46
2. Betsy Haverkamp (GR South Christian)12 ....19:15
3. Maria Zeiler (Hillsdale) 19:36
4. Megan Smedley (Buchanan) 19:37
5. Rhonda Wolfe (Sturgis) 19:39
6. Michelle St Louis (Sturgis) 19:57
7. Kelli DeCamp (Jackson) 20:07
8. Nicole Randolph (Tecumseh) 20:19
9. Elke Thompson (Royal Oak) 20:20
10. Jenny Coykendall (Wyoming Godwin Hts)9 ....20:24
11. Melissa Hayward (Parma Western) 20:24
12. Cymbre Fleming (South Haven) 20:32

1993 CLASS B GIRLS

Caledonia won its first state title in any sport. Said coach Dave Hodgkinson, "They went out and ran as fast as they could today. We don't worry about places or times, just to be the best runners that we can become."

Kelly Smith defended her title with a massive 52-second margin. The Colorado-bound star had mixed feelings about moving on. "It is kind of sad to think about because I'll be at a different school [next year] with different teammates."

Grand Rapids Golf Club, Grand Rapids, Nov. 6 ⊠
1993 GIRLS CLASS B TEAMS
1. Caledonia 58
2. Gaylord 122
3. Saline 195
4. Fremont 206
5. Petoskey 233
6. Chelsea 258
7. Big Rapids 263
8. Hudsonville 268
9. West Branch Ogemaw Heights 306
=10. Caro 359
=10. Dearborn Divine Child 359
12. Yale 365
13. Jackson Lumen Christi 370
14. Zeeland 378
15. Paw Paw 391
16. Grand Rapids South Christian 406

17. Sparta	423
18. Flint Powers	441
19. Plainwell	485
20. Richland Gull Lake	486
21. Bloomfield Hills Andover	508
22. Lansing Catholic	513
23. Gladwin	541
24. Clawson	574
25. Perry	584
26. Stockbridge	640
27. Trenton	652
28. Ludington	673
29. Carleton Airport	709
30. Algonac	781

1993 GIRLS CLASS B TEAM RACE

1. Kelly Smith (Petoskey)12	18:28
2. Katie Sobczak (Caledonia)10	19:20
3. Sarah Flegel (Caledonia)11	19:27
4. Rita Arndt (Saline)	19:41
5. Michelle Harkema (GR South Christian)11	19:42
6. Stacey Lenard (Hudsonville)11	19:43
7. Molly Galsterer (Caro)	19:43
8. Summer Adlof (Big Rapids)	19:53
9. Jenny Spiller (Yale)	19:57
10. Stephani Young (Gaylord)	20:00
11. Shannon Houseman (Caledonia)9	20:02
12. Melissa Hand (Chelsea)	20:05
13. Ann Byland (Fremont)	20:10
14. Karyn Duba (Caledonia)	20:10
15. Kristie DeYoung (GR South Christian)	20:11
28. Sarah Parbel (Caledonia)10	20:38
30. Beth Parbel (Caledonia)9	20:43
43. Meredith Denison (Caledonia)12	20:53

1993 GIRLS CLASS B INDIVIDUAL RACE

1. Kate Fall (Vassar)10	19:12
2. Maria Zieler (Hillsdale)	19:27
3. Kelli DeCamp (Jackson Northwest)	19:35
4. Jenny Coykendall (Wyoming Godwin Hts)10	19:37
5. Laura Deneau (Warren Woods Tower)11	19:40
6. Rhonda Wolfe (Sturgis)	19:42
7. Kellie Anderson (Brooklyn Columbia Central)10	19:47
8. Christine Freeman (Oxford)	19:48
9. Erin Deming (Essexville Garber)	19:51
10. Amy Farmer (St Joseph)	19:55
11. Missy Guetschow (Vicksburg)	20:00
12. Elizabetgh Kelm (Stevensville Lakeshore)10	20:01
13. Amber Crenshaw (Coldwater)	20:02
14. Jenny Lilly (Croswell-Lexington)	20:02
15. Heidi Schmidt (Brooklyn Columbia Central)	20:03

1994 CLASS B GIRLS

Caledonia won Class B in one of the most impressive team performances in the state's history. The Scots put six runners under 20-minutes, while the rest of the teams combined could only manage three. The team placed runners 2-3-4-5-7. Coach Dave Hodgkinson said he would gladly race the Class A winners: "We wouldn't be afraid to run anyone. That's what it's all about."

During the regular season, the Fighting Scots won 10 duals with a 15-50 score. The only meet score that wasn't "perfect" went 15-49.

Carrie Gould won her third state title—but her first for Flint Powers. The previous two she had won in Class C for Burton Bendle.

Grand Rapids Golf Club, Grand Rapids, Nov. 5 ☐
1994 GIRLS CLASS B TEAMS

1. Caledonia	21
2. Gaylord	83
3. Fremont	182
4. Flint Powers	238
5. Ludington	266
6. Jackson Lumen Christi	281
7. West Branch Ogemaw Heights	297
8. Grand Rapids South Christian	305
9. Grosse Ile	322
10. Stockbridge	338
11. Tecumseh	347
=12. St Joseph	356
=12. Sparta	356
14. Dearborn Divine Child	365
15. Paw Paw	376
16. Cadillac	379
17. Caro	386
18. Parma Western	417
19. Clawson	448
20. Hastings	471
21. Madison Heights Lamphere	481
22. Petoskey	535
23. Carleton Airport	544
24. Lakeville	561
25. Lansing Catholic	614
26. Royal Oak Dondero	616
27. Holland Christian	652

Keri Bloem (right) and Barb Warner lead Caledonia with a 2-3 finish.

1994 GIRLS CLASS B TEAM RACE

1. Carrie Gould (Flint Powers)11	18:55
2. Keri Bloem (Caledonia)10	19:19
3. Barb Warner (Caledonia)10	19:22
4. Shannon Houseman (Caledonia)10	19:23
5. Sarah Parbel (Caledonia)11	19:34
6. Veronica Quackenbush (Ogemaw Heights)10	19:40
7. Katie Sobczak (Caledonia)11	19:48
8. Audrey Warner (Caledonia)10	19:48
9. Gina Jackson (Ludington)10	19:55
10. Kate Halgren (Gaylord)12	20:09
11. Crystal Porta (Gaylord)10	20:17
12. Genny Yavello (Dearborn Divine Child)10	20:28
13. Michelle Harkema (GR South Christian)12	20:30
14. Kelsie Gould (Flint Powers)9	20:34
15. Sarah Flegel (Caledonia)12	20:35

1994 GIRLS CLASS B INDIVIDUAL RACE

1. Laura Deneau (Warren Woods Tower)12	19:24
2. Stacey Lenard (Hudsonville)12	19:29
3. Jeannie Spink (Chelsea)	19:41
4. Erin Deming (Essexville Garber)	19:49
5. Kate Fall (Vassar)11	19:49
6. Jenny Spiller (Yale)11	19:54
7. April Barfoot (Whitehall)	20:01
8. Kellie Anderson (Brooklyn Columbia Central)11	20:05
9. M. Laughmunn (Stevensville-Lakeshore)	20:09
10. Shannon Ottenweller (GR Catholic Central)	20:09
11. Danielle Risner (Albion)	20:10
12. Rhonda Wolfe (Sturgis)	20:11
13. Kelli DeCamp (Jackson Northwest)	20:12
14. Norma Haddon (Beaverton)12	20:13
15. Tami Lauritzen (Wyoming Park)11	20:19

1995 CLASS B GIRLS

Caledonia produced another boggling performance, a 28-point score that left runner-up Gaylord a record 162 points behind.

Carrie Gould made it four-straight individual titles, two in Class C and two in Class B. The next spring she would win her fourth state title on the track, taking the Class B 1600 in 5:03.9. In 1997 she would win the Mid-American cross country title for Eastern Michigan.

Grand Rapids Golf Club, Grand Rapids, Nov. 4 ☐
1995 GIRLS CLASS B TEAMS

1. Caledonia	28
2. Gaylord	190
3. Chelsea	198
4. Fremont	211
5. Jackson Lumen Christi	255
6. Shepherd	255
7. Grosse Ile	266
8. Ida	273
9. Hillsdale	296
10. Flint Powers	303
11. Paw Paw	306
12. Richland Gull Lake	310
13. Coopersville	3154
14. Ludington	315
15. Sparta	323
16. Gladwin	428
17. Holland Christian	480
18. Haslett	485
19. Dearborn Divine Child	486
20. Ionia	492
21. Algonac	500
22. Petoskey	504
23. Fowlerville	540
24. Clawson	544
25. Carlton Airport	566
26. Whitehall	602
27. Royal Oak Dondero	668

1995 GIRLS CLASS B TEAM RACE

1. Carrie Gould (Flint Powers)12	18:00
2. Julie David (Coopersville)10	18:03
3. Keri Bloem (Caledonia)11	18:08
4. Liz Fortuna (Caledonia)10	18:14
5. Shannon Houseman (Caledonia)11	18:14
6. Angie Lefere (Jackson Lumen Christi)11	18:19
7. Brooke Wierenga (Caledonia)9	18:41
8. Chrystal Porta (Gaylord)11	18:47
9. Sarah Parbel (Caledonia)12	18:51
10. Kelsie Gould (Flint Powers)10	18:56
11. Jeannie Spink (Chelsea)10	19:02
12. Janice Denney (Clawson)10	19:06
13. Audrey Warner (Caledonia)11	19:12
14. Laura Bartelson (Richland Gull Lake)12	19:16
15. Kristin Pauken (Hillsdale)10	19:17
32. Barbara Warner (Caledonia)11	19:56

1995 GIRLS CLASS B INDIVIDUAL RACE

1. Kate Fall (Vassar)12	18:26
2. Erin White (Battle Creek Pennfield)10	18:47
3. Kim Browning (Onsted)12	18:53
4. Christenell Freeman (Oxford)	19:00
5. Veronica Quackenbush (Ogemaw Heights)11	19:02
6. Cami Moll (Hudsonville)	19:03
7. Danielle Risner (Albion)	19:03
8. Melisssa Laughhunn (Stevensville Lakeshore)	19:04
9. Charissa Shaw (Hastings)	19:04
10. Laurie Meyers (Battle Creek Harper Creek)10	19:10
11. Erin Deming (Essexville Garber)	19:15
12. Jessica Davis (Middleville TK)	19:17
13. Amber Crenshaw (Coldwater)	19:18
14. Jody Thompson (West Branch Ogemaw Hts)	19:19
15. Becky Keller (Oxford)	19:21

1996 CLASS B GIRLS

In the first year at Michigan International Speedway, Caledonia won a record fourth straight B title, as Bethany Brewster of Valley Lutheran took the individual race by 57 seconds. In a holdover from the separate races of previous yeas, 7th-placer Julie David of Coopersville was given a first-place medal as the "individual winner."

Veronica Quackenbush pulled away from Caledonia's Shannon Houseman on the final stretch to seal a 3-second win.

Michigan Int. Speedway, Brooklyn, Nov. 2 ⊠
1996 GIRLS CLASS B TEAMS

1. Caledonia 53
2. Grand Rapids West Catholic 136
3. Fremont 181
4. Jackson Lumen Christi 214
5. Shepherd 247
6. Ludington 277
7. Dearborn Divine Child 286
8. West Branch Ogemaw Heights 291
9. Chelsea 296
10. Parma Western 297
11. Whitehall 316
12. Gaylord 343
13. Vicksburg 357
14. Grosse Ile 383
15. Flint Powers 383
16. Haslett 391
17. Durand 415
18. Algonac 444
19. Grand Rapids Catholic Central 459
20. Caro 479
21. Bloomfield Hills Andover 507
22. St Joseph 534
23. Clawson 537
24. Gladwin 540
25. Ida 586
26. Richland Gull Lake 605
27. Auburn Hills Avondale 644

1996 GIRLS CLASS B INDIVIDUALS

1. Veronica Quackenbush (Ogemaw Heights)12 18:06
2. Shannon Houseman (Caledonia)12 18:09
3. Angie Lefere (Jackson Lumen Christi)12 18:18
4. Katie Clifford (GR West Catholic)12 18:22
5. Liz Fortuna (Caledonia)11 18:37
6. Brooke Wierenga (Caledonia)10 18:48
7. Julie David (Coopersville)11 18:57
8. Harmony Dykhuis (Fremont)9 19:01
9. Keri Bloem (Caledonia)12 19:07
10. Rashel Bayes (Sparta)12 19:08
11. Tami Lauritzen (Wyoming Park) 19:09
12. Jeannie Spink (Chelsea)11 19:11
13. Cathy Piotrowski (Algonac)10 19:13
14. Anne McGrath (GR Catholic Central) 19:14
15. Genny Yavello (Dearborn Divine Child)12 19:18
16. Alaina Stuart (Parma Western)9 19:24
17. Nicole Sackrider (Battle Creek Harper Creek) 19:27
18. Laurel Myers (Battle Creek Harper Creek)11 19:28
19. Tracey Graw (Wyoming Godwin Heights)11 19:29
20. Laura Saxton (Ludington)11 19:29
21. Jodi Vermeulen (Holland Christian)10 19:29
22. Beth Boruta (GR West Catholic)12 19:30
23. Janice Denney (Clawson)11 19:31
24. Kelly Kemmis (Ogemaw Heights)10 19:32
25. Michelle Rice (Whitehall)10 19:33
26. Karen LeRoy (Oxford)9 19:33
27. Jenny Ziegler (Jackson Lumen Christi)11 19:34
28. Rebecca Keller (Oxford) 19:36
29. Courtney Daunt (Flint Powers)10 19:41
30. Amy Farmer (St Joseph) 19:42
33. Jenny Sprague (Caledonia) 20:01
40. Beth Parbel (Caledonia) 20:11
53. Sarah Grow (Caledonia) 20:36

1997 CLASS B GIRLS

Fremont, coached by legendary runner Herb Lindsay, took both the overall win and had the top runner in sophomore Harmony Dykhuis, who triumphed in 19:42.

"We've had five girls who have been running strong all season long," said Lindsay. "Battling Whitehall, we knew who our competition was from early in the season. We knew they were the team to beat today."

Michigan Int. Speedway, Brooklyn, Nov. 1 ⊠
1997 GIRLS CLASS B TEAMS

1. Fremont 111
2. Whitehall 118
3. West Branch Ogemaw Heights 142
4. Grand Rapids Catholic Central 166
5. Battle Creek Harper Creek 171
6. Parma Western 204
7. Holland Christian 290
8. Chelsea 298
9. Flint Powers 319
10. Cedar Springs 325
11. Richland Gull Lake 348
12. Carleton Airport 361
13. Corunna 374
14. Dearborn Divine Child 380
15. Grand Rapids West Catholic 380
16. Shepherd 422
17. Haslett 426
18. Monroe Jefferson 450
19. Hemlock 456
20. Stevensville Lakeshore 457
21. Oxford 483
22. Petoskey 493
23. Essexville Garber 516
24. Algonac 534
25. Plainwell 541
26. Clawson 553
27. Bloomfield Hills Andover 624

1997 GIRLS CLASS B INDIVIDUALS

1. Harmony Dykhuis (Fremont)10 19:42
2. Miranda Makovic (Stevensville Lakeshore)11 19:51
3. Mary Reynolds (GR Catholic Central)11 20:04
4. Jillian Duff (Whitehall)10 20:07
5. Jennifer Cook (Fowlerville)10 20:09
6. Melissa Miller (Portland) 20:11
7. Jessica Kraft (WB Ogemaw Heights)9 20:17
8. Kelsie Gould (Flint Powers) 20:19
9. Michelle Rice (Whitehall)11 20:20
10. Jessica Davis (Middleville TK) 20:22
11. Jenny Ziegler (Jackson Lumen Christi) 20:22
12. Abigail Nelkie (WB Ogemaw Heights)9 20:23
13. Karyn Hren (Fremont)9 20:24
14. Jessica Kellogg (Delton Kellogg)9 20:27
15. Tanya Fraser (Spring Lake) 20:27
16. Karen Leroy (Oxford)10 20:28
17. Laurel Myers (Battle Creek Harper Creek)12 20:29
18. Rebecca Porinsky (Dexter) 20:30
19. Jeannie Spink (Chelsea) 20:30
20. Jessica Gilbert (Corunna)12 20:32
21. Danielle Quisenberry (Middleville TK)10 20:33
22. Tami VerMeulen (Holland Christian)11 20:35
23. Amber Terry (Vicksburg)11 20:39
24. Rebecca Keller (Oxford) 20:40
25. Char Brandow (Cedar Springs)12 20:41
26. Katie Klaver (Wyoming Park) 20:44
27. Amanda Portis (Richland Gull Lake)10 20:47
28. Kristy Debski (Sparta) 20:48
29. Sarah Pepera (Ortonville Brandon)11 20:50
30. Tiffeny Kotecki (Fremont) 20:51
56. Kari Dawe (Fremont)10 21:21
92. Lori Nieboer (Fremont)9 21:40
155. Shelly Noland (Fremont)10 22:21
176. Billie Hall (Fremont)10 22:32

1998 CLASS B GIRLS

Corunna's Jamie Krzyminski won the B title in a sprint dual with Bishop Foley's soccer star Nicole Breger, who had led much of the later stages of the race. It was Krzyminski's first season of running. "I'm kind of in shock right now," she said. "This whole season has just been great. To come here and win is really exciting."

It was sophomore Breger's last season of running. She ended up concentrating on soccer. She later played for the University of Texas and won All-Big 12 honors twice.

Whitehall, coached by Kathy Hector, won its first-ever team title after a near-miss the year before.

Michigan Int. Speedway, Brooklyn, Nov. 7 ⊠
1998 GIRLS CLASS B TEAMS

1. Whitehall 85
2. West Branch Ogemaw Heights 95
3. Corunna 149
4. Fremont 182
5. Monroe Jefferson 203
6. Parma Western 222
7. Flint Powers 233
8. Ludington 253
9. Jackson Lumen Christi 280
10. Haslett 316
11. Wayland 335
12. Richland Gull Lake 362
13. Gladwin 367
14. Holland Christian 382
15. Grand Rapids West Catholic 393
16. Carleton Airport 415
17. Middleville Thornapple-Kellogg 417
18. Cedar Springs 434
19. St Clair 435
20. Dearborn Divine Child 493
21. Shepherd 513
22. Bad Axe 530
23. Saginaw Nouvel 552
24. Vicksburg 567
25. Ida 597
26. Algonac 649
27. Richmond 669
28. Bloomfield Hills Andover 725

Jamie Krzyminski won by a second.

1998 GIRLS CLASS B INDIVIDUALS

1. Jamie Krzyminski (Corunna)11 17:54
2. Nicole Breger (Madison Heights Foley)10 17:55
3. Harmony Dykhuis (Fremont)11 18:05
4. Sarah Pepera (Ortonville Brandon)12 18:20
5. Mary Reynolds (GR Catholic Central)12 18:31
6. Colleen Lange (Corunna)12 18:35
7. Sara Dillman (Marshall)12 18:35
8. Rachel Cox (Battle Creek Lakeview)11 18:40
9. Danielle Quisenberry (Middleville TK)11 18:41
10. Katie Vyncke (Marysville)11 18:41
11. Kara Hollern (GR Catholic Central)10 18:42
12. Lisa Fishel (Whitehall)12 18:42
13. Michelle Rice (Whitehall)12 18:45
14. Abigail Nelkie (WB Ogemaw Heights)10 18:45
15. Sarah Sterenberg (Hamilton)10 18:45
16. Jessica Kraft (WB Ogemaw Heights)10 18:47
17. Liz Fortuna (Caledonia)12 18:50
18. Abby Barnett (Battle Creek Lakeview)11 18:51
19. Kim Cocco (Grand Rapids S Christian)12 18:52
20. Brooke Wierenga (Caledonia)12 18:53
21. Carrie Smeltzer (Monroe Jefferson)10 18:55
22. Julia Wagner (Battle Creek Pennfield)12 18:56
23. Sarah Grygiel (Wayland)12 18:57
24. Jeannie Seckinger (Haslett)11 18:58
25. Nichelle Carpenter (Flint Powers)11 19:00
26. Sarah Roberts (Vicksburg)11 19:04
27. Amy Tomlinson (Wyoming Kellogsville)9 19:07

28. Heidi Johnson (Ludington)9....19:07
29. Charla Eustice (Cheboygan)12....19:08
30. Jessica Kellogg (Delton Kellogg)10....19:11
32. Jillian Duff (Whitehall)11....19:15
35. Stefanie DeLong (Whitehall)10....19:20
68. Katrina Alvesteffer (Whitehall)10....19:48
76. Ginger Russell (Whitehall)12....19:56
160. Eva Spiece (Whitehall)10....20:41

1999 CLASS B GIRLS

Tammy Benjamin's Middleville Thornapple-Kellogg team rose to the top to win the final Class B title by more than 50 points.

Corunna's Jamie Krzyminski dominated in defending her title. She excelled even more at Michigan State, placing 3rd in the 2004 NCAA 10,000 and 8th in the Olympic Trials 10,000 that same year.

Michigan Int. Speedway, Brooklyn, Nov. 6 ⊠
1999 GIRLS CLASS B TEAMS
1. Middleville Thornapple-Kellogg....112
2. Flint Powers....174
3. Richland Gull Lake....181
4. Big Rapids....199
5. Parma Western....236
6. Fremont....237
7. Whitehall....239
8. Monroe Jefferson....249
9. Gaylord....257
10. Wyoming Kelloggsville....303
11. Sparta....315
12. Milan....329
13. West Branch Ogemaw Heights....357
14. Dearborn Divine Child....384
15. Holland Christian....385
16. Frankenmuth....389
17. St Clair....431
18. Haslett....449
19. Portland....464
20. Jackson Lumen Christi....476
21. Trenton....495
22. Lansing Catholic....499
23. Hamilton....515
24. Detroit Country Day....571
25. Bloomfield Hills Andover....585
26. Gladwin....628
27. Clawson....673

1999 GIRLS CLASS B INDIVIDUALS
1. Jamie Krzyminski (Corunna)12....18:19
2. Danielle Quisenberry (Middleville TK)12....18:31
3. Jessica Kraft (WB Ogemaw Heights)11....18:36
4. Abigail Nelkie (WB Ogemaw Heights)11....18:37
5. Jeannette Seckinger (Richland Gull Lake)12....18:40
6. Rachel Kirvan (Lansing Catholic)11....18:52
7. Melissa Quisenberry (Middleville TK)10....18:53
8. Krishawna Parker (Detroit Crockett)10....18:54
9. Melissa Miller (Portland)12....18:55
10. Carrie Smeltzer (Monroe Jefferson)11....19:02
11. Kalli Williams (Dexter)9....19:02
12. Anne Venier (Monroe Jefferson)11....19:05
13. Melissa Nasers (Battle Creek Pennfield)11....19:12
14. Amanda Huck (Fowlerville)9....19:12
15. Jenny Cook (Fowlerville)12....19:15
16. Amy Tomlinson (Wyoming Kelloggsville)10....19:18
17. Heidi Saunders (Plainwell)12....19:19
18. Erica Mahler (Muskegon Orchard View)9....19:20
19. Lori Nieboer (Fremont)11....19:22
20. Sarah Jaquith (Petoskey)9....19:23
21. Stefanie DeLong (Whitehall)11....19:23
22. Kathryn Vyncke (Marysville)12....19:24
23. Elizabeth Whiting (Parma Western)12....19:24
24. Emily VanSumeren (Parma Western)10....19:26
25. Jessica Kellogg (Delton Kellogg)11....19:30
26. Megan Schneider (Pontiac Notre Dame)11....19:30
27. Stacey Kandas (Trenton)10....19:31
28. Carolyn Thoma (Flint Powers)10....19:32
29. Jill LeBlanc (Richland Gull Lake)10....19:33
30. Katie Touran (Petoskey)12....19:35
46. Katie Richter (Middleville TK)11....19:57
62. Christine Dood (Middleville TK)10....20:09
82. Elise Nyland (Middleville TK)9....20:19
143. Theresa Miller (Middleville TK)9....20:47
155. Jen Verkerke (Middleville TK)11....20:50

2000 D2 GIRLS

The move to Divisions didn't have a huge effect on the state's second-largest classification. Middleville Thornapple-Kellogg defended its title with a 16-point win over Flint Powers; at 170 points it was the highest winning score in meet history.

Abigail Nelkie and Jessica Kraft pulled off a 1-2 finish for 14th place Ogemaw Heights. Nelkie took off from the start, leading at 1M in 5:38 and having a 9-second margin at 2M (11:33).

Abigail Nelkie (right) and Jessica Kraft led a powerful 1-2 finish for Ogemaw Heights.

Michigan Int. Speedway, Brooklyn, Nov. 4 ⊠
2000 GIRLS DIVISION 2 TEAMS
1. Middleville Thornapple-Kellogg....170
2. Flint Powers....186
3. Ludington....227
4. Richland Gull Lake....229
5. Mt Pleasant....234
6. Trenton....242
7. Battle Creek Lakeview....262
8. Big Rapids....291
9. Monroe Jefferson....294
10. St Clair....297
11. Sparta....311
12. Plainwell....315
13. Cedar Springs....324
14. West Branch Ogemaw Heights....329
15. Holland Christian....332
16. Lowell....334
17. Dexter....363
18. Birmingham Marian....365
19. Mason....417
20. Birmingham Seaholm....420
21. Farmington....441
22. Dearborn Divine Child....446
23. Pontiac Notre Dame....494
24. Stevensville Lakeshore....517
25. Farmington Hills Harrison....660
26. Corunna....706
27. St Clair Shores Lake Shore....760

2000 GIRLS DIVISION 2 INDIVIDUALS
1. Abigail Nelkie (WB Ogemaw Heights)12....18:06
2. Jessica Kraft (WB Ogemaw Heights)12....18:17
3. Carrie Smeltzer (Monroe Jefferson)12....18:24
4. Jill LeBlanc (Richland Gull Lake)11....18:44
5. Rebecca Walter (Birmingham Groves)11....18:45
6. Melissa Nasers (Battle Creek Lakeview)12....18:49
7. Anne Venier (Monroe Jefferson)12....18:50
8. Sara Lunning (Ludington)11....18:53
9. Mimi Speyer (Grand Rapids Christian)12....18:55
10. Meagan Webb (Battle Creek Harper Creek)9....18:56
11. Heidi Johnson (Ludington)11....19:07
12. Callie Adamson (Big Rapids)12....19:07
13. Megan Newton (East Lansing)10....19:07
14. Lindsay Mosher (Birmingham Seaholm)10....19:10
15. Melissa Quisenberry (Middleville TK)11....19:12
16. Jennifer Waters (Birmingham Marian)10....19:13
17. Katy Jackson (Grosse Ile)11....19:13
18. Kathleen Smith (Flint Powers)10....19:14
19. Carrie Davis (Eaton Rapids)10....19:14
20. Nicolette Merritt (Greenville)10....19:16
21. Becky Tirrell (Charlotte)11....19:18
22. Bethany Hofman (Holland Christian)10....19:20
23. Stephanie Kandas (Trenton)10....19:20
24. Kelli Gilliand (Trenton)9....19:20
25. Stacey Kandas (Trenton)11....19:21
26. Sarah DeBruyn (Comstock)12....19:21
27. Jackie Gaydos (Allen Park)10....19:22
28. Alison McMullin (Battle Creek Lakeview)12....19:26
29. Sarah Jaquith (Petoskey)10....19:30
30. Tricia Miedema (Caledonia)9....19:32
39. Jessica Stortz (Middleville TK)9....19:42
63. Katie Richter (Middleville TK)12....20:00
66. Jennifer Verkerke (Middleville TK)12....20:01
92. Elise Nyland (Middleville TK)10....20:18
136. Christine Dood (Middleville TK)11....20:44
145. Amber DeMaagd (Middleville TK)12....20:50

2001 D2 GIRLS

A third-straight for Middleville Thornapple-Kellogg, handily defeating Stevensville Lakeshore by 48 points. Individually, Rebecca Walter of Groves won big.

"I wanted top open it up as quickly as I could, so I tried to do it right away and hold on," she said of leading from the start, hitting splits of 5:31 and 11:45. "Winning was awesome. It was like I was in a dream."

Michigan Int. Speedway, Brooklyn, Nov. 3 ⊠
2001 GIRLS DIVISION 2 TEAMS
1. Middleville Thornapple-Kellogg....156
2. Stevensville Lakeshore....204
3. Birmingham Marian....205
4. Mt Pleasant....221
5. Lowell....226
6. Petoskey....265
7. Richland Gull Lake....269
8. Gaylord....272
9. Ludington....276
10. Chelsea....299
11. Dearborn Divine Child....299
12. Flint Powers....309
13. Battle Creek Lakeview....313
14. Trenton....330
15. Holland Christian....338
16. Grosse Ile....365
17. Eaton Rapids....390
18. Bloomfield Hills Andover....404
19. Whitehall....442
20. Fruitport....444
21. Birmingham Seaholm....458
22. Corunna....474
23. Flint Kearsley....477
24. Plainwell....478
25. Madison Heights Lamphere....580
26. Ypsilanti....624
27. St Clair Shores Lakeview....778

2001 GIRLS DIVISION 2 INDIVIDUALS
1. Rebecca Walter (Birmingham Groves)12....18:41
2. Michelle Diverio (Battle Creek Lakeview)10....19:17
3. Katie Prast (Bay City Glenn)11....19:18
4. Megan Newton (East Lansing)11....19:19
5. Kathleen Smith (Flint Powers)11....19:21
6. Jennifer Waters (Birmingham Marian)11....19:24
7. Heidi Johnson (Ludington)12....19:24
8. Carrie Davis (Eaton Rapids)11....19:24
9. Amber Myers (Jackson Northwest)10....19:26
10. Melissa Quisenberry (Middleville TK)12....19:30
11. Bethany Hofman (Holland Christian)11....19:34
12. Elise Rouwhorst (Fruitport)9....19:35
13. Colleen Duff (Birmingham Marian)12....19:35
14. Meagan Webb (Battle Creek Harper Creek)10. 19:36
15. Sarah Jaquith (Petoskey)11....19:37
16. Mallory Edmonds (Coopersville)10....19:37
17. Elizabeth Webster (Dearborn Divine Child)12... 19:38
18. Katie Erdman (Cadillac)12....19:38
19. Sarah Moore (Coldwater)9....19:38

20. Tricia Miedema (Caledonia)10 ....19:39
21. Kathryn Harriger (Gaylord)9.....................19:40
22. Rachel Gutierrez (Linden)10.....................19:40
23. Kelly Carter (Sparta)11...........................19:40
24. Kelly Sampson (Detroit Renaissance)9 ....19:41
25. Liz VanderLaan (GR Catholic Central)11 ....19:42
26. Lisa Wojciakowski (Lowell)11 ....19:42
27. Katy Jackson (Grosse Ile)12.....................19:46
28. Andrea Karl (Marine City)12.....................19:47
29. Jill LeBlanc (Richland Gull Lake)11 ....19:48
30. Alice Gauvin (Chelsea)10 ....19:49
45. Natalie Hoag (Middleville TK)9 ....20:14
59. Kaleigh Page (Middleville TK)9 ....20:23
69. Christine Dood (Middleville TK)12...............20:28
78. Jessica Stortz (Middleville TK)10................20:33
97. Elise Nyland (Middleville TK)11..................20:45
187. Theresa Miller (Middleville TK)11...............22:01

2002 D2 GIRLS

Jackie Gaydos of Allen Park and Laura Malnor of East Grand Rapids waged a see-saw battle throughout the race, with Caitlin Clifford of Lahser staying close. The pack stayed close together through a 2M split of 11:45. Gaydos took off in the final 400 to win by 11 seconds.

Battle Creek Lakeview, coached by Becky Turbin, won its first team title. "You couldn't ask for a better season," she said.

Michigan Int. Speedway, Brooklyn, Nov. 2
2002 GIRLS DIVISION 2 TEAMS
1. Battle Creek Lakeview 169
2. Petoskey...207
3. St Joseph..216
4. Lowell..217
5. Grand Rapids Christian 238
6. Chelsea 243
7. Dearborn Divine Child............................264
8. Remus Chippewa Hills 273
9. Mt Pleasant 273
10. Gaylord 294
11. Holland Christian 303
12. Sparta 303
13. Spring Lake 323
14. Milan 333
15. Dexter 337
16. Richland Gull Lake 371
17. Flint Powers 414
18. Croswell-Lexington 422
19. Fremont 433
20. Ypsilanti 471
21. Stevensville Lakeshore..........................500
22. Birmingham Seaholm 503
23. Flint Kearsley 510
24. Ionia 537
25. Detroit Renaissance 573
26. Birmingham Marian 586
27. Bloomfield Hills Andover 738
28. St Clair Shores Lakeview 800
29. Royal Oak Dondero 871

2002 GIRLS DIVISION 2 INDIVIDUALS
1. Jackie Gaydos (Allen Park)12 ....17:59
2. Laura Malnor (East Grand Rapids)9 ....18:10
3. Kelly Sampson (Detroit Renaissance)10 ......18:36
4. Caitlin Clifford (Bloomfield Hills Lahser)9.......18:38
5. Chelsea McVay (Croswell-Lexington)9 ....18:51
6. Megan Newton (East Lansing)12................18:53
7. Angela Martinez (Milan)9........................18:54
8. Sarah Jaquith (Petoskey)12.....................19:00
9. Rachel Severin (Chelsea)9 ....19:00
10. Kelsey Devereaux (Jackson Northwest)9.....19:00
11. Michelle Diverio (Battle Creek Lakeview)11 ...19:01
12. Jennifer Hamilton (Battle Creek Lakeview)10 ....19:05
13. Jennifer Waters (Birmingham Marian)12 ......19:07
14. Bethany Hofman (Holland Christian)12........19:07
15. Tracy Fry (Remus Chippewa Hills)9 ....19:07
16. Jessica Stortz (Middleville TK)11...............19:13
17. Diane Hamilton (Battle Creek Lakeview)10 .....19:15
18. Kelly Carter (Sparta)12 ....19:15
19. Erin Webster (Dearborn Divine Child)12 ....19:19
20. Jennifer Ludington (Croswell-Lexington)12 ....19:20
21. Kaitlin Darnell (Dearborn Divine Child)10......19:21
22. Colleen O'Shea (St Joseph)12..................19:22
23. Carrie Davis (Eaton Rapids)12 ....19:22
24. Kristin Hooker (Flint Kearsley)10 ....19:24
25. Kelsey Muczynski (Richmond)10................19:24
26. Katie Harriger (Gaylord)10 ....19:26
27. Tricia Miedema (Caledonia)11 ....19:27
28. Rachel Jeltema (Spring Lake)10................19:28
29. Faith Kejbou (Warren Fitzgerald)12 ....19:28
30. Emma Hummel (DeWitt)11 ....19:28
75. Lindsay Grosteffon (Battle Creek Lakeview)9....20:06
148. Clarissa Krajewski (Battle Creek Lakeview)11 ....20:56
159. Kelsey Nyberg (Battle Creek Lakeview)10 ....21:03
171. Brooke Ruble (Battle Creek Lakeview)9..........21:12

2003 D2 GIRLS

With three freshmen on the team, East Grand Rapids went from not qualifying the year before to the top of the podium.

Caitlin Clifford of Bloomfield Hills Lahser had a big lead early, but Laura Malnor gradually whittled it away, catching up after they entered the stadium. She ran 17:55 to lead her team, coached by Nick Hopkins, to the win.

Michigan Int. Speedway, Brooklyn, Nov. 1
2003 GIRLS DIVISION 2 TEAMS
1. East Grand Rapids................................ 79
2. Grand Rapids Christian 119
3. Battle Creek Lakeview 207
4. Monroe Jefferson 228
5. East Lansing 231
6. Dexter 262
7. Petoskey..264
8. Remus Chippewa Hills 279
9. St Joseph 300
10. Richland Gull Lake 302
11. Grand Rapids South Christian 311
12. Gaylord 314
13. Milan 333
14. Flint Kearsley 369
15. Birmingham Seaholm 376
16. Trenton 394
17. Sparta 426
18. Flint Powers 443
19. Whitehall 444
20. Spring Lake 448
21. Bloomfield Hills Lahser 491
22. Vicksburg 509
23. Detroit Renaissance 543
24. Ortonville Brandon 581
25. Birmingham Marian 584
26. Livonia Ladywood 613
27. Royal Oak Dondero 632

2003 GIRLS DIVISION 2 INDIVIDUALS
1. Laura Malnor (East Grand Rapids)11 ....17:55
2. Bekah Smeltzer (Monroe Jefferson)9..........18:01
3. Kelly Sampson (Detroit Renaissance)11 ......18:10
4. Caitlin Clifford (Bloomfield Hills Lahser)10 .....18:18
5. Jessica Armstrong (Wayland)9 ....18:20
6. Amber Myers (Jackson-Northwest)12..........18:35
7. Chelsea McVay (Croswell-Lexington)10 ......18:36
8. Kelsey Devereaux (Jackson Northwest)10....18:38
9. Nikki Brown (East Grand Rapids)9 ....18:39
10. Jenna Matthews (Otsego)9....................18:44
11. Katie Okonowski (Dearborn Divine Child)11...18:46
12. Ellen French (Birmingham Seaholm)9 ....18:48
13. Michelle Diverio (Battle Creek Lakeview)12 ...18:50
14. Alicia Hoffman (Monroe Jefferson)11..........18:50
15. Rebecca Winchester (Middleville TK)9 ....18:51
16. Lori Burgess (GR South Christian)10..........18:52
17. Kristin Hooker (Flint Kearsley)11 ....18:54
18. Becca Bauman (GR Catholic Central)11......18:56
19. Amanda McKenzie (Chelsea)9.................18:59
20. Hannah Stone (Lapeer East)10 ....18:59
21. Dana Bialek (East Lansing)9 ....19:02
22. Emma Hummel (DeWitt)12 ....19:03
23. Katie Harriger (Gaylord)11 ....19:03
24. Carrie Hoogland (Grand Rapids Christian)11....19:04
25. Natli Nalli (Dexter)11.............................19:04
26. Kelli Gilliand (Trenton)11 ....19:06
27. Meghan Wafer (Redford Thurston)12..........19:06
28. Raeanne Lohner (East Grand Rapids)11......19:06
29. Leah Elenbaas (Greenville)11 ....19:08
30. Jessica Koster (Grand Rapids Christian)10....19:09
43. Jessica Brenner (East Grand Rapids)10 ......19:26
55. Mary Thomson (East Grand Rapids)12 ....19:40
82. Kristina Buschle (East Grand Rapids)9 ....19:54
104. Jenny Lohner (East Grand Rapids)12 ....20:11

2004 D2 GIRLS

Bekah Smeltzer of Monroe Jefferson, runnerup the year before, ran with Vicksburg frosh Molly Waterhouse for the first two miles before pulling away to a 16-second win. Smeltzer had won the 1600 and 3200 on the track the previous spring.

East Grand Rapids defended with a 61-point margin over crosstown rival Grand Rapids Christian.

Jefferson's Bekah Smeltzer won with a powerful final mile.

Michigan Int. Speedway, Brooklyn, Nov. 6
2004 GIRLS DIVISION 2 TEAMS
1. East Grand Rapids................................92
2. Grand Rapids Christian 153
3. Dexter 211
4. Monroe Jefferson 216
5. Grand Rapids South Christian 229
6. Chelsea 230
7. Forest Hills Northern 236
8. Milan 257
9. Remus Chippewa Hills 307
10. St Joseph 314
11. Spring Lake 315
12. Battle Creek Lakeview 319
13. Ortonville Brandon 322
14. Gaylord 353
15. East Lansing 363
16. Detroit Renaissance 370
17. Vicksburg 372
18. Petoskey 410
19. Richland Gull Lake 451
20. Sparta.. 469
21. Flint Powers 487
22. Flint Kearsley 512
23. Birmingham Seaholm 528
24. Bloomfield Hills Lahser 611
25. Ypsilanti 614
26. Royal Oak Dondero 615
27. Livonia Ladywood 628

28. Birmingham Marian......682

2004 GIRLS DIVISION 2 INDIVIDUALS
1. Bekah Smeltzer (Monroe Jefferson)10......17:52
2. Molly Waterhouse (Vicksburg)9......18:08
3. Jessica Armstrong (Wayland)10......18:10
4. Rachel Severin (Chelsea)11......18:26
5. Laura Malnor (East Grand Rapids)12......18:28
6. Nikki Brown (East Grand Rapids)10......18:33
7. Lori Burgess (GR South Christian)11......18:34
8. Jennifer Hamilton (Battle Creek Lakeview)12......18:41
9. Alicia Hoffman (Monroe Jefferson)12......18:44
10. Jenna Matthews (Otsego)10......18:46
11. Rachel Swaney (Fremont)12......18:47
12. Rebecca Stringer (Royal Oak Dondero)10......18:52
13. Cheal Prahl (Greenville)9......18:56
14. Amanda McKenzie (Chelsea)10......18:57
15. Becca Bauman (GR Catholic Central)12......18:59
16. Erin LaFave (Bloomfield Hills Lahser)9......18:59
17. Jessica Koster (Grand Rapids Christian)11......18:59
18. Rebecca Winchester (Middleville TK)10......19:01
19. Diane Hamilton (Battle Creek Lakeview)12......19:04
20. Katherine McCarthy (Kenowa Hills)11......19:06
21. Stephanie McCarthy (Kenowa Hills)11......19:06
22. Raeanne Lohner (East Grand Rapids)12......19:07
23. Jennifer Anderson (GR Christian)9......19:09
24. Kaitlin Diemer (GR South Christian)9......19:10
25. Katie Okonowski (Dearborn Divine Child)12......19:10
26. Chelsea McVay (Croswell-Lexington)11......19:11
27. Jennifer Boven (Spring Lake)9......19:11
28. Ramzee Fondren (Detroit Renaissance)9......19:12
29. Candice Babcock (Charlotte)10......19:12
30. Melany Mioduszewski (Dexter)10......19:12
33. Kristina Buschle (East Grand Rapids)10......19:25
68. Erin Cvengros (East Grand Rapids)11......20:04
159. Bianca Stubbs (East Grand Rapids)10......21:19
167. Jessica Brenner (East Grand Rapids)11......21:26

2005 D2 GIRLS

Bekah Smeltzer lost 7 weeks of summer training to a stress fracture above her right ankle, but came back to defend her title in a sprint finish with Erin LaFave of Lahser. At the line, the margin was razor thin, 17:43.95-17:44.00.

Said Smeltzer, "I was heading to the finish line and I heard the crowd start screaming. I knew I had to keep kicking. I didn't find out who won until a half hour later."

LaFave, who is deaf, signed through her mother/interpreter, "I wanted to finish first so bad. I didn't think I'd be first though, but I pushed hard at the end and did everything I could."

Michigan Int. Speedway, Brooklyn, Nov. 5 ⊠
2005 GIRLS DIVISION 2 TEAMS
1. Grand Rapids Christian......108
2. Grand Rapids South Christian......164
3. Forest Hills Northern......218
4. East Lansing......237
5. Chelsea......242
6. Gaylord......252
7. Dexter......256
8. Ortonville Brandon......263
9. Milan......284
10. East Grand Rapids......302
11. Mt Pleasant......325
12. Monroe Jefferson......335
13. St Clair......354
14. Spring Lake......357
15. Forest Hills Eastern......383
16. Remus Chippewa Hills......395
17. Birmingham Seaholm......418
18. Stevensville Lakeshore......426
19. Bloomfield Hills Cranbrook......441
20. Allegan......463
21. Battle Creek Lakeview......477
22. Fenton......512
23. Tecumseh......517
24. Harper Woods Regina......544
25. Bloomfield Hills Lahser......628
26. Livonia Ladywood......679
27. Birmingham Marian......680

2005 GIRLS DIVISION 2 INDIVIDUALS
1. Bekah Smeltzer (Monroe Jefferson)11......17:44
2. Erin LaFave (Bloomfield Hills Lahser)10......17:44
3. Brooke Eilers (Holland Christian)10......17:56
4. Jazmine Ford (Comstock Park)11......18:01
5. Thereseann Zimmerman (Gaylord)12......18:15
6. Amanda Mckenzie (Chelsea)11......18:18
7. Andrea Schedlbauer (Caledonia)10......18:21
8. Jessica Armstrong (Wayland)11......18:25
9. Lori Burgess (GR South Christian)12......18:26
10. Megan Josey (Spring Lake)12......18:28
11. Rebecca Winchester (Middleville TK)11......18:30
12. Meggan Freeland (Parma Western)9......18:34
13. Magan Antor (Sparta)11......18:37
14. Hannah Stone (Lapeer East)12......18:42
15. Ramzee Fondren (Detroit Renaissance)10......18:43
16. Alyssa Penning (Grand Rapids Christian)9......18:44
17. Rebecca Stringer (Royal Oak Dondero)11......18:45
18. Rachel Severin (Chelsea)12......18:47
19. Katherine McCarthy (Kenowa Hills)12......18:47
20. Kelsey Burgess (GR South Christian)9......18:48
21. Shannon Mathews (Bloomfield H Cranbrook)......18:48
22. Rebekah Bentle (Parma Western)10......18:49
23. Stephanie Essenmacher (Battle C Lakeview)11......18:49
24. Chelsey McVay (Croswell-Lexington)12......18:49
25. Jennifer Anderson (Grand Rapids Christian)10......18:53
26. Gina Valgol (Harper Woods Regina)9......18:56
27. Jessica Koster (Grand Rapids Christian)12......18:59
28. Samantha Draney (Allegan)11......19:00
29. Crystal Stanley (Lansing Sexton)......19:02
30. Stephanie McCarthy (Kenowa Hills)12......19:02
59. Leah Warners (Grand Rapids Christian)9......19:40
67. Tina Bolt (Grand Rapids Christian)11......19:48
85. Kelly VanderLaan (Grand Rapids Christian)11......19:59
93. Andrea Beukema (Grand Rapids Christian)11......20:02

2006 D2 GIRLS

Doug Jager's Grand Rapids Christian squad came out 13 points ahead of defender East Grand Rapids.

Parma Western's Meggan Freeland captured the win in 18:04 ahead of Lahser's Erin LaFave, who had finished second the previous year. "I accept it, even though it's frustrating," said LaFave.

Michigan Int. Speedway, Brooklyn, Nov. 4 ⊠
2006 GIRLS DIVISION 2 TEAMS
1. Grand Rapids Christian......134
2. East Grand Rapids......147
3. East Lansing......149
4. Gaylord......175
5. Dexter......249
6. Milan......258
7. Spring Lake......279
8. Forest Hills Eastern......293
9. Chelsea......323
10. Grand Rapids South Christian......336
11. Sparta......346
12. Goodrich......361
13. Hamilton......361
14. Ortonville Brandon......390
15. Wayland......390
16. Birmingham Seaholm......397
17. Stevensville Lakeshore......415
18. Petoskey......418
19. Parma Western......425
20. Owosso......453
21. Marshall......464
22. Bloomfield Hills Lahser......469
23. Croswell-Lexington......486
24. Algonac......516
25. St Clair......575
26. Harper Woods Regina......623
27. Madison Heights Lamphere......699

2006 GIRLS DIVISION 2 INDIVIDUALS
1. Meggan Freeland (Parma Western)10......18:04
2. Erin LaFave (Bloomfield Hills Lahser)11......18:11
3. Bekah Smeltzer (Monroe Jefferson)12......18:19
4. Alyssa Penning (Grand Rapids Christian)10......18:24
5. Alex Mathews (Birmingham Seaholm)9......18:24
6. Samantha Hunt (Gaylord)10......18:25
7. Rebecca Winchester (Middleville TK)12......18:27
8. Sloan Secord (Gaylord)11......18:28
9. India Peek Jensen (Spring Lake)9......18:30
10. Magan Antor (Sparta)12......18:33
11. Maddi Reeves (East Lansing)10......18:34
12. Amanda Mckenzie (Chelsea)12......18:36
13. Brooke Eilers (Holland Christian)11......18:38
14. Jenna Matthews (Otsego)12......18:38
15. Emily Wilson (Milan)12......18:38
16. Dana Bialek (East Lansing)12......18:49
17. Beka Bentle (Parma Western)11......18:50
18. Gina Valgoi (Harper Woods Regina)10......18:53
19. Molly Waterhouse (Vicksburg)11......18:54
20. Erin Fedewa (St Johns)11......18:59
21. Jessica Armstrong (Wayland)12......19:00
22. Raeanne Lohner (E Grand Rapids)12......19:00
23. Kelsey Burgess (GR S Christian)10......19:00
24. Amber Kassuba (Gaylord)10......19:00
25. Danielle Hicks (Marshall)10......19:01
26. Jessica Vickers (Dexter)12......19:01
27. Andrea Hoffman (Monroe Jefferson)11......19:01
28. Alison Tuuk (GR Christian)12......19:01
29. Amanda Putt (Tecumseh)11......19:02
30. Kelsey Meyers (Goodrich)12......19:05

2007 D2 GIRLS

Sloan Secord led her Gaylord teammates to the title in a 10-point victory over Forest Hills Eastern. "It was really exciting because we all worked so hard," she said. "We started in the summer with team camp and it was exciting to see how the team progressed."

Michigan Int. Speedway, Brooklyn, Nov. 3 ⊠
2007 GIRLS DIVISION 2 TEAMS
1. Gaylord......131
2. Forest Hills Eastern......141
3. Grand Rapids Christian......174
4. Bloomfield Hills Lahser......208
5. East Lansing......225
6. Milan......281
7. Dexter......284
8. East Grand Rapids......292
9. Flint Powers......308
10. Croswell-Lexington......335
11. Birmingham Seaholm......346
12. Marshall......351
13. Otsego......352
14. Remus Chippewa Hills......357
15. St Clair......365
16. Fremont......366
17. Parma Western......388
18. Vicksburg......394
19. Sparta......432
20. Tecumseh......451
21. Hamilton......471
22. Trenton......485
23. Dearborn Divine Child......494
24. Sturgis......558
25. Madison Heights Lamphere......616
26. Warren Regina......637
27. Warren Woods-Tower......696

2007 GIRLS DIVISION 2 INDIVIDUALS
1. Sloan Secord (Gaylord)12......17:50
2. Maddi Reeves (East Lansing)11......18:05
3. Meggan Freeland (Parma Western)11......18:12
4. Jordan Tomecek (Milan)10......18:13
5. Alyssa Penning (GR Christian)11......18:22
6. Allyson Winchester (Middleville TK)9......18:23
7. Alyssa Dyer (Forest Hills Eastern)9......18:24
8. Erin LaFave (Bloomfield Hills Lahser)12......18:35
9. Margaret Lindman (East Lansing)10......18:37
10. Amber Kassuba (Gaylord)11......18:39
11. Kelsey Burgess (GR South Christian)11......18:42
12. Beka Bentle (Parma Western)12......18:43
13. Leah O'Connor (Croswell-Lexington)10......18:50
14. Katelyn Cnossen (Sparta)10......18:50
15. Remme Cortright (Dexter)12......18:52
16. Danielle Partain (Corunna)12......18:53

17. Molly Waterhouse (Vicksburg)12 .... 18:53
18. Amanda Balk (Stevensville Lakeshore)11 .... 18:53
19. Carly Plank (GR Northview)11 .... 18:54
20. Amanda Brewer (Ionia)9 .... 18:56
21. Alexandria Vintevoghel (Marine City)10 .... 18:58
22. Morgan Stuut (Three Rivers)9 .... 19:02
23. Taylor Pogue (Goodrich)10 .... 19:04
24. Courtney Clancy (Richland Gull Lake)11 .... 19:04
25. Samantha Hunt (Gaylord)11 .... 19:05
26. Amanda Putt (Tecumseh)12 .... 19:06
27. Ashley Botham (Forest Hills Eastern)12 .... 19:06
28. Ellen Junewick (Forest Hills Eastern)9 .... 19:07
29. Jennifer Anderson (GR Christian)12 .... 19:08
30. Andrea Hoffman (Monroe Jefferson)12 .... 19:09
78. Amanda Olds (Gaylord)9 .... 19:52
87. Anna Kassuba (Gaylord)9 .... 19:55
88. Savannah Hypio (Gaylord)10 .... 19:55
110. Maria Kulka (Gaylord)12 .... 20:11

2008 D2 GIRLS

After being ranked behind Grand Rapids Christian all season, East Grand Rapids rose to the occasion and scored a 68-point win at MIS. Said Lauren Grunewald in third, "They gave us a ton of motivation to go out there and show everyone that we could beat them again."

Individually, Milan's Jordan Tomacek got out fast and never looked back, hitting 5:32 and 11:19 at the mile marks en route to a 17:41 course record victory. "I went out at a good pace," she said, "because I didn't want to get boxed in like last year, when I freaked out a little bit."

Milan's Jordan Tomaceck led from start to finish. (Pete Draugalis photo)

Michigan Int. Speedway, Brooklyn, Nov. 1
2008 GIRLS DIVISION 2 TEAMS
1. East Grand Rapids 98
2. Grand Rapids Christian 166
3. Williamston 168
4. Gaylord 208
5. Grand Rapids Forest Hills Eastern 239
6. Petoskey 257
7. East Lansing 273
8. DeWitt 277
9. Fremont 294
10. Hamilton 313
11. Milan 317
12. Dexter 337
13. Dearborn Divine Child 353
14. Sturgis 368
15. Flint Powers 381
16. Birmingham Seaholm 384
17. Battle Creek Harper Creek 398
18. Richland Gull Lake 402
19. Otsego 413
20. Marshall 443
21. Pontiac Notre Dame 490
22. Goodrich 499

23. Trenton 501
24. Marine City 538
25. Carleton Airport 593
26. Madison Heights Lamphere 712
27. Croswell-Lexington 778

2008 GIRLS DIVISION 2 INDIVIDUALS
1. Jordan Tomecek (Milan)11 .... 17:41
2. Allyson Winchester (Middleville TK)10 .... 17:55
3. Lauren Grunewald (East Grand Rapids)11 .... 18:21
4. Kaitlyn Patterson (Cadillac)12 .... 18:22
5. Taylor Pogue (Goodrich)11 .... 18:23
6. Morgan Stuut (Three Rivers)10 .... 18:24
7. Maddi Reeves (East Lansing)12 .... 18:26
8. Emma Drenth (Williamston)11 .... 18:29
9. Kelsey Burgess (GR South Christian)12 .... 18:38
10. Alyssa Penning (Grand Rapids Christian)12 .... 18:39
11. Gina Valgoi (Warren Regina)12 .... 18:45
12. Meggan Freeland (Parma Western)12 .... 18:47
13. Ann Marie Arseneau (Sturgis)11 .... 18:48
14. Kassidy Clark (East Grand Rapids)9 .... 18:51
15. Jessie Baloga (East Grand Rapids)9 .... 18:52
16. Cassie Peterson (Byron Center)10 .... 18:52
17. Taylor Smith (Otsego)10 .... 18:53
18. Molly Touran (Petoskey)12 .... 18:54
19. McKenzie Mora (Flint Powers)10 .... 18:55
20. Crysta Paganelli (Grand Rapids Northview)9 ... 18:58
21. Emily Oren (Hamilton)9 .... 18:58
22. Louisa Coppola (Warren Wood-Tower)11 .... 18:58
23. Margaret Lindman (East Lansing)11 .... 18:59
24. Karissa Kalisz (Marshall)10 .... 18:59
25. Rachele Schulist (Zeeland West)9 .... 19:02
26. Courtney Clancy (Richland Gull Lake)12 .... 19:02
27. Libby Salemi (St Johns)10 .... 19:02
28. Chloe Gilbert (Owosso)10 .... 19:02
29. Amanda Olds (Gaylord)10 .... 19:02
30. Alex Keyser (Sturgis)11 .... 19:03
64. Brianna Clifford (East Grand Rapids)11 .... 19:34
73. Katie Samuelson (East Grand Rapids)11 .... 19:40
81. Kathleen Stubbs (East Grand Rapids)11 .... 19:45
175. Nicole Dear (East Grand Rapids)11 .... 20:53

2009 D2 GIRLS

East Grand Rapids, coached by Nick Hopkins, defended its title with a thin 12-point margin over Hamilton.

Taylor Pogue of Goodrich went out fast on a windy day and suffered in the final stages. Lauren Grunewald of East Grand Rapids passed her with 150 to go. However, Grunewald was having problems of her own with heat exhaustion, and Pogue passed her back. "Honestly, when she first passed me, I thought that was it," said Pogue. "I heard people cheering for me, and it gave me the extra push to go for it."

Michigan Int. Speedway, Brooklyn, Nov. 7
2009 GIRLS DIVISION 2 TEAMS
1. East Grand Rapids 96
2. Hamilton 108
3. Grand Rapids Christian 146
4. Williamston 153
5. East Lansing 199
6. Otsego 225
7. Forest Hills Eastern 282
8. Dexter 287
9. Cedar Springs 291
10. Jackson Northwest 300
11. Spring Lake 347
12. DeWitt 350
13. Bloomfield Hills Lahser 367
14. Sturgis 367
15. Dearborn Divine Child 396
16. Sparta 410
17. Gaylord 424
18. Mt Pleasant 455
19. St Clair 472
20. Marine City 481
21. Flint Powers 485
22. Bloomfield Hills Marian 525
23. Grosse Ile 554
24. Linden 601
25. Yale 603

26. Trenton 622
27. Lapeer East 647

Taylor Pogue of Goodrich won in 2009. (Pete Draugalis photo)

2009 GIRLS DIVISION 2 INDIVIDUALS
1. Taylor Pogue (Goodrich)12 .... 18:11
2. Lauren Grunewald (East Grand Rapids)12 .... 18:19
3. Taylor Smith (Otsego)11 .... 18:33
4. Rachele Schulist (Zeeland West)10 .... 18:37
5. Kristen Yarows (Dexter)12 .... 18:48
6. Lauren Halm (Williamston)12 .... 18:56
7. Allyson Winchester (Middleville TK)11 .... 18:59
8. Emma Drenth (Williamston)12 .... 19:01
9. Jessie Baloga (East Grand Rapids)10 .... 19:02
10. Ashley Montgomery (Mt Pleasant)9 .... 19:02
11. Alyssa Dyer (Forest Hills Eastern)11 .... 19:04
12. Hannah Grischke (Williamston)10 .... 19:04
13. India Peek Jensen (Spring Lake)12 .... 19:08
14. Molly Oren (Hamilton)9 .... 19:09
15. Breeann Ovokaitys (Cedar Springs)12 .... 19:10
16. Crysta Paganelli (GR Northview)10 .... 19:11
17. Alex Trecha (East Lansing)10 .... 19:12
18. Julia Bos (Grand Rapids Christian)9 .... 19:16
19. Erica Crane (Dearborn Divine Child)12 .... 19:18
20. Louisa Coppola (Warren Woods-Tower)12 . 19:19
21. Katie Wieler (Cedar Springs)9 .... 19:22
22. Chloe Gilbert (Owosso)11 .... 19:22
23. Ericka Snyder (Marine City)11 .... 19:22
24. Emily Oren (Hamilton)10 .... 19:24
25. Cathy Coryell (Hamilton)9 .... 19:27
26. Carla Jones (East Lansing)9 .... 19:31
27. Kassidy Clark (East Grand Rapids)10 .... 19:35
28. Sarah Oren (Hamilton)12 .... 19:38
29. Alex Keyser (Sturgis)12 .... 19:40
30. Morgan Stuut (Three Rivers)11 .... 19:42
47. Kathleen Stubbs (East Grand Rapids)12 .... 19:58
60. Breezy Clifford (East Grand Rapids)12 .... 20:12
117. Katie Samuelson (East Grand Rapids)12 .. 20:58
118. Jill McLain (East Grand Rapids)11 .... 20:58

2010 D2 GIRLS

With four girls breaking 17:50, Rachel Schulist of Zeeland West led one of the fastest D2 races ever on a day of lightning-fast course conditions. That gave her a rare claim to fame, as her farther Martin won the 1976 Class C individual title for Whitehall.

"I just let it go and did what I could do," she said. "I wanted to hang with the girls and see how it felt." She broke Jordan Tomacek's 2008 course record by a second.

Grand Rapids Christian narrowly held off Hamillton for the team win, 111-116.

Michigan Int. Speedway, Brooklyn, Nov. 6
2010 GIRLS DIVISION 2 TEAMS
1. Grand Rapids Christian 111
2. Hamilton 116
3. East Grand Rapids 177
4. East Lansing 202
5. Forest Hills Eastern 220
6. Cedar Springs 236
7. Otsego 246
8. Ionia 274
9. Mt Pleasant 291
10. St Johns 301
11. Warren Regina 306
12. Bloomfield Hills Andover 317
13. Dearborn Divine Child 330
14. Bloomfield Hills Lahser 369
15. Holland Christian 373
16. Sturgis 382
17. Fremont 397
18. Gaylord 409
19. Marine City 421
20. St Clair 421
21. Chelsea 423
22. Linden 474
23. Richland Gull Lake 545
24. Corunna 556
25. Carleton Airport 639
26. Milan 720
27. Goodrich 734

Rachele Schulist followed her father's footsteps in winning at the big meet. (Pete Draugalis photo)

2010 GIRLS DIVISION 2 INDIVIDUALS
1. Rachele Schulist (Zeeland West)11 .... 17:40
2. Allyson Winchester (Middleville TK)12 .... 17:43
3. Megan O'Neil (Remus Chippewa Hills)9 .... 17:48
4. Julia Bos (Grand Rapids Christian)10 .... 17:49
5. Molly Oren (Hamilton)10 .... 18:00
6. Cathy Coryell (Hamilton)10 .... 18:21
7. Makenzie Evers (Plainwell)9 .... 18:22
8. Jessie Baloga (East Grand Rapids)11 .... 18:23
9. Katie Weiler (Cedar Springs)10 .... 18:28
10. Alyssa Dyer (Forest Hills Eastern)12 .... 18:28
11. Taylor Smith (Otsego)12 .... 18:30
12. Ashley Montgomery (Mt Pleasant)10 .... 18:30
13. Julie Oosterhouse (Byron Center)12 .... 18:32
14. Cassidy Hass (Mason)10 .... 18:35
15. Emily Oren (Hamilton)11 .... 18:35
16. Kelsie Schwartz (Warren Regina)9 .... 18:36
17. Chloe Gilbert (Owosso)12 .... 18:36
18. Claire Gilbert (Owosso)10 .... 18:37
19. Morgan Wixson (Remus Chippewa Hills)12 . 18:37
20. Hannah Grischke (Williamston)11 .... 18:38
21. Casey Lawson (Middleville TK)10 .... 18:39
22. Jacquelynn Overbeek (Hamilton)12 .... 18:39
23. Brittany Beeler (Spring Lake)10 .... 18:41
24. Liza Gunnink (Grand Rapids Christian)12 ... 18:42
25. Amanda Balczak (Cedar Springs)10 .... 18:43
26. Brianna Kalisz (Marshall)10 .... 18:47
27. Ann Marie Arseneau (Sturgis)12 .... 18:47
28. Clara Cullen (Forest Hills Eastern)10 .... 18:50
29. Amanda Brewer (Ionia)12 .... 18:53
30. Mado Glew (East Lansing)9 .... 18:58
52. Dana Veen (Grand Rapids Christian)12 ...... 19:24
59. Erika Overbeck (Grand Rapids Christian)12 19:27
62. Lauren McCarthy (GR Christian)12 .... 19:29
65. Kimby Penning (Grand Rapids Christian)12 19:30
158. Cassie Jager (Grand Rapids Christian)9 ... 20:29

2011 D2 GIRLS

East Grand Rapids scored its fifth title, finishing 23 points ahead of Cedar Springs. Julia Bos of Grand Rapids Christian won the individual crown in a course record 17:25. "I was kind of surprised about how slowly the lead pack took it out," she said. "I like them to go out too fast and then try to catch them."

Bos led at the mile in 5:48, then ripped off the next two splits in 5:26 and 5:15. In second and third, Kenzie Weiler and Ali Weirsma also dipped under the old course standard.

Michigan Int. Speedway, Brooklyn, Nov. 5
2011 GIRLS DIVISION 2 TEAMS
1. East Grand Rapids 153
2. Cedar Springs 176
3. Forest Hills Northern 195
4. Hamilton 213
5. Grand Rapids Christian 230
6. Fremont 261
7. East Lansing 265
8. Bloomfield Hills Lahser 278
9. Chelsea 278
10. Richland Gull Lake 296
11. Grand Rapids South Christian 296
12. Dearborn Divine Child 312
13. Plainwell 320
14. Forest Hills Eastern 326
15. Bloomfield Hills Cranbrook-Kingswood 338
16. DeWitt 339
17. Mason 341
18. Warren Regina 380
19. Cadillac 430
20. Pontiac Notre Dame 457
21. Bloomfield Hills Andover 465
22. Williamston 486
23. Owosso 556
24. Corunna 580
25. Yale 601
26. New Boston Huron 634
27. Milan 635

2011 GIRLS DIVISION 2 INDIVIDUALS
1. Julia Bos (Grand Rapids Christian)11 .... 17:25
2. Kenzie Weiler (Cedar Springs)9 .... 17:36
3. Ali Wiersma (Allendale)12 .... 17:37
4. Rachele Schulist (Zeeland West)12 .... 18:15
5. Molly Oren (Hamilton)11 .... 18:17
6. Katie Weiler (Cedar Springs)11 .... 18:23
7. Karrigan Smith (St Johns)9 .... 18:23
8. Sara Barron (Pontiac Notre Dame)12 .... 18:25
9. Megan O'Neil (Remus Chippewa Hills)10 .... 18:30
10. Kassidy Clark (East Grand Rapids)12 .... 18:31
11. Anna Kreslins (Fremont)9 .... 18:31
12. Alexis Miller (GR South Christian)9 .... 18:32
13. Brittany Beeler (Spring Lake)11 .... 18:33
14. Emily Starck (Remus Chippewa Hills)9 .... 18:36
15. Emily Oren (Hamilton)12 .... 18:36
16. Cassie Bloch (Warren Regina)10 .... 18:37
17. Cathy Coryell (Hamilton)11 .... 18:39
18. Clara Cullen (Forest Hills Eastern)11 .... 18:41
19. Jessie Baloga (East Grand Rapids)12 .... 18:42
20. Claudia Vredeveld (Forest Hills Northern)11 18:44
21. Devon Sutton (Ludington)11 .... 18:46
22. Meg Darmofal (Mason)9 .... 18:49
23. Rachel Durbin (Armada)11 .... 18:54
24. Jackie Bredenberg (Bloomfield H Lahser)9 . 18:54
25. Casey Lawson (Middleville TK)11 .... 18:57
26. Morgan Posthuma (Forest Hills Northern)9 . 18:57
27. Mado Glew (East Lansing)10 .... 18:59
28. Mandy Paull (Cheboygan)9 .... 19:00
29. Jessica Delaney (Jackson Northwest)11 ..... 19:00
30. Gabrielle Perrin (Vicksburg)9 .... 19:01
61. Becca Solberg (East Grand Rapids)9 .... 19:42
63. Mckayley Gourley (East Grand Rapids)10 ... 19:42
102. Sarah Lime (East Grand Rapids)9 .... 20:06
177. Susan Hoffman (East Grand Rapids)11 ..... 21:04

Julia Bos won two straight for Grand Rapids Christian. (Pete Draugalis photo)

2012 GIRLS

Forest Hills Eastern won its first title. Coach Jeremy Hurley's squad topped Spring Lake by 57 points.

Julia Bos repeated as the individual champion: "It was pretty good," she said. "I didn't PR, which I was kind of hoping to, but I'm still happy with it."

Michigan Int. Speedway, Brooklyn, Nov. 3
2012 GIRLS DIVISION 2 TEAMS
1. Forest Hills Eastern 93
2. Spring Lake 150
3. Grand Rapids Christian 182
4. Middleville Thornapple-Kellogg 186
5. East Grand Rapids 231
6. Forest Hills Northern 233
7. Richland Gull Lake 236
8. Cedar Springs 275
9. Warren Regina 277
10. Bloomfield Hills Cranbrook-Kingswood 332
11. Sparta 351
12. Fremont 362
13. Bloomfield Hills Lahser 370
14. Vicksburg 404
15. Jackson Northwest 410
16. Pontiac Notre Dame 415
17. Linden 437
18. Marshall 459

19. Chelsea	464
20. St Joseph	466
21. Dearborn Divine Child	470
22. Grosse Ile	481
23. Plainwell	483
24. Croswell-Lexington	557
25. Yale	559
26. Corunna	656
27. Owosso	686

2012 GIRLS DIVISION 2 INDIVIDUALS
1. Julia Bos (Grand Rapids Christian)12	17:21
2. Kenzie Weiler (Cedar Springs)10	17:50
3. Molly Oren (Hamilton)12	18:04
4. Elena Miller (Bloomfield Hills Lahser)12	18:08
5. Kelli Nesky (Hudsonville Unity Christian)10	18:10
6. Clara Cullen (Forest Hills Eastern)12	18:11
7. Megan O'Neil (Remus Chippewa Hills)11	18:15
8. Meg Darmofal (Mason)10	18:16
9. Rachel Durbin (Armada)12	18:18
10. Lindsey Carlson (Charlotte)9	18:20
11. Makenzie Evers (Plainwell)11	18:20
12. Gabrielle Perrin (Vicksburg)10	18:23
13. Peyton Boughton (Sturgis)11	18:24
14. Ashley Montgomery (Mt Pleasant)12	18:25
15. Carlyn Arteaga (Spring Lake)10	18:28
16. Sydney Elmer (Linden)11	18:30
17. Karrigan Smith (St Johns)10	18:30
18. Mikayla Hostetler (Richland Gull Lake)10	18:32
19. Katie Weiler (Cedar Springs)12	18:33
20. Alana O'Mara (Bloomfield Hills Lahser)12	18:35
21. Brittany Beeler (Spring Lake)12	18:36
22. Becca Schott (Coldwater)12	18:37
23. Emily Starck (Remus Chippewa Hills)10	18:38
24. Melissa Winchester (Middleville TK)10	18:39
25. Shelby Waterson (DeWitt)10	18:39
26. Alexis Miller (GR South Christian)10	18:40
27. Lindsey Brewis (Dearborn Divine Child)11	18:41
28. Mary Kostielney (Forest Hills Eastern)11	18:43
29. Audri Bornamann (Battle Crk Pennfield)11	18:46
30. Karin Lee (Byron Center)9	18:47
38. Lauren Allard (Forest Hills Eastern)9	18:59
44. Abagail Bowman (Forest Hills Eastern)10	19:12
52. Angela Ottenwess (Forest Hills Eastern)12	19:21
98. Taylor Sterenberg (Forest Hills Eastern)10	19:56
118. Bethany Bartlett (Forest Hills Eastern)11	20:06

2013 D2 GIRLS

Grand Rapids Christian had graduated two-time individual champ Julia Bos, but still came up with enough firepower to win by 94 points on the muddy course.

Kenzie Weiler of Cedar Springs came from behind after 3M to catch Country Day's Jackie Bredenberg before the line, 17:55.1-17:55.9.

"It was probably the best competition that I've ever run against at the state meet," said Weiler. "There were so many good girls—even down to the last minute of the race… Coming into the home stretch, I just knew I wasn't done yet."

Michigan Int. Speedway, Brooklyn, Nov. 2
2013 GIRLS DIVISION 2 TEAMS
1. Grand Rapids Christian	109
2. Spring Lake	205
3. Otsego	213
4. Linden	216
5. East Grand Rapids	219
6. Grand Rapids South Christian	226
7. Warren Regina	229
8. Sparta	231
9. Richland Gull Lake	290
10. Forest Hills Northern	308
11. DeWitt	309
12. Vicksburg	337
13. Middleville Thornapple-Kellogg	343
14. Chelsea	348
15. Cedar Springs	356
16. Dearborn Divine Child	420
17. Essexville Garber	429
18. Croswell-Lexington	436
19. Pontiac Notre Dame	446
20. Grosse Ile	455
21. Whitehall	481
22. Charlotte	490
23. Bloomfield Hills Cranbrook-Kingswood	532
24. Detroit Country Day	549
25. Goodrich	583
26. Riverview	651
27. Bloomfield Hills Marian	832

Kenzie Weiler (left) overtook Country Day's Jackie Bredenberg on the final stretch. (Pete Draugalis)

2013 GIRLS DIVISION 2 INDIVIDUALS
1. Kenzie Weiler (Cedar Springs)11	17:56
2. Jackie Bredenberg (Detroit Country Day)11	17:56
3. Karrigan Smith (St Johns)11	18:04
4. Meg Darmofal (Mason)11	18:22
5. Morgan Posthuma (Forest Hills Northern)11	18:22
6. Alexis Miller (GR South Christian)11	18:41
7. Audrianna Bornamann (Battle C Pennfield)12	18:44
8. Megan O'Neil (Remus Chippewa Hills)12	18:51
9. Alexis Smith (Gaylord)10	18:58
10. Dillon McClintock (Owosso)11	18:59
11. Megan Aalberts (Otsego)9	19:01
12. Rachel Warners (GR Christian)11	19:02
13. Lindsey Carlson (Charlotte)10	19:06
14. Gabrielle Perrin ((Vicksburg)11	19:08
15. Erika Freyhof (Hamilton)9	19:08
16. McKayla Guy (Linden)10	19:12
17. Layna Steele (Vicksburg)9	19:14
18. Teresa Myles (Belding)11	19:15
19. Cassie Bloch (Warren Regina)12	19:15
20. Katie Verhulst (Grand Rapids Christian)11	19:16
21. Kayla Kraft (St Johns)12	19:18
22. Tegan Jackson (Kentwood Grand River)11	19:18
23. Kelli Nesky (Hudsonville Unity Christian)11	19:18
24. Shelby Waterson (DeWitt)11	19:24
25. Makenzie Evers (Plainwell)12	19:25
26. Jenna Jeczmionka (Essexville Garber)9	19:25
27. Claire Ford (BH Cranbrook-Kingswood)11	19:26
28. Lily Cesario (Petoskey)9	19:27
29. Peyton Boughton (Sturgis)12	19:29
30. Erin O'Keefe (Spring Lake)10	19:30
34. Claire Brouwer (Grand Rapids Christian)10	19:39
46. Lindsey Fox (Grand Rapids Christian)11	19:46
67. Leah Bishop (Grand Rapids Christian)10	20:01
77. Megan Schenkel (Grand Rapids Christian)9	20:07
163. Kat Jonker (Grand Rapids Christian)12	21:05

2014 D2 GIRLS

Karrigan Smith of St. Johns and defending champion Kenzie Weiler battled each other from the start, with Smith drafting most of the way before kicking to the win in the final stretch.

"Given the windy conditions, I knew I would have to have some help cutting through the wind, so that's why I stayed behind Kenzie the whole time. I knew at the end I was going to need something special to get her because she's such a great competitor."

The two would go on to be teammates at Michigan State.

Grand Rapids Christian won its third title in five years. "Last year we won," said senior Claire Brouwer, "but I think this year we deserved it a lot more because of the training. It was kind of nerve-wracking as we knew defending was a possibility but we didn't want to get ahead of ourselves."

Michigan Int. Speedway, Brooklyn, Nov. 1
2014 GIRLS DIVISION 2 TEAMS
1. Grand Rapids Christian	87
2. Otsego	145
3. DeWitt	156
4. St Joseph	186
5. East Grand Rapids	200
6. Chelsea	208
7. Cedar Springs	255
8. Grand Rapids Forest Hills Northern	270
9. Whitehall	281
10. Linden	292
11. Middleville Thornapple-Kellogg	294
12. Grand Rapids South Christian	304
13. Spring Lake	319
14. Warren Regina	325
15. Bloomfield Hills Cranbrook-Kingswood	355
16. Gaylord	397
17. Essexville Garber	403
18. Adrian	513
19. Detroit Country Day	522
20. Ann Arbor Richard	523
21. Grosse Ile	529
22. Pontiac Notre Dame	542
23. Carleton Airport	591
24. Flint Powers	601
25. Marysville	617
26. Williamston	628
27. Ortonville Brandon	631

Karrigan Smith (right) outlasted defending champion Kenzie Weiler (center) and Morgan Posthuma. (Pete Draugalis photo)

2014 GIRLS DIVISION 2 INDIVIDUALS
1. Karrigan Smith (St Johns)12	18:11
2. Kenzie Weiler (Cedar Springs)12	18:14
3. Morgan Posthuma (Forest Hills Northern)12	18:25
4. Megan Aalberts (Otsego)10	18:35
5. Erin O'Keefe (Spring Lake)11	18:36
6. Kelli Nesky (Hudsonville Unity Christian)12	18:40
7. Erika Freyhof (Hamilton)10	18:46
8. Melissa Winchester (Middleville TK)12	18:51
9. Claire Brouwer (Grand Rapids Christian)11	18:53

10. Carlyn Arteaga (Spring Lake)12 .... 18:58
11. Sarah Goble (Petoskey)12 .... 18:58
12. Maya Hector (Whitehall)10 .... 18:59
13. Lindsey Fox (Grand Rapids Christian)12..... 19:00
14. Rachel Warners (Grand Rapids Christian)12 19:01
15. Jessica Harris (Whitehall)12 .... 19:02
16. Maegen Hopkins (Chelsea)12 .... 19:04
17. Gabrielle Perrin (Vicksburg)12 .... 19:04
18. Shelby Waterson (DeWitt)12 .... 19:05
19. Hannah Adler (DeWitt)9 .... 19:05
20. Alexis Miller (GR South Christian)12 .... 19:06
21. Gabrielle Morton (St Clair)9 .... 19:08
22. Jackie Bredenberg (Detroit Country Day)12 19:08
23. Alexis Smith (Gaylord)11 .... 19:09
24. Dillon McClintock (Owosso)12 .... 19:11
25. Savannah Ferrara (Linden)12 .... 19:11
26. Layna Steele (Vicksburg)10 .... 19:11
27. Teresa Diehl (Warren Regina)11 .... 19:12
28. Claire Ford (BH Cranbrook-Kingswood)12.. 19:16
29. Katie Vitou (DeWitt)9................................... 19:18
30. Kaitlin Newton (St Joseph)9 .... 19:20
36. Michelle Koetje (Grand Rapids Christian)11 19:27
51. Megan Schenkel (GR Christian)10 .... 19:40
76. Camilla Bjelland (GR Christian)10 .... 20:01
97. Jenna Bishop (Grand Rapids Christian)9 .... 20:16

2015 D2 GIRLS

Hamilton's Erika Freyhof led from the start to capture her first title by over 100m. "It felt good," she said. "I just worked hard and it became a reality."

Freyhof would later star at Nebraska, making All-Region in NCAA cross country in 2018 and '19.

The previous year's runner-up, Steve Long's Otsego Bulldogs defeated both of the powerhouse programs from Grand Rapids.

Hamilton's Erika Freyhof won by more than 100 meters. (Pete Draugalis photo)

Michigan Int. Speedway, Brooklyn, Nov. 7
2015 GIRLS DIVISION 2 TEAMS
1. Otsego.. 97
2. East Grand Rapids 180
3. Grand Rapids Christian 199
4. Linden... 205
5. DeWitt... 224
6. St Joseph... 232
7. Gaylord 239
8. Flint Powers 263
9. Whitehall... 277

10. Grand Rapids South Christian 329
11. Warren Regina... 333
12. Forest Hills Eastern...................................... 339
13. Richland Gull Lake....................................... 346
14. Middleville Thornapple-Kellogg.................... 348
15. Chelsea 369
16. Big Rapids.. 412
17. Holland Christian.. 420
18. Ann Arbor Richard 422
19. Hamilton 457
20. Goodrich... 465
21. Croswell-Lexington 476
22. Allendale... 506
23. Alma 546
24. Adrian 586
25. Pontiac Notre Dame..................................... 638
26. Marysville 654
27. Essexville Garber... 659

2015 GIRLS DIVISION 2 INDIVIDUALS
1. Erika Freyhof (Hamilton)11 ....18:01
2. Kayla Windemuller (Holland Christian)10....... 18:23
3. Alia Frederick (Linden)11............................. 18:31
4. Alexis Smith (Gaylord)12 .... 18:33
5. Megan Aalberts (Otsego)11 .... 18:39
6. Sophia Hirzel (Otsego)11............................. 18:43
7. Makayla Perez (Allen Park)10 .... 18:48
8. Julia Vanitvelt (Flint Powers)11 .... 18:51
9. Anna Fischer (St Joseph)10 .... 18:53
10. Ashley Shipps (DeWitt)9 .... 18:54
11. Lauren Biggs (Ludington)11 .... 18:54
12. Claire Brouwer (Grand Rapids Christian)12.18:54
13. Hannah Adler (DeWitt)10.............................. 18:55
14. Madison Goen (GR Kenowa Hills)12........... 18:55
15. Meg Scheske (Sturgis)9 .... 18:55
16. Katelyn Smith (Gaylord)12 .... 18:55
17. Gabrielle Morton (St Clair)10 .... 18:57
18. Sydney Kreger (Grosse Ile)12 .... 18:57
19. Kaitlin Newton (St Joseph)10 .... 19:00
20. Audrey Steiert (Linden)9.............................. 19:00
21. Maya Hector (Whitehall)11 .... 19:00
22. Rebecca VanderKooi (GR So Christian)10 .19:01
23. Makenzie Wank (Richland Gull Lake)9 ....19:01
24. Teresa Diehl (Warren Regina)12................. 19:02
25. Megan Schenkel (GR Christian)11 .... 19:02
26. Tannah Adgate (Middleville TK)12 .... 19:03
27. Maddie Marciniak (Otsego)10 .... 19:03
28. Madison Hammer (Big Rapids)9.................. 19:06
29. Kate O'Connell (East Grand Rapids)10........ 19:07
30. Taylor Ganger (Linden)12............................ 19:09
39. Sydney Kubiak (Otsego)9 .... 19:20
45. Gracie VerHage (Otsego)10 .... 19:27
52. Erica Drobny (Otsego)11 .... 19:32
58. Madison Secord (Otsego)12........................ 19:36

2016 D2 GIRLS

Otsego made it two straight, delivering a winning margin of 139 points, the second-biggest ever; the Bulldogs' 48-point score was the fourth-lowest in meet history. Said lead runner Megan Aalberts, "This year we kind of stressed individual success to get the best place we could do, and then as a team the rest would come together."

After winning two state track titles in the spring, individual champion Kayla Windemuller of Holland Christian made the hard decision to give up basketball and focus on cross country. "It was a hard decision, but the mental focus on cross country was the right decision."

Michigan Int. Speedway, Brooklyn, Nov. 5
2016 GIRLS DIVISION 2 TEAMS
1. Otsego.. 48
2. East Grand Rapids 187
3. Grand Rapids Christian 208
4. Flint Powers 215
5. Cadillac... 233
6. Whitehall... 249
7. Dearborn Divine Child.................................. 261
8. Ann Arbor Richard 298
9. DeWitt... 313

10. St Johns.. 315
11. St Joseph... 316
12. Linden... 326
13. Adrian 364
14. Forest Hills Eastern...................................... 381
15. Grand Rapids South Christian 407
16. St Clair 407
17. Holland Christian.. 462
18. Grand Rapids Catholic Central 469
19. Middleville Thornapple-Kellogg 476
20. Goodrich... 478
21. Warren Regina... 480
22. Zeeland West 487
23. Alma 494
24. Remus Chippewa Hills................................. 514
25. Allendale... 597
26. Bloomfield Hills Marian 655
27. Marysville 674
28. Parma Western 694
29. Owosso... 763

Kayla Windemuller of Holland Christian won by a big margin. (Pete Draugalis photo)

2016 GIRLS DIVISION 2 INDIVIDUALS
1. Kayla Windemuller (Holland Christian)11....... 18:07
2. Anna Fischer (St Joseph)11 .... 18:31
3. Erika Freyhof (Hamilton)12........................... 18:33
4. Makenna Veen (Plainwell)9 .... 18:45
5. Julia Vanitvelt (Flint Powers)12 .... 18:45
6. Megan Aalberts (Otsego)12 .... 18:48
7. Jillian Lange (Goodrich)10........................... 18:50
8. Cecilia Stalzer (Mason)10 .... 18:52
9. Sophia Hirzel (Otsego)12............................. 18:57
10. Taryn Chapko (St Johns)9........................... 19:07
11. Lauren Biggs (Ludington)12 .... 19:08
12. Ashley Shipps (DeWitt)10............................ 19:08
13. Olivia Miller (Forest Hills Eastern)10 .... 19:09
14. Haley Aho (Dearborn Divine Child)9 .... 19:09
15. Sydney Kubiak (Otsego)10.......................... 19:13
16. Meg Scheske (Sturgis)10 .... 19:14
17. Alia Frederick (Linden)12 .... 19:19
18. Erica Drobny (Otsego)12 .... 19:20
19. Maddie Marciniak (Otsego)11 .... 19:21
20. Gabrielle Morton (St Clair)11 .... 19:22
21. Emily Deline (Carleton Airport)11 .... 19:23
22. Kate O'Connell (East Grand Rapids)11....... 19:23
23. Audrey Steiert (Linden)10............................ 19:24
24. Molly Thompson (Paw Paw)10 .... 19:25
25. Katie Vitou (DeWitt)11.................................. 19:25
26. Paige Deitering (Flint Powers)11 .... 19:25
27. Miranda Banks (Carleton Airport)11............. 19:26
28. Analynne Klotz (Cadillac)11 .... 19:30
29. Lidia Clarizio (Haslett)11 .... 19:33

30. Seanna Schmidt (Milan)9	19:34
79. Gracie VerHage (Otsego)11	20:18
148. Molly Farrell (Otsego)11	21:05

2017 D2 GIRLS

New to Division 2, Lansing Catholic made a big impression, topping Grand Rapids Christian by 68 points.

Senior Olivia Theis, who had been runnerup the year before in Division 3, went out with the pack in 5:40 and then steadily sped up, hitting 2M in 11:09 (5:29) and her final mile in 5:11 en route to a 16:52.1. That gave her a winning margin of 43 seconds over Mason's Cecilia Stalzer in addition to an All-Division course record.

"I had no idea what the time I was at or anything," she said. "I knew there was a space between me and the next person so I was hoping as long as nothing went wrong that I could get the title."

The Cougars, coached by former Michigan State star Tim Simpson, put three in the top six.

Michigan Int. Speedway, Brooklyn, Nov. 4

2017 GIRLS DIVISION 2 TEAMS

1. Lansing Catholic	77
2. Grand Rapids Christian	145
3. DeWitt	197
4. Otsego	218
5. Dearborn Divine Child	241
6. Holland Christian	293
7. Pontiac Notre Dame	297
8. Chelsea	300
9. Allendale	303
10. Forest Hills Eastern	335
11. Mason	343
12. Spring Lake	346
13. Linden	351
14. Ann Arbor Richard	359
15. Cadillac	376
16. Flint Powers	386
17. South Haven	387
18. Goodrich	422
19. Petoskey	445
20. Wayland	459
21. Parma Western	464
22. Zeeland West	464
23. Frankenmuth	471
24. Whitehall	534
25. Marysville	591
26. Croswell-Lexington	622
27. Alma	647
28. Imlay City	705

2017 GIRLS DIVISION 2 INDIVIDUALS

1. Olivia Theis (Lansing Catholic)12	16:53
2. Cecilia Stalzer (Mason)11	17:36
3. Lauren Cleary (Lansing Catholic)11	17:44
4. Kayla Windemuller (Holland Christian)12	17:51
5. Makenna Veen (Plainwell)10	17:56
6. Jaden Theis (Lansing Catholic)10	18:19
7. Jillian Lange (Goodrich)11	18:27
8. Kaitlyn St. Bernard (Monroe Jefferson)12	18:30
9. Paisley Sipes (South Haven)12	18:32
10. Meghan Langworthy (Big Rapids)11	18:33
11. Taryn Chapko (St Johns)10	18:35
12. Rylee Cronkright (Wayland)10	18:40
13. Ashley Shipps (DeWitt)11	18:41
14. Jennifer Ohlsson (Pontiac Notre Dame)10	18:41
15. Katie Vitou (DeWitt)12	18:44
16. Sadie Heeringa (Grand Rapids Christian)12	18:48
17. Claire McNally (Ann Arbor Richard)12	18:50
18. Molly Thompson (Paw Paw)11	18:50
19. Hannah Adler (DeWitt)12	18:52
20. Lucy Petee (Mason)10	18:54
21. Audrey Renaud (Dearborn Divine Child)11	18:54
22. Gracie VerHage (Otsego)12	18:56
23. Ruby Strahan (Ludington)10	18:57
24. Madelyn Marciniak (Otsego)12	18:58
25. Analynne Klotz (Cadillac)12	18:59
26. Seanna Schmidt (Milan)10	19:04
27. Alexandra Case (Pontiac Notre Dame)11	19:04
28. Jami Reed (Forest Hills Eastern)11	19:05
29. Caroline Hirth (Chelsea)12	19:06
30. Sydney Kubiak (Otsego)11	19:08
33. Grace Frost (Lansing Catholic)12	19:16
63. Rachel Reid (Lansing Catholic)10	19:36
197. Addison Puck (Lansing Catholic)9	21:21
218. Maya Hecksel (Lansing Catholic)12	21:47

Olivia Theis powered her way to a course record in 2018. (Pete Draugalis photo)

2018 D2 GIRLS

Lansing Catholic's Jaden Theis took control of the race from the start in her attempt to follow her sister as state champion. She hit the mile in 5:31 with her teammate, senior Lauren Cleary, running strong in second. The two were the only representatives of the Lansing Catholic team that had won the title a year earlier.

Theis, a junior, continued to pull away, hitting two miles in 11:17. Plainwell's Makenna Veen had moved into second by that point, just ahead of Cleary as they both ran over 100m behind Theis.

Entering the stadium, a wobbly Cleary collapsed and was not able to finish the race. Up front, Theis slowed a bit in comparison to Veen, running 6:10 for the third mile (vs. 6:03) but handily won the crown in 18:01.9. It was the first time in state history that one sister followed another as state champion.

Margaret Coney, in 5th at 18:39, led an impressive 51-point effort for East Grand Rapids.

Michigan Int. Speedway, Brooklyn, Nov. 3
Mostly cloudy, muddy, 40°, breezy.

2018 GIRLS DIVISION 2 TEAMS

1. East Grand Rapids	51
2. DeWitt	159
3. Petoskey	169
4. Dearborn Divine Child	244
5. Grand Rapids Christian	258
6. St Johns	260
7. Holland Christian	266
8. Grosse Ile	278
9. Otsego	285
10. Fremont	290
11. Forest Hills Eastern	294
12. Goodrich	350
13. Milan	356
14. Cadillac	356
15. Freeland	396
16. Pontiac Notre Dame	413
17. Zeeland West	418
18. Marshall	441
19. Mason	460
20. Flint Powers	476
21. Bloomfield Hills Marian	479
22. Parma Western	528
23. Frankenmuth	539
24. Zeeland East	564
25. Croswell-Lexington	579
26. Marysville	592
27. Warren Regina	626

Jaden Theis won in 2018, making it three straight for the Theis family and Lansing Catholic. (Pete Draugalis photo)

2018 GIRLS DIVISION 2 INDIVIDUALS

1. Jaden Theis (Lansing Catholic)11	18:02
2. Makenna Veen (Plainwell)11	18:17
3. Taryn Chapko (St Johns)11	18:36
4. Kendall Schopieray (Cadillac)9	18:37
5. Margaret Coney (East Grand Rapids)11	18:39
6. Madelyn Frens (Grand Rapids Christian)9	18:41
7. Emma Squires (Petoskey)10	18:46
8. Gillian Fiene (Holland Christian)11	18:49
9. Michelle Kuipers (Holland Christian)11	18:50
10. Sophia DiPiazza (Allendale)11	18:51
11. Ainsley Workman (East Grand Rapids)9	18:52
12. Meg Scheske (Sturgis)12	18:53
13. Jillian Lange (Goodrich)12	18:54
14. Ashley Shipps (DeWitt)12	18:55
15. Katie Hessler (East Grand Rapids)11	18:57
16. Mackenzie Hill (Plainwell)9	19:00
17. Erika Machan (Coldwater)11	19:00
18. Jennifer Ohlsson (Pontiac Notre Dame)11	19:01
19. Seanna Schmidt (Milan)11	19:02
20. Anna Petr (East Grand Rapids)11	19:03
21. Audrey Whiteside (East Grand Rapids)12	19:05
22. Meghan Langworthy (Big Rapids)12	19:08
23. Sofia Perez (DeWitt)12	19:10
24. Kaitlyn Hynes (DeWitt)10	19:11
25. Jamie Reed (Forest Hills Eastern)12	19:12
26. Alexandra Case (Pontiac Notre Dame)12	19:13
27. Cecilia Stalzer (Mason)12	19:14
28. Kiera Hansen (Freeland)9	19:14
29. Kori Baymann (Allendale)11	19:16

2019 D2 GIRLS

East Grand Rapids, coached by Daniel Rietberg, delivered a historic team performance, putting five in the top 14 to score a stunning 36 points, beating No. 1-ranked Petoskey by 56. The Pioneers tied the third-lowest score in meet history.

Senior Anna Petr keyed the win with an 18:00 victory, despite hanging back from the leaders throughout the race. She didn't catch defending champion Jaden Theis until the final stretch.

Said Petr, "I was not expecting this coming into today. I know there are a ton of girls good and competitive, and I'm just happy I was able to be up there and compete with them."

Michigan Int. Speedway, Brooklyn, Nov. 2
2019 GIRLS DIVISION 2 TEAMS
1. East Grand Rapids 36
2. Petoskey 92
3. Otsego 200
4. Forest Hills Eastern 246
5. Cadillac 249
6. Frankenmuth 270
7. Holland Christian 287
8. Plainwell 290
9. Dearborn Divine Child 307
10. Spring Lake 315
11. Tecumseh 316
12. Grand Rapids Christian 320
13. Flint Powers 348
14. Freeland 372
15. Warren Regina 401
16. Allendale 423
17. St Johns 426
18. Coldwater 439
19. Grand Rapids South Christian 471
20. Whitehall 479
21. Mason 483
22. Linden 484
23. Macomb Lutheran North 555
24. Pontiac Notre Dame 587
25. Bloomfield Hills Marian 592
26. Zeeland East 636
27. Marysville 659

2019 GIRLS DIVISION 2 INDIVIDUALS
1. Anna Petr (East Grand Rapids)12 ...... 18:00
2. Jaden Theis (Lansing Catholic)12 ...... 18:03
3. Makenna Veen (Plainwell)12 ...... 18:05
4. Elka Machan (Coldwater)12 ...... 18:27
5. Emma Squires (Petoskey)11 ...... 18:28
6. Gillian Fiene (Holland Christian)12 ...... 18:31
7. Hannah Bodine (East Grand Rapids)11 ...... 18:32
8. Katie Hessler (East Grand Rapids)12 ...... 18:33
9. Jennifer Ohlsson (Pontiac Notre Dame)12 ...... 18:35
10. Ainsley Workman (East Grand Rapids)10 ...... 18:36
11. Michelle Kuipers (Holland Christian)12 ...... 18:36
12. Taryn Chapko (St Johns)12 ...... 18:45
13. Grace Pettit (Plainwell)9 ...... 18:49
14. Abigail Petr (East Grand Rapids)9 ...... 18:52
15. Ryann Jibson (Whitehall)10 ...... 18:54
16. Hannah Pricco (Lansing Catholic)9 ...... 18:55
17. Kiera Hansen (Freeland)12 ...... 18:56
18. Joy Wolfe (Otsego)10 ...... 18:56
19. Gabbie Michael (Frankenmuth)11 ...... 18:56
20. Sarah Liederbach (Petoskey)11 ...... 18:57
21. Madison Price (Trenton)12 ...... 18:57
22. Taylor Mater-Gerth (Fremont)10 ...... 18:58
23. Julia Finley (Belding)10 ...... 18:58
24. Claudia Stachura (Otsego)10 ...... 18:59
25. Landyn Howell (Forest Hills Eastern)12 ...... 18:59
26. Haleigh Bissett (North Branch)10 ...... 19:00
27. Noel Vanderwall (Petoskey)10 ...... 19:00
28. Olivia Waalkes (Grand Rapids Christian0)11 ...... 19:01
29. Cambrie Smith (Petoskey)11 ...... 19:02
30. Chelsea Glessner (Otsego)9 ...... 19:03
30. Lully Evans (Corunna)10 ...... 19:18
38. Margaret Coney (East Grand Rapids)12 ...... 19:20
53. Hannah Bodine (East Grand Rapids)10 ...... 19:48
56. Camryn Bodine (East Grand Rapids)9 ...... 19:52
69. Katie Edison (East Grand Rapids)9 ...... 19:57

CLASS B/D2 STATISTICS

TOP 25 CLOCKINGS AT MIS
16:53 Olivia Theis (Lansing Catholic)12 2017
17:21 Julia Bos (Grand Rapids Christian)12 2012
17:25 Bos 2011
17:36 Kenzie Weiler (Cedar Springs)9 2011
17:36 Cecliia Stalzer (Mason)11 2017
17:37 Ali Weirsma (Allendale)12 2011
17:40 Rachele Schulist (Zeeland West)11 2010
17:41 Jordan Tomacek (Milan)11 2008
17:43 Alyson Winchester (Middleville TK)12 2010
17:44 Bekah Smeltzer (Monroe Jefferson)11 2005
17:44 Erin LaFave (Bloomfield H Lahser)10 2005
17:44 Lauren Cleary (Lansing Catholic)11 2017
17:48 Megan O'Neil (Remus Chippewa H)9 2010
17:49 Bos 2010
17:50 Sloan Secord (Gaylord)12 2007
17:50 Weiler 2012
17:51 Kayla Windemuller (Holland Chr)12 2017
17:52 Smeltzer 2004
17:54 Jamie Krzyminski (Corunna)11 1998
17:55 Nicole Breger (Madison Hts Foley)10 1998
17:55 Laura Malnor (East Grand Rapids)11 2003
17:55 WInchester 2008
17:56 Brooke Eilers (Holland Christian)10 2005
17:56 Weiler 2013
17:56 Jackie Bredenberg (Det. Country D)11 2013
17:56 Makenna Veen (Plainwell)10 2017

BIGGEST WINNING MARGINS
68   Mary Ann Opalewski/Cindy Nelson 1976
53.1 Kelly Smith/Katie Sobczak ...... 1993 T
43.8 Olivia Theis/Cecilia Stalzer 2017
37.8 Tere Stouffer/Cathy Buckart ...... 1983 T
37   Nicole Randolph/Rhonda Wolf ...... 1991 I

SMALLEST WINNING MARGINS
0.0 Bekah Smeltzer/Erin LaFave 2005
0.4 Kelly Smith/Laura Bell ...... 1990 T
0.8 Kenzie Weiler/Jackie Bredenberg 2013
1   Jamie Krzyminski/Nicole Breger 1998
2.5 Karrigan Smith/Kenzie Weiler 2014
2.7 Rachele Schulist/Alyson Winchester 2010

LOWEST WINNING SCORES
21 Caledonia 1994
28 Caledonia 1995
36 Hillsdale 1975
36 East Grand Rapids 2019
48 Otsego 2016
51 East Grand Rapids 2018
52 Hillsdale 1976
53 Caledonia 1996
58 Caledonia 1993
62 Livonia Ladywood 1977
62 Livonia Ladywood 1980

HIGHEST WINNING SCORES
170 Middleville Thornapple-Kellogg 2000
169 Battle Creek Lakeview 2002
156 Middleville Thornapple-Kellogg 2001
153 East Grand Rapids 2011
144 Jackson Lumen Christi 1990
141 Jackson Lumen Christi 1986
141 Chelsea 1989
134 Grand Rapids Christian 2006
131 Gaylord 2007
122 Carleton Airport 1978

CLOSEST TEAM FINISH
1   Jackson Lumen Christi/Caledonia 1990
5   Chelsea/Fremont 1989
5   GR Christian/Hamilton 2010
7   Fremont/Whitehall 1997
10 White Hall/Ogemaw Heights 1998
10 Gaylord/Forest Hills Eastern 2007

BIGGEST WINNING TEAM MARGIN
162 Caledonia/Gaylord 1995
139 Otsego/East Grand Rapids 2016
108 East Grand Rapids/DeWitt 2018
94   GR Christian/Spring Lake 2013
91   Milan/East Grand Rapids 1988

Caledonia's 1994 team won with a record-low 21 points.

GIRLS CLASS C / DIVISION 3

Bath state C-D champions
The first champions in C-D.

1975 CLASS C-D GIRLS

The first de-facto state meet was organized on a 2.25M course by the coaches and Ann Arbor's Pioneer and Huron high schools. Coached by Howard Roberson, the Bath girls had no seniors on the squad. Results are missing, and it is unknown if there were other teams with complete squads beyond the first two.

Cheryl Kerkaert, the first C-D champion, had solid track credentials, having won the '75 Spartan Relays indoor two mile in 11:51.9.

Pioneer HS, Ann Arbor, November 8 ☐
1975 GIRLS CLASS C-D TEAMS
1. Bath...18
2. Detroit Country Day..................................ns
Other schools with entries: Fennville, Hale, Lansing Catholic, Montrose, Whittemore-Prescott.

1975 GIRLS CLASS C-D INDIVIDUALS
1. Cheryl Kerkaert (Bath)11..............................nt
2. Connie Swain (Fowlerville)...........................nt
5. Cherie David (Bath)......................................nt
6. Tammy Canfield (Bath).................................nt
9. Kathy Nichols (Bath).....................................nt
12. Sharon Jubb (Bath)......................................nt
? Ardel Bernard (Bath).....................................nt

1976 CLASS C GIRLS

The second state meet organized by the Ann Arbor coaches was much better attended. Bath defended its title by a 4-point margin over a tough Fowlerville squad. The distance was 3M.

Pioneer HS, Ann Arbor, November 3 ☐
1976 GIRLS CLASS C TEAMS
1. Bath...47
2. Fowlerville..51
3. Mt Clemens Lutheran North.......................72
4. Eau Claire..80
5. Detroit Country Day....................................99
6. Fennville...162
7. Union City...174
8. Whittemore-Prescott.................................191

1976 GIRLS CLASS C INDIVIDUALS
1. Nora Green (Shepherd)10...................19:13
2. Cheryl Kerckaert (Bath)12...................19:20
3. Leanh Dunklee (Montrose)..................19:31
4. Sue Trull (Buchanan)..........................19:35
5. Kathy Seibel (Decatur).........................20:02
6. Mary Spencer (Fowlerville)..................20:14
7. Kathy Nichols (Bath)............................20:19
8. Kim Webber (Montrose).......................20:21
9. Linda Craig (Freeland)........................20:23
10. Cyndy Kaiser (Mt Clemens Lutheran North)...20:27
11. Dee Cook (Detroit Country Day)...........20:38
12. Colleen Swain (Fowlerville).................20:49
13. D. Berkshire (Kalkaska)......................20:51
14. Ellen Southern (Kalkaska).................20:52
15. Amalie White (Shepherd)....................20:57
16. Ellen Moul (Comstock Park)...............20:59
17. Brenda Mueller (Mt Clemens Lutheran North)...21:05
18. Cherie David (Bath).............................21:18
19. Faith Otte (Eau Claire).........................21:28
20. Joan Blough (Eau Claire)....................21:31
24. Jeanne Hanson (Bath).........................21:48
35. Tammy Canfield (Bath)........................23:01

1977 CLASS C GIRLS

Decatur pulled in two basketball girls to clinch a state title by a mere 5 points. One of them, Judy Davis in 33rd place, had never run a cross country race before. The other, Kathy Stanbeck, placed 9th.

Said coach Ken Klinkers, "Judy had never run in a meet before, but she had run the course. She's one of those 100% people. I had hoped she could break 21 minutes and she did."

Potterville, Oct. 22 ☐
1977 GIRLS CLASS C TEAMS
1. Decatur...41
2. Mt Clemens Lutheran North.......................46
3. St Louis..91
4. Bath..110
5. Carrollton..136
6. Yale...175
7. Eau Claire..185
8. Whitehall...185
9. Napoleon..187
10. Bellevue..214
11. Whittmore Prescott..................................250
12. Kalkaska..295

1977 GIRLS CLASS C INDIVIDUALS
1. Nora Green (Shepherd)11...................17:57
2. Kathy Siebel (Decatur).........................18:06
3. Mary Perez (Decatur)...........................18:46
4. Anne Pewe (Olivet)..............................18:52
5. Cindy Kaiser (Mt Clemens Lutheran North)...19:09
6. Sue Urich (Mt Clemens Lutheran North)...19:10
7. Cindy Woodrow (Carrollton).................19:12
8. Karen Majchrowski (East Jackson)......19:19
9. Kathy Stanbeck (Decatur)....................19:21
10. Julie Stansberry (Yale)9......................19:26
12. Susan Trull (Buchanan)..........................nt
13. Beth Evon (St Louis)...............................nt
15. Kathy Nichols (Bath)...............................nt
16. Linda Strasser (Decatur).........................nt
33. Judy Davis (Decatur)...............................nt

1978 CLASS C GIRLS

The first year of MHSAA-sponsored girls cross country combined all the classes into one race. See Class A for the results of the MHSAA race.

Potterville decided to again host separate races by class, called the "Girls' State Open Cross Country Championships." The prime motivator, especially for smaller schools, was that so few of them would qualify for the MHSAA meet at a regionals dominated by Class A schools.

On the Class C level, most of the state's top teams competed at Potterville (7 of 12 from the previous year's meet, including the top 3).

St. Louis beat Decatur by a slim two points. Two weeks later Decatur would be the top Class C school (8th) at the MHSAA's all-class championship, finishing 39 points ahead of St. Louis. DeWitt, which did not participate here, was the 3rd Class C school at the MHSAA meet, ahead of Three Oaks River Valley, the only other C team there.

Shepherd's Nora Green won for the third straight year. She would later win All-MAC honors in cross country twice for Central Michigan.

Potterville HS, Potterville, October 21 ☐
1978 GIRLS CLASS C TEAMS
1. St Louis..105
2. Decatur..107
3. Mt Clemens Lutheran North.....................119
4. Three Oaks River Valley..........................159
5. Breckenridge..185
6. Whitehall...211
7. Napoleon..292
8. Vandercook Lake.....................................306
9. Williamston..312
10. Shepherd..313
11. Whittemore-Prescott................................368
12. Bellevue..387
Incomplete squads: Buchanan, Carson City-Crystal, Clare, Dundee, Flint Burton Bendle, Hart, Homer, Ida, Kalkaska, Montrose, Olivet, Vermontville Maple Valley, Shelby.

1978 GIRLS CLASS C INDIVIDUALS
1. Nora Green (Shepherd)12...................17:14
2. Gail Burch (Whitehall)9...........................nt
3. Sheila Varga (Three Oaks River Valley)......17:59
4. Anne Pewe (Olivet).................................nt
5. Kathy Seibel (Decatur).............................nt
6. Cheri Warchock (Kalkaska).....................nt
7. Beth Evon (St Louis)...............................nt
8. Geri Gaines (Breckenridge)....................nt
9. Cathy Stambeck (Decatur).....................nt
10. Sandy Mead (Shelby).............................nt
11. Debbie Marbeiter (Buchanan)................nt
19. Linda Strasser (Decatur).........................nt

1979 CLASS C GIRLS

Finally Class C had a MHSAA title race. Mt. Clemens Lutheran North, coached by Stephen Siekmann, would claim the first sanctioned win, topping Clare by 33 points.

The previous year's runnerup, Gail Burch of Whitehall, won by a monster 50-second margin in 17:44 on the 3M course. Connie Kidder of Burton Bendle took the individual race in 18:10.

County Clare GC, Clare, Nov. 3 ☐
1979 GIRLS CLASS C TEAMS
1. Mt Clemens Lutheran North......................64
2. Clare...97
3. DeWitt...115
4. Royal Oak Shrine.....................................129
5. Shepherd..134

6. St Louis 155
7. Whitehall 163
8. Vandercook Lake 167
9. Reed City 229
10. Buchanan 237
11. St Joseph Lake Michigan Catholic 239
NS—Mason County Central (4 finishers).

1979 GIRLS CLASS C TEAM RACE
1. Gail Burch (Whitehall)10 .... 17:44
2. Anne Simon (Shepherd) 18:34
3. Jackie Hinken (Reed City) 18:46
4. Michelle Barnett (Mason County Central) 18:58
5. Deanna Macreno (Royal Oak Shrine) 19:12
6. Liz Jensen (DeWitt) 19:20
7. Amy Anderson (St Louis) 19:25
8. Deborah Webb (Mt Clemens Lutheran North) 19:36
9. Susan Urich (Mt Clemens Lutheran North) 19:39
10. Linda Richardson (Clare) 19:39
11. Karla Schillinger (Mt Clemens Lutheran North) .. 19:44
12. Marsha Rider (Vandercook Lake) 19:46
13. Liz Bransdorfer (Clare) 19:47
14. Cynthia Kaiser (Mt Clemens Lutheran North) 19:48

1979 GIRLS CLASS C INDIVIDUAL RACE
1. Connie Kidder (Burton Bendle) 18:10
2. Ann Kennedy (Breckenridge) 19:15
3. Bonnie Leckrone (Benzie Central) 19:29
4. Monice Gordon (Roscommon) 19:31
5. Ann Lymangrover (Edwardsburg) 19:33
6. Jennie Hunter (Freeland) 19:44

1980 CLASS C GIRLS

Gail Burch won the team race in Class C, becoming the second girl to win three titles. She didn't take the lead until the last half of the race.

Undefeated St Louis hoped to keep its streak going here, but Williamston grabbed places 8-11, plus 29th.

Said Williamston coach Paula Crowe, "We faced St. Louis High four times and lost four times. We knew who we had to beat."

Frosh Linda Hagenbarth dominated the individual race.

County Clare GC, Clare, Nov. 1 □
1980 GIRLS CLASS C TEAMS
1. Williamston 67
2. St Louis 80
3. Mason County Central 124
4. Napoleon 150
5. Vandercook Lake 154
6. Wyoming Lee 162
7. Sandusky 190
8. Mt Clemens Lutheran North 202
9. St Joseph Lake Michigan Catholic 205
10. Whitehall 209
11. Berrien Springs 218
12. Muskegon Oakridge 259
13. Kalamazoo Christian 293
14. Capac 315

1980 GIRLS CLASS C TEAM RACE
1. Gail Burch (Whitehall)11 .... 18:54
2. Cindy Reed (Napoleon)10 .... 19:14
3. Brenda Essenmacher (Sandusky)10 .... 19:23
4. Karen Mauer (Mason County Central) 20:08
5. Michele Nate (Wyoming Lee) 20:13
6. Michelle Howard (Vandercook Lake) 20:15
7. Tyanna Weller (SJ Lake Michigan Catholic) 20:18
8. Kathy Moore (Williamston) 20:18
9. Sue Rutledge (Williamston) 20:19
10. Cindy Bjorkquist (Williamston) 20:20
11. Kara Rosendale (Williamston) 20:22
12. LoAnn Omans (St Louis)10 .... nt
13. Sharon Cavanaugh (St Louis)12 .... nt
14. (Wyoming Lee) .... nt
16. Jill Ball (St Louis)9 .... nt
19. Janell Best (St Louis)12 .... nt
20. Pam Farrar (St Louis)11 .... nt
29. Sandy Eyster (Williamston) 21:13
43. Gayle Bond (Williamston) 21:58

57. Lynette Van Ostran (Williamston) 22:33

1980 GIRLS CLASS C INDIVIDUALS
1. Linda Hagenbarth (Watervliet)9 .... 19:01
2. Heather Bauman (Lansing Catholic) 19:35
3. Kristen Atlee (Haslett) 19:38
4. Ann Lymangrover (Edwardsburg) 19:56
5. Donna Donakowski (Dearborn Hts Riverside)10 . 19:59
6. Pam Chron (Burton Atherton) 20:00
7. Connie Bailey (Freeland) 20:02
8. Bobby Jo Dawson (Shelby) 20:13
9. Anne Green (Shepherd) 20:15
10. Ann Beaujean (Harper Woods Lutheran) .... nt

1981 CLASS C GIRLS

DeWitt took its first girls state title, guided by coach Barry Kloenhammer. Cindy Reed of Napoleon, the Class C two mile champion the previous spring, beat 3-time defender Gail Burch by three seconds.

Watervliet HS, Watervliet, Oct. 31 □
1981 GIRLS CLASS C TEAMS
1. DeWitt 121
2. Whitehall 125
3. Williamston 132
4. Harbor Beach 134
5. Mt Clemens Lutheran North 145
6. Benzie Central 158
7. Napoleon 168
8. Kalamazoo Christian 201
9. Lakeview 201
10. St Joseph Lake Michigan Catholic 214
11. St Louis 226
12. Vandercook Lake 250
13. Cass City 261
14. Edwardsburg 313

1981 GIRLS TEAM RACE
1. Cindy Reed (Napoleon)11 .... 19:31
2. Gail Burch (Whitehall)12 .... 19:34
3. Michelle Volmering (Harbor Beach) 20:03
4. LoAnn Omans (St Louis)11 .... 20:30
5. Carol Roberts (Mt Clemens Lutheran North) 20:33
6. Sharon Nichlas (DeWitt) 20:38
7. Catherine Rowley (Kalamazoo Hackett) 20:38
8. Jill Ball (St Louis) 20:39
9. Duncan (Napoleon) 20:41
10. Hogerheide (Kalamazoo Christian) 20:46
11. Rosendale (Williamston) 20:50
18. Kelly Quimby (DeWitt) .... nt
29. Teresa Kirchen (DeWitt) .... nt
32. Tammy Brown (DeWitt) .... nt
36. Debbie Hammon (DeWitt) .... nt

1981 GIRLS INDIVIDUALS
1. Brenda Essenmacher (Sandusky)11 ...... 20:07
2. Ruth Richardson (Clare)12 .... 20:15
3. Kelli Johnson (Quincy) 20:18
4. Karen Maurer (Mason County Central) .. 20:19
5. Deb Spierling (Union City) 20:20
6. Lynda Hagenbarth (Watervliet)10 .... 20:26
7. Sue Straton (Reed City) 20:28
8. Kim Manor (Freeland) 20:29
9. Alia Newman (Detroit Country Day) 20:29
10. Kirky Atlee (Haslett) 20:31
11. Jodi Proctor (Carson City-Crystal) 20:32
12. Milanda Brauker (Union City) 20:33
13. Michelle Belknap (Reese) 20:38

1982 CLASS C GIRLS

Cindy Reed of Napoleon defended her title with a 54-second margin over Brenda Essenmacher of Sandusky on a snowy course. Essenmacher's coach, Wayne Roberts, said, "Brenda ran good, but there was snow all over the place and there was bad footing."

Benzie Central won its first team crown.

The race for individual runners was won by Riverside's Donna Donakowski, who joined her brother Gerard as a state champion (Class B

'76-77). Oldest brother Bill was runnerup in in in '75 and both brothers went on to world class careers. "My older brothers never pushed me into track, but it's true what they've done has inspired me," she told the *Detroit Free Press*. "Lately though, they've begun to push me harder."

Watervliet HS, Watervliet, Nov. 6 □
1982 GIRLS CLASS C TEAMS
1. Benzie Central 60
2. DeWitt 98
3. Bath 108
4. Cass City 119
5. Kalamazoo Hackett 162
6. Sandusky 168
7. Clare 170
8. Muskegon Oakridge 200
9. Byron 249
10. Napoleon 256
11. Vandercook Lake 260
12. Union City 260
13. Kalamazoo Christian 299
14. Berrien Springs 423

1982 GIRLS TEAM RACE
1. Cindy Reed (Napoleon)12 .... 19:37
2. Brenda Essenmacher (Sandusky)12 .... 20:31
3. Mary Jo Robotham (Benzie Central) 20:39
4. Laurie Wentzel (Bath) 20:40
5. Catherine Rowley (Kalamazoo Hackett) 20:41
6. Carrie Lautner (Cass City) 20:41
7. Kim Sanchez (Benzie Central) 20:45
8. Renee Stimpfel (Cass City) 20:50
9. Monica Orchard (Sandusky)9 .... 21:02

Donna Donakowski was the only girl on the Riverside team.

1982 GIRLS INDIVIDUAL RACE
1. Donna Donakowski (Dearborn Hts Riverside)11. 19:59
2. Linda Hagenbarth (Watervliet)11 .... 20:23
3. Jennie Hunter (Freeland) 20:30
4. Kim Mahar (Freeland) 20:35
5. Jodi Proctor (Carson City-Crystal) 20:41
6. Michele Volmering (Harbor Beach) 20:44
7. Heather Habkirk (Detroit Lutheran West) 20:55
8. Sarah Sargent (Midland Bullock Creek) 20:58
9. Laura Bucholtz (Harbor Beach) 21:00
10. Tabitha Schinke (Lakeview) 21:01
11. Barb Gagan (Lake Fenton) 21:06

1983 CLASS C GIRLS

Watervliet's Linda Hagenbarth had won the individual race as a 9th-grader and was determined to do so again one more time. "I knew this was my last chance. I wasn't sure that I had won it until I crossed the finish line. Everyone was screaming and I didn't realize there were runners close behind."

Jolene Crooks led her Benzie Central teammates to a second-straight win, racing past frosh Suzy Stanberry of Capac in the final quarter mile.

Katke Golf Course, Big Rapids, Nov. 5
1983 GIRLS CLASS C TEAMS
1. Benzie Central 67
2. DeWitt 81
3. Mt Clemens Lutheran North 113
4. Bath 115
5. Capac 145
6. Muskegon Oakridge 188
7. Cass City 193
8. St Joseph Lake Michigan Catholic 207
9. Kalamazoo Christian 228
10. St Louis 242
11. Bangor 252
12. Middleville Thornapple-Kellogg 259
13. Breckenridge 266
14. Ida 377

1983 GIRLS CLASS C TEAM RACE
1. Jolene Crooks (Benzie Central)12 ....19:41
2. Suzy Stanberry (Capac)9 ....19:49
3. Kari Quimby (DeWitt) 19:54
4. Laurie Wentzel (Bath) 20:18
5. Alicia Witchell (Bath) 20:19
6. Colleen Quimby (DeWitt) 20:21
7. Kim Sanchez (Benzie Central)11 ....20:23
8. Becky Hoose (Bangor) 20:24
11. Irene Bacolar (St Joseph Lake Mi Catholic)........20:36
14. Robetham (Benzie Central) 20:48
16. Long (Benzie Central) 20:52
29. Nugent (Benzie Central) 21:25
55. Leckrone (Benzie Central) 22:24

1983 GIRLS CLASS C INDIVIDUAL RACE
1. Linda Hagenbarth (Watervliet)12 ....19:45
2. Jodi Proctor (Carson City-Crystal) 19:47
3. Lourene Foster (Marlette) 19:53
4. Penny Pennington (Marlette) 20:01
5. Laura Buchholtz (Harbor Beach) 20:12
6. Terri Forrest (Union City) 20:15
7. Lisa Salyers (Sandusky) 20:18
8. Casey Thorpe (Kalkaska) 20:21
9. Casey O'Neill (Blissfield) 20:21
10. Aliu Newman (Detroit Country Day) 20:25
11. Karen Mauer (Mason) 20:29
12. Kloss (Perry) 20:30
14. Wendy Murray (Niles Brandywine) 20:48

1984 CLASS C GIRLS

Casey Thorpe of Kalaska had the fastest time of the day at 19:46 to win the individual run. The team run went to Michigan Center's Julie Barry in 19:49.

Bath, coached by Mel Comeau, won its first team title since 1976, surprising many even though it was the Bees' third-straight undefeated regular season

Katke Golf Course, Big Rapids, Nov. 3
1984 GIRLS CLASS C TEAMS
1. Bath 69
2. Capac 116
3. Michigan Center 174
4. Perry 178
5. Benzie Central 203
6. Burton Bendle 212
7. Muskegon Oakridge 217
8. Carson City-Crystal 232
9. Bangor 239
10. St Louis 248
11. Harbor Beach 250
12. Kalamazoo Christian 265
13. Ida 286
14. Niles Brandywine 295
15. Blissfield 315
16. Caledonia 327
17. Detroit Country Day 315

1984 GIRLS CLASS C TEAM RACE
1. Julie Barry (Michigan Center) 19:49
2. Kathleen O'Neill (Blissfield) 19:50
3. Jodi Proctor (Carson City-Crystal) 19:50
4. Penny Pennington (Carson City-Crystal) 19:55
5. Lisa Kloss (Perry) 20:08
6. Lisa Behnke (Capac) 20:09
7. Michelle Stressman (Muskegon Oakridge) ...20:13
8. Alicia Mitchell (Bath) 20:15
9. Kim Sanchez (Benzie Central) 20:26
10. Laurie Wentzel (Bath) 20:27
11. Teresa Barber (Burton Bendle) 20:28
12. Wendy Murray (Niles Brandywine) 20:29
13. Pam Pollie (Caledonia) 20:34
14. Becky Hoose (Bangor) 20:38
16. LeAnn House (Bath) ....nt
17. Deb Nichols (Bath) ....nt
18. Christine Abendroth (Bath) ....nt
?. Aaron Neely (Bath) ....nt
?. Karen Snyder (Bath) ....nt

1984 GIRLS CLASS C INDIVIDUAL RACE
1. Casey Thorpe (Kalkaska) 19:46
2. Kim Fox (Mayville) 19:55
3. Irene Bacolar (St Joseph Lake Mich Catholic) ...20:17
4. Kristin Johnson (Mason County Central) 20:29
5. Sarah Collins (Jonesville) 20:33
6. Sue Miller (Breckenridge) 20:37

1985 CLASS C GIRLS

Capac won its first title, topping Bath by 22 points. Wendy Murray of Brandywine led the first two miles of the team run before Cathy Ackley of Hart passed her to take the win.

"At the state meet, you either poke or you peak," said Capac coach Fred Hunt. "We peaked." The Chiefs won despite their regional champion, Lisa Behnke, twisting an ankle in midrace and finishing 23rd.

Rolling Hills GC, Cass City, Nov. 2
1985 GIRLS CLASS C TEAMS
1. Capac 99
2. Bath 121
3. Mason County Central 123
4. Niles Brandywine 129
5. DeWitt 175
6. Onsted 177
7. Detroit Country Day 183
8. Bangor 183
9. Shepherd 200
10. Edwardsburg 222
11. Vandercook Lake 230
12. Benzie Central 231
13. Concord 246
14. Mayville 302
NS (incomplete teams)—Hart, Michigan Center.

1985 GIRLS CLASS C TEAM RACE
1. Cathy Ackley (Hart)10 ....19:39
2. Wendy Murray (Niles Brandywine) 19:49
3. Suzy Stanberry (Capac)11 ....19:54
4. Deb Nichols (Bath) 19:58
5. Janelle Balogh (Mayville) 20:06
6. Julie Allen (Shepherd) 20:05
7. Missy Malowey (DeWitt) 20:10
8. Tara McCutcheon (Benzie Central) 20:12
9. Kristin Johnson (Mason County Central) 20:22
10. Hameera Newman (Detroit Country Day) ..20:23
11. Ngina Burgette (Detroit Country Day) 20:25
14. Michelle Newman (Niles Brandywine) 20:34
16. Becky Hoose (Bangor) 20:38
19. Nancy Herman (Capac)9 ....20:47
23. Lisa Behnke (Capac)11 ....21:07
24. Kathy Bartling (Capac)10 ....21:08
36. Elena Chavez (Capac)11 ....21:35
64. (Capac) ....nt
76. (Capac) ....nt

White Pigeon frosh Stacy Kilburn had the fastest time in 1985.

1985 GIRLS CLASS C INDIVIDUAL RACE
1. Stacey Kilburn (White Pigeon)9 ....19:06
2. Jodie Shay (Bellevue)9 ....19:18
3. Casey O'Neill (Blissfield) 19:44
4. Cindy Nieboer (Kalamazoo Christian) 20:03
5. Jenkie Ornee (Belding) 20:05
6. Sara Collins (Jonesville) 20:13
7. Lisa Kloss (Perry) 20:22
8. Sharon Shuboy (Mancelona) 20:28
9. Susie Paetschow (Clare) 20:31

1986 CLASS C GIRLS

"We showed today we are not a one-person team," said Capac coach Fred Hunt of the Chiefs' successful title defense. "We don't rely on just one runner or even the top 5. This was an 11-person effort. We had 11 good girls to develop a top 7 and that sure helps."

Jeanne Spitler of Montague (18:34) won a speedy individual run, with seven runners faster than the winning time in the team race.

Rolling Hills GC, Cass City, Nov. 1
1986 GIRLS CLASS C TEAMS
1. Capac 115
2. Grandville Calvin Christian 158
3. Onsted 172
4. Bath 182
5. Bronson 214
6. Kalamazoo Christian 216
7. Benzie Central 220
8. Buchanan 220
9. DeWitt 237
10. Ida 238
11. Carson City-Crystal 251
12. Detroit Country Day 262
13. Shepherd 274
14. Perry 277
15. Mason County Central 296
16. Whittemore-Prescott 296
17. Clare 347
18. Mayville 347

1986 GIRLS CLASS C TEAM RACE
1. Rachelle Bydlowski (Ida)9 ....19:37
2. Martha Cameron (Buchanan)9 ....19:45
3. Cindy Nieboer (Kalamazoo Christian)11 .....19:49
4. Julie Allen (Shepherd)12 ....19:54

5. Suzy Stansberry (Capac)12	20:00
17. Angie Behnke (Capac)9	20:32
23. Lisa Behnke (Capac)12	20:51
34. Elena Chavez (Capac)12	21:07
36. Nancy Herman (Capac)10	21:11
45. Sharon Gott (Capac)10	21:31
57. April Kepler (Capac)10	21:54

1986 GIRLS CLASS C INDIVIDUAL RACE

1. Jeanne Spitler (Montague)12	18:34
2. Stacey Kilburn (White Pigeon)10	18:51
3. Kathleen O'Neill (Blissfield)12	19:17
4. Cathy Ackley (Hart)11	19:20
5. Jody Shay (Bellvue)10	19:25
6. Kris Butler (Galesburg-Augusta)11	19:34
7. Nichole Butler (Galesburg-Augusta)11	19:34
8. Jenny Pratt (Parchment)12	19:40
9. Ketlina Kirberg (Leslie)11	19:42
10. Becky Duda (Goodrich)11	19:43
11. Angela Moore (Detroit Lutheran West)10	19:43
12. Teresa Barber (Burton Bendle)11	19:54
13. Marti Swiderski (Haslett)12	19:56
14. Sarah Collins (Jonesville)12	20:00
15. Ginger Goostrey (Michigan Center)11	20:02

1987 CLASS C GIRLS

"What do I think? I think we won it!" Barry Kloenhamer, the DeWitt coach, was more than thrilled that his Panthers scored a 49-point win over Burton Atherton to capture their first state crown.

In the individual run, Stacy Kilburn of White Pigeon rolled to an 18:37 victory topping Goodrich's Becky Duda by 26 seconds.

Bath HS, Bath, Nov. 7

1987 GIRLS CLASS C TEAMS

1. DeWitt	78
2. Burton Atherton	127
3. Grandville Calvin Christian	159
4. Carson City-Crystal	202
5. Tawas City	207
6. Addison	215
7. Benzie Central	220
8. Bath	220
9. Bronson	237
10. Rogers City	240
11. Buchanan	241
12. Charlevoix	245
13. East Jordan	250
14. Onsted	285
15. Detroit Country Day	301
16. Quincy	314
17. Ida	325
18. Beaverton	386

1987 GIRLS CLASS C TEAM RACE

1. Dodie Wiler (Bronson)10	19:45
2. Monica Beck (Rogers City)12	19:52
3. Rachelle Bydlowski (Ida)10	19:55
4. Nichole Hutchins (Bronson)9	19:59
5. Jena Vite (Buchanan)10	20:00
6. Stacie Glomson (Burton Atherton)10	20:01
7. Melissa Moloney (DeWitt)12	20:02
8. Terri Osborn (DeWitt)10	20:02
9. Maureen McBride (DeWitt)10	20:03
18. Stacy Kemler (DeWitt)10	20:35
36. Stacy Cook (DeWitt)12	21:12
59. Barb Babcock (DeWitt)	21:56
97. Traci Ruiz (DeWitt)	23:09

1987 GIRLS CLASS C INDIVIDUAL RACE

1. Stacey Kilburn (White Pigeon)11	18:37
2. Becky Duda (Goodrich)12	19:03
3. Cathy Ackley (Hart)12	19:25
4. Teresa Barber (Burton Bendle)12	19:37
5. Michelle Snyder (Godwin Heights)12	19:40
6. Kerry Little (Vandercook Lake)9	19:44
7. Joy Perkins (Elk Rapids)10	19:47
8. Andrea Ripley (Olivet)9	19:48
9. Kathy O'Boyle (Breckenridge)10	19:50
10. Rebecca Woodliff (Homer)11	19:54
11. Susan Peterson (Blanchard-Montabella)12	19:57
12. Angela Moore (Detroit Lutheran West)11	19:58
13. Lori Belleville (Whittemore-Prescott)12	19:58
14. Dondi Myers (Niles Brandywine)11	19:59

1988 CLASS C GIRLS

Stacy Kilburn of White Pigeon won her third Class C crown on a very muddy course that slowed times considerably. She would go on to win the 1993 Mid-American Conference title for Western Michigan.

Mayville, coached by Dave Patterson, won its first team title, setting a record for the highest winning team score.

Bath HS, Bath, Nov. 5

1988 GIRLS CLASS C TEAMS

1. Mayville	128
2. Ida	153
3. DeWitt	162
4. Carson City-Crystal	177
5. Tawas City	191
6. Grandville Calvin Christian	193
7. Burton Atherton	216
8. Benzie Central	221
9. Southfield Christian	224
10. Charlevoix	226
11. Bath	242
12. Muskegon Oakridge	253
13. Vandercook Lake	254
14. Bronson	290
15. Addison	292
16. Beaverton	305
17. Watervliet	345
18. Quincy	359

Teri Osborn – DeWitt.

1988 GIRLS CLASS C TEAM RACE

1. Teri Osborn (DeWitt)11	20:56
2. Laurel Hay (Tawas City)11	21:02
3. Tammy Baumer (Burton Atherton)12	21:04
4. Kerry Little (Vandercook Lake)12	21:08
5. Rachelle Bydlowski (Ida)11	21:10
6. Julie Bush (Charlevoix)10	21:13
7. Andrea Foote (Mayville)12	21:16
8. Tammy Colb (Southfield Christian)9	21:22
9. Gail LaBair (Mayville)11	21:27
17. Mandi Snyder (Mayville)11	21:47
43. Sarah Brown (Mayville)9	22:46
52. Jamie Freeland (Mayville)11	23:00
56. Jenny Smith (Mayville)11	23:06

1988 GIRLS CLASS C INDIVIDUAL RACE

1. Stacey Kilburn (White Pigeon)12	20:07
2. Renae Essanmacher (Harbor Beach)9	20:20
3. Holly Johnson (East Jordan)10	20:37
4. Andrea Ripley (Olivet)10	20:47
5. Megin Cronin (Harbor Beach)10	20:54
6. Jenny Stuht (Laingsburg)10	20:56
7. Pam Dickman (St Louis)12	20:58
8. Angela Moore (Detroit Lutheran West)12	21:05
9. Gina Glover (Kingsley)9	21:11
10. Marci Hohlbein (Shepherd)12	21:21
11. Charlene Merten (Hart)12	21:27

1989 CLASS C GIRLS

Southfield Christian won its first title by just 4 points over Olivet. Coached by Jim Wood, the Eagles scored 102 points.

Olivet junior Andea Ripley won the team run in 18:47, with a lead of over 300m at the finish.

Torrey Pines Golf Course, Lake Fenton, Nov. 4

1989 GIRLS CLASS C TEAMS

1. Southfield Christian	102
2. Olivet	106
3. Williamston	122
4. Laingsburg	167
5. Shelby	184
6. Mayville	190
7. Kingsley	217
8. Grandville Calvin Christian	234
9. Burton Atherton	244
10. Quincy	269
11. Shepherd	280
12. St Louis	280
13. Elk Rapids	281
14. Vandercook Lake	305
15. Edwardsburg	319
16. St Joseph Lake Michigan Catholic	322
17. Schoolcraft	345
18. Bath	403

1989 GIRLS CLASS C TEAM RACE

1. Andrea Ripley (Olivet)11	18:47
2. Jenny Stuht (Laingsburg)11	19:37
3. Amy Hayes (Shelby)10	19:53
4. Stephanie Crum (Laingsburg)9	20:09
5. Tammie Cobb (Southfield Christian)10	20:11
6. Michelle Harrier (Shepherd)12	20:17
7. Danielle Choate (Vandercook Lake)11	20:18
8. Charleen Long (Southfield Christian)10	20:23
9. Tammy Heisler (Olivet)11	20:25
10. Stacie Glomson (Burton Atherton)12	20:26
14. Anna Kraftson (Southfield Christian)	nt
37. Ann Samuelson (Southfield Christian)	nt
38. Joy Wright (Southfield Christian)	nt

1989 GIRLS CLASS C INDIVIDUAL RACE

1. Holly Johnson (East Jordan)11	19:34
2. Valentine Stumpf (Roscommon)11	19:37
3. Cindy Furlong (Vermontville Maple Valley)11	20:06
4. Kathy Norquist (Bridgman)11	20:15
5. Rachelle Bydlowski (Ida)12	20:18
6. Julie Bush (Charlevoix)11	20:21
7. Patti Silva (Union City)10	20:23
8. Jackie Cullom (Muskegon Oakridge)12	20:23
9. Jenny Doyle (Burton Bendle)10	20:26
10. Kim Cooley (Dundee)11	20:26

1990 CLASS C GIRLS

Ninth grader Megan Smedley of Buchanan captured the team run title. According to coach Mike Rouse, she was behind in the early going. "She was patient and waited for the right time to move. She caught back up to the lead runners about halfway through the race and then she just pulled away."

"I was worried at first," said Smedley, "but I ran my own race."

Olivet, coached by Matt Baldus, moved up to the top of the podium in the closest Class C finish ever, just one point ahead of Southfield Christian. Temperatures were in the mid-70s at race time and a numer of athletes collapsed with heat issues.

Torrey Pines Golf Course, Lake Fenton, Nov. 3

1990 GIRLS CLASS C TEAMS

1. Olivet ... 113
2. Southfield Christian ... 114
3. Edwardsburg ... 138
4. Laingsburg ... 147
5. Burton Bendle ... 212
6. Ida ... 223
7. Leslie ... 243
8. Byron ... 244
9. Williamston ... 262
10. Elk Rapids ... 265
11. Shelby ... 269
12. Grandville Calvin Christian ... 273
13. Charlevoix ... 276
14. Buchanan ... 277
15. Napoleon ... 288
16. St Joseph Lake Michigan Catholic ... 307
17. Centreville ... 307
18. St Louis ... 394

NS—Coleman (4 finishers).

1990 GIRLS CLASS C TEAM RACE

1. Megan Smedley (Buchanan)9 ... 18:51
2. Andrea Ripley (Olivet)12 ... 19:14
3. Stephanie Crum (Laingsburg)11 ... 19:36
4. Jessica Maddux (Ida)9 ... 19:37
5. Jenny Stuht (Laingsburg)12 ... 19:41
6. Tori Edwardson (Elk Rapids) ... 19:56
7. Amy Hayes (Shelby)11 ... 20:12
8. Jenny Milliken (Edwardsburg)11 ... 20:13
15. Tammy Heisler (Olivet)12 ... 20:33
25. Angie Suntken (Olivet)9 ... 21:06
35. Sandy Munro (Olivet)12 ... 21:37
36. Stacy Southward (Olivet)10 ... 21:38
57. Monnette Wallace (Olivet)11 ... nt
94. Erin Gilding (Olivet)9 ... nt

1990 GIRLS CLASS C INDIVIDUAL RACE

1. Kelly Wynn (Addison)12 ... 19:23
2. Holly Johnson (East Jordan) ... 19:36
3. Heather Grigg (Onsted)11 ... 19:48
4. Becky Wing (Bellevue)10 ... 19:48
5. Jennifer Miller (GP University Liggett)11 ... 19:55
6. Patti Silva (Union City)11 ... 20:00
7. Amanda Foutch (Burton Atherton)10 ... 20:08
8. Mary Veselenak (Rogers City) ... 20:08
9. Stacy VanErp (Bad Axe)9 ... 20:11
10. Andrea Little (Vandercook Lake)9 ... 20:13
11. Kym Cooley (Dundee)12 ... 20:14
12. Mari Chandler (Tawas City) ... 20:16

1991 CLASS C GIRLS

It was a historic day for the Smedley family as both Megan and her brother Mike won Class C titles. "It's wonderful," she said. I can't describe it. Mike and I have run hard for this."

The weather conditions were challenging, with temperatures close to freezing and winds gusting to nearly 50mph. "I tried to keep my pace," said Smedley, "but the wind was so strong it nearly blew me over."

Southfield Christian captured the win, this time by a massive 102 points, the biggest margin in meet history.

Memorial Park, Frankenmuth, Nov. 2 □
1991 GIRLS CLASS C TEAMS

1. Southfield Christian ... 53
2. Onsted ... 155
3. Blissfield ... 180
4. Burton Atherton ... 190
5. Frankenmuth ... 203
6. Williamston ... 207
7. Howard City Tri-County ... 216
8. Capac ... 233
9. Clare ... 237
10. Shepherd ... 250
11. Napoleon ... 251
12. Benzie Central ... 254
13. Carson City-Crystal ... 258
14. Quincy ... 294
15. Kalamazoo Hackett ... 306
16. Buchanan ... 344
17. Elk Rapids ... 360

1991 GIRLS CLASS C TEAM RACE

1. Megan Smedley (Buchanan)10 ... 19:22
2. Jennifer Barber (Frankenmuth)12 ... 20:16
3. Laura Wright (Southfield Christian) ... 20:17
4. Heather Brigg (Onsted) ... 20:18
5. Michelle Neer (Kalamazoo Hackett) ... 20:38
6. Joy Wright (Southfield Christian) ... 20:50
13. Anna Kraftson (Southfield Christian) ... 21:13
14. Sarah Decker (Southfield Christian) ... 21:14
17. Charleen Long (Southfield Christian) ... 21:22

1991 GIRLS CLASS C INDIVIDUAL RACE

1. Amy Hayes (Shelby)12 ... 19:38
2. Jenny Stoffel (SJ Lake Michigan Catholic)12 ... 19:40
3. Lorenda Godefroidt (St Louis)11 ... 19:47
4. Jennifer Miller (GP University Liggett)12 ... 19:58
5. Renae Essenmacher (Harbor Beach)12 ... 20:00
6. Rebecca Wing (Bellevue) ... 20:04
7. Andrea Ranck (Coleman) ... 20:12
8. Amanda Gould (Burton Bendle) ... 20:20
9. Trish Clarke (Coleman) ... 20:26
10. Stacey Brockway (Addison) ... 20:35
11. Shanna Ferrigan (Bath) ... 20:39
12. April Barfoot (Whitehall) ... 20:40
13. Jessica Maddox (Ida) ... 20:43
14. Kelly Taylor (Hemlock) ... 20:44
15. Melissa Coomer (Centerville) ... 20:46

1992 CLASS C GIRLS

Onsted, coached by Jim Hill, captured its first crown by just 4 points, topping Carson City-Crystal 136-140; it was the highest Class C winning total ever. Carrie Gould of Burton Bendle won the team run in 19:24, outsprinting Whitehall's April Barfoot on the final stretch.

Memorial Park, Frankenmuth, Nov. 7 □
1992 GIRLS CLASS C TEAMS

1. Onsted ... 136
2. Carson City-Crystal ... 140
3. Ida ... 152
4. Williamston ... 183
5. Suttons Bay ... 188
6. Whitehall ... 200
7. Burton Atherton ... 200
8. Edwardsburg ... 218
9. Grand Rapids South Christian ... 224
10. Reese ... 238
11. Burton Bendle ... 238
12. Vermontville Maple Valley ... 241
13. Addison ... 257
14. Clare ... 273
15. Colon ... 278
16. Centreville ... 298
17. Laingsburg ... 303

1992 GIRLS CLASS C TEAM RACE

1. Carrie Gould (Burton Bendle)9 ... 19:24
2. April Barfoot (Whitehall) ... 19:29
3. Traci Knudsen (Suttons Bay)10 ... 19:35
4. Rebecca Walz (Onsted) ... 20:04
5. Kathryn Murphy (Vermontville Maple Valley)9 ... 20:06
6. Stacey Brockway (Addison) ... 20:13
7. Leah Nilsson (Williamston)9 ... 20:13
8. Kim Browning (Onsted) ... 20:16
9. Laura Wright (GR South Christian) ... 20:18
10. Jessica Maddox (Ida) ... 20:35
11. Erica Davis (Colon)11 ... 20:38
12. Amanda Gould (Burton Bendle) ... 20:39
13. Erica Stanton (GR South Christian) ... 20:43
31. Carolyn Walz (Onsted) ... 21:32
36. Stephanie Series (Onsted) ... 21:44

1992 GIRLS CLASS C INDIVIDUAL RACE

1. Becky Wing (Bellevue)12 ... 19:44
2. Dana Silva (Union City) ... 20:08
3. Christie Achenbach (Unionville-Sebewaing) ... 20:12
4. Sarah Krebs (Laker) ... 20:25
5. Kelly Taylor (Hemlock) ... 20:29
6. Lorenda Godefroidt (St Louis) ... 20:33
7. Jeni Brewer (Southgate Aquinas) ... 20:39

1993 CLASS C GIRLS

Carrie Gould defended her title in 19:10, and with sister Amanda placing 9th, Burton-Bendle, coached by Mike Gould, won its first title by just four points over Addison, setting a high score record for the Class C meet.

Bendle's Carrie Gould became a 4-timer All-MAC pick for Eastern Michigan.

Candlestone Golf Club, Lowell, Nov. 6 □
1993 GIRLS CLASS C TEAMS

1. Burton Bendle ... 149
2. Addison ... 153
3. Ida ... 169
4. Vermontville Maple Valley ... 163
5. Onsted ... 188
6. Colon ... 197
7. Reese ... 205
8. Clare ... 219
9. Carson City ... 224
10. Hemlock ... 229
11. Newaygo ... 234
12. Whitehall ... 245
13. Buchanan ... 292
14. Suttons Bay ... 309
15. Beaverton ... 335
16. Quincy ... 344
17. Byron ... 418
18. Grand Rapids South Christian ... 418
19. Saginaw Michigan Lutheran ... 447
20. Grandville Calvin Christian ... 515

1993 GIRLS CLASS C TEAM RACE

1. Carrie Gould (Burton Bendle)10 ... 19:10
2. Traci Knudsen (Suttons Bay) ... 19:27
3. Kimberly Browning (Onsted) ... 19:38
4. Melllisa Laughlynn (Buchanan) ... 19:39
5. April Barfoot (Whitehall) ... 19:41
6. Kristi Davenport (Addison) ... 19:51
7. Megan Smedley (Buchanan) ... 19:56
8. Jessica Maddux (Ida) ... 19:59
9. Amanda Gould (Burton Bendle) ... 20:00
10: Kathryn Murphy (Vermontville Maple Valley)10. 20:10
11. Kelly Taylor (Hemlock) ... 20:22
12. Bambi Valdez (Whitehall) ... 20:26
13. Erica Davis (Colon)12 ... 20:29
23. Jennifer Plute (Burton Bendle) ... 21:07
32. Jessica Knowles (Burton Bendle) ... 21:17

1993 GIRLS CLASS C INDIVIDUAL RACE

1. Christie Achenbach (Unionville-Sebewaing)10 ... 19:56
2. Dana Silva (Union City) ... 20:05
3. Kristi Davis (Bronson) ... 20:09
4. Jessica McKnight (Williamston)11 ... 20:18
5. Tina Richards (East Jordan) ... 20:21
6. Angie Sell (Blissfield) ... 20:22
7. Leah Nilsson (Williamston)10 ... 20:24
8. Melissa Webster (Montose) ... 20:26

1994 CLASS C GIRLS

Kimberly Browning of Onsted won the Team race and quipped, "It's not cold enough, but the mud is great."

The team title went to Dave Burke's Shepherd squad in a close 142-149 finish with Hemlock.

Lowell HS, Lowell, Nov. 5 □
1994 GIRLS CLASS C TEAMS
1. Shepherd 142
2. Hemlock 149
3. Addison 155
4. Ida 170
5. Carson City-Crystal 172
6. Morley-Stanwood 191
7. Vermontville Maple Valley 197
8. Saginaw Valley Lutheran 213
9. Clare 214
10. Charlevoix 231
11. Reese 238
12. Quincy 285
13. Suttons Bay 300
14. Williamston 317
15. Lutheran Westland 339
16. Burton Atherton 367
17. Union City 412
18. Elk Rapids 442
19. Southlfield Christian 475
20. Grandville Calvin Christian 589
21. Wyoming Kelloggsville 597
22. Buchanan 611

1994 GIRLS CLASS C TEAM RACE
1. Kristy Davenport (Addison)10 .... 20:11
2. Kathryn Murphy (Vermontville Maple Valley)11 ... 20:41
3. Gern Rollins (Ida) 20:52
4. Kelly Taylor (Hemlock) 20:59
5. Leah Nilsson (Williamston)11 .... 21:01
6. Nichole Ruhanen (Reese) 21:06
7. Bethany Brewster (Saginaw Valley Lutheran)9 .. 21:18
8. Jodi Werman (Lutheran Westland) 21:20
9. Amber Abbott (Carson City-Crystal) 21:25
10. Melissa Priebe (Reese) 21:26
11. Rebekah Schultz (Hemlock) 21:32
12. Traci Knudsen (Suttons Bay) 21:39
13. Melissa Culver (Morley-Stanwood) 21:40
14. Stephanie Wohlgamuth (Quincy) 21:49
15. Faith Quillin (Ida) 21:52
16. Stephanie Curtiss (Shepherd) 21:54
17. Chelsea Gorkiewicz (Charlevoix) 21:56
30. Jalayne Powers (Shepherd) 22:44
34. Tara Maas (Shepherd) 22:50
38. Stacey Guthrie (Shepherd) 22:58

1994 GIRLS CLASS C INDIVIDUAL RACE
1. Kimberly Browning (Onsted)11 .... 20:37
2. Christie Achenbach (Unionville-Sebewaing)11 ... 20:55
3. Abbi Rysztak (Benzie Central) 22:02
4. Nikki Deja (Midland Bullock Creek) 22:08
5. Kristi Davis (Bronson) 22:11

1995 CLASS C GIRLS

Carson City-Crystal won its first title with a low 61 points, beating Charlevoix by 69. Said coach Gordie Aldrich of the win, "We certainly hope there will be more."

Kathryn Murphy of Vermontville Maple Valley moved up from the runnerup spot to capture the team run in 18:57, defeating defending champion Kristy Davenport. "Beating the girl who beat her last year had to be gratifying," said coach Gary Hamilton.

Lowell HS, Lowell, Nov. 4
1995 GIRLS CLASS C TEAMS
1. Carson City-Crystal 61
2. Charlevoix 130
3. Clare 140
4. Shelby 182
5. Blissfield 200
6. Addison 212
7. Kalamazoo Christian 216
8. Bear Lake 227
9. Vermontville Maple Valley 251
10. Quincy 262
11. Hemlock 263
12. Saginaw Valley Lutheran 278
13. Haslett 281
14. Williamston 305
15. Newaygo 326
16. Lutheran Westland 370
17. Freeland 392
18. Colon 438
19. Buchanan 510
20. Bendle 513
21. New Lothrop 526

Maple Valley's Kathryn Murphy dominated in 1995.

1995 GIRLS CLASS C TEAM RACE
1. Kathryn Murphy (Vermontville Maple Valley)12 ... 18:57
2. Kristy Davenport (Addison)11 .... 19:01
3. Leah Nilsson (Williamston)12 .... 19:16
4. Marisa Ryan (Carson City-Crystal)9 ...... 19:31
5. Melonnie Furghason (Blissfield) 19:38
6. Jodie Werman (Lutheran Westland) 19:46
7. Megan Warnke (Saginaw Valley Lutheran) ... 19:46
8. Rebekah Schultz (Hemlock) 19:50
9. Erinn Boot (Kalamazoo Christian) 20:07
10. Amber Abbott (Carson City-Crystal)10 .. 20:10
13. Sarah Christensen (Carson City-Crystal)12 ... 20:23
16. Jamie Shepler (Carson City-Crystal)9 ... 20:38
18. Michelle Swift (Carson City-Crystal)9 ... 20:41

1995 GIRLS CLASS C INDIVIDUAL RACE
1. Abbi Rysztak (Benzie Central)12 .... 19:50
2. Christie Achenbach (Unionville Sebewaing)12 ... 20:01
3. Rachel Laansma (Allendale)10 .... 20:02
4. Shannon Gleesing (Breckenridge) 20:15
5. Heidi Wright (Southfield Christian) 20:15
6. Becky Miller (Pewamo-Westphalia) 20:18
7. Mackenzie Woodring (Holton) 20:23
8. Melissa Culer (Morley-Stanwood) 20:28
9. Nicole Ruhanen (Reese) 20:34
10. Michelle Kline (Napoleon) 20:38

1996 CLASS C GIRLS

In the first year at MIS, the individual and team runs were finally combined. However, with the medals already on hand, the MHSAA still recognized the winners of each race, separated only on paper.

Overall winner Bethany Brewster of Saginaw Valley Lutheran won "individual" honors in 18:01. More than 300 meters back, runnerup Kristin Bishop of Kalamazoo Christian was officially recognized as the team race champion.

Carson City-Crystal, coached by Mark Ryan, successfully defended its team title on a cold day with light snow flurries.

Michigan Int. Speedway, Brooklyn, Nov. 2 ⊠
1996 GIRLS CLASS C TEAMS
1. Carson City-Crystal 64
2. Kalamazoo Hackett 107
3. Kalamazoo Christian 122
4. Blissfield 153
5. Shelby 165
6. Hemlock 208
7. Benzie Central 223
8. St Louis 252
9. Vermontville Maple Valley 275
10. Charlevoix 293
11. Lutheran Westland 313
12. McBain 319
13. Freeland 321
14. Hudson 348
15. Jonesville 377
16. Mayville 394
17. Buchanan 425
18. Southfield Christian 440
19. Lake Fenton 446
20. Bangor 472
21. Schoolcraft 475

1996 GIRLS CLASS C INDIVIDUALS
1. Bethany Brewster (Saginaw Valley Lutheran)11 . 18:01
2. Kristin Bishop (Kalamazoo Christian)10 . 18:58
3. Jenny Gerteisen (Kalamazoo Hackett)9 .. 18:58
4. Jodi Werman (Lutheran Westland) 19:04
5. Erinn Boot (Kalamazoo Christian) 19:06
6. Eiren Delong (Kalamazoo Hackett) 19:15
7. Melonnie Furgason (Blissfield) 19:20
8. Jessica Ringle (Carson City-Crystal) 19:20
9. Marisa Ryan (Carson City-Crystal)10 .... 19:22
10. Megan Warnke (Saginaw Valley Lutheran) .. 19:27
11. Michelle Swift (Carson City-Crystal) 19:30
12. Kristy Davenport (Addison) 19:38
13. Dienna Daughenbaugh (Freeland) 19:39
14. Lindsye Wade (Benzie Central) 19:46
15. Kylie Schultz (Clare) 19:50
16. Sarah Peterson (St Louis) 19:52
17. Jessica Lopez (Shelby) 19:55
18. Shane Prielipp (Blissfield) 19:55
19. Kate Veldman (Three Oaks River Valley) .. 20:00
20. Kerry Shurtz (Kalamazoo Hackett) 20:01
27. Amber Abott (Carson City-Crystal) 20:13
32. Amorena Newman (Carson City-Crystal) .. 20:22
34. Jamie Shepler (Carson City-Cystal) 20:24
38. Jennifer Ringle (Carson City-Crystal) ... 20:29

1997 CLASS C GIRLS

Bethany Brewster of Saginaw Valley Lutheran once again won, this time by an impressive 42 seconds over Carson City-Crystal's Marisa Ryan.

"It was slippery out there," Brewster said of the mud. "It made the footing difficult. You almost had to pick up your other leg to keep going. The course was a little more difficult this year."

After the state finals in track, Brewster would sign with Wisconsin, where she won 11 Big 10 titles in cross country and track.

Kalamazoo Hackett, coached by Lowie van Staveren, won a close team race against Benzie Central, 118-124.

Michigan Int. Speedway, Brooklyn, Nov. 1 ⊠
1997 GIRLS CLASS C TEAMS
1. Kalamazoo Hackett 118
2. Benzie Central 124
3. Kalamazoo Christian 152
4. Blissfield 158
5. Jonesville 162
6. Carson City-Crystal 212
7. McBain 242
8. Saginaw Valley Lutheran 251
9. Vermontville Maple Valley 265

10. Shelby	280
11. Sandusky	293
12. Freeland	298
13. Hudson	306
14. Mason County Central	323
15. Manchester	353
16. Buchanan	357
17. Hopkins	361
18. Southfield Christian	415
19. Laingsburg	431
20. Three Oaks River Valley	472
21. Lutheran Westland	479
22. St Louis	502

1997 GIRLS CLASS C INDIVIDUALS
1. Bethany Brewster (Saginaw Valley Lutheran)12	18:47
2. Marisa Ryan (Carson City-Crystal)11	19:29
3. Naomi Wendland (Saginaw Michigan Luth)11	19:34
4. Katie Veldman (Three Oaks River Valley)11	19:40
5. Erinn Boot (Kalamazoo Christian)11	19:44
6. Jenny Gerteisen (Kalamazoo Hackett)11	19:55
7. Heidi Wright (Southfield Christian)11	20:02
8. Nicole Suitor (Freeland)9	20:14
9. Kristin Warner (Jonesville)9	20:16
10. Melissa Byrne (McBain)9	20:16
11. Arika Peck (Kalamazoo Hackett)11	20:16
12. Caryn Waterson (Benzie Central)9	20:16
13. Kara Brown (Blissfield)9	20:27
14. Stephanie Lauer (Concord)11	20:30
15. Gabrielle Maggi (Rogers City)11	20:32
16. Jenny Stoyk (Hudson)9	20:34
17. Stephanie Patterson (Mayville)10	20:37
18. Dawn VanderVlucht (Vermontville Maple Val)9	20:38
19. Megann Root (Dundee)9	20:39
20. Michelle Swift (Carson City-Crystal)9	20:40
34. Emily Farrer (Kalamazoo Hackett)	21:05
36. Eiren Delong (Kalamazoo Hackett)11	21:08
94. Sarah Slosberg (Kalamazoo Hackett)	22:05
149. Julie Deppen (Kalamazoo Hackett)	22:51

1998 CLASS C GIRLS

The middle mile made the difference for Michigan Lutheran's Naomi Wendland. The senior was 8 seconds behind Carson City-Crystal's Marisa Ryan at the mile mark, but passed her before 2M and went on to win by 80m.

Benzie Central won its third title, beating Pittsford in a 2-point race.

Michigan Int. Speedway, Brooklyn, Nov. 7
1998 GIRLS CLASS C TEAMS
1. Benzie Central	132
2. Pittsford	134
3. Kalamazoo Hackett	178
4. Kent City	195
5. Blissfield	205
6. Kalamazoo Christian	210
7. Charlevoix	212
8. Concord	247
9. Southfield Christian	269
10. Laingsburg	290
11. Unionville-Sebewaing	297
12. Elk Rapids	303
13. Leslie	330
14. St. Louis	339
15. Vermontville Maple Valley	340
16. Sanford Meridian	346
17. Manchester	365
18. Mayville	375
19. Dundee	406
20. Freeland	411
21. Buchanan	422

1998 GIRLS CLASS C INDIVIDUALS
1. Naomi Wendland (Saginaw Mich Lutheran)12	18:10
2. Marisa Ryan (Carson City-Crystal)12	18:23
3. Caryn Waterson (Benzie Central)10	19:01
4. Heidi Wright (Southfield Christian)12	19:09
5. Gabrielle Maggi (Rogers City)12	19:12
6. Sarah Peterson (St Louis)12	19:13
7. Kim Hoover (Berrien Springs)10	19:14
8. Stephanie Patterson (Mayville)11	19:16
9. Nicole Suitor (Freeland)10	19:22
10. Keely Bigelow (Benzie Central)11	19:23
11. Katie Veldman (Three Oaks)12	19:23
12. Jennifer Leichtman (Ann Arbor Greenhills)9	19:23
13. Arika Peck (Kalamazoo Hackett)12	19:24
14. Megan Eaton (Buchanan)12	19:25
15. Kelly Johnson (Kent City)12	19:26
16. Megann Root (Dundee)10	19:26
17. Ashley Vercler (Constantine)9	19:26
18. Amy Averill (Southfield Christian)12	19:27
19. Beth Ferdinand (Suttons Bay)10	19:28
20. Tricia Hodge (Charlevoix)12	19:29
31. Sarah Warnke (Benzie Central)11	19:45
84. Erica Evans (Benzie Central)10	20:50
104. Sarah Tarsney (Benzie Central)9	21:06
150. Lindsey Wade (Benzie Central)12	21:46
180. Patti Herron (Benzie Central)11	22:37

1999 CLASS C GIRLS

The final Class C championship saw Kalamazoo Hackett, coached by Mike Northuis, roll to a 78-point win over Pittsford.

Caryn Waterson of Benzie Central didn't finish her regional race because of dehydration and low blood sugar, but she bounced back to win her first state title in a close finish with Lauren Fairbanks of Rogers City.

"I'm just grateful for the chance to run at the state finals," she said. "My team got me there after I didn't finish at the regional… So my team deserves most of the credit."

Caryn Waterson of Benzie Central bounced back from a bad regional experience.

Michigan Int. Speedway, Brooklyn, Nov. 6
1999 GIRLS CLASS C TEAMS
1. Kalamazoo Hackett	107
2. Pittsford	185
3. Benzie Central	185
4. Kent City	190
5. Suttons Bay	198
6. Kalamazoo Christian	204
7. Southfield Christian	215
8. St Louis	223
9. Sanford Meridian	229
10. Maple City Glen Lake	256
11. Concord	294
12. Laingsburg	304
13. Bath	305
14. Blissfield	306
15. Vandercook Lake	343
16. Berrien Springs	349
17. Lutheran Westland	354
18. Mayville	357
19. Erie-Mason	375
20. Unionville-Sebewaing	434
21. Almont	558

1999 GIRLS CLASS C INDIVIDUALS
1. Caryn Waterson (Benzie Central)11	18:56
2. Lauren Fairbanks (Rogers City)9	18:58
3. Katie Forsyth (Bath)9	19:19
4. Shannon Stanglewicz (St Louis)10	19:24
5. Nicole Suitor (Freeland)11	19:35
6. Stephanie Patterson (Mayville)12	19:40
7. Leanna Wolf (Mason County Central)10	19:45
8. Kayla Rousos (Kalamazoo Hackett)9	19:46
9. Chase Edwards (Maple City Glen Lake)9	19:48
10. Erin Booth (Homer)9	19:50
11. Kendra Huff (Whitmore Lake)12	19:53
12. Jennifer Lietchman (Ann Arbor Greenhills)10	19:54
13. Dawn Essenmacher (Pittsford)10	19:54
14. Sarah VanderPlas (Kalamazoo Christian)11	19:55
15. Leah Roche (Kent City)12	19:57
16. Jillian Harkey (Southfield Christian)12	19:59
17. Jackie Cyr (Boyne City)12	19:59
18. Christine Andres (Traverse City St Francis)10	19:59
19. Colleen Brady (Jonesville)11	19:59
20. Sarah Taylor (Unionville-Sebewaing)11	20:00
23. Carrie Drake (Kalamazoo Hackett)9	20:03
38. Alissa Dall (Kalamazoo Hackett)10	20:24
43. Amanda James (Kalamazoo Hackett)9	20:35
67. Kaitlyn McGahey (Kalamazoo Hackett)9	20:55
72. Kristen DeLong (Kalamazoo Hackett)9	21:01
110. Claire Gushurst (Kalamazoo Hackett)10	21;24

2000 D3 GIRLS

The switch to divisions had an effect, as the top three teams in D3 had all competed in Class B the previous year.

Ninth-grader Nicole Bush of Kelloggsville produced a stunning 17:53 to capture the title and the course record, leading her teammates to the team crown as well. "It was hard," said Bush, "because I was by myself for most of the last mile."

Michigan Int. Speedway, Brooklyn, Nov. 4
2000 GIRLS DIVISION 3 TEAMS
1. Wyoming Kelloggsville	80
2. Lansing Catholic	90
3. Whitehall	174
4. Kalamazoo Hackett	220
5. Edwardsburg	222
6. Gladwin	232
7. Suttons Bay	234
8. Milan	234
9. Jackson Lumen Christi	246
10. Muskegon Orchard View	251
11. Hillsdale	286
12. Tawas City	306
13. Boyne City	312
14. Benzie Central	326
15. Berrien Springs	328
16. Kent City	386
17. Shepherd	402
18. Ida	412
19. Essexville Garber	426
20. Stanton-Central Montcalm	431
21. Erie-Mason	545
22. Goodrich	547
23. Lake Fenton	602
24. Clawson	647
25. Bad Axe	675
26. Otisville Lakeville	719

NS--Vassar (four finishers).

2000 GIRLS DIVISION 3 INDIVIDUALS
1. Nicole Bush (Wyoming Kelloggsville)9	17:53
2. Krishawna Parker (Detroit Crockett)11	18:18
3. Rachel Kirvan (Lansing Catholic)12	18:45
4. Curry Breedlove (Sanford Meridian)11	18:48

5. Jessie Rodgers (Clare)9..................................18:57
6. Natoshia Bauer (Onsted)10.............................18:57
7. Amy Tomlinson (Wyoming Kelloggsville)11..........18:59
8. Arianne Field (Kalamazoo Hackett)11................19:01
9. Lesley Jurasek (Albion)11................................19:13
10. Nicole Suitor (Freeland)12...............................19:14
11. Danielle Smith (Ida)11....................................19:15
12. Katie Chenoweth (Lansing Catholic)12.............19:16
13. Emily Glancy (Tawas City)12...........................19:22
14. Kerri Sheriff (Muskegon Orchard View)12.........19:23
15. Jenna Heitchue (Richmond)10.........................19:25
16. Meagan Strohkirch (Gladwin)12......................19:27
17. Heather Postema (Kent City)12.......................19:29
18. Kati Swenor (Charlevoix).................................19:29
19. Sarah Vanderplas (Kalamazoo Christian)..........19:30
20. Suzanne Popranwa (Lansing Catholic)11.........19:31
22. Alexis Smith (Wyoming Kelloggsville)12..........19:37
41. Erin Hop (Wyoming Kelloggsville)12...............20:04
65. Erin Tomlinson (Wyoming Kelloggsville)10......20:31
175. Mollee Gierz (Wyoming Kelloggsville)10.......21:59
222. Andrea Panzica (Wyoming Kelloggsville)11....22:52

2001 D3 GIRLS

"I was a little surprised to see people behind me," Nicole Bush said. "Last year there was a gap, but I know there were others who wanted to win this race."

The Kelloggsville soph won in 18:40, beating Megan Young of Detroit Country Day and Krishawna Parker of Crockett.

Said Kelloggsville coach Ray Antel, "Parts of the course were just a thick carpeting of sand and mud. We knew it was out there. I guarantee you Nicole is disappointed with her time, but it was great to get a second state championship out of her."

Conditions were wet and warm as Spring Lake, coached by Scott Hector, captured its first title with 176, the highest winning total ever.

Michigan Int. Speedway, Brooklyn, Nov. 3
2001 GIRLS DIVISION 3 TEAMS
1. Spring Lake...176
2. Hanover-Horton...202
3. Tawas City..213
4. Hillsdale..229
5. Boyne City..234
6. Laingsburg...235
7. Albion...240
8. Williamston..246
9. Blissfield..272
10. Stanton-Central Montcalm................................290
11. Elk Rapids..293
12. Suttons Bay..297
13. Kalamazoo Hackett..317
14. Frankenmuth..341
15. Lansing Catholic..355
16. Essexville Garber..363
17. Kalamazoo Christian...412
18. Caro...413
19. Wyoming Kelloggsville......................................420
20. Delton Kellogg...423
21. Ida..468
22. Perry...517
23. Standish-Sterling..522
24. Cass City...547
25. Erie-Mason...552
26. Detroit Country Day..587
27. Goodrich...595

2001 GIRLS DIVISION 3 INDIVIDUALS
1. Nicole Bush (Wyoming Kelloggsville)10.............18:40
2. Megan Young (Detroit Country Day)9.................18:45
3. Krishawna Parker (Detroit Crockett)12...............18:50
4. Jaime Watson (Allendale)9.................................18:59
5. Lesley Jurasek (Albion)12..................................19:01
6. Christine Alcenius (Hanover-Horton)12...............19:06
7. Arianne Field (Kalamazoo Hackett)12................19:18
8. Emilie Erler (Tawas City)12................................19:29
9. Elizabeth Ulrich (Charlevoix)11..........................19:31
10. Katherine Rice (Williamston)10........................19:39
11. Jessie Rodgers (Clare)10.................................19:42
12. Jesse Lord-Wilder (Perry)10.............................19:44
13. Danielle Stein (Kalkaska)10.............................19:45
14. Lindsey Forche (Blissfield)9.............................19:47
15. Charity Mead (Stanton-Central Montcalm)11....19:53
16. Jane Stieber (Boyne City)10.............................19:54
17. Julie Pelak (Capac)12.......................................19:58
18. Kristen Poulos (Goodrich)11.............................19:59
19. Jenna Heitchue (Richmond)11.........................19:59
20. Simone Schelle (Jackson Lumen Christi)10.....20:00
34. Rachel Jeltema (Spring Lake)10.......................20:29
41. Jill Overacker (Spring Lake)10..........................20:36
66. Jeana Rokos (Spring Lake)12..........................21:06
71. Jodie Mohrhardt (Spring Lake)12.....................21:09
74. Aarika Woodard (Spring Lake)12......................21:10
191. Julie Jackson (Spring Lake)9.........................23:05

2002 D3 GIRLS

Nicole Bush of Kelloggsville stormed to title No. 3, passing the 1M in 5:32—the fastest split in any division, and hitting 2M in 11:37. Under cloudy skies with temperatures just above freezing, Bush held on to win by nearly 100m over Jaime Watson of Allendale.

Hillsdale took the team victory with a 27-point margin over Hanover-Horton.

Michigan Int. Speedway, Brooklyn, Nov. 2
2002 GIRLS DIVISION 3 TEAMS
1. Hillsdale..152
2. Hanover-Horton...179
3. Whitehall...194
4. Williamston...195
5. Blissfield...200
6. Clare...210
7. Jackson Lumen Christi..220
8. Saginaw Swan Valley..223
9. Essexville Garber..241
10. Goodrich...302
11. Onsted..332
12. Charlevoix..385
13. Laingsburg...393
14. Elk Rapids..395
15. Kent City..415
16. Lansing Catholic..420
17. Delton Kellogg...434
18. Perry...435
19. Detroit Country Day..447
20. Grand Rapids Baptist.......................................449
21. Kalamazoo Christian...458
22. Frankenmuth..478
23. Benzie Central...504
24. Kalamazoo Hackett..515
25. Cass City...570
26. Erie-Mason...608
27. Bad Axe..754

2002 GIRLS DIVISION 3 INDIVIDUALS
1. Nicole Bush (Wyoming Kelloggsville)11.............18:29
2. Jaime Watson (Allendale)10..............................18:46
3. Kristen Poulos (Goodrich)12..............................18:55
4. Danielle Stein (Kalkaska)11...............................19:02
5. Natoshia Bauer (Onsted)12................................19:04
6. Megan Young (Detroit Country Day)10...............19:06
7. Lindsey Forche (Blissfield)10.............................19:10
8. Kate Rice (Williamston)11..................................19:14
9. Mickayla Grosskopf (Corunna)10.......................19:15
10. Jessie Rodgers (Clare)11.................................19:19
11. Jennifer Phelan (Hanover-Horton)11................19:20
12. Jenny Nilsson (Williamston)10.........................19:22
13. Erin Batt (Hillsdale)10......................................19:22
14. Libby Carpenter (Whitehall)12..........................19:22
15. Elizabeth Ulrich (Charlevoix)12........................19:26
16. Cassie Wilkins (East Jackson)12.....................19:29
17. Rachel White (Hillsdale)12...............................19:31
18. Mollie Ringer (Kent City)9................................19:32
19. Meghan Soltis (Albion)11.................................19:35
20. Leah Reames (Kalamazoo Christian)9.............19:37
27. Sarah Jackson (Hillsdale)11............................20:07
77. Deeann Hassenzahl (Hillsdale)11....................20:48
83. Kathy Kehn (Hillsdale)12..................................20:54
105. Andrea Lytle (Hillsdale)11..............................21:08
134. Jessica Russell (Hillsdale)9...........................21:28

Kelloggsville's Nicole Bush went on to star at Michigan State and become a world-class steeplechaser.

2003 D3 GIRLS

The story of the meet revolved around defending champion Nicole Bush going for her fourth-straight title. The Kelloggsville star had run 17:41 earlier in the season, and though she won her regional race, she reportedly struggled the last 200m.

She led for the first two miles when trouble hit. "Going up the hill my thighs started burning, but I ignored it," she recounted. "I thought I could stretch it out on the downhill. But then it got worse. I thought, 'This isn't good.'"

Jaime Watson of Allendale, runnerup the previous year, passed Bush on the downhill leading back to the stadium and went on to win in 18:13. Bush, apparently hit by dehydration again, struggled just to finish. She crossed the line in second-to-last.

"I think other people took it harder than I did," she said. "I wasn't guaranteed to win going in. It's not the end of the world. I've had good things happen in my life in and out of running. But it would have been nice."

Watson would go on to a solid career at Liberty University, though not in cross country, where she only ran one collegiate race. On the track she honed her speed and ran 53.61 for the 400 and 2:05.42 for the 800; she won Big South conference titles in both.

Bush won the Big 10 cross country title for Michigan State and in 2009 was named the Spartan's female athlete of the year. That came the year after she placed 4th in the Olympic Trials steeplechase.

Goodrich, coached by John Shaw, won its first team title with a convincing 52-point margin over defending champ Hillsdale.

Michigan Int. Speedway, Brooklyn, Nov. 1
2003 GIRLS DIVISION 3 TEAMS
1. Goodrich...62
2. Hillsdale..114

3. Jackson Lumen Christi 178
4. Elk Rapids 199
5. Williamston 217
6. Kent City 226
7. Hanover-Horton 229
8. Essexville Garber 284
9. Blissfield 304
10. Grand Rapids Baptist 339
11. Charlevoix 352
12. Newaygo 355
13. Allendale 357
14. Clare 365
15. Kalamazoo Christian 367
16. Lansing Catholic 374
17. Perry 395
18. Morley-Stanwood 409
19. Saginaw Swan Valley 428
20. Schoolcraft 454
21. Kalamazoo Hackett 468
22. Boyne City 474
23. Grosse Ile 583
24. Bad Axe 597
25. Monroe St. Mary Catholic Central 643
26. Frankenmuth 645
27. Armada 668

Jaime Watson of Allendale later ran for Liberty University.

2003 GIRLS DIVISION 3 INDIVIDUALS
1. Jaime Watson (Allendale)11 ....18:13
2. Kayla O'Mara (Goodrich)9 ....18:26
3. Erin Batt (Hillsdale)11 ....18:32
4. Thereseann Zimmerman (Boyne City)10 ..18:33
5. Megan Young (Detroit Country Day)11 ...18:51
6. Kaitlin O'Mara (Goodrich)9 ....18:52
7. Leah Reames (Kalamazoo Christian)10 ..18:53
8. Danielle Stein (Kalkaska)12 ....18:59
9. Sarah Dugan (Freeland)10 ....19:06
10. Brittney Hohn (Morley-Stanwood)9 ....19:07
11. Jennifer Nilsson (Williamston)11 ....19:08
12. Bethany Hammer (Elk Rapids)9 ....19:10
13. Janee Jones (Goodrich)11 ....19:26
14. Mollie Ringer (Kent City)10 ....19:27
15. Sarah Jackson (Hillsdale)12 ....19:27
16. Melloni Diem (Montrose)9 ....19:29
17. Jessie Rodgers (Clare)12 ....19:32
18. Jacinda Bingoff (Stockbridge)11 ....19:33
19. Adrienne Pastula (Hillsdale)9 ....19:34
20. Hannah Wittbrodt (Elk Rapids)9 ....19:43
32. Samantha Minkler (Goodrich)10 ....19:55
35. Kelsey Meyers (Goodrich)9 ....20:03
85. Natalie Cook (Goodrich)10 ....20:52
207. Molly Downer (Goodrich)12 ....23:12
237. Nicole Bush (Wyomiong Kelloggsville)12 ...29:30

2004 D3 GIRLS

Goodrich put three into the top 8 to successfully defend the title, led by individual winner Janee Jones, who won by a massive 47 seconds. Jones was the only senior on the Goodrich squad.

"The first mile I felt pretty good," said Jones. "Then it started to get windy, so the last mile and a half was a lot harder and I tried to hang in there. I took it out pretty slow, but nobody else went with me."

Michigan Int. Speedway, Brooklyn, Nov. 6 ☒
2004 GIRLS DIVISION 3 TEAMS
1. Goodrich 69
2. Jackson Lumen Christi 119
3. Williamston 144
4. Hillsdale 165
5. Elk Rapids 214
6. Macomb Lutheran North 231
7. Blissfield 270
8. Allendale 298
9. Charlevoix 305
10. Stockbridge 308
11. Whitehall 331
12. Harbor Springs 379
13. Kent City 385
14. Kalamazoo Christian 394
15. Monroe St. Mary 398
16. Clare 419
17. Bad Axe 426
18. Freeland 436
19. Ann Arbor Richard 448
20. Stanton-Central Montcalm 471
21. Frankenmuth 494
22. Delton Kellogg 498
23. Saginaw Nouvel 519
24. Morley-Stanwood 521
25. Schoolcraft 625
26. Armada 625
27. St. Louis 673

2004 GIRLS DIVISION 3 INDIVIDUALS
1. Janee Jones (Goodrich)12 ....18:08
2. Leah Reames (Kalamazoo Christian)11 ..18:55
3. Erin Batt (Hillsdale)12 ....18:58
4. Jaime Watson (Allendale)12 ....19:04
5. Megan Young (Detroit Country Day)12 ...19:07
6. Kayla O'Mara (Goodrich)10 ....19:14
7. Kyle Dexter (Williamston)12 ....19:17
8. Kaitlin O'Mara (Goodrich)10 ....19:19
9. Hilary Snyder (Jackson Lumen Christi)9 ..19:21
10. Adrienne Pastula (Hillsdale)10 ....19:22
11. Lindsey Forche (Blissfield)12 ....19:23
12. Morgan Royal (Hemlock)11 ....19:24
13. Melloni Diem (Montrose)10 ....19:29
14. Mikinzie Stuart (Saginaw Nouvel)12 ....19:30
15. Jacinda Bingoff (Stockbridge)12 ....19:32
16. Mollie Ringer (Kent City)11 ....19:33
17. Carissa Hudson (Macomb Lutheran North)9 ..19:33
18. Brittany Hohn (Morley-Stanwood)10 ....19:36
19. Bethany Hammer (Elk Rapids)10 ....19:37
20. Alise Nilsson (Williamston)12 ....19:38
23. Kelsey Krych (Goodrich)10 ....19:42
49. Kelsey Meyers (Goodrich)10 ....20:17
50. Mary Haiderer (Goodrich)9 ....20:21
125. Samantha Minkler (Goodrich)11 ....21:23

2005 D3 GIRLS

Goodrich again came to the big show with some top-end firepower, putting three into the top 10.

Mikal Beckman of Newaygo stunned many with her quick improvement. A year before she had finished 51st. "Over the summer I felt since I was going to do cross country and basketball I needed to get in shape. I found myself giving my all to running," she explained of her decision to drop basketball.

"I was pretty surprised," she said of her win. "I was expecting people to be with me the last mile. I was looking forward to having someone there to give me that little push."

Michigan Int. Speedway, Brooklyn, Nov. 5 ☒
2005 GIRLS DIVISION 3 TEAMS
1. Goodrich 118
2. Jackson Lumen Christi 147
3. Hillsdale 150
4. Elk Rapids 176
5. East Jordan 214
6. Whitehall 289
7. Macomb Lutheran North 290
8. Kalamazoo Christian 291
9. Freeland 307
10. Otsego 316
11. Clare 324
12. Hanover-Horton 329
13. Schoolcraft 334
14. Benzie Central 341
15. Armada 374
16. Frankenmuth 414
17. Perry 415
18. Morley-Stanwood 419
19. Erie-Mason 431
20. Grandville Calvin Christian 446
21. Shepherd 458
22. Monroe St Mary 475
23. Saginaw Swan Valley 497
24. Ovid-Elsie 553
25. Ithaca 593
26. Kalamazoo Hackett 647
27. Onsted 662
NS. Kalamazoo Christian (two finishers).

2005 GIRLS DIVISION 3 INDIVIDUALS
1. Mikal Beckman (Newaygo)11 ....18:04
2. Kristi Werner (East Jordan)11 ....18:28
3. Aubree Danielson (Whitehall)9 ....18:30
4. Devyn Ramsey (Benzie Central)9 ....18:40
5. Kaitlin O'Mara (Goodrich)11 ....18:45
6. Ylva Elhammer (Otsego)9 ....18:45
7. Kelsey Meyers (Goodrich)11 ....18:52
8. Bethany Hammer (Elk Rapids)11 ....18:57
9. Elizabeth Horcha (Durand)10 ....18:58
10. Kelsey Krych (Goodrich)11 ....18:59
11. Brittany Hohn (Morley-Stanwood)11 ....18:59
12. Adrienne Pastula (Hillsdale)11 ....18:59
13. Sam Schmiedeknecht (Whitehall)9 ....19:01
14. Carissa Hudson (Macomb Luthern North)10 ..19:03
15. Amanda Hammer (Elk Rapids)9 ....19:06
16. Ashley Quick (Harbor Springs)12 ....19:08
17. Lindi Edger (Charlevoix)11 ....19:10
18. Mollie Ringer (Kent City)12 ....19:14
19. Leah Reames (Kalamazoo Christian)12 ..19:17
20. Alisha Nussbaum (Hillsdale)11 ....19:18
42. Mary Haiderer (Goodrich)10 ....19:51
109. Samantha Miinkler (Goodrich)12 ....20:40
132. Kayla O'Mara (Goodrich)11 ....20:57
141. Laura Haiderer (Goodrich)12 ....21:03

2006 D3 GIRLS

Jackson Lumen Christi, coached by Mike Woolsey, captured its first title in 15 years. Junior Hillary Snyder placed 3rd, and a solid pack of four came in the 19:50s to seal a 13-point win over Leroy Pine River.

"We ran a pretty good pack," said Woolsey. "Running in a pack gives us a scoring and a mental edge."

Individually, sophomore Devyn Ramsey of Benzie Central may have been the first to sing her way to a state title. "I try to stay right behind the first person to that point," she told the *Detroit Free Press*, "so they are thinking about me the whole time and not the race. I was thinking about how much I really wanted to win, and I was singing to myself a little, actually—just little pieces of all my favorite songs."

Michigan Int. Speedway, Brooklyn, Nov. 4 ☒

2006 GIRLS DIVISION 3 TEAMS
1. Jackson Lumen Christi 136
2. Leroy Pine River 149
3. Allendale 155
4. Monroe St Mary 187
5. Elk Rapids 201
6. Macomb Lutheran North 214
7. Williamston 223
8. Whitehall 239
9. Hillsdale 242
10. Flint Powers 269
11. Schoolcraft 335
12. Clare 337
13. Benzie Central 356
14. Lansing Catholic 371
15. Grand Rapids West Catholic 411
16. Morley-Stanwood 417
17. Freeland 423
18. Ann Arbor Richard 463
19. Blissfield 494
20. Durand 529
21. Armada 532
22. Perry 548
23. Frankenmuth 580
24. Essexville Garber 604
25. Kalamazoo Christian 637
26. Buchanan 648
27. Edwardsburg 655
28. Saginaw Nouvel 684

2006 GIRLS DIVISION 3 INDIVIDUALS
1. Devyn Ramsey (Benzie Central)10 .... 18:32
2. Adrienne Pastula (Hillsdale)12 .... 18:38
3. Hillary Snyder (Jackson Lumen Christi)11 .... 18:42
4. Amanda Hammer (Elk Rapids)10 .... 18:50
5. Camille Borst (Allendale)9 .... 18:57
6. Aubree Danielson (Whitehall)10 .... 19:00
7. Devan John (Allendale)9 .... 19:01
8. Emma Drenth (Williamston)9 .... 19:08
9. Anne Bellino (Monroe St Mary)12 .... 19:09
10. Kristi Werner (East Jordan)12 .... 19:11
11. Lauren Halm (Williamston)9 .... 19:11
12. Alissa Ott (Detroit Country Day)11 ..... 19:14
13. Chelsie Fuller (Freeland)11 .... 19:14
14. Bethany Hammer (Elk Rapids)12 .... 19:17
15. Mikal Beckman (Newaygo)12 .... 19:19
16. Lindsay Sanders (Schoolcraft)10 .... 19:19
17. Audrey Pastula (Hillsdale)11 .... 19:20
18. Amber Hutson (Hanover-Horton)11 .... 19:21
19. Alisha Nussbaum (Hillsdale)12 .... 19:21
20. Alina Dhaseleer (Charleviox)11 .... 19:22
45. Cara Cremeans (Jackson Lumen Christi)10 ..... 19:51
46. Theresa Walsh (Jackson Lumen Christi)11 ..... 19:55
48. Kristine Knapp (Jackson Lumen Christi)12 ..... 19:56
50. Kelly Crowley (Jackson Lumen Christi)12 ..... 19:57
108. Audrey Spring (Jackson Lumen Christi)10 ....20:52
130. Allison Tompkins (Jackson Lumen Christi)10 ..21:06

2007 D3 GIRLS

Lumen Christi won again, but by a tiny 2-point margin. "The kids followed the race plan completely," remarked coach Mike Woolsey. "We knew it would be close but not this close."

Devan John of Allendale won the race, passing leader and defending champion Devyn Ramsey in the final strides. "I didn't think I was going to get her," she said. "She had a pretty good lead going into the last stretch, the final mile, but I guess I really wanted to kick it in."

Michigan Int. Speedwar, Brooklyn, Nov. 3 ⊠
2007 GIRLS DIVISION 3 TEAMS
1. Jackson Lumen Christi 101
2. Leroy Pine River 103
3. Williamston 114
4. Schoolcraft 131
5. Benzie Central 159
6. Allendale 195
7. Ida 240
8. Macomb Lutheran North 265
9. Grand Rapids West Catholic 267
10. Whitehall 299
11. Freeland 331
12. Shepherd 371
13. Hanover-Horton 379
14. Kalamazoo Christian 385
15. Monroe St Mary 394
16. Armada 399
17. Perry 399
18. Leslie 406
19. Kingsley 471
20. Detroit Country Day 485
21. Caro 492
22. Lansing Catholic 501
23. Hillsdale 549
24. Kalamazoo Hackett 643
25. Grosse Ile 646
26. Madison Heights Foley 678
27. Saginaw Swan Valley 696
28. Riverview Richard 829

2007 GIRLS DIVISION 3 INDIVIDUALS
1. Devan John (Allendale)10 .... 18:16
2. Devyn Ramsey (Benzie Central)11 ...... 18:16
3. Lia Jones (Leroy Pine River)12 .... 18:30
4. Emma Drenth (Williamston)10 .... 18:49
5. Cara Cremeans (Jackson Lumen C)11 .... 18:50
6. Amaya Ayers (Laingsburg)10 .... 18:55
7. Alissa Ott (Detroit Country Day)12 ...... 18:57
8. Audrey Pastula (Hillsdale)12 .... 18:58
9. Hilary Snyder (Jackson Lumen Christi)12 .... 18:58
10. Lauren Halm (Williamston)10 .... 18:59
11. Alina Dhaseleer (Charleviox)12 .... 19:03
12. Amelia Bannister (Albion)11 .... 19:04
13. Rachel Whitley (Leroy Pine River)11 .. 19:04
14. Krista Broekema (Schoolcraft)9 .... 19:06
15. Deanna Pineda (Montague)12 .... 19:07
16. Amanda Hammer (Elk Rapids)11 .... 19:08
17. Amanda Paris (Hemlock)11 .... 19:08
18. Megan Rodgers (Clare)11 .... 19:10
19. Betsey Hudson (Schoolcraft)11 .... 19:11
20. Becca Holmquist (Leroy Pine River)12 .... 19:11
40. Bekah Stanton (Jackson Lumen Christi)9 .... 19:46
41. Theresa Walsh (Jackson Lumen Christi)12 ..... 19:46
42. Jill McEldowney (Jackson Lumen Christi)9 ..... 20:00
43. Audrey Spring (Jackson Lumen Christi)11 ...... 21:09
174. Sarah Deagostino (Jackson Lumen Christi)10 21:40

Devan John won three in a row for Allendale (Pete Draugalis photo)

2008 D3 GIRLS

Once again Devan John beat Devyn Ramsey for the win, but this time the Allendale junior carried a big lead to the finish to triumph, 18:07-18:35.

John and Ramsey had run neck-and-neck for the first 2M before John pulled away. "She ran really good," said John of her rival, "especially for someone hurt that bad."

Ramsey, troubled all season by what doctors thought might be a pinched nerve in her leg, got a sweet consolation, leading her Benzie Central teammates to the team victory. "It's my last year. I couldn't go out not running. That would've hurt even more."

Ramsey would go on to become an All-MAC athlete for Toledo.

Michigan Int. Speedway, Brooklyn, Nov. 1 ⊠
2008 GIRLS DIVISION 3 TEAMS
1. Benzie Central 91
2. Leslie 120
3. Allendale 122
4. Jackson Lumen Christi 164
5. Hanover-Horton 178
6. Kent City 218
7. Macomb Lutheran North 225
8. Schoolcraft 271
9. Elk Rapids 277
10. Grand Rapids West Catholic 294
11. Portland 301
12. Clare 329
13. Lansing Catholic 331
14. Cass City 393
15. Monroe St Mary 395
16. Caro 402
17. Ida 474
18. Michigan Center 475
19. Almont 478
20. Freeland 510
21. Midland Bullock Creek 531
22. Buchanan 540
23. Vassar 549
24. Standish-Sterling 589
25. Blissfield 629
26. Lake Fenton 633
27. Delton Kellogg 684

2008 GIRLS DIVISION 3 INDIVIDUALS
1. Devan John (Allendale)11 .... 18:07
2. Devyn Ramsey (Benzie Central)12 ...... 18:35
3. Amanda Hammer (Elk Rapids)12 .... 18:37
4. Olivia Sydow (GR West Catholic)12 ..... 18:42
5. Anna Rudd (Leslie)12 .... 18:46
6. Lindsey Berdette (Hanover-Horton)9 ... 18:49
7. Michaela Carnegie (Benzie Central)10 .18:51
8. Ali Wiersma (Allendale)9 .... 18:55
9. Brittany Slinker (Dundee)9 .... 18:55
10. Sadie Ringer (Kent City)9 .... 18:57
11. Amaya Ayers (Laingsburg)11 .... 19:03
12. Audrey Tremaine (Leslie)9 .... 19:06
13. Rachel Whitley (Leroy Pine River)12 . 19:07
14. Shannon Morehouse (Clawson)12 .... 19:07
15. Camille Borst (Allendale)11 .... 19:10
16. Hilary Kast (Hillsdale)10 .... 19:10
17. Meagan Rodgers (Clare)12 .... 19:12
18. Brittany Anderson (Leroy Pine Riv)11 19:14
19. Lindsay Sanders (Schoolcraft)12 .... 19:14
20. Krista Broekema (Schoolcraft)10 .... 19:15
35. Theresa Warsecke (Benzie Central)9 .19:37
36. Taylor Nye (Benzie Central)10 .... 19:37
43. Marika Grabowski (Benzie Central)10 19:50
63. Jill Lousignau (Benzie Central)11 .... 20:04
96. Amber Peabody (Benzie Central)9 ..... 20:35

2009 D3 GIRLS

Devan John of Allendale captured her third-straight title on a breezy day. "It was tough with the wind," she said. "I tried to get out a little bit early. I don't like the wind."

Hanover-Horton, coached by Dean Blackledge, won its first title, topping Allendale by 11.

Michigan Int. Speedway, Brooklyn, Nov. 7 ⊠
2009 GIRLS DIVISION 3 TEAMS
1. Hanover-Horton 63
2. Allendale 74
3. Benzie Central 110

4. Leslie ... 120
5. Jackson Lumen Christi ... 199
6. Kent City ... 210
7. Macomb Lutheran North ... 232
8. Lansing Catholic ... 275
9. Caro ... 283
10. Schoolcraft ... 285
11. Grand Rapids NorthPointe Christian ... 386
12. Freeland ... 395
13. Portland ... 400
14. Essexville Garber ... 431
15. Ida ... 441
16. Leroy Pine River ... 452
17. Berrien Springs ... 459
18. Hillsdale ... 479
19. Manchester ... 489
20. Kingsley ... 519
21. Blissfield ... 531
22. Bad Axe ... 536
23. Sanford Meridian ... 540
24. Bangor ... 555
25. Almont ... 596
26. Whitmore Lake ... 649
27. Durand ... 729
28. Lake Fenton ... 755

2009 GIRLS DIVISION 3 INDIVIDUALS
1. Devan John (Allendale)12 ... 18:31
2. Megan Heeder (Lansing Catholic)11 ... 19:06
3. Ali Wiersma (Allendale)10 ... 19:09
4. Michaela Carnegie (Benzie Central)11 ... 19:11
5. Raquel Serna (St Louis)9 ... 19:15
6. Taylor Nye (Benzie Central)11 ... 19:21
7. Megan Hubbard (Hanover-Horton)9 ... 19:28
8. Audrey Tremaine (Leslie)10 ... 19:29
9. Lindsey Burdette (Hanover-Horton)10 ... 19:30
10. Camille Borst (Allendale)12 ... 19:32
11. Colleen Grassley (Monroe St. Mary's)11 ... 19:33
12. Amanda Valliere (Midland Bullock Creek)9 .. 19:36
13. Brittany Anderson (Leroy Pine River)12 ... 19:36
14. Brittany Slinker (Dundee)10 ... 19:36
15. Amaya Ayers (Laingsburg)12 ... 19:36
16. Grace Campbell (GR NorthPointe Chr)12 ... 19:40
17. Rachel Durbin (Armada)9 ... 19:43
18. Krista Broekema (Schoolcraft)11 ... 19:44
19. Emily Short (Tawas City)11 ... 19:45
20. Kaylee Carew (Kent City)11 ... 19:46
21. Emily Wrozek (Hanover-Horton)11 ... 19:47
24. Sharon Morgan (Hanover-Horton)11 ... 19:50
28. Lindsey Chinavare (Hanover-Horton)10 ... 19:59
35. Kelly Morgan (Hanover-Horton)11 ... 20:09
108. Sierra Melling (Hanover-Horton)10 ... 21:25

2010 D3 GIRLS

Ali Wiersma made it four years in a row with an Allendale runner on top of the podium. The junior followed in Devan John's footsteps to win her first title. "This feels wonderful," she said. "I trained a ton over the summer because I knew this day was what it was all about."

Once again, Hanover-Horton won the team title. Said coach Dean Blackledge, "We had five all-state runners a year ago and we wanted to do better, and we did with six this year."

Michigan Int. Speedway, Brooklyn, Nov. 6
2010 GIRLS DIVISION 3 TEAMS
1. Hanover-Horton ... 88
2. Benzie Central ... 129
3. Kent City ... 188
4. Stockbridge ... 267
5. Jackson Lumen Christi ... 278
6. St Louis ... 281
7. Flint Powers ... 292
8. Leslie ... 307
9. Shepherd ... 323
10. Grandville Calvin Christian ... 327
11. Lansing Catholic ... 342
12. Schoolcraft ... 367
13. Clare ... 374
14. Dundee ... 384
15. Perry ... 392
16. Caro ... 393
17. Monroe St Mary ... 429
18. Hillsdale ... 467
19. Charlevoix ... 470
20. Manton ... 490
21. Blissfield ... 521
22. Ida ... 525
23. Cass City ... 531
24. Parchment ... 536
25. Macomb Lutheran North ... 541
26. Tawas CIty ... 596
27. Delton Kellogg ... 605
28. Allendale ... 623
29. Freeland ... 658

With Ali Wiersma's 2010 win, Allendale had won four individual titles in a row.
(Pete Draugalis photo)

2010 GIRLS DIVISION 3 INDIVIDUALS
1. Ali Wiersma (Allendale)11 ... 18:01
2. Lindsey Burdette (Hanover-Horton)11 ... 18:07
3. Megan Heeder (Lansing Catholic)12 ... 18:12
4. Breanne Lesnar (Freeland)12 ... 18:19
5. Michaela Carnegie (Benzie Central)12 ... 18:43
6. Emily Short (Tawas City)12 ... 18:45
=7. Kelly Schubert (Manistee)11 ... 18:46
=7. Colleen Grassley (Monroe St. Mary)12 ... 18:46
9. Rachel Stathakis (Macomb Lutheran N)12 ... 18:47
10. Audrey Tremaine (Leslie)11 ... 18:48
11. Kaylie Rhynard (Shepherd)9 ... 18:48
12. Callyanne Wyma (St Louis)12 ... 18:55
13. Teha Ames (Shepherd)12 ... 18:56
14. Krista Broekema (Schoolcraft)12 ... 18:56
15. Taylor Nye (Benzie Central)12 ... 18:57
16. Emma Frost (Lansing Catholic)10 ... 19:01
17. Stephanie Ingraham (Manton)12 ... 19:02
18. Shannon Richardson (Hanover-Horton)9 ... 19:03
19. Jenny Frantz (Ovid-Elsie)11 ... 19:03
20. Ashley Russo (Kent City)9 ... 19:04
21. Kelly Morgan (Hanover-Horton)12 ... 19:05
27. Emily Wrozek (Hanover-Horton)12 ... 19:11
29. Sharon Morgan (Hanover-Horton)12 ... 19:12
30. Megan Hubbard (Hanover-Horton)10 ... 19:12
79. Sierra Melling (Hanover-Horton)11 ... 20:10

2011 D3 GIRLS

With Allendale being bumped up to Division 2, the 4-year individual winning streak ended. This time, Manistee senior Kelly Schubert rose to the top with a sterling 17:59 performance.

In the team standings, Benzie Central scored a 20-point win over Kent City, with 2-time defending champion Hanover-Horton in third. Said lead Benzie runner Theresa Warsecke,

"We won my freshman year and Amber and I, the two seniors, wanted that again. It made us want it that much more after finishing second last year."

Manistee's Kelly Schubert.
(Pete Draugalis photo)

Michigan Int. Speedway, Brooklyn, Nov. 5
2011 GIRLS DIVISION 3 TEAMS
1. Benzie Central ... 126
2. Kent City ... 146
3. Hanover-Horton ... 166
4. Jackson Lumen Christi ... 190
5. Harbor Springs ... 197
6. Charlevoix ... 212
7. Flint Powers ... 228
8. Grandville Calvin Christian ... 235
9. Clare ... 254
10. Macomb Lutheran North ... 264
11. Caro ... 266
12. Shepherd ... 307
13. St. Louis ... 312
14. Stockbridge ... 320
15. Bath ... 332
16. Ann Arbor Richard ... 419
17. Allen Park Cabrini ... 428
18. Sandusky ... 457
19. Monroe St Mary ... 471
20. Schoolcraft ... 517
21. Delton Kellogg ... 522
22. Durand ... 552
23. Hart ... 581
24. Parchment ... 583
25. Freeland ... 694
26. Hemlock ... 757
27. Almont ... 793

2011 GIRLS DIVISION 3 INDIVIDUALS
1. Kelly Schubert (Manistee)12 ... 17:59
2. Raquel Serna (St Louis)11 ... 18:24
3. Ashley Sorge (Ida)9 ... 18:29
4. Lindsey Burdette (Hanover-Horton)12 ... 18:30
5. Kaylie Rhynard (Shepherd)10 ... 18:34
6. Gina Patterson (Macomb Lutheran North)9 ... 18:34
7. Emma Frost (Lansing Catholic)11 ... 18:44
8. Megan Hubbard (Hanover-Horton)11 ... 18:45
9. Amber Way (Charlevoix)9 ... 18:55
10. Theresa Warsecke (Benzie Central)12 ... 18:58
11. Annie Fuller (Manistee)9 ... 19:02
12. Mickey Ludlow (Jackson Lumen Christi)12 .. 19:04
13. Jenny Frantz (Ovid-Elsie)12 ... 19:09
14. Lindsay Poll (Stockbridge)11 ... 19:11
15. Audrey Tremaine (Leslie)12 ... 19:13
16. Jessica Disselkoen (Grandville Calvin C)12 ... 19:15
17. Jeanne Wilson (Kent City)12 ... 19:15
18. Olivia Certa (Charlevoix)11 ... 19:17
19. Shannon Richardson (Hanover-Horton)10 ... 19:17
20. Alia Benedict (Manchester)9 ... 19:18
26. Bryce Cutler (Benzie Central)10 ... 19:21
48. Amber Peabody (Charlevoix)12 ... 20:00
55. Makayla Huddleston (Benzie Central)10 ... 20:05
57. Rachael Peabody (Benzie Central)10 ... 20:05

{ 173 }

| 67. Charlotte Warsecke (Benzie Central)9 | 20:10 |
| 124. Savannah Hayden (Benzie Central)9 | 20:51 |

2012 D3 GIRLS

Gina Patterson of Macomb Lutheran North seemed genuinely stunned when she won by 16 seconds. "I just came out here and was looking forward to having a great experience," she said. Her 17:44 broke a 12-year-old D3 record.

"I just wanted to go out with the first runners and let it unfold from there. It broke into just me and [Raquel Serna of St. Louis] and I kind of separated from there. I kept looking back thinking, 'Is this going too fast? What's going to happen?' Once we started getting farther and farther away, I was okay."

Lumen Christi won another close one, this time by 4 points over Grandville Calvin Christian.

Gina Patterson won by 90 meters in 2012. (Pete Draugalis photo)

Michigan Int. Speedway, Brooklyn, Nov. 3
2012 GIRLS DIVISION 3 TEAMS
1. Jackson Lumen Christi	167
2. Grandville Calvin Christian	171
3. Caro	201
4. Benzie Central	204
5. Lansing Catholic	237
6. Hanover-Horton	241
7. Macomb Lutheran North	275
8. Bath	288
9. Shepherd	299
10. Mason County Central	332
11. Newaygo	340
12. Clare	357
13. Manistee	360
14. Flint Powers	364
15. Stockbridge	393
16. Hillsdale	395
17. Sandusky	401
18. Grand Rapids NorthPointe Christian	415
19. Essexville Garber	421
20. Ann Arbor Richard	421
21. Hopkins	422
22. Allen Park Cabrini	455
23. Ida	459
24. Dundee	483
25. Saginaw Nouvel	565
26. Hartford	583
27. Delton Kellogg	626

2012 GIRLS DIVISION 3 INDIVIDUALS
1. Gina Patterson (Macomb Lutheran North)10	17:44
2. Raquel Serna (St Louis)12	18:00
3. Annie Fuller (Manistee)10	18:11
4. Amber Way (Charlevoix)10	18:14
5. Allison Vroon (Holland Black River)10	18:22
6. Julia Jeczmionka (Essexville Garber)10	18:25
7. Kaylie Rhynard (Shepherd)11	18:26
8. Ashley Sorge (Ida)10	18:34
9. Megan Hubbard (Hanover-Horton)12	18:36
10. Alyssa Bennett (Benzie Central)11	18:38
11. Madeline Richards (Hillsdale)11	18:42
12. Ashley Russo (Kent City)11	18:44
13. Ashley Lindeman (Manistee)9	18:45
14. Rachael Weber (Hopkins)10	18:51
15. Kathy Middaugh (Newaygo)12	18:57
16. Allison Dorr (Birch Run)11	18:57
17. Monica Ellicott (Caro)10	18:57
18. Bryce Cutler (Benzie Central)11	18:58
19. Emma Frost (Lansing Catholic)12	19:01
20. Taylor Thrush (Shepherd)10	19:02
23. Caitlin Clark (Jackson Lumen Christi)10	19:10
24. Aubrey Penn (Jackson Lumen Christi)10	19:11
48. Jensen McEldowney (Jackson Lumen C)9	19:47
56. Leanne Leuthard (Jackson Lumen C)12	19:55
82. Anna Berkemeier (Jackson Lumen C)12	20:17
134. Emily Yoxheimer (Jackson Lumen C)10	20:57
187. Jacqueline Miller (Jackson Lumen C)12	21:58

2013 D3 GIRLS

Shepherd won its first title since 1994. Coach Carey Hammel's Bluejays topping perennial powerhouse Benzie Central by 66 points. Said Hammel, "They went out and they executed the plan and it just can't get any better than this."

Gina Patterson of Lutheran North took her second-straight title, passing Charlevoix's Amber Way to take the win, 18:03-18:05. "I wasn't comfortable at all. I thought she had it, actually."

Michigan Int. Speedway, Brooklyn, Nov. 2
2013 GIRLS DIVISION 3 TEAMS
1. Shepherd	120
2. Benzie Central	186
3. Macomb Lutheran North	214
4. Hopkins	220
5. Caro	230
6. Hanover-Horton	240
7. Grandville Calvin Christian	249
8. Manistee	252
9. Clare	257
10. Ithaca	260
11. Jackson Lumen Christi	283
12. Ann Arbor Richard	285
13. Lansing Catholic	294
14. Kalamazoo Hackett	320
15. Flint Powers	359
16. Holland Black River	369
17. Hart	390
18. Quincy	406
19. Ida	442
20. Erie-Mason	462
21. Frankenmuth	560
22. Grand Rapids Covenant Christian	565
23. Freeland	571
24. Schoolcraft	594
25. Reese	611
26. Capac	794
27. Almont	837

2013 GIRLS DIVISION 3 INDIVIDUALS
1. Gina Patterson (Macomb Lutheran North)11	18:03
2. Amber Way (Charlevoix)11	18:05
3. Allison Vroon (Holland Black River)11	18:38
4. Ashley Sorge (Ida)11	18:45
5. Ashley Russo (Kent City)12	18:50
6. Annie Fuller (Manistee)11	18:52
7. Kaylie Rhynard (Shepherd)12	18:56
8. Rachael Weber (Hopkins)11	18:56
9. Ashley Lindeman (Manistee)10	18:57
10. Jasmine Harper (Clare)9	18:58
11. Courtney Allen (Ithaca)9	19:09
12. Katelyn Hutchinson (Shepherd)9	19:13
13. Hannah Davis (St Louis)12	19:20
14. Abigail Gilmore (Lansing Catholic)9	19:21
15. Shannon Richardson (Hanover-Horton)12	19:22
16. Emily Sievert (Frankenmuth)12	19:22
17. Kaitlyn Beyer (Carson City-Crystal)11	19:23
18. Bryce Cutler (Benzie Central)12	19:25
19. Stephanie Schaub (Benzie Central)10	19:25
20. Monica Ellicott (Caro)11	19:27
44. Kylie Hutchinson (Shepherd)9	20:15
47. Rachel Mathers (Shepherd)9	20:21
49. Taylor Thursh (Shepherd)11	20:22
53. Taylor Priest (Shepherd)12	20:28
83. Sarah Bellinger (Shepherd)10	20:45

2014 D3 GIRLS

A first-ever state title for Ithaca made head coach Gene Lebron happy. "I honestly think being ranked first all year kind of helped," he told RunMichigan.com. "Being ranked No. 1 from the beginning kind of helped us settle in… They bought into everything that we were preaching—believing in each other and doing all the little things."

Holly Bullough of Traverse City St. Francis edged Charlevoix's Amber Way by 0.2 seconds, staging a huge come-from behind sprint. "I'm more of a finisher than a beginner. I conserve my energy so I can finish stronger."

Holly Bullough (left) outkicked Amber Way in the final stretch. (Pete Draugalis photo)

Michigan Int. Speedway, Brooklyn, Nov. 1
2014 GIRLS DIVISION 3 TEAMS
1. Ithaca	147
2. Shepherd	158
3. Manistee	163
4. Jackson Lumen Christi	164
5. Hart	177
6. Lansing Catholic	195
7. Grandville Calvin Christian	229
8. Caro	239
9. Macomb Lutheran North	259
10. Holland Black River	262
11. Grand Traverse Academy	276
12. Leslie	300
13. Hopkins	321
14. St. Louis	321
15. Clare	370

16. Hanover-Horton	390
17. Grand Rapids West Catholic	481
18. Watervliet	510
19. Blissfield	519
20. Delton Kellogg	535
21. Otisville LakeVille	536
22. Erie-Mason	558
23. Reese	558
24. Ida	570
25. Adrian Madison	573
26. Roscommon	660
27. Capac	790
28. Byron	793

2014 GIRLS DIVISION 3 INDIVIDUALS
1. Holly Bullough (Traverse City St Francis)11	17:52
2. Amber Way (Charlevoix)12	17:52
3. Annie Fuller (Manistee)12	18:16
4. Allison Vroon (Holland Black River)12	18:17
5. Gina Patterson (Macomb Lutheran North)12	18:30
6. Ashley Sorge (Ida)12	18:53
7. Kayla Keane (East Jordan)12	18:56
8. Kaitlin Beyer (Carson City-Crystal)12	18:59
9. Sierra Albus (Hart)10	19:01
10. Taylor Thrush (Shepherd)12	19:04
11. Jasmine Harper (Clare)10	19:05
12. Courtney Allen (Ithaca)10	19:07
13. Alex Love (Ovid-Elsie)12	19:09
14. Abby Fifarek (Grand Traverse Academy)12	19:11
15. Jennie Gottardo (Hart)12	19:15
16. Haley Dack (Leslie)11	19:16
17. Sophia Bradley (St Louis)12	19:18
18. Remington Hobson (Montrose)9	19:19
19. Olivia Theis (Lansing Catholic)9	19:23
20. Logan Luckett (Elk Rapids)11	19:29
33. Amelia Freestone (Ithaca)10	19:56
46. Hannah Thayer (Ithaca)12	20:17
51. Blaire Showers (Ithaca)11	20:23
61. Alyssa Mankey (Ithaca)11	20:29
106. Kurstin Kalisek (Ithaca)11	21:08
120. Erica Sheahan (Ithaca)11	21:15

2015 D3 GIRLS

Holly Bullough led a Traverse City St. Francis charge to the top. The Glads topped Benzie Central by 72 points.

Bullough, a senior, successfully defended her title by charging out at the start, passing 1M in 5:24. "I was trying to get out front, trying to lead everyone." She had her eyes on the All-Division course record, it turns out. "To get 16:54, which I was trying to get, I needed like a 5:15. So it was a little bit slower, but I felt good when I did it." Even so, she nailed the D3 record with her 17:42.

Bullough was running on a fractured second metatarsal in her foot, and had been crosstraining for weeks. "I kind of felt it the last mile."

Michigan Int. Speedway, Brooklyn, Nov. 7
2015 GIRLS DIVISION 3 TEAMS
1. Traverse City St Francis	69
2. Benzie Central	141
3. Shepherd	181
4. Lansing Catholic	202
5. Ithaca	209
6. Grandville Calvin Christian	219
7. Holland Black River	240
8. Jackson Lumen Christi	283
9. Pewamo-Westphalia	298
10. Blissfield	300
11. Hart	325
12. St. Louis	332
13. Clare	336
14. Leslie	341
15. Hanover-Horton	355
16. Hopkins	389
17. Olivet	396
18. Charlevoix	432
19. Frankenmuth	470
20. Wixom St Catherine	506
21. Watervliet	553
22. Livonia Ladywood	573
23. Reese	594
24. Bridgman	624
25. Delton Kellogg	660
26. Otisville LakeVille	696
27. Montrose	758
28. Marlette	787

2015 GIRLS DIVISION 3 INDIVIDUALS
1. Holly Bullough (Traverse City St Francis)12	17:42
2. Adelyn Ackley (Hart)9	18:19
3. Amber Gall (Shepherd)9	18:25
4. Katelyn Duffing (Traverse City St Francis)9	18:36
5. Emmalyne Tarsa (Traverse C St Francis)11	18:43
6. Klaudia O'Malley (McBain)9	18:53
7. Jasmine Harper (Clare)11	18:55
8. Lainey Veenkant (Clare)9	18:58
9. Olivia Theis (Lansing Catholic)10	18:59
10. Laura Velderman (Hopkins)9	19:04
11. Brooklyn Filipiak (St Louis)9	19:06
12. Joyana Tarsa (Traverse C St Francis)10	19:06
13. Abigail Gilmore (Lansing Catholic)11	19:14
14. Casey Reed (Blissfield)9	19:15
15. Kelli Smith (GR NorthPointe Christian)12	19:16
16. Logan Luckett (Elk Rapids)12	19:17
17. Haley Hegenauer (Shepherd)9	19:17
18. Courtney Allen (Ithaca)11	19:22
19. Lauren Cleary (Lansing Catholic)9	19:23
20. Bethany McNair (Kingsley)10	19:29
66. Lauren Bramer (Traverse C St Francis)10	20:24
100. Christine Scerbak (TC St Francis)9	20:50
131. Emma Fifarek (Traverse C St Francis)11	21:09

2016 D3 GIRLS

St. Francis won title No. 2, but this competition was much closer, as Lansing Catholic finished only 11 points behind.

Adelyn Ackley of Hart topped Olvia Theis of Lansing Catholic in a blistering finish, 17:40.6-17:41.3. "Everyone was kind of expecting me to beat her and I wasn't sure, because she beat me once and I beat her once," said Ackley, who nipped the D3 course record by a second.

Michigan Int. Speedway, Brooklyn, Nov. 5
2016 GIRLS DIVISION 3 TEAMS
1. Traverse City St Francis	77
2. Lansing Catholic	88
3. Benzie Central	125
4. Saugatuck	152
5. Shepherd	160
6. Clare	166
7. Hart	168
8. Grandville Calvin Christian	175
9. Charlevoix	290
10. Blissfield	317
11. Grand Rapids Covenant Christian	324
12. Wixom St Catherine	355
13. Olivet	367
14. Jackson Lumen Christi	399
15. Ithaca	417
16. Hopkins	423
17. Sanford Meridian	465
18. Frankenmuth	471
19. Leslie	484
20. Quincy	515
21. Adrian Madison	533
22. Hemlock	538
23. Bangor	582
24. Marine City	632
25. Brown City	650
26. Lawton	721
27. Almont	784

2016 GIRLS DIVISION 3 INDIVIDUALS
1. Adelyn Ackley (Hart)10	17:41
2. Olivia Theis (Lansing Catholic)11	17:42
3. Lauren Cleary (Lansing Catholic)10	18:25
4. Klaudia O'Malley (McBain)10	18:38
5. Amber Gall (Shepherd)10	18:44
6. Jaden Theis (Lansing Catholic)9	18:55
7. Alayna Ackley (Hart)11	19:13
8. Joyana Tarsa (Traverse City St Francis)11	19:14
9. Jasmine Harper (Clare)12	19:15
10. Remington Hobson (Montrose)11	19:22
11. Katelyn Duffing (Traverse C St Francis)10	19:24
12. Lainey Veenkant (Clare)10	19:25
13. Thea Johnson (Saugatuck)10	19:27
14. Michelle Bollini Charlevoix)11	19:30
15. Courtney Krupp (New Lothrop)11	19:31
16. Haley Hegenauer (Shepherd)10	19:33
17. Lauren Freeland (Kent City)10	19:35
18. Hunter Luke (Byron)9	19:37
19. Emmalyne Tarsa (Traverse C St Francis)12	19:38
20. Lucy Karpukhno (Benzie Central)11	19:38
35. Libby Gorman (Traverse City St Francis)9	20:14
38. Christine Scerbak (TC St Francis)10	20:18
64. Madelyn Taylor (Traverse C St Francis)10	20:39
111. Emma Fifarek (Traverse C St Francis)12	21:24

2017 D3 GIRLS

Adelyn Ackley successfully defended, and this time she took her Hart teammates to the top of the podium as well. The junior won by 27 seconds over Shepherd's Amber Gall.

Hart, coached by Terry Tatro, made the most of the Ackley family, with three sisters in the top 7 and cousin Lynae Ackley finishing 20th. It was Hart's first team title in any sport. Said Tatro, "It's so exciting. All our meets, it's like an Ackley family reunion."

"I went out pretty hard," said the champion, "just to get out of the crowd but it felt pretty easy at first. The second mile was definitely the hardest."

Michigan Int. Speedway, Brooklyn, Nov. 4
2017 GIRLS DIVISION 3 TEAMS
1. Hart	55
2. Benzie Central	124
3. Grandville Calvin Christian	137
4. Saugatuck	178
5. Clare	195
6. Pewamo-Westphalia	231
7. Charlevoix	237
8. Shepherd	241
9. Traverse City St Francis	244
10. Jackson Lumen Christi	328
11. Hanover-Horton	388
12. Harbor Springs	399
13. Leslie	399
14. Kent City	425
15. Byron	425
16. Wixom St Catherine	447
17. Bloomingdale	468
18. Blissfield	473
19. Reese	474
20. Grand Rapids Covenant Christian	488
21. Bangor	545
22. Montrose	559
23. Grass Lake	573
24. Dundee	603
25. Sanford Meridian	604
26. Grosse Pointe Woods University Liggett	695
27. Bad Axe	702
28. Madison Heights Foley	794

2017 GIRLS DIVISION 3 INDIVIDUALS
1. Adelyn Ackley (Hart)11	17:50
2. Amber Gall (Shepherd)11	18:17
3. Lauren Freeland (Kent City)11	18:45
4. Klaudia O'Malley (McBain)11	18:47
5. Thea Johnson (Saugatuck)11	18:49
6. Savannah Ackley (Hart)9	18:52
7. Alayna Ackley (Hart)12	18:52
8. Isabella Lindsay (North Muskegon)10	18:58
9. Michelle Bollini (Charlevoix)12	19:01
10. Judy Rector (Hanover-Horton)11	19:01
11. Casey Reed (Blissfield)12	19:05
12. Lainey Veenkant (Clare)11	19:08
13. Jelena Prescott (Bad Axe)10	19:09
14. Courtney Krupp (New Lothrop)12	19:11
15. Paige Swiriduk (Manton)10	19:11

16. Lucy Karpukhno (Benzie Central)12 .... 19:15
17. Paige Johnston (Benzie Central)10 .... 19:18
18. Remington Hobson (Montrose)12 .... 19:21
19. Katelyn Duffing (Traverse C St Francis)11 .. 19:23
20. Lynae Ackley (Hart)9 .... 19:24
37. Brenna Aerts (Hart)10 .... 19:52
55. MacKenzie Stitt (Hart)9 .... 20:12
85. Layla Creed (Hart)9 .... 20:37

Adelyn Ackley won three titles for Hart—the last two leading her team to the win. (Pete Draugalis photo)

2018 D3 GIRLS

Adelyn Ackley, Amber Gall and Judy Rector set out to dominate the race, and ran together through the mile mark (5:38). Ackley and Gall pulled away in the middle of the race, Ackley hitting 2M in 11:19 with Gall a couple strides behind.

On the finishing stretch, the Hart senior showed her speed, building up more than a 10-second margin to win her third-straight victory in 17:42.8. Gall had more of a struggle with the mud—a patch at the 3M mark had turned into a quagmire by the fourth race of the day—the afternoon races would be routed around it.

"It's a pretty awesome feeling," said Ackley. "I'm really glad I could be a state champion three times."

The Hart squad, featuring three Ackleys, put 5 in the top 14 for an impressive 43 points. It was the lowest winning score since Decatur's 41 in 1977 (pre-MHSAA).

Michigan Int. Speedway, Brooklyn, Nov. 3 ✠
Mostly cloudy, muddy, 40°, breezy.
2018 GIRLS DIVISION 3 TEAMS
1. Hart 43
2. Grandville Calvin Christian 143
3. Pewamo-Westphalia 152
4. Clare 183
5. Traverse City St Francis 208
6. Shepherd 223
7. Kent City 233
8. Benzie Central 246
9. McBain 285
10. St Louis 295
11. Harbor Springs 302
12. Charlevoix 340

13. Byron 359
14. Ithaca 378
15. Hanover-Horton 385
16. Grand Rapids Covenant Christian 401
17. Bloomingdale 414
18. Jackson Lumen Christi 436
19. Stockbridge 492
20. Galesburg-Augusta 546
21. Hartford 559
22. Quincy 585
23. Allen Park Cabrini 593
24. Marine City 616
25. Ida 654
26. Dundee 658
27. Grosse Pointe Woods University Liggett 695

2018 GIRLS DIVISION 3 INDIVIDUALS
1. Adelyn Ackley (Hart)12 .... 17:43
2. Amber Gall (Shepherd)12 .... 17:54
3. Lauren Freeland (Kent City)12 .... 18:41
4. Judy Rector (Hanover-Horton)12 .... 18:47
5. Klaudia O'Malley (McBain)12 .... 18:49
6. Lani Bloom (Ithaca)9 .... 19:05
7. Savannah Ackley (Hart)10 .... 19:16
8. Libby Munderloh (St Louis)9 .... 19:17
9. Lainey Veenkant (Clare)12 .... 19:22
10. Audrianna Enns (Hart)9 .... 19:27
11. Xochitl Garcia (Bronson)12 .... 19:27
12. Katelyn Duffing (Traverse City St Francis)12 .. 19:32
13. Lynae Ackley (Hart)10 .... 19:32
14. MacKenzic Stitt (Hart)10 .... 19:35
15. Isabella Lindsay (North Muskegon)11 ...... 19:35
16. Libby Gorman (Traverse City St Francis)11 .... 19:39
17. Abby Ignasiak (Kent City)11 .... 19:40
18. Layla Martini (Kent City)10 .... 19:47
19. Aubrey George (Pewamo-Westphalia)11 .... 19:48
20. Rylee Tolson (Stockbridge)9 .... 19:49
24. Breanna Aerts (Hart)11 .... 19:54
119. Sadie Sorensen (Hart)9 .... 21:27

2019 D3 GIRLS

Rylee Tolson of Stockbridge, only 20th the year before as a frosh, hung with the lead pack through 2M in 12:06 before making her break near 2.5M to win by 7 seconds in 18:32.

"It's overwhelming," said Tolson. "I'm still trying to process everything." Of the course, she said, "It's muddy and completely gross and nasty. It's okay, it really was worth it."

Hart won its third-straight, halving the score of runner-up Shepherd.

Michigan Int. Speedway, Brooklyn, Nov. 2 ✠
2019 GIRLS DIVISION 3 TEAMS
1. Hart 77
2. Shepherd 134
3. Grandville Calvin Christian 137
4. Traverse City St Francis 176
5. Pewamo-Westphalia 179
6. Ithaca 215
7. Benzie Central 234
8. Clare 256
9. St Louis 276
10. Grand Rapids Covenant Christian 279
11. McBain 281
12. Harbor Springs 327
13. Charlevoix 340
14. Kent City 370
15. Byron 378
16. Reese 410
17. Galesburg-Augusta 421
18. Saugatuck 424
19. Jackson Lumen Christi 481
20. Richmond 532
21. Blissfield 540
22. Clinton 645
23. Hanover-Horton 650
24. Bronson 671
25. Coloma 683
26. Ida 728
27. Grosse Pointe Woods University Liggett 811

2019 GIRLS DIVISION 3 INDIVIDUALS

1. Rylee Tolson (Stockbridge)10 .... 18:32
2. Maddy Bean (Richmond)12 .... 18:39
3. Allison Chmielewski (Roscommon)10 .... 18:41
4. Savannah Ackley (Hart)11 .... 18:49
5. Audrianna Enns (Hart)10 .... 18:57
6. Libby Gorman (Traverse City St Francis)12 .. 18:57
7. Ava Maginity (Boyne City)9 .... 19:06
8. Maye Burns (Harbor Springs)10 .... 19:09
9. Allissa Ash (Byron)12 .... 19:12
10. Libby Munderloh (St Louis)10 .... 19:14
11. Clara Krupp (New Lothrop)10 .... 19:17
12. Sophia Rhein (Traverse City St Francis)9 .... 19:21
13. Abbigail Kiaunism(Reed City)11 .... 19:26
14. Lynae Ackley (Hart)11 .... 19:27
15. Isabella Lindsay (North Muskegon)12 ...... 19:27
16. Layla Martini (Kent City)11 .... 19:31
17. Aubrey George (Pewamo-Westphalia)12 .. 19:33
18. Lani Bloom (Ithaca)10 .... 19:33
19. Leanne Krombeen (Grandville Calvin Chr)10 .... 19:34
20. Madde Skeel (Shepherd)11 .... 19:34
38. MacKenzie Stitt (Hart)11 .... 20:12
49. Breanna Aerts (Hart)12 .... 20:21
54. Layla Creed (Hart)11 .... 20:30
95. Lauren VanderLaan (Hart)10 .... 20:58

CLASS C/D3 STATISTICS

TOP 25 CLOCKINGS AT MIS
17:41	Adelyn Ackley (Hart)9	2016
17:42	Holly Bullough (TC St Francis)12	2015
17:42	Olivia Theis (Lansing Catholic)11	2016
17:43	Ackley	2018
17:44	Gina Patterson (Macomb Luth N)10	2012
17:50	Ackley	2017
17:52	Bullough	2014
17:52	Amber Way (Charlevoix)12	2014
17:53	Nicole Bush (Wyoming Kelloggsville)9	2000
17:54	Amber Gall (Shepherd)12	2018
17:59	Kelly Schubert (Manistee)12	2011
18:00	Raquel Serna (St Louis)12	2012
18:01	Bethany Brewster (Sag Valley Luth)11	1996
18:01	Ali Wiersma (Allendale)11	2010
18:03	Patterson	2013
18:04	Mikal Beckman (Newaygo)11	2005
18:05	Way	2013
18:07	Devan John (Allendale)11	2008
18:07	Lindsey Burdette (Hanover-Horton)11	2010
18:08	Janee Jones (Goodrich)12	2004
18:11	Annie Fuller (Manistee)10	2012
18:12	Megan Heeder (Lansing Catholic)12	2010
18:13	Jaime Watson (Allendale)11	2003
18:14	Way	2012
18:16	John	2007
18:16	Devyn Ramsey (Benzie Central)11	2007
18:16	Fuller	2014

BIGGEST WINNING MARGINS
65	Connie Kidder/Ann Kennedy	1979 I
56.6	Bethany Brewster/Kristin Bishop	1996
54.0	Cindy Reed/Brenda Essenmacher	1982 T
53.9	Megan Smedley/Jennifer Barber	1991 T
50	Gail Burch/Anne Simon	1979 T
50	Andrea Ripley/Jenny Stuht	1989 T

SMALLEST WINNING MARGINS
0.2	Julie Barry/Kathleen O'Neill	1984 T
0.2	Holly Bullough/Amber Way	2014
0.7	Devan John/Devyn Ramsey	2007
0.7	Adelyn Ackley/Olivia Theis	2016
1.3	Linda Hagenbarth/Jodi Proctor	1983 I

LOWEST WINNING SCORES
41	Decatur	1977
43	Hart	2018
47	Bath	1976
53	Southfield Christian	1991
55	Hart	2017

60	Benzie Central	1982	136	Onsted	1992	4	Southfield Christian/Olivet	1989
61	Carson City-Crystal	1995	136	Jackson Lumen Christi	2006	4	Onsted/Carson City-Crystal	1992
62	Goodrich	2003	132	Benzie Central	1998	4	Burton Bendle/Addison	1993
63	Hanover-Horton	2009	128	Mayville	1988	4	Jackson Lumen Chr/Grandville Calvin	2012
64	Mt Clemens Lutheran North	1979	126	Benzie Central	2011			
64	Carson City-Crystal	1996						

HIGHEST WINNING SCORES

176	Spring Lake	2001
167	Jackson Lumen Christi	2012
152	Hillsdale	2002
149	Burton Bendle	1993
147	Ithaca	2014
142	Shepherd	1994

CLOSEST TEAM FINISH

1	Olivet/Southfield Christian	1990
2	St Louis/Decatur	1978
2	Benzie Central/Pittsford	1998
2	Jackson Lumen Chr/Leroy Pine River	2007
4	Bath/Fowlerville	1976
4	DeWitt/Whitehall	1981

BIGGEST WINNING TEAM MARGIN

102	Southfield Christian/Onsted	1991
100	Hart/Grandville Calvin Christian	2018
78	Kalamazoo Hackett/Pittsford	1999
72	TC St Francis/Benzie Central	2015
69	Carson City-Crystal/Charlevoix	1995
69	Hart/Benzie Central	2017

The Decatur 1977 squad won with the lowest score in meet history: 41 points.

GIRLS CLASS D / DIVISION 4

1976 CLASS D GIRLS
This early state finals was a small affair organized by the coaches at Ann Arbor's Huron and Pioneer high schools. The previous year the event had featured a C/D race. This first D only competition hosted three scoring teams and 11 additional individuals, for a total of 30 runners.

Pioneer HS, Ann Arbor, November 3 ☐
1976 GIRLS CLASS D TEAMS
1. Potterville...25
2. Burr Oak..47
3. Hale...54

Cheryl Watters of Sacred Heart was the first Class D state champion of the pre-MHSAA sponsorship days.

1976 GIRLS CLASS D INDIVIDUALS
1. Cheryl Watters (Mt Pleasant Sacred Heart)9......19:13
2. Jane Nabozny (Burr Oak)...........................20:04
3. Kim Rhoda (Mendon).................................20:55
4. Carrie Morrissey (Potterville).....................20:57
5. Annette Hackworth (Potterville).................21:10
6. Cathy Kuripla (Potterville)........................21:25
7. Beth Lori (Centreville)...............................21:45
8. Teresa Hermatz (Mesick)...........................22:09
9. Janet Chappell (Battle Creek St Phillip).....22:19
10. Brenda Horton (Centreville).....................22:25
11. Diane Smith (Hale)...................................22:34
12. Betsy Duren (Ann Arbor Greenhills)........22:52
13. Cheri Hackworth (Potterville)...................22:59
14. Pat Hackett (Burr Oak)..............................23:00
15. Bonnie Schroeder (Hale)..........................23:46

1977 CLASS D GIRLS
Potterville, host of the meet, won its second straight under the coaching of Tom Swanson, who said, "I knew they were getting better all year and knew they could win if they all ran well."

Julie Lantis would go on to star for Southwestern Michigan JC and Illinois, where she won All-Big 10 honors.

Potterville, Oct. 22 ☐
1977 GIRLS CLASS D TEAMS
1. Potterville...69
2. Burr Oak..83
3. Ann Arbor Greenhills..............................87
4. Detroit Country Day................................96
5. Mendon..101
6. Pittsford...103
7. Lansing Christian..................................105

1977 GIRLS CLASS D INDIVIDUALS
1. Julie Lantis (Grass Lake)11....................19:07
2. Mary Mullally (Flint Holy Rosary)..........19:11
3. Katy Topp (Ann Arbor Greenhills).........19:22
4. Jane Nabozny (Burr Oak).......................19:28
5. Cheryl Watters (Mt Pleasant Sacred Heart)10.....19:34
6. Martha Kundrat (Potterville)..................19:48
7. Segrid Lana (Pittsford)...........................20:01
8. Kim Roda (Mendon)................................20:08
9. Dee Cook (Detroit Country Day)...........20:15
10. Pam Maguire (Akron-Fairgrove)...........20:22
12. Betsy Duren (Ann Arbor Greenhills)....nt
13. Annett Hackworth (Potterville).............nt
23. Michelle Wickwire (Potterville)............nt
24. Kathy Roos (Potetrville)........................nt
32. Patti Conarton (Potterville)...................nt

1978 CLASS D GIRLS
The first year of MHSAA-sponsored girls cross country combined all the classes into one race. See Class A for the results of the MHSAA race.

Potterville decided to again host separate races by class, called the "Girls' State Open Cross Country Championships." On the Class D level, most of the state's top teams competed (5 of 7 from the previous year's meet).

Potterville HS, Potterville, October 21 ☐
1978 GIRLS CLASS D TEAMS
1. Akron-Fairgrove......................................74
2. Potterville...78
3. Detroit Country Day..............................115
4. Flint Holy Rosary..................................129
5. St Joseph Lake Michigan Catholic......155
Incomplete squads: Ann Arbor Greenhills, Burr Oak, Colon, Grass Lake, Kingston, Pittsford.

1978 GIRLS CLASS D INDIVIDUALS
1. Robin Magee (Ann Arbor Greenhills)10..............18:49
2. Julie Lantis (Grass Lake)12..................nt
3. Martha Kundrat (Potterville)................nt
4. Jane Nabozny (Burr Oak).....................nt
5. Mary Mullally (Flint Holy Rosary).......nt
6. Jane Sarna (Akron-Fairgrove).............nt
7. Pam Maguire (Akron-Fairgrove).........nt
8. Susie Selfridge (Potterville)................nt
9. Dee Cook (Detroit Country Day)........nt
10. Sigrid Lama (Pittsford)........................nt

1979 CLASS D GIRLS
Potterville HS, Potterville, Nov. 3 ☐
1979 GIRLS CLASS D TEAMS
1. Ann Arbor Greenhills..............................82
2. Flint Holy Rosary...................................83
3. Kingston...154
4. Lansing Christian.................................164
5. Manton...173
6. Akron-Fairgrove....................................176
7. Detroit Country Day..............................184
8. Dansville..198
9. Mt Pleasant Sacred Heart....................219
10. Grass Lake...220
11. Saranac..223
12. Potterville..231
13. Centreville...280
NS—Bloomfield Hills Roeper (4 finishers).

1979 GIRLS CLASS D INDIVIDUALS
1. Robin Magee (Ann Arbor Greenhills)11.........18:04
2. Julie Lantis (Grass Lake)......................18:57
3. Karen Bleicher (Flint Holy Rosary).....19:09
4. Jill Barden (Kingston)...........................19:12
5. Mary Mullally (Flint Holy Rosary).......19:27
6. Cheryl Watters (Mt Pleasant Sacred Heart)12.....19:39
7. Beth Britton (Kingston).........................20:17
8. June Johnson (Mt Pleasant Sacred Heart).....20:30
9. Teresa Casey (Ann Arbor Greenhills)..20:38
10. Martha Kundrat (Potterville).............20:43
11. Amy Cornelisse (Saranac)..................20:51
12. Dee Cook (Detroit Country Day).......20:53
13. Heidi Whitmore (Manton)....................21:10
14. Pamela Maguire (Akron-Fairgrove)...21:12
15. Margaret Dixon (Saranac)...................21:14

1980 CLASS D GIRLS
Bruce Dyer's Greenhills squad won for the second straight year, with senior Robin Magee grabbing a third-straight individual title. That spring Magee would win Class D state titles at 1600 (5:06.3) and 3200 (11:31.3); that gave her a total of 8 state titles in track and cross country by the time she graduated.

Potterville HS, Potterville, Nov. 1 ☐
1980 GIRLS CLASS D TEAMS
1. Ann Arbor Greenhills..............................61
2. Flint Holy Rosary...................................75
3. Akron-Fairgrove....................................120
4. Detroit Country Day..............................145
5. Dansville..152
6. Kingston...187
7. Pontiac Catholic...................................208
8. Lansing Christian.................................220
9. Grass Lake..228
10. Mesick..231
11. Mt Pleasant Sacred Heart..................273
12. Bridgman..302
13. Morenci...305
14. Mendon..307
15. Bloomfield Hills Roeper.....................376

1980 GIRLS CLASS D INDIVIDUALS
1. Robin Magee (Ann Arbor Greenhills)12........19:13
2. Lisa Einhauser (Pontiac Catholic).......19:32
3. Jill Barden (Kingston)...........................20:05
4. Karen Majehrowacki (Grass Lake).....20:18
5. Alia Newman (Detroit Country Day)...20:24
6. Jodi Watters (Mt Pleasant Sacred Heart)......20:24
7. Sabrina Batchelder (Potterville)..........20:28
8. Edith Torres (Flint Holy Rosary).........20:43
9. Julie Tym (Bridgman)............................20:58
10. Daphne Fozarsi (Akron-Fairgrove)....21:00
11. Becky Fulling (Dansville)....................21:03

12. Shirley Brower (Dansville) 21:05
13. Sara Salgat (Flint Holy Rosary) 21:09
14. Sandy Irani (Ann Arbor Greenhills) 21:10
15. Jenny Cox (Ann Arbor Greenhills) 21:16
16. Kris Cowan (Ann Arbor Greenhills) 21:23
20. Lucy Chambers (Ann Arbor Greenhills) 21:38

1981 CLASS D GIRLS

Wyoming Lee coach Art Kraal went to his team after the race and told them they had lost. "I thought it would take between 80 and 85 points to win, and we had 96. But it's hard to tell team places in a race like this." Turns out he jumped the gun, and 96 points was indeed good enough to take home the team trophy.

Allendale's Gina VanLaar finished first in 19:52.

Johnson Park, Wyoming, Oct. 31 ☐
1981 GIRLS CLASS D TEAMS
1. Wyoming Lee 96
2. Akron-Fairgrove 108
3. Dansville 127
4. Colon 144
5. Flint Holy Rosary 147
6. Mt Pleasant Sacred Heart 158
7. Suttons Bay 163
8. Lansing Christian 168
9. Kingston 187
10. Fowler 197
11. Ann Arbor Greenhills 244
12. Grass Lake 294
13. Pontiac Catholic 306
14. Morenci 323

1981 GIRLS CLASS D INDIVIDUALS
1. Gina VanLaar (Allendale)10 19:52
2. Becky Pulling (Dansville) 20:07
3. Emily Feldpausch (Fowler) 20:13
4. Jenny Franssen (Concord)9 20:20
5. Jane Johnson (Mt Pleasant Sacred Heart) 20:26
6. J. Barden (Kingston) 20:34
7. T. Casey (Ann Arbor Greenhills) 20:44
8. Deborah Taylor (Wyoming Lee)10 20:49
9. L. LaValle (Colon) 20:52
10. J. McIntyre (Pontiac Catholic) 20:54
11. Batchelder (Potterville) 20:57
12. J. Sullivan (Battle Creek St Philip) 21:00
13. Sue Shackleton (Colon) 21:05
14. J. Quillen (Mt Pleasant Sacred Heart) 21:06
15. Mary Foster (Mancelona) 21:08

1982 CLASS D GIRLS

Ice and snow slowed runners on the course. Defending champion Gina VanLaar of Allendale hyperventilated less than a mile from the finish, and had to be carried from the course. The doctor who treated her speculated that the frigid air hurt her lungs, so she wasn't breathing as she usually did. Individual runner-up Karen Amundson was leading past the mile mark when she slipped and fell.

Johnson Park, Wyoming, Nov. 6 ☒
1982 GIRLS CLASS D TEAMS
1. Concord 68
2. Wyoming Lee 97
3. Akron-Fairgrove 108
4. Fowler 110
5. Dansville 126
6. Colon 145
7. Suttons Bay 172
8. Ann Arbor Greenhills 207
9. Kingston 212
10. Centreville 226
11. Mancelona 242
12. Manton 283
13. Grass Lake 343

1982 GIRLS CLASS D TEAM RACE
1. Jenny Franssen (Concord)10 19:33
2. Sue Shackleton (Colon)12 20:00
3. Julie Peterson (Suttons Bay) 20:06
4. Deborah Taylor (Wyoming Lee)11 20:51
5. E. Feldpaush (Fowler) 21:01
6. Sandy Telgenhoff (Wyoming Lee)12 21:20
7. D. Fogarski (Akron-Fairgrove) 21:22
8. Terri Baird (Concord)12 21:24
9. JoAnne Falbe (Wyoming Lee)12 21:35
10. B. Pulling (Dansville) 21:36
11. S. Brower (Dansville) 21:38
12. Kathy Shackleton (Colon)11 21:41
13. Jeanne Gilliland (Ann Arbor Greenhills) 21:43
14. Cindy Franssen (Concord)12 21:42
16. Annalisa Bauman (Concord)9 22:02
29. Chris Fedor (Concord) 23:06
40. Jill Nichols (Concord)9 nt
72. Sue Wood (Concord)11 nt

1982 GIRLS CLASS D INDIVIDUAL RACE
1. Sabrina Batchelder (Potterville)11 21:09
2. Karen Amundson (Battle Creek St Phillip) 21:16
3. Shelley Spratt (Southfield Christian) 21:50

1983 CLASS D GIRLS

Gina Van Laar, the only member of Allendale's cross country team, recaptured the individual title she had won as a sophomore, finishing with a monstrous lead of more than two minutes. The team race was exceptionally close, with Kingston and Danville having to go to the tie-breaking 6th runner. Kingston's Banowski finished 79th, 38 seconds ahead of Dansville's 6th.

Kingston's 1983 champions.

Great Lakes Bible College, Lansing, Nov. 5 ☒
1983 GIRLS CLASS D TEAMS
1. Kingston 118
2. Dansville 118
3. Concord 136
4. Akron-Fairgrove 143
5. Southfield Christian 152
6. Fowler 161
7. Ann Arbor Greenhills 167
8. Flint Holy Rosary 172
9. Mancelona 173
10. Colon 198
11. Wyoming Lee 207
12. Suttons Bay 269
13. Centreville 304
14. Camden-Frontier 337
15. Hanover-Horton 387
16. Lansing Christian 433

1983 GIRLS CLASS D TEAM RACE
1. Larissa Szporluk (Ann Arbor Greenhills)12 19:27
2. Jenny Franssen (Concord)11 19:45
3. Jeanne Gilliland (Ann Arbor Greenhills) 19:56
4. Debbie Taylor (Wyoming Lee) 20:05
5. Lisa Meier (Kingston)9 20:13
6. Tracey Harper (Southfield Christian) 20:16
7. Shelly Spratt (Southfield Christian) 20:22
8. Beth Wirth (Fowler) 20:34
9. Carol George (Fowler) 20:43
10. Bleicher (Flint Holy Rosary) 20:52
11. Beecky Pulling (Dansville) 20:56
12. Deb Moore (Kingston)10 20:58
13. Sue Shackleton (Colon) 21:02
17. Karen Laycock (Kingston)12 21:17
18. Michelle Landram (Kingston)11 21:18
66. Monica Tait (Kingston)10 23:49
79. Missy Banowski (Kingston)10 24:56

1983 GIRLS CLASS D INDIVIDUAL RACE
1. Gina VanLaar (Allendale)12 18:53
2. Julie Quillen (Mt Pleasant Sacred Heart) 20:57
3. Jodi Watters (Mt Pleasant Sacred Heart) 21:14

1984 CLASS D GIRLS

Concord, coached by Chuck King, returned to the top of the podium by virtue of a narrow 3-point win over Southfield Christian.

Ninth graders won both of the races, with Jenny Gradowski of Suttons Bay the fastest at 19:31.

Grace Bible College, Lansing, Nov. 3 ☒
1984 GIRLS CLASS D TEAMS
1. Concord 99
2. Southfield Christian 102
3. Fowler 103
4. Suttons Bay 122
5. Akron-Fairgrove 139
6. Kingston 142
7. Colon 159
8. Wyoming Lee 203
9. Mason County Eastern 205
10. Kingsley 211
11. Lansing Christian 264
12. Covert 265

1984 GIRLS CLASS D TEAM RACE
1. Jenny Gradowski (Suttons Bay)9 19:31
2. Michelle Wait (Covert) 19:56
3. Dawn Harkema (Lansing Christian) 20:09
4. Jenny Franssen (Concord)12 20:10
5. Lisa Meier (Kingston)10 20:19
6. Beth Wirth (Fowler) 20:22
7. Carol George (Fowler) 20:33
8. Michelle Landram (Kingston)12 20:44
9. Deb Lundquist (Mason County Eastern) 20:46
10. Nina Dunkerson (Southfield Christian) 20:56
11. Carrie Beller (Akron-Fairgrove) 21:00
12. Kathy Hubbard (Concord)10 21:02
16. Annalisa Bauman (Concord)11 21:19
32. Jean Dobons (Concord) 22:21
35. Tanya Hill (Concord)10 22:31
46. Tanya Fedor (Concord)9 23:49
54. Leslie Ledyard (Concord)10 24:29

1984 GIRLS CLASS D INDIVIDUAL RACE
1. Theresa Padilla (Camden-Frontier)9 20:01
2. Jeanne Gilliland (Ann Arbor Greenhills) 20:15
3. Jordi Yarwood (Frankfort) 20:46

1985 CLASS D GIRLS

Suttons Bay soph Jenny Gradowski successfully defended her title, and this time celebrated the victory of her team as well, coached by Terry Ebright. The Norsemen edged Akron-Fairgrove by 2 points, 82-84.

West Shore CC, Muskegon, Nov. 2 ☐
1985 GIRLS CLASS D TEAMS
1. Suttons Bay 82
2. Akron-Fairgrove 84
3. Kingston 112
4. Wyoming Lee 116
5. Bridgman 126
6. Colon 152
7. Fowler 162
8. Mason County Eastern 169
9. Detroit Bethesda 173
10. Kingsley 207
11. Vestaburg 298
12. Springport 319

1985 GIRLS CLASS D TEAM RACE
1. Jenny Gradowski (Suttons Bay)10 20:17
2. Lisa Meier (Kingston)11 21:37
3. Robin Aldrich (Akron-Fairgrove) 22:00

4. Lisa Popa (Suttons Bay)9 ... 22:20
5. Tracey Mott (Colon)10 ... 22:29
6. Trudy Svoboda (Bridgman) ... 22:37
7. Jackie Hays (Bridgman) ... 22:40
8. Peggy Gehart (Detroit Bethesda)10 ... 22:54
9. Jeanine Knight (Kingsley)11 ... 22:57
10. Lori Chantiny (Kingston)10 ... 22:57
11. Delaine Harned (Mason County Eastern) ... 23:05
14. (Suttons Bay) ... nt
31. (Suttons Bay) ... nt
32. (Suttons Bay) ... nt
37. (Suttons Bay) ... nt

1985 GIRLS CLASS D INDIVIDUAL RACE

1. Theresa Padilla (Camden-Frontier)10 ... 20:50
2. Michelle Waite (Covert) ... 21:28
3. Andrea Barnes (Pathfinder) ... 21:53
4. Kirsten Moyes (North Muskegon) ... 22:31

1986 CLASS D GIRLS

Jenny Gradowski won title No. 3 for Suttons Bay, though her defending teammates fell to second as Warren Bethesda Christian took the win by 21 points.

"I knew we would be pretty good," said coach Chuck Meredith. "We only lost two girls last year, and we picked up one this year. A couple of them worked really hard this summer."

West Shore CC, Muskegon, Nov. 1 ☒
1986 GIRLS CLASS D TEAMS

1. Warren Bethesda Christian ... 89
2. Suttons Bay ... 110
3. Akron-Fairgrove ... 119
4. Mancelona ... 135
5. Concord ... 139
6. Fowler ... 174
7. Manton ... 223
8. Webberville ... 231
9. Kingston ... 239
10. Mesick ... 258
11. Saginaw Michigan Lutheran ... 288
12. Lansing Christian ... 315
13. Springport ... 328
14. North Muskegon ... 338
15. Springfield ... 345
16. Lutheran Westland ... 385

=17. Kingsley ... 386
=17. Portland St Patrick (5 finishers) ... 386

1986 GIRLS CLASS D TEAM RACE

1. Jenny Gradowski (Suttons Bay)11 ... 20:10
2. Lisa Popa (Suttons Bay)10 ... 20:19
3. Joy Perkins (Manton) ... 20:55
4. Lisa Meier (Kingston)12 ... 20:59
5. Chris Durbin (Mancelona) ... 21:19
6. Dawn Harkema (Lansing Christian) ... 21:24
7. Dawn King (Concord)10 ... 21:33
8. Kim Richards (Mesick) ... 21:34
9. Jenny Hartwig (Concord)10 ... 21:35
10. Kirsten Moyes (North Muskegon) ... 21:42
11. Becky Underwood (Bethesda Christian)11 ... 21:44
12. Robin Aldrich (Akron-Fairgrove) ... 21;44
13. Jayneed Gantz (Webberville) ... 21:57
15. Carrie Abraham (Bethesda Christian) ... 22:04
18. Kate Bulat (Bethesda Christian) ... 22:19
21. Peggy Gehart (Bethesda Christian)11 ... 22:25
24. Allison Garwood (Bethesda Christiian) ... 22:40
93. Felicia Pruitt (Bethesda Christian) ... 31:16

1986 GIRLS CLASS D INDIVIDUAL RACE

1. Theresa Padilla (Camden-Frontier)11 ... 21:25
2. Christy Ochua (Bridgman) ... 21:59
3. Trudy Suoboda (Bridgman) ... 22:29

1987 CLASS D GIRLS

Suttons Bay won the Class D crown with the lowest score ever, 38 points. Theresa Padilla of Camden-Frontier won a record fourth-straight title.

Kelli Gilchrist of Colon won the team race in her first season of running. "I thought she'd be in the top three, but her to win it was unexpected," said coach John Van Winkle.

Wyoming HS, Wyoming, Nov. 7 ☐
1987 GIRLS CLASS D TEAMS

1. Suttons Bay ... 38
2. Akron-Fairgrove ... 69
3. Fowler ... 103
4. Concord ... 135
5. Colon ... 146
6. Lansing Christian ... 154
7. Mesick ... 181
8. Schoolcraft ... 188
9. Kingsley ... 191
10. Kingston ... 241
11. North Muskegon ... 256

1987 GIRLS CLASS D TEAM RACE

1. Kelli Gilchrist (Colon)10 ... 20:44
2. Lisa Popa (Suttons Bay)11 ... 20:57
3. Dawn Harkema (Lansing Christian)12 ... 21:05
4. Theresa Bischoff (Akron-Fairgrove)11 ... 21:16
5. Shannon Tenbrook (Suttons Bay)10 ... 21:17
6. Lisa Rademacher (Fowler)10 ... 21:18
7. Gwen McNeil (Suttons Bay)9 ... 21:19
8. Jenny Gradowski (Suttons Bay)12 ... 21:26
9. Traci Eickenroth (Mesick)10 ... 21:33
10. Julie Lillrose (Akron-Fairgrove)11 ... 21:34
11. Katie Martin (Colon)9 ... 21:45

? Jean Cookman (Suttons Bay) ... nt
? Alyson Miller (Suttons Bay) ... nt

1987 GIRLS CLASS D INDIVIDUAL RACE

1. Theresa Padilla (Camden-Frontier)12 ... 20:04
2. Jennifer Gerlach (Lutheran Westland)9 ... 20:55
3. Christy Ochoa (Bridgman)11 ... 21:41
4. Becky Underwood (Warren Bethesda Chr)11 ... 21:56

1988 CLASS D GIRLS

Fowler, coached by Kim Spalsbury, beat defending champion Suttons Bay by 12 points to claim the win. "What made this so special," he said, " is that we brought both trophies home. I'm extremely pleased with our performance. Although I knew we had the talent to win, I was really holding my breath."

Memorial Park Frankenmuth, Nov. 5 ☒
1988 GIRLS CLASS D TEAMS

1. Fowler ... 85
2. Suttons Bay ... 97
3. Potterville ... 100
4. Lutheran Westland ... 104
5. Schoolcraft ... 112
6. Mesick ... 131
7. Akron-Fairgrove ... 132
8. Colon ... 155
9. Battle Creek St Phillip ... 180

1988 GIRLS CLASS D TEAM RACE

1. Katie Martin (Colon)10 ... 21:19
2. Shannon TenBrock (Suttons Bay)11 ... 21:21
3. Sandy Oliphant (Schoolcraft)11 ... 21:36
4. Jane Cookman (Suttons Bay)10 ... 21:47
5. Lisa Popa (Suttons Bay)12 ... 21:51
6. Lynette Feldpausch (Fowler)11 ... 22:18
7. Mary Lantinga (Battle Creek St Philip)11 ... 22:21
8. Jennifer Gerlach (Lutheran Westland)10 ... 22:28
9. Lisa Rademacher (Fowler)11 ... 22:37
10. Nikki Bennett (Potterville)10 ... 22:47
11. Kara Brink (Akron-Fairgrove)9 ... 22:51
17. Cristen Hoerner (Fowler)12 ... 23:36
24. Wendy Myers (Fowler)9 ... 24:24
29. Kelly Nobis (Fowler)11 ... 25:03
31. Heather Risselada (Fowler)9 ... 25:20
34. Melinda Koenigsknecht (Fowler)12 ... 25:32

1988 GIRLS CLASS D INDIVIDUAL RACE

1. Barbara Hall (Warren Bethesda Christian)11 ... 21:43
2. Cindy Butler (Wyoming Lee)9 ... 22:43
3. Djorariah Stevens (Alanson Littlefield)10 ... 22:49
4. Brenda Czinder (North Muskegon)9 ... 22:50

1989 CLASS D GIRLS

Fowler held on to the trophy, putting together a low 42-point performance to edge the strong run by Lutheran Westland.

Mary Lantinga of Battle Creek St. Philip won by nearly a quarter mile with her sterling 19:32 performance. "She did what she was supposed to do," said coach Earl Wilson. "That's take control of the race early. Like I told her, don't look back, and run for time."

Memorial Park, Frankenmuth, Nov. 4 ☐
1989 GIRLS CLASS D TEAMS

1. Fowler ... 42
2. Lutheran Westland ... 52
3. Potterville ... 84
4. Akron-Fairgrove ... 118
5. Wyoming Lee ... 132
6. Mesick ... 144
7. Battle Creek St Philip ... 144
8. Buckley ... 185

NS—Webberville (4 runners finished).

1989 GIRLS CLASS D TEAM RACE

1. Mary Lantinga (Battle Creek St Philip)12 ... 19:32
2. Jennifer Gerlach (Lutheran Westland)11 ... 20:53
3. Lynette Feldpausch (Fowler)12 ... 21:00
4. Laura Irrer (Fowler)9 ... 21:01
5. Ellen Anderson (Lutheran Westland)12 ... 21:07
6. Nikki Bennett (Potterville)11 ... 22:01
7. Jade Turcotte (Akron-Fairgrove)12 ... 22:16
8. Tammy Halsey (Potterville)9 ... 22:21
9. Lisa Rademacher (Fowler)12 ... 22:28
10. Lisa Thelen (Fowler)9 ... 22:30
11. Renee Ruth (Lutheran Westland)10 ... 22:43
16. Wendy Myers (Fowler) ... nt

1989 GIRLS CLASS D INDIVIDUAL RACE

1. Jane Cookman (Suttons Bay)11 ... 20:16
2. Barb Hall (Bethesda Christian)12 ... 21:29
3. Katie Martin (Colon)11 ... 22:09
4. Sandy Wescott (Hale)12 ... 22:27

1990 CLASS D GIRLS

Potterville, coached by Joe Wood, put together a solid 46-point run to top the two-time defending champs. Ninth-grader Erica Davis won the team race by two seconds.

Colon's Erica Davis.

Memorial Park, Frankenmuth, Nov. 3 ☐
1990 GIRLS CLASS D TEAMS

1. Potterville ... 46
2. Fowler ... 73
3. Pittsford ... 106
4. Webberville ... 132
5. Manton ... 141
6. Colon ... 167
7. Grass Lake ... 192
8. Mesick ... 193

9. Wyoming Lee ... 208
10. Bellaire ... 211
11. Buckley ... 259
12. Ann Arbor Greenhills ... 272
NS—Ann Arbor Richard (4 finishers).

1990 GIRLS CLASS D TEAM RACE
1. Erica Davis (Colon)9 ... 20:28
2. Nikki Bennett (Potterville)12 ... 20:32
3. Tammy Halsey (Potterville) ... 20:48
4. Laura Irrer (Fowler)10 ... 21:00
5. Trisha Law (Colon) ... 21:10
6. Jennifer Mulder (Wyoming Lee) ... 21:42
7. Sheri Thelen (Fowler) ... 21:49
8. Jennifer Barnard (Bellaire) ... 21:54
9. Marissa Smith (Pittsford) ... 21:56
10. Pamela Martin (Webberville)12 ... 22:28
11. Suzanne Wolcott (Potterville) ... 22:42
12. Staci Fogg (Potterville) ... 22:49
18. Julie VanDergriff (Potterville) ... nt
30. Shannon Sterle (Potterville) ... nt
44. Heidi Metzmaker (Potterville) ... nt

1990 GIRLS CLASS D INDIVIDUAL RACE
1. Jane Cookman (Suttons Bay)12 ... 21:14
2. Erica Powers (Central Lake) ... 22:08
3. Mary McLaughlin (North Muskegon) ... 22:29
4. Jennifer Petipren (Akron-Fairgrove) ... 22:32
5. Stephanie Zilch (Camden-Frontier) ... 22:35

1991 CLASS D GIRLS

Akron-Fairgrove, coached by Jerry Lasceski, won its first girls' title with a powerful 42-point margin over Pittsford.

Erica Davis won her second title despite fracturing her foot earlier in the season. "Last year I didn't feel any pressure because I didn't figure on accomplishing what I did," she said. "This year, however, I do feel the pressure… I really need to put the pain in my foot in the back of my mind because it will really affect my run if I don't."

Bath HS, Bath, Nov. 2 □
1991 GIRLS CLASS D TEAMS
1. Akron-Fairgrove ... 69
2. Pittsford ... 111
3. Colon ... 129
4. Potterville ... 132
5. Manton ... 134
6. Fowler ... 138
7. Schoolcraft ... 160
8. Grass Lake ... 162
9. Ann Arbor Greenhills ... 225
10. Central Lake ... 241
11. Whitmore Lake ... 249
12. Ann Arbor Richard ... 262
13. Buckley ... 308

1991 GIRLS CLASS D TEAM RACE
1. Erica Davis (Colon)10 ... 20:04
2. Sarah Petipren (Akron-Fairgrove) ... 20:12
3. Trisha Law (Colon) ... 20:59
4. Jennifer Petipren (Akron-Fairgrove) ... 21:08
5. Gene Blouw (Manton) ... 21:12
6. Sarah Shay (Central Lake) ... 21:16
7. Julie Copley (Ann Arbor Richard) ... 21:23
8. Sarah Parks (Grass Lake) ... 21:24
9. Michelle Hammon (Pittsford) ... 21:25
10. Christi Deck (Pittsford) ... 21:26
11. Yvonne Oliphant (Schoolcraft) ... 21:30
12. Sheri Thelen (Fowler) ... 21:31

1991 GIRLS CLASS D INDIVIDUAL RACE
1. Tracy Knudson (Suttons Bay)9 ... 20:33
2. Sara Bolford (Wyoming Lee) ... 20:56
3. Autumn Hunter (Reading) ... 21:08

1992 CLASS D GIRLS

With Colon's move to Class C, 2-time champ Erica David lost her chance to add to her winning streak. In her stead, Bath's Shana Ferrigan took the win in 20:08. "She's really a different athlete," said Bath coach Mel Comeau. "The bigger the meet, the better she does."

Schoolcraft, coached by Rob Kauffman, took an impressive win with a 55-point performance. The winning margin of 74 points was the biggest in Class D history.

Bath HS, Bath, Nov. 7 □
Cloudy, mid-30s.
1992 GIRLS CLASS D TEAMS
1. Schoolcraft ... 55
2. Potterville ... 129
3. Fowler ... 134
4. Grass Lake ... 138
5. Pittsford ... 145
6. Akron-Fairgrove ... 151
7. Bath ... 152
8. Ann Arbor Richard ... 162
9. Manton ... 168
10. Reading ... 193
11. Bear Lake ... 283
12. Central Lake ... 287
13. McBain ... 334

1992 GIRLS CLASS D TEAM RACE
1. Shana Ferrigan (Bath)11 ... 20:08
2. Heather Triezenberg (Schoolcraft) ... 20:32
3. Sarah Parks (Grass Lake) ... 20:44
4. Sheri Thelen (Fowler) ... 20:45
5. Autumn Hunter (Reading) ... 20:47
6. Tammy Halsey (Potterville) ... 20:49
7. Liz Tvedten (Bath) ... 21:07
8. Yvonne Oliphant (Schoolcraft)10 ... 21:16
9. Michelle Hammond (Pittsford) ... 21:20
10. Farrah Petipren (Akron-Fairgrove) ... 21:27
11. Emily Palmer (Schoolcraft) ... 21:39
14. Laura Oliphant (Schoolcraft) ... 21:42
19. Marcie Weslock (Schoolcraft)10 ... 21:49

1992 GIRLS CLASS D INDIVIDUAL RACE
1. Katy Speer (Whitmore Lake)10 ... 20:41
2. Britta Ultz (Burr Oak) ... 20:47
3. Rachel Zilka (Camden-Frontier) ... 20:49
4. Rachel Murnaw (Wyoming Lee) ... 20:49
5. Stephanie Klein (Mendon)9 ... 20:55
6. Priva Berx (Ann Arbor Greenhills) ... 21:14

1993 CLASS D GIRLS

Ninth-grader Betsy Speer of Whitmore Lake beat her sister, defending champ Katy Speer, for the title in the team race. Coach Larry Steeb's Trojans ran to their first team title with a record low score of 27 points. It helped to have 4 runners in the top 5.

Pando Recreation Area, Wyoming, Nov. 6 □
1993 GIRLS CLASS D TEAMS
1. Whitmore Lake ... 27
2. Fowler ... 92
3. Reading ... 109
4. Grass Lake ... 130
5. Bear Lake ... 165
6. Buckley ... 168
7. Akron-Fairgrove ... 179
8. Fairview ... 180
9. Potterville ... 193
10. Battle Creek St Phillip ... 251
11. Wyoming Lee ... 264
12. Central Lake ... 278
13. McBain ... 293

1993 GIRLS CLASS D TEAM RACE
1. Betsy Speer (Whitmore Lake)9 ... 20:41
2. Katy Speer (Whitmore Lake)11 ... 22:01
3. Melissa Wolk (Whitmore Lake) ... 22:11
4. Kerri Thelen (Fowler)10 ... 22:37
5. Kari Smith (Whitmore Lake) ... 22:39
6. Rachel Mumaw (Wyoming Lee)10 ... 22:41
7. Sarah Shay (Central Lake) ... 22:45
8. Autumn Hunter (Reading) ... 22:53
9. Michelle Rector (Reading) ... 22:57
10. Cheryl Frederickson (Fairview) ... 23:00

1993 GIRLS CLASS D INDIVIDUAL RACE
1. Stephanie Klein (Mendon)10 ... 21:41
2. Rachael Zitka (Camden-Frontier) ... 21:55
3. Nichole Offer (Warren Bethesda Christian) ... 22:09
4. Britta Ultz (Burr Oak) ... 22:30
5. Kristi High (Grand Rapids Baptist) ... 22:47

1994 CLASS D GIRLS

Stephanie Klein of Mendon won the individual run in 20:21, just a second faster than Whitmore Lake soph April Jackson ran in the team race.

Bear Lake, coached by Ken Overla, unseated defender Whitmore Lake in a low-scoring team race, 37-49.

Christian Reformed Rec. C, Kentwood, Nov. 5 □
1994 GIRLS CLASS D TEAMS
1. Bear Lake ... 37
2. Whitmore Lake ... 49
3. Fowler ... 96
4. North Muskegon ... 120
5. Grass Lake ... 182
6. Wyoming Lee ... 206
7. Buckley ... 210
8. Fairview ... 232
9. Ann Arbor Richard ... 238
10. Central Lake ... 252
11. Bath ... 291
12. Grand Rapids Baptist ... 295
13. Auburn Hills Oakland Christian ... 311
14. Manton ... 318

1994 GIRLS CLASS D TEAM RACE
1. April Jackson (Whitmore Lake)10 ... 20:22
2. Cindy Roberson (Bath)10 ... 20:41
3. Katy Speer (Whitmore Lake)12 ... 20:52
4. Natalie Reed (Bear Lake) ... 21:04
5. Heather Matesich (Bear Lake) ... 21:07
6. Rachel Mumaw (Wyoming Lee)11 ... 21:15
7. Betsy Speer (Whitmore Lake)10 ... 21:24
8. Wendy Lautner (Bear Lake) ... 21:25
9. Amanda Reed (Bear Lake) ... 21:29
10. Sarah Wirth (Fowler) ... 21:37
11. Rebecca Reed (Bear Lake) ... 21:41
33. Becky Swenson (Bear Lake) ... 23:18

1994 GIRLS CLASS D INDIVIDUAL RACE
1. Stephanie Klein (Mendon)11 ... 20:21
2. Brook Creed (Walkerville)10 ... 21:03
3. Michelle Klein (Mendon)9 ... 21:06
4. Amy Pair (Genesee) ... 21:33

1995 CLASS D GIRLS

Larry Steeb's Whitmore Lake squad moved to the top of the podium again after the previous year's second place. The Trojans—all underclassmen—tallied 56 points to top Mendon by 32. Lead runner Betsy Speer also returned to the top spot after a year away.

Christian Reformed Rec. C, Kentwood, Nov. 4 □
1995 GIRLS CLASS D TEAMS
1. Whitmore Lake ... 56
2. Mendon ... 88
3. Grass Lake ... 130
4. Fowler ... 131
5. Pittsford ... 180
6. Wyoming Tri-Unity Christian ... 203
7. Fairview ... 212
8. Central Lake ... 218
9. Ann Arbor Richard ... 226
10. Buckley ... 226
11. North Muskegon ... 256
12. Wyoming Lee ... 262
13. Mason County Eastern ... 274
14. Genesee ... 317
15. Wolverine ... 324

Larry Steeb guided Whitmore Lake to three team titles.

1995 GIRLS CLASS D TEAM RACE
1. Betsy Speer (Whitmore Lake)11 ....19:38
2. Stephanie Klein (Mendon)12 ....19:59
3. Michelle Klein (Mendon)10 ....20:06
4. April Jackson (Whitmore Lake)11 ....20:32
5. Kasey Culp (Mendon)10 ....20:39
6. Michelle Rector (Pittsford) 20:42
7. Janel DeGennarro (Wyoming Lee) 20:44
8. Sarah Wirth (Fowler)..20:50
9. Melissa Wolk (Whitmore Lake)11 ....20:52
10. Lindsay Carrier (Wyoming Tri-Unity Christian) ...20:56
11. Regina Andalaro (Grass Lake)12 ....20:58
12. Kari Smith (Whitmore Lake)11 ....21:02
13. Lisa Watt (Wolverine)..21:02
14. Amie Shay (Central Lake) 21:06
15. Denise Kellogg (Buckley) 21:10
30. Nicole Weaver (Whitmore Lake)10............................ nt

1995 GIRLS CLASS D INDIVIDUAL RACE
1. Brook Creed (Walkerville)10 ....20:05
2. Trudy Chase (Walkerville)9 ....20:13
3. Britta Ultz (Burr Oak)12 ....20:59
4. Holly Koshar (Lawrence) 21:29
5. Elizabeth Campbell (Ann Arbor Greenhills)9 ....21:40

1996 CLASS D GIRLS

In the first year at Michigan International Speedway, cold weather was the order of the day. The team and individual races were finally combined, but officials gave two sets of awards to the winners anyway. Seventh-placer Jennifer Kamps of North Muskegon was named the individual champion. No one else from the individual race finished in the top 15.

Kasey Culp took the win with a big finishing kick in the last 50. "I got closer and I thought to myself, 'Wow, I can win this race,'" she said. The margin was the closest ever: 19:51.1-19:51.7.

Whitmore Lake won the team race again, the third time in four years.

Michigan Int. Speedway, Brooklyn, Nov. 2
1996 GIRLS CLASS D TEAMS
1. Whitmore Lake 52
2. Mendon 82
3. Wyoming Tri-Unity Christian 104
4. Grass Lake 181
5. Mason County Eastern 188
6. Bear Lake 198
7. Buckley 204
8. Walkerville 210
9. Traverse City St Francis 226
10. Ann Arbor Richard 238
11. Ann Arbor Greenhills 262
12. Ubly 271
13. Fowler 277
14. Central Lake 295

1996 GIRLS CLASS D INDIVIDUALS
1. Kasey Culp (Mendon)11 ....19:52
2. Betsy Speer (Whitmore Lake)12 ....19:52
3. April Jackson (Whitmore Lake)12 ....19:54
4. Trudy Chase (Walkerville)10 ....20:02
5. Sarah Carter (St Joseph Lake Mich Catholic) 20:02
6. Michelle Klein (Mendon)11 ....20:10
7. Jennifer Kamps (North Muskegon)9......................20:27
8. Lindsay Carrier (Wyoming Tri-Unity Christian)....20:35
9. Brook Creed (Walkerville)11 ....20:37
10. Kathy Haley (Traverse City St Francis)..............20:38
11. Liz Campbell (Ann Arbor Greenhills) 20:48
12. Melissa Wolk (Whitmore Lake)12 ....20:53
13. Lena Rice (Mendon)10 ....20:53
14. Andrea Holt (Wyoming Tri-Unity Christian)9 ......20:54
15. Kari Brown (Buckley)9 ....21:02
16. Kari Smith (Whitmore Lake)12 ....21:02
25. Nicole Weaver (Whitmore Lake)11 ....21:21
28. Kendra Huff (Whitmore Lake)9 ....21:29
85. Liz Schroeder (Whitmore Lake) 23:22

1997 CLASS D GIRLS

Kasey Culp led her mendon teammates, coached by Art Bombrys, to the win, beating Tri-Unity Christian 50-60 with defending champ Whitmore Lake in third.

Said Culp of her repeat win, "I love getting muddy. It makes it more fun to run in. This is so unreal. Winning probably won't sink in until tomorrow morning when I wake up."

Michigan Int. Speedway, Brooklyn, Nov. 1
1997 GIRLS CLASS D TEAMS
1. Mendon 50
2. Wyoming Tri-Unity Christian 60
3. Whitmore Lake 123
4. Grass Lake 148
5. Walkerville 174
6. Fulton 184
7. Mio 209
8. Atlanta 229
9. Litchfield 233
10. Mason County Eastern 247
11. Akron-Fairgrove 251
12. Auburn Hills Oakland Christian 300
13. Wolverine 303
14. Buckley 309
15. Adrian Lenawee Christian 323

1997 GIRLS CLASS D INDIVIDUALS
1. Kasey Culp (Mendon)12 ....19:52
2. Brook Creed (Walkerville)12 ....20:15
3. Michelle Klein (Mendon)12 ....20:17
4. Lindsey Carrier (Wyoming Tri-Unity Christian).... 20:20
5. Silke Roedder (Wyoming Tri-Unity Christian).......20:36
6. Trudy Chase (Walkerville)11 ....21:01
7. Jill Wieman (North Muskegon) 21:11
8. Lena Rice (Mendon)11 ....21:21
9. Tina Petipren (Akron-Fairgrove)10 ....21:22
10. Stephanie Carpenter (Mio)11 ....21:27
11. Heather Hampton (Fulton) 21:30
12. Nicole Weaver (Whitmore Lake) 21:32
13. Kendra Huff (Whitmore Lake) 21:33
14. Christina Stephenson (Mendon) 21:33
15. Gretchen Shoup (Mason County Eastern) 21:41
34. Mindy Zinemaster (Mendon)11 ....22:22
39. Tiffany Nemire (Mendon)11 ....22:38
47. Elyssa Vernon (Mendon) 22:59

1998 CLASS D GIRLS

Even with Kasey Culp graduated, Mendon won again, nipping Bear Lake by 11 points. Akron-Fairgrove's Tina Petipren—the only girl on her team—won decisively by 26 seconds. "It's just fantastic to watch her go out there and run," said coach Jerry Lasceski.

In second place, Tiffany Seitz produced her first sub-20 on the perfect day.

Michigan Int. Speedway, Brooklyn, Nov. 7
1998 GIRLS CLASS D TEAMS
1. Mendon 106
2. Bear Lake 117
3. Grass Lake 129
4. Litchfield 139
5. North Muskegon 169
6. Fulton-Middleton 175
7. Buckley 182
8. Wolverine 189
9. Wyoming Tri-Unity Christian 192
10. Atlanta 215
11. Potterville 223
12. Auburn Hills Oakland Christian 252
13. New Lothrop 283
14. Rochester Hills Lutheran Northwest 328
15. Adrian Lenawee Christian 371

Tina Petipren of Akron-Fairgrove shattered the Class D course record by 35 seconds.

1998 GIRLS CLASS D INDIVIDUALS
1. Tina Petipren (Akron-Fairgrove)11 .... 19:17
2. Tiffany Seitz (New Buffalo)12 .... 19:43
3. Candi Mason (Potterville)12 .... 20:05
4.Trudy Chase (Walkerville)12 .... 20:15
5. Andrea Holt (Wyoming Tri-Unity Christian)11 ...... 20:17
6. Carol Licht (Atlanta)12... 20:19
7. Stephanie Carpenter (Mio)12 .... 20:25
8. Sarah Kostrzeba (Center Line St Clement)11 .... 20:26
9. Jennifer Kamps (North Muskegon)11 .... 20:30
10. Heather Hampton (Fulton-Middleton)11............. 20:33
11. Jessica Salvano (Lawrence)10............................ 20:35
12. Kelli O'Rourke (Wolverine)10 .... 20:39
13. Lena Rice (Mendon)12 .... 20:44
14. Angela Pitts (Litchfield)10 .... 20:47
15. Regina Andaloro (Grass Lake)12 .... 20:50
20. Mindy Zinemaster (Mendon)12............................ 20:58
28. Tiffany Nemire (Mendon)12 .... 21:23
46. Elizabeth Sacksteder (Mendon)11....................... 22:05
55. Keri McClish (Mendon)10 .... 22:34
65. Dana Kline (Mendon)11 .... 23:00
109. Christy Pearson (Mendon)12 .... 25:29

1999 CLASS D GIRLS

In the final Class D championship before the sport in Michigan went to a divisional format, Mt. Pleasant's Sacred Heart Academy, coached by Mark Zitzelsberger, came away with a 24-point win over Colon.

Atlanta's Kimi Landane was the big revelation of the meet, with a stunning victory in 18:24 that left the opposition far behind.

Michigan Int. Speedway, Brooklyn, Nov. 6
1999 GIRLS CLASS D TEAMS
1. Mt Pleasant Sacred Heart 92

2. Colon 116
3. North Muskegon 130
4. Mason County Eastern 133
5. Bear Lake 133
6. Buckley 161
7. Litchfield 175
8. Wyoming Tri-Unity Christian 194
9. Auburn Hills Oakland Christian 202
10. Mendon 208
11. Lawrence 221
12. New Lothrop 239
13. Rochester Hills Lutheran Northwest 276
14. Adrian Lenawee Christian 342
15. Marine City Mooney 395

Atlanta's Kimi Landane became the last Class D champion.

1999 GIRLS CLASS D INDIVIDUALS

1. Kimi Landane (Atlanta)12 18:24
2. Sarah Hinkley (Reading)11 19:08
3. Sabrina Mitchell (Bear Lake)10 19:51
4. Karen Latus (New Buffalo)11 20:10
5. Michelle Rolf (Rcohester Hills Lutheran NW)10 20:28
6. Jessica Pifer (Buckley)12 20:31
7. Jennifer Kamps (North Muskegon)12 20:33
8. Anna Holtz (Wyoming Tri-Unity Christian)12 20:39
9. Joey Pribble (Lansing Christian)11 20:44
10. Kelli Zoellner (Harper Woods Lutheran East)9 20:45
11. Sarah Kostrzeba (Center Line St Clement)12 20:45
12. Heather Doerr (Mt Pleasant Sacred Heart)9 20:47
13. Krista DeWys (Mason County Eastern)12 20:48
14. Gretchen Shoup (Mason County Eastern)12 20:50
15. Sarah Converse (Litchfield)9 20:51
18. Liz Burdick (Mt Pleasant Sacred Heart)10 21:03
29. Emily Sias (Mt Pleasant Sacred Heart)9 21:23
41. Ashley Alwood (Mt Pleasant Sacred Heart)9 21:55
54. Kacey Neyer (Mt Pleasant Sacred Heart)12 22:26
125. Jill Thering (Mt Pleasant Sacred Heart)9 28:29

2000 D4 GIRLS

The move to a divisional format had a big effect on the race for the smallest schools, as a significant number of schools that had formerly been Class C moved down. It showed in the results, as the highest-placing team from the previous year's D race, defending champion Mt. Pleasant Sacred Heart, could only finish 11th.

Maple City Glen Lake, coached by Byran Burns, won the first Division 4 title with a score of 116.

Sophomore Lauren Fairbanks of Rogers City overcame the lead of Jennifer Leichtman at the 2M mark to set the course record with her 18:20. "We went back and forth all the way into the stadium," said Fairbanks. "I looked back once, which I really shouldn't have done, but I really didn't have much left."

Michigan Int. Speedway, Brooklyn, Nov. 4
2000 GIRLS DIVISION 4 TEAMS

1. Maple City Glen Lake 116
2. Ann Arbor Greenhills 148
3. Bath 189
4. East Jordan 190
5. Concord 194
6. Pittsford 219
7. Hanover-Horton 255
8. Rogers City 277
9. Lutheran Westland 281
10. Bellevue 301
11. Mt. Pleasant Sacred Heart 301
12. St. Louis 317
13. Southfield Christian 333
14. Bear Lake 368
15. Colon 419
16. Buckley 434
17. Auburn Hills Oakland Christian 450
18. Ubly 452
19. Lawrence 453
20. New Lothrop 464
21. Wolverine 508
22. North Muskegon 531
23. Mendon 535
24. Grand Rapids Baptist 538
25. Genesee 548
26. Harper Woods Lutheran East 593

No score--Grosse Pointe Woods University Liggett.

2000 GIRLS DIVISION 4 INDIVIDUALS

1. Lauren Fairbanks (Rogers City)10 18:20
2. Jennifer Leichtman (Ann Arbor Greenhills)12 18:26
3. Sabrina Mitchell (Bear Lake)11 18:43
4. Katie Forsyth (Bath)10 18:59
5. Holly Piffer (Buckley)10 19:02
6. Caitlin Kelly (Kinde-North Huron)10 19:06
7. Shannon Stanglewicz (St Louis)11 19:20
8. Sarah Hinkley (Reading)12 19:20
9. Theresa Kuehne (Lutheran Westland) 19:27
10. Chase Edwards (Maple City Glen Lake)10 19:27
11. Robyn Schmidt (Maple City Glen Lake)11 19:34
12. Leelanee Sterett (Manton)9 19:38
13. Lisa Booth (Homer)10 19:39
14. Kelly Zoellner (HW Lutheran East) 19:40
15. Chris Alcenius (Hanover-Horton)11 19:41
43. Megan Kiem (Maple City Glen Lake)9 20:35
53. Liz Huron (Maple City Glen Lake)11 20:45
66. Adele Wiejaczka (Maple City Glen Lake)11 20:58
100. Janet VanZoeren (Maple City Glen Lake)11 21:38
104. Lindsey Webber (Maple City Glen Lake)9 21:45

2001 D4 GIRLS

Ann Arbor Greenhills came away with a big win, topping defending champion Maple City Glen Lake by 72 points. Said coach Josh Scully, "It was unbelievable. I told them they could do it."

Caitlin Kelly of Kinde-North Huron led from the mile mark, but almost didn't make it to the finish, falling just steps before the line before getting up to cross it. "It feels unbelievable. Giving everything was worth it," she said.

Michigan Int. Speedway, Brooklyn, Nov. 3
2001 GIRLS DIVISION 4 TEAMS

1. Ann Arbor Greenhills 74
2. Maple City Glen Lake 146
3. Concord 195
4. Mt. Pleasant Sacred Heart 210
5. Traverse City St. Francis 248
6. Rogers City 283
7. Ubly 290
8. Pittsford 293
9. Lutheran Westland 316
10. Brown City 323
11. East Jordan 337
12. Whitmore Lake 350
13. Kinde-North Huron 360
14. Bath 371
15. Bellevue 383
16. Pewamo-Westphalia 396
17. Colon 399
18. Bear Lake 401
19. Harbor Springs 407
20. Mendon 428
21. Lawton 447
22. Saugatuck 467
23. Litchfield 474
24. Harper Woods Lutheran East 575
25. North Muskegon 604
26. Auburn Hills Oakland Christian 607

2001 GIRLS DIVISION 4 INDIVIDUALS

1. Caitlin Kelly (Kinde-North Huron)11 18:55
2. Holly Pifer (Buckley)11 19:06
3. Katie Forsyth (Bath)11 19:11
4. Sabrina Mitchell (Bear Lake)9 19:16
5. Cassidy Edwards (Maple City Glen L)9 19:29
6. Jennifer Leichtman (Ann Arbor Greenhills)12 19:45
7. Dawn Essenmacher (Pittsford)12 19:46
8. Leelannee Sterrett (Manton)10 19:51
9. Laysie Skinner (Colon)11 19:55
10. Lauren Fairbanks (Rogers City)11 19:59
11. Camille Doan (Concord)11 20:04
12. Kaitlin Harvey (Tekonsha)11 20:04
13. Kelli Zoellner (HW Lutheran East)11 20:04
14. Theresa Iwinski (Brown City)10 20:06
15. Sarah Couyoumjian (Ann Arbor Greenhills)11 20:07
23. Rebecca Sameroff (Ann Arbor Greenhills)11 20:21
24. Katie Olson (Ann Arbor Greenhills)10 20:25
30. Laurie Baumann (Ann Arbor Greenhills)11 20:39
68. Marianna Kerppola (Ann Arbor Greenhills)11 21:46
69. Alexa Wahr (Ann Arbor Greenhills)9 21:46

2002 D4 GIRLS

Ann Arbor Greenhills won a second-straight, holding off the challenge of Suttons Bay by 53 points.

Defending champ Caitlin Kelly of Kinde-North Huron led through miles of 5:45 and 6:00, with Laura Rolf of Lutheran Northwest staying close behind. Inside the stadium, Rolf made her move, and finished with a D4 course record 18:17.

In 27th place, Kelcie Spruyt-Daniels won All-State honors. At age 12 and in 7th grade, she is the youngest-ever MHSAA medalist.

Michigan Int. Speedway, Brooklyn, Nov. 2
2002 GIRLS DIVISION 4 TEAMS

1. Ann Arbor Greenhills 93
2. Suttons Bay 146
3. Traverse City St. Francis 170
4. Bear Lake-Onekama 209
5. Rogers City 222
6. Harbor Springs 225
7. Bath 229
8. Saugatuck 240
9. Concord 287
10. Ann Arbor Richard 291
11. Mt. Pleasant Sacred Heart 302
12. Southfield Christian 304
13. Brown City 314
14. Ubly 317
15. Potterville 344
16. Kinde-North Huron 354
17. Mendon 386
18. Pewamo-Westphalia 456
19. Rochester Hills Lutheran Northwest 473
20. Colon 477
21. Centreville 486
22. Pittsford 505
23. Ellsworth 565
24. Lawton 578
25. Grosse Pointe Woods Univ. Liggett 766

2002 GIRLS DIVISION 4 INDIVIDUALS

1. Laura Rolf (Rochester H Lutheran Northwest)10 18:17
2. Caitlin Kelly (Kinde-North Huron)12 18:24
3. Cassidy Edwards (Maple City Glen Lake)10 18:56
4. Tricia Rozeboom (Saugatuck)9 19:15
5. Laycie Skinner (Colon)12 19:20
6. Alexa Glencer (Ann Arbor Greenhills)9 19:26
7. Kaitlin Harvey (Tekonsha)12 19:26
8. Lauren Fairbanks (Rogers City)12 19:35
9. Katie Forsyth (Bath)12 19:36
10. Shelly Millard (Mendon)12 19:37
11. Theresa Iwinski (Brown City)11 19:38
12. Cassie Niersel (Harbor Springs)10 19:39

13. Margot McGlothlin (Suttons Bay)12 .... 19:40
14. Samantha Mitchell (Bear Lake-Onekama)10 ..... 19:42
15. Erin Booth (Homer)12 .... 19:45
21. Katie Olson (Ann Arbor Greenhills)11 .... 20:01
26. Laurie Baumann (Ann Arbor Greenhills)12 .... 20:10
30. Sarah Couyoumjian (Ann Arbor Greenhills)12..20:12
48. Rebecca Sameroff (Ann Arbor Greenhills)12....20:57
51. Alexandra Ford (Ann Arbor Greenhills)9........... 21:00
101. Marianna Kerppola (Ann Arbor Greenhills)12..21:52

2003 D4 GIRLS

A determined effort by Traverse City St. Francis beat the 2-time defending champs from Ann Arbor Greenhills, 135-152. It was the highest scoring win yet.

Laura Rolf pulled away from the field after a 5:47 mile to produce an 18:30 and win her second-straight title, with Greenhills' Katie Olson in second.

Michigan Int. Speedway, Brooklyn, Nov. 1
2003 GIRLS DIVISION 4 TEAMS
1. Traverse City St. Francis 135
2. Ann Arbor Greenhills 152
3. Big Rapids Crossroads 166
4. Potterville 228
5. Ann Arbor Richard 229
6. Ubly 229
7. Hudson 231
8. Southfield Christian 239
9. Bear Lake 257
10. Harbor Springs 290
11. Saginaw Valley Lutheran 293
12. Beal City 317
13. Bath 317
14. Pittsford 339
15. Rochester Hills Lutheran Northwest 356
16. Lutheran Westland 385
17. Morenci 396
18. Saugatuck 461
19. Hudsonville Freedom Baptist 489
20. Royal Oak Shrine 500
21. Ellsworth 532
22. Saginaw Michigan Lutheran 550
23. Bellevue 584
24. Colon 603
25. Lawton 626
26. East Jordan 628
27. Centreville 682
28. Auburn Hills Oakland Christian 692

2003 GIRLS DIVISION 4 INDIVIDUALS
1. Laura Rolf (Rochester Hills Lutheran NW)11 .... 18:30
2. Katie Olson (Ann Arbor Greenhills)12 .... 18:53
3. Jackie Rivard (Ubly)11 .... 18:54
4. Kylee Kubacki (Ubly)9 .... 19:04
5. Cassidy Edwards (Maple City Glen Lake)11 ...... 19:06
6. Kailah Gerig (Sand Creek)10 .... 19:07
7. Rebecca Monroe (Big Rapids Crossroads)10..... 19:14
8. Katie Rolf (Rochester Hills Lutheran NW)12 ...... 19:22
9. LaTricia Rozeboom (Saugatuck)10 .... 19:24
10. Alexa Glencer (Ann Arbor Greenhills)10 .... 19:32
11. Audrey Dahlgren (Potterville)10 .... 19:36
12. Jenelle Keinath (Saginaw Valley Lutheran)11 .. 19:40
13. Wendi Kirwin (Walkerville)12 .... 19:41
14. Lindsay Gordon (Pittsford)10 .... 19:42
15. Megan Carter (Southfield Christian)9 .... 19:43
28. Teresa Dawson (Traverse City St Francis)12 .... 20:14
30. Jena Brown (Traverse City St Francis)10 .... 20:19
33. Kelly Biedron (Traverse City St Francis)11 .... 20:21
37. Colleen Griffin (Traverse City St Francis)10 ...... 20:39
47. Kristine Perria (Traverse City St Francis)9 .... 20:50
81. Molly Maxbauer (Traverse City St Francis)12 ... 21:32
117. Krysta Zakrzewski (Traverse C St Francis)12..22:18

2004 D4 GIRLS

Big Rapids Crossroads, coached by Kendall Schroeder, won its first title with a 115-point performance. The team was led by 7th-placer Rebecca Monroe.

Marissa Treece of Maple City Glen Lake, who had won the 3200 title the previous spring as a 9th-grader, left Jackie Rivard of Ubly behind in the final 800 to win her first title in 18:21.

Marissa Treece won three titles for Glen Lake.

Michigan Int. Speedway, Brooklyn, Nov. 6
2004 GIRLS DIVISION 4 TEAMS
1. Big Rapids Crossroads 115
2. Southfield Christian 146
3. Ann Arbor Greenhills 169
4. Potterville 190
5. Ubly 211
6. Traverse City St Francis 212
7. Grand Rapids NorthPointe Christian 218
8. Saginaw Valley Lutheran 228
9. Hudson 239
10. Maple City Glen Lake 294
11. Mason County Eastern 366
12. Lutheran Westland 370
13. Bath 374
14. Rogers City 375
15. Fowler 377
16. Beal City 380
17. Fairview 400
18. Saginaw Michigan Lutheran 406
19. Concord 424
20. Lawrence 454
21. Rochester Hills Lutheran Northwest 504
22. Pittsford 522
23. Ellsworth 523
24. Ottawa Lake Whiteford 550
25. Hartford 568
26. Centreville 659
27. Auburn Hills Oakland Christian 685

2004 GIRLS DIVISION 4 INDIVIDUALS
1. Marissa Treece (Maple City Glen Lake)10 .... 18:21
2. Jackie Rivard (Ubly)12 .... 18:31
3. Tricia Rozeboom (Saugatuck)11 .... 18:54
4. Alexa Glencer (Ann Arbor Greenhills)11 .... 19:15
5. Marcia Silveria (Ann Arbor Greenhills)9 .... 19:18
6. Katie Rolf (RH Lutheran Northwest)10 .... 19:23
7. Rebecca Monroe (Big Rapids Crossroads)11 ... 19:31
8. Kailah Gerig (Sand Creek)11 .... 19:34
9. Kylee Kubacki (Ubly)10 .... 19:45
10. Valerie Allen (Southfield Christian)11 .... 19:46
11. Audrey Dahlgren (Potterville)11 .... 19:50
12. Alexandra Ford (Ann Arbor Greenhills)11 .... 19:50
13. Jenelle Keinath (Saginaw Valley Lutheran)12 .. 19:52
14. Cassidy Edwards (Maple City Glen Lake)12 ..... 19:57
15. Chelsea Lehrbass (Mason County Easterm)9 .. 20:02
18. Stacy Leyder (Big Rapids Crossroads)11 .... 20:14
22. Katie Thorne (Big Rapids Crossroads)10 .... 20:16
44. Nicole Erler (Big Rapids Crossroads)11 .... 21:00
45. Rachel Thorne (Big Rapids Crossroads)9 .... 21:01
198. Caryn Reynolds (Big Rapids Crossroads)11 ... 24:44

2005 D4 GIRLS

"I felt good," said Marissa Treece, "but I was kind of scared that they were going to come back on me. I didn't know how quick they were."

The Maple City Glen Lake junior defended her title with a 17:58 D4 course record.

Big Rapids Crossroads successfully defended its team title.

Michigan Int. Speedway, Brooklyn, Nov. 5
2005 GIRLS DIVISION 4 TEAMS
1. Big Rapids Crossroads 132
2. Traverse City St Francis 159
3. Ann Arbor Greenhills 176
4. Southfield Christian 181
5. Saginaw Valley Lutheran 213
6. Ubly 229
7. Grand Rapids NorthPointe Christian 240
8. Hesperia 246
9. Hudson 266
10. Rogers City 281
11. St Joseph Lake Michigan Catholic 299
12. Potterville 308
13. Concord 335
14. Maple City Glen Lake 346
15. Battle Creek St Philip 355
16. Hillsdale Academy 357
17. Fowler 363
18. Unionville-Sebewaing 394
19. Vandercook Lake 413
20. Mason County Eastern 454
21. Beal City 478
22. Ellsworth 525
23. Three Oaks River Valley 548
24. Centreville 578
25. Fairview 584
26. Auburn Hills Oakland Christian 787
27. Royal Oak Shrine 867

2005 GIRLS DIVISION 4 INDIVIDUALS
1. Marissa Treece (Maple City Glen Lake)11 .... 17:58
2. Kaylee Kreft (Rogers City)9 .... 18:37
3. Kylee Kubacki (Ubly)11 .... 18:38
4. Alexa Glencer (Ann Arbor Greenhills)12 .... 18:38
5. Rebecca Monroe (Big Rapids Crossroads)12 ... 18:50
6. Tricia Rozeboom (Saugatuck)12 .... 18:54
7. Heather Strong (Fulton-Middleton)9 .... 19:03
8. Kailah Gerig (Sand Creek)12 .... 19:07
9. Lacey Kreft (Rogers City)12 .... 19:09
10. Rachel Ham (Hudson)12 .... 19:11
11. Megan Carter (Southfield Christian)11 .... 19:13
12. Valerie Allen (Southfield Christian)12 .... 19:14
13. Emily Peil (Saginaw Valley Lutheran)9 .... 19:18
14. Katie Thorne (Big Rapids Crossroads)11 .... 19:25
15. Alexandra Ford (Ann Arbor Greenhills)12 .... 19:25
31. Nicole Erler (Big Rapids Crossroads)12 .... 20:02
51. Rachel Thorne (Big Rapids Crossroads)10 ..... 20:54
69. Stacy Leyder (Big Rapids Crossroads)12 .... 21:09
91. Jessica Aguirre (Big Rapids Crossroads)10 ..... 21:29
166. Caryn Reynolds (Big Rapids Crossroads)12 .. 23:10

2006 D4 GIRLS

With 105 points, Grand Rapids NorthPointe Christian won its first title. Coached by Todd Schenck, the Mustangs had two runners in the top 11.

Maple City Glen Lake's Marissa Treece won her third straight in a meet record 17:55 after passing the mile marks in 5:41 and 11:32. She would go on to a successful career at Notre Dame, winning All-Big East honors in track.

Michigan Int. Speedway, Brooklyn, Nov. 4 ⊠
2006 GIRLS DIVISION 4 TEAMS
1. Grand Rapids NorthPointe Christian....105
2. Potterville....126
3. Harbor Springs....127
4. Battle Creek St Philip....137
5. Saginaw Valley Lutheran....169
6. Ubly....171
7. Southfield Christian....291
8. Hudson....298
9. Beal City....303
10. Unionville-Sebewaing....311
11. Hesperia....319
12. Fowler....324
13. Mendon....340
14. Ann Arbor Greenhills....342
15. Traverse City St Francis....361
16. Big Rapids Crossroads....373
17. Maple City Glen Lake....417
18. Hillsdale Academy....428
19. Bear Lake-Onekama....443
20. Whitmore Lake....446
21. Lawton....571
22. Allen Park Cabrini....575
23. Saugatuck....597
24. Ellsworth....598
25. Rogers City....630
26. Lawrence....680
27. Royal Oak Shrine....747

2006 GIRLS DIVISION 4 INDIVIDUALS
1. Marissa Treece (Maple City Glen Lake)12....17:55
2. Megan Carter (Southfield Christian)12....18:53
3. Rebecca Campbell (GR NorthPointe Chr)12....19:01
4. Kylee Kubacki (Ubly)12....19:01
5. Heather Strong (Fulton-Middleton)10....19:07
6. Melinda Palinkas (Saranac)9....19:21
7. Cayla Nousain (Concord)10....19:37
8. Brooke Simon (Fowler)10....19:42
9. Chloe Peckels (Battle Creek St Philip)11....19:45
10. Sara Turschak (Unionville-Sebewaing)10....19:46
11. Grace Campbell (GR NorthPointe Christian)9....19:48
12. Alivia Murphy (Harbor Springs)10....19:53
13. Kari Johnson (Central Lake)11....19:56
14. Jessica Hall (Harbor Springs)9....20:01
15. Emily Peil (Saginaw Valley Lutheran)10....20:02
35. Karly Sikma (GR NorthPointe)11....20:38
45. Heather Carlson (GR NorthPointe)12....20:53
47. Erin Kole (GR NorthPointe Chr)10....20:54
147. Jessi Byl (GR NorthPointe Chr)12....22:40
158. Betsy Witte (GR NorthPointe Chr)12....22:56

2007 D4 GIRLS

NorthPointe Christian stayed on top for another year, beating challenger Harbor Springs by 14 points. "We were all nervous, but we pulled it together," said senior Karlyn Sikma.

In her first run on the MIS course, North Muskegon frosh Lindsay Neal put together a good one. "I was really nervous when I got here," she said. "It was so big. I was freaking out." Of her win in 18:30: "I'm in shock."

Michigan Int. Speedway, Brooklyn, Nov. 3 ⊠
2007 GIRLS DIVISION 4 TEAMS
1. Grand Rapids NorthPointe Christian....109
2. Harbor Springs....123
3. Manton....173
4. Southfield Christian....224
5. Ann Arbor Greenhills....254
6. Battle Creek St Philip....269
7. Ubly....281
8. Potterville....309
9. Harbor Beach....312
10. Hesperia....319
11. Saginaw Valley Lutheran....322
12. Unionville-Sebewaing....341
13. Bear Lake-Onekama....367
14. St Louis....400
15. Royal Oak Shrine....402
16. Mendon....415
17. Fowler....420
18. Jonesville....427
19. Saugatuck....433
20. Maple City Glen Lake....437
21. Concord....438
22. Waterford Our Lady of the Lakes....448
23. White Cloud....469
24. Pittsford....526
25. Lawton....540
26. Rogers City....552
27. Hartford....577
28. Ellsworth....628

2007 GIRLS DIVISION 4 INDIVIDUALS
1. Lindsay Neal (North Muskegon)9....18:30
2. Cayla Nousain (Concord)11....18:45
3. Melinda Palinkas (Saranac)10....18:51
4. Amber Therrien (Maple City Glen Lake)12....19:00
5. Grace Campbell (GR NorthPointe Christian)10....19:16
6. Heather Strong (Fulton-Middleton)11....19:22
7. Rachel Carter (Southfield Christian)11....19:22
8. Chloe Peckels (Battle Creek St Philip)12....19:27
9. Sara Turschak (Unionville-Sebewaing)11....19:31
10. Allison Varney (Jonesville)9....19:31
11. Alivia Murphy (Harbor Springs)11....19:34
12. Megan Crandall (Beal City)10....19:35
13. Karlyn Sikma (GR NorthPointe Christian)12....19:38
14. Felicia Peacock (Hesperia)11....19:41
15. Rachael Brushaber (Harbor Springs)9....19:43
17. Anna Duckworth (GR NorthPointe Christian)10 19:46
62. Emilee Belk (GR NorthPointe Christian)9....20:58
69. Erin Kole (GR NorthPointe Christian)11....21:07
137. Amanda Roels (GR NorthPointe Christian)11 .21:53
144. Kristie Sikma (GR NorthPointe Christian)10....21:59

2008 D4 GIRLS

A solid pack made the victory happen for Harbor Springs, with lead runner Maddie Buntin placing 15th. Said coach Emily Kloss, "We've been trying to move up each time—now let's see if we can stay there for a while. We have a good balance of ages and we rearely have the same top seven finish in the same order. That's a strength in that we always have someone pick it up."

The race was won by Sacred Heart's Bridget Bennett in 18:37, who had been disqualified in the previous year's race. The junior, running on a possible stress fracture in her foot, said, "When we got to the 2M mark I noticed we weren't at the pace I wanted, so I just took off from there."

Michigan Int. Speedway, Brooklyn, Nov. 1 ⊠
2008 GIRLS DIVISION 4 TEAMS
1. Harbor Springs....91
2. Manton....103
3. Hesperia....127
4. Grand Rapids NorthPointe Christian....138
5. Fowler....205
6. Royal Oak Shrine....264
7. Saugatuck....290
8. Battle Creek St Philip....303
9. Harbor Beach....320
10. Bear Lake-Onekama....347
11. Pewamo-Westphalia....349
12. Concord....363
13. Mt Pleasant Sacred Heart....366
14. Lawton....369
15. Traverse City St Francis....438
16. Hillsdale Academy....444
17. Unionville-Sebewaing....458
18. Southfield Christian....483
19. Waterford Our Lady of the Lakes....486
20. Sand Creek....491
21. Onaway....502
22. Mendon....510
23. Wolverine....522
24. Ann Arbor Greenhills....523
25. Mayville....538
26. Centreville....554
27. Waldron....583

2008 GIRLS DIVISION 4 INDIVIDUALS
1. Bridget Bennett (Mt Pleasant Sacred Heart)11....18:37
2. Melinda Palinkas (Saranac)11....18:49
3. Lindsay Neal (North Muskegon)10....18:52
4. Alexandrea Wessels (Harbor Beach)11....19:00
5. Nicole Wurster (Homer)11....19:06
6. Megan Crandall (Beal City)11....19:12
7. Grace Campbell (GR NorthPointe Christian)11....19:12
8. Sara Turschak (Unionville-Sebewaing)12....19:13
9. Heather Strong (Fulton-Middleton)12....19:19
10. Rachel Carter (Southfield Christian)12....19:20
11. Winonah Krug (Newport Lutheran South)11....19:27
12. Sonny Jenkins (Manton)10....19:33
13. Lisznai Elyse (Hillsdale Academy)8....19:37
14. Jennifer Messing (Ubly)12....19:38
15. Maddie Buntin (Harbor Springs)9....19:39
22. Caitlin Reeves (Harbor Springs)12....19:54
26. Alivia Murphy (Harbor Springs)12....20:00
33. Grace Carbeck (Harbor Springs)9....20:11
42. Katie Hoffman (Harbor Springs)10....20:24
47. Rachael Brushaber (Harbor Springs)10....20:35

2009 D4 GIRLS

Harbor Springs made it two in a row, putting two in the top 8 to key a 66-point performance to beat No. 1-ranked Manton by 30 points.

Sacred Heart's Bridget Bennett went out conservatively before breaking away with a 5:51 middle mile to take the win in 18:36. "When you're trying to do it a second time, it's like, 'Am I deserving of this?' Many people don't get to do this once," said Bennett. "I doubted myself a lot. I guess God had it in the plan for me today."

Michigan Int. Speedway, Brooklyn, Nov. 7 ⊠
2009 GIRLS DIVISION 4 TEAMS
1. Harbor Springs....66
2. Manton....96
3. Saugatuck....188
4. Mt Pleasant Sacred Heart....188
5. Traverse City Grand Traverse Academy....213
6. Royal Oak Shrine....219
7. Hesperia....248
8. Beal City....248
9. Boyne Falls....262
10. Saranac....278
11. Pewamo-Westphalia....297
12. Battle Creek St Phillip....334
13. North Muskegon....339
14. Bath....364
15. Concord....397
16. Lutheran Westland....405
17. Wolverine....428
18. Kalamazoo Christian....448
19. Sand Creek....460
20. St Joseph Lake Michigan Catholic....469
21. Mayville....516
22. Ann Arbor Greenhills....526
23. Traverse City St Francis....532
24. Auburn Hills Oakland Christian....583
25. Rochester Hills Lutheran Northwest....615
26. Centreville....653

2009 GIRLS DIVISION 4 INDIVIDUALS
1. Bridget Bennett (Mt Pleasant Sacred Heart)12....18:36
2. Lindsay Neal (North Muskegon)11....19:19
3. Nicole Wurster (Homer)12....19:29
4. Melinda Palinkas (Saranac)12....19:43
5. Emily Kwekel (Bellaire)11....19:45
6. Rhi Cullip (Harbor Springs)9....19:50
7. Alexandrea Wessels (Harbor Beach)12....19:52
8. Maddie Buntin (Harbor Springs)10....19:59
9. Lauren Cody (Lawton)10....19:59
10. Megan Crandall (Beal City)12....20:06
11. Stephanie Ingraham (Manton)11....20:08
12. Maggie Kolb (Beal City)9....20:11
13. Natalie Perry (Adrian Lenawee Christian)9....20:12
14. Melanie Glinski (Sand Creek)12....20:16
15. Alexa Rumsey (Hesperia)9....20:16
25. Grace Carbeck (Harbor Springs)10....20:38

26. Kendal McCarthy (Harbor Springs)11 ....20:38
38. Jessica Hall (Harbor Springs)12 ....21:01
49. Kaitlyn Alessi (Harbor Springs)9 ....21:20
175. Katie Hoffman (Harbor Springs)11 ....24:07

2010 D4 GIRLS

It was a nail-biter, but Hesperia managed to knock Harbor Springs off the top of the podium in a close 107-111.

Ninth-grader Kirsten Olling of Breckenridge produced an 18:10 to win the title over North Muskegon's Lyndsay Neal, who placed 1-3-2-2 in her four runs at MIS. The race got close in the second mile. Said Olling, "When I realized she was just a second behind me, then I started picking it up again. There was never any point of reassurance that I was running by myself."

Michigan Int. Speedway, Brooklyn, Nov. 6
2010 GIRLS DIVISION 4 TEAMS
1. Hesperia	107
2. Harbor Springs	111
3. Saugatuck	149
4. North Muskegon	171
5. Traverse City Grand Traverse Academy	177
6. Mt Pleasant Sacred Heart	243
7. Royal Oak Shrine	249
8. Lutheran Westland	267
9. Fowler	272
10. Bear Lake-Onekama	277
11. Hillsdale Academy	288
12. Traverse City St Francis	324
13. Concord	331
14. Kalamazoo Christian	333
15. Johannesburg-Lewiston	337
16. Pittsford	366
17. Ottawa Lake Whiteford	435
18. Grosse Pointe University Liggett	488
19. Auburn Hills Oakland Christian	507
20. Mayville	522
21. Saginaw Arts & Sciences	544
22. Wolverine	547
23. St Joseph Lake Michigan Catholic	557
24. Centreville	578
25. New Lothrop	594
26. Ann Arbor Greenhills	690

2010 GIRLS DIVISION 4 INDIVIDUALS
1. Kirsten Olling (Breckenridge)9	18:10
2. Lindsay Neal (North Muskegon)12	18:24
3. Alexa Rumsey (Hesperia)11	18:55
4. Taylor Bolinger (Fulton-Middleton)9	19:00
5. Rhi Cullip (Harbor Springs)10	19:04
6. Brianne Feldpausch (Fowler)12	19:20
7. Erica Westbrook (Boyne Falls)10	19:22
8. Emily Kwekel (Bellaire)12	19:27
9. Katharine Jones (Mt Pleasant Sacred Heart)9	19:27
10. Tobi Schoedel (Bear Lake)12	19:27
11. Nicole Zeinstra (Holland Black River)11	19:28
12. Heather Price (Saugatuck)11	19:28
13. Lauren Jenkins (Saugatuck)9	19:29
14. Gabbie Bates (Hesperia)11	19:35
15. Amanda Reagle (Homer)9	19:37
42. Jacklyn Yates (Hesperia)11	20:28
43. Donna Aslakson (Hesperia)11	20:29
60. Lauren Zeerip (Hespieria)9	20:48
80. Jasmine Hall (Hesperia)10	21:10
102. Haley Wiseman (Hesperia)11	21:28

2011 GIRLS

Hesperia, coached by Douglas Baird, won again, becoming the fourth-straight school to win the D4 crown twice in a row.

Another repeater was individual winner Kirsten Olling of Breckenridge. "I was really hoping to run a 16:59," she admitted, noting that the conditions weren't ideal. "But what can you do? It's cross country, it's a mentally tough sport. So you just have to keep on going no matter what happens."

Michigan Int. Speedway, Brooklyn, Nov. 5
2011 GIRLS DIVISION 4 TEAMS
1. Hesperia	67
2. North Muskegon	103
3. Saugatuck	159
4. Traverse City Grand Traverse Academy	183
5. Concord	239
6. Homer	245
7. Breckenridge	258
8. Johannesburg-Lewiston	280
9. Pittsford	301
10. Beal City	318
11. Potterville	319
12. Bear Lake	333
13. Royal Oak Shrine	348
14. Lansing Christian	355
15. Lutheran Westland	422
16. Kalamazoo Hackett	429
17. Sand Creek	439
18. Traverse City St Francis	462
19. Ellsworth	479
20. Auburn Hills Oakland Christian	480
21. Ottawa Lake Whiteford	503
22. Mayville	517
23. Saginaw Arts & Sciences	521
24. Lawton	528
25. Centreville	533
26. Rogers City	550
27. Grosse Pointe University Liggett	603

2011 GIRLS DIVISION 4 INDIVIDUALS
1. Kirsten Olling (Breckenridge)10	18:03
2. Nicole Zeinstra (Holland Black River)12	18:41
3. Alexa Rumsey (Hesperia)12	18:46
4. Meridith DeLuca (Johannesburg-Lewiston)11	18:48
5. Taylor Smith (Blanchard-Montabella)10	19:08
6. Taylor Bolinger (Fulton Middleton)10	19:10
7. Shaley Albaugh (Hillsdale Academy)11	19:12
8. Heather Price (Saugatuck)12	19:15
9. Gabbie Bates (Hesperia)12	19:18
10. Kate McLain (Kalamazoo Christian)10	19:20
11. Lauern Jenkins (Saugatuck)10	19:30
12. Katelyn VanMorick (Evart)12	19:37
13. Leah DeSimpelare (Unionville-Sebewaing)9	19:39
14. Lucy Ankenbauer (Kalamazoo Hackett)9	19:39
15. Erica Westbrook (Boyne Falls)11	19:41
25. Donna Aslakson (Hesperia)12	20:00
30. Lauren Zeerip (Hesperia)11	20:06
36. Jasmine Hall (Hesperia)11	20:17
68. Jacklyn Yates (Hesperia)12	21:04
72. Mary Tozer (Hesperia)9	21:11

*Breckenridge's Kirsten Olling, winning No. 3.
(Pete Draugalis photo)*

2012 D4 GIRLS

Homer won its first-ever title, coached by Rebecca Willis. The Trojans put three in the first 18.

Breckenridge's Kirsten Olling made it three in a row, despite a mid-season diagnosis of anemia. "I was actually worried I was going to lose it. I was really worried today. By the mile I pretty much knew I'd be okay."

Michigan Int. Speedway, Brooklyn, Nov. 3
2012 GIRLS DIVISION 4 TEAMS
1. Homer	118
2. Bear Lake	142
3. Harbor Springs	157
4. Beal City	160
5. Saugatuck	162
6. North Muskegon	206
7. Traverse City St Francis	243
8. Royal Oak Shrine	253
9. Lutheran Westland	265
10. Breckenridge	265
11. Hesperia	315
12. Traverse City Grand Traverse Academy	333
13. Kalamazoo Hackett	351
14. Pittsford	362
15. Pewamo-Westphalia	371
16. Concord	390
17. Morenci	406
18. Mancelona	433
19. Johannesburg-Lewiston	473
20. Kalamazoo Christian	475
21. Reading	501
22. Waterford Our Lady of the Lakes	591
23. Ubly	610
24. New Lothrop	613
25. Saginaw Michigan Lutheran	615
26. Grosse Pointe University Liggett	621
27. St Joseph Lake Michigan Catholic	649

2012 GIRLS DIVISION 4 INDIVIDUALS
1. Kirsten Olling (Breckenridge)11	18:00
2. Holly Bullough (Traverse City St Francis)9	18:32
3. Tessa Fornari (Waterford Our Lady Lakes)9	18:39
4. Taylor Smith (Blanchard-Montabella)11	18:55
5. Kendra Colesa (Deckerville)11	19:00
6. Lauren Jenkins (Saugatuck)11	19:15
7. Moriah Hill-Green (Potterville)11	19:17
8. Hannah Steffke (Beal City)9	19:26
9. Jessica Reagle (Homer)10	19:27
10. Rhi Cullip (Harbor Springs)12	19:29
11. Jenna Wisner (Lutheran Westland)9	19:31
12. Ruth Letherer (Pittsford)10	19:33
13. Kate McLain (Kalamazoo Christian)11	19:45
14. Avery Lowe (North Muskegon)10	19:49
15. Larissa Langerak (GR Covenant Christian)9	19:52
19. Bailey Manis (Homer)10	20:00
23. Amanda Reagle (Homer)11	20:05
45. Kayla Kline (Homer)9	20:38
70. Johnica March (Homer)12	21:02
145. Alexis Mestdagh (Homer)	22:17
181. Kirsten King (Homer)9	23:11

2013 D4 GIRLS

"It makes me happy and proud to think that I am one of the few that have done it," said Kirsten Olling of Breckenridge of her fourth-straight victory in 17:45, breaking the course record for D4 by 10 seconds.

"The course was all muddy; it was a true cross country course. There was mud, there was water, it was great really."

Beal City, coached by Dave King, topped Breckenridge for the team win, 120-136.

Michigan Int. Speedway, Brooklyn, Nov. 2
2013 GIRLS DIVISION 4 TEAMS
1. Beal City	120
2. Breckenridge	136
3. Bear Lake	158
4. Pewamo-Westphalia	160

5. Homer 165
6. Sandusky 185
7. Saugatuck 213
8. Traverse City St Francis 259
9. Blanchard-Montabella 260
10. Unionville-Sebewaing 303
11. Concord 325
12. Grand Traverse Academy 339
13. Reading 361
14. Mendon 406
15. Royal Oak Shrine 420
16. North Muskegon 432
17. Lutheran Westland 444
18. Waterford Our Lady of the Lakes 459
19. Ubly 471
20. Britton Deerfield 500
21. Sand Creek 527
22. Kalamazoo Christian 544
23. Indian River Inland Lakes 569
24. Johannesburg-Lewiston 590
25. Rogers City 620
26. Auburn Hills Oakland Christian 631
27. St Joseph Lake Michigan Catholic 737

2013 GIRLS DIVISION 4 INDIVIDUALS

1. Kirsten Olling (Breckenridge)12 17:45
2. Tessa Fornari (Waterford Our Lady/Lakes)10 18:42
3. Holly Bullough (Traverse City St Francis)10 19:00
4. Kendra Colesa (Deckerville)12 19:13
5. Kayla Keane (East Jordan)11 19:19
6. Amanda Reagle (Homer)12 19:22
7. Jenna Wisner (Lutheran Westland)10 19:23
8. Isabella Tremonti (Bellaire)12 19:25
9. Lauren Jenkins (Saugatuck)12 19:26
10. Hannah Steffke (Beal City)10 19:27
11. Taylor Smith (Blanchard-Montabella)12 19:28
12. Kate McLain (Kalamazoo Christian)12 19:35
13. Betsy Arens (Pewamo-Westphalia)12 19:46
14. Terasa Eidenier (Reading)10 19:46
15. Alexis McConnell (Mt Pleasant Sacred Heart)9 19:47
19. Hannah Neyer (Beal City)12 19:57
30. Emily Steffke (Beal City)11 20:13
58. Ariel Salter (Beal City)9 20:53
66. Brenda Faber (Beal City)9 21:05
70. Haley Neyer (Beal City)11 21:12
230. Rachel Schwerin (Beal City)11 25:44

2014 D4 GIRLS

Ava Strenge of Battle Creek St. Philip—only 73rd the year before—ran neck-and-neck with Sacred Heart's Alexis McConnell before outsprinting her on the final stretch to win in 18:55.

"The best I expected to be was in the top 10, so it was a real surprise. When we hit the 4K mark, I kind of thought, 'Maybe if I push it, I've got a shot.' It certainly felt like my best race. I went out and gave it my all."

Beal City held off Kalamazoo Hackett to hold on to the trophy for another year.

Michigan Int. Speedway, Brooklyn, Nov. 1 ☒
2014 GIRLS DIVISION 4 TEAMS

1. Beal City 94
2. Kalamazoo Hackett 108
3. Mt. Pleasant Sacred Heart 130
4. Harbor Springs 156
5. Bear Lake-Onekama 180
6. Reading 243
7. Breckenridge 252
8. Saugatuck 256
9. Manton 340
10. Ubly 350
11. New Lothrop 384
12. Royal Oak Shrine 399
13. Maple City Glen Lake 400
14. Hillsdale Academy 414
15. Blanchard-Montabella 426
16. Wixom St. Catherine 427
17. Fowler 435
18. Britton Deerfield 442
19. Waterford Our Lady of the Lakes 459
20. Muskegon Western Michigan Christian 467
21. Mendon 501
22. Rogers City 506
23. Grosse Pointe Woods University Liggett 513
24. Riverview Richard 521
25. North Muskegon 536
26. Indian River Inland Lakes 565
27. Kalamazoo Christian 796

2014 GIRLS DIVISION 4 INDIVIDUALS

1. Ava Strenge (Battle Creek St Philip)10 18:55
2. Alexis McConnell (Mt Pleasant Sacred Ht)10 18:59
3. Mary Ankenbauer (Kalamazoo Hackett)9 18:59
4. Avery Lowe (North Muskegon)12 19:15
5. Emily Steffke (Beal City)12 19:15
6. Hannah Steffke (Beal City)11 19:26
7. Kaitlin Grigg (Maple City Glen Lake)12 19:35
8. Tessa Fornari (Waterford Our Lady/Lakes)11 19:35
9. Lucy Ankenbauer (Kalamazoo Hackett)12 19:36
10. Jenna Wisner (Lutheran Westland)11 19:41
11. Andrea Jagielski (Hillsdale Academy)10 19:42
12. Caitlin Henne (Springport)9 19:43
13. Bailley McConnell (Mt Pleasant Sacred Ht)9 19:48
14. Alicia Roney (Waldron)11 19:49
15. Paisley Sipes (Saugatuck)9 19:53
27. Hayley Neyer (Beal City)12 20:18
41. Madeline Steffke (Beal City)9 20:41
55. Ariel Salter (Beal City)10 20:56
93. Brenda Faber (Beal City)10 21:42
212. Rachel Schwerin (Beal City)12 24:37

2015 D4 GIRLS

Powered by the McConnell family, Mt. Pleasant Sacred Heart roared to a 52-point winning performance. Junior Alexis placed 4th, sophomore Bailey 5th and frosh Cammie 17th. Another 9th-grader, Scout Nelson, was 10th.

The individual race was won by Tessa Fornari of Waterford's Our Lady of the Lakes. "I'm so proud that I made it to this point after four years… I just sprinted as fast as I could that last 800 because I knew that I wanted it."

Tessa Fornari held on to beat defending champion Ava Strenge. (Pete Draugalis photo)

Michigan Int. Speedway, Brooklyn, Nov. 7 ☒
2015 GIRLS DIVISION 4 TEAMS

1. Mt Pleasant Sacred Heart 52
2. Harbor Springs 119
3. Saugatuck 124
4. Beal City 156
5. Kalamazoo Hackett 246
6. Hudson 274
7. Manton 301
8. Fowler 306
9. Concord 314
10. Frankfort 354
11. Hillsdale Academy 355
12. Ubly 361
13. Waterford Our Lady of the Lakes 371
14. New Lothrop 375
15. Grosse Pointe Woods University Liggett 385
16. Sand Creek 434
17. White Cloud 437
18. Battle Creek St Philip 443
19. Blanchard-Montabella 452
20. Mason County Eastern 472
21. Indian River Inland Lakes 504
22. Byron Center Zion Christian 513
23. Southfield Christian 547
24. Royal Oak Shrine 553
25. Mendon 569
26. Riverview Richard 577
27. East Jordan 641

2015 GIRLS DIVISION 4 INDIVIDUALS

1. Tessa Fornari (Waterford Our Lady/Lakes)12 18:15
2. Ava Strenge (Battle Creek St. Philip)11 18:24
3. Mary Ankenbauer (Kalamazoo Hackett)10 18:43
4. Alexis McConnell (Mt Pleasant Sacred H)11 18:56
5. Bailley McConnell (Mt Pleasant Sacred H)10 19:12
6. Caitlin Henne (Springport)10 19:13
7. Samantha Saenz (Concord)10 19:13
8. Paisley Sipes (Saugatuck)10 19:14
9. Riley Rutherford (Battle Creek St. Philip)12 19:20
10. Scout Nelson (Mt Pleasant Sacred Heart)9 19:20
11. Hannah Steffke (Beal City)12 19:20
12. Jenna Wisner (Lutheran Westland)12 19:23
13. Kensington Garvey (Blanchard-Montab)12 19:24
14. Chloe Brittain (Breckenridge)10 19:26
15. Haili Gusa (Ubly)9 19:26
17. Cammie McConnell (MP Sacred Heart)9 19:32
26. Lauren MacDonald (MP Sacred Heart)9 20:00
36. Megan Nowak (Mt Pleasant Sacred H)10 20:27
47. Rowan Fitzpatrick (MP Sacred Heart)10 20:45

2016 D4 GIRLS

Senior Ava Strenge of Battle Creek St. Philip roared back to recapture the title she first won as a sophomore. "I'm not really a good sprinter," she said, "so I wanted a good lead so they wouldn't pass me in the straightaway.

Mt. Pleasant Sacred Heart was better than ever, notching a record-low score of 34 points to beat runner-up Pewamo-Westphalia by 82 points, the biggest margin in meet history. Three McConnell sisters placed in the top 5, with a new one, freshman Desiree, in 26th.

Michigan Int. Speedway, Brooklyn, Nov. 5 ☒
2016 GIRLS DIVISION 4 TEAMS

1. Mt Pleasant Sacred Heart 34
2. Pewamo-Westphalia 116
3. Harbor Springs 151
4. Breckenridge 239
5. Hillsdale Academy 243
6. Kalamazoo Hackett 276
7. Manton 289
8. Indian River Inland Lakes 302
9. Muskegon Western Michigan Christian 311
10. Hudson 335
11. Bear Lake-Onekama 347
12. Sand Creek 353
13. Carson City-Crystal 365
14. Ubly 377
15. Lake Leelanau St Mary 387
16. Fowler 413
17. Grosse Pointe Woods University Liggett 438
18. Potterville 462
19. Ellsworth 464
20. Battle Creek St Philip 470
21. Royal Oak Shrine 473
22. Waterford Our Lady of the Lakes 512
23. Kingston 513
24. White Cloud 553

25. Holton 583
26. Southfield Christian 600
27. Marcellus 610

2016 GIRLS DIVISION 4 INDIVIDUALS
1. Ava Strenge (Battle Creek St Philip)12 .... 18:28
2. Bailley McConnell (Mt Pleasant Sacred H)11 18:56
3. Samantha Saenz (Concord)11 .... 19:05
4. Alexis McConnell (Mt Pleasant Sacred H)12. 19:10
5. Cammie McConnell (MP Sacred Heart)10 ... 19:11
6. Aubrey George (Pewamo-Westphalia)9 .... 19:22
7. Andrea Jagielski (Hillsdale Academy)12 ...... 19:22
8. Alyssa Kihnke (Harbor Springs)11 .... 19:23
9. Megan Nichols (Auburn Hills Oakland Chr)12 19:29
10. Mary Ankenbauer (Kalamazoo Hackett)11 .. 19:30
11. Lauren MacDonald (MP Sacred Heart)10 ... 19:41
12. Chloe Brittain (Breckenridge)11 .... 19:56
13. Kylie Sikkema (Marion)12 .... 20:00
14. Haili Gusa (Ubly)10 .... 20:00
15. Ellie Fleming (Harbor Springs)10 .... 20:01
20. Scout Nelson (Mt Pleasant Sacred H)10 .... 20:10
25. Desiree McConnell (MP Sacred Heart)9 .... 20:15
31. Rowan Fitzpatrick (MP Sacred Heart)11 .... 20:28

Senior Ava Strenge recaptured the title she first won as a sophomore. (Pete Draugalis)

2017 D4 GIRLS

Mt. Pleasant Sacred Heart, coached by Mark Zitzelsberger, won a third-straight time, its 39-point tally besting runner-up Ubly by 99 points, a meet record winning margin.

Samantha Saenz of Concord put together a 28-second win to capture the top spot in 18:17. The senior explained that she dedicates her races to her sister, who died the year before. "Ever since she passed it's been hard on my family... I really run for her."

Michigan Int. Speedway, Brooklyn, Nov. 4 ☒
2017 GIRLS DIVISION 4 TEAMS
1. Mt. Pleasant Sacred Heart 39
2. Ubly 138
3. Lansing Christian 141
4. Hudson 210
5. Breckenridge 211
6. Lake Leelanau St. Mary 251
7. Deckerville 276
8. Sand Creek 304
9. Fowler 314
10. Pittsford 316

11. East Jordan 316
12. Frankfort 370
13. Carson City-Crystal 378
14. Plymouth Christian 400
15. Bridgman 403
16. White Cloud 406
17. Bear Lake-Onekama 417
18. Ellsworth 417
19. Kalamazoo Hackett 447
20. Hudsonville Libertas Christian 453
21. Centreville 464
22. Gobles 466
23. Waterford Our Lady of the Lakes 532
24. Lutheran Westland 570
25. Rogers City 599
26. Big Rapids Crossroads 630
27. Rochester Hills Lutheran Northwest 696

2017 GIRLS DIVISION 4 INDIVIDUALS
1. Samantha Saenz (Concord)12 .... 18:17
2. Bailley McConnell (Mt Pleasant Sacred H)12.18:45
3. Scout Nelson (Mt Pleasant Sacred Heart)11..18:47
4. Mary Ankenbauer (Kalamazoo Hackett)12....18:58
5. Madison Volz (Lansing Christian)9 .... 19:03
6. Anna Mason (Hudsonville Libertas Chr)11 .. 19:13
7. Haili Gusa (Ubly)11 .... 19:16
8. Desiree McConnell (MP Sacred Heart)10 ... 19:21
9. Hanna Grant Lake (Leelanau St. Mary)12....19:28
10. Olivia Hankey (Waterford Our Lady/Lks)12..19:32
11. Chloe Brittain (Breckenridge)12 .... 19:41
12. Josie Aardema (Muskegon WM Chr)11 ... 19:42
13. Lexi Kinnas (Lansing Christian)9 .... 19:42
14. Skylar Thompson (Concord)9 .... 19:43
15. Ellie Kendell (Royal Oak Shrine)10 .... 19:45
19. Lauren MacDonald (MP Sacred Heart)11 .. 19:57
23. Rowan Fitzpatrick (MP Sacred Heart)12 ... 20:02
36. Sara Peltier (Mt Pleasant Sacred Heart)10 ..20:32
128. Michele Reinke (MP Sacred Heart)10 ..... 22:21

2018 D4 GIRLS

All eyes were on Abby VanderKooi, the frosh phenom who had broken 17:00 in three races during the season, reportedly the first time a 9th grader had ever done that in U.S. history. She didn't waste time here, moving to a huge lead in the opening minutes and never looking back through splits of 5:33 and 11:21. She won in 17:48, with a margin of nearly a quarter mile.

VanderKooi explained that it was her first race on the course but she knew it well: "I've been coming to this race since I was very, very little" to watch her brother run. "I wouldn't have minded running a little faster, but it was very muddy. This is the muddiest course I've ever run on."

The team race was close, with Mt. Pleasant Sacred Heart holding off Saugatuck, returning to this division after two years in Div. 3. The defenders packed three in the top 10 to triumph by 13 points for a record fourth in a row.

Michigan Int. Speedway, Brooklyn, Nov. 3 ☒
Mostly cloudy, muddy, 40°, breezy.
2018 GIRLS DIVISION 4 TEAMS
1. Mt Pleasant Sacred Heart 69
2. Saugatuck 82
3. Muskegon Western Michigan Christian 199
4. Hillsdale Academy 235
5. Pittsford 245
6. Frankfort 275
7. Fowler 278
8. Ubly 278
9. East Jordan 298
10. Hudson 312
11. Plymouth Christian 320
12. Lansing Christian 322
13. Lake Leelanau St Mary 369
14. Battle Creek St Phillip 389
15. Bridgman 390
16. Carson City-Crystal 400

17. Ellsworth 410
18. Royal Oak Shrine 439
19. Breckenridge 454
20. Marcellus 458
21. Saginaw Michigan Lutheran 497
22. Maple City Glen Lake 499
23. Dryden 504
24. Potterville 516
25. Clarkston Everest Collegiate 529
26. Johannesburg-Lewiston 569
27. Athens 677

2018 GIRLS DIVISION 4 INDIVIDUALS
1. Abby VanderKooi (Muskegon W Mich Christ)9 ... 17:48
2. Madison Volz (Lansing Christian)10 .... 19:03
3. Ellie Kendell (Royal Oak Shrine)11 .... 19:14
4. Thea Johnson (Saugatuck)12 .... 19:27
5. Riley Ford (Marlette)11 .... 19:35
6. Desiree McConnell (MP Sacred Heart)11 ...... 19:45
7. Taylor Conner (Saugatuck)12 .... 19:47
8. Scout Nelson (MP Sacred Heart)12 .... 19:51
9. Renee Osborne (Pittsford)12 .... 19:51
10. Lauren McDonald (MP Sacred Heart)12 ...... 19:51
11. Natalie Martinson (Saugatuck)12 .... 19:52
12. Caleigh Winters (Potterville)11 .... 19:56
13. Haley Rowbotham (Mayville)10 .... 19:59
14. Skylar Thompson (Concord)10 .... 20:00
15. Haili Gusa (Ubly)12 .... 20:07
18. Cammie McConnell (MP Sacred Heart)12 .... 20:14
54. Riley Hacker (MP Sacred Heart)9 .... 21:27
93. Sara Peltier (MP Sacred Heart)11 .... 22:09
145. Michele Reinke (MP Sacred Heart)11 .... 23.03

2019 D4 GIRLS

Abby VanderKooi, the sophomore defending champ from Muskegon Western Michigan Christian, came in as the overwhelming favorite and ran like it. At the mile (5:36), she led by more than 150m. At 2M (11:28) she led by more than 300. She finished in 18:11 to win her second title.

"I didn't feel as good this year, but the conditions were about the same as last year," said VanderKooi. She added that the course was very soft, especially in the final stretch. "I kind of struggled the last mile, especially that last section."

Bridgman, coached by Spencer Carr, edged 4-time defending champs Sacred Heart, 132-148.

Abby VanderKooi won her second in 2019. (Pete Draugalis photo)

Michigan Int. Speedway, Brooklyn, Nov. 2 ☒

2019 GIRLS DIVISION 4 TEAMS
1. Bridgman 132
2. Mt Pleasant Sacred Heart 148
3. Kalamazoo Christian 174
4. Hillsdale Academy 219
5. Hudson 221
6. Battle Creek St Phillip 254
7. Adrian Lenawee Christian 258
8. Muskegon Western Michigan Christian 309
9. East Jordan 310
10. Clarkston Everest Collegiate 317
11. Allen Park Cabrini 318
12. Harbor Beach 344
13. Johannesburg-Lewiston 366
14. Owendale-Gagetown 371
15. Carson City-Crystal 375
16. Deckerville 397
17. Beal City 400
18. Frankfort 421
19. Fowler 431
20. Ellsworth 436
21. Fruitport Calvary Christian 463
22. Leland 500
23. Maple City Glen Lake 505
24. Morrice 525
25. Royal Oak Shrine 546
26. Saranac 550
27. Marcellus 679

2019 GIRLS DIVISION 4 INDIVIDUALS
1. Abby VanderKooi (Muskegon W Mich Christ)10 .. 18:11
2. Riley Ford (Marlette)12 .... 19:23
3. Madison Volz (Lansing Christian)11 .... 19:31
4. Makenna Scott (Maple City Glen Lake)10 .... 19:32
5. Skylar Thompson (Concord)11 .... 19:39
6. Karsyn Stewart (Bridgman)11 .... 19:39
7. Erika Van Loton (Westland Huron Valley)9 .... 19:52
8. Kaylee Locke (Beal City)9 .... 19:54
9. Haley Rowbotham (Mayville)11 .... 19:55
10. Rachal Weber (Beal City)10 .... 19:55
11. Arie Hackett (Bridgman)10 .... 19:59
12. Olivia Ervin (Mt Pleasant Sacred Heart)9 .... 20:02
13. Desiree McConnell (Mt Pleasant Sacred H)12 .. 20:10
14. Miriam Murrell (Gaylord St Mary)8 .... 20:12
15. Alexis Tracey (Brethren)11 .... 20:16
39. Summer Fast (Bridgman)9 .... 21:00
68. Jane Kaspar (Bridgman)10 .... 21:44
81. Mikaela Owen (Bridgman)12 .... 21:56
221. Grace Fenech (Bridgman)10 .... 26:01
223. Alexa Ackerman (Bridgman)11 .... 26:02

CLASS D/D4 STATISTICS

TOP 25 CLOCKINGS AT MIS
17:45 Kirsten Olling (Breckenridge)12 2013
17:48 Abby VanderKooi (Musk WM Christ)9 ... 2018
17:55 Marissa Treece (Maple City Glen Lk)12 2006
17:58 Treece 2005
18:00 Olling 2012
18:03 Olling 2011
18:10 Olling 2010
18:11 VanderKooi 2019
18:15 Tessa Fornari (Waterford OLLakes)12 .. 2015
18:17 Laura Rolf (RH Lutheran NW)10 2002
18:17 Samantha Saenz (Concord)12 2017
18:20 Lauren Fairbanks (Rogers City)10 2000
18:21 Treece 2004
18:24 Kimi Landane (Atlanta)12 1999
18:24 Caitlin Kelly (Kinde-North Huron)12 2002
18:24 Ava Strenge (Battle Creek St Philip)11 . 2015
18:26 Jennifer Leichtman (AA Greenhills)12 .. 2000
18:28 Strenge 2016
18:30 Rolf 2003
18:30 Lindsay Neal (North Muskegon)9 2007
18:31 Jackie Rivard (Ubly)12 2004
18:32 Holly Bullough (TC St Francis)9 2012
18:36 Bridget Bennett (MP Sacred Heart)12 .. 2009
18:37 Kaylee Kreft (Rogers City)9 2005
18:37 Bridget Bennett (MP Sacred Heart)11 .. 2008

BIGGEST WINNING MARGINS
123.4 Gina VanLaar/Julie Quillen .... 1983 I
81   Mary Lantinga/Jennifer Gerlach .... 1989 T
80.7 Jenny Gradowski/Lisa Meier .... 1985 T
80.0 Betsy Speer/Katy Speer .... 1993 T
75.6 Abby VanderKooi/Madison Volz 2018

SMALLEST WINNING MARGINS
0.6   Kasey Culp/Betsy Speer 1996
2.0   Katie Martin/Shannon TenBrock .... 1988 T
3.6   Ava Strenge/Alexis McConnell 2014
4   Julie Lantis/Mary Mullally 1977
4   Erika Davis/Nikki Bennett .... 1990 T

LOWEST WINNING SCORES
25   Potterville 1976
27   Whitmore Lake 1993
34   Mt Pleasant Sacred Heart 2016
37   Bear Lake 1994
38   Suttons Bay 1987
39   Mt Pleasant Sacred Heart 2017
42   Fowler 1989
46   Potterville 1990
50   Mendon 1997
52   Whitmore Lake 1996
52   Mt Pleasant Sacred Heart 2015

HIGHEST WINNING SCORES
135   Traverse City St Francis 2003
132   Big Rapids Crossroads 2005
132   Bridgman 2019
120   Beal City 2013
118   Kingston 1983
118   Homer 2012
116   Maple City Glen Lake 2000
115   Big Rapids Crossroads 2004
109   GR NorthPointe Christian 2007
106   Mendon 1998

CLOSEST TEAM FINISH
0   Kingston/Dansville 1983
1   Ann Arbor Greenhills/Flint Holy Rosary 1979
2   Suttons Bay/Akron-Fairgrove 1985
3   Concord/Southfield Christian 1984
4   Akron-Fairgrove/Potterville 1978
4   Hesperia/Harbor Springs 2010

BIGGEST WINNING TEAM MARGIN
99   MP Sacred Heart/Ubly 2017
82   MP Sacred Heart/Pewamo-Westphalia . 2016
74   Schoolcraft/Potterville 1992
72   Ann Arbor Greenhills/Maple City Glen L 2001
67   MP Sacred Heart/Harbor Springs 2015

1980 Champions: Ann Arbor Greenhills

XC! High School Cross Country in Michigan

GIRLS UP CLASS AB / DIV. 1

1978 UP GIRLS

Eight of 14 invited schools made it to the first UP finals for girls. Marquette captured the crown with a slim four-point margin. Coach Dale Phillips said, "We had some injuries, but they came back and showed me a lot of guts."

Gladstone GC, Gladstone, Oct. 18
1978 GIRLS UP TEAMS
1. Marquette 41
2. Ishpeming 45
3. Gwinn 80
4. Calumet 89
5. Hancock 126

1978 GIRLS UP INDIVIDUALS
1. Penny Martin (Marquette)12 .... 19:41
2. Nancy Liljequist (Ishpeming) 19:57
3. Karen Schei (Marquette)12 .... 20:08
4. Leah Johns (Wakefield) .... nt
5. Kim Peterson (Gwinn) .... nt

1979 UP GIRLS

Kim Peterson broke the Gladstone course record that Penny Martin had set the previous year. Ishpeming moved up to the top spot in the closest of team races, winning by one point over Gwinn and Marquette.

The Ishpeming championship squad of 1979.

Gladstone GC, Gladstone, Oct. 17
1979 GIRLS UP TEAMS
1. Ishpeming 66
2. Gwinn 67
3. Marquette 67
4. Hancock 122
5. Rock Mid-Peninsula 183

1979 GIRLS UP INDIVIDUALS
1. Kim Peterson (Gwinn)12 .... 19:38
2. Mary Radecki (Rudyard) 19:43
3. Penny Tussing (Chassell) 19:54
4. Kara Braak (Marquette) 20:00
5. Kyrin Smith (Marquette) 20:04

1980 UP GIRLS

Ishpeming got lucky in Class C-D. Rival Negaunee ran 1-2 and put three runners in the top six, but didn't have the five necessary to get a team score. In Class A-B, Marquette had five of the top six finishers. That added up to a perfect 15, since third-placer Denise Gentile didn't count in team scoring because Menominee failed to field a full team. Missing from the race was injured Kim Peterson of Gwinn, who had dominated UP running all fall. The races was held on a 3M course.

Gladstone GC, Gladstone, Oct. 15
1980 GIRLS UP CLASS AB TEAMS
1. Marquette 15
2. Calumet 63
3. Gwinn 73
4. Gladstone 96
5. Escanaba 123

1980 GIRLS UP CLASS AB INDVIDUALS
1. Kara Braak (Marquette)10 .... 19:10
2. Kyrin Smith (Marquette)10 .... 19:26
3. Denise Gentile (Menominee)11 .... 19:53
4. Kelly Russell (Marquette) 20:17
5. Lisa Schwindt (Marquette) 20:25

1980 GIRLS UP CLASS CD TEAMS
1. Ishpeming 21
2. Hancock 57
3. Ishpeming Westwood 79
4. Chassell 90
5. Mid-Peninsula 128

1980 GIRLS UP CLASS CD INDIVIDUALS
1. Sue Terres (Negaunee) 19:38
2. Sue Luokkala (Negaunee) 19:55
3. Nancy Lilequist (Ishpeming) 20:09
4. Ann Cevigney (Ishpeming) 20:25
5. Tammy Hanlon (Ishpeming) 20:33

1981 UP GIRLS

Marquette captured the top two places to key an overwhelming team win in A-B. "They just ran their hardest," said coach Dale Phillips. The top three runners from 1980 repeated their positions a year later.

Marquette Golf and CC, Marquette, Oct. 14
1981 GIRLS UP CLASS A/B TEAMS
1. Marquette 23
2. Gladstone 68
3. Menominee 78
4. Gwinn 94
5. Escanaba 98

1981 GIRLS UP CLASS A/B INDIVIDUALS
1. Kara Braak (Marquette)11 .... 19:12
2. Kyrin Smith (Marquette)11 .... 19:42
3. Denise Gentile (Menominee)12 .... 19:56
4. Shari Ahola (Gwinn) 20:14
5. Liz Sarvello (Marquette)11 .... 20:26

1981 GIRLS UP CLASS C/D TEAMS
1. Negaunee 55
2. Ishpeming Westwood 57
3. Calumet 58
4. Ishpeming 105
5. Painesdale-Jeffers 111

1981 GIRLS UP CLASS C/D INDIVIDUALS
1. Beth Collins (Negaunee)10 .... 18:45
2. Ann Cevigney (Ishpeming) 19:32
3. Rachelle Olsen (Ishpeming Westwood) .. 19:40
4. Sue Terres (Isphemimg Westwood)12 ... 19:45
5. Julane Andrews (Painesdale-Jeffers) .. 19:53

1982 UP GIRLS

Marquette scored a perfect 15 against the four-team Class A competition. Kara Braak ran to 5th place in her second race since a September stress fracture.

Days River Golf Club, Gladstone, Oct. 13
1982 GIRLS UP CLASS A/B TEAMS
1. Marquette 15
2. Menominee 71
3. Gladstone 78
4. Escanaba 80

1982 GIRLS UP CLASS A/B INDIVIDUALS
1. Shelly Loukkala (Marquette)9 .... 18:24
2. Kyrin Smith (Marquette)12 .... 18:54
3. Lisa Schwindt (Marquette)11 .... 19:20
4. Liz Sarvello (Marquette) 19:21
5. Kara Braak (Marquette) 19:39

1982 GIRLS UP CLASS C/D TEAMS
1. Negaunee 34
2. Ishpeming Westwood 72
3. Painesdale-Jeffers 80
4. Calumet 107
5. Ishpeming 110

1982 GIRLS UP CLASS C/D INDIVIDUALS
1. Beth Collins (Negaunee) 18:07
2. Tracy Babcock (Iron Mountain)10 ..... 18:40
3. Wendy Babcock (Iron Mountain)9 .... 19:06
4. Lesley Coduti (Negaunee) 19:36
5. Stephanie Todd (Chassell) 19:38

1983 UP GIRLS

The Babcock sisters produced the two fastest times of the day in leading Class C-D. Negaunee added the women's title to go with the men's it had won. Marquette won Class A-B with five runners in the top seven. "It was a tremendous performance by the girls in those weather conditions," said coach Dale Phillips. Conditions were "sloppy", with plenty of standing water and mud on the course.

Marquette Golf and CC, Marquette, Oct. 12
1983 GIRLS UP CLASS A/B TEAMS
1. Marquette 22
2. Menominee 76
3. Gladstone 77
4. Gwinn 91
5. Escanaba 100

1983 GIRLS UP CLASS A/B INDIVIDUALS
1. Kris Koski (Gwinn)9 .... 20:47
2. Shelly Luokkala (Marquette)10 .... 20:53
3. Jennifer Smith (Marquette)9 .... 21:29
4. Katherine Cooper (Marquette) 21:39
5. Julie Weinfurter (Kingsford) 21:44

1983 GIRLS UP CLASS C/D TEAMS
1. Negaunee 46
2. Ishpeming Westwood 67
3. Iron Mountain 87
4. Calumet 138
5. Stephenson 143

1983 GIRLS UP CLASS C/D INDIVIDUALS
1. Traci Babcock (Iron Mountain)11 ...... 19:42
2. Wendy Babcock (Iron Mountain)10 .. 19:48
3. Jessica Green (Ishpeming Westwood)9 .. 20:19
4. Stephanie Todd (Chassel) 20:23
5. Beth Collins (Negaunee) 20:33

1984 UP GIRLS

Painesdale-Jeffers won its first Class D title. Said coach Terry LaJeunesse, "The girls were ready to run yesterday; they were anxious to get out on the course."

Marquette Golf and CC, Marquette, Oct. 10
1984 GIRLS UP CLASS A/B TEAMS
1. Marquette 23
2. Escanaba 52

3. Gladstone 71
4. Menominee 84

1984 GIRLS UP CLASS A/B INDIVIDUALS
1. Julie Weinfurter (Kingsford)12 ....20:19
2. Lorraine Boucher (Escanaba) 20:30
3. Jennifer Smith (Marquette)10 ....20:42
4. Kelley Abramson (Marquette) 20:51
5. Monica Metivier (Escanaba) 20:55

1984 GIRLS UP CLASS C TEAMS
1. Ishpeming Westwood 42
2. Negaunee 67
3. Calumet 70
4. Iron Mountain 77
5. Stephenson 99

Traci Babcock later ran for Michigan.

1984 GIRLS UP CLASS C INDIVIDUALS
1. Traci Babcock (Iron Mountain)12 ....18:07
2. Wendy Babcock (Iron Mountain)11 ....18:25
3. Jesse Green (Ishpeming Westwood)10 ....18:48
4. Brita Sturos (Calumet) 19:38
5. Heidi Robson (Ishpeming Westwood) 19:53

1984 GIRLS UP CLASS D TEAMS
1. Painesdale-Jeffers 30
2. Chassell 40
3. Hancock 56
4. Crystal Falls-Forest Park 89

1984 GIRLS UP CLASS D INDIVIDUALS
1. Stephanie Todd (Chassell) 19:46
2. Maria Skates (Hancock) 20:36
3. Jenny Asiala (Painesdale-Jeffers)9 ....21:38
4. Kim DeForge (Painesdale-Jeffers) 21:48
5. Jill Aho (Chassell) 22:04

1985 UP GIRLS

Lorraine Boucher came through in Class A-B with her first win of the season. She had been troubled by tendinitis in her hip all fall. "I was really nervous before the meet but I felt confident after the first mile," she said.

Gladstone Golf Course, Gladstone, Oct. 19
1985 GIRLS UP CLASS A/B TEAMS
1. Marquette 21
2. Escanaba 78
3. Menominee 80
4. Gwinn 92
5. Gladstone 93

1985 GIRLS UP CLASS A/B TEAMS
1. Lorraine Boucher (Escanaba) 18:55
2. Jennifer Smith (Marquette)11 ....19:02
3. Laura Coughlin (Marquette)10 ....19:14
4. Kalley Abramson (Marquette) 19:31
5. Michelle Chause (Marquette) 19:49

1985 GIRLS UP CLASS C TEAMS
1. Calumet 31
2. Stephenson 47
3. Ishpeming Westwood 55
4. Houghton 134
5. Ishpeming 137

1985 GIRLS UP CLASS C INDIVIDUALS
1. Wendy Babcock (Iron Mountain)12 ....17:40
2. Brita Sturos (Calumet)10 ....18:16
3. Heidi Robson (Ishpeming Westwood) 18:56
4. Karla Parks (Calumet) 19:11
5. Terri Jeschke (Stephenson) 19:22

1985 GIRLS UP CLASS D TEAMS
1. Painesdale-Jeffers 24
2. Rock-Mid Peninsula 50
(only two schools fielded complete teams)

1985 GIRLS UP CLASS D INDIVIDUALS
1. Stephanie Todd (Chassell) 20:21
2. Kim DeForge (Painesdale-Jeffers) 20:49
3. Patty Thurber (Rock-Mid Peninsula) 20:56
4. Jennifer Asiala (Painesdale-Jeffers) 21:07
5. Nora Pietila (Painesdale-Jeffers) 22:10

1986 UP GIRLS

Undefeated Marquette dominated, winning easily despite the fact that two top runners were out with injuries. Said Coach Dale Phillips, "The girls have been undefeated and we knew we were a heavy favorite. We ran without Kelly [Abramson] and Leslie Davis."

Gladstone Golf Course, Gladstone, Oct. 18
1986 GIRLS UP CLASS A/B TEAMS
1. Marquette 19
2. Menominee 78
3. Sault Ste Marie 82
4. Escanaba 106
5. Gwinn 115

1986 GIRLS UP CLASS A/B INDIVIDUALS
1. Laura Coughlin (Marquette)11 ....19:10
2. Lisa Werner (Marquette)11 ....19:32
3. Jennifer Smith (Marquette)12 ....19:34
4. Karen Anderson (Sault Ste Marie) 19:51
5. Laura Ernsberger (Gwinn) 20:08

1986 GIRLS UP CLASS C/D TEAMS
1. Ishpeming Westwood 42
2. Calumet 55
3. Houghton 65
4. Negaunee 92
5. Hancock 97

1986 GIRLS UP CLASS C/D INDIVIDUALS
1. Brita Sturos (Calumet)11 ....19:17
2. Heidi Robson (Ishpeming Westwood) 19:24
3. Ann Bastian (Hancock) 20:11
4. Jamie Coduti (Negaunee) 20:13
5. Debbie Jobst (Houghton) 20:19

1987 UP GIRLS

Marquette won its ninth straight by piling up the best score possible. Not only did the Redettes tally 1st through 5th for 15 points, they added 6th and 7th place as well. "This is something that we've done all year long," said coach Dale Phillips. An upset in Class C-D saw defending champion Brita Sturos passed by two rivals in the final sprint. Soph Jamey Coduti of Negaunee grabbed the win. "The wind and cold slowed me down," said Coduti, "but I didn't let it get to me. I'm happy, but I'm really tired."

Marquette Golf and CC, Marquette, Oct. 24
1987 GIRLS UP CLASS A/B TEAMS
1. Marquette 15
2. Sault Ste Marie 62
3. Menominee 79
4. Kingsford 116
5. Gladstone 130

1987 GIRLS UP CLASS A/B INDIVIDUALS
1. Kelly Abramson (Marquette)12 ....18:57
2. Laura Coughlin (Marquette)12 ....19:17
3. Lisa Werner (Marquette)12 ....19:23
4. Michelle Chause (Marquette) 19:42
5. Anna Goodwin (Marquette) 19:58

1987 GIRLS UP CLASS C/D TEAMS
1. Calumet 66
2. Hancock 78
3. Iron Mountain 108
4. Negaunee 127
5. Houghton 127

1987 GIRLS UP CLASS C/D INDIVIDUALS
1. Jamey Coduti (Negaunee)10 ....19:14
2. Anne Borowski (Ironwood) 19:17
3. Brita Sturos (Calumet)12 ....19:18
4. Kimberly Lawton (Hancock) 19:22
5. Heidi Robson (Ishpeming Westwood) 19:39

1988 UP GIRLS

Class C-D saw one of the tightest team finishes ever. Stephenson won with 82 points and was followed by Calumet, Houghton and Ironwood, all with 83 points!

Marquette Golf and CC, Marquette, Oct. 22
1988 GIRLS UP CLASS A/B TEAMS
1. Marquette 21
2. Sault Ste Marie 60
3. Menominee 68
4. Kingsford 92
5. Gladstone 129

1988 GIRLS UP CLASS A/B INDIVIDUALS
1. Carla Johnson (Marquette)10 ....19:33
2. Sarah Hynnek (Menominee)12 ....19:45
3. Debbie Townsend (Marquette)12 ....19:50
4. Anne Goodwin (Marquette)10 ....20:17
5. Wendy Price (Marquette)11 ....20:20

1988 GIRLS UP CLASS C/D TEAMS
1. Stephenson 82
2. Calumet 83
3. Houghton 83
4. Ironwood 83
5. Hancock 103

1988 GIRLS UP CLASS C/D INDIVIDUALS
1. Debbie Bastian (Hancock)10 ....19:33
2. Jamey Coduti (Negaunee)11 ....19:51
3. Debbie Jobst (Houghton)12 ....20:04
4. Anne Borowski (Ironwood)10 ....20:14
5. Reva Rogers (Houghton)11 ....20:15

1989 UP GIRLS

Marquette won its tenth-straight title, led by junior Carla Johnson. Christie Nutkins of Newberry won in C/D. During the season she had nearly won the Lower Peninsula Michigan-Huron Shores League race, where she had been allowed to run as an exhibition competitior.

Gladstone Golf & CC, Gladstone, Oct. 21
1989 GIRLS UP CLASS A/B TEAMS
1. Marquette 22
2. Ironwood 70
3. Sault Ste Marie 80
4. Kingsford 82
5. Escanaba 108

1989 GIRLS UP CLASS A/B INDIVIDUALS
1. Carla Johnson (Marquette)11 ....20:54
2. Carol Anderson (Marquette)9 ....21:29
3. Joy Makinen (Ironwood)10 ....21:31
4. Hayley Murphy (Marquette) 21:46
5. Anne Goodwin (Marquette)11 ....21:47

1989 GIRLS UP CLASS C/D TEAMS
1. Calumet 41
2. Houghton 65
3. Hancock 73
4. Stephenson 76
5. Iron Mountain 139

1989 GIRLS UP CLASS C/D INDIVIDUALS
1. Christie Nutkins (Newberry) 21:12
2. Christine Heikkila (Calumet) 21:22
3. Kim Lawton (Hancock)11 .... 21:51
4. Reva Rogers (Houghton)12 .... 22:00
5. Carrie Nakkula (Calumet)10 .... 22:07

1990 UP GIRLS

Marquette's Carla Johnson became the first-ever three-time winner of a UP girls title. Said coach Dale Phillips, "She ran an intelligent race. She let Bobie and LaMaide go out quickly, and that took a lot out of them. She kept closing the gap."

Said Phillips, "There were two inches of snow on the course and some rain. The times were slow." The Marquette girls all wore spikes for the first time in the season. "It gave them a little confidence because the course was very slippery and slick on the corners. It gave them a psychological edge."

Gladstone Golf & CC, Gladstone, Oct. 20
1990 GIRLS UP CLASS A/B TEAMS
1. Marquette 24
2. Ironwood 64
3. Sault Ste Marie 98
4. Escanaba 107
5. Kingsford 117

1990 GIRLS UP CLASS A/B INDIVIDUALS
1. Carla Johnson (Marquette)12 .... 20:43
2. Mary LaMaide (Menominee)11 .... 21:01
3. Bobie Rodriguez (Marquette)10 .... 21:16
4. Lisa Larson (Marquette) 21:19
5. Angel Kusz (Ironwood) 21:23

1990 GIRLS UP CLASS C/D TEAMS
1. Hancock 41
2. Calumet 61
3. Iron Mountain 75
4. Stephenson 80
5. Ishpeming Westwood 98

1990 GIRLS UP CLASS C/D INDIVIDUALS
1. Christie Nutkins (Newberry) 20:49
2. Carrie Nakkula (Calumet)11 .... 20:50
3. Teri Lawton (Hancock) 21:03
4. Amy Larson (Ishpeming Westwood) 21:22
5. Lisa Wiitala (Hancock) 21:44

1991 UP GIRLS

All nine Class D girls teams ran the combined C-D race under protest. Said Rock-Mid Peninsula coach Verne Nelson, "The state bulletin says, 'if three or more schools are competing in a class, there shall be a separate race.' We were led to believe through our pre-race information there would be separate races for Class C and D. We believe this is illegal."

Countered meet director Boris Martycz, "I don't have any opinions either way. I'm just following the instructions from the state and trying to do the best job that I can."

Marquette won its 12th straight Class A-B state title, breaking the national record for consecutive wins. Coach Dale Phillips predicted that prospects for Number 13 looked good: "Of the eight girls we dressed, six are back next year." Team leader Amy Lassila led from wire-to-wire.

Marquette Golf and CC, Marquette, Oct. 1
1991 GIRLS UP CLASS A/B TEAMS
1. Marquette 19
2. Escanaba 66
3. Ishpeming Westwood 83
4. Sault Ste Marie 120
5. Gwinn 122

1991 GIRLS UP CLASS A/B INDIVIDUALS
1. Amy Lassila (Marquette)12 .... 19:47
2. Jolene Bennon (Ishpeming Westwood)10 ... 20:20
3. Bobie Rodriguez (Marquette)11 .... 20:30
4. Denise Wilcox (Marquette) 20:37
5. Lisa Larson (Marquette) 20:38

1991 GIRLS UP CLASS C/D TEAMS
1. Calumet 62
2. Ironwood 67
3. Stephenson 78
4. Superior Central 95
5. Hancock 129

1991 GIRLS UP CLASS C/D INDIVIDUALS
1. Liz Wilson (Houghton) 20:02
2. Carrie Nakkula (Calumet) 20:05
3. Angel Kusz (Ironwood)10 .... 20:18
4. Joy Makinen (Ironwood) 20:24
5. Tammy Anderson (Ishpeming) 20:33

1992 UP GIRLS

Westwood's Jolene Bennon knocked 40 seconds off the course record set earlier in the year. "There was a lot of pressure on today," she said. "It was a fast race." Marquette won its 13th straight A-B title.

Presque Ile Park, Marquette, Nov. 7
1992 GIRLS UP CLASS A/B TEAMS
1. Marquette 37
2. Escanaba 71
3. Ishpeming Westwood 72
4. Gladstone 108
5. Menominee 117

1992 GIRLS UP CLASS A/B INDIVIDUALS
1. Jolene Bennon (Ishpeming Westwood)11 ... 18:38
2. Lucy Lea (Marquette)9 .... 18:40
3. Lisa Hansen (Escanaba) 19:24
4. Amy Larson (Ishpeming Westwood) 19:31
5. Anderson (Marquette) 19:35

1992 GIRLS UP CLASS C/D TEAMS
1. Calumet 66
2. Stephenson 74
3. Ishpeming 102
4. Ironwood 104
5. Rock-Mid Peninsula 144

1992 GIRLS UP CLASS C/D INDIVIDUALS
1. Myra Peterson (Calumet)9 .... 18:42
2. Liz Wilson (Houghton) 18:59
3. Angel Kusz (Ironwood)11 .... 19:22
4. Tara Leppanen (Ishpeming) 19:29
5. Beth Durocher (Ishpeming) 19:37

1993 UP GIRLS

Marquette had won 13 straight state titles, but Westwood finally snapped the streak by scoring its first-ever victory. Said Marquette coach Dale Phillips, "We can't complain. We've had a lot of injuries and sickness this year. We're just glad to be here at all." Menominee ran a close third despite the fact its top runner, Kelli Haglund, couldn't run after two nights in a hospital. She had become "ill and disoriented" during her conference meet. Times were slower this year, because 140 yards had been added to the course to make it more accurate.

Presque Ile Park, Marquette, Oct. 23
1993 GIRLS UP CLASS A/B TEAMS
1. Ishpeming Westwood 54
2. Marquette 62
3. Menominee 67
4. Kingsford 93
5. Escanaba 105

1993 GIRLS UP CLASS A/B INDIVIDUALS
1. Lucy Lea (Marquette)10 .... 20:03
2. Angela Sandretto (Ishpeming Westwood)9 ... 20:29
3. Denelle Allsworth (Gladstone)12 .... 20:30
4. Hannah Rife (Marquette) 20:45
5. Linette Schmidt (Kingsford) 20:52

1993 GIRLS UP CLASS C/D TEAMS
1. Calumet 37
2. Stephenson 89
3. Houghton 96
4. Rock-Mid Peninsula 104
5. Ironwood 112

1993 GIRLS UP CLASS C/D INDIVIDUALS
1. Myra Peterson (Calumet)10 .... 19:40
2. Liz Wilson (Houghton) 19:44
3. Faye Peterson (Rock-Mid Peninsula)9 .. 19:58
4. Angel Kusz (Ironwood)12 .... 20:21
5. Marissa Lupino (Ironwood)9 .... 20:29

1994 UP GIRLS

Faye Peterson captured Mid-Peninsula's first state crown. She admitted, "The little hills weren't bad, but the big one got me."

Marquette returned to the top of the podium with a 24-point win over Menominee.

Gladstone Golf & CC, Gladstone, Oct. 22
1994 GIRLS UP CLASS A/B TEAMS
1. Marquette 27
2. Menominee 51
3. Ishpeming Westwood 95
4. Kingsford 102
5. Gladstone 119

1994 GIRLS UP CLASS A/B TEAMS
1. Lucy Lea (Marquette)11 .... 20:20
2. Tarra Hodge (Menominee)10 .... 21:17
3. Angela Sandretto (Ishpeming-Westwood)10 ... 21:28
4. Jenny Morris (Marquette) 21:55
5. Michele Scherer (Marquette) 22:02

1994 GIRLS UP CLASS C TEAMS
1. Calumet 31
2. Stephenson 53
3. Ironwood 89
4. Houghton 109
5. Ishpeming 120

1994 GIRLS UP CLASS C INDIVIDUALS
1. Myra Peterson (Calumet)11 .... 21:16
2. Kate Hamblen (Stephenson) 21:36
3. Manssa Lupino (Ironwood)10 .... 21:44
4. Natalie Seel (Houghton) 22:10
5. Emily Pleshe (Calumet) 22:27

1994 GIRLS UP CLASS D TEAMS
1. Painesdale-Jeffers 26
2. Republic-Michigamme 64
3. Rock-Mid Peninsula 74
4. Eben Junction-Superior Central 89
5. Carney-Nadeau 99

1994 GIRLS UP CLASS D INDIVIDUALS
1. Faye Peterson (Rock-Mid Peninsula)10 ... 21:29
2. Jaclyn DeMars (Republic-Michigamme) .. 22:34
3. Vicki Stemhagen (Painesdale-Jeffers) .. 23:05
4. Sara Wesa (Painesdale-Jeffers) 23:10
5. Renee Johnson (Painesdale-Jeffers) ... 23:11

1995 UP GIRLS

Rock-Mid Peninsula scored its first-ever team win, a year after Faye Peterson captured the school's first individual title. "I'm still pretty numb," said coach Duane England. "I swore we could have flown as high as a B-52."

Red Fox Run Golf Course, Sawyer, Oct. 21
1995 GIRLS UP CLASS A/B TEAMS
1. Marquette..31
2. Menominee..46
3. Ishpeming Westwood..73
4. Kingsford...97
5. Gladstone..140

1995 GIRLS UP CLASS A/B INDIVIDUALS
1. Angela Sandretto (Ishpeming Westwood)11.......20:13
2. Lucy Lea (Marquette)12....................................20:17
3. Tarra Hodge (Menominee).................................20:50
4. Laura Burnette (Ishpeming Westwood)..............20:58
5. Jenny Morris (Marquette)...................................21:11

1995 GIRLS UP CLASS C TEAMS
1. Calumet..41
2. Stephenson..43
3. Ironwood..58
4. Hanock..127
5. Ishpeming...132

1995 GIRLS UP CLASS C INDIVIDUALS
1. Elizabeth Pietila (Hancock)10............................20:10
2. Myra Peterson (Calumet)12...............................20:48
3. Jenny Shull (Ironwood)10..................................21:05
4. Dussie Lord (Stephenson).................................21:22
5. Kelly Johnson (Calumet)....................................21:25

1995 GIRLS UP CLASS D TEAMS
1. Rock-Mid Peninsula..29
2. Carney-Nadeau..39
3. Eben-Superior Central.......................................58

1995 GIRLS UP CLASS D INDIVIDUALS
1. Faye Peterson (Rock-Mid Peninsula)11............21:39
2. Autumn Ahlgren (Rock-Mid Peninsula).............22:13
3. Theresa Brimmer (Engadine)............................22:36
4. Kristen Mattila (Republic Michigamme).............22:40
5. Valerie Quist (Carney-Nadeau)..........................23:09

1996 UP GIRLS

Ironwood won its first Class C title with a record-low 21 points. Said coach Bruce Beckman, "They placed first in eight of the nine invitationals they entered."
Faye Peterson of Rock-Mid Peninsula finished her career with three-straight wins.

Red Fox Run Golf Course, Sawyer, Oct. 19
1996 GIRLS UP CLASS A/B TEAMS
1. Marquette..52
2. Menominee..53
3. Ishpeming Westwood..70
4. Escanaba..110
5. Sault Ste Marie...140

1996 GIRLS UP CLASS A/B INDIVIDUALS
1. Angela Sandretto (Ishpeming Westwood)12......20:15
2. Krista O'Dell (Escanaba)9.................................20:38
3. Michelle Paul (Gladstone)9................................20:55
4. Hannah Wolfe (Menominee)...............................21:03
5. Lisa Abramson (Sault Ste Marie).......................21:05

1996 GIRLS UP CLASS C TEAMS
1. Ironwood...21
2. Calumet..57
3. Stephenson..62
4. Rudyard..117
5. Newberry..155

1996 GIRLS UP CLASS C INDIVIDUALS
1. Ann Somerville (Ironwood)11............................19:25
2. Elizabeth Pietila (Hancock)11............................19:49
3. Richelle Robinson (St Ignace)11......................21:03
4. Tara Makinen (Ironwood)..................................21:04
5. Kate Hambien (Stephenson).............................21:06

1996 GIRLS UP CLASS D TEAMS
1. Painesdale Jeffers..29
2. Republic-Michigamme..46
3. Rock-Mid Peninsula..47
4. Pickford..110

1996 GIRLS UP CLASS D INDIVIDUALS
1. Faye Peterson (Rock-Mid Peninsula)12............20:50
2. Theresa Brimmer (Engadine)11........................21:12
3. Jane Rautiola (Painesdale-Jeffers)9.................21:22
4. Autumn Ahlgren (Rock-Mid Peninsula).............21:59
5. Renee Johnson (Painesdale-Jeffers)................22:06

1997 UP GIRLS

Krista O'Dell of Escanaba built up a 59-second margin on the field to win her first title. Menominee captured the A-B team trophy for the first time.

Red Fox Run Golf Course, Sawyer, Oct. 18
1997 GIRLS UP CLASS A/B TEAMS
1. Menominee..44
2. Marquette..52
3. Escanaba..65
4. Sault Ste Marie...124
5. Gladstone...125

1997 GIRLS UP CLASS A/B INDIVIDUALS
1. Krista O'Dell (Escanaba)10...............................19:38
2. Jenna Weber (Kingsford)12...............................20:37
3. Erin Bourion (Menominee)10..............................20:40
4. Emily Anderson (Marquette)..............................20:44
5. Hannah Wolfe (Menominee)...............................20:48

1997 GIRLS UP CLASS C TEAMS
1. Ironwood...33
2. Calumet..63
3. Stephenson..68
4. Ishpeming Westwood..77
5. Newberry..133

1997 GIRLS UP CLASS C INDIVIDUALS
1. Ann Somerville (Ironwood)12............................19:04
2. Chelsea Finco (Ironwood)10.............................20:06
3. Hannah Vissering (Ishpeming Westw)9............20:42
4. Julie Juntilla (Calumet).....................................21:10
5. Allison Philippo (Stephenson)...........................21:11

1997 GIRLS UP CLASS D TEAMS
1. Republic Michigamme...25
2. St Ignace..51
3. Rock-Mid Peninsula..57

1997 GIRLS UP CLASS D INDIVIDUALS
1. Jane Rautiola (Painesdale-Jeffers)10...............20:25
2. Trisha Nyland (Crystal Falls-Forest Park)11.....20:51
3. Jamie Cooper (Carney Nadeau)12....................22:05
4. Theresa Warlin (Republic-Michigamme)............22:06
5. Melanie Dillon (Republic Michigamme)..............22:31

Marquette soph Emily Anderson dominated.

1998 UP GIRLS

Athletes made Upper Peninsula history by complaining about the heat for once. Temperatures rose into the mid-60s on race day, as Menominee defended its Class A-B crown with a 20-point margin over rival Marquette.

Red Fox Run Golf Course, Sawyer, Oct. 17
1998 GIRLS UP CLASS A/B TEAMS
1. Menominee..37
2. Marquette..57
3. Escanaba..88
4. Sault Ste Marie...108
5. Gladstone...123

1998 GIRLS UP CLASS A/B INDIVIDUALS
1. Emily Anderson (Marquette)10..........................19:37
2. Lindsey Olson (Escanaba)10.............................19:53
3. Hannah Wolfe (Menominee)12...........................20:22
4. Tracy Wills (Menominee)...................................20:25
5. Hannah Vissering (Ishpeming Westwood).........20:41

1998 GIRLS UP CLASS C TEAMS
1. Stephenson..44
2. Calumet..45
3. Ironwood..64
4. Houghton..103
5. Newberry..131

1998 GIRLS UP CLASS C INDIVIDUALS
1. Randi Johnson (St Ignace)11............................20:52
2. Trisha Nylund (Crystal Forest- Forest Park)12..21:12
3. Chelsea Finco (Ironwood)11..............................21:13
4. Laura Lankton (Houghton)................................21:14
5. Julie Juntilla (Calumet).....................................21:24

1998 GIRLS UP CLASS D TEAMS
1. Republic-Michigamme..33
2. Chassell...37
3. Rock-Mid Peninsula..88
4. Carney-Nadeau..89
5. Superior Central...96

1998 GIRLS UP CLASS D INDIVIDUALS
1. Jane Rautiola (Painesdale-Jeffers)11...............20:34
2. Jolinda Tervo (Chassell)10................................22:56
3. Janette Koski (Chassell)10................................23:00
4. Mary Daavettila (Painesdale-Jeffers)................23:12
5. Melanie Dillon (Republic-Michigamme)..............23:17

1999 UP GIRLS

Horrid conditions that included rain, snow, and 60mph wind gusts made the performance of the Anderson twins all the more impressive. Emily and Katie ran side-by-side the entire way, topping the rest of the field by over a minute in 18:45. That wasn't enough for Marquette to top rival Menominee, as the Maroons won in a tie-breaker.

Pictured Rocks CC, Munising, Oct. 23
1999 GIRLS UP CLASS A/B TEAMS
1. Menominee..44
2. Marquette..44
3. Escanaba..65
4. Sault Ste Marie...86
5. Gladstone...128

1999 GIRLS UP CLASS A/B INDIVIDUALS
1. Emily Anderson (Marquette)11..........................18:45
2. Katie Anderson (Marquette)11..........................18:45
3. Mandi Long (Menominee)11...............................20:07
4. Krista O'Dell (Escanaba)...................................20:49
5. Mary Miller (Sault Ste Marie).............................20:49

1999 GIRLS UP CLASS C TEAMS
1. Stephenson..31
2. Ironwood..45
3. Calumet..78
4. Hancock...81
5. Houghton..148

1999 GIRLS UP CLASS C INDIVIDUALS
1. Hanna Vissering (Ishpeming Westwood)11 ....20:48
2. Chelsea Finco (Ironwood)12 ....21:01
3. Lisa Granskog (Stephenson)12 ....21:17
4. Kate Godin (Stephenson) 21:39
5. Anna Hagstrom (Ironwood) 21:50

1999 GIRLS UP CLASS D TEAMS
1. Republic-Michigamme 30
2. Pickford 40
3. Eben-Superior Central 54

1999 GIRLS UP CLASS D INDIVIDUALS
1. Jane Rautiola (Painesdale-Jeffers)12 ....21:44
2. Leslie Slater (Pickford)10 ....22:58
3. Rachel Morrison (Pickford)10 ....23:03
4. Hannah Wojcik (Eben-Superior Central) 23:05
5. Kristen Mettila (Republic-Michigamme) 23:23

2000 UP GIRLS

Katie Anderson of Marquette got the win this time, running a minute faster (albeit in much better conditions) than she did the previous year.

"We have a lot more depth than last year," said winning Marquette coach Dale Phillips, and the two Andersons have really taken charge as seniors."

Pictured Rocks CC, Munising, Oct. 23

2000 GIRLS UP DIVISION 1 TEAMS
1. Marquette 23
2. Sault Ste. Marie 52
3. Menominee 71
4. Calumet 92
5. Escanaba 145

2000 GIRLS UP DIVISION 1 INDIVIDUALS
1. Katie Anderson (Marquette)12 ....17:45
2. Emily Anderson (Marquette)12 ....18:42
3. Mandi Long (Menominee)12 ....19:42
4. Natalie Cahill (Sault)11 ....20:12
5. Christty Griffen (Marquette) 20:19

2000 GIRLS UP DIVISION 2 TEAMS
1. Stephenson 28
2. Ishpeming Westwood 63
3. Ironwood 64
4. St Ignace 109
5. Newberry 109

2000 GIRLS UP DIVISION 2 INDIVIDUALS
1. Amber Smith (Westwood)9 ....19:43
2. Hanna Vissering (Westwood)12 ....20:02
3. Teresa Morstad (Norway)12 ....20:45
4. Tiffany Tessmer (Stephenson) 21:03
5. Joanna Grille (Stephenson) 21:06

2000 GIRLS UP DIVISION 3 TEAMS
1. Carney-Nadeau 30
2. Pickford 41
3. Eben-Superior Central 67
4. Republic Michigamme 78

2000 GIRLS UP DIVISION 3 INDIVIDUALS
1. Hannah Wojcik (Superior Central)11 ....21:53
2. Nicole Hansen (Crystal Falls-Forest Park) 22:11
3. Laurie Tuinstra (Carney-Nadeau) 22:26
4. Trisha Hernandez (Carney-Nadeau) 22:30
5. Carly Benson (Carney-Nadeau) 22:32

2001 UP GIRLS

Natalie Cahill, still a running rookie, captured the D1 title. She told *The Evening News*: "Last year was my first year of running. I've learned not to give up. This year when I got passed, I was able to stay with the runner."

In D3, freshman Dani Holmgren lost 15 yards after taking a wrong turn, but still won. "I probably starting pulling away after the guy made me come back and go around [the flag] for the second time," she said. "I got kind of an adrenalin rush."

Gladstone Golf Club, Gladstone, Oct. 20

2001 GIRLS UP DIVISION 1 TEAMS 1
1. Marquette 25
2. Sault Ste Marie 47
3. Calumet 99
4. Menominee 128
5. Gladstone 148

2001 GIRLS UP DIVISION 1 INDIVIDUALS
1. Natalie Cahill (Sault Ste Marie)12 ....20:14
2. Christy Griffen (Marquette) 21:28
3. Charlotte Delorey (Marquette) 21:35
4. Casey Andrews (Marquette) 21:46
5. Kayce Lawrence (Sault Ste Marie) 21:58

2001 GIRLS UP DIVISION 2 TEAMS
1. Stephenson 42
2. Ironwood 57
3. Hancock 101
4. Rudyard 113
5. Newberry 114

2001 GIRLS UP DIVISION 2 INDIVIDUALS
1. Amber Smith (Ishpeming Westwood)10 ....19:45
2. Stephanie Folkersma (Rudyard) 21:28
3. Emmy Hagstrom (Ironwood) 21:35
4. Joanna Grille (Stephenson) 22:02
5. Ginger Polich (Ironwood) 22:24

2001 GIRLS UP DIVISION 3 TEAMS
1. Eben-Superior Central 34
2. Pickford 55
3. Carney-Nadeau 57
4. Rapid River 85
5. Republic Michigamme 105

2001 GIRLS UP DIVISION 3 INDIVIDUALS
1. Dani Holmgren (Rapid River)9 ....21:08
2. Trisha Hernandez (Carney-Nadeau)12 ....21:21
3. Rosanna Chapman (Pickford) 22:43
4. Hannah Wojcik (Eben-Superior Central) 22:53
5. Nichole Hansen (Crystal Falls-Forest Park) 22:57

Westwood's Amber Smith won four straight.

2002 UP GIRLS

Amber Smith of Westwood captured her third D2 title in dominating fashion, her 18:49 winning by a quarter mile. Six weeks later she would be runner-up in the Footlocker Midwest Regional before placing 4th at Nationals.

Gladstone Golf Club, Gladstone, Oct. 19

2002 GIRLS UP DIVISION 1 TEAMS 1
1. Marquette 61
2. Sault Ste Marie 73
3. Escanaba 74
4. Calumet 83
5. Gladstone 103

2002 GIRLS UP DIVISION 1 INDIVIDUALS
1. Kayce Lawrence (Sault Ste Marie)12 ....20:39
2. Angela Gaudette (Kingsford) 21:00
3. Jennifer Corbiere (Sault Ste Marie) 21:07
4. Kaye Helminen (Calumet) 21:16
5. Casey Andrews (Marquette) 21:21

2002 GIRLS UP DIVISION 2 TEAMS
1. Ironwood 48
2. Stephenson 61
3. Hancock 84
4. Ishpeming Westwood 103
5. Newberry 108

2002 GIRLS UP DIVISION 2 INDIVIDUALS
1. Amber Smith (Ishpeming Westwood)11 ....18:49
2. Stephanie Folkersma (Rudyard) 20:26
3. Emmy Hagstrom (Ironwood) 20:49
4. Laura Aderman (Stephenson) 21:32
5. Sara Grabavcich (Ironwood) 21:35

2002 GIRLS UP DIVISION 3 TEAMS
1. Pickford 45
2. Rapid River 56
3. Eben Junction-Superior Central 61
4. Painesdale-Jeffers 90
5. Carney-Nadeau 98

2002 GIRLS UP DIVISION 3 INDIVIDUALS
1. Dani Holmgren (Rapid River)10 ....20:53
2. Laura Kangas (Chassell)10 ....21:16
3. Michelle Hall (Rapid River)9 ....21:27
4. Shalyn Beauchamp (Rock-Mid Peninsula) 21:40
5. Mandy Smith (Painesdale-Jeffers) 21:52

2003 GIRLS

In her finale hurrah, Amber Smith of Westwood won D2 by nearly two minutes. In an unusual twist, she reported that she had received most of her workouts from former UP great Emily Anderson. She finished her Westwood career with four state XC wins and 12 individual LP titles in track (four straight in the 800/1600/3200). Add a 4x8 win and she is one of the most heavily decorated athletes in Michigan history, with 17 wins. She would go on to run at Colorado, where she struggled with persistent injuries.

Fountain XC Course, Banat, Oct. 18

2003 GIRLS UP DIVISION 1 TEAMS 1
1. Marquette 41
2. Calumet 69
3. Gladstone 106
4. Ironwood 119
5. Escanaba 126

2003 GIRLS UP DIVISION 1 INDIVIDUALS
1. Kylee St Arnaud (Marquette)9 ....19:24
2. Stephanie Ostrenga (Escanaba)11 ....20:34
3. Danielle Mitchell (Kingsford)10 ....20:35
4. Kaye Helminen (Calumet) 21:07
5. Claire Vallin (Marquette) 21:08

2003 GIRLS UP DIVISION 2 TEAMS
1. Stephenson 42
2. Hancock 65
3. Rudyard 79
4. Ishpeming Westwood 87
5. Norway 125

2003 GIRLS UP DIVISION 2 INDIVIDUALS
1. Amber Smith (Ishpeming Westwood)12 ....17:54
2. Laura Aderman (Stephenson) 19:48
3. Amanda Newlin (Stephenson)9 ....19:51
4. Christina Mishica (Hancock)9 ....20:44
5. Charlotte Folkersma (Rudyard)11 ....21:20

2003 GIRLS UP DIVISION 3 TEAMS
1. Rapid River 37
2. Painesdale-Jeffers 70
3. Chassell 78
4. Pickford 95
5. Carney-Nadeau 104

2003 GIRLS UP DIVISION 3 INDIVIDUALS
1. Laura Kangas (Chassell)11 ..... 20:03
2. Michelle Hall (Rapid River)10 ..... 20:42
3. Dani Holmgren (Rapid River)11 ..... 21:52
4. Sara Bailley (Rapid River)11 ..... 21:56
5. Nichole Hansen (Crystal Falls-Forest Park) 22:03

2004 UP GIRLS

Kylie St. Arnauld of Marquette defended her D1 title in 19:17. She was just as well known for her hockey feats. In D2, Rudyard and Ironwood tied for runner-up, but with no sixth runner, Ironwood lost the tiebreaker. In D3, Dani Holgren came back from her loss as a junior to win her third state title.

Fountain XC Course, Banat, Oct. 23
2004 GIRLS UP DIVISION 1 TEAMS 1
1. Marquette 31
2. Calumet 72
3. Gladstone 86
4. Kingsford 108
5. Escanaba 119

2004 GIRLS UP DIVISION 1 INDIVIDUALS
1. Kylee St Arnaud (Marquette)10 ..... 19:17
2. Stephanie Ostrenga (Escanaba)12 ..... 20:04
3. Danielle Mitchell (Kingsford)11 ..... 20:32
4. Karen Koljonen (Calumet)11 ..... 20:44
5. Andrea Millimaki (Marquette)9 ..... 20:47

2004 GIRLS UP DIVISION 2 TEAMS
1. Stephenson 54
2. Rudyard 75
3. Ironwood 75
4. Ishpeming Westwood 104
5. Munising 116

2004 GIRLS UP DIVISION 2 INDIVIDUALS
1. Amanda Newlin (Stephenson)10 ..... 19:34
2. Christina Mishica (Hancock)10 ..... 19:59
3. Stephanie Folkersma (Rudyard)12 ..... 20:33
4. Erika Peterson (Ironwood)9 ..... 20:35
5. Megan Davis (Munising)12 ..... 21:14

2004 GIRLS UP DIVISION 3 TEAMS
1. Cedarville 41
2. Rapid River 48
3. Painesdale-Jeffers 96
4. Carney-Nadeau 103
5. Pickford 110

2004 GIRLS UP DIVISION 3 INDIVIDUALS
1. Dani Holmgren (Rapid River)12 ..... 20:01
2. Karissa Schlosser (Cedarville)9 ..... 20:09
3. Laura Kangas (Chassell)12 ..... 20:45
4. Laura Sexton (Powers North Central)11 ..... 20:51
5. Lauren Izzard (Cedarville)11 ..... 21:18

2005 UP GIRLS

Ninth-grader Nikki Kiilunen won for Calumet, but the Copper Kings lost the team race to perennial champion Marquette.

Michigan Tech, Houghton, Oct. 22
2005 GIRLS UP DIVISION 1 TEAMS
1. Marquette 30
2. Calumet 55
3. Kingsford 73
4. Gladstone 92
5. Escanaba 124

2005 GIRLS UP DIVISION 1 INDIVIDUALS
1. Nikki Kiilunen (Calumet)9 ..... 20:06
2. Andrea Millimaki (Marquette)10 ..... 20:45
3. Jeanee Bennetts (Escanaba)10 ..... 21:00
4. Kylee St. Arnaud (Marquette)11 ..... 21:04
5. Karen Koljonen (Calumet)12 ..... 21:04

2005 GIRLS UP DIVISION 2 TEAMS
1. Ironwood 39
2. Stephenson 60
3. Newberry 71
4. Hancock 94
5. Ishpeming Westwood 111

2005 GIRLS UP DIVISION 2 INDIVIDUALS
1. Amanda Newlin (Stephenson)11 ..... 20:21
2. Christina Mishica (Hancock)11 ..... 20:45
3. Erika Peterson (Ironwood)10 ..... 21:38
4. Cori Glime (Newberry)11 ..... 22:01
5. Sonia Oja (Ironwood)12 ..... 22:04

2005 GIRLS UP DIVISION 3 TEAMS
1. Cedarville 56
2. Powers-North Central 61
3. Rapid River 78
4. Rock Mid-Peninsula 111
5. Painesdale-Jeffers 134

2005 GIRLS UP DIVISION 3 INDIVIDUALS
1. Michelle Hall (Rapid River)12 ..... 20:37
2. Jasmine Ledy (Pickford)9 ..... 20:57
3. Brooke Verbrigghe (Superior Central)10 ..... 21:19
4. Billie McLeod (Cedarville)9 ..... 21:30
5. Ashley Sweeney (Cedarville)9 ..... 22:14

2006 UP GIRLS

The fastest runner of the year came from the smallest division, as Katie Granquist from North Central, a ninth-grader, won D3 by over a minute with her 20:26.

Michigan Tech, Houghton, Oct. 21
2006 GIRLS UP DIVISION 1 TEAMS
1. Marquette 33
2. Calumet 94
3. Sault Ste Marie 94
4. Houghton 106
5. Ironwood 118

2006 GIRLS UP DIVISION 1 INDIVIDUALS
1. Andrea Millimaki (Marquette)11 ..... 20:55
2. Lindsay Kiilunen (Calumet)9 ..... 21:08
3. Jeanee Bennetts (Escanaba)11 ..... 21:16
4. Colleen Peterson (Marquette)11 ..... 21:17
5. Lauren Reckker (Marquette)10 ..... 21:21

2006 GIRLS UP DIVISION 2 TEAMS
1. Stephenson 40
2. Rudyard 67
3. Ishpeming Westwood 72
4. Hancock 93
5. St. Ignace 107

2006 GIRLS UP DIVISION 2 INDIVIDUALS
1. Amanda Newlin (Stephenson)12 ..... 20:28
2. Jamie Honkala (Westwood)9 ..... 21:49
3. Christina Mishica (Hancock)12 ..... 22:04
4. Willow Carmody (Munising)10 ..... 22:24
5. Olivia Orr (Hancock)11 ..... 22:28

2006 GIRLS UP DIVISION 3 TEAMS
1. North Central 46
2. Cedarville 53
3. Pickford 66
4. Superior Central 82
5. Rapid River 88

2006 GIRLS UP DIVISION 3 INDIVIDUALS
1. Katie Granquist (Powers-North Central)9 ..... 20:26
2. Jasmine Ledy (Pickford)10 ..... 21:47
3. Amber Granquist (Powers-North Central)12 ..... 21:53
4. Billie McLeod (Cedarville)10 ..... 22:13
5. Ashley Sweeney (Cedarville)10 ..... 22:44

2007 UP GIRLS

Abbey Kelto of Munising won D2 in 19:54, the fastest time of the day, as Ironwood won the D2 team race by a 40-point margin.

Sault Ste Marie, Oct.20
2007 GIRLS UP DIVISION 1 TEAMS
1. Marquette 42
2. Houghton 57
3. Kingsford 108
4. Gladstone 114
5. Calumet 121

2007 GIRLS UP DIVISION 1 INDIVIDUALS
1. Kelly Lufkin (Houghton)12 ..... 19:57
2. Emily Humes (Houghton)9 ..... 20:00
3. Katie Holway (Marquette)11 ..... 20:04
4. Lindsey Lusard (Gladstone)9 ..... 20:12
5. Celeste Santi (Kingsford)9 ..... 20:16

2007 GIRLS UP DIVISION 2 TEAMS
1. Ironwood 39
2. Newberry 79
3. Ishpeming Westwood 99
4. St Ignace 101
5. Stephenson 122

Munising's Abbey Kelto became an NCAA qualifier for Central Michigan.

2007 GIRLS UP DIVISION 2 INDIVIDUALS
1. Abbey Kelto (Munising)10 ..... 19:54
2. Alyssa Chapman (Westwood)9 ..... 20:25
3. Emily Keskey (Ironwood)9 ..... 20:40
4. Erika Peterson (Ironwood)12 ..... 21:12
5. Kari Strand (Ironwood)11 ..... 21:32

2007 GIRLS UP DIVISION 3 TEAMS
1. Powers-North Central 54
2. L'Anse 56
3. Chassell 61
4. Rapid River 81
5. Painesdale-Jeffers 105

2007 GIRLS UP DIVISION 3 INDIVIDUALS
1. Erin Holmberg (Rapid River)9 ..... 20:14
2. Katie Granquist (North Central)10 ..... 20:59
3. Paige Koskinen (L'Anse)12 ..... 22:23
4. Brianna Anderson (Rapid River)11 ..... 22:30
5. Erin Connor (L'Anse)11 ..... 22:45

2008 UP GIRLS

Abbey Kelto of Munising fought off a challenge by Rapid River's Erin Holmberg to win her second D2 title by 8 seconds.

Sault Ste Marie, Oct. 18
2008 GIRLS UP DIVISION 1 TEAMS
1. Marquette 65
2. Gladstone 76
3. Houghton 77
4. Calumet 94
5. Kingsford 108

2008 GIRLS UP DIVISION 1 INDIVIDUALS
1. Teri Brown (Kingsford)12 .... 19:14
2. Lindsey Lusardi (Gladstone)10 .... 19:27
3. Alicia Romano (Marquette)11 .... 19:44
4. Nikki Kiilunen (Calumet)12 .... 19:59
5. Emily Lawton (Kingsford)10 .... 20:01

2008 GIRLS UP DIVISION 2 TEAMS
1. Ironwood 61
2. L'Anse 69
3. Munising 88
4. Rapid River 135
5. West Iron County 158

2008 GIRLS UP DIVISION 2 INDIVIDUALS
1. Abbey Kelto (Munising)11 .... 19:00
2. Erin Holmberg (Rapid River)10 .... 19:08
3. Jaclyn Waara (West Iron County)9 .... 19:53
4. Alyssa Chapman (Ishpeming Westwood)10 .. 19:55
5. Nicole Elmblad (St Ignace)10 .... 20:22

2008 GIRLS UP DIVISION 3 TEAMS
1. Powers North Central 26
2. Painesdale-Jeffers 55
3. Chassell 65
4. Cedarville 69

2008 GIRLS UP DIVISION 3 INDIVIDUALS
1. Lauren Spranger (Superior Central)9 .... 19:22
2. Katie Granquist (North Central)11 .... 19:42
3. Allison Fallon (Chassell)9 .... 20:25
4. Ali Rittenger (Eben-Superior Central)9 .... 21:24
5. Brandi Kopitz (Pickford)10 .... 21:26

2009 UP GIRLS

Calumet's Tara Kiilunen, the younger sister of '05 champ Nikki Kiilunen, won the D1 title in 19:37. She led her teammates to the team win, scoring a remarkable 32 points to upend Marquette.

Abbey Kelto of Munising won her third-straight in D2. In track, she won a total of 14 UP titles. She would later qualify for NCAA Div. I cross country nationals for Central Michigan.

Sault Ste Marie, Oct. 24
2009 GIRLS UP DIVISION 1 TEAMS
1. Calumet 32
2. Marquette 66
3. Houghton 80
4. Menominee 122
5. Gladstone 137

2009 GIRLS UP DIVISION 1 INDIVIDUALS
1. Tara Kiilunen (Calumet)9 .... 19:37
2. Lindsay Kiilunen (Calumet) 20:03
3. Alicia Romano (Marquette)12 .... 20:05
4. Emily Humes (Houghton) 20:08
5. Lindsey Lusardi (Gladstone)11 .... 20:21

2009 GIRLS UP DIVISION 2 TEAMS
1. Ironwood 58
2. Rudyard 59
3. L'Anse 67
4. St Ignace 84
5. Stephenson 110

2009 GIRLS UP DIVISION 2 INDIVIDUALS
1. Abbey Kelto (Munising)12 .... 19:39
2. Sarah Cullip (St Ignace) 20:31
3. Leah Jarvie (Rudyard) 20:55
4. Nicole Elmblad (St Ignace)11 .... 21:07
5. Paige Koskinen (L'Anse) 21:17

2009 GIRLS UP DIVISION 3 TEAMS
1. Eben-Superior Central 63
2. Painesdale-Jeffers 85
3. Pickford 87
4. Cedarville 100
5. Powers-North Central 117

2009 GIRLS UP DIVISION 3 INDIVIDUALS
1. Lauren Spranger (Eben-Superior Central)10 . 20:44
2. Brandi Kopitz (Pickford)11 .... 20:51
3. Brittany Richard (Cooks-Big Bay de Noc)10 . 21:27
4. Ali Rittenger (Eben-Superior Central)10 .... 21:35
5. Katie Granquist (Powers-North Central)12 .. 21:56

2010 UP GIRLS

Tara Kiilunen won her second-straight D1 race, leading her Calumet teammates to their second-straight team title.

Escanaba, Oct. 23
2010 GIRLS UP DIVISION 1 TEAMS
1. Calumet 51
2. Marquette 95
3. Houghton 103
4. Menominee 115
5. Kingsford 135

2010 GIRLS UP DIVISION 1 INDIVIDUALS
1. Tara Kiilunen (Calumet)10 .... 18:38
2. Rachel Poyhonen (Calumet)11 .... 19:22
3. Lindsey Lusardi (Gladstone)12 .... 19:33
4. Emily Humes (Houghton) 19:38
5. Julia Lean (Calumet) 19:43

2010 GIRLS UP DIVISION 2 TEAMS
1. Rudyard 42
2. Ironwood 46
3. L'Anse 63
4. Painesdale-Jeffers 100
5. St Ignace 127

2010 GIRLS UP DIVISION 2 INDIVIDUALS
1. Sarah Cullip (St Ignace)10 .... 19:27
2. Leah Jarvie (Rudyard)10 .... 19:41
3. Jessica Gering (Ironwood)9 .... 19:48
4. Jaclyn Waara (West Iron County)11 .... 20:58
5. Rebecca Malaski (Rudyard)12 .... 21:08

2010 GIRLS UP DIVISION 3 TEAMS
1. Dollar Bay 49
2. Cedarville 62
3. Eben-Superior Central 90
4. Baraga 103
5. Powers North Central 118

2010 GIRLS UP DIVISION 3 INDIVIDUALS
1. Erin Holmberg (Big Bay de Noc)12 .... 19:51
2. Brandi Kopitz (Pickford) 20:26
3. Lauren Spranger (Eben-Superior Central)11 . 20:36
4. Allison Fallon (Dollar Bay)11 .... 20:58
5. Ashley Hill (Munising) 21:16

2011 UP GIRLS

Tara Kiilunen won her third-straight D1 crown, but this time, it wasn't enough to lift Calumet to the team win.

Pictured Rocks GC, Munising, Oct. 22
2011 GIRLS UP DIVISION 1 TEAMS
1. Marquette 46
2. Menominee 64
3. Calumet 67
4. Houghton 82
5. Sault Ste Marie 100

2011 GIRLS UP DIVISION 1 INDIVIDUALS
1. Tara Kiilunen (Calumet)11 .... 19:13
2. Rachel Poyhonen (Calumet)11 .... 20:10
3. Alex Bott (Marquette)12 .... 20:10
4. Addy Grier-Welch (Houghton)12 .... 21:22
5. Calla Martysz (Marquette)9 .... 20:36

2011 GIRLS UP DIVISION 2 TEAMS
1. Rudyard 54
2. West Iron County 64
3. Ironwood 79
4. L'Anse 93
5. St Ignace 100

Sarah Culip of St Ignace won big in D2.

2011 GIRLS UP DIVISION 2 INDIVIDUALS
1. Sarah Cullip (St Ignace)11 .... 19:16
2. Leah Jarvie (Rudyard)11 .... 19:54
3. Jessica Gering (Ironwood)10 .... 20:21
4. Abbey Trembreull (L'Anse)10 .... 20:30
5. Gabrielle Young (Newberry)9 .... 20:38

2011 GIRLS UP DIVISION 3 TEAMS
1. Cedarville 40
2. Eben-Superior Central 52
3. Dollar Bay 82
4. Baraga 112
5. Munising 117

2011 GIRLS UP DIVISION 3 INDIVIDUALS
1. Lauren Spranger (Eben-Superior Central)12 . 20:57
2. Erin Currie (Cedarville)12 .... 21:00
3. Lucia Nye (Dollar Bay)12 .... 21:44
4. Brittany Richard (Big Bay de Noc)12 .... 21:48
5. Alexis Scott (Cedarville)9 .... 21:58

2012 UP GIRLS

Calumet returned to the top of the D1 heap, led by 4-time champion Tara Kiilunen and sister Leah. The fastest time of the day came in D3 with the 19:36 performance of Sarah Cullip.

Pictured Rocks GC, Munising, Oct. 20
2012 GIRLS UP DIVISION 1 TEAMS
1. Calumet 41

2. Escanaba 62
3. Sault Ste Marie 84
4. Marquette 96
5. Menomineeq 101

2012 GIRLS UP DIVISION 1 INDIVIDUALS
1. Tara Kiilunen (Calumet)12 ....19:45
2. Leah Kiilunen (Calumet) 19:50
3. Kameron Burmeister (Menominee)11 ....19:54
4. Aimee Giese (Escanaba) 20:08
5. Calla Martysz (Marquette)10 ....20:21

2012 GIRLS UP DIVISION 2 TEAMS
1. Newberry 50
2. Ironwood 52
3. Hancock 79
4. L'Anse 112
5. Norway 118

2012 GIRLS UP DIVISION 2 INDIVIDUALS
1. Jessica Gering (Ironwood)11 ....20:41
2. Hannah Palmeter (Ironwood)12 ....21:28
3. Rebekah Serbinski (West Iron County)12 ....21:32
4. Natalie Beaulieu (Newberry)9 ....21:41
5. Bridgette Stoetzer (Newberry) 21:42

2012 GIRLS UP DIVISION 3 TEAMS
1. St Ignace 40
2. Dollar Bay 74
3. Rudyard 81
4. Munising 89
5. Cedarville 101

2012 GIRLS UP DIVISION 3 INDIVIDUALS
1. Sarah Cullip (St Ignace)12 ....19:36
2. Lillian Calcaterra (St Ignace) 20:48
3. Leah Jarvie (Rudyard)12 ....20:54
4. Kaylee Hoolsema (Rudyard) 21:27
5. Emily Chartrand (Brimley) 21:33

2013 UP GIRLS

Marquette put together a 1-2-3 sweep to win D1 with a sparkling 27-point tally. Senior Kameron Burmeister led the way in 19:37. She would become an All-American for Northern Michigan and in 2020 competed in the Olympic Trials Marathon.

Gentz's Homestead GC, Harvey, Oct. 19
2013 GIRLS UP DIVISION 1 TEAMS
1. Marquette 27
2. Calumet 89
3. Escanaba 112
4. Sault Ste Marie 113
5. Menominee 138

2013 GIRLS UP DIVISION 1 INDIVIDUALS
1. Kameron Burmeister (Menominee)12 ....19:37
2. Lindsey Rudden (Marquette)10 ....19:43
3. Amber Huebner (Marquette)9 ....19:57
4. Leigha Woelffer (Gladstone)9 ....20:05
5. Nichole Mackey (Marquette) 20:23

2013 GIRLS UP DIVISION 2 TEAMS
1. Hancock 43
2. St Ignace 60
3. Newberry 69
4. Norway 117
5. Ironwood 117

2013 GIRLS UP DIVISION 2 INDIVIDUALS
1. Abbey Trembruell (Hancock)12 ....21:05
2. Lilly Calcaterra (St Ignace)11 ....21:13
3. Natalie Beaulieu (Newberry)10 ....21:26
4. Kyra Johnson (Norway)10 ....21:31
5. Jessica Gering (Ironwood)12 ....21:38

2013 GIRLS UP DIVISION 3 TEAMS
1. Munising 46
2. Cedarville 54
3. Dollar Bay 55
4. Rudyard 82
5. Brimley 104

2013 GIRLS UP DIVISION 3 INDIVIDUALS
1. Kaylee Hoolsema (Rudyard)11 ....20:33
2. Marissa Immel (Munising) 21:17
3. Emma Bohn (Cedarville)9 ....21:20
4. Emily Chartrand (Brimley)11 ....21:20
5. Carli Gratopp (Paradise) 21:33

2014 UP GIRLS

"I wasn't expecting this at all," Leigha Woelffer told John Vrancic. "I thought Amber [Huebner] was right behind me. In the last half-mile, I was almost in shock." The Gladstone sophomore got a little lucky, as Lindsey Rudden of Marquette had been in the lead until missing a turn and having to run 200m extra. "I feel real bad for Lindsey," said Woelffer. "She deserved to win."

Gentz's Homestead GC, Harvey, Oct. 18
2014 GIRLS UP DIVISION 1 TEAMS
1. Marquette 36
2. Sault Ste Marie 42
3. Calumet 97
4. Escanaba 128
5. Gladstone 155

2014 GIRLS UP DIVISION 1 INDIVIDUALS
1. Leigha Woelffer (Gladstone)10 ....19:53
2. Amber Huebner (Marquette)10 ....19:58
3. Michaela Rushford (Sault Ste Marie)12 ......20:00
4. Courtney Arbic (Sault Ste Marie)10 ....20:01
5. Mackenzie Kalchik (Sault Ste Marie)9 ....20:12

2014 GIRLS UP DIVISION 2 TEAMS
1. Ishpeming 32
2. Hancock 52
3. Ishpeming Westwood 55
4. West Iron County 91

2014 GIRLS UP DIVISION 2 INDIVIDUALS
1. Kathryn Etelamaki (Ishpeming Westwood)11 20:52
2. Tori Harris-Hogaboom (West Iron County)12 21:37
3. Olivia Holmberg (Manistique)12 ....21:44
4. Kyra Johnson (Norway)11 ....21:45
5. Khora Swanson (Ishpeming)10 ....21:53

2014 GIRLS UP DIVISION 3 TEAMS
1. Chassell 60
2. St Ignace 86
3. Dollar Bay 93
4. Newberry 117
5. Cedarville 122

2014 GIRLS UP DIVISION 3 INDIVIDUALS
1. Natalie Beaulieu (Newberry)11 ....20:57
2. Alyssa Webber (Munising)9 ....21:11
3. Emma Bohn (Cedarville)10 ....21:17
4. Emily Chartrand (Brimley)12 ....21:38
5. Lela Rautiola (Chassell)8 ....21:43

2015 champ Lindsey Rudden later ran for MSU.

2015 UP GIRLS

Marquette senior Lindsey Rudden finally got the title she missed the previous year. On a rainy day, the MSU-bound runner won by six seconds, saying, "It's overdue."

Beachamp's Grove, Flat Rock, Oct. 24
2015 GIRLS UP DIVISION 1 TEAMS
1. Marquette 40
2. Sault Ste Marie 49
3. Negaunee 97
4. Calumet 115
5. Houghton 131

2015 GIRLS UP DIVISION 1 INDIVIDUALS
1. Lindsey Rudden (Marquette)12 ....19:00
2. Clara Johnson (Negaunee)11 ....19:06
3. Kathryn Etelamaki (Ishpeming Westwood)12 19:10
4. Mackenzie Kalchik (Sault Ste Marie)10 ......19:22
5. Holly Blowers (Marquette)12 ....19:28

2015 GIRLS UP DIVISION 2 TEAMS
1. Ishpeming 31
2. Hancock 49
3. Wakefield-Marenisco/Bessemer 83
4. St Ignace 89
5. Norway 118

2015 GIRLS UP DIVISION 2 INDIVIDUALS
1. Khora Swanson (Ishpeming)11 ....20:57
2. Taylor Pertile (Hancock)12 ....21:16
3. Mariah Bertucci (Ishpeming)10 ....21:44
4. Melissa Wanink (Wakefield-Marenisco/B)10 21:46
5. Madisyn Wright (Hancock)12 ....21:47

2015 GIRLS UP DIVISION 3 TEAMS
1. Chassell 67
2. Munising 69
3. Cedarville 92
4. Dollar Bay 105
5. Brimley 114

2015 GIRLS UP DIVISION 3 INDIVIDUALS
1. Natalie Beaulieu (Newberry)12 ....19:25
2. Shitaye Sam (Chassell)12 ....19:47
3. Alyssa Webber (Munising)10 ....19:58
4. Emma Bohn (Cedarville))11 ....20:56
5. Lauren Halvorsen (Brimley)11 ....21:30

2016 UP GIRLS

Sault Ste. Marie won its first girls' title, beating Marquette by 19 points. "This is huge for our program," said coach Jim Martin.

Marquette senior Becci McNamee, coming off illness, ran her fastest race ever for the win. "I don't think anybody outside of Marquette expected me to win this race, especially by that much," she told John Vrancic.

Beachamp's Grove, Flat Rock, Oct. 22
2016 GIRLS UP DIVISION 1 TEAMS
1. Sault Ste Marie 34
2. Marquette 53
3. Houghton 114
4. Menominee 124
5. Gladstone 137

2016 GIRLS UP DIVISION 1 INDIVIDUALS
1. Becci McNamee (Marquette)12 ....19:07
2. Courtney Arbic (Sault Ste Marie)12 ....19:34
3. Emily Paupore (Negaunee)9 ....19:46
4. Clara Johnson (Negaunee)11 ....19:47
5. Peyton Johnson (Kingsford)10 ....19:52

2016 GIRLS UP DIVISION 2 TEAMS
1. Ishpeming 62
2. Munising 70
3. Hancock 101
4. St Ignace 124
5. Newberry 134

Coach Jim Martin and his 2016 championship team from the Soo.

2016 GIRLS UP DIVISION 2 INDIVIDUALS
1. Alyssa Webber (Munising)11 .... 19:59
2. Madeleine Peramaki (Munising)10 .... 20:33
3. Lily Wieringa (Wakefield-Marenisco/Bess)12 20:45
4. Emmuy Kinner (West Iron County)12 .... 21:12
5. Emily Carey (Ironwood)10................................ 21:16

2016 GIRLS UP DIVISION 3 TEAMS
1. Cedarville.. 34
2. Chassell... 46
3. Dollar Bay.. 81
4. Rock-Mid Peninsula 00
5. Stephenson 90

2016 GIRLS UP DIVISION 3 INDIVIDUALS
1. Lela Rautiola (Chassell)10 .... 20:13
2. Emma Bohn (Cedarville)12............................. 20:28
3. Gracia Asiala (Painesdale-Jeffers)10 .... 20:47
4. Danika Walters (Eben-Superior Central)9 ..... 21:09
5. Cami Daavettila (Dollar Bay)12....................... 21:15

2017 UP GIRLS

"I wanted to take off hard," said Emily Paupore of Negaunee, "but my first mile was slower than I wanted…. My pacing wasn't good today, although it feels great to win it."

Pictured Rocks GC, Munising, Oct. 21
2017 GIRLS UP DIVISION 1 TEAMS
1. Marquette 47
2. Sault Ste Marie 61
3. Negaunee 94
4. Menominee 131
5. Escanaba 150

2017 GIRLS UP DIVISION 1 INDIVIDUALS
1. Emily Paupore (Negaunee)10....................... 19:23
2. Ericka Asmus (Marquette)10........................ 19:56
3. Mackenzie Kalchik (Sault Ste Marie)12 .... 20:22
4. Nicole Kamin (Escanaba)9............................ 20:44
5. Clarity Gipp (Calumet)9................................. 20:48

2017 GIRLS UP DIVISION 2 TEAMS
1. St Ignace 34
2. Ishpeming 61
3. Ishpeming Westwood 77
4. Hancock 88
5. Newberry 99

2017 GIRLS UP DIVISION 2 INDIVIDUALS
1. Tessa Leece (Ishpeming Westwood)10 .... 20:55
2. Elizabeth Becker (St Ignace)11 .... 21:10
3. Emmalee Hart (St Ignace)9.......................... 21:16
4. Emily Carey (Ironwood)11............................. 21:26
5. Hallie Marshall (St Ignace)9 .... 21:44

2017 GIRLS UP DIVISION 3 TEAMS
1. Chassell.. 40
2. Rock-Mid Peninsula 72
3. Munising 74
4. Cedarville.. 84
5. Painesdale-Jeffers 112

2017 GIRLS UP DIVISION 3 INDIVIDUALS
1. Daisy Englund (Rock-Mid Peninsula)10 ....20:32
2. Madeleine Peramaki (Munising)11 ....20:38
3. Lela Rautiola (Chassell)11.............................20:43
4. Alyssa Webber (Munising)12..........................20:52
5. Landry Koski (Rock-Mid Peninsula)9..............20:56

2018 UP GIRLS

The Sault Ste. Marie girls joined the boys team in carrying off D1 trophies. Coach Jim Martin was thrilled: "This is one for the record books."

The day was cold and windy, as noted by defending champion Emily Paupore of Negaunee. "My original plan was to run this in about 18:40, but once we got here I kind of knew that wasn't going to happen."

Pictured Rocks GC, Munising, Oct. 20
2018 GIRLS UP DIVISION 1 TEAMS
1. Sault Ste Marie.......................................56
2. Marquette..66
3. Houghton...66
4. Ishpeming Westwood..............................88
5. Menominee 128

2018 GIRLS UP DIVISION 1 INDIVIDUALS
1. Emily Paupore (Negaunee)11 ....19:59
2. Ericka Ausmus (Marquette)11 ....20:31
3. Anabel Needham (Houghton)12 ....20:35
4. Tessa Leece (Ishpeming)11 ....20:41
5. Maria Velat (Houghton)9................................20:47

2018 GIRLS UP DIVISION 2 TEAMS
1. Hancock 26
2. St Ignace 62
3. Munising 79
4. Newberry 96
5. West Iron County 96

2018 GIRLS UP DIVISION 2 INDIVIDUALS
1. Elizabeth Becker (St Ignace)12 ....20:46
2. Madeleine Peramaki (Munising)12 ....21:09
3. Emily Carey (Ironwood)12 ....21:18
4. Abby Racine (Ishpeming)9............................21:37
5. Kalli Chynoweth (Hancock)9..........................21:38

2018 GIRLS UP DIVISION 3 TEAMS
1. Chassell..25
2. Cedarville..84
3. Rock-Mid Peninsula 95
4. Dollar Bay..115
5. Engadine 122

2018 GIRLS UP DIVISION 3 INDIVIDUALS
1. Danika Walters (Eben-Superior Central)11 ....20:38
2. Daisy Englund (Rock-Mid Peninsula)11 ....20:58
3. Lela Rautiola (Chassell)12.............................21:33
4. Landry Koski (Rock-Mid Peninsula)10...........21:44
5. Paige Sleeman (Chassell)9 ....21:50

2019 UP GIRLS

Emily Paupore of Negaunee won her third-straight in D1, telling John Vrancic, "Honestly, this was one of my toughest races this year. This wasn't my best race, but I'm thankful to end with a U.P. championship."

In D3, Chassell also made it three-straight.

Gentz's Homestead GC, Harvey, Oct. 19
2019 GIRLS UP DIVISION 1 TEAMS
1. Marquette..61
2. Kingsford...65
3. Sault Ste Marie.......................................74
4. Houghton...115
5. Menominee 116

2019 GIRLS UP DIVISION 1 INDIVIDUALS
1. Emily Paupore (Negaunee)12 ....19:19
2. Melanie Wenzel (Kingsford)11.......................20:27
3. Hayden Buck (Menominee)10 ....20:50
4. Olivia Moffitt (Marquette)11............................20:51
5. Sarah Kulas (Kingsford)11.............................21:05

Emily Paupore of Negaunee won by over a minute.

2019 GIRLS UP DIVISION 2 TEAMS
1. Hancock 34
2. St Ignace 56
3. Ishpeming 84
4. Ironwood 104
5. West Iron County 106

2019 GIRLS UP DIVISION 2 INDIVIDUALS
1. Maylie Kilpela (Hancock)9 ....21:17
2. Hattie Cota (Munising)9 ....21:44
3. Taylor Longtine (Ishpeming)10 ....22:01
4. Hallie Marshall (St Ignace)11 ....22:13
5. Sierrah Driscoll (Hancock)10 ....22:20

2019 GIRLS UP DIVISION 3 TEAMS
1. Chassell.. 36
2. Rock-Mid Peninsula 73
3. Cedarville.. 90
4. Newberry 98
5. Stephenson 111

Mid-Peninsula's Landry Koski.

2019 GIRLS UP DIVISION 3 INDIVIDUALS
1. Landry Koski (Rock-Mid Peninsula)11 ....21:32
2. Lilianna Cason (Cedarville)9 ....21:43
3. Daisy Englund (Rock-Mid Peninsula)12........21:50
4. Natalie Miller (Pickford)12 ....22:01
5. Kamryn Sohlden (Chassell)10 ....22:08

LEGACY RATINGS

For some reason, cross country coaches and fans love ratings. They excitedly debate which are the best teams of their conference, the best teams of the decade and the best of all-time. Yet the perfect measuring stick is hard to find. Comparing different teams from different eras is the ultimate in apples-to-oranges comparisons. So much changes from year to year: course conditions, weather, coaches and, of course, the athletes themselves.

In the early 1960s, Birmingham coach Kermit Ambrose had a good run of victories at the state level and he felt that teams that performed well over the course of a decade deserved special recognition. He created the Top Teams of the Decades, a compilation that is still around today. It gave points to programs that placed in the top 10 at the state finals and tallied the points by class/division. Kermit was a dear friend and I wish he were still around so I could get his feedback on the new Legacy Ratings. I've created them to create a more accurate and fair method to compare teams across the years.

The Top Teams of the Decades compilations tended to work against teams that move up or down in divisions (the Saugatucks of the world) because their points would be split between two different tallies. Or teams that had great streaks that were split by decades (say 2006-2015); their totals would be cut in half. The most notable fix I wanted to make was to give all teams recognition for making it to the finals. It's HARD to get a team to the top level, and teams that place outside the top 10 deserve to be ranked.

Kermit Ambrose in 1962, giving Seaholm's MVP Award—the Kermit Ambrose Award—to Dave Kennedy. Today, MITCA's highest award for coaching excellence is named for Ambrose.

The Legacy Rating is very simple. Teams get a point for finishing with a score at the finals, and they get a point for every team they beat. So in the typical modern 27-team final, 1st place gets 27 points, last gets 1 point. It is a straightforward reflection of how a team does every year at the finals. Moving up or down in division doesn't matter. Each year's score reflects how the team did against similar-sized schools. So the Legacy Ratings are able to show all Lower Peninsula schools on the same list and is the truest measure possible of a school's dominance in MHSAA final competition.

We present two versions here: all-time (1922-2019) and 21st Century (2000-2019). The word "legacy" is key because the all-time listing, for instance, reflects the entire history of the school's cross country program at the finals. The structure of the ratings makes comparison across the many generations much more fair. For instance, there are schools that scored "easy" wins back in the 1940s, when sometimes only two teams would show up for a Class B final. The winning team only gets 2 points in those cases. A modern win (27ish) points is much more valuable. Thus it's also a reflection of the scale of participation in cross country in this state and how it has grown.

Like any rating, these are just for fun. My hope is that these Legacy Ratings also give credit to the schools that over the decades have also put a priority on cross country, even though coaches change and times change.

LEGACY RATINGS
TOP 100 ALL-TIME BOYS TEAMS

1. Ann Arbor/Pioneer 1132.5
2. Milford 808
3. Fremont 804
4. Benzie Central 690
5. White Lake Lakeland 657
6. Grand Rapids Christian 648
7. Jackson Lumen Christi 625
8. Rockford 622
9. Detroit Catholic Central 590
10. Monroe 574.5
11. Saline 571
12. Bear Lake/Onekama 523
13. St Joseph 514
14. Traverse City/Central 496
15. Charlevoix 487
16. Dearborn 483.5
17. Concord 476
18. Shepherd 466
19. Dearborn Divine Child 447
20. Stockbridge 440
21. Chelsea 436
22. Otsego 420.5
23. Napoleon 415
24. Grand Blanc 410.5
25. Flint Kearsley 400
26. Jackson 388.5
27. Sturgis 385
28. Potterville 384
29. Williamston 379
30. Harbor Springs 377
31. Kalamazoo Central 373
32. St Clair 371
33. Birmingham/Baldwin/Seaholm 366
34. Dexter 365
35. Grand Rapids Catholic Central 363
36. Linden 358
37. Flint Powers 351
38. Big Rapids 344
39. Novi 342
=40. Carson City-Crystal 339
=40. Portage Northern 339
=40. Sparta 339
43. Grosse Pointe North 338
=44. Mason County Central 335
=44. Petoskey 335
46. Clare 323
47. Corunna 320
=48. Grand Ledge 319
=48. Hemlock 319
50. Brighton 318

51. Lansing Catholic 316
52. Grandville Calvin Christian 314
53. St Louis 313
54. Caledonia 309
55. Coldwater 308
56. Pinckney 304
=57. Lake Orion 303
=57. Saugatuck 303
59. Ann Arbor Richard 297
60. Swartz Creek 283
61. Walled Lake/Walled Lake Central 281.5
62. Grand Rapids West Catholic 280
63. Pontiac/Pontiac Central 278.5
64. Caro 273
=65. Mt Pleasant Sacred Heart 271
=65. Richland Gull Lake 271
67. East Grand Rapids 268
68. Hudson 266
69. Hesperia 265
70. Okemos 264
71. Flint Central 263
72. Sandusky 262
73. Holly 258
74. Alma 257
75. Plymouth 256.5
=76. Hillsdale 254
=76. Temperance Bedford 254
=78. Mendon 251
=78. Rochester Adams 251
80. Bangor 250
=81. Ann Arbor Huron 249
=81. Pewamo-Westphalia 249
83. Ypsilanti/Ypsilanti Central 246.5
84. Bath 246
85. Fenton 245
86. Kalamazoo Hackett 241
87. Farmington 239
88. Kalamazoo Christian 237
89. Gaylord 236
90. Bloomfield Hills Lahser 235
=91. Hazel Park 234
=91. Kalamazoo Norrix 234
93. Cedar Springs 232
94. Saranac 229
95. Vicksburg 226.5
96. Charlotte 222
97. Haslett 221
98. Grand Haven 220
99. Bridgman 218
100. Wyoming Rogers 217

LEGACY RATINGS
TOP 100 BOYS TEAMS OF 21st CENTURY

1. Benzie Central....................431
2. Milford 420
3. Saline 408
4. Fremont 402
5. Rockford 390
6. Grand Rapids Christian....382
7. Bear Lake/Onekama 380
8. Harbor Springs 377
9. Ann Arbor/Pioneer...........362
10. Chelsea 355
11. Dexter............................351
12. St Clair 348
13. Lansing Catholic............311
14. Saugatuck 303
15. Jackson Lumen Christi..299
16. Shepherd.......................298
17. Pinckney........................294
18. Potterville......................292
19. Concord.........................284
20. Flint Powers 277
21. Williamston 266
22. Linden 263
=23. Mt Pleasant Sacred Heart...............255
=23. Traverse City/Central 255
25. White Lake Lakeland 254
26. Mendon 251
27. Hesperia 245
28. Lake Orion.....................244
29. Detroit Catholic Central.243
=30. Grandville Calvin Christian 237
=30. Hudson........................237
32. Corunna 231
33. East Grand Rapids........229
34. Stockbridge 225
35. Sparta............................217
36. Hanover-Horton.............216
37. Grand Rapids West Catholic............214
38. Otsego...........................212
=39. Bridgman......................208
=39. Saginaw Heritage.........208
41. Pewamo-Westphalia.....194
42. Bloomfield Hills Lahser .191
43. Charlevoix 188
44. Hillsdale.........................185
45. Petoskey 184
46. Hemlock........................183
47. Caro...............................182
48. Kalamazoo Hackett.......181
=49. Erie-Mason..................180
=49. Traverse City West 180
51. Grand Blanc 176

52. Fenton...........................174
53. Saranac.........................173
54. DeWitt............................168
55. Bangor 167
56. Beal City........................165
57. Mason County Central ..161
58. St Joseph......................159
59. St Louis 158
60. Clarkston.......................157
=61. Forest Hills Northern ...155
=61. Northville.....................155
63. Evart..............................154
=64. Ann Arbor Huron.........153
=64. Dearborn Divine Child.153
=66. Freeland......................151
=66. Richland Gull Lake 151
=66. Vandercook Lake.........151
69. Kent City 150
70. Clare 147
71. Ionia 144
72. Plymouth.......................137
73. Grand Rapids Covenant Christian....136
74. Novi 135
=75. Forest Hills Eastern 134
=75. Unionville-Sebewaing.134
77. North Muskegon 131
78. Holland Black River......130
79. St Johns........................127
80. Ann Arbor Richard........126
=81. Allendale.....................122
=81. Breckenridge...............122
=81. Portage Northern 122
=84. Caledonia....................120
=84. Coldwater....................120
=84. Ubly..............................120
=87. Sturgis.........................119
=87. Waterford Mott.............119
=89. Cedar Springs.............118
=89. East Jordan.................118
=89. Temperance Bedford..118
=92. Rochester Adams........117
=92. Whitmore Lake.............117
94. Haslett...........................115
95. Ellsworth 114
96. Southfield Christian......113
=97. Romeo.........................112
=97. Walled Lake Central ...112
=99. Big Rapids 111
=99. Jonesville....................111
=99. Spring Lake.................111

LEGACY RATINGS
TOP 100 ALL-TIME GIRLS TEAMS

1. Jackson Lumen Christi 826
2. Brighton 723
3. Traverse City/Central 717
4. Grand Rapids Christian 656
5. Milford 640
6. Rockford 619
7. Ann Arbor Pioneer 618
8. Saline 603
9. Grosse Pointe South 563
10. Sterling Heights Stevenson 539
11. Benzie Central 520
12. Chelsea 496
13. Flint Powers 482
14. East Grand Rapids 480
15. Gaylord 450
16. Troy 447
17. Rochester Adams 421
18. Grand Haven 420
19. Clarkston 402
20. Fremont 398
21. Dearborn Divine Child 394.5
22. Shepherd 387
23. Whitehall 378
24. Birmingham Seaholm 373
25. Clare 368
26. Harbor Springs 366
27. Richland Gull Lake 353
28. Hillsdale 350
29. Petoskey 347
30. Traverse City St Francis 345
31. Milan 344
32. Hanover-Horton 339
33. Fowler 334
34. Livonia Stevenson 331
35. Saugatuck 317
36. Mt Pleasant Sacred Heart 306
37. Grandville Calvin Christian 305
=38. DeWitt 297
=38. East Lansing 297
=38. Lansing Catholic 297
=41. Concord 296
=41. Williamston 296
43. Dexter 292
44. Southfield Christian 288
45. Otsego 275
46. Blissfield 274
47. Kalamazoo Hackett 272
48. Livonia Churchill 270
49. Dearborn Edsel Ford 269
50. Kalamazoo Christian 268
51. Grand Rapids South Christian 266
52. Northville 265
=53. Ann Arbor Greenhills 264
=53. Ubly 264
=55. Ann Arbor Huron 263
=55. Rochester 263
57. Bath 260
58. Forest Hills Eastern 259
59. Temperance Bedford 255
60. St Louis 254
61. Charlevoix 250
=62. Caledonia 245
=62. Kent City 245
=64. Grandville 239
=64. Pittsford 239
66. Holland Christian 238
67. Potterville 227
68. Royal Oak Shrine 226
69. Portage Northern 225
70. Caro 224.5
=71. Macomb Lutheran North 224
=71. Spring Lake 224
73. Ida 221
74. Troy Athens 217
75. Carson City-Crystal 213
76. Pewamo-Westphalia 206
77. Beal City 205
78. Gladwin 204
=79. Hudson 203
=79. Mt Pleasant 203
=79. Salem 203
82. Bear Lake 200
83. St Joseph 198.5
84. Grosse Pointe North 198
85. Manton 194
=86. Lutheran Westland 190
=86. Pinckney 190
88. Sparta 189.5
89. Suttons Bay 184
90. Allendale 181
=91. Ann Arbor Richard 177
=91. Middleville/Thornapple-Kellogg 177
=93. Elk Rapids 176
=93. Goodrich 176
95. Kalamazoo Norrix 175
96. Cedar Springs 172
=97. Grand Rapids Catholic Central 171
=97. Hesperia 171
99. Schoolcraft 170
100. Okemos 169

LEGACY RATINGS
TOP 100 GIRLS TEAMS OF 21st CENTURY

1. Rockford..................................462
2. Grand Rapids Christian.............455
3. Saline......................................448
4. Traverse City Central................445
5. East Grand Rapids...................417
6. Jackson Lumen Christi..............411
7. Harbor Springs........................366
8. Benzie Central.........................350
9. Milford....................................347
10. Traverse City St Francis..........339
11. Hanover-Horton......................337
12. Clarkston...............................330
13. Brighton.................................320
14. Saugatuck..............................317
15. Birmingham Seaholm..............301
16. Clare.....................................289
17. Flint Powers...........................288
18. Grand Haven.........................286
19. Lansing Catholic....................279
20. Mt Pleasant Sacred Heart.......272
21. Troy......................................271
22. Grosse Pointe South..............266
=23. Northville.............................262
=23. Shepherd.............................262
=25. Otsego.................................261
=25. Ubly....................................261
=27. Ann Arbor Pioneer................259
=27. Forest Hills Eastern..............259
29. Bear Lake Onekama..............242
30. Grandville Calvin Christian.....237
31. Rochester Adams..................233
32. Whitehall...............................228
=33. Macomb Lutheran North......224
=33. Spring Lake........................224
35. Gaylord.................................222
36. Dexter...................................221
37. Dearborn Divine Child............219
38. Livonia Churchill....................218
39. East Lansing.........................216
40. Chelsea................................212
41. Kent City...............................209
42. Concord................................208
43. Pewamo-Westphalia..............206
44. Beal City...............................205
=45. Hillsdale..............................203
=45. Salem..................................203
47. Ann Arbor Greenhills.............201
48. Williamston...........................197
49. DeWitt..................................186
=50. Fowler.................................185
=50. Hudson...............................185
52. Grand Rapids South Christian..........182
53. Allendale..............................181
=54. Blissfield.............................177
=54. Kalamazoo Hackett.............177
=54. Sterling Heights Stevenson..........177
=57. Goodrich............................176
=57. Royal Oak Shrine................176
=59. Petoskey............................175
=59. Richland Gull Lake.............175
61. Hesperia..............................171
62. Milan....................................169
63. Charlevoix............................168
64. Forest Hills Northern.............165
65. Southfield Christian...............162
66. Pinckney..............................161
67. Pittsford...............................155
68. Potterville.............................154
69. Hillsdale Academy................152
70. Ann Arbor Richard................151
71. Caro....................................150
=72. Akron-Fairgrove..................149
=72. Battle Creek St Philip..........149
=72. Grand Rapids NorthPointe Christ...149
=72. Grandville...........................149
76. Manton.................................148
77. Holland Christian..................147
78. Kalamazoo Christian............146
=79. Battle Creek Lakeview........145
=79. Elk Rapids..........................145
=81. Breckenridge......................142
=81. Lutheran Westland.............142
83. Leslie...................................141
84. St Louis...............................139
=85. Schoolcraft.........................138
=85. St Joseph..........................138
87. Cedar Springs.....................136
88. Middleville Thornapple-Kellogg........135
89. Bath.....................................133
=90. Sparta.................................130
=90. Warren Regina...................130
=92. Maple City Glen Lake.........129
=92. Okemos..............................129
94. Linden..................................127
95. Hamilton...............................125
=96. Ithaca..................................122
=96. Livonia Stevenson..............122
=96. Rochester...........................122
99. East Jordan.........................121
100. Freeland............................120

ALL-TIME LEGACY RATINGS BY SCHOOL
► BOYS ◄

The Pioneers of Ann Arbor, 1953.

Addison 74
   1970CD, 1972CD, 1973CD, 1975C, 1989C,
   1996C, 1999C, 2000D3, 2018D4
Adrian 123
   1951B, 1952B, 1954B, 1966A, 1968A, 1969A
   1975A, 1976A, 1979A, 1985A, 1986A, 1991A
   2010D2, 2019D2
Adrian Lenawee Christian 40
   2007D4, 2008D4
Adrian Madison 85
   1959CD, 1961CD, 1962CD, 1963CD, 1964CD
   1967CD, 2014D3
Akron-Fairgrove 95
   1972CD, 1976C, 1977D, 1978D, 1983D, 1985D
   1987D, 1988D, 1990D, 1991D, 1992D, 1993D
   1994D
Alanson 11
   1928CD, 1929CD, 1980D, 1988D, 1989D
Alba 12
   1962CD, 1963CD, 1985D
Albion 147
   1993B, 1997B, 1998C, 1999C, 2003D3, 2005D3
   2006D3, 2008D3, 2009D3, 2010D4, 2011D4
   2012D4
Albion-Starr Commonwealth 13
   1947CD, 1948CD
Algonac 40
   1986B, 1989B, 1991B, 1992B

Allegan 57
   1949B,1950B,1952B,1953B,1954B,1968B,
   1990B,1993B,2000D2,2002D2,2017D2
Allen Park 32
   1956A, 1957A, 2014D2, 2015D2
Allen Park Cabrini 111
   1975C, 1976C, 1978C, 1979C, 1980C, 1981C
   1998C, 1999C, 2000D4, 2001D4, 2002D4,
   2010D3, 2019D4
Allendale 158
   1982D, 1998C, 1999C, 2002D3, 2003D3,
2004D3
   2005D3, 2006D3, 2009D3, 2010D3, 2019D2
Alma 257
   1940B,1941B,1947B,1948B,1949B,1950B,
   1951B,1952B,1953B,1954B,1958B,1965B,
   1966B,1971B,1972B,1975B,1976B,2006D2,
   2007D2,2008D2,2009D2,2010D2,2018D2,
   2019D2
Almont 44
   2009D3, 2010D3, 2011D3, 2013D3, 2014D3
   2015D3, 2016D3, 2017D3
Alpena 82
   1974A,1976A,1977A,1979A,1999A,2016D1,
   2018D1
Ann Arbor/Pioneer 1132.5
   1922,1923,1924,1925,1926,1927,1928A
   1930A,1933A,1934A,1935A,1937A,1939A
   1940A,1941A,1945A,1946A,1947A,1948A
   1949A,1950A1,1950A2,1951A,1952A
   1953A,1954A,1958A,1959A,1960A,1963A
   1964A,1965A,1966A,1968A,1970A,1971A
   1972A,1973A,1975A,1979A,1980A,1983A
   1984A,1985A,1986A,1987A,1988A,1989A
   1990A,1991A,1992A,1993A,1994A,1995A
   1996A,1997A,2000D1,2001D1,2003D1
   2004D1,2005D1,2006D1,2007D1,2008D1
   2009D1,2010D1,2011D1,2012D1,2013D1
   2014D1,2016D1,2017D1,2018D1,2019D1
Ann Arbor Richard 297
   1976D, 1977D, 1978D, 1979D, 1980D, 1981D
   1982D, 1983D, 1984D, 1985D, 1986D, 1990D
   1991D, 1994D, 1995D, 1996D, 2000D4, 2001D4
   2002D4, 2003D4, 2004D4, 2005D4, 2007D4
   2008D4, 2009D4, 2017D3, 2018D3
Ann Arbor Huron 249
   1969A, 1970A, 1973A, 1975A, 1987A, 1989A
   1993A, 2002D1, 2003D1, 2004D1, 2005D1
   2007D1, 2008D1, 2009D1, 2010D1
Ann Arbor Richard 147
   1977D, 1978D, 1979D, 1980B, 1981D, 1982D
   1985C, 1987C, 1988D, 1989D, 1990D, 1991D
   1992C, 1992D, 1994D, 1995D, 1996D, 1997C
   2003D4, 2007D3, 2008D3, 2012D3, 2014D2
Ann Arbor Skyline 91
   2014D1, 2015D1, 2017D1, 2018D1, 2019D1
Ann Arbor St Thomas 119
   1961CD, 1962CD, 1963CD, 1964CD, 1965CD
   1967CD, 1968CD, 1970CD, 1971CD
Armada 55
   2003D3, 2004D3, 2008D3, 2009D3, 2014D2
   2018D2, 2019D2

Athens 12
   2002D4
Atlanta 9
   1997D, 1999D
Auburn Hills (Heights) Avondale 35
   1952B, 1971B, 1972B
Auburn Hills Oakland Christian 34
   1999D, 2002D4, 2003D4, 2004D4, 2006D4
   2010D4, 2011D4, 2015D4, 2017D4
Bad Axe 33
   1940B, 1999B, 2000D3, 2001D3, 2017D3
Bangor 250
   1966CD, 1970CD, 1977C, 1978C, 1979C,
   1985C, 1993C, 1994C, 1995C, 1996C, 1997C,
   1998C, 2000D3, 2001D3, 2005D3, 2006D3,
   2007D3, 2008D3, 2009D3, 2012D3, 2014D3,
   2015D3, 2016D3, 2017D3, 2018D3
Bangor Glenn 6
   2005D2
Bath 246
   1974C, 1975C, 1976C, 1982C, 1983C, 1984C,
   1985C, 1991C, 1992D, 1993C, 1994D, 1995C,
   1997C, 1998C, 2001D4, 2002D4, 2003D4,
   2016D3
Battle Creek Central 173.5
   1922, 1924, 1944A, 1945A, 1946A, 1947A,
   1948A, 1949A, 1950A1, 1950A2, 1951A, 1952A,
   1953A, 1955A, 1972B
Battle Creek Harper Creek 92
   1968B, 1970B, 1974B, 1976B, 1977B, 1978B,
   1988B, 2016D2, 2019D2
Battle Creek Lakeview 99.5
   1968A, 1970A, 1974C, 1979A, 1980A, 1981B,
   1982B, 1990B, 1992A, 1998B
Battle Creek Springfield 10
   1961CD
Battle Creek St Philip 74
   1968CD, 1969CD, 1970CD, 1980D, 1983D,
   1984D, 2016D4, 2017D4
Bay City Central 89
   1949A, 1950A1, 1950A2, 1951A, 1952A, 1970A,
   1971A
Bay City Handy 41
   1949A, 1950A1, 1951A, 1952A, 1972A, 1988B
Bay City Western 81
   1997A, 2007D1, 2008D1, 2010D1, 2015D1,
   2016D1
Beal City 165
   2002D4, 2013D4, 2014D4, 2015D4, 2016D4,
   2017D4, 2018D4, 2019D4
Bear Lake/Onekama 523
   1975D, 1976D, 1977D, 1978D, 1979D, 1989D,
   1990D, 1991D, 1992D, 1993D, 1994D, 1996D,
   1997D, 1998D, 1999D, 2000D4, 2001D4,
   2002D4, 2003D4, 2004D4, 2005D4, 2006D4,
   2007D4, 2008D4, 2009D4, 2010D4, 2011D4,
   2012D4, 2013D4, 2014D4, 2015D4, 2016D4,
   2017D4, 2018D4
Beaverton 96
   1987C, 1988C, 1989B, 1990B, 2002D3, 2003D3,
   2004D3, 2016D3
Belding 5

1992B
Bellaire 5
    1961CD
Belleville 84
    1949B, 1950B, 1951B, 1952B, 1953B, 1971A,
    1991A, 1993A
Bellevue 88
    1967CD, 2003D4, 2004D4, 2005D4, 2008D4,
    2009D4
Benton Harbor 29
    1928A, 1941A, 1947A, 1950A1, 1951A
Benzie Central 690
    1973CD, 1975C, 1976C, 1980C, 1981C, 1982C,
    1983C, 1984C, 1985C, 1986C, 1987C, 1989C,
    1994C, 1995C, 1996C, 1997C, 1998C, 1999C,
    2000D3, 2001D3, 2002D3, 2003D3, 2004D3,
    2005D3, 2006D3, 2007D3, 2008D3, 2009D3,
    2010D3, 2011D3, 2012D3, 2013D3, 2014D3,
    2015D3, 2016D3, 2018D3, 2019D3
Berkley 42
    1965A, 1991A, 1992A, 1993A
Berrien Springs 63
    1998C, 1999C, 2006D3, 2016D3, 2017D3,
    2018D3, 2019D2
Big Rapids 344
    1975B, 1977B, 1978B, 1986B, 1987B, 1988B,
    1990B, 1991B, 1992B, 1996B, 1997B, 1998B,
    1999B, 2000D2, 2001D2, 2002D2, 2004D2,
    2009D2, 2015D2, 2018D2
Birch Run 13
    1946CD, 1947CD, 1948CD, 1949CD, 1950CD,
    1951CD
Birmingham/Baldwin/Seaholm 366
    1927B, 1928B, 1943B, 1944B, 1945B, 1946B,
    1947B, 1948B, 1949B, 1950B, 1951B, 1952A,
    1953A, 1954A, 1955A, 1956A, 1957A, 1958A,
    1959A, 1960A, 1961A, 1962A, 1963A, 1964A,
    1966A, 1970A, 1971A, 2000D2, 2004D2,
    2005D2, 2006D2, 2013D1, 2015D1, 2016D1
Birmingham Groves 24
    1973A, 1975A, 1979A, 1989A
Blanchard Montabella 12
    1940CD, 1941CD, 2009D4
Blissfield 17
    1970B, 1973CD, 2015D3
Bloomfield Hills 7
    1959B, 1993B
Bloomfield Hills Andover 15
    1992B, 1993B, 1994B, 1997B, 1998B, 2012D2
Bloomfield Hills Cranbrook 192
    1945B, 1946B, 1947B, 1948B, 1980B, 1984B,
    1985B, 1987B, 1988B, 1989B, 1991B, 1992B,
    1993B, 1996B, 2000D2, 2001D2, 2005D2,
    2006D2, 2013D2, 2014D2
Bloomfield Hills Lahser 235
    1971A, 1979A, 1987A, 1999A, 2001D2, 2002D2,
    2003D2, 2004D2, 2005D2, 2006D2, 2007D2,
    2009D2, 2011D2, 2012D2
Bloomingdale 29
    2009D3, 2018D3, 2019D3
Boyne City 14
    1959CD, 2014D3

Boyne Falls 49
    1990D, 1991D, 1992D, 1993D, 1994D, 1995D,
    2003D4, 2011D4, 2013D4
Breckenridge 203
    1976C, 1977C, 1978C, 1994C, 1995C, 1998C,
    2001D4, 2011D4, 2012D4, 2014D4, 2018D4,
    2019D4
Brethren 13
    2005D4
Bridgeport 7
    1983A, 1987A
Bridgman 218
    1989C, 1990C, 2003D4, 2007D4, 2008D4,
    2009D4, 2010D4, 2011D3, 2013D3, 2014D3,
    2015D3, 2017D4, 2018D4, 2019D4
Brighton 318
    1975B, 1976A, 1977A, 1978A, 1979A, 1981A,
    1983A, 1984A, 1991A, 1992A, 1993A, 1994A,
    1995A, 1996A, 2006D1, 2010D1, 2016D1,
    2017D1, 2018D1, 2019D1
Britton Deerfield 5
    2013D4
Bronson 22
    1984C, 2002D3, 2004D3, 2015D3
Brooklyn/Columbia Central 29
    1935CD, 1936CD, 1938CD, 1994B
Brown City 137
    1958CD, 1959CD, 1960CD, 1961CD, 1962CD,
    1963CD, 2000D4, 2001D4, 2002D4, 2003D4,
    2004D4, 2007D4, 2010D4
Buchanan 24
    1979C, 1991C, 1992B
Buckley 70
    1970CD, 1973CD, 1974D, 1993D, 1994D,
    1995D, 1997D, 1998D, 1999D, 2000D4, 2001D4
Burr Oak 40
    1989D, 1990D, 1992D, 1993D, 1994D
Burton Atherton 36
    1957CD, 1958CD, 1959CD, 1960CD, 1995C,
    1992C
Burton Bendle 9
    1936CD, 1969CD
Byron 17
    2009D3, 2011D3, 2014D3, 2018D3, 2019D3
Byron Center 46
    1964CD, 1965CD, 2008D2, 2010D2
Cadillac 165
    1977B, 1978B, 1979B, 1980B, 1981B, 1982B,
    1989B, 1990B, 1992A, 1993A, 1994B, 2001D2,
    2002D2, 2008D2
Caledonia 309
    1981C, 1986B, 1987B, 1989B, 1990B, 1991B,
    1992B, 1994B, 1995B, 1996B, 1999B, 2006D2,
    2007D2, 2008D1, 2009D1, 2010D1, 2011D1,
    2015D1, 2016D1, 2018D1, 2019D1
Camden-Frontier 140
    1954CD, 1955CD, 1956CD, 1957CD, 1958CD,
    1959CD, 1960CD, 1961CD, 1962CD, 1963CD,
    1964CD, 1990D, 1991D, 1992D, 1993D, 1995D
Canton 61
    1980A, 1989A, 1990A, 1994A, 2001D1, 2007D1
Capac 110

1964CD, 1976C, 1977C, 1978C, 1982C, 1985C, 1986C, 2003D3, 2004D3, 2005D3, 2006D3, 2013D3
Carleton Airport 75.5
1975B, 1976B, 1977B, 1979B, 1983B, 2000D2, 2001D2, 2003D2, 2004D2, 2005D2, 2006D2, 2007D2, 2008D2, 2009D2
Caro 273
1979B, 1980B, 1981B, 1983B, 1984B, 1989B, 1994B, 2000D2, 2001D3, 2007D3, 2008D3, 2009D3, 2012D3, 2013D3, 2014D3, 2015D3, 2016D3, 2017D3, 2018D3, 2019D3
Carrollton 10
1974B, 2013D3, 2014D3
Carson City-Crystal 339
1962CD, 1971CD, 1972CD, 1973CD, 1974C, 1985C, 1986C, 1988C, 1990C, 1991C, 1992C, 1993C, 1994C, 1995C, 1996C, 1997C, 2003D3, 2004D3, 2005D3, 2007D3, 2017D4, 2019D4
Carsonville-Port Sanilac 26
1997D, 2000D4, 2003D4, 2010D4, 2011D4, 2009D4
Cass City 131
1981C, 1982C, 1983C, 1984C, 2005D3, 2006D3, 2007D3, 2008D3, 2015D3, 2016D4, 2017D4
Cedar Springs 232
1965B, 1977B, 1989B, 1990B, 1991B, 1992B, 1993B, 1994B, 1995B, 2003D2, 2011D2, 2012D2, 2017D2, 2018D2, 2019D1
Center Line 119
1980B, 1983B, 1984B, 1985B, 1986B, 1990B, 2002D2, 2003D2
Central Lake 67
1949CD, 1995D, 1996D, 1997D, 2001D4, 2002D4, 2009D4
Centreville 73
1975D, 1931CD, 1974D, 1976D, 1980D, 1981D, 1982D, 1987C, 1989C, 1990C, 1992C, 2014D4
Charlevoix 487
1977C, 1978C, 1979C, 1980C, 1981C, 1982C, 1983C, 1984C, 1985C, 1986C, 1987C, 1988C, 1989C, 1990C, 1991C, 1992C, 1993C, 1994C, 2000D3, 2001D3, 2008D3, 2009D3, 2011D3, 2013D3, 2015D3, 2016D3, 2017D3, 2018D3, 2019D3
Charlotte 222
1938B, 1940B, 1941B, 1943B, 1944B, 1945B, 1946B, 1947B, 1948B, 1949B, 1955B, 1967B, 1968B, 1969B, 1970B, 1971B, 1972B, 1973B, 1978B, 1979B, 1980B
Chelsea 436
1980B, 1981B, 1982B, 1985B, 1992B, 1994B, 1999B, 2000D2, 2002D2, 2003D2, 2004D2, 2005D2, 2006D2, 2007D2, 2008D2, 2009D2, 2010D2, 2011D2, 2012D2, 2013D2, 2014D2, 2015D2, 2016D2, 2017D2, 2018D2, 2019D2
Chesaning 59
1938CD, 1970B, 1979B, 1984B, 2009D3, 2011D3
Clare 323
1974C, 1975C, 1976C, 1978C, 1977C, 1979C, 1987C, 1988C, 1990C, 1991C, 1992C, 1993C, 1995C, 2000D3, 2009D3, 2011D3, 2012D3, 2013D3, 2014D3, 2015D3, 2016D3, 2017D3, 2018D3
Clarkston 199
1970A, 1999A, 2000D1, 2004D1, 2005D1, 2008D1, 2011D1, 2012D1, 2014D1, 2015D1, 2016D1, 2017D1, 2018D1, 2019D1
Clarksville 10
1929CD, 1931CD
Clawson 58
1994B, 1995B, 1996B, 1997B, 1998B
Clinton 55
1964CD, 1977C, 1978C, 1983C, 1984C, 2011D3, 2019D3
Clinton Township Chippewa Valley 5
1987A
Clio 141
1960B, 1961B, 1963A, 1964B, 1967A, 1980A, 1986A, 1987A, 1990A, 2011D2, 2012D2, 2013D2, 2014D2, 2015D2, 2016D2
Coldwater 308
1924, 1923, 1956B, 1969B, 1983B, 1989B, 1991B, 1992B, 1993B, 1994B, 1995B, 1997A, 1998B, 1999B, 2002D2, 2003D2, 2004D2, 2005D2, 2006D2, 2015D2, 2016D2
Coleman 17
2002D4, 2003D4
Colon 120
1985D, 1986D, 1987D, 1989D, 1997D, 2002D4, 2003D4, 2004D4, 2005D4, 2006D4, 2007D4
Columbiaville 1
1948CD
Comstock Park 5
1994C
Concord 476
1966CD, 1969CD, 1972CD, 1973CD, 1974C, 1975D, 1976D, 1977D, 1978D, 1980C, 1981D, 1982D, 1983D, 1984D, 1985C, 1986D, 1987D, 1988C, 1994C, 1995C, 1997C, 2000D4, 2006D4, 2008D4, 2009D4, 2010D4, 2011D4, 2012D4, 2013D4, 2014D4, 2015D4, 2016D4, 2018D4, 2019D4
Constantine 56
1996C, 2001D3, 2002D3, 2003D3, 2004D3
Coopersville 3
1963B
Corunna 320
1971B, 1974B, 1986B, 1996B, 1997B, 1998B, 2001D2, 2002D3, 2003D3, 2004D2, 2005D2, 2006D2, 2010D2, 2013D2, 2014D2, 2015D2, 2016D2, 2017D2, 2018D2, 2019D2
Covert 76
1957CD, 1958CD, 1959CD, 1960CD, 1961CD, 1962CD, 1963CD, 1964CD, 1965CD
Croswell/Croswell-Lexington 154
1930CD, 1931CD, 1948B, 1949B, 1950B, 1951B, 1960B, 1963B, 1994B, 1996B, 2002D2, 2003D2, 2009D2, 2010D2, 2011D2, 2012D2, 2013D2, 2015D2, 2016D2, 2017D2
Crystal 5

1956CD, 1957CD, 1958CD
Dansville 75
   1969CD, 1971CD, 1972CD, 1973CD, 1974D,
   1975D, 1976D, 1981D, 2017D4, 2019D4
Davison 131.5
   1948B, 1949B, 1951B, 1952B, 1954B, 1980A,
   1981A, 1985A, 1988A, 1998A, 2019D1
Dearborn 483.5
   1926, 1927B, 1928B, 1929B, 1930B, 1931B,
   1934B, 1935B, 1936A, 1937A, 1938A, 1939A,
   1940A, 1941A, 1943A, 1944A, 1945A, 1946A,
   1947A, 1948A, 1949A, 1950A1, 1951A, 1952A,
   1953A, 1955A, 1956A, 1957A, 1958A, 1959A,
   1960A, 1962A, 1967A, 1969A, 1970A, 1971A,
   1972A, 1973A, 1975A, 1979A, 1980A, 1983A,
   1984A, 1985A, 1986B, 1987B, 1988B, 1989B,
   1990A, 1992A, 1994A, 1999A, 2000D1, 2019D1
Dearborn Divine Child 447
   1971B, 1975B, 1977B, 1978B, 1979B, 1980B,
   1981B, 1982B, 1983B, 1984B, 1985B, 1986B,
   1987B, 1988B, 1989B, 1990B, 1991B, 1992B,
   1993B, 1994B, 1997B, 1999B, 2000D2,
   2002D2, 2003D2, 2005D2, 2009D2, 2010D2,
   2011D2, 2012D2, 2013D2, 2014D2, 2016D2,
   2017D2, 2018D2, 2019D2
Dearborn Edsel Ford 208
   1956A, 1957A, 1960A, 1973A, 1974A, 1976A,
   1977A, 1978A, 1981A, 1982A, 1983A, 1984A,
   1985A, 1986A
Dearborn Fordson 209
   1928B, 1929B, 1930A, 1975A, 1976A, 1978A,
   1979A, 1983A, 1984A, 1988A, 1990A, 1992A,
   1993A, 1994A, 1996A, 1997A, 1998A, 2002D1,
   2007D1
Dearborn Heights Annapolis 16
   1968B, 2002D3, 2006D2
Dearborn Heights Crestwood 60
   1990B, 1995B, 1997B, 1998B, 2002D2, 2003D2,
   2004D2
Dearborn Heights Riverside 77
   1962B, 1963B, 1964B, 1965B, 1966B, 1967B
Dearborn St Alphonsus 26
   1970CD, 1975C, 1976C
Deckerville 40
   2013D4, 2017D4, 2019D4
Delton Kellogg 27
   1981B, 2003D3, 2010D3
Detroit Austin 51
   1974B, 1975B, 1976B
Detroit Benedictine 5
   2000D4, 2001D4
Detroit Cass Tech 18
   1926, 1927A, 1928A, 1984A
Detroit Catholic Central 590
   1951A, 1964A, 1968A, 1974A, 1979A, 1982A,
   1983A, 1984A, 1985A, 1987A, 1988A, 1989A,
   1991A, 1992A, 1993A, 1994A, 1995A, 1996A,
   1997A, 1998A, 1999A, 2000D1, 2001D1,
   2002D1, 2003D1, 2005D1, 2007D1, 2008D1,
   2009D1, 2010D1, 2014D1, 2015D1, 2019D1
Detroit Central 8
   1924, 1923, 1962A
Detroit Chavez Academy 1
   2005D4
Detroit Cody 4
   1961A
Detroit Communication Media Arts 5
   2008D3
Detroit Cooley 3
   1969A, 1971A
Detroit Country Day 31
   1962CD, 1978D, 1979D, 1980D, 2004D3,
   2010D2, 2011D2, 2014D2
Detroit Crockett 4
   2006D3
Detroit DePorres 3
   1978D
Detroit East Catholic 41
   1969B, 1970B, 1973CD, 1978D
Detroit Eastern 50
   1922, 1925, 1926, 1923, 1927A, 1928A, 1929A
Detroit Holy Redeemer 67
   1927B, 1928B, 1979C, 1989D, 1993D, 1994D,
   1995D, 1996D, 1997D, 1998D, 1999D, 2000D4,
   2001D4, 2002D4, 2004D4
Detroit Lutheran West 60
   1964B, 1968B, 1982C, 1983C, 1984C, 1985C,
   1986C
Detroit Mumford 12
   1966A, 2006D1, 2007D1
Detroit Murray-Wright 10
   1983A, 1988A
Detroit Northeastern 2
   1922, 1923
Detroit Northern 8
   1925, 1927A, 1928A
Detroit Northwestern 64
   1922, 1924, 1925, 1926, 1923, 1928A, 1929A,
   1961A, 1962A
Detroit Osborn 3
   1991A
Detroit Redford 72
   1926, 1928A, 1961A, 1962A, 1964A, 1965A,
   1966A
Detroit Servite 9
   1963B
Detroit Southeastern 41
   1923, 1924, 1925, 1926, 1927A, 1928A, 1929A
Detroit St Anthony 39
   1966B, 1967B, 1968B
Detroit St Charles s3
   1948CD
Detroit St Joseph 21
   1951A, 1952A, 1963B
Detroit Temple Christian 3
   1976D
Detroit U-D Jesuit 137
   1959A, 1963A, 1968A, 1979B, 1980B, 1985B,
   1986B, 1988A, 1990A, 1997A, 2000D1, 2001D1,
   2002D1, 2003D1, 2004D1, 2005D1, 2006D1,
   2007D1, 2011D1
Detroit Western 16
   1926, 1927A
Detroit Weston Prep 1

2008D4

DeWitt 168
1961CD, 1962CD, 1963CD, 1964CD, 1969CD,
1975C, 1976C, 1977C, 1978C, 1980C, 1981C,
1983C

Dexter 365
1954CD, 1955CD, 1995B, 1996B, 2001D2,
2002D2, 2003D2, 2004D2, 2005D2, 2006D2,
2007D2, 2009D2, 2010D1, 2011D1, 2012D1,
2015D1, 2016D1, 2018D1, 2019D1

Dryden 21
2018D4

Dundee 108
1999C, 2000D3, 2003D3, 2006D3, 2012D3,
2013D3, 2014D3, 2015D3, 2016D3, 2017D3,
2018D3, 2019D3

Durand 34
1988B, 2004D3, 2006D3, 2009D3

East Grand Rapids 268
1965B, 1972B, 1985B, 2001D2, 2002D2,
2003D2, 2004D2, 2005D2, 2012D2, 2013D2,
2014D2, 2015D2, 2016D2, 2017D1, 2018D2,
2019D2

East Jackson 163
1939CD, 1940CD, 1941CD, 1947CD, 1957CD,
1958CD, 1959CD, 1960CD, 1961CD, 1967B,
1968CD, 1969CD, 1977C, 1978C, 1979C

East Jordan 192
1994C, 1997C, 1998C, 1999C, 2000D4, 2001D4,
2017D4, 2018D4, 2019D4

East Kentwood/Kentwood 210
1961CD, 1963B, 1975A, 1976A, 1979A, 1980A,
1982A, 1983A, 1984A, 1985A, 1987A, 1988A,
1994A, 1998A, 2008D1, 2009D1, 2011D1,
2013D1, 2017D1

East Lansing 157
1948B, 1959A, 1960A, 1965A, 1966A, 1967A,
1972A, 1982A, 1983A, 1993A, 2000D2, 2001D2,
2003D2, 2008D2, 2010D2

East Pointe/East Detroit 32
1975A, 1988A, 1989A, 1990A, 1992A

Eaton Rapids 80
1949B, 1994B, 1995B, 1996B, 2006D2, 2007D2

Eau Claire 57
2006D4, 2010D4, 2011D4, 2012D4, 2014D4,
2015D4

Ecorse 29
1934B, 1959B, 1960B, 1961B, 1966B, 1967A,
1982B

Edwardsburg 140
1954CD, 1955CD, 1975C, 1976C, 1977C,
1980C, 1981C, 1982C, 1983C, 1984C, 1985C,
1986C, 1987C, 1988C, 1989C, 1991B, 1992C,
1996B

Elk Rapids (inc. Cherryland) 98
1968CD, 1969CD, 1975D, 2001D3, 2006D3,
2007D3, 2008D3

Elkton-Pigeon-Bayport 6
1982C, 1994C

Ellsworth 114
2004D4, 2005D4, 2006D4, 2007D4, 2010D4,
2014D4, 2015D4, 2016D4, 2017D4, 2018D4

Elsie 12
1963CD

Erie-Mason 199
1992C, 1995C, 1997C, 1998C, 2000D3, 2003D3,
2004D3, 2005D3, 2006D3, 2009D3, 2011D3,
2012D3, 2015D3, 2016D3, 2017D3, 2019D3

Essexville Garber 205
1964CD, 1980B, 1981B, 1982B, 1983B, 1984B,
1985B, 1986B, 1987B, 1988B, 1990B, 1998B,
2001D3, 2002D3, 2003D3, 2004D3, 2013D2,
2015D2, 2017D2

Evart 154
2009D4, 2010D3, 2011D4, 2012D4, 2013D4,
2014D4, 2015D4, 2016D4

Fairview 133
1964CD, 1968CD, 1969CD, 1971CD, 1979D,
1980D, 1982D, 1987D, 1989D, 1990D, 1991D,
1993D, 1995D, 1996D, 2003D4, 2005D4,
2014D4, 2016D4

Farmington 239
1949B, 1950B, 1951B, 1952B, 1954B, 1955B,
1956B, 1969A, 1970A, 1974A, 1977A, 1984A,
1985A, 1986A, 1987A, 2000D2

Farmington Hills Harrison 19
1986B, 1991B, 2002D2, 2005D2, 2006D2

Farwell 13
1990C, 2012D3

Fennville 100
1960CD, 1961CD, 1962CD, 1963CD, 1964CD,
1971CD, 1984C

Fenton 245
1950B, 1951B, 1953CD, 1962B, 1965B, 1968B,
1969B, 1970B, 1974B, 1978B, 2002D2, 2003D2,
2004D2, 2005D2, 2006D2, 2007D2, 2008D2,
2015D1, 2017D1, 2018D1, 2019D1

Ferndale 122.5
1927B, 1928B, 1931A, 1932A, 1933A, 1934A,
1935A, 1938A, 1939A, 1940A, 1965A, 1967A,
1983A, 1987A, 1993A, 2004D2, 2006D2,
2007D2, 2011D2, 2013D2, 2014D2

Flat Rock 38
1990C, 1991C, 1992C, 1993C, 1996C, 2013D2

Flint Ainsworth 83
1976B, 1977B, 1978B, 1979B, 1981B, 1982B,
1984B, 1985B

Flint Carman-Ainsworth 7
1994A, 1997A

Flint Central 263
1924, 1927A, 1928A, 1930A, 1931A, 1932A,
1933A, 1934A, 1935A, 1936A, 1937A, 1938A,
1939A, 1940A, 1941A, 1943A, 1946A, 1947A,
1948A, 1949A, 1950A1, 1951A, 1952A, 1957A,
1958A, 1960A, 1961A, 1963A, 1965A, 1966A

Flint Hamady 10
1964CD, 1976B

Flint Holy Rosary 19
1975D, 1978D, 1981D

Flint Hoover 2
1940CD

Flint Kearsley 400
1941CD, 1943CD, 1944B, 1945B, 1946B,
1947B, 1948B, 1952B, 1953B, 1968A, 1969A,

1970A, 1971A, 1972A, 1973A, 1975A, 1976A,
1977A, 1978A, 1979A, 1980A, 1981A, 1982A,
1984A, 1985A, 1989A, 1991A, 1992A, 1993A,
1994A, 1995A, 1996A, 2000D2, 2007D2

Flint Northern 192
1929A, 1930A, 1931A, 1932A, 1934A, 1937A,
1938A, 1939A, 1945A, 1946A, 1947A, 1948A,
1949A, 1950A1, 1951A, 1952A, 1956A, 1973A,
1974A, 1978A, 1986A

Flint Powers 351
1972B, 1975B, 1976B, 1997B, 1998B, 1999B,
2000D2, 2001D2, 2002D2, 2003D2, 2004D2,
2005D2, 2006D3, 2007D2, 2008D2, 2009D2,
2010D3, 2016D2, 2017D2, 2018D2, 2019D2

Flint Southwestern 32
1959A, 1960A, 1962A

Flint Technical 10
1948B, 1949B

Flint Utley 12
1947CD, 1948CD

Flushing 54
1962B, 1964B, 1965B, 1966B, 1991A, 1992A,
2005D1, 2007D1

Forest Hills Central 47
1978B, 1983B, 1987B, 2002D1, 2018D1

Forest Hills Eastern 134
2006D2, 2007D2, 2008D2, 2009D2, 2011D2,
2013D2, 2015D2, 2016D2

Forest Hills Northern 159
1983C, 2004D2, 2005D2, 2009D2, 2010D2,
2011D2, 2012D2, 2013D2, 2014D2

Fowler 176
1985D, 1986D, 1987D, 1988D, 1989D, 1990D,
1991D, 1992D, 1993D, 1994D, 1995D, 1996D,
1997D, 1998D, 1999D, 2008D4

Fowlerville 20
1930CD, 1931CD, 1955CD, 1964CD, 1993B

Frankenmuth 74
1987B, 1993B, 2002D3, 2008D3, 2009D3,
2010D3, 2011D3

Frankfort 16
2014D4, 2015D4, 2016D4, 2019D4

Fraser 4
1986A

Freeland 193
1978C, 1979C, 2004D3, 2005D3, 2006D3,
2008D3, 2009D3, 2010D3, 2011D3, 2012D3,
2013D3

Freesoil 11
1964CD

Fremont 804
1946B, 1949B, 1976B, 1978B, 1979B, 1980B,
1982B, 1983B, 1984B, 1985B, 1986B, 1987B,
1988B, 1989B, 1991B, 1992B, 1993B, 1994B,
1995B, 1997B, 2000D2, 2001D2, 2002D2,
2003D2, 2004D2, 2005D2, 2006D2, 2007D2,
2008D2, 2009D2, 2010D2, 2014D2, 2015D2,
2016D2, 2017D2, 2018D2, 2019D2

Fruitport 44
1985B, 1986B, 2016D2

Fulton-Middleton 29
1970CD, 1975D, 1977D, 1979C

Galien 22
1964CD, 1998D, 1999D

Garden City East 15
1976A, 1977A

Gaylord 236
1951CD, 1952CD, 1982B, 1988B, 1992B, 1993B,
1994B, 1995B, 1996B, 1998A, 1999B, 2003D2,
2009D2, 2010D2, 2011D2, 2012D2

Gaylord St Mary 10
2002D4

Genesee 6
1997D, 1998D

Gibraltar Carlson 34
1984B, 1986A, 1987A

Gladwin 42
1991B, 1998B, 1999B, 2000D3, 2006D3

Glen Arbor Leelanau 9
1961CD

Gobles 40
2002D4, 2004D4, 2005D4, 2017D4, 2018D4

Goodrich 88
1984C, 1993C, 1994C, 1995C, 1996C, 2000D3,
2001D3, 2002D3, 2018D2, 2019D2

Grand Rapids West Michigan Aviation 17
2016D3

Grand Blanc 410.5
1945B, 1946B, 1967A, 1968A, 1969A, 1972A,
1974A, 1975A, 1976A, 1977A, 1978A, 1979A,
1981A, 1982A, 1983A, 1984A, 2000D1, 2001D1,
2002D1, 2003D1, 2004D1, 2008D1, 2009D1,
2010D1, 2011D1, 2012D1, 2013D1, 2014D1,
2016D1

Grand Haven 220
1977A, 1978A, 1989A, 1990A, 1994A, 1995A,
1996A, 1997A, 2005D1, 2010D1, 2011D1,
2012D1, 2014D1, 2015D1, 2016D1, 2017D1,
2018D1

Grand Ledge 319
1952B, 1956B, 1957B, 1959B, 1972A, 1974A,
1986A, 1987A, 1988A, 1989A, 1990A, 1994A,
1995A, 1996A, 1997A, 1998A, 1999A, 2000D1,
2001D1, 2003D1, 2007D1, 2012D1

Grand Rapids Baptist 30
2000D4, 2001D3

Grand Rapids Catholic Central 363
1948A, 1949A, 1950A2, 1951A, 1952A, 1953A,
1956A, 1957A, 1958A, 1965A, 1974B, 1975B,
1981B, 1982B, 1983B, 1984B, 1989B, 1993B,
1994B, 1996B, 1997B, 1998B, 2002D2, 2003D2,
2009D2, 2013D2

Grand Rapids Central 19.5
1954B, 1956A, 1959A, 1960A, 1961A

Grand Rapids Central Christian 3
1971B

Grand Rapids Christian 648
1958A, 1959A, 1960A, 1961A, 1963A, 1964A,
1966A, 1967A, 1970B, 1977B, 1978B, 1979B,
1980B, 1981B, 1982B, 1985B, 1989A, 1990A,
1991A, 1992A, 1993A, 1999A, 2001D2, 2002D2,
2003D2, 2004D2, 2005D2, 2006D2, 2007D2,
2008D2, 2009D2, 2010D2, 2011D2, 2012D2,

2013D2, 2014D2, 2015D2, 2016D2, 2017D2, 2018D2, 2019D2
Grand Rapids Covenant Christian 136
   2003D4, 2004D4, 2005D4, 2006D4, 2007D4, 2014D3, 2015D3, 2019D3
Grand Rapids Creston 35
   1956A, 1968A, 1969A, 1970A
Grand Rapids East Christian 41
   1965B, 1966B, 1967B
Grand Rapids Kenowa Hills 31
   1988B, 2009D1, 2012D1
Grand Rapids NorthPointe Christian 43
   2004D4, 2010D3, 2011D3
Grand Rapids Northview 41
   1967B, 1968B, 1972B
Grand Rapids Ottawa Hills 27
   1950B, 1954A, 1968A, 1976A
Grand Rapids South 22.5
   1928A, 1930A, 1931A, 1951A
Grand Rapids South Christian 128
   1959B, 1962B, 1963B, 1964B, 1975B, 1983C, 1987B, 1988B, 1993B, 2008D2, 2011D2, 2014D2, 2017D2, 2018D2
Grand Rapids Union 144
   1950A1, 1951A, 1952A, 1953A, 1954A, 1955A, 1956A, 1967A, 1969A, 1970A, 1971A, 1981A, 2000D1, 2001D1
Grand Rapids West Catholic 280
   1970B, 1972B, 1973B, 1974B, 1986B, 2001D3, 2002D3, 2003D3, 2004D3, 2005D3, 2006D3, 2007D3, 2008D3, 2009D2
Grand Traverse Academy 46
   2010D4, 2011D4, 2012D4, 2013D4
Grandville 59
   1982C, 1986A, 1993A, 1994A, 2001D1, 2011D1, 2013D1, 2019D1
Grandville Calvin Christian 314
   1976C, 1978C, 1980C, 1981C, 1983C, 1985C, 1988C, 1993C, 2008D3, 2009D3, 2010D3, 2011D3, 2012D3, 2013D3, 2014D3, 2015D3, 2018D3, 2019D3
Grant 74
   1990C, 1992B, 1995B, 2017D3, 1991C
Grass Lake 143
   1974D, 1975D, 1989D, 1990D, 1991D, 1992D, 1993D, 1994D, 1995D, 1996D, 1997D, 1998D, 2000D4
Greenville 42
   1966B, 1971B, 1973B, 1976B, 1987B, 2002D2
Grosse Ile 174
   1950CD, 1967B, 1968B, 1969B, 1972B, 1973B, 1992B, 1993B, 1994B, 1995B, 1996B, 2000D2, 2001D2, 2002D2, 2007D3, 2015D2, 2016D2, 2017D2, 2018D2
Grosse Pointe North 338
   1969A, 1970A, 1971A, 1972A, 1973A, 1974A, 1975A, 1976A, 1977A, 1978A, 1979A, 1980A, 1981A, 1982A, 1985A, 1986A, 1987A, 1989A, 1990A, 1993A, 1994A, 1998A, 1999A, 2002D1, 2003D1, 2004D1, 2005D1, 2006D1, 2008D1, 2014D1, 2016D1, 2017D1, 2018D1, 1997A
Grosse Pointe South 103

1978A, 1983A, 1984A, 1985A, 1986A, 1988A, 1989A, 1991A, 1992A, 1993A, 1994A, 1995A, 1996A, 1997A, 1998A, 1999A, 2000D1, 2001D1, 2002D1, 2003D1, 2004D1, 2005D1, 2006D1, 2007D1, 2008D1, 2010D1, 2011D1, 2012D1
Grosse Pointe St Paul 20
   1968CD, 1969CD
Grosse Pointe Woods University Liggett 31
   1960CD, 1961CD, 1963CD, 1964CD, 2001D4, 2002D4, 2012D4, 2013D4, 2014D4, 2015D4, 2016D4, 2000D4
Hale 81
   1959CD, 2002D4, 2003D4, 2004D4, 2016D4
Hamilton 26
   2015D2, 2016D2
Hamtramck 5
   1948A, 1950A1, 1952A
Hanover 6
   1931CD
Hanover-Horton 216
   2000D4, 2007D3, 2012D3, 2013D3, 2014D3, 2015D3, 2016D3, 2017D3, 2018D3, 2019D3
Harbor Springs 377
   2000D4, 2001D4, 2002D4, 2003D4, 2004D3, 2006D4, 2007D4, 2008D4, 2009D4, 2010D4, 2012D4, 2014D4, 2015D4, 2016D4, 2017D3, 2018D3, 2019D3
Harper Woods 6
   1993B
Harper Woods Gallagher 80
   1965B, 1966A, 1967A, 1973B, 1974B, 1975B, 1976B, 1977B, 1978B
Harper Woods Lutheran East 7
   1971B, 1972CD
Harper Woods Notre Dame 104
   1968A, 1969A, 1970A, 1971A, 1983A, 1984A, 1985A, 1987A, 1994B, 1995B, 1996B, 1997B, 1999B, 2000D2, 2001D2
Harrison 18
   1995C, 2007D3
Hart 134
   1978C, 2002D3, 2003D3, 2006D4, 2017D3, 2018D3, 2019D3
Hartford 26
   1971CD, 1980C, 1984C, 1988C, 1994C, 1995C
Hartland 155
   1979B, 1980B, 1984B, 1985B, 1986B, 1987B, 2011D1, 2012D1, 2013D1, 2019D1
Haslett 221
   1957CD, 1958CD, 1959CD, 1960CD, 1961CD, 1962B, 1963B, 1964B, 1965CD, 1979C, 1990B, 1995B, 1997B, 2001D2, 2002D2, 2010D2, 2011D2, 2018D2, 2019D2
Hastings 32
   1947B, 1985B, 2019D2
Hazel Park 234
   1943A, 1944A, 1945A, 1946A, 1947A, 1948A, 1949A, 1950A1, 1950A2, 1951A, 1952A, 1953A, 1954A, 1955A, 1956A, 1957A, 1958A, 1965A, 1966A, 1967A, 1968A, 1983A, 1984A, 1985A, 1987A, 1992A, 2003D2, 2004D2, 2005D2
Hemlock 319

1946CD, 1947CD, 1948CD, 1949CD, 1974B, 1981B, 1982B, 1985B, 1987B, 1996C, 1997B, 1998C, 1999C, 2000D3, 2001D3, 2002D3, 2004D3, 2005D3, 2010D3, 2011D3, 2012D3, 2013D3, 2015D3

Hesperia 265
1974D, 1998C, 1999C, 2002D3, 2004D4, 2005D4, 2006D4, 2007D4, 2008D4, 2009D4, 2010D4, 2011D4, 2012D4, 2016D4, 2017D4

Highland Park 19
1925, 1926, 1927A, 1928A, 1929A

Hillsdale 254
1984B, 1985B, 1986B, 1987B, 2001D3, 2003D3, 2004D3, 2005D3, 2007D3, 2008D3, 2009D3, 2010D3, 2011D3

Hillsdale Academy 102
2007D4, 2008D4, 2010D4, 2013D4, 2014D4, 2017D4, 2018D4, 2019D4

Holland 113
1952A, 1955A, 1983A, 1985A, 1986A, 1989A, 1990A, 1991A, 1996A

Holland Black River 130
2011D4, 2013D3, 2014D3, 2015D3, 2016D3, 2017D3, 2018D3

Holland Christian 137
1960B, 1964B, 1966B, 1981B, 1985B, 1998B, 1999B, 2000D2, 2005D2, 2018D2, 2019D2

Holland West Ottawa 71
1999A, 2003D1, 2004D1, 2005D1, 2006D1, 2007D1, 2008D1

Holly 258
1973B, 1976B, 1977B, 1978B, 1980A, 1981B, 1982B, 1983A, 1984A, 1985A, 1988A, 1989A, 1993A, 1995A, 2013D1, 2014D1

Holt 127.5
1957CD, 1963B, 1969B, 1976B, 1977B, 1978B, 1979B, 1986A, 1993A, 1994A, 1995A, 1997A

Holton 41
2009D4, 2015D4, 2016D4

Homer 22
1964CD

Howard City Tri County 54
1996C, 1997B, 1999B, 2000D3, 2016D2

Howell 178.5
1946B, 1947B, 1948B, 1949B, 1950B, 1951B, 1952B, 1953B, 1954B, 1956B, 1957B, 1958B, 1959B, 1960B, 1961B, 1962B, 1966B, 1970A, 1978A, 1982A, 1984A, 2004D1, 2005D1, 2006D1

Hudson 266
1970CD, 1978C, 1985C, 1988C, 1993C, 2002D3, 2003D4, 2004D4, 2005D4, 2006D4, 2007D4, 2009D4, 2011D4, 2013D4, 2014D4, 2015D4, 2016D4, 2017D4, 2018D4

Hudsonville 58
2006D1, 2007D1, 2011D1, 2012D1, 2013D1, 2014D1, 2018D1

Hudsonville Unity Christian 34
1989B, 1998B, 2015D2

Ida 180
1974C, 1994C, 1995B, 1996B, 1997B, 1998B, 1999B, 2000D3, 2001D3, 2002D3, 2009D3, 2010D3, 2011D3, 2012D3, 2013D3, 2018D3

Imlay City 23
1941CD, 1943CD, 1944CD, 1945CD, 1946CD, 1997B, 1998B, 1999B

Indian River Inland Lakes 11
2013D4, 2015D4

Inkster 19
1955B, 1957A, 1985B

Inkster Cherry Hill 13
1975A, 1977B, 1978B

Ionia 210
1987B, 1988B, 1989B, 1991B, 1993B, 1994B, 2000D2, 2001D2, 2008D2, 2009D2, 2010D2, 2011D2, 2012D2

Iron Mountain 12
1937B, 1938B, 1939B

Ithaca 85
1948CD, 1949B, 2007D3, 2012D3, 2017D3, 2018D3

Jackson 388.5
1932A, 1933A, 1934A, 1935A, 1936A, 1938A, 1939A, 1940A, 1941A, 1943A, 1944A, 1945A, 1946A, 1947A, 1948A, 1949A, 1950A1, 1950A2, 1951A, 1952A, 1953A, 1954A, 1955A, 1956A, 1957A, 1958A, 1974A, 1976A, 1977A, 1978A, 1979A, 1980A, 1981A, 1996A

Jackson Christian 12
2002D4, 2013D4

Jackson Lumen Christi 625
1968B, 1973B, 1974B, 1977B, 1978B, 1979B, 1980B, 1981B, 1983B, 1984B, 1985B, 1986B, 1987B, 1988B, 1991B, 1992B, 1993B, 1996B, 1997B, 1998B, 2001D3, 2002D3, 2003D3, 2004D3, 2005D3, 2006D3, 2007D3, 2008D3, 2009D3, 2010D3, 2011D3, 2012D3, 2013D3, 2014D3

Jackson Northwest 24.5
1960CD, 1973B, 1975B, 1996B

Jackson Parkside 32
1964A, 1965A, 1966A

Jenison 33
1979A, 1982A, 1984A, 2004D1

Johannesburg-Lewiston 25
2017D4, 2018D4, 2019D4

Jonesville 208
1990C, 1993C, 1994C, 1995C, 1996C, 1997C, 1998C, 1999C, 2000D4, 2001D4, 2002D4, 2003D4, 2014D3, 2017D3, 2018D3, 2019D3

Kalamazoo Central 373
1922, 1924, 1925, 1926, 1927A, 1928A, 1929A, 1930A, 1931A, 1932A, 1933A, 1934A, 1935A, 1936A, 1937A, 1938A, 1939A, 1940A, 1941A, 1943A, 1944A, 1945A, 1946A, 1947A, 1948A, 1949A, 1950A1, 1951A, 1952A, 1953A, 1954A, 1955A, 1957A, 1962A, 1963A, 1964A, 1991A, 1995A, 2002D1, 2003D1, 2017D1

Kalamazoo Christian 237
1971B, 1972CD, 1973CD, 1976C, 1980C, 1981C, 1982C, 1990C, 1991C, 1992C, 1993C, 1995C, 1998C, 1999C, 2005D3, 2012D4, 2013D4, 2014D4, 2015D4, 2018D4, 2019D4

Kalamazoo Hackett 241

1994C, 1995C, 1996C, 1997C, 1999C, 2000D3,
2001D3, 2002D3, 2005D3, 2006D3, 2007D3,
2008D3, 2009D3, 2010D3, 2011D4, 2012D4,
2015D4, 2016D4

Kalamazoo Norrix 234
1962A, 1965A, 1966A, 1967A, 1969A, 1971A,
1973A, 1975A, 1976A, 1977A, 1978A, 1980A,
1981A, 1982A, 1983A, 1985A, 1986A, 1987A,
1988A

Kalamazoo St Augustine 13
1949CD, 1950CD, 1951CD, 1952CD, 1953CD

Kalamazoo Western State/University 24
1934CD, 1964CD

Kalkaska 78
1987C, 2002D3, 2003D3, 2005D3, 2006D3

Keego Harbor 10
1952CD, 1953CD, 1954CD, 1955CD

Kent City 175
1963CD, 1975C, 1976C, 1979C, 2003D3,
2004D3, 2005D3, 2006D3, 2007D3, 2008D3,
2009D3, 2017D3, 2018D3

Kingsley 115
1967CD, 1974D, 1975D, 1976D, 1977D, 1978D,
1979D, 1980D, 1981D, 1983D, 1984D, 1985D,
1986D, 1987D, 1989C, 1991C, 2010D3, 2011D3

Kingston 3
2016D4

L'Anse Creuse 3
1994A

Laingsburg 17
1998C, 1999C, 2008D3

Lake City 23
1963CD, 1964CD, 1965CD, 2000D3

Lake Fenton 81
1975B, 2000D3, 2001D3, 2002D3, 2003D3,
2005D3, 2016D2, 2017D2, 2018D2, 2019D2

Lake Leelanau St Mary 11
2018D4

Lake Odessa/Lakewood 102
1954CD, 1955CD, 1957CD, 1958CD, 1961CD,
1962CD, 2000D2, 2001D2

Lake Orion 303
1996A, 1998A, 1999A, 2000D1, 2001D1,
2004D1, 2005D1, 2006D1, 2007D1, 2008D1,
2009D1, 2010D1, 2011D1, 2013D1, 2014D1,
2015D1, 2016D1

Lakeview 22
1980C, 1991C, 1992C, 1993C

Lambertville 8
1936CD, 1937CD, 1938CD, 1939CD

Lansing Catholic 316
1989B, 2004D3, 2005D3, 2006D3, 2007D3,
2008D3, 2009D3, 2010D3, 2011D3, 2012D3,
2013D3, 2014D3, 2015D3, 2016D3, 2017D2,
2018D2

Lansing Central 28
1933A, 1936A, 1937A, 1938A

Lansing Christian 92
1977D, 1978D, 1979D, 1980D, 1981D, 1982D,
1983D, 2014D4, 2015D4, 2016D4

Lansing Eastern 167
1932A, 1933A, 1934A, 1935A, 1937A, 1938A,
1939A, 1940A, 1943A, 1944A, 1945A, 1947A,
1948A, 1952A, 1954A, 1955A, 1956A, 1957A,
1981A, 2002D1

Lansing Everett 88.5
1947B, 1948B, 1949B, 1950CD, 1951CD,
1952CD, 1953CD, 1955CD, 1956CD, 1957B,
1958B

Lansing Resurrection 8
1949B, 1957B

Lansing Sexton 46
1952A, 1953A, 1954A, 1959A, 1962A

Lansing St Mary 10
1937CD, 1938CD

Lansing Waverly 43
1965B, 1966B, 1985A, 1987A

Lapeer East 4
2008D2

Lawrence 66
1998D, 1999D, 2000D4, 2004D4, 2005D4,
2006D4, 2007D4, 2008D4, 2019D4

Lawton 171
1963CD, 1964CD, 1965CD, 1966CD, 1967CD,
1978D, 2000D4, 2001D4, 2002D4, 2003D4

Leroy Pine River 14
2005D3

Leslie 152
1979C, 1986C, 1987C, 1989C, 1990C, 1991C,
1992C, 1993C, 1994C, 1995C, 1996C, 1997C,
1999C, 2017D3

Lincoln Alcona 2
1930CD

Lincoln Park 180.5
1940A, 1941A, 1943A, 1944A, 1945A, 1946A,
1947A, 1948A, 1949A, 1950A1, 1951A, 1952A,
1954A, 1955A, 1957A, 1958A, 1959A, 1962A,
1968A, 1969A, 1971A

Linden 358
1952CD, 1972B, 1973B, 1974B, 1980B, 1981B,
1983B, 1990B, 1991B, 2006D2, 2007D2,
2008D2, 2009D2, 2010D2, 2011D2, 2012D2,
2013D2, 2014D2, 2015D2, 2016D2, 2017D2,
2018D2, 2019D2

Litchfield 64
1969CD, 1995D, 1996D, 1997D, 1998D, 1999D

Livonia Bentley 52
1951B, 1952B, 1953B, 1954B, 1962A, 1973A

Livonia Churchill 84
1975A, 1982A, 1983A, 1999A, 2001D1, 2004D1,
2006D1

Livonia Clarenceville 31
1950CD, 1952B, 1956B, 1965B, 1973B

Livonia Franklin 3
1988A

Livonia Stevenson 91
1971A, 1972A, 1973A, 1976A, 1977A, 2000D1,
2002D1, 2003D1, 2012D1, 2016D1

Lowell 67
1951B, 1954B, 1955B, 1956B, 1957B, 1958B,
1962B, 1990B, 1994B, 1995B, 2004D2

Ludington 38
1973B, 1977B, 1979B, 1980B, 2013D2

Ludington St Simon 1

1941CD

Lutheran Westland 121
1987D, 1988D, 1989D, 1993C, 1995C, 1997C, 1998C, 1999C, 2003D4, 2004D4, 2007D4, 2010D4, 2011D4, 2012D4, 2015D4, 2017D4, 2018D4

Mackinaw City 48
1931CD, 2004D4, 2005D4, 2006D4, 2007D4, 2011D4

Macomb Dakota 15
2009D1, 2010D1, 2016D1

Macomb L'Anse Creuse North 32
2003D1, 2004D1, 2005D1, 2010D1, 2014D1

Macomb Lutheran North 35
2005D3, 2006D3, 2007D3, 2008D3, 2011D3, 2012D3, 2013D3, 2014D3, 2016D2

Madison Heights Foley 17
1979B, 2016D3, 2018D3, 2019D3

Madison Heights Lamphere 15
1995B, 2000D2, 2001D2, 2007D2

Mancelona 61
1977D, 1978D, 1979C, 1980C, 1984D, 1986D, 2012D4

Manchester 18
1973CD, 1974C, 1975C, 1976C, 1977C, 1996C

Manistee 21
2012D3, 2019D3

Manton 126
1982D, 1983D, 1988D, 1989D, 1990D, 1991D, 1992D, 1994D, 2013D4, 2014D4, 2015D4, 2016D4, 2017D3

Maple City Glen Lake 39
2000D4, 2002D4, 2017D4, 2019D4

Marcellus 15
1995C, 2001D4, 2004D4

Marine City 10
2010D2, 2011D2, 2012D2

Marion 8
2002D4

Marlette 126
1977C, 1978C, 1979C, 1981C, 1983C, 1987C, 1988C, 1989C, 1990C, 1991C, 1999C, 2005D3, 2011D3, 2012D3, 2013D3, 2015D3

Marshall 80
1964B, 1965B, 1975B, 1977B, 1978B, 1981B, 1995B, 2017D2, 2019D2

Marysville 98
1957B, 1958B, 1980B, 1981B, 1982B, 1983B, 1991B, 1996B, 1998B

Mason 170
1975B, 1976B, 1980B, 1982B, 1983B, 2010D2, 2011D2, 2012D2, 2013D2, 2017D2

Mason County Central 335
1970CD, 1972CD, 1974C, 1975C, 1976C, 1977C, 1979C, 1984C, 1985C, 1986C, 1988C, 1989C, 1990C, 1994D, 1996C, 1997C, 2003D3, 2004D3, 2008D3, 2009D3, 2010D3, 2012D3, 2013D3, 2014D3, 2015D3

Mason County Eastern 110
1981D, 1985D, 1986D, 1987D, 1988D, 1992D, 1995D, 1999D, 2004D4, 2005D4, 2006D4, 2010D4, 2018D4, 2019D4

Mattawan 111
1977C, 1978C, 1979C, 1980C, 1982C, 2003D2, 2005D2, 2008D2, 2010D2

Mayville 148
1966CD, 1967CD, 1969CD, 1970CD, 1971CD, 1972CD, 1974C, 1975C, 1976C, 1989C, 1990C, 1991C, 1992C, 1993C, 2005D4, 2006D3, 2018D4

McBain 158
1955CD, 1956CD, 1957CD, 1960CD, 1967CD, 1992D, 1993D, 1995C, 1996C, 1999C, 2001D4, 2006D4, 2016D3, 2018D3

Memphis 12
2017D3, 2019D3

Mendon 251
2000D4, 2004D4, 2005D4, 2006D4, 2007D4, 2008D4, 2009D4, 2010D4, 2011D4, 2012D4, 2013D4, 2014D4, 2015D4, 2016D4, 2017D4, 2018D4, 2019D4

Merrill 41
1946CD, 1947CD, 1948CD, 1949CD, 1950CD, 1952CD

Merrill Sacred Heart 4
1948CD

Merritt 2
1951CD

Mesick 8
1987D, 1988D

Michigan Center 21
1975C, 1984C, 1986C, 1991C

Midland 141
1945A, 1946A, 1947A, 1948A, 1949A, 1950A1, 1950A2, 1951A, 1952A, 1953A, 1954A, 1958A, 1961A, 1964A, 1973A, 1975A, 1979A, 1999A

Midland Bullock Creek 98
1967B, 1968B, 1969B, 1970B, 1975B, 1978B, 1982C, 1983C, 2013D3

Midland Dow 26
1997A, 1998A, 1999A, 2009D1

Milan 32
1948CD, 2011D2, 2012D2, 2013D2

Milford 808
1930CD, 1948B, 1949B, 1950B, 1952B, 1953B, 1954B, 1955B, 1959B, 1960B, 1961B, 1963B, 1964A, 1976A, 1979A, 1980A, 1981A, 1982A, 1983A, 1984A, 1986A, 1988A, 1989A, 1990A, 1991A, 1994A, 1997A, 1998A, 1999A, 2000D1, 2001D1, 2002D1, 2003D1, 2004D1, 2005D1, 2006D1, 2007D1, 2008D1, 2009D1, 2010D1, 2011D1, 2012D1, 2013D1, 2015D1, 2016D1, 2017D1, 2018D1

Monroe 574.5
1925, 1928B, 1929B, 1930A, 1931A, 1932A, 1933A, 1934A, 1935A, 1936A, 1937A, 1938A, 1939A, 1940A, 1941A, 1945A, 1946A, 1947A, 1948A, 1950A1, 1954A, 1959A, 1961A, 1983A, 1984A, 1985A, 1986A, 1987A, 1988A, 1989A, 1990A, 1991A, 1992A, 1993A, 1994A, 1995A, 1996A, 1997A, 2004D1, 2005D1, 2006D1, 2008D1, 2009D1, 2015D1

Monroe Catholic Central 43
1971B, 1972B, 1979B, 1983B, 1984B

Monroe Jefferson 34
    1989B, 2001D2, 2011D2
Monroe St Mary 86
    1990B, 1991B, 2004D3, 2007D3, 2008D3,
    2009D3, 2010D3, 2016D3
Montague 61
    1961CD, 1962CD, 1964CD, 1969CD, 2019D3
Montrose 81
    1968CD, 1973CD, 1975C, 2015D3, 2017D3,
    2018D3, 2019D3
Morenci 34
    1964CD, 2001D4, 2009D4
Morley-Stanwood 28
    2001D3, 2003D3
Morrice 27
    1983D, 1984D, 1987D, 2019D4
Mt Clemens 93
    1925
    1928A, 1929B, 1930A, 1935B, 1953A, 1956A,
    1961A, 1964A, 1965A, 1966A, 1972A, 1975A,
    1976A, 1987B, 1988B
Mt Clemens Lutheran North 16
    1981C, 1988B, 1989B
Mt Morris 20
    1926, 1948B, 1949B, 1950B
Mt Morris St Mary 5
    1938CD
Mt Pleasant 125.5
    1948B, 1949B, 1950B, 1951B, 1952B, 1954B,
    1955B, 1956B, 1973B, 1980B, 1983B, 1984B,
    2003D2, 2010D2
Mt Pleasant Sacred Heart 271
    1976D, 1977D, 2000D4, 2001D4, 2006D4,
    2009D4, 2010D4, 2011D4, 2012D4, 2013D4,
    2015D4, 2016D4, 2017D4, 2018D4, 2019D4
Muskegon 25
    1957A, 1958A, 1959A, 1960A
Muskegon Catholic 60
    1969B, 1970B, 1971B, 1972B, 1973B
Muskegon Christian 73
    1958CD, 1960CD, 1961CD, 1963CD, 1964CD,
    1970CD
Muskegon Heights 33
    1962CD, 1964A, 1965A, 1967B
Muskegon Mona Shores 62
    1988A, 1991A, 2001D1, 2002D1, 2003D1,
    2004D1
Muskegon Oakridge 65
    1977C, 1979C, 1980C, 1981C, 1983C, 1984C,
    1985C, 1993C
Muskegon Orchard View 72
    1996B, 1997B, 1998B, 2006D2
Muskegon Western Michigan Christian 71
    1973CD, 1974C, 2017D4, 2018D4, 2019D4
Napoleon 415
    1930CD, 1931CD, 1934CD, 1935CD, 1936CD,
    1937CD, 1938CD, 1939CD, 1940CD, 1941CD,
    1943CD, 1944CD, 1945CD, 1946CD, 1947CD,
    1948CD, 1949CD, 1950CD, 1951CD, 1952CD,
    1953CD, 1954CD, 1958CD, 1959CD, 1960CD,
    1961CD, 1962CD, 1963CD, 1964CD, 1965CD,
    1966CD, 1967CD, 1968CD, 1980C, 1981C,
    1982C, 1983C, 1988C, 1989C, 1990C, 1992C,
    2005D3, 2010D3, 2012D3, 2013D3, 2015D3,
    2019D3
New Baltimore Anchor Bay 27
    1976B, 1977B
New Boston Huron 40
    1971B, 1975B, 1976B, 1979B
New Buffalo 98
    1994D, 1995D, 1996D, 1997D, 1998D, 1999D,
    2001D4, 2013D4
New Haven 11
    1967CD
New Lothrop 6
    1998D, 1999D, 2012D4
New Lothrop Maple Grove 9
    1950CD
New Lothrop St Michael 107.5
    1951CD, 1952CD, 1953CD, 1954CD, 1955CD,
    1956CD, 1957CD, 1958CD, 1959CD, 1960CD,
    1961CD, 1963CD
Newaygo 42
    1989C, 1993C, 2011D3, 2012D3, 2013D3
Newport Lutheran South 2
    2007D4, 2010D4
Niles 151
    1992A, 1931B, 1934B, 1935B, 1936B, 1937B,
    1938B, 1939B, 1940B, 1941B, 1947B, 1948B,
    1949B, 1950B, 1951B, 1952B
Niles Brandywine 37
    1967B, 1981C, 1982C, 1985C
North Branch 26
    1968CD, 1969CD, 1996B
North Farmington 10
    1961CD, 1980A, 1994A
North Muskegon 134
    1966CD, 1969CD, 2007D4, 2008D4, 2009D4,
    2010D4, 2011D4, 2014D4, 2016D3
Northville 190
    1970B, 1977A, 1978A, 1980A, 2007D1, 2012D1,
    2013D1, 2014D1, 2015D1, 2016D1, 2018D1,
    2019D1
Novi 342
    1990A, 1998A, 1999A, 2000D1, 2001D1,
    2002D1, 2003D1, 2004D1, 2005D1, 2006D1,
    2008D1, 2009D12014D1, 2015D1, 2016D1,
    2017D1
Okemos 264
    1957CD, 1965B, 1966B, 1971B, 1982B, 1983B,
    1984B, 1985A, 1986B, 1987A, 1990A, 2000D1,
    2005D1, 2008D1, 2009D1, 2010D1, 2011D1,
    2014D1, 2016D1, 2017D1
Olanson 4
    1930CD
Olivet 53
    1979C, 1980C, 1986C, 1988C, 2016D3
Onaway 22
    1963CD, 2008D4, 2009D4
Onsted 164
    1978C, 1981C, 1982C, 1986C, 1987C, 1989C,
    1990C, 1991C, 1992C, 1993C, 1994C, 2001D3,
    2002D3, 2003D3, 2004D3, 2016D3, 2017D3,
    2018D3

Orchard Lake 26
    1975A, 1982C
Orchard Lake St Mary's 200
    1957CD, 1958CD, 1959CD, 1960CD, 1965CD,
    1966CD, 1971CD, 1981C, 1983C, 1984C,
    1985C, 1988C, 1989C, 1990C, 1994C, 1998B,
    2001D2, 2002D2, 2003D2, 2004D2, 2009D2,
    2012D2, 2013D2, 2014D2, 2015D2
Ortonville Brandon 47
    1990B, 1991B, 1992B, 1993B
Oscoda 6
    1997B
Otsego 420.5
    1950B, 1951B, 1952B, 1953B, 1954B, 1955B,
    1956B, 1957B, 1960B, 1961B, 1962B, 1970B,
    1971B, 1975B, 1977B, 1978B, 1979B, 1980B,
    1981B, 1985B, 1994B, 2007D2, 2008D2,
    2010D2, 2012D2, 2013D2, 2014D2, 2015D2,
    2016D2, 2018D2, 2019D2
Ottawa Lake Whiteford 22
    2009D4, 2014D4, 2015D4
Ovid-Elsie 46
    2000D3, 2001D3, 2014D3
Owosso 10
    2012D2
Oxford 176
    1967B, 1968B, 1969B, 1970B, 1971B, 1985B,
    1987B, 1989B, 1990B, 1991B, 1992B, 1993B,
    1994B, 1995B, 2000D2, 2001D2, 2013D1
Parchment 14
    1975B, 2019D3
Parma Western 65
    1929CD, 1983B, 1997B, 2014D2, 2015D2,
    2016D2, 2017D2, 2018D2
Paw Paw 7
    1973B, 1993B
Pellston 9
    2013D4
Pentwater 42
    1988D, 1989D, 1990D, 1998D, 1999D
Perry 87
    1967CD, 1989B, 1998B, 1999B, 2000D3,
    2001D3, 2010D3, 2011D3
Petoskey 335
    1948B, 1950B, 1951B, 1952B, 1983B, 1984B,
    1985B, 1995B, 1996B, 1997B, 1998B, 1999B,
    2000D2, 2001D2, 2002D2, 2003D2, 2004D2,
    2005D2, 2006D2, 2007D2, 2013D2, 2014D2,
    2019D2
Petoskey St Francis 4
    1952CD
Petoskey St Michael 24
    2019D4
Pewamo-Westphalia 249
    1958CD, 1959CD, 1960CD, 1977C, 2010D4,
    2011D3, 2012D4, 2013D4, 2014D3, 2015D3,
    2016D4, 2017D3, 2018D3, 2019D3
Pinckney 304
    1988B, 2003D1, 2004D1, 2005D1, 2006D1,
    2007D1, 2008D1, 2009D1, 2010D1, 2011D1,
    2012D1, 2013D1, 2014D1, 2015D1
Pinconning 7
    1972B
Pittsford 92
    1964CD, 1991D, 1992D, 1993D, 1995D, 1996D,
    1997C, 2005D4
Plainwell 113
    1955CD, 1959B, 1965B, 1966B, 1967B, 1968B,
    1976B, 1977B, 1978B, 1984B, 1986B, 1990B,
    1991B
Plymouth 256.5
    1936B, 1940A, 1944B, 1945B, 1946B, 1947B,
    1948B, 1949B, 1950B, 1951B, 1952A, 1956A,
    1960A, 1961A, 2006D1, 2008D1, 2009D1,
    2010D1, 2013D1, 2017D1, 2018D1, 2019D1
Plymouth Christian 105
    1998D, 2011D4, 2012D4, 2014D4, 2015D4,
    2016D4, 2017D4, 2018D4, 2019D4
Pontiac/Pontiac Central 278.5
    1926, 1927A, 1928A, 1947A, 1948A, 1949A,
    1950A1, 1950A2, 1951A, 1952A, 1953A, 1954A,
    1955A, 1956A, 1957A, 1958A, 1959A, 1965A,
    1966A, 1967A, 1974A, 1975A, 1988A
Pontiac Christian 3
    1982D
Pontiac Dublin 4
    1949CD, 1950CD
Pontiac Northern 69
    1965A, 1968A, 1969A, 1970A, 1971A
Pontiac Notre Dame 91
    2008D2, 2013D2, 2014D2, 2015D2, 2016D2,
    2017D2
Port Huron 28
    1924, 1978B, 1979B, 1995A, 1996A
Port Huron Northern 90
    1978A, 1979A, 1986A, 1990A, 1991A, 1992A,
    1993A, 2012D1, 2014D1, 2019D1
Portage/Portage Central 86
    1952B, 1954B, 1955B, 1956B, 1988A, 1997A,
    1998A, 2009D1, 2010D1, 2012D1, 2014D1,
    2015D1, 2016D1, 2017D1
Portage Northern 339
    1972A, 1973A, 1974A, 1977A, 1978A, 1979A,
    1983A, 1984A, 1985A, 1987A, 1989A, 1990A,
    1991A, 1992A, 1999A, 2000D1, 2001D1,
    2003D1, 2005D1, 2006D1, 2007D1, 2008D1,
    2012D1, 2016D1, 2018D1
Portland St Patrick 35
    1961CD, 1962CD
Potterville 384
    1976D, 1977D, 1979D, 1980D, 1981D, 1982D,
    1985D, 1987D, 1988D, 1989D, 1990D, 2004D4,
    2005D4, 2006D4, 2007D4, 2008D4, 2009D4,
    2010D4, 2011D4, 2013D4, 2014D4, 2015D4,
    2016D4, 2017D4, 2018D4
Quincy 13
    1981C, 1991C, 1996C
Ravenna 1
    1969CD
Reading 59
    1983D, 1987D, 1988D, 1990D, 1991D, 1992D,
    1993D, 2001D4
Redford Borgess 9
    1970A, 1971A, 1972A

Redford Thurston 14
   1958A, 1960A, 2003D2
Redford Union 111.5
   1944B, 1945B, 1946B, 1947B, 1948B, 1951B,
   1952B, 1954B, 1956B, 1957A, 1966A, 1967A, 1
   968A, 1969A, 1974A, 1981A, 1982A, 1984A
Reed City 62
   1970CD, 1982C, 1983B, 1984B
Reese 152.5
   1962CD, 1963CD, 1964CD, 1965CD, 1966CD,
   1969CD, 1975C, 1979C, 1980C, 2002D3,
   2003D3, 2007D4, 2010D3, 2012D3, 2014D3
Remus Chippewa Hills 138.5
   1961CD, 1962CD, 1963CD, 1964CD, 1965CD,
   1966CD, 1967B, 2000D2, 2006D2
Richland Gull Lake 271
   1978B, 1979B, 1989B, 1995B, 1996B, 1997B,
   1998B, 1999B, 2000D2, 2001D2, 2002D2,
   2003D2, 2004D2, 2010D2, 2011D2, 2012D2,
   2014D2, 2015D2
Richmond 37
   1999B, 2004D3, 2006D2, 2008D2
River Rouge 103
   1931B, 1934A, 1936A, 1938A, 1939A, 1940A,
   1941A, 1943B, 1944B, 1945B, 1946B, 1947B,
   1948B, 1954B, 1955B, 1956B, 1957B, 1958B
Riverview 47
   1961B, 1962B, 1969B, 1970B, 2012D2
Riverview Richard 39
   1978B, 1981B, 1991C, 2001D3, 2005D3,
   2006D3, 2007D3, 2014D4, 2015D4
Rochester 180
   1981A, 1982A, 1984A, 1985A, 1986A, 1994A,
   1995A, 1998A, 2002D1, 2003D1, 2004D1,
   2008D1, 2014D1
Rochester Adams 251
   1969B, 1975A, 1985A, 1990A, 1992A, 1993A,
   1994A, 1996A, 1997A, 1999A, 2001D1, 2005D1,
   2006D1, 2007D1, 2008D1, 2009D1, 2015D1
Rochester Hills Lutheran Northwest 22
   1999D, 2009D4, 2013D4, 2014D4, 2017D4,
   2018D4, 2019D4
Rochester Hills Stoney Creek 80
   2005D1, 2006D1, 2009D1, 2010D1, 2017D1,
   2018D1, 2019D1
Rockford 622
   1974B, 1975B, 1976B, 1977B, 1979A, 1980A,
   1981A, 1984A, 1988A, 1995A, 1996A, 1997A,
   1998A, 1999A, 2000D1, 2001D1, 2002D1,
   2003D1, 2004D1, 2005D1, 2006D1, 2007D1,
   2008D1, 2009D1, 2010D1, 2011D1, 2012D1,
   2013D1, 2014D1, 2015D1, 2016D1, 2017D1,
   2018D1, 2019D1
Rogers City 170
   1970B, 1971B, 1972CD, 1973CD, 1978C,
   1980C, 1981C, 1982C, 1983C, 1986C, 1998C,
   2000D4, 2010D4, 2011D4, 2012D4
Romeo 112
   2011D1, 2012D1, 2013D1, 2017D1, 2018D1,
   2019D1
Romulus 45
   1930CD, 1931CD, 1936CD, 1937CD, 1946CD,
   1954B, 1955B, 1956B
Roscommon 10
   2009D3, 2010D3
Royal Oak 209.5
   1926, 1927B, 1928B, 1929A, 1932A, 1937A,
   1938A, 1939A, 1940A, 1941A, 1943A, 1944A,
   1945A, 1946A, 1947A, 1948A, 1949A, 1950A1,
   1951A, 1952A, 1953A, 1956A, 1957A, 2009D1,
   2011D1, 2012D1, 2015D1, 2018D1, 2019D1
Royal Oak Dondero 90
   1967A, 1969A, 1977A, 1978A, 1980A, 1981A,
   1990A, 1991A
Royal Oak Kimball 196
   1963A, 1964A, 1965A, 1966A, 1967A, 1968A,
   1969A, 1970A, 1972A, 1973A, 1976A, 1977A,
   1978A, 1985A, 1986A, 2004D2, 2005D2
Royal Oak Shrine 181
   1972B, 1973B, 1974B, 1975B, 1977C, 1981B,
   1982B, 1983B, 1985B, 2004D4, 2005D4,
   2006D4, 2008D4, 2009D4, 2010D4, 2011D4,
   2012D4, 2013D4
Saginaw 5
   1938A, 1947A
Saginaw Eastern 7.5
   1937A
Saginaw Eisenhower 67
   1973B, 1974B, 1975A, 1977B, 1980B, 1981B
Saginaw Heritage 208
   2007D1, 2008D1, 2009D1, 2010D1, 2011D1,
   2012D1, 2013D1, 2015D1, 2016D1, 2017D1,
   2018D1, 2019D1
Saginaw Hill 132
   1944A, 1945A, 1946A, 1947A, 1948A, 1949A,
   1950A1, 1951A, 1952A, 1955A, 1956A, 1957A,
   1989A
Saginaw Michigan Lutheran 63
   1986D, 2003D4, 2004D4, 2005D4, 2008D4,
   2012D4, 2013D4
Saginaw Nouvel 1
   2008D3
Saginaw Swan Valley 31
   2005D3, 2006D3, 2007D3
Saginaw Valley Lutheran 135
   1980D, 1993C, 1994C, 1995C, 1996C, 1997C,
   1998C, 2004D4, 2006D4, 2007D4
Salem 179
   1987A, 1989A, 1990A, 1995A, 1997A, 1998A,
   2002D1, 2003D1, 2004D1, 2005D1, 2007D1,
   2012D1, 2017D1, 2018D1
Saline 571
   1982B, 1984B, 1985B, 1987B, 1988B, 1989B,
   1990B, 1991B, 1995A, 1998A, 1999A, 2000D1,
   2001D1, 2002D1, 2003D1, 2006D1, 2007D1,
   2008D1, 2009D1, 2010D1, 2011D1, 2012D1,
   2013D1, 2014D1, 2015D1, 2016D1, 2017D1,
   2018D1, 2019D1
Sand Creek 100
   1931CD, 2003D4, 2008D4, 2009D4, 2010D4,
   2011D4, 2012D4, 2013D4, 2015D4, 2016D4,
   2017D4, 2019D4
Sandusky 262

1983C, 1985C, 1986C, 1987C, 1988C, 1989C, 1990C, 1991C, 1992C, 1993C, 1994C, 1995C, 1996C, 1997C, 1998C, 1999C, 2000D3, 2013D4, 2014D3, 2016D3, 2018D3
Sanford Meridian 94
1991B, 1992C, 1995C, 1996C, 1997C, 1998C, 1999C, 2000D3, 2008D3, 2016D3, 2019D3
Saranac 229
1930CD, 1931CD, 1961CD, 1962CD, 1963CD, 1964CD, 1979D, 2000D4, 2001D4, 2002D4, 2005D4, 2006D4, 2007D4, 2008D4, 2009D4, 2012D3, 2018D4
Saugatuck 303
2001D4, 2006D4, 2007D4, 2008D4, 2010D4, 2011D4, 2012D4, 2013D4, 2014D4, 2015D4, 2016D3, 2017D3, 2018D4, 2019D3
Sault Ste Marie 5
1931B
Schoolcraft 72
1964CD, 1988D, 1990C, 1991D, 2000D3, 2004D3, 2007D3, 2008D3, 2010D3, 2011D3, 2012D3, 2013D3
Shepherd 466
1964CD, 1965CD, 1966CD, 1967CD, 1968CD, 1969CD, 1970CD, 1971CD, 1973CD, 1976C, 1981C, 1984C, 1986C, 1987C, 1994C, 1995B, 2002D3, 2003D3, 2004D3, 2005D3, 2006D3, 2007D3, 2008D3, 2010D3, 2014D3, 2015D3, 2016D3, 2017D3, 2018D3, 2019D3
South Haven 104
1931B, 1956B, 1957B, 1958B, 1959B, 1991B, 1992B, 1998B, 1999B, 2006D2, 2012D2, 2013D2
South Lyon 23
2005D1
South Lyon East 1
2010D2
Southfield 3
1955A, 1982A
Southfield Christian 152
1976D, 1977D, 1978D, 1981D, 1982D, 1983D, 1984D, 1987C, 2001D4, 2002D4, 2003D4, 2004D4, 2005D4, 2006D4, 2007D4, 2008D4, 2009D4, 2010D4, 2014D4, 2016D4
Southfield Lathrup 14
1978A, 1982A
Southgate Aquinas 8
1986B, 1987B
Sparta 339
1961B, 1962B, 1965B, 1966B, 1967B, 1968B, 1969B, 1975B, 1988B, 1996B, 1997B, 1999B, 2001D2, 2002D2, 2003D2, 2004D2, 2005D2, 2006D2, 2007D2, 2008D2, 2010D2, 2011D2, 2014D2, 2015D2, 2016D2, 2019D2
Spring Arbor 73
1950CD, 1951CD, 1952CD, 1953CD, 1954CD, 1955CD, 1956CD, 1957CD, 1958CD, 1959CD
Spring Lake 169
1982B, 1984B, 1993B, 1996B, 2000D3, 2001D3, 2007D2, 2015D2, 2016D2, 2017D2, 2018D2, 2019D2
Springport 95
1961CD, 1963CD, 1964CD, 1965CD, 1966CD, 1978C, 1979C
St Clair 371
1983B, 1984B, 1986B, 2000D2, 2001D2, 2002D2, 2003D2, 2004D2, 2005D2, 2006D2, 2007D2, 2008D2, 2009D2, 2010D2, 2011D2, 2012D2, 2013D2, 2014D2, 2015D2, 2016D2, 2017D2, 2018D2, 2019D2
St Clair Shores Lake Shore 3
1976A, 2007D2
St Clair Shores Lakeview 6
2002D2, 2013D1, 2014D1
St Clair Shores South Lake 4
1968A
St Johns 185
1958B, 1959B, 1960B, 1961B, 1979B, 1995A, 1996A, 1998A, 2008D2, 2012D2, 2014D2, 2015D2, 2016D2, 2017D2, 2018D2, 2019D2
St Joseph 514
1968A, 1969A, 1970A, 1971A, 1972A, 1974A, 1975A, 1980B, 1982B, 1983B, 1984B, 1986B, 1987B, 1988B, 1991B, 1992B, 1993B, 1994B, 1995B, 1996B, 1997B, 1998B, 1999B, 2000D2, 2007D2, 2009D2, 2010D2, 2011D2, 2012D2, 2013D2, 2014D2, 2016D2
St Joseph Lake Michigan Catholic 43
1974C, 1975C, 1982C, 1983C, 1986C, 1987C, 1993D, 2002D4, 2005D4, 2009D4
St Louis 313
1968B, 1969B, 1975C, 1977C, 1978C, 1979C, 1980C, 1981C, 1996C, 1997C, 1999C, 2000D4, 2004D3, 2005D4, 2006D4, 2007D4, 2013D3, 2019D3
Standish Sterling 5
2015D3
Stanton-Central Montcalm 21
1975C, 2005D3
Sterling Heights 133
1979A, 1980A, 1981A, 1989A, 1996A, 1998A, 1999A, 2000D1, 2001D1, 2002D1, 2003D1, 2004D1
Sterling Heights Ford 107
1980A, 1987A, 1988A, 1989A, 1990A, 1991A, 1994A, 1995A, 1997A, 1998A, 2006D1
Sterling Heights Stevenson 125
1977A, 1978A, 1981A, 1982A, 1983A, 1987A, 1988A, 1989A, 1991A, 1992A
Stevensville Lakeshore 33
1969B, 1970B, 1979B, 1985B, 1987B, 2001D2
Stockbridge 440
1979C, 1980C, 1981C, 1987C, 1988C, 1989B, 1993B, 1994B, 1995B, 1996B, 1997B, 1999B, 2000D3, 2001D3, 2002D3, 2009D3, 2011D3, 2012D3, 2013D3, 2014D3, 2015D3, 2016D3, 2017D3
Sturgis 385
1952B, 1965B, 1966B, 1967B, 1969B, 1970B, 1971B, 1972B, 1973B, 1974B, 1975B, 1976B, 1980B, 1981B, 1982B, 1983B, 1985B, 1986B, 1987B, 1988B, 1989B, 2001D2, 2006D2, 2008D2, 2009D2, 2011D2, 2012D2, 2013D2, 2014D2, 2015D2

Suttons Bay 121
1981D, 1984D, 1987D, 1989D, 1990D, 1991D,
1992C, 1993C, 2007D4, 2008D4, 2009D4
Swartz Creek 283
1958CD, 1966B, 1967B, 1978A, 1982A, 1983A,
1984A, 1985A, 1986A, 1987A, 1988A, 1989A,
1990A, 1991A, 1992A, 1993A, 1994A, 1995A,
1996A
Tawas City 17
1999B, 2001D3
Taylor Center 7
1970A
Tecumseh 51
1981B, 1990B, 1999B, 2000D2, 2007D2,
2008D2
Temperance Bedford 254
1974A, 1975A, 1980A, 1981A, 1982A, 1987A,
1992A, 1993A, 1995A, 1996A, 1998A, 1999A,
2000D1, 2001D1, 2002D1, 2008D1, 2009D1,
2010D1, 2011D1, 2014D1, 2015D1, 2016D1,
2017D1, 2018D1
Three Oaks River Valley 56.5
1975C, 1979C, 1986C, 1996C, 1997C, 2003D3
Three Rivers 99
1926, 1928B, 1929B, 1930B, 1984B, 2000D2,
2004D2, 2005D2, 2006D2, 2007D2
Traverse City/Central 496
1966A, 1980A, 1981A, 1986A, 1989A, 1990A,
1991A, 1992A, 1993A, 1994A, 1995A, 1996A,
1997A, 1998A, 1999A, 2000D1, 2001D1,
2002D1, 2003D1, 2004D1, 2006D1, 2007D1,
2011D1, 2012D1, 2013D1, 2014D1, 2015D1,
2017D1, 2018D1, 2019D1
Traverse City St Francis 90
1996D, 2003D4, 2007D4, 2008D4, 2012D4,
2016D3, 2017D3, 2018D3, 2019D3
Traverse City West 180
2000D1, 2001D1, 2002D1, 2003D1, 2004D1,
2005D1, 2006D1, 2010D1, 2013D1, 2014D1,
2015D1, 2016D1, 2017D1
Trenton 183.5
1943B, 1946B, 1947B, 1948B, 1949B, 1950B,
1951B, 1952B, 1953B, 1955B, 1956B, 1965A,
1994B, 1995B, 1998B, 1999B, 2007D2,
2008D2, 2009D2, 2010D2
Troy 138
1977B, 1978B, 1981A, 1982A, 1986A, 1988A,
1989A, 1995A, 1996A, 1999A, 2000D1,
2001D1, 2002D1, 2007D1, 2009D1, 2012D1,
2013D1, 2015D1, 2017D1, 2019D1
Troy Athens 117
1993A, 1994A, 1995A, 1996A, 1997A, 2001D1,
2002D1, 2003D1, 2004D1, 2005D1, 2006D1
Tustin 25
1954CD, 1963CD, 1964CD
Ubly 120
2001D4, 2002D4, 2006D4, 2008D4, 2014D4,
2015D4, 2016D4, 2017D4, 2000D4
Union City 19
1976C, 1983C, 1988C
Unionville-Sebewaing 216
1974C, 1980C, 1982C, 1984C, 1985C, 1986C,
1987C, 1997C, 2001D4, 2005D4, 2006D4,
2008D4, 2010D4, 2011D4, 2012D4, 2018D4,
2019D4
Utica 4
2015D1
Utica Eisenhower 119
1984A, 1985A, 1986A, 1997A, 1998A, 1999A,
2000D1, 2001D1, 2002D1, 2007D1
Van Dyke Lincoln 8
1940B, 1941A, 1951A
Vanderbilt 8
1998D
Vandercook Lake 211
1969CD, 1970CD, 1971CD, 1982C, 1985C,
1998C, 2000D4, 2001D4, 2002D4, 2003D4,
2004D4, 2005D4, 2006D4
Vassar 53
1971B, 1972B, 1973CD, 1988B, 1992B, 1994B,
2000D3
Vicksburg 226.5
1957B, 1962B, 1963B, 1964B, 1965B, 1966B,
1967B, 1968B, 1969B, 1972B, 1974B, 1982B,
1983B, 1984B, 1985B, 2004D2, 2005D2,
2007D2, 2008D2, 2009D2, 2011D2, 2017D2
Walkerville 47
1980D, 1996D, 1997D, 2016D4, 2017D4
Walled Lake/Walled Lake Central 281.5
1948B, 1949B, 1950B, 1951B, 1952B, 1953B,
1954B, 1955B, 1956B, 1957A, 1959A, 1978A,
1985A, 1986A, 1997A, 2004D1, 2005D1,
2014D1, 2016D1, 2018D1, 2019D1
Walled Lake Northern 36
2010D1, 2012D1, 2013D1
Walled Lake Western 52
1990A, 1991A
Warren 5
1990B
Warren Cousino 114
1972A, 1973A, 1974A, 1979A, 1980A, 1983A,
1984A, 1991B, 1992B, 1993A, 1995A, 1996A,
1997A, 1998A
Warren DeLaSalle 132
1974B, 1986A, 1988A, 1990A, 1991A, 1992A,
1993A, 1994A, 2000D1, 2006D1, 2007D1,
2008D1, 2009D1, 2013D1, 2019D1
Warren Fitzgerald 66
1974A, 1982B, 1986B, 1987B, 1988B, 1989B
Warren Mott 11
1999A, 2011D1
Warren Tower 78
1977A, 1978A, 1981A, 1982A, 1983A
Warren Woods-Tower 4
1984A, 1999B
Waterford Mott 123
1977A, 2010D1, 2011D1, 2012D1, 2013D1,
2014D1
Waterford Our Lady of the Lakes 15
2011D4, 2012D4
Watervliet 121
1970CD, 1971CD, 1972CD, 1973CD, 1974C,
1978C, 2011D3, 2012D3, 2013D3, 2014D3,

2015D3
Wayland 19
    1997B, 1995B
Wayne/Wayne Memorial 137
    1934B, 1935B, 1936B, 1937B, 1938B, 1939B,
    1940B, 1941B, 1944B, 1950A1, 1951A, 1957A,
    1958A, 1960A, 1973A, 1974A, 1976A, 1977A,
    1978A, 1981A, 1982A, 1983A, 2013D1
Wayne St Mary 15
    1962CD, 1970CD
Webberville 33
    1985D, 1988D, 1989D, 2019D4
West Bloomfield 114
    1966B, 1967B, 1971A, 1972A, 1973A, 1976A,
    1978A, 1979A, 1982A, 1992A, 2003D1
West Branch Ogemaw Heights 150
    1991B, 1992B, 1993B, 1994B, 1995B, 1996B,
    1997B, 1998B, 2008D2, 2009D2, 2017D2
Westland Glenn 21
    1973A, 1975A, 1983A, 1984A
Westland Lutheran 7
    1994C
White Cloud 29
    1973CD, 1974C, 1975C, 1987D, 2017D4
White Lake Lakeland 657
    1980A, 1983A, 1984A, 1985A, 1986A, 1987A,
    1988A, 1989A, 1990A, 1991A, 1992A, 1993A,
    1994A, 1995A, 1996A, 1997A, 1998A, 2000D1,
    2001D1, 2002D1, 2004D1, 2005D1, 2006D1,
    2007D1, 2008D1, 2010D1, 2011D1, 2014D1,
    2015D1, 2016D1, 2017D1
White Pigeon 24
    1962CD, 1964CD, 1968CD
Whitehall 48
    1947CD, 1972B, 2000D3, 2007D3, 2012D2,
    2013D2
Whitmore Lake 191
    1986D, 1987D, 1988D, 1990D, 1991D, 1992D,
    1996D, 1997D, 2004D4, 2006D4, 2007D3,
    2008D3, 2009D3, 2010D3, 2017D3, 2019D4
Whittemore-Prescott 5
    1964CD
Williamston 379
    1960CD, 1970CD, 1980C, 1984C, 1985C,
    1986C, 1987C, 1988C, 1989C, 1998B, 1999B,
    2000D3, 2001D3, 2002D3, 2003D3, 2004D3,
    2005D3, 2006D3, 2007D3, 2008D2, 2009D2,
    2015D2
Wolverine 39
    1996D, 1997D, 1998D, 2008D4
Wyandotte 288
    1927B, 1928B, 1929A, 1934A, 1935A, 1938A,
    1939A, 1940A, 1941A, 1944A, 1945A, 1946A,
    1947A, 1948A, 1949A, 1950A1, 1951A, 1952A,
    1954A, 1956A, 1957A, 1958A, 1960A, 1963A,
    1964A, 1965A, 1966A, 1967A, 1972A, 1988A,
    1995A, 1996A, 1996A, 1997A, 1998A, 1999A,
    2011D1, 2012D1, 2013D1
Wyandotte Mt Carmel 3
    1999D, 2000D4
Wyoming Godwin Heights 46
    1958B, 1988C, 1989C, 1990B
Wyoming Kelloggsville 67
    1973B, 1976B, 1996C, 1997C, 2000D3, 2002D3
Wyoming Lee 183
    1954CD, 1955CD, 1964CD, 1966CD, 1967CD,
    1968CD, 1970CD, 1971CD, 1972CD, 1973CD,
    1975C, 1977C, 1978C, 1979C, 1982D, 1994D,
    1995D
Wyoming Park 63
    1960B, 1961B, 1962B, 1963B, 1975B, 1979B,
    1995B
Wyoming Potter's House 23
    2019D4
Wyoming Rogers 217
    1956CD, 1957CD, 1958CD, 1963B, 1964B,
    1965B, 1966B, 1968B, 1969B, 1976B, 1978B,
    1979B, 1980B, 1981B, 1984B, 1985B, 1986B
Wyoming Tri-Unity Christian 19
    2003D4, 2004D4
Yale 65
    1993B, 2001D3, 2002D3, 2009D2, 2015D2,
    2017D2, 2018D2, 2019D2
Ypsilanti/Ypsilanti Central) 246.5
    1927B, 1928B, 1934B, 1935B, 1936B, 1937B,
    1938B, 1939B, 1940B, 1941B, 1943B, 1944B,
    1945B, 1946B, 1947B, 1948B, 1949B, 1950A1,
    1950A2, 1951A, 1952A, 1955A, 1959A, 1960A,
    1961A, 1962A, 1967A, 1996B, 2004D2, 2005D2
Ypsilanti Lincoln 23
    1982B, 1988B, 1993B
Ypsilanti Roosevelt 16
    1928CD, 1929CD, 1930CD, 1948CD
Zeeland 118
    1968B, 1969B, 1970B, 1974B, 1976B, 1992B,
    1993B, 1994B, 1996A, 2000D1, 2002D1
Zeeland East 34
    2011D2, 2017D2, 2018D2
Zeeland West 67
    2012D2, 2014D2, 2017D2, 2018D2, 2019D1

ALL-TIME LEGACY RATINGS BY SCHOOL
► GIRLS ◄

Jackson Lumen Christi's 1983 squad.

Addison 77
    1987C, 1988C, 1992C, 1993C, 1994C, 1995C
Adrian 19
    1977A, 2014D2, 2015D2, 2016D2
Adrian Lenawee Christian 25
    1997D, 1998D, 1999D, 2019D4
Adrian Madison 11
    2014D3, 2016D3
Akron-Fairgrove 149
    1978D, 1979D, 1980D, 1981D, 1982D, 1983D,
    1984D, 1985D, 1986D, 1987D, 1988D, 1989D,
    1991D, 1992D, 1993D, 1997D
Albion 21
    2001D3
Algonac 69
    1983B, 1989B, 1990B, 1991B, 1992B, 1993B,
    1995B, 1996B, 1997B, 1998B, 2006D2
Allegan 15
    1980B, 1989B, 2005D2
Allen Park Cabrini 59
    1983B, 1988B, 2006D4, 2011D3, 2012D3,
    2018D3, 2019D4
Allendale 181
    2003D3, 2004D3, 2006D3, 2007D3, 2008D3,
    2009D3, 2010D3, 2015D2, 2016D2, 2017D2,
    2019D2
Alma 97
    1977B, 1979B, 1983B, 1984B, 1985B, 1987B,
    1988B, 1990B, 2015D2, 2016D2, 2017D2
Almont 17
    1999C, 2008D3, 2009D3, 2011D3, 2013D3,
    2016D3
Alpena 24
    1998A, 1999A, 2009D1
Ann Arbor Greenhills 264
    1977D, 1979D, 1980D, 1981D, 1982D, 1983D,
    1990D, 1991D, 1996D, 2000D4, 2001D4,
    2002D4, 2003D4, 2004D4, 2005D4, 2006D4,
    2007D4, 2008D4, 2009D4, 2010D4
Ann Arbor Huron 263
    1975A, 1976A, 1977A, 1978all, 1980A, 1981A,
    1982A, 1983A, 1984A, 1985A, 1986A, 1989A,
    1992A, 1994A, 2000D1, 2001D1, 2002D1,
    2006D1, 2007D1, 2008D1
Ann Arbor Pioneer 618
    1975A, 1976A, 1977A, 1978all, 1979A, 1983A,
    1984A, 1985A, 1987A, 1988A, 1989A, 1990A,
    1991A, 1994A, 1997A, 1998A, 1999A, 2000D1,
    2001D1, 2002D1, 2004D1, 2005D1, 2006D1,
    2008D1, 2009D1, 2010D1, 2013D1, 2014D1,
    2015D1, 2016D1, 2017D1, 2018D1, 2019D1
Ann Arbor Richard 177
    1991D, 1992D, 1994D, 1995D, 1996D, 2002D4,
    2003D4, 2004D3, 2006D3, 2011D3, 2012D3,
    2013D3, 2014D2, 2015D2, 2016D2, 2017D2
Ann Arbor Skyline 5
    2017D1
Armada 37
    2003D3, 2004D3, 2005D3, 2006D3, 2007D3
Athens 1
    2018D4
Atlanta 14

1997D, 1998D
Auburn Hills Avondale 1
    1996B
Auburn Hills Oakland Christian 53
    1994D, 1997D, 1998D, 1999D, 2000D4, 2001D4,
    2003D4, 2004D4, 2005D4, 2009D4, 2011D4,
    2013D4, 2010D4
Bad Axe 34
    1998B, 2000D3, 2002D3, 2003D3, 2004D3,
    2009D3, 2017D3
Bangor 40
    1983C, 1984C, 1985C, 1996C, 2009D3, 2016D3,
    2017D3
Bath 260
    1975CD, 1976C, 1977C, 1982C, 1983C, 1984C,
    1985C, 1986C, 1987C, 1988C, 1989C, 1992D,
    1994D, 1999C, 2000D4, 2001D4, 2002D4,
    2003D4, 2004D4, 2009D4, 2011D3, 2012D3
Battle Creek Central 6
    1985A
Battle Creek Harper Creek 34
    1997B, 2008D2
Battle Creek Lakeview 154
    1999A, 2000D2, 2001D2, 2002D2, 2003D2,
    2004D2, 2005D2, 2008D1, 2016D1
Battle Creek St Philip 156
    1988D, 1989D, 1993D, 2005D4, 2006D4,
    2007D4, 2008D4, 2009D4, 2015D4, 2016D4,
    2018D4, 2019D4
Bay City Western 89
    1984A, 1985A, 1986A, 2007D1, 2013D1,
    2015D1, 2017D1, 2018D1, 2019D1
Beal City 205
    2003D4, 2004D4, 2005D4, 2006D4, 2009D4,
    2011D4, 2012D4, 2013D4, 2014D4, 2015D4,
    2019D4
Bear Lake-Onekama 316
    1992D, 1993D, 1994D, 1995C, 1996D, 1998D,
    1999D, 2000D4, 2001D4, 2002D4, 2003D4,
    2006D4, 2007D4, 2008D4, 2010D4, 2011D4,
    2012D4, 2013D4, 2014D4, 2016D4, 2017D4
Beaverton 9
    1987C, 1988C, 1993C
Bellaire 3
    1990D
Belleville 31
    1986A, 1992A, 1993A, 1995A, 1996A, 1998A
Bellevue 39
    1977C, 1978C, 2000D4, 2001D4, 2003D4
Benton Harbor 4
    1981A
Benzie Central 520
    1981C, 1982C, 1983C, 1984C, 1985C, 1986C,
    1987C, 1988C, 1991C, 1996C, 1997C, 1998C,
    1999C, 2000D3, 2002D3, 2005D3, 2006D3,
    2007D3, 2008D3, 2009D3, 2010D3, 2011D3,
    2012D3, 2013D3, 2015D3, 2016D3, 2017D3,
    2018D3, 2019D3
Berkley 92
    1981A, 1982A, 1983A, 1984A, 1988A, 1992A,
    1993A, 1994A, 1999A, 2017D1
Berrien Springs 35
    1980C, 1982C, 1999C, 2000D3, 2009D3
Big Rapids 140
    1983B, 1991B, 1992B, 1993B, 1999B, 2000D2,
    2015D2
Big Rapids Crossroads 94
    2003D4, 2004D4, 2005D4, 2006D4, 2017D4
Birmingham Groves 2
    2002D1
Birmingham Marian 44
    2000D2, 2001D2, 2002D2, 2003D2, 2004D2,
    2005D2
Birmingham Seaholm 373
    1982A, 1983A, 1991A, 1995A, 1996A, 1997A,
    1998A, 2000D2, 2001D2, 2002D2, 2003D2,
    2004D2, 2005D2, 2006D2, 2007D2, 2008D2,
    2009D1, 2011D1, 2012D1, 2013D1, 2014D1,
    2015D1, 2016D1, 2017D1, 2018D1, 2019D1
Blanchard Montabella 41
    2013D4, 2014D4, 2015D4
Blissfield 274
    2019D3, 1984C, 1991C, 1995C, 1996C, 1997C,
    1998C, 1999C, 2001D3, 2002D3, 2003D3,
    2004D3, 2006D3, 2008D3, 2009D3, 2010D3,
    2014D3, 2015D3, 2016D3, 2017D3
Bloomfield Hills 26
    2013D1, 2017D1, 2018D1, 2019D1
Bloomfield Hills Andover 75
    1986A, 1991B, 1992B, 1993B, 1996B, 1997B,
    1998B, 1999B, 2001D2, 2002D2, 2010D2,
    2011D2
Bloomfield Hills Cranbrook 58
    2005D2, 2011D2, 2012D2, 2013D2, 2014D2
Bloomfield Hills Lahser 139
    1980A, 1982A, 1984A, 1986A, 1992A, 2003D2,
    2004D2, 2005D2, 2006D2, 2007D2, 2009D2,
    2010D2, 2011D2, 2012D2
Bloomfield Hills Marian 21
    2009D2, 2013D2, 2016D2, 2018D2, 2019D2
Bloomfield Hills Roeper 1
    1980D
Bloomingdale 23
    2017D3, 2018D3
Boyne City 43
    2000D3, 2001D3, 2003D3
Boyne Falls 18
    2009D4
Breckenridge 152
    1978C, 1983C, 2011D4, 2012D4, 2013D4,
    2014D4, 2016D4, 2017D4, 2018D4
Bridgman 70
    1980D, 1985D, 2015D3, 2017D4, 2018D4,
    2019D4
Brighton 723
    1978all, 1979A, 1980A, 1981A, 1982A, 1983A,
    1984A, 1985A, 1987A, 1989A, 1990A, 1991A,
    1992A, 1993A, 1994A, 1995A, 1996A, 1997A,
    1998A, 1999A, 2000D1, 2001D1, 2002D1,
    2003D1, 2004D1, 2006D1, 2007D1, 2008D1,
    2009D1, 2010D1, 2011D1, 2012D1, 2013D1,
    2014D1, 2015D1, 2016D1, 2017D1, 2018D1,
    2019D1
Britton Deerfield 18

2013D4, 2014D4
Bronson 33
   1986C, 1987C, 1988C, 2019D3
Brown City 33
   2001D4, 2002D4, 2016D3
Buchanan 78
   1979C, 1986C, 1987C, 1988B, 1990C, 1991C,
   1993C, 1994C, 1995C, 1996C, 1997C, 1998C,
   2006D3, 2008D3
Buckley 66
   1989D, 1990D, 1991D, 1993D, 1994D, 1995D,
   1996D, 1997D, 1998D, 1999D, 2000D4
Burr Oak 8
   1976D, 1977D
Burton Atherton 71
   1987C, 1988C, 1989C, 1991C, 1992C, 1994C
Burton Bendle 55
   1984C, 1990C, 1992C, 1993C, 1995C
Byron 64
   1982C, 1990C, 1993C, 2014D3, 2017D3,
   2018D3, 2019D3
Byron Center Zion Christian 6
   2015D4
Cadillac 155
   1982B, 1985B, 1986B, 1988B, 1992A, 1994B,
   2011D2, 2016D2, 2017D2, 2018D2, 2019D2
Caledonia 245
   1984C, 1989B, 1990B, 1991B, 1992B, 1993B,
   1994B, 1995B, 1996B, 2010D1, 2011D1,
   2012D1, 2017D1, 2018D1, 2019D1
Camden-Frontier 3
   1983D
Canton 65
   1987A, 1988A, 1989A, 2001D1, 2002D1, 2007D1
Capac 73
   1980C, 1983C, 1984C, 1985C, 1986C, 1991C,
   2013D3, 2014D3
Carleton Airport 115
   1976B, 1977B, 1978all, 1978B, 1979B, 1980B,
   1993B, 1994B, 1995B, 1997B, 1998B, 2008D2,
   2010D2, 2014D2
Caro 224.5
   1984B, 1985B, 1987B, 1988B, 1991B, 1993B,
   1994B, 1996B, 2001D3, 2007D3, 2008D3,
   2009D3, 2010D3, 2011D3, 2012D3, 2013D3,
   2014D3
Carson City-Crystal 213
   1984C, 1986C, 1987C, 1988C, 1991C, 1992C,
   1993C, 1994C, 1995C, 1996C, 1997C, 2016D4,
   2017D4, 2018D4, 2019D4
Cass City 49
   1981C, 1982C, 1983C, 2001D3, 2002D3,
   2008D3, 2010D3
Cedar Springs 172
   1992B, 1997B, 1998B, 2000D2, 2009D2,
   2010D2, 2011D2, 2012D2, 2013D2, 2014D2
Central Lake 22
   1991D, 1992D, 1993D, 1994D, 1995D, 1996D
Centreville 42
   1979D, 1982D, 1983D, 1990C, 1992C, 2002D4,
   2003D4, 2004D4, 2005D4, 2008D4, 2009D4,
   2010D4, 2011D4, 2017D4

Charlevoix 250
   1987C, 1988C, 1990C, 1994C, 1995C, 1996C,
   1998C, 2002D3, 2003D3, 2004D3, 2010D3,
   2011D3, 2015D3, 2016D3, 2017D3, 2018D3,
   2019D3
Charlotte 6
   2013D2
Chelsea 496
   1983B, 1984B, 1985B, 1986B, 1987B, 1989B,
   1990B, 1991B, 1992B, 1993B, 1995B, 1996B,
   1997B, 2001D2, 2002D2, 2004D2, 2005D2,
   2006D2, 2010D2, 2011D2, 2012D2, 2013D2,
   2014D2, 2015D2, 2017D2
Chesaning 2
   1979B
Clare 368
   1979C, 1982C, 1986C, 1991C, 1992C, 1993C,
   1994C, 1995C, 2002D3, 2003D3, 2004D3,
   2005D3, 2006D3, 2008D3, 2010D3, 2011D3,
   2012D3, 2013D3, 2014D3, 2015D3, 2016D3,
   2017D3, 2018D3, 2019D3
Clarkston 402
   1982A, 1986A, 1987A, 1995A, 1996A, 2001D1,
   2002D1, 2003D1, 2004D1, 2005D1, 2006D1,
   2007D1, 2008D1, 2011D1, 2012D1, 2013D1,
   2014D1, 2015D1, 2016D1, 2017D1, 2018D1,
   2019D1
Clarkston Everest Collegiate 21
   2018D4, 2019D4
Clawson 33
   1989B, 1993B, 1994B, 1995B, 1996B, 1997B,
   1999B, 2000D3
Clinton 6
   2019D3
Clio 102
   1979A, 1982A, 1983A, 1984A, 1985A, 1988A,
   1989A, 1980A, 1981A
Coldwater 56
   1985B, 1986B, 1988B, 2019D2
Coloma 3
   2019D3
Colon 135
   1981D, 1982D, 1983D, 1984D, 1985D, 1987D,
   1988D, 1990D, 1991D, 1992C, 1993C, 1995C,
   1999D, 2000D4, 2001D4, 2002D4, 2003D4
Concord 296
   1982D, 1983D, 1984D, 1985C, 1986D, 1987D,
   1998C, 1999C, 2000D4, 2001D4, 2002D4,
   2004D4, 2005D4, 2007D4, 2008D4, 2009D4,
   2010D4, 2011D4, 2012D4, 2013D4, 2015D4
Coopersville 15
   1995B
Corunna 73
   1989B, 1997B, 1998B, 2000D2, 2001D2,
2010D2, 2011D2, 2012D2
Covert 1
   1984D
Croswell-Lexington 70
   1979B, 1980B, 2002D2, 2006D2, 2007D2,
   2008D2, 2012D2, 2013D2, 2015D2, 2017D2,
   2018D2
Dansville 53

1979D, 1980D, 1981D, 1982D, 1983D
Davison 52
    1980A, 1981A, 2003D1, 2012D1, 2014D1
Dearborn 71
    1985A, 1986B, 1987B, 1988B, 2003D1
Dearborn Divine Child 394.5
    1977B, 1978B, 1979B, 1980B, 1983B, 1984B,
    1985B, 1987B, 1988B, 1989B, 1990B, 1991B,
    1993B, 1994B, 1995B, 1996B, 1997B, 1998B,
    1999B, 2000D2, 2001D2, 2002D2, 2007D2,
    2008D2, 2009D2, 2010D2, 2011D2, 2012D2,
    2013D2, 2016D2, 2017D2, 2018D2, 2019D2
Dearborn Edsel Ford 269
    1982A, 1983A, 1984A, 1985A, 1986A, 1987A,
    1988A, 1989A, 1990A, 1991A, 1992A, 1993A,
    1996A, 1997A, 1998A, 1999A
Dearborn Heights Crestwood 2
    1987B
Dearborn St Alphonsus 1
    1985B
Decatur 39
    1977C, 1978all, 1978C
Deckerville 33
    2017D4, 2019D4
Delton Kellogg 50
    2001D3, 2002D3, 2004D3, 2008D3, 2010D3,
    2011D3, 2012D3, 2014D3, 2015D3
Detroit Bethesda 4
    1985D
Detroit Cass Tech 3
    1988A
Detroit Country Day 88
    1975CD, 1976C, 1977D, 1978D, 1979D, 1980D,
    1984C, 1985C, 1986C, 1987C, 1999B, 2001D3,
    2002D3, 2007D3, 2013D2, 2014D2
Detroit Kettering 4
    1986A
Detroit King 1
    2005D1
Detroit Mumford 3
    2006D1
Detroit Pershing 1
    1987A
Detroit Redford 1
    1991A
Detroit Renaissance 23
    2002D2, 2003D2, 2004D2
Detroit Northern 11
    1981B
DeWitt 297
    1978all, 1979C, 1981C, 1982C, 1983C, 1985C,
    1986C, 1987C, 1988C, 2008D2, 2009D2,
    2011D2, 2013D2, 2014D2, 2015D2, 2016D2,
    2017D2, 2018D2
Dexter 292
    1980B, 1981B, 1982B, 1983B, 2000D2, 2002D2,
    2003D2, 2004D2, 2005D2, 2006D2, 2007D2,
    2008D2, 2009D2, 2010D1, 2011D1, 2012D1,
    2013D1, 2014D1
Dryden 5
    2018D4
Dundee 30
    1998C, 2010D3, 2012D3, 2017D3, 2018D3
Durand 28
    1996B, 2006D3, 2009D3, 2011D3
East Grand Rapids 480
    1987B, 1988B, 1989B, 1990B, 2003D2, 2004D2,
    2005D2, 2006D2, 2007D2, 2008D2, 2009D2,
    2010D2, 2011D2, 2012D2, 2013D2, 2014D2,
    2015D2, 2016D2, 2017D1, 2018D2, 2019D2
East Jordan 127
    1987C, 2000D4, 2001D4, 2003D4, 2005D3,
    2015D4, 2017D4, 2018D4, 2019D4
East Kentwood 163
    1982A, 1984A, 1987A, 1988A, 1991A, 1992A,
    1993A, 2006D1, 2008D1, 2009D1, 2011D1
East Lansing 297
    1977A, 1978all, 1979A, 1980A, 1985A, 1989A,
    1990A, 2003D2, 2004D2, 2005D2, 2006D2,
    2007D2, 2008D2, 2009D2, 2010D2, 2011D2,
    2012D1, 2013D1
Eaton Rapids 11
    2001D2
Eau Claire 11
    1976C, 1977C
Edwardsburg 69
    1981C, 1985C, 1989C, 1990C, 1991B, 1992C,
    2000D3, 2006D3
Elk Rapids 176
    1989C, 1990C, 1991C, 1994C, 1998C, 2001D3,
    2002D3, 2003D3, 2004D3, 2005D3, 2006D3,
    2008D3
Ellsworth 74
    2002D4, 2003D4, 2004D4, 2005D4, 2006D4,
    2007D4, 2011D4, 2016D4, 2017D4, 2018D4,
    2019D4
Erie-Mason 38
    1999C, 2000D3, 2001D3, 2002D3, 2005D3,
    2013D3, 2014D3
Essexville Garber 151
    1982B, 1983B, 1985B, 1986B, 1997B, 2000D3,
    2001D3, 2002D3, 2003D3, 2006D3, 2009D3,
    2012D3, 2013D2, 2014D2, 2015D2
Fairview 36
    1993D, 1994D, 1995D, 2004D4, 2005D4
Farmington 138
    1985A, 1986A, 1987A, 1989A, 1994A, 1995A,
    2000D2, 2001D1, 2003D1, 2015D1
Farmington Hills 12
    1977A
Farmington Hills Harrison 5
    1986B, 2000D2
Farmington Hills Mercy 53
    1978all, 1979A, 1982A, 1987A, 1988A, 1993A,
    2004D1
Fennville 3
    1976C
Fenton 59
    1979B, 2005D2, 2017D1, 2018D1, 2019D1
Flint Carman-Ainsworth 3
    1991A
Flint Holy Rosary 47
    1978D, 1979D, 1980D, 1981D, 1983D
Flint Kearsley 100

1978all, 1984A, 1985A, 1988A, 1989A, 1990A, 1992A, 1993A, 2001D2, 2002D2, 2003D2, 2004D2

Flint Northern 43
1981A, 1982A

Flint Powers 482
1981B, 1982B, 1983B, 1992B, 1993B, 1994B, 1995B, 1996B, 1997B, 1998B, 1999B, 2000D2, 2001D2, 2002D2, 2003D2, 2004D2, 2006D3, 2007D2, 2008D2, 2009D2, 2010D3, 2011D3, 2012D3, 2013D3, 2014D2, 2015D2, 2016D2, 2017D2, 2018D2, 2019D2

Flushing 159
1978all, 1981A, 1983A, 1986A, 1992A, 1993A, 1994A, 1995A, 1996A, 1997A, 1998A, 1999A, 2006D1, 2007D1, 2014D1, 2016D1

Forest Hills 3
1980B

Forest Hills Central 27
2002D1, 2013D1, 2015D1

Forest Hills Eastern 259
2005D2, 2006D2, 2007D2, 2008D2, 2009D2, 2010D2, 2011D2, 2012D2, 2015D2, 2016D2, 2017D2, 2018D2, 2019D2

Forest Hills Northern 165
2001D1, 2004D2, 2005D2, 2011D2, 2012D2, 2013D2, 2014D2, 2018D1, 2019D1

Fowler 334
1981D, 1982D, 1983D, 1984D, 1985D, 1986D, 1987D, 1988D, 1989D, 1990D, 1991D, 1992D, 1993D, 1994D, 1995D, 1996D, 2004D4, 2005D4, 2006D4, 2007D4, 2008D4, 2010D4, 2014D4, 2015D4, 2016D4, 2017D4, 2018D4, 2019D4

Fowlerville 21
1976C, 1987B, 1989B, 1995B

Frankenmuth 132
1991C, 1999B, 2001D3, 2002D3, 2003D3, 2004D3, 2005D3, 2006D3, 2013D3, 2015D3, 2016D3, 2017D2, 2018D2, 2019D2

Frankfort 66
2015D4, 2017D4, 2018D4, 2019D4

Fraser 2
2003D1, 2004D1

Freeland 147
1995C, 1996C, 1997C, 1998C, 2004D3, 2005D3, 2006D3, 2007D3, 2008D3, 2009D3, 2010D3, 2011D3, 2013D3, 2018D2, 2019D2

Fremont 398
1978B, 1979B, 1988B, 1989B, 1990B, 1991B, 1992B, 1993B, 1994B, 1995B, 1996B, 1997B, 1998B, 1999B, 2002D2, 2007D2, 2008D2, 2010D2, 2011D2, 2012D2, 2018D2

Fruitport 8
2001D2

Fruitport Calvary Christian 7
2019D4

Fulton-Middleton 20
1997D, 1998D

Galesburg-Augusta 19
2018D3, 2019D3

Gaylord 450
1987B, 1988B, 1989B, 1990B, 1991B, 1992B, 1993B, 1994B, 1995B, 1996B, 1998A, 1999B, 2001D2, 2002D2, 2003D2, 2004D2, 2005D2, 2006D2, 2007D2, 2008D2, 2009D2, 2010D2, 2014D2, 2015D2

Genesee 4
1995D, 2000D4

Gladwin 204
1979B, 1980B, 1981B, 1982B, 1983B, 1984B, 1987B, 1988B, 1989B, 1991B, 1993B, 1995B, 1996B, 1998B, 1999B, 2000D3

Gobles 6
2017D4

Goodrich 176
2000D3, 2001D3, 2002D3, 2003D3, 2004D3, 2005D3, 2006D2, 2008D2, 2010D2, 2013D2, 2015D2, 2016D2, 2017D2, 2018D2

Grand Blanc 128
1982A, 1983A, 2002D1, 2004D1, 2006D1, 2007D1, 2008D1, 2010D1, 2019D1

Grand Haven 420
1978all, 1979A, 1980A, 1987A, 1988A, 1989A, 1994A, 1995A, 1997A, 1998A, 2000D1, 2001D1, 2002D1, 2003D1, 2004D1, 2005D1, 2006D1, 2007D1, 2008D1, 2009D1, 2010D1, 2011D1, 2012D1, 2013D1, 2014D1, 2015D1, 2016D1, 2017D1

Grand Ledge 115
1975A, 1978all, 1987A, 2001D1, 2005D1, 2006D1, 2007D1, 2008D1, 2009D1, 2010D1, 2011D1, 2012D1

Grand Rapids Baptist 32
1994D, 2000D4, 2002D3, 2003D3

Grand Rapids Catholic Central 171
1983B, 1984B, 1985B, 1986B, 1987B, 1988B, 1989B, 1990B, 1996B, 1997B, 2016D2

Grand Rapids Christian 656
1979B, 1980B, 1981B, 1982B, 1983B, 1984B, 1985B, 1986B, 1987B, 1988B, 1996A, 2002D2, 2003D2, 2004D2, 2005D2, 2006D2, 2007D2, 2008D2, 2009D2, 2010D2, 2011D2, 2012D2, 2013D2, 2014D2, 2015D2, 2016D2, 2017D2, 2018D2, 2019D2

Grand Rapids Covenant Christian 62
2013D3, 2016D3, 2017D3, 2018D3, 2019D3

Grand Rapids Kenowa Hills 16
2014D1

Grand Rapids NorthPointe Christian 149
2004D4, 2005D4, 2006D4, 2007D4, 2008D4, 2009D3, 2012D3

Grand Rapids Ottawa Hills 5
2018D1

Grand Rapids South Christian 266
1989B, 1991B, 1992C, 1993B, 1993C, 1994B, 2003D2, 2004D2, 2005D2, 2006D2, 2011D2, 2013D2, 2014D2, 2015D2, 2016D2, 2019D2

Grand Rapids West Catholic 117
1996B, 1997B, 1998B, 2006D3, 2007D3, 2008D3, 2014D3

Grand Traverse Academy 118
2009D4, 2010D4, 2011D4, 2012D4, 2013D4, 2014D3

Grandville 239

1985A, 1989A, 1990A, 1991A, 1992A, 1993A,
2002D1, 2003D1, 2004D1, 2005D1, 2006D1,
2009D1, 2012D1, 2013D1, 2014D1, 2015D1

Grandville Calvin Christian 305
1986C, 1987C, 1988C, 1989C, 1990C, 1993C,
1994C, 2005D3, 2010D3, 2011D3, 2012D3,
2013D3, 2014D3, 2015D3, 2016D3, 2017D3,
2018D3, 2019D3

Grass Lake 112
1979D, 1980D, 1981D, 1982D, 1990D, 1991D,
1992D, 1993D, 1994D, 1995D, 1996D, 1997D,
1998D, 2017D3

Greenville 92
1984B, 1985B, 1986B, 1987B, 1988A, 1990A,
1995A

Grosse Ile 165
1984B, 1989B, 1990B, 1991B, 1992B, 1994B,
1995B, 1996B, 2001D2, 2003D3, 2007D3,
2009D2, 2012D2, 2013D2, 2014D2, 2018D2

Grosse Pointe North 198
1979A, 1980A, 1981A, 1982A, 1983A, 1984A,
1985A, 1986A, 1987A, 1988A, 1989A, 1990A,
1991A, 1992A, 1994A, 1997A, 1999A, 2001D1,
2002D1, 2003D1, 2004D1, 2005D1, 2006D1,
2007D1, 2008D1, 2010D1, 2011D1, 2013D1,
2014D1, 2015D1

Grosse Pointe South 563
1980A, 1981A, 1982A, 1983A, 1984A, 1985A,
1986A, 1987A, 1988A, 1989A, 1990A, 1991A,
1992A, 1993A, 1994A, 1995A, 1996A, 1997A,
1998A, 1999A, 2000D1, 2001D1, 2002D1,
2003D1, 2004D1, 2005D1, 2006D1, 2007D1,
2008D1, 2009D1, 2010D1, 2011D1, 2012D1,
2013D1, 2014D1, 2015D1, 2016D1

Grosse Pointe Woods University Liggett 47
2002D4, 2010D4, 2011D4, 2012D4, 2014D4,
2015D4, 2016D4, 2017D3, 2018D3, 2019D3

Hale 1
1976D

Hamilton 130
1999B, 2006D2, 2007D2, 2008D2, 2009D2,
2010D2, 2011D2, 2015D2

Hanover-Horton 339
1983D, 2000D4, 2001D3, 2002D3, 2003D3,
2005D3, 2007D3, 2008D3, 2009D3, 2010D3,
2011D3, 2012D3, 2013D3, 2014D3, 2015D3,
2017D3, 2018D3, 2019D3

Harbor Beach 73
1981C, 1984C, 2007D4, 2008D4, 2019D4

Harbor Springs 366
2001D4, 2002D4, 2003D4, 2004D3, 2006D4,
2007D4, 2008D4, 2009D4, 2010D4, 2011D3,
2012D4, 2014D4, 2015D4, 2016D4, 2017D3,
2018D3, 2019D3

Harper Woods Lutheran East 4
2000D4, 2001D4

Hart 161
2011D3, 2013D3, 2014D3, 2015D3, 2016D3,
2017D3, 2018D3, 2019D3

Hartford 14
2004D4, 2007D4, 2012D3, 2018D3

Hartland 133
1980B, 1981B, 1982B, 1983B, 1984B, 1985B,
2009D1, 2011D1

Haslett 71
1995B, 1995C, 1996B, 1997B, 1998B, 1999B

Hastings 33
1976B, 1977B, 1992B, 1994B

Hazel Park 7
1979A, 1989A, 1990A

Hemlock 100
1980B, 1982B, 1984B, 1993C, 1994C, 1995C,
1996C, 1997B, 2011D3, 2016D3

Hesperia 171
2005D4, 2006D4, 2007D4, 2008D4, 2009D4,
2010D4, 2011D4, 2012D4

Hillsdale 350
1975B, 1976B, 1977B, 1978all, 1978B, 1979B,
1980B, 1984B, 1985B, 1991B, 1995B, 2000D3,
2001D3, 2002D3, 2003D3, 2004D3, 2005D3,
2006D3, 2007D3, 2009D3, 2010D3, 2012D3

Hillsdale Academy 152
2005D4, 2006D4, 2008D4, 2010D4, 2014D4,
2015D4, 2016D4, 2018D4, 2019D4

Holland 26
1989A, 1993A, 2000D1

Holland Black River 53
2013D3, 2014D3, 2015D3

Holland Christian 238
1980B, 1981B, 1983B, 1986B, 1992B, 1994B,
1995B, 1997B, 1998B, 1999B, 2000D2, 2001D2,
2002D2, 2010D2, 2015D2, 2016D2, 2017D2,
2018D2, 2019D2

Holland West Ottawa 152
1991A, 1992A, 1994A, 1995A, 1996A, 2005D1,
2006D1, 2007D1, 2016D1, 2017D1, 2018D1,
2019D1

Holly 47
1987A, 1990A, 1991A

Holt 69
1977B, 1978B, 1979B, 1980B, 1994A, 2002D1

Holton 3
2016D4

Homer 72
2011D4, 2012D4, 2013D4

Hopkins 78
1997C, 2012D3, 2013D3, 2014D3, 2015D3,
2016D3

Howard City Tri-County 11
1991C

Howell 23
1985A, 2018D1, 2019D1

Hudson 203
1996C, 1997C, 2003D4, 2004D4, 2005D4,
2006D4, 2015D4, 2016D4, 2017D4, 2018D4,
2019D4

Hudsonville 134
1992B, 1993B, 1996A, 2010D1, 2011D1,
2012D1, 2013D1, 2014D1, 2016D1, 2017D1,
2018D1

Hudsonville Freedom Baptist 10
2003D4

Hudsonville Libertas Christian 8
2017D4

Ida 221
    1983C, 1984C, 1986C, 1987C, 1988C, 1990C,
    1992C, 1993C, 1994C, 1995B, 1996B, 1998B,
    2000D3, 2001D3, 2009D3, 2010D3, 2012D3,
    2013D3, 2014D3, 2018D3, 2019D3, 2008D3,
    2007D3
Imlay City 3
    1988B, 2017D2
Indian River Inland Lakes 34
    2013D4, 2014D4, 2015D4, 2016D4
Ionia 44
    1982B, 1995B, 2002D2, 2010D2
Ithaca 122
    2005D3, 2013D3, 2014D3, 2015D3, 2016D3,
    2018D3, 2019D3
Jackson 74
    1982A, 1986A, 1987A, 1988A, 2005D1
Jackson Lumen Christi 826
    1979B, 1980B, 1981B, 1982B, 1983B, 1984B,
    1985B, 1986B, 1987B, 1988B, 1989B, 1990B,
    1991B, 1992B, 1993B, 1994B, 1995B, 1996B,
    1998B, 1999B, 2000D3, 2002D3, 2003D3,
    2004D3, 2005D3, 2006D3, 2007D3, 2008D3,
    2009D3, 2010D3, 2011D3, 2012D3, 2013D3,
    2014D3, 2015D3, 2016D3, 2017D3, 2018D3,
    2019D3
Jackson Northwest 131
    1977B, 1978B, 1979B, 1981B, 1982B, 1984B,
    1988B, 1989B, 1990B, 2009D2, 2012D2
Jackson Parkside 15
    1980A, 1981B
Jenison 80
    1993A, 1994A, 1995A, 2013D1, 2019D1
Johannesburg-Lewiston 62
    2010D4, 2011D4, 2012D4, 2013D4, 2018D4,
    2019D4
Jonesville 36
    1996C, 1997C, 2007D4
Kalamazoo Central 3
    1977A
Kalamazoo Christian 268
    1980C, 1981C, 1982C, 1983C, 1984C, 1986C,
    1995C, 1996C, 1997C, 1998C, 1999C, 2001D3,
    2002D3, 2003D3, 2004D3, 2005D3, 2006D3,
    2007D3, 2009D4, 2010D4, 2012D4, 2013D4,
    2014D4, 2019D4
Kalamazoo Hackett 272
    1982C, 1991C, 1996C, 1997C, 1998C, 1999C,
    2000D3, 2001D3, 2002D3, 2003D3, 2005D3,
    2007D3, 2011D4, 2012D4, 2013D3, 2014D4,
    2015D4, 2016D4, 2017D4
Kalamazoo Norrix 175
    1976A, 1977A, 1979A, 1981A, 1982A, 1983A,
    1986A, 1987A, 1988A, 1989A, 1990A, 2000D1,
    2001D1
Kalkaska 1
    1977C
Kent City 245
    1998C, 1999C, 2000D3, 2002D3, 2003D3,
    2004D3, 2008D3, 2009D3, 2010D3, 2011D3,
    2017D3, 2018D3, 2019D3
Kinde-North Huron 24
    2001D4, 2002D4
Kingsley 41.5
    1984D, 1985D, 1986D, 1987D, 1989C, 2007D3,
    2009D3
Kingston 82
    1979D, 1980D, 1981D, 1982D, 1983D, 1984D,
    1985D, 1986D, 1987D, 2016D4
Laingsburg 94
    1989C, 1990C, 1992C, 1997C, 1998C, 1999C,
    2001D3, 2002D3
Lake Fenton 10
    1996C, 2000D3, 2008D3, 2009D3
Lake Leelanau St Mary 50
    2016D4, 2017D4, 2018D4
St Joseph Lake Michigan Catholic 11
    1980C, 1981C
Lake Orion 60
    2007D1, 2010D1, 2013D1, 2014D1, 2015D1,
    2017D1, 2018D1
White Lake Lakeland 10
    2004D1
Lakeview 9
    1981C, 1987B
Otisville LakeVille 4
    1994B
Lansing Catholic 297
    1993B, 1994B, 1999B, 2000D3, 2001D3,
    2002D3, 2003D3, 2006D3, 2007D3, 2008D3,
    2009D3, 2010D3, 2012D3, 2013D3, 2014D3,
    2015D3, 2016D3, 2017D2
Lansing Christian 97
    1977D, 1979D, 1980D, 1981D, 1983D, 1984D,
    1986D, 1987D, 2011D4, 2017D4, 2018D4
Lansing Everett 4
    1977A, 1986A
Lapeer East 1
    2009D2
Lawrence 23
    1999D, 2000D4, 2004D4, 2006D4
Lawton 43
    2001D4, 2002D4, 2003D4, 2006D4, 2007D4,
    2008D4, 2011D4, 2016D3
Leland 6
    2019D4
Leroy Pine River 67
    2006D3, 2007D3, 2009D3
Leslie 162
    1990C, 1998C, 2007D3, 2008D3, 2009D3,
    2010D3, 2014D3, 2015D3, 2016D3, 2017D3
Lincoln Park 2
    1995A
Linden 141
    1978B, 1979B, 2009D2, 2010D2, 2012D2,
    2013D2, 2014D2, 2015D2, 2016D2, 2017D2,
    2019D2
Litchfield 32
    1997D, 1998D, 1999D, 2001D4
Livonia Churchill 270
    1981A, 1982A, 1983A, 1984A, 2000D1, 2001D1,
    2002D1, 2003D1, 2004D1, 2005D1, 2006D1,
    2007D1, 2008D1, 2009D1, 2011D1, 2012D1,
    2014D1, 2016D1

Livonia Franklin 9
    2010D1
Livonia Ladywood 93
    1977B, 1980B, 1981B, 1982B, 1986B, 2003D2,
    2004D2, 2005D2, 2015D3
Livonia Stevenson 331
    1976A, 1977A, 1978all, 1980A, 1984A, 1985A,
    1990A, 1991A, 1994A, 1995A, 1996A, 1997A,
    1998A, 1999A, 2000D1, 2001D1, 2002D1,
    2003D1, 2004D1, 2005D1, 2006D1, 2007D1
Lowell 109
    1980B, 1989B, 1990B, 1999A, 2000D2, 2001D2,
    2002D2
Ludington 127
    1993B, 1994B, 1995B, 1996B, 1998B, 2000D2,
    2001D2
Lutheran Westland 190
    1986D, 1988D, 1989D, 1994C, 1995C, 1996C,
    1997C, 1999C, 2000D4, 2001D4, 2003D4,
    2004D4, 2009D4, 2010D4, 2011D4, 2012D4,
    2013D4, 2017D4
Macomb L'Anse Creuse North 2
    2008D1, 2014D1
Macomb Lutheran North 224
    2004D3, 2005D3, 2006D3, 2007D3, 2008D3,
    2009D3, 2010D3, 2011D3, 2012D3, 2013D3,
    2014D3, 2019D2
Madison Heights Foley 33
    1977B, 1978B, 1979B, 1980B, 1986B, 2007D3,
    2017D3
Madison Heights Lamphere 16
    1994B, 2001D2, 2006D2, 2007D2, 2008D2
Mancelona 36
    1982D, 1983D, 1986D, 2012D4
Manchester 23
    1997C, 1998C, 2009D3
Manistee 61
    2012D3, 2013D3, 2014D3
Manton 194
    1979D, 1982D, 1986D, 1990D, 1991D, 1992D,
    1994D, 2007D4, 2008D4, 2009D4, 2010D3,
    2014D4, 2015D4, 2016D4
Maple City Glen Lake 141
    1999C, 2000D4, 2001D4, 2004D4, 2005D4,
    2006D4, 2007D4, 2014D4, 2018D4, 2019D4
Marcellus 10
    2016D4, 2018D4, 2019D4
Marine City 34
    1989B, 1990B, 1991B, 1992B, 2008D2, 2009D2,
    2010D2, 2016D3, 2018D3
Marine City Mooney 1
    1999D
Marlette 1
    2015D3
Marshall 51
    2006D2, 2007D2, 2008D2, 2012D2, 2018D2
Marysville 135
    .... 1980B, 1981B, 1982B, 1983B, 1984B, 1985B,
    1986B, 1988B, 1989B, 1990B, 2014D2,
    2015D2, 2016D2, 2017D2, 2018D2, 2019D2
Mason 122
    1982B, 1983B, 1985B, 1990B, 1997A, 2000D2,
    2011D2, 2017D2, 2018D2, 2019D2
Mason County Central 55
    1980C, 1985C, 1986C, 1997C, 2012D3
Mason County Eastern 73
    1984D, 1985D, 1995D, 1996D, 1997D, 1999D,
    2004D4, 2005D4, 2015D4
Mattawan 53
    1989B, 1990B, 1991B
Mayville 69
    1985C, 1986C, 1988C, 1989C, 1996C, 1998C,
    1999C, 2008D4, 2009D4, 2010D4, 2011D4
McBain 45
    1992D, 1993D, 1996C, 1997C, 2018D3, 2019D3
Mendon 146
    1977D, 1980D, 1995D, 1996D, 1997D, 1998D,
    1999D, 2000D4, 2001D4, 2002D4, 2006D4,
    2007D4, 2008D4, 2013D4, 2014D4, 2015D4
Mesick 32
    1980D, 1986D, 1987D, 1988D, 1989D, 1990D
Michigan Center 25
    1984C, 2008D3
Middleville/Thornapple-Kellogg 177
    1983C, 1998B, 1999B, 2000D2, 2001D2,
    2012D2, 2013D2, 2014D2, 2015D2, 2016D2
Midland 91
    1976A, 1977A, 1978all, 1995A, 1996A, 1997A,
    1998A, 2005D1, 2009D1, 2010D1
Midland Bullock Creek 40
    1976B, 1977B, 1978B, 1985B, 1986B, 1987B,
    2008D3
Midland Dow 95
    1976A, 2001D1, 2009D1, 2010D1, 2011D1,
    2012D1, 2013D1, 2015D1, 2016D1
Milan 344
    1976B, 1978B, 1979B, 1980B, 1981B, 1986B,
    1987B, 1988B, 1989B, 1990B, 1992B, 1999B,
    2000D3, 2002D2, 2003D2, 2004D2, 2005D2,
    2006D2, 2007D2, 2008D2, 2010D2, 2011D2,
    2018D2, 1977B
Milford 640
    1975B, 1976A, 1979A, 1980A, 1981A, 1983A,
    1984A, 1985A, 1986A, 1989A, 1990A, 1991A,
    1992A, 1993A, 1994A, 1996A, 1997A, 1999A,
    2000D1, 2001D1, 2002D1, 2003D1, 2004D1,
    2005D1, 2006D1, 2007D1, 2009D1, 2010D1,
    2012D1, 2013D1, 2014D1, 2015D1, 2016D1,
    2017D1, 2018D1, 2019D1
Mio 9
    1997D
Monroe 148
    1984A, 1988A, 1990A, 1991A, 1992A, 1993A,
    1994A, 1997A, 2009D1, 2010D1, 2015D1
Monroe Jefferson 138
    1997B, 1998B, 1999B, 2000D2, 2003D2,
    2004D2, 2005D2
Monroe St Mary 136
    1977B, 1978B, 1982B, 1992B, 2004D3, 2006D3,
    1991B, 2003D3, 2005D3, 2007D3, 2008D3,
    2010D3, 2011D3
Montrose 9
    2015D3, 2017D3

Morenci 27
    1980D, 1981D, 2003D4, 2012D4
Morley-Stanwood 54
    1994C, 2003D3, 2004D3, 2005D3, 2006D3
Morrice 4
    2019D4
Mt Clemens 25
    1985B, 1987B, 1988B, 1990A
Mt Clemens Chippewa Valley 69
    1983A, 1989A, 1990A, 1991A, 1992A, 1994A
Mt Clemens Lutheran North 112
    1976C, 1977C, 1978C, 1979C, 1980C, 1981C,
    1983C, 1984B, 1986B, 1987B
Mt Morris 21
    1979B, 1980B, 1981B
Mt Pleasant 203
    1987A, 1989A, 1990A, 1991A, 1993A, 1997A,
    1998A, 2000D2, 2001D2, 2002D2, 2005D2,
    2009D2, 2010D2
Mt Pleasant Sacred Heart 306
    1979D, 1980D, 1981D, 1999D, 2000D4, 2001D4,
    2002D4, 2008D4, 2009D4, 2010D4, 2014D4,
    2015D4, 2016D4, 2017D4, 2018D4, 2019D4
Muskegon Catholic 50
    1981B, 1982B, 1983B
Muskegon Mona Shores 9
    1978all
Muskegon Oakridge 37
    1980C, 1982C, 1983C, 1984C, 1988C
Muskegon Orchard View 17
    2000D3
Muskegon Western Michigan Christian 72
    2014D4, 2016D4, 2018D4, 2019D4
Napoleon 45
    1977C, 1978C, 1980C, 1981C, 1982C, 1990C,
    1991C
New Baltimore Anchor Bay 1
    1995A
New Boston Huron 9
    1990B, 2011D2
New Lothrop 52
    1995C, 1998D, 1999D, 2000D4, 2010D4,
    2012D4, 2014D4, 2015D4
Newaygo 50
    1993C, 1995C, 2003D3, 2012D3
Niles Brandywine 15
    1984C, 1985C
North Farmington 4
    2001D1
North Muskegon 153
    1986D, 1987D, 1994D, 1995D, 1998D, 1999D,
    2000D4, 2001D4, 2009D4, 2010D4, 2011D4,
    2012D4, 2013D4, 2014D4
Northville 265
    1984A, 2001D1, 2006D1, 2009D1, 2010D1,
    2011D1, 2012D1, 2013D1, 2014D1, 2015D1,
    2016D1, 2017D1, 2018D1, 2019D1
Novi 139
    1983B, 1985A, 1989A, 1994A, 1995A, 1996A,
    1997A, 2004D1, 2008D1
Okemos 169
    1978B, 1983B, 1990A, 1991A, 1992A, 1994A,
    1997A, 2000D1, 2003D1, 2004D1, 2005D1,
    2006D1, 2007D1, 2008D1, 2011D1, 2016D1,
    2019D1
Olivet 62
    1989C, 1990C, 2015D3, 2016D3
Onaway 7
    2008D4
Onsted 97
    1985C, 1986C, 1987C, 1991C, 1992C, 1993C,
    2002D3, 2005D3
Ortonville Brandon 55
    2003D2, 2004D2, 2005D2, 2006D2, 2014D2
Oscoda 16
    1976B, 1977B
Otisville LakeVille 38
    1989B, 1990B, 1991B, 2000D3, 2014D3, 2015D3
Otsego 275
    1984B, 1985B, 2005D3, 2007D2, 2008D2,
    2009D2, 2010D2, 2013D2, 2014D2, 2015D2,
    2016D2, 2017D2, 2018D2, 2019D2
Ottawa Lake Whiteford 21
    2004D4, 2010D4, 2011D4
Ovid-Elsie 4
    2005D3
Owendale-Gagetown 14
    2019D4
Owosso 26
    1987A, 2006D2, 2011D2, 2012D2, 2016D2
Oxford 80
    1984B, 1985B, 1997B, 2011D1, 2012D1, 2016D1
Parchment 10
    2010D3, 2011D3
Parma Western 138
    1981B, 1994B, 1996B, 1997B, 1998B, 1999B,
    2006D2, 2007D2, 2016D2, 2017D2, 2018D2
Paw Paw 46
    1993B, 1994B, 1995B
Perry 123
    1984C, 1986C, 1991B, 1992B, 1993B, 2001D3,
    2002D3, 2003D3, 2005D3, 2006D3, 2007D3,
    2010D3
Petoskey 347
    1981B, 1984B, 1985B, 1987B, 1988B, 1989B,
    1990B, 1991B, 1993B, 1994B, 1995B, 1997B,
    2001D2, 2002D2, 2003D2, 2004D2, 2006D2,
    2008D2, 2017D2, 2018D2, 2019D2
Pewamo-Westphalia 206
    2001D4, 2002D4, 2008D4, 2009D4, 2012D4,
    2013D4, 2015D3, 2016D4, 2017D3, 2018D3,
    2019D3
Pinckney 190
    1993A, 1994A, 1995A, 2007D1, 2008D1,
    2009D1, 2010D1, 2011D1, 2015D1, 2016D1,
    2017D1, 2018D1
Pittsford 239
    1977D, 1990D, 1991D, 1992D, 1995D, 1998C,
    1999C, 2000D4, 2001D4, 2002D4, 2003D4,
    2004D4, 2007D4, 2010D4, 2011D4, 2012D4,
    2017D4, 2018D4
Plainwell 116
    1990B, 1991B, 1992B, 1993B, 1997B, 2000D2,
    2001D2, 2011D2, 2012D2, 2019D2

Plymouth 20
   2018D1, 2019D1
Plymouth Christian 31
   2017D4, 2018D4
Pontiac Catholic 11
   1980D, 1981D
Pontiac Central 13.5
   1975A, 1976A, 1977A, 1978all
Pontiac Notre Dame 88
   2000D2, 2008D2, 2011D2, 2012D2, 2013D2,
   2014D2, 2015D2, 2017D2, 2018D2, 2019D2
Port Huron 36
   1987A, 1989A, 1992A, 1999A
Port Huron Northern 90
   1988A, 1989A, 1991A, 1993A, 1994A, 1995A,
   1996A, 1997A, 1998A
Portage Central 111
   1992A, 1995A, 1997A, 1998A, 1999A, 2000D1,
   2001D1, 2002D1, 2003D1
Portage Northern 225
   1978all, 1979A, 1980A, 1981A, 1982A, 1983A,
   1984A, 1985A, 1986A, 1987A, 1990A, 1991A,
   1996A, 2003D1, 2004D1, 2015D1
Portland 42
   1999B, 2008D3, 2009D3
Portland St Patrick 1.5
   1986D
Potterville 227
   1976D, 1977D, 1978D, 1979D, 1988D, 1989D,
   1990D, 1991D, 1992D, 1993D, 1998D, 2002D4,
   2003D4, 2004D4, 2005D4, 2006D4, 2007D4,
   2011D4, 2016D4, 2018D4
Quincy 69
   1987C, 1988C, 1989C, 1991C, 1993C, 1994C,
   1995C, 2013D3, 2016D3, 2018D3
Reading 59
   1992D, 1993D, 2012D4, 2013D4, 2014D4
Redford Borgess 5
   1987A, 1988B
Redford Union 152.5
   1975A, 1976A, 1977A, 1978all, 1979A, 1980A,
   1981A, 1982A, 1984A, 1988A, 1990A
Reed City 3
   1979C
Reese 71
   1992C, 1993C, 1994C, 2013D3, 2014D3,
   2015D3, 2017D3, 2019D3
Remus Chippewa Hills 97
   1981B, 2002D2, 2003D2, 2004D2, 2005D2,
   2007D2, 2016D2
Richland Gull Lake 353
   1980B, 1981B, 1982B, 1983B, 1984B, 1985B,
   1986B, 1988B, 1990B, 1993B, 1995B, 1996B,
   1997B, 1998B, 1999B, 2000D2, 2001D2,
   2002D2, 2003D2, 2004D2, 2008D2, 2010D2,
   2011D2, 2012D2, 2013D2, 2015D2
Richmond 10
   1998B, 2019D3
Riverview 5
   1983B, 2013D2
Riverview Richard 7
   2007D3, 2014D4, 2015D4

Rochester 263
   1978all, 1979A, 1980A, 1984A, 1985A, 1986A,
   1990A, 1995A, 1996A, 1997A, 1998A, 1999A,
   2000D1, 2003D1, 2005D1, 2006D1, 2007D1,
   2008D1, 2009D1, 2014D1
Rochester Adams 421
   1983A, 1987A, 1988A, 1989A, 1992A, 1993A,
   1994A, 1995A, 1996A, 1997A, 1998A, 1999A,
   2000D1, 2001D1, 2002D1, 2003D1, 2004D1,
   2005D1, 2006D1, 2007D1, 2008D1, 2011D1,
   2012D1, 2015D1, 2019D1
Rochester Hills Lutheran Northwest 36
   1998D, 1999D, 2002D4, 2003D4, 2004D4,
   2009D4, 2017D4
Rochester Hills Stoney Creek 33
   2005D1, 2009D1, 2010D1, 2017D1, 2019D1
Rockford 619
   1993A, 1994A, 1995A, 1996A, 1997A, 1998A,
   1999A, 2000D1, 2001D1, 2002D1, 2003D1,
   2004D1, 2005D1, 2006D1, 2007D1, 2008D1,
   2009D1, 2010D1, 2011D1, 2012D1, 2013D1,
   2014D1, 2015D1, 2016D1, 2017D1, 2018D1,
   2019D1
Rogers City 122
   1987C, 2000D4, 2001D4, 2002D4, 2004D4,
   2005D4, 2006D4, 2007D4, 2011D4, 2013D4,
   2014D4, 2017D4
Romeo 141
   1983A, 1998A, 1999A, 2000D1, 2001D1,
   2002D1, 2009D1, 2016D1, 2018D1, 2019D1
Roscommon 3
   2014D3
Royal Oak 2
   2019D1
Royal Oak Dondero 24
   1976A, 1977A, 1979A, 1994B, 1995B, 2002D2,
   2003D2, 2004D2
Royal Oak Kimball 40
   1976A, 1977A, 1979A, 1981A, 1983A
Royal Oak Shrine 226
   1979C, 1981B, 1982B, 1983B, 2003D4, 2005D4,
   2006D4, 2007D4, 2008D4, 2009D4, 2010D4,
   2011D4, 2012D4, 2013D4, 2014D4, 2015D4,
   2016D4, 2018D4, 2019D4
Saginaw Arts & Sciences 11
   2010D4, 2011D4
Saginaw Carrollton 8
   1977C
Saginaw Heritage 10
   2015D1, 2016D1
Saginaw Hill 1
   1978all
Saginaw Michigan Lutheran 37
   1986D, 1993C, 2003D4, 2004D4, 2012D4,
   2018D4
Saginaw Nouvel 15
   1998B, 2004D3, 2006D3, 2012D3
Saginaw Swan Valley 37
   1975B, 2002D3, 2003D3, 2005D3, 2007D3
Saginaw Valley Lutheran 142
   1994C, 1995C, 1997C, 2003D4, 2004D4,
   2005D4, 2006D4, 2007D4

Salem 234
   1984A, 1990A, 1996A, 2003D1, 2004D1,
   2005D1, 2009D1, 2010D1, 2012D1, 2013D1,
   2014D1, 2015D1, 2016D1, 2017D1, 2018D1,
   2019D1
Saline 603
   1978B, 1982B, 1984B, 1985B, 1986B, 1987B,
   1988B, 1992B, 1993B, 1998A, 1999A, 2000D1,
   2001D1, 2002D1, 2003D1, 2004D1, 2005D1,
   2006D1, 2007D1, 2008D1, 2009D1, 2010D1,
   2011D1, 2012D1, 2013D1, 2014D1, 2015D1,
   2016D1, 2017D1, 2018D1, 2019D1
Sand Creek 82
   2008D4, 2009D4, 2011D4, 2013D4, 2015D4,
   2016D4, 2017D4
Sandusky 72
   1980C, 1982C, 1997C, 2011D3, 2012D3,
   2013D4
Sanford Meridian 40
   1998C, 1999C, 2009D3, 2016D3, 2017D3
Saranac 22
   1979D, 2009D4, 2019D4
Saugatuck 317
   2001D4, 2002D4, 2003D4, 2006D4, 2007D4,
   2008D4, 2009D4, 2010D4, 2011D4, 2012D4,
   2013D4, 2014D4, 2015D4, 2016D3, 2017D3,
   2018D4, 2019D3
Schoolcraft 170
   1987D, 1988D, 1989C, 1991D, 1992D, 1996C,
   2003D3, 2004D3, 2005D3, 2006D3, 2007D3,
   2008D3, 2009D3, 2010D3, 2011D3, 2013D3
Shelby 70
   1989C, 1990C, 1995C, 1996C, 1997C
Shepherd 387
   1978C, 1979C, 1985C, 1986C, 1989C, 1991C,
   1994C, 1995B, 1996B, 1997B, 1998B, 2000D3,
   2005D3, 2007D3, 2010D3, 2011D3, 2012D3,
   2013D3, 2014D3, 2015D3, 2016D3, 2017D3,
   2018D3, 2019D3
South Haven 12
   2017D2
South Lyon 16
   1985A, 1998A
Southfield Christian 288
   1983D, 1984D, 1988C, 1989C, 1990C, 1991C,
   1994C, 1996C, 1997C, 1998C, 1999C, 2000D4,
   2002D4, 2003D4, 2004D4, 2005D4, 2006D4,
   2007D4, 2008D4, 2015D4, 2016D4
Southgate Aquinas 16
   1991B
Sparta 189.5
   1993B, 1994B, 1995B, 1999B, 2000D2, 2002D2,
   2003D2, 2004D2, 2006D2, 2007D2, 2009D2,
   2012D2, 2013D2
Spring Lake 224
   2001D3, 2002D2, 2003D2, 2004D2, 2005D2,
   2006D2, 2009D2, 2012D2, 2013D2, 2014D2,
   2017D2, 2019D2
Springfield 4
   1986D
Springport 7
   1985D, 1986D

St Clair 101
   1998B, 1999B, 2000D2, 2005D2, 2006D2,
   2007D2, 2009D2, 2010D2, 2016D2
St Clair Shores Lake Shore 1
   2000D2
St Clair Shores Lakeview 12
   1980A, 1981A, 2001D2, 2002D2
St Johns 77
   1993A, 1997A, 2010D2, 2016D2, 2018D2,
   2019D2
St Joseph 198.5
   1981B, 1982B, 1983B, 1994B, 1996B, 2002D2,
   2003D2, 2004D2, 2012D2, 2014D2, 2015D2,
   2016D2
St Joseph Lake Michigan Catholic 45
   1978D, 1979C, 1983C, 1989C, 1990C, 2005D4,
   2009D4, 2010D4, 2012D4, 2013D4
St Louis 254
   1977C, 1978all, 1978C, 1979C, 1980C, 1981C,
   1983C, 1984C, 1989C, 1990C, 1996C, 1997C,
   1998C, 1999C, 2000D4, 2004D3, 2007D4,
   2010D3, 2011D3, 2014D3, 2015D3, 2018D3,
   2019D3
Standish-Sterling 15
   1986B, 2001D3, 2008D3
Stanton-Central Montcalm 50
   1986B, 1991B, 2000D3, 2001D3, 2004D3
Sterling Heights 11
   1999A, 2000D1
Sterling Heights Ford 31
   1984A, 1990A, 1996A, 1997A
Sterling Heights Stevenson 548
   1982A, 1983A, 1984A, 1985A, 1986A, 1987A,
   1988A, 1989A, 1990A, 1991A, 1992A, 1993A,
   1994A, 1995A, 1996A, 1997A, 1998A, 1999A,
   2000D1, 2001D1, 2002D1, 2003D1, 2004D1,
   2005D1, 2006D1, 2009D1, 2010D1, 2011D1,
   2012D1, 2013D1, 2014D1, 2019D1
Stevensville Lakeshore 68
   1997B, 2000D2, 2001D2, 2002D2, 2005D2,
   2006D2
Stockbridge 103
   1993B, 1994B, 2004D3, 2010D3, 2011D3,
   2012D3, 2018D3
Sturgis 97
   1986B, 1987B, 1988B, 2007D2, 2008D2,
   2009D2, 2010D2
Suttons Bay 184
   1981D, 1982D, 1983D, 1984D, 1985D, 1986D,
   1987D, 1988D, 1992C, 1993C, 1994C, 1999C,
   2000D3, 2001D3, 2002D4
Swartz Creek 79
   1986A, 1987A, 1988A, 1991A, 1994A, 1995A,
   1996A, 1999A, 2000D1
Tawas City 72
   1987C, 1988C, 2000D3, 2001D3, 2010D3
Tecumseh 50
   1977B, 1978B, 1994B, 2005D2, 2007D2, 2019D2
Temperance Bedford 255
   1981A, 1982A, 1983A, 1985A, 1986A, 1987A,

1995A, 1996A, 1997A, 1998A, 1999A, 2000D1,
2003D1, 2004D1, 2005D1, 2009D1, 2011D1,
2012D1, 2013D1, 2017D1, 2018D1, 2019D1

Three Oaks River Valley 23
    1978all, 1978C, 1997C, 2005D4

Three Rivers 6
    1981B, 1982B

Traverse City/Central 717
    1978all, 1981A, 1983A, 1984A, 1986A, 1988A,
    1989A, 1990A, 1991A, 1992A, 1994A, 1996A,
    1997A, 1998A, 1999A, 2000D1, 2001D1,
    2002D1, 2003D1, 2004D1, 2005D1, 2006D1,
    2007D1, 2008D1, 2009D1, 2010D1, 2011D1,
    2012D1, 2013D1, 2014D1, 2015D1, 2016D1,
    2017D1, 2018D1, 2019D1

Traverse City St Francis 345
    1996D, 2001D4, 2002D4, 2003D4, 2004D4,
    2005D4, 2006D4, 2008D4, 2009D4, 2010D4,
    2011D4, 2012D4, 2013D4, 2015D3, 2016D3,
    2017D3, 2018D3, 2019D3

Traverse City West 133
    1999A, 2000D1, 2001D1, 2002D1, 2003D1,
    2004D1, 2008D1, 2011D1, 2017D1, 2018D1

Trenton 110
    1980A, 1986A, 1987A, 1988A, 1993B, 1999B,
    2000D2, 2001D2, 2003D2, 2007D2, 2008D2,
    2009D2

Troy 447
    1986A, 1987A, 1988A, 1989A, 1991A, 1992A,
    1993A, 1994A, 1995A, 1996A, 1998A, 1999A,
    2001D1, 2002D1, 2003D1, 2004D1, 2005D1,
    2006D1, 2007D1, 2008D1, 2009D1, 2010D1,
    2011D1, 2012D1, 2013D1, 2015D1, 2016D1,
    2017D1, 2018D1, 2019D1, 2000D1

Troy Athens 217
    1980A, 1981A, 1982A, 1983A, 1989A, 1990A,
    1991A, 1993A, 1994A, 1995A, 1997A, 1998A,
    2000D1, 2002D1, 2003D1, 2004D1, 2005D1,
    2006D1

Ubly 264
    1996D, 2000D4, 2001D4, 2002D4, 2003D4,
    2004D4, 2005D4, 2006D4, 2007D4, 2012D4,
    2013D4, 2014D4, 2015D4, 2016D4, 2017D4,
    2018D4

Union City 11
    1976C, 1982C, 1994C

Unionville-Sebewaing 87
    1998C, 1999C, 2005D4, 2006D4, 2007D4,
    2008D4, 2013D4

Utica 28
    1988A, 2006D1

Utica Eisenhower 89
    1984A, 1985A, 1992A, 1993A, 1994A, 2004D1,
    2013D1

Vandercook Lake 57
    1978C, 1979C, 1980C, 1981C, 1982C, 1985C,
    1988C, 1989C, 1999C, 2005D4

Vassar 11
    1992B, 2008D3

Vermontville Maple Valley 86
    1992C, 1993C, 1994C, 1995C, 1996C, 1997C,
    1998C

Vestaburg 2
    1985D

Vicksburg 113
    1979B, 1984B, 1986B, 1987B, 1992B, 1996B,
    1998B, 2003D2, 2004D2, 2007D2, 2012D2,
    2013D2

Waldron 1
    2008D4

Walkerville 18
    1996D, 1997D

Walled Lake Central 41
    1981A, 1985A, 1986A, 2000D1

Walled Lake Northern 35
    2005D1, 2010D1, 2013D1, 2014D1

Walled Lake Western 62
    1980A, 1991A, 1992A, 2007D1

Warren Bethesda Christian 18
    1986D

Warren Cousino 19
    1979A, 1981A, 1998A

Warren Mott 22
    1982A, 1988A, 1989B, 1990B, 1993A, 1996A,
    2000D1

Warren Regina 150
    1986A, 2002D1, 2005D2, 2006D2, 2007D2,
    2010D2, 2011D2, 2012D2, 2013D2,
    2014D2, 2015D2, 2016D2, 2018D2, 2019D2

Warren Woods-Tower 1
    2007D2

Waterford Kettering 14
    1985A

Waterford Mott 104
    2008D1, 2009D1, 2010D1, 2011D1, 2012D1,
    2014D1, 2015D1, 2016D1, 2017D1

Waterford Our Lady of the Lakes 67
    2007D4, 2008D4, 2012D4, 2013D4, 2014D4,
    2015D4, 2016D4, 2017D4

Watervliet 21
    1988C, 2014D3, 2015D3

Wayland 40
    1998B, 2006D2, 2017D2

Webberville 20
    1986D, 1990D

West Bloomfield 146
    1979A, 1986A, 1987A, 1988A, 1989A, 1990A,
    1992A, 1993A

West Branch Ogemaw Heights 162
    1992B, 1993B, 1994B, 1996B, 1997B, 1998B,
    1999B, 2000D2

Westland Glenn 12
    1977A, 1983A

White Cloud 33
    2007D4, 2015D4, 2016D4, 2017D4

White Lake Lakeland 45
    1976A, 1977A, 2008D1, 2016D1, 2018D1

Whitehall 35
    1977C, 1978C, 1979C, 1980C, 1981C

Whitehall 343
    1992C, 1993C, 1995B, 1996B, 1997B, 1998B,
    1999B, 2000D3, 2001D2, 2002D3, 2003D2,
    2004D3, 2005D3, 2006D3, 2007D3, 2013D2,
    2014D2, 2015D2, 2016D2, 2017D2, 2019D2

Whitmore Lake 97
    1991D, 1993D, 1994D, 1995D, 1996D, 1997D,
    2001D4, 2006D4, 2009D3
Whittemore-Prescott 8
    1976C, 1977C, 1978C, 1986C
Williamston 296
    1978C, 1980C, 1981C, 1989C, 1990C, 1991C,
    1992C, 1994C, 1995C, 2001D3, 2002D3,
    2003D3, 2004D3, 2006D3, 2007D3, 2008D2,
    2009D2, 2011D2, 2014D2
Wixom St Catherine 50
    2014D4, 2015D3, 2016D3, 2017D3
Wolverine 38
    1995D, 1997D, 1998D, 2000D4, 2008D4,
    2009D4, 2010D4
Woodhaven 63
    1988A, 1991A, 2007D1, 2008D1, 2011D1,
    2012D1, 2014D1
Wyandotte 14
    1999A, 2008D1, 2015D1, 2016D1
Wyoming Kelloggsville 55
    1994C, 1999B, 2000D3, 2001D3
Wyoming Lee 79
    1980C, 1981D, 1982D, 1983D, 1984D, 1985D,
    1989D, 1990D, 1993D, 1994D, 1995D
Wyoming Park 16
    1981B
Wyoming Rogers 7
    1982B
Wyoming Tri-Unity Christian 51
    1995D, 1996D, 1997D, 1998D, 1999D
Yale 125
    1977C, 1980B, 1981B, 1985B, 1986B, 1987B,
    1988B, 1989B, 1990B, 1991B, 1992B, 1993B,
    2009D2, 2011D2, 2012D2
Ypsilanti 16
    2001D2, 2002D2, 2004D2
Zeeland 17
    1993B
Zeeland East 6
    2018D2, 2019D2
Zeeland West 26
    2016D2, 2017D2, 2018D

1957 Class A State Finals

Hillsdale won the first-ever Class B race in 1975.

Traverse City girls won the 1991 Class A title.

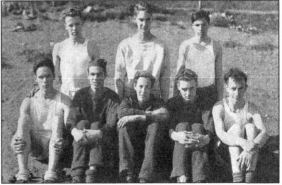
Grand Rapids South tied for the 1930 Class A win.

Michigan at Mideast Meet of Champions

Since 1987, Michigan has sent a team of its top seniors to Indian Riffle Park in Kettering, Ohio, on the third weekend of November to race against teams representing Ohio and Indiana. Over the years, other states have participated also: Illinois, Kentucky, Pennsylvania.

Team Michigan has always been selected through a qualifying race. In the early years, it was held in conjunction with the TAC/USA Junior Olympic race (TAC/USA was the forerunner of USATF). More recently, the qualifying race has been organized by MITCA coaches and held the Saturday following the state finals at a variety of sites. For years it was held at Jackson's Sharp Park. The last few editions have been held on the course at Shepherd High School.

Results of many of the early years could not be found; so corrections and results are welcome to make the compilation complete.

MITCA – Team Michigan Qualifying Race Winners

Boys
Year	Winner	Time
1992	Clint Verran (Lake Orion)	nt
1995	Abdul Alzindani (Dearborn Fordson)	nt
1999	Jake Flynn (Benzie Central)	15:16
2000	Jason Stover (Williamston)	15:38
2001	Tim Ross (Caledonia)	15:23
2010	Austin Whitelaw (Monroe)	15:56
2011	Evan Chiplock (Saginaw Heritage)	15:41
2012	Connor Mora (Cedar Springs)	15:36
2013	Dan Sims (Northville)	16:21
2014	Jesse Hersha (Concord)	15:50
2015	Logan Kleam (Woodhaven)	15:52
2016	Noah Jacobs (Corunna)	15:27
2017	Shuaib Aljabaly (Coldwater)	15:13
2018	Harrison Grzymkowski (White Lake Lakeland)	15:28
2019	Brendan Favazza (Clarkston)	15:32

Girls
Year	Winner	Time
1992	Lorenda Godefroidt (St Louis)	nt
1999	Emily Blakeslee (Rockford)	18:14
2010	Alissa Williams (East Kentwood)	18:23
2011	Lindsey Burdette (Hanover Horton)	18:23
2012	Raquel Serna (St Louis)	18:31
2013	Kirsten Olling (Breckenridge)	18:41
2014	Gina Patterson (Macomb Lutheran North)	18:26
2015	Samantha Hanson (Sterling Heights Stevenson)	19:05
2016	Erika Freyhof (Hamilton)	18:07
2017	Rachel McCardell (Birmingham Seaholm)	17:49
2018	Madeline Rehm (White Lake Lakeland)	17:58
2019	Maryam Sheena (Walled Lake Western)	18:27

MIDEAST BOYS

1987 – 2nd place – 35
3. Jon Gill (Ferndale) 15:45
4. Paul Butterfield (Bridgeport) 15:45
5. Jim Huff (Bloomfield Hills Lahser) 15:50
9. Eric Sorensen (Utica Eisenhower) 15:54
(results incomplete)

1988 – 2nd place – 45
1. Brian Grosso (Walled Lake Western) 15:32
3. Jason Colvin (Ann Arbor Pioneer) 15:47
(results incomplete)

1989 – 2nd place – 59
4. Bill Stricklin (Sterling Heights Ford) 15:36
(results incomplete)

1990 – 4th place - 70
1. Brian Hyde (East Kentwood) 15:19
8. Ben Goba (Farmington) 15:39
16. Trevor Smith (Allegan) 15:52
21. James Neumann (Center Line) 15:56
24. Doug Corcoran (Reading) 16:02
26. Chris Priestaf (Dearborn Edsel Ford) 16:03
28. Mike Milliman (Ann Arbor Pioneer) 16:07
29. Jeff Grosso (Walled Lake Western) 16:09
35. Kris Eggle (Cadillac) 16:24
46. Marc Norman (Warren) 17:30

1991 – 2nd place – 50
4. Jeff Christian (Beaverton) 15:33
8. Bill Crosby (Walled Lake Western) 15:39
9. Marzuki Stevens (Bloomfield Hills Cranbrook) 15:39
13. Michael Ball (Hudson) 15:47
16. Brian Pickl (Milford) 15:51
19. Ryan Burt (Dearborn Divine Child) 15:56
22. Edward Reilly (Royal Oak Dondero) 15:58
24. Barry Deese (Linden) 16:00
35. Chris Rudolph (Sterling Heights Ford) 16:15
47. James Sweetman (Walled Lake Western) 16:36

1992 – 3rd place – 70
8. Clint Verran (Lake Orion) 16:16
10. Jim Marcero (Monroe St Mary) 16:16
(results incomplete; also on team—Chris Johnson (Saginaw Michigan Lutheran, Matt Rodeheffer (Hancock), Mark Goodfellow (Oxford), Rob Busquaert (St Clair Shores Lakeview), Boyce Littlefield (Hartford), Gary Kinnee (Flint Kearsley), Jim Park (Ann Arbor Pioneer), Eric Bierstetel (Fowler)

1993 – 3rd place – 82
(no MI runners in top 5)

1994 – 1st place – 33
2. Todd Snyder (Ann Arbor Pioneer) — 15:20
5. Stetsen Steele (Dearborn) — 15:27
6. Steve Schell (Dearborn Fordson) — 15:28
7. Jeff Ferrell (Waterford Mott) — 15:31
13. Justin Curry (Carson City-Crystal) — 15:42
(results incomplete)

1995
1. Abdul Alzindani (Dearborn Fordson) — 15:28
(results incomplete)

1996 – 3rd place – 101
24. Lyle Mayers (Charlotte) — 16:08
32. Tom Boring (Stockbridge) — 16:18
(results incomplete; no MI runners in top 5)

1997 – 2nd place – 59
3. Nick Brockway (Richland Gull Lake) — 15:50
11. Ryan Mol (Rockford) — 16:04
12. Jamey Lister (Stockbridge) — 16:04
16. Justin Momany-Pfruender (Midland) — 16:11
17. Nick Gow (White Lake Lakeland) — 16:11
25. Corey Kellicut (Grand Ledge) — 16:19
27. Jed Hindes (Fremont) — 16:21
34. Dave Cook (Portage Northern) — 16:26
35. Rob Block (Livonia Stevenson) — 16:27
45. Nate Hanes (Concord) — 16:42

1998 – 4th place – 58
6. Adam Cross (Rochester Adams) — 15:47
7. Ben Evans (Birmingham Rice) — 15:47
9. Jared Aldrich (Corunna) — 15:48
(results incomplete)

1999 – 1st place 33
4. Ryan Cole (Sanford-Meridian) — 15:26
5. Todd Mobley (Walled Lake Central) — 15:26
6. Andy Marsh (Grand Ledge) — 15:30
7. Tom Greenless (Milford) — 15:32
11. Justin Perez (Flint Powers) — 15:39
12. Jake Flynn (Benzie Central) — 15:40
18. Tristan Perlberg (Saginaw Valley Lutheran) — 15:53
24. Aaron Rogers (Berrien Springs) — 15:56
25. Andy Martin (Rockford) — 15:57
26. Adam Booth (Homer) — 16:05
(Sophomore Dathan Ritzenhein won the Challenge Race in 15:46)

2000 – 2nd place – 52
3. Jason Stover (Williamston) — 15:33
5. Brian Maat (Holland Christian) — 15:40
11. Pat Klein (White Lake Lakeland) — 15:50
15. Brian Smith (Rockford) — 15:57
18. Blake Terhune (Traverse City Central) — 15:58
20. Andy Duemling (Ubly) — 15:59
22. John Cook (St Clair) — 16:00
24. Joe Swendrowski (Rockford) — 16:01
26. Matt Daly (Detroit Catholic Central) — 16:03
42. Kyle Fujimoto (Rockford) — 16:24

2001 – 1st place – 40
1. Tim Ross (Caledonia) — 15:10
4. Andrew Bauer (Bloomfield Hills Lahser) — 15:26
8. Adam Ludwig (St Joseph) — 15:31
11. Matt French (Howell) — 15:34
16. Michael Putzke (New Buffalo) — 15:42
19. Daniel Murray (Birmingham Rice) — 15:45
20. Jason Schoener (Grand Blanc) — 15:45
24. Scott Kallgren (Trenton) — 15:50
39. Nick Oertel (Goodrich) — 16:06
40. Aaron Nasers (Battle Creek Pennfield) — 16:07

2002 – 3rd place – 71
5. Jeff Byrne (Bay City Glenn) — 15:48
12. Steve Czymbor (Hemlock) — 16:03
15. Kevin Gienapp (Brighton) — 16:05
26. Jonathan Hodge (Grosse Ile) — 16:14
34. Chris Mehay (New Baltimore Anchor Bay) — 16:20
42. Jeff Draggich (Sterling Heights) — 16:35
43. Mark VanderMeer (Wyoming Park) — 16:37
48. Greg Schmit (Leslie) — 16:49
51. Eric Huffman (Swartz Creek) — 16:58

2003 – 1st place – 36
2. Frank Tinney (Ann Arbor Huron) — 15:28
5. Josh Perrin (Hillsdale) — 15:46
7. Luke Walker (Flint Powers) — 15:48
8. Liam Boylan-Pett (Bath) — 15:50
14. David Bills (Williamston) — 15:53
17. Seth Thibodeau (Milford) — 16:02
30. Don Letts (Portage Northern) — 16:14
31. Michael Barrows (Flint Powers) — 16:15
35. Jeff Hubbard (Ann Arbor Pioneer) — 16:23
44. Tim Kenny (Traverse City West) — 16:43

2004 – 1st place – 35
2. Dan Cramer (Cedar Springs) — 15:45
5. Nick Katsefaras (Pinckney) — 15:50
7. Ian Boyle (Pinckney) — 15:57
10. Riak Mabil (Grand Ledge) — 15:59
11. Morty Stensones-Fornaess (Ann Arbor Pioneer) — 16:01
12. Adam Daoud (Ann Arbor Huron) — 16:02
21. Josh Hofbauer (Harbor Springs) — 16:12
35. Curtis Vollmar (Grand Blanc) — 16:30
36. Robert Gunn (Detroit Central) — 16:31
41. Carter Bishop (Saline) — 16:40

2005 – 4th place – 108
1. Landon Peacock (Cedar Springs) — 15:23
17. Patrick Grosskopf (Corunna) — 16:05
29. Christopher Pankow (Williamston) — 16:22
30. Mike Quick (Bloomfield Hills Lahser) — 16:23
31. Ian Gerard (Chelsea) — 16:23
32. Sam Breen (Woodhaven) — 16:24
34. Michael Mayday (Hanover Horton) — 16:28
35. Andrew Ropp (Flint Powers) — 16:30
39. Loren Ahonen (Temperance Bedford) — 16:38
45. Peter Christmas (Ann Arbor Pioneer) — 16:56

2006 – 4th place – 118
20. Aaron Simoneau (Manistee) — 16:28
21. Tyler Emmorey (Cedar Springs) — 16:29
22. Paul Grieve (Kalkaska) — 16:31
24. Ryan Neely (Dexter) — 16:31
31. Robert Fisher (Grosse Pointe North) — 16:45
40. Brandon Griffin (Erie Mason) — 16:50
44. Neil Grundman (Croswell-Lexington) — 16:56
49. Cole Sanseverino (Monroe) — 17:13
53. Billy Neri (Blissfield) — 17:22
54. Eric Stouten (Sparta) — 17:22

2007 – 2nd place – 51
2. Maverick Darling (Ovid-Elsie)	15:05
4. Bobby Aprill (Dexter)	15:23
10. Justin Heck (Monroe)	15:37
13. Addis Habtewold (St Clair)	15:40
22. Matt Lutzke (Williamston)	15:49
26. Mike Katsefaras (Pinckney)	15:51
38. Nathan Martin (Three Rivers)	16:09
41. Josh McAlary (Jackson Lumen Christi)	16:19
43. Ike VanDoorne (Grant)	16:21
48. Dan Nix (Williamston)	16:29

2008 – 4th place – 61
5. Dan Culbertson (Ann Arbor Pioneer)	15:59
7. Michael Murphy (Birmingham Rice)	16:03
10. Tec Adams (Harbor Springs)	16:09
16. Ryan Ziolko (Lake Orion)	16:13
23. Sam Aklilu (East Kentwood)	16:19
26. Joe Maki (Flint Powers)	16:23
30. Jon Hurrell (Bay City Western)	16:26
32. Edwin Gay (Grosse Pointe South)	16:32
35. Mike Reimann (Rochester Adams)	16:39
38. Brett Burdick (Grand Blanc)	16:44
44. Nick Petro (Monroe)	17:11

2009 – 3rd place – 57
2. Nathan Karr (Ann Arbor Pioneer)	15:42
6. Ian Hancke (Haslett)	15:50
14. Adam Kern (Ann Arbor Pioneer)	15:58
16. Nick Perry (Woodhaven)	16:02
19. Alex Wilson (Kent City)	16:03
24. Matthew Hoshal (East Lansing)	16:16
26. Ben Carruthers (Dexter)	16:18
28. Tanner Pesonen (Pinckney)	16:19
29. Nathaniel Ellsworth (Saginaw Heritage)	16:20
35. Paul Lewis (Albion)	16:28

2010 – 3rd place – 95
1. Austin Whitelaw (Monroe)	15:22
15. Jeff Sattler (Byron Center)	15:48
22. Taylor Compton (Hamilton)	15:57
23. Cameron Dobson (Croswell-Lexington)	15:59
34. Blake Bitner (GR Kenowa Hills)	16:13
35. Spencer Pageau (Jackson Lumen Christi)	16:14
37. Colin Creagh (Lanse Creuse North)	16:17
40. Nick Culbertson (Macomb Dakota)	16:31
41. Jordan Staley (Macomb Dakota)	16:32
42. Blake Yard (South Lyon)	16:35
46. Andrew Alvarez (Hillsdale Academy)	16:45
47. Justin Krauss (Perry)	16:55

2011 – 2nd place – 48
3. Nicholas Soter (Dearborn Divine Child)	15:53
4. Evan Chiplock (Saginaw Heritage)	15:53
10. Zachary Kughn (Grand Blanc)	16:06
11. Garret Zuk (White Lake Lakeland)	16:06
20. Thomas Girardot (Birmingham Brother Rice)	16:21
24. Michael Cox (Pinckney)	16:25
32. Derek Gielarowski (Plymouth)	16:34
33. Paul Ausum (Milford)	16:40
34. Joshua Kersjes (Grandville Calvin Christian)	16:47
37. Spencer Nousain (Concord)	16:57
40. Ryan Beyea (Haslett)	17:17

2012 – 1st place – 42
1. Nick Raymond (Erie-Mason)	15:25
4. Connor Mora (Cedar Springs)	15:40
9. Jeff Bajema (GR Kenowa Hills)	15:54
11. Alex Whitmer (Mason)	15:55
17. Zachary Nowicki (Grandville Calvin Christian)	16:02
18. Roger Phillips (Linden)	16:02
19. Cody Snavely (Milford)	16:04
23. Bryce Stroede (Hanover Horton)	16:06
25. Nathan Burnand (Waterford Mott)	16:11
34. Sean Kelly (Saugatuck)	16:17

2013 – 4th place – 77
10. Dan Sims (Northville)	16:08
12. Costa Willets (Ann Arbor Pioneer)	16:09
14. Alec Toreki (Romeo)	16:12
18. Trevor Holowaty (St Clair)	16:19
23. Alex McCormick (Haslett)	16:26
24. Calum Ahmed (Royal Oak)	16:26
33. Dietrich Hittner (East Lansing)	16:34
36. Clayton Springer (Saugatuck)	16:39
37. Zachary Hardway (Hillsdale)	16:40
38. Justin Kiprotich (East Kentwood)	16:40

2014 – 2nd place – 39
1. Jesse Hersha (Concord)	15:27
3. Nick Schmidt (Davison)	15:47
8. Matt Thomas (Port Huron Northern)	15:57
9. Jacob Greer (Midland)	15:58
18. Austin Sargent (Cedar Springs)	16:11
19. Dominic Davis (Wyandotte)	16:11
21. Parker Eisengruber (Saginaw Heritage)	16:17
27. Codey Cook (St Johns)	16:20
28. Alec Keaton (Allen Park)	16:21
29. Damien Halverson (Hesperia)	16:24

2015 – 3rd place - 67
4. Logan Kleam (Woodhaven)	15:51
7. James McCann (Holland Black River)	16:00
12. Joost Plaetinck (Novi)	16:05
20. Austin Wicker (Pinckney)	16:24
24. Mark Freyhof (Hamilton)	16:35
27. Jake Lee (Fenton)	16:37
35. Andrew Bill (Berkley)	16:44
36. Dilon Lemond (Holly)	16:44
39. Antonio Wenglikow (Bay City Western)	16:58
41. Jesse Saxton (Grant)	17:05
42. Ryan Hildebrandt (Hemlock)	17:06
43. Chaz Jeffress (Salem)	17:11

2016 – 1st place – 2016
1. Noah Jacobs (Corunna)	15:41
2. Riad Rababeh (Dearborn)	15:41
3. Matt Schram (Rochester Adams)	15:55
5. David Mitter (Howell)	16:01
7. Christian Hubaker (Grand Ledge)	16:03
11. Lewis Tate (Paw Paw)	16:09
12. Steven Stine (Fraser)	16:09
19. Evan Goodell (St Louis)	16:20
25. Brian Njuguma (Bridgman)	16:27
33. Brayden Huddleston (Benzie Central)	16:40
34. Jacob Ferguson (Davison)	16:43
36. Zach Pettinga (Saugatuck)	16:46

2017 – 1st place – 35
2. Shuaib Aljabaly (Coldwater)	16:00
3. Drew Wenger (White Lake Lakeland)	16:02
6. Abdi Ahmed (Forest Hills Northern)	16:03

9. CarLee Stimfel (Cass City)	16:24
15. Dayton Brown (Rockford)	16:32
24. Reid Parsons (Comstock Park)	16:45
26. Landon Melling (Hanover Horton)	16:49
29. Fraser Wilson (Kent City)	16:52
32. Chris Davis (Fowlerville)	16:58
33. Austin Remick (Rochester)	16:59

2018 – 1st place – 32
3. Aden Smith (Alpena)	16:04
4. Harrison Grzymkowski (White Lake Lakeland)	16:04
7. Yami Albrecht (Caro)	16:09
8. Evan White (Milford)	16:10
10. Josh Smith (Alpena)	16:11
14. Sam Martens (Holland)	16:15
19. Ransom Allen (Ithaca)	16:31
21. Alec Miracle (Birmingham Brother Rice)	16:32
24. Carson Rabbitt (Chelsea)	16:35
28. Foster Thorburn (Chelsea)	16:41
30. Jakob Sayers (Birmingham Seaholm)	16:46
35. Luke Haran (Salem)	16:51

The record-setting victorius 2019 squad.

2019 – 1st place - 18
1. Andrew Nolan (Lake Orion)	15:47
2. Tyler Buchanan (Linden)	15:49
4. Justin Hill (Walled Lake Central)	15:58
5. Luke Perelli (Detroit Catholic Central)	15:58
6. Andrew Lane (East Lansing)	16:01
8. Scott Spaanstra (Brighton)	16:08
9. Nathan Larson (Dexter)	16:08
17. Hunter Fougner (Waterford Mott)	16:19
19. Shawn Little (Dowagiac)	16:24
22. Scott Masterson (Oxford)	16:28
26. Karsin Dass (Ann Arbor Huron)	16:33
27. Jason Milliss (Davison)	16:33

MIDEAST GIRLS

1987 – 3rd place – 56
2. Seana Arnold (Ann Arbor Pioneer)	18:22
5. Danielle Harpell (Ann Arbor Pioneer)	18:36
(results incomplete)	

1988 – 1st place – 41
5. Stacy Kilburn (White Pigeon)	19:14

(results incomplete)

1989 – 5th place – 107
(no MI runners in top 5)

1990 - 3rd place – 45
2. Laura Bell (Otisville LakeVille)	18:24
6. Amy Lathrop (Jackson Northwest)	18:39
10. Sylvia Marino (Ann Arbor Pioneer)	18:55
13. Julie Banks (Utica)	19:04
14. Erica Adams (Gladwin)	19:11
15. Colleen Danes (Dearborn Edsel Ford)	19:12
18. Julie Hay (Three Rivers)	19:16
21. Wendy Johnecheck (Petoskey)	19:30
23. Carrie Vanisacker (Monroe)	19:32
30. Julie Jorgenson (Muskegon Mona Shores)	19:48

1991 – 5th place – 85
4. Molly Lori (East Kentwood)	18:18
14. Jenny Kornacker (Richland Gull Lake)	19:09
16. Jennifer Barber (Frankenmuth)	189:13
23. Renae Essenmacher (Harbor Beach)	19:25
28. Amy Hayes (Shelby)	19:32
31. Jennifer Miller (Grosse Pointe Woods University Liggett)	19:34
32. Tracy Priska (Sterling Heights Stevenson)	19:36
34. Amy Parker (Troy)	19:42
37. Jenny Stoffel (St Joseph Lake Michigan Catholic)	19:52
53. Julie Kokoczka (Jackson Lumen Christi)	21:02

1992 – 2nd place – 46
2. Lorenda Godefroidt (St Louis)	18:57
5. Edith Kortekaas (Hastings)	19:15
6. Annie Erlewine (Big Rapids)	19:18

(results incomplete; other team members—AJ Koritnik (Livonia Stevenson), Becky Wing (Bellevue, Emily Shively (North Farmington), Sharmilla Prasad (Farmington Mercy), Ann Welch (Monroe St Mary), Deb Barton (Holly), Amanda Foutch (Burton Atherton)

1993 – 1st place - 41
1. Christy Goodison (Sterling Heights Stevenson)	18:40
2. Megan Smedley (Buchanan)	19:04

(results incomplete)

1994 – 4th place – 93
9. Laura Deneau (Warren Woods Tower)	18:44
15. Stacey Lenard (Hudsonville)	19:01

(results incomplete)

1995 – 1st place – 41
29. Laura Harger (Holt)	19:37
34. Leah Nilsson (Williamston)	19:49
38. Kathryn Murphy (Vermontville Maple Valley)	19:54

(results incomplete)

1996 – 5th place – 91
5. Shannon Houseman (Caledonia)	18:41

(results incomplete)

1997 – 1st place – 28
2. Bethany Brewster (Saginaw Valley Lutheran)	18:33
3. Ann Somerville (Ironwood)	18:42
5. Jonnie Vasse (Grosse Pointe South)	18:55
7. Sharon Dickie (Grand Blanc)	18:58
11. Erin Leonard (Ann Arbor Pioneer)	19:05
18. Kasey Culp (Mendon)	19:11

23. Rachel Smith (Monroe)	19:17
27. Kelly Travis (Livonia Stevenson)	19:21
31. Hidi Jasch (Holland)	19:41
34. April Smith (Charlotte)	19:48

1998 – 4th place – 96
(results incomplete; no MI runners in top 11)

1999 – 1st place – 45
3. Jamie Krzyminski (Corunna)	18:15
6. Emily Blakeslee (Rockford)	18:18
9. Kimi Landane (Atlanta)	18:28
14. Danielle Quisenberry (Middleville Thornapple-Kellogg)	18:46
20. Jeanette Seckinger (Richland Gull Lake)	18:50
26. Michelle Suszek (Alpena)	19:12
33. Marne Smiley (Sterling Heights Stevenson)	19:28
35. Melissa Miller (Portland)	19:31
36. Krista O'Dell (Escanaba)	19:33

2000 – 1st place – 41
1. Katie Boyles (Rochester Adams)	18:02
7. Jessica Kraft (West Branch Ogemaw Heights)	18:39
9. Abigail Nelke (West Branch Ogemaw Heights)	18:44
11. Michelle Kinkela (Sterling Heights Stevenson)	18:51
13. Carrie Smeltzer (Monroe Jefferson)	18:59
16. Anne Venier (Monroe Jefferson)	19:06
24. Caryn Waterson (Benzie Central)	19:18
35. Kristyn Kern (White Lake Lakeland)	19:40
36. Miriam Speyer (Grand Rapids Christian)	19:41
40. Kellie Nicholson (Temperance Bedford)	19:56

2001 – 3rd place – 92
10. Katie Danyko (Sterling Heights Stevenson)	18:25
13. Heidi Johnson (Ludington)	18:37
16. Lesley Jurasek (Albion)	18:42
26. Chris Alcenius (Hanover Horton)	18:54
27. Amy Baker (Ann Arbor Huron)	18:55
28. Jentry Soule (Grand Haven)	18:56
31. Natalie Cahill (Sault Ste Marie)	19:03
32. Leigha Christian (Rochester)	19:04
35. Andrea Moreland (Rochester Adams)	19:15
41. Melissa Quisenberry (Middleville Thornapple-Kellogg)	19:26

2002 – 4th place – 84
3. Jackie Gaydos (Allen Park)	18:27
9. Katie Kelly (Kinde-North Huron)	18:48
23. Jennifer Culbertson (Macomb Dakota)	19:25
24. Rachel Ward (Brighton)	19:26
25. Rachel Bumann (Brighton)	19:28
37. Beth Ann Lannen (Jackson)	19:50
38. Faith Kejbou (Warren Fitzgerald)	19:51
40. Laura Fisher (Grosse Pointe North)	19:53
42. Sarah Jaquith (Petoskey)	19:57
50. Nicole Blake (Sterling Heights Stevenson)	20:37

2003 – 5th place – 150
19. Lisa Senakiewich (Davison)	19:00
30. Susie Rivard (Brighton)	19:17
31. Rachael Button (Farmington)	19:27
33. Amber Myers (Jackson Northwest)	19:31
37. Michelle Diverio (Battle Creek Lakeview)	19:36
38. Mo Kuhta (Clarkston)	19:37
39. Meghan Wafer (Redford Thurston)	19:39
44. Lisa Canty (Milford)	20:04
46. Libby Carpenter (Whitehall)	20:19
48. Kelly Higgins (Corunna)	20:37

2004 – 4th place – 64
3. Heather Sirko (Livonia Stevenson)	18:37
6. Laura Malnor (East Grand Rapids)	18:47
15. Becca Bauman (Grand Rapids Catholic Central)	19:06
17. Erin Batt (Hillsdale)	19:15
23. Geena Gall (Grand Blanc)	19:23
24. Alicia Hoffman (Monroe Jefferson)	19:26
28. Gillian Nordquist (Clarkston)	19:31
36. Anne Oltman (Clarkston)	20:00
37. Michelle Mercier (Muskegon Reeths Puffer)	20:04
40. Janee Jones (Goodrich)	20:12

2005 – 3rd place – 67
2. Kellee Lemcke (Sterling Heights Stevenson)	18:24
14. Lori Burgess (Grand Rapids South Christian)	19:08
15. Erica D'Angelo (Mt Clemens Chippewa Valley)	19:12
17. Kristina Olson (Jackson)	19:13
19. Rachel Severin (Chelsea)	19:15
23. Alexa Glencer (Ann Arbor Greenhills)	19:28
36. Lyndsay Smith (Clarkston)	19:41
38. Sara Leblein (Lake Orion)	19:48
42. Kylen Cieslak (Livonia Churchill)	19:59
44. Rebecca Monroe (Big Rapids Crossroads)	20:00

2006 – 2nd place – 45
6. Emily Langenberg (Grand Ledge)	19:11
7. Carlie Green (Milford)	19:11
8. Bekah Smeltzer (Monroe Jefferson)	19:14
10. Adrienne Pastula (Hillsdale)	19:23
14. Jessica Armstrong (Wayland Union)	19:31
18. Amanda McKenzie (Chelsea)	19:43
20. Hannah Cavicchio (Salem)	19:45
38. Megan Carter (Southfield Christian)	20:20
41. Shannon Kohlitz (Jackso)	20:26
32. Adrian Dent (Sterling Heights Stevenson)	20:29

2007 – 1st place – 40
3. Tiffany Abrahamian (Rochester)	18:13
4. Katie Haines (Rockford)	18:20
5. Sloan Secord (Gaylord)	18:21
13. Lindsey Gakenheimer (Monroe)	18:42
15. Jen Rock (Utica Eisenhower)	18:45
16. Erin LaFave (Bloomfield Hills Lahser)	18:47
17. Rachel McFarlane (Livonia Churchill)	18:48
23. Lia Jones (Leroy Pine River)	19:00
28. Alissa Ott (Detroit Country Day)	19:17
36. Molly Waterhouse (Vicksburg)	19:33

2008 – 1st place – 27
2. Cally Macumber (Rochester Adams)	18:12
4. Audrey Huth (Utica)	18:20
5. Lindsey Hilton (Rochester Adams)	18:29
7. Courtney Calka (Livonia Stevenson)	18:34
9. Meggan Freeland (Parma Western)	18:41
12. Kaitlyn Patterson (Cadillac)	18:48
17. Alyssa Penning (Grand Rapids Christian)	18:57
18. Danielle Tepper (Grandville)	18:58
21. Ellory Green (Brighton)	19:00
26. Amanda Mergaert (Utica)	19:12
32. Rachel Quaintance (Walled Lake Northern)	19:29
40. Tiffany Kincaid (Clarkston)	19:54

2009 – 3rd place – 55
5. Devan John (Allendale)	18:44
8. Melinda Palinkas (Saranac)	18:54

13. Rachel Steilberg (Grandville) 18:56
14. Krista Parks (East Kentwood) 18:57
15. Kristen Yarows (Dexter) 18:58
17. Amaya Ayers (Laingsburg) 19:07
22. Brittany Anderson (Leroy Pine River) 19:18
23. Breeann Ovokaitys (Cedar Springs) 19:19
27. Lauren Halm (Williamston) 19:25
35. Emma Drenth (Williamston) 19:32

2010 – 4th place – 84
10. Alissa Williams (East Kentwood) 18:12
12. Megan Heeder (Lansing Catholic) 18:14
19. Ann Marie Arseneau (Sturgis) 18:29
21. Anna Pasternak (Hartland) 18:34
22. Taylor Smith (Otsego) 18:34
27. Emily Short (Tawas) 18:48
34. Chloe Gilbert (Owosso) 18:55
35. Teha Ames (Shepherd) 18:56
36. Jacquelynn Overbeek (Hamilton) 18:58
39. Morgan Wixson (Remus Chippewa Hills) 19:12
42. Shivani Kaushal (Grand Blanc) 19:14
43. Bianca Kubicki (Canton) 19:21

2011 – 3rd place – 56
2. Rachele Schulist (Zeeland West) 18:54
9. Natalie Smith (Clarkston) 19:22
11. Nicole Zeinstra (Holland Black River) 19:22
16. Amy Creutz (Saline) 19:35
18. Heather Price (Saugatuck) 19:40
23. Jenny Frantz (Ovid-Elsie) 19:49
26. Emily Oren (Hamilton) 19:57
28. Lindsey Burdette (Hanover Horton) 20:00
31. Mickey Ludlow (Jackson Lumen Christi) 20:18
34. Rosanna Neuhausler (Ann Arbor Pioneer) 20:25
39. Hannah Grischke (Williamston) 20:46
42. Katie Hoevet (Ann Arbor Pioneer) 21:42

2012 – 4th place – 100
8. Raquel Serna (St Louis) 18:31
16. Katie Weiler (Cedar Springs) 18:48
21. Gabrielle Thivierge (Rochester Adams) 18:59
27. Erin Dunne (Northville) 19:07
28. Allison Lunau (Brighton) 19:11
29. Rachel Durbin (Armada) 19:14
30. Jessica Gaines (Sterling Heights Stevenson) 19:17
33. Daya Waugh (Waterford Mott) 19:23
35. Megan Hubbard (Hanover Horton) 19:28
38. Jessica Delaney (Jackson Northwest) 19:34
43. Jemma Howlett (Bloomfield Hills Cranbrook) 19:45
44. Christine Micale (Macomb Dakota) 19:45

2013 – 2nd place – 45 (on tiebreaker)
1. Megan O'Neil (Remus Chippewa Hills) 18:15
2. Kirtsen Olling (Breckenridge) 18:31
12. Audrianna Bormaman (Battle Creek Pennfield) 18:54
13. Nicole Kowalchick (Rochester Hills Stoney Creek) 18:55
17. Ashley Russo (Kent City) 19:04
30. Morgan Harney (Rockford) 19:36
32. Shannon Richardson (Hanover Horton) 19:38
34. Rachel Walny (Mt Clemens Chippewa Valley) 19:44
35. Nicole Poca (Erie Mason) 19:48
36. Marissa McGahan (Brighton) 19:56
43. Kayla Kraft (St Johns) 20:10
44. Lauren Jenkins (Saugatuck) 20:11

2014 – 3rd place – 60

5. Gina Patterson (Macomb Lutheran North) 18:34
8. Annie Fuller (Manistee) 18:49
12. Hannah Lonergan (Novi) 18:54
14. Sophia Bradley (St Louis) 18:58
21. Taylor Thrush (Shepherd) 19:11
24. Madison Paquette (Milford) 19:17
28. Jessica Harris (Whitehall) 19:23
29. Avery Lowe (North Muskegon) 19:27
30. Alexis Miller (GR South Christian) 19:35
36. Madison Marciniak (Bay City Western) 19:49

2015 – 4th place – 98
8. Samantha Hanson (Sterling Heights Stevenson) 18:57
12. Kayla Dobies (Macomb Dakota) 19:10
19. Allison Shannon (Sterling Heights Stevenson) 19:25
26. Alyssa Schwartz (Grand Rapids South Christian) 19:46
33. Emily Fluent (Lake Orion) 19:57
34. Ashley Lindeman (Manistee) 19:59
35. Kensington Garvey (Blanchard-Montabella) 20:03
38. Laura Estrada (Bay City Western) 20:12
39. Audrey Pohl (Pewamo-Westphalia) 20:15
40. Alicia Roney (Waldron) 20:52

2016 – 1st place – 41
3. Erika Freyhof (Hamilton) 18:34
7. Olivia Schroder (Caledonia) 18:46
9. Christina Sawyer (Tecumseh) 18:51
10. Julia Vanitvelt (Flint Powers) 18:53
12. Maggie Pawelczyk (Wyandotte) 18:57
19. Jenna Magness (Grand Ledge) 19:03
22. Jessi Lindstrom (Flushing) 19:11
31. Jasmine Harper (Clare) 19:22
32. Alexis McConnell (Mt Pleasant Sacred Heart) 19:22
35. Claire Kendall (Berkley) 19:32
46. Faith Kiprotich (East Kentwood) 20:07
47. Reanna Raymond (Grosse Pointe South) 20:16

2017 – 3rd place – 51
4. Rachel McCardell (Birmingham Seaholm) 19:02
5. Samantha Saenz (Concord) 19:07
11. Emily Rooney (Birmingham Seaholm) 19:34
14. Olivia Clymer (White Lake Lakeland) 19:46
17. Rachel Kempf (Saginaw Heritage) 19:51
18. Camryn Gabriel (Rockford) 19:53
21. Katie Vitou (DeWitt) 20:02
23. Lucy Karpukhno (Benzie Central) 20:06
27. Maija Rettelle (Midland Dow) 20:13
30. Lynsey Amthor (Saginaw Heritage) 20:16

The winning 2018 squad.

2018 – 1st place – 35
1. Madeline Rehm (White Lake Lakeland)		18:26
3. Noelle Adrieans (Pinckney)		18:34
5. Victoria Heiligenthal (Milford)		18:39
12. Jillian Lange (Goodrich)		18:54
14. Maddy Boyd (Alpena)		18:57
15. Lauren Freeland (Kent City)		19:03
16. Klaudia O'Malley (McBain)		19:04
17. Elizabeth Bulat (Rochester)		19:07
22. Abby Inch (Farmington)		19:14
26. Grace Nolan (Clarkston)		19:29
28. Elizabeth Dalrymple (Clarkston)		19:35
29. Jami Reed (Forest Hills Eastern)		19:39

2019 – 2nd place - 37
1. Maryam Sheena (Walled Lake Western)	18:25
3. Taryn Chapko (St Johns)	18:30
7. Emily Paupore (Negaunee)	18:46
11. Michelle Kuipers (Holland Christian)	19:07
15. Madison Price (Trenton)	19:20
18. Landyn Howell (Forest Hills Eastern)	19:24
19. Kiera Snyder (Port Huron Northern)	19:29
22. Jenna Picard (Bay City Western)	19:38
23. Ahna Vanderwall (Petoskey)	19:39
24. Allissa Ash (Byron)	19:42
25. Brooke Soper (Okemos)	19:42

Michigan at Foot Locker Nationals

Originally called the Kinney Cross Country Championships, the meet changed names in 1993 when Foot Locker came on board as the title sponsor. It has annually been the national championship for individuals in cross country.

With 9 titles won (7 boys, 2 girls), Michigan has showed itself as one of the top states in the nation for cross country. Only California has more boys titles (8) and overall titles (18).

Since 1981, the Midwest Regional has been in Kenosha, Wisconsin, on the UW-Parkside campus, held Thanksgiving weekend. In 1979-80, there were five regions, each qualifying 7 runners. Starting in 2005, the number of regional qualifiers went from 8 to 10. Each athlete's regional result is shown in parentheses.

BOYS

1979 (San Diego)
No qualifiers

1980 (San Diego)
11. Mark Smith (Cadillac)12   15:27
    (MW 3rd – 14:53)

1981 (San Diego)
No qualifiers

1982 (San Diego)
19. Phil Schoensee (Center Line)11   15:17
    (MW 6th – 15:44)

1983 (San Diego)
6. Rusty Korhonen (Forest Hills Central)12   15:10
    (MW 5th – 15:32)
8. Phil Schoensee (Center Line)12   15:14
    (MW 6th – 15:34)
21. Jeff Mundt (Anchor Bay)12   15:44
    (MW 7th – 15:41)
23. Bill Taylor (Charlevoix)12   15:46
    (MW 4th – 15:31)

1984-1985 (San Diego)
No qualifiers

1986 (San Diego)
2. Todd Williams (Monroe)12   14:49
    (MW 1st – 15:13)
16. Cliff Dwelle (Lake Orion)12   15:25
    (MW 4th – 15:28)
27. Chris Tolonen (Ann Arbor Pioneer)12   15:48
    (MW 8th – 15:30)

1987 (San Diego)
No qualifiers

1988 (San Diego)

1. Brian Grosso (Walled Lake Western)12   15:03
   (MW 3rd – 15:47)
18. Jason Colvin (Ann Arbor Pioneer)12   15:35
    (MW 2nd – 15:44)
29. Phil Sanborn (Monroe)12   16:10
    (MW 6th – 15:52)

1989 (San Diego)
26. Rob Huff (Bloomfield Hills Lahser)12   15:51
    (MW 2nd – 16:04)

1990-1993 (San Diego)
No qualifiers

1994 (San Diego)
8. Steve Schell (Dearborn Fordson)12   15:12
   (MW 6th – 15:22)
22. Abdul Alzindani (Dearborn Fordson)11   15:32
    (MW 5th – 15:21)
23. Tom Chorny (Fruitport)12   15:33
    (MW 7th – 15:23)

1995 (San Diego)
1. Abdul Alzindani (Dearborn Fordson)12   15:12
   (MW 4th – 15:37)
5. Joe Leo (Detroit Catholic Central)12   15:26
   (MW 3rd – 15:36)

1996 (San Diego)
32. Christian Dullock (Jackson)12   18:01
    (MW 7th – 16:02)

1997 (Orlando)
24. Nick Gow (White Lake Lakeland)12   16:30
    (MW 6th – 15:56)

1998 (Orlando)
4. Jason Hartmann (Rockford)12   15:33
   (MW 2nd – 15:10)
8. Dathan Ritzenhein (Rockford)10   15:47
   (MW 3rd – 15:12)
27. Jake Flynn (Benzie Central)11   16:32
    (MW 7th – 15:17)

1999 (Orlando)
1. Dathan Ritzenhein (Rockford) 11   14:29
   (MW 1st – 14:55)
18. Todd Mobley (Walled Lake Central)12   15:20
    (MW 8th – 15:24)
21. Tom Greenless (Milford)12   15:30
    (MW 7th – 15:23)

In 2000, Dathan Ritzenhein became the first Michigander to win the Foot Locker title twice.

2000 (Orlando)
1. Dathan Ritzenhein (Rockford)12   14:35
   (MW 1st – 14:35)
8. Tim Moore (Novi)11   15:13
   (MW 2nd – 15:08)
24. Sean Moore (Saline)12   15:43
    (MW 6th – 15:17)

2001 (Orlando)
1. Tim Moore (Novi)12   14:50
   (MW 1st – 15:15)
5. Tim Ross (Caledonia)12   14:58
   (MW 6th – 15:40)
28. Adam Ludwig (St Joseph)12   16:03
    (MW 5th – 15:37)

2002 (San Diego)
No qualifiers
(MW top finisher: 15. Frank Tinney – Ann Arbor Huron 16:01)

2003 (San Diego)
24. Neal Naughton (Walled Lake Western)12   15:45
    (MW 5th – 15:23)
27. Justin Switzer (Waterford Kettering)11   15:59
    (MW 8th – 15:26)

2004 (San Diego)
7. Justin Switzer (Waterford Kettering)12   15:35
   (MW 5th – 15:37)
18. Dan Roberts (Vicksburg)11   15:53
    (MW 7th – 15:42)
21. John Black (Bloomfield Hills Rice)12   15:56
    (MW 4th – 15:34)

2005 (San Diego)
5. Landon Peacock (Cedar Springs)12   15:15
   (MW 2nd – 15:01)
(Daniel Roberts moved to Colorado and placed 12th in 15:27)

2006 (San Diego)

No qualifiers
(MW top finisher: 13. Bobby Aprill – Dexter 15:30)

2007 (San Diego)
10. Maverick Darling (Ovid-Elsie)12   15:23
    (MW 3rd 15:07)

2008 (San Diego)
No qualifiers
(MW top finisher: 11. Ben Miller – Warren DeLaSalle 15:30)

2009 (San Diego)
39. Nathan Karr (Ann Arbor Pioneer)12   16:35
    (MW 4th – 15:46)

2010 (San Diego)
35. Caleb Rhynard (Shepherd)12   15:59
    (MW 10th – 15:13)

2011 (San Diego)
27. Evan Chiplock (Saginaw Heritage)12   15:53
    (MW 6th – 15:18)

2012 (San Diego)
20. Nick Raymond (Erie-Mason)12   15:44
    (MW 3rd – 15:02)
29. Connor Mora (Cedar Springs)12   15:58
    (MW 8th – 15:09)

2013 (San Diego)
1. Grant Fisher (Grand Blanc)11   15:07
    (MW 1st – 15:02)
21. Ryan Robinson (Waterford Mott)11   15:49
    (MW 10th – 15:22)

In 2014, Grant Fisher became the second Michigander to win Foot Locker twice.

2014 (San Diego)
1. Grant Fisher (Grand Blanc)12   15:03
    (MW 1st – 15:00)
16. Jesse Hersha (Concord)12   15:33
    (MW 2nd – 15:09)

2015 (San Diego)
23. Isaac Harding (Rockford)12   15:45
    (MW 9th – 15:19)

2016 (San Diego)
14. Noah Jacobs (Corunna)12   15:25
    (MW 4th – 15:08)
17. Mitchell Day (Alpena)12   15:32
    (MW 8th – 15:13)

2017 (San Diego)
27. Shuaib Aljabaly (Coldwater)12   16:16
    (MW 9th – 15:10)

2018 (San Diego)
4. Carter Solomon (Plymouth)11   15:26
    (MW 4th – 16:14)
9. Evan Bishop (East Grand Rapids)11   15:32
    (MW 3rd – 16:10)
17. Zachary Stewart (Brighton)11   15:57
    (MW 10th – 16:20)
27. Brendan Favazza (Clarkston)11   16:12
    (MW 9th – 16:23)

2019 (San Diego)
2. Carter Solomon (Plymouth)12   15:17
    (MW 9th – 16:00)
6. Evan Bishop (East Grand Rapids)12   15:24
    (MW 6th – 15:55)
19. Jack Spamer (Brighton)12   15:43
    (MW 8th – 15:59)
20. Brendan Favazza (Clarkston)12   15:45
    (MW 7th – 15:58)
26. Zach Stewart (Brighton)12   15:56
    (MW 5th – 15:54)
28. Nathan Walker (Fremont)11   16:00
    (MW 3rd – 15:53)
32. Michael Hancock (Dearbon Divine Child)12   16:13
    (MW 2nd – 15:52)

GIRLS

1979 (San Diego)
No qualifiers

1980 (San Diego)
20. Pat Hamparian (Brighton)11   18:39
    (MW 6th – 17:53)
26. JoAnn Lanciaux (Fremont)12   19:22
    (MW 7th – 17:55)

1981-1982 (San Diego)
No qualifiers

1983 (San Diego)
21. Michelle Bews (Birmingham Seaholm-Australia)12   18:18
    (MW 8th – 18:24)

1984 (San Diego)
6. Mary Peruski (Dearborn Edsel Ford)12   17:34
   (MW 3rd – 17:49)

1985 (San Diego)
20. Denys Adams (Okemos)12   18:02
    (MW 4th – 18:31)
21. Kristin Salt (Dearborn Edsel Ford)11   18:07
    (MW 7th – 18:41)

1986 (San Diego)
10. Kristin Salt (Dearborn Edsel Ford)12   17:48
    (MW 7th – 18:33)

1987-1989 (San Diego)
No qualifiers

1990 (San Diego)
19. Molly Lori (East Kentwood)11   18:29
    (MW 4th – 18:40)

1991 (San Diego)
9. Molly Lori (East Kentwood)12   18:18
   (MW 6th – 20:45)
26. Christy Goodison (Sterling Heights Stevenson)10   19:15
    (MW 4th – 20:40)

1992 (San Diego)
6. Kelly Smith (Petoskey)11   18:04
   (MW 4th – 19:15)

1993 (San Diego)
7. Eileen Fleck (East Lansing)12   17:59
   (MW 7th – 18:21)
30. Christy Goodison (Sterling Heights Stevenson)12   19:08
    (MW 2nd – 18:13)

1994 (San Diego)
30. Katie Sobczak (Caledonia)11   18:29
    (MW 8th – 18:18)

1995 (San Diego)
No qualifiers
(MW top finisher-10. Shannon Houseman-Caledonia) 18:35

1996 (San Diego)
4. Sharon Van Tuyl (Portage Northern)11   18:05
   (MW 5th – 18:46)

1997 (Orlando)
21. Bethany Brewster (Saginaw Valley Lutheran)12   18:47
    (MW 7th – 18:44)

1998 (Orlando)
No qualifiers
(MW top finisher: 16. Jamie Krzyminski –Corunna 18:34)

1999 (Orlando)
10. Kalin Toedebusch (Rockford)11   17:39
    (MW 4th – 17:59)

2000 (Orlando)
5. Kalin Toedebusch (Rockford)12   17:32
   (MW 5th – 17:49)
10. Katie Boyles (Rochester Adams)12   17:39
    (MW 3rd – 17:45)

16. Linsey Blaisdell (Rockford)12   17:54
    (MW 6th – 17:50)

2001 (Orlando)
25. Nicole Bohnsack (Rockford)10   18:15
    (MW 2nd – 18:08)
29. Amber Smith (Ishpeming Westwood)10   18:35
    (MW 3rd – 18:21)

2002 (San Diego)
5. Amber Smith (Ishpeming Westwood)11   17:48
   (MW 2nd – 18:10)
31. Nicole Bohnsack (Rockford)11   20:51
    (MW 7th – 18:31)

2003 (San Diego)
No qualifiers
(MW top finisher: 10. Amber Smith – Ishpeming Westwood 17:57)

2004 (San Diego)
20. Bekah Smeltzer (Monroe Jefferson)10   18:33
    (MW 9th – 18:21)
35. Molly Waterhouse (Vicksburg)9   19:30
    (MW 10th 18:24)

2005 (San Diego)
No qualifiers
(MW top finisher-13. Mikal Beckman-Newaygo 18:07)

2006 (San Diego)
28. Marissa Treece (Maple City-Glen Lake)12   18:52
    (MW 9th – 18:03)

2007 (San Diego)
26. Katie Haines (Rockford)12   18:35
    (MW 9th – 17:58)
32. Meggan Freeland (Parma Western)11   18:47
    (MW 10th – 18:00)

2008 (San Diego)
3. Megan Goethals (Rochester)11   17:30
   (MW 1st – 17:31)
21. Becca Addison (Grand Haven)12   18:24
    (MW 5th – 17:44)
22. Jordan Tomecek (Milan)11   18:25
    (MW 9th – 18:03)

Megan Goethals won by inches in 2009.

2009 (San Diego)
1. Megan Goethals (Rochester) 12   17:07
   (MW 1st – 17:24)
30. Shannon Osika (Waterford Mott)10   18:29
   (MW 10th – 18:37)
35. Sara Kroll (Livonia Churchill)12   18:36
   (MW 7th – 18:15)

2010 (San Diego)
7. Erin Finn (West Bloomfield)10   17:38
   (MW 4th – 17:29)
8. Shannon Osika (Waterford Mott)11   17:46
   (MW 3rd – 17:27)
11. Gabi Anzelone (Grand Blanc)12   17:46
   (MW 2nd – 17:26)
18. Brook Handler (Rochester)12   18:02
   (MW 8th – 17:36)

2011 (San Diego)
2. Erin Finn (West Bloomfield)11   17:24
   (MW 3rd – 17:34)
10. Julia Bos (Grand Rapids Christian)11   17:40
   (MW 2nd – 17:14)
14. Lindsey Burdette (Hanover-Horton)12   17:56
   (MW 9th – 17:43)
25. Taylor Manett (Rockford)12   18:17
   (MW 4th – 17:35)

2012 (San Diego)
No qualifiers
(MW top finisher: 12. Erin Finn-West Bloomfield 17:46)

2013 (San Diego)
24. Lauren Brasure (Rockford)12   18:13
   (MW 6th – 17:47)
31. Kirsten Olling (Breckenridge)12   18:29
   (MW 8th – 17:52)

2014 (San Diego)
7. Audrey Belf (Birmingham Seaholm)12   17:51
   (MW 4th – 17:31)
39. Sarah Kettel (Capital Homeschool)11   19:51
   (MW 8th – 17:49)

2015 (San Diego)
7. Madison Troy (Grandville)10   17:42
   (MW 6th – 17:32)
35. Emma Wilson (Romeo)12   18:33
   (MW 9th – 17:45)

2016 (San Diego)
5. Anne Forsyth (Ann Arbor Pioneer)11   17:46
   (MW 1st – 17:18)
14. Olivia Theis (Lansing Catholic)11   17:56
   (MW 5th – 17:41)

23. Kyla Christopher-Moody (West Bloomfield)10   18:05
   (MW 10th – 17:49)
34. Ava Strenge (Battle Creek St Phillip)12   18:24
   (MW 9th – 17:48)

2017 (San Diego)
3. Olivia Theis (Lansing Catholic)12   17:23
   (MW 1st – 17:14)
10. Adelyn Ackley (Hart)11   18:00
   (MW 8th – 17:44)
25. Ericka VanderLende (Rockford)11   18:39
   (MW 5th – 17:38)
26. Cecilia Stalzer (Mason)11   18:41
   (MW 7th – 17:44)
30. Rylee Robinson (Waterford Mott)11   18:48
   (MW 10th – 17:46)

2018 (San Diego)
3. Abby VanderKooi (Western Michigan Christian)9   17:14
   (MW 4th – 18:16)
6. Jaden Theis (Lansing Catholic)11   17:30
   (MW 8th – 18:49)
10. Ericka VanderLende (Rockford)12   17:44
   (MW 5th – 18.20)
16. Adelyn Ackley (Hart)12   18:06
   (MW 6th – 18:37)

Zofia Dudek became the second Michigan girl to win at Foot Locker.

2019 (San Diego)
1. Zofia Dudek (Ann Arbor Pioneer)12   16:45
   (MW 2nd – 17:21)
3. Abby VanderKooi (Muskegon WM Christian)10   16:56
   (MW 1st – 17:18)
18. Audrey Dadamio (Birmingham Seaholm)11   17:59
   (MW 10th – 18:15)

Michigan at NXN – NIKE XC Nationals

Nike Team Nationals started in 2004 to provide a de-facto national team championship, something the Foot Locker series did not offer. From 2004-13 it was held in Oregon at Portland Meadows Golf Course. In 2014 it moved to Glendoveer Golf Course in Portland.

In 2008 the name was changed to Nike Cross Nationals (NXN) and individual qualifiers were allowed—the top 5 from each regional who weren't on a qualifying club.

In 2018 an additional 5 individuals were invited to Nationals on an at-large basis.

Long-standing MHSAA policy forbids national competitions for school teams, though it is allowed for individuals. All Michigan competitors have competed in NXN as individuals, except for the Northville girls in 2015, who defied the MHSAA and qualified as a team. The returning girls missed some of their meets the following season as part of an MHSAA suspension.

BOYS

2004-2011
No qualifiers

2012
dnf—TJ Carey (Lake Orion)12 – Injured during race
   (MW 3rd – 15:33.7)

2013
No qualifiers

2014
55. Ryan Robinson (Waterford Mott)12   16:11
   (MW 2nd – 15:03.1)

2015
10. Morgan Beadlescomb (Algonac)12   15:20.4
   (MW 7th – 15:18.5)

2016-2017
No qualifiers

2018
9. Corey Gorgas (Saugatuck)12   15:10.7
   (MW 3rd – 15:20.8)
13. Nick Foster (AA Pioneer)12   15:15.7
   (at-large invitee)
20. Evan Bishop (East Grand Rapids)11   15:20.9
   (at-large invitee)

2019
17. Jack Spamer (Brighton)12   15:23.1
   (MW 5th – 15:09.6)
33. Evan Bishop (East Grand Rapids)12   15:40.2
   (MW 4th – 15:05.8)
39. Brendan Favazza (Clarkston)12   15:43.4
   (MW 6th – 15:10.0)
48. Michael Hancock (Dearborn DC)12   15:50.5
   (at-large invitee)

GIRLS

2004-2008
No qualifiers

2009
17. Michelle Moriset (Troy)12   18:13.2
   (MW 4th – 18:10.4)

2010
No qualifiers

2011
65. Avery Evenson (Hartland)11   18:57
   (MW 3rd – 18:36.6)

2012-13
No qualifiers

2014
14. Audrey Belf (Birmingham Seaholm)12   17:46
   (MW 2nd – 17:30.6)
23. Sarah Kettel (Capital Homeschool)11   18:12
   (MW 1st – 17:28.8)
42. Rachel Bonner (Port Huron)11   18:32
   (MW 4th – 17:38.1)

Northville 2015 – the only Michigan team to ever make it to NXN. (Kim Harris photo)

2015
12. Madison Troy (Grandville)10   17:24.2

(MW 4th – 17:29.1)
50. Lexa Barrott (Northville) 18:12.0
(MW 20th – 18:12.3)
99. Olivia Harp (Northville) 18:50.3
(MW 53rd – 18:43.2)
105. Ana Barrott (Northville) 18:55.3
(MW 56th – 18:43.8)
157. Cayla Eckenroth (Northville) 19:26.0
(MW 183rd – 20:00.1)
159. Emma Hermann (Northville) 19:28.9
(MW 70th – 18:50.8)
183. Hailey Harris (Northville) 20:00.4
(MW 55th 18:43.7)
189. Rachel Zimmer (Northville) 20:18.1
(MW 255th – 20:26.5)
(The Northville teaqm placed 17th overall at NXN with 360 points.)

2016
14. Anne Forsyth (AA Pioneer)11 17:58.6
(MW 3rd – 17:09.1)

2017
No qualifiers

2018
8. Ericka VanderLende (Rockford)12 17:27.7
(at-large invitee)

2019
dnc—Zofia Dudek (Ann Arbor Pioneer)12—bypassed NXN so she could represent Poland in the European XC Championships in Lisbon, Portugal, where she finished 5th in 14:22 on the 4.3K course. She had won the NXN Midwest race in 16:49.3.

Michigan High Schoolers Who Represented the U.S. in International XC Competition

Dathan Ritzenhein won the World bronze in 2001.

Every year, Team USA competes in at least one international championship in cross country. The most prestigious of these is the World Cross Country Championship, which has been held since 1903 (since 1973 it has been sponsored by the IAAF/World Athletics). Currently the Worlds are held every two years. The NACAC (North American-Central American-Caribbean) includes all the Western Hemisphere nations and has been held annually since 2005. The Pan-American Cross Country Cup started in 2015; it also involves Western Hemisphere nations and some years is run concurrently with the NACAC race.

High schoolers typically compete in the U20 race, which means that they are racing against college freshmen and some sophomores. In the case of Kathy Moore (1968) and Pam Bagian (1970), there were no U20 championship races at the time, so they raced against senior women.

Qualification is at the USATF National U20 Cross Country Championships (note—NOT through the Junior Olympics program).

Lincoln Park's Pam Bagian competed at the 1970 World Championships.

1968 - Kathy Moore (Lincoln Park)9 – placed 6th in the AAU Women's Nationals in November 1967 in New York City and was named to the World XC Team for the competition in Blackburn, England, but was struck by appendicitis and unable to make the trip.

1970 - Pam Bagian (Lincoln Park)12 placed 3rd in 11:15 for 2M in the AAU Women's Nationals in November 1969 in St Louis. At the World Cross Country meet in Fredericksburg, Maryland, she placed 14th, running 15:45 for 4K.

1974 – Pat Davey (Birmingham Brother Rice)12 – Placed 10th in the World Junior XC race in Monza, Italy, running 21:59 for 7.1K.

1987 – Todd Williams (Monroe HS)12 – Finished 2nd in the Junior race at the Cross Country Trials in Dallas, running 25:33 for 8K. Then placed 23rd in the World Junior XC race in Warsaw, Poland, running 23:30 for 7.05K.

2001 – Dathan Ritzenhein (Rockford HS)12 – Placed 2nd in the Junior race at the U.S. XC Trials in Vancouver, Washington, running 24:11 for 8K. Won the bronze medal at the World Junior XC race in Oostende, Belgium, in 25:46 on the 7.7K course.

2002 – Tim Moore (Novi HS)12 – Won the Junior race at the USATF XC Champs in Vancouver, Washington, in 24:48 for 8K. Placed 54th (25:47 for 7.974K) at the World Junior XC race in Dublin, Ireland.

2013 – Erin Finn (West Bloomfield HS)12 - Selected for US National Junior Team and won the NACAC XC Championships in Mandeville, Jamaica, in 14:09 for 4.1K. Placed 2nd (20:49 for 6K) in the USATF Junior Nationals in St Louis a week later. At the World XC in Bydgoszcz, Poland, she placed 34th in 20:03 for 6K.

Pinckney's Noelle Adrieans placed 9th at the 2019 NACAC Championships in Trinidad. (Iris Albrecht photo)

2019—Noelle Adriaens (Pinckney)12 – placed 9th (21:53 for 6K) in the USATF Junior Nationals in Tallahassee, then placed 9th (23:01 for 6K) in the NACAC Championships in Trinidad.

2020—Evan Bishop (East Grand Rapids)12—Was runner-up at the USATF Junior Nationals in San Diego in 26:22 for 8K. Then finished 2nd (27:20 for 8K) in the Pan-American XC Championships in Victoria, Canada.

The author, at left, doing color commentary at the 2018 Lower Peninsula Finals. At right is Rudy Godefroidt, head official. Godefroidt has been MITCA's Coach of the Year and also has won the MHSAA's Forsythe Award.

About the Author

Jeff Hollobaugh became a fan as a 15-year-old distance runner in Allen Park. After going to Western Michigan University, he was hired as statistician by *Track & Field News*, the Bible of the Sport. That started his career as a sportswriter and editor. In his first stint with *T&FN*, he stayed for 7 years and after several years as managing editor returned to Michigan.

He taught for 15-plus years at the community college and high school level and has coached everything from munchkins to a national champion. Along the way, he covered 7 Olympic Games and 14 World Championships for *T&FN*. He has worked as an information specialist for the World Championships and the 1996 Olympic Games. In 2016 he returned to *T&FN* as associate editor. His writing has also been published by ESPN.com, the Detroit Free Press, RunMichigan, Michigan Runner, USATF and the IAAF.

In 1996 Hollobaugh founded www.michtrack.org to share his enthusiasm for Michigan track history and records. A longtime announcer of the MHSAA Finals in cross country and Div. I track, he also announces for the University of Michigan and Aquinas College, as well as many major high school events. A resident of Dexter, Hollobaugh and his wife Karen have two daughters and a dog named Huckleberry.

Made in the USA
Monee, IL
24 May 2020